Letters from Assyrian Scholars to the Kings Esarhaddon and Assurbanipal

Part II: Commentary and Appendices

Letters from Assyrian Scholars to the Kings Esarhaddon and Assurbanipal

Part II: Commentary and Appendices

Simo Parpola

Winona Lake, Indiana
Eisenbrauns
2007

This edition reprinted 2007 by Eisenbrauns
Winona Lake, Indiana, U.S.A.
by permission of Ugarit-Verlag (Münster) and
the editors of Alter Orient und Altes Testament.

Printed in the United States of America.

www.eisenbrauns.com

Library of Congress Cataloging-in-Publication Data

Parpola, Simo.
Letters from Assyrian scholars to the kings Esarhaddon and Assurbanipal / [compiled] by Simo Parpola.
p. cm.
Romanized Assyro-Babylonian and English.
Reprint. Originally published: Kevelaer: Butzon & Bercker, 1970–1983.
Includes bibliographical references and indexes.
ISBN 978-1-57506-137-5 (v. 1 : hardback : alk. paper)
ISBN 978-1-57506-138-2 (v. 2 : hardback : alk. paper)
ISBN 978-1-57506-139-9 (set: hardback : alk. paper)
1. Assyro-Babylonian letters. 2. Esarhaddon, King of Assyria, d. 668 B.C.—Correspondence. 3. Assurbanipal, King of Assyria, fl. 668–627 B.C.—Correspondence. I. Esarhaddon, King of Assyria, d. 668 B.C. II. Assurbanipal, King of Assyria, fl. 668–627 B.C. III. Title.
PJ3889.P3 2007
492′.1—dc22

2007017026

The paper used in this publication meets the minimum requirements of the American National Standard for Information Sciences—Permanence of Paper for Printed Library Materials, ANSI Z39.48-1984. ♾™

To my wife

Sisko

who shared the moments of joy and frustration
experienced during the writing of this volume

FOREWORD

The manuscript of this volume was essentially completed and submitted to press in July 1978. Since then, only minor alterations to the text were possible. Some additions and corrections that have occurred to me while the book was in press could, however, be included at the end of the volume (see p. 507 ff.). These additions are referred to in the commentary by asterisks placed at the ends of the relevant commentary entries.

The purpose and the scope of the commentary are assessed in the introduction to the volume. As for the introduction, which replaces the one presented in 1971 as my doctoral dissertation (and originally intended to be reprinted here), it should be taken for what it is: an *introduction* to the present commentary and the letters in general. It is not intended as a serious study of the matters it deals with, which would actually call for several separate monographs. Its purpose is simply to present to others certain ideas and personal views that have gradually taken shape in the course of my prolonged preoccupation with the correspondence, in the hope that they will make the nature of this correspondence clearer to the casual user of the book and provide a starting point to those who will pursue these matters more seriously.

It is impossible to give proper credit here to all the persons who in a way or another have contributed to the writing and publication of this book. Their help is gratefully acknowledged in the commentary in appropriate contexts. Here I would specially like to record my gratitude to

- Professor Hermann Hunger (Vienna), for his encouragement, criticism, and help with the astronomical literature,
- Drs. Edmond Sollberger and Christopher Walker (British Museum), who were always ready to help when I needed collations,
- Professor Manfried Dietrich, who as editor could not have been more co-operative and patient, and
- the Finnish Academy and Societas Scientiarum Fennica, which provided financial assistance towards defraying the printing costs of this book.

May I finally express the hope that the present study will succeed in drawing greater attention to these letters and encouraging their use as a historical source. They would deserve it.

Chicago, April 1982 Simo Parpola

TABLE OF CONTENTS

INTRODUCTION

The scope and purpose of the present volume

The present volume provides a detailed and systematic commentary to the corpus of letters edited in *AOAT* 5/1. It has two basic purposes: (1) to make the information of the corpus more readily available to those who wish to utilize it, and (2) to form an adequate and reliable starting point for future research on this valuable but difficult body of texts.

The most serious and vexing problem these letters present is their chronology. All but four of them are undated, and the kings to whom they are addressed are never identified by name. Without a date, a letter is deprived of its historical context; and without context, the present letters in particular become a collection of isolated jigsaw-puzzle pieces – pieces that are difficult to understand, often fail to make sense and can only give a hint of the events, processes and settings that once engendered them.

These puzzle pieces are difficult to understand also because they are so damaged, fragmentary and small. There are only 41 complete and 86 well-preserved texts in the corpus, vs. 241 fragmentary ones, and only 31 letters have a length of more than 40 lines, while 191 have only 19 lines or less. The name of the sender has been lost in 150 letters. In addition, many of the letters deal with obscure technical matters, and their language, Neo-Assyrian tinted with scholarly terminology and idioms, abounds in grammatical and lexical difficulties. All this adds up to make large parts of the corpus, without explanatory comments, virtually nonsensical and therefore useless.

Naturally, there are ways to amend the situation. The corpus contains many useful chronological clues that can be used for determining the dates of individual letters – most importantly, a large number of astronomical observations offering unique opportunities for absolute dating. The technical contents of the letters can be elucidated with the help of the vast body of Mesopotamian scholarly literature. The grammatical problems can be studied in the light of a large and constantly growing corpus of other Neo-Assyrian texts. And finally, the *LAS* corpus itself is sufficiently large and chronologically compact to provide ground for reconstructing the contexts of the letters from the internal evidence of the corpus – especially when supplemented with the evidence provided by the related segments of the Ninevite royal archives, i.e., contemporary astrological reports, extispicy queries and reports, letters, legal and administrative documents, etc.

During the well over a hundred years now that have elapsed since the first specimens of the *LAS* corpus were published, the letters have been the object of numerous studies. But while these studies have done a lot in drawing attention to the information potential of the corpus, they have failed to solve the basic problems that hamper its effective utilization. For this, they have all been too limited in scope, concept and effort. The astronomical evidence of the letters, for instance, requires extensive preliminary studies in contemporary chronology and prosopography before it can be successfully exploited. In particular, a reliable identification of an astronomical phenomenon reported in a broken letter is often possible only if the identity of the writer can be securely determined first, and this in turn is only possible through a detailed distinctive feature analysis encompassing the whole corpus. Similarly, a successful exploitation of the clues offered by external evidence requires a systematic, sustained and time-consuming search through a vast amount of cuneiform (and non-cuneiform) sources of all types and periods, the great majority of which are poorly edited and, above all, poorly indexed. None of the scholars who have studied the corpus have taken the trouble of executing these imperative, preliminary tasks. As a result, at the time I started working on this commentary, the object of study looked like a swamp veiled in a mist of ill-founded hypotheses and subjective interpretations, and offering but a few *secure* footholds in an almost endless sea of uncertainties. This verdict applies particularly to the chronology of the corpus. The monumental work of Waterman offered nothing sound in this respect.

The only useful studies were a handful of articles on individual letters by Schnabel (1924), Schott and Schaumberger (1938 and 1941) and Hartman (1962). But that was by far too little to significantly improve the situation.

I am aware that the corpus still remains a "swamp" after the completion of the present study. The present commentary, too, contains a lot of hypotheses, unanswered questions and plain mistakes. However, it does represent a serious attempt to remove the *basic* obstacles to understanding along the lines just described, and I do feel that the "swamp" is now much better mapped out than before and the number of secure footholds in it greatly increased. Other scholars with different qualifications and lines of approach will hopefully push the understanding of the corpus further. I hope I have grounded the results which I consider valid well enough to make them a solid basis for others to build on, and marked uncertain hypotheses and open questions clearly enough as such to help them fulfill the purpose they serve for: to provide incentive for further research.

On the chronology of the letters

A full discussion of the chronology of the *LAS* correspondence cannot be undertaken here for two reasons. Firstly, these letters form only a small segment of a much larger whole, the Sargonid royal correspondence, which again is but a fraction of a larger whole, the imperial archives of Nineveh. A proper discussion of the basic problems encountered in the course of the chronological analysis of the corpus, such as its curious chronological structure (see App. I 4), would accordingly have to take as its starting point the chronological structure of the whole archives, which has never been adequately studied. To present such a study within the present introduction would not only be completely out of its scope, but also tedious and space-comsuming in the extreme. Secondly, it must be remembered that the chronological structure of the *LAS* corpus and its implications cannot be assessed on the basis of unambiguous dates inscribed on the texts themselves, but on the basis of dates that have been painstakingly established from the chronological evidence readable from the letters – evidence that can at times be extremely complex, and certainly greatly varies in quality and quantity from letter to letter. Thus, while a large number of the dates assigned to the letters in this study can be considered certain (cf. App. I 1), many of the dates assigned involve a degree of probability or conjecture. The borderline between certainty and probability is not always easy to draw; and doing so is certainly not possible within the confines of the present introduction. The following discussion will therefore limit itself to the most essential facts emerging from the chronological analysis of the corpus.

The most central – and most curious – fact is that about 80% of the whole correspondence (which, as stated in Pt. I, is supposed to cover the whole Sargonid dynasty) appears to date from the reign of Esarhaddon; about 20% can with certainty be assigned to the reign of Assurbanipal, and one letter (*LAS* 105) seems to have been addressed to Sin-šarru-iškun. The reasons for this curious state of affairs are not entirely clear. The fact that virtually all letters dealing with medical and exorcistic matters (which account for more than 45% of the whole corpus) can be securely dated to Esarhaddon's reign would seem to indicate that this part of the correspondence was largely a product of Esarhaddon's failing health (see commentary on *LAS* 246), and should accordingly be considered as something exceptional. The numerous astrological letters addressed to Esarhaddon may also have been – at least to a good part – occasioned by the peculiar psychosomatic disposition of that ruler. However, this still does not explain why there are so few letters addressed to other Sargonid kings in the corpus, especially since incidental passages in the *ABL* corpus (see commentary to *LAS* 41) prove that the other kings, too (especially Sennacherib), regularly received letters and reports from scholarly experts. Cf. Appendix Q, and note the astrological report to Sargon mentioned in App. J, as well as the remarks of A.L. Oppenheim in *Centaurus* 14 (1969), 120 f. There simply is no way getting around the fact that many more letters of the *LAS* type, addressed to different Assyrian rulers, must have existed. Where all these letters are now can only be guessed. Many of them may have been destroyed (partly perhaps on purpose) already in antiquity, many may simply not yet have hit the spade of the archaeologist.

The extant corpus is by no means uniform and includes, besides letters exchanged between the king (or the crown prince/queen mother acting for the king) and scholars attached to the court in Niniveh, also random petitions by unemployed scholars, and a number of occasional reports on lunar observations from scholars stationed in various other cities of Assyria. However, by far the largest part of the correspondence (325 letters, close to 90% of the whole corpus) comes from persons whose relationship to the king must be regarded as *close*. About 70% of the letters from these men can be dated, and interestingly enough, surprisingly many of them (in all, more than 160 letters) appear to date from a relatively limited time span, a period of four years at the end of the reign of Esarhaddon (672-669 BC). What's more, these letters are not at all evenly distributed over the period concerned but form clear *clusters* separated from one another by irregular intervals of time (see Chart 1 below). All letters in each of these "clusters" share the

Chart 1: CLUSTERS OF LETTERS

Year	Month	Sender	Letters	Subject
674	IX-XII	Nabû-zēru-līšir	30 + 31 + 32	substitute king ritual
672	II	Marduk-šākin-šumi	195 + 197 + 198	funeral of queen
		+Ištar-šumu-ēreš	+ 4	
672	IV	Ištar-šumu-ēreš	1 + 2 + 3	treaty of succession
672	V	Adad-šumu-uṣur	129 + 132 (+ 171)	nomination of crown prince (uncertain)
671	VIII-X	Ištar-šumu-ēreš	26 + 27	substitute king ritual
		+Adad-šumu-uṣur	+134	
		+Urad-Nanâ	+ 249	
		+Mār-Ištar	+ 277 + 292	
671	VII	Balasî	57	
		+Nabû-aḫḫē-erība	+ 58	
		+Mār-Ištar	+ 276 + 281	crown of Nabû
671	XII-670 III	Marduk-šākin-šumi	185	substitute king ritual
		+unknown	+ 232	
		+Nabû-nāṣir	+ 218	
		+Mār-Ištar	+ 279 + 280	
670	IV-V	Balasî + Nabû-aḫḫē-erība	51	king falls ill
		+Adad-šumu-uṣur	+ 123 + 124 + 130 + 133 + 143 + 151	
		+Marduk-šākin-šumi	+ 180 + 181 + 183	
		+Urad-Nanâ	+ 246 + 247 + 256?	
		+Urad-Ea	+ 273	
670?	VI-VII	Ištar-šumu-ēreš	16	earthquake (uncertain)
		+Adad-šumu-uṣur	+ 147 + 148	
670	VI-VII	Adad-šumu-uṣur	159 + 160	Naqia falls ill
		+Marduk-šākin-šumi	+ 184 + 186 + 187	
		+Nabû-nādin-šumi	+208	
		+Nabû-nāṣir + Urad-Nanâ	+ 222	
670	VIII	Balasî + Nabû-aḫḫē-erība	10 +	postponement of festival because of intercalation
		+Marduk-šākin-šumi	+ 190	
		+Mār-Ištar	+ 284 + 287	
670/69	XII-I	Marduk-šākin-šumi	163+164+173+174+175+176+177	antiwitchcraft rituals
669	III-	Ištar-šumu-ēreš	12	visit of crown prince connected with sighting of Mercury and opposition of Mars
		+Balasî	+ 45 + 46 + 53 + 66	
		+Nabû-aḫḫē-erība	+ 70 + 65 + 69 +	

669	IV	Adad-šumu-uṣur	233	Mars + Spica
		+Marduk-šākin-šumi	149	
669	V-VI	Ištar-šumu-ēreš	28 + 25	
		+Adad-šumu-uṣur	135+136+137+138+139+166 +167+152+154+155+156	substitute king ritual, earthquake
		+Urad-Nanâ	257 + 153	and diarrhoea of the king's
		+Balasî	35 + 234	grandchild
667	IV	Balasî	40	
		+Nabû-aḫḫē-erība	+ 60 + 61	lunar eclipse
667/6	X-IV	Adad-šumu-uṣur	120 + 121 + 122 + 125	petitions for Urad-Gula
666	VI-VII	Akkullānu	298 + 299	substitute king ritual

same topic, which they treat from different angles; these can be events of short duration, like bad omens, or situations or chains of events lasting for several weeks; but whichever the case, any kind of topic can attract quite large clusters (up to 16 letters) consisting of either a series of letters from a single author, or of several parallel (and overlapping) series of letters from different scholars. Some clusters touch each other or overlap chronologically so as to make it possible for one to get a detailed, albeit fragmentary picture of developments at the Assyrian court over a period of several successive months. In some clusters, letters follow each other in rapid succession: several in a row within a few days. All this strongly suggests that at least for the years 672-669, and probably for some years before and after that time period (say, 675-666), the corpus as we have it fairly closely reflects the true extent of the correspondence the Assyrian king had with his scholarly counsellors at that time, and that not too much of that correspondence has been lost. This conclusion is substantiated by references to previous and future letters in the corpus, about 60% of which are identifiable in the extant material (see App. P 6), by the considerable number of parallel letters and reports from two closely cooperating astrologers (see Chart 2), and by the fact that spectacular astronomical events (such as eclipses) are very well covered in the present corpus for the period 675-666 BC, but not for the time falling outside of these time brackets. Additional evidence to the same effect could be presented. Hence the chronological structure of the corpus does *not* seem to imply that a lot of letters from the periods separating the clusters have been perished or not found, but rather that very *few* *LAS*-type letters (or no letters at all) were written during the intervening periods – probably because there was little or no incentive to a correspondence between the king and his scholars in those times.

On the correspondents

By their fields of specialization, the scholars featuring in the *LAS* correspondence can be divided into five groups:

(1) "Scribes" (*ṭupšarru*) – experts in the art of interpreting celestial, terrestrial and teratological portents, and establishing the calendar and the ominous significance of days and months;

(2) "haruspices" (*bārû*) – experts in the art of prognosticating future, primarily by studying the exta of sheep sacrificed to the oracle gods;

(3) "exorcists" (*āšipu*) – experts in the art of manipulating supernatural forces (such as illness-causing demons) by magical means;

(4) "physicians" (*asû*) – experts in the art of curing diseases by means of drugs and other physical remedies,

(5) "chanters" (*kalû*) -- experts in the art of soothing angered gods (and thus averting calamities) by means of elaborate chants and lamentations.

Chart 2: PARALLEL LETTERS AND REPORTS

	Balasî		Nabû-aḫḫē-erība	Date (B.C.)
(1)	*RMA* 183A	=	*LAS* 328	? 672-02
(2)	*RMA* 256B	=	*RMA* 258	? 672-08
(3)	*RMA* 234A	=	*RMA* 237	671-03-26
(4)	*LAS* 34	=	*LAS* 59	671-07
(5)	*LAS* 57	=	*LAS* 58	? 671-08
(6)	*LAS* 41	=	*RMA* 274G	670-12-02
(7)	*RMA* 88	=	*RMA* 103	669-03-15
(8)	*LAS* 66	=	*LAS* 65	669-03-26
(9)	*LAS* 46	=	*LAS* 69+71	669-03-30
(10)	*LAS* 40	=	*LAS* 61	667-04-21
(11)	*RMA* 68	=	*RMA* 70	667-07-04
(12)	*LAS* 38	=	*LAS* 349	? 670-04-20
(13)	*RMA* 247I	=	*RMA* 274E	undatable
(14)		*LAS* 51		670-05-03
(15)		*LAS* 52		undatable
(16)		*LAS* 53		? 669-03-23
(17)		*LAS* 54		669-03-13
(18)		*LAS* 55+?43		undatable
(19)		*LAS* 56		undatable
(20)	*RMA* 91	? =	*RMA* 96	undatable

By their relationship to the king, the scholars can be divided into two groups: the "inner circle", and the "outer circle" of scholars.

The "inner circle" consists of 16 men:

* Nabû-zēru-lēšir, the Chief Scribe (*rab ṭupšarrī*) and Master (*ummânu*) of Esarhaddon, author of three letters to the king dealing with the substitute king ritual;

* Ištar-šumu-ēreš, son of the preceding, Chief Scribe and Master of Esarhaddon and Assurbanipal, and the author of altogether 72 letters and reports to the king dealing mainly with astrological and hemerological matters and omen interpretation at large;

* Balasî, title unknown, teacher (*ummânu*) of the crown prince Assurbanipal (*LAS* 34), and author of 47 letters and reports dealing with astrology, hemerology and omen interpretation at large;

* Nabû-aḫḫē-erība, contemporary and colleague of the preceding, author of 60 letters and reports largely paralleling and duplicating those of Balasî;

* Marduk-šumu-uṣur, the chief haruspex (*rab bārê*) of Esarhaddon and Assurbanipal, author of five official letters and one personal petition to the king;

* Marduk-šākin-šumi, the chief exorcist (*rab āšipī*) of Esarhaddon and Assurbanipal, author of 43 letters of medical and magical content;

* Adad-šumu-uṣur, the personal exorcist of Esarhaddon and chief [. . .] (*ADD* 448) of Assurbanipal, author of 48 letters and reports dealing with medicine (mostly the health of royal children), magic, astrology and hemerology, and two petitions to Assurbanipal;

* Urad-Gula, son of the preceding, deputy chief physician (*šaniu rab asê*) under Sennacherib, exorcist (*āšipu*) under Esarhaddon, author of 6 professional letters on exorcistic matters and one personal petition (*ABL* 1285);

* Nabû-nādin-šumi, exact position unknown (possibly deputy chief exorcist), author of 15 letters to the king almost exclusively dealing with apotropaic (*namburbi*) rituals;

* Nabû-nāṣir, exorcist, associate of Adad-šumu-uṣur, author of 12 medical letters almost exclusively dealing with the health of royal babies;

* Urad-Nanâ, the chief physician (*rab asê*) of Esarhaddon (and Assurbanipal?), author of 14 letters on the health of the royal family;

* Ikkāru, physician (rank unknown, predecessor of Urad-Nanâ?), author of five medical letters;

* Urad-Ea, the chief chanter (*galamāḫu*) of Esarhaddon and the chanter priest of the moon-god of Harran, author of seven short letters dealing with lamentation rites and three astrological reports;

* Nabû-zēru-iddina, son and successor of the preceding under Assurbanipal, author of two fragmentary letters;

* Akkullānu, astrologer (exact title unknown) and priest of Assur, author of 35 letters and reports dealing with astrological and cultic matters.

In addition. there are the 24 letters of Mār-Ištar, Esarhaddon's special ("eye and ear") agent in Babylonia. Despite his area of activity, this man must be regarded as an extension of the "inner circle", for many of his letters deal with astrological and magical matters also forming the subject of the "inner circle" correspondence. Note the title "scribe" accorded to him in *ADD* 769 (App. N 27).

This survey suffices to make it clear that the "inner circle" was made up of high-ranking men. Eight of them bear titles showing them to be the supreme scholars of the realm in their special disciplines; two of them were important enough to deserve a place in the Assyrian king lsit (see Appendix N 1). The rest were certainly no small fish either. *Mār-Ištar* was the key figure in the reorganization of the cultic services and the rebuilding of the destroyed temple areas of Babylon, Borsippa, Akkad, Uruk and other Babylonian cities under Esarhaddon. *Akkullānu* held the extremely influential position of the "temple enterer" in the temple of Assur, empowering him to supervise the celebration of national festivals, check the conduct of the Assur clergy and to impose loyalty oaths on other nations (App. N 56). *Balasî* was the teacher of the crown prince Assurbanipal and evidently a personal friend and favorite of the king himself (see *LAS* 34+49 and 51). His colleague and close associate *Nabû-aḫḫē-erība* enjoyed a similar position (cf. *LAS* 59 and 349); *RMA* 55 (see under *LAS* 12) shows that he was in no way considered inferior to the mighty chief scribe Ištar-šumu-ēreš. The exorcist and former deputy chief physician *Urad-Gula* enjoyed special privileges (cf. *ABL* 1285) as the son of the venerable Adad-šumu-uṣur, who as the personal exorcist and close confidant of Esarhaddon ranked even higher at court than the chief exorcist Marduk-šākin-šumi (cf. under *LAS* 164). Nothing certain is known about the titles of the remaining three men. But it should be noted that in the introductory section of *LAS* 222, the name of *Nabû-nāṣir* p r e c e d e s that of the chief physician Urad-Nanâ – a convention evidently connoting superiority in rank. The physician *Ikkāru* may well have been the predecessor of Urad-Nanâ in the office of the chief physician: in *LAS* 260, he appears in charge of other physicians, and none of his letters appear to postdate 672 (while no letters of Urad-Nanâ appear to antedate 671). Clearly, then, a prominent position must be postulated for *Nabû-nādin-šumi* as well, considering the number of his letters and the frequency in which he his mentioned in the letters of his colleagues (App. N 64, 70-72), even though his exact status cannot be determined as yet.

What all this amounts to imply is that even though the Assyrian court housed a great many of scholarly experts specializing in the same disciplines as the "inner circle", and even though many more similar experts were scattered all around the empire, only very few select "wise men" could be engaged in any sort of "regular" correspondence with the king. And while lesser scholars could occasionally write a letter to the king or occasionally even receive a letter from the king, such exchange of letters was bound to remain highly restricted and exceptional. Revealingly, only *one* letter from the deputy chief physician Bānî is extant, and there are *no letters at all* from the deputy chief scribe

Nabû-mušēṣi, even though that man has left us as many as 17 *reports*. The situation is thus exactly parallel to that observable in the extant correspondence of King Sargon II: it consists virtually exclusively of letters exchanged between the king and his grandees (provincial governors and other officials of comparable or superior rank), with only occasional letters from deputy governors and other lower level officials.

As to be expected, the same situation also holds for the "outer circle" component of the *LAS* correspondence: the letters written by scholars not resident in Nineveh. They appear all to originate either with whole *teams* of scholars or the foremen of such scholar teams (*rab eširti*). The "outer circle" correspondence differs from its "inner circle" counterpart in that it was clearly more sporadic and ephemeral in nature, and probably largely owed its existence to royal orders seeking to confirm or calibrate inconclusive lunar (and solar) observations made at the capital (cf. *LAS* 119 and 323, also *RMA* 274). But the important thing is that here too only high-ranking scholars (or corporate bodies of scholars) appear as the king's correspondents.

That the king would engage in correspondence only with a limited number of high-ranking or otherwise important persons may seem the most natural and self-evident thing on the earth, but it is important to make the point formally since the recognition of the fact has great practical relevance. As many as 150 letters (a full 40%) of the *LAS* corpus lack the name of the sender. Since, as pointed out above, all but one letters of the corpus appear to date from a limited period of time of about 30 years (674-648), the bulk coming from a still more limited period (672-669), most if not all of the 150 letters with lost sender name should have been authored by the same limited array of prominent scholars who authored the rest of the correspondence. This conclusion has been fully validated by a detailed distinctive-feature analysis of the corpus. 82% of the letters lacking indication of authorship can be assigned to known writers on the basis of such an analysis, mostly with absolute certainty (see App. M 2). The fact that 27 letters still remain unassigned (see App. M 3) does not imply that their writers are to be sought outside the known roster of senders but is largely due to the fragmentary condition of the relevant texts and/or their lack of distinctive features preventing an even tentative assignation. (The reliability of the distinctive feature analysis in the identification of senders has since the appearance of Pt. I been strikingly confirmed not only by joins such as *LAS* 34 + 49, 69 + 71, and 218 + 221, but also by the joins 110 + 300 and 129 + 339, which were only discovered after a refined analysis of the relevant fragments. Note also the proportionally good match between the number of letters assigned to a given sender and the size of his assured letter dossier, shown in the right-hand columns of App. M 2).

A closer look at the "inner circle" reveals an interesting thing about this group of prominent scholars. In the brief survey of the "circle" given above attention was already drawn to three cases of father-son-relationship existing between the members of the circle (1. Nabû-zēru-lēšir, chief scribe – son: Ištar-šumu-ēreš, chief scribe; 2. Adad-šumu-uṣur, king's exorcist – son: Urad-Gula, deputy chief physician/exorcist; 3. Urad-Ea, chief chanter – son: Nabû-zēru-iddina, chief chanter). Actually, there are even more family links within the circle. From *ABL* 1285, a letter written by Urad-Gula but too late identified as such to be included in the present edition, it appears that the writer's father, that is Adad-šumu-uṣur, was a brother of Nabû-zēru-lēšir, the chief scribe just mentioned (see App. N 73; a thorough re-edition of *ABL* 1285 is in preparation by the present writer). Accordingly, Urad-Gula was a cousin of Ištar-šumu-ēreš, the next-to-be chief scribe. Since Adad-šumu-uṣur is (from a colophon recently published by H. Hunger) known to have been the son of the eminent scribe Nabû-zuqup-kēnu (see App. N 2), who himself was a descendant of Assurnasirpal II's chief scribe Gabbi-ilāni-ēreš, four members of the "inner circle" (i.e., more than 25% of it) can be shown to belong to the same prestigious family line with continuous scribal tradition extending over a period of 250 years at least and probably longer. A similar prestigious family line (with different scholarly specialization) is also attested for the chief chanter Urad-Ea, and probably for the other eminent scholars as well, even though the relevant evidence is as yet lacking.

The recognition of the family ties between the members of the "inner circle" opens interesting perspectives. It seems evident, in the first place, that the important court offices of scholarly advisors were in the hands of a few privileged families, a veritable scholarly "mafia", which monopolized these offices from generation to generation.

This does not mean that the position of the father would have been automatically inherited by the son, as in the cases of Ištar-šumu-ēreš and Nabû-zēru-iddina; the fact that Ištar-šumu-ēreš's grandfather (cf. App. N 9) Nabû-zuqup-kēnu did not hold the office of the chief scribe, as well as the fate of Urad-Gula (see *LAS* 120-121 and *ABL* 1285), shows that the appointments to the office were made by the king, who in making his choice presumably took into consideration the individual qualifications of the available candidates (cf. *LAS* 280 r25 ff, 309 r.1 ff., 310:5' ff., *ABL* 565, etc.). But being the son of an office-holder certainly greatly helped in the appointment process (cf. simply the passages just referred to), and a son's failure to regain his father's position must have been rather exceptional and regarded as a major catastrophe (cf. *LAS* 121 r14 ff. and discussion sub *LAS* 120). And if such a thing happened, the elect would in any case have had to come from some other old family with scholarly traditions.

In the second place, the stemma of the Adad-šumu-uṣur family as reconstructed in Chart 3 reveals an interesting fact about the scholarly orientation of this family. As can be seen, starting with Nabû-zuqup-kēnu the family's focus in scholarly specialization (which until then seems to have been centered on *ṭupšarrūtu*) was split between *āšipūtu* and *ṭupšarrūtu*. Adad-šumu-uṣur, who started his career as a *ṭupšarru*, occupied at the court of Esarhaddon the post of the king's personal *āšipu*, while his brother perpetuated the family tradition as the chief *ṭupšarru*. In the next generation, the split is carried further. Adad-šumu-uṣur's son Urad-Gula acquires the skills of not only an *āšipu* but also those of the closely related discipline of *asûtu*; of Nabû-zēru-lēšir's two sons, one (Ištar-šumu-ēreš) continues the father's speciality (*ṭupšarrūtu*), the other (Šumāju) becomes an exorcist. The reason for this broadening of professional competence probably lies in the intense competition and struggle for court positions between rivalling scholarly families. Since the available positions were limited in number and only open for the very best, young scholars not able to succeed their fathers but aspiring for a position at the court were literally forced to strive for maximum scholarly excellence (*ummânūtu*). This situation naturally encouraged "interdisciplinary" study, reading beyond one's primary field of specialization and/or eventually specializing in a discipline different from that of the father. Such an interdisciplinary competence is observable not only with the scholars already mentioned but also other writers of the *LAS* correspondence (note the chanter Urad-Ea writing astrological reports [App. Q 5.1], Marduk-šākin-šumi quoting from hemerological literature [*LAS* 196 r.5-10], etc.), and no doubt was regarded as an essential requirement of true scholarship.

Echoes of rivalry, competition and struggle for jobs are a priori not likely to be found in the *LAS* correspondence, with its writers safely anchored in the highest positions available, but they are all the same there. Promoted by the king, the court scholars owed everything they possessed (fame, respect, privileges, even their living) to him, and were (at least theoretically) in constant danger of losing everything, should the royal favour for some reason turn against them. This basic insecurity is given concrete expression in the concluding part of *LAS* 41: "The king my lord must have already discharged me! In anxiety and fear, I have nothing to report"; cf. also *LAS* 241 and the discussion sub *LAS* 51. And it is more indirectly yet unmistakably manifested in the general mental disposition that permeates and tinges the entire correspondence: humbleness and servile fear towards the monarch, and arrogance, contempt and hatred towards colleagues and other persons fealt as a potential threat to one's own position. For the former no examples need to be quoted, for the latter, cf. *LAS* 36 r.11 ff, 121 r.14 ff, 224, 264, and especially the ironical and sarcastic comments in *LAS* 12 r.3 ff and 65:8 ff and r.19 ff.

Against this background, it is difficult to understand the frequently expressed and apparently wide-spread notion of the role of the scholars in the Sargonid court (especially at the time of Esarhaddon), viz, that they would have been or somehow become a sombre and powerful background force behind the king shrewdly directing and manipulating the political and military decisions of the latter by the authority of the arcane disciplines they represented (cf. e.g. Olmstead, History of Assyria [1923] 347; von Soden, *Herrscher* [1964] 125, Landsberger, *Bischof* [1965] 14[8]; Labat, *Fischer Weltgeschichte* 4 [1967] 81). A critical scrutiny of the evidence shows that such a view is altogether untenable. There is, of course, nothing to deny the fact that since many of the scholars (the "scribes" and haruspices) were specifically attached to the king's service to prognosticate the future, they naturally came to play an important role in the political decision-making process. However, it is important to realize the overwhelmingly passive and "academic" nature of their advisory role. As shown in detail in Appendix P, virtually all letters of the *LAS* corpus are to

Chart 3: THE STEMMA OF THE ADAD-ŠUMU-UṢUR FAMILY

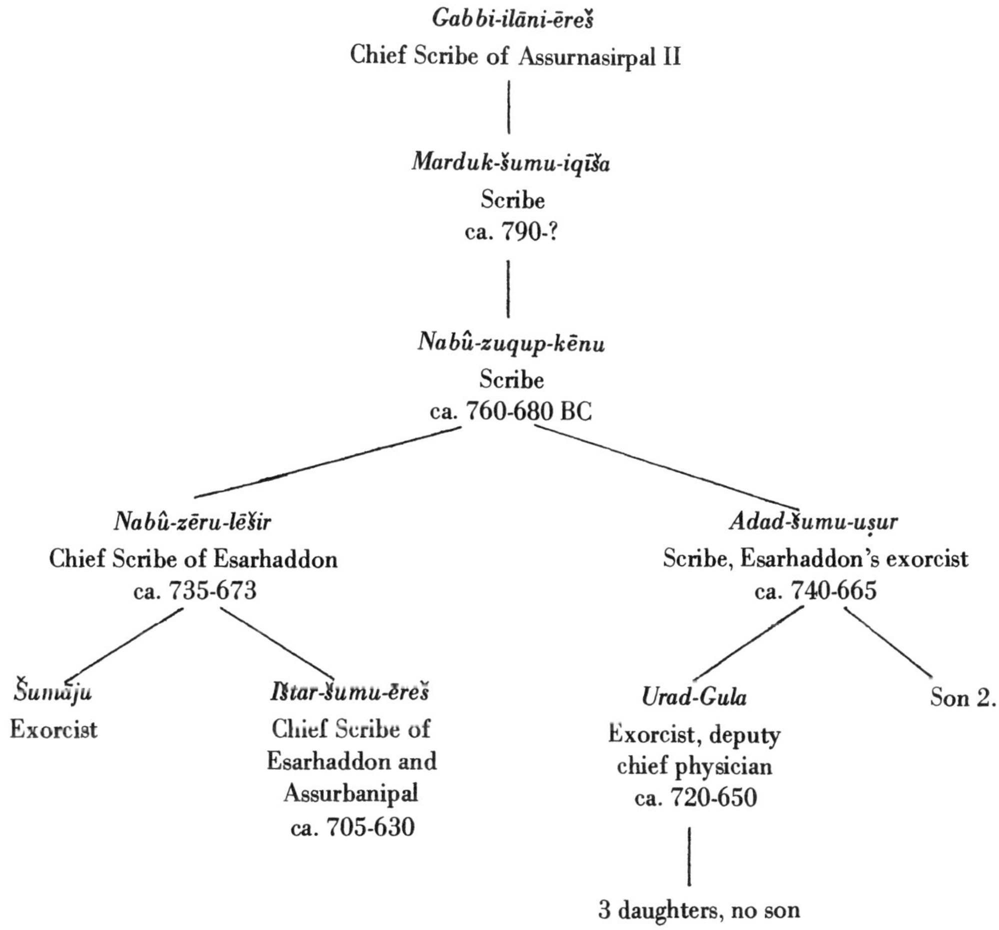

be understood as *responses to external pressure exerted on the scholars either by the king* (demanding answers to specific questions) *or by circumstances* (omens, cases of illness, etc., necessitating prompt professional action). Whichever the case, the content and direction of the scholar's answer was in all its essential features dictated by the relevant scholarly literature, not by his personal views or ambitions. In other words, the scholar's role was basically that of an automate or a robot anabling the ruler to protect his person and to further his personal desires (*ṣibūtu*) with the help of the Mesopotamian "wisdom". Any attempt to deviate from this basic role would have been harshly dealt with by the king.

This does not mean that high-ranking scholars would not have tried their best to influence the king to their own advantage. The letters are simply too full of flatteries (see on *LAS* 229) and little scholarly tricks designed to keep the king happy and in good mood (see, e.g. *LAS* 38 and 45) to make one believe this. But it is also evident that all this little cunning and scheming was not at all aimed at influencing or dictating the imperial policies but simply at furthering the writers' material well-being and security. *The happier and less worried the king*, the better for his servants. It should be remembered that the latter were basically very much afraid of their lord, who is often portrayed as a quick-tempered "image of Marduk" (cf. notes on *LAS* 51:7f. and 125:18f., also 247:19ff.). For this reason, all the professional advices and suggestions for action the scholars felt obliged to make are always couched in the most cautious and respectful terms, and accompanied by remarks such as "the king my lord may act as he pleases / as it is acceptable to him", "if the king my lord says so", "if it is acceptable to the king", "what could I say" (*LAS* 199:14) or "what can I say, an old man who has no reason" (143 r2 ff.). Note especially *LAS* 3:8ff. ("the 20th, 22nd and

25th days are auspicious for taking the oath (but) we shall arrange it *whenever* the king my lord orders"; similarly 72 r5f) and the commentary on *LAS* 166 r5ff. It may well be that these demonstrations of humility were deliberate and calculating. But they serve to underline the social chasm that separated the allegedly Machiavellian circle of scholars from the person of the king.

It should also be noted that despite the existence of the "inner circle", there probably was relatively little direct contact between the scholars and the king. There is every reason to believe that even though the former were attached to the king's service, they did not permanently reside in the palace area but in their own houses situated in downtown Nineveh (cf. *LAS* 2, 147:9ff, 248 r5ff), which they would only occasionally leave for visits to the palace (the term for this is *erābu* "to enter (the king's audience)", cf. *LAS* 39 r5, 185 r27, 246 r13, 252 r19, 349 r12) or wherever the king would decide to send them. Cf. *LAS* 19, 29, 181, 186, 206, 211, 217, 226, 232, 249, 271, 272, 306 and 335, written during or after missions to Assur, Babylonia, Egypt(?), Calah, Tarbisu, Sippar(?), Calah, Akkad, Kurbail, Harran, Tarbiṣu and Arbela respectively, and *LAS* 125 r7ff 142, 147, 158, 247 r27f and 250 r8ff etc., – referring to patient calls outside the palace area. Regular presence at the royal audience (*mazzāz-pānūtu*) appears to have been a privilege the inner circle was entitled to (cf. *LAS* 2, 34, 59, 121, 122 and 125 etc.), but the possibility of their forming a clicque constantly present in the palace and exerting a permanent influence upon the king is absolutely out of the question.

Thus the relationship between the king and the scholars, as evidenced in the *LAS* correspondence, can be most appropriately defined as one between master and servants – the very way in which it is defined by the scholars themselves at the beginning of every single letter of the correspondence. However, it is good to remember, at the same time, that the same relationship also held between the king and the most potent men of the empire, the provincial governors and other holders of top military and administrative offices. They addressed the king in the same way in their letters, and were as dependent on the whimsies of their autocratic lord. Yet, as long as they could bask in the sunshine of the royal favour, they were mighty and important men indeed – and so were the top scholars. The importance of their position can be gauged from the mention of the chief scribe alongside the king in king lists (App. N 1), or from the well-known passage in the inscriptions of Sargon II where the scholars of Babylon head the delegation welcoming Sargon as the new king of Babylon (Lie *Sg.* 55:371f.), or from the "Vassal-treaties" of Esarhaddon where scholars are listed after the royal family and provincial governors as potential king-makers (*VTE* 79). Cf. also the story of Ahiqar. And it is easy to understand how and why they were so important. For one thing, the top scholars of the realm epitomized Mesopotamian wisdom and enjoyed great respect as the linear followers of the legendary seven sages of the period before the Flood, and their famous historical predecessors (cf., e.g., W.G. Lambert, "Ancestors, authors and canonicity", *JCS* 11 [1957], 1 ff.). Secondly, and certainly more importantly, their services were simply indispensable to the king. They provided the royal family with medical care (physicians and exorcists), protection against witchcraft, malicious demons, and angry gods (exorcists and chanters), and a possibility to lift the veil of future when important issues were at stake (haruspices) or when curious portents were observed (scribes). And of course, without the scribes there would have been no royal libraries, no royal inscriptions, no regulation of the lunar calendar, no knowledge of the auspiciousness of days and months for royal enterprises.

For these reasons, the king must have deeply respected his scholarly advisors, even if he did not always adequately remunerate them for their services. And the master-servant relationship existing between him and the scholars did not hinder a certain degree of intimacy and a sort of affection developing between the two parties. Cf., on the one hand, the touching and/or affectionate words of the king collected in App. P 5.4-5, and on the other hand letters like *LAS* 51 and 143, showing that the scholars were capable of feeling a true concern over the health of their lord. These occasional touches of human feelings should not, however, obscure the fact that in the main the tone of the letters is matter-of-fact.

In their professional work the *LAS* scholars appear to have been (in the highest degree of the term's implication) "men versed in the Scriptures". Everything in their correspondence makes it patently clear that their learning, way of thinking and professional competence were based on and moulded by an intensive study of the "Scriptures", the professional lore accumulated by earlier generations of scholars. This lore, which consisted of innumerable disconnected observations haphazardly noted nown over the centuries, had gradually grown into a coherent system of interpreting and coping with the world conceived as a place dominated by gods and demons. Much of it would have to be dismissed today as unscientific, but there is no question that the "Scriptures" were regarded by our scholars and their contemporaries as the ultimate source of wisdom, the validity of which was never seriously questioned. It is important to stress this basic fact, as it implies that any attempt to evaluate the technical contents of the letters without recourse to the "Scriptures" is likely to lead to grossly incorrect results. See, for a warning example, the commentary on the "dental diagnosis" in *LAS* 216.

As to be expected, the letters bear witness not only of an extensive application of the scholarly lore into praxis but also of its teaching and transmission to future generations (cf. *LAS* 34, 85, 116, 319, 320, 331 and 358). But it would be a mistake to infer from what has been just said that the *LAS* scholars were merely blindly accepting and putting into practical use the teachings and recognitions of their forefathers. They were also actively involved in the process of adding to and further developing the scientific knowledge of their time. Because of the nature of the *LAS* correspondence, this aspect of their scholarly activity is easily overlooked, but it emerges clearly from an analysis of the astrological letters of the corpus and the subsequent development of astronomy. Much of the efforts of the contemporary astrologers appears to have been directed towards predicting astronomical phenomena (particularly eclipses of the moon and the sun, and planetary phases) in advance, evidently with an eye to capitalize on the king's desire to attach to his service the best prognosticators available. Many of these predictions can be shown to have been based on really primitive methods directly derived from the "Scriptures" (cf., e.g., *RMA* 30 r6-7, based on the omen quoted ibid. Obv.8), but many turn out to involve more sophisticated methods not to be found in the "Scriptures" (knowledge of planetary and lunar periods, understanding of the variations in lunar velocity and latitude etc.); see commentaries on *LAS* 41-42, 53 and 62-66, and cf. *RMA* 155, 33, 272 and especially 274). The astronomical knowledge making such predictions possible can only have been acquired through systematic/intensive study and recording of astronomical phenomena (cf. discussion sub *LAS* 105). Systematic collection of observational data had already been explicitly prescribed for practicing astrologers in the second tablet of the astronomical treatise Mul Apin dating from the end of the second millennium B.C.; and there can be little doubt that the drive for further research was greatly intensified in the Sargonid period owing to the vehement scholarly competition discussed above. This development continued under the Neo-Babylonian kings, and eventually led to the birth of mathematical astronomy at the turn of the 5th century.

Considered as a whole, the *LAS* corpus can thus without exaggeration be said to illuminate virtually every aspect of the activities of ancient Mesopotamian scholars: their family background and social position, their schooling, professional work and research activities, their role at the royal court, political influence and relation to the king, and last but not least, even their life and personality. All these matters are naturally also elucidated by other sources (cf. App. N and Q, not to speak of the vast corpus of Mesopotamian scientific texts and references to scholars in texts not included in the two appendices just mentioned), but by far not in a comparable variety and abundance in detail. It is just this variety and abundance of detail information, the countless problems it poses, and the possibility to resurrect some of the scholars as living individuals that makes this corpus such an exciting and truly challenging object of study. In containing a lot of information directly taken from the Mesopotamian scholarly lore and at the same time focusing attention to its practical application and to the men involved in the creation of that lore, these letters form a bridge between the monotonous scientific texts and the real life. The letters in App. Q show that the emerging picture can in its main features be regarded as valid for Mesopotamia at large, not just for the Sargonid period. Considering the fact that the roots of modern science are largely to be sought in ancient Mesopotamia, the value of the corpus for the history of sciences hardly needs stressing.

EXCURSUS: THE SUBSTITUTE KING RITUAL

By the *substitute king ritual* is understood an arrangement in which, briefly put, the ruling king temporarily abdicates his throne for a surrogate who, having ruled his predetermined period, is put to death, after which the king reascends his throne and continues ruling as if nothing had happened. This rite forms the subject of one of the most familiar tales in the Arabian Nights, and from incidental and garbled statements made by ancient historiographers (see below, p. XXIX ff) is has long been known (or suspected) that the ritual was from time to time actually practiced in ancient oriental courts. The historicity of these more or less anecdotal reminiscences was put beyond all doubt by the discovery of the Nineveh letter archives, which contain numerous references to a substitute king (*šar pūḫi*) ruling in the king's place, and above all by the publication in 1957 and 1967 of two sets of ritual texts (Akkadian and Hittite) showing that the rite was known and practiced all over the ancient Near East, not just in Sargonid Assyria. These texts revealed many previously unknown facts about the ritual and its function, but they also presented many problems, some of which have proved very difficult to solve. Despite much discussion (see Bibliography under Bottéro 1978, Böhl 1953, Dhorme 1941, Kümmel 1967, Labat 1946, Lambert 1957/8 and 1959/60, Landsberger 1965, Parpola 1971, Schott 1941/2, von Soden 1936 and 1956), there still exists much unclarity about the exact circumstances calling for the performance of the ritual, about the frequency at which it was performed, and – since the ritual instructions are badly broken – even about the general course of the ritual. This underlines the importance of a thorough and systematic analysis of the information provided by the *LAS* corpus – for the 30 letters of the corpus pertaining to the ritual (*LAS* 25-28, 30-32, 77, 134-139, 166-67, 179, 185, 205, 232, 235-6, 249, 257, 278-80, 292, 298-99, 317 and 334) not only are (along with *ABL* 735 and a few administrative documents from Calah, see below, p. XXVII) the only as yet available *direct* documentation of the performance of the ritual; they also contain a wealth of information furnishing, when properly organized, an answer to all the puzzles it initially presents.

The individual *šar pūḫi* letters are thoroughly analyzed and discussed in the commentary. The present chapter provides, by way of a synthesis, a discussion of the ritual as a whole, and a catalogue of all attested instances of its performance – including ones recorded in non-cuneiform sources. The numbers in square brackets in the following discussion refer to entries in this catalogue. No systematic stand is taken on the research hitherto done (cf. above), which is taken as the point of departure to the present study.

The ritual: discription and discussion

The need for a substitute king was created by evil omens, specifically *eclipses*, portending the death of the king. This is made quite clear by the ritual tablet [3], which defines the cause of the ritual as "the evil portent of evil and unlucky signs, eclipses of the moon, the sun, Jupiter, Venus, Mercury and Saturn, [and Mars]" (A 9-13). In fact, every single performance of the ritual featured in the *LAS* correspondence can be traced back to an eclipse, either a lunar or [11, 13] a solar one. And while no "planetary eclipses" (i.e., occultations of planets behind the moon) can as yet be shown to have triggered the ritual, there is no reason to doubt that they may occasionally have done so (cf. discussion sub *LAS* 14).

Not every eclipse, however, called for the performance of the ritual. One important restriction derived from an omen included in Tablet XX of *Enūma Anu Enlil*:

> "If an eclipse (of the moon) takes place and the planet Jupiter is present in that eclipse, the king is safe; a noble dignitary will die in his stead."
>
> (*ACh* 2 Spl. 29:14)

This omen implied, as pointed out in three messages to the king where it is quoted (*LAS* 298, *ABL* 1006 and *RMA* 272), that there was no need to enthrone a substitute if Jupiter had been visible during the eclipse since the god's presence indicated that the sign did not, as usual, concern the king but one of his magnates. A similar restriction also applied to solar eclipses:

> "If an eclipse (of the sun) takes place and Venus and Jupiter are visible, the king is safe, but the country will be attacked by an enemy."
>
> (*ACh* Šamaš 8:6, see App. F 4.5)

A further restriction resulted from the analysis of the eclipses themselves. While every eclipse (excepting the cases just mentioned) in principle signified that a powerful king was to die (cf., e.g., *ACh* Spl. 22 ii 4', "If the moon is eclipsed on the 14th of Simānu, a famous king will die", and ibid. iii 12', "If an eclipse occurs from the 1st to the 30th of Du'ūzu, . . . a great king will die"), the identity of the king and the land in question had in each case to be established separately by taking into consideration the month, day, and hour of the eclipse, the area of the moon's or the sun's disc affected by the eclipse, and the direction in which the eclipse shifted (see App. F 4). Of overriding importance was the message sent by the eclipsed disc, which was divided into four quadrants, each corresponding to a specific quarter of the world (Amurru, Elam, Subartu, Akkad); the other factors were of subordinate interest. The darkening of a quadrant implied a threat to the relevant country. Thus, a total eclipse spelled danger to all kings of the world, while e.g. an eclipse touching only the upper part of the moon or the sun signified that a king of the West (Amurru) was going to die. The kings of Assyria were in danger whenever the lowermost quadrant (Subartu/Assyria) was eclipsed. For Esarhaddon, who was the king of both Assyria and Babylonia, even eclipses with darkened right-hand quadrant (Akkad/Babylonia) posed a mortal danger.

Accordingly, the need for a substitute king theoretically arouse in Assyria whenever the portion of the lunar or solar disc representing Subartu (in the case of Esarhaddon: Subartu *and* Akkad) was eclipsed and the planet Jupiter was not simultaneously visible. How this theory was converted into practice can be seen from the following analysis of 16 consecutive eclipses in the reigns of Esarhaddon and Assurbanipal:

Eclipse	Quadrants eclipsed	Visibility of Jupiter	Substitute king required (and attested)
680 Jul 11 /Duz 14	Amurru	–	no
679 Jun 1 / Sim 14	Subartu	–	yes
679 Jun 17 (Sun)	ALL	–	yes (*LAS* 30f.?)
678 May 22 / Sim 14	ALL	+	NO (*ABL* 1006, *RMA* 270)
677 Nov 3 / Ara 14	Subartu + Elam	–	yes (*LAS* 136:12)
674 Sep 3 / Ulu 15	ALL	–	yes (*LAS* 30f.?)
673 Feb 27 / Add 14	Elam + Amurru	–	NO (*RMA* 272B)
671 Jul 2 / Duz 14	ALL	–	yes (*LAS* 26f., 249, 278, 292)
671 Dec 27 / Kan 15	ALL		yes (*LAS* 185, 232, 270f., 317)
670 Dec 17 / Kis 15	Amurru	–	NO (*LAS* 41, 62, 164, 173ff.)
669 May 27 (Sun)	Subartu + Amurru	–	yes (*LAS* 28, 104)
669 June 10 / Sim 14	Subartu	–	yes (*LAS* 25, 77, 234f., 257)
667 Apr 21 / Nis 16	ALL	+	NO (*LAS* 40, 61)
667 Oct 15 / Taš 14	ALL	+	NO (*RMA* 272A, 273)
666 Apr 10 / Nis 15	Subartu + Akkad	+	no (but enthroned by error! See *LAS* 298)
666 Oct 4 / Taš 14	Amurru + Akkad	–	no

As can be seen, of these 16 eclipses, eight (exactly one half) called for the enthronement of a substitute king in Assyria. In all these cases (insofar as our evidence goes), a substitute was actually enthroned. Conversely, excepting one case explicitly labelled a mistake (*LAS* 298), eclipses interpreted as harmless according to the above principles never triggered the ritual. This veritably perfect fit between theory and praxis proves that the factors considered really played the central role in deciding whether the king needed a substitute or not.

As soon as the need for a substitute had been established, the king was notified. In *LAS* 185 [10] and 134 [9], this was done by the chief exorcist alone; in *LAS* 28 [11] and 31 [7], by a group of several high-ranking scholars, including the chief exorcist, the chief scribe and the chief chanter. The latter probably was the normal practice (cf. [15]). Note that *LAS* 185 represents a special case, in which the suggestion to enthrone a substitute was exceptionally presented to the king already *before* the eclipse had actually taken place. Normally the need for the substitute could only be determined *post eventum*. In any case, the idea of enthroning a substitute never came from the king himself but from his counselors, even in the abnormal case of [12] (see discussion sub *LAS* 298). And while the king was formally given the option to decide whether the ritual be performed or not (cf. *LAS* 185 r.17), it was surely taken for granted that the answer was always in the affirmative (cf. [15]!).

Having got the go-ahead signal, the chief exorcist picked up a suitable substitute – a prisoner of war [4], a prisoner [15], a criminal condemned to death [16], a political enemy of the king [10], a gardener [1] or a simpleton (*LAS* 280 r.13ff) – in a word, a person whose life did not matter much or who would have deserved death anyway. The man was taken to the palace (*LAS* 279:7, [6]), treated with wine, washed and anointed, clad in the king's robes, furnished with the diadem and other royal insignia, and eventually seated on the royal throne ([1, 15-16, 19]; cf. *LAS* 134 and Ritual Tablet, [3], B 5-6, and see note on *LAS* 185 r.18). A "girl" (*LAS* 139) or "virgin" (Ritual Tablet, Col. A 20) was at the same time seated at his side as his "queen" (cf. [4]and *LAS* 30 and 280), and a statuette was presented as a substitute to the Netherworld gods [4].

At this moment, the substitute and the real king formally reversed their roles. The changed status of the latter is reflected in the fact that after the enthronement of the substitute, he was no more to be addressed as "king" [4] but as "Peasant" or "Farmer" (LÚ.ENGAR, cf. App. L 1 and 6) or simply as "my lord" (*LAS* 26-28). And while relevant evidence is lacking, it seems reasonable to assume that he did not wear any external marks of kingship or go near the throne as long as the substitute was occupying it, and otherwise, too, kept a low profile. It goes without saying, of course, that this reversal of the roles was only symbolic. In the eyes of his aides, the king was still very much the real king, as indicated by several letters (*LAS* 134-136, 249, 278-79 and 292) written while a substitute king was on the throne but nevertheless (inadvertently) addressed to the *king*, not the "farmer".

That the "reversal of roles" was only partial is also indicated by the fact that merely putting a substitute king on the throne was just not enough. One had also to make sure that the fate portended by the eclipse really was to befall him and not the real king, under whose rule the portent had occurred. To this end, the eclipse omens, along with other recently observed evil portents, were written down and (immediately after the enthronement) recited to the substitute king and his queen, who had to repeat them "in front" of Šamaš, the celestial judge (*LAS* 26, 30 and 279). The importance of this recitation ceremony (supervised by the chief scribe and complemented with exorcistic rites) is borne out by the fact that it had to be performed even in the (rare) case when the substitute had been enthroned *before* the eclipse had actually taken place (*LAS* 279). It made the substitute to "accept" from the officiating scholar the signs that had been originally sent to the king (*LAS* 30). To make sure that the omens would irrevocably remain affecting the substitute, the document where they were written was physically *attached* to his garments (*LAS* 26).

The ceremony just described reveals an important thing about the rationale behind the whole ritual. The danger looming before the king, as portended by the eclipse, was not just something that would befall *any* king [of Assyria]; it was the fate decreed by the gods to the ruling king *personally* as a punishment for his conduct as king. This fate could not be evaded by just suddenly abdicating the throne; it could only be evaded by having somebody to take upon himself the signs sent to the king, to accept responsibility for the king's sins, to be atoned only by death [4].Thus the function of the substitute king was basically that of a *scapegoat*, the innocent sufferer, not that of a puppet king. He had to be a king, because otherwise the scriptures would not come true, but otherwise the aspect of kingship was secondary. The whole ritual was functionally equivalent to the *pūḫi amēli* ("man's substitute") ritual described in commentary to *LAS* 140, in which a virgin kid was sacrificed to save a deadly sick patient. For the aspect of "sin" associated with the ritual cf. discussion sub *LAS* 35 (and 321).

The fate portended by the eclipse was to befall the king within 100 days from the occurrence of the eclipse (see note on *LAS* 135 r.6). Accordingly, the "reign" of the substitute king theoretically could, and in certain cases [9] certainly did last for a long as a hundred days. It could, however, and probably often did end considerably earlier. [10] certainly lasted less than a hundred days, [11] for 47 days, [12] for 20 days, the case planned in *LAS* 205 for only 7 days, and [19] (if the tradition is correct) for only 3 days. This variation in the duration of the ritual shows that the length of the substitute's reign was of no great importance in itself, and depended in each case on external circumstances. For instance, if other eclipses were liable to occur after the initial eclipse, as in the case of [11], the reign was certain to last for at least a month, so that the "evil" of all potential eclipses would befall the same substitute. If, on the other hand, no eclipses or other unlucky celestial portents were to be expected within a hundred days from the initial eclipse, there was no pressing need to extend the substitute's reign to its theoretical maximum; it was left to the king to decide whether he should "go to his fate" early or "complete his 100 days" (cf. *LAS* 135).

A special case was constituted by eclipses calling for repetition of the enthronement rites. According to *LAS* 298:11f. and 19ff., the substitute had to be enthroned in the residence of the ruler. For Esarhaddon (and other Assyrian kings who also held the kingship of Babylon), this meant that each time the lunar quadrant corresponding to Babylonia was eclipsed, a substitute had to be placed on the throne in Babylon as well. And if the quadrants of *both* Assyria and Babylonia were eclipsed, as actually happened three times in Esarhaddon's reign, the *same* substitute had to be enthroned *both* in Nineveh *and* in Babylon. Since the latter city was in ruins and thus not yet suited for a royal residence city in Esarhaddon's reign, the scene of the enthronement rites in Babylonia was in this reign the ancient capital of the Sargonic empire, Akkad (cf. *LAS* 134, 249, 279, 280, 298 and *CT* 53 206; it is uncertain whether Akkad was already the scene of the ritual in *LAS* 30). It seems that in the case of such double enthronements, the reign of the substitute was preferred to extend to its full length. *LAS* 26 indicates that the re-enthronement of the substitute in Akkad too place 50 days after the first enthronement in Nineveh, and *LAS* 292 shows that it ended after the full 100 days, so that the substitute came to spend exactly the same number of days both in Assyria and Babylonia. This appears to have been the case in *LAS* 30, too. On the other hand, in *LAS* 279 [10] the substitute was transferred to Akkad immediately after his enthronement in Nineveh. This may well have been due to the inflamed political situation in Assyria at the moment (cf. commentary on *LAS* 247, and also *LAS* 185r.25 and 280 r7ff.).

Until quite recently, nothing certain was known about the status of the substitute king during his "reign". The allegations of the Greek and Persian historians [16, 19] and the tradition of the Arabian Nights that he enjoyed full royal powers is now to some extent confirmed by the Nimrud wine lists published by Kinnier Wilson [5a, 6a]. These show that the substitute king had a sizeable entourage, about 1/10 of the size of the royal court, which included musicians, cooks, confectioners and other personnel designed to entertain the body and soul of the mock king. The lists also show that a sumptuous banquet (*naptunu*) was a regular feature of the substitute king's day, and that he was (at least in a certain measure) able to travel around. But they also reveal something that could not be a priori expected, viz. that as much as 1/3 of the substitute's "entourage" (about 100 men) consisted of bodyguards. Since the real king was certainly not in the least concerned about keeping his surrogate alive, this large number of armed attendants can only have served the function of keeping the surrogate under close surveillance, to prevent any attempt to perpetuate the example set by Illil-bāni [1]. It is hence clear that whatever "royal power" the substitute king possessed was only illusory; he seems to have been permitted to display a considerable amount of royal pomp in the public, and to enjoy a comfortable life, but the real power stayed with the king.

The king himself was certainly, to some extent, inconvenienced by the substitute's reign. Not only was he forced to maintain a costly mock court for the substitute king and to withdraw from public life, but he was also strongly adviced to stay within the confines of the palace and not to leave for the open country until the 100-day term of the eclipse was over (*LAS* 280 r.13, 299 r.7). The same injunction also concerned the other members of the royal family (cf. *LAS* 249). Otherwise, however, at least the private life of the monarch seems to have continued as usual. He kept receiving letters and even conducting administrative business with his officials (cf., e.g., *LAS* 278 and 292).

When the time came to terminate the ritual, both the substitute king and his queen were put to death. The ritual tablet [3] prescribes this explicitly ("The man given as substitute for the king will die, and the king and his country will be well", Col. A 6'f.), and all sources attesting to the performance of the ritual (with the understandable exception of [1]) imply the same. Exactly how the substitute met his death is unclear in most instances, and may have varied depending on the case. It is suggested in the commentary to *LAS* 280 that the method preferred in Sargonid Assyria was an overdosis of "soporific"; but [16] suggests that harsher methods were normally resorted to, and this may well have been the case. The expression "to go to one's fate" used when referring to the substitute king's death (*LAS* 135, 166, 249, 280 and 292) does not imply that the event itself was a matter which one preferred not to talk about directly, but rather that it was regarded as something decreed by fate and thus not to be avoided. The manner of death did not matter greatly.

The only extant description of the burial of a substitute king is provided by Mār-Ištar in *LAS* 280. This letter tells that the substitute was buried with royal honours. He and his queen were balsamized, bewailed and publicly displayed just like any other royal dead (cf. commentary on *LAS* 4 and 195), and their corpses were deposited in a mausoleum (KI.MAḪ) specifically built for the occasion. A tomb (lit. a "resting place", *maṣallu*) of the substitute king is also mentioned in *LAS* 32. It may be, of course, that the publicity given to the burial of the substitute in *LAS* 280 was exceptional and dictated by the political necessitites of the day (cf. ibid., r.8); but the possibility that the burial of the substitute king was a public event comparable to that of the king cannot be excluded for the present (however unlikely it may appear).

At the time of and following the burial many magical rites were performed. The ritual tablet (Col. A 18f.) prescribes the preparation of a figurine of "everything that is evil" (*ṣalam mimma lemnu*) which the substitute was supposed to take with himself to the Netherworld. *LAS* 280 states that "all kinds of exorcistic rites, including the elaborate rituals of *bīt rimki* and *bīt salā mê*" (actually prophylactic rites performed on the occasion of an eclipse) were performed at the burial. This may be exaggeration, but both the ritual tablet (Col. B 9ff.) and *LAS* 179 make it clear that the royal exorcists had a lot to do after the substitute's death. The palace of the king had to be surrounded with all kinds of prophylactic figurines designed to drive off evil forces threatening the king's peace of mind, and the king himself was to be cleansed immediately after the substitute king had "gone to his fate" (ritual tablet, col. B 8'; *LAS* 166:11;cf. also [15b]). We do not know how this purification was effected (it may have involved a shaving ritual, a bath in the Tigris, the donning of new garments, and a lot of incense burning, or a combination of all these cleansing methods), but it may be assumed that it was at least as much intended to clean the king's conscience as his (probably very little stained) body. One may speculate that the performance of the ritual, which indeed, as often emphasized (cf., e.g., von Soden, 1954, p. 125), came close to a human sacrifice, was bound to leave an undeletable impression on the king's psyche – cf. the testimony of the Alexander biographers, below [15].

Catalogue of sources and references to the ritual

1. Chronicle of Early Kings (Grayson, *TCS* 5 p. 155, No. 20), A 31-36: King Erra-imitti (of Isin, 1868-61) had the gardener Illil-bāni seated on his throne as a substitute statue (NU NÍG.SAG.GIL-e) and placed his royal tiara upon his head. Erra-imitti died in his palace while swallowing hot porridge. Illil-bāni who was sitting on the throne did not leave it, and was accepted as the king (1860-1837 BC).

For royal inscriptions of Illil-bāni see E. Solberger and J.R. Kupper, *IRSA* p. 179f.

1a. Agathias Scholasticus (died A.D. 582), *Hist.* II 25:

As the dynasty of the family of Semiramis ended with this Beleus, a certain man named Belētaras, who was a gardener and the keeper and overseer of the royal orchards, by accident plucked for himself the kingship and founded his own dynasty, as noted by Bion and Alexander Polyhistor (1st cent. B.C.)

It is generally agreed (cf. Labat, *RA* 40 124) that this anecdote is based on the chronicle entry just quoted, probably through the intermediary of Berossus. How the name Illil-bāni came to be replaced by Belētaras (= Bēl-ēṭer) remains a mystery.

2. The OB/MB epistolary formula *ana dinān bēlīja lullik* "I am ready to die as my lord's substitute" (see *CAD* D p. 148 and E. Salonen, *StOr* 37 103f.).

Possibly an indirect indication that the ritual was repeatedly practiced in the OB/MB period, cf. *LAS* 280:9 and r.19; cf. also below, [21].

3. W.G. Lambert, "A part of the ritual for the substitute king", *AfO* 18 (1957-58) 109-112; additions, *AfO* 19 (1959-60), 119.

The extant copies come from the library of Assurbanipal, but the text itself was certainly composed much earlier, probably in the Kassite period or under the Isin II dynasty (at the latest). The existence of the Hittite rituals [4] even suggests an OB prototype.

4. H.M. Kümmel, *Ersatzrituale für den hethitischen König* (StBoT 3 [1967]).

The texts published in this book date from about 1350-1250 B.C., see Kümmel p. 188. Their Babylonian origin is put beyond all doubt by the Akkadograms *PU-UḪ-ŠU/ŠÚ* and *LÚ PU-ḪI-ŠU* used for writing the Hittite word for the substitute king, as well by several other Mesopotamian features and ritual termini (e.g. *LÚ A-ŠI-PI* "exorcist" and *MÁŠ.ḪUL.DÚB.BA.ḪI.A* "scapegoat") occurring in the texts.

5. ND 3484 (D.J. Wiseman, *Iraq* 15 pl.15):

Administrative text mentioning a substitute king (MAN! *pu-ḫi*, coll. J.W. Kinnier Wilson, *CTN* 1 p. 111) in Rev. 11. The tablet, which comes from an archive dating to the reign of Adad-nērārī III, appears to contain an eponym date in r.9f.: *lim-mu* TA DI x / $^{\text{I.d}}$MAŠ-MAN-PAP "eponymy . . . Ninurta-šarru-uṣur". This date presents serious problems. Since there was no such eponym as Ninurta-šarru-usur in the reign of Adad-nērārī III or even his successor Shalmaneser IV, the sign MAŠ must be miscopied for either PA or ŠÚ, which would both yield acceptable eponyms, Nabû-šarru-uṣur (786 B.C.) and Marduk-šarru-uṣur (784 B.C.). The problem is that there were no eclipses calling for a substitute, and consequently no substitute king, in either year. Accordingly, the date possibly represents an *urki* date, and should be emended to read *lim-mu ša*! *ur*!-*ki*! or EGIR) $^{\text{I.d}}$PA/ŠÚ-MAN-PAP. This would date the text to either 785 or 783 B.C. However, there were no really suitable eclipse in these years either. In 785 B.C., there were only the solar eclipse of August 16, during which Jupiter was not visible (but which might not have been observed in Mesopotamia since it started only 15 minutes before sunset), and a lunar one on August 30, during which Jupiter was clearly visible all the time; and in 783 B.C., no eclipses at all took place. This state of affairs prevents a reliable dating of the document for the time being. In addition to the problems already mentioned, one has also to take into consideration the fact that the order of eponyms in the last years of Adad-nērārī III is far from assured (cf. Gurney, *AnSt* 3 21). Moreover, there is the possibility that all the eponym dates in question have to be lowered by a year; see below, [6]. In any case, the principles followed in the Sargonid period would only have called for the enthronement of a substitute in 782 and (possibly) in 785 BC.

5a. ND 10026 (J.M. Kinnier Wilson, *CTN* 1 p. 111 and pl. 45f.):

Text recording the issue of wine (from palace wine-cellars) in the eponym year of [ ]-šarru-uṣur (GEŠTIN^{MEŠ} KÚ ⌜*ša*⌝ [*lim-me* $^{\text{I.d}}$DN]-MAN-PAP, Obv.1). The reverse pertains to the substitute king (MAN *pu-ḫi*, lines 12, 14 and 16):

1 homer 7 seahs issued to (*pānāt*) the substitute king in the centre of the city, for two [. . . .];

5 homers 1 seah 5 liters in the city of Ubasê, issued to the substitute king, for two journeys;

14 homers 5 seahs in the Armoury (*ekal māšarti*);

in all 21 homers 3 seahs 5 liters for the substitute king.

The total amount of wine consumed is almost exactly 10 times more than the amount consumed by the court of the substitute king in a day according to [6a]. This may imply that the reign of the substitute in this case lasted for about ten days (of which only the first one was spent in the royal palace in the centre of Calah). If so, the reign in question cannot be identical with the one attested in [6] and [6a], and should accordingly (along with [5]) be dated to 785 B.C.

6. ND 3483 (D.J. Wiseman, *Iraq* 15 pl. 15):

Text recording issues of victuals to the (court of the) substitute king (LUGAL *pu-ḫi*, lines 3, 5, 7 and 14) from the 22nd to the 24th of Du'ūzu, eponym year of Ninurta-nāṣir ($^{\text{I.d}}$MAŠ!-PAP-*ir*), i.e. 783 BC. However, there were no eclipses in that year. On the other hand, a substitute king must have been enthroned on account of the total lunar eclipse of June 1 (Simanu 14/15), -781, during which Jupiter was not visible. This creates a problem for the Assyrian chronology. Are all the dates in the early 8th century to be lowered by one year?

6a. ND 6213 + 6227 (J.W. Kinnier Wilson, *CTN* 1 No. 33, pl. 14f.):

Text detailing rations of wine issued to the court of the substitute king (MAN *pu-ḫi*) on Ābu 22 (year not specified), in all 2 homers 1 seah and 8 liters, or about 10% of the daily wine consumption of the royal court. Accepting tentatively Kinnier Wilson's hypothesis that the standard daily ration of wine per person was one cup of ca. 0.2 l, the court of the substitute king would have comprised about 320 persons, most of whom (100) would have been bodyguards (*ša qurbūti*, Obv. 4), the rest consisting of lackeys, charioteers, musicians, bakers, confectioners, and the staff of the palace superintendent. One important magnate is mentioned in Col. ii 4 as recipient of wine rations: Ṣilli-Ištar, the eponym of 787 BC. This same man also figures in *CTN* 1 No. 4, dating from 780 BC. Since the date mentioned in the heading (Ābu 22) is only a month later than the one mentioned in ND 3483 [6], it is extremely likely that both texts pertain to the same substitute king. The reign of this substitute (which started on June 1 = Simānu 14/15, 782 BC) would accordingly have lasted for at least 67 days.

7. *LAS* 30-32:

Letters pertaining to a substitute king enthroned in Nineveh following the lunar eclipse of June 1, -678, or the lunar eclipse of September 3, -673, and re-enthroned 50 days later in Babylonia. See, in detail, commentary to *LAS* 30 and Addenda, p. 516.

8. *LAS* 136:12:

Passage referring to a substitute king enthroned on account of the lunar eclipse of November 3, -676.

9. *LAS* 26f., 249, 278 and 292:

Letters pertaining to a substitute king enthroned in Nineveh following the total lunar eclipse of July 2, -670, re-enthroned in Akkad 50 days later, and put to death after a 100-day reign.

Two other letters, *LAS* 134 and *CT* 53 206, may also pertain to this case. Cf. *CT* 53 206:3'f ([*ina* ^{URU}]URI [*e-ta-rab*] ⌜*i*⌝-*t*[*u*]-*ši-bi*) with *LAS* 279:10 (*a-na* ^{URU}*Ak-kad e-ta-rab it-tu-ši-ib*) and 298:8 (*ina* ŠÀ ^{URU}*Ak-ka-di it-tu-šib*), and note also the end of the letter, which may be restored: *šum-mu be-*[*lí i-qab-bi ina*] É.GAL [. . .] "if my lo[rd] (i.e., the farmer) [commands, . . . in] the palace . . ." (r4 f.). The rest of the letter deals with building activities in Akkad (^{URU}URI, Obv.5').

10. *LAS* 185, 279f., 232 and 317:

Letters pertaining to a substitute king enthroned in Nineveh slightly before the total lunar eclipse of December 27, -670, transferred to Akkad and re-enthroned there 5 days later, and put to death in January/February, 670 BC. The identity of this substitute king is known: Damqî, the son of the "bishop" of Akkad (*LAS* 280:24).

11. *LAS* 25, 28, 77, 135ff., 166f., 234f. and 257:

Letters pertaining to a substitute king enthroned in Nineveh on account of the solar eclipse of May 27, -668, and put to death after a "reign" of 47 days. This substitute king stayed in Nineveh for the whole of his reign.

12. *LAS* 298f. and 205:

Letters pertaining to a short (20-day) reign of a substitute king in the city of Akkad three months after the lunar eclipse of April 10, -665. This eclipse would not have called for a substitute king, for the planet Jupiter was visible during the eclipse. See commentary on *LAS* 298.

13. *LAS* 334: Letter addressed to the "farmer" in early May, 657 BC, and thus indirectly attesting to the enthronement of a substitute king on account of the solar eclipse of April 15, -656.

14. Herodotus, *Hist.* VII 15 and 17:

Then Xerxes, greatly frightened at the vision, sprang from his coach, and sent a messenger to call Artabanus, who came at the summons, when Xerxes spoke to him in these words: "Artabanus, . . . ever since I repented and changed my mind a dream has haunted me, which disapproves my intentions and has just gone from me with threats ["Know that unless you go forth to the war, this thing shall happen to you – as you are grown mighty and puissant in a short space, so likewise shall you within a little time be brought low indeed."]Now if this dream is sent to me from god, and if it is indeed his will that our troops should march against Greece, you too will have the same dream come to you and receive the same commands as myself. And this will be most sure to happen, I think, *if you put on the dress which I wear*, and then, after *taking your seat upon my throne*, lie down to sleep on my bed." . . .

Artabanus, thinking to show Xerxes that his words were nought, obeyed his orders. Having put on the garments which Xerxes was wont to wear, and, taken his seat upon the royal throne, he lay down to sleep upon the king's own bed. As he slept, there appeared to him the very same dream which had been seen by Xerxes; it came and stood over Artabanus, and said: "So you are the man who, as if concerned for Xerxes, seek to dissuade him from leading his armies against the Greeks! *But you shall not escape*, either now or in time to come, because you sought to prevent *that which is fated to happen.* As for Xerxes, it has been plainly told to himself what will befall him, if he refuses to perform my bidding." In such words the vision threatened him, and then endeavoured to burn out his eyes with red-hot irons . . .

This is properly speaking not an instance of the substitute king ritual, but it contains all the essential elements of it: A divine message threatening the king, the magical transfer of the king's person upon another individual by robing and enthronement rites, and the irrevocability of the fate decreed by the gods both for the king and the substitute. If Herodotus heard this anecdote from Persian informants, it would certainly imply that the substitute king ritual was regularly practiced in the court of Xerxes (486-465 BC).

15. Plutarch (d. A.D. 120), *Lives*, Alexander LXXIII-IV:

As he was upon his way to Babylon, Nearchus . . . came to tell him he had met with some *Chaldean diviners*, who had *warned* him against Alexander's going thither. Alexander, however, took no thought of it, and went on, and when he came near the walls of the place, he saw a great many crows fighting with one another, some of whom fell down just by him . . . Besides this, he was disturbed by many other prodigies . . . And one day after he had undressed himself to be anointed, and was playing at ball, just as they were going to bring his clothes again, the young men who played with him perceived a *man clad in the king's robes with a diadem upon his head, sitting silently upon his throne.* They asked him who he was, to which he gave no answer a good while, till at last, coming to himself, he told them his name was Dionysius, that he was of Messenia, that for some crime of which he was accused he was brought thither from the seaside, and had been kept long in prison, that Serapis appeared to him, had freed him from his chains, conducted him to that place, and *commanded him to put on the king's robe and diadem, and to sit where they found him, and to say nothing.* Alexander, when he heard this, *by the direction of his soothsayers, put the fellow to death,* but he lost his spirits, and grew diffident of the protection and assistence of the gods, and suspicious of his friends . . . When once Alexander had given way to fears of supernatural influence, his mind grew so disturbed and so easily alarmed that, if the least unusual or extraordinary thing happened, he thought it a prodigy or a presage, and *his court was thronged with diviners and priests whose business was to sacrifice and purify and foretell the future.*

This episode, which took place shortly before Alexander's death in June, 323 BC, was recognized to pertain to the substitute king rites by Th. Jacobsen, *ZA* 52 (1957) 139[115], and indubitably gives a reliable account of the events. As noted by Kümmel [4], it is also told by two other Greek historians:

15a. Arrian (died ca. AD 170), *Anabasis of Alexander*, VII 24:

But Alexander's own end was now near. Aristobulos [contemporary of Alexander] says that the following occurrence was a prognostication of what was about to happen. He was distributing the army which had come with Peucestas from Persia, . . . and becoming thirsty he retired from his seat and thus left the royal throne empty. On each side of the throne were couches with silver feet, upon which his personal Companions were sitting. A certain man of obscure condition (some say that he was even one of the men kept under guard without being in chains), seeing the throne and the couches empty, . . . walked through the line of eunuchs, ascended the throne, and sat down upon it. According to a Persian law, they did not make him rise from the throne, but rent their garments and beat their breasts and faces as if on account of a great wail.

When Alexander was informed of this, he ordered the man who had sat upon his throne to be put to the torture, with the view of discovering whether he had done this according to a plan concerted by a conspiracy. But the man confessed nothing, except that it came into his mind at the time to act thus. Even more for this reason the *diviners* explained that this occurrence boded no good to him.

15b. Diodorus Siculus (died ca. 20 B.C.), *Library of Universal History*, XVII 116; As the king was having himself anointed and the royal garment and the diadem were lying on a couch beside the throne, a native prisoner freed himself from his chains and, unnoticed by the guards, made his way through the doors into the hall without anybody trying to stop him. He went to the throne, dressed in royal robes, put on the diadem, sat upon the throne and remained quiet. When the incident was noticed, the king, though frightened by it, went to the throne and, concealing his fright, calmly asked the man who he was and for what purpose he had done it. As he answered that he was aware of no reason whatever, the king consulted the soothsayers about the omen and then, by their direction, put the man to death so as to make the unlucky portents turn against him. Himself, he dressed again in his robes and sacrificed to the protective gods, but felt restless. He remembered the prophecy of the Chaldeans and castigated the philosophers who had persuaded him to enter Babylon, admiring the skill of the Chaldeans and their vision. . .

16. Dio Chrysostomus (died ca. A.D. 115), *De Regno*, IV 66-68:

"You, too", continued Diogenes, "have a fiery temperament, the same kind of a dangerous and violent sting. Why don't you throw away what you are now wearing, put on a simple smock-frock and serve those who conduct themselves better as rulers, instead of running about with that riduculous diadem? Or are you perhaps planning next to grow a comb and a tiara like a cock? Don't you know the Sakaia rites performed by the Persians, against whom you are now planning to march?"

Alexander immediately asked what kind of a ceremony that was, for he wanted to learn everything about the Persians.

"They take a prisoner condemned to death, seat him upon the throne of the king, robe him in royal garments and let him issue orders, drink and revel, yes, during those days he is even allowed to amuse himself with the king's concubines, and nobody prevents him from doing what he wants. Then, however, he is dragged out, whipped, and hanged.

What do you think this festival stands for? And why do the Persians celebrate it? Isn't the idea as follows: the power and title of the king is often grabbed by stupid and vicious men, who for a while indulge in revelries and soon find an infamous end. Therefore, it also is natural that the ignorant fool rejoices and congratulates himself when freed from his chains, but the one who knows laments bitterly, resists being taken along, and would much rather remain in chains as before. You, too, fool, don't try to be a king before you have got reason! Until then it is better to give no commands but live a life of one's own in a smock-frock."

The origin of this anecdote is unknown, but it certainly represents a tradition not dependent on the following one.

17. Athenaios Naucratica (ca. A.D. 230), *Deipnosophistai*, XIV 639c (fragm. 16M): In the first book of the Babyloniaka, Berossus tells that from the sixteenth day of the month Loos there went on for five days in Babylon a festival called the Sakaia, during which it was customary that masters were given commands by servants, one of whom was led out of his house clad in robes resembling those of the king, and he says that this one was called Zoganes. The said festival is also mentioned by Ctesias in the second book of his Persika.

This passage probably refers to the Babylonian New Year's festival and has (despite the name Sakaia which it shares with the preceding entry) nothing to do with the substitute king ritual.

18. Suetonius (died A.D. 150), *Vitae*, Claudius XXIX 3:

But it is beyond all belief, that at the marriage which Messalina had contracted with her paramour Silius he [Claudius] signed the contract for the dowry with his hand, being induced to do so on the ground that the marriage was a feigned one, designed *to avert and turn upon another a danger which was inferred from certain portents to threaten the emperor himself.*

Cf. XXVI 2: But when he learned that besides other shameful and wicked deeds she had actually married Gaius Silius, and that a formal contract had been signed in the presence of witnesses, he put her to death.

That this garbled account may attest to the ritual of the substitute king practiced in the court of Claudius (A.D. 41-54) was pointed out by C.J. Gadd, *AfO* 18 (1957-58), 218. By marrying the empress Messalina, Silius had conveniently become a *substitute emperor.*

19. John Malcom, *The History of Persia*, Vol. I (London 1829), p. 346:

While engaged in preventing the inroads of the Usbegs, . . . he (= Abbas the Great) was suddenly called from all considerations of foreign or domestic policy, by *a prediction of his astrologers; who, from the aspect of the heavenly bodies, had discovered that a most serious danger impended over the sovereign of Persia.* Abbas was not exempt from the superstition of the age in which he lived, and did not hesitate to adopt the strange expedient by which his counsellors proposed to avert the dreaded omen. *He abdicated the throne*; and a person of the name of Yusoofee, whom Persian authors take care to tell us was *an unbeliever* (probably a Christian), *was crowned*; and for three days, if we are to believe these historians [Zubd-ul-Tuarikh], *he enjoyed not only the name and state, but the power of the king.* The cruel farce ended as was to be expected. Yusoofee *was put to death; the decree of the stars was fulfilled by this sacrifice*; and Abbas, who reascended his throne in a most propitious hour, was promised by his astrologers a long and glorious reign.

This incident took place in 1591 (A.H. 1000), less than 300 years ago!

20. E.W. Lane, *The Arabian Nights* (London 1889), Vol. 2, p. 312 ff:

The Story of Abu-l-Ḥasan the Wag, or the Sleeper Awakened.

Even though this story, placed in the reign of Harun ar-Rashid, unlike the substitute king ritual has a happy end, it can hardly be doubted that it has been inspired by the ritual.

21. A.H. Layard, *Nineveh and Its Remains* (London 1849), p. 271:

When Keritli Oglu, Mohammed Pasha, first came to Mosul, this sect [the Yezidis] was amongst the objects of his cupidity and tyranny. He seized by treachery, as he supposed, their head or high priest; but Sheikh Nasr had time to *escape the plot against him, and to substitute in his place* the second in authority, who was carried as prisoner to the town. Such is the attachment shown by the Yezidis to their chief, that the deceit was not revealed, and *the substitute bore with resignation* the tortures and imprisonment inflicted upon him.

While this episode has nothing to do with the substitute king ritual as such, it does illustrate the mental climate that fostered the performance of the rite in the Near East from the earliest times on, and furnishes a living example of what the letter formula cited under [2] could have meant in practice.

ABBREVIATIONS

The *bibliographical* abbreviations used in this book are for the most part identical with those listed in R. Borger, *Handbuch der Keilschriftliteratur* (*HKL*, Berlin and New York 1967-1975), Bd. 2, p. xi ff. and in the *Chicago Assyrian Dictionary* (*CAD*, Chicago 1956ff.); for abbreviated titles of monographs cited with the author's name see the Bibliography and *HKL* under respective authors. Abbreviations *not* found in *HKL* or *CAD* are as follows:

ABB	Behrens 1906
AfO Bh	*Archiv für Orientforschung.* Beiheft
Asb	Streck 1916
EAE	Enūma Anu Enlil
Farber *Atti Ištar*	Farber 1977
Finkelstein Memorial Volume	*Essays on the Ancient Near East in Memory of Jacob J. Finkelstein*, Memoirs of the Connecticut Academy of Arts and Sciences 19. Hamden, Conn. 1977
Fs Baumgartner	*Hebräische Wortforschung*, Festschrift zum 80. Geburtstag von Walter Baumgartner. Vetus Testamentum Supplement 16. Leiden 1967
Fs Christian	*Vorderasiatische Studien*. Festschrift für Prof. Dr. Viktor Christian. Wien 1956
Fs Friedrich	Festschrift Johannes Friedrich zum 65. Geburtstag am 27. August 1958 gewidmet. Heidelberg 1959
IBA	Inbu Bēl Arḫi
IE	Labat 1965
KAI	H. Donner + W. Röllig, *Kanaanäische und aramäische Inschriften.* Wiesbaden 1964-1968
Lexicon	L. Koehler + W. Baumgartner, *Lexicon in Veteris Testamenti Libros.* 2nd ed. Leiden 1958
Muss-Arnolt	W. Muss-Arnolt, *Assyrisch-englisch-deutsches Handwörterbuch.* Berlin 1905
NL	H.W.F. Saggs, *The Nimrud Letters, 1952*: *Iraq* 17 (1955) 21ff. and 126ff., etc.
PICO	Proceedings of the . . .th International Congress of Orientalists
PKTA	Ebeling 1950
Pract. Voc.	B. Landsberger + O.R. Gurney, Practical Vocabulary of Assur: *AfO* 18 (1957/8), 328ff.
RCAE	Waterman 1930-1936
RépG	D.O. Edzard et al., *Répertoire Géographique des Textes Cunéiformes.* Wiesbaden 1974ff.
SACA	M. Zeitlin, *Le style administratif chez les Assyriens.* Paris 1910
Studi Volterra	Studi in onore di Eduardo Volterra, vol. 6. Milano 1973
Ungnad *Glossar*	A. Ungnad, *Neubabylonische Rechts- und Verwaltungsurkunden, Glossar.* Leipzig 1937
Unity and Diversity	H. Goedicke + J. Roberts (ed.), *Unity and Diversity*. Essays in the History, Literature, and Religion of the Ancient Near East. Baltimore 1975
VTE	Wiseman 1958
Warfare	Y. Yadin, *The Art of Warfare in Biblical Lands.* London 1963
ZRG	*Zeitschrift für Religionsgeschichte*

The other abbreviations are either self-explanatory or commonly used and largely agree with the conventions of the *CAD* and *AHw.* (W. von Soden, *Akkadisches Handwörterbuch*, Wiesbaden 1959ff.). Note, however, the following:

A.R.	right ascension
l.	line
itr.	intransitive
mod.	modern
q.v.	quod vide
Šš(m)k	Šamaš-šumu-ukīn
stat.	stative
st. cstr.	status constructus
Tgl	Tiglath-Pileser III
tr.	transitive
unp.	unpublished

Writers of letters are frequently abbreviated to their first initial (e.g., Marduk-šākin-šumi → M.), if the name in question appears in a repetitive or otherwise unequivocal context.

COMMENTARY TO LETTERS 1-345

1

B i b l i o g r a p h y :[1]
(I) [= F u l l e d i t i o n s with transliteration, translation (and commentary):] L. Waterman, *RCAE* [I-III (1930-31) no.] 386.
(II) [= S t u d i e s a n d d i s c u s s i o n s:][2] E. Dhorme, *RHR* 116 (1937) 6; A.L. Oppenheim, *JAOS* 61 (1941) 258; Böhl, *Opera Minora* (1953) 393f.; D.J. Wiseman, *Iraq* 20 (1958) 8^{76}, 81.

C o p y :[3]
R.F. Harper, *ABL* IV no. 386.

P h o t o g r a p h :
RCAE IV pl. 10.

A d d r e s s e e :
Esarhaddon.

D a t e a n d d i s c u s s i o n :
Probably Nisannu 7, eponymy of Nabû-bēlu-uṣur = April 10, 672 BC. The day and month are obtained from Obv. 22 and Rev.13; the year depends on the identification of the treaty (*adê*: see on Obv.9) referred to in the letter. Though the purpose of this treaty is not explicitly stated, there are several (mostly indirect, but nevertheless weighty) grounds for seeing in it the oath of allegiance by which Esarhaddon settled his succession in 672 BC (= the so-called "Vassal-Treaties of Esarhaddon" *VTE*, published by Wiseman, loc.cit.):

(1) The treaty involved the adjuration of *scribes* (and other scholars: *LAS* 2) coming from *all* important cities of Assyria proper; this implies that a treaty relating to the internal affairs of Assyria is in question, and excludes e.g. a covenant made with a foreign power.

(2) The *scene* of the oath-taking was, as in the case of the Vassal-Treaties, Calah/Nimrud: see note on Obv.10. As Calah at the time concerned wasn't the capital of Assyria, its choice as the scene of the ceremonies must be somehow related to the purpose of the treaty: this points definitely to a treaty bearing on the royal succession, Calah being the *centre* of the Assyrian cult of Nabû (see presently).

(3) The treaty was to be "entered into" under the statues of *Bēl and Nabû* (Obv.22f); this tallies with the fact that the extant copies of the Vassal-Treaties come from the throne-room of the *Nabû* temple of Calah, where the kind resided during his visits to the temple and which was also (occasionally) visited by the god himself (see Wiseman, *op.cit.* p.1f and Mallowan, *Nimrud* I p. 240ff). As such, it was the most convenient scene for a treaty concerning the royal succession, the presiding god Nabû being the son of Marduk, i.e., the "celestial *crown prince*". See on 46 r9 and 318:4, and cf. also below, note to Obv.22f.

(4) The sender (Ištar-šumu-ēreš) is known to have been active as royal counselor between 678 and 650 BC (see Appendix 02); his datable letters and reports cover the time between 672 and 657 BC. This implies that the king addressed can be only Esarhaddon or Assurbanipal. But there is no evidence that Assurbanipal had his

---

1 From 1930 on, with the exception of a few earlier studies of permanent value. For literature up to 1930 see the edition of Waterman.

2 Omitting, for obvious reasons, standard reference works such as *AHw*, *CAD* and *RlA*.

3 References to *Harper's* copies otherwise omitted, since already given in Pt.1.

subjects swear allegiance to any of his sons before 650 BC;[4] hence, if a treaty concerning the royal succession is in question, the addressee can be only Esarhaddon.

It is true that the days (Nisannu 8 and 15) mentioned in the letter do not coincide with the days on which the Vassal-Treaties of Esarhaddon were actually concluded, viz. Ajāru 12 (cf. Streck, *Asb* p.2 i 12), 16 (Wiseman, *VTE* p. 79:669', text ND 4336C) or 18 (ibid., texts °54F and °54D; Borger, *Ash* p.72:40). But then the letter does not report on the actual oath-taking but only suggests for consideration some days on which the *scribes* could enter in the treaty. It is conceivable that scribes who would draw up treaty documents in their home towns should be adjured before the rest of the population; and as the dates quoted above show, the adjuration of all Assyria (and her vassals) was not a matter accomplished in a single day. Besides, there is no guarantee that the dates proposed in the present letter remained final: the king may have preferred later ones (cf. 15f, r1f!). Anyway, it is significant that the dates are not later but *earlier* than the ones on which the population and the vassals entered the treaty.

Disregarding the implications of arguments (2) and (3), it could be objected that there are at least two treaties pertaining to the internal affairs of Assyria that could be in question equally well as the "Vassal-Treaties"; viz. the adjuration of Assyrian magistrates effected after the rebellion of 670 BC (see on *LAS* 284) and the treaty of Zakūtu on behalf of Assurbanipal (*ABL* 1239 + 83-1-18,266). However, these alternatives not only fail to account for the scene of the oath-taking ceremonies but are unsatisfactory in other respects, too: there is nothing in the letter even vaguely pointing to a time of internal instability such as prevailed in Assyria in early Nisannu, 670 (see commentary to *LAS* 247); the letter is addressed to *king* not to queen mother, as one would expect in the case of the Zakūtu treaty; and the planets Jupiter and Venus, before which this treaty was concluded (*ABL* 1239: 25), are not even mentioned in the present letter. All in all, the letter makes sense only in the historical context of the "Vassal-Treaties", and its dating to early April, 672, may thus be considered if not certain, so at least plausible. Further evidence in favour of this dating is provided by *LAS* 2, q.v.

Notes:

9. *a-de-e*: on this term see, most recently, M. Weinfeld, "Covenant terminology in the ancient Near East and its influence on the West", *JAOS* 93 (1973) 190-199 and H. Tadmor, *Unity and Diversity* (1975). For a bibliography of NA treaties see S. Parpola, *AOAT* 6 p.XXIV; add Borger, *WZKM* 55 73f (cf. *JCS* 19 76); Deller + Parpola, *Or* NS 37 (1968) 464ff; Millard, *Iraq* 32 (1970) 174; Ebeling, *SVAT* (1954) no.2; and K.3374, K.4439, 83-1-18, 266, 83-1-18,493, Bu. 91-5-9,22 and 131 (unp.). For references to treaties in Sargonid letters see *ABL* 90, 129, 1008, 1029 (time of Sargon); *ABL* 213, 328, 539, 555, 831, 948, 1110+, *LAS* 129, 133, 211, 284 (time of Ash); and *ABL* 202, 280, 350(?), 998, 1341(?), 1404 (time of Asb); for refs. in Sargonid inscriptions see *CAD* A/1 s.vv. *adû* A and B.

10. *it-tal-ku-u-*[*né*] "they have come": this remark settles the question of the scene of the treaty ceremonies (above, date 2). The city in question *cannot* be Nineveh, Kalizi, Arbela or Assur, since scribes from these cities had *come* (or were expected to come) for the treaty; it can only be Calah, since scribes from that city could enter the treaty (21ff) but are *not* mentioned among the people who had to make a special trip to the scene of the ceremonies.

13f. These lines, explaining the delay of the scribes of Assur, are probably to be restored ^{LÚ}[TU.É^{M}]^{EŠ} ^{14}*šu-nu-*[*ú-n*]*i* "they are [temple-enterer]s", or similarly; note that the letter was written during the great New Year's festival of the city of Assur (cf. van Driel, *CA* 145f and 163f), in whose celebration the scribes of the city (many of whom served in the Assur temple) almost certainly had to participate in official capacity.

22. *UD 8.KÁM:* the 8th of Nisannu was not a favourable day according to Mesopotamian hemerological traditions, nor was the 15th (r6; see Labat, *RA* 38 [1944] 20); thus, it is curious that the writer could propose

4 It would rather seem that *no* such oath was taken before the death (or expatriation) of Assurbanipal. Note that Aššur-etel-ilāni in his account of his accession (Postgate, *NARGD* no. 13 and 14) does not mention that allegiance was sworn to him in his father's lifetime (*NARGD* 14:11 refers to an oath taken after A.'s accession); correspondingly, the treaty of Sîn-šarru-iškun (Weidner, *AfO* 13 215[69]) was not concluded before the accession of this king but only afterwards, as clearly shown by line 3 of the text.

oath-taking ceremonies for these days, for such ceremonies had normally to be arranged on *favourable* days (cf. *LAS* 3 and pertinent commentary). Did the scribes generally have a "day off" (cf. 11. 21 and r5) every seventh day (or perhaps better, every "evil" day; cf. 185:21) coinciding with the principal lunar phases, and couldn't they conveniently enter the treaty on normal "weekdays" when they had other things to do? Cf. r3f.

22f. *"Under Bēl and Nabû"* [i.e., under the (statues of the) celestial king and crown prince]: on the significance of this remark for the identification of the treaty in question see above, Date (3).[5] The use of the preposition *šapla* in lieu of *(ina) pān* may imply that the statues concerned were of gigantic stature. This would account for the massive podium and pavement slabs in the Nabû sanctuary (Mallowan, *Nimrud* I 262f) and also agree with the description of the statue of Bēl given by Herodotus (I 183: "twelve cubits [6 m] high . . ."); as far as is known, Bēl did not have a temple of his own in Calah, so his statue was probably brought there from elsewhere, most likely from Assur where the Babylonian god was in "exile" (cf. *ABL* 213 [a letter from Assur to Esarhaddon] Obv.7ff: "As to the king's writing to me: 'Let the gods come for the treaty . . .'").[6] It isn't, of course, excluded that the passage implies an act of proskynesis or prostration before the divine statues, cf. *a-zi-iz ina tar-ṣi-šá ak-mì-is šá-pal-šá* "I stood before her, I knelt down to (lit. *under*) her" (Piepkorn, *AS* 5 64:27, referring to Ištar).

r5. *li-ri-qu-u-né*: translate "let them *get* free (again)" rather than ". . . be free" (Pt.I). Cf. above, note on Obv.22.

r8. *am-ma-ka*: probably referring to the statues of Bēl and Nabû mentioned above, or more generally to the Nabû temple in Calah.

r12. *bi-ib-la-a-ni*: since the following quotation occurs in an almost identical form in two different hemerological texts (cf. Labat, *HMA* 58;15,I UD *15*.KÁM *šá* ^{d}NIN.É.AN.NA ^{16}KI.MIN *la i-tam-ma* DINGIR DIB *su* and the *Babylonian Almanac* [Labat, *RA* 38 23], entry for Nisannu 15: [*la i-tam-ma*] DINGIR DIB-*su*), the term *biblu* was probably a collective designation for hemerologies in general rather than "texts of the iqqur īpuš type" (thus *CAD* B 222*b*). The *Babylonian Almanac* seems to have been called "Abšegeda" in *ABL* 1092:16.

r19. *"Before the stars"*: cf. *ina* IGI ^{d}SAG.ME.GAR ^{d}*Dil-bat* $^{14 MUL}$UDU.IDIM.SAG.UŠ ^{MUL}UDU.IDIM.GU$_4$.UD $^{15 MUL}$*Ṣal-bat-a-nu* ^{MUL}KAK.SI.SÁ "In the presence of Jupiter, Venus, Saturn, Mercury, Mars, and Sirius", *VTE* 13ff. All these stars, with the exception of Mars, were "present" during the Vassal-Treaty ceremonies, Mercury from Ajāru 9 on (and previously from Addāru II 13 till Nisannu 9), see App. C and D. *

2

Bibliography:
(I) Waterman, *RCAE* 33 (cf. IV 232); Pfeiffer, *SLA* 211.
(II) Dhorme, *RHR* 116 (1937) 5; Wiseman, *Iraq* 20 (1958) 3, 8[76].

Copy:
Cf. also S.A. Smith, *PSBA* 10 (1888) 309f, pl. 3.

Photo:
RCAE IV pl.6 (Obv. only).

Addressee:
Esarhaddon.

Date:
Nisannu 15, eponymy of Nabû-bēlu-uṣur = April 18, 672 BC. For the month and day cf. obv.12 and r1f; for the

[5] Though Nabû was also the patron god of the scribal craft, the mention of Bēl makes it unlikely that this was the actual reason why the scribes had to be adjured before this particular god.

[6] This interpretation is naturally not weakened by the fact that certain Mesopotamian divine statues were certainly human-sized (see e.g. Layard, *Nineveh and Its Remains* II, plate facing p.451).

year, see commentary to *LAS* 1.[7] The dating to 672 BC is substantiated by the fact that while the writer obviously mentions in ll.6-9 all classes of "wise men" living at the royal court and in downtown Nineveh, he does not mention interpreters of dreams. This would be anachronistic in a letter written after 672, as it is known that Esarhaddon attached to his court Egyptian dream interpreters in 671 BC (Borger, *Ash* § 80 i 9; for the reading LÚ*ḫar-ṭi-bi* cf. idem, *AfO* 18 [1957/58] 116). Note that Egyptian dream interpreters are listed along with scribes, exorcists, physicians, haruspices, augurs and chanters in the text *ADD* 871 edited in Appendix N 4, dating from about 650 BC.

N o t e s :

r1f. *ú-ma-a iš-ši-a-ri*: render "today and tomorrow" rather than "now . . . ". See note to 198 r13.

3

B i b l i o g r a p h y :
(I) Waterman, *RCAE* 384; Pfeiffer, *SLA* 341.
(II) Dhorme, *RHR* 116 (1937) 5; Labat, *Royauté* (1939) 308; Böhl, *Opera Minora* (1955) 393f; Wiseman, *Iraq* 20 (1958) 3[18].

P h o t o :
RCAE IV pl.10 (obv. only).

A d d r e s s e e :
Esarhaddon.

D a t e :
Uncertain. The sequence of favourable days occurring in the letter (20-22-25) fits only two months, Ajāru (tradition of Assur) and Addāru (actually 20-22-24-25, the Babylonian Almanac), see Labat, *RA* 38 (1944) 20f. Since the letter agrees orthographically with the two preceding numbers, and since both Addāru (the 12th month) and Ajāru (the 2nd month) are sufficiently close to Nisannu to explain the orthographical similarities, the letter can be tentatively dated either about Addāru 19 = February 21, or Ajāru 19 = May 21, 672. The former date would then be more probable in view of the fact that the latest attested date for the Vassal Treaties is Ajāru 18, see under *LAS* 1. But, as appears from the preceding, the evidence is extremely slim and other possibilities cannot be excluded.

D i s c u s s i o n :
The importance of taking the treaty oath on a favourable day is also stressed in royal inscriptions, e.g. Borger, *Ash* p.40:15ff and Streck, *Asb* p.2:11ff.

4

B i b l i o g r a p h y :
(I) Waterman, *RCAE* 670 (cf. IV 186).
(II) Dhorme, *RHR* 116 (1937) 8 and *RA* 38 (1941) 60f.

A d d r e s s e e :
Esarhaddon(?).

D a t e :
Obscure. The term *šuruptu* and *taklimtu* (see on Obv.13 and 17) as well as the purificatory ceremonies performed for the king (see on r5f) make it certain that the letter deals with the funeral of a member of the royal family, or

[7] The association of the letter with no.1 is made certain by the subject matter, handwriting (cf. *RCAE* IV pls. 1 and 6), orthography (cf. the blessing formulae with that of no.8, etc.) and last but not least, by the fact that the date Nisannu 15 was explicitly suggested in *LAS* 1.

of a substitute king (cf. *LAS* 280), but it seems impossible to establish with certainty the identity of the deceased and thus give the letter an exact date. One can only eliminate possibilities. Though exact details as to the time which generally elapsed between death and burial in Assyria are lacking,[8] it can be taken for granted that the deceased could not be publicly displayed longer than a week after the death,[9] and as the ceremony proposed for the 5th in r8'ff certainly only slightly postdated the display ceremony, it can be concluded, with great probability, that the deceased had died before the 3rd of the current month but not before the 26th of the preceding month. This would exclude the wife of Esarhaddon, who died on Addāru 5/6[10], 672, and certainly Esarhaddon himself, who died on Araḫsamna 10,[11] 669; further, the substitute kings of 669 and 666 BC (who died on Du'ūzu 15 and Ābu 5, respectively, see on *LAS* 166 and 298), and of Du'ūzu-Tašrītu and Kanūnu-Šabāṭu, 671 BC (who where buried in Akkad while the king was in Nineveh and therefore could not be "displayed" in the king's presence, cf. *LAS* 280). What is left? Considering the known time limits of Ištar-šumu-ēreš's floruit (ca. 678-650 BC), which eliminate the possibility that the letter refers to the burial of Sennacherib or Assurbanipal, at least a royal infant (cf. *LAS* 171, reign of Esarhaddon) and the queen mother Naqia, who died in the early years of Assurbanipal (date and year unknown); perhaps also other members of the royal family of whose deaths we are not informed. In view of all this, even the identity of the king to whom the letter was addressed (Esarhaddon or Assurbanipal) remains uncertain, though the reference to the Babylonians (Obv.7ff) points to the reign of Esarhaddon.

Notes:

7ff. Cf. *CT* 22 1:3ff, "(converse with) PN_1, PN_2, PN_3 and (other) scholars (^{LÚ*}*um-ma-nu*) of Borsippa whom you know (*šá at-ta ti-du-ú*)." The identity of the two Babylonians mentioned here cannot be established with certainty, since their professional status is not known and the names in question are very common. The likeliest candidates are Bēl-nāṣer the astrologer (author of several reports and one letter to Esarhaddon, floruit 677-672; see App. J3 and Q4-5), the only Babylonian scholar of this name known as a contemporary of Ištar-šumu-ēreš, and if the identification of Bēl-nāṣer is correct, Bēl-īpuš the haruspex, mentioned in a report of the former (^{Id}EN-DÙ-*uš* DUMU DIN.TIR^{KI} ^{LÚ}ḪAL, *RMA* 18 r3f). But why had *Babylonian* scholars (including an astrologer and a haruspex) to be consulted about details of burial ceremonies? Was the deceased perhaps a native of Babylonia?[12]

10. *ú-da-kan-ni* = "(who) are known to you"; not "(who) know you" (*CAD* I/J 25*b* after Waterman) = **ú-du-(u-)kan-ni*. Cf. the parallel *CT* 22,1 cited in the preceding note; further, *a-na* LUGAL *bi-li-ni lu ud-da-áš-šú ki-i* "let it be known to the king, our lord, that . . . ", *ABL* 415 r1f; [*ša a*]*-na* EN-*já ú-du-n*[*i*] "which is known to my lord", *LAS* 27:13; (NB) DUB^{MEŠ} *aq-ru-tu ša mi-dak-ku-nu-ši-ma* "the precious tablets which are known to you", *CT* 22 1 r7f; *lu me-dak-kun-ú-šu* let it be known to you", *ABL* 401:9; *lu mi-di* "let it be known (to the king)" (passim); etc. all passages showing clearly that the present occurrence of *ú-da* is a(n indeclinable) stative corresponding both in meaning ("known") and usage (datival suffixes) to the likewise indeclinable NB stative *mīdi*. Cf. *GAG* §§ 78b and 106q.

12. Idiomatic for "an hour after sunrise"; literally "the day will rise for half a *bēru* (6th part of the distance between sunrise and sunset)". For "day" = "sun" cf. 64:17; the verb *šaqû* used in the idiom actually referred to the rising of heavenly bodies (cf. 41:4, 119:9.11, 139 r2, 300:7, *RMA* 91 r5, 94:6, 181 r5, etc.) and therefore was only used to indicate early morning hours; cf. note to 252:10ff.

13. *tak-lim-tu*: referring to public exhibition of the (treated and decorated body of the) deceased to mourners (in the case of a royal death, certainly not only to the closest relatives). See Dhorme, *RA* 38 (1940) 57ff, and cf. *LAS* 280:14f and K 164.1ff (= *ZA* 45 [1939] 42ff; cf. 43 [1936] 256f). In *LAS* 5-6 the term refers to cultic exhibition of a dead god. It is interesting that the exhibition was, according to the present text, to take

[8] In ancient Israel, the dead were buried very quickly, mostly already on the day of the death (cf. Deut. 21:23). This was necessary because of the hot climate, and the same certainly was the case in Mesopotamia, too.

[9] Cf. Gilg M ii 7ff, "seven days and seven nights I (Gilgameš) wept for him (Enkidu), until a maggot dropped out of his nose", given as example of an unusually long delay of burial.

[10] See Grayson, *TCS* 5 p.85:22 and 127:23 but cf. below, note to obv.7ff.

[11] Ibid. p.86:31.

[12] Esarhaddon's wife was born in Babylonia, see Winckler, *AOF* I 417 and Borger, *Studien* p.66[12]. Should the date of her death given in the chronicles be taken to refer to the date of her burial?

place several times during the morning, each time probably lasting only for a few minutes. The reasons for this remain obscure (several groups of mourners?).[13]

17. [*šu*]-*ru-up-tú*: "funeral burning", an exact counterpart of Bibl. *šᵉrēpāh* (2 Chr. 16:14, 21:19); see discussion sub *LAS* 195 and cf. 280:16 and K. 164:16 (*ZA* 45 42ff). The term has nothing to do with the ritual *šurpu*, just as the term *maq(a)lûtu* (see on 167 r7) has nothing to do with *maqlû* (208:7). Notice the suffix -*ka* referring to the king, and cf. note on 196:13.

r5. *Torches* and censers (r11) were the magical means by which Assyrian exorcists purified places and objects (cf. 172 r6ff, 206 r10, and the numerous examples cited in *CAD* G 113f),[14] and they very probably had the same function in the present instance, too. Obviously the king had to be cleansed from the contamination resulting from physical (or even indirect) contact with the corpse.[15]

r7. While *(ina) qanni* certainly means "at, by, on the border" (cf. *AHw* 897*b*), *a-na qa-an-ni* used with the verb *uṣû*, as here, equally certainly does not mean "(to go) to the border" (thus *CAD* E 391*b*), or the like, but simply "(to go) out". The semantic shift from "at, by" to "out(side of)" may have been helped by passages where *qanni* stands in opposition to *libbi* or *qabsi* "inside", e.g. *LAS* 38 r1f (*qa-an-ni* URU contrasted with *lib-bi* URU)[16]; cf. also 45 r1ff, *la ina qa-an-ni ú-ṣa . . . ina qa-ab-si* É.GAL *ina pa-an* LUGAL *er-rab*, and *CT* 53 76 B 8f, [*l*]*a e-rab ina qa-an-ni ma-d*[*ak-ti*] ⁹[*is-s*]*e-e-šú du-ub-ba* "he may not enter (the camp), speak to him outside the camp!" Note also KÁ.GAL *ša qa-ni* "outer gate" (*Iraq* 4 189 r11; opp. KÁ.GAL *qab-si-te* ibid.10) = Bab. KÁ.GAL *ka-wi-tum* "outer gate" (*CAD* K 127*a*).

r11. The reading NÍG!.NA has now been verified by Sollberger (collation 19.1.1976).

5

Bibliography:
(I) Waterman, *RCAE* 35.
(II) Dhorme, *RHR* 116 (1937) 6 and *RA* 38 (1940) 60; Labat, *Royauté* (1939) 122 and 215; Jacobsen, *Unity and Diversity* (1975) 72.

Date:
Late Du'ūzu, same year as *LAS* 8 (670/669 BC)? This is just a guess, based on the orthographical affinities of the letter with *LAS* 8 (q.v.); note the spellings ᴵ15-MU-KAM (without the final -*eš*), *šùl-mu* and *lu-ú-kal-li-mu* which the letter shares with *LAS* 8, 9, 21(?) and 23(?), as against ᴵ15-MU-KAM-*eš* and *šul-mu* in *LAS* 1-3, 13, 25 and 29; since *LAS* 8 was written in early Du'ūzu (cf. ibid., r1-4) and the present letter towards the end of the same month (cf. note on obv.7ff), the letters are at least theoretically sufficiently close to one another to share a uniform orthography; cf. notes on the dates of *LAS* 3 and 246, and cf. also the discussion on the following number.

Discussion:
This letter was apparently written to remind the king of a previous royal decree concerning the date of the Tammuz festival at Arbela (r1ff) and conflicting with another, freshly issued order (obv.5ff). Why such a reminder, if the celebration of the festival had already begun (cf. obv.7, "today . . .")? The likeliest answer is that the writer simply wanted to make sure that the important ceremonies of Arbela (cf. on r2) would not be performed on the

---

[13] If this hypothesis is correct, then the deceased might have been the queen mother (possibly also born in Babylonia, cf. Borger, op.cit. p.66) whose death certainly attracted incomparably much more attention than a royal infant's. But also the death of the queen (cf. preceding note) was an event of great publicity.

[14] Cf. *ina še-eḫ-ti šá te-li-si tu-še-taq* ᵈGIŠ.BAR *li-l*[*il ta-qab-bi*] "you carry out a purification by censer and say: May fire purify", *PKTA* 10:14. Note also the antiseptic properties of certain types of incense, on which see Thorwald, *Macht und Geheimnis der frühen Ärzte* (1967) 92f.

[15] Cf. *LAS* 195 r9 (purification) and the Biblical passages (Deut.21 etc.) referring to pollution caused by death.

[16] Incidentally, note that NA *qanni* has an exact counterpart in Urartian (cf. e.g. *ABL* 148:4 *qa-an-ni* URU *Ṭu-ru-uš-pa-a* with Urart. *ka-ni* URU *Ṭu-uš-pa*). Is NA *qanni* hence a loan from Hurrian/Urartian, or vice versa?

same days as the corresponding ceremonies in the other cities of Assyria, which lasted from Du'ūzu 26 to Du'ūzu 28 (*LAS* 6).

Notes:

7ff. Comparison with *LAS* 6 makes it certain that the "displays" (*tak-lim-a-ti*) mentioned here refer to the festival of Tammuz (celebrated in late Du'ūzu), more exactly to the exhibition of (a statue of) the (dead) god (lying on biers) to his devotees (mourners, sick people hoping for miraculous cure, etc., see on the following number). Note that the present letter lacks introductory blessing: is this due to the fact that the time of the festival was in Assyria an official period of mourning (*tādertu*)? Cf. note to *LAS* 61:5ff.

r1f. *tak-lim-a-ti la-bir-a-ti* "the old displays": referring, as appears from r8, to ceremonies at Arbela, the time-honoured centre of the cult of Tammuz (and Ištar) in Assyria. The celebration of the festival in this city obviously differed in details (and prestige) from the way in which it was celebrated in other Assyrian cities. For another example of the adjective *labīru* "old" referring to cultic services of great antiquity cf. *CT* 53 965 r4 f, *la dul-lu la me-me-e-ni*[5] *la-a la-bi-ru šu-ú* "it is not a ritual, it is nothing, it is not old (, your father has instituted it)". Note also *rim-ka-a-ni* GIBIL^{MEŠ} (BM 121206 viii 4' [= *CA* p. 86ff] and *PKTA* 15 iv 17'ff) referring to "new ablutions" of divine statues instituted by Sennacherib (in contrast to established ceremonies of old).

6

Bibliography:

(I) Waterman, *RCAE* 1097 (cf. IV 196).
(II) Ebeling, *TuL* (1931) 60f; Labat, *Royauté* (1939) 122f and 215; Dhorme, *RA* 38 (1941) 60; Jacobsen, *Unity and Diversity* (1975) 72.

Writer:

Identified as Ištar-šumu-ereš on the following grounds: 1) Affinity with the preceding letter (the subject matter is not taken up in other letters of the present corpus);[17] 2) orthography (KÁM, *šá*, *an-nim-ma*, cf. Appendix M 6; *kil-lu*$_4$ cf. 343:11.r10); 3) handwriting (personal collation 25.3.1968). The letter does not contain any features contradicting this assignation.

Discussion and possible date:

It is easy to see that the letter furnishes information on the celebration of the Tammuz festival in different cities of Assyria, but for what purpose was this information needed? The easiest solution would be to assume that the king to whom the letter was addressed had not previously familiarized himself with the dates on which this annual festival was celebrated; in view of the career of Ištar-šumu-ēreš (672-648), the king would then be Assurbanipal, and the date of the letter, Du'ūzu, 668. Such a solution, however, might well be an oversimplification.[18] Cf. discussion of the date of the preceding number.

From the viewpoint of the study of Assyrian cult, it is a pity that the letter is so laconic and fragmentary; nevertheless, the data it gives on the local variations of the Tammuz festival are interesting and largely unknown from other sources (cf. *LKA* 69 and 70 [an exorcistic ritual purporting to cure dangerously ill people on the days of the festival]; *LKA* 72 = Ebeling, *TuL* no.10 [a cultic commentary on the ceremonial acts performed during the festival]; *LKU* 51:27ff [detailing the celebration of the festival in Uruk]; the final section of "Ištar's Descent into the Nether World", *ANET*[2] 106ff, etc.; and *LAS* 347).

Notes:

7'ff. The dates of the festival at Assur given here are consistent with those found in *LKA* 69 (Du'ūzu

---

17 · Except no. 347 (see Additions) which probably also originates from Ištar-šumu-ēreš.

18 Note, e.g., that *LAS* 343, also written by Ištar-šumu-ēreš and dealing with the celebration of a festival in various cities of Assyria, was almost certainly addressed to Esarhaddon, judging by the reference to the king's sons ibid. obv.7.

26-28);[19] the cultic acts performed on the individual days, however, appear from *LKA* 69 to have been more variable than the present letter gives to understand (26th: appearance of Ištar, miraculous cure of illness; 27th: days of the "pens" [TÙR^{MEŠ}] of Tammuz; 28th: preparation of the bier for Tammuz). Should one restore ^{d}*15* at the end of l. 7' ("they introduce [Ištar] and perform the display ceremony") by analogy with *LKA* 69?

r1'. *kil-lu*$_4$: referring to the mourning of Tammuz, a prominent feature of the festival (cf. Ezek. 8:14, *LKA* 69:4f, etc.).

pa-šá-ru: unclear whether referring to the release of Ištar from Hades (mimed by cultic acts) or to the cure of the sick, associated with this event. Cf. UD *23*.KAM *pa-šar* GÌR^2 (referring to Assur) in *CA* 102:41', and *ABL* 366r2 (Nabû GÌR^2-*šú i-pa-áš-šar* "releases his feet"). Jacobsen (1975) takes *pašāru* in the sense of "dehulling (grain)", referring to the cultic commentary *LKA* 72, which reads: "His (= Dumuzi's) death is when they grind the roasted grain that has been thrown on Dumuzi on the millstones . . ."

7

Bibliography:

(I) Waterman, *RCAE* 36.
(II) Behrens, *ABB* (1906) 29f; Dhorme, *RHR* 116 (1937) 6.

Addressee:

Esarhaddon.

Date:

672-669 BC. Note the reference to the statues of the two crown princes (Assurbanipal and Šamaš-šumu-ukīn) in r6'f;[20] a more exact date does not seem possible in lack of more definite historical and chronological indications. Given the possibility, however, that the dispatchment of the statues to Harran was connected with the restoration of Eḫulḫul (cf. on *LAS* 8, and note the pertinence of *LAS* 286 to the restoration of Esangil), a dating to 670-669 BC would seem more plausible than an assignation to the early half of the 4-year period in question.

Notes:

6. As appears quite clearly from rev.3'ff, the statues mentioned here were not meant to be set up as mere objects of art, nor as objects of *worship* (though deified royal statues, especially those of ancient kings, *were* worshiped in Assyrian temples, cf. simply *CAD* S 81*b*), but, on the contrary, as incessant supplicants of the moon-god of Harran, hoped to render the king the blessings mentioned in r9'ff. Cf. Borger, *Ash* 87 r3f, *ṣa-lam* LUGAL-*ti-ja mu-sa-pu-u* DINGIR-*ti-šú-un mu-te-riš ba*-TI-*ja* ^{4}*ù ṣa-lam* ^{I}*Aš+šur*-DÙ-A DUMU *re-du-ti-ja ab-ta-ni ṣe-ru-uš-šú-* "a statue of my kingship, supplicating to their divinity and begging for my life, and a statue of Assurbanipal, my successor, I fashioned upon it"; similarly Streck, *Asb* p.270 iv 3 (*ṣa-lam* LUGAL-*ti-ja mu-sa-ap-pu-u* DINGIR-*ti-šú-un ma-ḫar-šú-un ul-ziz*), etc.

15. *pi-ši*[*r-šú*] "its interpretation": here not referring to an entry in an omen text, as usual, but almost certainly to an entry in the menology *Iqqur Īpuš*.[21] Accordingly, menologies, or "monthly prognostications" (Isa. 47:13), were probably regarded as a certain kind of *omens*, which explains why they indeed were styled like omens ("If he destroyes and rebuilds in month so-and-so, . . . "). On the reading *pi-šir-šú* (not *pi-šar-šú*) see note on 13:23.

---

[19] The duplicate *LKA* 70 has however, for unclear reasons, Du'ūzu 27-29, the days on which the festival was celebrated in Arbela.

[20] That only *two* sons of the king were meant is implied by the fact that the statues were to be placed *before and* [*behind*] the moon-god; that the sons in question were *crown princes* appears from the very fact that their statues could be set up in temples besides statues of the king. Cf. note to obv.6.

[21] Cf. notes on 8 r1f and 72:9.

r3'f. Cf. *LAS* 286 r5f, "I placed the statues of the king . . . on the right and left side (of the goddess Tašmētu)", but note that most often the royal statues seem to have *faced* the god they were adoring (in addition to the Asb passage quoted above, cf. e.g. *ABL* 951:19, "the king's father placed royal statues on the pedestal, one in front of Bēl, another in front of Nabû"). The present arrangement (the god's statue being surrounded by *four* statues in opposite points of compass) may have symbolized incessant adoration (cf. r10'; one statue for each lunar phase).

By "big royal statues" the writer probably meant something like the statue of Shalmaneser III shown in Strommenger + Hirmer, *The Art of Mesopotamia* (London 1964) pl. 207 (measuring 6.3 feet in height); the statuettes of the princes may have resembled the statue of Assurnasirpal II found in the Ninurta temple of Calah, ibid. pl. 197 (height 3.3 feet only).

r7'. At the end of the line restore *ina* [EGER (^{d}*30*)] "behind (the moon-god)", and cf. above, sub date.

r10'. *ar-ḫi-šá-am la na-par-ka-a*: an allusion to En. El. V 14, and a favoured cliché in Sargonid royal inscriptions (examples in *CAD* A/2 258); the same also applies to the following lines (cf. crit. app. and Borger, *Ash* p.7:27). A chief scribe, Ištar-šumu-ēreš was certainly responsible for the composition of many royal inscriptions; this circumstance most naturally accounts for the formulation of the present passage, though similar clichés also occur in letters of other scholars (e.g. *LAS* 123-124 passim, 125:13 and 28ff).

r11'ff. The idea of these lines is that the moon was hoped to make its (heliacal) risings and its settings (on the days of opposition) as "regular" as possible; cf. Borger, *Ash* p.2 i 31, ^{d}[*30 u* ^{d}U]TU DINGIR^{MEŠ} *maš-šu-ú-te* ^{32}*áš-[šu d]e-en kit-te* ^{33}*ù mi-šá-ri* ^{34}*a-n[a* KUR] *u* UN^{MEŠ} *šá ra-ku* ^{35}ITU-*š[a]m-ma ḫar-ra-an kit-te* ^{36}*ù mi-šá-ri ṣab-tu-ma* ^{37}UD [*1*].KÁM UD *14*.KÁM ^{38}*ú-[s]a-di-ru ta-mar-tú* "In order to grant the country and its inhabitants just and righteous judgments, the twin gods Sîn and Šamaš followed every month the path of justice and righteousness, appearing regularly on the 1st and 14th day".[22] Cf. also Streck, *Asb* p. 172 r64ff: "May [Sîn and] Nusku [joyfully look at] my good deeds, . . . make signs of good portent appear [in the sky], . . . let the foundations of my royal throne grow old . . ., affect the defeat of my enemies . . ." (etc., in an inscription describing the restoration of Eḫulḫul, the moon-temple of Harran).

r17'. [*la*] *i-pa-ra-ka-a* "will not cease": this verb is out of the place in this context, and makes the preceding passage a clear anacoluthon (deliberate or unintentional? Note *la na-[par-ka-a]* in r10').

8

Bibliography:
(I) Waterman, *RCAE* 673 (cf. IV 260); Pfeiffer, *SLA* 340.
(II) Dhorme, *RHR* 116 (1937) 9; Labat, *Royauté* (1939) 192.

Copy:
Cf. Zeitlin, *SACA* (1910), no. 22.

Photograph:
RCAE IV pl.13 (obv. only).

Addressee:
Esarhaddon.

Date and discussion:
Early Du'ūzu (cf. r1-4), 670/669 BC. Despite the lack of specific details, it is virtually certain that the cella of Nusku referred to in the letter was situated either in Assur or Harran, for these were the only cities in which sanc-

22 Alluding to the following frequently quoted omens: "If the moon appears on the 1st day, there will be reliable speech and the land will be happy"; "If the moon and the sun are in opposition on the 14th day, there will be reliable speech, and the land will be happy" (*RMA* passim). The moon's appearance on the 1st day also portended long reign, cf. sub *LAS* 100.

tuaries of Nusku were – according to royal inscriptions – restored in the reigns of Esarhaddon and Assurbanipal. In Esarhaddon's building inscriptions, Nusku is mentioned only in connection with the restoration of Esarra,[23] which was initiated in 680/679 BC (cf. Borger, *Ash*, Ass.A), then interrupted for several years, resumed in 671 (cf. ibid, AsBbE, p. 86ff), and finally completed at the beginning of Assurbanipal's reign (cf. Streck, *Asb* p. 147 x 10f). Assurbanipal, on the other hand, refers to a chapel of Nusku only in two inscriptions describing the restoration of Eḫulḫul, the moon-temple of Harran, which was completed in his accession year (669).[24] It is not possible to decide for certain which case is meant here, though the fact that *atmunu* usually refers to the main cult-room of the temple[25] makes the latter alternative seem more attractive.[26]

Notes:

9. For ^{d}PA+KU = *Našuḫ* (^{d}*Na-šuḫ*, ^{d}*Na-šu-ḫu*, ^{d}*Na-áš-ḫu*, ^{d}*Nu-uš-ḫu*) in Aramaic (and partly Akkadian) personal names of the Harran region see, provisionally, K. Deller, *Or* NS 34 (1965) 474. Reading the god's name *Nusku* (cf. *Nu-us-ku* S^{b}B 210, *Nu-uš-ku* Ea I 270, etc.) is of course also possible, supposing that the temple in question was not situated in Harran.

14. *šatbû*: literally, "to make rise"; taken as a building term on the ground of Rev.9f, where the verb appears in parallelism with *epāšu*. An Aramaism? Cf. Hebr./Aram. *qām* "to rise", Hiph. "to set up, erect, found" (lit. "to make rise").

r1f, and r7. Cf. *KAR* 177 ii 11f, BARAG GIBIL-*eš* ^{ITU}BÁR ^{ITU}GUD ^{ITU}SIG$_4$ ^{ITU}KIN ^{ITU}ZÍZ ^{ITU}ŠE ŠE "should he restore a shrine: Nisannu, Ajāru, *Simānu, Ulūlu,* Šabāṭu and Addāru are favourable months" (Labat, *HMA* p. 151ff and id., *MIO* 5 [1957] 315ff, appendixes to *Iqqur Ipuš*). The 17th of Simānu is, despite the allegation of the text, otherwise not attested as a favourable day; cf. Labat, *RA* 38 (1941) 21. The figure *17* should, consequently, probably be emended to *27*! (cf. r4) or *16*! (cf. the figures quoted by Labat, loc.cit.).

9

Bibliography:
(I) Waterman, *RCAE* 31; Pfeiffer, *SLA* 260.
(II) Dhorme, *RHR* 116 (1937) 7.

Copy:
Cf. S.A. Smith, *PSBA* 10 (1888) 71, pl. IX.

Photograph:
RCAE IV pl.6 (obv. only).

Discussion:
The word *izzirtu* (obv.9, rev.2) is best attested referring to curses concluding royal (building) inscriptions (cf. *CAD* I/J 319f), and it is hence possible that the present letter pertained to an ancient inscription searched for during the clearing of the foundations of a dilapidated public building. Was the building in question the cella of Nusku discussed sub *LAS* 8? Note the orthographical affinities of that letter with the present text, and cf. note on date of *LAS* 5.

---

23 Borger, *Ash* p.3 v 3ff, *i-na* ITU *šal-me* ^{4} *u*$_4$*-mu še-me-e* (–––) ^{9} *uš-še-e-šú* (–––) ^{10} *ad-di* (–––) vi ^{28} ^{d}*A-šur*$_4$ LUGAL DINGIR.MEŠ ^{29} *i-na at-ma-ni* ^{30} *be-lu-ti-šu ṣi-i-ri* ^{31} *ú-šar-ma-a* ^{32} *pa-rak da-ra-a-te* ^{33} ^{d}NIN. URTA ^{d}PA+KU ^{34} DINGIR^{MEŠ} ^{d}15.MEŠ ^{35} ZAG *u* KAB ^{36} *i-na man-zal-ti-šú-nu ú-kin* "I laid its (Ešarra's) foundations in a propitious month, on a propitious day (–––) and had Aššur, the king of the gods, take his seat of eternity in the august cella of his lordship, placing Ninurta, Nusku and the other gods and goddesses on their stands to (his) right and left."

24 SAG *šar-ru-ti-ja* É.KUR *šú-a-tú a-na si-ḫi-ir-ti-šú* . . . [*ú*]-*šak-lil*, Streck, *Asb* p.170:51.

25 Cf. the dictionaries and von Soden, *RAI* XX (1975) 134.

26 In Harran, Nusku had a temple of his own called Emelamanna, on which see Streck, *Asb* p.762. For the god's cella in Ešarra cf. van Driel, *CA* p.37f.

10

Bibliography:

(I) Waterman, *RCAE* 1141.

(II) Deller, *AOAT* 1 (1969) 61.

The text has now (19.1.1976) been joined to 83-1-18,513 (unp.) providing the missing halves of all lines extant in 83-1-18,151 but not missing top and bottom of the original tablet. For a new transliteration and translation see New Joins (p. 373).

Copy of 83-1-18,513:

CT 53, pl. 209 no. 942.

Writer:

Nabû-aḫḫē-erība and Balasî. This assignation seems assured by the gloss *ur-ḫu* in rev.3', cf. Appendix M 6.[27] The spelling *be-li* (obv.8), on the basis of which the letter was in Pt.I attributed to Ištar-šumu-ēreš (cf. App. M 6), is not attested in letters of Nabû-aḫḫē-erība and Balasî; but since it is on the other hand, by no means *exclusively* restricted to letters of Ištar-šumu-ēreš (cf. 31:3 and 32:1 [Nabû-zēru-līšer]; 116:6 [Marduk-šumu-uṣur]; 124:11, 167: 1.5 [Adad-šumu-uṣur]; 220:3 [Nabû-nāṣer]; 225:6 [Urad-Gula]; and 241:11 [unknown writer]), it cannot be considered as distinctive as the gloss which is a feature only attested in letters and reports of Balasî and Nabû-aḫḫē-erība. See also note on r4'.

Date:

Ulūlu II (= September), 670 BC. Cf. obv.11 and rev.2'ff showing that the letter was written in a leap year containing an intercalary *Ulūlu*, and note that 670 was the only leap year during the attested career of Balasî (674-665) meeting this requirement (see App. A1).

Discussion:

This letter evidently concerns a prospective royal pilgrimage to a sacred city of Assyria, probably Assur, Arbela, or Calah (cf. *LAS* 146, *ABL* 333 and 1285; less likely to Babylon, since that city was usually not spelt with the determinative URU [obv.7], cf. *AOAT* 6 s.v. Bābili). Since the time of the journey was left open, it was hardly occasioned by a public festival but rather by personal needs, and the possibility therefore exists that the letter is related to *LAS* 72, q.v.

Notes:

10. *ina É-an-ni*: lit. "inside", probably idiomatic for "out of sight" (sc. of the common people). The grounds for this caution remain unclear (hemerological?).

r4'. *da-ri-ir*: the first attestation of the stative of *darāru* "to intercalate" (cf. *da-ra-ri* 38 r10, *lid-ru-ru* 325 r8). Note that the verb is (save for *ABL* 971 r1) hitherto only attested in letters of Balasî.

r6'. *ITU e-ri-ib-a-ni* "(in) the coming month"; cf. UD 5.KAM *ša e-rib-a-ni*, *AfO* Bh 6 no. 9:3f, and note also *LAS* 69 r8' (ITUBÁR *e-tur-bu*), 65 r12 ([ITU *ša*] *er-rab-an-n*[*i*]), and 287 r10 (ITU *ša e-ra-ban-ni*). The final -*i* (for expected -*u*, cf. on 25 r8') may be due to the preposition *ina* (implied, here omitted as unnecessary) but is also explainable otherwise (cf. note on 174 r12).

11

Bibliography:

(I) Waterman, *RCAE* 1145.

Writer:

Ištar-šumu-ēreš, judging from the handwriting (personal collation) and the spelling *be-li* in ibv.5' (cf. App. M 6).

[27] Cf. also obv.11f with 72:11ff, r2f and r10f.

Discussion:
Though not fully clear in details, owing to its fragmentariness, this letter evidently pertains to the cult (*par-ṣi*) of Venus (^{MUL}*Dili-bat*), on which see the commentary to *LAS* 308. Obv.2'ff (and rev.2ff) indicates that the present ceremonies were linked with the heliacal rising of the planet as *evening* star (cf. notes to r5 and 69 r4').[28]

Notes:

2'-5'. Possibly quoting an Ištar prophecy, the suffix *-ja* (4') referring to the goddess.

7'. Probably [^{MUL}*Dili-ba*]*t ša sin-niš* "feminine Venus", see note to 69 r4'. *ak-li* perhaps = pl. of *ak(a)lu* "(sacrificial) bread" (cf. 309 r19, *ABL* 65 r8, *BA* 2 628:27, etc) rather than = *aklu* "overseer" (*CAD* A/1 p.277ff; cf. Postgate, *GPA*, commentary to no.15:52). Cancel the translation in Pt.I.

r5'. *nap-ḫa-ta*: to be analysed as {napḫat+a} = stat. sg. 3 fem. of *napāḫu* „to be lighted, to rise" (referring to heavenly bodies) + the ventive suffix *-a(m)*, which the verb regularly takes in the meaning concerned (cf. *AHw* 732*b*). This interpretation seems obligatory in view of the spelling *nap-ḫa-ta-ni* in obv.3', which shows that the final *-a* had morphemic relevance and was not due to prosodic factors (cf. note to 18 r8) nor to orthographic conventions (Deller's "inverse spellings"): without the ventive suffix, the paradigmatic subjunctive form would have been **napḫat-ūni*. Obviously, one has to reformulate *GAG* § 82d, according to which "im Stativ gibt es besondere Ventivformen nur bei der 3. Ps. *mit Ausnahme der 3. f. Sg.*" Another similar case is *še-ṣu-a-ta-ni* in *KAV* 205:6, to be analysed as {šēṣuat+a(m)+ni}, cf. *ša-ak-nu-tu-ni* ibid.7.

12

Bibliography:
(I) Waterman, *RCAE* 37 (cf. IV 173).
(II) Dhorme, *RHR* 116 (1937) 7; Meier, *AfO* 12 (1937/39) 240.

Date:
Addāru 25, eponymy of Šulmu-Bēl-lašme = March 24, 669 BC. For the month and day see obv.11f; the year follows from the connection of the letter with *LAS* 65, whose date is discussed in detail in commentary to *LAS* 70.

Addressee:
Esarhaddon.

Discussion:
Rev.8ff of this letter deals with an omen concerning Venus (not related to a recent observation), Obv.6ff with a forecast predicting the heliacal rising of Mercury in the coming month (Nisannu) and attributed to an unnamed colleague of Ištar-šumu-ēreš. Even though a substantial portion of the text is now lost, it seems certain that the writer categorically rejected the forecast as faulty and irritatingly amateurish.[29] In this he was definitely right, for Mercury was in fact due to appear much earlier – according to the tables of Schoch (1928), already on March 24 (Addāru 25), 669, the very date of the present letter. In view of the well-known difficulties encountered by Mesopotamian astrologers in predicting the heliacal phenomena of Mercury exactly (see sub *LAS* 53), the surety by which Ištar-šumu-ēreš could turn down his colleague can only imply that he had personally succeeded in observing the rising of Mercury before writing the present letter.

Evidently Ištar-šumu-ēreš did not bother to detail to the king the grounds on which he was able to reject the prediction but simply satisfied himself with observing the fact and mocking his colleague. This had unfortunate consequences. The king, who was not himself able to read the letter, mistook the Venus-omen explained in r8ff for

[28] For a religious ceremony possibly connected with this event see *KAR* 139, analyzed by Oppenheim, *History of Religions* 5 (1966), 250-265.

[29] Note the scornful proverb cited in rev.3ff. Since the Venus omen is only introduced in rev.8, this proverb must pertain to the communicator of the Mercury forecast (unless a new topic was introduced in the preceding fragmentary lines, which seems very unlikely). Cf. also Obv.14f with 65:15f and r2f, and 66:10ff.

a real observation and, believing that Ištar-šumu-ēreš had totally excluded the possibility that Mercury would rise soon, and assuming that he had instead observed *Venus*, sent to Nabû-aḫḫē-erība and Balasî to confirm this observation (*LAS* 65-66).[30] Both astrologers naturally indignantly refuted the impossible observation, Nabû-aḫḫē-erība mockingly suggesting that the "cheater" be promoted, and demanding to see first thing in the morning the report which the man had sent to the king. The chain of misunderstandings finally led to a quarrel between Nabû-aḫḫē-erība and Ištar-šumu-ēreš, reported in *RMA* 55:

Obv.1	^{d}*3[0 u$_4$-mu] ú-šal-lam*	"The moon-god will complete [the
2	*ša b[a-a-di] re-eš* MU.AN.NA	day; t[onight] is the New Year's
3	SIG$_5$ *š[a* LUGAL] EN-*ja*	day; good luck t[o the king], my lord.
4	*ina* UGU $^{\text{M[UL]}}$UDU.IDIM.GU$_4$.UD	As to the planet Mercury on which
5	*ša* LUGAL *be-lí iš-pur-an-ni*	the king, my lord, wrote to me,
6	*it-ti-ma-li* ^{Id}*15*-MU-APIN-*eš*	yesterday Ištar-šumu-ēreš had
7	*ina* ŠÀ É.GAL *ṣa-a-su*	an argument with Nabû-aḫḫē-erība
8	*a-na* ^{Id}PA-PAP^{MEŠ}-SU *ig-di-ri*	in the palace. After-
Rev.1	*i-da-a-ti ina nu-bat-ti*	wards, in the evening, both
2	*it-ta-al-ku gab-bi-šú-nu it-ta-aṣ-ru*	went to make the observa-
3	*e-ta-am-ru ip-tu-šu*	tion, saw (it) and were satisfied.
4	*ša* ^{I}*B[a]-la-si-i*	From Balasî."

According to the report, the argument had taken place on Addāru 29. This is exactly what one would expect on the grounds of *LAS* 65 r4ff, where Nabû-aḫḫē-erība asks for permission to glance over the words of the "incompetent" astrologer "tomorrow", i.e. on the 28th of Addāru. For the evidence associating *RMA* 55 with the present letter and *LAS* 65-66, see in more detail under *LAS* 70.

On the basis of the foregoing, one should beware of taking too literally the isolated passages in the present corpus where the scholars have to correct surprising statements attributed to their colleagues; such cases may well be due to misunderstandings on the king's part. A clear example of such a misunderstanding seems to be furnished by *LAS* 46.

Notes:

10. *"Which month do you have now?":* This question is probably to be taken at its face value: the king, who did not possess a modern pocket almanac and was not even aided by the moon (which was at the time concerned only visible just before dawn), simply wanted to know how long he still had to wait for the month Nisannu to begin; possible he also wanted to know how long in advance the prediction was made. The same question also in *LAS* 65, 106 and 329.

r3-6. This passage not only *sounds* like a proverb but is actually *defined* as such in rev.7', cf. *LAS* 145 r9ff; note also the language (Standard Babylonian) typical of Akkadian proverbs. The passage is accordingly to be added to the corpus of "proverbs quoted in letters and elsewhere" (Lambert, *BWL* 280ff). For another proverb quoted by Ištar-šumu-ēreš (and missing in *BWL*) see commentary to *LAS* 182; cf. also 281 r12ff (with comment) and 322:4'ff.

r10ff. In its complete form, the omen here quoted reads: I ^{MUL}*Dil-bat ina še-re-e-ti i-kun* (UN^{MEŠ}) KUR DÙ.A.BI NINDA *nap-šá* KÚR^{MEŠ} LUGAL^{MEŠ} KÚR^{MEŠ} SILIM^{MEŠ} "If Venus is stationary in the morning, (the people of) all countries will have much food to eat (and) hostile kings will be reconciled", *ACh* Ištar 2:6; Spl. 34:8-9.

[30] Note the date of the letters (Addāru 27) which is exactly what one would expect supposing that the king received *LAS* 12 on Addāru 26 and immediately wrote to the two scholars; the quotation MUL *Dili-bat nam-rat* [*ina* ITU.Š]E *nam-rat* (65:7f), which clearly refers to r8ff of the present letter (combined with Obv.11); and the fact that the Venus omen of the present letter is also discussed in *LAS* 65:18ff in response to the king's letter.

The appended commentary is likewise given in a slightly abbreviated form. Cf. *ACh* Ištar 2:7f, *ina šu-ut* AN-*e* (var. 2 Spl. 41:1, *ina* KASKAL *šu-ut* ^{d}*A-nim*) KUR-*ma* GÍD *na-ma-ru* GÍD *a-ma-ru ina a-ma-ru ki-na-at* KI. GUB-*sà* GI.NA [8] *: ina* ^{d}UTU.ŠÚ.A KUR-*ma še-e-ru na-ma-ru* ŠE.ER.ZI ÍLA-*ma* "she (Venus) lights up in the path of the Anu stars; GÍD = to be bright, GÍD = to see; she is stable to behold, her stand is stable. Dito, she is lighted in the west; *šēru* (morning) means 'to be bright', she is of great luminosity."

The omen itself seems to have originally referred to the stationary phase of Venus as *morning star* (i.e. at the end of its inferior conjunction); this is actually how it is interpreted in *LAS* 69:19. However, the commentary extends its significance to cover *both* stationary points of the planet, i.e. also the moment it appears as *evening star* (before the inferior conjunction). It is perhaps no coincidence that Ištar-šumu-ēreš here presents only the latter interpretation, for though Venus was not visible, *Mercury* was as a matter of fact rising as evening star (cf. above discussion). Note also the point made in the commentary about the "homophony" of *namāru* "to be bright" and *amāru* "to see", and cf. *namrat* ("it is visible", but also "it is bright") in 65:7.

13

Bibliography:
(I) Waterman, *RCAE* 519.
(II) Behrens, *ABB* (1906) 109; Weidner, *OLZ* 16 (1913) 209f; Landsberger, *LSS* 6/1-2 (1915) 126; Dhorme, *RHR* 116 (1937) 7f; Labat, *Royauté* (1939) 321; Oppenheim, *JAOS* 61 (1941) 264 and 64 (1944) 193; Weidner, *AfO* 14 (1941/44) 180; Elman, *JANES* 7 (1975) 23 ff.

Photograph:
RCAE IV pl. 12 (obv. only).

Date:
Probably mid-January, 671 BC = late Kanūnu, eponymy of Nabû-bēlu-uṣur. This date is based on the following (admittedly rather complicated) evidence. Firstly, the letter quotes and interpretes three planetary omens derived from retrogradations of Mars and Jupiter:

(1) Mars emerges from Scorpio, retrogrades and re-enters Scorpio (Obv.21 ff);
(2) Mars retrogrades from the head of Leo and touches Cancer and Gemini (Rev.3 ff);
(3) Jupiter passes Regulus, retrogrades passing Regulus again, and then moves forward passing Regulus for the third time (Rev.12 ff).

Between 680 and 645 BC – the absolute time limits of the career of Ištar-šumu-ēreš (see Appendix 0) – respective retrogradations were observable only on three separate occasions:

Mars (1): April 5 through June 20, 667 BC;
Mars (2): November 17, 659, through February 6, 658 BC;
Jupiter (3): November 26, 679, through March 26, 678 BC.[31]

The fact that the three retrogradations concerned span a period of over 20 years and in addition are all separated from one another by an interval of approximately 10 years makes it clear that the writer cannot in all cases refer to actual, recently observed omens; rather, the passage Obv.21 – Rev.24 has to be understood as a systematic presentation and discussion of *all evil omens* derived from the retrogradations of outer planets, intended to demonstrate the king that he had without reason accused the writer of leaving out of consideration an "evil" omen, which actually was not evil at all (see Obv.5-8, and cf. commentary to *LAS* 41). Accordingly, *none* of the omens mentioned in the letter constituted the immediate reason for its writing, and the above dates of the three retrogradations have thus nothing to do with the date of the letter itself. Nevertheless, they offer *indirect* assistance to the dating. On the one hand, the incidental remark that the writer had personally discussed the last (Jupiter) omen with the king to whom the letter was addressed (Rev.23 ff) not only gives the letter a terminus post quem

[31] See Appendices C and D.

(678 BC)[32] but also a terminus ante quem (669 BC, the year in which Esarhaddon died). The concomitant reference to the deceased "servant of the king" even implies a lower terminus post (674 BC), see note on r24. On the other hand, the very fact that the writer deals exclusively with retrogradations of Mars and Jupiter indicates that either of these planets was retrograde while the letter was written, even though the event in question was not considered evil-boding.

The broad time brackets 674-669 BC thus obtained can be narrowed down on the basis of Rev.25f, "Saturn, too, will 'push itself' this very month". This is tantamount to saying that the planet Saturn had passed a stationary phase and was about to enter a retrograde period, like the other planet considered earlier in the letter (see note on r26); in other words, while the letter was written, either Mars or Jupiter was retrograding, and Saturn was soon expected to do the same. This immediately rules out the possibility that the retrograding planet was Jupiter, since Jupiter and Saturn did not retrograde simultaneously or in close succession between 674 and 669 BC. By contrast, the retrograde phases of Mars and Saturn overlapped thrice (in 674/3, 671 and 669) during these years, as follows:[33]

	MARS		SATURN	
	stationary	retrograde	stationary	retrograde
674	± Nov 30	beginning Dec 5	Nov 20 - Dec 25	beginning Jan 1
671	± Jan 4	beginning Jan 10	Dec 15 - Jan 20	beginning Jan 25
669	± Feb 15	beginning Feb 20	Jan 10 - Feb 15	beginning Feb 20

Holding that the letter was written in a situation where Mars was retrograde while Saturn was still stationary, as deduced above, the last case is evidently out of the question. Both others seem possible at the first glance. However, on closer examination it becomes evident that the case of 674/3 must also be left out of consideration. At the end of December, 674, Mars was retrograding from the "head" of Leo (longitude 105°) towards Cancer, which it was due to reach at the end of the next month; even though it ultimately did not "touch" Gemini, the situation resembled the second Mars-omen discussed in the letter, and under such circumstances the writer could certainly not have presented the omen concerned as calmly as he actually does. By contrast, in January 671, Mars was retrograding from Virgo towards Leo — an event considered harmless from the astrological point of view and thus perfectly fitting the implications of the letter.

Addressee:
Esarhaddon.

Notes:

9 ff. An exceptionally solemn oath; normally only two gods (maximum) are mentioned in the introductory clause. Cf. *LAS* 249 r4-6, *ABL* 541 r2-7, and 695 r7-10 (oath introduced by *ina libbi ilāni attama*); *LAS* 214 r6-9, 321:3, *ABL* 841:14-18, and *NL* 54 r1-10 = *Iraq* 21 p. 163 (introduced by DN_1 DN_2 *ilānīka/ja lū ūdû*); *LAS* 219 r2-4, 254 r9-11, *ABL* 390 r10-12, 556:18-20, 1285 r26-29, and *Iraq* 20 p.191 r11-12 (introduced by (DN_1 DN_2) *ilānīku/ju*); and *LAS* 199:16-r6, *ABL* 211 r6-8, 884 r3, 896:12-13, 972:3-5 and 1432:11 (introductory clause omitted altogether).

23. *pi-ŠAR šú*: better *pi-šìr-šú*. While **pišar-* is theoretically acceptable as a stat. cstr. form of *pišru* besides *pišir-* in view of the frequent *a/i* alternation in the environment C-C liquid/nasal/dental (e.g., *tarṣi/tirṣi, ilku/alku, pinnigu/pannigu, adru/idru, siman/simin, nēmal/nēmil*; cf. Matouš + Petraček, *ArOr* 24 (1956) 1 ff), it is nowhere attested in unequivocal spelling (**pi-šá-ar-šú*, etc.); wherever such spellings occur, the form is always unquestionably *pišir-* (cf. *pi-še-er-šu/šú*, *LAS* 35 r4, 234:4', 300:8, 302:11, 326:6). The syllabic value SAR = *šìr* is unequivocally attested in the present corpus e.g. in (*ú-še-šìr-am-ma*, *LAS* 153 r2, and *pi-šìr-a-ti*, 185:12' and 186 r11

[32] Sic; even though Jupiter retrograded in Leo also in 667/666 and 655/654 BC, it did not pass Regulus thrice in those years, as the omen quoted in the present letter presumes. Before 679/678, the omen was also observable in 691/690 BC; but at that time, Ištar-šumu-ereš had certainly not yet entered the king's service.

[33] Cf. Appendices C and D. The dates given here are only approximative, corresponding to the difficulty of determining the beginnings of the retrograde periods precisely with the naked eye.

(<*pišrāti*,[34] with an anaptyptic *-i-* inserted between *š* and *r* in accordance with the rule formulated in the note to *LAS* 39:11).

21-27. As pointed out above (sub Date), the retrogradation discussed here was not observable (in recent time) before the letter was written, but only a couple of years afterwards; the conjunction *kīma* "when" doesn't accordingly here refer to the past but has an indefinite meaning ("whenever"), and is more or less here equivalent to the conjunction *šumma* "if" occurring in r13 (cf. note to 156:11). An actual, *observed* retrogradation of Mars in Scorpio is referred to in *RMA* 33, 68, 70 and 236G (all dating from 667 BC); cf. especially *RMA* 70 r2 ff, MUL*Ṣal-bat-a-nu is-su-uḫ-ur* 3 *ut-ta-mì-iš ina pa-na-tu-uš-šu* | *ina* ŠÀ MULGÍR.TAB 4 *il-lak lum-nu šu-ú* 5 *ma-šar-tú ár-ḫi-iš lu-gam-mì-ru* 6 *uṣ-ṣu-ú ša* LUGAL EN-*ja lu-u ú-qur* 7 *a-du né-mar-u-ni a-ke!-e ša il-lak-u-ni* 8 *iz-za-zu-u-ni* "Mars has turned round, set in motion, (and) is going forwards inside Scorpio — an ill-portending sign. The muster (of troops) should be finished quickly, (and) the outside visits of the king, my lord, should be kept to a minimum untill we see how it goes and stands".[35]

r2. *ša pi-i um-ma-ni šu-u*: literally, "it is according to the masters"; referring to authoritative oral tradition (sayings of ancient scholars) circulated in written form. See, in detail, Yaakov Elman, "Authoritative Oral Tradition in Neo-Assyrian Scribal Circles", *JANES* 7 (1975) 19 ff, especially 26 ff.

r3-7. Cf. note to Obv.21-27; no astrological reports pertaining to this case of retrogradation are extant, but its special ominousness is also evidenced (albeit indirectly) by *RMA* 235, a report from Akkullānu probably written a couple of months before the opposition of Mars in 672 BC: MUL*Ṣal-bat-a-nu* MULAL.LUL *ik-ta-*[*šad*] 2 *ina* ŠÀ-*šú e-ta-rab ma-ṣar-tu at-ta-*[*ṣar*] 3 *la in-né-mid la i-zi-iz* KI.TA *il-*[*ta-pat*] 4 *il-lak ú-ṣu-um-ma re-e-ḫe a-na a-*[*ma-ri*] 5 *ki-ma it-tu-ṣi pi-šìr-šú ana* LUGAL EN-*já a-*[*šap-pa-ra*] "Mars has reached Cancer (and) entered it. I have kept watch; it has not become fixed nor stationary (but only) to[uched] the lower part (of the constellation), and keeps going. The exit only remains to be ob[served]. As soon as it has emerged, I shall se[nd] the pertinent solution to the king, my lord" (Rev.1 ff).

r16 ff. This omen is also quoted in *RMA* 272 r4 ff: I MULSAG.ME.GAR *ik-*KUR-*am-ma* MULLUGAL DIB-*iq-ma ip-ni-šú* EGIR-*nu* MULLUGAL 5 *šá* MULSAG.ME.GAR DIB-*šú-ma ip-nu-šú* KUR-*ma* (glossed *i-kas-šá-dam-ma*) MULSAG.ME.GAR DIB-*iq-ma ana ri-bi-šú il-lak* 6 *taš-nun-tu* GÁL-*ma a-a-ab* ZI-*ma* AŠ.TE DIB-*bat 2-iš* KUR *ina-an-ziq* "If Jupiter reaches, passes and gets ahead of Regulus, and afterwards Regulus, which Jupiter passed and got ahead of, reaches and passes Jupiter, beginning to set, there will be rivalry, and an enemy will come up and seize the throne; alternatively, the land will groan." The report in question contains numerous other astronomical omens, observations and forecasts, on the basis of which it is certainly datable between the 18th and 25th of November, 679 BC, i.e. immediately before Jupiter began retrograding in the way described in the omen (cf. above, sub Date).

r17. *ša* MUL*LUGAL*: a lapsus for MULLUGAL *ša* (cf. *RMA* 272 r4-5). A similar scribal error also occurs in *RMA* 244:8 ([MUL] UDU.SAG.IDIM.UŠ for MULUDU.IDIM.SAG.UŠ).

r23. *"The servant of the king"*: almost certainly referring to Nabû-zēru-līšer, the father of Ištar-šumu-ēreš and his predecessor as the chief scribe and *ummânu* of Esarhaddon: the wording of the passage implies that a well-known and respected person was in question; nobody deserved to be called *the* servant of the king better than his personal counselor; the context shows that the man was a "scribe"; and it is known from *LAS* 31 that Ištar-šumu-ēreš did work with his father, just as the present passage implies. None of the extant letters of Nabû-zēru-līšer appear to postdate 674 BC; his death therefore probably occurred in 673. Note that the earliest datable letters written by Ištar-šumu-ēreš alone (in the capacity of the chief scribe) date from early 672 BC (see *LAS* 1-3).

r26. *ra-man-šú i-da-'i-ip*: literally, "will push himself". In the present context, the meaning intended can only be "to begin to move" (after a stationary phase).[36] The verb usually found in this technical meaning in astro-

34 Written *pi-iš-ra-a-te* in *KAR* 141:8.

35 A report from Nabû-aḫḫē-erība; cf. its "doublet" *RMA* 68, from Balasî. Both reports were written on Du'ūzu 1 = July 5, 667 BC; the muster mentioned in *RMA* 70 probably referred to preparations for a campaign to Egypt, cf. sub *LAS* 73.

36 Another technical meaning of *ramanšu da'āpu*, much more frequently attested than the present one, was "to collapse" (referring to buildings). See Deller and Parpola, *RA* 60 (1966) 66; cf. also *LAS* 19 r10'. This meaning is naturally excluded here.

nomical contexts was *nammušu* (cf. e.g. the passage quoted under note to Obv.21-27); perhaps the choice of the present expression was prompted by mythological considerations, cf. B. Alster, "Ninurta and the Turtle", *JCS* 24 (1972), 121:40-44.

r29. *is lip*: obscure; one would expect either *il-lak* "it goes" or *e-tiq* "it passes".

14

Bibliography:
(I) Waterman, *RCAE* 565; Pfeiffer, *SLA* 327.
(II) Oppenheim, *JAOS* 61 (1941) 260.

Writer:
The assignation of this letter to Ištar-šumu-ēreš (based on the handwriting, which resembles that of *LAS* 4, the affinities of the text with *LAS* 13 and 15,[37] the introductory formula, which excludes Balasî and Nabû-aḫḫē-erība,[38] and orthographical considerations[39]; see also notes to Obv.6 and 15) is not absolutely certain; the writer can also be Akkullānu. Cf. *LAS* 300+110 and 302 (subject matter, dividing lines, phraseology), 303 and 314 (introductory formula), and *RMA* 235, quoted in note to *LAS* 13 r3-7 (note especially *RMA* 235 r4 = present letter, r11 f; *RMA* 235 r5 = present letter, r3-5; and *RMA* 235 r2 = present letter, r3). The fact that the phrase *anniu piširšu* occurs in the letters of Akkullānu in the spelling *pi-še-er-šu* only (302:11, cf. 300:8) is not against his authorship, since the spelling *pi-šìr-šu* occurring here is found in his *reports* (e.g., *RMA* 235 r5). The plene writing *le-E-mur* (r14) is comparable with *le E pu šu* (299 r9), *ta-A-mur* (110 r5), and *le-E-*[*mur*] (331 r8), and the wish in Obv.6-8 with 298 r29'f, 301:8ff, and 302:6ff. The exclamation "perhaps the king will not believe me!" (r6) also fits well in the mouth of Akkullānu, cf. 298 r18'ff, 302 r11'ff, 305 r5'ff, etc.*

Date:
Not determined, but certainly determinable with absolute precision. An occultation of Jupiter behind (nearly) full moon (cf. on r13f) is a very rare event and as such identifiable with certainty, provided that the approximate time limits of the observation are known. In the present case, one can set as such time limits the years 680 and 645 BC, as all other datable letters and reports of Ištar-šumu-ēreš and Akkullānu were certainly written within those years and there is no other evidence either that these scholars were active as royal counselors beyond the years concerned. Jupiter passes full or nearly full moon approximately every thirteenth month; thus within the period indicated, such a passing was observable 34 times (e.g. in August 672, September 671, October 670, Deember 669, January 667, February 666, etc.), and on one of these occasions, when the latitudes of the moon and Jupiter coincided with a precision of 15', the occultation anticipated in the letter took place. The moment in question could, I believe, relatively easily be identified with the help of computer-generated tables giving lunar and planetary longitudes and latitudes with the required precision at fice-day intervals for the period concerned, such as have been compiled by Bryant Tuckerman for the Neo-Babylonian and later periods;[40] unfortunately no such tables are available for the Sargonid age at present, and as it is very time-consuming to compute the necessary data manually, I have not made a serious attempt to solve the problem for the time being.[41] *

37 Note especially the dividing lines and the phrase *an ni u pi šìr šu* found in both letters.

38 Neither of these scribes inserted the conjunction *u* between ᵈPA and ᵈAMAR.UD. For Ištar-šumu-ēreš, cf. *LAS* 12, 19 and 26 (EN-*já*).

39 Note especially the spelling *le-E-mur* (r14), to be compared with *le-e-pu-šu* 1 r4, *le-e-ru-bu* 1:19.r10, etc., but not paralleled in letters of Nabû-aḫḫē-erība and Balasî. The spelling *be-lí* (Obv.14, Rev.6, for I.'s usual *be-LI*) also in *LAS* 13 passim.

40 B. Tuckerman, *Planetary, lunar and solar positions 601 B.C. to A.D. 1 at five-day and ten-day intervals* (Philadelphia 1962).

41 RMA 235A, a report by Bēl-šum-iškun datable to 675 BC (see App. J1), refers to an occultation of Jupiter said to have taken place thrice(!) after the lunar eclipse of Arahsamna = November, 677 BC. The precise time when this occultation occurred, and whether it can be identified with the occultation meant in the present letter, remain to be established.*

Discussion:

The occultation anticipated in the letter is reported as occurred in two astrological reports, *RMA* 192 and 193, the former (unsigned, Assyrian script) very plausibly identifiable as the report promised in the present letter, r3-5, the latter (Babylonian script) signed by a certain Ṭābīja, the author of 7 further reports to king (*RMA* 12, 71, 73, 222, 243A, 260, and Ki 1904-10-9,28), one of which (*RMA* 222) is datable to 668 BC. Beyond omens, these reports contain little information useful for the identification of the event. The month in question is not specified; but *RMA* 193 quotes, following omens derived from the occultation, ones pertaining to the opposition of the moon and the sun on the 14th day. As astronomical omens generally seem to have been reported in chronological order (cf. e.g. *RMA* 272), this may imply that the occultation had occurred shortly *before full moon* (observed on the 14th), as also suggested by the present letter (cf. on r13 f).

The omens derived from the event differ slightly in the two reports, but they were consistently ill-portending, especially to the king of Assyria (cf. the present letter, Obv.14-20). *RMA* 192 gives more omens, and reads:

(1-3) "If Jupiter stands in the middle of the moon, the king will die in that year; dito, the moon and the sun will be eclipsed, (and) a great king will die";

(4-7) "If Jupiter enters into the moon, there will be famine in the Westland; the king of Eastland will be slain with weapon; in Subartu (Assyria) a nobleman will rebel against his lord."

(r1-2) "If Jupiter enters the moon, the rate of exchange of the land will deteriorate";

(r3-4) "If Jupiter emerges from the rear side of the moon, there will be hostility in the country."

Occultations of planets constituted a potential cause for the enthronement of a substitute king (see Intr., p. 56 f); in the present case, however, it is unlikely that any substitute was needed since the omens, though bad, did not explicitly predict the death of king of Assyria.

Notes:

6. *šùl-mu ša a-dan-niš*: similar expressions are [*râmu*] *ša a-dan-niš*, *RMA* 247:4 (Ištar-šumu-ēreš), [*d*]*u-un-qu* [*š*]*a a-dan-niš*, *LAS* 199:16f, [*ṭa-ab-t*]*a-nu ša a-dan-niš*, 212:10, and *šá-a-r*[*u*] *dan-nu ša a-dan-niš*, *CT* 53 197:6.

12f. Quoted from *ACh* Ištar 19:1, I ^{MUL}SAG.ME.GAR *ana* EGER ^{d}*30* GUB *nu-*KÚR*-tú ana* MAN *ina* KUR GÁL-*ši*, "If Jupiter stands at the rear side of the moon, there will be hostility against the king in the country". Cf. also *RMA* 192 r3f, I ^{MUL}SAG.ME.GAR *ana ku-tal 30* È ^{4} *nu-*KÚR*-ti ina* KUR GÁL-*ši*, "If Jupiter emerges from the rear side of the moon, there will be hostility in the country." The expression "at the rear side of the moon" has to be understood in light of the apparent (westward) motion of the moon, see Largement, *ZA* 52 (1957) 259; Jupiter was accordingly to be seen to the east of the moon, where it of course had to be in order to be overtaken by the moon.

14f. Restore LUGAL *be-lí* ⸢*a*⸣-[*bu-tú*] ^{15} *in!-nu-*⸢*u!*⸣[42] [*ši-i*] "O king, my lord, [this is] a m[atter] concerning us" on the basis of *LAS* 299:8'ff, *a-bu-tu an-ni-tú us-se-ṣi-a . . . in-nu-u* "I have brought up this matter . . . , it concerns us". Cf. also *it-tu iš-šá-n*[*u-u*] "a portent concerning them", *RMA* 74 r2, referring to Amurru.[43]

19f. Restore (probably) *lum-nu* [*ša* KUR SU.BIR$_4$^{KI}] ^{20} *šu-ú-*[*tu*] "it is an ill portent [to Subartu (Assyria)]." Cf. *LAS* 298:13 (*lum-nu ša* KUR URI^{KI}) and ibid. r24'f (H[UL] *ša* KUR SU.[BIR$_4$^{KI}]), and see Discussion.

r6ff. This passage clearly implies that eunuchs (^{LÚ}SAG) were in Assyria commonly regarded as men in whom the king trusted most, a fact strongly suggesting that ^{LÚ}SAG (= *šá-re-šú*, Igituḫ Short Version 232) has indeed universally to be taken to mean "eunuch" (as required by linguistic considerations [cf. Hebr./Aram./Arab. *sarîs* "eunuch", a loanword from Assyrian], and numerous other reasons [see below]), and not just a type of go-

42 Sic; collated by E. Sollberger (19. 1. 1976). The traces would also permit reading *in-nu-t*[*ú*] (to conform with the gender of *abutu*), but *LAS* 299:8'ff and 45:17f (*in-nu-ú zi-it-ti-in-ni*) show that the form *innû* was used for both Masc. and Fem.

43 The report in question is signed by ^{LÚ}GAL-A.BA "the chief scribe", i.e. Ištar-šumu-ēreš.

vernment official (as most recently argued – with some reservations – by Oppenheim, "A Note on *Ša Rēši*", Gaster Festschrift [1973] 325ff). Cf. Herodotus VIII 105: "Among the barbarians, eunuchs are, in respect to their uncompromising fidelity, held in higher esteem than the uncastrated", and more fully, Xenophon, *Cyropaedia* VII 60 ff: "(When starting to organize his bodyguard, Cyrus realized that he would hardly find among married men servants in whose loyalty he could absolutely trust;) but as he observed that *eunuchs* were not susceptible to any such affections [as married men], he thought that they would esteem most highly those who were in the best position to make them rich and to stand by them, if ever they were wronged, and to place them in offices of honour; and no one, he thought, could surpass him in bestowing favours of that kind. Besides, inasmuch as eunuchs are object of contempt to the rest of mankind, for this reason, if for no other, they need a master who will be their patron . . . But he did not admit what many might very easily be inclined to suppose, that eunuchs are weaklings . . . On the contrary, they showed both in times of war and hunting that they still preserved in their souls a spirit of rivalry; and of their fidelity they gave the best proof upon the fall of their masters, for *no one ever performed acts of greater fidelity in his master's misfortunes than eunuchs do.* And if it is thought with some justice that they are inferior in bodily strength, yet on the field of battle steel makes the weak equal to the strong. *Recognizing these facts, he selected eunuchs for every post of personal service to him,* from the door-keepers up."

For further evidence showing that ^{LÚ}SAG = *ša-rēši* means "eunuch" and nothing else, note that the Middle Assyrian court statutes (*AfO* 17) state explicitly that the *ša-rēšēn* had to be castrated (*marrur*)[44]; that homosexuals were punished by turning them into *ša rēšēn* (*KAV* 1 II 54.97); that *šūt rēši* are called *la ālidi* "unable to beget"(*CT* 23 10:14), that clauses referring to children and grandchildren are missing in Neo-Assyrian contracts in which eunuchs appear as possible violators of the deed; that the prophecy quoted in note to *LAS* 129:8 carefully distinguishes between "the sons of the bearded" (= uncastrated court-officials) and "the successors (*ḫalputu*) of the eunuchs"; and note the sculptural evidence discussed by Reade, *Iraq* 34 (1972) 87 ff (cf. also the remarks of Layard, *Nineveh and Its Remains* II (1850) 325f.). For the social and political role of eunuchs in Mesopotamia, cf. also Herodotus III 48 ff; 77 ff; 92; VI 9 and 32; Diodorus XVI 47ff; Ktesias F 15, 54 ff, etc.

r9. *i-da-at* ^{d}*30*: in view of the context, certainly = *ku-tal*/EGER ^{d}*30* of the omens quoted above, and hence to be translated "the rear side of the moon". *i-da-at* is here possibly a neologism derived from the preposition *(id)dāt* "after" (*CAD* D 121f), meaning originally "(what comes) after (something)".

r11f. One "span" or "half-cubit" (NA *rūṭu* < *(amma)r-ūṭu*, see Landsberger, *WZKM* 56, 110) = 15 "fingers" (*ubānu*) of 5' = 1°25' (i.e., three apparent diameters of the moon). Cf. *15* ŠU.SI = ½ $^{\text{ú-ṭu}}$ KÙŠ, *RA* 23 p.33 no.49:3, and see Thureau-Dangin, *RA* 28 (1931) 23 ff on the measures *ubānu* and *ammatu* (5' and 2°30') used in Mesopotamian astronomy to express small angular distances. The moon pacing daily a distance of ca. 13° (i.e., ca. 30' in an hour), it can be concluded that the occultation was to take place approximately 3 hours after the writing of the letter.

r13f. *"He should stand in shadow"*: This remark (together with the previous remark that the observer should be sharp-eyed) implies that the occultation took place at (nearly) full moon. The same is also implied by *RMA* 193, see above, sub Discussion.

15

Bibliography:
(I) Waterman, *RCAE* 385.
(II) G. Meier, *Or*NS 8 (1939) 306.

Copy:
Cf. Harper, *ZA* 8 (1893) 350f.

---

44 Cf. Oppenheim, *JANES* 5 (1973) 330, and *CAD* M/2 p. 223b. It has to be pointed out, however, that the suggested interpretation of *marrur* is uncertain and other renderings (like "hardened") are not excluded.

Discussion:

The central issue of this letter (and in effect, of the royal letter quoted in Obv.7-10 and 12-?13) seems to be: Is an incident (described in the king's letter) to be regarded as ominous, and in particular, is it to be interpreted in light of a particular omen, the protasis of which (quoted in Obv.7f) differs slightly from the actual incident? The issue is admittedly trivial, and the significance attached to it probably due to special circumstances: the incident had apparently happened while the king was embarking on an important journey, perhaps on a military expedition, as suggested by r13-16. After presenting a detailed analysis of the case (Obv.14 ff), the scholar concludes that it has indeed to be regarded as ominous (r1 f) and goes on to present the traditional interpretation of the protasis cited by the king, which is not lucky at all (r8-10). If I understand correctly the continuation, the king is then advised to call off the planned expedition on the grounds that he would be defeated by the enemy kings, as predicted by the omen (see notes on r11 ff).

Of the two kings to whom the letter can have been addressed (Esarhaddon and Assurbanipal), only the latter mentions in his inscriptions the Nabataeans (r11), and the incident in question took place relatively late in his reign, see Streck, *Asb* p. CCLXXXV and Weippert, *WO* 7 (1973) 72. But it would be risky and probably wrong to associate the present letter with this episode. Expeditions against the Nabataeans may have been planned much earlier, only to be subsequently cancelled, perhaps for reasons as trivial as those given in the present letter.

Notes:

7. *ú-la*: interpretation unclear; possibly an emphatic variant of the negation *la*, in which case the passage should be rendered: "Doesn't (the omen so-and-so) apply to what emerged from under the chariot? It does (*ina muḫ-ḫi šu-u*)." However, this (OA) negation is otherwise not attested in Neo-Assyrian. All other NA attestations of *ú-la* are to be taken as variants of the conjunction *ulâ* "or" (otherwise spelled *ú-la-a*), cf. *ABL* 523 r8 ff, EN.NUN-*ka tu-uk-*[*tin*] ^{9} *te-ti-qa tal-la-ka* ^{10} *ú-la i-ti-is* EN.[NUN-*ka*] ^{11} *ú-ṣur* EN KUR *ta-t*[*aq-qa-nu-ni*] "(if) you have secured your position, you (may) come over here, *otherwise* stay (where you are) and be on your guard until the country is safe"; *LAS* 187 r2 ff, *ja-um-ma* ^{3} [*šu-u du*]*l-li ú-la šu-mu* . . . ^{6} *a-qab-ba-áš-ši ta-zak-kar* "(as to the names . . .) [it is a ri]tual of mine; *or* I shall tell the names . . . to her (and) she will pronounce them"; *CT* 53 78+426 r1 ff, [*i*]-*lak a-na me-eḫ-ri-šu i-qab-bi ma-a ina* IGI LUGAL ^{2} *la qa-bi ú-la* LUGAL *be-lí bir-ti* IGIx2^{MEŠ}*ša* ^{L}[^{Ú}*N]AM^{MEŠ} ^{3} *ina muḫ-ḫi lu-ma-di-du* "he will go and tell his comrade: 'It was not communicated(?) to the king.' Alternatively, O king my lord, let it be made clear to the governors that . . ." Cf. also the two attestations of *ú-la-ma-a* "or/lest" (< **ula+ma*?) in *NL* 14:28 (*Iraq* 17 pl.30) and *CT* 53 92:8' (*ḫa-na-k*[*a*] $^{8'}$ *le-ku-lu ú-la-ma-a a-du be-lí* ^{9} [*ina* ^{U}]^{RU}$_{A}$^{MEŠ}-*dur-na-ni lil-li-ku-né*). The meaning "or" (etc.) does not fit in the present context, however.

10. *tu-ṣu-u-ni*: in view of r4 (and the fact that ^{d}NIN.KILIM = *šikkû* "mongoose" is at least formally masculine) one would rather expect *ú-ṣu-u-ni*. The feminine prefix is perhaps due to the formulation of the question: does a protasis referring to *legs* apply to what emerges from under *a chariot*? Here the stress is on the difference between legs and chariot (note the lengthening of the final vowel in ^{GIŠ}GIGIR-*e*); the identity of the animal (which is not questionable) is of secondary importance. The king may in fact have intentionally formulated his question in an abstract way, not referring to the mongoose specifically but to the situation in general, without any reference to the animal. From this point of view, the feminine prefix would be understandable; abstract words and "things" in general were feminine in Akkadian.

For the rest of the line cf. above, note on Obv. 7.

12 ff. These lines probably specified the position of the king's legs on the chariot; the fragmentary exposition cannot be reconstructed reliably.

r1 f. The idiom *ana X kullu* "to regard as" also occurs in *LAS* 325:6; cf. Oppenheim, *JNES* 35 (1974) 205[31]. Note also *a-na it-tum ul iṣ-ṣab-bat*, *RMA* 236:2-3.

r2. *šu-u* [^{d}*NIN.KILIM*]: this word order also in Streck, *Asb* p.30 iii 96, *ù šu-u* $^{I.d}$GIŠ.NU$_{11}$-MU-GI.NA ŠEŠ *la ke-e-nu* "but that deceitful brother of mine, Šamaš-šumu-ukīn . . ." In the present context, *šu-u* may also mean "that is (to say)", serving as a bridge to the following sentence which specifies the event considered ominous (mongoose approaching the chariot from the left and passing under it); cf. note on 298 r21'.

Taken as an omen, the incident was definitely ill-portending. Apart from the omen quoted in Rev.8-10, it may be noted that mongoose was considered a portentuous animal (note simply the spelling of the name of name of the animal with the determinative ^{d}) and that the left side (Latin *sinister!*) was in the Mesopotamian omen theory generally interpreted as unlucky (see I. Starr, "Pars familiaris and pars hostilis in Mesopotamian extispicy", in press).

r8-10. This omen does not seem to be otherwise attested; nevertheless, it was almost certainly quoted from the 32nd tablet of *Šumma Ālu*, which contained mongoose omens according to the catch-line of Tablet XXXI (*CT* 38 pl.43; cf. *KAR* 394 ii 2').

r11. Cancel the nonsensical rendering of this line in Pt. I, and render instead: *a-ḫu-lam-ma* ^{LÚ}*Na!* (text MA)*-ba!-aja-ti* [12] *ni-iq-bi* "Let us say 'mercy' to the Nabataeans" (i.e. let us 'pardon' them, dropping the campaign being prepared against them). The passage is admittedly extremely difficult, and even the interpretation proposed here is not unproblematical. It is based on the following considerations:

(1) *a-ḫu-lam-ma*: An ambiguous word, cf. the different translations in *AHw*. ("weit weg", p.22*b* s.v. *aḫula*) and *CAD* ("alas! woe!", A/1 p.213 s.v. *aḫūla*; "possibly the expression is to be connected with *aḫulap* as a late popular etymology influenced by *aḫullâ*"). Actually, *both* renderings are correct, for the word is a merger of two etymologically distinct lexemes (*aḫu+ullâ+ma*, lit. "at the other side [of the river]", and *aḫulap+ma* "mercy!", or the like); the former meaning is attested in *ABL* 615 r3 ff, PAP *17* UDU *ša* É ^{d}*Da-gan* [4] *ina pa-an* LUGAL*-ma ḫa-na-ak* [5] *la ú-še-ti-qu* [6] *a-na a-ḫu-lam-ma* [. . .] || *a-na a-hu-la*, *ABL* 879:5 (referring to Elam, cf. ibid.10), and possibly in *LAS* 320:4', the latter in the NA personal name *Aḫulamma* (^{I}*A-ḫu-lam-ma*, *ADD* 711 r7; *AR* 55:18; *RA* 22, 147:13; VAT 10007 r8 and 16502:10, ^{I}PAP*-lam-ma*, VAT 9783a 9, b 7, and 14454:1.9.16.38, see Deller, *OrNS* 34, 267) to be compared with the OB *Aḫulap* names cited in *CAD* A/1 214f (*Aḫulapja*, *Aḫulap-mītim*, *Aḫulap-wēdim*, etc.). In the present context, a local adverb is obviously out of the question, whereas the meaning "mercy!" fits well: note that the word is immediately followed by the verb *qabû*, and cf. the numerous examples of the expression *aḫulap qabû* in NA royal inscriptions referring to the pardoning of enemies, listed in *CAD* A/1 214.

(2) ^{LÚ}*Na!-ba!-aja-ti*: This reading seems obligatory, despite some epigraphic difficulties (cf. the collation in Pt.I p.295; the crucial signs were recollated at my request by E. Sollberger in January, 1976. The sign following LÚ is unquestionably MA or ÁŠ, and can only be taken as NA by assuming scribal sloppiness; the following sign () is not SIL but BA lacking the final vertical, cf. *LAS* 2 = *ABL* 33:6 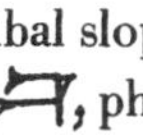, photo *RCAE* IV pl. 6). Accepting that the interpretation hesitatingly attempted in Pt.I (LÚ*-ma sil-ija-ti*) is abortive, as seems clear, the only alternative left is to take the signs as a gentilic referring to the "enemy kings" mentioned in r13. The only known NA gentilic ending in *-aja-ti* is the well-known ^{LÚ}*Na-ba-aja-ti* (see *AOAT* 6 s.v., and cf. ibid., Reverse Index), and the possibility that an unknown gentilic is in question is extremely slight considering that the people concerned had several "kings".

(3) *ni-iq-bi*: certainly to be taken as cohortative ("we should say/let us say"). The preterite was obsolete in NA positive-assertive main clauses, and the lack of an interrogative word/vowel lengthening indicates that the passage was not to be understood as a question.

r12 f. The rendering of this passage proposed in Pt.I also needs modification: the negation *la* does not belong with *u-la-a* "why" but to the following nominal clause, which it marks as interrogative (for similar cases cf. e.g. *LAS* 171 r1-2 and 181 r6-7); *a-ta-a* is to be understood as a one-word question motivated by the preceding sentence (cf. 290 r29'). Render accordingly: "Why (so)? Are they not enemy kings?" The latter question is a rhetorical one, intended to emphasize the "self-evident" fact that since the king's adversaries were also kings, he would run the risk of being defeated by them, as predicted by the omen, if engaging in battle with them. The end of the letter (r14-16) states this even more explicitly: "They will not submit under the king's chariot." This last sentence cannot be taken as a question since the word order is normal and no interrogative words or vowel lengthenings are present.

16

Bibliography:

(I) Waterman, *RCAE* 34.

(II) Oppenheim, *JAOS* 61 (1941) 266.

Date:

Possibly Du'ūzu 14 = June 22, 670 BC. See Discussion.

Discussion:

Chances to identify the earthquake reported in this letter (which could provide a clue to its dating) are theoretically extremely slim, considering the commonness of earthquakes in the geographical area concerned. Nevertheless, a suggestion to this effect can be made on the basis of contemporary reports and letters dealing with earthquakes (*RMA* 262D, 263, 264, 265, 265A, 265B, 265C, 266, 266A, 266B, 267; K 1345; *LAS* 35, 137, 138, 147, 148, 234; BM 123358 = *Iraq* 4, p. 189) and the omens cited in the present letter, Obv.11-12 and Rev.8'. Most of the reports mentioned, and some of the letters, not only specify the month in which the earthquake they report occurred but also give some data as to the time of day concerned; at least 8 different earthquakes are referred to in these texts:

	Month	Year	Time	Text	Writer
(1)	Nisannu	657	night	*RMA* 264, 265	Ištar-šumu-ēreš, Aplâ
(2)	Simānu	669		*LAS* 234, (137f)	Balasî, (Adad-šumu-uṣur)
(3)	Du'ūzu 14		day	*RMA* 265A	Šāpiku
(4)	Du'ūzu		night	*RMA* 265B	[. . .]
(5)	Tašrītu			*RMA* 265C	Rēmūtu
(6)	Kanūnu		night	*RMA* 266	chief scribe
(7)	Šabāṭu		night	*RMA* 266A, 267	[Nabû-iqīša], Ištar-šumu-ēreš
(8)	Addāru	657		*RMA* 264	Ištar-šumu-ēreš

Supposing that the earthquake under consideration is to be identified with one of the above cases, it is immediately clear that at least nos. 1, 4, 6 and 7 are out of the question since all of them took place at night, whereas the present letter refers to an earthquake in the daytime. Nos. 2, 5 and 8 must be left out of consideration because the fragmentary apodoses in Obv.11-12 cannot be reconciled with any earthquake omens associated with the months Simānu, Tašrītu and Addāru (cf. *ACh* Adad 20:38; Sin 35:11; Labat, *IE* §§ 100:3 and 101:3 [Simānu]; *RMA* 265C:1-3; *ACh* Adad 20:42; Sîn 35:27; *IE* §§ 100:7 and 101:7 [Tašrītu]; and *ACh* Adad 20:47; Sîn 35:48; *IE* §§ 100:12 and 101:12 [Addāru]. Only no.3 can be plausibly identified with the present case: it occurred in the daytime, and both omens quoted in the pertinent report are also found in the present letter (see notes on Obv. 12 and Rev.8'). The omen quoted in Obv.11 remains unexplained; it could perhaps be matched with an omen pertaining to the month Kanūnu (see note), but in that case the omen in Obv.12 would in turn remain unexplained. Thus it can be concluded that the earthquake under consideration probably occurred in the month Du'ūzu.

RMA 265A cannot be dated, but another report by the same writer (*RMA* 167) is datable to March, 669 BC, i.e. in the last year of Esarhaddon; none of his other reports can be dated to Assurbanipal's reign, and so there is at least some reason to suppose that even the earthquake reported in *RMA* 265A (and in the present letter) occurred toward the end of Esarhaddon's reign. For evidence suggesting that it is to be placed in 670 BC see the commentary to *LAS* 147.

Notes:

5f. Cf. *ABL* 438:17ff, *ša* LUGAL *be-lí iš-pur-an-ni* [18] *ma-a mi-nu i-ba-áš-ši* [19] *ú-de-e* [I]*Aš+šur*-EN-LAL [r.1] *e-pu-uš*.

7. *NAM.BÚR.BI ḪUL ri-i-bi*: this apotropaion is also mentioned in *LAS* 35 r12.22, 147:12 and 148 r2; the ritual tablet is fragmentarily preserved in *KAR* 7. Cf. commentary on *LAS* 137.

ba-ši: to my knowledge, the only attestation of the "normal" stative of *bašû* in Neo-Assyrian. For Neo-Babylonian, see *CAD* s.v. *bašû* (passim).

8. *É.GAL ma-šar-[t]e*: probably referring to the "armoury" of Nineveh (mod. Tell Nebî Yūnus) restored by Esarhaddon in 673/2 BC (cf. Borger, *Ash* p.59 ff), less likely to that of Calah (Fort Shalmaneser). The present passage is probably to be taken as a recommendation for the king to change his residence temporarily from the acropolis to the southern outskirts of Nineveh; the grounds for this are given in the following lines (cf. the omen Obv.12).

10. The beginning of the line is possibly to be restored simply as [*ši-i*].

11. Cf. *RMA* 266:7f, I *ina* ^{ITU}AB *ri-i-bu* ŠÚ-*ub* [8] LUGAL *ina* URU KÚR-*šú* TUŠ-*ab* "If there is an earthquake in Kanūnu, the king will take residence in the city of his enemy"; similarly *ACh* Sîn 35:40, BE (*ina* ^{ITU}AB) *ri-i-bu i-ru-ub* LUGAL *ina* URU KÚR *uš-ša-ab*; *RMA* 266A:4f and 267:14 f, I *ina* ^{ITU}ZÍZ KI *i-ru-ub ina* É.GAL NUN KÚR TUŠ-*ab* NUN *ana* KÚR-*šú i-qal-lil* "If the earth quakes in Šabāṭu, an enemy will dwell in the palace of the prince, the prince will count for less than his enemy" (restorations partly from *ACh* Adad 20:46); *LAS* 234: 5'ff, I *er-ṣe-tú ina* ^{ITU}SIG$_4$ *i-ru-ub šu-bat na-me-e na-du-u-ti ina a-mat* ^{d}EN*.LÍL *uš-ša-bu*. To my knowledge, these are the only earthquake omens containing the verb *wšb* in the apodosis; only the first could *possibly* be reconciled with the omen quoted here. But cf. above, sub Discussion.

12. Cf. *RMA* 265A r3 ff, I KI-*tim ina* ^{ITU}ŠU *i-nu-uš* NUN *ina* KUR IDIM [. . .] *i-rab-*[. . .] "If the earth trembles in Du'ūzu, the prince in the palace(?) . . . . . "; Labat, *IE* § 100:4, I *ina* ^{ITU}ŠU LUGAL/MAN KUR IDIM/DUGUD KUR *i-qàl-lil* "If (there is an earthquake) in Du'ūzu, the king of the country will count for less than a nobleman of the country"; and ibid. § 101:4, I *ina* ^{ITU}ŠU (KI *i-ru-ub*) LUGAL *ina* ŠÀ KUR-*šú i-qal-lil* "If (the earth quakes) in Du'ūzu, the king will be vilified inside his palace". The present line could plausibly be restored after *RMA* 265A r3f (read *ina*! KUR! IDIM! for M[U] BI); *IE* § 101:4 would account for the change of residence recommended in Obv.8f.

r2'-4'. These lines remain unclear.

r8'. This omen also in *ACh* Adad 20:51 (I KI *ina kal* UD *i-nu-uš* BIR-*aḫ* KUR), *RMA* 262D:1-2 (I KI-*tim ina kal* UD-*mi i-nu-uš* BIR-*aḫ* KUR), 263:1-3, and 265A r1-2.

17

Bibliography:
(I) Waterman, *RCAE* 675.

Notes:

9. *Aššur-mukīn-palēja*: This son of Esarhaddon was consecrated by Assurbanipal as high priest of the god [. . .] in his first year (Streck, *Asb* p.250:16), and appears later as donator of literature to the royal libraries (*ADD* 1053, dated 648 BC) and as a treaty partner of Assurbanipal's successor Sîn-šarru-iškun (*BRM* 4 50:4, ca. 627 BC). The present letter could thus, theoretically, date from any phase of Ištar-šumu-ēreš's long career (678-650 BC, cf. Appendix 0). However, it is likelier that it is approximately contemporary with the other letters of the present corpus mentioning Aššur-mukīn-palēja, which all belong to the last years of Esarhaddon (or possibly to the very first year of Assurbanipal). Cf. *LAS* 46 (669 BC) and 52, from Balasî; *LAS* 69+71 (669 BC) and 72, from Nabû-aḫḫē-erība; *LAS* 145 (669 BC) and 352, from Adad-šumu-uṣur; *LAS* 157, 218 (670 BC), 219 and 240, from Nabû-nāṣer; and *LAS* 250 (672-669 BC), from Urad-Nanâ; the letters of Balasî, Nabû-aḫḫē-erība and Adad-šumu-uṣur (*LAS* 145) pertain to visits of the prince to his father, the rest to his health. The present letter almost certainly belongs to the former category.

r2'. *né-e-su-ku*: G Prs./Pret. of *'sk* "to assign"? Otherwise only D forms of this verb are attested in NA.

18

Bibliography:
(I) Waterman, *RCAE* 1375.

Discussion:

Owing to the breaks, this letter necessarily remains partly unclear. The obverse clearly dealt with (divine?) statue(s), cf. *LAS* 7, 58-59, 276, 281, etc. On the reverse, however, this matter has been dropped: it seems that someone (the writer himself?) is seeking admission to the king's audience, a privilege which the king appears to have denied anyone who did not visit him while he was merely crown prince (r10-17). This suggests that the letter was addressed to Assurbanipal shortly after the death of Esarhaddon and accordingly has to be placed in late 669 BC.

Notes:

r8. *la-aṣ-ba-TA le-[pu-uš]*: cf. *la-ṣa-ba-TA . . . la-áš-pur* "let me seize *and* send", *ABL* 1369 r2 ff; *ú-ṣa-bi-TI . . . na-ṣa* "he seized *and* brought", *ABL* 599:12'f; *li-ib-tu-QU . . . lid-din* "let him separate (a piece of land) *and* give (it to my messenger)", *ABL* 480 r6 f, etc. As illustrated by these parallels, the final vowel attached to *laṣbat* has nothing to do with the ventive suffix but corresponds semantically to the enclitic particle *-ma* "and", which in its coordinative function had become almost completely obsolete in Neo-Assyrian. The loss of the particle was compensated by prosodic means, raising the pitch (and, concomitantly, lengthening the vowel) of the syllable previously followed by *-ma*; closed syllables were thereby usually opened by means of paragogic vowels in accordance with the law formulated in note to *LAS* 259 r9 f (*ṭāb* > *ṭāba*, etc). For more examples of these "coordinative" vowels, see notes on *LAS* 252:11 and 280:23; cf. also on 58 r6, 246:12 and r1, and 248:13.

r9. *ṣi-ib-tu ú-ṣ[a-ab]*: if correctly restored, this seems to be the first attestation of the (OA/OB) expression *ṣibtam waṣābum* in Neo-Assyrian. Cf. note on 315 r10 f.

r13. *ina ga ri du* [. . .]: unclear. Perhaps simply an error for *ina* É *re-du-[u-ti]* "in the Succession Palace"?

19

Bibliography:
(I) Waterman, *RCAE* 1378.
(II) Dhorme, *RHR* 116 (1937) 9.

Discussion:

The restoration of [*ma-a*] in line 6 is of course only conjectural; the passage could also (and perhaps more plausibly, cf. Rev) be rendered: "I have seen the [. . .] on which the king wrote to (or sent) me to Assur". However that may be, the letter is clearly a (preliminary) report on investigations conducted by the writer (by the king's order) in a temple or temples in Assur, perhaps in the context of the restoration work carried out by Esarhaddon in that city, and is accordingly possibly related with *LAS* 8-9.

Date:
Possibly 669 BC; see on r9'.

Notes:

r2'-5'. Probably quoting words of a priest; cf. 277:7ff and 309 r1 ff. The restoration of r3' proposed in Pt.I is very uncertain and probably wrong. In r5' Harper's *uq-ṭa-li-lu*! (text 1B)-[*u*]*ni* "they have diminished (the quantity of gold)" is preferable to the interpretation given in Pt.I.

r6'. Cf. *EA* 27:26f, *ki-i a-na ši-ip-ki tù-ur-ru . . . gam-ru-ma*, referring to statues of gold.

r8'. *qa-a-tú ina lìb-bi tal-lik-u-ni*: an idiom apparently not attested elsewhere (cf. the dictionaries); lit., "where the hand has moved". Cf. notes on *aḫu* + *alāku* (212 r4) and *ubānu* + *alāku* (39 r11).

raq-qa-aq: "*very* thin", an intensive form of *raqqu* "thin" (see *GAG* § 55m); cf. *ABL* 467:25f, GIŠŠÚ.AMEŠ . . . *ša me-eḫ-ri ši-na* 26 *ra-qa-qa a-dan-niš* "these stools of *meḫru*-wood are extremely delicate". The meaning of the present passage is clear: contrary to the gold-work of old, the cultic objects manufactured in the days of the writer were not cast but (made of wood and) only plated with gold, probably owing to shortage of sufficient amounts of the precious metal. The implication seems to be: these cheap objects should be replaced by worthy ones as soon as possible.

r9'. *É dMAR.TU*: This temple, also called É-níg-ba-dù-a (cf. é-níg-ba-dù-a / É *nap-ta-ni nid-pi-i'* / É dMAR.TU, *KAV* 42 ‖ 43 r24), had previously been restored by Tiglatpileser I (12th cent. BC), cf. Unger, *RlA* I p.179*b*. The restoration referred to here is not recorded in any building inscriptions of Esarhaddon of Assurbanipal; this may imply that the work was completed late in Esarhaddon's last year (669 BC), too late to be recorded in the inscriptions of this king and too early for Assurbanipal to take the credit for the completion of the project to himself.

r10'. *É dA-nù*: certainly referring to the famous Anu-Adad temple of Assur (É *dA-nù* dIM *šá* URUŠÀ-URU, *3 R* 66 ii 24f). The housing of Amurru in this temple is natural in view of the fact that Amurru was considered an aspect of Adad (cf. dMAR.TU = dIM *šá a-bu-be*, *CT* 24 pl. 40:8).

20

Bibliography:
Waterman, *RCAE* 41.

Notes:

6. *is-su ḫa-r[am-me]* "recently, of late": this translation is grounded in note to *LAS* 176:6.

r4'ff. All restorations here are very uncertain and should be treated with caution.

21

Bibliography:
Waterman, *RCAE* 677.

Discussion:

For another letter of Ištar-šumu-ēreš to the mother of Esarhaddon (Naqia/Zakūtu) see *LAS* 230 (and cf. *ABL* 254, 263, 303, 324, 368, 569 and 917, likewise addressed to the queen mother); the possibility is not excluded that both fragments are actually parts of the same tablet. While the purpose of these letters remains unclear owing to their fragmentary condition, the fact that they are the *only* letters to the queen mother in the present corpus suggests that they were written in an exceptional situation, possibly immediately after the death of Esarhaddon (early November, 669 BC) when Naqia temporarily held the reins of the empire (cf. *ABL* 1239).[45]

On Naqia in general see the literature mentioned sub *LAS* 230.

Notes:

r2'. *dNIN.LÍL*: Instead of Ninlil, the name of this goddess in Neo-Assyrian texts should be read as Mullissu (> Greek *Mylitta/Molis*), see provisionally Postgate, *BSOAS* 34 (1971), 390.*

r4'f. The text of these lines, misprinted in Pt.I, should read as follows: UDMEŠ GÍDMEŠ DÙG+G[A *lìb-bi*] 5 HUL *lìb-bi* x [. . . .].

45 Hardly during her illness in 670 BC, on which see sub *LAS* 222.

25

Bibliography:
(I) Waterman, *RCAE* 38.
(II) Dhorme, *RHR* 116 (1937) 7; Oppenheim, *JAOS* 64 (1944) 190f; von Soden, *Fs Christian* (1956) 101; Kümmel, *StBoT* 3 (1967) 173ff, 180.

Date:
Approximately Simānu 13, eponymy of Šamaš-kāšid-ajābī = June 9, 669 BC. See in detail sub *LAS* 77.

Addressee:
Esarhaddon.

Notes:

r1'. Notice the difference between the tenses of the conditional sentences here and in line 6':
šum-ma i-⸢*šá*⸣*-*[*kan*] (Prs., the king speaking);
šum-ma is-sa-kan (Pf., words of the writer).

This difference has no modal implications, but is to be explained purely on the temporal basis. The general rule governing the use of tenses in NA conditional sentences is that the present refers to the future, the Pf. to the past; to express precedency in time in relation to the main clause, Pf. was used (cf. the use of Pf. as a futurum exactum, discussed in note to *LAS* 34:8).[46] The aspect of will was expressed by the present or the precative, as usual; all other modal implications were to be read from the context. For example:

I. Conditional sentence: P r s.

šum-ma šu-u i-da-an [12] *a-na-ku la-din* "if he will give, I shall give", *ABL* 167 r12-13;

šúm-ma qa-ra-bu [15] *tu-up-pa-áš ep-šá* "if you will (= want to) fight, fight!", *ABL* 174:14-15;

šúm-mu LUGAL *be-lí i-qa-bi* [2] *ina* É *Aš+šur nu-še-ri-ib-ši* "if the king, my lord, says (= wants), we shall bring it into the temple of Aššur!", *ABL* 433 r1-2; similarly *ABL* 371 r11f, 683 r7f, 1092:19, *LAS* 38:20-22, 177: 10f, 246 r5f;

šúm-ma LUGAL *be-lí* [9] SAG*-su-nu i-na-ši* [10] *pa-an* ^{LÚ}*mu-šar-kis*^{MEŠ} [11] *ina* ^{URU}*Kal-ḫa šú-nu* "in case the king wants to summon them, they are at the disposal of the recruiting sergeants in Calah", *ABL* 127r 8-11;

šum-mu tal-la-ka [9] *a-na* ^{URU}*Kal-ḫa a-na* ^{I}*A-ḫu-ni* [10] *liš-pa-ru-né* "if she (wants to) come, let them write to Calah to Aḫūnī", *LAS* 186 r8ff;

šum-ma i-qal-lil [4] *pi-še-er-šú ri-i-bu šu-u* "if he will come to naught, its explanation can be the earthquake only", *LAS* 35 r3-4;

LUGAL *be-lí ṭè-e-mu* [11] *liš-kun šum-ma ú-ṣu-u* [12] *šum-ma li-zi-zu* "the king, my lord, should give orders whether they should come out or stay (inside the armoury)", *ABL* 375 r10-12;

šúm-ma šal-ma-a-ti ni-mat-ta-aḫ [8] *šúm-ma 1-et a-na 2-šú ni-ba-taq* [9] *mi-i-nu šá ši-ti-i-ni* LUGAL *be-lí* [10] *liš-pu-ra* "the king, my lord, should send definite instructions as to whether we (should) lift them intact or cut each in two", *ABL* 467 r7-10;[47]

II. Conditional sentence: P f.

a) denoting past time

šum$_4$*-ma ina ta-ḫu-me-ku-nu* [3] *ina* ^{URU}ḪAL.ṢU^{MEŠ}*-ku-nu* [4] *aḫ-ti-ṭi ina* ŠU^2*-ja* [5] *ba-i-a* "if I have violated your territory or forts, take me to account", *ABL* 548 r2-4;

---

[46] In negative sentences the Pf. is replaced by Prt. as usual.

[47] Similarly *mi-i-nu ša ši-te-i-*[*ni*] [8] *šum-mu* TA* *e-mu-qe-e-šú il-la*⸢*-ka*⸣ [9] *šum-mu za-ku-u šu-u-tu il!-la!-ka ma-a ár-ḫiš* [10] *ina* UGU DUMU.LUGAL *a-šá-pa-ra* "I shall quickly send to the crown prince a definite report as to whether he will come with his troops or whether he is 'clean'" *ABL* 198 r7-10.

šum-ma PN *si-par-ri* AN.BAR [7] *a-sa-kan si-par-ri* AN.BAR-*e-šú* [8] *li-[i]p-ṭu-ru* "if I have put PN in irons, let them release his irons", *ABL* 154:6-8;

b) denoting future time

šúm-ma [6] UN^{MEŠ} *ú-se-bi-la ina* UGU LUGAL *be-lí-a* [8] *ú-še-ba-la-áš-šú-nu* "if he sends people, I shall send them over to the king, my lord", *ABL* 128 r5-8;

šúm-ma i-tal-ku-né [18] *[i-tu-ṣ]u-u-né ina* UGU LUGAL *ú-še-bal-šú-nu* "if they return, coming out (of their hiding place), I shall send them over to the king, my lord", *ABL* 310 r17-18;

šúm-mu la iš-mu-né [7] *ina* UGU LUGAL EN-*a a-šap-pa-ra* "if they will not obey them, I shall write to the king, my lord", *ABL* 610 r6-7;

šúm-ma is-sa-kan šúm-ma la iš-kun [10'] *mi-i-nu ša ši-ti-i-ni a-na* MAN EN-*já* [11'] *a-šap-pa-ra* "I shall send the king, my lord, a definite report as to whether it (the eclipse) takes place or not", *LAS* 278 r9'-11'. (Cf. above, I, last example).

Accordingly, in the present case, Pf. is required in Rev.6 because the expected eclipse would have taken place before the action denoted by the verb *i-na-sa-ḫa* in Rev.9'; whereas in Rev.1 the verb is in the present, because information concerning the eclipse could be given even before the event had actually occurred.

r3' ff. Cf. App. F 4. For the full wording of the omens here paraphrased see *RMA* 271.*

r7'. *kaqquru* "area, region" was the technical term for "moon quadrant" (see App. F 4); in the eclipse of June 10, 669, only the quadrant of Subartu/Assyria was eclipsed. For the transliteration *kaq-qu-ru* (not **qaq-qu-ru*) see E.E. Knudsen, "Cases of free variants in the Akkadian *q* phoneme", *JCS* 15 (1961) 84 ff. Note, however, that *kaqquru* cannot be considered a *free* variant of *qaqquru* in Neo-Assyrian, since there are no explicit spellings of this word with an initial *q* (**qa-qu-ru* etc.) in Neo-Assyrian texts. By contrast, all unequivocal spellings we have show an initial *k*, e.g. *ka-aq-qí-ri, LAS* 45:20; *ka-qí-ri*, 280 r13; and *ka-qu-ru, LAS* 10+ r8', *ABL* 100 r8, and 433 r5.

r8'. *šá-a-RI*: a lapsus for *šá-a-ru*. The Nom./Gen. distinction was otherwise on the whole well maintained in the present corpus, and the few exceptions to the rule are usually attributable to Babylonian influence (cf. on 280:23).

26

Bibliography:
(I) Waterman, *RCAE* 676.
(II) Oppenheim, *JAOS* 64 (1944) 194; Böhl, *Opera Minora* (1953) 417; von Soden, *Fs Christian* (1956) 104f.

Date:
About Ulūlu 19 = September 5, 671. This date is based on the following reasoning. Obv.8-9 is almost certainly a reference to a planet issuing from the "breast" of a zodiacal constellation. "Breast" (*irtu*) is known as a part of two zodiacal constellations only, Leo (^{MUL}GABA-UR.GU.LA, Gössmann, *Planetarium* p. 67) and Scorpio (^{MUL}GABA-GÍR.TAB, ibid. p.31). The planet in question can hardly have been but Venus, Mars or Jupiter (Saturn moves too slowly in relation to the zodiac to be considered seriously, Mercury too quickly); the traces in Obv. 8 fit only Mars ([^{MUL}*Ṣal*]-*bu*[*t-u-n*]*u*). Rev.3 refers to the enthronement of a substitute king (cf. 30:6 ff and 279: 10 ff), hence the observation under consideration must have been made relatively soon after it. Altogether 6 separate performances of the substitute king ritual during the career of Ištar-šumu-ēreš are known, beginning respectively in Ulūlu/September, 674 (*LAS* 30-31), Du'ūzu/July, 671 (*LAS* 249 and 292), Kanūnu/December, 671 (*LAS* 185, 232 and 279-280), Ajāru/May, 669 (*LAS* 25, 28, 77, 135-139, etc), Du'ūzu/July, 666 (*LAS* 298), and Nisannu/April, 657 BC (*LAS* 334). Mars was not even near Leo or Scorpio at any of these dates. But it is known that on three occasions, following the total lunar eclipses of September 674, July 671 and December 671, the substitute king initially enthroned in Nineveh was taken to Babylonia and re-enthroned there (see *LAS* 30, 134, 249,

279 and 292).[48] In the last case the re-enthronement followed very soon after the initial enthronement (*LAS* 280); the date of the other re-enthronements is unknown, yet it would be logical to assume that the substitute king, under normal conditions, spent half his reign in Nineveh and the other half in Akkad. Thus the three re-enthronements in question would have occurred respectively about October 23, 674, August 21, 671, and January 1, 670. The middlemost date fits perfectly, whereas the other two fail completely. On August 21 = Ulūlu 4, 671, Mars was already very close to Scorpio, and by September 5 = Ulūlu 19 (i.e. only two weeks after the hypothetical date of enthronement) it had reached Antares, the star identified as the breast of Scorpio (see note on 235 r4 and, for the position of Mars at the time concerned, Stahlman + Gingerich, *Solar and Planetary Longitudes,* p.225). The agreement with the present letter is thus perfect. Moreover, it is known for certain from *LAS* 277 (written on September 27, 671, or slightly earlier) and 292 (written on October 7, same year) that the exit of Mars from Scorpio was indeed followed closely during the time the substitute king was resident in Akkad in fall 671. By contrast, as already stated, no other known enthronement of the substitute king provides an explanation for Obv.8-9. The dating to 671 is finally also supported by the fact that the king is in the present letter addressed not as "Farmer", as in *LAS* 25 (669 BC) and 31 (674 BC), but merely as "my lord".[49]

Addressee:
Esarhaddon.

Notes:

8f. Restore (in accordance with the above discussion): [^{MUL}*Ṣal*]-*ba*[*t-a-n*]*u* [T]A* ŠÀ *ir-ti* ^{9} [*ša* ^{MUL}GÍR.TAB *ú*]-*ṣa-a* "Mars is issuing from the breast [of Scorpio]". There is no place for [*ma-a*] in the beginning of line 8; the passage is accordingly *not* a quotation from the king's letter.

r1'ff. See discussion sub *LAS* 27. On the practice of having the substitute king "take on himself" all the bad omens threatening the safety of the king even at his re-enthronement, see in more detail *LAS* 279:11 ff and 30:6 ff.

r8'. Cancel the translation of this line in Pt.I and render: "I attached (them) to his seam". While the meaning of *ag-da-da-ad* in the preceding line remains uncertain,[50] the idea of the passage is clear: the evil omens previously recited to the substitute king were written down (on a papyrus or pergament scroll, or a perforated cuneiform tablet) and attached to the garment of the substitute, to make sure that he was constantly "afflicted" by them. On the magical doctrine underlying the procedure, see Contenau, *Magie* p. 127 ff.

27

Bibliography:
Previously unpublished.

Copy:
CT 53, pl. 141 no. 593.

Date and discussion:

About Ulūlu 4 = August 21, 671 BC. The omission of the word "Farmer" in Obv.13, as well as the affinities of Obv.6f with 26 r1'-4', indicate that this fragment is approximately contemporaneous with *LAS* 26; and Obv.10-13, where the writer asks the king to communicate to him all the evil omens he is possibly aware of, shows

[48] In only one case (*LAS* 279) it is explicitly stated that the substitute king enthroned in Nineveh was the same as the one enthroned in Akkad. But since Esarhaddon was king of both Assyria and Babylonia, it was obligatory that one man only functioned as his substitute in both countries in the other case, too.

[49] This form of address is, it is true, also used in *LAS* 28. But in that case, the title "Farmer" could not be used anyway, since the substitute king had not yet been enthroned and the king thus had not yet changed status, whereas in the present case no such obstacle was in the way.

[50] Cf. *AHw* p.273a; possibly to be read *aq-ṭa-da-ad* "I bowed".

that the letter was written at the time of the re-enthronement of the substitute king in question. The grounds for dating this re-enthronement to Ulūlu 4 = August 21, 671, are presented sub *LAS* 26. The temporal distance of the two letters would thus be about two weeks. This agrees well with the proposed dating, supposing that *LAS* 26 was written soon after the writer received the king's answer to the present letter. Judging from *LAS* 279:6-10, journey from Nineveh to Akkad took normally about 5 days,[51] which would imply that the king's letter reached Ištar-šumu-ēreš only about 10 days after the dispatchment of the present letter (unless of course the mail was delivered by special couriers).

On the basis of Obv.10, where Ištar-šumu-ēreš refers to signs he has personally observed, it is probable that at the moment of enthronement he recited to the subsitute king only whatever omens he was himself aware of, and later supplemented the inventory by the omens communicated in the king's letter. This would account for the two separate recitation ceremonies mentioned in *LAS* 26 r1' ff.

Addressee:
Esarhaddon.

Notes:

1. The title ^{LÚ}ENGAR restored in this line in Pt.I has to be cancelled on the basis of Obv.13 and *LAS* 26, where it is missing. Cf. note on 28:1.

28

Bibliography:
(I) Waterman, *RCAE* 674.

Date:
Ajāru 29, eponymy of Šamaš-kāšid-ajābi = May 27, 669 BC. Cf. *LAS* 104, and note that there were only three solar eclipses visible in Nineveh between 680-663 BC, viz. those of June 17, -678; May 27, -668; and August 28, - 663. The first possibility can be ruled out since Ištar-šumu-ēreš heads the writer team of the letter (see sub *LAS* 31); the last is extremely improbable as no other letter of the present corpus is datable to 664 BC.

Addressee:
Esarhaddon.

Notes:

1. Cancel the restoration [^{LÚ}ENGAR]; since the substitute king had not yet been enthroned (r4), the king was certainly called simply "lord" (as in *LAS* 26-27); note that [^{LÚ}ENGAR] cannot be restored in Obv.6ff.

12. For [*šum-ma* UD *30*].KÁM* (Pt.I) restore [*ma-a* UD *29*].KÁM*, and translate: "A solar [eclipse occurred on the 29]th".

---

[51] Cf. Rassam, *Asshur and the Land of Nimrod* (1897), p.193, describing his journey from Baghdad to Mosul, which he accomplished in six days on horseback: "As I wished to proceed as fast as I could, I chose the *quickest* mode of travelling, though not the easiest, in having recourse to the Government postal service, by which means I was enabled to make long stages at a quick pace, partly gallopping, and partly trotting. At each station we changed horses and escort. Though the distance from Baghdad to Mossul via Karkook and Arweel (the ancient Arbela) is only one hundred hours, or three hundred miles, I accomplished it in six days, allowing a good margin for detentions and necessary night rest. Some part of the road was rather muddy and difficult to ride through, in consequence of the frost and the heavy rains that fell during the winter."

29

Bibliography:

(I) Waterman, *RCAE* 32.

(II) Landsberger, *BBEA* (1965) 68; Deller, *AOAT* 1 (1969) 54; Borger, *BiOr* 29 (1972) 36.

Date and discussion:

Ajāru 18, eponymy of Šamaš-kāšid-ajābi = May 16, 669 BC. For the day see Obv.7; the month and year obtain from the following considerations. As first noticed by Landsberger (1965), the letter makes sense only in the context of an unsuccessfull attempt to return the statue of Marduk (cf. Obv.7ff) to Babylon (Rev.7 ff). It is certain that the returnal of the god (carried away from Babylon under Sennacherib) was being planned and prepared intensively at the end of the reign of Esarhaddon: at least two separate oracle queries pertaining to the transportation of the god (by boat) to Babylon were ordered by this king (see *AGS* 104 f), and in one query (*AGS* 106) the king asks whether he should personally go to meet the god in his cella in Babylon; an inscription of Esarhaddon (Borger *Ash*, AsBbE) describes the god's return as a *fait accompli*, and another (Ass.C, possibly by the same scribe as AsBbE; see Borger, op.cit. p.7, note to iii 11) even fixes the date of the god's departure from Assur at Ajāru ⌜8⌝ (r. iii 13; ll. 4f ibid. refer to an oracle query to Šamaš, line 6 mentions the month (^{ITU}GUD), and ll. 9ff describe the mouth-washing ceremony performed to the god in the Assur temple on the 7th [of Ajāru], just before the departure [to Babylon]). This date of departure would perfectly tally with the date mentioned in the present letter, considering that the town where Bēl and his escort were said to be sojourning was situated some 350 km south of Assur (cf. note to Obv.8); and the year in question would be 669 BC, as the temple area of Babylon was still under construction in Tašrītu 670 and hence not yet suited for the returnal ceremonies (see under *LAS* 284). The dating of the incident to 669 BC is further supported by the reference to strong floods in the inscription just discussed (Ass.C iii 7f), cf. notes to *LAS* 291:8ff and 294.

The statue was, of course, eventually returned only in the first year of Assurbanipal.[52] The date on which this happened (Ajāru 24/5) would also perfectly fit the situation described in the present letter. However, two details in the letter make it improbable that it refers to this latter enterprise. First, there is the reference to the crown prince (= Šamaš-šumu-ukīn) in Obv.11. Even granting that Šamaš-šumu-ukīn was recognized as king of Babylon only after Marduk's arrival in Babylon (cf. Streck, *Asb* p. CCLVI) and could thus still be referred to as the crown prince before Ajāru 24/5, 668, it is still difficult to imagine how two persons *under the jurisdiction of the governor of Šamaš-nāṣir* (Obv. 12, cf. relevant note) could have belonged to the household of Šamaš-šumu-ukīn in Ajāru 668, when he had *certainly* been for some time resident in Nineveh (cf. *AGS* 149) and *probably* had already switched his court to Babylon in anticipation of his imminent enthronement. By contrast, the reference fits perfectly the situation prevalent in Esarhaddon's two last years, cf. sub *LAS* 280:10f; one could hypothesize that the two men, employed as grooms at Šamaš-šumu-ukīn's court at Laḫīru, had come to Labbanat as members of a princely delegation charged with disembarking Bēl and the other gods from the ships and taking them to Babylon by land. Secondly, the incident reported in the letter is actually much better understandable in the context of a suddenly and unexpectedly interrupted expedition (see presently), and it is certain that the return of the statue attempted in 669 BC *had* indeed been unexpectedly interrupted; otherwise it would remain unexplicable how the inscriptions Ass. C and AsBbL came to be composed.

Why, then, was the expedition called back just before it would have reached its destination? The answer is, again following Landsberger, very likely provided by the incident reported to the king in the present letter,

---

[52] MU SAG $^{\mathrm{I.d}}$GIŠ.NU$_{11}$-MU-GI.NA *ina* ^{ITU}GUD ^{d}EN *u* DINGIR^{MEŠ} šá KUR URI^{KI} *ul-tu* URU.ŠÀ.URU *ú-ṣu-nim-ma ina* ^{ITU}GUD UD ⌜24⌝.KÁM *ana* DIN.TIR^{KI} TU^{MEŠ}*-ni* "In the accession year of Šamaš-šumu-ukīn, Bēl and the gods of Akkad set out from the city of Assur in the month Ajāru and entered Babylon on the 24th of Ajāru", Grayson, *TCS* 5 p.86:34-36 (Chronicle 1); the same statement is also found in Chronicles 14 (ll. 35-36) and 16 (5-7), see op.cit. pp.127 and 131, with the modification that the date of Bēl's arrival in Babylon is given as Ajāru 25 in Chron.14. Assurbanipal describes the return of the god in detail in his inscription L^4 (Streck, *Asb* p.252 ff, csp. 262 ff). An oracle query pertaining to the matter, dated Nisannu 23, 668 BC, has also been preserved (*AGS* 149).

Obv.9 - Rev.17; notice the end of the letter: "What is it that the king says?" (scil. "Should the undertaking be interrupted or not?"). What the writers themselves thought about the incident is nowhere explicitly stated, but the accurate details given on the background of the two men involved in it imply that considerable significance was attributed to it. The same is suggested by the remark "everything is fine" in Obv.9, which was quite clearly occasioned by the following story. Accordingly, this must have been considered alarming, at least in some sense, and probably even ominous. What had happened, actually? A man attending to a pompously harnessed horse due to draw Bēl's chariot from the riverside to the city of Labbanat (see note to Obv.13) suddenly gets mad and, helped by his comrade, mounts the sacred animal. But not enough with that; when he is taken down and questioned for his odd behaviour, he begins to deliver an oracular – virtually nonsensical – message from Bēl and Zarpānītu, the two chief participants of the expedition. The situation is thus closely reminiscent of the passages in Assyrian royal inscriptions (particularly those of Esarhaddon and Assurbanipal) referring to spontaneous oracular utterances and prophetic messages received by the king (or his officials) in times of distress or in the context of important enterprises, and valued as messages from the gods themselves. Such messages were often conveyed by ecstatic prophets (*maḫḫû, raggimu*) appearing in crowds (cf. e.g. Borger, *Ash* p.45, and Piepkorn, *AS* 5 p.68), but it has to be noted that even common men (*iltēn eṭlu*, etc.) appear as deliverers of oracles (*egerrû*) or oracular dreams (see Streck, *Asb* p.20:95 ff, 32:118 ff, 48:95 ff, 166:13 ff, and cf. Oppenheim, *Dreams* p.249 f). Whether or not these oracles were heeded depended, of course, on their content and the contextual situation. In the present case, the message was definitely evilboding (at least to the king of Assyria): Babylon, and with it of course also the temple of Bēl, was going to be looted by a man bearing the name of an ancient Babylonian king. The situation itself was extremely precarious (the supreme god of the Babylonian pantheon travelling through uninhabited regions!), particularly to Esarhaddon, to whom the event at the same time signified the fulfilment of his dreams and the end of a troublesome political commitment; his attitude is clearly displayed by his prayer to Marduk in Assur, Borger *Ash* p.82 (cf. Landsberger, *BBEA* p.21). All the necessary conditions therefore exist for the incredible conclusion that the king indeed called off the expedition at that late stage for such a seemingly insignificant reason!

Notes:

8. ^{URU}*La-ab-ba-na-at*: "Eine sonst wenig bekannte Grenzstadt zwischen Assyrien und Babylonien am Tigris (Tigl.III Tontafel S. 56 8). Man mag vermuten, daß hier Bēl seine Prachtgaleere, die ihn Tigris abwärts brachte, verließ und zu Lande weiter transportiert werden sollte." (Landsberger, op.cit., fn. 136). This hypothesis is supported by *ABL* 1102 r4 f. referring to a road leading from Labbanat to Babylon (KASKAL.2 *ul-tu* ^{5} DIN.TIR^{KI} *a-di* ^{URU}*La-ab-ban-at*). The town or better the fort of Laʾbanat (cf. *bir-tu ša La-ab-ba-na-at* Rost *Tgl* p.56: 8, and ^{URU}*bir-tu ša La-ab-na-at*, ibid. XXXIV 7) must have situated pretty close to modern Baghdad, since the expedition had yet to pass Dūr-Kurigalzi = mod. ʿAqar Qūf, see note to Rev.14-17.

9. *Bēl-erība*: An individual with this name belonging to the house of Kurigalzu was a figure of some importance in the reign of Marduk-zākir-šumi I (ca. 850-820 BC); cf. VS I 35:27. This circumstance and the fact that Bēl occurs as an element of the name may have influenced the content of the oracle concocted by the man or contributed to its credibility.

10. The sign following LÚ is, according to recent (January, 1976) collation by Sollberger, simply an archaizing ÌR "servant" ().

11. *DUMU.MAN*: in this context, naturally the crown prince of Babylon = Šamaš-šumu-ukīn. See above, sub Discussion.

12. ^{URU}*Šá-maš-PAP-er*: exact location unknown but certainly in the Diyāla region (in the vicinity of Laḫīru). References in *AOAT* 6 p.330 f.

13ff. Cancel the rendering in Pt.I and translate instead: "A strong horse harnessed in trappings[53] of the land of Kush". This expression may provide as clue to the meaning of the enigmatic "Kushite" horses (KUR^{MEŠ} *Ku-sa-a-a*) itemized in the horse-reports of Nabû-šumu-iddina/Nādinu.[54] These are taken by Salonen, *Hippologica*

[53] On *tallultu*, a type of harness or trappings of draught-horses, see Salonen, *Hippologica* p.112 f.

[54] See *ABL* 60 ff (etc.), and cf. Postgate, *TCAE* (1974) 7 ff; Fales, *Assur* 1/3 (1974) 15 ff, and Parpola, *ZA* 65 (1975) 294.

p.36, for a breed imported to Assyria from Susiana, an interpretation difficult to accept since the reports show that the horses concerned came to Nineveh from all parts of Assyria, even from the West,[55], and there is absolutely no evidence that *Kūsu*, the Assyrian name of Ethiopia/Nubia (Bibl. Kush), was ever used to refer to Susiana.[56] It is equally difficult to believe that a breed imported from Nubia is in question; but the fact that *all* "Kushite" horses, like the horse mentioned here, are classed (together with KUR^{MEŠ} *Me-sa-a-a*) as draught-horses (^{ANŠE}KUR.RA^{MEŠ} *ša ni-i-ri*),[57] makes one ask whether the designation "Kushite" does not actually in the reports, too serve as an identification of the *harness* the horses were *wearing, and not* as a breed identifier. This possibility is not so unlikely as it might seem at the first sight; note the following facts. 1) Even though "Kushite" horses are listed in hundreds as draught-horses they never appear as riding-horses; that is difficult to explain supposing a foreign breed is in question (even granting that certain breeds are more fitting for use as draught-horses than others), but only natural if the identification *Ku-sa-a-a* refers to a specific type of harness. 2) That a "Kushite" type of harness, distinct from other types of harness, *was* used in the period concerned appears with certainty from the present passage. 3) The horse here mentioned was doubtless intended to draw the chariot of Bēl (cf. *LAS* 175) to Babylon; the reference to the harness of the horse very probably served to make this clear to the king, and it may so be concluded that horses harnessed in the "Kushite" way were primarily used for drawing chariots; there was thus plenty of room for hundreds of "Kushite" horses, just as the statistics in the reports indicate. The origin of the term "Kushite" is this usage of course remains to be clarified.

15. *e-rab URU*: lit., "entering of the city", a technical term for the ceremonial arrival of a religious procession in a cult centre; see note on 196:4' and 170:5. In the present context, the city to be "entered" was certainly Babylon (the fort of Labbanat is out of the question because Bēl and his escort already were there). The translation of the line given in Pt.I has accordingly to be cancelled; render instead: "The strong horse harnessed . . . for the (ceremonial) entry into the city (of Babylon)". On the word order, see notes on 214 r3' and 247:16'ff.

16. *a-na* ^{URU}*La-ab-ba-na-at* "in Labbanat": sic, not *to* L. Cf. above, and see note to 39 r3.

17. [*i*]*-za-zu-u-né*: to be taken, like *iz-za-az* in 290:8, as a 'prefixed stative' (*GAG* § 78b) referring to the *past*, and not to be rendered with the present as done in Pt.I. The expression *uzuzzu* + *ina muḫḫi* (Obv.13), lit. "to stand upon (something)", means idiomatically "to be busy with, to attend to", see *AHw.* 409*b* sub I 6. The translation of Obv.13-17 should accordingly be modified to read: "(B. and N., servants of the governor of Š.) *were attending* in Labbanat *to* a strong horse", etc.

r5f. *iṣ-ṣab-tu-neš-šú us-sa-an-ni-qu-šú*: this expression also in *ABL* 144:7 ff, 152:11 and 599:12 ff. Cf. above, sub Discussion.

r10. *ina UGU áš-li*: the same expression also in *ABL* 473:17 and *CT* 53 594:3'(*ina* UGU] *áš-li il-*[*la-ka*). The contexts imply an idiomatic meaning like "straight" (lit. "along the measuring rope").

r11. *Kurigalzu*: the name of two kings of the Kassite dynasty, see Brinkman, *Materials and Studies for Kassite History*, Vol. I (1976), 205 ff. A person with this name is also known as a man of some importance under Esarhaddon and/or Assurbanipal, cf. *ABL* 1394 r2 ff (^{I}*Ku-ri-gal-zu* [3] DUMU ^{LÚ}GAR-NÁM*-ni* [4] *maḫ-ri-i pa-liḫ* [5] DINGIR *u* LUGAL *šu-ú* "K., the son of our previous commandant, is a man fearing the god and the king"), *ABL* 1185:13 (^{I}*Ku-ri-gal-zu* DIN.TIR$^{KI.MEŠ}$ "K. and the citizens of Babylon"), *ABL* 1460 r2 f (^{I}TUKU*-ši-*[DINGIR] . . . ^{I}*Ku-ri-gal-*[*zu*] "Rāši-[ili][58] . . . (and) K."), and *ABL* 345, a letter from K. concerning economic matters. It does not seem excluded that a descendant of the old dynasty is in question.

r14-17. Obviously an attempt to give a rational explanation to the oracular "message". The solution suggested is simply to relate each word of the oracle allegorically to the realia of the undertaking: "Babylon" means Bēl; "loot" means robbers (*parriṣūti*); "Kurigalzu" means Dūr-Kurigalzu,[59] a city yet to be passed by the expedition

[55] Cf. *ABL* 394:7-11, 575:7f, etc.

[56] Cf. *AOAT* 6 s.v. Kūsu.

[57] E.g., *ABL* 394:7-10.

[58] Probably identical with the priest R. involved in the organization of Bēl's cult in Assur and returnal to Babylon (see *ABL* 475, 496-498, 501, etc.).

[59] Sic; the sign preceding *Ku-* in r16 is definitely [BÀ]D, not DIŠ.

on its way to Babylon.[60] "Straight" (*ina muḫḫi ašli*) may have been taken in various senses (either locally ["on the way to"] or modally ["irrevocably"], etc.). The implication that the procession would run the risk of being attacked at Dūr-Kurigalzu is obvious, and the fact that the interpretation was considered worth of reporting to the king shows that it furnished matter for serious refelction to the men in charge of the undertaking.

30

Bibliography:

(I) Waterman, *RCAE* 223 (cf. IV 177, 241); Pfeiffer, *SLA* 249.

(II) Nougayrol, *RA* 36 (1939) 35; Labat, *Royauté* (1939) 358; Oppenheim, *JAOS* 64 (1944) 191; Böhl, *Opera Minora* (1953) 420f; von Soden, *Fs Christian* (1956) 102; Brinkman, *OrNS* 34 (1965) 247; Landsberger, *BBEA* (1965) 51[91]; Kümmel, *StBoT* 3 (1967) 171ff; Oppenheim, *Centaurus* 14 (1969) 128[12]; Leichty, *TCS* 4 (1970) 13; Dietrich, *AOAT* 7 (1970) 34, 41, 150ff.

Copy:

Cf. Winckler, *SKT* II pl.13.

Photo:

RCAE IV pl.7 (Obv. only).

Date:

Araḫsamna 5, eponymy of Šarru-nūrī = October 23, 674 BC. This date is based on the following evidence. Firstly, the letter certainly dates from Esarhaddon's reign: Nabû-zēru-līšer, who here clearly writes in the capacity of the Chief Scribe (cf. *LAS* 26-27), held this office only under Esarhaddon (cf. Assur 14616c IV 13 and *KAV* 182 IV 4', edited in App. N1.1). The reference to the rebellious plans of Ṣallāju on the reverse gives the letter a very probable terminus ante quem (Addāru 8 = February 21, 673 BC); see note on r1. A very plausible terminus post quem (March, 678 BC) is furnished by the reference to the three Chaldean nobles in r3-5, see respective note. While the time brackets 678-673 thus obtained are not absolutely certain, they nevertheless provide a useful teststone to the identification of the eclipse which caused the enthronement of the substitute king figuring in the letter.

No solar eclipses were observable in Mesopotamia between 678 and 670 BC (see App. E); the eclipse in question was consequently lunar.[61] The fact that a substitute king was needed for Babylonia implies that the right side of the moon had been eclipsed, and in addition, that the planet Jupiter had not been visible during the eclipse (see Intr., p.57 ff and cf. App. F3). These two requirements are met by only one lunar eclipse between 680 and 672 BC, that of September 3,-673 (see App. F2 and 3). This was a total eclipse and so required the enthronement of a substitute king not only in Akkad but in Nineveh, too; and in the reign of Esarhaddon who at the same time was king of both Assyria and Babylonia, the practice was that the same substitute functioned as the king of both countries, residing the first half of his 100-day reign in Nineveh and the last half in Akkad (see, in detail, discussion under *LAS* 26). The present letter would consequently pertain to recoronation ceremonies in Akkad 50 days after the occurrence of the said eclipse, i.e. on October 23 = Araḫsamna 5, 674 BC. This date fits perfectly all data of the letter. Firstly, it explains the curious outcry of the substitute king in Obv.15f: since the day of the coronation was 50 days removed from the eclipse, there was – contrary to his previous coronation immediately preceded by a shattering omen visible to everybody – no apparent motivation for the ceremony. Secondly, the very fact that the substitute wondered at his transfer to Akkad indicates that the case had no precedents in recent memory and thus implies that the lunar eclipse in question was the first total one in Esarhaddon's reign requiring the enthronement of a substitute king. And finally, the date places the information on the plans of Ṣallāju in a meaningful historical context, the present letter preceding only by four months the Assyrian intervention in Bīt-Awukāni. Cf. the relation of the letters of Nabû-rēḫtu-uṣur to the quelling of the conspiracy of Sāsî, discussed under *LAS* 247.

---

60 Note the location of 'Aqar Qūf between the Diyala crossing and Babylon, and cf. the description of Sennacherib's way to Babylon on his campaign to the Sealand, *OIP* 2 p.73 ff.

61 Eclipses of planets, which are also mentioned in the substitute king ritual tablet (*AfO* 18 110, col. A 11-12), can be left out of consideration for reasons stated in discussion on *LAS* 14.

Addressee:
Esarhaddon.

Notes:

10f. *NAG-ú* . . . *TU*$_5$ . . . *ŠÉŠ*^{MEŠ}*-šú*: in view of *LAS* 280:14f (*dam-mu-qu ka-an-nu-u . . . qa-ab-ru ba-ki-i-u*), to be taken as forms of 3 Pl. Stative, and to be read respectively as *šaqiū, ramkū, paššū*; the signs *ú* and *šú* are phonetic complements. The persons intended are, of course, the substitute king and his queen.

11f. *"I made them eat those birds"*: this measure can hardly have been part of the coronation ceremonies which must have reached their climax at the anointment of the substitute and his wife (cf. e.g., *VAB* 2 no.51:6, Ì^{MEŠ} *a-na* SAG.DU-*šu iš-ku-un-šu* "he crowned him king", lit. "he put oil on his head"), and therefore in all probability belonged to the rites performed in order to have the substitute "take on himself" the omens threatening the safety of the king. The birds in question were, accordingly, presumably ominous (or had been involved in an ominous incident; cf., e.g., Plutarch, *Lives* VII, Alexander LXXIII: "Certain Chaldeans had met him and advised that Alexander should keep away from Babylon. Alexander paid no heed to this, but continued on his march; and when he was arrived at the walls, he saw many ravens flying about and clawing one another, and some fell dead at his feet" – an omen immediately preceding the enthronement of a substitute king); by having the substitutes literally *eat* them, the persons in charge of the ceremonies probably wanted to make sure that the evil of the birds would irrevocably and concretely attach to the substitute king and his queen instead of the true king and his wife. Cf. note on 26 r8'.

14. *"The substitute king cried out"*: surely an exceptional incident; the substitute kings were expected to keep their mouths shut while exercising their duty (cf. "a man clad in the king's robes with a diadem upon his head, sitting silently upon his throne . . . asked who he was . . . gave no answer", Plutarch, loc.cit.; "sat upon the throne and remained quiet", Diodorus XVII 116). On the content of the outcry see above, sub Date; see also below, note on Obv.17f.

15. The emendation *la* <*ṭa*>*-ab-tu* adopted in Pt.I following von Soden (*Fs Chıistian*, 102) is not necessary; read with Landsberger (*BBEA*, p. 51) ISKIM *la-ap-tu* "ominous sign". While ISKIM is certainly feminine in Obv.6 (cf. the suffix *-ši-na* in Obv.7) and has accordingly there to be read *ittu*, and while this reading also applies to many cases where ISKIM is followed by the verb *lpt* (cf. ISKIM-*šú la-ap-ta-at*, *LAS* 109:17'f, and *it-tu*$_4$ *ul ta-lap-pat*, *RMA* 108:6), *LAS* 325 r2 (ISKIM-*šú la i-lap-pa-*[*at*], cf. ISKIM *ka-aja-ma-nu*, ibid. r7) shows that it is perfectly possible to take ISKIM as masculine in the present case. Whether this means that ISKIM is here to be read *giskimmu* (a Sum. LW otherwise attested only in literary contexts) remains uncertain, cf. notes on 152:13ff and 325 r2.

16. For *ina lìb-bi-*⌜*ma*⌝ (Pt.I) read *ina lìb-bi-*⌜*šu*⌝! (cf. collation Pt.I p.295 and photo *RCAE* IV pl.7). The suffix *-šu* refers to ISKIM; the particle *-ma* would not be motivated in the context.

17. *"And he spoke"*: That a man forced to die for the king still remains so loyal to his lord as to voluntarily expose to him a conspiracy which, if allowed to mature, might have saved his life, may seem strange to us but probably was more natural in the eyes of the contemporaries. Note that a similar mental attitude is still attested for Mesopotamia of the 19th century by Layard, *Nineveh and Its Remains I*, p. 271: "The substitute bore with resignation the tortures and imprisonment inflicted upon him . . ." Whence the substitute had received his information remains unclear, though the matter was presumably explained in Obv.19-21 which could be fancifully restored: *ina ba-*⌜*a*⌝*-*[*di ša* UD x.KÁM]^{20} *ma-a* GEŠT[IN^{MEŠ} *ni-si-ti*] ^{21} *ṭa-*[*a'-ta-a-ti*], and translated: "In the eve[ning of the . . th, we were drinking w]ine; Ṣallāju gave b[ribes] to his servant N., and in that context (*ina libbi*) asked about (the fate of) Nikkal-iddina . . ."

r1. *Ṣallāju*: a powerful figure in the politics of Babylonia under Esarhaddon, who ca.673 ended up in an open revolt against the Assyrians, see Dietrich, *AOAT* 7 (1970) 39 ff. While there is no mathematical proof for the contention of Dietrich that Ṣ. was the official in charge of Bīt-Awukāni, this is made extremely likely by the fact that no more than 4 month after the dispatchment of the present letter, which contained aggravating charges against Ṣ., Assyrian troops invaded Bīt-Awukāni; cf. Grayson, *TCS* 5 p.126, Chron.14:20, MU ⌜7⌝.KÁM ^{ITU}ŠE UD *8*.KÁM ERIM^{MEŠ} KUR *Aš+šur a-na* ^{URU}*Šá*-LÚ^{MEŠ} D[U^{ME}]^{Š}*-ku* "In the 7th year (of Esarhaddon), on the

8th of Addāru (= February 21, 673 BC), the army of Assyria m[arche]d to Ša-amīlē", and see Luckenbill, *OIP* 2 p.53:43 for Ša-amīlē (^{URU}*Šá-a-me-le-e*) as one of the fortified cities of Bīt-Awukāni (URU^{MEŠ} *dan-nu-ti šá* KUR*É-A-mu-ka-a-ni*, ibid.47).

r3-5. The three men mentioned here were Chaldean nobles holding key administrative positions in Babylonia in the beginning of Esarhaddon's reign but later removed from their offices and/or deported to Assyria. On Nikkal-iddina, governor of Ur, fired 675 at the latest, see Brinkman, *Or*NS 34 (1965) 246 ff; on Šamaš-ibni, head of Bīt-Dakūri, deported in 678, see Grayson, *TCS* 5 p.83, entry for Esarhaddon's 3rd year, and Borger, *Ash* pp.32 and 52; on Na'id-Marduk, governor of Sealand, discharged 675 at the latest, see Borger, *Ash* p.47 and Dietrich, *AOAT* 7 p.23ff, and cf. note on *LAS* 282 r14'. There is a definitely possibility, noted by Dietrich p.34f, that all the three men were already fired in 678; cf. *RMA* 272, a report datable with certainty between the 18th and 25th of November, 679 (see note to 13r16ff): "All these portents . . . concern Babylonia and its nobles; none of the evil signs pertain to the king, my lord . . . The nobles of Babylonia appointed by your father destroyed Babylon and carried off its valuables, that's why these evil signs have appeared. The troops of the king should go, seize them, and put other persons in their stead. If the king does not act swiftly, the enemy will come and change them" (Rev.7ff); note also *ABL* 1006 = *RMA* 268, a report on the total lunar eclipse of Simānu 14 = May 22, 678 BC: "Let the chief exorcist act as he deems best, and let the king once again remove one of the noblemen of Chaldea, Aram or [. . .] from his office . . ." (Obv.18 ff). The fact that all three men are here mentioned together *by name* makes it certain that their eventual fate was already known to Ṣallāju and so provides the letter with a convenient terminus post quem; the reference to them can thus only have been a reference to their humiliating fate, obviously meant to spur the anti-Assyrian feelings of the listeners and thus prepare ground for the planned uprising (cf. r6-7).

31

Bibliography:
(I) Waterman, *RCAE* 332.

Addressee:
Esarhaddon.

Date:
Ulūlu 15, eponymy of Šarru-nūrī = September 3, 674 BC. The composition of the writer collegium (chief scribe, chief exorcist, head of the stargazers of Nineveh [Nabû-šumu-iddina], chief chanter and junior chief scribe) and the way in which the king is addressed can only imply that the letter was, at the same time, 1) a report of the occurrence of an alarming eclipse (cf. *LAS* 28 and 77) and 2) an announcement that the collegium had immediately enthroned a substitute to eliminate the danger threatening the king; had the substitute not yet been enthroned, the king should have been addressed differently (cf. sub *LAS* 28). The eclipse in question can only be that of September 3, 673, discussed sub *LAS* 30, or an earlier eclipse during which Jupiter was not visible.[62] The odds are for the former alternative, considering that there is a gap of three years before one finds a suitable eclipse preceding September 674 (November 3, 677; cf. App. F1). The letter thus predates *LAS* 30 by about 50 days.

32

Bibliography:
(I) Waterman, *RCAE* 1376.

Addressee:
Esarhaddon.

[62] Later eclipses are out of the question for reasons stated in note to 13 r23. The eclipse of February 23, -672, during which Jupiter was visible and in which the quadrant of Subartu was not eclipsed did not necessitate the enthronement of a substitute.

Date:

Probably about Kislīmu 25, eponymy of Šarru-nūrī = December 11, 674 BC. While the letter is not addressed to "Farmer", the fact that it is written together with the exorcist Adad-šumu-uṣur, who also figures in the writer team of *LAS* 31, considered in conjunction with the reference to a tomb (KI.MAH, r3'; note also *ma-ṣa-al-lu*, Obv. 12) makes it more than likely that it, like *LAS* 280, pertained to the burial of a substitute king. This, in turn, must be identical with the one figuring in *LAS* 30-31 (see on *LAS* 31). The date December 11, 674 is based on the assumption that the reign of the substitute king was of normal length, that is, 100 days. The king could of course be addressed normally after the 100-day period was over.

34(+)49[63]

Bibliography:

(I) Waterman, *RCAE* 604 (cf. IV 258); Pfeiffer, *SLA* 103.
(II) Behrens, *ABB* (1906) 76[1]; Schott, *ZA* 44 (1938) 198[1]; G. Meier, *AfO* 12 (1939) 239; Oppenheim, *JAOS* 61 (1941) 259; Deller, *Or*NS 34 (1965) 266, and *AOAT* 1 (1969) 62.

Date:

Early Du'ūzu = late June, 671 BC; see under *LAS* 59.

Writer:

The assignation of this letter to Balasî can be regarded as absolutely certain on the ground of the subject matter (see Discussion) and the spelling *an-ni-i-e* occurring in Obv. 16. See Appendix M 6, and cf. *LAS* 35:15, 39 r6, 40:5, 41 r9, 45 r6, 50:13, *RMA* 88 r10 and 208A r3. An additional feature pointing to Balasi can be seen in the blessing of Obv.11-13, which recurs in almost identical form in 36 r4-8, 40:10-r2' and 50 r6-12 (cf. also 44:7ff).

Addressee:

Esarhaddon.

Discussion:

This letter is a virtual duplicate of *LAS* 59, from Balasî's colleague Nabû-aḫḫē-erība. The existence of two nearly identical letters from different authors is naturally explained by the royal message quoted in Obv.7, which was possibly distributed in identical copies to several scholars serving the king (thus Deller 1969), but it also attests to the exceptionally close collaboration of these two astrologers: there is hardly any doubt that they had worked out the content of their answers together. The best indication of this collaboration is of course provided by the numerous joint letters of Balasî and Nabû-aḫḫē-erība (*LAS* 10, 43, 51-56), but it should be noted that even many of their private letters are nearly identical in content: see *LAS* 38 = *LAS* 349; *LAS* 40 = *LAS* 61; *LAS* 41 = *LAS* 62; *LAS* 46 = *LAS* 69+71; *LAS* 66 = *LAS* 65; *RMA* 68 = *RMA* 70; *RMA* 88 = *RMA* 103; *RMA* 183A = *LAS* 328; *RMA* 234A = *RMA* 237; *RMA* 256B = *RMA* 258; *RMA* 274E = *RMA* 2740; note also the pair of 'joint letters', *LAS* 57 = *LAS* 58!

Addressee:

Esarhaddon.

Notes:

8. A comparison with 59:9 (*ma-a ina ḫa-ra-am-me* [10] *ina pu-tú-ú-a* [11] *ta-za-az*) shows that the Pf. *ta-ti-ti-sa* "you have stayed" here actually denotes future time. The possibility of a linguistic lapsus is excluded since the tense is repeated in Rev.2 (*ni-ti-ti-zi*) also referring to future time, cf. *az-za-az*, 59:16. Two explanations of this odd fact seem possible: either the Gtn present of *uzuzzu* "to stand" was in NA formed in a way not distinguishable from G perfect, or then the present passage has to be regarded as one of the rare cases in which the Akkadian perfect refers to the future (cf. Hecker, *GKT* § 76d for isolated OA examples). Such a usage is otherwise (excepting the phrase *ūmâ annūrig assapra*, where the Pf. expresses simultaneous action) very poorly attested in Neo-Assyrian;

[63] This indirect join confirmed by E. Sollberger, January 19, 1976.

the present writer has noticed only the following two examples: *an-nu-ri ka-rim* [7] *i-la-ka* LÚUŠMEŠ [8] *a-na e-ṣa-di i-tal-ku-u* "(they way) is now blocked, (but) will the drivers later on go to the harvest?", *KAV* 214:6 ff; *šúm-mu la-áš-šú ḫal-qa-ni* [TA*] ŠU²-*ka* [30] *ni-iḫ-ti-liq* "if you will not, we shall be lost and (forced to) disappear [from] your service", *KAV* 197:19 f. In 83-1-18,162:11f (LÚ*EN-NAM . . . [12] *iq-ṭi-ba-na-ši ma-a ina* ŠÀ É.GAL [13] *a-ta-mar-ku-nu gul-gul-lat-ku-nu* [14] *ú-mar-ra-qa*) the scribe has probably simply omitted *šumma* or *kīma*.

15. *ki ma-ṣi ina* u_4*-me an-ni-i-e*: this idiom is not attested elsewhere, but its meaning is quite clear from the following parallels:

> *šá-ni-ú ina* u_4*-mi an-ni-e* "it's (for) the 2nd (day) today (that)", *ABL* 514 r13 and *LAS* 143:14
> *šá-al-šú ina* u_4*-me an-ni-i-e, LAS* 51:12-13 and
> *3-šú ina* u_4*-me an-ni-i* "it's (for) the 3rd (day) today" 312:5;
> *14 ina* u_4*-me an-ni-i* "it's 14 (days) today (since)" 148:12;
> ITU *ina* u_4*-me an-ni-i* "today a month (has passed since)" *ABL* 203:11;
> *an-nu-rig 8* MU.AN.NA "now it's the 8th year (since) *LAS* 309 r22.

As in the first four of these examples, the word *ūmī* "days" has to be understood as omitted after *ki ma-ṣi*: "how many (days)"[64] = "how long", an elliptic expression for indefinite time. This temporal use of *kī maṣi* is also attested in *ABL* 493 r21: (*ú-ma-a*) *a-na ki ma-ṣi i-tur-ru* "(now) they have returned for how long (I don't know)". The expression is of course exaggerated in the present context, for the king had only been absent for three months; cf. *LAS* 59 r3 ff.

18. The syntactical function of *ina muḫ-ḫi šu-u* here is to underline the adverbial status of the preceding relative clause within the whole utterance. Anaphoric prepositional expressions of this kind were inserted in the main clause always when the preceding relative clauses were of a complicated structure, even if one thus had to repeat the preposition heading the latter, e.g.:

> *ina* UGU *ša* d*30* UD *13*.KÁM *in-na-mer-u-ni*
> *ina* UGU *šu-u* MULUDU.IDIM.SAG.UŠ *ina* TÙR d*30 it-ti-it-zi* "on account of the fact that the moon was seen (opposite the sun) on the 13th day on account of that Saturn (now) stood in the moon's halo" (*RMA* 180:7-8);
> *ina* ŠÀ *ṭup-pi* [6] *an-ni-i-e ša a-na* [7] LUGAL EN-*ja ú-še-bi-la-an-ni* [8] *ina lìb-bi šu-mu* [9] *ki-i šá-ṭir-u-ni* [10] *ú-kal-lam, LAS* 39 r5ff.

Other similar examples are found in *LAS* 15:9 f, 180:10 ff, 186: r4 ff, 195 r8 ff, and 216 r2 ff.

r2 f. Cf. *man-nu* DINGIR-*ú-a man-nu* EN-*a* IGI²-*ja it-ti man-nu ki-i šak-nu* [7] *al-la* LUGAL EN-*a* "Who is my god? Who is my lord? How could I be devoted to anyone else than the king, my lord?", *RMA* 124 r6 f. The same exclamation also in *LAS* 59:17 ff.

r6 ff. Compare this passage with Assurbanipal's account of his education (Streck *Asb*, p.252 ff); that the king indeed had been instructed in the interpretation of (astrological) omens is also shown by *LAS* 331, see under relevant commentary; cf. also sub *LAS* 318 and 320. Whether the letters sent by Assurbanipal as crown prince (*ABL* 1001, 1026, 1257; *CT* 53 26(?), 147 and 469) were really written by the prince himself is uncertain; their cursive hand and many abbreviations suggest that at least some of them were written down according to dictation.

r9. *liginnu qabû*: literally, "to recite a school tablet". This expression could refer to both teacher and pupil, and so mean idiomatically both "to teach" and "to learn". See G. Meier, *AfO* 12 (1937/39) 238[15].

35

Bibliography:

(I) Waterman, *RCAE* 355 (cf. III 373, IV 248); Pfeiffer, *SLA* 273; Oppenheim, *Letters* (1976) 162 (translat. only).
(II) Behrens, *ABB* (1906) 14[5]; Dhorme, *RHR* 116 (1937) 23f; Schott, *OLZ* 40 (1937) 362; G. Meier, *Or*NS 8 (1939) 306ff; Labat, *Royauté* (1939) 338 and 344; Nougayrol, *RA* 36 (1939) 31f.

[64] Cf. *ad ki ma-ṣi* UDMEŠ "for how many days", *Arch.* 79 pl.49 ii 15 (Epic of Tukulti-Ninurta I).

Photo:
RCAE IV pl.9 (Obv. only).

Date:
Perhaps early Simānu = early June, 669 BC. See note to Obv.8ff.

Discussion:

This letter is important for the unique glimpse it provides of the "deep structure" of the Mesopotamian omen exegesis which we otherwise know only surfacially. The picture conveyed by the text is this. In Sargonid Assyria, omens were – just as in contemporary Israel – given a *moral* content and understood as signs of divine pleasure or displeasure with the *conduct of the king*. All the "signs" infallibly led to the end specified in the sacred literature, *except if* they were counteracted with special apotropaic rituals, created by the gods themselves. But performing these rituals (which always involved prayers and offerings) was by no means *enough*: the king was also supposed to *revalue* his way of life, "to be on his guard" (Rev.22).

It remains uncertain whether this moral requirement was from the beginning inherent in the thinking of the persons responsible for the interpretation and nullification of omens, or whether it resulted from an attempt to explain why the experts were not always capable of averting the evil, despite the blameless performance of the appropriate magical rituals.

Notes:

6. The term *pišru* "interpretation, solution" is here used in a way that can be regarded as exactly opposite to its normal usage.

Normally, the thing to be "solved" was an ominous sign (*ittu*), often translated "omen" but to be sharply distinguished from the term *šumu* "omen" occurring here. The relationship of the three terms is usually as follows:

ittu "isgn", "omen"	always referring to *observed* ominous natural phenomena (identical with the *protasis* of omen texts, but not a designation of this)[65]
pišru "interpretation"	the 'scientific' interpretation of the former, usually given in the form of a direct quotation from the omen texts (factually identical with an omen *apodosis*)[66]
šumu "omen", "name (of the sign)", "line"	always referring to an entry in traditional omen literature (= *protasis* + *apodosis*)[67]

In the present letter, however, *pišru* denotes the solution of a *šumu* and, as appears from Rev.4, leads to the identification of the relevant *ittu*, contrary to the normal practice according to which one proceeded from *ittu* to *šumu* through *pišru*. It is important to note that in our text *pišru* is factually identical with the content of the protasis concerned, which should warn against taking the meaning of *pišru* too narrowly, e.g. as a technical term for "prediction".

8 ff. The apodosis quoted here recurs in Tablet XXII of *Enūma Anu Enlil* dealing with a set of astrological and meteorological omens month by month; the omen in question pertained to the month Simānu, and read in its entirety as follows:

BE *ri-i-bu i-ru-ub* LUGAL KUR *it-ti* IDIM^{MEŠ}-*šú i-qal-lil*

"If there is an earthquake (in Simānu), the king of the land will come to naught with his dignitaries" (*ACh* Sîn 35:11); cf. I *ri-bu ina* ^{ITU}SIG$_4$ *i-ru-ub* LUGAL KI IDIM^{MEŠ} *ma-gal i-qal-lil*, Lacheman, *RA* 34 (1937) 3:11.[68]

---

[65] For examples see *CAD* I/J 306 ff.

[66] See *AHw* 868b; for occurrences in the present edition, see Pt.I, p.318 s.v.

[67] Cf. *LAS* 13 r1, 39 r8, 44 r4, *RMA* 235 r2, 268 r5, etc. See also Oppenheim, *Centaurus* 14 (1969), p.8 n.9, and for the occurrences of *šumu* in colophons, Hunger, *AOAT* 2 (1968), p.2.

[68] Note also *ACh* Sin XXVII 22, [I *ina* IT]U.SIG$_4$ UD *14*.KAM AN.MI GAR-*ma ina* IM.4 SAR-*ma* UD LUGAL KI ID[IM.MEŠ-*šú iqallil*].

This would imply that the earthquake concerned occurred in the month Simānu and is hence perhaps identical with the earthquake referred to in *LAS* 234 which is datable to 669 BC. On the other hand, the fact that the apodosis is here characterized as belonging to the "monthly omens" suggests that is may also originate in the menological omen collection *Iqqur Īpuš*, where a similar apodosis follows an earthquake omen associated with the month Du'ūzu:[69]

I *ina* ^{ITU}ŠU (*ri-i-bu i-ru-ub*) LUGAL (/MAN KUR) IDIM/DUGUD KUR *i-qàl-lil* (§ 100);
I *ina* ^{ITU}ŠU (KI *i-ru-ub*) LUGAL *ina* ŠÀ KUR-*šú i-qal-lil* (§ 101).

The letter could thus also (though less plausibly) date from Du'ūzu 670? BC. See on *LAS* 16 and 147.

11. Cf. *damū iššakkanū* "there will be bloodshed", *YOS* 10 31 xii 44 (OB ext., see *CAD* D 79*b*). For *muṭê* "losses" (scil. in authority, wealth etc.) see note to *LAS* 58:19.

r1. The emendation *il-*<*lu*>*-ku* is based on the context: a verb is required, and only a form of *alāku* fits the signs and makes satisfactory sense. True, no emendation at all is necessary, if *il-ku* is interpreted as a variant spelling of 3 Pl. Stat. /*alkū*/ (pronounced [elku])[70]; the translation would remain the same. – The reading *il-qú* proposed in *CAD* B 168*b* and elsewhere (with the translation "they have taken") conflicts with NA orthography (which did not recognize the value KU = *qú*) and grammar (no Pret. in positive main clauses, except in questions!) and consequently cannot be accepted.

r5. *ú-de-šú* "alone" (not "since" [*RCAE*] or "recently" [Oppenheim 1967]!) has naturally to be connected with the earthquake (*rību*) and not with the following verb. Cf. *LAS* 12 r1, 223 r13.19, 224 r15', etc., also *ABL* 414:4-7, ^{URU}*Ḫe-e-sa* É *mar-di-ti-ja*! (wr. E) ^{5} UN^{MEŠ} *ina lìb-bi la-áš-šu* ^{6} ^{LÚ}GAL *kal-li-e* ^{LÚ}GAL *rak-si* ^{7} *ú-de-šú-nu ina lìb-bi* "The city of Ḫêsa serves as my road station, (but) there is not (enough) personnel there; the head of the post riders and the chief of the mercennaries alone live there (and they cannot be alert the whole time)"[71].

r9. *īpuš Ea ipšur Ea*: a magical formula often pronounced in the course of apotropaic rituals (*namburbi*, cf. Rev.12), but also attested in other exorcistic rituals.[72] Cf. *i-pu-uš* ^{d}*É-a ip-šur* ^{d}*É-a* DUG$_4$.GA "you (= the exorcist) say 'Ea has done, Ea has undone'", *LKA* 116:16 (= Ebeling, *RA* 48 140, *namburbi* against fungus on wall); similarly *LKA* 120:69' and K.137+2788 (= *ACh* Spl Ištar 33 + unp.), lines 27 and 65, cited by Meier, *Or*NS 8 307[3]; DÙ-*uš* ^{d}*É*[*a ip-šur*] ^{d}*É-a* DÙG$_4$.[GA-*ma*] "he recites (7 times) Ea did it, Ea undid it", *Or*NS 42 (1973) 510f; DÙ-*uš* ^{d}*É-a ip-šur* ^{d}*É-a 7-šú* DUG$_4$.GA-*ma*, ibid 509:26; [*i-p*]*u-uš* ^{d}*É-a ip-šur* ^{12} [^{d}*É-a ir*]*-ku-us* ^{d}*É-a* DU$_8$ DUG$_4$.[G]A "you say: 'Ea has done, Ea has undone; Ea has bound, <Ea> has released'", *AMT* 42,5:11f (medical rit.); UR$_5$.GIM DUG$_4$.GA ^{13} ÉN DÙ-*uš* ^{d}*É-a ip-šur* ^{d}*É-a pa-ṭar lum-ni šup-šu-ḫi uz-zu* ^{14} *pu-su-us ki-ṣir lum-ni* ^{d}*É-a it-ti-ka-ma* "you say as follows: 'Incantation. Ea has done, Ea has undone. It is in your power, O Ea, to undo evil, to soothe anger, to destroy evil knots!", *CT* 23 1, Obv.12 ff (medical rit.); see also *5 R* 51 iii 7. The formula of course need not have any magical implications in the present context.

r19 f. *uznē pattû* = lit. "to open the ears", idiomatically "to inform", see Oppenheim, *JAOS* 61 (1941) 263 (cf. also Lambert, *BWL* p.289[8]). An important parallel to our passage is furnished by *RMA* 57 (from Nabû-aḫḫē-erība) also dealing with a "sign" sent to the king:

Obv.! [I *30* UD] *28*.KÁM IGI.[LAL] ^{2} [SI]G$_5$ KUR URI^{KI} ḪUL KUR N[IM.MA^{KI}] ^{3} [*ša*] UD *28*.KÁM ^{d}*30*⌜*e*⌝-⌊*mur-u-ni*⌋ ^{4} ⌊IGI⌋+UM![*it*]*-tú me-ḫer*$^{\textit{me-ḫe-er}}$ IGI+UM$^{\textit{it-ti}}$ *š*[*a* UD *12*.KÁM] ^{5} [*š*]*u-u*
Rev.! *ša a-na* LUGAL EN-*ja áš-pu*[*r-an-ni*] ^{2} *mu-uk* PI^{MEŠ} $^{\textit{uz-ni}}$*ša* LUGAL [EN-*ja*] ^{3} DINGIR^{MEŠ}*-ni ú-pat-t*[*i-u*] ^{4} *šúm-ma me-me-ni a-na* [LUGAL DU-*ka*] ^{5} TA* ŠÀ-*šú i-da-bu-ub ina* [. . .] ^{6} *i-ḫar-ru-pu* | IGI+UM$^{\textit{it-tú}}$ | TA* Š[À AN-*e*] ^{7} [*i-š*]*ap-par-u-né ma-a* [. . . . .]

"[If the Moon] appe[ars] on the 28th day, (that means) good luck for the land of Akkad, bad luck for E[lam]. –

---

69 Thus also *ACh* Adad 20:39.

70 Cf., e.g., *al-ku*, var. *il-ku*, *AKA* p.241:50.

71 Correct the rendering in *CAD* K 84*b*.

72 E.g. *šurpu* p.12 r II 10', ÉN [DÙ] ^{d}*1 ip-šur* ^{d}*1*; *KAR* 78:6', [ÉN *i-p*]*u-uš* ^{d}*é-a ip-šur* ^{d}*É-a* ‖ 82–5–22,546 r5' (bīt salā' mê).

[The fact that] the Moon was sighted on the 28th (means) that this sign counterbalances the sign of [the 12th day]."[73]

"When I wrote to the king, my lord, (saying) 'the gods will open the ears of the king, [my lord]', (I meant that) if anything [should happen] to [the king] (so that) he would become worried, [the gods] would hurriedly send a sign from [the heaven] (saying) [. . . . " (Rest broken).

The general idea of this report is thus the same as in our letter.

r21. *upnē patû*: cf. Landsberger, *MAOG* 4 (928) 298: "Die assyrischen Denkmäler liefern . . . Material auch für den spezifisch assyrischen Bittgestus, das *upnē petû*: Während die Rechte den Segensgestus in der erwähnten spezifischen Form ausführt, wird der linke Unterarm waagerecht mit geöffneter Hand gehalten, aber auch beide Arme in der letztbeschriebenen Haltung kommen vor." The latter form of the gesture is illustrated e.g. by the reliefs of Sennacherib pertaining to the siege of Lachish (A. Parrot, *Nineveh and Babylon*, p.41; cf. p.35), to be compared with Streck *Asb* p.24 iii 7: *áš-šú ba-laṭ* ZI-*tì-šú up-na-a-šú ip-ta-a ú-ṣal-la-a* EN-*ja* "he opened his fists and prayed my majesty to save his life."

r22. The reading *lu e-ti-ik* "he should be on his guard" (not **lu e-ti-iq* "it may by-pass" *CAD* E 390ab, etc.) is certain on the ground of *LAS* 279 r12 f (MAN *be-lí lu-u e-ti-ik-ma* EN.⸢NUN⸣ *lu-u dan-na-at*) and the parallel passages in *RMA* 103 r3 and 268 r9-10. Note also the explicit spelling with <k> in *LAS* 72 r18 (*lu et-ku*). – For the apotropaic ritual here referred to see *LAS* 137 and pertinent notes.

36

Bibliography:

(I) Waterman, *RCAE* 353 (cf. IV 247); Pfeiffer, *SLA* 334; Oppenheim, *Letters* (1967) 166 (translat. only).
(II) Behrens, *ABB* (1906) 74f; Oppenheim, *Centaurus* 14 (1969) 115 ff.

Photograph (of Obverse):
RCAE IV pl.8.

Discussion:

See Oppenheim 1969. It seems likely that the favourable omens quoted in the obverse encouraged the writer to present his petition in this context, even though the petition is formally presented as a separate message.

Notes:

7-r3. All these omens are, with the highest degree of probability, quoted from *Šumma Ālu*, Tablets LXVI and LXVII, even though the relevant portions of the Series itself have not been preserved (or identified to date). Cf. *CT* 39, Pl.23 f, containing omens derived from the behaviour of falcons, and ibid. Pl.25, dealing with ravens and eagles.

r9. On the probable location of the province (or perhaps better, the feudal benefice) of the Chief Cupbearer (some 75 km NW of Nineveh, between Nisibin and the Tigris) see Forrer, *Provinzeinteilung*, 21 ff; cf. also *AOAT* 6, 289.*

r12. *GIŠ.SAR*^{MEŠ}*-ja iṣ-ṣa-aḫ-tu*: cf. ND.2734+:50, *man-nu ša* A.ŠÀ.GA *ṣa-ḫi-tú-u-ni i-bat-taq* "wer immer ein Feld begehrt, schneidet (von dem herrenlosen Land ein Stück) ab", Deller *Or*NS 33 (1964) 90. *iṣ-ṣa-aḫ-tú* (hitherto misread as *PA-ṣa-aḫ-tú*, cf. e.g. *AHw* 839*b* [1969] and Oppenheim 1967) is the first prefixed form of *ṣaḫātu* "to desire, want" (NA only, replacing older *ḫašāḫu*) attested so far; the context confirms the meaning assigned to the verb by Deller, loc. cit.

---

[73] Cf. *RMA* 119 r1-2, [^{d}*30* U]D *12*.KAM IGI-*ma* ḪUL KUR URI^{KI} ² SIG$_5$ NIM.MA^{KI} "the Moon's appearance on the 12th signifies bad luck for Akkad, good luck for Elam".

On the relative size of Balasî's landed possessions, cf. note to *LAS* 114:7.

r15. *T[A* qa]-ni*: see note to *LAS* 239:5'.

37

Bibliography:

(I) Waterman, *RCAE* 75; Postgate, *TCAE* (1974) 248; see ibid. pp.68f, 94, 102 and 248.

Writer:

Certainly not Balasî the astrologer; in addition to the arguments to this effect presented by Postgate (the subject matter and the difference of the greeting formula from that found in the letters of the astrologer), note also the occurrence of the sign LÚ* in Obv.6.9 (against LÚ of the astrologer). Legal documents from Nineveh refer to two other individuals named Balasî, a bodyguard occurring as witness in texts dated between 640 and 620 BC (*AR* 57, 129, 210, 231, 341, 377, 396, 628 and 632, dates according to Falkner, *AfO* 17 118 ff) and a "majordomo" ([1]*Ba-la-si* GAL-É), mentioned in *ADD* 128 = *AR* 322:15 (665 BC); the content of the present letter points to the household manager rather than the bodyguard. The writer of the letter is apparently also referred to in another letter (*ABL* 413) as a person responsible for issuing working materials from the palace to a weaving establishment (Obv. 6 ff: *ina* UGU *ša* LUGAL *be-lí* [7] *a-na* ÌR-*šú iš-pur-an-ni* [8] *ma-a ina* UGU [TÚG]BAR.DUL$_5$ [MEŠ] [9] *a-na* [I]*Ba-la-si-i* [10] *šá-'a-al* TA* *a-a-ka* [11] *id-da-nu-ni šup-ra* [12] *a-na* [I]*Ba-la-si-i as-sa-'a-al* [r1] *ma-a* SÍG SA$_5$ [2] TA* ŠÀ É.GAL *ni-dan* "in re what the king, my lord, wrote to his servant, viz. 'Ask Balasî about the *kusītu* garments, and write whence they issue them', I have (now) asked Balasî; he said: 'We give red wool from the Palace' . . .").

Discussion:

The interpretation of this document involves various difficulties, but it seems probable that the articles mentioned in it were items regularly delivered to the palace by state-employed shepherds in compensation for the military service (*ilku*) of which they were relieved, to be later distributed as standard military equipment to Assyrian troops. These deliveries were normally collected by the official *abarakku* ("steward") mentioned in Obv.6; it is accordingly a little surprising that the writer of the present letter considered it necessary to ask the king to remind the *abarakku* of a duty which he obviously would have fulfilled anyway. Perhaps the items mentioned were urgently needed for a special purpose before the time they were usually collected. For details see Postgate, op.cit., pp. 68f, 84ff and 102; cf. especially the texts ND 3467, edited ibid., p.399f, and ND 10009 and 10012, published (in copy) in Kinnier Wilson, *NWL* pl.46f and 50f and discussed by Postgate, op.cit. p.74 ff.

Notes:

7f. The articles *sāgu* and *mazā'u* appear together in several texts referring to the basic equipment of Assyrian soldiers (e.g., *AfO* Bh 6 no.48:10(!)-11; ND 3467:5-6; *ADD* 1036 ii 13 and 1095:14; *NL* 25:13-14); the former probably denotes the broad linen belt of Assyrian soldiers often depicted in sculptures (cf. Ungnad, *AfO* Bh 6 p.34 *ad* line 12), the latter a kind of water-skin (cf. Postgate, op.cit. p.69; note that the word is replaced in *NL* 25:14 by [KUŠ]*ḫintu* "leather bag, water-skin").

r1. The emendation *[i]-na!-áš-šú-u-ni* suggested in Pt.I is not feasible; according to collation by E. Sollberger (Jan.19, 1976) the tablet indeed reads *[i]-ba-áš-šú-u-ni*, as copied by Harper.[74] The rendering of the passage has accordingly to be changed slightly; for „they should not sell anything *they bring*" read ". . . anything there is" (*[am-mar i]-ba-áš-šú-u-ni*).

[74] The reading *i-na!-áš-šú-u-ni* is abortive also because *našû* "to bring" requires the ventive ending, and the form should therefore be *i-na-áš-šú-u-ni-ni*, cf. *am-mar i-na-ši-ú-ni-ni*, *KAV* 98:18.

38

Bibliography:

(I) Waterman, *RCAE* 74 (cf. IV 174).

(II) Behrens, *ABB* (1906) 69f; Labat, *Royauté* (1939) 214; Meier, *Or*NS 8 (1939) 308f; Oppenheim, *JAOS* 61 (1941) 263.

Copy:

Cf. Harper, *Hebraica* 10 (1889) 198.

Date:

Late Nisannu, eponymy of Šulmu-Bēl-lašme = early April, 670 BC. See note on Rev.10 ff.

Addressee:

Esarhaddon.

Discussion:

The incident discussed in this letter also forms the subject matter of a letter written by Balasî's colleague Nabû-aḫḫē-erība, overlooked in Pt.I but edited below, p.363, as *LAS* 349 (q.v.). The wording of *LAS* 349:9-11 suggests that the destruction of the field by the lightning took place approximately at the time of harvest; this fits perfectly the dating of the letter to Nisannu, as the first crops of the year seem to have been harvested in Assyria approximately at that time (cf. ND 2094:7, *ina* ^{ITU}GUD *ša* EGIR *i-bu-ri* ^{8} *ú-ga-ma-ra ú-ṣa*; also *LAS* 110+300 [written in May], r1-2; EBUR *šá* KUR URI^{KI} *ina* ^{ITU}BARAG ^{12} *in-né-eṣ-ṣi-d*[*u*], *ABL* 815 r11 f, etc.).

Notes:

6. *Ḫariḫumba*: a town otherwise known only from two administrative documents from Calah (ND 440 = *Iraq* 13 110 and ND 3483 = *Iraq* 15 154, and therefore probably located within the territory controlled by the prefect of that city. The texts themselves do not contain any concrete evidence as to the location of the town, except that ND 440 also mentions ^{URU}*Ši-iš-li*, a town also to be located in the vicinity of Calah (see J.N. Postgate, *Iraq* 32 (1970) 139, note to line 9').

7 ff. Cf. Job 1:16, *'š 'lhym nplh mn-hšmym wtb'r bṣ'n wbn'rym wt'klm* "God's fire fell from heaven, struck the sheep and the shepherds and burnt them up" (referring to the second trial of Job). It is certain that strokes of lightning were conceived as divine punishments in Assyria, too, as in ancient Israel; cf. Streck *Asb* p.32 iii 124 "I (= the moon god) will grant them an evil death, I will put an end to their lives with a flaming sword, the thunderbolt, and (with) famine and pestilence."

11. On *qatinnu* "tiller" (or the like) see, provisionally, van Driel, *CA* p.188[70]; cf. Fales, *CCENA*, nos. 11 iii 2, and 23:29.

17 f. *ḪUL mì-qit-ti i-šá-ti*: referring to the apotropaia against 'evil of lightning' published by Caplice, *Or*NS 36 (1967) 287 ff (cf. Obv.1', *šum-ma mi-iq-ti* [*i-šá-ti* . . .] and Rev.24', *ana* ḪUL IZI.ŠUB.BA *ana* NA NU TE-*e*) and ibid, 294 ff, and Ebeling, *RA* 48 (1954) 84f (*ana* ḪUL IZI.ŠUB.BA-*e ana* NA etc., Obv.3 and 6). Note also the hand-lifting prayer published by Ebeling, *AGH* 25.[75]

r1-8. These omens are based on *Šumma Ālu* Tablet LV (*CT* 39 pl.1 ff) though the quotations are, significantly enough, not quite exact.[76] Cf. *CT* 39 pl.4:31 ff:

I A.ŠÀ URU ^{d}IM RA-*iṣ* NA BI MU 3.KÁM *ina ku-ri u* ZARAḪ [DU^{MEŠ}]

---

[75] Hardly pertaining to the present incident, even though written for a certain ^{I}*Ba-la-si* (*ana-ku* ^{I}*Ba-la-si* DUMU DINGIR-*šu* . . . ^{15} *ina* ḪUL IZI.ŠUB.BA *ša* ina É-MU GÁL-*a* ^{16} *pal-ḫa-ak ad-ra-ak u šu-ta-du-rak* . . . , Obv. 14 ff). The text originates in Assur.

[76] The omission of the vertical wedge (I), usually preceding verbatim quotations, in Rev.1 may be quite intentional. The wedge is otherwise omitted only in *LAS* 1r.14 and 64r.12.

I *ina* GÌR.BAL-*šu* IZI *mim-ma ú-qal-li* ŠÀ A.ŠÀ NA BI ÚŠ
I *ṭi-bi-iḫ* ^{GIŠ}GIGIR *iš-kun* IBILA BI *iš-šal-lal* NA BI ÚŠ

"If Adad devastates a field of a city, the man concerned will live 3 years in utter misery."

"If during the devastation lightning burns anything, this man will die in his field."

"If he (Adad) puts down a . . . of (his) chariot, the heir concerned will be carried away and the said man himself will die."

It is evident why the writer has melted all three omens together: all apodoses except the first one would have unnecessarily frightened the king – or at least Balasî seems to have thought so (cf. commentary to *LAS* 41!). The additional remark that the omen did not concern the king of course served the same purpose.

r3. *magarru*, given only the meaning "wheel" in *AHw* 575a, certainly means here "chariot"; cf. the third omen quoted above (^{GIŠ}GIGIR).

r10 ff. *"This is indeed a leap year"*: The subsequent reference to the expected heliacal rising of Jupiter (r13 ff) makes it possible to identify the leap year concerned and thus give the letter an exact date. As the *place* of the intercalary month was still open to discussion (cf. r20), i.e., it was still possible to choose between an intercalary Ulūlu or Addāru, the letter must have been written during the first half of the year (Nisannu to Ulūlu); and in principle, either the first or the fifth month should be in question, otherwise the question of intercalation would not have been at all timely.[77] A checking of the heliacal settings and risings of Jupiter in the five leap years (676, 673, 670, 668 and 665 BC, cf. App.A1) included in the period covered by the correspondence of Balasî gives the following result (cf. App. C4):[78]

LEAP YEAR	E LAST AND	M FIRST OF JUPITER	
676	Tašrītu 16	Araḫsamna 20	(8th month)
673	Kislīmu 14	Kanūnu 19	(10th month)
670	Nisannu 12	Ajāru 22	(2nd month)
668	Simānu 15	Du'ūzu 20	(4th month)
665	Ulūlu 21	Tašrītu 25	(7th month)

Years 676, 673 and 665 can be immediately elimated on the above grounds; and year 668 is out of the question since *LAS* 326 (q.v.) shows that in that year the whole matter of intercalation was taken up only in Šabāṭu (11th month) and then not by the king but by Balasî himself.

r17 ff. Exactly how the heliacal risings of Jupiter regulated the practice of intercalation remains obscure, but the present passage makes it clear that it did affect the choice between an intercalary Ulūlu and Addāru; the role played by the planet in the matter is certainly related to the fact that it was Jupiter = Marduk who "established the patterns of the year" (*Enūma Eliš* V 5). Note that the intercalation rules of Mul Apin (see Hunger + Reiner, *WZKM* 67 [1975] 21 ff), which Balasî had certainly followed in deciding that the year in question was intercalary (cf. sub *LAS* 326), did not specify when an Ulūlu or an Addāru had to be intercalated. The theoretical basis of the choice is therefore still unknown. One can only state that "in the earlier periods there is a marked preference for second Ulūlus. A gradual shift from Ulūlus to Addarus in later periods can be seen. When an Addaru is missed for any reason, ––– an Ulūlu is often inserted in the following year to bring the calendar up to date more quickly" (Parker + Dubberstein, *Babylonian Chronology*, p.2 f).

77 That the month concerned was Nisannu is made likely by the fact that Balasî was able to tell assuredly that the year was intercalary. Cf. the well-known "Pleiaden-Schaltregel" (Schaumberger, *SSB* 3. Erg. 340 ff): "If Moon and Pleiades are in conjunction on the third day of Nisannu, this is a leap year".

78 To obtain the probable dates for the risings and settings of the planet in Nineveh, the dates given in the Appendix (for Babylon) have been slightly modified. Cf. sub *LAS* 51.

39

Bibliography:

(I) Waterman, *RCAE* 688.

(II) Behrens, *ABB* (1906) 78f; Oppenheim, *JAOS* 64 (1944) 194, *AS* 16 (1965) 256, and *Centaurus* 14 (1969) 119, 128[12]; Leichty, *TCS* 4 (1970) 9f.

Photograph:

RCAE IV pl.13 (obverse only).

Discussion:

See Leichty 1970, also for other contemporary letters and reports referring to or quoting teratological omens. Notice, however, that (contra Leichty) the present letter does not pertain to an earlier *report* on an anomalous birth but to an entire *tablet* of the anomaly series itself (*ṭup-pu ša* BE *iz-bi*, see on Obv.5f).

Notes:

5-12. Cancel the rendering of this passage given in Pt.I and read and translate instead: *ina* UGU ⌜*ṭup*!⌝-[*pi*] [6] *ša* BE *iz*-[*bi ša*] ⌜LUGAL *be-lí*⌝ [7] *iš-pur-an-ni ma-a* ⌜*a*⌝-[*mur*] [8] *ina* ŠÀ BE *iz*⌜-*bé*⌝-*e* ⌜*x*⌝[. .] [9] *i-šaṭ-ṭar 1-en* [*šu*!]-⌜*ú*⌝ [10] *ṭup-pu*! *ša id*?-⌜*a*⌝-*t*[*e*? *ina lìb-b*]*i* [11] *šá-aṭ-ṭa-ra-a-ni* [12] *an-nu-rig a-na* LUGAL [13] *us-se-bi-la* "As to the tab[let] of *Šumma Izbu* [concerning which] the king, my lord, wrote to me: 'Look (at it)! [Who would] write [. . .] in *Šumma Izbu*?'; (there is) a particular tablet [in] which the . . . s are written, (and) I am now sending it to the king, my lord." Details below.

5. *ina UGU* ⌜*ṭup*!⌝-[*pi*]: sic according to photo; cf. Obv.10.

6. *BE iz-bi*: the normal spelling of the title of the series *Šumma Izbu* in the colophons of the work itself (cf. *TCS* 4 pp.52, 65, 73, etc.) and elsewhere (cf. *CAD* I/J 318); the presence of BE also in ll. 8 and r1 confirms that it is indeed the series in general that is meant here, not just a case of prodigy birth recently reported to the king.

7. ⌜*a*⌝-[*mur*]: sic rather that ⌜*a*⌝-[*ke-e*] (Pt.I). For similarly worded royal orders see *LAS* 7, 8, 13, 142, 149, 173, 203-205, 207, 209, 211, 223 and 259; the restoration proposed in Pt.I is improbable since the lengthening of the final vowel of *izbi* in Obv.8 indicates that the interrogative sentence lacked a specific question word (cf. note on 321:1f).

8f. Restore possibly *ina* ŠÀ BE *iz*-⌜*bé*⌝-*e* ⌜X⌝[*.man-nu*] [9] *i-šaṭ-ṭar*; the reading of the sign following *e* remains obscure.

9f. *1-en* ⌜*šu*!⌝-[*ú*] *ṭup-pu*!: sic according to photo; cf. *1-en šu-ú li-li-su* URUDU "one particular bronze kettle-drum", *ABL* 1092 r13.

10. The reading of the signs following *ša* remains unclear; on the basis of the context, one would expect *ṣâti* "archaisms"; the traces, however, seem to read neither ⌜*ṣa-a-te*⌝ nor ⌜UD.UL.DÙ.A^{MEŠ}⌝ (nor UL^{MEŠ}) but either ⌜*da-a*-X⌝ (= ?*dâti* "information", cf. *CAD* s.v. *di'atu*) or ⌜*id-a*-X⌝ (= ? *idāti* "omens", cf. *CAD* s.v. *ittu*).

11. *šá-aṭ-ṭa-ra-a-ni*: either Pl. of *šaṭ(ṭ)āru* "writing, document, etc." (thus von Soden, *AHw*. 1203*b* [1976]; Leichty, *TCS* 4 [1970] 10, *et alii*) or 3f Pl. Stat. + Subj. of *šaṭāru* G "to write" (thus Behrens, *ABB* [1906] 78[2]). In favour of the former interpretation one may note the occurrence of *ša(ṭ)ṭāru* in colophons of literary texts besides *ṭuppu* (cf. *a-na pi-i ṭup-pi ša-ṭa-ri ša* PN . . . *ša-aṭ-rat* "written according to a tablet written by PN", *KAR* 15 r13f = Hunger, *AOAT* 2 p.30, cf. ibid. p.175*b*) and the fact that *šaṭṭāru*, otherwise attested only twice in Neo-Assyrian letters (cf. *šaṭ-ṭa-ru*, *ABL* 438:15 and r9, and *šá-ṭa-a-ri*, *LAS* 198 r4), indeed took the plural suffix *-āni*, at least in LB (cf. *ša-ṭa-ra-nu*, *šá-ṭa-ra-nu*^{MEŠ} and the other spellings listed in *AHw* l.c.). However, one should note that if this *morphologically* tempting interpretation is accepted, one is immediately faced with certain lexical, logical and syntactic difficulties. Taking *šaṭṭarāni* as a noun would require that the passage concerned is

translated "one tablet of [. . .] *and* (the) 'writings' I am now sending to the king", where 'writings' should have the technical meaning "explanatory comments", or the like – a meaning not otherwise attested for *ša(ṭ)ṭāru* (and logically improbable, since Balasi later only refers to the *tablet* he has sent and promises to give explanatory comments orally). And finally, there is the syntactic difficulty that *annūrig* as an adverb of time should be placed at the beginning of the sentence and not be preceded by two objects, as the interpretation under consideration would require. This rule seems to have been followed quite strictly in Neo-Assyrian; as far as the present writer has been able to ascertain, *annūrig* could only be preceded by particles (*ū*, etc.), other adverbs (*ūmâ*) and an emphasized subject, as in *LAS* 186 r12f (*ù a-na-ku an-nu-rig ṭup-pa-a-ni* etc.) and *ABL* 396 r5 ff (*ma-a* $^{\mathrm{I.d}}$AMAR+UD-MU-SUM-*na an-nu-rig i-da-tú-u-a il-la-ka*). In *ABL* 331:8 ff (PN_1 . . . PN_2 . . . PN_3 ^{r3} PAP *3* ERIM^{MEŠ} 4 ^{URU}*Si-na-a-a šu-nu* ^{5} *la* ^{KUR}*Ḫa-ma-ta-a-a šu-nu* ^{6} *an-nu-rig* ^{7} UGU LUGAL EN-*a* ^{8} *ú-se-bi-la*), a passage closely paralleling the present one, the 3 persons mentioned in Obv.8 - Rev.5 logically constitute the object of *ú-se-bi-la*, but *syntactically* Obv.8 - Rev.5 is an independent clause asyndetically coordinated with Rev.6-8. Such a construction cannot be assumed in the present case, if *šaṭṭarāni* is taken to be a noun.

By contrast, all these difficulties are avoided if *šá-aṭ-ṭa-ra-a-ni* is taken as the predicate of the relative clause qualifying *ṭup-pu* in Obv.10 and explained as an alloform of paradigmatic/šaṭrāni/. The intrusive -*ṭa*-can be easily accounted for in the light of parallel examples, which show that an anaptyptic vowel (always of the same quality as the preceding one) was frequently inserted into the consonant cluster separating two potentially stressed syllables *in case the stress was for some reason shifted to or placed on the second syllable*. Typical examples of the workings of this 'law' are *diglī́ja* > *di-gi-li-ja*, *LAS* 294 r2; *ḫiblā́ti* > *ḫi-bi-la-te*, *ABL* 463 r2; *(ša-)qurbū́ti* > ^{LÚ}*qur-ru-bu-ú-tu*, VAT 170:9.11 (*VS* 5 72); *maqlūtu* > *ma-qa-lu-tú*, *LAS* 167 r7, *ABL* 606 r4; *meḫrī́šu* > *me-ḫe-ri-šu*, *ABL* 85 r8; *nakrū́te* > *na-ka-ru-te* passim (but always *na-ak-ru* = *nákru*); *taḫrúbu* > *ta-ḫa-ru-bu*, *ABL* 311:5; *iḫrū́bu* > *i-ḫi-ru-bu*, ND 2677 r5 (but *iḫ-ru-ub* = *íḫrub*, *ABL* 1235:6), and so on. A secondary consonantal gemination (such as in our case) sometimes accompanied the anaptyxis, probably to avoid the sequence of two open short syllables; cf. *ṣil-li-ba-a-ni*, *LAS* 181:6 = *ṣi-il-ba-ni*, 246 r9.

Exactly parallel stative forms (however without an expressly indicated consonantal gemination) are, e.g., *pa-qa-da-a-ni*, *ABL* 434:10 (for *paqdā́ni*), and *ta-da-nu-u-ni*, *ABL* 532 r13, 602:6 (for *tadnū́ni*).

r1. "*Šumma Izbu is difficult to 'decipher'*": The writer probably refers to the fact that the Series contained a number of obsolete words, expressions and sign values which had to be separately explained in a commentary attached to the work (see Leichty, *TCS* 4 p.211 ff). Cf. note to r11 ff.

r3. *a-na 1-en* u_4*-mu*: here certainly "*on* the first day", not "*till* the first day"; in other words, *a-na* here stands for expected *ina* (cf. *ina 2-i* u_4*-me*, *ABL* 1372:13; *ina* UD *29*.KAM, *LAS* 96:11, etc.). It is a well-known fact that in Neo-Assyrian orthography <ina> often stands for expected /ana/ (many examples e.g. in Johns, *ADD* 252 ff; cf. also note to 79 r4) but the reverse case is left without any notice in the standard grammars (von Soden, *GAG* and Ylvisaker, *LSS* 5/6). Nevertheless, it is well attested, especially in indications of time, but also elsewhere, e.g.

a-na UD *2*.KÁM*, *LAS* 173 r10;
a-na UD *24*.KÁM* ibid. 7;
a-na UD *7*.KÁM*-*im-ma*, 176 r5;
a-na ši-a-ri ibid. 8 (cf. *iš-ši-a-r[i]* ibid. 11);
a-na ba-a-di, *ABL* 101:11, *LAS* 165 r4, *ABL* 366:6, 373 r10,
a-na šá-al-še, *ABL* 311:11, similarly *LAS* 210 r1;
a-na ^{URU}*arrap-ḫa* "in Arrapḫa", *NL* 72:4 (*Iraq* 27 pl.3);
a-na de-e-ni-šú "in his case", *ADD* 503:16';
a-na ma-te-ni "in our country", *ABL* 124:5;
a-na ḫa-an-ši u_4*-me-šú* "in his fifth day", *ABL* 1372 r6;
a-na ma-ḫe-er-te, *ABL* 387 r16 (cf. *ina ma-ḫer-ti* 252:12);
a-na ^{ITU}ZÍZ "in Šabāṭu", *ABL* 91 r10;
a-na si-mìn "at the time (of)", *ABL* 503 r14;

a-na DIN.TIR^{KI} "in Babylon", *ABL* 212:24;
a-na lìb-bi ta-ḫu-me "within the territory", *ABL* 484 r7;
a-na UGU "concerning", *ABL* 173:9, 860:6 (for usual *ina* UGU);
a-na pa-zu-ur-ti "secretly", *AfO* Bh 6 No. 4:4.

Cf. also the adverbial expressions surveyed in note to *LAS* 158:6. As parallel examples are also to be found in Old and Middle Assyrian (e.g., *a-na* u_4*-um e-ṭá-ri-im, CCT* 4 no.22a:4; *a-na ad-ra-ti* "at threshing time", *KAJ* 77:6, beside *i-na ad-ra-ti* ibid. 69:7, etc.), it is clear that the use use of *a-na* for expected *ina* can at least partially be explained idiomatically, particularly in temporal expressions. On the other hand, there is reason to believe that the semantic distinction between the prepositions *ina* and *ana* was (at least partially) lost already in Middle Assyrian, probably as a result of a phonetic merger of the two prepositions in certain environments (e.g., the proclitic forms *an+* and *in+*).[79] Cf., e.g. the interchange of *ina* and *ana* in *PKTA* 19*a* ii 12'ff:

ša-nu-te-šu i-ḫa-bu a-na ^{d}*a-šur i+na* UGU *e-bi-ir-te* (line 12'),
ša-la-⌜*šu*⌝*-šu i-ḫa-bu a-na* ^{d}*a-šur a+na* UGU *e-bi-ir-t*[*e*] (line 14').

Examples like these suggest that *ina* and *ana* still existed in MA and NA as phonologically distinct linguistic units but had lost their semantic distinction, so that the two prepositions could occur as free variants of each other in virtually every context; the NA spellings *ina* and *a-na* could thus be taken to stand for spoken [ina] and [ana], i.e. as reflections of two distinct pronunciations of a single preposition. On the other hand, the fact that */ina/ is very rarely spelled *i-na* in NA,[80] coupled with the fact that the sign AŠ = *ina* can equally well be read *anà* (cf. AŠ = *i-na*, AŠ = *a-na*, Izi E 168(a)), makes it possible that *ina* and *ana* had *totally* merged in NA (also phonetically) and that virtually all spellings with AŠ = *ina* actually stand for *an(a)*. The truth probably lies halfway between these two possibilities.

r5. *i-tar-ba*: an unconventional spelling for 1st Sg. Pf. of *erābu* G, possibly reflecting more truly the actual pronunciation than the conventional spelling *e-tar-ba*. Other similar cases are *i-ru-bu, ABL* 883 r9; *i-rab, KAV* 215:9; *i-tar-bu, LAS* 339 r4; *i-ta-rab, CA* p.90 vii 25'.29' (beside *e-ta-rab,* ibid. 27'); *i-mu-ru-ni, KAV* 197: 27; *i-ma-ru-ni, ABL* 463 r7, etc.; conversely, one finds *e-rab-bi* for expected /irabbi/ in *ADD* 88:7, *e-tú-ru* for expected /ittūrū/ in *ABL* 484:8, etc.

r5-8. *ina ŠÀ ṭup-pi . . . ina lìb-bi*: on this expression see note to *LAS* 34:18.

r9. *ki-i šá-ṭir-u-ni "how* (the omen) is written": sic, not "*that* (this line) is written there" (Leichty 1970). See Dietrich, *AOAT* 1 (1969) 76f on the positional difference between NB *kī* "how" and *kī* "that"; the rule formulated there also holds for NA.

r11f. Literally, "before whom the (teacher's) finger has not 'gone' ", probably standing idiomatically for "who has not been specifically intructed in reading (*Šumma Izbu* omens)"; correct the rendering in Pt.I.[81] Leichty (1970) restores in line 12 [*im*]*-tal-li-ku-u-ni* and translates "what a finger in front of him cannot show him", but this is unacceptable since *malāku* Gt is otherwise not attested in Neo-Assyrian.[82]

---

79 Cf. Arab. *'anta, 'anti* > Iraqi-Arab. *'inta, 'inti,* class. *kalimatun* > dial. *kilme,* (Iraqi) *cilma,* etc. Contextual factors would account for the predominance of *i*-spellings in the proclitic forms of the prepositions, while elsewhere *a*-spellings predominate (see note to *LAS* 158:6.

80 In my statistics, there are only 27 attestations of *i-na* against 1641 of *a-na* and 1210 of *ina* (= AŠ). Most scribes writing *i-na* also wrote *a-na* (i.e., the two prepositions contrast in their letters, see e.g. *LAS* 124 and *ABL* 1110), but note *i-na mi-i-ni* (= *ana mīni, ammīni*) in *ABL* 474+ r5.

81 The idiom *ubānu* + *alāku* does not seem to occur elsewhere; cf. *qātu* + *alāku* (*LAS* 19 r8') and *aḫu* + *alāku* (212 r4).

82 For Bab. *malāku* Gt "to take counsel" one finds in NA *malāku* N (cf. *LAS* 185 r5f and *AHw* 594*a*). Cf. Deller, *OrNS* 34 (1965) 271: "Rez. ist der Auffassung, daß das nA keine Stammformen mit einfachem *ta*-Infix (Gt, Dt, Št, NT) bildet. Es gibt nur von Gt-Stämmen abgeleitete Nomina (wie *taḫāzu, ana mitḫar*), einen Dtt-Stamm und Stammformen mit *-tan-* Infix."

40

Bibliography:

(I) Waterman, *RCAE* 691.

Date:

Nisannu 16, eponymy of Gabbāru = April 21, 667 BC. This date follows from the statement in Obv.7-9 that Jupiter, Venus and Saturn were "present" in the lunar eclipse reported. Such a situation prevailed only once between 680-663, as appears from the following survey based on App. F1 and F3 (+ = visible, - = invisible).

Date of eclipse	Venus	Jupiter	Saturn
679 NOV 26	-	-	-
678 MAY 22	-	+	+
677 NOV 3	+	-	-
674 SEP 3-4	-	-	-
673 FEB 27	+	-	+
671 JUL 2	-	-	+
671 DEC 27-28	-	-	+
670 DEC 17	-	-	+
669 JUN 11	-	-	-
667 APR 21	+	+	+
667 OCT 15	I	I	-
666 APR 10	-	+	+
666 OCT 4	-	-	-
664 AUG 13	-	-	-

The present letter accordingly deals with the same eclipse as *LAS* 61, from Nabû-aḫḫē-erība. For other synchronic letters and reports from Balasî and Nabû-aḫḫē-erība, see commentary to *LAS* 34.

Addressee:

Assurbanipal.

Discussion:

Notice the remark "the king should not be afraid of this eclipse" directed to *Assurbanipal* — a welcome reminder that not all undatable letters of the present corpus referring to a king scared by omens (e.g. *LAS* 204) necessarily were addressed to Esarhaddon.

41

Bibliography:

(I) Waterman, *RCAE* 687 (cf. IV 186, 260); Pfeiffer, *SLA* 315; Oppenheim, *Letters* (1967) 161f.
(II) Schott, *OLZ* 40 (1937) 363; Labat, *Royauté* (1939) 329; Schott, *ZA* 47 (1941/2) 100; Oppenheim, *JAOS* 61 (1941) 259.

Copy:

Cf. Zeitlin, *SACA* (1910), no. 23.

Date:

Araḫsamna 26, eponymy of Šulmu-Bēl-lašme = December 1, 670 BC. See note to r6.

Addressee:

Esarhaddon.

Discussion:

This letter provides, in addition to its astronomically interesting details, a rare (albeit indirect) glimpse of the the air of flattery that must have surrounded the Sargonid kings: knowing and/or fearing that his servants may, in an effort to please him or keep him happy, conceal unpleasant news from him, the king (morbidly interested in astrological omens which he views as signs from gods, cf. sub *LAS* 246), here blames his astrologer for *lack of reports*!! The implications of the situation are illustrated by another letter (*ABL* 1216) dating from ca. 680 BC:[83]

Rev. 1 ^{I}*Kal-bi* DUMU-*šú šá* ^{Id}AG*-KAR-*er a-na tar-ṣi* LUGAL AD-*ka ri-ik-s[u it-ti]*
2 ^{LÚ}DUB.SAR^{MEŠ} *ù* ^{LÚ}ḪAL^{MEŠ} *šá la* LUGAL AD-*ka ki-i ú-r[ak-ki-su]*
3 *um-ma ki-i it-tu la ba-ni-ti ta-at-tal-ku a-na* LUGAL *n[i-qab-bi]*
4 *um-ma it-tu e-ši-ti ta-at-tal-ka ṭup-pi a-na ṭup-pi [lum-na-a-ni]*
5 *gab-bi-šú-nu i-da-ku ki-i it-tu šá ina muḫ-ḫi-šú la ba-na-a-[tu illiku]*
6 *ù šu-ú mim+ma šá la ba-na-a ár-ka-niš a-lu-u ki-i il-li-[ku* AD-*ka um-ma it-tu]*
7 *šá i-na muḫ-ḫi-ja la ba-na-a-tu tal-li-kám-ma la taq-ba-a-ni* [. . . . .]
8 *di-ib-bi an-nu-ti* ^{LÚ}DUB.SAR^{ME} : ^{LÚ}ḪAL^{ME} *ina* ŠU^{2}-*šú-nu ki-i iṣ-ba-tu* [^{d}EN ^{d}AG* DINGIR^{MEŠ}-*ka*]
9 *lu-ú i-du-ú ki-i it-tu ma-la a-na ṭar-ṣi* LUGAL AD-*ka tal-li-[ku iq-ta-bu-u]*
10 LUGAL AD-*ka la bal-ṭu-ma ù* LUGAL-*u-tú la i-pu-šú-ma*

"After Kalbu the son of Nabû-ēṭer[84] under your royal father made the following arrangement with (all) the scribes and haruspices, without (the knowledge of) the king, your father:

'If an untoward sign appears, [let's tell] the king:

"An obscure sign has appeared."',

they systematically (= *ṭuppi ana ṭuppi*) censored (= *idakkū*, lit. "kept removing") all [unfavourable predictions], if a sign untoward to him (= Sennacherib) [occurred], or if there was anything else untoward. Afterwards (however), as the *alû*-disease (cf. sub *LAS* 172) "came", [your royal father told them]:

'[A sign] that is untoward to me has appeared, and you have not told me! [. . . . .]'

The scribes and haruspices took notice of these words and, [your gods Bēl and Nabû] be my witnesses, they [reported] every sign that appeared in the time of your royal father; and was your royal father (still) not (fully) alive and did he not exercise the kingship?"

It is hardly necessary to add that the endeavour of courtiers to conceal bad omens from despots is universal and parallel examples can be found in courts of almost any time and place. Cf. simply Herodotus, *Historiae* VII 6: "For that reason he (= Onesikritos) announced his predictions whenever he entered into the presence of the king (= Xerxes). But if they contained anything that meant bad luck for the barbarian, he told nothing about the matter, but picked out and read only the most lucky passages." A quite recent parallel is found in Albert Speer's *Erinnerungen* (Berlin 1969), p. 129(!):

> "In der Reichskanzlei gab es seit Jahrzehnten eine Marmorbüste Bismarcks von Reinhold Begas. Einige Tage vor der Einweihung fiel sie beim Umzug in die neuen Räume den Arbeitern zu Boden, so daß der Kopf abbrach. Eine üble Vorbedeutung, wie mir schien. Und da ich zudem Hitlers Erzählung kannte, daß genau zu Beginn des Ersten Weltkrieges der Reichsadler vom Postgebäude herabgestürzt sei, verheimlichte ich das Unglück und ließ durch Breker eine genaue Kopie anfertigen, die wir mit Tee etwas patinierten."

Notes:

9. *ta-ta-ma-RA*: the paragogic vowel (-*a*) is here not due to interrogative intonation (cf. note to 208 r8), but to the special emphasis placed on the verb, and has to be explained in the light of note to 18 r8 (*tātamāra* = *tātamár-ma*). Cf. *ABL* 996 r1, *i-su-ri* ^{2} *i-ba-áš-ši* ^{3} *né-ma-RA*, ABL 996 r3; LÚ *ut-ru i-ba-ši* ^{5} *is-se-šú i-za-ZA* 309 r4-5; *ibašši lā ēpuš ina adê at-ta-la-KA*, *LAS* 211:12; similarly, with *laššu*, ABL 312:8, *la-áš-šu la ta-ri-ṢI*, and 103+: 11 *la-áš-šú* ^{12} *la ni-qar-ri-BI*. That the penultimate vowel was in all cases long (though not written so) is indicated by occasional spellings such as *a-ta-ma-a-ra* (*CT* 53 930:7).

---

[83] On the dating of the document see Labat, "Esarhaddon et la ville de Zaqqap", *RA* 53 (1959) 113 ff. The beginning of the letter is translated ibid., p.115f.

[84] Identified as the *ummânu* of Sennacherib in the kinglist of Assur (Appendix N, no.1).

r1 ff. This section shows, as clearly as one could wish, that the lunar and solar theory was in the Sargonid period not yet sufficiently developed to enable the astrologers to compute the possible times of occurrence of solar eclipses (that is, the moments of the conjunctions of the sun and the moon), let alone to predict whether these would occur or not.[85] Instead, the sun was watched intensively during the new moon periods before and after an expected lunar eclipse.[86] Accordingly, it can be concluded that while the present letter was written, a lunar eclipse was expected to occur in the month Kislimu – a fact that makes it possible to date the letter exactly. As appears from App. F1, the only lunar eclipse between 681 and 661 BC to take place in Kislimu was that of December 17, -669. The preceding conjunction occurred on December 2, which consequently must be the approximate date of the letter. (Incidentally, a solar eclipse indeed occurred on that date, though it could not be seen in Mesopotamia.)

r6. *UD 26.KÁM**: this date implies that the moon had already disappeared on the 25th; accordingly, the beginning of Araḫsamna, 670, had been misplaced owing to weather. Cf. *RMA* 85; also *LAS* 119 and relevant notes.*

r17. For the idiom *našû rammû*, lit. "lift up and let fall", see Deller, *Or*NS 30 (1961) 347. Some additional examples: GÍR *me-me-ni* [19] *la-a qur-bu i-ti-ši* [20] *ur-ta-mi-ú-šú-nu* "no sword was drawn, they let them go (voluntarily)", *ABL* 144:18 ff; *at-ti-ši an-na-ka ur-ta-am-me* "I left (the stools) here" 467 r1; *dul-lu it-ta-ṣu* [13] *ur-ta-am-me-u* "(the servants) quitted the work", 885:12 f; KÁ.GAL-*ma* [37] *ša* É-*ni la ar-ṣip a-ti-ši* [38] ⌜*ur*⌝-*ta-am!-mi!* "I did not even brick up the inner gate, (but) quitted (the work) instantly", ND 2715:36 ff (*Iraq* 17 pl. XXX). See also *LAS* 241 r4 f.

r18. *ḫi-ip lìb-bi*: cf. Arab. *ḫāfa* (*ḫiftu*) "to fear, be afraid", *ḫauf* "anxiety, fear". The expression "fear of the heart" may be compared with *ti-ri-ik lìb-bi* "throbbing heart", *LAS* 247:18, and *ḫu-up lib-ba-te* "injured pride", 120 r3. Despite the alluring parallel *ku-su-up lìb-bi* "broken heart" in *LAS* 246 r10, the word *ḫīpu* cannot in the present expression be regarded as a derivate from the verb *ḫapû* "to break"; cf. the context in *LAS* 264 r15.

42

Bibliograpy:

(I) Waterman, *RCAE* 351.

Discussion:

This letter is of interest because of the two eclipse predictions it contains. As pointed out in Introduction, p. 16 ff, mathematical procedures were not involved in either case. The exclusion of the lunar eclipse was possible by means of periodically arranged lists of eclipses reaching back till year 747 at least; in addition to the thumb rule that the moon may be eclipsed every sixth synodic month, the scholars of this period certainly had recognized the 47-month eclipse period[87] and probably also the 18-year "Saros".[88] The prediction concerning the solar eclipse (Rev.3f) agrees with what was already observed in note to *LAS* 41 r1 ff: the writer clearly did not feel safe to predict whether the eclipse would take place or not; he only affirms that the sun was being ob-

[85] Computation of the moment of conjunction requires a sufficiently accurate knowledge of the variations of the lunar and solar velocity, which certainly was not acquired before the end of the Neo-Babylonian period (though data on the lunar velocity were systematically collected already in the Sargonid period, cf. notes to *LAS* 105). Correct predictions of solar eclipses require sufficiently accurate knowledge of the actual distances of the sun and the moon from the earth, as well as an idea of the relative sizes of these bodies, – in other words, a level of knowledge that was never attained by Mesopotamian astronomers. Cf. O. Neugebauer, *Exact Sciences*, p.119.

[86] Cf. *LAS* 290:8-11.

[87] See van der Waerden, *Anfänge der Astronomie* (1968) 122 ff.

[88] Sic; while the utility of the "Saros" can be disputed, its recognition by the Assyrians can hardly be doubted (notwithstanding Willy Hartner, "Eclipse periods and Thales' prediction of a solar eclipse – historical truth and modern myth", *Centaurus* 14 (1969) 60 ff).

served intensively during the whole period of the moon's invisibility, that if the eclipse does not occur during that time, it will not occur at all. For other similar reports from Balasî, see *RMA* 274I and O.

Notes:

13. *da-a'-nu-tú-[ni]*: irregular Stat. 3f Sg. (+ Subj.) of *da'nu/dannu* "strong", certainly to be connected with *ma-ṣar-ti* in Obv.9; translate "(the watch) is strong", and cancel the italicized nonsense in Pt.I. The form is irregular only in the sense that the vowel of the Fem. *-at-* has been assimilated to *u* (as in Middle-Assyrian) though the vowel harmony was in general not operative in Neo-Assyrian in pre-stressed positions; the variant root *d'n* itself was not rare at all in Neo-Assyrian but seems to have alternated freely with *dnn*. Thus, while the stative *dannat* is attested more frequently that *da'nat* (occurring only here; but cf. note to 206:8), the attestations of the stative *dā(')na* (*da-a'-na LAS* 39 r1, 109:17, 312:10, *da-a-na*, ABL 242:12, 526:15 etc., both < *dân* < **da'an*, cf. note to *LAS* 206:8f) outnumber those of *dann* (written *da-an*, e.g. *LAS* 142:15, *ABL* 479 r2, or KALAG-*an*, *ABL* 482:11, 544 r6, etc.).

14. [u_4]-*mu ša ši-i-[a-ri] šu-ú ú-de-e-šú*: this somewhat clumsy expression of course means that the "watch" was going to last only till the evening of the following day, on which the crescent of the moon was accordingly expected to appear. For the syntax (noun + *šū* + *udêšu*) cf. *LAS* 35 r4 f (with note); the expression *ūmu ša šijāri* is paralleled by *mūšu ša timāli* "night of yesterday", *ABL* 371 r6 f and *LAS* 235 r1.

43

Bibliography:
Previously unpublished.

Copy:
CT 53 pl.39 no.115.

Writer:
The grounds for assigning this fragment to Balasî are the same as given in commentary to *LAS* 34 (*an-ni-i-e*, etc.). The plural suffix in line 1' points to a joint authorship with Nabû-aḫḫē-erība; the letter may actually be part of the same tablet as *LAS* 55.

Notes:

5' ff. This is the only explicit mention of the astronomical treatise Mul Apin (see provisionally, Weidner *AJSL* 40 [1923/4] 186 ff) in the present corpus, even though the text was certainly industriously utilized in the Sargonid period (for another quotation from the text, see 67 r1-5; cf. also sub *LAS* 289:5ff and 344-345). The passage quoted here belongs to the first tablet of the work, to a section giving the heliacal risings of 36 important constellations and stars (cf. note to 319 r6) in terms of a sidereal year of 365 days beginning with the rising of Aries; cf. *CT* 33 pl.3 ii 36, I *ina* ^{ITU}BÁR UD *1*.KÁM $^{\mathrm{MUL.LÚ}}$ḪUN.GÁ IGI.LAL ^{36} 1 *ina* ^{ITU}BÁR UD *20*.KÁM ^{MUL}ZUBI IGI.LAL ^{37} I *ina* ^{ITU}GUD UD 1.KÁM ^{MUL}MUL IGI.LAL, etc. The date of composition of Mul Apin can be approximately fixed at 1300-1000 BC (see van der Waerden, *JNES* 8 [1949] 6, and id., *Anfänge der Astronomie* [1968], 70 ff); at that time, the constellations mentioned in the present letter rose as follows:

Aries (α Arietis)	= April 6.
Auriga (α Aurigae)[89]	= April 22.

For the Sargonid Era, however, the relevant dates are a little later (Aries = April 9, Auriga = April 24); see Appendix H.

7'. [*iq-ṭ*]*i-bi*: see note to *LAS* 298 r8'f.

---

89 On the identication ^{MUL}ZUBI = Auriga see Weidner, *RlA* 3 p.136 s.v. *gamlu*.

44

Bibliography:
(I) Waterman, *RCAE* 352 (cf. IV 247); Pfeiffer, *SLA* 321.
(II) Oppenheim, *JAOS* 61 (1941) 257.

Photograph (Obverse only): *RCAE* IV pl. 8.

Notes:

11 ff. Cf. [MU]L*Dil-bat pa-ni-šú* 7 *[a-n]a du-un-qi is-sa-kan*, *LAS* 69 r6f (referring to an impending heliacal rising of Venus, regarded as an suspicious sign). The literal translation of the expression (for *šakānu* + *pānī* in general see Oppenheim, *JAOS* 61 [1941] 257) would be "the god DN has set his face towards good", that is, DN is favourably disposed; note that the sign SIG_5 here has to be read *dunqu* in accordance with *LAS* 69 r6 f, and not *dummuqu* as assumed in *CAD* D 63*a* (cancel the translation ibid.).

The present passage very concretely illustrates the lucky character of the beginning of the month ("the moon's birthday", *ú-mu i-lit-ti* d*30, Babyl.* 6 pl.2 r16) as opposed to the preceding three days of the moon's absence, a time of death (cf. [UD-*um*] *ki-is-pi* = *bu-ub-bu-lum* "day of offerings to the dead = *bubbulu*, *CT* 18 pl.23 K 4397:13). Cf. *LAS* 51:16ff and note to 45 r8; on the ideas associated with the crescent moon (youthfulness, life, good health etc.) see Tallqvist, *Månen i myt och dikt, folktro och kult* (*StOr* 12, 1948) passim.

r4 f. Delete the rendering in Pt.I and read instead: $[u]_4$*-mu un-ni-i-u* 5 *[l]a!-mì-i-ni* "this day is a holiday (lit. 'evil'), so I shall write (only) tomorrow". On the "evil days" (1st, 7th, 14th, 19th, 21st and 28th of each month) cf. notes on 185:21 and 1:22; *la-mì-i-ni* = Stat. 3m Sg. of *lamānu* + paragogic vowel and vowel lengthening due to the rule formulated in note to *LAS* 18 r8.

45

Bibliography:
(I) Waterman, *RCAE* 356; Pfeiffer, *SLA* 328.
(II) Behrens, *ABB* (1906) 70f; Dhorme, *RHR* 116 (1937) 23; Schott, *OLZ* 40 (1937) 362; Labat, *Royauté* (1939) 335, 364f.

Date:
Approximately Addāru 23, eponymy of Šulmu-Bēl-lašme = c. March 22, 669 BC. This date is obtained from Obv. 8-11 and Rev.5-8, according to which the letter was written in the month Addāru and the planet Mars was anticipated to remain exceptionally bright till the coming Ajāru. A checking of the retrograde periods of Mars between 680-660 BC (App. C3) shows that these data fit only the year 669: the first stationary point of the planet occurred then on Šabāṭu 16, the opposition on Addāru 23, and the second stationary point on Ajāru 3. Since the writer could predict that Addāru would be 30 days long (r8), the letter must have been written after the opposition of the sun and the moon (= Addāru 16, cf. *RMA* 88), but of course before the end of the month.

Addressee:
Esarhaddon.

Discussion:

This letter becomes truly understandable only when it is studied in the context of the other contemporary letters listed in the commentary to *LAS* 70 (q.v.). It is important to realize above all, that the crown prince referred to in the letter (and in *LAS* 46, etc.) probably was *not* Assurbanipal, as one would be inclined to think at the first sight, but Šamaš-šumu-ukīn (see on *LAS* 70 r11f), and that the prospective visit of the prince did not just imply as short trip from one palace to another within the citadel area of Nineveh but a journey from Babylonia to Assyria. This explains why the king was so sensitive about the correct timing of the visit: Mars was generally considered an ill-boding planet (see von Weiher, *AOAT* 11 p.76ff), particularly to inhabitants of Babylonia. See in more detail below.

Notes:

12 ff. This question is attributed to the king in *CAD* B 1f (1965), but that is impossible since words of Balasî precede, and the question itself is not introduced by the particle *mā*; note also the word LUGAL in line 13.[90] The passage has to be understood as a rhetorical question leading to the scholar's answer; comparable bridge passages are also found in *LAS* 8 r5f, 148:10, 173:10, etc.

17 ff. *"Have we got not profit from it?"*: a rhetorical question referring to the fact that from the astrological point of view, the brightness of Mars at the time concerned was profitable to Assyria. Cf. *RMA* 167 r7, ^{d}*Ṣal-bat-a-*[*nu ina*] ^{KUR}SU.BIR$_4$ ^{KI} *ba-'i-il* [8] *ù šá-ru-*[*ru*] *na-ši* SIG$_5$ *šá* ^{KUR}SU.BIR$_4$^{KI} "Mars' being bright and clothed in brilliance in Subartu means good luck for Subartu (= Assyria)"; the writer of this report, commenting on a conjunction of Saturn and Mars (taking place while our letter was written![91]), apparently considered Mars the star of Subartu (or Elam), since he specifies Saturn as the star of Amurru (^{MUL}UDU.IDIM.SAG.UŠ MUL *šá* ^{KUR}MAR.TU^{KI} ibid. r9), an attribute otherwise attached to Mars.[92] However, the omen was interpreted to the advantage of Assyria whatever the differences in tradition: cf. *RMA* 107 r5, ^{MUL}*Ṣal-bat-a-nu* MUL MAR.TU[^{KI}] [6] ḪUL *šá* ^{KUR}MAR.TU^{KI} u NIM.MA[^{KI}] [7] ^{MUL}UDU.IDIM.SAG.UŠ MUL KUR URI^{KI} [8] SIG$_5$ *šá* LUGAL *be-lí-*[*ja*] "Mars is the star of Amurru: bad luck for Amurru and Elam. Saturn is the star of Akkad: good luck for the king, my lord."

For the case of Šamaš-šumu-ukīn, however, the brightness of Mars was of course of dubious advantage: as an Assyrian, he could consider it as a good omen; but in his official position as the crown prince of Babylon, he was bound to take into consideration the fact that for Babylonians, the brightness of Mars signified ill fortune. Cf. *RMA* 232 r3, I^{d}*Ṣal-bat-a-nu ú-ta-na-at-ma* SIG$_5$ *ib-il-ma a-ḫi-tú* "If Mars becomes dim, (this is) favourable, (if) it becomes bright, (that is) unfavourable."

20 ff. *"He will not return to the area of Subartu"*: a remark virtually inexplicable unless it is assumed that the prince in question was resident in Babylonia. For the passage on the whole, see note on *LAS* 280 r11-13.

r2. *la me-me-ni*: an ellipsis for "there is no danger". Cf. ḪUL *ina* ŠÀ É.GAL *la me-me-ni*, 38:13.

r8 and 9. The idiom ^{d}*30 u$_4$-mu ú-šal-lam* (also in 46 r13, 70 r13, *RMA* 51, 54, 55 etc.) and its counterpart ^{d}*30 u$_4$-mu ú-tar-ra* (*RMA* 53:3, 62 r5, 70:7 etc.), "the Moon will complete/reject the (30th) day", served as technical expressions for indicating the two normal lengths of lunar months (see Schaumberger, *ZA* 47 [1941/42] 128[1]); since the lunar months began immediately with the appearance of the crescent, the expression "in month MN" in this context always refers to the *following* month. The significance attached in the letters to appearances of the crescent making the month 30 days long is doubtless related to the sacred number of the moon, 30; by making the length of the month correspond with his mystic number, the moon god was thought to display his good will toward the king (cf. note on *LAS* 44:11 ff). The omen was regarded as particularly auspicious if the "completion" of the month happened on New Year's day (*rēš šatti*). Cf. *RMA* 16, reporting on the appearance of the moon under similar circumstances: *ina* SAG MU.AN.NA [2] ^{d}*30* ISKIM SIG$_5$*-tì* [3] *ša* GÍD.DA *u$_4$-me* BALA [4] *a-na* LUGAL *be-lí-ja* [5] *i-sa-ap-ra* "the Moon has sent the king, my lord, on the New Year's Day a good omen portending a reign of long duration" (Rev.1-5); ^{d}*3*[*0 u$_4$-mu*] *ú-šal-lam* [2] *ša b*[*a-a-de*] *re-eš* MU.AN.NA [3] SIG$_5$ *š*[*a* LUGAL] EN-*ja* (translated sub *LAS* 12); similarly *RMA* 183A.

---

90 A prediction like "Mars will be bright till the month of Ajaru" presupposes too detailed a knowledge about the phases of Mars and the planet's variable velocity to be assignable to the king. Logic, too, implies that the quotation from the king's speech ends in line 9.

91 See under *LAS* 54.

92 Cf. *RMA* 101 r2, MUL *Ṣal-bat-a-nu* MUL KUR MAR^{KI}, and Borger *Ash* p.2 ii 6, MUL *Ṣal-bat-a-nu pa-ri-is pur(u)-se-e* KUR MAR.TU^{KI}.

46

Bibliography:

(I) Waterman, *RCAE* 354;

(II) Behrens, *ABB* (1906) 85 f, and G. Meier, *Or*NS 8 (1939) 305.

Date:

Nisannu 1, eponymy of Šamaš-kāšid-ajābī = March 30, 669 BC. The evidence on which this date is based will be assessed in detail in the commentary on *LAS* 70.

Addressee:

Esarhaddon.

Discussion:

This letter continues with the subject of the preceding number, which, as noted sub *LAS* 45, was written only a week earlier. Notice that *LAS* 69+71, from Balasî's associate Nabû-aḫḫē-erība, runs exactly parallel to the present letter and was also written on the same day. Cf. above, remarks on the writer of *LAS* 34.

Notes:

7. The restoration of this line is based on *LAS* 138:8 f, *iš-pu*]*r-an-ni ma-a iq-ṭi-bu-nê* [*ma-a*]. See also our letter, Obv.18-20.

8. Whoever communicated this hemerological prescription to the king (Nabû-aḫḫē-erība?) must have made a mistake (or rather, the king probably had misunderstood what he heard, see, sub *LAS* 12), for the prohibition actually concerned the 2nd, not the 1st of Nisannu; see *LAS* 70:10', where the relevant passage is quoted correctly. Balasi probably corrected the mistake in line 9 which may be restored: UD 2.KÁM* *šu-ú* [*ina lìb-bi qa-bi*] "this (injunction) [concerns] the 2nd day" (cf. 20 r7-8).

12 f. The rest of Obverse dealing with the properties of the 1st and 4th of Nisannu, the king's words quoted in these lines most likely were something like "which one (of them) [is more favourable]?" and the scholar's answer, "both are [favourable]." The words *i*[*š-lim*] and *šá-a*[*l-mu-ti*] restored at the ends of the lines fit the traces and also make satisfactory sense, *šalmu* being a synonym of *ṭābu* in the technical meaning "favourable" (cf. Borger *Ash* p.4 v 3, and passim), but I cannot explain the preterite *i*[*šlim*]; read rather ⸢*i*⸣!-[*šal-lim*]?

14 ff. *ūmu eššu* "new day" as a designation of the *4th* day is completely unknown from other cuneiform documents, to judge from the examples of *eššu* in time indications given in *CAD* E p.376a (the Nuzi passage quoted ibid. refers to the 1st day). Therefore, and also in view of the gloss *iš-še-i*[*š*][93] (accidentally)erased in line 15, I would suggest that this "new day" actually is only an unusual form, perhaps a folk etymology, of the well-known *eššēšu*-day (see *CAD* E p.371 ff). Notice especially that in the hemerology from which the foregoing quotation originates, the 4th day of Nisannu is explicitly characterized as the *eššēšu*-day of Nabû (UD 4.KÁM UD ÈŠ.ÈŠ ^{d}*Na-bi-um* ½ UD ŠE "the 4th day: *eššēšu*-day of Nabû – half a day favourable", *KAR* 178 i 31 f).

r1-6. This section may be compared with 45:15-r5. Cf. also 148 r6 ff, and notice the differences in the constructions of *qurbu*: here with *ina* ŠÀ, there with *ina* UGU.

r9. Mercury was the astral embodiment of Nabû, the firstborn son of Marduk (see Gössmann, *Planetarium*, p. 25; Schott, *ZA* 43 [1936] 134; Tallqvist, *Götterepitheta*, p. 319 and 380 ff);[94] the astrological dogma that

[93] Perhaps better *iš-še-*⸢*e*⸣-[*š*]*ú*; cf. *iš-še-e-šú*, Borger *Ash* p.81:40.

[94] The equation ^{MUL}UDU.IDIM.GU$_4$.UD = ^{d}*Nabû* is, as far as I know, not attested lexically (cf. Schott, *ZA* 43 [1936] 134) but can be deduced indirectly. See, above all, the hymn to Nabû published by Lambert, *AfO* 18, 385ff, where the god is addressed as ^{d}GU$_4$.UD and "the star of east and west". A point worth noticing is that Nabû (lit. "herald", cf. Mercury as herald of the gods) was worshiped in the Sargonid period as a swift god (cf. ^{d}AG *ša li-is-me*, Frankena, *Tākultu* p.124:111, and *u*$_4$*-mu li-is-mu ša* ^{d}AG, *STT* 87 r8'), a property that is evidently related to the swift motion of the *planet* Mercury. Note also the logographic spelling of Nabû: ^{d}PA = the "staff-god", and cf. Mercury's staff!

it was the star of the crown prince is a corollary of this, and is also attested in *LAS* 70 r7-8 and 71 r6. For the brightness of the planet at the time concerned, see the commentary on *LAS* 70.

48

Bibliography:

(I) Waterman, *RCAE* 929.

Discussion:

According to re-collation of the tablet by Sollberger (January, 1976), the first sign of r1' is possibly to be read ⸢LUGAL⸣ rather than ⸢LÚ⸣. The line should accordingly be translated "let the king, my lord, come tomorrow", and the letter would, like *LAS* 10+, concern a trip of the *king* himself, not one of his sons, as most letters of this type. This interpretation would actually also provide a satisfactory explanation for the blessing r3'-4', which in other similar contexts (52 r13ff, 69+71 r29-30, 70 r1-2) pertains to the person embarking on the travel. Rev.5f should then be translated: "I shall (*a-mur*, cf. 64 r6) see his (the king's) success."

50

Bibliography:

(I) Waterman, *RCAE* 76 (cf. IV 234); Pfeiffer, *SLA* 306.
(II) Landsberger, *MAOG* 4 (1928) 319; Dhorme, *RHR* 116 (1937) 22; Labat, *Royauté* (1939) 334; Oppenheim, *JAOS* 64 (1944) 191, and *AfO* 17 (1954/6) 49 ff.

Discussion:

Cf. *LAS* 217 and 219. The present letter is of interest in two respects: (1) It shows that hemerological considerations were involved in the performance of dream-rituals, and (2) that the relevant information was, as expected, furnished by "scribes". The recommendation found here that the ritual should be performed on the 13th, while the moon was gibbous, was certainly motivated by the wide-spread association of the god of dreams with the moon (cf. ^{d}ZA.QAR *na-áš-par-ti* ^{d}ŠEŠ.KI "Zaqīqu, message of the Moon god", *PSBA* 40 pl.7 r8). In *LAS* 219 the ritual was also performed while the moon was gibbous, on the 16th.[95]

Notes:

7. *ge-en-ti*: the only word found in the dictionaries that could be connected with this hapax legomenon is *igimtu* (*CAD* I/J 40*b* "wrath"; *AHw* 367*a*: "Zorn"), of which *gintu* would be a plausible NA form (for the apocope of the initial vowel cf. *ikkilu* > *killu*, *adduräru* > *duräru*, *alaḫḫinu* > *laḫḫinu* etc.). The meaning does not fit the context particularly well, however.

10. *mu-šu-ta-t*[*i*]: a hapax legomenon of uncertain derivation. The word which one would expect here on the ground of the context is "dream-ritual" or the like (see Discussion), and since *egerrû* is intimately connected with *šuttu* "dream", it is perhaps possible to see in *mu-šu-ta-ti* a denominative of *šuttu* with the meaning just indicated. The word would then be analyzable as *muš(u)tattu*, a *muprast*-formation (*GAG* § 56d) comparable to *munattu* "Morgenschlummer" (*AHw* 672*a*) or *nubattu* "Abend, Abendopfer" (*AHw* 800*a*).[96] The anaptyptic vowel inserted between *š* and *t* (a consonant cluster not tolerated in Neo-Assyrian) is phonetically justifiable since a stressed syllable follows, see note to 39:11 (at the end). As for the final -*t*[*i*], it is possible to assume that the word occurs here in the plural, since **muš(u)tatāti* would in any case normally have yielded **muš(u)tāti* by haplology (cf. **uptatatarrisū* > *uptatrisu*, Deller *AOAT* 1 [1969] 53).

---

[95] The full moon day may have been avoided because of its association with lunar eclipses.

[96] The fact that *šuttu* "dream" goes back to **šuntu* is no obstacle; cf. *uššušu*, a denominative from *eššu* (= **edšu*) "new", discussed in note to 188 r6.

12-15. Cf. I UD *13*.KÁM *šá* ᵈ*30* ᵈMAḪ UD ŠE ⁹ ᵈ*30* AGA *taš-reḫ-ti ana* KUR *na-šu-u* (var. ÍL-*ši*) "the 13th day, of the Moon and Bēlet-ilī, (is) a favourable day; the Moon displays the crown of splendour to the country", *4 R* 32 ii 8-9 (*Inbu Bēl Arḫi*, Tablet VIII = Ulūlu II; the entry for the 13th day appears to have been identical in all months, cf. Langdor, *Babylonian Menologies* p.72 ff [Nisannu] and Landsberger, *LSS* 6/1-2 (1915), p.103). *agû tašreḫti* "crown of splendour" occurs otherwise only in another entry of the *Inbu*-series, that for the 11th day (*e-nu-ma* ITU AGA *taš-re-eḫ-ti na-šu-u* GURUN *ḫa-du-u*, *4 R* 32 ii 2, etc.). The gibbous moon indeed resembles the tiaras worn by the Mesopotamian gods, see Schaumberger, *SSB* 3. Ergänzungsheft, p. 277.

r2 ff. Opposition of the sun and the moon on the 14th was regarded as a good omen (see note to 7 r11'), but it must not be confused with the *(e)gerrû* (r4) which referred to a totally different type of divine message. See note to 217 r1-2 and, exhaustively, A.L. Oppenheim, "Sumerian: i n i m . g a r , Akkadian: *egirrû* = Greek : *kledon*", *AfO* 17 (1954-56) 49-55. The date is here singled out simply because it was on the *full moon* days that the dream god Zaqīqu (also called messenger of Moon) was thought to be particularly active. See commentary on *LAS* 219.

51

Bibliography:

(I) Waterman, *RCAE* 78; Pfeiffer, *SLA* 265; Behrens, *ABB* (1906) 72 ff (no.6); Oppenheim, *JAOS* 61 (1941) 265 (translation only).
(II) Ylvisaker, *LSS* 5/6 (1912) 47[3]; Weidner, *HBA* (1915) 55; Dhorme, *RHR* 116 (1937) 22 f; Labat, *Royauté* (1939) 308, 320; Böhl, *Opera Minora* (1953) 403; Landsberger, *AfO* 18 (1957-58) 338; Deller, *AOAT* 1 (1969) 54.

Date:

Ajāru 24(?), eponymy of Šulmu-Bēl-lašme = May 4(?), 670 BC. See note to Rev.6.

Addressee:

Esarhaddon.

Discussion:

To understand this letter correctly it is essential to realize that its recipient was seriously ill at the time the letter was written. This appears not only from *LAS* 143, a letter from Esarhaddon's personal exorcist Adad-šumu-uṣur, written a day before the present letter,[97] but also from several other letters showing that Esarhaddon,

[97] The central position of the verb *adāru* (which can mean both "to be dark/eclipsed" and "to mourn") in *LAS* 143 could also suggest a different interpretation: the king was mourning a recently deceased close relative of his. Cf. commentary on *LAS* 197. This interpretation would be supported by the fact that Jupiter indeed rose heliacally (cf. r6) soon after the death of Esarhaddon's queen (Addāru 5/6 = February 7/8, 672 BC), exactly at the time the king was going through his mourning ritual, which probably involved at least partial abstinence from food (see under 197). However, two tiny details make it unlikely that the case of Addāru/February, 672, is in question. First, Obv.16 – Rev.7 indicates that the writers associated the king's fasting with the disappearance of the moon, hinting that the king would give up his fast as soon as the moon would become visible; but on Addāru 12 = February 14, the date on which Jupiter rose in 672 BC, the moon was almost full! It could be objected that Obv.16ff can perfectly well be taken as a reference to the past ("When the moon became visible in the beginning of the month, the king *said*", etc.). But how then to explain the remark in Rev.6f, "the king may demand food for the entire year hereafter", clearly motivated by the 12-month period of visibility of Jupiter? If Jupiter = Moon, doesn't this remark imply that the king would likewise have "demanded food" for each entire *month* (= the period of Moon's visibility) following the appearance of the moon? A fast associated with the moon was actually motivated only on the *ūm bubbuli*, the period of the moon's invisibility, cf. note on *LAS* 44:11 ff.
Secondly, it can be regarded as certain that the king was seriously ill while the letter was written. The writers of both the present letter and *LAS* 143 would have endorsed a fast of *one* day but not a longer one; it is hardly thinkable that they would have interfered with the demonstrations of grief of the king already on the *second*

whose health had been ailing from the beginning of his reign, experienced a severe attack of illness in the spring of 670 BC: see in detail sub *LAS* 246-247. This attack of illness accounts for the king's isolation and lack of appetite[98] referred to here and in *LAS* 143 and 246/7, and there is no need whatever to assume that the king's three-day fast was a *periodic* necessity imposed on him by the official cult, as virtually all scholars who have commented on this letter have done. On the contrary the fact that in both *LAS* 51 and 143 the writers ***do their best*** to make the king ***give up*** his fast (explicitly characterized as ***unhealthy*** in *LAS* 143) clearly shows that whatever the king was doing happened at his own will and was not dictated by any cultic necessity; and, as a matter of fact, there is no further reference to royal (cultic) fasting in contemporary texts.[99] The seriousness of the king's physical condition is reflected by the very fact that Balasî and Nabû-aḫḫē-erība (two astrologers, no doctors!) ventured to write to him *spontaneously* in a matter like this; for trying to influence the king without being *specifically* asked for it was a kind of thing that could easily provoke royal anger, as clearly implied by the beginning of the present letter (see presently)!

N o t e s :

7 f. Cf. LUGAL ***be-lí*** [4] ***re-ma-nu šu-ú*** "the king, my lord, is merciful", *ABL* 228 r3 f (preceding a petition addressed to the king); ***ù en-na*** LUGAL ***be-lí-já*** [13] ***re!-[m]a-nu-ú šu-u*** "but now, the king, my lord, is a merciful (person)", *ABL* 587:12 f (cf. ibid. r12 f); LUGAL ***re-ma-nu at-ta*** "you are a merciful king", 499:13 (preceding a petition).[100] As a matter of principle, mercifulness was a royal characteristic on the basis of his equation to Marduk (see note to *LAS* 125:18; cf. En. el. VII 27 ff: ***(Marduk) šá an*** DINGIR.DINGIR ***ka-mu-ti ir-šu-ú ta-aja-ru*** . . . [30] ***re-mé-nu-ú ša bu-ul-lu-ṭu ba-šu-ú it-ti-šu*** "(Marduk) who pardoned the bound gods . . . the merciful one[101], in whose power it is to dispense life"); it is not difficult to see why he was reminded of this characteristic especially in precarious situations like the present one (cf. also the passage *RMA* 170:5 ff, quoted in note to 125:18).

9. ***issēn ūmu e-ṣe-e*** = naturally "isn't one day enough" (lit. "is one day too little", ***ēṣê*** < ***ēṣe*** < ***(w)īṣ*** "(it) is little", with interrogative intonation[102]); the different translations presented in *CAD* A/1 119b ("enough that"), I/J 59a ("is one day not too little") and elsewhere are incorrect.

12. ***adi mati*** (for the form *immati* occurring here see note to 72 r4) was an exclamation connoting distress, and corresponds exactly to Bibl. ***ʿad matai*** (when used without an accompanying verb). Cf. the commentary item ***a-ḫu-la-pi : a-di ma-ti*** "alas = how long" (Lambert, *BWL* p.50:37), and note the alternation of ***adi mati*** with ***aḫulap*** in the penitential psalms of the ***kalû***-chanters (e.g., Reisner, *SBH* p.53:24; ***4*** R^2 10 r22, 29** r8). A Biblical passage comparable to the present one is Ps. 6:3 "my soul quivers in dismay, and thou, O lord – how long?". Cf. also Streck *Asb* p.252 r14 EN ***im-mat*** DINGIR ***an-na-a te-ep-pu-šá-an-ni*** "how long, O my god, will you treat me like this" (the king complaining about his miserable health).

For the translation of ***šá-al-šú*** (not from ***šaʾālu*** "to ask"!) see Deller 1969 and cf. note to *LAS* 34:15.

15. On ***muškēnu*** "poor man, beggar" (> Aram. ***meskēnā*** > Arab. ***miskīn*** etc., however without the pejorative connotations of French ***mesquin***) see W. von Soden, "***Muškēnum*** und die Mawālī des frühen Islam ", *ZA* 56 (1964) 133 ff. But the context implies that the term here means an ascetic (practicing a self-imposed fasting), hence the translation "dervish".

---

day (cf. *LAS* 143:14), if he had been in good health. *LAS* 159, which certainly is approximately contemporaneous with *LAS* 143, actually explicitly refers to the "illness of the king", and the word "illness" also occurs in *LAS* 143 in a revealing context (r15-18); cf. also below, n.98. But nothing in *LAS* 197-198, written after the death of Esarhaddon's queen, indicates that the king was ill at the time concerned.

98 Note that refusal (or inability) to eat could alone be considered a symptom of serious illness. Cf. *ABL* 341:8ff, ***ú-ma-a*** GEMÉ ***ša*** LUGAL [9] MÍ.^{d}BA.Ú-***ga-me-lat*** [10] ***mar-ṣa-at a-dan-niš la ku-sa-pi ta-kal*** "Now, a female servant of the king (named) Bābu-ĝāmilat is seriously ill, she doesn't (or can't) eat bread".

99 The royal hemerology ***Inbu Bēl Arḫi*** and corresponding compendia only forbade eating certain dishes on certain (evil) days. The mourning fast discussed in commentary on *LAS* 197 does not seem to have been ritually prescribed.

100 Note also "King Esarhaddon is merciful" (***rḥmn hw***) in the sayings of Aḥiqar, Pritchard *ANET*^{2} p.428***a***.

101 Cf. Allah's standard attribute ***ar-Raḥmānu*** and its connotations.

102 See note to 208 r8. Incidentally, the fact that the paragogic vowel could be lengthened (as in ***ṭāba*** > ***ṭa-ba-a***) shows that it had become more or less stabilized despite its final position.

16 ff. See note on *LAS* 44:11 ff.

r1. *ú-šar-ra*: the etymology of the verb is uncertain,[103] but the reading and translation seem assured on the ground of the context and the following passage in the *aluzinnu* text *2 R* 60 No.1 ii 9'f:

bu-bu-ta ra-ba-ku	*a-ka-la ṭa-ab-a!-ku*
10 qa uš-tar-ra	*30 qa a-pat-tan*
"I am great in hunger (but)	better in eating;
"I can *miss* 10 loaves (but	then) I can *eat* 30 loaves."

In this example, *uštarra* (a Dt-form) is clearly the opposite of *apattan* "I eat", and the meaning "to fast" is confirmed by the occurrence of *bubūtu* "hunger" in the preceding line (opposed to *akālu* "eating"). That the verb does not occur here in the Dt-stem is due to the fact that the reflexive *ta*-infix had become obsolete in Neo-Assyrian (cf. note to 39 r12) and the function of this infix is here covered by the pronoun *ramunu* "self" (*raminī* "myself"). Cf. Syr. *š'rā et*pe. "to be interrupted, dismissed"?

r5. Cf. dSAG.ME.GAR MUL *šá* d*30 šú-u* "Jupiter is the star of the Moon", BM 121206 viii 55' (van Driel, *CA* [1969] p.96), and dUD.AL.TAR : d*30* "the 'Martial One' (Jupiter) = the Moon", *ACh* Ištar 7:43. Jupiter's equation with the moon is a "logical" corollary of another astrological dogma according to which the two great outer planets Jupiter and Saturn, were "twins", like the sun and the moon;[104] since Saturn was considered the nightly sun[105], "logic" implied Jupiter's being the "nightly moon".

r6. This line furnishes the clue for the exact dating of the letter. The statement that Jupiter will be visible for a whole year (this is naturally implied here) is possible only on the condition that the planet had just risen heliacally; on the other hand, this must have happened at the end of the month, since the moon was absent (or at least waning). A comparison with *LAS* 143 shows, furthermore, that a year in Esarhaddon's reign (i.e., before 668) is in question[106], and as all other datable letters of Balasî, Nabû-aḫḫē-erība and Adad-šumu-uṣur seem to postdate 675 BC (cf. App. 0), the letter can with a very high degree of probability be assigned to the period 674-669 BC. In these years, Jupiter rose in Nineveh as follows (cf. App. C4):

[674	no heliacal rising observed]	
673	January 6	= Kanūnu 21
672	February 14	= Addāru 12
671	March 27	= Nisannu 5
670	May 4	= Ajāru 24 (Babylon: Ajāru 22)[107]
669	June 6	= Simānu 8 (Babylon: Simānu 6)[107]

As appears from this survey, the only year in which the rising of Jupiter took place close enough to the disappearance of the moon (26th or 27th)[108] is, within the period concerned, 670 BC. That this year indeed is in

[103] Neither *šrī* G "to be rich" (Arab. *ṯariya*) nor *šr'* D "to begin" (= Hebr./Aram.) can be in question.

[104] See E. Weidner, *HBA* p.55, and cf. Borger *Ash* p.2 i 31.

[105] See notes to *LAS* 326.

[106] Note the reference to the "charge" and the absence of an elaborate introductory formula typical of the letters addressed to Assurbanipal.

[107] The dates in the parentheses are based on actual observations made in Babylonia and reported in *LAS* 289; for Nineveh, approximately 2 days later dates must be assumed (see Schaumberger, *ZA* 47 [1943/4] 122f). According to the tables of Schoch (1928). Jupiter should have been observable in Babylon in the said years already on Ajāru 19 and Simānu 3 (see App. C4); hence all the dates of the m first of Jupiter at Babylon given in App. C4 have been raised by 5 days to obtain the corresponding date for Nineveh (given in the present list).

[108] They may have gained this insight from a passage in Mul Apin and *Enūma Anu Enlil* ("Mercury appears every month and disappears again every month either in the sunset or in the sunrise", *CT* 33 pl.3 ii 16f and *ACh* Spl. 53:26) which does not apply to the latitude of Nineveh. Cf. Schaumberger, *SSB* 3 Erg. 286f: "Für Babel ergibt sich als durchschnittliche Dauer der Unsichtbarkeit [von Merkur] bei der oberen Konjunction 36,7, bei den unteren 24,3, als Durchschnitt beider 30,5 Tage, d.i.. ca 1 Monat. Bei einem Umlauf des Planeten dauern also die beiden Unsichtbarkeitsperioden zusammen durchschnittlich zwei Monate . . . "

question is confirmed by two other letters (*LAS* 132 and 247) linking Esarhaddon's attack of illness with a coup d'état quelled in April, 670 BC; see, in detail, commentary to *LAS* 247.

53

Bibliography:
(I) Waterman, *RCAE* 692.

Addressee:
Esarhaddon.

Date:
Probably Addāru 26, eponymy of Šulmu-Bēl-lašme = March 25, 669 BC, i.e. slightly before *LAS* 65 ff. A connection of the present letter with the group of letters discussed under *LAS* 70 is probable, though of course by no means certain, in view of the eagerness of the king to confirm a Mercury observation made in Babylon, which would be understandable in the context of *LAS* 65 ff (see under *LAS* 70 on the planned visit of Šamaš-šumu-ukīn to Nineveh). But if the letter coheres with *LAS* 65 ff, it must predate them by at least a day since the two writers here state they could not yet observe Mercury, whereas while writing *LAS* 65 ff they definitely had observed it. Assuming that the rising of Mercury could not be observed in Babylon earlier that on the 23rd (see on *LAS* 65), and assuming further that it took at least two days before the messanger sent to report the observation could reach Nineveh, the date of the letter would then be firmly fixed at March 25 = Addāru 26.

Notes:

r3 f. *"Perhaps he has really observed it"*: This remark implies that the writers were aware of the fact that the latitude of Babylon was better suited for sighting Mercury than that of Nineveh.[108]

Furthermore, r9 ff shows that they also were perfectly well aware of the relatively great anomaly (e = 0,20561) and inclination ($i = 7^{o}0' 11''$) of the orbit of Mercury, which made even moderately accurate predictions of the planet's appearances impossible before the time of Ptolemy.[109] Such an insight is actually only possible on the basis of extensive, systematically collected observational data, and it would thus seem very likely that such systematic observational data on Mercury were already available (in written form) in the Sargonid Era.[110]

r5 f. *[IG]I×2-šú ina muḫ-ḫi ta-tu-qut*: this expression in only attested here and in Rev.11 f; the context suggests an idiomatic meaning "to observe by chance".

r10. The verb *nasāku* seems to occur only here as an astronomical terminus technicus (cf. *AHw* 752 f), but in view of the context it can be hardly be doubted that the term refers to an abnormally long angular distance of Mercury from the ecliptic. Instead of *na-si-ku* (for expected *nasik*), it is preferable to read *na-si-ki!* with a paragogic vowel to be explained according to the rule formulated in note to *LAS* 18 r8.[111]

54

Bibliography:
(I) Waterman, *RCAE* 79.

Addressee:
Esarhaddon.

---

[109] Cf. O. Neugebauer, *Exact Sciences,* p.200 ff. The word *ḫarip* "early" has to be understood "earlier than average"; for *nasik* see note to r10.

[110] The existence of such observational texts has now been actually confirmed by the fragments published by Reiner and Pingree in *RA* 69 (1975) 175ff.

[111] The passage has now (19.1.76) been collated and the reading -ki confirmed by E. Sollberger.

Date:

Addāru 14, eponymy of Šulmu-Bēl-lašme = March 13, 669 BC.

Discussion:

Though this letter is badly broken, sufficiently much of it remains to show that it dealt with the conjunction of Saturn and Mars discussed by Schaumberger and Schott, "Die Konjunktion von Mars und Saturn im Frühjahr 669 v. Chr. nach Thompson, Reports Nr. 88 und anderen Texten", *ZA* 44 (1938) 271 ff.[112] That a *conjunction of planets* is in question appears from the Reverse where the *daily motion* and the remaining *distance* of the heavenly bodies in question is specified; the first of these is identifiable as Saturn on the ground of the sign preserved at the end of Obv.7. The second (of which only the determinative MUL remains in Obv.8) must also have been an outer planet in view of the relatively slight daily motion of the system indicated in Rev.7'[113]; since Jupiter and Saturn were not in conjunction between 680-663 B.C. (cf. App. D), the only alternative left is Mars. As a matter of fact, the data of our letter correspond exactly to what can be inferred from the positions of Mars and Saturn in the middle of March 669:[114]

March 13	♂	$\lambda = 176.89^{o}$	$\beta = 3.27^{o}$
	♄	$\lambda = 176.9^{o}$	$\beta = 2.85^{o}$
March 14	♂	$\lambda = 176.7^{o}$	$\beta = 3.21^{o}$
	♄	$\lambda = 176.8^{o}$	$\beta = 2.85^{o}$
March 15	♂	$\lambda = 176.5^{o}$	$\beta = 3.15^{o}$
	♄	$\lambda = 176.7^{o}$	$\beta = 2.85^{o}$
March 16	♂	$\lambda = 176.28^{o}$	$\beta = 3.08^{o}$
	♄	$\lambda = 176.6^{o}$	$\beta = 2.85^{o}$

This can be put graphically as follows:

FIGURE 1. The conjunction of ♂ and ♄ in March 669

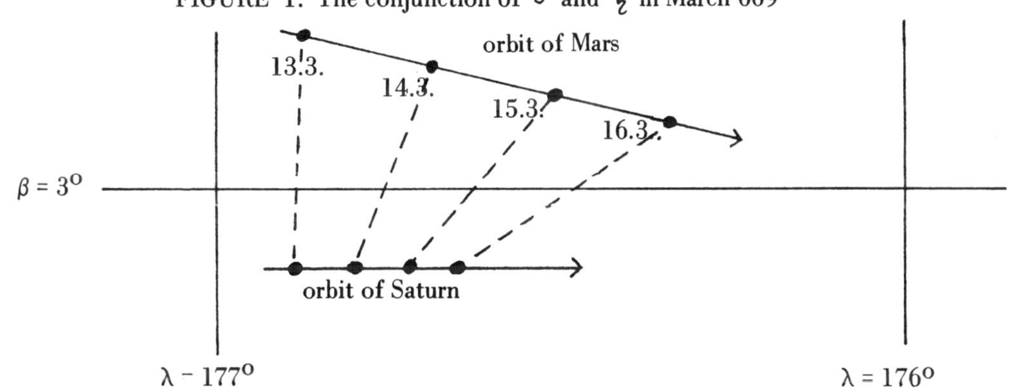

As appears from this figure, the distance of the planets on March 13 was approximately 25 minutes = 5 fingers, as stated in our letter, the minimum distance (22' = c. 4 fingers) was reached on March 15 (cf. ^{MUL}*Ṣal-bat-a-nu | er-bi | ú-ba-ni* TA* IGI ^{MUL}UDU.IDIM.SAG.UŠ ^{9} *pa-a-te la iṭ-ḫi* "Mars is at the distance of 4 fingers from Saturn and has not approached" *RMA* 88:8f, Balasî reporting on the situation of March 15). At this time, the daily motion of Saturn was 6' = 1 finger, whereas Mars was retrograding at the speed of 2 fingers a day (1 fin-

[112] The list of pertinent texts given ibid. does not include the present letter.

[113] The inner planets move much too swiftly (except for a short time in the vicinity of their inferior conjunctions) to be taken into consideration seriously.

[114] The values for March 14-15 are based on the computations of Schaumberger, art.cit., p.283, those of March 13 and 16 have been extrapolated.

ger in relation to Saturn). It may be pointed out that this situation did not repeat at a later date (nor before): on January 23, the planets had been at the distance of 5 fingers from each other, but at that time the daily motion of Mars was about 2 fingers, whereas Saturn was stationary; on June 6, the planets were in conjunction again, but that occasion does not fit the data of the letter at all, the distance of the planets being as great as 3° = 36 fingers. See Schaumberger, art. cit. p.282 ff for more details.

Notes:

r1'. For *ubānu* "finger" as an astronomical measure (= 5') see Thureau-Dangin, "Les mesures angulaires '*ammatu*' et '*ubānu*'," *RA* 28 (1931) 23ff. The broken numeral in this line cannot be ⌜2⌝, since the distance of Mars and Jupiter was on no occasion between 680-663 less than 3 fingers (= 15').

r2'. Cf. *LAS* 14 r11 f.

57

Bibliography:
(I) Waterman, *RCAE* 689.

Writer:
In spite of its apparent 'joint authorship', this letter was quite obviously written by Balasî *alone.* It forms a pair with the following number, which formally also is a 'joint' letter but certainly was written by Nabû-aḫḫē-erība alone; and as many individual letters of B. and N. form similar pairs (see the list in commentary to *LAS* 34), it appears likely that the present two 'joint' letters were also written separately (though simultaneously) by the two scholars, hence *LAS* 57 by Balasî.[115]

Date:
Probably late Du'ūzu = Mid-July, 671 BC. See under *LAS* 58.

Addressee:
Esarhaddon.

Notes:

10f, r2. All the stones mentioned in this letter were jewellery used in the ornamentation of divine statues: for ^{NA_4}IGI$^{2.MEŠ}$ and ^{NA_4}*šanṭuppu* see notes to No.58; ^{NA_4}*ašgikû* (tentatively identified as arsenic by R.C. Thompson, *DACG* p.54 f) and especially its variety ^{NA_4}*eli-ašgikû* (cf. ^{NA_4}.ÁŠ.GI$_4$.GI$_4$: *áš-ki-ku-u*, ^{NA_4}UGU.ÁŠ.GI$_4$.GI$_4$: *e-li* MIN, Ḫḫ XVI 353 f) were with preference used for precious necklaces and divine tiaras, see the examples collected in *CAD* A/2 p. 427 s.v. and notice the famous passage *Gilg.* IX vi 32, where [^{NA_4}] UGU.ÁŠ.GI$_4$.GI$_4$ appears as a jewel tree. *Ašgikû*-gems are also mentioned in *LAS* 281:13 in connection with the crown of Nabû.

58

Bibliography:
(I) Waterman, *RCAE* 404; Pfeiffer, *SLA* 251.

Writer:
Nabû-aḫḫē-erība. Cf. note on Rev.6 and discussion sub *LAS* 57.

---

[115] Note that of the 'joint' letters at least *LAS* 51 (cf. the spelling *an-ni-i-e* in l.13)was also written by Balasî; and as the name of Balasî there precedes that of Nabû-aḫḫē-erība, whereas the order of the names is reversed in *LAS* 58 written by N., it seems likely that also *LAS* 52-56 (i.e. all other joint letters of B. and N.) were written by Balasi. Consequently, in these joint letters the first sender name indicates the writer of the letter; yet this was not a universal rule, see note on the writer of *LAS* 164.

Addressee:
Esarhaddon.

Date:
Late Du'ūzu = Mid-July, 671 BC(?). This date is obtained from *LAS* 276 and 281 likewise referring to a tiara of Nabû, the former (where the tiara is mentioned in a context implying that its fashioning had not yet begun) written on Ābu 2 = July 22, 671, the latter (stating that the tiara had been completed) in March 670. It is entirely unlikely that our letter would deal with a different object, especially since the reference to the crown prince (= Assurbanipal) in Obv.13 proves for certain that the text dates from the period 672-669 BC.[116] In this chronological context, the fashioning of a magnificent crown for Nabû can hardly be dissociated from the restoration of Borsippa which appears to have begun immediately after Esarhaddon's 2nd Egyptian campaign and continued, simultaneously with the rebuilding of Esangil, at least through the year 670 (see *LAS* 281 ff), obviously with the purpose of getting the scenery ready for the return of Bēl to Babylon, scheduled for early 669 BC (see *LAS* 29, and relevant notes). As the stones to be used for the tiara obviously still were in Nineveh while the present letter was written, it should antedate *LAS* 276 by a couple of days at least.

Notes:

8. ^{NA_4}*.IGI*^{2}*.MEŠ*: lit. "eye-stones", by which were meant eye-shaped beads made of precious stones such as agate and chalcedony, white at base and furnished with a brown or black centrepiece representing the pupil, and mostly bearing a dedicatory inscription to a deity. See in detail W.G. Lambert, "An eye-stone of Esarhaddon's queen and other similar gems", *RA* 63 (1969) 65 ff. The function of these objects is disputed, but it is certain that the belonged to the decoration of divine statues and, as even the present context implies, were probably mounted on tiaras. Cf. note on 276:11.

17. The rendering of the line given in Pt.I is not entirely certain: the verb *e-ta-aṭ-ra* (from *eṭāru* "to take away; to save", cf. *ṭuppam e-ta-aṭ-ru-né* etc. *CAD* E p.402) could possibly also be read *e-ta-at-ra* (from *utāru* "to exceed, surpass") and translated "the (supply of) obsidian has increased, there is more obsidian (available now)"[117], scil. after the conquest of Egypt. On ^{NA_4}.KA = *ṣurru* "obsidian" see Oppenheim, *Glass* pp.14 f and 17; note that a lexical passage (Hh XVI 391 ff) lists white, black, red, yellow and multicolored varieties of this "stone", which would allow for its use both for the eyeballs and the pupils of the "eye-stones" in question.

19. No Neo-Assyrian attestations of *muṭê* (pl. tantum; < *muṭā'ē* < OA/MA *muṭā'ū*) are quoted in the *AHw* (p.691b), but this must be simply due to oversight. In addition to the present passage, the word is also attested in *LAS* 35:11 and (written LAL-*e*) in *ABL* 167:13.18, 971:5 and many administrative texts (cf. Postgate, *GPA* p.165); all these examples agree with the meaning and usages of OA *muṭā'ū* "deficit", discussed by Veenhof, *Aspects of Old Assyrian Trade . . .* (Leiden 1972), 17 ff and 46 ff.

r3. *šá-an-ṭup/dup-pu*: this word also occurs (among other ornaments and precious objects) in two Cassite treasure inventories, Clay *PBS* 2/2 105:45 (*2 ša-an-ṭup-pi* BABBAR.DIL[118] *iḫ-zu* KÙ.GI "two *šanṭuppus* of *pappardillu*-stone in gold mountings") and Legrain, *PBS* 13 80:26. Exact meaning unclear; possibly a head ornament, if a loan-word from Sumerian (*šan* < Sum. /šaŋ/ "head").

r6. *le-pu-u-šú*: this curious plene writing is otherwise attested only in *LAS* 60 r10, *RMA* 96:4 and *ABL* 1447 = *RMA* 252D r3, all from Nabû-aḫḫē-erība, and it thus conclusively proves that the present letter, unlike all other joint letters of Balasî and Nabû-aḫḫē-erība, was actually written by him (cf. under *LAS* 57; another feature pointing to N. here is the phrase Obv.10-15, cf. *LAS* 69+71 r29f and 70 r1 4). The lengthening of the penultimate vowel is difficult to explain. It could functionally correspond to the enclitic particle *-ma* "and", linking the three *šumma* clauses together (cf. note on 18 r8; in *LAS* 60, *RMA* 96 and *ABL* 1447, the lengthening would correspond to *-ma* with an iterative or emphasizing meaning), but in corresponding cases it was normally the *final* syllable

[116] Cf. *LAS* 276:17 ff!

[117] Cf. *CAD* Ṣ 258a. This interpretation would, it is true, leave the ventive ending unexplained: not a single instance of **wtr* + vent. is quoted in *CAD* A/2 p.487-492. Perhaps the final *-a* is not ventive at all but has to be explained differently (cf. *e-tak-la*, *ABL* 138:16; *a-ṣab-ta*, 150 r3, etc.).

[118] On this stone (a close "relative" of *ṣurru* and *mušgarru*) see Oppenheim, *Glass* p.15.

that was lengthened. A lengthening of the penultimate vowel is, however, also attested in *RMA* 112 r11 (*ip-ti-e-te*) and 274G:4 (*ir-ti-i-bi* "it set *and* skipped the eclipse"), both from Nabû-aḫḫē-erība.

59

Bibliography:

(I) Waterman, *RCAE* 80 (cf. IV 234); Pfeiffer, *SLA* 159.
(II) Behrens, *ABB* (1906) 76 f; Schott, *ZA* 44 (1938) 198[1] : Oppenheim, *JAOS* 61 (1941) 259; Deller, *Or*NS 31 (1962) 233 and AOAT 1 (1969) 62.

Addressee:

Esarhaddon.

Date:

Early Du'ūzu, eponymy of Kanūnāju = late June, 671 BC. Comparison of the letter with *LAS* 34 (q.v.) assures the time brackets 672-669 BC;[119] and the only occasion within that time span which could have kept Esarhaddon out of Assyria for months (cf. 34:15f) and timed his returnal to occur in the 4th month (= Du'ūzu) was the Egyptian campaign of 671 BC, in which the king is known to have partaken in person[120] and which lasted from Nisannu to late Du'ūzu. Cf. the relevant entry in the Babylonian Chronicle (Grayson, *TCS* 5 p.85:23-27; Borger, *Ash* p.124):

MU *10*.KAM ^{ITU}BARAG ERIM KUR *Aš+šur ana Mi-ṣir* DU *ḫe-pí*
^{ITU}ŠU UD *3*.KÁM UD *16*.KÁM UD *28*.KÁM
3-šú di-ik-tum ina KUR *Mi-ṣir di-kát*
UD *22*.KÁM *Me-em-pí* URU LUGAL-*tú* [*ṣ*]*a-bit*
LUGAL-*šú ul-te-zib* DUMU-*šú u* Š[EŠ-*šú ina* ŠU^{2} *ṣa-a*]*b-tu*

"The 10th year: In the month Nisannu, the troops of Assyria went to Egypt. On the 3rd, 16th and 28th of Du'ūzu, three times there was a massacre in Egypt. On the 22nd, Memphis, the royal residence, was taken; its king escaped, but his son and brother were taken captives."

However, it should be noted that the present letter was certainly written *before* the campaign had been definitely finished, i.e. before Du'ūzu 28: if the king had left Egypt only at that date, he could not have returned to Nineveh in the fourth month, as the letter states. Actually, it seems that the king's return took place quite early in Du'ūzu, as no reference is made in the letter to the total lunar eclipse of Du'ūzu 14 or its consequences (the enthronement of a substitute king; cf. *LAS* 249 and 292). This conclusion is also supported by *LAS* 278, see relevant commentary.

Notes:

r3 f. *a-na 4 ITU (ra-ab-bi ur-ḫi)*: not "for 4 months" (Pt.I) but "until the 4th month". The gloss *ra-ab-bi* cannot be taken as a special NA form of the numeral "four" (thus von Soden, GAG §69c:9, *AHw* 232*b* and 934*a*; *CAD* A/2 p.259, lex.sect., etc.), since other passages (e.g., *RMA* 88:8, *ABRT* I 6 r8) show that this NA form was *erbi* or *erbe*; moreover, the text does not read "months" (ITU^{MEŠ}) but "month" (ITU; cf. *LAS* 309 r22, *8* MU.AN.NA "the eighth year", but 114:8, *14* MU.AN.NA^{MEŠ} "14 years"). The correct interpretation (as already

[119] Note the ref. in *LAS* 34 r6 to the crown prince [Assurbanipal].

[120] Cf. *ABL* 276:5f, *ul-tù* LUGAL EN ^{6} *a-na* KUR *Mi-ṣir il-lil-lik* ^{7} *ina* ITU.ŠU AN.MI *iš-kun-nu* "after the king, my lord, went to Egypt and an eclipse occurred in the month Du'ūzu . . . "; *AGS* 68:2ff, [$^{\text{I.d}}$*Aš+šur*-ŠEŠ-SUM-*na* LUGAL] KUR *Aš+šur* KI *li-iṣ-rim lik-*[*pi*]*d-ma* . . . ^{3} [*ana na*]*-gi-i šá* KUR *Mi-ṣir* . . . *lil-lik-ma* "may Esarhaddon, king of Assyria, plan and go to the territory of Egypt?"; and Borger, *Ash* p.112:6ff, *ina 10-e* KASKAL.*2-ja* . . . ^{10} *ina* ITU.BARAG . . . *ul-tú* URU-*ja Aš+šur at-tu-muš* . . . ^{15} *a-na* KUR *Me-luḫ-ḫa uš-te-še-ra ḫar-ra-nu* "In my 10th campaign, . . . I departed from my city Assur in the month Nisannu . . . and headed for the country of Meluḫḫa (= Kush)".

noticed by Ylvisaker, *LSS* 5/6 [1912] 28) is, of course, that *ra-ab-bi* is the Neo-Assyrian form of the ordinal "fourth", going back (through assimilation *b'* > *bb*) to original *rab'i.* Cf. *GAG* §70c for the pattern of NA ordinals (*paris*) and Deller, *RA* 61 189 for the assimilation *b'* > *bb.*

60

Bibliography:
(I) Waterman, *RCAE* 1096; Pfeiffer, *SLA* 261.
(II) Oppenheim, *Centaurus* 14 (1969) 127[8].

Sender:
The assignation of this letter to Nabû-aḫḫē-erība can be regarded as absolutely certain on the ground of three characteristic spellings otherwise attested only in his letters: *ur-ke-e-et* Obv.16 (cf. *LAS* 69 r12'); [*le*]-*pu-u-šu* Rev. 10 (cf. note to 58 r6); and *ki ša* Rev.8 (cf. App. M 6).

Addressee:
Assurbanipal (see below).

Date:
Appr. Nisannu 18, eponymy of Gabbāru = April 23, 667 BC. The fact that the letter provides information regarding the praxis of communicating interpretations of lunar eclipses to the *father* of the king can only imply that the king in question had just experienced the *first* eclipse of the moon in his reign, and since the career of Nabû-aḫḫē-erība is documented only for 674-666 BC, and no letters of the present corpus demonstratably predate 674 BC, this king can only be Assurbanipal. The first lunar eclipse in his reign occurred on April 21, -666, but since this eclipse is *reported* in *LAS* 61 (q.v.), the present letter cannot have been written on the date of the eclipse itself but probably one or two days later.

Notes:

7. *u'iltu*: the NA term for tablets of the "report" type, i.e. horizontally oblong one-column ones, as opposed to vertically oblong one-column tablets used for writing letters (*egirtu*), cf. Oppenheim 1969 (l.c.) and note also *LAS* 40 r3, 61 r4, 110 r6 and 81-2-4,61 r29 (*šá-ṭa-ru šá ú-il-ti*), not quoted by Oppenheim.[121] The term did not, however, refer to "reports" only but could denote any tablets of this form (*ADD* 976 = *AfO* Bh 3, no. 52, designated as *ú-ìl-ti* [I]*Mu-šal-lim*-X[ ] (Rev.10), is a horizontally oblong one-column tablet listing incipits of literary compositions). The origin of the term seems to be in Babylonian bills of exchange thus designated and having the same characteristic format.[122]

r1. *"On the bank of the river"*: a location convenient for washing away the pollution caused by the eclipse. Cf. on *LAS* 160 r6, 185:17, 195 r7f, 205:11f, 210 r4 and also 61:5ff.

r2. [LÚ]*ERIM*[MEŠ]: as shown by the corresponding predicate (r6) and the pron.suffix in r4, this is either a "rebus" spelling for *ummânu* "scholar" (for ERIM[MEŠ] = *ummānu* "army" see *CAD* Ṣ 54b; cf. also ERIM-*ni* = (glossed:) *um-ma-*[*ni*] in a report from Nabû-aḫḫē-erība, *RMA* 246B:4 f), or else the NA word for "man" has to be posited as *ṣabū̆* (with a long final *u*) against Bab. *ṣābu.*[123] For examples of the use of the sign MEŠ to indicate a long vowel see note to *LAS* 223:9 ff. *

r5. *qersu*: a word attested only in Neo-Assyrian (cf. *AHw* 918*a* and Ebeling, *Or*NS 22 [1953] 35), and of an obscure etymology (if a WSem. loanword, cf. possibly Bibl. *qäräš* "board; prow(?)" and Ug. *qrš* "abode"). From the contexts in which it occurs (note, in addition to the passages listed in *AHw.* also Ebeling, *Or*NS 22 37

[121] The most important passage is *RMA* 188 = *LAS* 324 r4, *ú-il-tu šá-ni-tú a-na-as-sa-ḫa* "I shall extract (quotations for) *another* report (and notify the king)". Oppenheim's interpretation of Obv.12f presented ibid. cannot be accepted.

[122] See Ungnad, *Glossar* p.1, under *u'iltu e'ēlu* (OB *e'iltu e'ēlu*, cf. *CAD* E 51f).

[123] Cf. OAkk *ṣabi'um*, Mari *ṣaba'um* (*CAD* Ṣ 54b).

r15)[124] it is, however, quite evident that it denotes a fenced area (mostly situated in the temple precincts) reserved for the performance of cultic and magical rituals demanding the highest secrecy: apotropaic rituals (*LAS* 137, 138, 167), extispicies (*LAS* 115), divine meal (K 10209 r23', there corresponding to *emāšu* of En.el. V 114), etc. This also explains its choice as the place where lunar eclipses were reported and interpreted to the king, a situation loaded with royal anxiety and trepidation.*

61

Bibliography:
(I) Waterman, *RCAE* 47 (cf. IV 232); Pfeiffer, *SLA* 325; Oppenheim, *Letters from Mesopotamia* (1967), p. 161 (transl. only).
(II) Ylvisaker, *LSS* 5/6 (1912) 22[9]; Schott, *OLZ* 40 (1937) 363; Labat, *Royauté* (1939) 337; Landsberger, *BBEA* (1965) 44[68].

Photograph:
RCAE IV pl.10 (Obv. only).

Date:
Nisannu 16, eponym year of Gabbāru = April 21, 667 BC. The way in which the lunar eclipse reported in this letter is described implies that it was total (this is the case in all eclipses beginning in the eastern quadrant and ending in the western one, cf. App. F2) and could not be seen from its beginning (only the *drifting* of the shadow from the east is reported); moreover, the planets Jupiter and Venus were visible until the end of the eclipse (Obv. 12-15). These data fit only one eclipse between 680 and 660 B.C., that of April 21, -666 (see App. F1 and F3), and the identification is confirmed by the parallel letter *LAS* 40 from Balasî reporting the same eclipse (q.v.). Note, furthermore, that *LAS* 60 (written slightly after the present letter) also refers to this same eclipse.

Recipient:
Assurbanipal.

Notes:

5 ff. Cf. *u₄-mu an-ni-u šá ta-d[er-ti]* [5] *šu-ú a-na e-pa-ši l[a ṭa-a-ba]* "this is a gloomy day, not fit for performing (rituals)", *LAS* 257 r4 f. The blessing (= "may Nabû and Marduk bless the king, my lord") is otherwise never omitted in Nabû-aḫḫē-erība's letters. The same holds for the letters of Balasî, except for *LAS* 40 dealing with the same exclipse as our letter, and generally for the whole selection of letters here edited: of the remaining four letters lacking the blessing, No. 83 also deals with an eclipse, 168 and 170 are fragmentary (but may have been of similar content[125], and only No. 5 is clearly neutral in this respect (yet it was also written on an *ūmu ša taderti*, the day of the death of Tammuz). This circumstance is explained by the fact that eclipses were considered manifestations of divine anger[126] making invocation of gods not seem appropriate on the relevant days. On the other hand, eclipses did not by any means *necessitate* omission of the blessing formulae: cf. *LAS* 77, 80, 83, etc.

16 ff. For the astrological interpretation of this eclipse see App. F4, and cf. *LAS* 279:15ff and discussion under *LAS* 279. The Jupiter-omen predicting safety of the king is quoted in *LAS* 298 r10' f.

62

Bibliography:
Waterman, *RCAE* 1069 (cf. IV 195).

---

[124] A number of attestations of (GIŠ) *qersu* (mostly in Pl.) in NA texts obviously refer to a wooden vehicle (drawn by asses), cf. *ABL* 100 r5, 784 r6.10, *ADD* 1036 ii 11, 1039 ii 3, ND 2451:13.14 (*Iraq* 23 28), 2643 r22 (*Iraq* 18 pl.9). This word may or may not be etymologically related to (GIŠ) *qersu* "sacred enclosure".

[125] Cf. *LAS* 168 with No. 28.

[126] See note to *LAS* 278:9.

Writer:

Certainly Nabû-aḫḫē-erība; note the explanatory glosses in Obv.11' and Rev.5' (cf. Appendix M 6.5). The handwriting, too, is unmistakably Nabû-aḫḫē-erība's.

Addressee:

Esarhaddon.

Date:

Kislīmu 13/14, eponymy of Šulmu-Bēl-lašme = December 16/17, 670 BC. For the identification of the lunar eclipse predicted in Obv.6' ff see note to *LAS* 41 r1 ff. That our letter was written immediately before the eclipse appears from the reference to the lunar halo in Obv.3', which implies that the moon was almost full. The correlation Kislīmu 14 = December 17 can be inferred from the fact that the preceding month (Araḫsamna) had only 29 days (cf. *RMA* 274G, to be quoted presently), which shows that the moment of conjunction (Dec. 2) must have fallen on the 28th of Araḫsamna (cf. 41 r6 ff).

Discussion:

This letter runs roughly parallel to No. 41, and much of what was said in the relevant comments applies here, too. Cf. also *RMA* 85 (from Rāši-ili). Note, incidentally, that contrary to *LAS* 63, Nabû-aḫḫē-erība here evidently did not venture predicting the watch in which the eclipse was going to take place.[127] This may have been due to atmospheric conditions (note the time of the year!) making it difficult to observe the risings of the moon in the days preceding the eclipse; cf. discussion sub *LAS* 63.

Notes:

3' ff. Altogether 8 reports of Nabû-aḫḫē-erība dealing with lunar halos have been preserved (see *RMA* 96-98, 103, 106, 112, 179, 180 and 246B), but none of them can be the halo-tablet (sic, not "report" = *u'iltu*!) mentioned here. The longitude of the moon on December 16, 670, was about 65°, and if one hypothesizes that the halo made a 22-degree circle around the moon (which is more common than a 46-degree circle),[128] the constellations of Gemini and Cancer (partly) would have been enclosed in it. Such a situation is actually reported in *RMA* 114 (from Bulluṭu).

10'. The restoration of this line is based on 63:4'-7' *mu-šu an-n[i-ú]* . . . *ma-ṣar-tu-šú*; the reading [*par-s*]*u* seems virtually certain in view of the gloss in the following line. For the meaning of *parsu* in the present context see Oppenheim, *Centaurus* 14 (1969) 119; in addition to the examples quoted there, note also *a-mat pa-ri-is-tú* [6] *šup-ra*, *ABL* 477:5 (cf. *a-mat pa-ri-is-*tu_4 [4] *a-na* LUGAL *al-tap-ra*, 1448 r3-4); *lum-nu par-su* "unequivocal evil", 137:10, and *dib-bi par-su-*tu_4 *šú-nu* "these are definite words", ibid. r1.

r8. The writer refers to the solar eclipse expected in *LAS* 41. This eclipse is very likely also referred to in *RMA* 274G, a report from Nabû-aḫḫē-erība reading as follows:

[EN.NUN] *šá* ^{d}*Šá-maš* [2] [^{ITU}APIN] UD *29*.KÁM* [3] [*ni*]-*ta-ṣar* [4] *ir-ti-i-bi* [5] [AN.MI] *us-se-et-iq* [6] [^{d}*30 ina*] ^{ITU}KAN [7] [u_4 *mu*] *ú tar ra* "We observed the Sun on the 29th of [Araḫsamna], it set (as usual), skipping [the eclipse]. [The Moon] will reject [the (30th) day] in Kislīmu."

63

Bibliography:

(I) Waterman, *RCAE* 869.
(II) Schott, *ZA* 44 (1938) 195.

---

[127] The restoration of [*la ni-ip*]-*ru-us* in line 14' appears fairly safe in view of ll. 10'-11'.

[128] The term *tarbaṣu* used in the present letter is generally taken to refer to the 22° circle only, see Kugler, SSB II 101f. The greater halo appears to have been called *supūru*, cf. *RMA* 117:7ff (AMÁŠ = TÙR *ra-bu-ú*) and Kugler, loc.cit.

Writer:

The explanatory glosses in Obv.6' indicate that this letter was written by Nabû-aḫḫē-erība; see already Schott (1938).

Date:

Probably Tašrītu 14 = October 15, 667. Only three eclipses occurred in the morning watch in years 680-663 (see App. F1); of these, the eclipse of June 11, 669 should be ruled out since it was not certainly predictable by means of eclipse periods (see Schnabel, *ZA* 35 [1924] 301f), and that of December 17, 670, because the writer was not able to predict its moment of occurrence with certainty in the preceding letter.

Discussion:

A point worth noticing in this letter is the surety with which the writer assigns the predicted eclipse to a definite night watch. The eclipse periods known in the Sargonid era (cf. notes to *LAS* 41) did not make such predictions possible, and it is certain that the astrologers of that time were not able to compute the moments of oppositions mathematically (cf. ibid.). On what grounds, then, was the present forecast made? The only explanation I can think of is that the hour of the opposition was approximated from the time the moon needed to appear before sunset a day or two before the expected eclipse. If the moon was near the ecliptic, two observations on successive days would have sufficed for determining the desired hour with reasonable accuracy. This method was certainly used at least in predicting the d a y s of oppositions in advance; cf. *RMA* 271A Obv.1 ff: [^{d}]*30 ina* ^{ITU}KIN UD *15*.KÁM ^{2} [KI] ^{d}*Šá-maš in-na-mar* . . . ^{r2} [AN.MI] *ú-še-taq la i-šá-kan* ^{3} *šá* ^{Id}PA-PAP^{MEŠ}-SU ^{4} UD *13*.KÁM "the Moon will be seen opposite to the Sun of Ulūlu 15; . . . [the eclipse] will pass by, it will not occur. From Nabû-aḫḫē-erība. On the 13th." Note also *RMA* 155 r1 ff (following report on full moon): "Let the king, my lord, not say: 'There were clouds, how did he observe id?' Tonight, when I observed its (the moon's) appearance, it appeared just before sunset and reached the region in which it will be seen (in opposition with the sun). It was a sign that it will be observed. In the morning, if the day is cloudless, the king will see . . . ."

64

Bibliography:

(I) Waterman, *RCAE* 405 (cf. III 374, IV 180, 250); Pfeiffer, *SLA* 330.
(II) Schott, *OLZ* 40 (1937) 364; Labat, *Royauté* (1939) 334; Oppenheim, *JAOS* 61 (1941) 263 and 64 (1944) 192.

Discussion:

"Dark" sunrises of the kind reported here are caused by heavy sandstorms filling the atmosphere with dust particles which scatter light so effectively as to give the sun and the sky near the horizon the abnormally red colouring referred to in Obv.20 and Rev.4.[129] It is uncertain whether Nabû-aḫḫē-erība was aware of the natural explanation of the phenomenon. This might be inferred from Rev.2-4, but as a matter of fact "dark" sunrises and sunsets are also linked with sandstorms in canonical omens, which are not based on cause-and-effect reasoning but observed natural phenomena.

Two other reports on "dark suns" have been preserved (see *RMA* 181 and *LAS* 109, the former pertaining to month Ajāru of an unknown year, the latter to Ajāru, 650 BC), but these have nothing to do with the present case. Since our letter does not contain any concrete chronological data (not even the name of the month in question is mentioned[130]), it cannot be dated even approximately.

Notes:

9-13. This omen is not attested elsewhere but it was certainly included in the series *Enūma Anu Enlil*, since no reference to the source was considered necessary. Cf. *LAS* 13 r1, 8, 15 (and note to r1), 12 r13-14, 110 r4-7,

[129] Cf. Kugler, *SSB* II 121.

[130] The reference to the path of the Anu stars (Rev.8, 12, 18) only excludes the months Simānu-Ābu and Kislīmu-Šabāṭu. Cf. Weidner, *HBA* I p.47.

r4-7, *RMA* 94 r5, 8 (*an-nu-ti ša* ÉŠ.GÀR; [8] *an-ni-ú a-ḫi-ú*) and 200:8, r4-5 (*an-ni-u ša iš*-[GÀR]; [r4] *an-ni-u ša pi-i ṭup-[pi]* [5] *ki-i* dPA-*ku-dúr*-PAP KURNIM.MA[KI] [6] *iḫ-pu-u-ni*).

14-16. Quoting *ACh* 2 Spl 39:8: I UD *a-der-ma* IM2 *ra-kib* ⌜*ú*⌝-[*kul-ti* . . . .].

r2-3. These lines are an allusion to *ACh* Šamaš 10:81, I (*20*) *ina la* ŠIDMEŠ-*šú* KA×MI *u a-šam-šá-a-tu* NIGINMEŠ-*da* ŠUB-*tì* ERIM-*ni* GÁL "If (the sun) is eclipsed at an unexpected time and dust storms whirl, the army will be defeated". Cf. also *ACh* Spl Šamaš 32:7, I *20 ina* KUR-*šú a-šam-š*[*á-tu*$_4$. . . .] "If, while the sun is rising, sandst[orms whirl . . . .]"; and Šamaš 16:6 f, I *20 ina* GÀL-*šú* ŠÚ-*ma a-šam-šá-tu*$_4$ "If the sun is eclipsed while it sets and sandstorms whirl", etc.

The long final vowels in *né-em-ma-ra* (Obv.21), *an-qu-ul-le-e* (Obv.22), *a-šá-an-šá-te-e* (Rev.2) and *su-u'-mu-u* (Rev.4) require more attention than appears from the translation given in Pt.I. The lengthening of morphically short vowels in Neo-Assyrian is always an indication of a special sentence intonation (e.g., interrogative[131], emotional[132], or coordinative[133]) affecting the meaning of the whole utterance and should actually be reflected in translation here, too. The context, unfortunately, is not particularly helpful in deciding which kind of sentence is in question. Since the statements presented here are not actual quotations, and since the event referred to had not yet occurred, it seems possible to regard this passage as an anticipation of the *rēḫti dibbī* "rest of the matter" to be assessed in another message according to Rev.5 ff; this would point to a sort of "list-intonation" attested in modern Arabic, cf. e.g. H. Palva, *StOr* 32 (1966), p. 130.

r6. The interpretation of the spelling *am-MUR* remains uncertain. It obviously stands for *ammar* "I shall see" (cf. *di-ib-bi gab-bu* LUGAL *le-e-mur*, ABL 1285:11 and *tu-u-ra am-mur* [16] *a-šap-pa-ra*, *LAS* 41 r15 f), and hence the possibility of a scribal mistake cannot be excluded. Alternatively the spelling could be taken to indicate a spoken [å] which undoubtedly occurred as an allophone of /a/ in similar environments. Cf. *qur-ru-bu*, *ABL* 241 r10 = /*qarrubū*/, [*qårrubu*]; URU*Si-pur LAS* 296 r6, *ABL* 320+8 etc. = URU*Si-par*, *ABL* 88 r5; URU*Bur-si-*[*ip*], *ABL* 1433:8, and *Bur-sip*KI, *2 R* 53 no. 1:3 = *Bar-sip*KI, BÁR.SIPAKI(Borsippa!), etc. See also W. Mayer, *AOATS* 2 p.13 for corresponding examples in Middle-Assyrian texts,[134] and cf. notes to *LAS* 35 r1 and 39 r3.

r12-17. The source of this quotation is unknown (probably *Enūma Anu Enlil*). The translation of lines 15f given in Pt.I (based on *LAS* 109:9'f) is very uncertain and perhaps to be modified after *CAD* K 263*b* ("the crisis moment has arrived, (the prognosis for) Elam became bad quite early"). Cf. *ūmē*[*ka imlû šanat*]*ka ikšudamma uk-ki-ba a-dan-ka* "the days [of your (life) are over, the year of] your (death) has come, the time appointed to you is here", Borger, *Ash* p.105 ii 32, and the similar passage in Streck, *Asb* p.178:15. In any case, the statement is obviously an equivalent of Rev.8-10 and 18-20, the only difference being that the evil is restricted to the morning-time (*kaṣâtiš* = *ana kaṣâti*!).

65

Bibliography:

(I) Waterman, *RCAE* 1132 (cf. IV 198f.).

(II) Deller, *Or*NS 30 (1961) 252 f. The piece 81-2-4, 420 has not been published or discussed before.

Writer:

This letter was assigned by Deller (1961) to Ištar-šumu-ēreš, which is however entirely unlikely since short vertical dashes separating words (here in Obv.10, 19 and Rev.9) are attested in none of the 37 letters and 32 reports of this writer. By contrast, they abound in the reports of Nabû-aḫḫē-erība: see *RMA* 43 r4, 57 r6, 62:3, 70 r3, 103: 4.11.r2.4.6.9.10, 112:4.9.r6, 139:8.r2, 191:2.5.7, 229:1.2.3, 237:2.7, 238:2.r2, 248:1 and 274E:3. Admittedly

131 See note to 208 r8.

132 Cf. the NA elegies *STT* 360 and K.890 (= Strong, *BA* 6 34), with spellings such as *mu-pi-šu-u*, *bak-ka-ni-i*, *up-na-ja-a* etc.

133 See note to *LAS* 18 r8.

134 Notice especially *e-mur* "he sees", *KAJ* 98:9, besides normal *e-mar* ibid. 93:13, 94:9, etc.

their use is also attested (in some measure) in letters and reports of Balasî, but since the present letter can be considered a doublet of *LAS* 66 (most likely) written by Balasî, its assignation to Nabû-aḫḫē-erība seems most natural in the light of the note on the writer of *LAS* 34 (q.v.). Other writers than these two are out of the question. Note, as a detail speaking for Nabû-aḫḫē-erība, that the word *anniu* is here written *an-ni-⟨i⟩-u* unlike in letters of Balasî, where the standard spelling is *an-ni-i-u* (see Introduction, p.30; exception: *LAS* 66 r13).

Date:

Addāru 27, eponym year of Šulmu-Bēl-lašme = March 26, 669 BC. For the month and day see r11 ff; the evidence placing the letter in 669 BC is discussed in detail in commentary to *LAS* 70.

Addressee:

Esarhaddon.

Discussion:

Between years 681 and 663, Venus did never rise heliacally in Aries in the month of Addāru;[135] the observation referred to in Obv.12f., if to be taken seriously, must accordingly be explained as due to a misunderstanding, an inability to distinguish between Venus and *Mercury,* as emphatically pointed out by the author of *LAS* 66 (cf. r26 ff); and as the latter planet was at the time concerned rising as a evening star exactly where the misguided astrologer had believed to observe Venus,[136] there is actually no reason to doubt the observation as such. According to the tables of Schoch (1928), the evening first of Mercury in 669 BC was observable at earliest on March 24' = Addāru 25; and as the observation mocked in the present letter must have been made on Addāru 26 (immediately after sunset, i.e., in the evening of March 24) *at the latest*, the atrologer in question, whatever his theoretical knowledge of planetary periods, must at least be credited with sharp eyes. Incidentally, the surety by which Nabû-aḫḫē-erība could rule out the possibility that the planet rising was Venus implies that he was aware of the periodicity of the Venus phenomena and probably utilized, like the compiler of the 63rd tablet of Enūma Anu Enlil, the 8-year Venus cycle for the prediction of the planet's appearances and disappearances. A person ignorant of this cycle could not have ruled out the possibility of the planet's being Venus, for the interval of invisibility of Venus at the superior conjunction can vary from 54 to 74 days, and the planet had already been 50 days absent at the time the observation was made (cf. App. C2).

Notes:

8. The integration [*la-a*] *: nam-rat* "it is [not] visible" proposed by Deller (1961) is unacceptable because the use of *:* as a word-boundary mark is otherwise not attested in Nabû-aḫḫē-erība's letters and reports.

18-21. On this passage see note to *LAS* 12 r10 ff.

r1. *lā kettu*: here clearly used as an adverb ("untruly, deceitfully"), cf. the corresponding adverbial use of *kettu* "truly" (examples *CAD* K 472*b*). The present meaning to be added to the dictionaries.

r5. For this form (*'tq* Š + vent. + pron. suff.) cf. *qabsi mātīšu lu-u-še-ti-qu-u-né-šú ABL* 1058 r8 and [*ina* URUBÀ]D-IEN-DINGIR-*aja* [16] [*ú-š*]*e-ta-qu-né-šá-nu-u-ni,* ND 2356:15 f (*Iraq* 28 pl.55 no.86). The idiom *šētuqu* + *ina libbi ēnē* "to glance over" seems to occur only here.

r14. [*i*]-*sa-na-al-li*: Gtn of *salû* "to lie", "to cheat". The meaning of this hitherto[137] misunderstood verb in the G-stem is evident from the parallelity of *ABL* 190:6 *ta-sa-la-'a-an-ni* with ib.17 *la ke-e-tu i-se-e-a ta-da-bu-ub* "you speak untruly with me" (context!); note also *ša a-na* LUGAL *be-lí-já* [10] *is-lu-ni* EME-*šú* TA* *ḫa-ru-ur-*

[135] See App.C2. The evening first of Venus in 673, which did occur on Addāru 27, took place not in Aries but in NE Fishes.

[136] That the "Venus" observation was also made in the evening appears from the Fem. predicate *nam-rat* in Obv. 7. See note to *LAS* 69+ r4'.

[137] Cf. Waterman, *RCAE* I (1930) p.105 "to be hostile", p. 127 "to rebel"; Pfeiffer, *SLA* (1935) p.147 "to slander"; von Soden, *ZA* 43 (1936) 29 "verächtlich behandeln"; Delitzsch, *Assyrisches Handwörterbuch* (1896) p.500 "vertrauensselig, hoffnungsvoll sein"; Muss-Arnholt, *A Concise Dictionary of the Assyrian Language* (1894-1905) p.761 "?"; Bezold, *Glossar* (1926), p.213 "dahinsiechen, gebrechlich sein".

ti-šú li-iš-du-du-u-né "let them pull the tongue out of the throat of the man who lied to the king, my lord", *ABL* 154:9 f; *aq-ṭi-ba-ak* [40] *la as-li-k[a]* [iv 1] *ú-ta-ki-i[l-ka]* [2] *la ú-ba-áš-[ka]* "I have spoken out to you, I have not lied to you; I have encourage you, I will not let you come to shame", K.4310 iii 39 ff (4 R^2 61); *a-na mì-i-ni ta-sa-al-li* [12] *a-na* LUGAL-*e* EN-*ja a-sa-al-li* "why do you lie to me? Would I lie to the king, my lord?", *LAS* 263:11 f. The frequentative Gtn-stem is best translated "to talk nonsense, rubbish", cf. (besides the present passage) *i-sa-na-li-i-[u] LAS* 281 r13; *is-sa-na-al-lu-ka*, *CT* 53, 397 r7; *i-sa-na-al-li ABL* 1454 r4; this meaning also suits the corresponding verbal noun *sil(i)āti*, which is only attested in the plural:[138] cf. *šu-mu an-ni-u si-li-a-te šu-u* [3] LUGAL *be-lí ina* UGU ŠÀ-*šú la i-šak-kan* "this omen is rubbish; the king, my lord, should not lay it on his heart" *RMA* 235 r2 f; *ú-da ki-i a-bu-tu ša áš-mu-[u-ni]* [8] *[s]i-li-E*[139]*-tu ši-ti-i-[ni]* "I know that the rumor I have heard is rubbish", *ABL* 1294 r7' f.; *si-il-a-te ši-na* "that is a lie", *LAS* 276 r3, similarly *[si-l]i-a-te ši-na* 298:15, and *si-li-'a-a-te ši-na* (sic!) in *ZA* 51 138:53.

r15. Cf. Hebr. *pḥz* "to be insolent" and Arab. *faḫaza* "to be boastful"; note also **pḫz* Š in *LAS* 281 r4 and 312 r14 (and cf. Hebr. *pḥz* Hi. "to cause to be loose").

r18. For the paragogic *-u* in *i-nàr-ru-ṭu* (corresponding to enclitic *-ma*) see note to *LAS* 18 r8.

r19. *lu-rab-bi-iš*: hardly from *rabāšu* "Einspruch erheben(?)" (*AHw* 934*a*, 3 attestations in Old Assyrian), since this verb is otherwise not attested in Neo-Assyrian and since it does not occur in the D-stem even in Old Assyrian. Rather, precative of **rbī* D "to make great" + pron. suff. of 3rd m Sg. (*-š* < *-šu* after long stressed vowel). Cf. *li-ik-liš*, *ABL* 426:11; *tu-se-li-iš*, ND 2316:5 (*Iraq* 16 pl.7); *i-du-ku-uš*, *ABL* 186 r9; *ú-sa-ga-li-uš*, 706 r4; *lu-bal-lit-ṭuš*, 427:10; *li-iṣ-ṣu-ru-uš*, *LAS* 72 r19 (also from Nabû-aḫḫē-erība), and *lu-gal-li-bu-uš*, 310:13'.[140] The ensuing translation "(the king) should make him great = promote him" is of course exactly opposite to what the miserable astrologer would actually have deserved; accordingly, we seem to have here a clear case of *irony*, and indeed an ironical remark such as "the king should not waver but *quickly promote* him" fits excellently the tenor of the letter. The word broken away before *lu-rab-bi-iš* can be actually restored as *[ár-ḫi]š* "quickly", the final vertical of *ḫiš* being still visible in Harper's copy. [Collated, June 1974]

66

Bibliogrphy:

(I) Waterman, *RCAE* 618 (cf. III 374, IV 185).
(II) Schott, *ZA* 44 (1938) 195 ff; Oppenheim, *JAOS* 64 (1944) 194.

Writer:

Balasî. Attribution to Nabû-aḫḫē-erība (Pt.I; Schott 1938) is also thinkable, as the letter contains many distinctive features of this man (introductory formula; astronomical contents; interlinear glosses; vertical dashes indicating word-division; and the spelling *an-ni-ú* in Rev.13, not attested in texts by Balasî); cf. on the preceding number. However, on closer examination the authorship of Balasî seems more probable, after all. Firstly, the spelling *iš-pu-ra-[an-ni]* (Obv.11, Rev.14) is not attested in the letters of Nabû-aḫḫē-erība (who always wrote *iš-pur-an-ni*),[141]

[138] Landsberger, *BBEA* p.54 translates correctly *sil'āte šina* "das sind Lügen"; the rendering of Oppenheim, *Centaurus* 14 118 (*šumu anniu siliāte šū* "this omen is worthless") is also acceptable. The coexistence of *siliāti* with **slī* Gtn (not G!) is certainly not accidental; notice that the plural sign MEŠ is also used in logographic spelling of Gtn-forms, as in DU^MEŠ^-*ak KAR* 148.10 (= *ittanallak*), DU^MEŠ^-*ki* (= *tattanallikī*) *Maqlû* IX 120, or simply DU^MEŠ^ (= *ittanallak*), *KAR* 428:33.

[139] Here an allograph of JA, cf. É *mar-di-ti-E* (= *ja*), *ABL* 414:4; ^KUR^*Nu-ri-E*, Streck *Asb* p.140:45 (for ^URU^*Nu-ri-ja*/ZALÁG-*ja* Borger, *Ash* p.60:71), etc. For other graphic mergers in NA script note TÚ = *te* ina *ni-ip-TÚ-te*, *ABL* 319:7 (conversely, TE = *tú* in *i-gír-TE* [Nom.!] *ABL* 313 r6); IQ = *qi* in *lip-IQ-dan-ni* 347:9 (but also QI = *iq*, as in *li-QI-bi* 190:15, *bu-ti-QI-te* 941:5, etc.).

[140] Similar apocopated forms are also attested in MA (see *AOATS* 2, §11.3) and certainly occurred more frequently in speech than the script would indicate.

[141] Note, however, *i[š-pu-r]a-an-ni*, *LAS* 73:8.

but occurs in *two* letters from Balasî (*LAS* 34:6 and 52:12).[142] Moreover, the letter begins exactly like *LAS* 46 (*ina muḫḫi . . . ša šarru bēlī išpuranni mā iqṭibûne mā* Obv.6-9 = 46:6-8), and Rev.13 ff resembles closely *LAS* 53 r1 ff; note also *ú-de-šú* r3 (= 35 r5) and the gloss *ka-ku-bu* in r10 (= 43:2') (against *ka-ka-bu RMA* 246A r2 and *ka-ak-ka-bu* 237:7, both from Nabû-aḫḫē-erība). Since explanatory glosses and vertical dashes are also attested in letters of Balasî, though only sporadically (see *LAS* 10+57, 326, and *RMA* 88:5), their presence can, in a controversial case like this, only be regarded to indicate an authorship of *either* Nabû-aḫḫē-erība *or* Balasî. The only really disturbing feature from the viewpoint of the attribution to Balasî is the spelling *an-ni-ú* in Rev.13, see Appendix M 6. This is however counterbalanced by the fact that if No.65 was written by Nabû-aḫḫē-erība, its virtual duplicate is most naturally assignable to Balasî (see sub *LAS* 34); in reverse case, No.65 should be assigned to the latter, which seems more improbable.

Date:

Addāru 27, eponym year of Šulmu-Bēl-lašme = March 26, 669 BC. Cf. above and *LAS* 65 r11.

Addressee:

Esarhaddon.

Discussion:

See under *LAS* 65.

Notes:

14. For *adannu* "astronomical period, cycle" cf. *CAD* A/1 p. 100 f. The word occurs in Neo-Assyrian in this (Babylonian) form only as an astrological terminus technicus; the Assyrian form (in non-technical contexts) was *edānu/edannu*, see Deller, *Or*NS 34 (1965) 264.

15. In this context, *da-aja-la-te* (a *parrāst/parāst*-formation from *dâlu* "to run/wander around"[143] is best taken as an astronomical terminus technicus for "synodic revolution", or the like; elsewhere, the word is attested in the meaning "(hunting) excursion". Cf. *mid-bar* [16] *[a]-na ša-ka-ni ša ma-da[k-ti]* [17] DUG+GA *a-na da-aja-la-te* [18] DUG+GA *-ma* "the (said) desert is fit for encamping, (and) it also is good for excursions" *CT* 53 76 "A" 15 ff *ina da-aja-la-te-šú šá ḫu-ri-ib-te lu-ur-me* GAZ-*ak* Scheil *Tn II* 80 = Schramm, *BiOr* 27 (1970) 152:80, similarly ibid. 81; NÍG.NA URUDU *ša da-aja-la-te* "a bronze censer for excursions", ND 2490+2460:35. Cf. also [*da*]-*aja-la-te ša* ^{d}*15*, Postgate, *NARGD* No.50:17', unless this example has to be restored [^{LÚ}GAL *da*]-*aja-la-te*.

17. *i-ga-ra-at*: in the absence of any further evidence of a verbal root **grd/t/ṭ*, probably Pl. of *igāru* "wall"; cf. *i-ga-ra-at* É and the other syllabic spellings listed in *CAD* I/J p.34 ff. Is the word here used as a terminus technicus for "(planetary) sphere"?

r5 ff. These fragmentary lines gain in importance when they are studied in light of the chronological evidence obtained from *LAS* 65. On March 26, 669, Venus was (with an elongation of less than 2° and a longitude of 3°20') invisible because of its proximity to the sun but located under the constellation of Aries (cf. r5ff, "presently if should be situated[144] (behind the sun) under [Aries]"); at the same time, Saturn (= the king's star, see *LAS* 326 and respective note) stood at the feet of Virgo, *exactly opposite to Venus* (with longitude 176°,7; cf. Rev.7-11).[145] It can hardly be doubted that the remarkably accurate picture the writer gives about the positions of the planets at the moment concerned reflects a sound empirical and theoretical knowledge of celestial mechanisms; would he otherwise have risked his reputation by rejecting an observation which could have been proved correct within a couple of days? As in *LAS* 65, the emphatic rejection of the possibility that the rising planet might be Venus implies that the writer knew and fully utilized for his predictions the 8-year Venus cycle; in addition, he

---

142 This circumstance has more significance than would appear at the first glance. In my statistics, there are only 13 attestations of the "syllabic" spelling *áš/iš-pu-ra-an-(na-ši-)ni* against a total of 151 attestations of the "morphemic" spelling *áš/iš-pur-a(n-na-ši)-ni.*

143 Cf. *GAG* §§55h and b ("deverbale Abstrakta"; "Nomina actionis von hohlen Wurzeln").

144 The precative probably underlines the *hypothetical* nature of the statement, the planet itself being not visible owing to its proximity to the sun.

145 For *ina pūt* "opposite to" see *AHw*. 884f; cancel the translation "in front of" given in Pt.I.

may have had a theory about the angular velocity of Venus making it possible for him to compute the planet's longitude (roughly) at any given time. In the absence of positive evidence, the existence of such a theory as early as in the 7th century may seem unlikely. But the possibility in itself is definitely not excluded. Mesopotamian mathematics had for centuries been fully developed to cope with the simple artihmetic progressions used in the computation of the ephemerides of Seleucid times; empirical data on the motion of Venus had been available from Old Babylonian times on (*EAE* 63); and the idea of planetary velocity changing in a "zig-zag" fashion, forming the theoretical basis of the Mesopotamian mathematical astronomy, is already attested (albeit in a crude form) in a Sargonid ivory prism used for the computation of the length of daylight in different seasons.[146]

67

Bibliography:
(I) Waterman, *RCAE* 647.
(II) Schott, *ZA* 44 (1938) 195 ff.

Addressee:
Esarhaddon.

Date:
March 25 (= Nisannu 3), 671 BC. See note to Obv.10f.

Discussion:

Cf. note on *LAS* 334:3 ff. At least one extant copy of the universal namburbi[147] has actual observations inserted in the standard list of evil ominous happenings given in the Ea-Šamaš-Asalluḫi-section of this ritual. See K.3844 + 82-2-23,57 (= *CT* 41 23 = Ebeling, *RA* 48 12 ff; cf. Weidner, *AfO* 16 56), the relevant lines of which read as follows (Col. i 6-15):

> "In the evil of the [moon] who appeared on the 30th of Ulūlu; in the evil of Mars who entered Cancer, emerged, proceeded into Leo, and stood to the right and left, front and back of Regulus; in the evil of the AŠ.LI-star, the glowing fireball that was seen on the path of the Anu-stars, that passed onto the path of the Enlil-stars and set; in the [evil] of Saturn who tarried in the sky, exceeded its period and did not appear [. . .]; [in the evil of Adad] who thundered in the month of Ulūlu . . . "[148]

Other similar namburbis have not been preserved, but the practice of inserting details referring to a particular situation in the standard wording of canonical texts is well attested in copies of other (exorcistic) compositions. See notes to *LAS* 185:23 ff. and *LAS* 334.

Notes:

9. *ša ta-mar-*[*a-ti*] is a *casus pendens* anticipating *pi-šìr-šú-nu* restored at the end of Obv.14; cf. *LAS* 108:3' f and 15' f.

10 f. The restoration of these lines is hypothetical, but very likely in view of the continuation. The omen quoted in Rev.1 ff shows that either Jupiter or Mercury, or both of them, must have been mentioned here

---

[146] See Langdon, *BMSC* p.55 ff and van der Waerden, *Anfänge der Astronomie*, pp.87 ff and 141.

[147] NAM.BÚR.BI ḪUL DÙ.A.BI, to be read *namburbi lumni kalāma*, see Zimmern, *ZA* 30 (1915/16) 219, and cf. DÙ.A.BI = *ka-la-mu* Ḫḫ II 215, Antagal A 140 etc. This ritual is certainly intended in our letter (cf. *LAS* 334), but it is uncertain whether the word DÙ.A.BI should be restored in Obv.7. The break itself would definitely allow for more signs than ḪUL, but if "everything" is restored, it would be difficult to account for the "anything" in the next line.

[148] Cf. the standard version in VAT 13652 (= *RA* 48,6 ff), K.2784+ K.7593 (= *BMS* 62) and 80–7–19,123 + 83–1–18,177 (= Langdon, *TI* pl.4; the name of Esarhaddon appears on the obverse). The reference to Mars fits only three years in the Sargonid period, viz. 721, 674 and 642 BC. I am unable to make out with certainty which of these years is in question.

(for "the star of Marduk" as a name of Jupiter *and* Mercury at the beginning of the year, see Schott, *ZA* 43 [1936] 126 ff; cf. MUL ^{d}AMAR+UD = ^{MUL}UDU.IDIM.GU$_4$.UD, *CT* 25 13 iv 2 and *RMA* 91 r3; MUL ^{d}AMAR+UD *a-na* ^{d}GU$_4$.UD *i-qab-bi, 3 R* 53 No.1 66f = *ACh* Ištar 25:67 f; MUL ^{d}AMAR+UD = *ni-bi-ri, CT* 33 2 (Mul Apin); *né-be-ru AfO* 19 112:25 (Ḫḫ); also RMA 94:7-r1): actually the traces in these lines favour the latter alternative, and the same is also implied by the fact that "the star of Marduk" is said to be ***black***; since it was a known characteristic of Mercury to "turn black" all stars in its immediate vicinity,[149] a "blackout" of the ***star of Marduk itself*** actually presupposes a conjunction of Jupiter and Mercury. The restoration is further supported by the fact that the conjunction of Jupiter and Mercury was indeed considered an evil portent calling for an apotropaic ritual; see *RMA* 195:8 ff "If Jupiter and Mercury are conjoined, there will be misfortune in the land", and cf. our letter, Rev.4 ff.

A suitable conjunction indeed occurred during the attested floruit of Nabû-aḫḫē-erība (674-666 BC). On March 22, 671, Jupiter was rising heliacally in SW Fishes (longit. 335°.8, see App. C4). At the same time, Mercury was setting, also in SW Fishes, and eventually disappeared into the rays of the sun approximately on March 26, 671 (longit. 336°.0, see App. C1). Shortly before that date, both planets must have been seen rising from the horizon in close succession just before sunrise, Jupiter being soon blotted out by the rapidly approaching Mercury. The date of the conjunction may thus be set at appr. March 25 = Nisannu 3 (cf. App. A3), i.e. at the beginning of the year, just as the letter implies. All in all, the wording of the letter fully fits this conjunction, and as no other suitable conjunction seems to have taken place between 680 and 663 BC (cf. App. C), the date March 25, 671, thus obtained for the letter would appear to be certain. The letter would hence slightly predate Esarhaddon's second campaign to Egypt.

13. *da-rat a-ḫe-e-iš*: otherwise attested only in *RMA* 70:7, a report also written by Nabû-aḫḫē-erība. The meaning "after each other, in succession, successively" assigned to the expression by Thompson (*RMA* p. xlvi) seems certain on the following evidence:

2 ITU^{MEŠ} *da-rat a-ḫe-e-iš* ^{8} *u$_4$-mu ut-ter^{er}-ra, RMA* 70:7 f; cf.
4 ITU^{MEŠ}*i-da-at a-*[*ḫe-e-iš*] ^{5} *u$_4$-mu us-sa-lim, RMA* 84:4 f; cf.
2 UD^{ME} *i-da-at a-ḫe-*⸢*e*⸣-[*iš*] ^{7} *ina* TÙR ^{d}*30 it-ti-it-*[*zi*], *RMA*

106 r6 f (the last two reports also originating with Nabû-aḫḫē-erība). Hence *da-rat* = *i-da-at* "after"; whether the former is to be taken as a variant of *dāt* (*AHw.* 165*b*, *CAD* D 121*b*)[150] or whether two distinct words are in question cannot be made out on the basis of the extant evidence. The lemma **darat* has in any case to be added to the *AHw* and *CAD*, which have, curiously enough, overlooked both of the known attestations of the word.

r1-4. Quoted from Mul Apin, Tablet II. Cf. I [MUL]⸢^{d}⸣AMAR+UD MI-*ma* IGI.LAL [M]U.BI ⸢A⸣.[S]ÌG GAL-*ši, STT* 331 r. i 21; [I] MUL ^{d}AMAR+UD MI-*ma* IGI [. . . . .], *ACh* 2 Spl 67 iv 1.

r6. This line should probably be restored TA* IGI *a-ḫe-*⸢*e*⸣-[*iš pa-ti-u*] "they keep away from each other", i.e. there is a difference in latitude between them. Cf. *RMA* 88:8 ff, "Mars keeps at a distance of 4 fingers from Saturn, it has not approached it" (TA* IGI ^{MUL}UDU.IDIM.SAG.UŠ ^{9} *pa-a-te la iṭ-ḫi*); similarly *RMA* 112 r11 f, *la iq-ri-ib* ^{12} [T]A* *pa-ni-šú ip-ti-e-ti.* Cf. also *RMA* 212:6 f, ^{MUL}UDU.IDIM.GU$_4$.UD [^{MUL}*Dil-bat*] ^{7} TA* IGI *a-ḫe-e-iš* ^{8} *e-*[*ta-a*]*t-qu* "Mercury [and Venus] have parted from each other."

r7. Instead of *la di-ḫu*[151] (Pt.I), read *la ṭe-ḫu-*[*u-né*] "they do not approach (each other)" on the basis of the parallel *RMA* 88:9 quoted in the preceding note.

---

149 E.g. ^{MUL}GU$_4$.UD *ina* ŠÀ ^{MUL}UR.GU.LA ^{2} *it-ti-ti-zi* ^{3} I ^{MUL}UR.GU.LA MI ^{4} *lìb-bi* KUR NU DÙG.GA "Mercury is standing in Leo: 'If Leo is black, the land will not be happy' ", *RMA 228*:1-4; cf. *RMA* 199A and 219, and see also note to *LAS* 70 r7-10.

150 Theoretically, both *da-rat* and *da-at* could be taken as renderings of spoken [dā'at], cf. Oppenheim, *Or*NS 42 (1973) 324 on NB *ma-ra* for Aram. *mā'ā.*

151 This reading based on *KAR* 44:8, Á.SÌG.GIG.GA$^{di-'u}$ GIG-*tum*^{MEŠ}; cf. present letter, Rev.4 f.

68

Bibliography:

(I) Waterman, *RCAE* 1449.

(II) Kraus, *Symbolae Koschaker* (1939) 52[4]; Schott, *ZA* 44 (1938) 195.

Copy:

Cf. G. Smith, *3 R* 51 no.8.

Writer:

To judge from the gloss *li-si* in Obv.3, probably Nabû-aḫḫē-erība (cf. App. M 6; thus already Schott 1938); less likely Balasî, cf. discussion under *LAS* 66. The phrase MULSN *ú-di-na la in-na-mar* (r1-3) recurs in identical orthography in *LAS* 65 (assigned to Nabû-aḫḫē-erība) and 66 (assigned to Balasî).

Addressee:

Esarhaddon.

Discussion:

The astronomical data found in this letter are not sufficient for dating it absolutely, but they can nevertheless be used to pinpoint the dates on which the letter was *most likely* written. The fact is that the fixed stars mentioned in the letter are *simultaneously* visible only at certain, limited times of the year; in the Sargonid Era these times were, according to Schoch's *Planetentafeln* (1927), Sp. XLIV, as follows:[152]

(1)	January 1 through 17	(17 days)
(2)	May 7 through 12	(6 days)
(3)	July 19 through August 7	(22 days)
(4)	November 16 through 24	(9 days)

Of these four periods, the wording of the letter makes the first most probable (see note to Obv.8). Supposing now that the letter dates from between 674 and 666, as all other (datable) letters and reports of Nabû-aḫḫē-erība, one can eliminate from the roster of possible dates all those years in which *Mercury* was visible between January 1 and 17 (cf. Rev.1 ff), viz. 674, 673, 670, 667 and 666 (see App. 3A). This leaves the years 672-671 and 669-668, in which the visibility of Mercury at the time concerned was as follows:

672 Jan 1-17	= Kan 28 - Šab 14[153]	Mercury e first Jan 28	= Šab 25
671 Jan 1-17	= Kan 9-25	e first Jan 12	= Kan 20
669 Jan 1-17	= Kan 1-17	m first Jan 14	= Kan 14
668 Jan 1-17	= Kan 12-28	m first Jan 4	= Kan 15

Since the letter explicitly states that Mercury was not *yet* visible, it has to be assumed that it was expected to appear before any of the fixed stars mentioned disappeared, i.e. before January 17, which excludes year 672; on the other hand, since the fixed stars had, according to the letter, already been visible "previously" (i.e. for some time), year 668 would also seem to be out of the question, Mercury appearing then *already* on January 4. This would leave Kanūnu, 671, or 669, as the most probable dates of the letter.[154]

Addressee:

Probably Esarhaddon (cf. discussion above).

Notes:

1'ff. On the identification of the stars mentioned here (MULKAK.SI.SÁ = Sirus, MULLI$_9$.SI$_4$ = Antares, MUL*Be-lit*-TI.LA = Vega) see Gössmann, *Planetarium*, sub nos. 212, 253 and 52; on MULKAK.SI.SÁ cf. also van

152 For more details, see notes below.

153 The Assyrian dates given here are based on App.2C.

154 Sirius, Antares, Vega and Mercury are also mentioned in another letter (*ABL* 648) as gods to whom burnt offerings had to be made, possibly because of a portentuous Mars observation (as in *RMA* 89 r10 ff). Mars was retrograde in Kanūnu 671 and in conjunction with Saturn in Kanūnu 669.

der Waerden, *Anfänge der Astronomie* p.69. The risings and settings of these stars at the latitudes of Nineveh and Babylon have been tabulated by Schoch (*Planeten-Tafeln* Sp.XLIV); the relevant figures for the 7th century BC are as follows:

	e last	m first	cosmic setting	acron. rising
Sirius	May 12	Jul 19	Nov 24	Dec 31
Antares	Oct 8	Nov 15	May 7	Apr 28
Vega	Jan 17	Nov 16	Aug 7	Apr 29

These figures may be compared with the data given in Mul Apin and the "Astrolabe" (MUL^{MEŠ} 3.TA.ÀM):[155]

"On the 15th of Du'ūzu (= Jul 20), Sirius, Hydra and Leo appear", *CT* 33 pl.4 ii 42 (Mul Apin I);
"On the 15th of Du'ūzu, the brightest star of Perseus culminates and Sirius lights up", ibid. pl.7 iv 21;
"On the 15th of Du'ūzu, Sirius appears and Aquarius sets", *KAV* 218 i 19 (Astrolabe);
"In Ṭebētu (= January), Aquarius appears and Sirius sets", ibid. i 31;
"In Araḫsamna (= November), Scorpio appears and Perseus sets", ibid. ii 27;
"In Ajāru (= May), Perseus appears and Scorpio sets", ibid. 15;
"On the 15th of Araḫsamna (= November 20), Vega and [. . .] light up", *CT* 33 pl.4 iii 4;
"On the 15th of Araḫsamna, Coma Berenices culminates and Vega lights up", ibid. pl.7 iv 26;
"When Canis Maior and Regulus light up (i.e., on Ābu 5 = August 10, cf. ibid. ii 44), Vega sets", ibid. pl. 5 iii 19.

Note that the Babylonian texts record only the heliacal risings and cosmic settings, referred to with the terms *nanmuru*/*napāḫu* and *rabû* respectively. Cf. following note.

8'. *in-na-me-ru-ni*: the verb *nanmuru* can in astronomical contexts mean either broadly "to be seen, observed" (referring to any kind of astronomical observation) or more narrowly "to become visible" (referring to heliacal risings of heavenly bodies): both renderings are theoretically possible in the present instance, but the odds are for the latter alternative. Not only does *in-na-mar* in Rev.3 definitely refer to the heliacal rising of Mercury, but this narrower meaning of the verb is also best attested elsewhere in the present corpus (cf. 38 r14, 43:4'. 8'.10', 51:17, 65:15.20, 66:20, 69 r4, 70 r10.12, 290 r2, 300:6; broad meaning only in 81 r5, 172 r15 and 291 r18); moreover, in Mul Apin (as also in LAS 43), *nanmuru* is exclusively used in this sense in contexts dealing with fixed stars. Accordingly, it seems likely that the stars mentioned in the present letter had risen relatively recently, and since both Antares and Vega rose in the middle of November, and only Sirius in the summer, one can conclude that the letter was written either between November 16 and 24, or between January 1 and 17 (cf. Discussion). The statement that all the stars had been sighted "previously" (*ina pa-ni-ti*) makes the former period seem less likely (it is hardly thinkable that the astrologer would have twice within a week reported the same sightings to the king), though it does not of course, rule it out completely.

69+71

Bibliography:
(I) Waterman, *RCAE* 82 and 1396 (cf. III 373, IV 174, 207).
(II) Schott, *ZA* 44 (1938) 195 ff; Labat, *Royauté* (1939) 302, 305; Oppenheim, *JAOS* 61 (1941) 259; Nougayrol, *RA* 36 (1942) 37; Landsberger, *WO* 3 (1964) 76. – The join (by myself) dates from February 7, 1971; a new transliteration and translation of the whole text, collated (in 1971) by E. Sollberger, is given on p.374ff, but for convenience the line numeration of Pt. I will be retained in the following (true line numbers in parentheses).

Date:
Nisannu 1, eponym year of Šamaš-kāšid-ajābī = March 30, 669 BC. The day and month are obtained from ll. 8, 1' (11) and 2'(12) (cf. Rev. 10 ff and *LAS* 46); for the year, see under *LAS* 70.

[155] The dates of Mul Apin refer to the situation in 1000 BC, when the morning first of Aries (April 6) better agreed with the spring equinox (Nisannu 1).

A d d r e s s e e :
Esarhaddon.

D i s c u s s i o n :

This letter was written on the same day and deals with virtually the same matters as *LAS* 46 (from Balasî), q.v. Furthermore, it postdates only by *a day LAS* 70, another letter of Nabû-aḫḫe-erība dealing with the same matters. One should note that the possibility that the letters might refer to different (albeit similar) situations in *different* years can be safely excluded (see, in detail, commentary to *LAS* 70 – moreover, the existence of 70 did by no means render 69+71 or 46 superfluous!).

N o t e s :

9 f. That this indeed is a quotation from the king's speech is confirmed by Rev.1'-3' (14-16) and 70:9-11. Obviously, *mā* here introduces an *oratio obliqua*, not an *oratio recta* as usual in Neo-Assyrian.

2'-13' (12-23). This quotation runs roughly parallel to the corresponding paragraphs of the "hemerologies of Assur" (*KAV* 178 i 1-30 = Labat, *HMA* p.146 ff), but it also differs from these much enough to make it probable that a different (version of the same) composition is in question. The tradition represented by our passage is much worse known than that of Assur, but seems to be attested in at least two Kuyunjik fragments dealing with Tašrītu and an unidentified month (see K.3765 = Virolleaud, *Babyl.* 4 108, and K. 2607 + K.6482 + K.8068 = *AMT* 6,6 + *Babyl.* 1 204f; cf. also K.3769 and K.6482 = *Babyl.* 4 104 ff).[156]

r1-4. The wording of this passage suggests that it was quoted from a commentary (*mukallimtu*) appended to the hemerology in question (cf. *LAS* 12 r13 ff); the hypothetical commentary is not otherwise known.

r6 f. On the brightness of Mercury at the time concerned (stellar magnitude -0,9) see Table II on p. 79, and cf. the discussion ibid. On the equation Mercury = crown prince (here, = Šamaš-šumu-ukīn), see note to 46 r1.

r2' (15). On this prince see note to *LAS* 17:9.

r4' (17). Note that MUL*Dil-bat* is here (as well as in Rev.6'.7'.11'; 65:23, 66:9.20, 120:11 etc.) m a s c u l i n e (*-šú*), whereas it is f e m i n i n e in LAS 11:3'.r5', 65:7, etc. This gender variation may at least partly be due to the fact that Venus was hermaphroditic in relation to the sun, being masculine as morning star, but feminine as evening star. Cf. Ptolemy, *Tetrabiblos* I 6: "They say, too, that the stars become masculine and feminine according to their aspects to the sun, for when they are morning stars and precede the sun, they become masculine, and feminine when they are evening stars and follow the sun." That this doctrine was current in Mesopotamia appears for certain from *ACh* Ištar 8:8f, UL MÍ*-a-ta* d*Dil-bat : sin-ni-šá-at*: TA dUTU.ŠÚ.A [È] 9 UL NITÁ*-a-ta* d*Dil-bat : zi-ka-rat :* TA dUTU.È.A ⸢È⸣-[*ma*].[157] However, at the time our letter was written, Venus had just passed its superior conjunction and was due to appear within a fortnight as *evening* star (see Discussion of *LAS* 70); the curious fact that it is here referred to as *masculine* is hard to explain. Perhaps the gender was determined by the last observation, which in this case pertained to a morning star.

Venus was considered a benevolent planet but this alone hardly explains the importance attached to its rising here. Cf. the synopsis of Venus-omina given in Gössmann, *Planetarium* p. 37 ff.

r9' f. This statement agrees perfectly with the dating of the letter to Nisannu 1 = March 30. At that date, the sun was almost exactly in the middle of Aries, and was soon to blot out the entire constellation (see App. B);

156 These fragments are styled and worded very much like the present passage. Cf., e.g., NA *šu-a-ti* GIM dUTU [*na-me-er*] K.3765;5' (our Obv.18f); I UD *9.*KÁM *ana* SILA NU È ibid.2' (our Obv.20); I *ina* ITUKIN UD *10.*KÁM *ana 30 liš-ken* K.3769:12' (our Obv.21 f), etc.

157 The dual character of the goddess Ištar (1. goddess of war = masculine = Ištar of Agade; 2. goddess of love = feminine = Ištar of Uruk) is also evidence of the hermaphroditic nature of the planet. Its continuous change from masculine to feminine and vice versa also explains the prominent role of transvestite (or hermaphrodite) temple personnel in the cult of Ištar, cf. the discussion in *CAD* K 558 s.v. *kurgarrû*, and note *Sumer* 11 pl.6 r6: "It is within your power, Ištar, to change men into women and women into men."

on the other hand, the bright stars at the head of the constellation were due to emerge from the rays of the sun within two weeks, on April 9 = Nisannu 11 (see commentary on *LAS* 106 and cf. note on r11').

r11' (24). *uṣ-ṣu-su* =/uṣût-su/ "its coming out" (cf. *CAD* A/2 385*a* s.v. *aṣūtu*, where only Babylonian refs. are cited; for the geminated *ṣ* cf. *uṣ-ṣu-u* = /uṣû/ (Inf. *wṣī*), *RMA* 70 r6, and *uṣ-ṣu-u-ni* = /ūṣûni/, *LAS* 67:14, both texts also written by Nabû-aḫḫē-erība). Since the verb *wṣī* is well attested as a term referring to the rising of the sun (*CAD* A/2 367) and eastern rising of planets (*LAS* 67:14), it seems certain that the present passage refers to the impending heliacal rising of Aries; Venus was going to rise in the western horizon (cf. on r4') and is therefore out of consideration. As implied by the context, the rising of Aries was regarded as an omen advantageous to Assyria; cf. *ACh* 2 Spl. 75:1, "When Aries appears, the king of Amurru will be slain with weapon", and note that in *RMA* 44 r7, where the same apodosis is quoted (see note to 70 r7-10), it is referred to as "a good omen of the king, my lord".

70

Bibliography:

(I) Waterman, *RCAE* 1383.
(II) Labat, *Royauté* (1939) 335 and 364; Oppenheim, *JAOS* 64 (1944) 196.

Photo:

King, *Cat. Spl.* pl. 1 (Obv. only).

Addressee:

Esarhaddon.

Date and Discussion:

Addāru 27, eponymy of Šulmu-Bēl-lašme = March 26, 669 BC. This date can be established with absolute certainty from a combination of the following data:

[1] The letter refers to a prince resident in Babylon and expected to visit a king (who clearly is his father[158]) in Nineveh;
[2] The planet Mercury is visible in Aries; at the same time
[3] Venus is *said* to be visible in *Babylon but not in Nineveh*;[159]
[4] The letter is written at the turn of the year (cf. r13f);
[5] The last month of the year (Addāru) will be 30 days long; and
[6] The day on which the letter is written is specified as auspicious (see r6).

The prince resident in Babylon [1] can of course only be Šamaš-šumu-ukīn, so the letter must have been written between Ajāru 18 = May 20, 672 (the official date of his nomination as the crown prince of Babylon, see sub *LAS* q and 129) and Araḫsamna 10 = November 1, 669 BC (the date of Esarhaddon's death). These time brackets, supplemented by the other details [4-6] found in the letter, suffice for identification of the year in which the planetary situation [2-3] holds. The following synopsis presents the essence of the necessary information:[160]

158 Cf. the blessing r1-4 with *LAS* 69+71 r29-30, 145 r5-6, 151:11-13, etc., where the object of the blessing certainly is the king's son. Note also the parallel formulation of the king's query here and in *LAS* 69+71, 145, 146, etc.

159 An odd statement: at the time of the vernal equinox, Venus would have been equally well visible in Nineveh as in Babylon. Probably [*in*]-*na-mar* in r12 has to be understood as referring to the future ("Venus *will* be visible in Babylon", scil. at the time of the prince's return). In any case, the qualification "in Babylon" clearly implies that the planet could not be seen in Nineveh (and hence not in Babylon either).

160 To be on the safe side, the table is not limited to the period 672-669 but covers the whole reign of Esarhaddon and the first year of Assurbanipal as well. The indications of visibility (+) and invisibility (-) are based on App. C, computed by means of Schoch's tables (1928); the letter being written around the vernal equinox, it was taken for granted that the *arcus visionis* used in these tables also apply to the horizon of Nineveh. The relevant values are (cf. Schoch, p.103):

Superior Conjunction	m last	e first	*Inferior Conjunction*	e last	m first
Mercury	9.5	10.5	Mercury	11.0	13.0
Venus	6.0	6.0	Venus	5.2	5.7

TABLE I. *Visibility of Mercury and Venus on the last days of the Assyrian lunar years, 680-668 BC*

	MERCURY	VENUS
March 31, 680	-	+
March 20, 679	-	+
March 9, 678	+ (Pisces 314°)	+
March 27, 677	-	-
March 17, 676	-	+
April 5, 675	+ (Taurus 27°)	+
March 26, 674	+ (Aries/Taurus 14°)	+
March 14, 673	-	+
April 2, 672	+ (Pisces 343°)	+
March 22, 671	+ (Pisces 330°)	+
March 11, 670	+ (Pisces 325°)	+
March 29, 669	+ (Aries/Taurus 16°)	- (e first April 8, 669)
March 18, 668	+ (Aries 8°)	+ (m first December 30, 669)

Even a superficial glance at the table suffices to show that the year in question must be 669 BC; in all other cases one of the criteria listed above fails. Year 669 also meets the requirements of criterion [5], for it is known from *LAS* 45 that Addāru 669 was 30 days long. It is true, of course, that by March 29, 669, Mercury no longer was within the confines of Aries (354°-7°); the letter must accordingly be dated a couple of days earlier. Theoretically the date could be either Addāru 26, 27 or 28 (cf. Table II), but the explicit remark that the day concerned was auspicious [6] shows that is can only be the 27th (see note on r6). At that date Mercury (at 10°) was still reasonably near Aries to be placed "within" the constellation (cf. 65:12).

Obtaining a reliable date for the present letter is of considerable importance because the text is topically related to several other letters of the corpus: *LAS* 46, 65, 66, 69+71, and *RMA* 55 (all from Balasî and Nabû-aḫḫē-erība; for *RMA* 55 see sub *LAS* 12). These texts not only refer to the sighting of Mercury and the simultaneous invisibility of Venus at the turn of the year (above, [2], [3] and [4]) but three of them also mention the specific length of Addāru [5] and the planned visit of the prince [1]. It cannot hence be doubted that they all pertain to the same historical situation and were written within a very short period of time, particularly as the chronological indications found in the letters suffice for placing them all between Addāru 27 and Nisannu 1.[161] Checking the Mercury observations reported in the texts by computation gives the final proof of the correctness of their dating to March, 669:

TABLE II. *Visibility of Mercury, March 25 through April 1, 669 BC*[162]

Julian date	Mar 24	Mar 25	Mar 26	Mar 27	Mar 28	Mar 29	Mar 30	Mar 31	Apr 1
longitude	6.2°	8.2°	10.1°	12.1°	14.1°	16.1°	18.0°	20.0°	22.0°
elongation from Sun	9.5°	10.5°	11.5°	12.5°	13.5°	14.5°	15.5°	16.5°	17.5°
magnitude	-1.7	-1.6	-1.5	-1.4	-1.2	-1.1	-0.9	-0.8	-0.7
Assyrian date	Add 25	Add 26	Add 27	Add 28	Add 29	Add 30	Nis 1	Nis 2	Nis 3
Observational data	Addāru 24: Western rising of Mercury observed in Babylon (*LAS* 53) Addāru 25: Mercury sighted in Nineveh (*LAS* 12) Addāru 27: Sighting of Mercury confirmed for Nineveh (*LAS* 66 and 67) Addāru 27: Mercury visible in Aries (*LAS* 70) Addāru 29: Visibility of Mercury raised beyond any doubt (*RMA* 55) Nisannu 1: Mercury shining brightly (*LAS* 46, 69+71)[163]								

161 *LAS* 46 is with certainty datable to Addāru/March, 669, on the basis of the Mars observation referred to in it.

162 At the time of the year concerned (vernal equinox), Mercury's latitude has very little bearing on its visibility and the relevant data have therefore been omitted here as unessential. The longitudes, elongations and stellar

Interestingly enough, these 6 texts are not the only ones in the extant correspondence of Balasî and Nabû-aḫḫē-erība that can be dated to the end of Esarhaddon's 11th year; at least 8 other letters and reports, 5 of them authored by B. and N., date from the same time. The following list surveys the texts in chronological order.

	Text	Writer	Date
1.	*LAS* 54	Balasî + Nabû-aḫḫē-erība	Addāru 14
2.	*RMA* 88	Balasî	Addāru 16[164]
3.	*RMA* 103	Nabû-aḫḫē-erība	Addāru 16
4.	*RMA* 89	Akkullānu	Addāru 16
5.	*LAS* 45	Balasî	Addāru 23 (appr.)
6.	*LAS* 12	Ištar-šumu-ēreš	Addāru 25
7.	*LAS* 53	Balasî + Nabû-aḫḫē-erība	Addāru 26(?)
8.	*LAS* 65	[Nabû-aḫḫē-erība]	Addāru 27
9.	*LAS* 66	[Balasî]	Addāru 27
10.	*LAS* 70	Nabû-aḫḫē-erība	Addāru 27
11.	*RMA* 55	Balasî	Addāru 30
12.	*LAS* 69+71	Nabû-aḫḫē-erība	Nisannu 1
13.	*LAS* 46	Balasî	Nisannu 1
14.	*LAS* 106	[ ]	Nisannu 9

This list contains only letters and reports written by Assyrian astrologers; contemporary reports of their Babylonian colleagues (e.g., *RMA* 167, 172 [= Addāru 16] and 44 [= Addāru 30]) were excluded. From the viewpoint of the chronological analysis of the Ninevite royal correspondance, the most important conclusion to be drawn from the list is that at least some scholars could send to the king as many as ***6 letters in half a month***, a rate that is in no proportion to the time span covered by the corpus of letters that has come down to us.

Notes:

r6. *"This day is good"*: this remark settles the question as to whether the letter was written on the 26th, 27th or 28th of Addāru (cf. above); of the three days, only the 27th was auspicious, the others not. Cf. I ^{ITU}ŠE *1 2 4 5 6 8 9 10 11 12 14 15 16 20 23 24 25 27 30* ŠE "In the month Addāru: (the days) . . . (specified) are favourable", *KAR* 177 v 33-35; similarly *MIO* 5 314. Cf. Labat, *RA* 38 (1944) 21.

r7-10. Cf. *RMA* 44 r6 ff, [^{MUL}UDU.ID]IM.GU$_4$.UD *ina* ^{d}UTU.ŠÚ.A *ina* ŠÀ $^{\text{MUL.LÚ}}$ḪUN.GÁ ^{7}[*in-na-m*]*er* SIG$_5$ *šá* LUGAL *be-lí-ja* ^{8} [*šu-ú*] LUGAL MAR.TU^{KI} *ina* ^{GIŠ}TUKUL ŠUB-*ut* ^{9} [*e-mu-qu šá* LUGAL] *be-lí-ja šá ina* ^{KUR}*Mi-ṣir* ^{10} [. . . . .] *i-kaš-šá-du* "[Mer]cury [has bec]ome visible in the west in Aries: a good omen to the king, my lord. The king of the West will be slain with weapon;[165] (that means), [the troops of the king], my lord, which are (stationed) in Egypt, will conquer [. . . .]." There can hardly be any doubt that this report refers to exactly the same situation as the present letter: note the ref. to Assyrian troops in Egypt, which assures a date after 671 BC, and the omen quoted in Rev.3ff (I *30 ina* ^{ITU}]BARAG *ina* UD *1*.KÁM* IGI-*ir* . . . "If the moon is sighted in the month of Nisannu on the 1st day, etc."), which implies that the report was written in the beginning of Nisannu and that the preceding month Addāru had contained 30 days.

r11f. *"In Babylon, the house of his dynasty"*: this remark shows that the crown prince concerned was not Assurbanipal but his brother Šamaš-šumu-ukīn (the crown prince of Babylon). Evidently the prince was at

---

magnitudes given in the table were computed with the help of P.V. Neugebauer, *Genäherte Tafeln für Sonne und Planeten* (1932). The visibility of the planet has to be judged in the light of the *arcus visionis* ($\gamma = 10.5^{\circ}$) referred to above, which in this case virtually coincides with the elongation figure.

163 The reference to the luminosity of Mercury made in these letters agrees with the fact that the luminosity of this planet is at its greatest at superior conjunction, before the greatest elongation is reached.

164 For the dating of Nos.2-4 see Schaumberger, *ZA* 44 (1938) 283 ff.

165 More fully, "If Aries is black, the king of the Westland will be slain in a battle" (K.230 r11 etc., see Gössmann, *Planetarium* p.92a). Cf. note to 67:10 f, and 69 r11'. The prediction reflects the astrological doctrine according to which Aries was the star of Amurru, see e.g. *RMA* 101 r4, $^{\text{MUL.LÚ}}$ḪUN.GÁ MUL MAR.TU^{KI}.

the time concerned resident in Babylonia, a detail which lends additional support to the date of the letter established above, cf. note on 280:10f. For *bēt abi* = "dynasty" see *CAD* A/1 p.73 f, and note also É *a-ba-nu gab-bi* "all the dynasties (of Chaldea)" in *CT* 54 22 r28.

72

Bibliography:

(I) Waterman, *RCAE* 406 (cf. IV 180, 250); Pfeiffer, *SLA* 342.
(II) Behrens, *ABB* (1906) 82[1], 84; Schott, *ZA* 44 (1938) 194 ff; Labat, *Royauté* (1939) 307.

Copy:

Cf. Delitzsch, *AL* (1912) 90g.

Date:

Possibly Tašrītu = October, 670 BC. See note on Obv.7.

Addressee:

Esarhaddon (note the ref. to Aššur-mukīn-palē'a, formulated in a way implying that the king addressed was the father of the prince; cf. 186:13 ff, etc.).

Notes:

7. *qarêtu*: literally "invitation" (a *parast* formation from *qarû* "to invite", cf. *AHw* 917f) and therefore perhaps a general term for "party", especially "drinking party" (cf. kaš-dé-a = *qé-re-e-tum*, *MSL* 5 p.11:35 [Ḫḫ I], etc.), but here definitely referring to a religious service, a banquet offered to gods; cf. Obv.10 (*qarêtu* = *parṣu*) and Obv.16 ff. Such divine banquets fell into two categories: banquets arranged at regular intervals within the framework of the official cult, and ones offered by private individuals outside the official cult for a variety of personal reasons. The former, probably imitating banquet scenes described in mythological texts such as *Enuma Eliš* III 130 ff, V 124 ff, and VI 70 ff, took place in a chapel called *akītu*, which usually was situated outside the city (and in any case outside the temple proper[166]) and therefore always was an event of great publicity in that it regularly involved a procession of divine statues to the feast-house and back.[167] This public festival cannot be in question here because the text makes it clear that the party concerned was arranged at the king's wish at an unusual time. The private *qarêtu* is known from two fragmentary ritual texts (Ebeling, *PKTA* pls.21-22 and 22b) and a few scattered references elsewhere (*ABL* 1285 r23, *ina* É *Kid-mur-ri e-ta-rab*! *qa-re-e-tu e-ta-pa-áš* "I entered Bēt Kidmūri [the temple of Ištar in Calah] and gave a party"; *ADD* 680:7ff, *šu-ú* MÍ-*šú* [8] *qa-re-e*(text JA)-*ti* [9] *e-ta-ap-šú*(text ŠE) "he (and) his wife gave a party"; cf. also the references in the hemerology *KAR* 178 to a "party of Nisaba" to be feasted on Simānu 30 [Col. vi 5] and to a "party of the god" to be feasted on Simānu 24 [v 66] and Du'ūzu 15 [vi 39]). These parties were more modest than the public ones; the giver of the party, assisted by a priest, was expected to offer a relatively limited inventory of food and drinks to the god(s) of a single temple

[166] Cf. Postgate, *Sumer* 30 (1974) 51 ff. For passages linking *qarêtu* and *akītu* see *KAH* II 119:8f (É *a-ki-ti i-sin-ni* [9] *qé-re-ti* AN.ŠÁR) and Luckenbill, *OIP* p.136:25 ff (*i-sin-ni qé-re-ti šá* LUGAL DINGIR.MEŠ AN.ŠÁR [26] *šá* . . . É *a-ki-it* [27] EDIN); *ABL* 858:8 ff, *iš-ši-ja-a-ri qa-ret* DINGIR.MEŠ [9] ᵈ*taš-me-tum da-at-tu* [10] *tu-ṣa-a* [11] *ina* ŠÀ É *á-ki-ti* [12] *tu-ú-šab*. Cf. also van Driel, *CA* p.161 f.

[167] Cf. *ABL* 65, 113, 134, 213, 366, 427, 858, 876, 1103, 1197; *LAS* 271, 272, 281, 282, 311; ND 2765 = Iraq 17 pl.33; *CT* 53 500 and 965. The processions mentioned in these letters, which mostly also mention the *akītu* house, were certainly not all related to the *qarêtu* feast, and feasts of individual gods were certainly timed differently depending on ancient cultic traditions. A *qarêtu* par excellance was the sumptuous *tākultu* meal offered to all gods of Assyria simultaneously in all cities of the empire, probably in connection with the New Year's festival (cf. preceding footnote). The purpose of this meal, explicitly stated several times in the prayers noted down in the ritual instructions, was to reward the king and country with longevity, prosperity, safety etc. in return for the sumptuous offerings the gods received. See in more detail Frankena, *Tākultu* (1956) and idem, *BiOr* 18 (1961), 199 ff; van Driel, *CA* p.160 ff. For economic texts recording issues of sacrificial bread (*liḫmu*) for the *qarêtu* of Ištar of Arbela see BT 116 and 117 (*Iraq* 25, 86ff).

and to perform a sheep sacrifice; in return, he was promised "life, name (and) seed" (*PKTA* Pl.22:7'). The context in *ABL* 1285 referred to above makes it indeed probable that private parties were offered to the gods primarily in the hope of long(er) life, public recognition and (additional) children. As Esarhaddon definitely did not lack the latter two, it is likely that the party considered in the present letter was motivated by reasons of health. It may have become timely after Esarhaddon fell ill in May, 670, and was perhaps intended as a kind of thanksgiving feast after the king's recovery (June 670; see sub *LAS* 151). On these premises, a connection with the pilgrimage postponed in *LAS* 10 (written in Ulūlu = August, 670) does not seem impossible; note that Tašrītu (September/October) was the first auspicious month after the king's recovery in which the feast could be arranged (see following note).

9. *GARZA il-qí*: an allusion to *KAR* 177 ii 35 f, LUGAL GARZA^{MEŠ} TI-*qí* ^{ITU}BÁR ^{ITU}GUD 36 ^{ITU}SIG$_4$ ^{ITU}APIN ^{ITU}ZÍZ ^{ITU}ŠE ŠE "(If) the king arranges (lit. 'takes') a cultic festival, the months Nisannu, Ajāru, Simānu, Tašrītu, Araḫsamna, Šabāṭu (and) Addāru are auspicious"; cf. ibid. 37 f, GARZA^{MEŠ} TI-*qí* ^{ITU}BÁR ^{ITU}GUD 38 ^{ITU}SIG$_4$ ^{ITU}DU$_6$ ^{ITU}APIN ^{ITU}ZÍZ ^{ITU}ŠE ŠE "(If) he (= a private person) arranges a cultic festival, the months Nisannu etc. (the same months as above) are auspicious" A similar passage also in Labat, *Iqqur Īpuš*, p.102 f (Nisannu, Ajāru, Simannu, Ṭebētu, Šabāṭu and Addāru specified as auspicious months).

14f. This sequence of auspicious days is not attested for any of the months mentioned above (cf. Labat, *RA* 38, 20f); the copy (not collated) is therefore probably not in order. A very similar sequence is attested for Tašrītu and Ṭebētu (13 - 14 - 17).

r5. Cf. *LAS* 3 r3f. On *am-ma-te* ~*im-mat* (etc.) see note on 158:6. The compound *in(a)+mati* has in Neo-Assyrian completely replaced older *mati* so that even forms such as *a-di im-ma-ti* (*LAS* 51:12) are possible. There is a definite possibility that this *immati* (which probably was pronounced [emmat]) lives on in Neo-Aram. *emmat* (= Syr. *ematī*), see Kaufman, *AS* 19 (1974) 58.

73

Bibliography:

(I) Waterman, *RCAE* 83.

Date:

Early Du'ūzu, eponymy of Gabbāru = early July, 667 BC. This date is made likely by the reference to the muster (*ma-šar-te*, scil. of troops) in Obv.6.11, which can hardly be separated from a similar reference in a report of Nabû-aḫḫē-erība dealing with Mars retrograding and stopping in Scorpio (*RMA* 70 r4f): "It is a bad omen; the muster (*ma-šar-tú*) should be finished immediately, and the king should be wary of going out until we find out how it goes and stands". This report can be dated with absolutely certainty to Du'ūzu 1 = July 4, 667 BC (see sub *LAS* 13), and it is hence probable that the muster mentioned in it belonged to preparations for a military campaign to Egypt which is known to have taken place in 667 (see Grayson, *TCS* 5 p.128, entry for Šamaš-šumu-ukīn's 1st year). That the present letter indeed dates from the same year is confirmed by the phrase *ki ša ina* IGI LUGAL [4] EN-*ja ma-ḫe-er-u-ni* (r3 f) which recurs (in identical orthography) in another letter of Nabû-aḫḫē-erība written in Nisannu/April, 667 (*LAS* 60 r8). Since the present letter is a reply to a letter of the king concerning the muster (plausible occasioned by *RMA* 70), it should postdate *RMA* 70 by a couple of days.

Addressee:

Assurbanipal.

Notes:

6. *ma-šar-te*: sic, cancel the nonsensical *ma-ḫer-te* in Pt.I. See above, and note that the syllable /ḫer/ is consistently spelled *he-er* in Nabû-aḫḫē-erība's orthography (cf. 59 r10, 60 r9, 72 r6 and 73 r4').

9. *šá-da-at-tu-nu*: meaning obscure, perhaps a cultic locus or seat. Otherwise attested only in *ABL* 333: 6f, *ki-i* LUGAL EN *ina* ^{URU}*Arba-ìl* [7] *ina muḫ-ḫi šá-ad-da-tu-u-nu kam-mu-su-u-ni* "as the king, my lord, was 'sitt-

ing' in Arbela on the š." (context unclear), and in *AGS* 108;19, *lu-ú i-na* UGU *šad-at-tu-ú-ni a-šar áš-bu* "(will Esarhaddon be attacked) upon the š. where his is 'sitting'" (context: "or on the royal throne where he is sitting, or upon a chariot, or while entering or going out on foot", etc.).

74

Bibliography:
(I) Waterman, *RCAE* 81.

Addressee:
Probably Esarhaddon.

Discussion:

The observation reported in this letter (full moon on the 13th) was considered a bad omen (cf. *RMA* 120: 1ff, I UD *13*.KÁM *30 u* ᵈUTU ² KI *a-ḫa-meš* IGI^MEŠ ³ KA NU GI.NA *a-lak-ti la ṭa-ab-ti* ⁴ *ina* KUR GÁL-*ši* ⁵ ᴸᵁKÚR *ina* KUR TI-*qí* "If the moon and the sun are seen in opposition on the 13th day, talk will be dishonest, bad habits will prevail in the country, (and) the enemy will take (advantage) of the country"), and called for the performance of a namburbi ritual (cf. *LAS* 172 r13ff, *ina* UGU *ša* UD *13*.KÁM *an-ni-i* ᵈ*30* ᵈUTU *is-sa-he-'i-iš in-na-mᵒ-ru-u-ni dul-lu-šú ša e-pa-a-še i-ba-áš-ši*). The fact that the case is otherwise reported in only 5 astrological reports (*RMA* 120-123A), most of which may be contemporary, suggests that it was of relatively rare occurrence, and the present letter may thus possibly be contemporary with *LAS* 172, which dates from 672-671 BC. To approximately the same time must be assigned *RMA* 180, another report of Nabû-aḫḫē-erība referring to the case under consideration in retrospect: *ina* UGU *ša* ᵈ*30* UD *13*.KÁM *in-na-mer-u-ni* ⁸ *ina* UGU *šu-u* ᴹᵁᴸUDU.IDIM.SAG.UŠ *ina* TÙR ᵈ*30 it-ti-it-zi* "It is because the moon was seen (in opposition with the sun) on the 13th that Saturn (now) has stood in the halo of the moon" (Obv.7f).[168] The present letter was consequently probably addressed to Esarhaddon.

77

Bibliography:
(I) Waterman, *RCAE* 816.
(II) von Soden, *Fs Christian* (1956) 105; Kümmel, *StBoT* 3 (1967) 174 f.

Copy:
Cf. G. Smith, *3R* 51 no.7 and Zeitlin, *SACA* (1910) no.27.

Date:
Simānu 14, eponymy of Šamaš-kāšid-ajābī = June 10, 669 BC. Even though the writer does not specify the month and watch in which the lunar eclipse he reports occurred, the fact that the letter is addressed to the "Farmer" implies that the eclipse concerned was preceded by a solar one. *LAS* 31 shows that Nabû-šumu-iddina was a contemporary of Nabû-zēru-līšer, Adad-šumu-uṣur, Ištar-šumu-ēreš and Urad-Ea; hence the present letter can with certainty be placed between 681 and 663 BC (cf. Appendix 0), and within these time brackets, only one lunar eclipse, that of June 10, -668, was immediately preceded by a solar one. See App. E-F; that this eclipse indeed occurred on the 14th day, as stated in the letter, appears from *RMA* 271; cf. also *LAS* 25.

Addressee:
Esarhaddon.

---

[168] In addition to Saturn, the text states that Regulus also was observed in the halo of the moon. This situation was in the 7th century possible only in Esarhaddon's reign (any time between 677 and 672) and 30 years later in the reign of Assurbanipal. Cf. App. D.

79

Bibliography:
(I) Waterman, *RCAE* 62; Pfeiffer, *SLA* 190.
(II) Aro, *Or*NS 22 (1963) 403.

Copy:
T.G. Pinches, *An Outline of Assyrian Grammar* (London 1910), p.61.

Notes:

r4. *šùl-mu ina É a-na UN*^{MEŠ}: cf. *lu-u šùl-mu ina* AMA-*ja* "greetings to my mother", *KAV* 215:3; IM ^{I}DÙG-É-*Aš+šur* ^{2} *ina* É *gab-bi* "tablet of PN to the whole family", *KAV* 199:1f (but ibid. 3, *lu-u šùl-mu A-NA ka-na-šú-nu*); *šùl-mu a-na* É.KUR^{MEŠ} ^{5} [*šùl-m*]*u ina* ^{URU}*Kal-ḫa* ^{6} [*šùl-mu*] *a-na* ^{MÍ}É.GAL "the temples are well, the city of Calah is well, the queen [is well]", *ABL* 232:4 ff, etc. The free variation of *ina* and *a-na* in these and similar examples, viewed against the scarcity of the spellings <i-na> and <ana> in NA texts, shows quite clearly that the prepositions *ina* and *ana* had (partially?) merged in Neo-Assyrian. Cf. note to *LAS* 39 r3.

80

Bibliography:
(I) Waterman, *RCAE* 882 (cf. IV 190).

Date:
May 13, 650 BC. The style of the report indicates temporal proximity to the letters of Nergal-šumu-iddina (82-84), hence a date ca. 650 BC. Between 660 and 640 BC, only two eclipses took place in the evening watch: those of July 2, -651, and May 13, -649 (see Kudlek + Mickler, *AOATS* 1, p. 147). Of the former (total), only the final phase was observable, hence the letter most likely refers to the latter.

Addressee:
Assurbanipal.

83

Bibliography:
(I) Waterman, *RCAE* 908.
(II) Deller, *Or*NS 33 (1964) 95.

Date:
June 7, 651 BC. According to Kudlek and Mickler (*AOATS* 1, p.40), only three solar eclipses were visible in Nineveh at noontime (*ina muṣulāli*[169]), within the period 680-645 covered by the present correspondence:

[1] April 15, -656 (JDN = 1481558, PMA = 0.84, TM = 11:09)[170];
[2] June 7, -650 (JDN = 1483802, PMA = 0,72, TM = 12:50);
[3] April 6, -647 (JDN = 1484836, PMA = 0.77, TM = 11:33).

If the wording of our text is taken seriously, only [2] can be in question. As a matter of fact, we possess an accurate description of [1](*RMA* 277R), according to which this eclipse did not take place "at noon", but "2½ double-hours after the sunrise" (= 10:45).

Addressee:
Assurbanipal.

[169] For the anaptyctic *-u-* see note to *LAS* 39:11 (at the end).
[170] JDN = Julian day number (serving for identification of the curves in the map p.191); PMA = maximal magnitude; TM = local time at the middle of the occultation.

85

Bibliography:
(I) Waterman, *RCAE* 346; Pfeiffer, *SLA* 307.
(II) Kümmel, *StBoT* 3 (1967) 175; Oppenheim, *Centaurus* 14 (1969), 106, 117 and 131[40]; Postgate, *TCAE* (1974) 78.

Discussion:
See Oppenheim, loc. cit.

Notes:

3. For the reading *Kàl-zi* (not *Kak-zi*) see note to 86:3.*

13 ff. The relevant omen is given in full in *LAS* 319:1-8.

r6. $^{\text{LÚ*}}$*di-da-bé-e*: this word, missing both in *CAD* and *AHw*, also occurs in *LAS* 310:10' (^{LÚ}*di-di-bu-ú*), 341 r1 (^{LÚ}*di-da-bé-*[e]), and *CT* 53 890:2' ([^{L}]$^{\text{Ú*}}$*di-da-b*[*é-e*]); the translation "apprentice, pupil" suggested here is based on the contexts. The word is clearly a loan from Sumerian, cf. Ur III d i$_4$ - d a b$_5$ - b a "eine Klasse von Minderfreien, Arbeiter" (see Falkenstein, *NG* I pp. 83, 87, 96 ff s.v. (TUR.)TUR-dìb-ba; for TUR = d i$_4$ see Å. Sjöberg, *MNS* I p.19).

86

Bibliography:
Waterman, *RCAE* 1037.

Notes:

3. The spelling ^{URU}*Ki-li-zi* occurring here gives the correct reading of the GN ^{URU}DÙ-*zi* in *LAS* 85:3: ^{URU}*Kàl-zi* or, perhaps better, ^{URU}*Kali-zi*; one should at long last give up the reading ^{URU}*Kak-zi* hitherto preferred in Assyriological publications.[171] The evidence for the reading ^{URU}*Kàl(i)-zi* and against ^{URU}*Kak-zi* is in detail as follows:

[1] Nos. 85 and 86 are virtual duplicates; consequently, the spellings ^{URU}*Ki-li-zi* and ^{URU}DÙ-*zi* are most naturally regarded as orthographic variants of the same city name.

[2] There are no explicit spellings justifying the reading *Kakzi*; the sign DÙ can equally well be read *kàl* (*kali*) as *kak* (*kaq, qaq*). Note that the syllabic value DÙ = *kàl* is well attested in spellings of the GN Calah: e.g. ^{URU}*Kàl-ḫa*, *ABL* 175:9, 211 r9, *ADD* 676:3; ^{URU}*Kàl-ḫi*, ADD 208:16, AR 31:4.5, *STT* 46 r35; ^{URU}*Kàl-ḫu*, *ABL* 545 r4; ^{URU}*Kàl-laḫ*$_4$, 3 R 2 no.5:5, etc., see *AOAT* 6, p.192. For the phonetic value DÙ = *kali* note, e.g., DINGIR^{MEŠ} KUR.KUR DÙ-*šú-nu*, *LAS* 126 r5, to be compared with DINGIR^{MEŠ} KUR.KUR^{MEŠ} *ka-li-šú-*[*nu*], *LAS* 123:17, etc.

[3] There are no other attestations of ^{URU}*Ki-li-zi* in Neo-Assyrian texts. Should this town be distinct from ^{URU}DÙ-*zi*, it would necessarily have been a pretty insignificant place, and could impossibly have housed a whole team of astrologers sending reports to the king. As appears from App. Q5 (and *LAS* 1), astronomical observations were indeed communicated to the court only from the major cities of Assyria (Nineveh, Assur, Calah, Arbela, ^{URU}DÙ-*zi*, Babylon, Borsippa, etc.); the reason is that professional astrologers necessarily needed a large stock of reference books (not available in every city) both for their daily use and teaching purposes (cf. *LAS* 85 r6 ff!), and above all, a ***carefully oriented observatory***, preferably a temple tower (only available in larger cities). These facilities were provided by ^{URU}DÙ-*zi* = mod. Qaṣr Šamāmok (see Furlani, *RSO* 15 [1935] 119), an im-

[171] The popularity of the reading *Kakzi* is illustrated e.g. by R. Ellis, *A Bibliography of Mesopotamian Archaeological Sites* (1972) p.74, s.v. Shimmama. The reading *Kalzi* is found in some publications (e.g., Thompson, *RMA* II [1900] p.136a; Schlobies, *MAOG* 1/3 p.20; Ebeling, *Or*NS 21 [1952] 129; Frankena, *Tākultu* [1954], p.120; Postgate, *NARGD* [1969], p.137), but has never been generally accepted.

pressive tell with remains of a temple tower, and known as an important cultic centre in the Neo-Assyrian period (see *AOAT* 6, p.193 f).

[4] There are no attestations of ^{URU}DÙ-*zi* in Old- and Middle-Assyrian texts; yet the size of Qaṣr Šamāmok implies that it must have been a significant place long before Neo-Assyrian times. On the other hand, the city *Kilizi/Kalizi* does figure in texts from the second millennium, and what is important, the available indications as to the location of this city are in accordance with its proposed identification with Qaṣr Šamāmok. See W. Hallo, *JCS* 18 (1964) 57 ff, §§70-71 (and relevant notes); E. Weidner, *AfO* 10 (1935) 21[172] and 21 (1963) 115 f.

For the *a/i* interchange in *Kalizi/Kilizi* see note to *LAS* 39 r3.

92

Bibliography:
(I) Waterman, *RCAE* 142; Pfeiffer, *SLA* 332.
(II) Oppenheim, *Centaurus* 14 (1969) 129, n.21.

Copy:
Delitzsch, *AL*^{5} (1912), 88a.

Discussion:

The incident reported in this letter was no doubt considered ominous – otherwise it would hardly have been reported to the king –, though I have not been able to identify the pertinent interpretation. No omens concerning foxes are included in Nötscher's edition of *Šumma ālu*[173]; for omens concerning wells, see *Šumma ālu*, Tablet XVII (*CT* 38 22-24). Note that a similar incident (fox entering Babylon) is also recorded in the astronomical diary VAT 4956 (= Weidner, *AfO* 16 [1953] Tf. XVII, Nisan) dating from the 37th year of Nebuchadnezzar (568 BC).

93

Bibliography:
(I) Waterman, *RCAE* 432.

Date:
December 17, 670 (or June 11, 669?). The identification of the lunar eclipse reported in this letter is facilitated by the existence of *LAS* 94, which quite obviously dates from approximately the same time (cf. *LAS* 96-99!), and can be assigned to years 672-669 BC on the ground of the fact that it is addressed to the crown prince (Assurbanipal; see note on 173:17). Only two lunar eclipses occurred in the morning watch within these years: those of December 17, -669, and June 11, -668. Of these two alternatives, the former is more probable; for one would expect the letter to be addressed to the "Farmer", were the latter in question (see on *LAS* 77). However, since the letter was sent from Arbela, it is not certain that the writer knew what was going at court, so the latter alternative cannot be certainly excluded.

Addressee:
Esarhaddon.

---

[172] Cf. ibid. fn.148: "Die Listen, in denen immer die gleiche Reihenfolge eingehalten wird, führen auf: die Städte Arba'il, Kilizu, Ḫalaḫḫu, Rimuššu . . ."

[173] If any fox-omens existed, which is by all means probable, these were certainly included in *Šumma ālu*, possibly in Tablets XXVIII-XXX or XLIII-XLIV (missing in Nötscher's edition).

94

Bibliography:
(I) Waterman, *RCAE* 982.

Date:
670 BC? Cf. commentary on the preceding letter; and see sub *LAS* 246, at the end of the discussion section, for the possibility that the letter was written during Esarhaddon's illness in mid-670 BC.

95

[Now joined to K 4719, a letter from [LÚ]GAL-*da-ni-ba-te*, and hence to be excluded from the present corpus.]

96

Bibliography:
(I) Waterman, *RCAE* 423 (cf. IV 252); Pfeiffer, *SLA* 298.
(II) Weidner, *OLZ* 15 (1915) 458; Labat, *Royauté* (1939) 213; Oppenheim, *Centaurus* 14 (1969) 106f.

Addressee:
Assurbanipal.

Date:
Addāru 1, eponymy of Sagab = March 1, 650 BC. Cf. App.A2.

97

Bibliography:
(I) Waterman, *RCAE* 829 (cf. IV 262); Pfeiffer, *SLA* 301.
(II) Ylvisaker, *LSS* 5/6 (1912) 70; Oppenheim, *Centaurus* 14 (1969) 106.

Copy:
Cf. G. Smith, *3R* 51 no.6; Delitzsch, *AL*[5] (1912) 92c; Zeitlin, *SACA* (1910) no. 26.

Photo:
RCAE IV pl.14 (obv. only).

Date:
Šabāṭu 1, eponymy of Bēl-Ḫarrān-šadû'a = January 21, 649 BC. Cf. App. A2.

Addressee:
Assurbanipal.

98

Bibliography:
Waterman, *RCAE* 671 (cf. IV 259); Pfeiffer, *SLA* 299.

Copy:
Cf. G. Smith, *3 R* 51 no.5; Zeitlin, *SACA* (1910) no. 25.

Photograph:
RCAE IV pl.13 (obverse only).

Date:
Du'ūzu 2, eponymy of Bēlšunu = July 5, 648 BC.

Addressee:
Assurbanipal.

100

Bibliography:
Previously unpublished.

Copy:
CT 53 pl.17 no.45.

Discussion:

In spite of its smallness, this fragment is significant in that it explains the meaning of a curious omen frequently quoted in astrological reports dealing with the appearance of the lunar crescent: I u_4-*mu a-na mi-na-ti-šú e-ri-ik* [4] BAL UD^MEŠ^ GÍD^MEŠ^,[174] usually translated "If the daylight is longer than its normal measure, there will be a reign of long duration" (*CAD* A/2 [1968] 224a and 285a; cf. *AHw* 64a "Wenn der Tag länger als (jeweils) normal dauert"). What this is supposed to mean remains obscure; *AHw*'s reference to Thompson, *RMA* p.117a explains nothing. Mesopotamian days lasted from sunset to sunset; they were hence true solar days, whose "normal measure" remained *unchanged* throughout the year – at least as far as the Assyrians could ascertain.[175] They had of course noticed the *seasonal* variation of the daylight, but the possibility is excluded that the omen concerned would simply refer to a "long" daylight exceeding the mean value of 12 hours.[176] Its explanation is rather to be sought in the fact that it is tightly linked with another omen referring to the appearance of the lunar crescent on the 1st of the month.[177] It appears a priori thinkable that the *last days* of the months were continued until the *sighting* of the crescent, being thus prolonged by an hour (approximately) over the "normal measure". However, this would leave unexplained why the omen is *never* quoted when the crescent is reported to have been observed on the 30th.[178] Moreover, it is perfectly clear that the days at the end of the month ended at sunset as normally; this is implied by the fact that the crescent terminating a 29-day month is said to have appeared on the 30th, not the 1st day of the following month.[179]

The puzzle is solved by the present fragment in which it is stated that *the 30th day became long because the (moon)god was not seen on the 30th.* Had the crescent been sighted, the day would obviously have become "short". In other words, there were two kinds of the 30th day: a "short" one, lasting about an hour only, and a "long" one, left "intact" by the moon god. Such a terminology is actually quite understandable in a lunar calendar in which the lengths of the months were determined not by computation but by actual observations. The omen in question must accordingly be translated: "If the (30th) day is lengthened to its (full) measure, there will be a reign of long duration." It is thus an equivalent of the idiom *Sîn ūmu ušallam* "the moon will supply (perhaps better: leave intact) the (30th) day" (opposite: *Sîn ūmu utarra* "the moon will repudiate the day") discussed in note to *LAS* 45 r8 f. Note *RMA* 36:1 ff, I u_4-*mu ana [minâtīšu īrik]* [2] BALA *[ūmī arkūti]* [3] *mi-na-at* ITU UD *30.*KÁM* *ú-šal-l[am]* "If the day [is lengthened] to [its full measure, there will be] a reign [of long duration]. (This means that) the 30th day completes the measure of the month." A similar comment is found in *RMA* 256 A: *an-ni-ú ta-mar-tú ša* UD *1.*[KÁM] "(If the moon etc.; if the day etc.): this pertains to the observation of (the moon on) the 1st day" (Obv.4). [The omen is once (*RMA* 135) quoted in a context other than the sighting of the crescent on the 1st day, viz. after full moon on the 14th; but the report in question was not written by a professional

[174] *RMA* 7:3-4; similarly (with slight orthographic variants) *RMA* 1-6, 8-22, and *passim*.

[175] The difference between the longest and shortest solar day is only 54 seconds, hardly to be detected by the inaccurate chronometers employed by the Assyrians.

[176] Cf. *RMA* 266, written in the month Kanūnu (December/January).

[177] I *30* UD *1.*KÁM IGI.LAL [2] KA GI.NA ŠÀ.KUR DÙG-*ab* "If the moon appears on the 1st, talk will be reliable and the country will be happy", *RMA* 21:1-2, etc. This omen always precedes the omen under consideration.

[178] See *RMA* 61-81, etc.

[179] It remains unclear, however, why *LAS* 91, 96-99, 102 etc invariably refer to watch of the moon on *the 29th.*

astrologer but by an exorcist (Adad-šumu-uṣur), so this exceptional case is probably simply due to a misunderstanding.]

101

Bibliography:
(I) Waterman, *RCAE* 1392; Pfeiffer, *SLA* 311.
(II) Labat, *Royauté* (1939) 213; Oppenheim, *JAOS* 64 (1944) 196.

Date:
Probably December 27, 670, or October 15, 667; less likely June 10, 669 BC. Cf. App. F1 for eclipses observable in the morning watch between 680 and 663 BC; the ref. to clouds points to winter or autumn rather than summertime.

102

Bibliography:
Previously unpublished.

Copy:
CT 53 pl.70 no.234.

Senders:
The scribes of Kalizi. This appears with full certainty from the handwriting, which is identical with that of *LAS* 86 (personal collation, May 6, 1974); see also note on Obv.1'f. The format of the tablet resembles that of *LAS* 86, which could provide the missing beginning of the letter, but the fragments do not join and actually do not seem to be parts of the same tablet.

Notes:

1'f. The tablet actually reads 1' *lik-ru-b*]*u*! 2' *m*[*a*!-*ṣar*]-⌜*tú*!⌝⌜*šá*!⌝ $^{d!}$*30*! 3' *ni-ta-ṣar* (cf. copy). This way of introducing a lunar observation is otherwise attested only in *LAS* 85-86.

6'ff. Restore (probably) *ki-ma ip-*[*ta-šar* ^{d}*3*]*0* 7' *né-ta-m*[*ar* (*la*) *a-ki* ^{d}]*30*! 8' *šá* UD *2*⌜*9*⌝.[KÁM* *šu*]-*u* 9' UD *3*.KÁM* (sic) [. . . .] ⌜1 *is-*[*ṣu-ri* . . . .] "when they dis[persed], we saw [the m]oon; [it] was [(not) like the] moon of the 29[th day]. The 3rd day (*or* three days) [. . . . .]. Per[haps . . . . " Cf. *LAS* 119 and relevant commentary; Obv.9' is possibly to be taken as a reference to the duration of the preceding *ūm bubbuli*.

104

Bibliography:
(I) Waterman, *RCAE* 470; Pfeiffer, *SLA* 275.
(II) Behrens, *ABB* (1906) 97; Dhorme, *RHR* 116 (1937) 17f; Labat, *Royauté* (1939) 334, 338; Oppenheim, *Centaurus* 14 (1969) 118.

Addressee:
Esarhaddon.

Date:
Ajāru 29[180], eponym year of Šamaš-kāšid-ajābi = May 27, 669 BC. The dating of this letter is made possible by the happy circumstance that only one solar eclipse was observable in Nineveh at sunrise in the reigns of Esarhad-

[180] The equation May 27 = Ajāru 29 is based on the *Table of Julian and Assyrian correlations* in App.A3. As a matter of fact, the report *RMA* 269, also referring to a solar eclipse at sunrise, explicitly states that the eclipse

don and Assurbanipal[181]; see Kudlek – Mickler, *AOATS* 1, p.40. The magnitude of the occultation at sunrise given ibid. (PMA = 0.17 at 4.92 a.m.) corresponds exactly to the value 2 fingers mentioned in our text.[182]

Notes:

8f. Cf. NAM.BÚR.BI-*šú-nu* [7] *i-ba-áš-ši* "there is an apotropaic ritual available against them", *ABL* 367 r6 f (referring to fungus and lichen on wall); [NAM.BÚR].BI-*šú la ib-ši* "there is no apotropaic ritual against this case", *LAS* 109:13' (referring to a 'dark' sunrise). The present passage could also be translated "its apotropaic ritual is not like that of a lunar eclipse", cf. the note on *laššu + lā* sub *LAS* 185:21 f. The implications of this remark remain unclear. It is true that the *Bīt rimki* ritual was performed only in the case of lunar eclipses, but the "universal" namburbi as well as the substitute king ritual also applied to solar eclipses and especially the one under consideration. Cf. *LAS* 28.

12. The omens relative to the eclipse in question are given in *RMA* 269. They were generally favourable, but one (Rev.9) portended death to the kings of Subartu (= Assyria) and Amurru and thus required the entronement of a substitute king.

105

Bibliography:
Waterman, *RCAE* 1444; Schaumberger, *ZA* 47 (1941-42) 127. Cf. Schaumberger, *ZA* 50 (1952) 220 f.

Addressee:
Sîn-šarru-iškun.

Date:
Simānu 14 = April 22, 621 BC. This date is of course derived from the eclipse reported in the letter, on whose identification see in detail Schaumberger 1952. The fact, however, that Schaumberger overlooked in his argumentation the Assyrian date Simānu 14 given in the tablet (miscopied by Harper/Waterman) makes the identification hard to accept at the first sight, and so necessitates a renewed analysis of the total evidence here. For if the correlation Simānu 14 = April 22 is accepted, the year 621 would have begun already on February 9 – an incredibly early date in view of the general rule that the beginning of the year had to be kept as close to the vernal equinox (March 28) as possible.[183] So early a New Year's day would imply that the ruling king had neglected his duty to keep the calendar up to date for several years, which is unlikely even in the stormy last years of the Assyrian empire.[184] It is hence of absolutely necessity to verify Schaumberger's (ungrounded) allegation that the description of the eclipse fits only one eclipse in the 7th century. The following chart[185] includes all those lunar eclipses visible in Nineveh from 700 to 612 which took place at a suitable time of the year[186] or in the constellation of Scorpio. The data of the present letter are given at the top of the chart to facilitate comparison.

---

took place on this date. One of the omens quoted in this report would seem to indicate that the eclipse was annular and hence rather to be identified with that of June 27,-660, but that particular eclipse occurred in the afternoon and is consequently out of the question.

181 A date later than 630 BC is excluded by the reference to Akkullānu in Obv.3.

182 For 1 "finger" = 1/10 (or 1/12) of apparent solar and lunar diameter, cf. Kugler, *SSB* II 17 and 61f, and van der Waerden, *Anfänge der Astronomie* (1968), 146.

183 See App.A. The earliest date to start a year between 626 BC and A.D. 75 was March 6 (in the 19th year of Nabopolassar = 607), see Parker-Dubberstein, *Babylonian Chronology*, p.27 ff. No year in Esarhaddon's reign began earlier than March 12, see App.A2.

184 The political situation in Assyria had more or less stabilized already in 625 after the turbulent period of anarchy following Assurbanipal's death (or dethronement); see von Soden, *ZA* 58 (1967) 241 ff. Moreover, the very existence of detailed eclipse reports of the present kind would seem to imply that intercalation of the year was not neglected at the time concerned.

185 Based in the main on the eclipse canon of Kudlek and Mickler, *AOATS* 1 (1971), p.146 f. The stellar positions are those given in P.V. Neugebauer, Tafeln zur astronomischen Chronologie I. *Sterntafeln von 4000 vor Chr. bis zur Gegenwart* (Leipzig 1912).

186 The ultimate possible limits for Simānu 14 are taken to be May 12 and July 2 (presupposing years starting on March 1 or April 23, respectively).

1. The eclipse as described in the present text

Date:	Simānu 14, implying that JD = May 12 to July 2
Place:	Scorpio, implying that L = 20°-50°[187]
Time:	Morning watch, implying that TM > 2.30[188]
Magnitude:	2 fingers, implying that PMA = appr. 0.2[189]
Eclipsed quadrant:	South, implying that P < 180.0 or > 360.0[190]
Culminating constellation:	δ Cygni (right ascension = 273.8)[191]

2. Eclipses to be considered

JD	L	TM	PMA	P	A.R. of culminating constellation
697 May 21	52.3	18.73	*0.27*	169.7	152.7
695 May 1	*32.2*	*3.89*	0.73	187.2	*270.5*
688 Jun 10	71.5	*2.11*	1.24	4.1	*283.1*
686 Apr 21	*23.4*	*3.07*	0.56	351.9	249.0
*679 Jun 2	62.7	*2.15*	*0.14*	*168.8*	*274.9*
678 May 22	52.7	19.35	1.51	177.6	162.6
671 Jul 2	92.1	21.02	1.48	182.1	227.7
*669 Jun 11	71.8	*2.33*	*0.05*	*11.9*	*286.8*
667 Apr 21	*23.4*	18.60	1.78	356.6	121.8
660 Jun 2	63.1	*2.78*	1.37	176.7	*285.4*
659 May 22	53.0	18.49	1.00	185.4	151.0
652 Jul 2	92.4	16.88	1.51	2.4	166.3
650 May 13	*44.3*	17.64	*0.27*	350.3	128.4
649 May 1	*33.9*	1.43	1.64	358.8	234.7
648 Apr 21	*23.2*	2.89	0.62	*6.9*	245.9
641 Jun 1	63.5	1.72	1.14	184.5	*268.4*
633 Jul 2	92.8	17.35	*0.31*	*10.2*	173.3
632 May 24	54.7	0.75	*0.12*	349.4	245.5
631 May 13	*44.3*	(8.11)	1.48	357.9	345.5
624 Jun 23	84.0	17.74	1.10	174.9	169.6
*621 Apr 22	*24.7*	*5.04*	*0.16*	*170.5*	*280.0*
612 May 12	*44.0*	(15.84)	0.93	*5.0*	102.2

It appears that besides the eclipse of April 621, only those of June 679 and 669 (marked with *) correspond closely enough to the description given in our letter to deserve serious attention. Both have the disadvantage that they did not take place in Scorpio, but in the adjacent constellation of Sagittarius; in addition, the eclipse of June 669 measured *1* finger rather than 2[192], and the star culminating in the middle phase of the eclipse was not δ but α Cygni (= Deneb), though these latter discrepancies with the text are perhaps not serious.[193] In any

[187] L = solar length at true conjunction. The *constellation* of Scorpio extends from δ Scorpii (A.R. = 203.2 in the 7th cent. B.C.) to G Scorpii (A.R. = 224.5); the *area* of Scorpion may however be allowed the extent 200-230° in view of the limits of the adjacent constellations (τ Librae = 197.0, γ Sagittarii – 230.0).

[188] TM = middle of occultation in true local time (in hours and fractional parts of them). The value 2.30^h represents the average beginning of the morning watch in Simānu; however, according to the ivory prism of Nineveh, the morning watch began in Nineveh 3 double-hours and 3,3 Assyrian minutes after sunset, i.e. at 1.33^h.

[189] PMA = maximal magnitude of occultation. If PMA < 1, the eclipse is partial, otherwise total.

[190] P = distance of the moon from the ascending node at true conjunction, in degrees.

[191] For the identification of the *kumāru* of Panther as δ Cygni see note to r2 f.

[192] The *Spezieller Kanon* of Neugebauer (1934) gives this eclipse the magnitude of 1 inch (= 1/12 of the apparent lunar diameter); the canon of Oppolzer (1887) reckons with a magnitude of 1,3 inches.

[193] The eclipse magnitudes given in Mesopotamian texts were only estimates and must be treated as such; see van der Waerden, *Anfänge der Astronomie*, p.101. As for the culminating constellation, we do not know whether it was observed at the beginning or the middle of the eclipse, though the *latter* alternative seems more probable.

case, the single advantage of these two early eclipses over that of April, 621, is that their Julian dates can with certainty be shown to correspond to the date Simānu 14 mentioned in the letter.[194] Under these circumstances, the choice between the three alternatives is clear; if the eclipses of June 679 or 669 are chosen, a serious observational error (Scorpio for Sagittarius) has to be assumed;[195] and since such an error is very hard to accept, one is left with the eclipse of April 621, despite the chronological problem mentioned above. This makes the present letter by far the latest letter of the present corpus, and one of the very few extant letters to Sîn-šarru-iškun known to date (cf. *ABL* 412, 469, 815, 1089, 1365 and 1366, all probably found in Calah).

Discussion:

This letter differs from the vast majority of the other Sargonid eclipse reports in one significant respect: it does not contain any omens, but gives only astronomically relevant information. Two other similar reports are known, both unfortunately fragmentary; see *LAS* 80 an 84.[196] The reason why we do not have more such reports from the Sargonid period is probably quite simply that the Assyrian rulers were not interested in purely astronomical matters but preferred interpreted omens. It would thus seem risky to draw from the scarcity of strictly observational astronomical texts in the Sargonid period the conclusion that the Sargonid ***astrologers*** themselves did not keep astronomical "diaries" (such as are known from the later periods; see e.g. B.L. van der Waerden, *Anfänge der Astronomie* (1968), 101 ff) for their own private purposes. The present letter, closely resembling Seleucid observation texts, though less specific, shows that such "diaries" may perfectly well have existed. As a matter of fact, at least one Sargonid observation text has actually been preserved (though not previously recognized as such): *ABL* 1408, containing observations on the risings and settings of the moon from the 11th to the [15th⸣(?) day of a month, and reading as follows:

ABL 1408 (Sm 2147)

Obverse	1	[ ] *u ni ri*
	2	[UD 29?.KÁM] AN.MI ^{d}UTU GAR-*an*
	3	[UD 1?].KÁM* *30* IGI
	4	[MI] *šá* UD *11*.KÁM
	5	[UD].ZAL *30* È
	6	[ ] UD *11*.KÁM
	7	[ ]-*i ma-'a-ad 30* ŠÚ
	8	[M]I! *šá* UD *12*.KÁM
Edge	9	[ ] UD.ZAL *30* È
Reverse	1	[UD *1*]2.KÁM IM.DIR GAR ŠÚ-*pat 30* NU IGI
	2	[ ]X MI *šá* UD *13*.KÁM
	3	[EN.NUN] UD.ZAL *30* È
	4	[UD *1*]3 IM.DIR GAR NU IGI
	5	[ ] *30* DIB
	6	[ ] MI *šá* UD *14*
	7	[EN.NUN UD].ZAL *30* È NIGÍN-*rat la iš-šur*
	8	[UD]⸢*15*⸣?.KÁM* X[X *i*]*na* IGI *20* DU

That this text (in the oblong form of the reports) refers to actual observations is clearly indicated by Obv.7 and Rev.1 ff, where we read: "(On the 11th day . . .), there was much [ ], the moon set; — on the 12th day, there were clouds, the weather was dusky and the moon was not seen; the moon came out (only) [ ] in the night of the 13th day, [in the] morning [watch]. The 13th day was cloudy, (the moon) was not seen; [the rising] of the moon passed by. [ ] In the night of the 14th day, the moon emerged in the [mo]rning ⸢watch; it was round(?) (*saḫrat*), it did not wane. [On the 1]5th(?) day [the moon] walked before the sun."

[194] See App.A2 and *RMA* 271.

[195] Sagittarius was called "the sting of Scorpio" (*zi-qit* ^{MUL}GÍR.TAB EN GAL-*ú* ^{MUL}PA.BIL.SAG, *RMA* 272:9), but it seems far-fetched to resort to such an interpretation here.

[196] It is not excluded that the present letter was written by either of the authors of these texts.

We should undoubtedly possess more similar texts if systematic excavations had ever been carried out in the downtown of Nineveh, where the houses of the leading astrologers were situated.

Notes:

r2 f. The *kumāru* of "Panther" (cf. U[D].KA.DU$_8$.⌜A⌝ = *nim-ru* "Panther", Nabnītu XXII 265) has been variously identified as γ, β, δ, or η Cygni; see Gössmann, *Planetarium* p.60 (with literature) and Schaumberger, *ZA* 50 (1952) 220f. Absolute preference must be given to the identification with δ Cygni, since the ancient sources explicitly state that the difference in right ascension between the *kumāru* and Vega was 20°, and 10° between Deneb and the *kumāru* (see Weidner, *HBA* p.132:18 ff). This fits well the actual distance of δ Cygni from Vega and Deneb, but does not hold good for β, γ, and η Cygni.[197] The position of δ Cygni at the flank of the constellation also fits the meaning "shoulder, edge" assignable to *kumāru* on the basis of non-astronomical texts (see *AHw* 927*b* s.v. *qumāru*; cf. also *CAD* K 532).

106

Bibliography:
Previously unpublished.

Copy:
CT 53 pl.209 no.945.

Date:
Probably Nisannu 9, eponymy of Šamaš-kāšid-ajābi = April 7, 669 BC. The Julian month and day are obtained from Obv.6 ff, according to which the heliacal rising of Aries was to be expected within two days; this happened in the Sargonid period approximately on April 9.[198]. The dating to 669 follows from the statement that Mercury was at the same time visible as [evening star] (Rev.3' f).[199] Checking through the years 680-663, to which time span the letter certainly must be assigned (see Introduction, p.48 ff), one finds that this requirement is only met in four years, namely *676, 675, 669*, and *668*, in which Mercury rose heliacally respectively on March 31, 16, 24 and 9, in all cases as evening star; in 679, 672 and 666, it was at the time concerned seen as morning star, and stayed invisible in the remaining years.[200] Years 676 and 668 can be eliminated since both began relatively early (March 18 and 19), and it would have been pointless to refer to the month Addāru in Obv.3' if the letter had been written at the end of Nisannu. Of the remaining two years, preference must be given to 669 because of the affinities of the letter to the other texts discussed in commentary on *LAS* 70 (q.v.). Note that Obv.3' ff actually implies that Mercury had been seen in Aries in the month Addāru.

Addressee:
Esarhaddon.

Notes:

1', 3'. Instead of the restorations suggested in Pt.I, restore *in-na-m*[*ir*!-*u-ni*] (collated) and [*it-ta-mar*] "it was visible" in accordance with the dating of the letter. *in-na-*[*mir-u-ni*] is preferable to *in-na-*[*mar-u-ni*] also because the present tense *innammar* is written *in-NAM-*[*mar*] in Rev.1.4.

r3-4, left out of the consideration in Pt.I, can with a fair degree of certainty be restored *ù šu-*[*t*]*ú*[*ina* ^{d}UTU.ŠÚ(.A)] ^{4} *in-nam-m*[*ar*] (coll.) and translated "(Mercury) itself is visible [in the west]". The remark "it (= Aries) is not Mercury" (*la-a* ^{d}GU$_4$.UD *š*[*u*!-*u-tu*], Rev.2) implies that Mercury was not visible as morning star;

[197] The right ascension of the stars concerned were in the 7th century as follows (according to P.V. Neugebauer, *Sterntafeln* [1912]): α Lyrae (Vega) = 256.9; α Cygni (Deneb) = 287.9; β Cygni (Albireo) = 270.1; γ Cygni = 281.9; δ Cygni = 273.8.

[198] See K. Schoch, *Planeten-Tafeln für Judermann* (1927), Sp. XLIV, Tafel A.

[199] For the restoration see relevant note.

[200] See Appendix C1.

however, Rev.4 shows that it was ***not invisible***, and must consequently have appeared as an evening star ***in the west***. This agrees with the situation on April 7, 669 (see above).

108

Bibliography:
Previously unpublished.

Copy:
CT 53 pl.72 no.241.

Writer:
Akkullānu(?). It is easy to see that the same scholar also wrote *LAS* 109; but orthographic and stylistic analysis of the two letters, as well as the date of *LAS* 109 (June, 650 BC) quite definitely bear out that none of the well-known astrologers of Esarhaddon can be in question, with the possible exception of Akkullānu who (from *LAS* 110+300) is known to have served Assurbanipal as late as 657 BC.[201] According to personal collation (May, 1974), the physical characteristics and the ductus of *LAS* 108 and 109 closely resemble those of *LAS* 331, whose author can indeed reasonably assuredly be identified as Akkullānu.

Addressee:
Assurbanipal.

Date:
About 650 BC; see under *LAS* 109.

Notes:

2'. This line actually reads NUN GABA.RI NU ⸢TUK (collated).

3' f. *ša* ⸢*ta-mar-ti*⸣ (*sic*, the first sign inadvertently omitted in Pt.I) is a *casus pendens* anticipating *pi-šèr-šú* in Obv.4'; cf. Obv.15' f and note to 67:9.

4'-6'. A slightly inaccurate quotation from *Enūma Anu Enlil*; cf. I *30 ina* ITUŠU *lu-u* UD *14*.KÁM* *lu-u* UD *15*.KÁM* ⁷ KI dUTU NU IGI-*ir* ⸢¹⸣ LUGAL *ina* É.GAL-*šú ú-ta-sar* "if the moon is not seen opposite the sun on the 14th *or the 15th* of Du'uzu, the king will be bound to his palace", *RMA* 166:6 ff, completing *ACh* 2 Spl 5:7; also *RMA* 169:1 ff, etc.

---

201 Ištar-šumu-ēreš is ruled out because he regularly introduces omen interpretations by *an-ni-u pi-šèr-šu* (*LAS* 13:23.r6, 14:10 f, *RMA* 264:2), whereas both *LAS* 108 and 109 have *ki-i an-ni-i pi-šèr-šu* (5 times). Moreover, Ištar-šumu-ēreš regularly uses the sign KÁM in writing Assyrian dates (*LAS* 1:22.r6.14.16, 2:12, 3:8-10, 5:12.r6.7, 12:12, 29.7, *RMA* 7:1, etc.; only once KAM [*LAS* 25 r3] and twice KÁM* [4 r8' and 8 r2]), whereas the author of *LAS* 108/9 consistently writes KÁM*. Balasî is out of the question because he consistently writes *pi-še-er-šu* (*LAS* 35 r4, 326:6, *RMA* 277F r3) and *an-ni-i-e* (see notes to *LAS* 34). Nabû-aḫḫē-erība wrote, instead of dUTU (*LAS* 108:5' and 109:8') always d*Šá-maš* (*LAS* 62:12', 64:15.16. r8.12, 71:8', *RMA* 179:1, 180:2', 244C r3, 271A:2.r1', 274H:2; the only exception is dUTU.È in *RMA* 204: 2) and, instead of *an-ni-i*, always *an-ni-(i-)e*. Mār-Ištar, who otherwise would seem a plausible candidate (particularly in view of *LAS* 289), must be excluded because of the spelling LÚKÚR occurring in *LAS* 108:8' and 109 L.E.1: in his letters LÚ is exclusively used for the writing of the *noun amēlu* "man" (see *LAS* 280 r15, 293 r12, 296 r4), while the *determinative* of professions etc. is always written with the graph LÚ*; cf. LÚ*KÚR *LAS* 291 r16, etc. As for Akkullānu, the orthography of *LAS* 108/9 is broadly identical with his, cf. Appendix M 6; true, the spellings *pi-šèr-šú*, UD . . . KÁM* and LÚ.KÚR are not attested in his letters (cf. *pi-še-er-šú* 300:8, UD . . . KÁM 298:6.7.r27f, 300:7, 302:12 etc., KÚR-*šú* 300:12), yet they do occur in his *reports*. Of the remaining Assyrian senders of astrological reports, *Šumāju* can be excluded on the ground of the writing *pi-šèr-šú* (cf. *an-ni-ú pi-še-er-šu*, *RMA* 207:2.7); the other reports do not contain any distinctive orthographical data.

6'-10'. Also quoted from *Enūma Anu Enlil*, see *ACh* Sîn 4:17 f and 2 Spl 18:14f. The wordings of these two copies differ slightly from each other (and from the present quotation, too), which is a clear indication that several different versions of the series existed side by side. More variants are known from astrological reports. The present version is also attested in *RMA* 157:1 ff[202]; the tradition of *ACh* 2 Spl 18:14 f (I UD *15*.KÁM *30 u 20 a-ḫa-meš* IGI^{MEŠ} ^{LÚ}KÚR *dan-nu* ^{GIŠ}TUKUL^{MEŠ}-*šú ana* KUR ÍL-*a* KÁ.GAL^{MEŠ} KÚ[R *inaqqar*) is followed by *RMA* 157D:1 ff and 159:1 ff. Cf. *ACh* Sîn 4:17 f: I UD *15*.KÁM KIMIN ^{LÚ}KÚR *dan-nu* ^{GIŠ}TUKUL^{MEŠ}-*šú ana* KUR ZI-*am* KÁ.GAL URU.MU *ina-qar*; similarly I UD *15*.KÁM *30 u 20* KI *a-ḫa-meš* [IGI^{MEŠ}] 2 ^{LÚ}KÚR *dan-nu* ^{GIŠ}TUKUL^{MEŠ}-*šú ana* KUR ÍL 3 KÁ.GAL URU-*ja* ^{LÚ}KÚR *ina-qar, RMA* 156:1 ff, also 160B:1 ff, 161:1 ff, 163:1 ff, 165:1 ff; I UD *15*.KÁM* *30 u 20 it-ti a-ḫa-meš* IGI[^{MEŠ}] 2 ^{LÚ}KÚR *dan-nu* ^{GIŠ}TUKUL^{MEŠ}-*šú* 3 *ana* KUR *i-na-áš-šá-a* 4 KÁ.GAL URU KÚR *i-naq-qar, RMA* 164:1 ff, also 158A:1 ff; I UD *15*.K[ÁM *30 u 2*]*0* KI *a-ḫa-meš* [IGI^{MEŠ}] 4 ^{LÚ}KÚR *dan-nu* [^{GIŠ}]TUKUL^{MEŠ}-*šú ana* KUR [*inašši*] 5 IGI KÁ.GAL.MU ^{LÚ}KÚR DIB-*ba*[*t*], *RMA* 158:3 ff.

10' ff. If these lines are correctly restored, which is hardly to be doubted in the light of the omen quoted in ll. 17'ff, the opposition of the moon and the sun had in the preceding year ***in 13 successive months*** taken place on the 15th day; such a situation is only possible after repeated failure to observe the lunar crescent at the proper time (leading to repeated misplacement of the beginning of the month) and, considering the intensity of celestial observation in the Sargonid period, must have been of extremely rare occurrence. Other similar cases are reported, but none of them covers as many months. Cf. *RMA* 164 (after the omen just considered): ^{ITU}GUD ^{ITU}SIG$_4$ ^{ITU}ŠU ^{ITU}NE ^{ITU}KIN 6 *5* ITU^{MEŠ} *an-nu-ti* 7 UD *14*.KÁM DINGIR KI DINGIR NU IGI-*i*[*r*] 8 LUGAL *lu-ú i-de u ḫa-si-*[*is*] "Ajāru, Simānu, Du'ūzu, Ābu, Ulūlu – in these months the god was not seen opposite the god on the 14th day; the king should know and remeber this!" Similarly *CT* 54 22:13ff(Dietrich, *AOAT* 7 p.158 f): *šad-da-qàd šá 5* ITU^{MEŠ} UD *15*.KÁM *30* KI ^{d}*20 in-na-mar* 14 ^{URU}*Ṣi-du-nu ul iz-bi-lu* URU *ul nu-pi-li* 15 UN^{MEŠ}-*šú ul* KUR-*du-né* "last year, (when) the moon and the sun in 5 (consecutive) months appeared in opposition on the 15th day, did Sidon not (have to) bear (the evil of this omen)? Was the city not devastated, (and) were its inhabitants not conquered?"

11'. After *ša-*[*ni-ti*] there is enough room for [*ki-ma*] which seems to be required by the context.

17'-19'. Quoted from *Enūma Anu Enlil*, cf. *ACh* Sîn 3:3 I *30 ina ta-mar-ti-šú ina* ^{d}UTU.È ŠÚ.ŠÚ-*bi* BAL LUGAL TIL MU^{MEŠ} *ip-pi-ri* GÁL^{ME} KUR-*su* SU.KÚ *dan-na* IGI-*mar*; also *ACh* 2 Spl 3:44 (I *30 ina* ^{d}UTU.È GAL^{ME} [B]AL LUGAL TIL MU⌜.AN.NA⌝^{ME} [. . . . .]). The expression *ina ṣīt šamši* must here be understood ***temporally***, not locally. Note the commentary on Sîn 3:3: *ina* ^{d}UTU GUB-*zi 30* IGI-*ma* KI *20* ŠÚ-*ma* : *ul-la-nu-um-ma ina* ^{d}UTU GUB-*zi 30 a-dir* "(this meens that) the moon is visible while the sun is up (and) sets opposite the sun; moreover, (it means that) the moon is eclipsed while the sun is up." This is a scholarly pun based on the double meaning of the logogram ŠÚ, "to set" (said of the sun) and "to be dark". Cf. $^{\text{šú-ú}}$ŠÚ = *e-re-bu ša* UD-*ši*, Ea I 342; $^{\text{šu-ú}}$ŠÚ = *a-da-ru*, A I/8:44, ŠÚ = *a-da-ri*, Erimḫuš V 120.

20'-21'. These lines pertain to the omen quoted in Obv 6' ff. Cf. *RMA* 156 r1 f (after the same omen): ^{ITU}SIG$_4$ KUR MAR.TU 2 UD *15*.KÁM* KUR MAR.TU "Simannu is (the month of) the Westland, the 15th is (the day of) the Westland." For Du'ūzu = Subartu see App. F4.4.

109

Bibliography:

(I) Waterman, *RCAE* 1134 (cf. IV 199).

Writer:

Akkullānu(?). See under *LAS* 108.

---

[202] I UD [*15*.K]ÁM *30 u 20* 2 KI *a-ḫa-meš* IGI.LAL^{MEŠ} 3 ^{LÚ}KÚR *dan-nu* 4 ^{GIŠ}TUKUL^{MEŠ}-*šú ina* KUR ÍL-*a* 5 BARAG^{MEŠ} DINGIR^{MEŠ} GAL^{MEŠ} *ina-qar.*

A d d r e s s e e :
Assurbanipal.

D a t e :
Approximately Simānu 13, eponymy of Bēl-Ḫarrān-šadû'a = June 10, 650 BC. See note to Rev.2 ff.

A d d r e s s e e :
Assurbanipal.

N o t e s :

1'-4'. These two omens (quoted from *Enūma Anu Enlil*, cf. the critical apparatus) probably refer to a meteor observed in the daytime; cf. *RMA* 164, 187, 200, 201, 201A, 202, and *ABL* 1237, all pretty certainly referring to meteors (e.g. *RMA* 201: *1* DANNA MI *it-ta-lak* [2] MUL GAL TA ^{IM}SI.SÁ [3] *a-na* ^{IM}GÀL.LU [4] *iṣ-ṣa-ru-ur* [4] *i-da-ti šá a-na* [6] ⌜*ṣi*⌝*-bu-ti ša* LUGAL [7] *ṭa-ba-ti* "at the first double-hour of the night, a great star flashed from the north to the south; this is a sign suiting the king's intentions!"). There do not seem to be any certain references to *comets* in Sargonid astrological letters and reports.

5' ff. Cf. in general the notes on *LAS* 64.

9' f. I have not been able to identify the source of this quotation; the restorations however seem certain in the light of the passages mentioned in the critical apparatus.

11'-13'. Cf. I *20 a-der* LUGAL URI^{KI} ÚŠ *šá-ru-ru-šú* ŠU[B^{MEŠ} *šá-ni*]*š* MI NAM!.[BÚR.BI-*šú* NU GÁL-*ši*], *ACh* 2 Spl 40:16.

16'. The preposition *ana* here indicates comparison; see note to *LAS* 143:17 ff.

r2 ff. According to our letter, Mars had moved onwards (*ú-tu-uk-kiš*, see on 289 r1) and reached its first stationary point in Capricorn some time after Ajāru 29 (cf. Obv.5'). This suffices for dating the letter with absolute certainty to 650 BC, for the same situation did not recur any other time between 722 and 612 (see Stahlman-Gingerich, *Solar and Planetary Longitudes*, p.219-233). In 650, the length of Mars at its first stationary point (June 9) was 282.°9, which agrees perfectly with the wording of the letter (*ina lìb-bi* ^{MUL}SUḪUR.MÁŠ KU$_6$ "in the *middle* of Capricorn", cf. App.B). Assurbanipal's 19th year began about March 30 (App.A2); hence June 9 = Simānu 12, which should be the approximate date of the letter since the present observation seems to be the last one communicated in it.

r5-8. An unidentified quotation (from *Enūma Anu Enlil*?). In r6 one has probably to restore *r*[*a-kib*], cf. *ACh* 2 Spl 68:16 and 69:4.

r10 f. Cf. I ^{MUL}*Ṣal-bat-a-nu* KUR$_4$-*ma* ŠE.ER.ZI ÍL-*ši* LUGAL NIM.MA^{KI} [. . .] [16] KALAG-*ma* NÍG.TUK [. . . .] [17] I ^{MUL}*Ṣal-bat-a-nu* ŠE.ER.ZI ÍL-*ši* LUGAL NIM.MA^{KI} x[. . . .] "If Mars is luminous and shines brightly, the king of the Eastland [. . .] will gain in strength and [. . . .] prosperity. If Mars shines brightly, the king of the Eastland [. . . . .].", *ACh* Spl 49:15 ff. Was the word "Eastland" intentionally omitted in our letter?

r12 f. Cf. *ACh* Ištar 20:85, I *miš-ḫu šá* ^{d}*Ṣal-bat-a-nu* IGI RI.RI.GA *ina* KUR GÁL : ŠUB-*tì bu-lì*, and 2 Spl 64 i 10: I *ina* AN-*e miš-ḫu šá* ^{d}*Ṣal-bat-a-nu* IGI ŠUB *bu-lì ina* KUR GÁL (56th tablet of *Enūma Anu Enlil*). The commentary section of the latter passage explains the term *mišḫu ša Ṣalbatānu* as follows. *ṣal-lum-mu-u : mi-šiḫ* ^{MUL}MIN (= *Ṣalbatānu*) *: zi-im* ^{MUL}MIN [12] ^{d}*Ṣal-bat-a-nu* ⌜*i*⌝*-ba-ìl-ma* "fireball = effulgency of Mars = glow of Mars (means that) Mars is bright."

110+300

See under *LAS* 300.

111

Bibliography:
(I) Thompson, *RMA* (1900) p.73 f (translit. only).

Writer:
Akkullānu(?). Cf. L.E.2 with *LAS* 307 r3', and note the date (666?) and the phrase *issuri* . . . (r1), typical of Akkullānu.

Discussion:

The omen quoted in Rev.5 ff is also found in *RMA* 207 and 207B, according to which our letter has been restored.[203] *RMA* 207, referring to an evening first of Venus, is datable to June 17, 666 on account of the fact that the event took place in the month Simānu and the planet was said to "reach Cancer within 5-6 days".[204]

Notes:

L.E.2. The exclamation *i-lu-um-ma* (not quoted in *CAD* and *AHw*) also occurs, in a similar environment, in *LAS* 307 r3'. Cf. Arab. *allāhumma* "O God", and MB *šarrumma* (*AHw* 1190a) "verily" (lit. "by king").

112

Bibliography:
Previously unpublished.

Copy:
CT 53 pl. 123 no.483.

Writer:
Probably Balasî, judging from the handwriting (coll. 1974).

113

Bibliography:
(I) Waterman, *RCAE* 773.

Photo:
RCAE IV pl.13 (obv. only).

Notes:

8. The identity of the person here mentioned is unclear. *Arbāju* (lit. "Arab") was a pretty common name (see Tallqvist, *APN* s.v. and *AOAT* 6, s.v. *Arubu*), but in this case a person of relatively high standing must be in question, since he is said to have employed a private haruspex. Two such individuals are known: a governor from the time of Esarhaddon (^{I}*Ar-ba-aju* ^{LÚ*}EN.NAM, *ADD* 857 ii 50), and a military official of Assurbanipal referred to in letters pertaining to the civil war of 652-648 B.C. (*ABL* 273, 543, 1108, 1244; *KAI* 233; cf. Donner-Röllig, *KAI* II p.287 ff). Since the writer of the letter was active both in the reigns of Esarhaddon and Assurbanipal (see Appendix 0), no clear decision can be made between these two alternatives.

---

203 Our text is classifiable as a letter on the ground of its shape. If it had the oblong form of the reports, far more signs should be restored in each line than is actually necessary.

204 On June 17, 666, the elongation of Venus from the sun was 6°, and her longitude 79° (Cancer = 85°-96°); by June 24, the latter value had changed to 85° as predicted in the report. The month Simānu began in 666 on May 25 (cf. App. 2C). A similar situation did not repeat between 680 and 663 B.C.

11 ff. *ṭēmu turru*, lit. "to return a statement", was in Neo-Assyrian often used idiomatically in the sense of "reporting"; cf. *ABL* 1201 r8, *ú-ma-a ṭè-mu te-re* [9] *šúm-mu i-ba-áš-ši* [10] *šúm-mu la-áš-šú*, etc. On the other hand, haruspical reports were also called "statements" (*ṭēmu*) : note the designation *bēl ṭēmi* referring to the "reporting" haruspex in *PRT* 106, 109, 111, etc., and cf. *ABL* 1247 r1 *u₄-mu-us-s[u]* [2] IdAG*-GÁL-*ši ba-ru-ú* [3] *ṭè-e-mu šá* É.GAL [4] *i-ḫa-ri-iṣ-ṣu* [5] *a-na* INÍG.GUB *i-šap-par* "every day, the haruspex Nabû-ušabši makes explicit the 'statement' concerning the palace and sends it to Kudurru". It is possible that *ṭēmu* here refers to an extispicy dealing with a campaign led by Arbāju.

r9. For the paragogic *-u* in *li-ip-ru-su* (= *liprūsu* < *liprús*) see note to *LAS* 246 r1.

114

Bibliography:

(I) Waterman, *RCAE* 421 (cf. IV 181,252); Pfeiffer, *SLA* 176.
(II) Ylvisaker, *LSS* 5/6 (1912) 69; Oppenheim, *JNES* 1 (1942) 371.

Copy:

See also Delitzsch, *AL*[5] (1912) 89d.

Photograph:

RCAE IV pl.11.

Addressee:

Assurbanipal.

Date and discussion:

667 BC, supposing that the king's father referred to in Obv.6 is Esarhaddon (Sennacherib would seem rather unlikely in view of the fact that the writer was still an active haruspex in 650 B.C.), and that the writer received his benefice in the king's first year, upon admission to the king's service. In other words, the letter would have been written in the second year of Assurbanipal. This dating seems maintainable despite the existence of *ABL* 916, a petition dating from the beginning of Esarhaddon's reign, the author of which (a certain Mardî)[205] likewise complains having lost his landed property to the governor of Barḫalzi.

Notes:

7. *"Ten homers of cultivated land"*: a relatively small estate, at least when compared with the estates listed in the Harran census, whose areas usually varied between 20 and 60 homers and in addition included vineyards, orchards, etc. Cf. Fales, *Censimenti*, Fig.3 (following p.136). Cf. also *LAS* 36.

Ḫalaḫḫu: an agriculturally important district probably situated between Nineveh and Dur-Šarrukīn; see Forrer, *Provinzeinteilung* p.112; *AOAT* 6, p.142; and most recently Postgate, *RlA* 4 p.58*b*.

13. *la*: certainly a scribal error for *ša*, cf. LÚEN.NAM *ša* KUR*Bar-ḫal-za*, ADD 447:3f and *ABL* 916:8. There is otherwise no evidence of the intrusion of Aram. *la* into Neo-Assyrian, contrary to Neo-Babylonian where the word had partly replaced *ultu* in certain expressions. – For the location of *Barḫalza* (NW of Nineveh) see Forrer, op.cit., 113f; the present passage strongly suggests that the "province" immediately bordered on Ḫalaḫḫu.

[205] Certainly identical with I*Mar-di-i* . . . ÌR *ša* LÚEN.NAM *ša* KUR*Bar-ḫal-za*, *ADD* 447 = *AR* 61:2-4 (dated 683 BC); also probably identical with Mardî the eunuch (I*Mar-di-i* LÚSAG) mentioned in *ABL* 841:7 and I*Mar-di-ja* LÚ*šá* IGI *ki-na-tu* [13] *šá* É LÚGAL.SAG, 1109 r12 f. The latter text is datable to 677-675 B.C. on the ground of the omens quoted on the obverse.

115

Bibliography:
(I) Waterman, *RCAE* 181 (cf. IV 176, 237); Pfeiffer, *SLA* 244.
(II) Behrens, *ABB* (1906) 51[2]; Labat, *Royauté* (1939) 217; Deller, *Or*NS 30 (1961) 348 f.

Copy:
See also S.A. Smith, *PSBA* 10 (1888), 66 f (pl.4).

Writers:
The authors of this letter also appear together in several haruspical queries dating from Esarhaddon's time, see *AGS* 6, 48, 88, 98, 108, 119, 120, 124 and 145; *PRT* 17, 44 and 81; Nāṣiru disappears with the accession of Assurbanipal, but Aqarâ is still mentioned in *ADD* 851 (ca.650 BC). For a letter from Aqarâ see *ABL* 1259, and for one from Nāṣiru, *ABL* 1261. Both are written in Babylonian and are petitions like *LAS* 114.[206]

Addressee:
Esarhaddon (judging by the fact that Nāṣiru does not figure in texts from Assurbanipal's time).

Notes:

8. *dullu* (lit. "service") here refers to an extispicy to be performed by the writer team; cf. *LAS* 246:18, LÚḪAL^{MEŠ} ^{19} *dul-lu ina muḫ-ḫi le-pu-*[*šú*] and 340:4 *ina* UGU *dul-li* ^{5} *ša* LÚḪAL.

9. *qorsu*: see note to *LAS* 60 r5.

12. *Sāsî*: a person frequently mentioned in contemporary letters and administrative documents, and certainly an important palace official; his exact administrative and professional status remains obscure, however. In two instances, he evidently is in charge of political hostages: cf. *ABL* 447:14 ff, "Kudurru and Kunāju have finished the series *Utukkī lemnūti*; their report is with Sāsî (*ṭè-en-šú-nu ina* IGI ^{I}*Sa-si-i*)"[207], and *ina* UGU ^{I}*Ku-na-aji* ^{7} ^{I}*Ku-dúr-ru šá* MAN EN *iq-bu-u-ni* ^{8} *ma-a šu!-pur liš!-ú-lu!* ^{9} *a-na* ^{I}*Sa-si-i* ^{10} *ma-a šu!-tú* [*ṭè*]*-en!-šú-*<*nu*> ^{11} *ú-da* "as regards Kunāju and Kudurru concerning whom the king, my lord, said to me: 'Send out (an order that) Sāsî be questioned, he knows about them", *ABL* 1257:6 ff (a letter from Assurbanipal to Ash, most probably written in 670 BC; collated). It is unclear whether this Sāsî is identical with the Sāsî involved in the conspiracy of 670 BC (see notes to *LAS* 247) and/or with ^{I}*Sa-si-i* LÚ*ḫa-za-nu* URU[. . . .] mentioned (together with Ištar-šumu-ēreš, Marduk-šākin-šumi and Adad-šumu-uṣur) in *ADD* 448:33.[208] *

116

Bibliography:
(I) Waterman, *RCAE* 722 (cf. III 374).
(II) Meier, *AfO* 12 (1937/9) 238; Elman, *JANES* 7 (1975) 25[21].

Discussion:

In the interpretation of this (owing to its fragmentariness, admittedly rather enigmatic) letter, the present writer follows G. Meier (1939) taking it as a request to modify the *curriculum of apprentice scribes*; the letter "zeigt, daß die den Schulbetrieb leitende und regelnde Zentralstelle der König selbst war" (ibid.). This interpretation is prompted by the fact that the tablets to be removed and substituted were of the *liginnu* type primarily used in elementary instruction (cf. *ABL* 308 and *LAS* 34, as well as the evidence presented by Meier, loc.cit.); and it can also be supported by Obv.15 f, if the word *iškāru* there is assigned the meaning "collection of (school-)texts"

[206] Cf. also *LAS* 36 and see the remarks of Oppenheim in *Centaurus* 14 (1969) 115 f.
[207] This text is edited in full in Appendix N (no.28); cf. *Iraq* 34 (1972) 33.
[208] Dated Šabāṭu 10 = January 26, [665 BC]. See Appendix N, no.17.

which it has in the "Exorcist's Manual" (*KAR* 44)[209] and similar contexts. On the other hand, the letter does not seem to make much sense unless an interpretation of this kind is accepted. Just consider the translation of Rev. 1 ff proposed in *CAD* Ṣ 119a: "May the king order excerpts of the two small tablets containing commentaries to be prepared and may he make available the two (tablets) on divination." Why should expert diviners turn to the king with such a request? Besides, rendering *našāru* with "to make excerpts" is out of the question. The technical term for "excerpting" was *nasāḫu* (cf. *LAS* 25 r9', 234 r5, 278 r5', 289 r12, 324 r5, and see *AHw* p.750 for more examples); and everywhere else in the present corpus the meaning of *našāru* is clearly "to remove, reduce" (cf. *LAS* 133 r16', 143 r13, 159:10, 305 r2'; more examples in *AHw* p.759).

Notes:

r4. For the spellings *li-iš-šur-ru* and *liš-KUN* (both for 3rd Masc. Pl.) see my remarks in *Iraq* 34 (1972) 25 ff.

117

Bibliography:

(I) Waterman, *RCAE* 923 (cf. IV 191, 265); Pfeiffer, *SLA* 248; Biggs, *ANET*³ (1969) 606 (transl. only).
(II) Behrens, *ABB* (1906) 20; Pfeiffer, *ANET*² (1955) 450; Labat, *Royauté* (1939) 38; J. Lewy, *HUCA* 19 (1946) 458 f; H. and J. Lewy, *Or*NS 17 (1948) 146; Böhl, *Opera Minora* (1953) 393; Oppenheim, *Dreams* (1956) 200.

Copy:

See also Strong, *Hebraica* 9 (1892) 1 ff, and Winckler, *SKT* II (1894) 9.

Date:

667 B.C. The reference to Esarhaddon's Egyptian campaign (in Obv.10 ff) assures the reign of Assurbanipal; on the other hand, the formulation of Obv.15 ff implies that Assurbanipal himself had not yet "expanded the territory of Aššūr", nor suffered any military setbacks. In particular, the letter must antedate the revolt that broke out in Egypt in 667 and the subsequent military campaign (cf. Grayson, *TCS* 4 p.128); for Obv.15 ("the *rest* of the countries . . .") implies that Egypt was still firmly in the hands of the Assyrians while the letter was written.

Discussion:

Notice that the letter was formally addressed not only to the king, but also to the god *Aššur*. The grounds for this remain obscure owing to the breaks. There is nothing in common between this letter and the other "letters to gods" discussed by A.L. Oppenheim in *JCS* 19 (1960) 133 ff.

Notes:

8. Just as *apkallu* "sage" here refers to Sennacherib, noted for his technical talent (cf. von Soden, *Herrscher* p.111 ff), so *Adapa* must be understood as a reference to Esarhaddon, who in his lifetime was repeatedly compared to this sage (see *LAS* 57 and 229; also Borger, *Ash* p.34:46). I consider the rendering NUN.ME UMUN A.DA.PÀ "the sage Umun-Adapa" proposed by Hallo, *JAOS* 83 (1963) 176[83] unacceptable in the present context; even though Adapa was sometimes referred to as Oannes-Adapa (e.g. ᴵUD-*an-na A-da-p*[*à*] *JCS* 16 64:6, *U*$_4$-*ma*-ᵈ*a-num A-da-pa ZA* 37 90[4]),[210] the former name was to my knowledge never written UMUN in 1st millennium texts. The interpretation of *u* as the connective "and" is fully justified by the context, cf. ᵈ*30 u* ᵈUTU (Obv.4), ᵈAG* *u* ᵈAMAR+UD, MU *u* NUMUN (Obv.5), AMA *u* NIN (Obv.6), ZU.AB *ù gi-mer um-ma-nu-*[*ti*] (Obv.9).

---

209 That text is entitled SAG^MEŠ ÉŠ.GÀR MAŠ.MAŠ-*ti šá a-na* NÍG.ZU *u* IGI.DU$_8$.A *kun-nu* MU.NE "these are the initial lines of the collection of exorcistic works that have been established for teaching and reference purposes". ÉŠ.GÀR MAŠ.MAŠ-*ti* should not be translated "Series of exorcism" in this connection, since no canonized corpus of the exorcistic listerature existed in the period concerned.

210 See also Borger, *JNES* 33/2 (1974) 186.

12ff. The meaning and implications of this passage are unclear. I cannot accept the astrological interpretation offered by the Lewys (1948) for the simple reason that the crowns mentioned in Obv.12 were clearly physical objects (cf. Obv.14). Equally unacceptable is the interpretation (most recently advanced in *CAD* K 117a) that a report on a *dream* is in question; the dream referred to in Obv.7 was seen by (or in the time of) *Sennacherib*, whereas our passage pertains to the time of *Esarhaddon* and is nowhere specified as a dream. It seems that the incident here reported really happened while Esarhaddon was passing Harrān; a symbolic representation of Sîn (seated upon a shepherd's staff, on which see below) wore exceptionally *two* crowns, as if the other were destined for the king who consequently was persuaded to put it on. The ominousity of the incident (which may well have been prearranged) probably lay in the significance of the moment and in its deviation from the normal cultic routine.

12. *GIŠŠIBIR*: staff functioning as a royal and divine emblem. For the reading of the logogram cf. ši-bir GIŠ.ŠIBIR(U.EN×GÁN) "*gi[š-pu-bur-ra-ku]* = *[ši-bir]-rum*, Diri IV 37; [ši-bir] ŠIBIR = *ši-bir-rum*, [uš-bar] ŠIBIR = *uš!* (text ZU)-*ba-rum* S^b^A 328 f; the meaning "staff" obtains from Antagal H 8, where the word is listed together with *ušpāru*, *ḫaṭṭu* and *palû* (^GIŠ^uš-bar = *uš-pa-ru*, ^GIŠ^PA = *ḫa-áṭ-ṭu*, bala = *pa-lu-ú*, ^ši-bir^šibir = *ši-bir-ru*, 5 ff). More specifically, the word must have denoted the type of staff worn by shepherds, cf. s u$_8$ - b a š i b i r - r a - n a d è - m u - u n - g i$_4$ - g i$_4$: *re-'u-ú ina ši-bir-ri-šú li-duk-ši* "may the shepherd (= Tammuz) kill her with his staff" *ASKT* p.120 r15 f. For attestations of the staff as a royal (and divine) emblem see *CAD* Ḫ 154f (s.v. *ḫaṭṭu*); in sculptures, *šibirru* may be plausibly identified with the long, narrow sceptre held by the king in audiences (cf. Hrouda, *Flachbild* p.105).

13. Cancel the equation Nusku = Mercury given in Pt.I (in accordance with the interpretation of the passage suggested by H. and J. Lewy in their article on Nusku, *Or*NS 17 [1948] 146 ff). The lunar character of the god is too obvious to be as completely denied as the Lewys contend; cf. ^d^A - b a - r a - l a ḫ$_4$ ^d^PA+KU [15] : ^d^*30* : ^d^AG "*Abaralaḫ*, (that is,) Nusku = Sîn = Nabû" 0.175:14f (= *RA* 16,145 ff); ^d^A - b a r - r a - l a ḫ$_4$ d u m u u$_4$ - 3 0 - k a m u$_4$ - n á - à m : ^d^PA+KU DUMU *še-la-še-e bu-um-bu-li* "Nusku, son of the 30th day, the day of the moon's disappearance" *RAcc.* 16:13 f (implying that Nusku was worshiped as the god of the lunar crescent). Most important, one cannot get around the fact that the cult of Nusku was centered in the "moon city" Harran (cf. note to *LAS* 8:9). Notice also the invocation of the god together with Sîn and Nikkal in *LAS* 273:5 f.

14. Cf. *LAS* 317 r6 ff.

119

Bibliography:

(I) Waterman, *RCAE* 894 (cf. III 375, IV 190, 264); Pfeiffer, *SLA* 303.
(II) Dhorme, *RHR* 113 (1936) 137f; Labat, *Royauté* (1939) 213; Deller, *AOAT* 1 (1969) 56.

Copy:

See also G. Smith, *3 R* 53 no.3.

Addressee:

Assurbanipal.

Date:

Probably Kislīmu 30, eponymy of Gabbāru = December 30, 667 BC. Note the affinities of the letter with *LAS* 120 (blessing formula, orthography, subject matter); the day is obtained from Obv.8, the month from the report *RMA* 76 quoted below. While the blessing formula occurring here is also found in a letter of Adad-šumu-uṣur written in Esarhaddon's reign (*LAS* 130), the fact that the letter concerned is addressed not to the king but to the *crown prince* (Assurbanipal) actually confirms that the present letter, too, dates from Assurbanipal's reign.

Discussion:

The lunar observation reported here is possibly also reported in *RMA* 76, by Bulluṭu.[211] The reverse of

[211] Cf. also *LAS* 102.

this report contains two omens related to the case, of which it appears that the month at the end of which the moon was sighted was Kislīmu; the obverse reads as follows:

UD *29*.KÁM *ni-ta-ṣar* IM.DIR *dan-[nat]* ² ᵈ*30 la né-mur* ³ UD *30*.KÁM *ni-ta-ṣar* ᵈ*30 né-ta-m[ar]* ⁴ *ma-ti-iḫ a-dan-niš* [0] ⁵ *ša* UD *29*.KÁM *šu-ú* [0] ⁶ *ina muḫ-ḫi qur-bu mì-i-nu* ⁷ *ša* LUGAL *be-lí i-qa-bu-u-[ni]* "We watched for (the moon) on the 29th, but the clouds were dense, so we did not see the moon. We watched again on the 30th and saw the moon. It was very high; (the clouds) of the 29th day have bearing on this (observation). What does the king, my lord, say?"

The question "what does the king say?" can only imply that in Sargonid Assyria, lunar months did not necessarily have to begin with the appearance of the crescent, but that the first day could be slightly adjusted if there was evidence that the crescent had been observed too late because of bad weather. The same is suggested even more explicitly by the present letter: "Let the king wait for the report of Assur; (only) afterwards should the king fix the (1st) day (of the month)." Whether or how often the king really took the trouble of adjusting the calendar by a specific order must, of course, remain a matter of speculation.

Notes:

8 ff. The interpretation of this observation (omitted!) would have run as follows:

I *30 ina* UD *30*.KÁM* IGI-*ir* ² *šu-ru-up-pu-ú* : GÙ-*mu* KÚR GÁL-*ši* I *30 ina* IGI.LAL-*šú šá-qu-ma* IGI-*ir* ⁴ KÚR *ina* KUR *i-leq-qe* I *30 ina* IGI.LAL-*šú ḫar-pí-iš na-an-mur* ⁶ ITU *ni-ziq-tum ub-ba-la*

"If the moon appears on the 30th day, there will be frost; ditto, clamour of the enemy (in the land). – If the moon at its appearance is high and (keeps) visible, an enemy will plunder in the land. – If the moon becomes visible earlier (than expected), the month will bring sorrow." (See *RMA* 59:1ff)

r1. This is a reference to the reports of Nabû'a of Assur (*LAS* 87-92 and *ABL* 817, 819-828). Note that these (calendrically probably very important) texts report dates on which the crescent and full moon were observed, whereas e.g. *LAS* 96-98 report that the crescent was not observed and therefore probably were meant to inform the king of the necessity to adjust the local calendar.

120

Bibliography:

(I) Waterman, *RCAE* 657 (cf. IV 186, 259); Pfeiffer, *SLA* 318; Oppenheim, *Letters* (1967) 157, no.94 (transl. only).

(II) Schott, *OLZ* 40 (1937) 363; Dhorme, *RHR* 113 (1936) 129f, 137f; Labat, *Royauté* (1939) 283; Oppenheim, *JAOS* 64 (1944) 194.

Copy:

See also Zeitlin, *SACA* (1910) no.24.

Addressee:

Assurbanipal.

Date:

Tašrītu 30, eponymy of Gabbāru = October 30, 667 BC. This date rests on the following evidence. According to the letter,

[1] an expected solar eclipse had not occurred;
[2] Venus was approaching Spica (Virgo);
[3] the heliacal rising of Mercury was impending.

These data fit perfectly the situation at the end of October, 667, and no other year between 680-663 BC. The sun had failed to make an eclipse on October 29 (a fortnight after the lunar eclipse of October 15[212]); Venus

[212] App. D; cf. *LAS* 41-42, 135-136, 290, etc.

was approaching Spica, her length on Oct. 30 being 165°.0 (Spica 167°.2);[213] and the heliacal rising of Mercury at Nineveh was really impending, as the planet had probably been visible at the latitude of Babylon already from October 26 on (see App. C2).[214] An *approximately* corresponding situation had prevailed on July 15, 669; but at that time the solar eclipse had passed by already three weeks earlier, and Venus, though on the borderline of Virgo (long. 136°), was still far away from Spica.

Discussion:

The above dating also fits perfectly the general background of the letter. Having presented his good "news" (see below), the writer feels safe enough to proceed with his actual matter, a petition on behalf of his son Urad-Gula. We know from other letters that the latter had been a servant of Esarhaddon and obviously in a fairly influential position, since he is mentioned relatively often (cf. *ABL* 1109, datable to 677-675 BC on the ground of the omens quoted in it; *ABL* 1285; and *LAS* 151, 174 and 224, the two latter ones datable to 672-669 BC). Our letter, however, shows that while it was written, Urad-Gula was *not* employed by the king: the king had not been reminded of him, and thus the poor servant was "falling out of the king's hands". Such a situation is best thinkable after a change of ruler, for the servants of the deceased king did not – for understandable reasons – inherit their old positions automatically, but had to be rehabilitated by the new king, who could leave "unsummoned" those he was not interested in (cf. *ABL* 954; *ABL* 1216:9 and 16; E. Weidner, *AfO* 17 286 f; Müller, *MVAeG* 41/3 14 iii 1 ff). The only hope of the "unsummoned" was to turn to the king personally (or through a mediator, as in *LAS* 227), trying to convince him of his competence (*LAS* 237) or appealing to the king's mercy.[215] The present letter did not have the desired effect; therefore the author wrote, probably some months later, another petition (*LAS* 121), presenting his case entirely differently.

Notes:

10 f. Cf. *ACh* Ištar 5:12, I ^{MUL}*Dil-bat ana* ^{MUL}AB.[SÍN TE . . . . .] [13] ^{d}*Dil-bat ana* ^{MUL}AB.SÍN [TE-*ma*]. ^{MUL}AB.SÍN here = Spica.[216]

12 ff. As in later astrology[217], Mercury in the Sargonid period was commonly considered an augur of rain and flood; hence the prediction given here, which certainly was thought to please the ruler. Cf. ^{MUL}GU$_4$.UD *mu-šá-az-nin* ŠÈG "Mercury, the one who brings rain" *RAcc.* p.138:306; I ^{d}UDU.IDIM *ina* ITU IGI.LAL [3] ŠÈG *u* A.[KAL] [4] I ^{d}UDU.IDIM *šum-ma ina* ^{ITU}GUD [5] *šum-ma ina* ^{ITU}SIG$_4$ IGI.LAL [6] A.KAL DU-*ma* A.ŠÀ A.GÀR *i-ma-gir* "If Mercury appears at the beginning of the month, there will be rain and flood. If Mercury appears either in Ajāru or Simānu, a flood will come and fields and commons will thrive," *RMA* 217:2ff, cf. 216C and 218; [I] ^{MUL}UDU.IDIM.GU$_4$.UD *ina* ^{d}UTU.ŠÚ.A TÙM [.] [2] TÙM-*ma* ŠÈG ŠUR-*nun* "If Mercury . . . . . disappears in the West, there will be rain", *RMA* 146 r1f, etc.[218] The remark "Adad will thunder" is explained by the fact that Mercury was also considered a star of Adad; cf. ^{MUL}UDU.IDIM.GU$_4$.UD MUL *šá* ^{d}IM "Mercury is the star of Adad", BM 121206 viii 59' (van Driel, *CA* p.96), and note that Adad shares with Mercury the epithet *mušaznin zunni* (cf. Tallqvist, *Götterepitheta* pp.95 and 248).

121

Bibliography:

(I) Fales, *ANL* 29 (1975) 453 ff; Waterman, *RCAE* 2 (cf. IV 173, 231); Pfeiffer, *SLA* 160; Oppenheim, *Letters*

[213] The length of Venus according the tables of Stahlman + Gingerich, the right ascension of Spica after P.V. Neugebauer's *Sterntafeln.*

[214] The prediction concerning the planet's appearance was certainly based on the thumb rule that Mercury is best visible around the equinoxes; notice its cautious formulation, and cf. commentary on *LAS* 53.

[215] Note that Urad-Gula very likely also wrote a personal petition: *ABL* 1285.

[216] Venus approaching (or moving in) *Virgo* was not an ominous event. Cf. on 233:11'. The present omen probably protended good crops.

[217] Cf. Ptolemy, *Tetrabiblos*, Proem, ch. 7. Also *TCL* 6 19:6ff (H. Hunger).

[218] On Nabû = Mercury = setting sun = west = evening = autumn = age = coolness = humidity, etc. (and similar astrological theorems concerning the other planets) see e.g. A. Jeremias, *Handbuch der altorientalischen Geisteskultur* ([2]Berlin/Leipzig 1929), 142 ff.

(1967) p.149f; Biggs, *ANET*^{3} (1969) 626f.
(II) Dhorme, *RHR* 113 (1936) 128f; Böhl, *Opera Minora* (1953) 403, 522^{75}; Deller, *AOAT* 1 (1969) 51, 53f.[219]

Photo:
RCAE IV pl.6 (Rev. only).

Copy:
Cf. S.A. Smith, *Die Keilschrifttexte Assurbanipals III* (1889) pl.10 f.

Addressee:
Assurbanipal.

Date:
Probably Nisannu, eponymy of Kanūnāju of the New Palace = April, 666 BC. This date is based on the following reasoning. A terminus *post quem* (Araḫsamna/November, 667) is obtained from *LAS* 120 which certainly predates the present letter.[220] Exactly how soon Adad-šumu-uṣur renewed his petition is a matter of conjecture but certain considerations make it likely that he did not do so immediately. Rev.6f of the present letter, which is best explained as a reference to the great New Year's reception of the king, would indicate that he waited till the beginning of the next year, and the same is suggested by Obv.10 implying that the king had been in power for at least two full regnal years. If the dating of *LAS* 119 to December 30, 667, is correct, the present letter would in any case postdate *LAS* 120 by at least two months, as it is extremely difficult to insert the correspondence *LAS* 121, 122, 125 between the formally remarkably homogenous *LAS* 119 and 120.

Discussion:

That this letter dates from the (beginning of the) reign of Assurbanipal has already previously been repeatedly suggested with reference to the *aurea aetas* theme developed on the obverse. The inscriptions of Assurbanipal stress the fact that the beginning of the king's reign was an exceptionally fortunate time to Assyria, which then experienced an economic boom as a result of copious rains and floods. Cf. e.g., Streck, *Asb* p.212: *ul-tu ina* ^{GIŠ}GU.ZA AD *ba-ni-ja ú-ši-bu* ^{d}IM ŠÈG^{MEŠ}*-šú ú-maš-ši-ra* ^{d}*É-a ú-paṭ-[ṭi-ra* A.KAL^{MEŠ}*-šú*] "after I had ascended the throne of my father and begetter, Adad released his rains and Ea let loose [his floods]" (K.2867 r2). The fullest account of these happy years (Prism B, paralleled by Prism D) agrees remarkably closely with the wording of the present letter:

mim-ma si-mat É.KUR *šá* KÙ.GI KÙ.UD *e-pu-[uš]*
e-li ša LUGAL^{MEŠ} AD^{MEŠ}*-ja ú-[rad-di]*
šat-tuk-ku gin-nu-u UGU *ša* u$_4$*-me ul-lu-u-[ti]*
ú-šá-tir-ma áš-rat DINGIR^{MEŠ} *áš-te-['a-a]*
at-tal-la-ka al-ka-[ka]-a-ti-šu-[un]
^{d}IM ŠÈG^{MEŠ}*-šú ú-maš-še-ra*
^{d}*É-a ú-[paṭ-ṭi-ra* A.K]AL^{MEŠ}*-[šú]*
5 KÙŠ ŠE.AM *iš-qu [ina* A]B.SÍN*-ni-[šú]*
e-ri-ik šu-bul-tu $\frac{5}{6}$ KÙŠ
SI.SÁ EBUR *na-pa-áš* ^{d}NISABA
ka-aja-na [ú-šaḫ-na-bu gi]-pa-ru
ṣip-pa-a-ti šu-ta-[am-mu-ḫa in]-bu
[MÁŠ.ANŠE *šu-te-šur ina ta-lit-ti*] *ina* BAL^{MEŠ}*-ja* ḪÉ.NUN *ṭuḫ-du*
[*ina* MU.AN.NA^{MEŠ}*-ja ku-um-mu-ru* ḪÉ.G]ÁL*-lu*
12 ANŠE ^{ŠE}PAD^{MEŠ} *2* [ANŠE GEŠTIN^{MEŠ}]
[*12 qa* Ì.GIŠ^{MEŠ} *1* GÚ.UN] SÍG^{MEŠ}
ina nap-ḫar KUR*-ja* KI.L[AM *nap-šu i-šam-mu*]

---

[219] For additional literature see Fales, l.c. 455 f.

[220] Note that *LAS* 122:16f is an almost literal allusion to the present letter (Rev.5f). Therefore *LAS* 120 cannot have been written after the present letter.

"I had made all kinds of gold and silver objects befitting the temples in greater amounts than any of my royal fathers, and I increased the regular temple offerings more than ever (cf. present letter, Obv.13 f); I visited the abodes of the gods and lived according to their ways (cf. Obv.13, 14f). Adad released his rains and Ea let loose his floods (cf. Obv.11 f); the grain grew 5 cubits tall in its furrow and the ear of barley reached five-sixths of a cubit in length; the grasslands constantly produced thriving crops and an abundance of cereals, the orchards abounded in fruit, and the cattle gave birth easily (cf. Obv.20 f). In my reign there was prosperity aplenty, in my years there was fullness to overflowing: 12 homers of barley went for 2 homers of wine, 12 litres of oil went for 1 talent of wool – there was an excellent rate of exchange in my whole country[221] (cf. Obv.12)" (Piepkorn, *AS* 5, p.28).

No comparable passages are to be found in the inscriptions of the other Sargonids. In the experience of the Assyrians themselves, the auspicious beginning of Assurbanipal's reign may indeed have seemed like a realization of an ancient prediction of a happy reign once coming upon the earth[222] and a fulfillment of the blessings said at the coronation of Assurbanipal.[223] The stressing of the "happy reign" theme in the king's own inscriptions and its formulation to correspond with the prophecies as closely as possible indicates, in any case, that at least the king himself considered the prophecies fulfilled in his reign. Adad-šumu-uṣur hence definitely pulled the right string in making it explicit that he recognized in his lord the expected "king of righteousness" – this was perhaps deliberate flattery, but all the more effective since it was based on reality.

The outcome of the writer's aspirations is to be seen in *LAS* 122 and 125.

Note, incidentally, that not only Urad-Gula (on behalf of whom the present letter was formally written) but also Adad-šumu-uṣur himself seems to have lost his former influential position as the king's personal exorcist under Assurbanipal. What else could Rev.14ff imply than that the writer no more had any occasion to converse with the king personally and perhaps was not even allowed to regularly enter the palace? Note also that the two "professional" letters sent by Adad-šumu-uṣur to Assurbanipal (*LAS* 119 and 120) do not concern exorcistic but astrological matters, i.e. affairs practiced by the writer in his youth (cf. *ADD* 350 and ND 5427 = Hunger, *ZA* 62 101, dated in the reign of Sargon). See also on 125 r11.

Notes:

6 f. Is this a reference to the royal name of the king (*Aššur-bāni-apli* = "Assur has created the heir")? Cf. the end of the following note. With the present passage in general cf. also Streck, *Asb* p.2 i 3 ff.

7-9. As this passage indicates, the choice of the Assyrian crown prince had to meet with the approval of Šamaš and Adad, which was obtained through inspection of the entrails of sacrifical sheep. This is also explicitly stated in royal inscriptions. Cf. Assurbanipal's own description of his nomination, running as follows:

---

221 Cf. K. Deller, "Getreidekursangaben in neuassyrischen Rechtsurkunden", *Or*NS 33 (1964) 257 ff. The most favourable rate of exchange attested in economic texts is 2 seahs (= 0.2 homer) of barley for 1 pound of copper; there were as a rule considerable local variations in the rate (ibid. p.260).

222 A.K. Grayson and W.G. Lambert, "Akkadian Prophecies" (*JCS* 18 7 ff), Text A, Col. ii 2-8: "[A prince will arise] and rule for eighteen years. The land will rest secure, fare well, (and its) people will [enjoy] prosperity. The gods will ordain good things for the land, favourable winds [will blow]. The . . . and the furrow will yield abundant crops. Šakkan (the god of beasts) and Nisaba (the god of grain) will . . . in the land. There will be rains and floods. The people of the land will enjoy themselves." Cf. Col. iii 2 ff: "That king will rule the (Four) Quarters [. . . . .]; his people will be filled with prosperity [. . . . .]. He will re-establish the regular offerings of the Igigi which had ceased [. . . . . .]. Favourable winds will blow, abundance . . [. . . . . .]. The cattle [will lie down] in green pastures. The winter-grass [will last] until summer (and) the summer-grass [will last until winter]. The offspring of the beasts [. . . .]."

223 "As corn and silver, oil and [the catt]le of Šakkan, and the salt of Bariku are good, so may the name of Assurbanipal, king of Assyria, prove to his gods; may eloquence, attention, truthfulness and righteousness be bestowed upon him; . . . may the city of Assur receive 30 kors of corn for 1 shekel of silver; may the city of Assur receive 3 seahs of oil for 1 shekel of silver; . . . may (the great gods) bless him every day, month and year . . . ; in his years, may they re[lease] rain from the sky and floods from the springs . . ." (E. Weidner, "Ein Segensgebet for Assurbânipal", *AfO* 13 [1939 40] 210-213, Obv.5-22).

it-ta-nap-la-as AD *ba-nu-u-a qar-ra-du-tú ša i-ši-mu-in-ni* DINGIR^{MEŠ} GAL^{MEŠ} [30] *ina qí-bit* DINGIR^{MEŠ} GAL^{MEŠ} *ina* UKKIN ŠEŠ^{MEŠ}-*ja* ⸢GAL⸣^{MEŠ} *ma-a'-diš i-ra-man-ni* [31] *áš-šú e-peš* LUGAL-*ti-ja im-hur* AN.ŠÁR LUGAL DINGIR^{MEŠ} EN *gim-ri* [32] *ú-ṣal-li* ^{d}NIN.LÍL ^{d}*Še-ru-u-a ru-bat i-la-a-ti be-let* GAŠAN^{MEŠ} [33] [*ú*]-*sa-ap-pi* ^{d}UTU ^{d}IM *ba-re-e šá-ma-me qaq-qar* DI.KUD *kib-ra-a-ti* --- ii [3] *ina* ^{ITU}GUD ITU ^{d}*É-a* EN *te-ni-še-e-ti pa-ti-q*[*u* DÙ *gim-ri*] [4] *e-ru-um-ma ina* É *re-du-u-ti a-šar ṭe-me u mil-*[*ki*] [5] *ina qí-bit* AN.ŠÁR AD DINGIR^{MEŠ} ^{d}AMAR.UD EN.EN.EN LUGAL DINGIR[^{MEŠ}] [6] *ú-šá-qa-an-ni* UGU DUMU^{MEŠ} LUGAL *šu-mì iz-kur ana* LUGAL-[*u-ti*]

"My father and begetter noticed the heroic nature which the great gods had provided me with, and thus he, by order of the great gods, loved me most in the assembly of my big brothers. On behalf of my (future) kingship he turned to the divine king Aššūr, the lord of the universe, prayed to the divine lady Mullissu-Šerū'a, the foremost among goddesses, and supplicated the cosmic diviners Šamaš and Adad, who pass judgement on the (Four) Regions. --- In Ajāru, the month of Ea, the lord of the mankind, and the creator of the entire universe, I entered the Succession Palace, the place of orders and counsels, and by order of Aššūr, the father of (all) gods, Marduk, the lord of lords and king of the gods, he advanced me above (all other) sons of the king and called my name to the kingship", Streck, *Asb* p.254 i 29 ff.[224]

A haruspical query concerning the introduction of a son of Esarhaddon to the Succession Palace (i.e. his offical proclamation as crown prince) has actually been preserved: *AGS* 107. The name of the prince in question, as given in the text, is *Sîn-nādin-apli*, an otherwise unknown individual. No corresponding document relating to the promotion of Assurbanipal is extant; in fact, the earliest references to Assurbanipal *by name* date from the time following the said event. This circumstance justifies a question already posed by G. Smith more than 100 years ago[225]: were Sîn-nādin-apli and Assurbanipal actually the same person? Does the former name represent the prince's original name, and was he *renamed* Assurbanipal (a name better befitting the future ruler of a mighty empire) only after his choice as heir to throne? Smith (and later Schrader) thought he was, but the idea was rejected by Knudtzon, *AGS* (1893) p.220, and quite emphatically by Streck, *Asb* p. CLXXXV, CCXLII and CCL; cf. also Klauber, *PRT* (1910) LXI[1]. Is it, however, so unthinkable after all? The objections of Knudtzon and Streck, rational as they are, prove nothing; by contrast, consider the following: 1) The eldest son of Esarhaddon was, as far as can be ascertained, not Sîn-nādin-apli but Šamaš-šumu-ukīn (cf. *LAS* 129:10 and relevant note); is it thinkable that the legitimate heirs' rights would have been wronged twice? 2) There is firm evidence that Assyrian princes were renamed after their nomination as heirs to throne (cf. simply *ABL* 1452 r1 ff for Esarhaddon = Aššur-etel-ilāni-mukīn-apli). 3) Isn't a name like "Aššur has created the heir" actually too presumptive to be originally given to a *minor* son of a king? Wouldn't it have implied that the king had displaced the legitimate heir already at the moment his younger brother was born? 4) Why has no query pertaining to Assurbanipal's promotion been preserved among the numerous queries from the years 673-669?

14 f. Literally, "the great gods of the heaven and earth have been *lifted up* in the time of the king."[226] Cf. *ú-ma-a* [LUGAL *be*]-*lí* [7] *a-na* AN-*e ú-se-la-a* "now, the king, my lord, has raised me to the heavens", *ABL* 861 r6 f, similarly *ABL* 85:9 f. For criticism of the translation "(all this) the great gods . . . have brought about" (*CAD* E 131*a*; Oppenheim 1967; Biggs 1969) see Deller, *AOAT* 1 (1969) 53.

18. Cf. Streck, *Asb* 260:13, *ina zi-kir* MU-*ja kab-ti ha-du-ú i-ri-šú kib-rat erbe* (TAB+TAB)-*tì* "the Four Regions rejoiced and exulted in the mention of my honourific name."

19. In view of the preceding line, the ring ceremony here referred to possibly formed part of marriage rites, as suggested by Deller, *loc.cit.* Cf. Syr. *qaddeš* "in matrimonium duxit", possibly a denominative from *q'dāšā* (pl. *q'dāšātā*) "earring" (Brockelmann, *Lexicon Syriacum*[2] 649*a*).

20 f. Cf. *ta-lit-ti* UR.MAH^{MEŠ} *qé-reb-ši-in i-šir-ma ina la-a me-ni iq-nin-*[*nu*] "the births of lions thrived in the (canebrakes) and they multiplied innumerably", Streck, *Asb* p.212 r4, referring to the first years of Assurbanipal.

[224] Esarhaddon's account of his nomination is quite parallel: "Though I was younger than my big brothers, my father and begetter, by order of Aššur etc., resolutely advanced me above all my brothers, saying: "This is my heir.' He consulted Šamaš and Adad through extispicy, and they replied in the affirmative: 'He is your successor'. . ." Borger, *Ash* p.40:8 ff.

[225] *History of Assurbanipal* (1871), 324.

[226] Thus already, Dhorme, *RHR* 113 (1936) 128.

21 f. Cf. *ḫi-ṭu dan-nu ina* É EN^{MEŠ}*-ja aḫ-ti-ṭi* [4] *ša du-a-ki a-na-ku la-a šá bal-lu-ṭi a-na-ku* [5] LUGAL *be-lí re-e-mu a-na kal-bi-šú is-sa-kan* "I committed a grave crime against the ruling house, I deserved to be killed, not to be kept alive, yet the king, my lord, had mercy on his servant", *ABL* 620:3' ff. This passage also recalls Isa. 61:1 ff.

24. There is no need to emend *tap-ta-ṭar* (collated) into *up!-ta-ṭar* (*CAD* Ṣ 7b), for "alternation from second to third person is a widely attested stylistic device, both in the namburbis and elsewhere in Akkadian and other Near Eastern literature; see the evidence gathered by O. Loretz, *Qohelet und der alte Orient* 213 f" (Caplice, *Or*NS 34 [1965] 120). This stylistic device is, besides Adad-šumu-uṣur (cf. *LAS* 122:14, 129:7-13, 21-r1 and r15-24), also attested in letters of other scholars (against Deller 1969, p.52). See *LAS* 194 r9' (Marduk-šākin-šumi); 4:17, 318 r4 (Ištar-šumu-ēreš); 34 r7, 35 r8, 48 r6', 50 r5 (Balasî); 14:8, 298:11 ff and r16', 299 r7', 300:14 (Ak-kullānu); and 219 r6 (Nabû-nāṣer).

r1-3. On the grammatical interpretation of these lines see Deller, *RA* 61 (1967) 189. Notice the structure of the triplet corresponding to the Mesopotamian rations system ŠE.BA – Ì.BA – SÍG.BA, "allowances of food, oil and clothing". Instead of *ub-bu-lu-ti* "the dried, the parched"[227], it is also possible to read *up-pu-lu-ti* "the lousy ones", see Jacobsen, *PAPS* 107 (1963) 477[11] ("there is no question that the anointing was meant, in part at least, to remove and keep off lice").

122

Bibliography:
(I) Waterman, *RCAE* 358 (cf. IV 248); Pfeiffer, *SLA* 162.
(II) Ylvisaker, *LSS* 5/6 (1912) 72; Dhorme, *RHR* 113 (1936) 130 ff; Heidel, *AS* 13 (1940) 265; Oppenheim, *JAOS* 61 (1941) 265; Deller, *AOAT* 1 (1969) 50f and 59; Fales, *ANL* 29 (1975) 479 ff.

Photograph:
RCAE IV pl.9 (reverse only).

Date:
Probably Nisannu, eponymy of Kanūnāju of the New Palace = April, 666 BC. See in detail under *LAS* 121. An indication that the letter dates from the beginning of Assurbanipal's reign is also to be seen in the fact that no sons of the king are mentioned in it. This would have been an unpardonable omission, had the letter been addressed to Esarhaddon.

Addressee:
Assurbanipal.

Notes:

4. For the reading *Zarpānītu* (not **Ṣarpānītu*) see Goetze, *JCS* 17 (1963) 84 f. Cf. *zrpnt*, *KAI* 222:8; ^{d}*Ze-er-pa-ni-tu*$_4$, DT.83 r4 (*PSBA* 17 133 ff); ^{d}*Zer-ba-ni-tu*, *STC* I 205:5; ^{d}NUMUN.DÙ-*tú/ti*, Borger *Ash* p.129, and note the folk etymology ^{d}*Zarpānītu ša kīma šumīšāma bānât zēri*, K.3371 (quoted in *CAD* Ṣ 112b).[228]

6. The reading ^{d}*La-aṣ* (not *^{d}*La-az*) is based on the spelling *lṣ* in *KAI* 222:9. Cf. also von Weiher, *AOAT* 11 (1971) 65.

14. The reading MÚŠ-*ka* ("your countenance") is here given as an alternative to the reading *šur-šu-ka* ("your roots") found in the earlier translations and studies; it is based on the parallel MÚŠ-*šú i-na-ḫi-su* "his appearance becomes poor" in Labat, *TDP* p.140 iii 54', cf. *lim-mi-ru zi-mu-ú-a*, King, *BMS* 8 r10, and the passages quoted in *CAD* Z 120 f. I do not contend that the other reading is excluded, though *šur-šu-ka* is an archaic form

[227] For *ubbulu* "dry" (said of human body) cf. *CAD* A/1 31a.

[228] For the interchange of *a* and *e* in this word see note to *LAS* 39 r3. Cf. *zerpat/zarpat* (e.g. *VS* I 86:14, *AJSL* 42 182:6, *ADD* 72 r8), *Manzarnê/Manzernê* (eponym of 684), etc.

and as such unacceptable in purely Neo-Assyrian contexts. In blessing formulae, however, the possibility of such forms (serving as stylistic devices) must be admitted, note the Babylonianisms occuring in *LAS* 123-124 and elsewhere (see notes to *LAS* 124). The general sense of the passage remains the same, whichever rendering is adopted: the king is clearly pictured as a tree offering shelter to his subjects. Cf. Dan. 4:20 ff: "The tree which you saw grow and become strong, reaching with its top to the sky and visible to earth's farthest bounds, its foliage lovely and its fruit abundant, a tree which yielded food for all, beneath which the wild beasts dwelt and in whose branches the birds lodged, that tree, O king, is you. You have grown and become strong. Your power has grown and reaches the sky; your sovereignty stretches to the ends of the earth." Cf. *LAS* 129:28 ff, 145:20 ff, 163 r10 ff, where however the "shadow of the king" possibly refers to the royal umbrella, see Oppenheim, *BASOR* 107 (1947) 7 ff.

r11-13. These lines are probably to be understood as a reference to the writer's burial described by means of a metaphor taken from rural life (cf. Deller, *AOAT* 1 50 f). Both *šapāku* and *kannušu* were agricultural terms: the former means "to cast, heap, pile up (grain)", the latter (in NA a LW from Aramaic)[229] otherwise exclusively "to harvest" (cf. Aram. *knš* pe. "to assemble", Hebr. *kns/š* [pi.] "to gather"); see the examples gathered in *CAD* K 116*b* (sub 4 a), and note in addition *uk-ta-ni-iš* *CT* 53 341:13' (following ^{ŠE}EBUR^{MEŠ} "crops" ibid.4'.6'). The present passage is actually exactly paralleled by a corresponding idiom in Babylonian, where *kms* D "to collect (grain, persons)" also means "to prepare for burial"; see *CAD* K 117*a*, sub 4 e.*

r12. *Dadâ*: probably identical with ^{I}*Da-da-a* ^{LÚ}MAŠ.MAŠ, a servant of Sennacherib mentioned in *ABL* 1216:14' together with the queen mother Naqia.[230] The name occurs otherwise only in *ABL* 968 r9.[231]

r14. *UŠ liš-kun*: sic according to collation (1968–3–22): the emendation *tè*$^{?}$<*-mu*> *liš-kun* found in earlier editions is consequently unnecessary. The reading of UŠ in the present context is hardly *šiddu* "length", as assumed in Pt.I on the basis of *ABL* 590 r1 f (*ši-du lu-ri-ku-na-ši*), but with Fales, *ANL* 29 p.495, probably *riddu.* I would, however, not follow Fales in his translation ("ai miei figli il re mio signore conceda la *successione*") but would rather choose the other meaning of *riddu*, "(gute) Führung, (gutes) Betragen" (*AHw* 981*a*), and translate "(let the king, my lord) in like manner give guidance (to my sons, etc.)".

r25. *li-iṭ-ṭu* "draft": thus following Landsberger, *BBEA* (1965) p.69 (*līṭu* = "Maquette" – "diese Bedeutung muß hier unbewiesen bleiben"); a translation like "picture, drawing" would perhaps be more appropriate, since the writer here certainly refers to a drawing such as often accompanied inscriptions on Assyrian royal steles (*asumittu*); cf. Hrouda, *Flachbild*, Tf. 46,3; 48,1-2; 49,1, and see *CAD* A/2 p.348. Cf. also *ABL* 497:6 *a-na muḫ-ḫi li-i-ṭu ša* ^{GIŠ}NÁ ^{7} *ša* ^{d}EN AN-*e* KI.TIM *ša* LUGAL EN-*a* ^{8} *iš-pu-ra um-ma šu-bi-la* "as to the *līṭu* of the bed of the Lord of Heaven and Earth, concerning which the king, my lord, wrote to me: 'Send it here' "; and *ABL* 685 r15 *li-ṭi ša* ^{URU}*bir-ti* ^{16} [*ina*] *maš*$^{!}$*-ki e-te-ṣi-ir* ^{17} [*a-na*] LUGAL *be-lí-ja* ^{18} [*ul*]-*te-bi-la* "I have drawn a picture of the fort on parchment and dispatched it to the king, my lord."

r29. *a-ḫi-ja* in this line has hitherto been translated "brother" (cf. e.g. *CAD* A/1 [1964] 202*a*, "I have heard it ten times from all my colleagues"), but the spelling of the word indicates that the correct rendering is "arm" (or metonymically "ability, strength"). The two homophones *aḫu* "brother" and *aḫu* "arm" were carefully kept apart in NA orthography, the former being always spelt with the logograms ŠEŠ or PAP, the latter either syllabically or with the sign Á. Cf. *a-ḫi-ja* "my arms" *LAS* 124 r5.6, 180:6, 235:6', ABL 885 r4; *a-ḫi-in-ni* "our arms" *LAS* 224 r9'. L.E. 1; *aḫ-šú* "his arm" *LAS* 212 r4'; *a-ḫa-šú-nu* "their arms", *ABL* 493 r24 (cf. ibid. r23). For writings with Á see *CAD* A/1 205f.

123

Bibliography:
(I) Waterman, *RCAE* 7.

[229] To be distinguished from Akk. *knš* D "to make submissive" (correct *CAD* K [1971] 146b !).

[230] The letter dates from 680 B.C.; cf. Labat, *RA* 53 (1959) 115 f.

[231] Concerning restoration of Babylon and hence probably dating from time after 671 B.C. or immediately after 681 B.C.

(II) Böhl, *Opera Minora* (1953) 402; Deller, *AOAT* 1 (1969) 55; Fales, *ANL* 29 (1975) 481, 489.

Addressee:
Esarhaddon.

Date:
Seemingly 666 BC (cf. *LAS* 121f, 125), but the spelling of the writer's name ($^{\text{I.d}}$IM-MU-*ú-ṣur*) as well as the reference to the *piqittu* (Obv.4) firmly place this letter in Esarhaddon's reign, more exactly in May 670 BC. See on *LAS* 151, and cf. *LAS* 133, 147, 158 (*-ú-ṣur*) and 143 and 215 (*piqittu* of *Šarrat parṣī*).

Addressee:
Esarhaddon.

Discussion:

This letter (and its continuation, *LAS* 124) was probably written to a sick king as part of his therapy. Cf. on *LAS* 151.

Notes:

4. *piqittu*: the meaning assigned to this word (recurring in similar contexts in several other letters of the present corpus, see below) in earlier translations and studies include "Verwaltung" (Behrens, *ABB* [1906] 82), "overseer" (ibid. 82[1]; Waterman, *RCAE* I [1930] p.253; Pfeiffer, *SLA* [1935] p.123), "minister" (Waterman, *op. cit.* p. 9), "administration" (Pfeiffer, *op. cit.* p.198), "personnel" (Oppenheim, *Letters* [1967] p.150), "team" (idem, *Centaurus* 14 [1969] 117); "Verwaltungs-, Betreuungsbereich" (von Soden, *AHw* Lfg.10 [1971] 865a) and "Beauftragte(?)" (ibid. 865b); Deller, *AOAT* 1 (1969) 55 leaves the word untranslated, but takes it as a designation of the crown prince. There are a number of reasons making it difficult to accept any of these renderings. First, the nominal pattern after which the word is formed does not point to a nomen *agentis* like "overseer", "personnel", but rather to a nomen *actionis* or object of an activity.[232] Secondly, study of the relevant contexts shows that no collective term like "administration" or "team" can be in question. There were three different *piqittus*, one of which was said to be teething (below, example [5]), another expressly designated as a child (example [12]), and the third quite obviously a small baby [7]. The evidence is in detail as follows:

A. The *piqittu* of the Queen of Cults[233] (mentioned in letters of Adad-šumu-uṣur and Nabû-nāṣer [1-6]).

[1] "The *piqittu* of the Queen of Cults is very well (*a-na* ^{LÚ}*pi-qit-ti ša* ^{d}GAŠAN GARZA *šul-mu a-dan-niš*); the king, my lord, can be happy. May the great gods of the cosmos let the king, my lord, see him prosper", *LAS* 151:6 ff (date: April, 670 BC);

[2-3] "The *piqittu* of the Queen of Cults (*pi-qit-ti ša* ^{d}GAŠAN GARZA) is very well; the king, my lord, can be very happy", 123:4 f, 143:10 ff (date: May, 670 BC);

[4] "The *piqittu* of the Queen of Cults (*pi-qi-te ša* ^{d}GAŠAN *par-ṣi*) is very, very well; the king, my lord, can be very happy. As for the *piqittu* of the Queen of Cults, the king will lift his grand-children into his lap", 215:7 ff;

[5] "The *piqittu* of the Queen of Cults (*pi-qit-te* [*š*]*a* ^{d}GAŠAN *par-ṣi*) is well. ––– His teeth were coming out, that's why he was feverish" 216:4 f, 13 ff (cf. relevant commentary);

[6] "The [*piqittu*] of the [Queen of Cults] is very, very well; the king, [my lord], can be [happy]. ––– [As for the *piqit*]*tu* of the Queen of Cults (^{d}GAŠAN *par-ṣi*), a happy dream concerning him has been seen, and I heard his utterance", 217:6 ff (cf. commentary).

---

232 See *GAG* §55c (*pirist* = "Nomina actionis von eigentlichen Verben, bisweilen mit Bedeutungsübergang ins Konkrete"). The translation best compatible with this definition is "charge". Cf. *ABL* 304:7, *ki-i pi-qit-ti ina pa-ni-ka* [8] *paq-du*, and 1018:4, GUD^{MEŠ} *pi-qi-tú ša ina* IGI-[*ja*].

233 Certainly an Ištar figure. Cf. Streck, *Asb* p.86 X 62, ^{d}*15 sa Arba-il*^{KI} ^{d}GAŠAN* GARZA^{MEŠ}, following ^{d}*15 šá* NINA^{KI} ^{d}*Šar-rat Kid-mu-ri*. According to the "Götteradressbuch" (Frankena, *Takultu* p.124:89), the goddess was worshiped in the Šarrat-nipḫa temple of Assur.

B. The *piqittu* of the Rear Palace[234] (mentioned in letters of Adad-šumu-uṣur; see, in detail, note to *LAS* 152:6):

[7] "The *piqittu* of the Rear Palace is well; he has lifted up[235] his head", *LAS* 126:5 ff (date: 669 BC);

[8-9] "The *piqittu* of the Rear Palace is well", 136:5 f (669 BC), 152:6 f;

[10] "As regards the *piqittu* [of] the crown prince's Rear Palace, we are doing our work, we are not negligent", 154:9 ff (note ibid. Obv.5 "(the prince) Aššur-etel-šamê-erṣeti-muballissu is well");

[11] "The *p[iqi]ttu* of the Rear Palace is well; we are performing our work unremittingly, we are not negligent", 155:7 ff.

C. The *piqittu* of the House of Urad-Dagūna[236] (mentioned in a letter of Adad-šumu-uṣur):

[12] "As regards the *piqittu* of the House of Urad-Dagūna, I was not told (about him) while I was there. Now I have (re-)entered (the house) and examined him. Is there a(ny) child which is not treated in this way?", 147 r4 ff.

D. [13] "All (or both) *piqittu*s are very well (*šùl-mu a-dan-niš* [9] *a-na* ^{LÚ}*pi-qit-ta-a-ti gab-bu*); the king, my lord, can be happy", 188:8 ff (Marduk-šākin-šumi).

All these passages are typical medical reports on the health of patients comparable with *LAS* 140 r1, 144:15, 172:5 (concerning the crown prince); 150:7 (Assurbanipal); 159:6, 160:7 (the queen dowager); 140:12, 150:9, 172:6 (Šamaš-šumu-ukīn); 150:11, 154:6 (Aššur-šar-šamê-erṣeti-muballissu); 142:7, 150:15 (Sîn-perʾī-ukīn), etc. Otherwise, only members of the royal family figure as patients, and there is nothing to indicate that the *piqittu*s constituted an exception; on the contrary, the remark "the king, my lord, can be happy" following each favourable report indicates that the king (in all cases Esarhaddon, cf. 1,3,7,8,10) was closely related to these patients.

The meaning of *piqittu* can accordingly be defined as follows: "a charge associated with a god (*Šarrat parṣī*) or a court (*Bīt kutalli, Bīt Urad-Dagūna*), specifically an *infant* member of the royal family." The fact that none of these patients had a *real* name makes it possible to be even more precise: all the *piqittu*s were little babies, one tended in the temple of Šarrat Parṣī in Assur in 670, another (a child of Assurbanipal) in the Rear Palace of Tarbiṣu in 669, and still another at the house of a scribe named Urad-Dagan probably in early 669. For the practice of entrusting (*paqādu*) royal babies to the care of goddesses note the following passage in the dialogue of Assurbanipal with Nabû (*ABRT* I 6 r 6 ff):

ṣe-eḫ-ru at-ta ^{I}AN.ŠÁR-DÙ-A *ša ú-maš-šir-u-ka ina* UGU ^{d}*šar-rat*-NINA^{KI} [7] *la-ku-u at-ta* ^{I}AN.ŠÁR-DÙ-A *ša áš-ba-ka ina bur-ki* ^{d}*šar-rat*-NINA^{KI} [8] *er-bi zi-ze-e-šá ina pi-ka šak-na 2 te-en-ni-iq 2 ta-ḫal-lap ana pa-ni-ka* "you were small, Assurbanipal, when I entrusted you to the Queen of Nineveh (= Ištar); you were a baby, Assurbanipal, when you were sitting in the lap of the Queen of Nineveh. Her four teats were placed in your mouth; you are sucking two, you are milking two to your face."

This passage can only be taken to imply that as a baby, Assurbanipal was left for nursing in the Ištar temple of Nineveh. Accordingly, the places mentioned above probably also housed nurses for royal sucklings. (It is, of course, clear that Assurbanipal cannot be identified with any of the "charges" here concerned.)

124

Bibliography:

(I) Waterman, *RCAE* 435 (cf. IV 253); Pfeiffer, *SLA* 164; Oppenheim, *Letters* (1967) 151 f, no.89 (translat. only).

[234] The crown prince's (= Assurbanipal's) palace in Tarbiṣu (mod. Šarīf Ḫān, 5 km NW of Nineveh), completed in 672 BC (see Borger, *Ash* p.71 ff and cf. *ADD* 1083).

[235] This phrase has to be taken quite literally: the baby(!) has grown enough to be able to lift his head! See respective note.

[236] Otherwise known only as the author of a fragmentary letter to the king dealing with scribal matters (Bu.91–5–9,81 = *LAS* 359).

(II) Dhorme, *RHR* 113 (1936) 132f; Labat, *Royauté* (1939) 232, 283; Deller, *AOAT* 1 (1969) 51, 61; Fales, *ANL* 29 (1975) 481, 490.

Copy:
See also Delitzsch, *AL*^{5} (1912) 90f.

Photograph:
RCAE IV pl.11 (obverse only).

Discussion:

As the words *an-ni-ú re-eḫ-ti da-ba-a-bi šá e-gér-ti pa-ni-it-ti* indicate, this tablet is a continuation of another letter, which can confidently be identified as *LAS* 123. Though the writer does not characterize his "previous letter" in any concrete way (cf. however below [2]), the coherence of *LAS* 123 and 124 can be proven as follows:

[1] Both tablets have exactly the same dimensions (see Pt. I, p.334)[237],

[2] *LAS* 123 contains only salutations and blessings; this implies that a continuation followed. The blessings of *LAS* 123 are referred to in *LAS* 124:12 f.

[3] The sign Ú is written with a superfluous wedge in both tablets (see 123 r4' and 15', 124:1.9.12.17 and r12).

[4] In both tablets, "the land of Akkad" is written syllabically (KUR *Ak-ka-di-i* 123:16.r8' and 124 r10); this spelling does not occur in any other Sargonid letter except *ABL* 1236, written in Babylonian (see *AOAT* 6, p.8 f). Similarly, both letters share the spellings KUR.KUR^{MEŠ} (123 r11 and 124:6, for normal KUR.KUR) and DÙG.GA (123 r13', 124 r9.11); both make use of the syllabic value KI = *qí* (123 r18', 124 r7).

[5] Both letters contain several Babylonianisms used as stylistic devices: there are 4 such forms in 123 (*nu-um-mur*, r14'; *šul-bur* & *ru-up-[pu-uš]*, r16; *šum-ú-du*, r17) and as many as 8 in 124 (*ki-ma*, *e-li*, *li-iṭ-bi* [for *lū taṭīb*], *az-ku-ru*, *li-iṣ-ṣi-pu*, *la-zi-iz-MA*, *gu-mur-ti*, and *áš-šu*). By contrast, in other letters of the present collection Babylonianisms occur only sporadically, and never more frequently than twice per letter (cf. *ar-ḫi-šá-am* and *na-da-an*, *LAS* 7 r9 and 14; *a-ma-ti*, 12 r5'; *ma-ḫar*, 26 r4 and 30:9; *it-ti*, 50 r3; *li-rap-pi-šú* and *mu-ma-'i-ru-te*, 122:14 and r21; *ma-la* and *it-ti*, 125:13 and r1; *e-pe-ši-šu* [also attested in MA], 157:5'; *e-pu-sa-ak-ki* [in quotation], 211:18; *il-du* (also MA), 247 r18; *it-ti* & *qaq-qa-ru*, 300+:5 and 29; *bu-luṭ*, 308:7; *nu-um-mur*, 310:4; *an-nu-ú* and *uš-ta-pal-u-ni*, 318 r9 and 10; *áš-šú*, 322:2; *an-nu-ú* in 152 r1 and *um-ma* in 334:5 are probably not pertinent, see relevant notes).

[6] Finally, there is an unusually high number of syllabic spellings in both letters.

Notes:

5-7. *"Good as oil ..."*: this comparison appears to have been very popular in the first millennium, and the benediction, too, recurs in slightly varying forms in several contemporary texts, especially in royal inscriptions. Cf., e.g., LUGAL-(*ú*-)*te* ^{11} GIM Ú (var. *ki-ma šam-me*) TI.LA ^{12} UGU UZU^{MEŠ} UN^{MEŠ} ^{13} *li-ṭib-ma*, Borger, *Ash* p.26:10 ff; *siq-ri pi-ja ke-e-nu-um ki-i ú-lu* Ì UGU *na-bi* MAH^{MEŠ} EN^{MEŠ}-*ja ma-a'-diš i-ṭí-ib-ma*, Lyon *Sg* p.9:55; *áš-ba* KUR.KUR *šub-tu né-eḫ-[tu ki]-ma ú-lu šam-ni taq-na kib-rat erbe-tim*, Streck *Asb* p.260:23; *ša* DINGIR^{MEŠ} GAL^{MEŠ} LUGAL-*us-su ki-ma ú-lu* ^{12} Ì^{MEŠ} *uš-ṭib-bu* UGU *gi-mir ma-ti-tan*, Böhl *AC* 25:11 f; GIM *ú-lu* Ú Ì.GIŠ *ṭib-bi* UGU UN^{MEŠ} DAGAL[^{MEŠ}], *KAV* 171.14, ^{LÚ}SIPA-*ut-ku ki-ma ú-lu ù* ÌxGIŠ! UGU *nap-ḫar kiš!-šat* ⌜UN⌝![^{MEŠ}] *li-iṭ-ṭib-bu*, *ABL* 1285:9 (letter to Assurbanipal); *a-mat* ^{d}7.BI *iq-bu-ú ki-i ú-lu* Ì.GIŠ UGU-*šú i-ṭib*, Cagni *Erra* I 93. The reading *li-iṭ-bi* (≦ *liṭīb*, rather than *li-it-bi* from *tabû* "to rise") adopted for the present passage is based on the above parallels. For the alternation *liṭbi* ~*liṭīb* cf. note on 151 r15.

r4 f. Cf. *ABL* 885 r4 f: *a-na-ku ina* ŠÀ *a-ḫi-ja* GÌR.2!-*ja* ^{5} *a-na* DUMU-LUGAL EN-*ja la-ap-làḫ* "I will serve (lit. fear) the crown prince, my lord, with my *arms and feet* ...."

r10 ff. *"It is said in a song from Babylonia"*: With the "song" the writer probably meant an epical poem sung or recited (as in the case of the Epic of Creation) to the accompaniment of music; however, I have

[237] Note that the lower edge of No.123 is broken away. The original length of the tablet must have been c. 74mm.

not been able to identify the source of the quotation. Cf. Streck, *Asb* p.258 ii 8': *ḫa-du-ú* NUN^{MEŠ} LÚ*šu-ut*-SAG *ú-pa-qu zi-kir šap-*[*ti-ja*] "the noblemen rejoiced, the eunuchs craved for the words of my lips. . ." On the subject of Babylonian "songs" see also Oppenheim, *Anc.Mes.*, p.22.*

125

Bibliography:

(I) Waterman, *RCAE* 6 (cf. III 373, IV 173, 231); Pfeiffer, *SLA* 161.
(II) Behrens, *ABB* (1906) 91; Ylvisaker, *LSS* 5/6 (1912) 67 f; Dhorme, *RHR* 113 (1936) 130, 133; Ebeling, *AfO* 14 (1941/4) 300; Oppenheim, *JAOS* 64 (1944) 190; Böhl, *Opera Minora* (1953) 402 f, 522[74]; Fales, *ANL* 29 (1975) 479 ff.

Date:

Nisannu/April, 666 BC. Comparison with *LAS* 122 (cf. 122:3-7 with 125:3-6; 122 r2-3 with 125:28-29; 122 r15-20 with 125:22-27; and 122 r26-30 with 125 r7-11) indicates that the present letter was written immediately after *LAS* 122, which in turn slightly postdated *LAS* 121; the dating of the latter to early 666 is made certain by *LAS* 120 (see pertinent commentary). For a detailed discussion of the relationship of *LAS* 121, 122 and 125 see Fales (1975).

Addressee:

Assurbanipal.

Notes:

7. *ṭābtānu*: a synonym of *bēl ṭābti* "benefactor", also attested in *LAS* 212:10 f, [*ṭa-ab-t*]*a-nu ša a-dan-niš ù ra-i-mu* [*ša* UN^{MEŠ}] || EN *ṭa-ab-ti-ja ša a-dan-niš šu-u, ABL* 221 r2 f. Words formed in a parallel way (*ṭābtu* "benefit" + individualizing morpheme *-ān-* [*GAG* § 56r]) are *nabalkattānu* "rebel" (Borger, *Ash* p.47:54) and *dannatānu maṣâtānu* "potent and influential person" (*ABL* 633:20); cf. also *si-im-ma-ta-nu-te, ABL* 1427:8.

12. *i-sa-ú* = /issa''ū/, Pf. 3m Pl. of *šamû* "to hear" (< *ištam'ū*); see Deller, *RA* 61 (1967) 189.

13. *ma-la šu-mu n*[*a-bu-u*]: a well-known "hymnic-epical" phrase, here probably used in order to render the diction of the letter additional elegance and given in its Babylonian form for the very same purpose. For other Babylonianisms in the present letter corpus see commentary to *LAS* 124.

18 f. *"The king is the very image of Bēl"*: cf. *šu-ú-ma ṣa-lam* ^{d}BE *da-ru-ú še-mu-u pi-i* UN^{MEŠ} "he (Tukulti-Ninurta) is the eternal image of Illil who listens to the words of (his) people", *AfO* 18 50 y 10. The present context confirms what was already suggested in the commentary to *LAS* 51:7 f, viz. that the king was likened to Marduk (or Bēl) especially when it was appropriate to extol his *goodness* and *mercifulness*, and it would accordingly seem that these indeed were characteristics most popularly associated with Marduk at the period concerned. Cf. the attributes of Marduk listed in Tallqvist, *Götterepitheta* p.371 and *CAD* G 22, s.v. *gamālu*, and note especially: "The merciful Lord, the warrior Marduk, was angry at night but relented in the morning. O King of the World! You are the very image of Marduk (LUGAL ŠÚ *ṣa-lam* ^{d}AMAR+UD *at-ta*); you were angry with your servants, we suffered the anger of the king our lord, (but) we (also) saw the king relent" (*RMA* 170:5 ff).

The king was, of course, also likened to other gods; cf., e.g., *LAS* 143 r4 f (King = Sun); 144 r6 f (*ša* LUGAL EN *iq-bu-u-ni ki-i ša* DINGIR *gam-rat*); 145 r12 f; and *ABL* 1221 r12 (LUGAL) *be-lí a-bat-su ki-i šá* DINGIR^{MEŠ} [*gam-rat*] "the word of the king, my lord, is as final as the gods' "). See also *LAS* 184 r7f and 230 r1 and the corresponding notes.

22. *ša* "that" in the sense of "because" also occurs in 34:14, 126 r17, and 152 r3.

r1. The blessing in this line is a direct adaptation of the poetical language of the royal inscriptions. Cf. DUMU^{MEŠ}-*šú* DUMU. DUMU^{MEŠ}-*šú it-ti ṣal-mat* SAG.DU *li-ku-nu* [60] *a-na du-ur da-ar*, Luckenbill, *OIP* 2 139:59 (Sennacherib), and see *CAD* D 108 and Ṣ 75 f for more similar examples.

r3 ff. Praying to the *name* of the great gods (*sic* according to collation) is reminiscent of the Biblical terminology, in which שֵׁם יהוה "often means not only the name, but the full being and power of Yahveh" (Koehler-Baumgartner, *Lexicon* p.984*a*); "later on, הַשֵּׁם ≈ God; God himself" (ibid. 984*b*). Our passage is paralleled by *LAS* 155 r1, DINGIR^{MEŠ} *nu-ṣal-la* "we pray to the gods" (omitting the word *šumu* "name"), which suggests that the equation "the name of God" = "God" existed in Assyria, too. Cf. also the idiom *šumu ša ilāni zakāru* "to mention the name of the gods" (e.g., *LAS* 124:14 and 126:8), to be compared with the Bibl. idioms quoted in Koehler-Baumgartner, loc.cit.

r11 f. At the first glance, this passage might be taken to imply that the co-operation of Adad-šumu-uṣur and Marduk-šākin-šumi began only after this particular royal order and that consequently all their joint letters (*LAS* 139, 163-166, 169; cf. also 162) would date from Assurbanipal's reign. However, a scrutiny of the dating criteria present in the letters concerned reveals that, on the contrary, *all* of them date from the reign of Esarhaddon. In these letters the name of Adad-šumu-uṣur always precedes that of Marduk-šākin-šumi, which indicates that the former (as the king's old personal exorcist) at that time ranked higher as the latter (the younger chief exorcist). In Assurbanipal's reign the rank order of the two must have been reversed. – For *uzuzzu* + *issi* "to stand by, assist" cf. *ABL* 447 r10 ff, "these 9 are those who are assisting the master (TA* *um-ma-a-ni iz-za-zu-ú-ni*) and working on the (series) "House of the Patient"".

r12 ff. For the end of the letter in general cf. Streck, *Asb* p.250:3, *a-na* DINGIR *u a-me-lu-tu*$_4$ *ana* ÚŠ *u* TI^{MEŠ} MUN DÙ-*uš* "I (Assurbanipal) did good to god and man, and to the dead and the living (alike)."

126

Bibliography:

(I) Waterman, *RCAE* 9 (cf. IV 232); Pfeiffer, *SLA* 163; Oppenheim, *Letters* (1967) 150.
(II) Oppenheim, *JAOS* 64 (1944) 190; de Liagre Böhl, *Opera Minora* (1953) 387; Aro, *StOr* 26 (1961) 145; Deller, *AOAT* 1 (1969) 55; Fales, *ANL* 29 (1975) 490.

Copy:

Cf. Pinches, *5 R* 53 no.3.

Photograph:

RCAE IV pl.6 (obv. only).

Addressee:

Esarhaddon.

Date:

Late June, 669 BC; see on *LAS* 154. The reference to the (crown) princes (DUMU^{MEŠ} LUGAL) in r7 assures the time brackets 672-669 BC, see on 173:17.

Notes:

6. *piqittu ša bēt kutalli*: a baby nurse in the "Rear Palace" of Tarbiṣu. See on *LAS* 123 and 152.[238]

7. *re-ši-šu* "his head": not to be explained as Gen. Sg. (+ poss.suff.) standing for *Nom.* Sg., as in the examples discussed by Deller and Parpola in *Or*NS 35 (1966) 121f,[239] but as Gen. *Du.* The idiom *rēšu našû* "to lift the head = to summon, to collect" was, it is true, regularly construed with *rēšu* in Sg. (cf. *re-es-su liššiū* 133 r22', and the numerous examples in Oppenheim, *JAOS* 61 252ff); but when *rēšu* occurred with pronominal suffixes referring to the subject of the sentence (as here), or in idioms *concretely* meaning "to raise or lower (one's own, or somebody else's) head", it was put in the dual. Cf. *BWL* 200:19, "the fox raised its head" (*iš-ši re-ši-šu*); ibid. 88:

[238] The king's blessings referred to in Obv.12f and Rev.17f may have been occasioned by the recovery of this patient. Cf. Rev.13-16.

[239] Note also *be-lí-ja* (Nom.) for normal *be-lí* in *ABL* 486:5, 885:16, 927:5, 1019 r4, 1026:4 etc.

293, "I did not raise my head" (*re-ši-ja ul ul-lu*); *CH* r. xxiv 63 ff, "Babylon, whose head Anum and Illil have raised" (*re-ši-šu ú-ul-lu-u*); numerous similar examples in *AHw.* 974*a* and Oppenheim, loc. cit.

r1-12. The three elaborate infinitive constructions making up this passage all pertain to *ik-ri-bi* "blessings" in Obv.15 (*ikribī . . . ša . . . ana qarrubi u ana sarruri u . . . ana tadāni*). The idea is that not only will the blessed person (= Adad-šumu-uṣur) profit by the benedictions, but the gods will also reward the b l e s s e r (i.e., Esarhaddon) a thousandfold (cf. 124:17ff, 125 r14ff). Cf. Landsberger, *MAOG* 4 (1928) 294: "Auch dieser Bedeutung von *karābu*, die sich oft nicht anders anders als durch "beten" übersetzen läßt, geht niemals das wesentliche Moment des Grüßens, die G e g e n s e i t i g k e i t , verloren: –– dem *karābu* des Menschen folgt als Lohn das *karābu* Gottes (*ana Sin likrub Sin awīla ikarrab* ["let him pray to Sin, Sin will bless the man"] III *R* 56, Nr. 6, 8f)."

r13. *né-me-qe ša* ᵈ*É-a u* ᵈ*Asal-lú-ḫi*: is this a (subconscious?) reminiscence of the incantation ÉN ᵈ*É-a u* ᵈ*Asal-lú-ḫi né-me-qa li-gam-me-ru-ni* "may Ea and Asalluḫi perfect my wisdom" mentioned in *CT* 22 1:16'f? The progressively assimilated final vowel in *né-me-qE* (for *-qu*) points to a long vowel in the penultima of this word, see Deller + Parpola, *Or*NS 36 (1967) 337f.[240] The underlying nominal pattern is, consequently, probably *maprās*, and the nominative of the word has to be posited as *nēmēqu* rather than *nēmequ* (*AHw.*). The pattern *maprās* (cf. *GAG* § 56b) also in *nēpēšu* "ritual" (*AHw* 778*b nēpešu*, but cf. *né-pe-e-še LAS* 280:18 and *né-pe-*⌜*e*⌝*-*[*še*] 208 r2), *mērēšu* "cultivation" (cf. *me-re-e-še ADD* 1169 r6), *māḫāzu, mākālu, maknāku*, etc.

127

See under *LAS* 339.

128

B i b l i o g r a p h y :
(I) Waterman, *RCAE* 1166 (cf. IV 201).
(II) Deller, *Or*NS 35 (1966) 317, and *AOAT* 1 (1969) 61.

W r i t e r :
Tentatively identified as Adad-šumu-uṣur on the basis of the affinities of the introductory blessing formula with the corresponding formulae in *LAS* 122-127; a similar (though more divergent) sequence of gods is otherwise found only in letters by Marduk-šākin-šumi. It should be noted, however, that certain orthographic and linguistic details make this assignation uncertain:

[1] The spelling *a-ki-i* (Rev.2') is otherwise attested in the present corpus in letters of Nabû-nādin-šumi only (203 r8, 205 r7 and 11, 212:11); Adad-šumu-uṣur wrote *a-ki* or *ki-i*;

[2] The form [*šum-m*]*u* (r7), if correctly restored,[241] would be a hapax legomenon in Adad-šumu-uṣur's letters, where only *šum-ma* is attested (119:14, 133 r7' and 8', 135:13, etc.);

[3] While Adad-šumu-uṣur appears to have consistently written ᵈNIN.URTA for *Ninurta* (cf. 122:6, 123:12, 125:5), the present letter has ᵈMAŠ (Obv.6);

[4] The letter also reads *a-šib* (Obv.7) where Adad-šumu-uṣur would have written *a-ši-bu-ti/te* (cf. 122:8, 123:15 and 16), and *a-ŠÁ-mu-ú-*[*ni*] for expected **a-šam-mu-u-ni* (cf. 133 r20'; see also below).

Note, in addition, that the gods Illil, Mulissu, Aja and [Šala], invoked in the blessing, are not mentioned at all in *LAS* 122-127.

---

[240] Note also MB *né-me-e-qí*, *EA* 357:84.

[241] Thinkable restorations would also be [*um-m*]*u* "fever" or [*šu-m*]*u* "omen", with [*šum-ma*] restored at the end of Rev.6.

Taking into consideration the relatively great instability of Adad-šumu-uṣur's orthography, the significance of these points should perhaps not be exaggerated, but they do cause difficulties. Assignation to Marduk-šākin-šumi or Nabû-nādin-šumi presents similar problems (*šum-mu* and *lib-bu* [r6'] not attested in the letters of the latter, *a-ki-i* and *lib-bu* not in those of the former). Perhaps the letter was, after all, written by Urad-Gula, who very probably also wrote *LAS* 127? The handwriting, however, does not point in this direction.

Discussion:

The interpretation of this letter, paradoxical as it may seem, entirely hinges on the way two separate words are understood. If the word *libbu* in r7' means "meaning" (see relevant note), then the verb *pašāru* in r4', 5' and 7' has to be rendered "to explain" (scil. omens, dreams, etc.), and vice versa. However, it is equally possible (and, in view of *LAS* 183 and 199, even more probable) that *pašāru* has to be taken here in its medical sense "to cure", in which case the translation of *libbu* would have to be "heart", "abdomen", or the like.[242] The fragmentary text does not permit a definite decision.

Notes:

r6'. [*E*]*N a-ge-e*: a standard epithet of the moon-god, sometimes also attached to Aššur; cf. Tallqvist, *Götterepitheta*, p.41.

lib-bu-šu: for the translation "meaning" given in Pt.I cf. *li-ib-bi a-wa-tim ul i-di* "I do not know the 'heart' of the matter", Laessøe, *Shemshara Tablets* 54 SH 921:23', but note the above reservations. Hardly to be read *nar-bu-šu*, *lub-bu-šu* or *lip-pu-šu*.

r10'. *iḫ-*⌜*du*⌝*-ṭu-u*: sic, but certainly simply a badly written *iḫ-te-ṭu-u* (thus Harper, with a question-mark) or *iḫ-ti-ṭu-u*.

129

Bibliography:

(I) Waterman, *RCAE* 595 (= K 1119) and 870 (= 82-5-22,107); Pfeiffer, *SLA* 151 (= 82-5-22,107); Oppenheim, *Letters* (1967) p.158 f (= 82-5-22,107); Deller, *AOAT* 1 (1969) 56 f (whole letter).
(II) Dhorme, *RHR* 113 (1936) 126 f; Oppenheim, *BASOR* 107 (1947) 9; Böhl, *Opera Minora* (1953) 394; von Soden, *Herrscher* (1954) 124; Wiseman, *VTE* (1958) 7 f; Fales, *ANL* 29 (1975) 490.

Copy:

CT 53 no.31.

Date:

Late Ajāru or early Simānu, eponymy of Nabû-bēlu-uṣur = May or June, 672 BC. See commentaries to *LAS* 1 and 171.

Writer:

Adad-šumu-uṣur. The grounds for this assignation should be obvious; however, taking into consideration the importance of the letter, it may be expedient to have the relevant facts explicitly put together. First, the writer calls himself "the old man of the king" (LÚ***par-šu-mu ša* LUGAL EN-*ja a-na-ku*), a statement otherwise only found in the correspondence of Adad-šumu-uṣur, where it occurs twice (126:14 ff and 144 r2 f). The introductory formula fits Adad-šumu-uṣur perfectly (cf. *LAS* 134 ff; note especially the omission of *u* "and" between ^{d}AG and ^{d}AMAR+UD; for the sign MAN in Obv.4 cf. 152:3). The same is true of the orthography of the letter: the spelling *an-ni-im-ma* (Obv.25) is also attested in 137 r11 and 145 r7 (while the word is spelled *an-NIM-ma* in the letters of Marduk-šākin-šumi); LUGAL-*ú-tú/te* (Obv.8.10) = 121:6.7,123 r4; *a-me-lu-te* (Rev.26) = 125 r15, 145 r10.11.12; *a-ni-nu* (Obv.13) = 121 r11, 125 r2, 155:9; *tu-us-sa-ad-gi-il* (Obv.7) ≈ *nu-us-sa-ad-gíl* 135:11. It is true that a few spellings differ from ones found in other letters by Adad-šumu-uṣur (e.g., *uk-ta-li-im* Obv.7 as against *uk-tal-lim*

[242] Referring to the king?

in 121 r7 and 122 r26, and *lu-ke-'i-in* in Obv.22 as against *lu-ke-in* in 119 r5), but this is only natural, especially bearing in mind the relative instability of Adad-šumu-uṣur's orthography (see Appendix M 6). Finally, the style of the letter is characteristically Adad-šumu-uṣur's; see on this point Deller (1969, p.51 f), and note especially Obv. 14 (= 121 r13), 15 (= 122 r6), 16-18 (= 123 r9-12 etc.), 21-22 (= 123 r5 f), 28-r1 (≠ 145:20 ff), and the antitheses, parataxes, parables and metaphors also characterizing the style of *LAS* 121 ff.

Addressee:
Esarhaddon.

Discussion:

The original way in which Esarhaddon decided to settle his succession has been the subject of much discussion, but the new information provided by the present letter, which until recently was available only in two disconnected fragments, necessitates taking up the question once more here. It is obvious that the letter was written immediately after the king had made his decision publicly known, and as such contains the only extant documentation of the immediate Assyrian reaction to the event.[243] The writer does not conceal that his immediate reaction was stupefaction ("what has not been done in heaven . . ."), which was perhaps not so much provoked by the fact that the realm was factually divided between two brothers than by the fact that the first-born son Šamaš-šumu-ukīn was given only the kingship of Babylon, whereas the kingship of Assyria was entrusted to the younger brother Assurbanipal.[244] The beginning of the letter was formerly taken as evidence of a strong *protest* against the supplanting of Šamaš-šumu-ukīn (see von Soden, *Herrscher im Alten Orient*, p. 124 and *Propyläen-Weltgeschichte* II, p.112; Wiseman, *Vassal-Treaties*, p.7f; Labat, *Fischer Weltgeschichte* 4, p.81). Now we know that just the opposite was the case. The writer says that when he (with his colleagues) heard the news, "he blessed the king and his heart was delighted"; the rest of the Assyrians, he continues, "let out a sigh of relief" (Rev.14), whereas the Elamites became "trembling and anxious" (Rev.6-10). These statements, if not mere flattery, imply that Assurbanipal was really universally considered abler and more talented than the legitimate heir Šamaš-šumu-ukīn (cf. von Soden, *op.cit.*, p.127: "Es kann nach den für diese Zeit recht ausgiebigen Quellen nicht zweifelhaft sein, daß Assurbanipal seinem Bruder an vielseitiger Begabung und Energie weit überlegen war; seine Ernennung zum Thronfolger hatte also durchaus im Interesse des Reiches gelegen."). It is also possible that the popularity of Assurbanipal was largely due to his well-known nationalistic stand (cf. von Soden, *op.cit.*, p.124; in addition to the evidence of the inscriptions, note also that the letters of Assurbanipal to Esarhaddon always open with an invocation of *Aššur*, Bēl and Nabû, not just Nabû and Marduk as usual at that time; see also *LAS* 130-131); in any case, it is hardly a coincidence that the name Aššur occurs 8 times in the present letter!

In his Tarbiṣu inscription, Esarhaddon plainly states that Assurbanipal was his favorite son ([I]*Aš+šur*-DÙ-IBILA DUMU.MAN GAL *ša* É *re-du-ti* DUMU *na-ram-ja*, Borger, *Ash* p.71 § 43:25), and this simple fact doubtless best accounts for his choice as the heir apparent. However, the present letter indicates that the choice could also be grounded by objective arguments; otherwise the reactions of the Elamites and the Assyrians (if correctly described) are unexplicable.

In the light of the present letter Assurbanipal's own account of his accession gains much in reliability; in fact, its general mood is just what breathes from the words of Adad-šumu-uṣur. "By order of the great gods, my father and begetter loved me more than the assembly of my older brothers; in the month Ajāru . . . I entered the Succession Palace, the place of command and counsel, and by order of Aššūr, the father of the gods, Marduk, the lord of lords and the king of the gods, he elevated me above (all) princes and called my name to the kingship. At my entrance in the palace, the whole 'camp' rejoiced (and) was filled with music; nobles and eunuchs exulted and craved for the words of my lips. I interceded for them in the presence of my father and begetter . . . The great gods looked with satisfaction upon my good deeds and by their august order I was happily seated on the throne of my father and begetter. Nobles and eunuchs craved for and loved my rule, the four quadrants of the earth rejoiced and exulted at the mention of my weighty name . . . " (Streck, *Asb* p.260 i 30 ff). Note especially the reference to the Elamite king later in the text, Col. ii 24.

---

243 Otherwise we have only Assurbanipal's self-description of his accession, for which see below.
244 See note on Obv.10.

Notes:

5-7. The exclamation "what has not been done (even) in heaven . . ."[245] is exaggerated, since Esarhaddon had himself passed over at least two of his brothers at his nomination as crown prince (cf. Borger, *Ash* p.40).

6,21. *kaq-qi-ri* "earth": when opposed to "heaven" (as here), normally spelt logographically KI.TIM. The present spelling and the lack of NA syllabic spellings of **erṣetu*, indicates that KI.TIM was always read *kaqquru* in NA. Cf. also *LAS* 212:6, *ki-i ša* AN-*e kaq-qu-ru da-ru-ú-ni* ≈ 122 r3 *a-du* AN-*e* KI.TIM *da-ru-u-ni* and note *ina šá-ma-me* (*ù*) *qaq-qa-ri* Borger, *Ash* p.16, Ep.12:13; p.45 ii 5; Streck, *Asb* p.180:19, etc. The existence of the reading *qaqqaru* is admitted in *CAD* E 313*b* but restricted to the cases where the sign KI lacks the complement TIM. However, TIM has here obviously not a phonetic, but a semantic function; the value TIM = *tì* does not belong to the Neo-Assyrian syllabary (spellings such as ḪUL-*tì* and KUR *Tam-tì* are traditional). For a discussion of "pseudo-phonetic" complements of the type TIM see E. Leichty, *TCS* 4, p.27 ff. Note also KI.TIM in Urartian inscriptions (Melikišvili, *St.Pohl* 7, p.70).

8. ^{TÚG}*pi*$^{!}$*-tu-tu*: sic after collation (Sollberger, Jan. 1976). The word is otherwise attested only twice (cf. *AHw* 871*a*) but the translation seems certain. The ornamental royal diadem was in Assyria, as in the whole ancient Near East, a distinctive symbol of the kingship, and both Šamaš-šumu-ukīn and Assurbanipal are depicted wearing it besides their father in the Zenjirli stele of Esarhaddon (see Unger, *RlA* II, p.202).[246] The girding with the diadem certainly symbolized the investment of the crown prince with the royal authority. Cf. *a-di ina* UGU DUMU^{MEŠ} *šá šá* SU$_6$^{MEŠ} *ina* UGU *ḫal-pe-te šá* ^{LÚ}SAG^{MEŠ} ^{5} [*at-t*]*a* LUGAL-*u-tú ina muḫ-ḫi-šú-nu tu-up-pa-šú-u-ni* ^{6} [*lu-taq-qi*]*-in-ka ina* É.UŠ-*u-ti* ^{7} [AD-*ka ina ri-š*]*á-a-ti* ^{TÚG}*pi-tu-tu i-rak-kas* "until you exercise the kingship over the sons of the bearded (courtiers) and the successors of the eunuchs, [I shall keep] you [sa]fe in the Succession Palace, [and your father] will joyfully gird (your temples) with the (royal) headband. . ." (Strong, *BA* 2, 645 = Craig, *ABRT* I Pl.26), also ^{TÚG}*pi-t*[*u-tu*] $^{6'}$[*ina* SA]G.DU-*šú i-rak-ka-su* "they gird his head with a diadem" (unp. cultic ritual, courtesy W.G. Lambert).

10. Šamaš-šumu-ukīn designates himself explicitly as "the first among the sons (DUMU.[UŠ SAG].KAL) of Esarhaddon" in BM 87229:9 (*CT* 10, Pl.4). Since Assurbanipal too explicitly states that he had older brothers ([*ina*] UKKIN ŠEŠ^{MEŠ}-*ja* [GA]L^{MEŠ}, Streck, *Asb* p. 258:30, for the translation see above), the long-lived debate about the age order of the two brothers (cf. Wiseman, *VTE* p.6 f) must be considered quite unessential. See already Streck, op.cit., p. CCXLIII f.

12f. In this metaphor (as in Semitic in general), the right hand signifies South (= Babylonia), the left Assyria. Cf. *Genesis* 48:13 f: "Then he took the two of them, Ephraim on his right at Israel's left and Manasseh on his left at Israel's right, and brought them close to him. Israel stretched out his right hand and laid it on Ephraim's head, although he was the younger, and, crossing his hands, laid his left hand on Manasseh's head; but Manasseh was the elder." The writer is obviously at pains trying to convince the king that he fully approved the doings of his majesty; the older son had been entrusted the kingship of Babylon, ergo been placed at the king's right side, ergo the king had acted correctly, according to the traditions, although he of course had decidedly violated the accepted order of succession, as plainly stated at the outset of the letter.

23f. Cf. *VTE* 1.54: KASKAL SIG$_5$ *ina* GÌR^{2} [[ ]]-*šú* [*l*]*a ta-šá-kan-a-ni* "(you swear that) you will set a fair path at his (= Assurbanipal's) feet."

25f. "*Your numerous sons*": Esarhaddon was indeed blessed with many children. Already Streck (*Asb* p. CCXLI ff) was able to list by name seven children of this king (against 6-7 known children of Sennacherib and 2 of Assurbanipal), and the number has since then increased so that one can now identify at least 9 of them by name and perhaps as many as 19 in more general terms:

[1]	Assurbanipal	(for references see Streck, *op.cit.*, p.691f)
[2]	Aššur-etel-šamê-erṣeti-muballissu	(cf. below, no. 5) ^{I}AN.ŠÁR-*e-tel*-AN-KI-TI.LA.BI, *LAS* 154:6, *VAB* 7,250:17 ^{I}*Aš+šur-e-tel*-AN-KI-TI.LA.BI, *ABL* 228:7, *AfO* 13, 214:21 [ ]-TI.LA.BI, *ADD* 970 i 4

[245] In heaven, the kingship always passed to the oldest son (cf. *En.El.* I 10ff; note also the late elevation of Nabû).
[246] Cf. now also Reade, *Iraq* 34 (1972) 93.

[3]	Aššur-mukīn-palē'a/palū'a[247]	^{I}*Aš+šur-mu-kin*-BAL-*ja*, *LAS* r6, 52:10, 69 r2, 72 r8, *AfO* 13, 214:20 ^{I}*Aš+šur-mu-kin*-BAL-*já*, *ADD* 1053 iv 1 [ ]-GIN-BAL-*já*, *ADD* 970 i 3 ^{I}AN.ŠÁR-*mu-kin*-BAL^{MEŠ}-*já*, *VAB* 7, 250:16 ^{I}*Aš+šur-mu-kin*-BAL^{MEŠ}-*ja*, *LAS* 218:6, 250 r11, *ABL* 113 r9 ^{I}*Aš+šur*-GIN-[BAL-*u*]-*a*, *BRM* 4 50:4 (627 BC) ^{I}*Aš+šur*-GIN-B]AL^{MEŠ}-*a*, *LAS* 352 r2' ^{I}*Aš+šur*-GIN-BAL^{MEŠ}-*ja*, *LAS* 145:7 ^{I}*Aš+šur-mu-kin*^{in}-BAL-*u-a*, *LAS* 157 r5, 219:2.r3 ^{I}*Aš+šur-mu-kin*-BAL-*u-a*, *LAS* 250:8 [ ]-*mu-kin*-BAL-*u-a*, *LAS* 240:8 ^{I}*Aš+šur-mu-kin*-[ ], *LAS* 17:9
[4]	Aššur-qā'iš-balāṭi	^{I}*Aš+šur*-BA-TI.LA, *AfO* 13, 214:19
[5]	Aššur-šarrāni-[muballis]su	^{I}*Aš+šur*-LUGAL-*a-ni*-[. .] .BI,*LAS* 218:8, possibly identical with [2][248]
[5a]	Aššur-šar-šamê-erṣeti-muballissu	^{I}*Aš+šur*!-LUGAL-AN-KI-TI.BI, *ABL* 113 r10 [ ]-LUGAL-AN-KI-[. .], *LAS* 150:11, probably identical with [2][249]
[5b]	Etlu-šamê-erṣeti-muballissu	[^{I}*E*]*t-lu*-AN-KI-TI.BI, *LAS* 251:7, an abbreviation for [2]?
[6]	Sîn-nādin-apli[250]	^{Id}*30*-SUM-*na*-IBILA, *AGS* 107:2; -A ibid.7
[7]	Sîn-perʾī-ukīn	^{Id}*30*-NUNUZ-GIN-*in*, *LAS* 142:7, 145:9, 150:15, 352 r3'
[8]	Šamaš-mētu-uballiṭ	^{Id}GIŠ.NU$_{11}$-UG$_{5}$.GA-TI.LA (letters by) *ABL* 341, 766, [1199] (mentioned in) *ADD* 946 ii 1, 970 i 5, *ABL* 1239:4 (eponym 637 B.C.) Falkner, *AfO* 17, 118 ff
[9]	Šamaš-šumu-ukīn	(for references see Streck, *Asb* p.721 f)
? [10]	Šarrat-sams[ī]	^{Id}*Šar-rat-sa-am-s*[*i*], *LAS* 157:2' (uncertain if a royal child)
[11]	Šērū'a-ēṭerat	$^{MÍ.d}$*Še-ru-u+a*-KAR-*at*, *ABL* 113 r8, *ADD* 970 i 2 ^{MÍ}*Še-ru-u-a*-⌜*e*⌝-[ ], *AfO* 13, 214:22 $^{MÍ.d}$EDIN-*e-ṭè-rat*, *ABL* 308 r1 $^{MÍ.d}$[ ], *LAS* 150 r11
[12]	. . . .	^{MÍ}x[ ], *AfO* 13, 214:23 (following Šerū'a-ēṭerat in a list of Esarhaddon's children).

Less certain, since not mentioned by name or in unequivocal context are:

[13] the child called *lakû* "babe" in *LAS* 219 r4, 250:13, 254:9;

[14-16] the three "charges" (*piqittu ša Šarrat parṣī, piqittu ša bēt kutalli, piqittu ša bēt Urad-Dāgūna*) mentioned in medical letters; see note on *LAS* 123:4; and

[17-18] the two unnamed patients housed in the "new Palace" (*2 ša ina bēti ešši*), mentioned together with Sîn-perʾī-ukīn in *LAS* 142:6.

---

[247] The name of this prince implies a date of birth after Esarhaddon's accession, i.e. after 681 BC.

[248] Cf. Streck, *Asb* p. CCXLIX.

[249] The logogram LUGAL would then have to be read *etellu* not *šarru* in this name. This is in fact quite possible, for though the equation LUGAL = *etellu* does not appear to be given in any syllabaries, it does occur in synonym lists (*e-tel-lum* = *šar-ru*, Malku I 5).

[250] Cf. note to *LAS* 121:7.

Finally, a child called [19] [^{I}. . .]*-ja-aḫ* has perhaps to be reckoned with in view of *LAS* 150:12 and 240 r3'.

Such a large number of children hardly had a single mother. The Vassal-Treaties of Esarhaddon, as a matter of fact, carefully differentiate between "sons born by the mother of Assurbanipal" and "the rest of the sons and offspring of Esarhaddon (ŠEŠ^{MEŠ}*-šú* DUMU AMA*-šú šá* ^{I}*Aš+šur*-DÙ-A *ù re-eḫ-ti* DUMU^{MEŠ} *ṣi-it lìb-bi šá* ^{I}*Aš+šur*-PAP-AŠ, *VTE* 496f. and 515f.). Cf. also commentary on *LAS* 195.

r2-4. A similar wish is found in *VTE*, ll.295-297: *a-bu-tú an-ni-tú šá ina* IGI DINGIR *u* LÚ*-ti maḫ-rat-u-ni ši-i ina pa-ni-ku-nu lu maḫ-rat* "may this matter which is acceptable to god and mankind, be acceptable to you also."

r9. *ú-na-ru-ṭ[u]*: lit. "they *make* tremble". The translation proposed in Pt.I, based on the context, presupposes that one has to restore [*ra-ma-an-šú*]at the end of line 8; cf. note on 51 r1.

r17f. Cf. *VTE* 8 ff, TA* *na-pa-aḫ* ^{d}UTU*-ši a-di ra-ba* ^{d}UTU*-ši am-mar* ^{I}*Aš+šur*-PAP-AŠ LUGAL*-tú . . . up-pa-áš-ú-ni*, and note also *ABRT* I 22 ii 3ff, *kip-pat erbe-ti* ^{d}*Aš+šur it-ta-na-šú* ⁴ TA* É *i-nap-pa-ḫa-an-ni* ⁵ É *i-rab-bu-u-ni* ⁶ LUGAL *mi-ḫir-šú la-áš-šú* "Assur has given him (= Esarhaddon) the entire world; from where he (= Assur) rises till where he sets, there is no king equal to him."

r24. *gur-šu*: meaning uncertain, probably "wedding night", "marriage", or the like.[251] The writer may, accordingly, here refer to prospective or impending marriages of the crown prince(s), which would agree with the implications of *LAS* 152 ff. (q.v.).

130

Bibliography:
(I) Waterman, *RCAE* 654.

Addressee:
Assurbanipal (as crown prince).

Date:
670 BC? Was this letter written in response to a call to attend the father of the prince who had suddenly fallen ill? The orthography agrees with that of *LAS* 143.

131

Bibliography:
(I) Waterman, *RCAE* 10.
(II) Deller, *AOAT* 1 (1069) 55.

Date:
Ca. 672-669 BC. Cf. sub *LAS* 129 and 130.

Addressee:
Assurbanipal.

Notes:

6. *Bēt rēdûti* "Succession Palace": the SW palace of Sennacherib at Kuyunjik (see Streck, *Asb* p.CCCLXXX ff, and cf. especially the epigraph *AfO* 8 p.200*a* , explicitly equating É *re-du-u-ti* with É IM *šu-u-ti* "the South" pa-

[251] Cf., in addition to the references cited in the dictionaries, especially *ABL* 65: 10, UD 4.KAM *gur-šu sa* ^{d}AG "(on the 3rd of Ajāru the bed of Nabû is prepared, Nabû enters the bedroom;) on the 4th, the 'marriage'(?) of Nabû takes place." The word is a *purs* formation from *garāšu* "to copulate", on which see, most recently, E. Reiner, *RA* 69 (1975) 95.

lace"). This palace, constructed by Sennacherib in the beginning of his reign (cf. *OIP* 2 p.94 ff), served as the official residence of the king and the administrative centre of the empire through the reigns of Sennacherib, Esarhaddon and Assurbanipal till the latter completed his North Palace (cf. Streck, loc.cit.); the practice of introducing the crown prince into this palace as an official token of his new status is attested in Assyria from the reign of Sargon on (cf. Streck, *Asb* p.4 i 23 ff. for Sennacherib residing in the *bēt rēdûti* as crown prince, and Borger, *Ash* p. 41:20 ff. for the introduction of Esarhaddon into the palace). On *rēdûtu* = "succession; government" see Streck, op. cit. p. 568 f; the name *bēt rēdûti* seems to have implicated both meanings. On the one hand, the attributes of *bēt rēdûti* in Borger, *Ash* p.41:21 f. and Streck, *Asb* p.254 ii 4, definitely favour a translation like "government Palace"; on the other hand, passages such as Piepkorn, *AS* 5, 84:37 (ANŠE[MEŠ] É *re-du-ti* "stud-asses", lit. "asses of the succession house") and Borger, *Ash* p.87 r4 ([I]*Aš+šur*-DÙ-IBILA DUMU *re-du-ti-ja* "Assurbanipal, my successor", lit. "my son of succession"; similarly, [I]*E-ri-si-in-ni* DUMU *re-d[u-ti-šú]*, *AfK* 2 102 iii 3, and [I]*Ú-šá-na-ḫu-ru* DUMU UŠ-*ti-su*, Borger, *Ash* p.99:43) make it perfectly clear that the idea of royal succession was inherent in the name of the palace, and may well have been the primary one attached to it.*

132

Bibliography:

(I) Waterman, *RCAE* no.614 (cf. III 374, IV 185); Deller, *AOAT* 1 (1969) 57 f.
(II) Zimmern, *ABB* (1906) 7; W.G. Lambert, *BWL* (1960) 315; M. Bayliss, *Iraq* 35 (1973) 124.

Addressee:

Esarhaddon.

Date:

Approximately May, 672 BC. Though no names are mentioned in it, the letter evidently pertains to the appointment of Assurbanipal as crown prince, and was in all probability written relatively soon after the event, like *LAS* 129. The woman whose ghost speaks in Rev.7f can only be Esarhaddon's main wife Ešarra-ḫamât, who deceased only three months before the treaty ceremonies (in Addāru 5 = February 8, 672 BC; cf. sub *LAS* 4). On this lady see W.G. Lambert, *RA* 63 (1969) 65 f.

Writer:

Probably Adad-šumu-uṣur, see Deller 1969. This assignation cannot, of course, be made 100-percent certain owing to the small size of the fragment; it should be noted, however, that virtually all the words occurring in it are attested in identical spelling in other letters by Adad-šumu-uṣur.

Discussion:

This letter is of importance to the understanding of the cult of dead kin in Mesopotamia, particularly its aspect of reciprocality. See, in detail, the article of Bayliss referred to above. Cf. also discussion sub *LAS* 195.

Notes:

r3 ff. For these words of the crown prince, cf. Streck, *Asb* p.2 i 5 ff.

r9 f. A free quotation from the "Counsels of Wisdom" (*BWL* p.104); the passage in question reads:

143	*pa-la-ḫu da-ma-qu ul-lad*	"Reverence begets favour;
144	*ni-qu-u ba-la-ṭu [u]t-tar*	"Sacrifice prolongs life.
145	*pa-liḫ* DINGIR[MEŠ] *ul i-še-es-su* x[x(x)]	"He who fears the gods is not slighted by [. . . . .]
146	*pa-liḫ* [d]*A-nun-na-ki ur-rak [*u_4*-mi-šú]*	"He who fears the Anunnaki extends [his days]."

Note that the word *pa-LAḪ* in the present letter could also be read *pa-liḫ*, as in the source passage.

133

Bibliography:
(I) Waterman, *RCAE* 656.
(II) Behrens, *ABB* (1906) 15 f; Oppenheim, *JAOS* 61 (1941) 252, and 88 (1968) 174; Deller, *AOAT* 1 (1969) 61.

Addressee:
Esarhaddon.

Date:
Probably late May, 670 BC. The reference to *weeping* [subjects of the king] (Rev.3) in connection with Rev.4' ("he will recover") and 16' (see relevant note) indicates that the letter dates from the time of Esarhaddon's illness in May, 670, on which see in detail the commentary on *LAS* 246 (cf. also sub *LAS* 143). The "secret service" information provided by the writer and the spelling of his name (-*ú-ṣur*) point in the same direction; see commentaries on *LAS* 247 and 147, respectively.[252] The quotation from the Vassal-Treaties found in Rev.19'ff assures the time brackets 672-669.

Notes:

r16'. *LUGAL in-na-šar-u-ni*: probably an ellipsis for "(the illness of) the king is being taken away", cf. [*a-ki*] ^{d}EN* *mur-ṣ*[*i*] MAN *iš-šur-u-ni*, 159:10.

r19'-21'. Despite the particle *mā*, these lines contain no direct quotation from the Vassal-Treaties but rather a free rendering of its main theme: the obligation of the treaty partners to keep the royal house informed on everything. Cf. *VTE* 73 ff: *šum-ma at-tu-nu a-bu-tú la* SIG_5-*tú* .... *ta-šam-ma-a-ni tu-pa-za-ra-a-ni* ... *la ta-qab-ba-a-ni* "(you swear) that you will neither listen to nor conceal any improper words . . . but will report these things"; similarly *VTE* 108 ff and passim in the treaty text. See, in general, Oppenheim, *JAOS* 88 174, also for other similar letters.

134

Bibliography:
(I) Waterman, *RCAE* 653.
(II) Dhorme, *RHR* 113 (1936) 136f; Labat, *Royauté* (1939) 354; von Soden, *Fs Christian* (1956) 104; Deller, *Or*NS 31 (1962) 232; Landsberger, *BBEA* (1965) 45[72]; Kümmel, *StBoT* 3 (1967) 172 ff; Deller, *AOAT* 1 (1969) 60.

Photo of Obverse:
RCAE IV Pl.13.

Date and discussion:

The reference to Akkad as the scene of the substitute king ritual dates this letter to 671 BC; see Intr., p. XXIV f and cf. commentary to *LAS* 292. The reign of Assurbanipal (666 BC) is out of the question in view of the introductory formula (cf. *LAS* 119ff).

Addressee:
Esarhaddon.

Notes:

10f. *ALAM LUGAL pu-u-ḫi*: Cf. on 298:5 and Intr., p.63.

[252] The circumstance that the information supplied in this letter would thus *postdate* the detection and crushing of the attempted coup d'état of 670 naturally in no way calls for an earlier date. The writer explicitly states that the informer had concealed the facts for a long time, and that meanwhile his mother and other persons had *died*, presumably because they had become entangled with the conspiracy.

r4. *bi-si*: a hapax legomenon, but probably only a variant of *basi* (*CAD* B 133b, *AHw* 110a) ~*bis* (*CAD* B 268a, *AHw* 130b). The interpretation of *ni-iš-ri* is more problematical. For *nišru* "reduction" see *AHw* 976b, to which the present example should be added, and cf. also *CT* 53 926 A 4 ff: *re-eḫ-tu* [5] [(.) *in*]*a* UGU *ni-iš-ri 2-i* [6] [0?] *ni-šá-ṭar nu-ga-mar.* Von Soden, *Fs Christian* p. 104 and *AHw* 130b, suggests reading *ni-iš-tal* and translating "(dann) wollen wir uns beraten", but his is incompatible with NA phonetics and morphology (see Deller 1969, p. 60; there are no finite Gt forms in NA). As an alternative, Deller (*loc.cit.*) proposes interpreting *ni-iš-ri* as cohortative fo a verb **šrī* G (Aram.?) which is not excluded but by no means necessary. In any case, the meaning of the line remains obscure.

r5. *ni-il-li-ik* "we shall go": scil. "to Akkad".

135

Bibliography:

(I) Waterman, *RCAE* 359 (cf. IV 248); Pfeiffer, *SLA* 313.
(II) Behrens, *ABB* (1906) 92[1] and 105[1]; Schott, *Quellen und Studien zur Geschichte der Mathematik* B 2 (1933), 365; Dhorme, *RHR* 113 (1936) 135f; Labat, *Royauté* (1939) 326 and 358; id., *RA* 40 (1946) 132f; Böhl, *Opera Minora* (1953) 417; von Soden, *Fs Christian* (1956) 102; Landsberger, *BBEA* (1965) 43[66]; Kümmel, *StBoT* 5 (1967) 174 ff, 180; Deller, *AOAT* 1 (1969) 59.

Addressee:

Esarhaddon.

Date and discussion:

Appr. Du'ūzu 10 = July 6, 669 BC. Cf. on *LAS* 166; full moon on the 16th of Du'ūzu would have portended imprisonment of the king of Assyria for a month (cf. *ACh* Sîn 4:18 and App. F4); this explains the direction given here that the substitute king may go to his fate on the 16th, *if* the opposition already occurs on the 15th (a harmless omen); otherwise, his reign would certainly have been extended considerably.

Notes:

14 f. *DINGIR*^{MEŠ} *a-ḫe-iš em-mu-ru,* lit. "(if) the gods see each other", referring to the opposition of the sun and the moon. This expression alternates in Assyrian letters and reports (e.g., *LAS* 74:8 ff, 85:10 ff, 88 r3 ff; also 82–5–22, 81 r1 ff = *Centaurus* 14 120) with the passive *Sîn u Šamaš issâḫē'iš innammurū* "the Moon and the Sun are seen with each other" (*LAS* 172 r14 f) and *ilu isse ili innammar* "the god is seen with the god" (*LAS* 81 r4 f; for more examples see *CAD* A/2 p. 27).

r6. *"Let him complete the 100 days"*: scil. until the evil portended has befallen him. Cf. *RMA* 270 r10: UD.DUG$_4$.GA EN.NUN AN.USÁN *ana* ITU *3*.KAM UD *10*.KAM "the term of (an eclipse occurring at) evening watch is 3 months and 10 days"; similarly *RMA* 271:10 UD.DUG$_4$.GA EN.NUN UD.ZAL.LI *ana* ITU [*3*.KÁM UD] *10*.KÁM "the term of the morning watch is 3 months and 10 days". Portents derived from stars were to be realized within a month: cf. *it-ti šá* MUL *a-di* ITU UD^{MEŠ} "a portent derived from a star is valid until a full month (has elapsed)", *RMA* 245 r6.[253]

136

Bibliography:

Deller, *AOAT* 1 (1969) 58.

---

[253] Cf. Littmann, *1001 Nächte* I, p.172: "Die Gefahr, die die Sterndeuter und Weisen für *den vierzigsten Tag* angegeben hatten . . . "

Copy:
CT 53 pl.20 no.49.

Writer:
Certainly Adad-šumu-uṣur in view of the reference to the "charge of the Rear Palace" (see note to *LAS* 123:4); cf. further the subject matter with *LAS* 134f and 137ff; the orthography agrees with A.'s.

Addressee:
Esarhaddon.

Date:
Approximately Simānu 26, eponymy of Šamaš-kāšid-ajābi = June 23, 669 BC. For the day cf. r2'f; the month and year follow from Obv.9 stating that the 100-day reign of the substitute king was due to end on Ulūlu [n+]6/⌜8⌝. Subtracting from this date a 100 days, it follows that the eclipse on account of which the substitute was enthroned occurred either at the end of Ajāru (solar eclipse) or in the middle of Simānu (lunar eclipse). Such eclipses occurred in the latter part of Esarhaddon's reign (where the letter is unquestionably placed by the reference to the "charge") only in 669 BC, cf. App. E/F. The solar eclipse mentioned by the writer in r2', was, of course, that expected *after* the lunar eclipse of Simānu 14, at the end of the month.

Notes:

9. The date can be restored either as *Ulūlu* [2]6 or *Ulūlu* ⌜*8*⌝. In the latter case, the substitute king's reign would have been scheduled to continue exactly 100 days after his enthronement following the solar eclipse of Ajāru (cf. *LAS* 28 and 104); in the former, it would have been due to last an additional 100 days after the lunar eclipse, in all 115 days.

11. *Bīt salā' mê* ("House of Water Sprinkling") was a purificatory ritual often performed together with *bīt rimki* after eclipses of the moon (cf. *LAS* 280:18 and the catalogue *BMS* p. xix combining these two rituals). According to the ritual tablet it was also to be performed yearly in the month Tašrītu (*enūma nēpēšī ša bīt salā' mê ina* ^ITU^*Tašrīti teppušu* "when you perform the rites of *Bīt salā' mê* in Tašrītu", K 2798+ Obv.1 = Meier, *AfO* 14 139²), as implied by the present passage; cf. also *LAS* 227:5 ff, and see note to 208 r2-3 for similar seasonal rites in general. It seems as if the king was worried that the performance of the ritual might not be of any avail to the royal family, should the substitute occupy the throne at the time concerned, and consequently he was perhaps urging his aides to depose the substitute as soon as possible; see in more detail sub *LAS* 166.

16 f. This is almost certainly a reference to the substitute king ritual performed on account of the lunar eclipse of Arahsamna 14 = November 3, 677 BC; cf. App. F2 and Intr., p. XXXIII.

137

Bibliography:
(I) Waterman, *RCAE* 4.
(II) Behrens, *ABB* (1906) 51² and 102⁶; Dhorme, *RHR* 113 (1936); Landsberger, *AfO* 12 (1937/9) 139; Böhl, *Opera Minora* (1953) 421; von Soden, *Fs Christian* (1956) 100 f; Kümmel, *StBoT* 3 (1967) 179 f.

Addressee:
Esarhaddon. See below, sub Date.

Discussion:

Despite the fact that the letter is addressed to "Farmer", its content probably has no connection with the substitute king ritual itself; the apotropaic rites described in it were intended to counteract the evil foreboded by an earthquake which had occurred during the reign of the substitute king.[254] Cf. the namburbi ritual trans-

[254] As the substitute king ritual was only devised to protect the king from the evil of eclipses, it probably was not thought sufficient to protect him from the evil of an earthquake, too.

lated below, written for the lamentation-chanter (*kalû*); the corresponding text for the exorcists is also extant (see *KAR* 7) but is too fragmentary to be properly compared with the present letter.

"If the earth quakes, there will be an enemy attack, the seat of the country will not be firm. If the earth shakes, there will be no stability in the entire country; the country will go out of its mind.

On an auspicious day the king cleans and purifies himself, and recites a penitential psalm to Anu, Illil and Ea. Thereafter, you set out two offering-arrangements to his god and goddess. Make offerings and set up a lament; have the king recite their conciliatory psalms.

In the morning, arrange three reed-altars to Anu, Illil and Ea. Make offerings. Set out shoulder-portions, intestinal tissue and roast; libate fine beer, wine and milk. Set up a lament; have the king recite the conciliatory psalms (beginning) *bar-ra umun e-ma-ta-KIL an-nam*, to Anu, *me-e u-mu-un-mu ši-šim*, to Illil and Ea, and *me-e an-sar*, to Šamaš. He prostrates, has himself shaved. Collect the hair of his body into a bottle and let it be abandoned at the border of the enemy. He goes straight to his palace. Make a big offering to Anu; set up a lament. Afterwards perform the lamentations and conciliatory psalms of these (gods) upon the royal cape in all cult centres. (If) you perform this, the evil will not get near the king" (Thureau-Dangin, *RAcc.* p.34:16 ff).

The shaving (*gallābūtu*) of a "patient" is prescribed in other namburbis as well (see Caplice, *OrNS* 36 21 ff and *CAD* G 18*a*), but none of these other namburbis contains the instruction to carry the shaved-off nails[255] to enemy territory. Though the ritual makes no explicit reference to the *qersu* and the reed-hut, as our letter does, one may suppose that these were mentioned in the corresponding *namburbi* of the exorcists.[256]

The hypothesis that the ritual described in the letter pertains to an earthquake is supported by *LAS* 234 mentioning an earthquake (in month Simānu) in connection with an eclipse. The latter is very probably to be identified as the lunar eclipse of June 11, -668, and since we know that the substitute king occupied the throne at that time (see sub *LAS* 26, 28 and 136), the occurrence of an earthquake during the time the king was called "farmed" is virtually certain. For another *namburbi* performed for a king called "farmer" see *LAS* 334.

Date:

Probably Simānu 12, eponymy of Šamaš-kāšid-ajābī = June 8, 669 BC. For the day see Obv.6; the month and year are obtained as follows. Since, according to the text quoted above, the ritual had to be performed on an *auspicious* day, one may suppose that the 13th day suggested in the letter was such, and had been selected by Adad-sumu-usur from one of the several canonical lists of auspicious days surveyed by Labat, *RA* 38, 13 ff. All these lists agree that the 13th day was auspicious only in the months Simānu, Du'ūzu, Araḫsamna, Kislīmu, and Ṭebētu. The remnants of the broken sign preceding the day in line 6 fit only Du'ūzu, Arahsamna and Ṭebētu, and taking into consideration the width of the break, Du'ūzu would epigraphically be the likeliest of these alternatives. However, a favourable 15th day (Rev.9) followed an auspicious 13th day in *Simānu and Araḫsamna only.* Since there is, in fact, no guarantee that the break contained any month name at all[257] (a thinkable restoration would be [*i-n*]*a*), it seems very likely indeed that the month in question was Simānu, as implied by *LAS* 234 (see above). This would mean that the earthquake had occurred before the lunar eclipse; and in Simānu, 669, the substitute king had in fact been enthroned already on account of the preceding solar eclipse, see commentaries on *LAS* 28 and 136 (and cf also sub *LAS* 25 and 77).

Notes:

6. In view of the *kalû* ritual cited above, it could be argued that *iš-ši-a-ri* here means "in the morning" rather than "tomorrow"; cf. *ši-a-ru nu-bat-tú* "morning and evening", *LAS* 126 r8 and 172 r12. However, such a rendering is not warranted by other NA occurrences of *iš-ši'āri*, which without an exception are to be translated

255 Instead of *nails* , the ritual text has MUNŠUB SU, literally "hair of the body". This may be interpreted as a broad designation of all outgrowths of the human body, including nails.

256 Note the frequent references to "unfrequented places" and *urigallu* standards in namburbi rituals. On the reed hut see note on Obv.7 f.

257 Such an indication would have been entirely redundant in the present context, the letter referring to the *following* day in the *middle* of the month.

"tomorrow" (cf. the refs. sub *LAS* 158); the NA expression for "in the morning" was *ina ša šērāti* (*LAS* 6:7', 50: 9, 64 L.E.21, 65:19, etc.), corresponding to MA *ina ši'ārāti* (Ebeling, *PKTA* p.59).

7f. *qersu*: see note on 60 r5; here certainly corresponding to the "unfrequented place" (KI GÌR TAR-*at*) of the namburbi rituals. The "reed hut" (*kikkisu*) is otherwise practically only known from the deluge stories in the epics of Atrahasis and Gilgameš (cf. *CAD* K 352) where it represents a place closely associated with the god Ea. This strongly supports the hypothesis presented above that the nail-cutting ceremony was occasioned by an earthquake, for it was precisely the god Ea who was considered the creator of earthquakes. Cf. *LAS* 35 r7 ff, and pertinent commentary.

138

Bibliography:

(I) Waterman, *RCAE* 183 (cf. III 373, IV 238); Pfeiffer, *SLA* 240.
(II) Behrens, *ABB* (1906) 51²; Dhorme, *RHR* 113 (1936) 139; Labat, *Royauté* (1939) 342; Böhl, *Opera Minora* (1953) 421; von Soden, *Fs Christian* (1956) 102; Deller, *AOAT* 1 (1969) 53.

Copy:

Cf. S.A. Smith, *PSBA* 10 157 f, pl. 1.

Discussion and date:

This letter clearly pertains to the same ritual as *LAS* 137, this time however not to be performed by the "Farmer", but (probably) by the two crown princes Assurbanipal and Šamaš-šumu-ukīn; cf. *LAS* 140, 173 and 185. Consequently, the letter was most likely written on the same day as no.137 (Simānu 12 = June 8, 669 BC), or slightly later.

139

Bibliography:

(I) Waterman, *RCAE* 15.
(II) Behrens, *ABB* (1906) 102; von Soden, *Fs Christian* (1956) 101; Kümmel, *StBoT* 3 (1967) 177, 179; Deller, *AOAT* 1 (1969) 58.

Date:

Approximately Simānu 9 = June 5, 669 BC? See note to r8 f.

Addressee:

Esarhaddon.

Discussion:

For lack of supplementary evidence, the exact "setting" of this letter inevitably remains unclear. However, since the letter is signed by two high-ranking exorcists[258] and addressed to the "Farmer", it can with reason be supposed to deal with some phase of the substitute king ritual. Von Soden (1956) has plausibly suggested that the "girl" referred to in Obv.6 was the queen of the substitute king, referred to as "virgin" (ᴹᴵ́KI.SIKIL) in the substitute king ritual tablet, *AfO* 18 109 ff, Col.A 20'; for the possibility that the logogram ᴹᴵ́GURUŠ.TUR (*batūssu*) found here actually means "virgin" rather than "girl", see *CAD* B 174*a*. Unfortunately, the fragmentary ritual tablet, in its present state of preservation, contains no more references to this "substitute queen", so one can only conjecture about the purpose of the visit alluded to in the present letter. Was the king perhaps ex-

[258] Note that of the two senders, it was certainly Marduk-šākin-šumi (the chief exorcist) who actually wrote down the letter. This is shown by the spelling *iq-bu-ni* in Obv.7 and the position of the preposition *ina* UGU in Obv. 6; see commentaries on *LAS* 149 and 164.

pected to have sexual intercourse with the girl? Note that in the *pūḫi amēli* ritual (*LAS* 140) the patient had to go to bed with the virgin kid given to Ereškigal as his substitute.

Notes:

10 f. These lines rendered according to Deller (1969); for *ḫa-ri-pa-a-ni* = Nom. Sg. (*-āni* for normal *-ānu*) see note to 174 r12. The interpretation proposed by von Soden, *AHw* 326*a* s.v. *ḫarīpu* ("since she is entirely stained with blood") cannot be accepted for various reasons, not least for lack of space for the integration [*malât*]*ūni* in line 11.

r1 f. Cf. *LAS* 4:12f and corresponding note. Though *šaqû* "to be high, to rise" was properly a verb ultimae *u*, the present spelling with *i* does not necessitate taking *liš-qi-a* as a precative of *šaqû* "to give to drink" (ult. *i*); cf. *i-man-NI-u*, *LAS* 251 r13, and *li-im-NI-i-u*, 276:22 (both from *mnu* "to count").

r6. The shaving ritual here mentioned probably had nothing to do with the earthquake namburbi discussed under *LAS* 137; nevertheless, its purpose doubtless was likewise purificatory, cf. the examples of *gallābūtu epēšu* in ritual contexts quoted in *CAD* G 17f, all of which formed part of elaborate magical cleansing ceremonies (also involving bathing in holy water and donning clean garments).[259] It seems evident that contact with the girl was considered contaminating, which supports the hypothesis that the queen of the substitute king indeed is in question.

r8 f. The nature of the nocturnal ceremony here referred to cannot be determined, but the date is interesting. If the "girl" indeed was the substitute queen, which seems likely, then she and her "husband" must have been resident in Nineveh in the early part (i.e., before the 11th) of the month (or the second month) following their enthronement, which had taken place at the middle or the end of the preceding month. This implies that the letter was written either in Ābu 671 or Simānu-Du'ūzu 669, since in 666 the substitute king was enthroned (and remained resident) in *Akkad*, whereas in Kanūnu 671 he was moved to Akkad hardly 6 days after his enthronement in Nineveh on Kanūnu 14; see Introduction, p. XXXV; substitute king rituals pre- or postdating 672 and 665 are out of the question, since the letter is signed by *both* Adad-šumu-uṣur *and* Marduk-šākin-šumi (cf. App. 0). As *LAS* 166 (also by A. and M., and addressed to the Farmer) dates from Du'ūzu 669, the odds are for this alternative, though it is of course impossible to rule out the other alternative (671) with *certainty*.

140

Bibliography:

(I) Waterman, *RCAE* 439; Pfeiffer, *SLA* 268.
(II) Behrens, *ABB* (1906) 102[6]; Ebeling, *TuL* (1931) 67; Dhorme, *RHR* 113 (1936) 136; Labat, *Royauté* (1939) 342; von Soden, *ZA* 43 (1936) 257, and *Fs Christian* (1956) 104; Kümmel, *StBoT* 3 (1967) 179; Deller, *AOAT* 1 (1969) 54.

Copy:

Cf. Lehmann, *Ššmk* II (1892) 74.

Date:

672-669 BC (note the ref. to *both* Assurbanipal and Šamaš-šumu-ukīn in r1 f), probably 672-671, since from early 670 on Šamaš-šumu-ukīn appears to have rather permanently resided in Babylonia (cf. on 280:10f).

Addressee:

Esarhaddon.

Discussion:

In spite of the reference to the "shaving" (Obv.12, cf. *LAS* 137-139) and the *pūḫi amēli* ritual (Obv.14, cf. respective note), this letter has nothing to do with the substitute king ritual. See von Soden, *Fs Christian* p.104.

[259] DT 80 is *not* a duplicate of K 2549+ etc (4 *R* Add.10) but fragment of a namburbi.

It seems that the spur to write the letter was given by the *pūt upni* incident reported in Obv.9 ff, whatever the exact nature of this incident actually was (cf. below).

Notes:

9. *i-lu* "god": sic, not *i-ṭib* (von Soden, *ZA* 43 257).[260] For other syllabic spellings of *ilu* in NA letters cf. *ABL* 705 r20, (ironically) *i-lu-u ina* IGI-*šu e-ra-ba* "is a god supposed to enter into his presence?" (collated), and *i-lu-um-ma* "by Jove" in *LAS* 111 and 307. Here possibly in the meaning "demon" (*CAD* I/J 101*b* mng. 4).

ina pu-ut up-ni: sic, not *pu-ut ÁR-ni* (Pt.I, and all earlier editions); cancel the translation "because of the sin" and render instead "(a god or demon has stood) in the *pūt upni* of the king".[261] The word *pūt upni* has nothing to do with "sin" but refers to a cultic object dedicated to a god or goddess, as clearly appears from the following passages: *kal-la-pu ši-bir-ti ina* UGU *pu-ut up-ni* [9] *i-tal-ka di-na-áš-šú* [r.1] *ina É-šár-ra li-lik* [2] *la-ṣa-ba-ta* "(this) messenger has come (to you = king) on account of the *pūt upni* (object); give (it) to him; let him (then) leave for Ešarra, (where) I will take it (into my possession)", *ABL* 1369:8 ff., god speaking; *2* ÁB KÙ.GI *2* ZAG *up-ni* KÙ.GI "two golden cows(?), two golden *pūt upnis*", *Iraq* 32 (1970) 156:14 (a text listing votive offerings to Nabû; also mentioning 2 *pūt upnis* made of silver); *1* ÁB.ÁB KÙ.UD [3] *1* ZAG *up-ni* KÙ.UD [4] *1 kap-pi* KÙ.UD [5] *ma-da-te* [6] PAP *dAš+šur* "1 ÁB.ÁB of silver, 1 *pūt upni* of silver, 1 cup of silver, of tribute; all this (belonging to) Assur", *ADD* 936+ i 2'ff. (cf. Postgate, *TCAE* p.316 ff.); this text lists further two pairs of ÁB and *pūt upni* made of gold and silver and dedicated, along with a royal statue made of silver, to the god Marduk (ii 8-12), and continues with similar dedications to other gods and goddesses (Ištar of Bēt Kidmūri, Ištar of Bēt Ēqi, Ninurta, etc.). The term might be taken as a *purs* formation of *upnē patû* "to pray" (lit. "to open one's fists" see note to 31 r21) and translated "prayer replica", though this seems rather bold in the lack of other attestations of a *purs* formation of *patû* (cf. *AHw* s.v. *petû* II and *pītu* I); note, however, the coexistence of *purs* and *pirs* nouns of the verbs *ḫepû* "break" and *ḫâpu* "fear" (*ḫīpu* "piece; panic", *CAD* Ḫ 196, and *ḫūpu* "twig; fear", ibid. 243).

The implication of the present passage seems to be that something unexplicable had happened to the king's *pūt upni*, an incident attributed to a supernatural being in want of a rational explanation. Possibly the object had somehow stained; that would explain the immediate need of a complete cleansing of the king.

14. *pu-u-ḫi LÚ a-na dEreš-ki-gal*: an exorcistic ritual involving the killing and burying of a virgin kid (MÍ=ÁŠ.GÀR UŠ.NU.ZU) instead of the patient to be cured. The text (*LKA* 79 and dupl. *KAR* 245; cf. the abbreviated version *LKA* 80) of the ritual has been edited by Ebeling in *TuL* (1931) 67 ff.; it is also mentioned in *LAS* 299 r5 f. From the nature of the ceremonies (wailing of the dead, funeral offerings etc.) and the very idea of the ritual it can be inferred that it was resorted to only when the condition of the patient was really serious; this again implies that at the time the present letter was written, the crown prince was (or had been) seriously ill. Cf. *LAS* 141, 144, 228, 252, 253, *AGS* 144 and BM 99062, also referring to serious illness of the crown prince (Assurbanipal). Perhaps it is legitimate to restore "crown prince" even in Obv.6 of the present letter (supposing that the *pūḫi amēli* ritual – where the patient was presumed to be able to walk – could be performed only after the fever of the prince had gone down sufficiently).

r3. *i-se-niš LA né-pa-áš* "we need NOT perform it at the same time": sic, despite the parallel *i-se-niš-MA a-sa-di-ir* [13] *mi-i-nu ša* LUGAL [13] *be-lí i-šap-par-an-ni*, *ABL* 71 r12 ff. (both passages collated by Sollberger [1976–1–19]). Obviously Šamaš-šumu-ukīn was in a better shape than his brother, and so the performance of the ritual for him was unnecessary despite the equal status of the brothers, which usually required their equal treatment (cf. e.g. *LAS* 185 r12, 249:7').

---

260 This interpretation is unacceptable both morphologically (the NA pf. of *ṭiābu* is *iṭṭūab* or *iṭṭība*, not **iṭṭīb*) and lexically (the posited idiom *ḫunṭu* + *ṭiābu* is not attested elsewhere).

261 The reading *pu-ut ÁR-ni* was chosen (and could be weakly defended) on the basis of the phrase *i-na pu-ut ḫi-ṭi-šu ḫi-iṭ-ṭu e-me-es-su* in Postgate, *NARGD* p.26:51, but this parallel is of no weight in comparison with the evidence showing that *p.* is a concrete object. Moreover, *ABL* 1369:8 *ina* UGU *pu-ut up-ni* shows that *ina pūt* cannot here be a preposition. The reading *UP-ni* not *ÁR-ni* is rendered likely by the sandhi spelling MÍ *pu-u-tu up-ni*-ZU in ND 3441:7.

141

Bibliography:

Previously unpublished.

Copy:

CT 53 pl.169 no.760.

Sender:

The assignation of this fragment to Adad-šumu-uṣur is based partly on the handwriting, which is distinctly A.'s (e.g. the form of ḪI and Ú), partly on the affinities with *LAS* 155 and 156.

Notes:

2'. *"There are lines in his chest"*: the patient meant is possibly the crown prince (Assurbanipal). See on *LAS* 252, and cf. especially ibid. Obv.9.

142

Bibliography:

(I) Waterman, *RCAE* 1; Pfeiffer, *SLA* 295.
(II) Dhorme, *RHR* 113 (1936) 133f; Deller, *AOAT* 1 (1969) 53.

Copy:

Cf. Delitzsch, *BA* 2 (1894) 22.

Photograph:

RCAE IV pl.6 (Obv. only).

Date:

(672-)669 BC. The reference to Sîn-per'i-ukīn (to be considered in light of similar refs. in *LAS* 145, 150 and 352) assures the reign of Esarhaddon, hence the terminus ante quem, November 669; the terminus post quem (673) is obtained from the reference to the New Palace in Obv.6 (see note). The orthography of the introductory formula points to (summer) 669, see commentaries to *LAS* 150 and 154.

Addressee:

Esarhaddon.

Notes:

6. *É GIBIL* "New Palace": here certainly referring to the "Armoury" (bēt mašarti) of Nineveh on Tell Nebī Yūnus, which was the only major palace restored by Esarhaddon in Nineveh; see note to *LAS* 16:8.[262] In itself, the term "New Palace" could of course refer to any recently completed palace, depending on the time and place in question; cf. É.GAL GIBIL *šá* URU*Kal-ḫa* "the New Palace of Calah", ND 2307:2 = *Iraq* 16 p.55, and É.GAL SUMUN "the Old Palace (of Calah)", ND 2309:7 (ibid.56), both texts dating from the latter part of Assurbanipal's reign, and especially the following extracts from *ADD* 953 and 1083 (these, too, dating from the reign of Assurbanipal):

ADD 953:	2	MÚRU URU*Ni-nu-a*	"Citadel of Nineveh"
	3	KUR *ma-šar-te* URU*Ni-nu-a*	"Armoury of ditto"[263]
	4	KUR *ki-ṣir* GIBIL	"New Garrison"
	5	É MÍÉ.GAL	"Palace of the Queen"
	6	KUR GIBIL URU*Kal-ḫa*	"New Palace of Calah"
ADD 1083 ii 13		É *ma-šar-te*	"Armoury"[263]

[262] Note the clear reference to the Armoury as "New Palace" in *ADD* 172:2f (LÚ.GAR-*nu šá* ANŠE.KUR.MEŠ *ša* É GIBIL). The text is dated in the eponymy of Šulmu-bēl-lašme = 670 BC.

[263] Note: not called *new* palace any more!

14 É *ki-ṣir* GIBIL	"New Garrison"
15 É GIBIL	"New Palace"
16 É UŠ-*u-te*	"Succession Palace"
17 É GIBIL MÚRU URU	"New Palace of the Citadel"
18 É *ku-tal*	"Rear Palace"

The semantic development "house" → "palace" evidenced here may be compared with Latin *domus* "house, palace" and Bibl. *bayit* "house, palace, temple" (Koehler-Baumgartner, *Lexicon* 122*b*).

12. [I]*Da-ni-i*: cf. [I]*Da-ni-i* [LÚ]A.BA (scribe) *ADD* 857 ii 40, and *a-na* [I]*Aš+šur*-PAP-*er a-n[a]* [I]*Da-ni-i* [8] LUGAL *li-iq-bi* "may the king (prob. Esarhaddon) speak to Aššur-nāṣer (= chief eunuch) and Dānî", *CT* 53 150 (r 7 – 8). Both texts written ca. 670 BC.

18. *li-ip-tu-šú* "his affliction": lit. "touch", here naturally referring to the "touch" of a disease-causing demon (cf. *ki-ma mi-i-nu il-ta-pat-su*, 172:11).

r8. *ú-pa-qá-da*: the syllabic value *qá* (= GA) is otherwise not attested in Neo-Assyrian; the present occurrence could be due to the influence of literary texts. Alternatively the spelling could be taken as evidence of a voiced pronunciation of /q/ in Neo-Assyrian, of which there are also other sporadic indications (cf. *a-qa-pu* 4 R^2 61 i 8 for usual *agappu* "wing", and *i-gi-ib* Langdon, *TI* pl. III ii 10', if for /iqib/ "heel"[264]). For the passage in general cf. *LAS* 167 r10, [LÚ]MAŠ.MAŠ *is-se-šu* [11] *ap-ti-qi-id* "I appointed an exorcist to help him"; notice the correspondence between *pqd* G + singular object and *pqd* D + plural object, and cf. Meyer, *AOATS* 2 § 68,2 and below, note on 278 r12'.

r9. *dullu* "work": a general term for any (exorcistic) activity, here certainly referring to the medical treatment of the patients. The suffix -*šunu* is ambiguous in this context: it may refer to the patients (cf. r6 and 203:14) but equally well to the exorcists (cf. 156 r1 and 223 r8').

143

Bibliography:

(I) Waterman, *RCAE* 5; Pfeiffer, *SLA* 264.
(II) Behrens, *ABB* (1906) 82f; Dhorme, *RHR* 113 (1937) 134; Labat, *Royauté* (1939) 320; Böhl, *Opera Minora* (1953) 403, 522[74]; Deller, *AOAT* 1 (1969) 52, 54f; Fales, *ANL* 29 (1975) 489.

Date:

Appr. Ajāru 23, eponymy of Šulmu-Bēl-lašme = May 3, 670 BC. The criteria suggesting this date are discussed in detail sub *LAS* 51, which was written a day after the present letter.

Addressee:

Esarhaddon.

Discussion:

See in general commentary to *LAS* 51. The arguments by which Adad-šumu-uṣur tries to induce the king to stop his isolation and fasting are partly medical (cf. r10 ff), but above all ideological: as a roi soleil, the king should not "keep in the dark" longer than just for half a day, the period the sun remains invisible daily. It is easy to understand that the sick king (cf. on *LAS* 246) was not to be influenced by such talk; as appears from *LAS* 51, he "kept in the dark" for at least one additional day. Yet in a different situation such ideological arguments would certainly have been taken quite seriously, as shown e.g. by the royal response to *LAS* 121 (cf. Fales, *ANL* 29 [1975] 453 ff) and the arguments by which the senders of *LAS* 51 tried to influence the king.

---

[264] The context would also permit reading *i-gi-ip* "wing" (for/agapp/), in which case one would have to explain the vowel change. GIŠ *pi-lag-gu* in K 3438a r3 has probably to be taken as a variant of *palaggu* "lyre" rather than of *pilaqqu* "spindle".

Notes:

14. On the rendering of this line see note to 51:12 and cf. r1ff.

15. ^{GIŠ}*BANŠUR*: here probably referring to the sanctified meal brought daily from the temple (of Assur) to the king's consumption, cf. Oppenheim, *Anc. Mes.* (1964) 189.

17 ff. *a-na* ^{d}*UTU . . . man-nu id-du-ru*: the preposition *ana* here certainly expresses comparison, as in *LAS* 109:16'f, *a-na* AN.MI *da-a'-na* "it is more dangerous than an eclipse", and in *gu-uš-šur ma-a'-diš a-na a-lid* AD-*šu* AN.ŠÁR "he was vastly superior to his own father Anšar", En. El. I 19.[265] *id-du-ru* is to be taken as verbal adjective of *adāru* A (cf. below) with an intensifying connotation; see *GAG* § 56 30a Iβ, and cf. the meanings of such adjectives as *pitqudu, šitmuru, bitrumu* etc. For the final (paragogic) vowel (< *iddûr*) see note to *LAS* 208 r8.

18. *"King of the gods"*: an epithet otherwise rarely attached to Šamaš (cf. Tallqvist, *Götterepitheta* p. 233f). Here it obviously served to direct attention to the equation "heavenly sun" (Šamaš) = "mundane sun" (King) employed in the argumentation.

r4 f. Other contemporary references to the king as roi-soleil are: LUGAL ^{d}UTU *ša* UN^{MEŠ} "the king is the sun of the people", *LAS* 117 r8'; LUGAL *be-lí* ^{d}UTU "the king, my lord, is the sun", *ABL* 633 + K 11448 r33; [*man-nu šu*]-⌈*ú*⌉ *a-na* ^{d}UTU-*šú mil-ku la mil-ku* ^{8} [*i-mal-li-k*]*a-a* "who would dare to give an untrue counsel to the sun?", *LAS* 321 r7; *ul-tu qí-rib tam-tim* ^{LÚ}KÚR^{MEŠ}-*ja ki-i-am iq-bu-u-ni* ^{25} *um-ma* KA$_{5}$.A *la pa-an* ^{d}UTU *e-ki-a-am il-lak* "from the midst of the sea my (i.e., Esarhaddon's) enemies were (heard) saying, 'where can the fox get away from the sun?'"; and of course the numerous passages where this idea is implied indirectly, viz. by the logographic spelling of the word "king" with the sign 𒌋𒌋 (MAN, *20*), which actually was the sacred number of the sun.[266] For the ideological background of the equation see Labat, *Royauté* p.229 ff; numerous additional examples from other periods are given by Seux, *Épithètes* royales p.283 ff.

r6. *ú-ta-da-ar*: Dtt present of *adāru* "to be dark", with haplology of the second *-ta-* (**ūtataddar*), possibly to avoid the sequence of three dental stops; cf. **uštatataminū* > *us-sa-at-mi-nu* (Dtt Pf. of *šmn*) in *ABL* 121 r2, and see Deller, *AOAT* 1 53, and above, note to *LAS* 50:10.

r7 ff. These lines were restored by Deller 1969 as [*še-tu-r*]*u la* DÙG+GA ^{8} [*ina le-a*]-*mu ša-ma-a-te* ^{9} [*ina ra-ma*]-*ki me*!-*e* "[exagge]ration is unhealthy; [by ta]king drugs (and) [wash]ing with water (the illness will soon be gone)". This certainly makes sense, and the restoration of line 7 seems plausible (despite the fact that the spacing of the signs indicates that more signs are missing), but the proposed readings in the following two lines are unacceptable for several reasons.[267] A more realistic rendering of r8 would seem to be [. . . *šùl*]-*mu šá ma-a-te* ^{9} [*i-ma-ṭi*] "the welfare of the country [will decline]", a reference to the harmful political consequences of the king's behaviour. The next lines might read [*ur*]-*ki* LAL-*e* ^{10} [*i-ḫal-liq a-kal*]etc. (". . . and af]ter declining, [it will be completely gone. Eating of] bread . . ."), but this is entirely hypothetical.

r14. This line could be an oblique reference to *Babylonian Theodicy* (Lambert, *BWL* p.63 ff.), col. vii 68: *il-lu nu-us-su-qu mi-lik-ka d*[*am-qu*] "choice friend, your advice is good."

144

Bibliography:

(I) Waterman, *RCAE* 3 (cf. IV 231); Pfeiffer, *SLA* 294.

(II) Dhorme, *RHR* 113 (1936) 134; Böhl, *Opera Minora* (1953) 403, 409 ff, 522[74], 524[95]; Finet, *AIPHOS* 14

[265] This usage has to be added to *GAG* §68.

[266] MAN = "king" attested 131 times in letters of the present corpus, particularly in those of Mār-Ištar (Adad-šumu-uṣur e.g. 129:4, L.E.1; 152:3; 156 r4; 159:10). For *20* = "sun" cf. 109:11', 185:15, 302:10 etc.

[267] More signs than assumed by the restorations are missing in both lines; *le-a-mu* is difficult both lexically (only one obscure NA attestation) and grammatically (*-mi* expected); one would expect *ŠAM-ma-a-te,* not *šá-ma-a-te*; the text has LAL-*e* not *me-e* (collated).

(1954-57) 137f; Thorwald, *Macht und Geheimnis* (1967) 162; Deller, *AOAT* 1 (1969) 54; Fales, *ANL* 29 (1975) 489, 492.

Copy:
Cf. S.A. Smith, *PSBA* 10 (1888) 155 ff, pl.5.

Date:
672-669 BC; cf. *AGS* 144 (quoted below) showing that the (crown) prince mentioned in the present letter indeed is to be identified with Assurbanipal. The present text is probably approximately contemporaneous with nos. 140, 228 and 252f; unfortunately none of these letters can be dated more precisely than the present one. [Cf. however under *LAS* 140].

Discussion:

This letter is clearly associated with *AGS* 144, an extispicy performed in order to find out whether it was really essential to have the crown prince Assurbanipal drink a drug purporting to cure him (*šu-z*]*u-ub-šú šá-lam* ZI^MEŠ^-*šú* ⁷ [*ša* ^I^*Aš+šur*-DÙ-A DUMU MAN (thus certainly to be restored on the basis of r9) *šá* É *re-du-ú*]-*ti i-na šá-qe-e šam-me an-na-a . . . qa-bi-i,* obv.6ff). One is hardly mistaken in conjecturing that the order to try the drug first on boy-servants, referred to in the present letter, was in some way motivated by the results of this inquiry. Doubtless the king feared that his heir might get poisoned. Cf. *VTE* p.47:259 ff: "(you swear) that you will not give Assurbanipal, the crown prince . . . a deadly drug to eat (or) drink" (*šam-mu ša mu-a-ti-šú tu-šá-kal-a-šú-u-ni ta-šá-qi-a-šú-u-ni*).

Notes:

8 ff. *"What the king said is right"*: sic, not "this drug . . . is good" (*AHw* [1974] 1157*a*, et alii; Finet, l.c. correctly). Cf. *ABL* 945:3, *ina* [UGU] ^LÚ^É-^I^*A-muk-a-na-a-a* ⁴ *ša* [*taš-pur-a*]-*ni* SIG$_5$ É *te-pu-šú-ni* "as to the man of Bīt-Awukkāni of whom you wrote, what you have done is fine (a lover of his lords acts in this way)"; the same word order also in *ABL* 417 r2f (*de-e-qe* ³ *ša taš-pur-an-ni*) and 303 r2f (SIG$_5$ *a-dan-niš* ³ *ki-i ša taq-bi-ni*). *Bēt* "where" is here clearly equivalent to *ša* "what"; cf. the above examples and Hebrew *ᵃšær* "where, what"; also *RMA* 89r10 (*ma-qa-lu-a-te bé-et* LUGAL *i*[*š-pur-an-ni*), *LAS* 57r8, and 230r2ff.

11. *^LÚ^GÀL^MEŠ^ "servants"*: more precisely "boy(servant)s", as *qallu* = "small" not "worthless". Cf. Lat. *puer*, Gk. *pais*, Fr. *garçon*, English "boy", etc.

145

Bibliography:
(I) Waterman, *RCAE* 652 (cf. IV 185, 259); Pfeiffer, *SLA* 345; Oppenheim, *LfM* (1967) 157f (no.96).
(II) Behrens, *ABB* (1906) 82[1]; Böhl, *MAOG* 11/3 (1937) 48f; Labat, *Royauté* (1939) 222; Oppenheim, *JAOS* 64 (1944) 194, *BASOR* 107 (1947) 9; Böhl, *Opera Minora* (1953) 403; Pfeiffer, *ANET*[1] (1950) 126; W.G. Lambert, *BWL* (1960) 281f; Deller, *AOAT* 1 (1969) 59f; Fales, *ANL* 29 (1975) 489f.

Date:
Probably Ajāru 9 = May 6, 669, or April 19, 670 BC. The reference to the king's children shows that this letter was addressed to Esarhaddon; it is very unlikely to antedate 672 BC (the terminus post quem of almost all letters of the present corpus); and years 672 and 671 seem to be excluded, since Esarhaddon was in these years too busy to receive the small (cf. r4) princes at the time indicated (672, Vassal-Treaties; 671, campaign to Egypt).

Discussion:

Cf. *LAS* 332, also by Adad-šumu-uṣur and listing favourable days of Ajāru beginning with the 10th of the month. This text may well be an "appendix" to the present letter, in which case both would probably date from Ajāru 9 = May 6, 669, or April 19, 670 BC.

Notes:

6ff. *ṭa-ba-a*: not connected (grammatically) with the continuation. Cf. *LAS* 146:7ff.

13f. "Ajāru is a good month, it has many favourable days": a survey of the Babylonian Almanac (Labat, *RA* 38 20) shows that this contention is indeed correct: only two months (Tašrītu and Addāru) had more, and as many as 6 months less favourable days; 3 months (Du'ūzu, Ulūlu and Araḫsamna) had an equal number (15) of such days.

15. The sense of this line remains obscure, but there is no doubt about its translation and grammatical interpretation. It is perhaps worth stressing that the rendering "I am dancing with joy" (Oppenheim [1947 and 1967], following Behrens, l.c.) is absolutely out of the question: the preterite was never used in positive non-interrogative main clauses in NA, and the first radical of *mtḫ* was never totally assimilated to the following *t* in the preterite, cf. *AHw* 632.

18f. Cf. Borger, *Ash* 81:9, *a-na-ku* [I]AN.ŠÁR-PAP-AŠ MAN ŠÚ MAN KUR *Aš+šur*[KI] [10] *am-ru ni-iš* IGI[2] AN.ŠÁR "I am Esarhaddon, king of the world, king of Assyria, the chosen of Aššūr" (lit. "the chosen in the eyes of A."). Note also the priestly PNN [I]*Am-ru-*[d]*A-šur*/[d]*Še-ru-u-a*, *KAV* 26 r6.10.[268]

20. On the "king's shadow" see Oppenheim 1947 and note to *LAS* 122:14.

r10ff. For detailed discussion on this difficult passage, see Lambert 1960 and Fales 1975 (both with literature); Lambert leaves open the question whether or not r11ff also belongs to the proverb. From the viewpoint of the NA grammar, the proverb comprises only r10 headed by the quotative particle *mā*; the immediate continuation (r11f) is a philosophic question posed by the writer on account of the proverb (note the lengthened final wovel in [LÚ]*a-me-le-e*); the rest (r12f) gives the 'logical' answer to the problem. Structurally, the passage corresponds to *LAS* 143:17 ff. As I understand it, the writer starts with the (implicit) proposition that the simple man (the writer himself) is only a shadow of the king (A < B); since the proverb quoted states that the same relation also holds between man and god (A < C), it 'follows' that B (king) = C (god). This kind of logic is well known from Akkadian commentaries and theological expositions of the 2nd and 1st millennia BC. Cf. e.g. the following passage: "Zababa [is said to be] Lord of the Lands by his name:

ZA = lord, $BA_4.BA_4$ = lands.

'Crusher of stones, Zababa' (quoting line 100 of the hymn of Bulluṭsa-rabi).
[Stone?] means the corpse-star, as it is said:
corpse-star means the body of the Asakku demon, thus stone means Asakku" (W.G. Lambert, *Or*NS 36 114).

r13. Cf. En. El. I 138, *m[e-l]am-ma uš-taš-šá-a i-li-iš um-taš-[šil]* "she endowed (them) with nimbus, made (them) like gods" (also ibid. II 24 and III 38); *ta-na-da-a-ti* LUGAL *i-liš ú-maš-šil* "I made praise for the king like god's", Ludlul II 31 (*BWL* p.41; a similar passage also ibid. p.108:1).

146

Bibliography:

(I) Waterman, *RCAE* 365 (cf. III 374, IV 249); Pfeiffer, *SLA* 344.
(II) Dhorme, *RHR* 113 (1936) 138; Labat, *Royauté* (1939) 366.

Date:

Mid-Šabāṭu (= early February), 671, or mid-Šabāṭu (= mid-February), 669 BC. For the month cf. r1 f.; the reference to the crown prince (Obv.8) places the letter between Ajāru (MAy) 672 and Araḫsamna (November) 669, cf. sub *LAS* 173:17. The only thinkable dates are thus Šabāṭu (February) 671, 670, and 669; and Šabāṭu 670 is

[268] The PN *Amar-ili* (*ABL* 179, 329 etc.) hardly renders the same idea, since probably identical with WSem. *'Āmar-'el.*

out of the question since the king was then living a shadow-life as "Farmer" (see Intr., p. XXIV) and was accordingly not able to perform the sacerdotal duties alluded to in the present letter.

Addressee:
Esarhaddon.

Notes:

11 ff. The royal visit to Assur referred to here was certainly occasioned by the important cultic festival which took place in that city annually from Šabāṭu 16 onwards and in which the king played a central part; see van Driel, *CA* 121 ff. and 141 ff: Ebeling, *Or*NS 21 (1952) 135 ff and 22 (1953) 39f; id., *TuL* p.37 ff; Virolleaud, *Babyl.* 1 p.206 f; and Langdon, *AJSL* 42 (1926) 110 ff.[269]

r1 f. Cf. note to 145:13 f. For the 17th of Šabāṭu the Babylonian Almanac has the expected entry: 17 ab-še-ge-da "the 17th is favourable". There were altogether 14 auspicious days in Šabāṭu: the 1st, 7th, 11th (semi-favourable), 14th, 15th, 17th, 19th, 21st, 22nd, 23rd, 25th, 26th, 28th, and 29th (semi-favourable).[270] The date mentioned here thus was the first favourable one following the king's arrival in Assur.

147

Bibliography:
(I) Waterman, *RCAE* 357.
(II) Dhorme, *RHR* 113 (1936) 140; Deller, *AOAT* 1 (1969) 59.

Addressee:
Esarhaddon.[271]

Date:
mid-Du'ūzu = late June, 670 BC(?). This (admittedly very uncertain) date is based on the following considerations. First, the fact that the letter is not addressed to the "Farmer" implies that the earthquake referred to in it cannot be identified with the earthquake discussed above, sub *LAS* 137-138, which occurred in June, 669. It could, however, well be identified with those mentioned in *LAS* 16 and 148. The latter text certainly dates from 672-669 BC, as shown by the ref. to the crown prince; the former cannot be placed in a definite year but probably dealt with an earthquake in the month Du'ūzu (see under *LAS* 16). If this earthquake is indeed in question here (as seems possible considering that the writer of *LAS* 16 implicitly suggested that the king contact an exorcist re the performance of the relevant apotropaic ritual – cf. the present letter, obv. 6f and 12), then the year concerned can have been only 672, 670 or 669 (671 is out of the question because of Esarhaddon's campaign to Egypt, which lasted till early Du'ūzu, and the immediately following substitute king ritual [*LAS* 249] – see above). Of these alternatives, 670 seems likeliest in view of the fact that the writing $^{I.d}$IM-MU-*ú-ṣur* (obv.2) occurs otherwise only in three letters (*LAS* 123, 133 and 150), two of which are datable to mid -670 (123 and 133). The third, which judging by its orthography very probably was approximately contemporaneous with the present letter, is unfortunately void of any dating criteria.

---

269 Notice that the festival was opened by a triumphal "entrance into the city" ([UD] *16*.KÁM *e rab* URU, A 125 i 5 = *CA* p.124) probably referring to the king's arrival in Assur, since he is not otherwise referred to in the ceremonies of the 16th day.

270 As the number of favourable days in Šabāṭu was not particularly high, "good" in the present context is to be taken to mean "passable, suitable" rather than "favourable".

271 The ref. to the "charge" (r4'), here certainly a small child (cf. LÚ.TUR, r10'), makes it extremely likely that the letter was addressed to Esarhaddon, see the evidence presented sub *LAS* 123. Note that all other datable refs. to "charges" are from years 670-669 BC, and that no extant letter of Adad-šumu-uṣur predates 672 BC.

Notes:

6ff. *"Why didn't you answer my letter?"*: From the continuation (obv.11 ff) it can be inferred that this unanswered letter (as well as probably the second royal message, too) dealt with the earthquake, its interpretation and the relevant apotropaic ritual. Obv.8 ff gives the writer's excuse for the delay of his answer, a laconic but interesting statement. It seems that upon receipt of the king's letter, Adad-šumu-uṣur had been detained, for some time, in the palace area, and for *this reason* could not answer the king's question promptly since the reference work he needed (a writing-board edition [cf. on 319r1] of a text dealing with earthquake omens, hence either *Enūma Anu Enlil* or *Iqqur Īpuš*) was in his downtown home. If this indeed is the correct interpretation of the passage – one cannot be absolutely sure because of its laconic formulation – two interesting conclusions are possible. First, Adad-šumu-uṣur (who by schooling was both excorcist *and* scribe) had not memorized the omen collection by heart, and certainly did not pretend to have done so, but relied entirely on written documentation. Second, at the time the present letter was written (last years of Esarhaddon), there was no central reference library in the palace area which the scholars could have freely utilized for consultation of the works they needed – in other words, no collection of literature comparable to the later Assurbanipal library. The same is also implied by scattered remarks such as "I will *search* and copy tablets (for such and such purposes)" in other letters of the present corpus (185:23ff, 186 r13ff).

8. *"These rams"*: Probably referring to sheep institutionally extracted by the Chief Cook from the provinces and delivered by him to the scholars of the palace for use in haruspical, exorcistic and cultic rituals. Cf. *ABL* 867:3'ff, UDU^{MEŠ} *an-nu-te ša* $^{\text{LÚ*}}$*um-ma-ni* $^{4'}$ *ša* TA* ^{URU}BÀD-*ia-ki-ni* $^{5'}$ *ú-ṣu-ni-ni* "these sheep given to (lit. of) the scholars, which were carried off (lit. came out) from Dūr-Jakīn"; *1 me* ⌜UDU⌝ *ma-da-te* ^{10} *2* UDU *2* ^{DUG}ŠAB ^{11} $^{\text{LÚ*}}$GAL-MU "100 tribute-sheep, 2 sheep and 2 jars (of wine): the Chief Cook", *ADD* 1036 i 9 ff; ^{LÚ}GAL MU *ša* É.[GAL] ^{24} TA* IGI ^{URU}*Ḫat-rak-k*[*a-a-a*] ^{25} ^{URU}*Ṣi-mir-ra-*[*a-a*] ^{26} *i-na-áš-ši-a i-d*[*a-an*] ^{27} PAB *ša* ^{I}MAN-GIN ^{28} *ir-ku-su-u-ni* "the Chief Cook of the Pa[lace] takes (the sheep) from the inhabitants of Hadrach and Simyra and delivers (them further): all this instituted by Sargon", *ADD* 1077 i 23 ff; cf. also *za-uz-zu* ^{2} *ša* MÁŠ GUD UDU^{MEŠ} ... ^{6} É ^{LÚ}GAL-MU^{MEŠ} "the distribution of the oxen and sheep taxes ..., (of) the household of the Chief Cook", *ADD* 754:1 ff. Another clear example of the verb *šēṣû* used in the sense of "taking out of a country" in *ABL* 165 r3f (^{ANŠE}KUR.RA^{MEŠ} TA* KUR-*i-ni* ^{4} *nu-se-ṣi-a*).

9. *ú-se-li*: either "I drove up" (cf. *Sg 8*:289.301, Borger *Ash* p.53 iii 82, Wiseman, *CCK* pl.12:68, Klauber *PRT* 10:4' etc. for other examples of *šēlû* + *ina libbi* meaning "to take, lead up") or, less likely, "I offered, dedicated" (cf. *LAS* 151 r12' and 281:27).

r2'. Cf. KEŠDA *ana* IGI ^{d}*Asal-lú-ḫi* KEŠDA-[*as*] "you set up an offering arrangement before Asalluḫi", *RA* 48 138:11, and similar passages in the namburbi rituals (*RA* 50 88:34 and *Or*NS 36 34:10 mention Ea and Asalluhi, *Or*NS 36 19:11, Ea, Šamaš and Asalluḫi). The spacing of the signs and the width of the break indicate that only Ea is to be restored in the present passage; yet the name of Šamaš is also expected to occur here, as the extant portion of the earthquake namburbi (*KAR* 7) contains a prayer to this god. On KEŠDA = *riksu* "offering arrangement" see Caplice, *SANE* 1/1 (1974) 10 f.

r3'f. *ki-i* [*an*]-⌜*ni*⌝-*i ta-ri-iṣ*: cf. *a-ke-e ta-ri-iṣ*, *LAS* 252:13f.

r5'. ^{I}*ÌR-*^{d}*Da-gu-na*: this man is otherwise known only from a fragmentary letter (Bu 91–5–9,81, published below p.367 as *LAS* 359) referring to *ṭupšarrūtu* "scribal art". The name is there spelled [^{I}ÌR]-^{d}[*D*]*a-ga-n*[*a*]: for the present spelling cf. É *du-ga-ni*, *LKA* 73:8 = É ^{d}*da-gan*, *CA* p.102:40', etc.

r7'. The position of this temporal clause in relation to the main clause (r6') is unusual, but not without parallels; cf. *i-si-ja a-na* ^{16} *ma-ṣar-ti li-zi-su* ^{17} *a-di* ^{GIŠ}ÙR^{MEŠ} *an-nu-te* ^{18} *ú-še-ṣu-u-ni* "they should stay with me as security troops until I have got these beams out (of the enemy territory)", *ABL* 138 r15 ff, and similar passages in *ABL* 433 r14 ff, 523 r10 f, 867:10f, 1360:10f, *LAS* 300+110:7, and 314 r4 ff.

r11'. For many examples of *epēšu* in the meaning "to treat" see *CAD* E 196f. The implication of the present passage seems to be that the child was properly treated in the house where he was being nursed. Or has it to be understood as an excuse for the postponement of the medical examination?

r15'. *dul-li "ritual"*: here naturally referring to the earthquake namburbi. The syllabic value ÁŠ = *ás* also in *a-ta-ÁŠ-ḫa, NL* 12 r36(*Iraq* 17 pl.30), and *ÁŠ-sa-al, NL* 96:7 (*Iraq* 36, 200). Cf. also *ú-tu-UŠ-si-ku, LAS* 276 r8, and *IŠ-sap-ra-a-né*, 211:7.r14.

148

Bibliography:
(I) Waterman, *RCAE* 1118.
(II) Meier, *Or*NS 8 (1939) 304.

Copy:
CT 53 pl. 50 no.153.

Sender:
Certainly Adad-šumu-uṣur. The assignation is consistent with the extant traces of the writer's name, the handwriting (personal collation), omission of the introductory blessing (cf. *LAS* 138, 156 and 158), subject matter (cf. *LAS* 146-147), and analysis of the orthography (cf. *ri-i-bi* 147:12; DUMU-LUGAL 130:1.2.6, 131:1.5, etc; u_4*-me* 126 r7, 129 r5, 135 r5, 143 r6; *an-ni-i* 122:18.25,27, 125 r16, 126:11, 133 r5, 140:5, etc; *ú-da* 125:17, 126 r13, 142:9; *mi-i-nu* 134 r5, 139:8, 140 r3, 144 r2; *pi-šìr-šú* 147:11; *ša qa-bu-u-ni* 145 r9; *qur-bu* 120:12; SIG_5*-iq* 144:8).

Addressee:
Esarhaddon.

Possible date:
Du'ūzu 28 = July 6, 670 BC.[272] See commentaries to *LAS* 16 and 147, and note Obv.12ff: "It is a fortnight since the earth quaked . . . "

Notes:

9. *iq-ṭi-bi-i*: this is as clear an example of the perfect tense used in a NA interrogative sentence as one can wish for, and consequently Deller's contention (*Or*NS 30 [1961] 349) that "nA ist das Perfect in Fragesätzen . . . nicht nachzuweisen" has to be refuted. Similar examples are easy to find; they are, however, confined to yes/no type (echo) questions. Cf. *it-tu-u me-me-ni e-ta-mar, LAS* 249:10'f; LUGAL *be-lí uz-nu is-sa-ka-a-na*, 298 r12', and *ina* UGU *a-bé-te-e an-ni-ti iq-ṭi-bu-né-ka*, ibid.14; TA* *ra-mì-ni-ka ta-di-li-bi*, 250 r8 f; *ak-tal(a)-šú-u* "could I prevent him?", *ABL* 409 r8 f; *e-tar-ba-a*, 428 r3 and *te-tar-ba-[a]*, 1153 r4; *i-tal-ku-u, KAV* 214:8; TA* IGI LUGAL-e . . . *up-ta-az-ze-er, LAS* 199 r13.

Here the purpose of the question clearly was to express astonishment: the earthquake didn't by any means obstruct the prince's freedom to move around, since the namburbi had been performed twice and the predictions were not sinister for the crown prince.[273]

12. Cf. note to 34:15.

14. *ri-i-bi*: Nom. Sg., the final *-i* being due to assimilation of *-u* to the long stressed penultimate vowel; see *Or*NS 36 337f. The same form also in *RMA* 266:6.

---

[272] The date cannot be Simānu = June 669, since the crown prince is permitted to go "outdoors", and hence no eclipse had occurred recently. Cf. *LAS* 249.

[273] Cf. note to 16:11f.

149

Bibliography:

(I) Waterman, *RCAE* 1099.
(II) Deller, *AOAT* 1 (1969) 60.

Sender:

Marduk-šākin-šumi. In Harper's "copy" the first element of the writer's name is (with reservations) given as ^{d}I[M], but my personal collation (1968–3–25) indicates that the probable reading is ^{d}A[MAR+UD] (see Pt.1, p.297). The restoration Ma[rduk-šākin-šumi] in Obv.2 thus imposes itself. The text in fact betrays an unmistakable scribal characteristic of Marduk-šākin-šumi: the placement of the word *lik-ru-bu* in the beginning of line 5 and the introduction of the actual message with *ina* UGU immediately following *lik-ru-bu* in the same line (cf. 173:5, 174:5, 176:5, 179:5, 181:5, 182:5, 183:5, 198:6, 199:5; cf. also 139:6, 164:6, 165:6 and 166:6, signed by both Marduk-šākin-šumi and Adad-šumu-uṣur but certainly originating from the hand of the former). In Adad-šumu-uṣur's letter this feature occurs only once (in *LAS* 145:5) and can accordingly be regarded as coincidental there. Moreover, the existence of *LAS* 233, written by Adad-sumu-usur and dealing with the same subject as the present letter, also favours the attribution to Marduk-šākin-šumi.

Addressee:

Esarhaddon.

Date:

Probably mid-Nisannu = mid-April, 669 BC. See commentary to *LAS* 233.

Notes:

5. For the restoration cf. the analogous passages in *LAS* 67 and 185.

7. Instead of [NAM.BÚR.BI-*šú*] restore rather [ŠU.ÍL.LÁ.KÁM^{MEŠ}-*šú*] "its hand-lifting prayers" in accordance with *LAS* 233 r4'.

r1. Probably [*a-na* MUL AB.SÍN] *i-kaš-šad* "it (Mars) will reach Spica", cf. *LAS* 233:9' and relevant note.

150

Bibliography:

Previously unpublished. Copy *CT* 53 pl.42 no.130.

Writer:

The attribution of this letter to Adad-šumu-uṣur is certain, for the first element of the name is unquestionably ^{d}I[M] and the content of the letter leaves no doubt as to the writer's profession. The handwriting is also distinctly Adad-šumu-uṣur's.

Addressee:

Esarhaddon.[274]

Date:

Probably 669 BC. Orthographical analysis of the correspondence of Adad-šumu-uṣur shows that the present form of his introductory blessing (*lu-u šul-mu* . . . ^{d}PA *u* ^{d}AMAR+UD, i.e. the sign *u* inserted both between *lu* and *šul*, and ^{d}PA and ^{d}AMAR+UD) occurs otherwise *only* in letters written in 669 BC (*LAS* 126, 135, 154, 155, 156; cf. also 142); and that letters predating 669 usually omit the sign *u* in *both* cases (i.e., they write *lu šul-mu* . . . ^{d}AG/^{d}PA ^{d}AMAR+UD; cf. 123, 129, 133(!), 143, 151, 152, 158, 159, 160; the only exceptions are 130, 134 and 147, which all have *lu-u* but no copula between the DNN), whereas letters written *after* 669 always have *u* in either po-

[274] The patients mentioned in the letter were all children of this king. Cf. note to 129:25f.

sition (see *LAS* 119-122 and 125). The spelling of the DN Aššur as AN.ŠÁR (in line 7) is also consistent with the suggested dating: the same spelling occurs in a letter also dating from 669 (*LAS* 154) and in another from 669 (*LAS* 121) but is not found in earlier letters (cf. *Aš+šur* *LAS* 129, 132, 145; ^{d}*Aš+šur* 123, 130). Finally, notice that the phrase "PN is well" in the present letter is *šulmu ana PN*, like in *LAS* 126, 136, 154 and 155 (all dating from 669 BC), whereas in *LAS* 123, 143, 151, 159 and 160 (670 BC) it is *ana PN šulmu.*

151

Bibliography:
(I) Waterman, *RCAE* 12 (cf. IV 173).
(II) Behrens, *ABB* (1906) 82[1] and 94[3]; Dhorme, *RHR* 113 (1936) 139f; Deller, *AOAT* 1 (1969) 56.

Addressee:
Esarhaddon.

Date:
April(?), 670 BC. This date is virtually certain in view of the exceptionally great affinities of the letter with *LAS* 143 (q.v.) and a number of other letters of Adad-šumu-uṣur (123, 130, 133, 159 and 160), all very probably written within the span of a few weeks. The evidence speaking for a close temporal coherence of these texts is as follows. First, all the texts (except the present one and *LAS* 160) are in a way or another associated with a serious attack of illness which Esarhaddon experienced in early May, 670 BC (see on *LAS* 246; *LAS* 143 is addressed to the sick king, 130 to the crown prince who probably had sent for Adad-šumu-uṣur because of his father's condition; 123, containing blessings and benedictions, is most plausibly taken as addressed to the king *during* his illness as part of his therapy; 159 refers to the king's recovery; and 133, referring to weeping [subjects of the king], seems to date from the time of his recovery, see ibid., not to r16'). *Secondly*, all the letters mentioned (with the exception of *LAS* 123, where the phrase may be restored in line 5) contain an invocation of "the great gods of Heaven and Earth" (DINGIR^{MEŠ} GAL^{MEŠ} *šá* AN-*e* (*u*) KI.TIM)[275], which is otherwise found only in letters addressed to Assurbanipal (119:5, 121:14, 122:7, 125:60 and exceptionally in 126 r3 and 129:17. *Thirdly*, the charge of Šarrat Parṣī whose health is reported in the present letter (obv.6f) also occurs in two other letters of the group under consideration (*LAS* 123:4f and 143:10f), and *these are the only letters of Adad-šumu-uṣur* in which this patient is mentioned. And finally, the letters are exceptionally uniform from the orthographical point of view. Leaving out of consideration *LAS* 130, which is addressed to the crown prince and has a different introductory formula, the salutation in all the letters is spelled *lu DI-mu* and followed by ^{d}AG ^{d}AMAR+UD without inserted *u* (compare the orthography of the letters dating from 669 BC and later, discussed in commentary to *LAS* 150); however, when the health of the patients is referred to, the spelling of /šulmu/ is consistently *ŠUL-mu* not DI-*mu* (143:11, 151:7, 159:8, 160:8). All the letters (excepting 133) contain the phrase "may . . . my lord be happy", spelled consistently *LIB-bu šá* (DUMU) LUGAL *be-lí-ja lu-u ṭa-a-ba*/DÙG.GA.[276] And it may added that two of the letters which do *not* mention the charge of Šarrat Parṣī, are addressed to a *recovered* king, and instead refer to an illness of the *queen mother* (*LAS* 159 and 160).

Considering now the temporal sequence of the letters, it is obvious that the letters referring to the queen mother are the last of the series, and those dealing with the charge of Šarrat Parṣī the first. In particular, the present letter should be the first of the whole series, since it obviously was written to a king still in good health, whereas both *LAS* 123 and 143 were addressed to a sick king (cf. above). Thus one obtains the following chronological sequence:

---

[275] 123:13f, 130:10, 143:4f, 151:10, 159:7, 160:4f.

[276] Only 123:5 has ŠÀ-*bu* for *lib-bu*; 159 r8' has EN-*já* for *be-lí-ja*; the spellings *ṭa-a-ba* and DÙG+GA both occur thrice.

TEXT	SUGGESTED DATE	KING'S CONDITION	OTHER PATIENTS MENT'D
151	April, 670	good	charge of Šarrat Parṣī
130	May 1, 670	serious	–
143	May 2, 670	serious	charge of Šarrat Parṣī
123	early May, 670	serious	charge of Šarrat Parṣī
133	late May, 670	improving	–
159	June (?), 670	improved	queen mother fallen ill
160	June (?), 670	good	queen mother recovering

Notes:

r1'f. This title (probably an exorcistic ritual) remains unidentified.

r2'ff. The beginning of this incantation is perhaps to be restored d*1*[*5 be-lit* MÚRU *u* MÈ] "Ištar, queen of Battle and Onslaught", considering the continuation and the great popularity of this particular epithet of Ištar (cf. e.g. *VTE* l. 453; *WO* 1 456 i 7; Thompson, *PEA* pl.2:74 and 4:38, and particularly Borger, *Ash* p.99 r55 f, d*15 be-lit* MÚRU *u* MÈ [56] *zik-ru-su sin-niš-a-niš lu-šá-lik-šú ina* KI.TA LÚKÚR-*šú lu-še-šib-šú ka-meš* "may Ištar, the queen of the battle and onslaught, turn his virility into femininity and submit him captive to his enemy"). The incantation itself remains unidentified. An unp. medical text contains an incantation beginning ÉN d⌜*15 be*⌝-*lit qab-l*[*u u* MÈ] (Sm. 460:8, cf. Bezold, *Cat.* IV 1409) but this cannot be meant here since the text continues: *muš-te-ši-rat* ⌜UN⌝MEŠ [. . .] [10] *na-šat* GIŠBAN *u iš-pat* "who sets aright the [scattered] people, carries the bow and quiver . . ." (ibid.9f; copy Geers).

r4'. Cf. Borger, *Ash* p.43 i 48f, *e-mu-qa-šu-un lil-lu-ta ú-šá-lik-ú-ma* [49] *šap-la-nu-ú-a ú-šak-me-su-šu-nu-ti* "they (the gods) turned their (the enemies') strength into weakness and made them kneel before me (Esarhaddon)".

r8'ff. Despite the fact that MÍ+KUR in NA texts often stands for MÍÉ.GAL "queen" (cf. simply *ABL* 1239+:1, *a-de-e ša* MÍ*Za-ku-u-te* MÍ+KUR *šá* I*30*-Š[EŠMEŠ-SU] "treaty of Zakūtu, queen of Sennacherib"), the meaning of the logogram in the present context certainly is "maid, female servant" (= GEMÉ). Cf. *ABL* 341:8ff, *ú-ma-a* MÍ+KUR (GEMÉ) *ša* LUGAL [9] MÍ.dBA.Ú*-ga-me-lat* [10] *mar-ṣa-at a-dan-niš* "now, a 'maid of the king' (named) Bābu-gāmilat is seriously ill", where MÍ+KUR cannot stand for "queen" since the name of the lady in question had to be specified explicitly; on the other hand, it is clear that a woman of a high social standing was in question, since she was to be attended by a court physician (ibid. 13f). A still clearer example is ND 2316:3ff (*Iraq* 16, pl.7); MÍ+KUR (GEMÉ) *ša* LUGAL [*š*]*a* É.GAL GIBIL [4] *ša* URU*Kal-ḫa* [*a*]*-na še-lu-te* [5] *tu-se-li-iš* "a 'maid of the king' of the new palace of Calah had dedicated her (to the temple) as a votary (of Mylitta)", where the 'maid' is identified with reference to a *particular palace* in Calah and thus certainly was just one among several other ladies of a similar status housed in different palaces of the king. Notice that in this text the 'maid' likewise appears as the promoter of a girl to the status of a temple votary (*šēlūtu*). In another text from Calah (ND 2309, *Iraq* 16 pl.7), a female household manager (*laḫḫinutu*) appears in the same function, acting for the female governor (*šakintu*) of the Old Palace of Calah (MÍ*laḫ-ḫi-nu-tu ša* . . . MÍ*šá-kín-tú ša* É.GAL SUMUN . . . *a-na še-lu-u-ti ša* dNIN.LÍL *ta-al-qi*). It appears hence possible that MÍ+KUR (GEMÉ) *ša* LUGAL, "a female servant of the king", is just a broad equivalent of a more exact administrative title like *laḫḫinutu* or *šakintu*, and applied to ladies in charge of the administration of the women's quarters of the royal palaces. A 'maid of the king' occurs also in ND 2308:4 (wr. MÍ+KUR *šá* MAN, context fragmentary).

The background of the present passage can be reconstructed as follows. The writer's son (Urad-Gula) has expressed his intention (*iq-ṭi-bi*) to dedicate a slave-girl of his to the (women's section of the) palace at Nineveh. The act of dedication has to be endorsed by the responsible administrative official, i.e., by the 'maid'. She contacts Adad-šumu-uṣur to find out whether the father (as the head of the family) wished to hand over the gift personally; and finally Adad-šumu-uṣur passes the matter to the king's notice, probably for no other reason than to draw attention to the "goodness" of his son, which otherwise might not have caught the king's eye. Cf. *LAS* 120-121.

r8'. For É = "palace" see note to 142:6.

r11'. *qa-li-su*: with von Soden (*Or*NS 37 [1968] 263), probably < Aram. *qallīl* "slight, light, swift" (*qallīssu* < **qallīltu*), as the Fem. of Akk. *qallu* would have been *qallutu* (cf. *AHw*. 894*a*). However, von Soden's further suggestion (ibid. and *AHw* 894*a*) that the word here is an adverb meaning "swiftly" seems unwarranted in the lack of exact Aram. and Akkadian parallels and in view of *ABL* 1308:4, where *a-bu-tu-u qal-li-su* certainly means "unimportant matter" (cf. Parpola, *OLZ* 1979, Sp. 31). A rendering like "tiny" (perhaps referring to the stature of the girl) would seem to be more to the point, and even the translation "slave girl" suggested in Pt.I does not seem to be out of consideration, cf. the semantic development "small" → "boy" → "boy servant" discussed in note to 144:11.

r14'. *an-ni-ja-ši*: sandhi for /an ijāši/ "to me", otherwise written either *a-na A+A-ši* or *a-na I+A-ši*; if the former spelling stands for /ajāši/, as generally assumed,[277] the latter should accordingly stand for /ijāši/, not for /jāši/ (as the word is lemmatized in *CAD* I/J 327, *AHw*. 412*b* etc.). In any case, the present form is not explainable without assuming the coexistence of /ijāši/ and /ajāši/ as free (or dialectal) variants of the same lexeme in NA as well as in earlier (and later) dialects of Akkadian (cf. the examples quoted in *CAD* loc.cit., and see also Gelb, *Or*NS 39 [1970] 538f on Mari *i-ja-ti*). A similar alternation also occurs in written forms of the words *ajābu* , *ajālu*, *ajāru*, *ajāka*, *ajānibu* and *ajārurūtu* (see the dictionaries), which clearly indicates a frequent assimilation of /a/ to /J/ in this particular environment. Cf. Hebr. *'ijjôb* and *'ijjâr*, which either represent an internal Hebrew development (< **'ajjôb*, **'ajjâr*) or direct loans from Akkadian (</ijjābu/ ~/ajjābu/, written respectively *I+A-a-bu* and *A+A-bu*/*a-ja-bu*; examples in *CAD* A/1 222 ff.).[278] If the same phonetic development also holds in the present instance, then the original form of the pronoun must be reconstructed as **a'āši* (> *ajāši* > *i(j)jāši*), which in fact is the form to be expected on the analogy of the corresponding suffixal forms of the same pronoun (poss.suff. [gen./pl.] *-a* : dat.suff. *-am* : indep. **a'āši*, cf. *-ka* : *-kum* : *-k(u)āši*, *-šu* : *-šum* : *š(u)āši*, etc.).

r15'. *šu-up-ru*: an alloform of /šupur/ "send!/write!" (wr. *šu-pur* in *LAS* 173 r4) possibly approximating spoken [šupr]. Similar forms are [*ḫu*]*-ur-ṣu*, *CT* 53 215:9; *mu-ut-ḫu*, *ABL* 581 r2'; *šu-uk-nu*, *ABL* 129 r20; *mu-uḫ-ru*, *STT* 88 X 44 and 4 *R* 66 viii 18; *kur-bu*, *PKTA* 11 r3; *ku-ur-ru*, *ABL* 1432 r12; *kur-ru*, *ABL* 471:9, *CT* 53 814, etc. (note also *šup-ru ABL* 388:9); notice the presence of a sonorous consonant in all the consonant clusters listed. Cf. Parpola, *Iraq* 34 (1972) 22 ff.

152

Bibliography:

(I) Waterman, *RCAE* 363; Pfeiffer, *SLA* 337.
(II) Dhorme, *RHR* 113 (1936) 135; Oppenheim, *JAOS* 64 (1944) 196; von Soden, *OLZ* 57 (1954) 483 (cf. *AHw* 466*b* and 846*b*); Deller, *AOAT* 1 (1969) 61.

Date:

June, 669 BC. See commentary to *LAS* 154 and below, note to obv.6f.

Addressee:

Esarhaddon.

Notes:

6f. *"Charge of the Rear Palace"*: An infant patient, probably a child of the crown prince Assurbanipal (see on *LAS* 123), whose state of health is also reported in *LAS* 126, 136, 154, 155 and (very probably) 156. The other letters show that the baby went through an extremely serious illness, and the present letter (which naturally in its entirety pertains to this patient) reveals the nature of the trouble: acute diarrhoea. Frequent evacuation through anus (r3ff) and heavy vomiting belong, as everybody knows, to the distinctive features of this disease,

[277] Cf. *a-na a-ja-ši* (var. *a-na I+A-a-ši*), *AKA* 303 ii 26.

[278] The development *ajā-* > *ijā-* here posited is actually easier to accept from the viewpoint of Akkadian phonology than the traditional interpretation I+A = /ja/, since word-initial /j/ was already early lost in Akkadian and is certainly attested only in loan words.

which, if not properly cured, may be deadly to sucklings under 3 months; and the remark that the patient had been sweating for two days (r6 f.) also agrees with this interpretation, the immediate and most essential objective in the cure of acute infant diarrhoea being to bring the patient's digestive system to balance by dietary means, primarily by having him drink only water for the first days.[279]

Diarrhoea of a baby may well last over two weeks, yet (especially in serious cases like the present one) hardly much longer since the baby would then lose too much weight.[280] Accordingly, all the letters referring to a critical condition of the patient (152, 154-156) probably were written within a relatively short period of time (perhaps only within a couple of days) and can be dated to June, 669 BC, on the basis of *LAS* 136 and orthographcial considerations (see on *LAS* 154).

8 ff. *"He has vomited gall"*: cf. I NA SAG ŠÀ-*šú* KÚ-*šú ina ge-ši-šú* ZÉ *im-ta-na-'i* NA BI *qer-bi-na* GIG "If a man's epigastrium hurts him (and if) he repeatedly ejects gall when he belches, that man suffers from an intestinal disease", *BKBM* pl.13:54 and 14:1; I NA NU *pa-tan* SAG ŠÀ-*šú i-kaz-za-as-su* KÚM ŠÀ TUKU^MEŠ^ *ina ge-ši-šu* ZÉ *i-ár-rù* NA BI *pa-⌜šit-tú⌝* [24] *tu-ga-na*! GIG "If a man's epigastrium hurts him (even) when he doesn't eat, (if) fever keeps burning his belly (and if) he ejects gall when he coughs up, that man suffers from the *pašittu* and *tugānu* diseases" ibid. pl.16:23 f; I *ina* GIG-*šú 1-šú 2-šú ina* IGI ZÉ *i-ḫa-ḫu* EGIR-*nu* MÚD *i-ḫa-ḫu* ÚŠ "If he during his sickness first vomits gall once or twice and later vomits blood, he will die", *TDP* 158:27. The verb *qâ'u* (cf. Hebr. *qy'*, Arab. *qā'a* "to vomit") occurring here is certainly the NA equivalent of the verbs *mâ'u, arû* and *ḫaḫû* occurring in the literary passages quoted above; cf. MÚD *i-ḫa-ḫu* = MÚD *i-qi-'a*, *STT* 403 r53 (comm. to *TDP*).

11. *pa-šu-ut li-ši-i*: interpretation uncertain (both words hapax legomena), perhaps an error for *pa-šu-ut-tu*! *ši-i* "it is the *pašuttu* (for *pašittu*, *AHw* 845*a*) disease". This interpretation seems attractive not only because of the parallel *BKBM* pl.16:23f quoted above but also because *pašittu* was a disease persecuting (often fatally) little babies and could thus very well have been associated with a serious diarrhoea of a suckling; cf. *li-ib-ši-ma i-na ni-ši pa-ši-it-tu* [4] *li-iṣ-bat še-er-ra* [5] *i-na bi-ir-ku a-li-it-ti* "let there be among the peoples the *Pašittu*-demon to snatch the baby from the lap of her mother", *Atraḫasīs* p.103 vii 3 ff. Note also *pašittu*'s frequent association with gall and bile: *pa-šit-tum im-tú : pa-šit-tum ša mar-tú ú-kal-la* "*pašittu* of venom = *pašittu* containing bile", *GC* II 406:4 (cf. Labat, *RA* 40 117, and note *im-tum* = *mar-tum* "venom = bile", Malku VIII 124); I NA ZÉ DIB-*su* "if a man has been seized by the bile (figured as a demon)", *BKBM* p.50:14, followed by I NA *pa-šit-tu* DIB-*su* "if a man has been seized by the *Pašittu*", ibid. 17: in *la-ma-as-tu mar-tu pa-ši-it-tu* (*MLVS* 2 3:1) and *mar-tam pa-ši-tam* ^d^DÌM.ME *ek-ke-em-tam* (*BiOr* 18 71:10) it is difficult to decide whether *martu* has to be taken as "daughter" (thus von Soden, *BiOr* 18 p.72) or "gall" (thus Labat, *RA* 40 p.117); perhaps both meanings were involved through a pun. In any case, spitting bile clearly constituted a good reason for attributing a disease to the *pašittu* demon, and the occurrence of the word in the present context would hence be perfectly natural. The equation *pašuttu* = *pašittu* must of course remain hypothetical until more spellings with *u* (which remains unexplainable) hopefully once become available.[281]

12. *ka-ṣir-tú*: probably for *kiṣirtu* "phlegm" (lit. "lump"), see *CAD* K s.v. and note especially *TDP* 180:25, I NA KÚM-*im* ŠÀ-*šú i-ta-na-aš ú-gan-na-aḫ u ki-ṣir-ta-šú* MI NA BI *ma-mit* GIG "if a man has a fever, his inside is weak, he has fits of coughing and retching, and his phlegm is black, that man has been seized by an oath"; *AMT* 81,8:15 mentions *kiṣirtu* in connection with *suālu* "sputum" and *ḫaḫḫu* "spittle, slime", *AMT* 81,3 r8 with *suālu* and *guḫḫu* "coughing and retching". It seems unlikely that the signs have to be read logographically ⌜KA×ÚŠ!⌝MUŠ BABBAR "white venom of snake", even though *imat marti* "spittle mixed with bile" has the connotation "poisonous foam" in *CT* 16 12 i 16f, and the demon Lamaštu (equated with *pašittu* in *CT* 17 25:5) was said to spit "snake venom" (in *LKU* 33:23, KA × ÚŠ MUŠ *i-mat-su*).

13 ff. *mar-tu a-na šap-liš it-tu-šib*: this remark certainly described the specific composition of the vomit and gave the reason why it was considered malignant (r1 f.), but its exact meaning is uncertain. Taken literally, the phrase would mean "the bile component (of the phlegm) 'settled' (= sank?) downward (= to the bottom?)",

---

279 Thus Dr. Juha Rantasalo (private communication).

280 Cf. note to *LAS* 167:12.

281 Theoretically, *pašuttu* could also be connected with Arab. *fsw* "furzen", Eth. *fasau* "Magenknurren" and regarded as the NA word for diarrhoea.

but that does not make good sense.[282] Could *ana šapliš ušābu* here occur in a transferred meaning? "He vomited phlegm, (and) bile formed the basic component of it" would make sense and would also account for the following comment (r1 f).

Note that *martu* is here *masculine* (*it-tu-šib*, GAR-*šú*), not feminine as usual (e.g. *VTE* l.646, [*ki-i*] *šá mar-tu mar-ra-tu-u-n*[*i*]). Cf. note on 325 r2 (*ittu* = m and f). Except possibly for *LAS* 318:6 (*ki-zir-tú šá-kin*), I know of no other cases in NA where words with the fem. gender morpheme would have been construed as masc.; corresponding cases of words without an overt fem. marker are more common (e.g. *ḫarrānu, kanīku, nāru, ṭuppu, urpu*; also *šinnu* in *CT* 17 50:17).

r1. *an-nu-ú*: this contracted form of *anniu* also in ND 2307:20 (*Iraq* 16 pl.7), ND 3467:23 (*Iraq* 15 pl. 13), *ABRT* I 22 ii 26, *PKTA* pl.10:30 || *STT* 88 X 54, and *LAS* 318 r9; the reverse contraction (i.e., *anniu* > *an-ni-i*, Nom. Sg.) was much more common in NA (e.g. *LAS* 125 r16, 172 r13, 181 r1, 185:18, 223 r16', 275 r5', 278 r11', 287:10; for more similar examples see note to 172 r6), though *most* commonly no contraction at all took place (the ratio is about 6:1 in favour of uncontracted forms of *anniu*).

r3. Cancel the translation "the one who purged . . . " given in Pt.I and translate instead: "Since he purged upward and downward (i.e. from his mouth and anus), he has been sweating for two days, and is (now) better." For *ša* = "since" see note to 125:22; for the literary background of the passage see on 153 r1 ff. The expression *a-na e-liš a-na šap-liš* "upward and downward" (referring to mouth and anus) occurs only here; it was perhaps influenced by the occurrence of *a-na šap-liš* in obv.14.

153

Bibliography:

(II) Deller, *AOAT* 1 (1969) 56.

Copy:

CT 53 pl.9 no.23.

Writer:

Urad-Nanâ. The attribution is certain: the sender is clearly a physician (he quotes recipe texts) and the spelling *an-ni-JA-e* in obv.4' has parallels only in letters of Urad-Nanâ, who was the only writer within the present corpus who used the sign JA for writing the glide /j/ in this particular word (cf. *an-ni-JA-u* 246:9.r2, 247:19, 248:12.r3; *li-si-JA-ú* 246:15; *uk-ta-si-JA-u* 247 r2, etc.).[283]

Addressee:

Esarhaddon.

Date:

June, 669. See commentary on the preceding letter.

Notes:

1' f. These lines can hardly (especially in view of r1 f) be dissociated from 152:13ff, and hence the passage should probably be restored: [*ina* UGU *mar-ti ša*] 1' ⌜*a-na e-liš*⌝ [*ú-šo-šìr-u*]*ni*, and translated: "[As to the bile which he purged] upwards (and) which 'settled' downwards" (cf. note on 153:13 ff). This would, it is true, force one to read *ú-šìb-u-ni* in l.2', i.e., to assign the sign ŠAB the value *šìb* which is otherwise attested only in 2nd millennium texts (cf. von Soden + Röllig, *AnOr* 42 p.30:154).

3'. *ina bu-ul-ṭi gab-bu*: lit. "in all recipes". *bu-ul-ṭi* is here in the plural, as in 246:10, 248:8, 250 r5, and 266:3' ff.

---

282 One would also expect *it-tu-rid* "descended" instead of *it-tu-šib*, supposing the verb refers to a motion of the bile.

283 JA is otherwise only exceptionally attested in this function (in 157 r1 and 199:9).

r1 ff. This statement indeed recurs in numerous recipes, though the implicit meaning there is slightly different from the one implied here. Cf. *AMT* 48,2:1 ff, "If a man's epigastrium repeatedly has a 'break', his epigastrium burns him, if he can't sleep day and night, (if he) has no appetite and feels feeble, that man has eaten or drunk 'charms'. To cure him, you pound *ariḫu*-plant, have him drink it in "drawn" wine, and he will purge from his anus and get well (*ina* KU-*šú* SI.SÁ-*ma* TI); "if ditto, you pound "sweet herb", have him drink it in "drawn" wine, and he will purge from his anus and get well" (*ina* KU-*šú* SI.SÁ-*ma* TI), ibid.5; "If a man suffers from colic (? *kīs libbi*), if his belly refuses to take food, etc., to cure him, you prepare a mixture of various liquids and drugs, have him drink it (early in the morning) before eating, and he will purge from his mouth and his anus (*ina* KA-*šú* *u* KU-*šú* SI.SÁ); you sprinkle him (with water) and he will get well", *BKBM* pl.I 26-30; "if ditto, you bray "mountain" salt and red salt in equal quantities and have him drink it in beer on an emptly stomach, he will (then) purge from his mouth and his anus, you will sprinkle him and he will get well (*ina* KA-*šú* *u* KU-*šú* SI.SÁ-*ma* *tu*-SUD-*ma* TI), ibid.31; similarly ibid.32; note also *ina* KU-*šú* *ú-šeš-še-ra-am-ma* TI, *AMT* 80,1:7, and *ina* KU-*šú* SI.SÁ-*ma* TI, *BKBM* pl.6:13. In all these examples, "purging from mouth and anus" clearly represents the intended *effect* of the medication, whereas in the present instance it is a symptom of a disease (cf. *LAS* 152) and as such actually would not have warranted the favourable prognosis given here. The phrase "purge from one's anus" also occurs in recipe texts in referring to a symptom of illness (e.g., *ir-ra-šu i-te-bu ina* KA-*šú* *ig-di-šá-a ina* KÚ-*šú* *uš-te-ši-ra*, *TDP* 168:11, listing symptoms of stomach infection [*sili'ti libbi*]), but in such cases the prognosis is not unconditionally favourable; in the example quoted it is entirely lacking. The fragmentariness of the context makes it impossible to ascertain whether the quotation was here used as a learned "trick" to calm the worried king, as in *LAS* 38 r1 ff.

154

Bibliography:

(I) Waterman, *RCAE* 658; Pfeiffer, *SLA* 293.
(II) Behrens, *ABB* (1906) 82[1]; Dhorme, *RHR* 113 (1936) 135; Schott, *OLZ* 40 (1937) 363; Böhl, *Opera Minora* (1953) 409 ff; Deller, *AOAT* 1 (1969) 61.

Date:

June, 669 BC. This date is suggested by two considerations, independent from each other. First, the charge of the Rear Palace occurs (apart from *LAS* 152 and 155, which are approximately contemporary with the present letter) otherwise only in *LAS* 126 and 136, the latter dealing with the substitute king ritual and datable to appr. June 23, 669; the date of the former is uncertain but may have been late June, same year. Secondly, the *orthography* of the salutation and blessing formula (*lu-u šùl-mu* . . . ^{d}AG *u* ^{d}AMAR+UD) also emphatically points to June-July, 669, cf. commentary to *LAS* 150. It is otherwise attested only in *LAS* 135, 155 and 156, the first of which deals with the substitute king ritual and probably dates from July 6, 669, while the others are virtually identical in contents with the present letter and hence very likely approximately contemporaneous with it (cf. on *LAS* 152).[284] Since letters of Adad-šumu-uṣur written in the early part of 669 (*LAS* 146 = February 669; 137-138 = (probably) June 8/9, 669) still display the orthography *lu šùl-mu* . . . ^{d}AG ^{d}AMAR+UD found in earlier letters (670 BC and earlier; see on *LAS* 151), it would seem that all the letters dealing with the illness of the charge of the Rear Palace postdate June 10, 669; and since the two letters mentioning the patient in contexts suggesting that he had recovered (or was recovering) from his illness date from June 23, 669, or later (*LAS* 126 and 136), it would seem that the letters dealing with his illness are all to be dated between June 10 and 23. The chronological sequence of the letters discussed in this note would then be approximately as follows:

---

[284] The salutation and blessing of *LAS* 136 was possibly also spelled in the same way. A slightly (but not significantly) different orthography (*lu šùl/šul-mu* . . . ^{d}PA *u* ^{d}AMAR+UD) occurs in *LAS* 126, 142 and 150, the first also mentioning the charge of the Rear Palace, the others not datable with certainty. See also the "joint" letter *LAS* 167.

TEXT	SUGGESTED DATE	INTRODUCTORY FORMULA	CONDITION OF PATIENT
137	June 8, 669	*lu* DI-*mu* . . . ^{d}AG ^{d}AMAR+UD	————————
138	June 9, 669	^{d}AG ^{d}AMAR+UD	————————
152	appr. June 15	*lu* DI-*mu* . . . ^{d}AG ^{d}AMAR+UD	serious
154	appr. June 15	*lu-u* DI-*mu* . . . ^{d}AG *u* ^{d}AMAR+UD	critical
155	appr. June 15	*lu-u šul-mu* . . . ^{d}AG *u* ^{d}AMAR+UD	critical
156	appr. June 15	^{d}AG *u* ^{d}AMAR+UD	critical
136	June 23, 669	[*lu-u* DI-*mu* . . . ^{d}AG *u* ^{d}AMAR+UD]	improving
126	late June, 669	*lu-u* DI-*mu* . . . ^{d}PA *u* ^{d}AMAR+UD	good
135	July 10, 669	*lu-u* DI-*mu* . . . ^{d}PA *u* ^{d}AMAR+UD	————————

Addressee:
Esarhaddon.

Notes:

6. *Aššur-etel-šamê-erṣeti-muballissu*: a son of Esarhaddon later consecrated (by Assurbanipal) as priest of Sîn in Harran; see Streck, *Asb* p.250:17 f. The other occurrences of the name are listed in note to 129:25f.

7. *ip-ta*<-*áš*>-*ḫa*: the suggested emendation now seems unnecessary in light of *AHw.* 810*a* s.v. *paḫāḫu.*

8. *ḫi-ṭu la-áš-šú*: here a medical terminus technicus indicating favourable prognosis, corresponding to *ḫīṭa ul išu* (wr. PA NU TUK) of the diagnostic-prognostic compendium *Bīt Marṣi* (Labat, *TDP* p.56:26.28, 100:10, 102 iii 6, 104:15, 108:13, etc.; see Ritter, *AS* 16 [1965] 302).

155

Bibliography:
(I) Waterman, *RCAE* 597 and 651 (cf. IV 186, 259); Pfeiffer, *SLA* 241; Deller, *AOAT* 1 (1969) 57.

Date:
June, 669 BC. See commentary to *LAS* 154.

Addressee:
Esarhaddon.

Notes:

r1. *"We pray to the gods"*: Was this remark directly occasioned by *TDP* p. 222:48, I ^{LÚ}TUR *ma-la* KÚ *i-ḫa-ḫu* KI.MIN *iṣ-ṣa-na-aḫ* ŠU^{2}-*šú u* GÌR^{2}-*šú it-te-ṣi-la-šú qí-bit-ka ana* ^{d}*30* GÁL-*ši* "If the baby vomits everything he eats, ditto, if he has diarrhoea, and his arms and feet tend to become paralyzed, you have to address a prayer to Sîn"? Cf. *LAS* 152 and relevant commentary. In any case, the condition of the patient must have been very serious.

156

Bibliography:
(I) Waterman, *RCAE* 360 (cf. III 374); Pfeiffer, *SLA* 56.
(II) Schott, *OLZ* 40 (1937) 361; Böhl, *Opera Minora* (1953) 387; Deller, *Or*NS 34 (1965) 266, and *AOAT* 1 (1969) 60.

Photograph:
RCAE IV pl.9 (Obv. only).

Date:

June, 669 BC. See commentary to *LAS* 154; even though the patient is here not explicitly identified as the charge of the Rear Palace, the connection of the letter with the preceding numbers can hardly be doubted.

Addressee:

Esarhaddon.

Notes:

11 ff. Cf. *ABL* 885:26, *ki-ma a-na-ku la-a e-pu-uš* ²⁷ *man-nu-um-ma le-e-pu-uš* "if I did not do (it), who would?", and *ki-ma a-ni-nu la né-pu-uš* [*mannumma lēpuš*] "If we didn't do, [who would]?", *ABL* 845:9. In all these examples (as also in *LAS* 13 r3 [cf. ibid.13!], 195r6 and 213 rl) *kīma* "when" has obviously undergone a semantic shift to "if"; cf. German *wenn* = "when", "if", and note to 144:8 ff (*bēt* "where" → "what").[285*]

13. Cf. *ABL* 455:8, *ša a-na* LUGAL EN-*ja la a-šam-*[*mu-u*]*-ni* ⁹ *a-na man-ni-ma aḫ-ḫur la-áš-me* "if I didn't obey the king, my lord, whom else then would I obey?"

157

Bibliography:

(I) Waterman, *RCAE* 636 (cf. III 374, IV 259); Pfeiffer, *SLA* 237.
(II) Oppenheim, *JAOS* 64 (1944) 194; von Soden, *Or*NS 24 (1955) 381; Deller, *AOAT* 1 (1969) 58.

Writer:

Nabû-nāṣer. Note the spellings *dul-LU* (Gen.) and *né-pe-ŠI*, characteristic of this writer, and the affinities of the letter with *LAS* 219. The subject matter, the reference to Aššur-mukīn-palū'a (cf. 218:6 and 219:6.r3) and the progressively assimilated final vowel in *tu-ú-ru* (obv.5', < *tūra*) confirm the identification. Despite superficial similarities with *LAS* 154-156, an assignation to Adad-šumu-uṣur is out of the question both for orthographic and linguistic reasons (cf. *tu-ú-RA* 143 r2, *né-pe-ŠE* 159 r4', [I]*Aš+šur*-GIN-BAL[MEŠ]*-ja* 145:7, *dul-li* 147:12.r15').

Addressee:

Esarhaddon.

Discussion:

This letter should be approximately contemporaneous with *LAS* 219 and 250, both referring to an illness of Aššur-mukīn-palū'a; unfortunately none of the letters contains chronological evidence pointing to a definite year. The reference to the crown prince (Assurbanipal) in 250:14 – without a simultaneous reference to Šamaš-šumu-ukīn – however very strongly suggests that the year in question was either 670 or 669. Cf. note to 280:10f.

Notes:

2'. [Id]*Šar-rat-sa-am-s*[*i*]: not otherwise known; possibly a royal child, though the syntactic position of the name makes such an interpretation rather dubious (one could, perhaps more plausibly, restore the end of line 1' as [*ina* ŠU²] instead of [*ina* UGU], which would make Š. a royal messenger: "[As regards . . .] of which the king, my lord, wrote to me [through] Š."; cf. e.g. *LAS* 226 r5'). Identical with the haruspex [Id]GAŠAN(*Šarrat*)-*sa-am-ma*-DINGIR-*a-a* occurring as reporter of extispicies in *PRT* 102:9 (652 BC) and 138 r3'?

4'. *ZI.KU.RU.DA*[MEŠ]: a whole family of dieseases caused by witchcraft, manifested in different ways (wandering eyes [*AMT* 13,4]; "seized" heart, blood running from mouth, stinging flesh [ibid. 42,5]; paralyzed [. . .], hurting teeth, fever [ibid. 90,1]); the remedy texts distinguish between "hand of Z." (*AMT* 44,4), "Z. of foe" (90,1 Rev.), "Z. of mongoose" (*DA* pl.42), "Z. of rat" (*AMT* 90,1), "Z. of bolt" (*AMT* 42,5), etc. The dis-

[285] Cf. also *šum-ma ka-ra-aš-ka . . . la e-ep-pa-aš ù mi-na-a e-ep-pu-us-sú-nu*, *EA* 29:146, where *šumma* replaces *kīma* of the present passage.

ease was cured both by medical and magical means. The former involved preparation of a mixture of drugs to be either drunk by the patient (*BAM* 203; *DA* pl.42:1ff; *AMT* 13,4, 84,9, 90,1 Rev.) or applied externally as an ointment (*AMT* 42,5, 99,2); the latter (which probably are meant here) closely resembled apotropaic namburbi rituals and always included a prayer recited by the patient to Šamaš, Sîn or some other deity. Cf. *AMT* 44,4 (nocturnal ritual on the roof, reed hut, *urigallu*-standards, etc.), 87,2 (slaughtering a pig, wrapping "sorceries" in its skin, prayer to Šamaš, etc.), 90,1 (offerings and prayers to Sîn), *DA* pl.42:8ff (a prayer scene before Big Dipper), etc.

6'. *"We called his name"*: A curious remark, in that in exorcistic rites the patients were usually expected to state their names *themselves* (in the context of a prayer formula). I have been able to find only *one* additional example in which the exorcist was supposed to utter the patient's name, and in that case the latter was obviously *unable* to speak himself. Cf. *LKA* 69:10 || 70 i 7f, MU ^{LÚ}GIG MU-*ár* ^{LÚ}GIG *šu-zi-bi* DUG$_4$.GA-*ma* "you utter the patient's name and say: 'Rescue the patient, (O Ištar)!", the ritual in question being intended to help a deadly sick patient seized by a ghost. Thus the condition of the patient referred to in the present letter may have been very serious. Note also MU-*šá i-za-ku-ru* "they utter her name" *ZA* 45, 44:33 (referring to a deceased); *aš-šu* NÍG.AG.A^{MEŠ} MU-*ku-nu lu-uz-*⸢*kur*⸣ "I am calling your name because of sorceries", *KAR* 227 iii 22 (referring to spirits of the dead); and the Netherworld associations of Syr. etc. *zakkūrā* "necromantic spirit, necromancer" (Zimmern, *Fremdwörter* p.67; Kaufman, *AS* 19 p.111, possibly a loanword from Akkadian), all examples suggesting that pronouncing a patient's name in exorcistic ritual had serious implications.

On the other hand, the passage also permits other interpretations. The patient may have been too small to speak for himself, or he may have been absent from the site of the ceremonies themselves. Cf. *LAS* 187 r3 ff and 201 r3' ff.

158

Bibliography:

(I) Waterman, *RCAE* 13.

(II) Labat, *Royauté* (1939) 342; Deller, *Or*NS (1966) 309, and *AOAT* 1 (1969) 56.

Date:

July, 670 BC(?). See commentary on *LAS* 147.

Addressee:

Esarhaddon.

Notes:

6. *a-sa-na-am-me*: cf. *LAS* 174, opened with exactly the same words as the present one. The idiomatic meaning of *assanamme* in both of these passages seems to correspond closely to Arab. *sam'an wa-ṭā'atan* "I hear and obey", a phrase often encountered in the *Arabian Nights* (e.g. Lane's [1889] translation, Vol. I, p.76); thus also *LAS* 318:14. A different shade of meaning is involved in Langdon, *TI* pl.2 ii 31 (*a-da-gal as-sa-nam-me* [32] *ú-ḫa-a-a-a-ṭa la ke-nu-ti* "I look around and listen, tracing the disloyal"), and obviously also in *LAS* 185 r21.

6 f. *a-še-'a-ar . . . al-lak*: cf. *ina ši-'a-a-ri al-lak*, 142 r5, and *ina ŠE a ri la-al-lik*, 147 r13'f (both letters by Adad-šumu-uṣur); also *a-š[i-j]a-ri lil-li-ka*, 48 r2'f. These parallels show, as already noted by Deller (1969), that *a-še-'a-ar* is a variant of the temporal adverb /ina ši'āri/ "in the morning", and there is no need to take it as a form of the verb *šêru* "Morgen werden" (*AHw.* 1219*b*) which is otherwise not attested in NA. All the phonetic peculiarities involved in the alternation /ina ši'āri/ ~/aš-ši'ār/ (replacement of *ina* by *ana*, proclisis of the preposition, and apocope of the final vowel) occur frequently in other temporal adverbs, too, and the coexistence of different variants of this sort in the idiolects of individual scholars is put beyond doubt by *LAS* 176, having *a-na ši-a-ri* (obv.8) beside *iš-ši-a-ri* (obv.11); the alternation <še> ~<ši> in the various spellings quoted above is purely orthographic.

The following table will clarify the issue.

ADVERB	FORMS WITH *AN(A)*		FORMS WITH *IN(A)*	
	ana	*an+*	*ina*	*in+*
aḫḫūr "yet"	*a-na ḫur* LAS 51 r6* *a-na ḫu-ru* ABL 1432 r3'	*aḫ-ḫur* passim		*i-ḫur ABL* 555r2 *iḫ-ḫur* passim
iddāt "afterwards"		*a-da-at ABL* 251 r7, 1086:5	*ina da-at ABL* 1244 r6	*i(d)-da-at LAS* 7 r11, *ABL* 628:14
			ina da-tú *CT* 53 39:12	*id-da-a-ti* passim *i-da-te LAS* 252:12
immāt "when (ever)"	*a-na ma-ti ABL* 1110 r16	*am-ma-te LAS* 72 r5	*ina ma-at CA* 98: 52'(!)	*im-ma-at LAS* 3 r3
	a-na ma-a-te LAS 12 r12		*ina ma-te- LAS* 294:13'	*im-ma-te/ti LAS* 38: 15, 173:9, and passim
iššaššūmi "the day before yesterday"	*a-na 3-ši u$_4$-me ABL* 132 r3	*e-šá-šu-u-me* BM 116230:30	*ina šal-ši u$_4$-me LAS* 129 r5	*i-ša-šu-me* ND 2648:5 *iš-šá-šú-me ABL* 605:7
iššiʾāri "tomorrow"	*a-na ši-a-ri LAS* 176:8	*a-še-ʾa-ar LAS* 158:6	*ina še-a-ri LAS* 147 r13	*i-ši-a-ri ABL* 100 r10, 1164:1
	a-na ši-ja-a-ri LAS 204:8	*a-š[i-j]a-ri LAS* 48 r1'	*ina ši-a-ri* passim	*i-ši-ʾa-a-ri ABL* 367 r10
			ina ši-ʾa-a-ri LAS 142 r5	*iš-ši-a-ri LAS* 2 r2
			ina ši-ja-a-ri LAS 248 r5 etc.	

7. *ku-u[s-si]-já* "my sedan chair": very probably *sic*, even though syllabic spellings of *kussû* are rare and one would rather expect the word to be written with the determinative GIŠ and a long final stem vowel. However, similar defective writings of morphemically long vowels do occur occasionally (e.g., *pi-ka*, *ABRT* I 6 r8; *pi-šú-nu*, *ABL* 434 r22; *ra-bé-šú*, *LAS* 64 r20) and the omission of the determinative constitutes no problem in itself; the traces can hardly be sensibly read otherwise (cf. Pt.I, p.297), and the same spelling actually recurs in lexical lists (cf. *ku-us-si gi-ir-ri*, Ḫg A I 34, and the other examples quoted in *CAD* K 588*a*). Finally, a ref. to a sedan chair makes good sense in the present context, Adad-šumu-uṣur being likely to use such a vehicle for any longer trips because of his age and prestigious position. Cf. *ABL* 1285 r18 ff: UN^{MEŠ} É *et-ti-qu dan-nu-ti ina* ^{GIŠ}GU.ZA^{MEŠ} 19 ^{LÚ}*2-ú-ti ina* $^{\text{GIŠ!}}$*sa!-par-ra!-ti* ^{LÚ}*ṣe-eḫ-ru-ti ina* ŠÀ ^{ANŠE}GÌR.NUN.NA^{MEŠ} "people pass my house, the mighty on sedan chairs, the second in rank in chaises, and even the small ones riding on mules (while the poor me must go on foot)."

159

Bibliography:

(I) Waterman, *RCAE* 660.

(II) Behrens, *ABB* (1906) 93[2]; Oppenheim, *JAOS* 64 (1944) 194.

Date:

June (?), 670 BC. See under date of *LAS* 151.

Addressee:

Esarhaddon.

Notes:

6ff. The obvious implication of this passage is that the queen mother was ill at the time the letter was written. Cf. commentary on *LAS* 222.

10. "[*When*] *Bēl took away the illness of the king*": This is almost certainly a reference to Esarhaddon's recovery from the attack of illness which he experienced in April, 670 BC (see under *LAS* 246). It is noteworthy that the exorcist explicitly ascribes the recovery to divine intervention and not to human skill. This seems to imply that the recovery had been quite sudden and that the disease had disappeared completely leaving behind no visible symptoms. Such a "miraculous" recovery actually fits well the hypothesis presented sub *LAS* 246 that Esarhaddon suffered from an extremely chronic rheumatoid disease characterized by alternating acute and latent periods. See discussion ibid.

r1. [*i*]*m-ra-ṣu-ni*: to judge from the prefix (*i-* not *ta-*), the writer here does not refer to the queen mother but to some other patient(s).[286] It is possible, however, that the continuation nevertheless pertains to the cure of the queen mother, since the present reference may have been of an equally general nature as those in *LAS* 247:9f and *RMA* 257:8ff (see sub *LAS* 182).

r4'. Delete the restoration and translation of this line proposed in Pt.I (*ušanni'ū* = Prt., not Prs. [= *ušannû*] as required by the translation, cf. note to 162:5). As the break did not necessarily contain a verb, several alternative restorations are possible, e.g. [*dul-lu šá d*]*i*!-'*u* "ritual against malaria", cf. 218:10 ff and 279 r14.[287]

r5'. Instead of a date, restore possibly [*šá ḫa-liq-ti* U]ZU! "(rites) [against the loss of f]lesh" (cf. 167:12) or the like.

r6'. *UŠ*$_{12}$*.BÚR.RU.DA*^{MEŠ}: incantations and rituals counteracting black magic (Akk. *kišpī pašāru*, lit. "to undo witchcraft"). Such antiwitchcraft magic was practiced both periodically (in the month Ābu, within the framework of the *Maqlû* ritual, for prophylactic purposes: see commentary to *LAS* 208) and occasionally, whenever need arose, for prophylactic, apotropaic and medical purposes (see commentary to *LAS* 173 on ušburrudas performed to nullify evil sorcery practiced during lunar eclipses; and *LAS* 218:18 on the namburbi ritual against witchcraft). The ušburrudas referred to in the present letter certainly belonged to the last category; in other words, they were intended to cure a definite *illness* ascribed to evil sorcery. Cf. *KAR* 80 (|| Langdon, *RA* 26 39 ff.), obv. 1 ff: "If a man's head aches, his face twitches, his nostrils ache, his saliva flows; if he forgets his words, his inwards are inflamed, his arms are paralyzed, his [hands] are numb, his feets sting him, and his ankles are "loose", that man has been subjected to the witchcraft and evil machinations of his enemy (NA BI EN DUG$_4$.DUG$_4$-*šú kiš-pi* NIGIN-[*šú*] [7] *kip-di* Ḫ[UL^{MEŠ} *ik-p*[*u-du-šú*, obv.8f); in order to undo this witchcraft . . . " (follows a ritual involving preparation of several images of the sorcerer and sorceress, a prayer to Šamaš, and subsequent burning and burial of the images made). Other texts describe symptoms of illnesses attributed to witchcraft in similar terms (cf. Schollmeyer, *SHG* no.21:9 ff || *LKA* 155 Rev.; *AMT* 86,1 ii 3 ff; 87,1:8'ff); one the whole, these descriptions give the impression that the patients in question suffered from mental and physical disorders (caused by continued severe stress?). Cf. Kinnier Wilson, *AS* 16 (1965) 296f.

For therapeutic *ušburrudas* (other than those already mentioned) see the numerous texts listed by Kinnier Wilson, loc.cit, fn.19; further, Ebeling, *Or*NS 22 358ff; Lambert, *AfO* 18 288 ff; *LKA* 158; *AMT* 87,5, 89,1, and 92,1. etc. Note that while most of these texts belonged to the corpus of the exorcists (*āšipūtu*), several recipes pertaining to the cure of bewitched persons were also incorporated in the lore of the physicians (*asûtu*). These mostly contained lists of drugs against witchcraft (Ú UŠ$_{12}$.BÚR.RU.DA) and directions for their use in salves and potions (e.g., *AMT* 87,5:1'ff; 87,1:8'ff; 86,1 ii 3 ff), but occasionally also quote incantations and rituals better known from the exorcistic texts (see e.g. *AMT* 86,1 ii 12 and 92,1 ii 11'ff, the latter passage duplicated by *BRM* 4 no.18:1'ff). It seems possible that the ušburrudas referred to in the present letter included texts from the lores of both crafts.

[286] True, Naqia was occasionally (because of her influential position?) addressed as if a man, cf. *ABL* 368:10 *ša* AMA MAN be-lí *IŠ-pur-an-ni.*

[287] This example is given here only to illustrate the range of possibilities, without any claim on correctness. Indeed, it is very unlikely to be correct, as the letter refers to therapeutic rituals whereas *LAS* 218 and 279 speak of phrophylactic and apotropaic ones.

160

Bibliography:

(I) Waterman, *RCAE* 549.

(II) Behrens, *ABB* (1906) 18; Dhorme, *RHR* 113 (1936) 148; Deller, *AOAT* 1 (1969) 55.

Date:

June (?), 670. See commentary to *LAS* 151.

Addressee:

Esarhaddon.

Notes:

r3'. The incantation-ritual mentioned here remains unidentified. For the various possibilities of restoration cf. *Exorcist's Manual* (*KAR* 44), 8f and 16f: Á.ZÀG.GIG.GA *di-'u*/GIG-*tum* MEŠ . . . [9] SAG.GIG.GA^MEŠ GÚ^sag-gig GIG.GA^MEŠ . . . . [16] IGI.GIG.GA.KE$_4$ ZÚ.GIG.GA.KE$_4$ . . . [17] ŠÀ.GIG.GA.KE$_4$ MUR.GIG.GA.KE$_4$ "wicked *asakku* demons, . . . headaches, aching necks, . . . (incantations for) sore eyes, toothache, . . . stomach troubles, diseased lungs . . ."

r4'. [*ÉN É*]*-a* ^d*UTU* ^d[*Asal-lú-ḫi*/^d*AMAR+UD*]: incantations beginning with these words are known from many different exorcistic rituals (e.g., the universal namburbi, bīt rimki, ušburruda, dingir-šadibba, bīt mēseri, see Kunstmann, *LSS* NF 2 (1932) 86 ff), but the one meant here does not seem to be otherwise known.

r5'. *ma-mit pa-š*[*á-a-ri*]: meant are exorcistic rituals and incantations used to cure diseases caused by (or attributed to) curses. For typical examples, see Reiner, *Šurpu* Appendix p.52 f; for symptoms of the relevant diseases, see Labat, *TDP* p.144:52'f (hand of C.; will die); 178:16 (running saliva, face covered by *aḫḫāzu*, . . . intestines: hand of Curse: will die); ibid. 17; and 180:20.21.25.28.32. These symptoms indeed suggest that the patients haunted by Curses (here the Queen Mother) suffered from psychic disorders, as argued in detail by Kinnier Wilson, *AS* 16 (1965) 294 ff.

r6'. *"You, River, Creator of Everything"*: an incantation forming a component of many namburbi rituals. Cf. *LKA* 123:12' ([ÉN *at-ti*] ÍD DÙ-*at* D[Ù.A.BI], evil of snakes); Ebeling, *RA* 50 88:25 (ÉN *at-ti*] ^dÍD DÙ-*at ka-*[*la-ma*], evil of monstrous birth; cf. Caplice, *Or*NS 34 127 and 130); Ebeling, *RA* 50 92:6 (ÉN *at-ti* ÍD *ba-na-te ka-la-m*[*a*], evil of dogs), cf. Caplice, *Or*NS 36 8:13 (ÉN *at-ti* ÍD *ba-na-ta ka-la-ma*, same namburbi); id., *Or*NS 36 290:29' (evil of lightning); *Or*NS 39 135:21 (evil of sorcery); *Or*NS 40 143:19 (evil of fungus); *Or*NS 42 509: 30' (idāti ittāti lemnēti), etc. In light of *LAS* 159, it seems likely that the incantation here mentioned belonged to the namburbi against witchcraft.

r7'. Probably to be restored simply *a-d*[*i* DÙ.DÙ.BI-*šú-nu*] "together wit[h their rituals]".

161

Bibliography:

(I) Waterman, *RCAE* 8.

(II) Deller, *AOAT* 1 (1969) 55.

Discussion:

This is a letter in an excellent state of preservation, except for two relatively small breaks on the left and right edges. Unfortunately these two breaks suffice to render the letter – which seems to list titles of little known exorcistic or medical compositions – virtually unintelligible; almost every line from obv.7 on remains a crux. This being so, it seems wisest to keep the commentary on this letter to a minimum rather than to present pages of hypotheses leading nowhere . The adjacent new copy will serve as a basis for further study and (hopefully) provoke brighter ideas in scholars knowing the Mesopotamian exorcistic and medical literature better than I do.[288]

LAS 161

Obv.

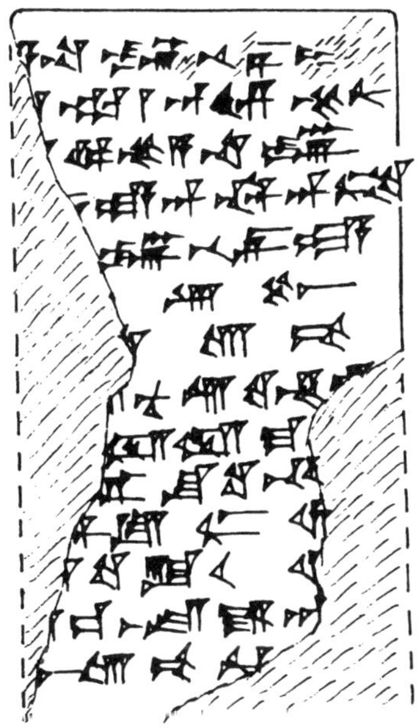

Rev. uninscribed

Notes:

7. Possibly [ÉN *ki-i*]*s lìb-bi* or the like. The restoration [*i-n*]*a* in Pt.I is justified inasmuch as the spelling *i-na* (otherwise rare in NA) also occurs (besides *ina*) in two letters of Adad-šumu-uṣur (124 r2 and 142:13), but it does not really make sense in this context.

8. On *é-nu-ru* incantations see Falkenstein, *LSS* NF 1 p.4 ff and id., *ZA* 45 22. The incantation UD EN.⌜NUN⌝ "day of the watch" (reading after Lambert, also EN.⌜LÍL⌝ possible) seems to be otherwise unknown.[289]

9. Instead of [NÍG].DÍM.DÍM.MA^{M}[EŠ] (on this physiognomic composition see Kraus, *ZA* 43 84 ff and *AfO* 11 219 ff; classed among exorcistic works in *KAR* 44:6), one may also consider restoring [AN].GIM.DÍM. MA.

11. Beginning obscure.[290] The latter part of the line probably reads ÁB K[Ù.GA] "pure cow", cf. Ì ÁB KÙ.GA "fat of a pure cow", *BIN* 2 22:195 (bil. incant.); GA ÁB KÙ.GA "milk of a pure cow", Küchler *BKBM* pl.5 iv 54 (catchline of *Suālu* Tablet I, var. GA ^{GUD}ÁB KÙ.GA, ibid. pl.6:1; the recipe in question pertains to the cure of stomach trouble [ŠÀ GIG]).

12. Beginning possibly [š]*u-tam-ṭu-u* "to be belittled" (Reiner), a rare verb occurring twice in the physiognomic omen series (*AfO* Bh 3 no.38a, 4, and *ZA* 43 102:26, cf. *AHw* 626*b*). Rest unclear (K[Ù.GI] "gold"?)

13f. These lines look like a commentary explaining the preceding unusual expression(s). Read [*q*]*i-is-su ša* ^{d}[.] "gift (*qīštu*) of . . . "??

162

Bibliography:

(I) Waterman, *RCAE* 1435.

(II) Böhl, *Opera Minora* (1953) 420; von Soden, *Fs Christian* (1956) 105; Kümmel, *StBoT* 3 (1967) 171.

---

288 I feel obliged to record here my gratitude to W.G. Lambert, E. Reiner and H. Hunger for their readiness to discuss this text at length with me, even though our discussions did not lead to any tangible results.

289 Cf. the én-é-nu-ru incantation in the *kīs libbi* recipe *BKBM* pl.I i4ff.

290 Hardly [TÚG]BAR.DUL$_5$ "*kusītu* garment".

Date:

Probably late June (= late Simānu), 669 BC. Since the king here entitles himself as "Farmer", and since the letter is written before a potential eclipse of the sun (obv.8 ff), it must date from the end of the first month of a sub-substitute king's reign, hence from late Du'ūzu or Kanūnu, 671, or late Simānu, 669 (see Intr., p. XXIII). While none of these three alternatives can be ruled out with absolute certainty, the odds are for the last of them: the title "Farmer" was most consistently used at that time, since the substitute king was then resident in Nineveh and his presence consequently strongly felt at court;[291] *LAS* 135 and 166, written by the two addressees to the "Farmer", are also to be placed in June/July, 669; and the worry about the potential solar eclipse, so clearly expressed in the present letter, is also well attested in other letters dating from June/July, 669, see *LAS* 135-136 and 290.

Sender:

Esarhaddon.

Discussion:

There is only one further letter in the present corpus which is likely to have been sent by the "Farmer" (*LAS* 242), and since it resembles pretty closely the present letter both in content and in physical appearance, and likewise is only partially preserved, one wonders whether the two fragments are not actually parts of the same tablet. This potential "sandwich" join was checked at my request by C.B.F. Walker, who writes (letter dated January 27, 1976): "K 1038 and 13906 do not join and to judge by the curvature and the amount of the core of the tablet surviving in each case I would say that they cannot belong to the same tablet." However, both fragments are very thin (Ø 9 and 11 mm maximum) flakes off the surface of the original tablet, and since their script, colour and dimensions are very alike (see Pt.I, pp. 335 and 338), I would not exclude the possibility of original coherence unless it can be definitely *dis*proved. Excepting these two fragments, the only extant royal letter addressed to Assyrian scholars is No. 226 of the present corpus. Most of the numerous other royal letters referred to elsewhere in this corpus (see App. P4) remain buried in the ruins of downtown Nineveh.

Notes:

5f. [*š*]*a-ni-'a . . . du-ub-ba*: a hendiadys (two imperatives, the verb *šannû* "to repeat" complementing and agreeing morphologically with the following verb) frequently encountered in Neo-Assyrian; cf. *lu-⸢šá⸣-an-ni-'u-u liš-ú-lu*, *TCS* 4 p.10; *lu-šá-ni-i' liš-pur*, *ABL* 1453+ r8'; *tu-šá-na-a . . . tu-šé-taq*, *STT* 88 r.X 13; *ú-sa-ni-i' . . . i-s*[*i-q*]*i*, ND 2462 r6f (*Iraq* 21 pl.45); [*u*]*s-sa-ni-i'* [*i*]*g-du-ru-ur*, *LAS* 235 r7 f; *ú-sa-ni-'u-ú iq-ṭi-bu-ni*, *ABL* 314:8f, etc. Not a variant of *šaniānu* "zum 2. Mal" (*AHw* 1163*b*).

The restoration ^{LÚ}*tur-*[*tan/ta-ni*] at the end of line 5 is supported by *LAS* 242:14', which reads (after collation) $^{\text{LÚ*}}$*tur-⸢ta⸣nu* (not ^{LÚ}TUR as given in Pt.I). Cf. *LAS* 165:6 (there also to be read ^{LÚ}*tur-*[*ta-nu*]?)

7. *pu-tu-ḫu ta-na-áš-ši*: cf. Ebeling, *SVAT* p.6 ad Z.35, and in detail Deller, *WZKM* 57 (1961) 38 ff.[292]; the attested meanings of the expression in NA letters are "to be responsible/take responsibility (for)" and "to guarantee (that)". Cf. *pu-tu-ḫu* ^{12} [$^{\text{NA4.d}}$AL]ÀD-^{d}LAMA^{MEŠ} . . . *na-ṣa-ku* "I assume the responsibility for the bull colossi (to be transported by ship)", *ABL* 103+985 r11-13; [*ket*]*-tu ana-ku pu-tu-ḫu* ^{16} [*a-na-áš*]*-ši šum-ma la* [*d*]*u-un-qu . . .* ^{18} *šu-tu-u-ni* "indeed, I guarantee that it is advantageous", *LAS* 199:15ff; *ma-a* ^{URU}*Ku-um-mu gab-bi-šú* ^{15} [^{L}]$^{\text{Ú*}}$*qe-e-pu la i-na-ši-ú ma-a a-né-*[*nu-ma*] ^{16} [*ni-n*]*a-ši ma-a pu-tu-ḫu na-ṣa-ni* "the city of Kummu

291 Actually, it seems that save for the two weeks following the shocking solar eclipse of May 27, 669, the use of the address "Farmer" was really customary only in the immediate proximity of eclipses.

292 The etymology considered by Ebeling and Deller (**pūḫ* Dt Inf.) is incorrect. The expression corresponds exactly to the Babylonian idiom *pūtu našû* "to be responsible for, to guarantee" (*AHw* 763*a* s.v. *našû* II G I 4; of the many examples given there note especially *pu-ú-tu* LUGAL *be-lí-ja na-šá-ku*, *RMA* 273 r13, and *pu-tú* [*a*]*-di 7-šú na-šá-ka* AN.MI *ul iš-šak-kan* "I guarantee 7 times that no eclipse will take place", *ABL* 1448) and has therefore every likelihood to be of the same origin; the etymological connection of *pūtuḫu* and *pūtu* is further borne out by spelling *pu-u-tú-ḫu* in ND 2338:21, showing that the first syllable of *putuḫu* was long, not short as assumed by Deller (and following him, by von Soden, *AHw* 885*a*). The element *-ḫu* (*ḫ* not geminated!) may be of Hurrian origin.

at large does not favour the presence of a royal delegate, but we support it (and) take the responsibility", *CT* 53 138:316; *pu-tu-ḫu ša* X[. . . . . *inašši*] "he is responsible for [. . .]" *CT* 53 37 r14. Accordingly, the present passage has to be rendered: "You will assume the responsibility in regard to the solar eclipse", whatever the implications of such a remark (see below). Note that the passage *cannot* be translated "you will be respondible *for* the eclipse", for this would have had to be expressed by a different construction (*pu-tu-ḫu* AN.MI . . . *ta-na-áš-ši*, cf. ND 2334:20 *pu-tú-ḫu te-lit ad-ri* [21] *i-na-áš-ši*, etc.). For the word order cf. *un-qu* KÙ.GI *na-aṣ ina muḫ-ḫi-ni*, ABL 582:5'ff; *is-sa-par-u-ni ina muḫ-ḫi-ja ma-a*, *ABL* 1049:3'f and 310 r14f; *ša* LUGAL *be-lí iq-bu-u-ni ina* UGU DUMU[ME] EN[ME]*-ka ma-a*, *LAS* 179:16f; *it-tal-ku-nu ina muḫ-ḫi-ja ma-a*, *ABL* 220 r4; *la-áš-*[*šú*] [8] [U]DU[MEŠ] *ina muḫ-ḫi-ja*, *AfO* Bh 6 no.106:9f; *mu-uk al-ka is-si-ja* [21] *ina* UGU *ka-ra-ri ša* URU_4, *ABL* 471:20f, etc.

Exactly what sort of "responsibility" the *turtānu* was supposed to assume remains obscure; perhaps simply the safeguarding of general law and order in lieu of the temporarily "disabled" king. The possibility is excluded that he was supposed to volunteer as a substitute king, because the king's title "Farmer" shows that a substitute had already been enthroned, and because the feared eclipse would thus have automatically "afflicted" the sitting substitute.

10. [*p*]*i-qi-ta-a-te*: if this is a reference to the "charges" (i.e. suckling patients) discussed in the commentary to *LAS* 123, its implications elude me. Note, however, the ref. to the "charge of the Rear Palace" in *LAS* 135 probably dealing with the same (expected) solar eclipse as the present letter.*

11. Restore simply [AN].MI ᵈUTU *i-šak-*[*kan*] "(Perhaps . . .) a solar eclipse will take place . . .". The normal word order would have been ᵈUTU AN.MI *i-šak-kan* (cf. 77 r1, 82:9 ff, 83:5 ff, 104:4 ff, 105:4'ff, 120: 8f, etc.), but the present wording – which may have been influenced by the occurrence of AN.MI ᵈ*Šá-maš* in line 8 – is also attested, in a similar context, in *LAS* 135:10 ff: *ina* IGI AN.MI [11] ᵈUTU *nu-us-sa-ad-gil* [12] AN.MI ᵈUTU *la iš-kun*.

163

Bibliography:

(I) Waterman, *RCAE* 364.

(II) Oppenheim, *BASOR* 107 (1947) 11; Deller, *AOAT* 1 (1969) 61.

Date:

Kanūnu 5, eponymy of Šulmu-Bēl-lašme = January 5, 669 BC. See commentary to *LAS* 173.

Addressee:

Esarhaddon.

Writer:

Adad-šumu-uṣur, in spite of 176:7-9! Note Obv.5 (ᵈAG ᵈAMAR+UD), etc.,[293] and cf. note on the writer of *LAS* 164.

Discussion:

This letter belongs to a lengthy correspondence (see sub *LAS* 173) concerning various practical questions relating to the performance of anti-witchcraft rituals for the royal family; it was immediately followed by *LAS* 176 and preceded by *LAS* 173, 164, 174 and 175? (in this order). The background of the matter discussed in the present letter is clarified by the previous correspondence. The ritual involved an exorcistic ceremony outside the palace, possibly on the roof or in a secluded place on the bank of the river (cf. AfO 18 288ff), and as the site was too small to accommodate all the people at the same time, the ceremony was performed in two rounds; for this purpose, the people involved were divided (probably by the king himself, cf. r3) into two groups, both of which were obviously originally meant to be treated within the same day (cf. 174:10ff). However, when the first group

[293] *lik-ru-bu* (Obv.7) not followed in the same line by *ina UGU*; *le-E-pu-šu* (r2.13) not attested in letters of M. (for A. cf. 136 r5. 145 r2.6, etc.).

had undergone the treatment, the second one did not automatically show up at the place of the ceremony and so the chief exorcist had to notify the king (cf. 175?); probably because of the vague answer received (pres. letter), the completion of the ritual was postponed to the following day. The fact that the writers, who had just supervised the performance of the first part of the ritual, could not tell exactly whom they had yet to treat indicates that the term "the king's people" (UN^{MEŠ} *ša* LUGAL) in 173:17f does not refer to the king's *nearest* relatives only but probably included at least his harem as well. In any case, a large number of people must have been involved.

Notes:

10 ff. The quotation from the king's letter ends comprises only lines 10-12, while lines 13 ff ("the others . . .") already belong to the answer of the scholars. Cf. *LAS* 176:7ff and 175:4'ff, and alter the translation given in Pt.I.

r4. *A+A-'u-ú-ti*: this spelling also occurs in K 4310 (*4 R*^{2}61) i 7 and 34 (*A+A-'u*), and clearly renders spoken [ai̯'u] (syllabified as *ai-u*; cf. *a-i-ú, LAS* 46:12, reflecting the same pronunciation). It is worth attention in two respects. First, it gives definite proof that the digraph A+A was in NA used to express the diphthong /ai̯/ and therefore has to be transliterated in certain (most?) contexts as *ai*.[294] Secondly, the spelling with <'> indicates that the diphthong /ai̯/ was not necessarily followed in prevocalic position by the glide /i̯/, and hence the pronoun concerned (and its derivates) should be lemmatized *ai̯u* (or *aju,* as in *CAD*) rather than *ajju* (as done in *AHw*).

164

Bibliography:

(I) Waterman, *RCAE* 11.
(II) Dhorme, *RHR* 113 (1936) 139; Deller, *AOAT* 1 (1969) 55.

Writer:

Despite the fact that the name of Adad-šumu-uṣur here precedes that of Marduk-šākin-šumi, the letter was certainly written by the latter. This appears not only from the handwriting, which is identical with that of *LAS* 173 (personal collation), but also from the orthography of the greeting and blessing formula (*lu-u šùl-mu . . .* ^{d}PA *u* ^{d}AMAR+UD, cf. *LAS* 173, 174, 176, 179-182, 197, 198, as against Adad-šumu-uṣur's usual *lu šùl-mu . . .* ^{d}AG ^{d}AMAR+UD), the sequence *lik-ru-bu ina UGU* in Obv.6 (see on *LAS* 149 and 244), and the spellings *ki-i an-ni-i* and *an-NIM-ma* (Obv.8, Rev.6), which are characteristic of Marduk-šākin-šumi (see Appendix M 6); for the content, cf. *LAS* 173. Note that most other joint letters of Adad-šumu-uṣur and Marduk-šākin-šumi (*LAS* 139 and 165-166) can also be attributed to M. on similar grounds. Presumably, Adad-šumu-uṣur's advanced age and position as the king's personal exorcist gave him authority over that of Marduk-šākin-šumi (despite the latter's high professional rank), and for this reason it was also considered appropriate that his name was mentioned first, even though he had personally not written the letter.[295]

Date:

End of Kislīmu/December, 670 BC. See under *LAS* 173 and below.

Discussion:

This letter was preceded by *LAS* 173 and followed by *LAS* 174, 175?, 163, 176 and 177; on the general setting see under *LAS* 163 and 173. The directions in Obv.10 – Rev.4 can hardly have been intended for anybody but the king himself; this would give the letter a terminus ante quem, Kanūnu 2 (cf. 173 r10 f). Correspondingly,

[294] The fact that the translit. *aju-'u-ú-ti* (Pt.I) is clearly nonsensical illustrates the point. I am now inclined to believe that at least most NA words written with a final A+A (gentilics etc.) indeed ended in *-ai*, despite the occasional spellings with case endings.

[295] But perhaps he had dictated it? Note that *LAS* 163, written by *Adad-šumu-uṣur*, may have been *dictated* by Marduk-šakin-šumi (cf. 163 r1-2 with 176:7-9!!).

the word *am-mu-ti* "the others" in Rev.6 would refer to the crown prince and the king's people, mentioned together also in 173:17f.

Notes:

9. [*ú-t*]*a-as-si-ik* "he assigned": logic would rather require [*NU-t*]*a-as-si-ik* "WE assigned", but this is hardly possible in view of the fact that the NA quotation particle of 1st person (plural) is otherwise regularly *nuk*/*muk*, not *mā* (r1.5); cf. provisionally Ylvisaker, *LSS* 5/6, p.63 f. I am aware of only one exception to this rule: *a-ni-ni* ⸢*ki*⸣ *an-ni-i* [12] *a-na* DUMU-TIN.TIR$^{KI.MEŠ}$ *ni-iq-ṭí-bi* [13] *ma-a* L[UG]AL *ina muḫ-ḫi-*⸢*ku*⸣*-nu i-*[*sa-ap*]*-ra-na-ši* "we spoke to the citizens of BAbylon as follows: 'The king has sent us to you, etc.' ", *NL* 1:11 ff (*Iraq* 17 pl.4); cf. ibid. 22ff, "we said to them (*a-ni-ni* [23] *ni-iq-ṭí-ba-šú-nu ma-a*): 'Open the gate, let us enter Babylon!', but they didn't agree", similarly ibid.31 ff. While these passages unquestionably show that *mā* could occasionally introduce oratio recta of 1st pl. also, they may, on the other hand, represent a special case which is not applicable to the present passage: the Assyrians in *NL* 1 were communicating with Babylonians and Chaldaeans and therefore may have used an interpreter; the particle *mā* may have served to indicate that the talking was actually not done by the writers themselves but by the interpreter. It may also be added that there is no *binding* need to restore [*nu-t*]*a-as-si-ik* in the present letter: the writers could perfectly well be quoting the words of a third party, e.g. a priest in charge of the scene of the ritual.

10. For ⸢*ša*⸣ restore rather ⸢É⸣ "as soon as he (scil. the king) has performed", etc. The subjunction *bēt* written É also in 179 r7.

10 f. In *LAS* 173 r1 ff, the tablets of ÉŠ.GÀR *mé-eḫ ri* (cf. present letter, r1) are contrasted with *šu-me-ra-ni ša uš$_{12}$-búr-ru-da-a-ni* "Sumerian (tablet)s of ušburruda-rituals". Accordingly, the present passage may perhaps be restored *uš$_{12}$-búr-ru-da-ni* [11] [EME].GI$_7$*-ti* "Sumerian ušburrudas", the spelling EME.KU(GI$_7$)*-ti* standing for *šumerūti*, Pl. of the adjective *šumeru* (cf. *CAD* A/1 p.272 s.v. *akkadû*, *AOAT* 6 p.338f s.v. *šumer*, and *LAS* 322:5').[296] On the Sumerian ušburrudas see note to 173 r1.

r1. *ša mé-eḫ-ri*: the pronoun *ša* ("that/those of") can here only refer to *uš$_{12}$-búr-ru-da-ni* in Obv.10, which means that the composition called *meḫru*, otherwise known only from 173 r8, largely if not exclusively consisted of anti-witchcraft incantations and rituals. The meaning of *meḫru* here remains obscure. On the one hand, the improbability of the idea that a composition consisting of several tablets (*LAS* 173) and playing such a central role in the ceremonies referred to here would have remained so poorly known , as well as the fact that the composition is clearly contracted with Sumerian incantations makes one wonder whether the term "*meḫru* (series)" in fact is not just a broad designation of a collection of Akkadian incantations and whether it should not be rendered plainly as "*refrain* series" or the like; cf. *AHw* 641 sub *meḫru* I 3 and see note on *LAS* 173 r1. In the lack of clear-cut evidence, the possibility that an unknown (or unidentified) series indeed is in question, as assumed in Pt.I, cannot be excluded, however; note the occurrence of *meḫru* 'opponent, adversity, mishap" in *Šurpu* and *Maqlû* (and various medical texts) besides all kinds of diseases attributed to witchcraft (*dipalû*, *epšetu*, *gimillu*, *kadibbidû*, *kišpu*, *râmu*, *ruḫû*, *rusû*, *upšašû*, *zēru*, *zikurudû*).

165

Bibliography:

(I) Waterman, *RCAE* 14.
(II) Deller, *AOAT* 1 (1969) 56.

Discussion and possible date:

This letter could be the answer to *LAS* 162, in which case it would probably date from late Simānu/June, 669 BC; but the fragmentary condition of both texts of course leaves this hypothesis entirely in the realm of spe-

[296] The restoration [*na-ṭ*]*u-ti* "geeignet" recently proposed by von Soden (*AHw* p.768) is not acceptable since neither the adj. nor the verb *naṭû* are otherwise attested in NA.

culation. Against the coherence of the two letters would seem to speak that the king is here not addressed as "Farmer"; but it has to be noted that the title "Farmer" is not used in *LAS* 135-136 either, both letters dating from approximately the same time as *LAS* 162.

Notes:

r5'. Cancel the translation of *lu la i-sa-am-mu-u* given in Pt.I, and render instead (in accordance with *AHw* 1020*a*), "they should not hesitate(?)."

166

Bibliography:
(I) Waterman, *RCAE* 362 (cf. IV 186).
(II) Landsberger, *LSS* 6/1 (1915) 104; Langdon, *Babylonian Menologies* (1933) 67; Dhorme, *RHR* 113 (1936) 138; von Soden, *ZA* 44 (1938) 184; Labat, *Royauté* (1939) 307; Oppenheim, *Or*NS 11 (1942) 127; Böhl, *Opera Minora* (1953) 421; von Soden, *Festschrift Christian* (1956) 102f; Kümmel, *StBoT* 3 (1967) 173, 176, 180; Deller, *AOAT* 1 (1969) 61; Oppenheim, *Centaurus* 14 (1969) 129[14].

Date:
Appr. Du'ūzu 12, eponymy of Šamaš-kāšid-ajābi = July 8, 669 BC. The relevant evidence is as follows. It is stated in Obv. 15 that the addressee had *at least* twice gone through a (purification) ritual following the execution of the substitute king. This proves , firstly, that the letter was addressed to Esarhaddon,[297] and secondly, that it cannot have been written before 671 BC, since the substitute king ritual had been performed only twice before that year in Esarhaddon's reign.[298] Within the time brackets 671-669 BC thus obtained, three different substitute kings were enthroned: one in Du'ūzu (July), 671, another in Kanūnu (December) of the same year, and a third in Ajāru (May), 669.[299] The first of these reigned for 100 days and was put to death on Tašrītu 22 = October 7, 671, or a few days later (see under *LAS* 292), and cannot hence be the person meant here (see Obv.6 ff). The decision between the two remaining alternatives can be made with the help of *LAS* 135. This letter, also by Adad-šumu-uṣur, refers to a watch for a solar eclipse and then goes on to suggest that the substitute king currently reigning may "go to his fate" on the 16th, *if* the full moon is observed on the 15th: alternatively, the substitute may complete his normal 100-day reign. That is exactly where the present letter begins: the king *endorses* the option of the 15th day (Obv.6f), *tells* that the substitute has to be executed and *not* allowed to complete his reign (Obv. 8f), and *affirms* he will perform his purificatory ritual on the 16th according to the established practice (Obv.9ff). The crucial 16th day also suggested in *LAS* 135 (albeit in a different sense) is reiterated twice in the letter; there cannot thus be any doubt that the present letter is connected with *LAS* 135. The orthography of the introductory salutation of *LAS* 135 links it up with the group of letters discussed in commentary to *LAS* 154, all datable to June 669; hence *LAS* 135, and consequently also the present letter, pertain to the case initiated by the eclipse of Ajāru/May, 669. The watch for the solar eclipse mentioned in *LAS* 135 occurred at the end of Simānu/June (see sub *LAS* 136 and 162), hence the full moon following which the substitute had to go to his fate certainly belonged to the month Du'ūzu/July. The present letter was probably written slightly before the full moon.

Addressee:
Esarhaddon.

Writer:
Marduk-šākin-šumi (see under *LAS* 164).

---

297 The last reference to Adad-šumu-uṣur (*ADD* 448) dates from 665 BC, his last letter to king (*LAS* 125) from 667 BC. By 665, only one substitute king ritual had been performed under Assurbanipal (see sub *LAS* 298). The next eclipse requiring the performance of the ritual came only in August, 664. The present letter should accordingly postdate even that case, and it is very unlikely that Adad-šumu-uṣur (born 730 at the latest, cf. ND 5427 and *ADD* 350) ever lived that long.

298 See *LAS* 136:12 (Araḫsamna 677) and *LAS* 30-31 (Ulūlu/Araḫsamna 674).

299 See under *LAS* 26.

Discussion:

Leaving out of consideration the mini-reign reported in *LAS* 298, which was due to a misunderstanding on the king's part, the present letter provides the only certain attestation of a substitute king ritual terminated before its normal end; in all other cases, except possibly in the case reported in *LAS* 280, the substitute obviously was allowed to "sit" full 100 days (cf. sub *LAS* 32, 292, 280 and 334). Accepting that the substitute began his reign on Ajāru 29, immediately after the solar eclipse (see on *LAS* 28), the ritual under consideration lasted only 47 days, i.e. not even half of its normal duration. Why? Two explanations seem possible. First, the king may have get *tired* of the *repeated* performance of the ritual in recent years, which certainly to some extent at least inconvenienced his life, and he may thus have wanted to finish the ritual as soon as possible. This is, however, improbable, knowing the psyche of Esarhaddon (cf. sub *LAS* 246); he must have been happy with all kind of protection and attention he could get. It is true that *LAS* 135:8ff and 134:9f clearly indicate that the king was getting impatient, but his impatience then was probably due to something else than just *boredom.* The beginning of the king's 12th year had been full of disappointments and frightening portents: cancellation of the returnal of Bēl to Babylon in mid-Ajāru (*LAS* 29), solar eclipse at the end of the same month (*LAS* 28 and 104); an ill-portending earthquake in the beginning of Simānu (*LAS* 35, 137 and 234), a lunar eclipse predicting evil to Assyria in the middle of the same month (*LAS* 25, *RMA* 271, etc.) and immediately after that, a sudden illness of a baby who apparently was very dear to the king (*LAS* 167, 152-156, 136 and 126). As a result of all this, he may have grown increasingly nervous and restless, unwilling to wait for months until the danger threatening him would be definitely eliminated; especially the last adversity, which was a decidedly personal one, may have given rise to a desire to get rid of the substitute as soon as possible (see on 136:11). That it was, in principle, possible to dethrone the substitute before his 100-day reign (cf. note on 135 r6) was over cannot be doubted, even though no clear statement to this effect is extant in the substitute king ritual tablet: otherwise Adad-šumu-uṣur could hardly have given the king this option in *LAS* 135.

Notes:

14. *e-pa-šú-u-ni*: despite the vocalization (and the three examples of frequentative Prs. referring to the past in *LAS* 60:14.15.r6), hardly = /eppašūni/ (Prs.) "they used to do": the present tense of *'pš* is in Marduk-šākin-šumi's orthography regularly — with only two exceptions — spelled with geminated *p* (cf. *ep-pa-áš*, 172 r11, 185:20.r2, 195:11; *ep-pu-šu*, 172:10, 237 B 7'; *te-ep-pa-áš*, 187:5.13; *né-ep-pa-áš*, 173 r15, 181:9, 183 r3, 191 r14, 342 r2, 355 r7; *né-ep-pa-šú-u-ni*, 196 r 14; the exceptions are *e-pu-šú*, 181 r2, and *né-pa-áš-u-ni*, 195 r8). More probably = /ēpašūni/ (Prt.), a variant of the "paradigmatic" preterite *e-pu-šú-u-ni* = /ēpušūni/ occurring in Obv.16. See Parpola, *Iraq* 34 (1972) 23 on the optional dissimilation *uCú* > *aCú* in Neo-Assyrian, and cf. Obv.18 (*iš-ka-nu-ni* < /iškunūni/).

17. *ṬE-mu* "order": possibly rather *šùl*(DI)-*mu* "safety/health". Note that *ṭēmu* is in other letters of Marduk-šākin-šumi consistently spelled with the sign NE (*ṭè-e-mu* 191 r5', 237 B 8', 342 r5; *ṭè-e-me* 184 r1, 186 r1), while the spelling *DI-mu* in his letters otherwise always stands for *šulmu* (139:4, 149:3, 164:4, 165:4, 172:3. 5.6, 173:3, 174:3, 176:3, 177:3, 178:3, 179:3, 180:3.r2, 181:3, etc.), and that the expression *šulmu šakānu* "to provide health/safety", with gods as subjects, also occurs in *LAS* 180 r1f (*Aš+šur* ^{d}UTU ^{d}EN ^{d}PA *šùl-mu i-šak-ku-nu*; cf. *ABL* 126:8 and 503:15). The reading *ṭēmu* is not entirely excluded, however; an exceptional spelling with DI also occurs in *LAS* 41 r18 (*ṭe-e-me*). By themselves, both *ṭēmu šakānu* ("as the gods have commanded . . .") and *šulmu šakānu* ("as the gods have provided safety . . .") would make equally good sense here, since the ritual concerned was apparently considered vital to the salvation of the king and was probably also regarded as a safety measure ordered by the gods themselves (cf. 35 r10 ff, 181 r10 ff, etc.).

r5. ^{LÚ}TUR^{MEŠ}*-im-ma* here certainly refers to apprentice scribes, not children in general (thus e.g. *CAD* Ṣ 183*a*); note the subsequent reference to the composition *Inbu Bēl Arḫi*, and cf. the frequent occurrences of *ṭupšarru ṣehru* "junior scribe" in colophons (Hunger, *AOAT* 2 p.173). The particle *-ma* attached to the word, left untranslated in Pt.I, served for emphasis: "As *even* the junior scribes have said . . ."

The month Du'ūzu did not contain an auspicious 16th day and an inauspicious 17th day (Rev.10-12) according to the tradition of the standard hemerologies (see Labat, *RA* 38, 21 f). But in the royal hemerology *Inbu Bēl Arḫi*, virtually every day of the year was marked as auspicious (UD ŠE; e.g., in the tablet for Ulūlu II,

4R pl.32 f, this remark is found 29 times and is missing only in the entry for the 25th day). The point of the passage hence clearly is: while normal practice would not have recommended choosing the 16th as the day for the king's ritual, the existence of *Inbu Bēl Arḫi* made it legitimate for the king to perform the ritual on whatever day he wished – in other words, *Quod licet Iovi, non licet bovi*. Seen in this light, the passage is at the same time an illustration of the enormous prestige of the king vis-à-vis his counselors (who preferred to comply with the royal wishes, even though these occasionally clashed with their scientific principles). Note that the original plan proposed in *LAS* 135 did not call for performing the king's ritual on the 16th.

r6. Against the emendation UD! ŠE suggested in Pt.I, the tablet reads, according to collation by Sollberger (January, 1976), clearly MÍ.ŠE as copied by Harper. Render: "It is marked as auspicious (*ana mitgurti*) in *IBA*".

r10. *id-da-a-ti*: here clearly in a modal meaning ("hence" < "thereafter"); the same usage also in 167 r14.

167

Bibliography:

(I) Waterman, *RCAE* 361 (cf. IV 241); Pfeiffer, *SLA* 272.

(II) Behrens, *ABB* (1906) 51f; Dhorme, *RHR* 113 (1936) 139; von Soden, *ZA* 44 (1938) 182; Böhl, *Opera Minora* (1953) 421; von Soden, *Fs Christian* (1956) 102; Deller, *AOAT* 1 (1969) 60.

Photo:

RCAE IV pl.9 (Obv. only).

Date:

Appr. Simānu 17 = June 12, 669 BC. This date is based on the following evidence: 1) The orthography of the greeting and blessing formula (^{d}AG *u* ^{d}AMAR+UD, *lu-U šul-mu*) strongly points to June, 669 (see commentary to *LAS* 154[300]). 2) The fact that the king is addressed as "Farmer" points to the same general date, see on *LAS* 162. 3) The references to the *bīt rimki* ceremony, burnt-offerings and acts of purification (r5 ff) imply that a lunar eclipse had recently occurred and (in the context of the substitute king ritual of 669 BC) place the letter in the middle of the month Simānu; see on *LAS* 25, 77, 136, 234, 235 and 257; note that in *LAS* 185, which refers to the performance of the *bīt rimki* ceremony in 671 BC, the king is *not* addressed as "Farmer". 4) A final confirmation of the date is provided by the ref. to exorcisms against "loss of flesh" in Obv.12, which makes sense only if taken to pertain to the diarrhoea patient mentioned in *LAS* 152-156 (see relevant comments).

Addressee:

Esarhaddon.

Notes:

12. For *ḫa-liq ti-bi u* (Pt.I) read *ḫa-liq-ti* UZU$^{!}$ "loss of flesh", a disease mentioned in a list of magical stones (*8* NA$_{4}^{\text{MEŠ}}$ *ḫa-liq-te* UZU "8 stones against Loss of Flesh", *BAM* IV 267:71, cf. Eypper, *Or*NS 44 [1975] 193) and in two catalogues of namburbi rituals (*šum-ma ina* É NA *lu* É.GAL LUGAL *ḫa-liq-ti* UZU DIB-*bat-su* "If in a house of a man or (in) a place of a king, Loss of Flesh seizes someone", Caplice, *Or* 34 [1965] 114, 4:7, and 42 [1973] 515:8'; cf. Eypper, loc. cit.). The present passage doubtless refers to same (exorcistic) rituals as the catalogues. Even though the relevant ritual text has not yet been identified, it can hardly be doubted that the term "Loss of flesh" meant "(morbid) loss of weight" (German "Abmagerung"), see Eypper, loc.cit. and cf. above, sub Date.

300 Despite the fact that Urad-Ea is given in Obv.3 as a co-author of the present letter, the true writer of the letter was certainly Adad-šumu-uṣur. Note the inadvertent omission of the plural sign in Obv.2 ("your *servant* Adad-šumu-uṣur"), the 1st person Sg. verbal forms in Rev.6, 7, 11 and 12, and the pronoun *anāku* "I" in Obv.12.

r7. *ma-qa-lu-tú* "burnt-offering": the NA equivalent of Bibl. *'ōlāh*[301], a type of offering favoured in times of distress: cf. *at-ta* UN^{MEŠ} KUR-*ka* [4] *3* UD^{MEŠ} *pa-an* ^{d}IM *di-at pa-ni bi-ki-a* [6] *sa-ri-ra* [7] KUR-*ku-nu* [r1] *ú-ga-ar-ku-nu* [2] *ka-pi-ra* [3] *ma-aq-lu-a-te* [4] *qu-lu-a* "you and your people, perform a public weeping before Adad, pray, cleanse your country and fields, and burnt burnt-offerings!", *AfO* Bh 6, no.5:3 ff; *ina* UGU *ma!-qa-lu-a-te bé-et* LUGAL *i*[*š-pur-an-ni up-ni-ja*] [11] *ap-te-te ina* UGU LUGAL DUMU.MAN ^{Id}GIŠ.N[U$_{11}$-MU-GI.NA] [12] *ú-sa-re-er* "as regards the burnt offerings about which the king wr[ote to me], I have 'opened [my fists]' and prayed for the king, the crown prince and Šamaš-[šumu-ukīn]", *RMA* 89 r10 ff (report on an ill-portening conjunction of Mars and Saturn).

r8. *tak-pir-tú*: referring to the cleansing ceremonies described in the *Ritualtafel* of Bīt Rimki (Zimmern, *BBR* 26 I 16 ff, II 1 ff, and V 34 ff). The phrase *takpirtu šētuqu* occurring here and in *LAS* 188 r2 and 10 corresponds to *takpirtu kuppuru* of the Ritualtafel, just as the phrase *ša tēlissi šētuqu* "to purify" in NA cultic texts replaces older (i.e., MA) *ša tēlilti ullulu*. Note that the execution of the ceremonies required the cooperation of an exorcist and a *kalû* chanter, and see commentary to *LAS* 185.

r14. *da-at an-ni-e* "thereafter": here probably in the modal sense "accordingly" (cf. 166 r10) rather than in the temporal sense best attested for *dāt* (cf. *CAD* D 121f). The whole passage would hence translate: "For 6 days do correspondingly, performing purification ceremonies after this (pattern)."

168

Bibliography:

(I) Waterman, *RCAE* 16.

Date and discussion:

Possibly Simānu = May, 670 BC. The fact that the letter is signed by influential scholars representing four different crafts (exorcist, chanter, scribe, astrologer/priest) indicates that it dealt with an extremely serious or important matter (cf. *LAS* 27-28, 31, and 170), and the occurrence of the term *paṭāru* "to solve, cure" in r.3' suggests that the subject matter was medical (see note to 171:10). The letter could thus date from the period of Esarhaddon's attack of illness in late spring, 670 BC (see on *LAS* 246). This hypothesis is supported by the rare syllabic value NE = ti_5 in Rev.2 (cf. Deller, *AOAT* 1 [1969] 47; add *ni-iq-ṭi*$_5$*-bi*, *ABL* 1238 r10), which also occurs in *LAS* 133, another letter of Adad-šumu-uṣur certainly datable to May, 670; and by the fragmentary word in Obv.10, which can be integrated to read [*ṣ*]*i*-[*ì*]*l-ba-a-ni* as in *LAS* 181:6 and 246 r9.[302] If this restoration is correct, the letter would be approximately synchronous with *LAS* 181 (writer: Marduk-šākin-šumi) and 246 (Urad-Nanâ); notice that neither Marduk-šākin-šumi nor Urad-Nanâ figure in the present writer team. Cf. also the following note and the commentary to *LAS* 61:5ff.

Notes:

r4'f. Possibly to be restored [LUGAL EN-*ni*] *ka-aja-ma-nu-um-ma* [5] [*lu la*] ⌈*ú*⌉*-du-ur* "[the king, our lord, should not] be continuously eclipsed" in accordance with *LAS* 143:19 ff (q.v.).

169

Bibliography:

(I) Waterman, *RCAE* 655.

[301] This equation cannot be grounded in detail here. Note, provisionally, *STT* 44:10f, "13 rams, 2 bulls, 2 male calves for the braziers, the burnt-offerings of the morning and evening."

[302] The syllabic value AN = *ìl* also e.g. in *LAS* 60:7 and 12.

Writer:
Nabû-nādin-šumi. Note the insertion of *a-dan-niš* before *lik-ru-bu* (Obv.7), comparable with 203:5, 205:5, 207:6, 208:6, etc., but not attested in any letters of Adad-šumu-uṣur or Marduk-šākin-šumi. The orthography of the salution and blessing formula agrees in other respects, too, with the conventions of Nabû-nādin-šumi.

Addressee:
Probably Esarhaddon. Note that all other letters in which Adad-šumu-uṣur and Marduk-šākin-šumi appear as joint authors (*LAS* 29, 139 and 163-165) date – insofar as ascertainable – from the two last years of Esarhaddon, and that there is no evidence that Adad-šumu-uṣur retained his position as king's personal exorcist (the office in which he clearly writes here, note the professions of the other two writers and the rank order of the names) after the accession of Assurbanipal: none of the 5 letters of A. addressed to Assurbanipal (*LAS* 119-122, 125) deal with exorcistic matters. The fact that Nabû-nādin-šumi is not mentioned in any extant letters of Adad-šumu-uṣur and Marduk-šākin-šumi dating from Esarhaddon's reign, while he does occur, together with Marduk-šākin-šumi, in a letter of Adad-šumu-uṣur written in late 667 BC (*LAS* 125), is probably coincidental and can hardly be taken as evidence for placing the present letter in Assurbanipal's reign. Note that Marduk-šākin-šumi, too, is never mentioned in Adad-šumu-uṣur's letters written to Esarhaddon, and vice versa, even though they wrote several joint letters to that king.

Notes:

r4'. *né-e-pa-*[*áš*]: this variant of /neppaš/ is also attested in *LAS* 277:6 and *ABL* 655 r3'; cf. *ta-a-din* for /taddin/, Bu 91-5-9,145 r11, *te-e-rab* for /terrab/, *ABL* 368 r8, 858:18, 1164:3, etc.

170

Bibliography:
(I) Waterman, *RCAE* 650 (cf. IV 185).
(II) Behrens, *ABB* (1906) 47[1].

Date:
Probably Ulūlu (= August), 670 BC. See note to Obv.5.

Writers:
Two persons with the name Nabû-mušēṣi are known as contemporaries of Adad-šumu-uṣur and Ištar-šumu- ēreš: N., deputy of the chief scribe (^{Id}PA-*mu-še-ṣi* ^{LÚ}2-*u* GAL.A.BA, *ADD* 857 i 39, time of Esarhaddon), the writer of several astrological reports (see App. 05), and N., scribe of the Aššūr temple (A.BA É ^{d}*Aš+šur*, K.11908 [Bez. *Cat.* 1204] and ^{LÚ}A.BA É.DINGIR, RMA 109 r6, the writer of *ABL* 209. Since Nabû-mušēṣi here *precedes* Ištar-šumu-ereš (the chief scribe), he can hardly be identified with the deputy scribe; the subject matter of the letter also points rather to the temple scribe.

Addressee:
Esarhaddon.

Notes:

5. ^{d}*Šatru*: a name of Ištar of Arbela obviously used only during the goddess' residence in Milqia, a small town near Arbela where the akītu temple of the city was situated; see Thureau-Dangin, *RAcc.* p.112 f, and cf. Streck, *Asb* p.248:6, ^{URU}*mil-qí-a* É.GAL EDIN *mu-šab* ^{d}*iš-tar an-ḫu-us-su ud-diš* [7] É *á-kit-su ar-ṣip* "I restored the town of Milqia, the palace of the steppe, the residence of Ištar, (re)building its akītu temple." Excepting *ABL* 1164, a brief note from Ištar-šumu-ēreš[303] explicitly equating Šatru with Ištar (^{d}*ša-at-ru* ^{d}INNIN, Obv.1f) and referring to the goddess' stay in Milqia and subsequent ceremonial return to Arbela, the name Šatru seems

[303] The note is unsigned but can be safely attributed to Ištar-šumu-ēreš on orthographic and palaeographic grounds (cf. the spellings *be-li* Obv.8 and Rev.3, *le-e-pu-šú* Obv.8, *te-e-rab* Obv.3, *ma-ḫi-ru-ni* Obv.7, and the forms of TA* and *ša*). For the text see below.

to be otherwise attested only in the following two epigraphs of Assurbanipal: *a-na-ku* ^{I}AN.ŠÁR-DU-A [LU]GAL KUR *Aš+šur*^{KI} *qé-reb* ^{URU}*Mil-qí-a* ^{23} SISKUR^{MEŠ} *taš-r[e-eḫ-ti] aq-qi* DÙ-*uš i-sin-ni* ^{d}*Šat-ri* "I, Assurbanipal, king of Assyria, offered sumptuous sacrifices in Milqia and celebrated the festival of Šatru", *AfO* 8 (1932/3) 182:22f; cf. *a-na-ku* ^{I}AN.ŠÁR-DÙ-A LUGAL KUR AN.ŠÁR^{KI} *ul-tu* SISKUR^{MEŠ} ^{d}*Šat-ri aq-qu-u e-pu-šu i-sin-ni* É *a-ki-ti* ^{44} *at-mu-ḫu* ^{KUŠ}*a-šá-a-ti* ^{d}*Iš-tar* ^{45} *ina* ŠÀ ^{I}*Du-na-ni* ^{I}*Sa-am-gu-nu* ^{I}IBILA-*ja u* KUD-*is* SAG.DU ^{I}*Te-um-man* ^{46} LUGAL KUR NIM.MA^{KI} *ša* ^{d}*Iš-tar* GAŠAN *im-nu-u qa-tu-u-a* ^{47} *e-reb* ^{URU}*Arba-ìl e-pu-uš ina* ḪÚL^{MEŠ} "having offered sumptuous sacrifices to Šatru, having performed the festival of *Bīt Akītu*, and having taken hold of the reins of (the chariot of) Ištar, I, Assurbanipal, king of Assyria, triumphantly entered the city of Arbela with Dunānu, Samgūnu, Aplâ and the severed head of Teumman, king of Elam, whom Ištar, my lady, had surrendered to me", ibid. 184:43 ff. These epigraphs certainly closely parallel the beginning of the present letter, and since even the above-mentioned text recording the restoration of Milqia dates from the reign of Assurbanipal, one would *prima facie* be inclined to associate the present letter with the particular event recorded in the epigraphs and to date it accordingly. However, on closer study this proves hardly possible. The episode in the epigraphs must be dated to about 653 on the basis of the reference to Teumman (see Streck, *Asb* p. CCCXV) and Dunānu and the other Gambulaeans (ibid. CCLXXXVII); but Adad-šumu-uṣur, one of the writers of the present letter, already calls himself "an old man" in a letter written in 672 BC (*LAS* 129), and the last reference to him as a living man dates from 665 BC (*ADD* 448). It is extremely unlikely that he would have been alive, let alone remained in the king's service, as late as 653 BC. Consequently, the letter must be dated earlier, and considering the chronological structure of Adad-šumu-uṣur's correspondence, the likeliest date is the latter part of Esarhaddon's reign, specifically Ulūlu 670 BC. See, in detail, commentary to *LAS* 196. The report *ABL* 1164 referred to above, by Ištar-šumu-ēreš, was probably also written at the same time, since Ištar-šumu-ērеš also figures among the senders of the present letter.[304]

171

Bibliography:

(I) Deller, *AOAT* 1 (1969) 58 f.
(II) Hecker, *WO* 6 (1971) 113 f.

Copy:

CT 53 pl.26 no.69.

Date:

Probably July, 672 BC, or later. Note the reference (Obv.20 ff) to an earlier letter concerning the king's personal relation to his sons, which the writer had, according to his own words, sent to the king in Simannu of the same year. This earlier letter could well be *LAS* 129, which was written soon after Assurbanipal's and Šamaš-šumu-ukīn's appointment as crown princes in Ajāru/May , 672. Cf. 129 r19-25 (especially r20-22) with Obv.17-23 (esp. 22-23) of the present letter; the expression "sons, your lords" (Obv.17) certainly refers to Asb and Ššmk as crown princes (see resp. note) and so places the letter firmly between 672 and 669 BC, and of the four possible occasions on which the "previous letter" thus could have been written (Simānu 672, 671, 670 and 669), the first seems by far

304 The text reads in its entirety as follows: *i-ši-a-ri* ^{d}*ša-at-ru* ^{2} ^{d}INNIN TA* ^{URU}*mì-il-qí-a* ^{3} *ta-ḫar-ru-pu pa-an* LUGAL *te-e-rab* ^{4} *i-da-a-ti* LUGAL *e-rab* ^{5} *ú-la-a* LUGAL *e-rab* ^{6} *i-da-a-ti* ^{d}INNIN *te-e-rab* ^{7} *ki-i šá ina pa-an* LUGAL EN-*ja ma-ḫi-ru-ni* ^{8} LUGAL *be-li liš-pur ina pit-ti le-e-pu-šú* r.1 *ú šu-ri* ^{d}INNIN TA* *am-mu-ka* ^{2} LUGAL TA* *an-na-ka* ^{3} *a-ke-e* LUGAL *be-li ina* ŠÀ IGI+2 *ša* ^{d}INNIN ^{4} *i-ma-qut ina muḫ-ḫi šu-u* ^{5} *a-na* LUGAL EN-*ja a-sa-ap-ra* "Tomorrow, (either) Šatru-Ištar will leave Milqia early and enter (the city of Arbela) before the king, whereupon the king will enter, or the king will enter (the city first) and Ištar thereafter. Let the king, my lord, write which way is preferable to the king, my lord. Perhaps Ištar (will set out) from that direction and the king from this direction; how will the king, my lord, present himself in the sight of Ištar? That is why I am writing to the king, my lord." The verb "enter" in ll.3-6 certainly refers to the ceremonial entry of the king and the goddess into the city after the akītu ceremonies, which is mentioned both in the epigraph *AfO* 8 184:43 ff (*e-reb* ^{URU}*Arba-ìl*) and *LAS* 196 (*e-rab* URU *ša* ^{URU}*Arba-ìl*); the text is in no way related to the Ištar ritual *KAR* 146 (= Ebeling, *OrNS* 21 [1952] 142 ff) where *erēbu* means "to enter (a temple or a chamber)".

the likeliest alternative.[305] For other (identified) references to previous letters in the present corpus, see 290:14-r1 (cf. 289:8'-15'), 298 r26'-28' (cf. 299), 292:11'f (cf. 277), 176:5-9 (cf. 163), 125:9-11 (cf. 122), 122:15-17 (cf. 121), 46:6-8 (cf. 71), 198:6-9 (cf. 197), etc.

Writer:

Adad-šumu-uṣur. The content of the letter implies that its author was either an exorcist or a physician; and the very confidential manner in which he puts forth his matter further implies that an influential man was in question, a fact which immediately narrows down the range of possible candidates to Adad-šumu-uṣur, Marduk-šākin-šumi and Urad-Nanâ. The last can be eliminated on the basis of the introductory blessing and orthographic details (*a-dan-niš* Obv.7 and *an-ni-e* Obv.8 as against Urad-Nanâ's *ad-dan-niš* and *an-ni-je-e*), but it is impossible to choose either of the two other alternatives with absolute certainty. Contrary to the position taken by me in Pt.I, the evidence seems, however, to favour Adad-šumu-uṣur. In addition to the arguments to this effect presented by Deller (1969), note the spelling *an-ni-e* (Obv.8; cf. 133 r18', 143:15, 167 r14) not found in letters of Marduk-šākin-šumi (there only *an-ni-i*, 5 attestations); the relative frequency of the personal pronoun *a-na-ku* (Obv.19) in the correspondence of Adad-šumu-uṣur (13 occurrences, all spelled *a-na-ku*, as against 6 in letters of Marduk-šākin-šumi, half of them spelled *ana-ku*, cf. 179 r14 and 199:14f); the opening of the letter with the phrase *ša LUGAL be-lí iš-pur-an-ni ma-a* (Obv.6f), found in 5 letters of Adad-šumur-uṣur (122:15f, 145:5f, 146:6ff, 147:5f and 352:6f) but in none of Marduk-šākin-šumi; the writing of the DN *Nabû* with the logogram ^{d}AG (Rev.3), common in the correspondence of Adad-šumu-uṣur (30 examples) but only 4 times attested in letters of M. (177:4, 186:5, 191:3, 195:4), as against 19 spellings with ^{d}PA; and the form *nu-uk* (Obv.22) for Marduk-šākin-šumi's *mu-uk* (176:8, 177 r6, 181 r8). The handwriting resembles more closely Adad-šumu-uṣur's than Marduk-šākin-šumi's; and finally, Obv.19-23 could plausibly be taken as a reference to *LAS* 129 r19-22 (cf. above). Against all this, the only piece of evidence which can be quoted in favour of the authorship of Marduk-šākin-šumi is the question in r1-2, which resembles 181r6-7, and the phrase *ša šarru bēlī iqbûni* in Obv.16, which occurs 11 times in his letters (139:7, 166:7, 173:6.r3, 180:5, 181:6.r4, 187:5.8, 190:17 and 195:17) but hardly anywhere else in the whole corpus. However, it does occur in two letters of Adad-šumu-uṣur (see 125 r8 and 144 r6) and so can also be evaluated as evidence pointing to the authorship of the latter.[306]

Addressee:

Esarhaddon.

Notes:

7-13. The rendering of this passage must be slightly modified according to the lines set by Deller (1969). The fact that the particle *mā* is not repeated after Obv.7 shows that the quotation from the king's speech ends with the word *né-pu-uš* in line 10; all that follows belongs to the answer of Adad-šumu-uṣur. Accordingly, insert quotation marks after "... this little one of mine?", delete the words in parenthesis ("I keep saying ..."), and render the sequel: "Should it have been cureable, you (= the king) would have given away half your kingdom and had it cured! (But) what can we do? O king, my lord, it is ....."

In any case, the meaning of the passage is clear. A child of the king had died recently, presumably of an incurable disease, and the father blamed himself and his doctors for insufficient effort to save the baby. The identity of the child remains unknown; there is no reason to connect the present passage with *LAS* 219 r3 ff, which refers to a later incident.

305 In Simannu 671, Esarhaddon was in the middle of his campaign to Egypt (see on *LAS* 59) and thus certainly had more urgent things to do than worry about than the careers of his sons; in Simannu, 670, he had just recovered, or was recovering, from a serious illness (see on *LAS* 151 and 246), had survived an attempted coup d'état (*LAS* 133 and 247), and had to worry about the health of his mother (see on *LAS* 151) but apparently had no trouble with his sons; and in Simannu, 669, the king and his ecorcists were preoccupied with the performance of the substitute king ritual and the illness of a royal suckling (cf. on *LAS* 154), while the two crown princes lived separately in their princedoms and therefore hardly could run into a situation fitting the tenor of the present letter.

306 Within the present corpus, the phrase is otherwise attested only in 41 r3 and 46 r7 (Balasî), 223:7.r4 (Urad-Gula), and 284:7 (Mār-Ištar).

10. For *paṭāru* "to solve" in the technical sense "to cure" see Ritter, *AS* 16 (1965) 307; cf. also *LAS* 182:8 and 246 r3. The pronoun *ši-i* at the end of the line, as well as the suffix *-ši* in line 12, must accordingly refer to a disease, the name of which remains unknown but surely was of the feminine gender (cf. *mišittu* "paralysis", *diliptu* "sleeplessness", *sili'tu* "infection" etc., all construed with the verb *paṭāru* in Labat, *TDP*).

11. *mi-šil ma-ti-i-ka lu ta-din* is, to the present writer's knowledge, the earliest occurrence of the familiar literary topos "(if you do this and that,) I shall give you (the princess and) half of my kingdom". *Ilias* 6:192f (*αὐτοῦ μιν κατέρυκε, δίδου δ' ὅ γε θυγατέρα ἥν, δῶκε δέ οἱ τιμῆς βασιληΐδος ἥμισυ πάσης*) is approximately contemporary, but less accurately datable. Later on the topos is found e.g. in Herodotus IX 34, Esther 5:3.6 ("Whatever you ask of me, up to half my kingdom, shall be given to you"), Mark 6:23 ("Whatever you ask I will give you, up to half my kingdom"), etc.

14 f. *alāku* "to go" in the sense of "to be possible/suitable" also occurs in *ABL* 312:10 ff (ÍD *da-a'-na* [11] *la a-na* ^{KUŠ}*maš-ki-ri ka-ra-ri* [12] *i-la-ka* "the river is fierce, it cannot be used for constructing (a bridge of) pontoons").*

17. *DUMU*$^{\textit{ME}}$ *EN*$^{\textit{ME}}$*-ka*: cf. [DUMU^{M}]^{EŠ} EN^{MEŠ}*-ja*, *LAS* 184:9; DUMU^{MEŠ} EN*-ja-a-ni* 187 r5; DUMU^{MEŠ} EN*-ja*, *ABL* 545:11; DUMU^{MEŠ} EN^{M}[^{EŠ}], *CT* 53 477 r5'; and LUGAL^{MEŠ}*-ni* DUMU^{MEŠ}*-ka*, *LAS* 129 r15, all refs. to Asb and Ššk. The curious pronominal suffix ("*your* lords", for "my lords") is possibly simply a scribal error.[307]

18. *tu-da-man-ni*: perhaps rather "makes me weep" (Deller 1969); for the rendering in Pt.I cf. *CAD* D 80*b*.

23. *qablē rakāsu* means originally "to gird up one's loins (for battle)", but then more generally "to get ready (for a difficult or dangerous action)", "to prepare (oneself)"; see Oppenheim, *Or*NS 14 (1945) 241 and Borger, *Or*NS 27 (1958) 148, and note, as a particularly clear example of the transferred meaning, *ABL* 893 r9 ff, *dul-lu šá* LUGAL [10] *ki-i lìb-bi šá* LUGAL *e-pu-uš* MÚRUB *šá dul-li* [11] *šá* LUGAL *be-lí-ja rak-sa.* Note also the opposite idiom "to ungird one's loins" = "to relax" (Oppenheim, *l.c.*; also in Greek, cf. "Xerxes *removed his girdle* there for the first time since he had fled from Athens, for it was only there that he could *feel safe* again", Herodotus VIII 120).

r1. *ba-zu-ḫ[a]-nu-u-a*: see Deller 1969, 59. The tablet seems actually to read *ba-zu-⌈za/šá⌉-nu-u-a.*

172

Bibliography:
(I) Waterman, *RCAE* 24 (cf. III 373).
(II) Behrens, *ABB* (1906) 25 and 90[1]; Dhorme, *RHR* 113 (1936) 144f; Labat, *Royauté* (1939) 212 and 293; Oppenheim, *JAOS* 61 (1941) 268; Ritter, *AS* 16 (1965) 319f; Deller, *OLZ* 134 (1965) 248.

Copy:
Cf. Lehmann, *Ššmk* (1892) pl.44.

Date:
672-669 BC, probably 672-671 in view of the joint ref. to the crown prince (= Asb) *and* Šamaš-šumu-ukīn (cf. commentary to *LAS* 140). *

Addressee:
Esarhaddon.

[307] Taking the passage to imply that the two princes Asb and Ššk were really considered "lords" of their father seems somewhat far-fetched.

Discussion:

Obv.7 - Rev.12 contain a summary of the ritual acts pertaining to the bilingual incantation *CT* 16, 27-29 = Thompson, *Devils* I p.128 ff. The instructions were possibly taken from a "ritual tablet" of the series *Utukkī lemnūti*;[308] this hypothetical tablet has not been preserved (or identified to date), but the corresponding portion of the incantation is worth quoting here in full for comparison with the present letter. Omitting the Sumerian, it reads:

53 *a-šip Eri-du*$_{10}$ *ša ši-pat-su nak-lat a-na-ku*
"I am an exorcist of Eridu whose incantation is elaborate."

55 *a-lu-ú lem-nu a-na na-sa-ḫi-ka i-rat-ka né-'i-i*
"Evil demon, to drive you out, to turn back your breast –

57 *a-šib na-me-e ana na-me-ka at-lak*
"inhabitant of wasteland, go back to your wasteland –,

59 EN GAL-*ú* ^{d}*É-a ú-ma-'e-er-an-*[*ni*]
"the great lord Ea has sent me,

61 TU$_6$.DUG$_4$.GA-*šú ana pi-ja ú-ṭib*
"has transferred his incantation into my mouth,

63 NÍG.NA *si-bit-ti-šú-nu šá par-ṣi el-lu-ti ana qa-ti-ja ú-ma-al-la*
"has put in my hands the seven censers of the holy cults;

65 *a-ri-ba iṣ-ṣu-ra na-gi!-ir* DINGIR^{MEŠ} *ina im-ni-ja at-mu-uḫ*
"in my right hand I hold the bird raven, the herald of the gods,

67 ŠÚR.DÙ^{MUŠEN} *iṣ-ṣu-ra mu-tal-la ina pa-ni-ka lem-nu-ti ina šú-me-li-ja ir-di-šú*
"with my left hand I have sent out the falcon, the noble bird, against your maliciousness;

69 *na-aḫ-lap-ta sa-an-ta šá pu-luḫ-ti aḫ-ḫa-lap-ka*
"I am covered with a frightful red cloak against you,

71 *ṣu-ba-ta sa-a-ma ṣu-bat nam-ri-ir-ri zu-mur* KÙ *ú-lab-biš-ka*
"I have put on against you a red garment, the garment of terrific splendour;

73 *ḫu-la-a ina ḫi-it-ti ša ba-a-bi a-lul-*[*la*]
"I have hung a mouse in the architrave of the door,

75 *pi-ri-i' bal-ti et-ti ina sik-ka-tì a-lul-l*[*a*]
"I have hung a shoot of the lone thornbush on a peg;

77 *ina qi-na-zi ki-ma i-me-ri mun-nar-bi zu-mur-ka ú-ṣar-ri-*[*ip*]
"with a whip I made your body burn like (that of) a straying donkey,

79 *ú-tuk-ku lem-nu na-an-si-iḫ a-lu-ú lem-nu te-bi*
"get out, evil devil! Depart, evil demon!"[309]

The statement found here that the incantation was used for exorcising epileptic patients (Obv.9) is interesting; the incantation itself only refers to the *alû* demon (passim), which accordingly seems to have been regarded one of the principal "causes" of epilepsy. Unfortunately the identity of the patient to be exorcised remains unclear.

Notes:

15. The logogram ^{TÚG}DÙL (sic) does not seem to be otherwise known (cf. Ḫḫ XIX and *ŠL* II/2 no. 329); the translation "cloak" in Pt.I is based on the corresponding passage in *Utukkī Lemnūti*, which has t ú g - g ú - è = *na-aḫ-lap-ta* for ^{TÚG}DÙL (ll. 68-69).

[308] The existence of a ritual tablet is indicated e.g. by K.4988+ (*CT* 17 49), an excerpt from the 10th tablet of the series with ritual instructions.

[309] The balance of the incantation (ll.80-91) has no direct connection with the present letter. For ll.92-101 see note r.9.

Note the reflexive meaning of *iš-šak-kan* (cf. *GAG* § 90f); similarly *il-la-biš* Obv.14 and *lip-pi-ši-iš* 246 r21 and 255 r4.

17. The emendation GARZA! suggested in Pt.I on the basis of *CT* 16 28:65 (cf. above) is not feasible (collation Sollberger 1976-1-19); read with Harper 7 KÁ^MEŠ "7 gates", perhaps referring to the seven gates of the Nether World at which Ištar was stripped of her divine powers (*parṣu*).

r4. This is the incipit of the incantation quoted above.

r5f. ^LÚ^*MAŠ.MAŠ 2-i*: perhaps better "assistant exorcist" than "another exorcist" (Pt.I); notice, however, that *šaniu* here certainly means "(an)*other*", not "second (in rank), deputy" (*AHw.* 1165*a* s.v. *šanû* I), since the latter meaning is only attested in substantive usage (e.g. ^LÚ*^*2-u ša* ^LÚ*^GAL-A.ZU, *ADD* 470 r19; ^LÚ^*2-u-šu*, *LAS* 311 r12). The form *2-i* (= *šanî*, Nom.!) is due not to "an indiscriminate use of the case-morphemes in Neo-Assyrian" (Moscati, *Comparative Grammar* p.95) but to vowel contraction (*i+u* > *î*); cf. note to 152 r1, and note also ^UDU^⌈*da-ri-i*⌉, *LAS* 309:11; *da-ri-i*, *ABL* 634:6 and *LAS* 309:16; *am-mì-i*, *ABL* 1385:14; *pa-ni-i*, *LAS* 296 r4', and *ur-ki-i* 286 r8', all Nom. Sg. forms standing for morphemic *-iu*.

r9. Referring to the latter part of the incantation *CT* 16, 27ff, beginning with line 92.

r13 ff. Referring to the incident reported in *LAS* 74?

r17. *Nabû-gāmil*: obviously an exorcist and therefore identical with the writer of *LAS* 227.

r20. The reading of the personal name in this line is not entirely certain, though *Urad-Ea* is absolutely the most likely alternative taking into consideration the co-operation of exorcists and appeasers in the performance of apotropaic rituals (cf. *LAS* 167, 185 and 335, and notes to *LAS* 137 and 268); the reading ^d*1* = Ea is assured for exorcistic texts by *BBR* 26 iii 44, cf. also Röllig, *RlA* 3 p.500. On the other hand, the only further attestation of ^d*1* in NA letters has certainly to be read Nabû, cf. ^d*1 u* ^dŠÚ *a-na* LUGAL EN-*já* ⁶ *lik-ru-bu* "may Nabû and Marduk bless the king, my lord", *CT* 53 151:5f. This reading is not entirely unthinkable in the present context either, if one takes it as an oblique reference to the following passage in a letter of Urad-Nabû to the King: *ú-ma-a* TA* ŠU² LUGAL EN-*ja lu-u la e-li* ¹¹ *1-en* ^LÚ^MAŠ.MAŠ *1-en* ^LÚ^A.ZU ¹² *ina* IGI-*ja lip-qid* T[A* *a-ḫa*]-*miš* ¹³ *dul-li le-pu-šu* "now, may I not get lost to the king, my lord! May he place an exorcist (and) a physician at my disposal, may they perform the ritual for me to[geth]er!" (*ABL* 1133 r10 ff).

173

Bibliography:
(I) Waterman, *RCAE* 18.
(II) Behrens, *ABB* (1906) 93f: Dhorme, *RHR* 113 (1936) 143f, 147f; Labat, *Royauté* (1939) 212.

Date:
Kislīmu 22, eponymy of Šulmu-Bēl-lašme = December 24, 670 BC. For the month and day cf. Obv.7 and Rev.10ff, and see note on Obv.13; the grounds for placing the letter in 670 BC are discussed in detail below.

Addressee:
Esarhaddon.

Discussion:

The subject matter of this letter is clear without more ado: performance of anti-witchcraft (*ušburruda*) rituals for the king, the crown prince and the royal family. But what was the reason making the performance of these rituals desirable? This question, bearing directly on the dating of the letter, is more difficult to answer and will therefore be studied at length below.

As pointed out in note to 159 r6', anti-witchcraft magic was practicied in Mesopotamia for three basic purposes: prophylactic, apotropaic and therapeutic. Rituals of the first and last category cannot be in question here. Prophylactic ušburrudas were performed on fixed calendar dates, whereas the dates of the rituals referred to here were entirely open to discussion; and as it is unthinkable that the whole royal family would have simultaneously displayed symptoms suggestive of illness caused by witchcraft, the possibility that medical ušburrudas are in question can be safely ruled out. It can thus be concluded that the rituals mentioned here were performed for *apotropaic* purposes and that they had been occasioned by an event making it seem likely that the king and his family had been subjected to the pernicious activity of sorcerers.

Various considerations suggest that the event concerned was an eclipse of the moon. First and foremost, lunar eclipses were in antiquity universally regarded as moments suitable for the practice of witchcraft, and for this reason the apotropaic ritual *bīt rimki*, performed for the protection of the king and his household from the "evil" of lunar eclipses, also contained a long cycle of ušburruda rituals and incantations (see Laessøe, *Bît rimki* p.94). But not enough with that; in addition to the standard anti-witchcraft rituals and incantations included in *every* performance of the *bīt rimki* ritual, eclipses occurring in months associated with death and netherworld (Ābu/August, the month of killing heat and dying vegetation, and Kislīmu/December, the month of the longest nights, the sun sojourning in the netherworld)[310] appear to have required intensified anti-witchcraft activity to match the potential intensification of black magic at the time concerned. This is implied by a series of tablets relating to the performance of two separate *bīt rimki* rituals for Šamaš-šumu-ukīn (*PBS* 1/1 nos. 13-18; *PBS* 1/2 nos. 108, 110, 119-121, 126, 129, 133; *PBS* 10/2 no.18; *RA* 16 p.67; *SFS* nos.2 and 6-8) respectively in Kislīmu (*PBS* 1/2 108) and Ṭebētu (*PBS* 1/2 120, cf. *SFS* 6), which include ušburrudas not found in the standard anti-witchcraft section of *Bīt rimki*; see *PBS* 1/1 13, 16; 1/2 120-121, 129, 133; 10/2 18; and cf. Laessøe, loc. cit. Two features in these sets of tablets are worth special attention: in so far as ascertainable, virtually every single incantation was written on a separate tablet and virtually every tablet was furnished with the name of Šamaš-šumu-ukīn[311], in some cases also with the date of the eclipse in question.[312] This means that for each performance of the ritual, a new copy of the canonical *Bīt rimki* series, plus the additional ušburruda tablets, had to be prepared, and considering the great number of individual prayers and incantations included in *bīt rimki* alone, the number of tablets to be copied for the ritual must have been great indeed. Thus it can be seen that every significant detail in the present letter (the *date* [a week after a potential lunar eclipse in Kislīmu; cf. *PBS* 1/2 120, dated Ṭebētu *24*, with the date Kislīmu 24 mentioned in Obv.7], the performance of ušburrudas for the king *and his household*, and the copying of *numerous* tablets for the ritual) supports the hypothesis that the ceremonies were occasioned by a lunar eclipse; by contrast, finding another rational explanation for the ceremonies does not seem possible to the present writer at least.

The eclipse in question would accordingly have occurred in Kislīmu. The reference to the crown prince (Obv.17, Rev.12) shows that the letter was written in Esarhaddon's reign (see respective note); in this reign, only one eclipse occurred in the month Kislīmu, viz. that of December 17, 670 BC (see App.F1). This eclipse did not require the enthronement of a substitute king, since only the lunar quadrant identified with Amurru was eclipsed (cf. App.F2), but it doutbless made scholars (and consequently, the king) feel insecure since the point at which the shadow of the earth last touched the lunar disc was identified with Akkad (whose king Esarhaddon was) and since the planets Jupiter and Venus were not visible during the eclipse (see App.F3 and F4). Moreover, as noted above, the month was opportune for the activity of witches. This eclipse accordingly qualifies well as a potential cause of the rituals referred to in the letter.

That the letter indeed was written in Kislīmu/December, 670 BC, is confirmed by the following considerations. The reference to the crown prince, as pointed out above, places the letter with certainty in Esarhaddon's reign, more exactly between Ajāru/May, 672 (the date of Assurbanipal's introduction into the Succession Palace), and Araḫsamna/November, 669 (date of Esarhaddon's death). Thus, the letter can theoretically date either from

[310] For Ābu cf. Abusch, *JNES* 33 (1974) 258 ff; for Kislīmu, cf. *KAV* 218 iii 6ff: "Kislīmu, the month in which the heroic Nergal rises from the netherworld, . . .", and similar passages.

[311] *PBS* 1/1 14 contains 3 short dingiršadibba incantations; the other tablets one incantation each. The name of Šamaš-šumu-ukīn is extant in *PBS* 1/1 14, 18; 1/2 108, 110, 119, 120; *PBS* 10/2 18; *RA* 16 67; *SFS* 2 and 6; it is certainly missing in *PBS* 1/1 13, 14, 17, and *PBS* 1/2 121 and 133, but may have been written in the balance of the tablets.

[312] *PBS* 1/2 108 and *SFS* 6.

Kislīmu 672, 671, or 670. In actual fact, however, only the last alternative stands closer examination. Firstly, while clearly implying that the rituals concerned the entire royal family, the writer repeatedly speaks of *one* crown prince only, whereas in *LAS* 185 pertaining to the performance of *bīt rimki* rituals and incantations in Kanūnu/ December, 671, he explicitly refers to *two* crown princes ("the crown prince and the crown prince of Babylon", 185 r12). That this is no mere accident is shown by the fact that the two princes are also mentioned in *LAS* 232, which is contemporaneous with *LAS* 185; but in *LAS* 186-187, written by Marduk-šākin-šumi in mid-670, he likewise speaks of *one* crown prince only (187 r4, "*the* crown prince"; 186:14, "Assurbanipal") whom he explicitly contrasts with "(all) his brothers" (ibid.). This is most naturally explained by assuming that in December, 671, both Assurbanipal and Šamaš-šumu-ukīn were resident in Assyria and therefore had both to be taken into consideration in the performance of the *bīt rimki* ritual, whereas from March 670 on, after Šamaš-šumu-ukīn's change of residence to Babylonia (see on 280:17), Assurbanipal was the only crown prince over whose health the Assyrian court exorcists had to be concerned. Secondly, Rev.4-10 of the present letter shows that the king was not resident in Nineveh while the letter was written and probably intended to stay away (in Calah?) till at least Kanūnu 2. However, in *LAS* 185 (written on Kanūnu 13, 671), he clearly is in Nineveh (cf. 185 r9 ff). While this latter argument is less binding than the former, it does support the conclusion that the present letter cannot have been written in late 671 and still less in the preceding year.

The possibility to determine the date of the letter exactly is of considerable importance in that five other letters of Marduk-šākin-šumi (*LAS* 163-164, 174 and 176-177) certainly, and one (*LAS* 175) probably, pertain to the same context situation as the present letter. In isolation, these letters would remain undated, but when associated with the present letter, many of them can be dated exactly. With one exception (*LAS* 164, which appears to have been written slightly before the treatment of the king scheduled in the present letter for the 2nd of Kanūnu), all these letters concern ušburruda rituals performed for the king's family and, judging from their contents and physical and orthographical affinities, were written within a very short period of time; *LAS* 163 and 176 date from the 5th of Kanūnu (cf. the date Kanūnu 6 suggested in the present letter, Rev.12 f), *LAS* 177 probably from the 7th of Kanūnu (cf. 176 r5), and *LAS* 174 very plausibly from the beginning of Kanūnu (see under this letter). *LAS* 175 should immediately precede 163 and 176. The chronological order of the letters would thus be as follows:

1)	*LAS* 173	Kislīmu 22 = December 24, 670
2)	*LAS* 164	appr. Kislīmu 29 = December 31, 670
3)	*LAS* 174	appr. Kanūnu 3 = January 3, 669
4)	*LAS* 175	Kanūnu 5 (?) = January 5, 669(?)
5)	*LAS* 163	Kanūnu 5 = January 5, 669
6)	*LAS* 176	Kanūnu 5 = January 5, 669
7)	*LAS* 177	Kanūnu 7 = January 7, 669

Reasons making this correspondence necessary were 1) the necessity to carry out the relevant ceremonies in two rounds because of the great number of the people involved (*LAS* 174), 2) the difficulties encountered in getting the second group of people to the scene of the ceremonies (*LAS* 163), 3) the mistake committed in *LAS* 163 in setting a date for the balance of the ceremonies, corrected in *LAS* 176, and 4) the re-opening of the ceremonies after a break of two days or more (*LAS* 177); see in more detail commentary to *LAS* 163. As noted above, the king was during the correspondence possibly absent from Nineveh.

Notes:

7. *a-na UD 24.KÁM*: the preposition *a-na* can here (and in r10) stand for /ina/ (cf. 39 r3), in which case one should translate "perform (it) *on* the 24th day". The translation given in Pt.I is, however, also possible, cf. 223:8, *a-na* u_4*-me né-pa-áš*, which, on the basis of the context, certainly means "we shall perform it *to* the day." In any case, the likeliest meaning of the present passage is: "Make it *ready* for the 24th day"; cf. the continuation.

8. Cf. *ABL* 467 r20 ff, *la-áš-šu* [21] *la nu-šá-an-ṣa ma-a* UD *10*.KÁM *ša* [ITU]NE [22] *la ni-il-la-ka* "we cannot make it, we shall not (be able to) come on the 10th of Ābu."

9f. Cf. Discussion. The tablets mentioned here probably included those of the series *Bīt rimki* as well as unserialized ušburrudas (possibly also tablets of *Maqlû*), and had to be recopied because the king's name (and the date of the eclipse) had to appear in the relevant incantations and prayers. Cf. note on 185:23 ff.

11. The writer here refers to images of sorcerers and sorceresses (and other adversaries) whose destruction formed an essential part of the rituals in question. They were made of various materials and were needed in great quantities. Thus an ušburruda ritual performed for Šamaš-šumu-ukīn against "the sorceress who made many charms" (*PBS* 10/2 18; most recent edition by W.G. Lambert, *AfO* 18 [1957/8] 288 ff) required the preparation of altogether 48 figurines made of 12 different materials, (clay, clay mixed with sulphur, tallow, residue of linseed, 3 different kinds of dough, tamarisk, cedar, bitumen and wax), all of which had to be burnt or otherwise destroyed during the recitation of the pertinent incantation; this ritual may well have been performed also in the present instance. The ušburruda tablet of *Maqlû* (Tablet II) refers to images made of tallow (II 18), bronze and sulphur (II 75), bronze (II 103), dough (II 125), clay (II 134), bitumen (II 148), residue of linseed (II 159), bitumen mixed with gypsum (II 181), bitumen mixed with tallow (II 205), tamarisk (II 229) and cedar (ibid.), each relating to a separate incantation. A set of similar images, though less variegated, was also needed in the *Bīt rimki* ritual (see Laessøe, op.cit., p. 28 ff). Since the situation described in the present letter presupposed that separate sets of the images be prepared not only for the king but also for the crown prince and the royal family, it is understandable that several days were needed for the making of the images alone, as pointed out in Obv.12f.

13. *ni-it-ti-ši*: not to be taken as a "futurum exactum" (cf. on 34:8) but simply as a normal perfect; cancel the translation of the passage in Pt.I and render instead: "Even the preparation of the images which the king saw (yesterday) took us 5-6 days to get ready with". This remark was certainly meant to make it clear that the copying of the tablets needed for the ritual would also take several days and that it would thus be impossible to start with the ceremonies themselves before the dates mentioned in Rev.10 ff. In addition, the passage also indicates on which day the letter was probably written. Supposing that the making of the figurines begun on the day of the eclipse, i.e. on Kislīmu 15(cf.App.F),the king would have been able to see them ready six days later, i.e. on Kislīmu 21; and as it is very likely that it was in this connection that the king gave the order to perform the ritual on the 24th (Obv.7), it follows from Obv.6 ("the king said *yesterday*") that the letter very probably was written on the 22nd of Kislīmu.

15. "*Kanūnu is a good month for performing ušburruda rituals*": the source on which this statement is based is unknown. The "Exorcist's Almanac" (*STT* 300), which gives auspicious dates for magical and exorcistic activities throughout the year, recommends Šabāṭu 27 and Addāru 26/27 for the performance of ušburrudas (Rev. 13-16). Cf. *LAS* 218:13 ff: "In Kanūnu, we performed . . . numerous ušburrudas." These ušburrudas were probably occasioned by the lunar eclipse of Kanūnu/December, 671 BC (see commentary on *LAS* 218).

17. *DUMU.MAN*: here certainly "*the* son of the king" = the crown prince; note the careful differentiation between this prince and the royal family (which must have included the rest of the king's numerous sons [see on 129:25f]) and the fact that the ritual in question was separately performed for him, as for the king. The interpretation DUMU.MAN/LUGAL = "*the* prince"' = "crown prince" also holds for all other letters of the present corpus. The official title of the Assyrian crown prince (*mār šarri rabiu*/*bēt rēdûti*) occurs only in two letters *addressed* to the crown prince (*LAS* 130-131); in all other letters, plain DUMU.MAN/LUGAL, without any further qualification, always refers to Assurbanipal (18 r14', 34 r6, 46:6f, 47:7ff, 58:13, 69:6ff, 71 r9, 94:1, 132 r4, 140 r1, 144:15, 146:8, 148:5, 154:10, 172:5, 174 r5, 185 r12, 187 r4, 228 r1, 238 r7', 247 r13, 249:7', 250:14, 252:8, 253:8, 264 r5, 318:4; note especially *pa-lu-u ša* LUGAL DUMU.LUGAL, 247 r13; DUMU.MAN contrasted with Aššur-mukīn-palū'a, 46, 69+71 and 250; with Šamaš-šumu-ukīn, 140, 172 and 249, cf. [^{I}*Aš+šur*]-DÙ-IBILA *ù* $^{I.d}$GIŠ.NU-MU-GI.NA, 224:5; with "his brothers", 58 and 187, cf. *ša* ^{I}*Aš+šur*-DÙ-IBILA *ša* ŠEŠ^{MEŠ}-*šú*, 186:14; Mercury star of the DUMU.LUGAL, 70 r8 and 71 r7) or, rarely, to Šamaš-šumu-ukīn (*LAS* 29, 45 and 70; identified as DUMU.MAN/LUGAL KÁ.DINGIR^{KI} in 185 r12, 281:6f and 295 A 8'), *never* to other sons of the king who, when referred to individually, are always identified by name (17:9, 46 r6, 52:10, 69 r2', 72 r8, 140 r2, 142:7, 145:7.9, 150:7 ff, 154:6, 157 r5, 218:6.8, 219:6.r3, 237 A 4', 240:8, 250:8.r11, 251:7, 258 r12.19, 280:11). Correspondingly, the plural DUMU^{MEŠ} LUGAL, when used without further qualifications such as *gabbu* "all" 187 r5, 250:14f), always refers to the two crown princes A. and Š. (7 r6'f, 126 r7, 171:17, 232:6f [cf. 185 r12], 276:18 and 343:7). The occurrences of DUMU.MAN/LUGAL in the present corpus can consequently be valued

as evidence for dating the respective letters between 672 and 669 BC; it must be stressed, however, that the equation DUMU.LUGAL = "crown prince" does not hold for NA non-epistolary texts where *mār šarri* may denote any son of the king.

r1f. *šu-me-ra-ni ša uš₁₂-búr-ru-da-a-ni*: very probably referring to bilingual (Sumero-Akkadian) ušburrudas such as *PBS* 1/2 122, *AJSL* 35 141f, *AMT* 92,1 ii 1'ff, etc.; the present writer has not been able to find a single ušburruda written exclusively in Sumerian. The possibility does not seem excluded that the term also covered bilingual incantations to Šamaš usually termed *ki-ᵈutu-kam*, which were recited in the seven "houses" of *Bīt rimki* in connection with purification rituals involving images of witches and enemies (cf., e.g., *PBS* 1/2 no.126 || *4R* 20 and 28, cf. Laessøe, *Bīt rimki* p.67) and were followed by Akkadian incantations likewise addressed to Šamaš. The latter could then perhaps be identified with the *meḫru* (refrain?) incantations mentioned in Rev.8 and 164 r1.

r5. *Nadīn-aḫḫē*: probably identical with a homonymous student working on the diagnostic series *Bīt Marṣi* in *ABL* 447 (time of Esarhaddon). An astrologer named N. occurs in *ADD* 851 i 2 (ca. 648 BC)in a list of scholars employed at court.

r8. *ÉŠ.GÀR mé-eḫ-ri*: see note on 164 r1.

r16. The expression *ina pān + infinitive + šakin* also occurs in *LAS* 286 r9'f; the contexts point to an idiomatic meaning like "to be inclined to do something". Cf. *a-na ṭu-bi šá-kin*, 185 r27.

174

Bibliography:

(I) Waterman, *RCAE* 17.

Date:

Ca. Kanūnu 3, eponymy of Šulmu-Bēl-lašme = January 3, 669 BC. See commentary on *LAS* 173; the date Kanūnu 3 is made likely by Rev.4 ff, which suggests that the ritual of the crown prince (scheduled in *LAS* 173 for the 4th of Kanūnu) had not yet been performed (the exorcists offered as replacements for the diseased exorcist of the crown prince were conceivably supposed to take care of the matter), and by the fact that the king's ritual (scheduled for Kanūnu 2) is not mentioned at all, which suggests that it had already been performed. In any case, the letter predates *LAS* 175, 163, 176 and 177, since the division of the king's family into two groups, there already carried into effect, is only proposed here (Obv.9 ff).

Addressee:

Esarhaddon.

Discussion:

See under *LAS* 163 and 173.

Notes:

8f. "*There is little room*": cf. *kaq-qu-ru ma-'a-ad* "there is much room", 318:11; *a-na ma-dak-ti* ⁸ *ka-qu-ru ma-a'-da* "there is much room for the camp", *ABL* 100 r7; *ka-qu-ru i-ba-ši* "there is room", *ABL* 433 r5; *áš-ru . . . i-mi-ṣa-an-ni-ma* "I had too little room", Borger *Ash* p.59:47. The verb *sadāru* "to arrange" naturally here implies directing the people to be exorcised to their proper places on the scene of the ritual (the roof of the palace?) and guiding them through their ritual acts, which presumably included recitation of antiwitchcraft incantations and a purificatory stripping ceremony (cf. 175:2', *PBS* 10/2 r40', *AfO* 18 288ff, etc.).

r2. ᴵᵈ[*PA-g*]*a*-[*mil*]: if correctly restored, certainly identical with the writer of *LAS* 227; also mentioned in 172 r17 and 238:11'.

r4. ^{I}*Re-mu-tú*: also known as an exorcist employed at the court of Assurbanipal ca. 648 BC (^{I}*Rém-u-tú* ... MAŠ.MAŠ, *ADD* 851 i 15). The fact that the man appears as a servant of *Assurbanipal* already in the present letter accounts for his long court career.

r6. ^{Id}*PA-SU-PAP*: also known from *LAS* 264 (r6) where found as an associate of a physician. The name has to be read *Nabû-rība-aḫu* (not Nabû-murīb-aḫi as suggested in Pt.I) on the basis of the spelling ^{Id}AG-*ri-ba*-ŠEŠ in K 9650 (unp., quoted *APN* p.157).

r7. ^{I}*Šu-ma-a son of Nabû-zēru-lišer*: see note on 211 r13.

r8. *Urad-Gula*: son of Adad-šumu-uṣur and the author of *LAS* 223-225 and 127(+)339. The exorcist Nabû-lē'ûtu (r9) recurs in 223 r6'.

r12. ⸢^{LÚ}⸣*ziq-na-nu*: taken as a spelling for /ša-ziqnāni/, Pl. of *ša-ziqni* "bearded one" = uncastrated courtier.[313] Note that the plural of *ša-rēši* "eunuch" (see under 14 r7) is likewise formed with the suffix *-āni* (cf. ^{LÚ}SAG^{MEŠ}*-ni*, *ABL* 322:4) and that the "prefix" *ša-* is frequently omitted in names of professions or concealed behind the determinative LÚ (^{LÚ}SAG = *ša-rēši*, ^{LÚ}EN.NUN = *ša-maṣṣarti*, ^{LÚ}BAD.ḪAL = *ša-pētḫalli*, etc.; note especially the frequent spelling ^{LÚ}*qur-bu-ti* for *ša-qurbūti* and ^{LÚ}*še-e-pi* [*ABL* 1217 r6'] for *ša-šēpi*). The unusual form of the plural suffix (*-ānu* for normal *-āni*) can be compared with *šu-ma-nu* (Pl. of *šumu* "name"), *ADD* 812: 15; note also the reverse case (*-āni* for expected *-ānu*) exemplified by *ḫa-ri-pa-a-ni*, 139:10, and *e-ri-ib-a-ni*, 10+ r6'.

175

Bibliography:
Previously unpublished.

Copy:
CT 53 pl.19 no.48.

Writer:
Certainly Marduk-šākin-šumi. The subject matter is paralleled (within the present corpus) only by *LAS* 163-164, 173-177 and 186-187; the phrase in Rev.2-4 recurs (in identical orthography) in 190 r10-12; the unusual spelling *ú-SAḪ-ki-[mu-u-ni]* (Obv.1', for *ušahkimūni*) can be compared with *lu-SAḪ-ki-im-šú*, 172 r18, and *ú-SAH-ka-mu ni*, 179 r8; and the spellings *EP-pa-a-šá* (Obv.7'), *an-nu-TIM-ma* (r1) and *šum-MU* (r6) are all distinctive features of M.'s orthography.

Date:
Kanūnu 5(?), eponymy of Šulmu-Bēl-lašme = January 5(?), 669 BC. See commentary on *LAS* 173; the date Kanūnu *5* is based on the hypothesis that the date on which the (first group of the) "king's people" was scheduled to go through the ritual, set in *LAS* 173 as Kanūnu 6, had later, for reasons stated in *LAS* 176, been altered to Kanūnu 5.

Discussion:
Cf. under *LAS* 163, 173 and 174. The reference to the garments (Obv.2') might *prima facie* seem to indicate that the letter coheres with *LAS* 186-187 rather than 163-164 and 173-177. However, the explicit reference to *two* groups of people in the present letter, which is lacking in 186-187, and the fact that the long blessing formula of 186-187 cannot have been included in the present letter (only about 8 lines are missing at the beginning of Obverse) make this possibility rather unlikely. As pointed out sub *LAS* 174, the garment ritual, though not mentioned in other letters of the correspondence initiated by *LAS* 173, very probably belonged to the rites alluded to in these letters, too.

---

313 Cf. the logographic spellings ^{LÚ}*ša*-SU$_{6}$^{MEŠ} in *ABL* 144:11 and *ša*-SU$_{6}$^{MEŠ} in *ABRT* I 26:4. The present example would be the only NA syllabic spelling of the plural of *ša-ziqni* of which I am aware.

Notes:

5'. Cancel the restoration [*pa-n*]*i-ú-ti* "the former (group of people)", which does not make sense in the present context, and restore instead, on the basis of 163:13, [*šá-n*]*i-ú-ti* "the others".

r5'ff. In view of the date of the letter, very probably a reference to the "Prunkwagen" of Marduk to be used in the (interrupted) journey of the god to Babylon four mounths later (see commentary to *LAS* 29). Cf. Streck, *Asb* p.148:32ff, GIŠGIGIR *ṣir-tu ru-kub* dAMAR+UD *e-tel-li* DINGIRMEŠ EN EN.EN *ina* KÙ.GI KÙ.UD NA_4MEŠ *ni-siq-ti ag-mu-ra nab-nit-sa* "with gold, silver, and choice stones I perfected the appearance of the lofty chariot, the vehicle of Marduk, king of the gods and lord of lords"; and note that several other letters of Marduk-šākin-šumi written in 670 BC (*LAS* 188-191) also refer to the cult of Marduk and objects of cult to be magically consecrated. The present passage would thus indicate that the chariot mentioned in the inscriptions of Assurbanipal had actually been completed in Esarhaddon's reign; cf. Landsberger, *BBEA* p.25f, on a similar "slip" of Assurbanipal regarding the cultic bed of Marduk.

176

Bibliography:

(I) Waterman, *RCAE* 20.
(II) Behrens, *ABB* (1906) 76[1]; Dhorme, *RHR* 113 (1936) 143; Labat, *Royauté* (1938) 308.

Date:

Kanūnu 5, eponymy of Šulmu-Bēl-lašme = January 5, 669 BC. See commentary on *LAS* 173 and cf. below, note on Obv.12.

Addressee:

Esarhaddon.

Notes:

6. *is-su ḫa-ra-am-me*: an adverb rendered "afterwards" in all standard lexica (cf. *CAD* Ḫ 89*b*, AHw 323*a*). However, the fact that the writer is here referring to a letter written not later but earlier in the same day (*LAS* 163) shows that this rendering is incorrect, notwithstanding the meaning "later (on)" firmly established for *ḫaramme(ma)* alone (see J. Lewy, *WO* 2 432 ff). Earlier letters are otherwise referred to in the present corpus with the adverb *ina pānīti* "formerly" (cf. 282 r3, 290:15f and r15f, 294 r12); that this adverb is not used here can only be due to the short time distance between *LAS* 163 and the present letter. Hence the meaning of *issu ḫaram-me* can very probably be established as "recently" (a meaning which incidentally does not seem to be covered by any other NA temporal adverb). For the semantic relationship between *ḫaramme(ma)* and *issu ḫaramme* cf. English *later (on)* : *of late.*

12. *"The day of the city god"*: a public holiday observed in Assyria on eight fixed calendar dates down to the Parthian times; see E. Weidner, "Der Tag des Stadtgottes", *AfO* 14 (1941/44) 340 ff. The evidence presented by Weidner makes it possible to reconstruct the dates concerned as follows (cf. especially *KAV* 79):

1) Tašrītu 8
2) Kislīmu 20
3) Kanūnu 6
4) Šabāṭu 20/22
5) Addāru 17-18
6) Nisannu 7
7) Ajāru 13
8) Ulūlu 14 and 17.

Since the rituals alluded to in the present letter had to be postponed because of the holiday till the 7th day, the inevitable conclusion is that the holiday in question took place before the 7th day of the month.

This makes it certain that the month in question was Kanūnu, as also implied by *LAS* 173 r12-13. Since, on the other hand, the letter was written a day *before* the holiday, it follows that its date can be assuredly established as Kanūnu 5.

r2. *al-tu-s*[*um*]: literally, "I ran", taken as a figurative expression for "I gave a hasty advice"; cf. *lasmu* adj. "prompt, quick". Restoring *al-tu-a*[*m*] (cf. *AHw* 560*a* s.v. *luāmum*) would not make sense in this context.

177

Bibliography:
(I) Waterman, *RCAE* 25.
(II) Behrens, *ABB* (1906) 93².

Date:
Kanūnu 7, eponymy of Šulmu-Bēl-lašme = January 7, 669 BC. See commentary on *LAS* 173. The date Kanūnu 7 is based on 176 r5; it is of course possible that the letter was actually written a couple of days later.

Addressee:
Esarhaddon.

Notes:

7. Restore *ni*-[*ib-ṭil-u-ni*] "(which) we interrupted" (cf. 176 r3 ff), and see *LAS* 219 r8 for another example of *baṭālu* used transitively.

12. *ṣur-ḫi*: in spite of the time of year (Kanūnu/January), here probably in the meaning "heat" or "heating" rather than "fever" (Pt.I). Note that elsewhere in the present corpus the word for "fever" is consistently *ḫunṭu* (cf. 140:8, 157:7, 180:10, 183:5.r3', 246 r2, 250:9 and 258:17) whereas the verb *ṣarāhu* elsewhere exclusively means "to be hot" (cf. 181:7f with note, 216:11, 255 r11 and 258 r10); the meaning "heat" also fits the other occurrence of *ṣurhu* in the corpus (181:11) which was likewise incorrectly rendered "fever" in Pt.I (cf. respective note). The implications of the passage remain obscure.

r2. Cancel the restoration *uq-ṭa-a*[*r-ri-ib*] suggested in Pt.I, which is grammatically impossible (negated past was never expressed through Pf. in Neo-Assyrian) and read instead *la ug-da-d*[*am-mir*] "it was not comp[leted]" (*gmr* Dtt).

r4. *ÉŠ.GÀR šu ri* [. . .]: unclear; possibly to be read *šu-ur!-*[*pu*][314] or ŠU GI[DIM!.MA]. Note that the promise to perform this ritual was given orally (*aq-bu-ni*, r6); this explains why no reference to it is made in the earlier correspondence.

178

Bibliography:
(I) Waterman, *RCAE* 21.
(II) Dhorme, *RHR* 113 (1936) 146; Oppenheim, *JAOS* 61 (1941) 263.

Copy:
Cf. S.A. Smith, *PSBA* 10 p.176, pl.11.

Discussion:

Compare with this letter *LKA* 136:14 ff, an exorcistic ritual to cure a person "gnashing his teeth":

---

314 Cf. note on 208:7.

"Take a human skull, spread a cloth over a chair, and place the said skull upon it. During three days make funerary offerings in the morning and evening. Recite the incantation (worded in lines 5-7) seven times "into" the skull, have the patient kiss the said skull seven and seven times before his bed, and he will get well. (Then) return the skull to the place you took it from."

While it is not certain that this ritual (cf. also *BAM* I 30) is meant in the text, this possibility remains open. That the skulls mentioned in the present letter also were human is rendered likely by the hesitation of the writer to take them into the *qersu* (cf. note on 60 r5) without the king's permission.

Notes:

r1. *nu-šá-URU-bi-iš*: sic. The syllabic value URU = al_x (< *ālu*) does not seem to be attested elsewhere but nevertheless perhaps deserves to be added to the syllabary of von Soden and Röllig (*AnOr* 42 p.5).

179

Bibliography:
(I) Waterman, *RCAE* 22.
(II) Falkner, *AfO* 17 (1954/56) 112f, n.22.

Discussion:

As can be seen without much difficulty, this letter concerns the burying of prophylactic figurines (*timru*, see on Obv.5) in various parts of the royal palace. The text contains too few details to make it possible to identify the ritual concerned with certainty, but it seems quite possible that the prophylactic ceremonies performed after the death of the substitute king, described in Col.B of the substitute king ritual tablet (W.G. Lambert, *AfO* 18, 109ff, and 19, 119), are in question (see notes below). If so, the letter most likely dates from late Du'ūzu/mid-July, 669 (cf. *LAS* 166), since in all other cases between 675 and 665 BC (= the period in which all but 16 datable letters of the present corpus belong) the substitute king was apparently put to death *in Akkad.* Cf. *LAS* 280, 292, 298 and 32, and see commentaries on *LAS* 26, 162 and 292.

Notes:

5. *tim-ra-a-ni*: to my knowledge, a hapax legomenon, but certainly a collective designation of figurines buried in ground for prophylactic purposes (*timru* = lit. "buried object", cf. *GAG* § 55c). For rituals involving the use of such figurines, see O.R. Gurney, "Babylonian prophylactic figures and their rituals", *AAA* 22 (1935) 31 ff; for excavated specimens, e.g. Lutz, *UCP* 9/7 (1930) 383f and Mallowan, *Nimrud* II (1966) 389 f. The substitute king ritual tablet prescribes (*AfO* 18 110 f) the burying of the following items: two raging dogs at [outer] gate (cf. Obv.9); two bulls of Šamaš at *papāḫu* chapel; two hydras at palace gate; two capricorns at bedroom (cf. r6); two kneeling figures in the middle of palace courtyard; and two lion-men at side entrance.

9. This line is very obliterated and hard to read in the original, and many of the extant traces allow different readings. According to personal collation, however, the signs preceding *te-te-*⌈*mer*⌉ are definitely not [GA]L-*lim*, as given in Pt.I, but almost certainly ⌈A.⌉AN (). The only locus in the prophylactic rituals which can be reconciled with these traces is KÁ DIL.ÀM "outer gate"; the correct reading of the line is hence almost certainly *ma-a* ⌈*ina* KÁ DIL.ÀM⌉ *te-te-*⌈*mir*⌉ "bury (them) at the outer gate". This could be quoted either from the substitute king ritual tablet (*2 ur-dím-me . . . i-na ba-a*[*b ka-mi-i t*]*e-tem-mir*, *AfO* 18 p.111:13) or from *KAR* 298 (Obv.28.32.36.39, Rev.22).

11-r1. The break here probably contained instructions parallel to those given in Rev.2-9; at the end of r1, restore [. . . *lit-me*]*-ru* (cf. r9).

r3 f. Cf. *LAS* 4 r8'ff, UD 5.KÁM *ki-ma* LUGAL *a-na qa-an-ni it-tu-ṣi* LÚMAŠ.MAŠ NÍG.NA GI.IZI.LÁ *lu-še-ti-iq* "on the 5th, when the king goes out of doors, an exorcist should move a censer (and) a torch past (the king)." Does the present passage refer to the same situation? The seemingly incidental remark about the king's exit from the palace may imply that he had previously not been permitted to leave the palace precincts for safety reasons; this would support the hypothesis that the letter pertains to the final phase of a substitute king ritual (cf. *LAS* 280 r11-13 with note).

r5. *É dan-ni* "main room": perhaps better "main building"; hardly to be read *É-tan-ni* "interiors" (cf. *É-an-ni*, *LAS* 10+:10). The building is not mentioned in the substitute king ritual tablet nor in other prophylactic rituals known to the present writer.

r6. *É KI.NÁ*^{MEŠ} "bedroom": corresponding to É *ma-a-a-[li]* of the substitute king ritual tablet (*AfO* 18 p.111:24). Cf. also *KAR* 298:11.14 (figurines buried *ina* SAG ^{GIŠ}NÁ "at the head of the bed").

r7 f. The rendering of this passage is based on the parallel *bé-et* LUGAL *i-qab-bu-ú-ni id-du-nu*, K 8669 ii 15 (cf. Müller, *MVAeG* 41/3 p.59 ff).

r11. Cf. *ina ma-at lìb-ba-šá-ni . . . lu še-ru-ub<-at>* "(the queen may be taken in whenever she so wishes", van Driel, *CA* p.98:52'f.

180

Bibliography:
(I) Waterman, *RCAE* 348 (cf. IV 180, 247); Pfeiffer, *SLA* 285.
(II) Schott, *OLZ* 40 (1937) 363; Böhl, *Opera Minora* (1953) 409 ff.

Photo:
RCAE IV pl.8 (Obv. only).

Date:
Probably Simānu/May, 670 BC. This date is based on the hypothesis that the letter pertains to the same attack of illness as *LAS* 51, 143, 181, and 246-247. Note the orthographical affinities with *LAS* 181.

Discussion:
See under *LAS* 246.

Notes:

8. *"I cannot open my eyes"*: cf. note on 183:5 f.

14. On the prognosis *laššu ḫīṭu* see note to *LAS* 154:8. Cf. 182:7ff, *la-áš-šú ḫi-ṭu* DINGIR^{MEŠ}*-ni ša* L[UGAL] *ár-ḫiš i-pa-aṭ-ṭu-ru.*

181

Bibliography:
(I) Waterman, *RCAE* 19.
(II) Dhorme, *RHR* 113 (1936) 141; Böhl, *Opera Minora* (1953) 409ff; Ritter, *AS* 16 (1965) 319.

Date:
Late Ajāru = early May, 670 BC. Cf. on *LAS* 246, with which the present letter evidently is approximately contemporary (note the king's fever and the *ṣillibānu*-treatment). The dating is confirmed by the reference to the enemy country (Egypt, r6) placing the letter after Du'ūzu 671, and by the time of the year (*ḫarpī* "early summer", obv.14).

Addressee:
Esarhaddon.

Discussion:

Contrary to what the faulty translation given in Pt.I (see below, on obv.7, 10f and 13) would seem to imply, this letter in its entirety concerns Esarhaddon, on whose illness see in detail sub *LAS* 246.

Notes:

6. *ṣil-li-ba-a-ni*: possibly = Syr. *ṣulbānā* "dry root of licorice" used as a poultice; see R.C. Thompson, *The Assyrian Herbal*, p.202b, but cf. *CAD* Ṣ 187 ("crosswise arrangement"). The word also occurs in *LAS* 246 r9 (*ṣi-il-ba-ni*) and *BBR* 67:5 (GIŠ*ṣil-li-ba-ni*, referring to an aromatic substance burnt in censers).

7. *ṣa-re-eḫ*: not "he is feverish" (Pt.I) but "it (= the poultice) is hot"; cf. below, obv.11, and 177:12, 216:11, 255 r11 and 258 r10. The passage refers to the king, cf. 246 r9ff.

8. *lu ṣa-re-eḫ*: either "it *should* be hot" (in order to provoke perspiration, cf. obv.12), or "even though it is hot" (Pt.I, cf. *GAG* §153c for *lū* used in this sense). The choice between these two alternatives depends on the rendering of the following line.

9. Postgate has recently (*Iraq* 35 [1973] 25⁹) pointed out that the traditional rendering of *basi* as "soon" should possibly be replaced by "so that", (as preposition) "for the purpose of". If so, the present line should be translated "to what purpose we are doing (this)", a rhetorical question answered in line 10f.

10f. Cancel the rendering of *la-a šu-tú ṣu-ur-ḫe-e* given in Pt.I, and translate instead: "Didn't he (=Urad-Nanâ) <opt for> heat, in saying (*mā*): 'It should make him sweat'?" The genitive[315] *ṣurḫê* (= /ṣurḫi/ + interrogative intonation) refers to the following *mā* clause; instead of *šu-tú*, one would expect *ša*, but this is excluded according to collation by Sollberger.

13. Render: "But why is he (= Esarhaddon) seized by ague?" The question is not part of the foregoing quotation.

r1. *mitḫar*: a terminus technicus for "steady (gleichmäßig, konstant) fever", see Labat, *RlA* 3 61*a*. Cf. also ibid. 61*b* for the terms *kuṣṣu, ḫunṭu, zūtu*.

r3. *ṭurru*: not "bandages" (Pt.I) but "string" (of perforated amulet stones hung around the neck), a well-known healing device of Mesopotamian exorcists. See Köcher, *AfO* 20 (1963) 156ff, and cf. note on 239:3'; for catalogues of amulet stones, see *BAM* IV 342-378. Here evidently a string of amulet stones obtained from Egypt is in question; the pronoun *ši-na* in Rev.9 has to be taken as referring to an implied *abnāti* "stones".

r10. *GIŠ.ḪUR*^MEŠ: uncertain whether referring to divine "patterns" (exorcistic literature, etc.) transmitted to the mankind in the beginning of times, or to the "patterns" (physical limitations, etc.) given to the king personally. The former alternative has been followed in the translation.

r14. *e-tu-ka-a-ni*: unclear, possibly Pl. of **etāku* (mng. unknown). The form cannot be taken as Stat. 1 Pl. of *'tk* "to be alerted" (with an anaptyptic vowel inserted between *t* and *k*), as done in Pt.I, since the anaptyptic vowel in question should be /e/ not /a/; see note on 39:11. Cf. *e-ta-ka-ni*, *ABL* 1451:4' (context fragmentary).

182

Bibliography:

(I) Waterman, *RCAE* 663.
(II) Schott, *OLZ* 40 (1937) 363; Dhorme, *RHR* 113 (1937) 141; G. Meier, *Or*NS 8 (1939) 304; Labat, *Royauté* (1939) 325.

Date:

Probably Ābu, eponymy of Nabû-bēlu-uṣur = August, 672 BC. It could be argued, on the basis of Obv.5, that this letter pertains to the same case of illness as *LAS* 181. However, it seems likelier that it is contemporaneous with

[315] Or is *ṣurḫu* "heat, fever" a plurale tantum? Cf. note on *LAS* 255:8.

the following report of Ištar-šumu-ēreš (*RMA* 257), which refers to an attack of illness in *Ābu/August* and is very likely datable to 672 BC on the basis of the thunderstorm reported in it:[316] *ina* UGU *la ṭu-ub* UZU *an-ni-i* [7] LUGAL *be-lí* TA* *lìb-bi-šú la i-da-bu-ub* [8] *mur-ṣu* MU.AN.NA *šu-ú* [9] UN^{MEŠ} *am-mar mar-ṣu-u-ni* [10] *gab-bu šul-mu* [11] *tu-ra-ma* LUGAL *be-lí* [12] *ša pa-lìḫ* DINGIR^{MEŠ} *šu-tu-u-ni* [13] u_4*-mu ù mu-šú* DINGIR^{MEŠ} *ú-ṣal-lu-u-ni* [r1] *ket-tu-ú me-me-ni* [2] *a-na* LUGAL EN-*ja ù* NUMUN-*šú il-la-ka* [3] *i-lu-ut-tu a-šir-tú* [4] *de-e-i-qi i-ba-aṭ-ti* [5] *šu-ú ki-i an-ni-i qa-a-bi* [6] *ma-gal a-še-er* UD^{MEŠ}-*šú* LUGÚD.DA^{MEŠ} [7] *im-da-na-ra-aṣ* UD^{MEŠ}-*šú* GÍD.DA^{MEŠ} "The king, my lord, should not worry about this illness: it is a disease of the season (= month Ābu), all the people who have been sick (with it) have got well. Moreover, the king, my lord, who is a god-fearing man and prays to the gods day and night – could anything possibly happen to the king, my lord, and to his seed? . . . (r3-4 unclear) . . . It is said as follows: 'He who is doing well dies young, he who is sickly lives long'."

[The proverb quoted in the report is not otherwise known; a Sumerian proverb (*tu-ra dùg-ga-àm peš*$_x$ (ŠÀ×TUR)-*dè gig-ga-àm*, Gordon, *Sumerian Proverbs* p.146 no. 1.193) resembles it externally, but renders an entirely different idea ("a sick person is relatively well – it is the woman in childbirth who is really ill").] – Unfortunately it cannot be made out with certainty whether the favourable prognosis given in the present letter was based on the writer's sincere evaluation of the patient's condition or whether it is rather to be viewed as an attempt to keep the king in good spirits despite his poor physical condition (cf. on *LAS* 246). If the latter is the case, then the writer may well have been aware of the interdependence of psychic and somatic disorders and could thus have followed in his prognosis a guideline similar to the "Hippocratic ethos" followed by his later colleagues from Classical antiquity till the present day.

183

Bibliography:

(I) Waterman, *RCAE* 664.

(II) Behrens, *ABB* (1906) 90f; Dhorme, *RHR* 113 (1936) 141; Ritter, *AS* 16 (1965) 320.

Date:

Late Ajāru = early May, 670 BC. Based on the hypothesis that the letter concerns the same case of illness as *LAS* 180-181, etc., which seems justified in view of Rev.2' (cf. note) and Obv.5f.

Addressee:

Esarhaddon.

Notes:

5 f. *ḫunṭu* [*ša*]⌜*e!*⌝-*na-a-te* "inflammation of eyes": sic according to collation by C.B.F. Walker (January 27, 1976); cancel the emendation [*eṣ*]-*ma!-a-te* suggested in Pt.I. Cf. *AMT* 20,2:7, I NA IGI²-*šú* GIG^{MEŠ}-*ma u ḫa-an-ṭa* "if the patient's eyes are sore and inflamed", and ibid. 16,1:9, I NA IGI²-*šú* UD.DA *ḫa-an-ṭa* "if the patient's eyes are inflamed from *ṣētu* fever". Cf. also 181:8 and 258:18, and see, on the whole, commentary on *LAS* 246.

7. *pašāru*: here in the technical sense "to cure", see Ritter, art.cit. 307.

r2. The name of the month can also be read ^{ITU}GU[D]! "Ajāru", which is expected, instead of ^{ITU}ZÍ[Z], which would be nonsensical here.

184

Bibliography:

Waterman, *RCAE* 1388.

---

[316] Cf. *RMA* 256B (Balasi), 258 (Nabû-aḫḫē-erība) and 235 (Akkullānu) certainly reporting on the same thunderstorm as *RMA* 257. These reports also contain a Mars observation which provides ground for their dating.

Writer:

The assignation of this letter to Marduk-šākin-šumi is certain on the ground of the spelling *is-sa-ḫe-'i-iš* in Rev.5 which occurs only in letters of this writer (see 172 r14, 191 r14' and 195 r2). Note also the affinities of Rev.1-3 with *LAS* 186 r1-2.

Addressee:

Esarhaddon.[317]

Date:

June, 670 BC.[318]

Notes:

r4f. [*ina q*]*a-an-ni* LÚGABA.RIMEŠ-*ja*: this expression has posed an intriguing problem of translation, despite the fact that the basic meanings and usages of both *qanni* ("at") and *meḫru* ("counterpart") are well known and the expression itself is attested several times in different contexts; cf. *AHw* 641*a*: "nA *qanni m*[*eḫri*] "eigenes Gebiet", but further down, p.897*b* sub *qanni* 5b: "Deutung unsicher". The present passage, where *meḫru* is spelled LÚGABA.RIMEŠ, i.e. with the plural sign and a Sumerogram usually meaning "opponent", establishes beyond doubt that *meḫru* cannot here refer to the writer himself ("eigen") but to some outsiders. The same is in fact implied by all other attestations of the phrase as well. Cf., in addition to *LAS* 264 r17, where *meḫru* indubitably refers to the colleagues of the writer (a physician), especially *ABL* 455:15 ff: *ina qa-ni mé-eḫ-re-e-a* 16 *dul-lu ep-pa-áš* 17 *la a-šá-re-du-um-ma* 18 *šá lìb-bi-šú-nu a-na-ku* 19 *la* ! *ma-ki-ju-ú a-na-ku* 20 [*a*]*-ki šá šu-nu ep-pa-šú-u-ni* 21 [*a-n*]*a-ku ep-pa-áš* "I do my work . . . (*qanni*) my colleagues; I am not the best of them, I am not the worst; I do as they do". From this passage one obtains the summary equation *ina qanni meḫrīja* ≈ *akī ša šunu*.

Note also ND 2635 (*NL* 43 = *Iraq* 20, pl.39) obv.11f: *ú-ma-a la ú-ṣi-u* 12 *qa-ni me-eḫ-ri-šú-nu la* ⌜*i*⌝-[*l*]*i-ku* "now, they have not come out and gone (at their work) . . . their colleagues". This passage refers to 40 men of the Gurru tribe who had formerly served the king but had at the time the letter was written refused to continue their work; here the word *meḫru* is perhaps more exactly rendered by "comrade" than by "colleague".[319]

As for (*ina*) *qanni*, the examples already quoted show quite clearly, I think, that the usual meanings "at, outside (of)" (cf. on *LAS* 4 r7) cannot be considered in the present instance. *ABL* 455:15ff suggests, as already pointed out, that (*ina*) *qanni* is here roughly synonymous with *kī ša* and could accordingly be rendered "like". Though such a translation also perfectly fits *LAS* 264 r17 and ND 2635:12, it does not fit the present passage where a local meaning like "with" is obviously required. Such a meaning is also required in the following two instances where *meḫru* "comrade" is replaced by *aḫā'iš* "each other":

qa-[*an*]*-ni a-ḫa-iš* 17 *it-tu-ṣu-ú-né* 18 *it-tal-ku-ú-né* "they 'came out' (= crossed the border) and were coming hither abreast of each other (when . . .)" *ABL* 138:17f;

qa-an-ni a-ḫe-iš ni-za-az 11' *né-pa-áš* "we are staying *side by side with* each other and performing (our work)" = "we are working in close co-operation", *LAS* 223 r10'f (cf. the present passage!).

This *qanni aḫā'iš* is clearly more or less synonymous with the common *issi aḫā'iš* "together" (lit. "with each other"), the only visible difference being that *qanni aḫā'iš* denotes a closer association than *issi aḫā'iš*; a translation like "*side* by *side* with" (cf. *CAD* A/1 168*a*) renders this idea most appropriately, just as the notion of "side" also underlies all other meanings of *qannu* (cf. the substantive usage of *q*., "border, seam, side"; the prepositional usages "at" [<on the *side* of] and "out*side* of"; the adverbial usage "out" [<out*side*]; and the subjunctive usage "as soon as" ["at the side of the moment when"] discussed in note to 239:5').[320] As this "basic" translation however does not satisfy all of the quoted instances of *qanni meḫri+*, it is evident that the meaning of the expres-

317 Note the ref. to the crown princes in Obv.9f.

318 See commentary to *LAS* 151.

319 The meaning "comrade" seems natural also in *ABL* 85 r6ff: *ki-ma i-šak-ki-ru* LÚ GÍR AN.BAR TA* *pa-an me-ḫe-ri-šu la ú-sa-aḫ-*<*ḫa*->*ra* "when they get drunk, none of them can keep his dagger off his comrade".

320 Why *issi qanni* (*AfO* Bh 6 no.106:12 and *Iraq* 16 38:43), lit. "with the side (of)", means "in behalf of, instead of", remains obscure.

sion is partly dependent on the context. In *LAS* 264 r7 the idea seems to be "let the king make me happy *at the side* of my colleagues (so that I may not be slighted among my equals)"; in the present letter and in *LAS* 223, where *qanni* occurs with the verb *uzuzzu* "to stand", the idea almost certainly is "to cooperate with"; cf. *uzuzzu* + *issi* "to assist", and OA *ina šaḫāt* NN *uzuzzum* "zur Seite treten" (Kienast, *ATHE* [1960] p.23).

The likeliest rendering of the present passage is accordingly (modifying slightly the translation given in Pt.I), "I am cooperating with my colleagues, we shall . . ." Meant are of course Adad-šumu-uṣur, Urad-Nanâ and Nabû-nāṣir: cf. *LAS* 159, 160, and 222.

r6. *ni-qab-bi* "we shall speak out": viz. to the queen mother.

r7 ff. *"The queen mother is wise as Adapa"*: a compliment otherwise granted only to kings. See on *LAS* 229 and cf. also commentary to *LAS* 230.

185

Bibliography:
(I) Waterman, *RCAE* 23 (cf. IV 173, 232); Pfeiffer, *SLA* 257; Behrens, *ABB* (1906) 87 ff.
(II) Schott, *OLZ* 40 (1937) 362; Dhorme, *RHR* 113 (1936) 141ff, 148; Labat, *Royauté* (1939) 213 and 338; Oppenheim, *JAOS* 61 (1941) 253, 266.

Addressee:
Esarhaddon.

Date:
Kanūnu 13, eponymy of Kanūnāju = December 25, 671 BC. This date (which can be regarded as certain) is obtained from the combined evidence of the following pieces of information:

[1] The cycle of prayers to the astral gods mentioned in Obv.5-12, as well as the one to the female deities referred to later in the text (r3-5), are attested as components of only one ritual, *Bīt rimki*, performed exclusively on account of lunar eclipses (in the eclipse-formula attacted to the relevant prayers *only* the moon is mentioned).

[2] The universal namburbi mentioned in Obv.13f likewise was a component of *Bīt rimki*, to be performed in connection with the prayer cycle just mentioned; see *BBR* 26 iii 23 and iv 23.

[3] In the other namburbi ritual mentioned in Obv.15f, both the moon and the sun had caused the evil to be averted.

[4] The execution of the ceremonies required the co-operation of an *exorcist* (Marduk-šākin-šumi) and a *kalû*-chanter (Urad-Ea), just as in No. 167 (q.v.); it took several days and was intended for the safety of the king (Rev.9).

[5] The letter was written in the evening of the 13th day (cf. Obv.18 ff, "*today* [= the 13th] I have performed such and such; but on an evil day [= the 14th, i.e., from tonight till tomorrow night] I cannot perform any prayers; therefore I shall go on with them only *tomorrow* night, on the eve of *the 15th day*").

[6] The fact that the two crown princes are mentioned (in Rev.8 and 12) fixes the date of the letter between 672 and 669 B.C.

[7] In suggesting that certain rituals be performed for the two princes, Marduk-šākin-šumi mentions only the prayers to the moon and the universal namburbi (Rev. 11f).

[8] In Rev.14 ff the writer refers to an unspecified but alarming lunar observation, on account of which he proposes that a substitute (king) should be put on the throne; this substitute would be "afflicted" *on the night* of the [th] day.

On the basis of these data it is easy to prove that the letter was written approximately a day before an expected lunar eclipse: the performance of the *Bīt rimki* ceremonies (above, [1], [2] and [4]) presupposes a lunar eclipse which, however, could not yet have occurred since the letter was written only on the 13th day [5] and since the substitute was to be "afflicted" only on a *coming* night [8]. That the "observation" (*tāmartu*) of the moon actually refers to this eclipse is clear from the fact that it was to be made in the nighttime and in the middle of the month. The apotropaic ritual concerning both the sun and the moon was accordingly intended to counteract the "evil" of the (ill-portending) opposition of the two bodies.

Secondly, it is virtually certain that the eclipse in question had been predicted for the 15th day. The substitute king was scheduled to be enthroned before the eclipse actually took place [8]; but when the chief exorcist was to *discuss* the matter with the king, the night of the 14th day had already passed! Hence the eclipse concerned can have occurred on the 15th *at the earliest* and on the 16th at the latest; the later date is only possible supposing a calendrical error.

Thirdly, the surety with which the eclipse could be predicted (the performance of the *Bīt rimki* ritual had already begun and enthronement of a substitute king was seriously considered) strongly suggests that the eclipse was TOTAL; cf. commentaries on *LAS* 41, 63 and 64, and note that the partial eclipse of Simānu/June 669 could not be predicted for certain (see *LAS* 25). Three other lunar eclipses occurred in Mesopotamia between 672 and 669 BC [6], of which two (Du'ūzu/July and Kanūnu/December, 671) were indeed total and only one (Kislīmu/December 670) partial; see App.F. The latter did not call for the substitute king ritual (see under *LAS* 173) whereas the other two did; but while the data of the present letter perfectly agree with the case of Kanūnu 671 (see *LAS* 279 and resp. commentary), the case of Du'ūzu 671 is out of the question since the eclipse then occurred *already on the 14th.*

Discussion:

The recognition that the letter was written before a predicted lunar eclipse is important in two respects. Firstly, the data of the letter can now be evaluated to provide information about little-known aspects of *Bīt rimki*. It appears 1) that the rites could commence even before the eclipse had actually occurred; 2) that the šuilla cycle *BBR* 26 iii 40 – iv 12 did not have to be performed without interruption but could be extended over several days; 3) that the order of individual prayers did not have to follow strictly the sequence prescribed in the ritual tablet (cf. on Obv.5ff); 4) that at least occasionally a new set of tablets containing the prayers had to be prepared for use in the ritual (see note to Obv.23 ff); and 5) that the recital of the prayers required the co-operation of a *kalû*-chanter who performed his ritual on the palace roof. Furthermore, the gap in *BBR* 26 iii 67ff can be partly restored on the ground of the incantations enumerated in Obv.5 ff. The information about the *substitute king ritual* is perhaps even more significant. It appears that the proposal to enthrone a substitute unambiguously originated, at least in the present case, with the chief exorcist Marduk-šākin-šumi (not with the king) and that the substitute was seated on the throne, if possible, already *before* the eclipse had taken place. In addition, Rev.21-27 illustrate the considerations involved in the choice of the substitute, see pertinent notes.

Notes:

5-12. Beginning the letter with this long list of rituals and prayers presumably served the purpose of assuring the king that effective countermeasures had been taken against the predicted eclipse and its "evil". Since the šuilla cycle of *Bīt rimki* did not begin with the prayers mentioned, it is reasonable to conclude that the prayers passed over here had already been performed earlier.

The list of prayers can be partly restored with the help of the ritual tablet of *Bīt rimki*, *BBR* 26, where the section concerning prayers to astral gods begins at Col. iii 60. Unfortunately *BBR* 26 is badly damaged at this particular point, the relevant text breaking off almost exactly where the present letter sets in (the prayer in *BBR* 26 iii 67 being addressed to Sirius according to Ungnad, *Or*NS 12 [1943] 198). Nonetheless, both texts supplement each other to some extent, though the order of individual prayers does not appear to have been the same (which is not really disturbing: the existence of at least two Assyrian versions of the ritual text itself has been posited by W.G. Lambert, *BiOr* 14 [1957] 229). The three lines following [^{MUL}]^{L}*Be*-[*lit*-TI.LA] probably contained prayers to stars such as MULSIPA.ZI.AN.NA (cf. *BBR* 26 iii 64), MULLI$_9$.SI$_4$, dEN.KUR.KUR and d*I-šum* (cf. *ABL* 648), MULMUL (*LSS* NF 2 p.62), etc.

On the hand-lifting prayers in general see W. Mayer, *St. Pohl* S.M. 5 (1976) 375 ff; and W. Kunstmann, *LSS* NF 2 (1932) 54-73. Of the *bīt rimki* prayers mentioned here, the following have been published to date: Moon = *BMS* 1 (Ebeling, *AGH* pp.6-8): *Nusku* = *AGH* 38-42; *Pleiades* = *AGH* 148-150 (cf. ibid. pp.62 and 144); *Sirius* = *BMS* 49 (*AGH* 144-146); *Mars* = *BMS* 46 (*AGH* 8-10 and 114-116).

It is noteworthy that the prayers to the female deities, which in the ritual tablet precede those to the stars, were in the present case performed collectively only after the latter had been done with. The grounds for this procedure remain unclear.

13f. For the wording of the "universal namburbi" see Ebeling, *RA* 48 (1954), 6 ff, and cf. Caplice, *SANE* 1/1 (1974) p.8f. The performance of this namburbi is prescribed in the ritual tablet of *bīt rimki* (*BBR* 26 iii).

15f. This namburbi is not otherwise known. The meaning assigned to *zinnatu* is based on Izi V 52 ff, i-si-iš = *ta-zi-[im-tum], zi-im-⌈ma⌉-[tum], zi-in-na-[tum]* (cf. *CAD* Z 122*b*).

18. *epāšu* "to perform" was an exorcistic terminus technicus covering *both* the performance of a given ritual act *and* the recitation of the accompanying incantation. In the present case, the ritual was very simple: the exorcist had to place a censer of juniper in front of the deities concerned and to libate fine beer before the recital of each prayer; e.g., *ana* IGI d*30* NÍG.NA ŠIM.LI GAR-*an* KAŠ.SAG BAL-*qí*, *BBR* 26 iii 52.

21 The injunction that an exorcist may not perform hand-lifting prayers on an "evil day" (UD.ḪUL.GÁL = *u$_4$-mu lem-nu*, Ḫḫ I 195; in view of the phonetic complement *-e*, however, the sumerogram has here to be read phonetically *uḫulgalê*, cf. UD.ḪUL.GÁL = ŠU-*lum*, Ḫḫ I 194, and the Ash passage quoted below) is not otherwise known. This may imply that the list of activities forbidden on the "evil days" (the 7th, 14th, 19th, 21st and 28th day of the lunar month) was in the religious circles of the Sargonid Assyria considerably larger than the traditional one found in *Inbu Bēl Arḫi* and related texts (see notes to *LAS* 198:10 and 210 r2-5). It is of course possible that the written injunctions were accompanied by complementary oral ones from the beginning, but it is not excluded either that the prohibitions tended to increase as time passed (cf. the development of the Jewish Sabbath).

On the "evil days" in general see Landsberger, *LSS* 6/1-2 (1915), 119-126. It should be noted that these days were not basically "inauspicious": every "evil day" is characterized in the series *Inbu Bēl Arḫi* as "auspicious" (UD ŠE). The attribute "evil" probably derives from a learned association of every 7th day of the month (the principal lunar phases) and their multiple (7X7 = 49 = 30+19: the 19th day) with the seven evil demons, through number symbolism; see Landsberger, loc. cit., and cf. Borger *Ash* p.104 ii 3: UD *21*.KAM UD.ḪUL.GÁL-*e u$_4$-mu lem-nu i-lit-ti a-sak-ki* "on the 21st day, the *uḫulgalû* (i.e.), evil day, birthday of the *asakku* demons" (thus *CAD* A/2 326*a*; cf. I/J 72*b*, where *ilitti asakkī* is translated "devil's offspring").

21f. *la DÙG+GA . . . la i-na-áš-ši*: lit., "it is not good, he may not lift (hands in prayer)", taken as a hendiadys for "it is not good/prepitious for him to perform prayers". The expression *lā ṭāba* + negated finite verb does not seem to be otherwise attested in NA, but it is paralleled by *laššu + negated finite verb* and *ibašši + positive finite verb*, where the statives *laššu* and *ibašši* likewise serve to modify (in these cases, to emphasize) the meaning of the following verb. For examples of *laššu lā* see *LAS* 173:8 and 9 r1; *ABL* 144 r5 (similarly 1085:5); 471:22 (similarly 222 r17f, 563 r1, 769 r4f); 547 r7f (similarly 610:9 and 885:20); 312:8; 1073 r4f; 251 r1f, and 315 r5; examples of *ibašši* in hendidys are to be found in *CAD* B, p.155. – Incidentally, the use of *i-na-áš-ši* instead of some other technical term indicates that ŠU.ÍL.LÁ.KÁM has to be read here *nīš qāti* rather than *šu'illāku*; cf. note to *LAS* 203 r1.

23 ff. The parallel passages in *LAS* 173 and 186 (cf. discussion on *LAS* 173) as well as the context itself assure that the tablets mentioned here were copied for immediate use in the ritual, not in the first place for inclusion in the royal libraries, as one might be inclined to think at the first sight.

Here too, as in No.173, the king's name and the specific circumstances involved (month etc.) were added to the standard prayers; cf. the tablets written for Šamaš-šumu-ukīn on a similar occasion, discussed in commentary to *LAS* 173. For a *bīt rimki* tablet with the name of Esarhaddon appearing on it (*anāku Aššur-aḫu-iddina mār ilišu*, etc.) see 83–1–18,177 (= Langdon, *TI* pl.IV).

r3. See note to Obv.5 ff. The actual order of these prayers, as prescribed in the ritual tablet, was as follows: *Zarpānītu* (cf. Mullo-Weir, *AfO* 18 [1957-58], 371f), *Ninlil* (cf. *BBR* 26 iii 42), *Gula* (iii 50), *Ištar* (iii 54), *Tašmētu* (iii 58); the prayer to *Nanai* is not included in the extant text. For the prayers themselves cf. E. Ebeling, *AGH* pp. 24 and 124-126 (*Tašmētu*); 30-32 and 46-48 (*Gula*); 60-62, 120, 130-136 (*Ištar*); and 68-70 (*Zarpānītu*); most of these, however, did not belong to the series *Bīt rimki*.

r6f. Cf. *RMA* 89 r10, [*up-ni-ja*] [11] *ap-te-te ina* UGU LUGAL DUMU.MAN ^{Id}GIŠ.N[U$_{11}$-MU-GI.NA] [12] *ú-sa-re-er* "I opened [my fists] and prayed for the king, the crown prince (and) Šama[š-šumu-ukīn]" (on account of a conjunction of Mars and Saturn). See also note to *LAS* 35 r21.

r13. *mīnu ḫīṭu*: lit. "what is the fault?", here certainly a rhetorical question meaning "it is not wrong (to take precautions)"; cf. Schott, *OLZ* 40 (1937) 362. The implication seems to be that while the *bīt rimki* ritual was supposed to protect the king and his "house", the two crown princes (who were not resident at court) *possibly* constituted a special case and therefore needed additional protection.

r18. Certainly referring to the enthronement of a substitute king. Cf. [*ina* É] *n*[*u-š*]*e-ši-bu-šú-ni* "when we enthroned him" (lit. "made him, scil. the substitute king, sit"), 26 r3; *mì-i-nu* ISKIM *la-ap-tu* . . . LUGAL *pu-u-ḫi tu-še-ši-ba* "what is the bad omen on account of which you have enthroned a substitute king?", 30:15f; *a-na še-šu-bi* [8] *ṭè-e-mu liš-ku-nu* "they should give order to enthrone (a substitute)", 134:7, cf. ib.r2' *nu-še-šib*; 298:10, *a-ta-a ina* ŠÀ ^{URU}*Ak-ka-di ú-še-ši-bu* "why did they enthrone (him) in Akkad?". The corresponding G-stem "to sit" (scil. on the throne) is used quite similarly: *ki ma-ṣi* UD^{MEŠ} [10] *lu-ši-ib* "how many days should he (the subsitute king) sit on the throne?", 135:9f; LUGAL [*pu-ḫi*] [6] *ša* UD *15*.KÁM* *ina* ^{UR}[^{U}NIN]A *ú-ši-b*[*u-u-ni*] "the [substitute] king who was seated on the throne in Nineveh on the 15th day", 279:5f; *ma-a 1 me u$_4$-me lu-ši-i*[*b*] "he should sit on the throne for a 100 days", 292:2'; *ina* ŠÀ ^{URU}*Ak-ka-di it-tu-šib*, 298:8. Note also *LAS* 136: 12, *a-ki ina* ^{ITU}APIN LUGAL *pu-u-ḫi* [13] *kam-mu-su-u-ni*, where *kammus* is the stative of *wšb*, corresponding to MA *ušib* (which was obsolete in NA). A study of the article *ašābu* in *CAD* A/2 suffices to show that this "technical" use of *wšb* (in the meaning "*to sit on the throne*") was confined to texts dealing with the substitute king ritual; in all other contexts the verb required in this meaning a specification like *ina kussê*, or the like.

r19. For other examples of *alāku* "to come" referring to time see *CAD* A/1 311*b*. The expression *liptu epāšu* "to bring about an 'affliction' ", which also occurs in r24 f, does not seem to be attested elsewhere; taking into consideration the implied meaning ("to *make* evil omens affect somebody") this of course is not by any means surprising!

r22f. Cf. *LAS* 163 r3-5, LUGAL *be-lí-ni ú-da ai-'u-ú-ti e-pu-šu-u-ni*; the restoration [*i da*]*-ba-bu-u-ni* is based on r25.

r25. [*d*]*a-bi-ba-nu-ti*: sic after collation; hapax legomenon, but certainly = Pl. of *dābibu* "talkative, gossipy person" (*CAD* D 16*a*) enlarged with the individualizing morpheme *-ān*, cf. *ḫādi'ānu* "ill-wisher" (*LAS* 121 r22), *ḫāripānu* "early bird" (139:10, *epišānu ša bārti* "one who foments rebellion" (*VTE* passim), *nabalkattānu* "insurgent" (Borger, *Ash* p.47 ii 54), etc. For the meaning "plotter" cf. *da-bi-bu par-ri-ṣu* "talkative = traitor", comm. to Šurpu II 63 (cited *CAD* l.c.), and *CAD* D 11 and 13*b* (*dabābu* mngs. 6 and 9). Before [*d*]*a* there is room for one sign only; the restoration [*ša*] is based on r19f.

The implication of the passage clearly is that the prospective substitute king should be chosen from among Babylonians fomenting rebellious (separatistic?) or criminal plans; the writer probably had in mind Babylonian noblemen or their sons held as hostages in Nineveh (cf. Parpola, *Iraq* 34 [1972] 33f). The suggestion did not necessarily have any political aims (though this is also possible, cf. note on 30 r3-5); it was apparently an established practice to choose the substitute from among criminals (see Intr., p. XXIV). In any case, the ultimate choice fell on a politically significant person: Damqî, the son of the bishop (*šatammu*) of Akkad, whose eventual death badly upset the inhabitants of Akkad. See *LAS* 279 and 280.

186

Bibliography:
(I) Waterman, *RCAE* 453 (cf. IV 253); Pfeiffer, *SLA* 258.
(II) Behrens, *ABB* (1906) 82[1], 99[4], 109; Dhorme, *RHR* 113 (1936) 140f, 148; Meier, *Or*NS 8 (1939) 304; Böhl, *Opera Minora* (1953) 401.

Writer:
Certainly Marduk-šākin-šumi. Note, in addition to the fact that the last element of the name is still extant (Obv. 2), the spelling *šum-mu* (Rev.8, for more usual *šum-MA* or *ŠÚM-mu/ma*) otherwise found (within the present corpus) only in letters of M.; the adverb *ina pu-ú-ti* (Rev.5), standing for *ina pitti* as in 181 r10 and 195 r12 (cf. note on r5); the affinities of Rev.1-2 with 184 r1-3, of Rev.13-18 with 185:23-27, of Rev.9-11 with 173 r5f, etc. *LAS* 187 displays two additional distinctive features of M.: the spelling *te-EP-pa-áš* (Obv.5'.14', cf. note on 166:14), and *iq-bu-u-ni* (Obv.6'.8', cf. under *LAS* 171).

Addressee:
Esarhaddon.

Provenance:
Calah (see note on r9).

Date and discussion:

Du'ūzu/Ābu, eponymy of Šulmu-Bēl-lašme = June/July, 670 BC. This tentative date is based on the following evidence. Firstly, the reference to Assurbanipal (as crown prince, cf. 187 r4) places the letter with *certainty* between 672 and 669, and the fact that Šamaš-šumu-ukīn is not mentioned at all (neither by name nor indirectly) makes it likely that the year in question was either 670 or 669 (see under *LAS* 173). Secondly, the introductory blessings of the present letter (and its companion *LAS* 187) greatly resemble those of *LAS* 188-193, of which 190 certainly dates from early Ulūlu/August, 670; the other letters (*LAS* 188-189 and 191-193) are in themselves undatable, but taking into consideration the fact that virtually all other letters of Marduk-šākin-šumi (*LAS* 139, 149, 164-166, 172-174, 176-185, 197-202, 244) are opened with the "standard blessing" *Nabû u Marduk ana šarri bēlīja likrubū*, it seems very likely that they too are approximately contemporaneous with *LAS* 190. If so, the entire group of letters under consideration should date from between Simānu/May and Kislīmu/December, 670, since letters immediately pre- and postdating these time limits are opened with the "standard blessing" (cf. *LAS* 181-182 and 173-177). In other words, all letters with the "amplified" blessing formula would seem to have been written within the months following Esarhaddon's recovery from his attack to illness of April-May, 670. A final impulse for garnishing the "standard blessing" with wishes of good health etc. may have been given by the illness of the king's mother in early Du'ūzu(?)/June, 670 (cf. commentary on *LAS* 151). Note that such wishes are also included in *LAS* 184 reporting on the recovery of the queen mother, which is opened with a slightly amplified variant of the "standard blessing".

The wording of *LAS* 186 and 187 is so vague that it is impossible to identify the rites mentioned in them with absolute certainty. But the data available make it very likely that rituals of the Maqlû and Šurpu type are in question (see below, notes on Rev.11f and 187:8' and 13'). Such rituals constituted an essential part of the cure of the queen mother in Du'ūzu(?)/June, 670 (see *LAS* 159 and 160); in addition, Maqlû and Šurpu were periodically performed at the end of the month Ābu for prophylactic purposes (see commentary on *LAS* 208). Both Du'ūzu and Ābu fall within the time limits just deduced, and the possibility that the present letter and *LAS* 187 were written in these months is enhanced by the prominent part played in them by the unnamed women mentioned in 186 r8ff and 187'5'ff,12' and r6, who can hardly be anybody but the queen mother herself. Note that Naqia is associated with the rites of Ābu in *LAS* 208, and that the section of *LAS* 184 explicitly concerning the queen mother opens with exactly the same words as the present letter; cf. also 160 r7'f with 187:5'.7', and 159 r6'ff with Rev. 13ff of the present letter.

Notes:

r1-6. The royal order (*ṭēmu*) here mentioned almost certainly concerned the therapy of the queen mother; note that Rev.7ff is an integral continuation of the present passage which in turn clearly coheres with *LAS* 184 r1 ff. The persons said to have verbatim repeated the order probably were the writer's colleagues mentioned in *LAS* 184; cf. *ni-qab-bi* "we shall speak out" (184 r7) with *iq-ṭi-bu-né* (Rev.6).

r5. *ina pu-ú-ti*: here (and in 181 r10 and 195 r12) for *ina pitti* "correspondingly". Cf. the context with *ABL* 308:8 ff, *ki-i ša* MÍAMA MAN [9] *taq-bu-u-ni* [10] *a-na-ku ina pi-te-ma* [r1] *aq-ṭi-bi* [2] SIG_5 *a-dan-niš* "just as the king's mother said, in the same manner I myself said; it is fine indeed."

r8f. Cancel the rendering in Pt.I and render instead: "If she (= the queen mother) comes *to Calah*, let them send Aḫūni here". The writer of the letter was clearly himself sojourning in Calah, note the ventive *liš-pa-ru-né* as opposed to *liš-pu-ru* (185 r10) and *la-áš-pur lil-lik* (173 r6); on the word order (*lišparūni ana Kalḫa*) see on 214 r3' and 247:16'ff; *ana Aḫūni* is a nota accusativi construction.

Aḫūni is not certainly identifiable; cf. Tallqvist, *APN* p.18 f. It is probable, however, that he was a Ninevite court exorcist, judging from the parallel passage in *LAS* 173 r5 f. Note that the name is not attested in any documents from Calah published to date (cf. Deller, *Or*NS 35 [1966] 179 ff; Postgate, *CTN* 2 [1973], index; and the indices in *Iraq* 12 ff).

r11 f. *ba-si pi-šìr-a-ti lu tak-ru-ur*: render "so she can throw the solvents", and cancel the rendering in Pt.I. For *basi* = "so (that)" see Postgate, *Iraq* 35 (1973) 25[9]; *pi-šìr-a-ti* is Pl. of *piširtu* "solution, solvent, *materia magica* for undoing illness (caused by witchcraft etc.)" (cf. *AHw.* 868*b*), not to be confused with the homophonous Pl. of *pišru* "(magical/astrological) solution, interpretation" (cf. *LAS* 35 r1). The term is primarily attested in ušburruda/namerimburruda rituals and incantations, including Maqlû and Šurpu; the relevant ritual involved throwing the *piširtu* (i.e., symbolic representations of the evil combatted) into fire, with the hope that the destruction of the evil would bring relief from disease in its trail. Cf. KI.NE *at-ta-paḫ at-ta-di pi-šir-ta* "I have kindled a brazier and thrown *piširtu* (on it)", Šurpu V/VI 174; KI.NE *al-ta-kan al-ta-rap pi-šìr-ta* "I have set up a brazier and burnt *piširtu*", *JNES* 15 138:110 (namehimburruda incant.); DINGIRMEŠ *ma-la al-su-u liš-ku-nu pi-šìr-ta* "may the gods whom I have invoked provide *piširtu*", ibid. 112; GIG *ma-me-tum* . . . DU_8*-ma* BÚR*-tum liš-šá-kin* "may the illness of (caused by) Curse be dispelled, may *piširtu* be provided", ibid.121; dUTU *pi-šir-ta li-bil-am-ma* "may Šamaš bring *piširtu* to me", Maqlû VII 151; *ana* BÚR*-ti* (var. *pi-še-er-ti*) *kiš-pi šá* NU ZU*-u* "for solution of unidentified charms", *BAM* 317 r4 || *KUB* 4 60:1' || *KUB* 4 99:4' || *LKA* 94 iii 7 (= Biggs, Šaziga p.14), etc. The phrase *piš(i)rāti karāru* "to throw solvents" (the NA equivalent of Babylonian *piširta nadû*, cf. above) is also attested in a NA absolution ritual on behalf of a "sinner" (*bēl arni*) (*ina* IGI dUTU *pi-iš-ra-a-te i-kar-ra-ar* "he throws solvents before Sun", *KAR* 141:8) and in *LAS* 187:12' ([*ina m*]*uḫ-ḫi pi-šìr-a-ti lu tak-ru-ur* "she should throw the solvents upon them", i.e. robes placed 'before' the sun); note also the Hittite equivalent *la-a-u-wa-a*[*r*] *ša-ra-a pé-eš-ši-ia-zi* "er wirft 'Lösung' darauf", *StBoT* 3 10:18', where *la-a-u-wa-ar* likewise means "(magical) solution" (H.G. Güterbock and Harry Hoffner Jr., orally). Throwing the solvents before the sun (upon the garments of the patients) served for magically deferring the case to the judgement of the god Šamaš (see note on 187:11'); the combustion of the materials probably took place immediately after this "court scene". It should be noted that at least in *KAR* it is clearly the patient who performs the throwing ritual; this supports the hypothesis presented above that the woman figuring in the present rites was the patient for whose benefit the ceremonies were performed and thus most likely the queen mother herself. On the nature of Naqia's illness see commentaries on *LAS* 159-160 and 222.

187

Bibliography:

(I) Waterman, *RCAE* 1126 (cf. IV 198).
(II) Oppenheim, *JAOS* 64 (1944) 195.

Writer:
Certainly Marduk-šākin-šumi; see under 186.

Addressee:
Esarhaddon.

Date:
Du'ūzu/Ābu, eponymy of Šulmu-Bēl-lašme = June/July, 670 BC. See under 186.

Discussion:

This letter probably immediately followed *LAS* 186, answering questions left open in the preceding letter. Note that while the writer constantly refers to *oral* questions of the king, the nature of these questions (they could have easily been answered orally) indicates that they had not been made in an eye-to-eye conversation with the writer. Consequently, they had probably been communicated to him orally by the messenger who had taken *LAS* 186 to the king.

Notes:

4'. *te-ra-BA*: comparison with Obv.6 (*le-ru-ub*) shows that the final *-a* is not the ventive ending but a paragogic vowel indicating question, due to the accentuation of the final syllable (*tērúb* > *tērûba*, see note on 208 r8). Consequently, the writer was not expected to enter the palace (in Nineveh) where the king was residing but a palace in Calah (as implied by 186 r8 f).

8'. *"Where do they place the robes?"*: the context implies that the robes belonged to the patient(s) present in the rites; it is hence almost certain that the function of the rites here referred to was a purificatory one, and that the garments in question had been taken off in order to symbolically release the patients from their previous contaminated state. Such purificatory stripping rituals (performed to the accompaniment of the incantation *ašḫuṭ ašḫuṭ* "I have taken off, I have taken off") are best known from anti-witchcraft magic (ušburruda, Maqlû); for references see W.G. Lambert, *AfO* 18 (1957/58) 288 and 297 f.

11'. *"Before the sun"*: this expression can mean either "in front of a cultic representation of the sun god" (see Caplice, *Or*NS 36 [1967] 7, on namburbi passages such as "you leave the presence of the sun and go off to the river") or "*sub divo*" (cf. Oppenheim, *JAOS* 61 [1941] 253[1], on passages describing oath-taking "before the sun", especially Strassmeier, *Nbn.*954:10f, *ki-i* UD *20.*KÁM *pe-tu-ú i-te-em-me ja-a-nu-ú* UD *20.*KÁM *šá* ITUGUD *i-te-em-me* "if the 20th [of Nisannu] is cloudless, he may take the oath, if not, he takes the oath on the 20th of Ajāru"). Whichever the case, the role of the sun in magical rituals (namburbi, ušburrudas, namerimburrudas, or whatever) was that of the Supreme Judge, who doomed the wicked and let free the innocent, and whom the exorcists approached to save their patients from the evil forces harassing them; cf. e.g. *KAR* 80:12 ("O Sun, . . . judge of the Igigi"; ušburruda), *RA* 50 p.35 ("O Sun, judge of Heaven and Earth"; namburbi), *PBS* 1/1 15:3 and dupls. ("O Sun, supreme judge of Heaven and Earth"; *bīt rimki*), *BAM* 140:18' ("O Sun, king of Heaven and Earth, you are the judge of god and man alike"; ušburruda), etc. The importance of this symbolic court of justice cannot be overstated; it unquestionably formed the backbone of the whole ritual.

13'. MÍ*qa-di-su* (= *qadištu*, lit. "sacred woman"; = Bibl. *qᵉdēšāh*), a hierodule serving in fertility rites and as a wet nurse, and very probably also practicing (cultic) prostitution,[321] is not the kind of person one would

[321] Cf. Renger, *ZA* 58 (1967) 179 ff and (for *qᵉdēšāh*) Driver, *Iraq* 6 (1939) 68[4]. That the *qadištu* practiced prostitution is clear from her association with *ḫarimtu* "whore" in the Middle Assyrian Laws (*KAV* 1 v 61ff, according to which unmarried *qadištu* were not permitted to veil themselves like respectable women but had to go unveiled like whores and slave-girls) and *Ana ittišu* Tablet VII iii 7ff || ii 23 ff (*MSL* 1 p.96 ff); not also *SBH* p.106:51ff (Ištar calling herself a whore/*ḫarimtu*) and *LKA* 37:6, *CT* 15 18:1f, and similar passages (Ištar calling herself *qadištu*). The primary difference between the terms *ḫarimtu* and *qadištu* seems to have been simply that women of the former class operated in brothels (*aštammu*) whereas the latter were attached to temples. For a fertility ritual involving the participation of several hierodules see *KAR* 154. The role of the *qadištus* as wet nurses is easily explicable by their frequent exposure to pregnancies; cf. Renger, art.cit. p.184.

expect to officiate in exorcistic rituals, but the fact that she *is* found in that function here actually strongly supports the hypothesis presented above (under commentary to *LAS* 186) that the rites alluded to in *LAS* 186-187 were anti-witchcraft in character. Disregarding an Assyrian ritual designed to undo lightheartedly sworn oath (VAT 10568a = Ebeling, *PKTA* pl.17 || *KAR* 134 || *PKTA* pl.18), where a ^{MÍ}*qa-diš-tu* (*PKTA* 17 r.IV 5) appears to be closely cooperating with an exorcist (^{LÚ}MAŠ.MAŠ, r.IV 7) in a context not recalling the present letter, and a passage in Šurpu (Tablet VIII 69)[322], the only references to hierodules in exorcistic texts are to be found in the composition Maqlû, and there the *qadištu*, impersonating both the witch and the goddess Ištar, figures prominently. Cf. Meier, *Maqlû* II 40 ff (|| *KAR* 226 ii 4 ff || *STT* 88 i 27'ff): ÉN ^{MÍ}UŠ$_{12}$.ZU *nir-ta-ni-tum . . .* ^{42} *a-ši-ip-tum eš-še-pu-ti* ^{43} ^{MÍ}MUŠ.LAH$_4$*-tum a-gu-gi-il-tum* ^{44} ^{MÍ}NU.GIG ^{MÍ}SAL+ME ^{45} ^{d}*15-i-tum kul-ma-ši-tum* ^{46} *ba-a-a-ar-tum šá mu-ši* "Incantation: O murderous witch . . . , female exorcist, ecstatic, snake charmer, sorceress, *qadištu*, nun, Ištar-woman, *kulmašītu*, who hunts by night . . . "; *KAR* 240:7 (|| *Maqlû* II 31'ff), *kiš-pi šá* ^{MÍ}*qa-diš-ti* "the sorceries of the *qadištu*"; and note especially three passages in Tablets V (51 ff) and VI (26ff and 37ff), where hierodules are invoked to bring their palm fibre mats (*pitiltu*) and small fir cones (*terinnat ašūhi*) to dispell evil sorceries (ÉN *at-ti man-nu* ^{MÍ}UŠ$_{12}$.ZU *šá* DÙ.DÙ-*šá 3* ITU^{MEŠ} *10* UD-*me* ½ UD-*me* ^{52} *ana-ku a-na-áš-šá-kim-ma* ^{ŠIM}GÚR.GÚR *ta-nat* KUR-*i* . . . ^{54} ŠU.SAR ŠU.SAR *šá* ^{MÍ}NU.GIG^{MEŠ} GIŠŠE.Ù.SUH$_5$ MIN *šá še-am ma-la-ti* ^{55} *an-nu-ú šá* ^{LÚ}UŠ$_{12}$.ZU-MU *u* ^{MÍ}UŠ$_{12}$.ZU-MU *he-pa-a ri-kiš-šú-un* ^{56} *ter-ra kiš-pu-šá ana me-he-e* "Incantation: whoever you are, witch, you who have practiced witchcraft against me for 3 months and ten and a half days. I lift up against you terebinth, . . . of the mountain, . . . the palm fiber mat, the palm fiber mat of the hierodules, the fir cone of ditto which is full of seeds: break this bond of my sorcerer and my sorceress, turn her sorceries into storm . . . !", *Maqlû* V 51-56; ÉN ^{ŠIM}GÚR.GÚR-*ma* ^{ŠIM}GÚR.GÚR ^{38} ^{ŠIM}GÚR.GÚR *ina* KUR^{MEŠ} KÙ^{MEŠ} *qud-du-šu-ti* ^{39} TUR^{MEŠ} *tir-hi šá e-né-ti* ^{40} TUR^{MEŠ} GIŠŠE.Ù.SUH$_5$^{MEŠ} *šá qa-aš-da-a-ti* ^{41} *al-ka-nim-ma šá* ^{LÚ}UŠ$_{12}$.ZU-MU *u* ^{MÍ}UŠ$_{12}$.ZU-MU ^{42} *dan-nu* GAZ-*a* KEŠDA-*sa* ^{43} *ù mim+mu ma-la te-pu-šá nu-tir a-na* IM "Incantation: Terebith, terebinth, terebinth (grown) in pure, holy mountains! Small pots of *entu*-priestesses! Small fir cones of hierodules! Come, break the strong bond of my sorcerer and sorceress, and we shall turn everything she has done into wind!", ibid. VI 37-41; similarly VI 26-36). While the ritual tablet of Maqlû does not specify that a hierodule *had* to participate in the rites (cf. Tablet IX 80 f. and 101 f., corresponding to Tablets V 51ff and VI 26ff, respectively), it seems, especially on the basis of the passage quoted last, that her presence may well have been desirable: the hierodule, impersonating the witch, provided a tangible object for exorcistic activity, whereas her accessories, the palm fibre mat and fir cone, probably symbolized the "bonds" of the sorcerers and were to be broken or unraveled in the course of the ceremonies (cf. *Šurpu* V 57.83.90).

r3. *ú-la*: probably for *ulâ* "or" (see note on 15:7); hardly = *ulla* (1 Sg. Prs. of *'lī* D).

L.E. Read [*ina* IGI ^{d}]UTU! *ni-šak-kan*, and cf. Obv.11.

188

Bibliography:
(I) Waterman, *RCAE* 970 (cf. IV 193, 265); Pfeiffer, *SLA* 267.

Writer:
Marduk-šākin-šumi (see commentary to *LAS* 186).

Date:
Approximately Ābu/August, 670 BC. See under *LAS* 186.

Addressee:
Esarhaddon.

---

[322] KI *ma-mit* DUMU.MÍ DINGIR^{MEŠ} ^{d}*kù-bi šá* NIN.DINGIR.RA SAL+ME ^{MÍ}NU.GIG *u kul-ma-ši-tu* MIN MIN MIN "Together with the oath of the daughters of the god, the premature child of an *entu*-priestess, a nun, a hierodule or a *kulmašītu*, ditto ditto ditto (= may your sin, your error, your oath . . . be released for you, be absolved for you)!"

Discussion:

As shown by line 6 of Reverse (see relevant note), the rites reported in this letter pertained to the "renewal" (*tēdištu*) and consecration (*mīs pî*) of statues, probably divine, and considering the date of the letter, it appears very likely that the statues in question actually belonged to the Babylonian gods whose "renewal" and consecration Esarhaddon describes in one of his late inscriptions (AsBb A), composed after the conquest of Egypt, i.e. in the latter part of 671 or later: ^{d}DINGIR-MAR.TU *mu-ul-lil* AN-*e u* KI-*tim mu-ub-bi-ib É-sag-gíl a-šib É-nam-tag-ga-du*$_8$*-a ud-diš* ^{d}*Ab-šú-šú* ^{d}*Ab-ta-gi*$_4$*-gi*$_4$ [41] *a-ši-ba É-giš-ḫur-an-ki-a* É ^{d}GAŠAN-NINA^{KI} *ù* DINGIR^{MEŠ} ^{d}IŠDAR^{MEŠ} *ma-la Aš+šur u* ^{d}AMAR+UD *iq-bu-u ud-diš-ma a-na áš-ri-šú-nu ú-tir* "I renewed the god Il-Amurru, who purifies Heaven and Earth, cleanses Esangil, and resides in Enamtaggadua; I renewed and returned to their places Abšušu and Abtagigi, who reside in Egišḫurankia, the temple of Bēlet-Ninâ, as well as all the gods and goddesses whom Aššur and Marduk had told (me to renew)", Borger *Ash* p.84:40 ff; for the approximate date of the inscription, cf. ibid., p.80:28 f. Note that the lines immediately following the passage just quoted refer to the returnal of the gods of Dēr, Uruk and Sippar-Arūru to their cities, all measures taken at approximately the same time, i.e. at the turn of the years 671/670 (see under *LAS* 190, 277 and 293).

Notes:

9'. ^{LÚ}*pi-qit-ta-a-ti gab-bu*: referring to sucklings identified as "the charge of the Queen of Cults" and "the charge of the Rear Palace", possibly also to "the charge of the house of Urad-Daguna", all under medical care in 670, see commentary on *LAS* 123.

r2. *tak-pir-tu (... us-se-tiq)*: cf. note on 167 r8. The purification rituals referred to here may have been those which had to be performed before the actual rites of renewal and consecration (see note on r6) took place; these rites are described in detail in *BBR* 31-37. On the other hand, since the present rites were performed in the "wing" of the eunuchs, and not in the house where the statues were subsequently renewed, it is also possible that the purification had nothing to do with the statues but was occasioned by the incident reported in *LAS* 342 (q.v.). Note, however, that if the man mentioned in line 5 was a eunuch, as seems likely, his house may well have situated in the "wing" of the eunuchs, which would make connection with the renewal ceremonies possible.

r3. *É-ŠU*^{2} *"wing"*: sic rather that "storehouse" (Pt.I), cf. van Driel, *CA* p.38 [but note also *ABL* 114:20, where É-ŠU^2 definitely means "storehouse"].

r5. ^{I}*Bal-ṭa-aju*: possibly identical with ^{I}*Bal-ṭa-aju* ^{LÚ}GAL-ŠE *ki-si-[te]* (*NARGD* 9:11.28.52 [657 BC]), a prominent eunuch of Assurbanipal (and Esarhaddon; cf. ibid., Obv.14). Also mentioned (in fragmentary context) in *ABL* 695 r5.

r6. *ú-ta-aš-ši-iš*: Pf. of **uššušu* "to renew", a back-formation from *eššiš* "anew" replacing older *uddušu*; cf. *IR* 68,1 ii 1 "I rebuilt (*uš-ši-iš-ma ēpuš*) a temple tower for Sin" with *VAB* 4 226 iii 4, "I rebuilt (*e-eš-ši-iš ēpuš*) Ebabbar together with its temple tower", both inscriptions of Nabunaid; cf. also *la-ab-ru ú-šiš ma-aq-tu ak-šír*, Borger *Ash* p.94 r6, paralleling *an-ḫu-sa ud-diš an-ša ak-ta-šir*, AOB 1 86 r3, etc. One would, of course, a priori expect a form like *ú-ta-ad-di-iš* (from *uddušu*), but as a matter of fact, this form is not supported by contemporary evidence (there are no certain attestations of *'dš* D in Neo-Assyrian). On the other hand, the context makes it certain that the D-stem of *ašāšu* "to cause distress" (*AHw* 79*b*, *CAD* A/2 424) cannot be in question.

For the ritual of renewing damaged divine statues (*ilu ša niqittu iršû*), see Ebeling, *TuL* p. 108 ff (No.27); note that the text repeatedly stresses that the place of the rites had to be carefully secluded from the outside world by means of curtains (*ina pān igāri šiddu tašaddad*, Obv.31; cf. Rev.7.9.16.17.18 and the diagrams accompanying the text), which would seem to correspond to Rev.4 (*pa-rik-tú par-kàt*) of the present letter (see note on 246 r12); note also the importance attached to reed altars (GI.DU$_8$) in the ritual, and cf. present letter, r9. For the *mīs pî* (KA.LUH.Ù.DA) ritual, see S. Smith, "The Babylonian ritual for the consecration and induction of a divine statue", *JRAS* 1925, 37-60 (= Ebeling, *TuL* p.100 ff) and Zimmern, *BBR* No.31-40, and cf. Oppenheim, *Anc.Mes.*, 185f.

r7. *(KA.LUḪ.Ù.DA) uq-ṭar-ri-ib*: the normal expression for "performing the mouth-washing ritual" was *KA.LUH.Ù.DA epēšu* (e.g., *BBR* 31-37:26, *TuL* p.103:12, and passim in these texts) but the present idiom is also attested in *BBR* 48:10 (KA.TUḪ.Ù.DA *tu-ṭaḫ-ḫa-šu-nu-ti, qarrubu* replacing *ṭaḫḫû* in Neo-Assyrian).

r7. *ṣa-lam* MU[L . . .] *ú-ta-aṣ-ṣir*: possibly to be connected with a section of the ***mīs pî*** ritual prescribing the setting up of several offering arrangements (*riksu*) to various stars (Jupiter, Venus, Moon, Saturn, Mercury, Sirius, Mars, Libra, Sun, Triangulum, Arcturus, etc; *TuL* p.105). It remains unclear, though, why the exorcist should have drawn a *picture* of these stars, which is not prescribed in the ritual tablet. Cf. the following note.

r8. *"I seated a dog (or dog[s]) upon it"*: certainly a reference to prophylactic dogs (made of clay) intended to protect the statues. Cf. *LKU* 33 r18 ff (2nd tablet of the series *Lamaštu*, restorations from duplicates): DÙ.DÙ.BI DUB SAR-*ar* UD.SAR AŠ.M[E. . . . . . .] [19] *ina muḫ-ḫi te-eṣ-ṣir ina* SAG [. . . . .] [20] *a!-ru-uh* ZI-*šú ú-ṣur* MU-*šú ṭu-*[. . . . . . .] [21] *2* UR.KU^{MEŠ} *šá* KÁ *ka-mi-i* [22] *ur-ru-uḫ* ZI-*šú a-na* EN.NUN [*la te-eg*]-*gi* [23] *2* UR.KU[^{MEŠ} *sa* KÁ É-*a-ni*] [24] *e tam-lik e-pu-uš* K[A-*ka si-kip lem-na*] [25] *2* UR.KU[^{MEŠ} *šá* KÁ É ^{GIŠ}NÁ] [26] ^{d}*30-re-'i-i* UR.KU *šá ap-ti* [*kalbī annūti . . . tu-še-eš*]-*ši-ib* "Its ritual: write a tablet, draw a crescent of the moon and a solar disc upon it, and [place it] at the head of [. . . .]. 'Destroy-his-life!' 'Guard-his-name!' [. . .] two dogs for the outer door. 'Destroy-his-life!' '[Do-not-neglect]-the-guard!' – two dogs for [the inner door]. 'Don't-hesitate! Open-your-mouth!' [Cast-down-the-evil!]' – two dogs [for the door of the bedroom]. Sin-rē'ī – the dog for the window. [Se]at [these dogs . . .]". A similar passage in *KAR* 298 (Rev.17-22; see Gurney, *AAA* 22 [1935] 72 f.) enumerates ten dogs by name, partly identical with those mentioned above; these were to be buried at the outer door, to keep off "evil foot". Many specimens of such terra-cotta dogs, inscribed with their names, and often coloured (white, red, black, green, or spotted), have been found in several Mesopotamian cities (Calah, Kish, Nineveh, Sippar); see Gurney, art. cit., pp. 41 and 72f; Scheil, *SFS* p.90 ff; Mallowan, *Nimrud* II p.431 and (photo) p. 433.

189

Bibliography:

Previously unpublished. Copy *CT* 53 pl.211, no.951.

Writer:

Marduk-šākin-sumi; assignation based on the affinities of the blessing formula with those of *LAS* 186-191. Cf. commentary on *LAS* 186.

Date:

Probably approximately Ulūlu/August, 670 BC. See under *LAS* 186.

Discussion:

The reference to Nergal suggests that this letter, too, dealt with cultic matters, perhaps of the same nature as in *LAS* 188 (Nergal is mentioned in *ABL* 474+659 among gods to be returned to Babylonia).

190

Bibliography:

(I) Waterman, *RCAE* 956.

Writer:

Certainly Marduk-šākin-šumi, cf. the blessing formula with 191:6-13; the same formula does not recur elsewhere.

Addressee:

Esarhaddon.

Date:

Ca. Ulūlu 1, eponymy of Šulmu-Bēl-lašme = August 7, 670 BC. This date is based on the following considerations. First, the writer states (Obv.17f) that the king had just decided to intercalate a second Ulūlu to bring the calendar up to date. Since the intercalation of the month was going to affect the celebration of a festival in Babylon (Rev. 3ff) and Dēr (Rev.8f), the king in question must be Esarhaddon.[323] The affinities of the long blessing formula with those of *LAS* 186-189 and 191-193 indicate further that the letter must be placed in one of the four last years of Esarhaddon (672-669 BC), since both *LAS* 186 and 187 refer to Assurbanipal in terms implying that the prince had already been officially recognized as the crown prince of Assyria (cf. note on 173:17 and, for a discussion of the blessing formulae of *LAS* 186-193, commentary on 186). On these premises, the leap year in question can now be identified with certainty. It is known from *ADD* 53 (= *AR* 258) that year 673 was a leap year and, in particular, one containing an intercalary Addāru. The intercalation under consideration must consequently have occurred either in 671 or 670. No texts written in the intercalary month concerned and dated by eponym, which would directly show which one of the two years is in question, have so far turned up[324], but there is iron-clad indirect evidence proving that the year was certainly 670. Firstly, *LAS* 289, written in Simānu/June, 669 BC, and reporting on a recently (Simānu 6) observed heliacal rising of Jupiter, states that the planet had in the previous year risen on Ajāru 23. Since the time separating two successive heliacal risings of Jupiter always is a minimum of 13 months, it follows that 670 must have been a leap year.[325] Correspondingly, *LAS* 279 and *ABL* 137, both certainly addressed to Esarhaddon (see under *LAS* 279), report a total lunar eclipse occurred in the month Kanūnu. A suitable identification is obtained only if 670 is taken as a leap year; if 671 had been intercalary, no lunar eclipses would have occurred in Kanūnu in Esarhaddon's reign.

Rev.3 ff implies that the present letter was written before the decision to intercalate had been communicated to Babylon. According to *LAS* 287, the relevant royal order arrived in Babylon on the night of Ulūlu 6. Assuming that the journey from Nineveh to Babylon usually took about 5 days (see commentary on *LAS* 27) and in any case a minimum of 2 days, it can be concluded that the latest possible date of the letter is Ulūlu 3. Possibly it was written a couple of days earlier, perhaps at the end of the preceding month (Ābu). Note that Obv.18 reads "We shall intercalate Ulūlu", not "this month", and that the matter of intercalation was taken up in *LAS* 325 at the end of Šabāṭu, i.e. in the month preceding the proposed intercalary month. By way of a compromise, the date Ulūlu 1 may, however, be accepted as the most probable date of the letter.

Discussion:

The Tašrītu festival of Babylon referred to in the letter has remained very imperfectly known up to the present date. According to private communication by W.G. Lambert, there exists in the collections of the British Museum a large tablet doubtless forming part of the "Festkalender" of Babylon (see Unger, *Babylon* p.267ff and Thureau-Dangin, *RAcc.* p.127ff), which gives in several columns detailed instructions about the cultic ceremonies performed in Babylon both in Tašrītu and the immediately preceding and following months. This tablet, which unfortunately remains unpublished, fixes the dressing ritual of Bēl, also mentioned in the present letter, on the 7th of Tašrītu (cf. ^{TÚG}*lu-bar-ri šá* UD 7 *šá* ^{ITU}DU$_6$ ^{d}EN *il-lab-šu*, Col. ii 6f) and the subsequent opening of the gate on the 8th (UD 8.KAM *ša* ^{ITU}DU$_6$ KI.MIN [= *ina še-rim* KÁ *ina* IGI ^{d}EN BAD-*te*], ibid. 10f). The text then goes on to state that a great meal was offered to Bēl following the opening of the gate, and a couple of lines later tells that sections from *Enūma Eliš* were recited to Bēl by a chanter (*nāru*) on the same day. The general outline of the ceremonies thus indeed resembled those of the New Year's festival of Nisannu (see *RAcc.*, loc.cit.); and as pointed out in Rev.6, even the procession of Bēl to the *akītu* house took place exactly on the same day (the 8th) as in Nisannu.

---

323 The first adjustment of the calendar after Esarhaddon's death happened in different years in Assyria (668/7, intercalary Addāru) and Babylonia (667/666, intercalary Ulūlu); see App.2C. This implies that the king of Assyria did not have any influence on the praxis of intercalation in Babylonia at that time.

324 BM 98975 = Ki 1904–10–9,4, an oracle query concerning the loyalty of an official, and certainly dating from the last years of Esarhaddon, mentions an intercalary Ulūlu and thus proves that the last leap year in Esarhaddon's year contained a second Ulūlu. The text is unfortunately not dated by *limmu* (courtesy J.Aro).

325 Cf. App. C4 and Schaumberger, *ZA* 47 (1941/2) 129.

Further detailed documentation relating to Tašrītu ceremonies in Babylon does not seem to be extant. But it is worth noting that the festival of the gods of Uruk in Tašrītu (*RAcc.* p.89 ff) also involved a dressing ceremony and a procession of gods to the *akītu*; cf. the remarks of Thureau-Dangin, op.cit. p.86f. A festival on the 8th of Tašrītu is also mentioned in *STT* 44:9', and a passage in *ABL* 951 (r2) may possibly be taken as an indirect reference to the ceremonies under consideration (*2-šú ina* ŠÀ MU.AN.NA *qab-li šá* ^{d}ŠÚ *ip-pa-ṭa-ra* "twice a year, the loins of Marduk are ungirded . . .").

The Tašrītu ceremonies must not be confused with the similar ones of *Ulūlu* which are referred to in two letters of Mār-Ištar (*LAS* 285 A 6'f and 287). While these also involved a dressing of Bēl and a gate-opening ceremony, the dates of these rituals differed from those of the Tašrītu festival (cf. *ABL* 496:8 ff, UD 3.KÁM *šá* ^{ITU}KIN ^{9} ^{TÚG}*lu-bu-uš-ti šá* ^{d}EN ^{10} UD 4.KÁM *pi-it* KÁ GAL-*ú šu-ú* "the dressing of Bēl takes place on the 3rd of Ulūlu, the great Opening-of-Gate on the 4th"; the same dates in *LAS* 285 and 287), and it cannot thus be doubted that the ceremonies concerned had a fully independent and permanent status in the Babylonian cultic year, different from that of the Tašrītu festival. However, this statement needs the qualification that both festivals probably *together* formed an integral whole, the former leading directly to the latter (just as Old Year abruptly changes to New) so that it was highly desirable to celebrate them in close succession, without an intervening month. This is the reason why it was so important to announce the intercalations of extra Ulūlus in proper time to the clergy in charge of the ceremonies. The same of course also applied to the New Year's festival of Nisannu (cf. note on 287: 9ff). Note that Tašrītu (lit. "Beginning") was, as in the Jewish calendar, considered New Year's month (cf. e.g. *RMA* 16:5, ^{ITU}ŠE ^{ITU}KIN SAG MU.AN.NA ^{6} *ki-i ša* ^{ITU}BÁR ^{ITU}DU$_{6}$ "(in this year) Addāru and Ulūlu are months beginning the year, just like (normally) Nisannu and Tašrītu"), certainly because the sun then crossed the celestial equator to begin its 6-month stay in the Abyss.[326]

Notes:

15. *da-re-e*: Inf. of *darû* "to intercalate", to be added (along with *nid-ri* Obv.18; *li-dir-i-u*, 285 A 4'; *šá-at-ti di-ri*, ibid.3') to the relatively few attestations of this verb listed in *CAD* (D 109*b*) and *AHw.* (167). Cf. also note on 10+ r4'.

17f. The king's decision to intercalate was possibly (at least partially) influenced by *ABL* 971, a letter referring to a "Festival of Babylon" and probably addressed to Esarhaddon; cf. Obv.16 ff: [DUMU]^{MEŠ} *ba-né-e ša* KÁ.DINGIR^{KI} ^{9} [DUMU]^{MEŠ} *ba-né-e ša* BÁR.SIPA^{KI} ^{10} [*a-n*]*a šul-me ša* LUGAL EN-*ja* ^{11} *i-tal-ku-ú-ni* ^{12} *ma-a i-si-nu šá* KÁ.DINGIR^{KI} ^{13} *šu-ú* ^{r1} *ma-a a-ke-e ni-id-ru-ur né-ti-iq* ^{2} *ma-a né-ru-ub* ^{UDU}SISKUR^{MEŠ} ^{3} *ina* IGI ^{d}EN *né-pu-uš* "Noblemen from Babylon and Borsippa have come to pay homage to the king, my lord. They say: 'The festival of Babylon is at hand; how do we intercalate? We should go and enter (Babylon), to make sacrifices before Bēl.' What does the king, my lord, say?" Cf. also *LAS* 285 A 4'f; for the factors affecting the decision as to whether a second Ulūlu or Addāru had to be intercalated, see note on 38 r17 ff.

19. Cf. *a-wa-tum ši-i ku-na-at*, Laessøe, *Det første assyriske imperium* (1966), Fig.22:4'. For the paragogic *-a* in *ku-un-na-TA*, see note on 18 r8.

20 r1. "May the king live forever (*lū dāri*) because of it": clearly a pun based on the homophony of *darû* "to intercalate" and *dārû* "everlasting".[327] A similar play with words occurs in *CT* 54 22 (cf. Dietrich *AOAT* 7 158f), Rev.11: LUGAL *be-lí-a lu-ú da-a-ru* ^{I}LUGAL-*lu-da-ru* ^{LÚ}*Mi-ṣir-a-a* "May the king my lord live forever! Šarru-lū-dāru, the Egyptian . . ." Cf. also *CT* 53 10 r13, *a-na-ga-ra* ^{LÚ}NAGAR^{MEŠ}-*ja* "Do I claim (half a penny for my services)? My carpenters (have run away). . ." The last sign of *da-a-IR* is certainly simply a badly written RI.

r3. The date here has to be restored as [UD 7.K]ÁM* on the basis of the ritual cited above, sub Discussion.

---

[326] Cf. En.el. V 125 ff, "When you rise from the Abyss to the assembly / let its sacred area be your nocturnal abode, to receive your assembly; / when you descend from the Heavens to the assembly / let its sacred area be your nocturnal abode, to receive your assembly; / let me call it Babylon, the house of the great gods."

[327] The real purpose of the exclamation should not be concealed behind the pun; it was clearly intended as a polite hint that the king's decision involved certain practical difficulties.

r5. Read (with Harper) UD *8*!.KÁM*, and see Discussion.

r6f. *"Bēl sets out"*: note that even though the statue of Marduk carried away by Sennacherib was still in "exile" in Assur (cf. sub *LAS* 29), Bēl could still be dressed and carried in procession in Babylon. This simply implies that a spurious statue was used in the ceremonies to keep the cult of the god alive,[328] and does not shatter the dating of the letter to Esarhaddon's reign, which rests on sound evidence. Cf. also *LAS* 287.

r8f. Note that according to *LAS* 277 r11 ff, the temple of Dēr was still under construction in Tašrītu/September, 671 BC, and that according to Esarhaddon's inscriptions (Borger, *Ash* p.84), the gods of the city (Ištarān, Šarrat-Dēri, Niraḫ, Bēlet-balāṭi, Kurunītu, Sakkut of Bubê and Mār-bīti) had been carried off to Assyria by Sennacherib. The present passage implies that the temple (whose construction was urged in *LAS* 277) had been completed and the gods returned to it by fall 670 BC.

r11 f. *"Let the king decide and send"*: certainly implying that an announcement of the intercalation should be sent to Babylon. Cf. *LAS* 287 and pertinent commentary.

r12. *Marduk-šarru-uṣur*: also known from *ADD* 857 ii 48, where called "bodyguard of the crown prince" (IdMES-MAN-PAP LÚ: DUMU.MAN) and probably from *ADD* 444 (660 BC), where mentioned together with Marduk-šākin-šumi and entitled "rein-holder" (IdAMAR+UD-MAN-PAP LÚDIB-KUŠPAMEŠ).

191

Bibliography:
(I) Waterman, *RCAE* 662 (cf. IV 186).

Date:
Ābu/Ulūlu, eponymy of Šulmu-Bēl-lašme = July/August, 670 BC. See under *LAS* 190; the blessing formula of the present letter parallels so closely that of 190 that the time difference between the two letters cannot have been more than a couple of days.

Addressee:
Esarhaddon.

Notes:

8. *ba-lá-ṭu*: the syllabic value LÁ occurs otherwise very rarely in Neo-Assyrian texts (the only occurrence noticed by the present writer is *Ah-lá-mu-ú*, *AGS* 108:10) but more frequently in magical and exorcistic literature (e.g., *Šurpu* VII 78 and VIII 88; *LKA* 43 r8; *KAR* 64:27, 73:30, 221:10 and 250:15). This little detail indicates that the present letter was written by a professional exorcist and therefore most probably by Marduk-šākin-šumi himself.

r9. *Adad* and *Šala*: gods worshiped in Assyria primarily in Kurba'il and Urakka (cf. *PKTA* 11 r13 ff, etc.). All the restorations on the reverse are uncertain and so the nature and purpose of the ritual referred to here necessarily remains obscure. Probably, however, a cultic ritual was in question; notice that it was scheduled to be repeated in Šabāṭu (ITUZÍZ-*ma*, r12'; the particle -*ma* indicates repetition and has to be rendered "again"), half a year after the dispatchment of the letter.

192

Bibliography:
(I) Waterman, *RCAE* 1075.

[328] The fact that M. considered it necessary to remind the king of the festival suggests that the statue and with it the cult of Marduk had been (re)introduced fairly recently.

Writer:
Identified as Marduk-šākin-šumi on the basis of the similarity of the blessing formula to those of *LAS* 189-191 (cf. especially 189); the formula does not recur elsewhere.

Date:
Du'ūzu/Ābu, eponymy of Šulmu-Bēl-lašme = June/July, 670 BC. See under *LAS* 189.

Addressee:
Esarhaddon.

Notes:

r5'. *pa-as-su-ra-a-[te] ša SIG₅ u ḫu-[ud lìb-bi]*: cf. 193:6'; 194 r4; Streck, *Asb* p.86 X 68, *ka-a-a-an pu-us-su-rat ḫa-de-e* [69] *ša ka-šad* LÚKÚR MEŠ*-ja ú-pa-sa-ru-in-ni* "(while in the Succession Palace, gods) constantly sent me happy news of victories over my enemies"; LÚA.KIN *pu-su-rat ḫa-de-e* [8] *ša a-tam-ra iq-ba-a ja-a-ši* "I met a messenger bringing good news, who spoke to me", Piepkorn, *AS* 5 p.12:7f; *áš-šu e-peš* LUGAL*-ti-ja pu-su-rat ḫa-[de-e] iš-tap-pa-ru* [UGU*-ja*] "(the kings of the Upper and Lower Sea) kept sending me good news because of my kingship", Streck, *Asb* p.260 ii 15; *pu-us-rat [du-un-q]i* ḪÚL*-e* "good and happy news", *PRT* 22:11 (time of Esarhaddon); note also *ABL* 943 (time of Assurbanipal) and *ABL* 153 (time of Sargon). In all the passages quoted above, excepting perhaps *ABL* 153, the content of the "happy news" is clearly political; unfortunately it is impossible to ascertain whether this is the case in the present letter, too. Esarhaddon does not seem to have experienced any particular political or military triumphs in mid-670.

193

Bibliography:
Previously unpublished.

Copy:
CT 53 pl.189 no.870.

Date:
Probably June/July, 670 BC. Cf. under *LAS* 192.

Notes:

8'. Cf. note on 258:9-11.

194

Bibliography:
(I) Waterman, *RCAE* 1184.

Discussion:

Whether this fragment was written by Marduk-šākin-šumi is very doubtful; the resemblance of Rev.4-7 to 192 r5'ff etc. may be quite fortuitous. Rev.8 recalls 299 r7.

195

Bibliography:
(I) Waterman, *RCAE* 378 (cf. IV 249); Pfeiffer, *SLA* 263.
(II) Behrens, *ABB* (1906) 98f; Dhorme, *RHR* 113 (1936) 146f; Deller, *Or*NS 31 (1962) 233.

Addressee:
Esarhaddon.

Date and discussion:

Ca. Addāru 9, eponymy of Atar-ili = February 11, 672 BC. This date is based on the hypothesis that the rites referred to in the letter are to be identified with those performed after the burial of Esarhaddon's queen, who died, according to the Babylonian Chronicle (Grayson, *TCS* 5 pp.85:22 and 127:23), on Addāru 5/6 of Esarhaddon's 8th year. In support of this hypothesis notice the following facts. 1) The term *šuruptu* "funeral burning" occurring in Obv.13 (see note) shows that rites connected with a burial certainly are in question. The available evidence suggests that the funeral burning was performed subsequent to the burial, which in turn took place a few days after the death (see commentary to *LAS* 4). Thus, if the death in question occurred on the 5th or 6th, the burial (preceded by a public display of the dead) would have taken place approximately on the 9th or 10th, and the funeral burning on the 10th or 11th, after which the persons who had participated in the ceremonies had to be kept in isolation for a while and thereafter purified magically. This reconstruction would agree with the date (14th day) mentioned in Rev.6, on which the women kept in custody while the letter was written were scheduled to go to (take a bath in) the river (cf. note on 205:11). 2) In so far as it is known, the *šuruptu* burning was performed only in connection with *royal* burials (including those of the substitute kings). The above reconstruction agrees with the date of the death of the said queen but not with that of Esarhaddon (who died on the 10th [of Arahsamna] on his way to Egypt); Assurbanipal and substitute kings are out of consideration for reasons stated in commentary to *LAS* 4. That a royal burial is in question is also made clear by the fact that the king was kept informed of the proceedings; note also Obv.14 possibly implying that the rites were performed in Assur (cf. note), the city where the members of Assyrian royal families were traditionally buried. 3) The letter has clear affinities with the ritual K 164 edited and discussed at length by von Soden, *ZA* 45 (1939) 42 ff, and Dhorme, *RA* 38 (1941) 57 ff. Against von Soden, this ritual (written in Neo-Assyrian on an *egirtu*-shaped tablet lacking colophon, and hence certainly composed for a unique occasion) is not to be regarded as a substitution ritual ("Ersatzopferritual") designed for a diseased crown prince, but, with Dhorme, as a funerary ritual for a member of the royal family, very probably the queen. The text consists of two sections, the first (lines 1-15) concerning the rites performed on the day of the display of the dead (*taklimtu*), the latter those performed on the day the funeral burning (*šuruptu*) took place. In both rituals women (including a daughter and daughter-in-law, scil. of the dead person) play a dominant role. The deceased in referred to as "she" in line 33 (MU-*šá i-za-ku-ru i-šá-tu um-mu-du* "they (masc. subject) pronounce her name and set fire to the utensils (*unūtu*)") and more explicitly as "queen" in 40-41:

> ^{MÍ}É.GAL^{MEŠ} *i-ra-ga-m[a ma-a] al-ka-ni* / ^{MÍ}É.GAL DUMU.MÍ *ki-na-*[.]x [*qa*]*b-bi-ra* "the queens cry out: 'Come on, bury (fem. subject) the queen, the daughter of *righ*[*teousness*]!'"[329]

The identity of the deceased also becomes apparent from the last lines of the text (48-51):

> *ki-ma ka-mì-iṣ ina pa-an* ^{d}*Šá-maš* [49] *ma-a ez-ḫa-at pa-aṭ-ra-at* [50] *ma-a mì-i-nu ez-ḫa-at pa-aṭ-ra-at ma-a* DINGIR^{MEŠ}*-ni-šá pal-ḫu* [51] *ma-a a-na* LUGAL NUMUN-*šú kur-bi* "When he (scil. the king) falls on his knees before Šamaš, (the following replication takes place): 'She was girt, (but now) she is released.' 'What is it, she was girt, she is released?'[330] 'Her gods have been feared.' 'Bless (sg. fem., referring to the deceased) the king and his seed!'"

Compare with passage *LAS* 132 r3ff certainly referring to the dead queen of Esarhaddon: "(The crown prince says:) 'Aššūr and Šamaš chose me as the crown prince of Assyria because of her (my mother's) *righteousness*.' (And) *her ghost blesses* him just as he has *feared* the ghost: 'May his descendants rule over Assyria!'"

---

[329] Von Soden's rendering of ^{MÍ}É.GAL ("Palastfrau", with the comment: "an unserer Stelle .... also nicht immer nur Bezeichnung für die Königin") is unacceptable, since the meaning of MÍ.É.GAL in all other contexts is assuredly "queen". The passage simply shows that the Assyrian kings could have more than one queens (possibly up to four, as in Ancient India; cf. also note on 129:25f, at end), one of which was in more prominent position than the others. In line 41, the likeliest restoration is DUMU.MÍ *ki-na-*[*a-t*]*e* (not collated); von Soden's DUMU.MÍ-*ki-na* "your (pl.) daughter" is hardly acceptable.

[330] The meaning of this enigmatic replique is clarified by Layard, *Nineveh and Babylon* (abr. ed.), p.120: "It is the will and mercy of God, *she is not dead but released!*" (an Iraqi Arab commenting on the death of a woman).

That the dead queen in K 164 is to be identified with Esarhaddon's main wife (Ešarra-ḫamât) is very likely considering that the text certainly was composed during the Sargonid Era, and that of all the 5 kings of this dynasty, only Esarhaddon is known to have lost his queen before his own death (Sennacherib's queen, Naqia, attestedly outlived both his husband and his son). Furthermore, the daughter and daughter-in-law mentioned in the text can without difficulty be identified as Ešarra-ḫamât's daughter Šērū'a-ēṭirat and Assurbanipal's wife Libbi-āli-šarrat (*ABL* 308:2). In any case, it can be deduced from the text that the following women were involved in the funerary rites of the queen: her daughter, her daughter-in-law, the other queens, and in addition the unnamed women (possibly royal concubines) referred to in lines 40-41 ("come, bury!"). All this agrees with the present letter where it is clearly stated that many women (status unspecified, but certainly in some way related to the king, cf. Obv.17), including a "female servant" or "queen" (MÍ+KUR, cf. note on 151 r8'ff), participated in the rites concerned. Their function was in all probability to serve and bewail the deceased; according to K 164, the daughter and daughter-in-law had to repeatedly wash, anoint and kiss the body of the dead, and line 41 makes it clear that the women also took care of the actual burial. This intimate contact with the deceased made them ritually impure, which in turn required that they were kept in an inaccessible place (cf. present letter, Obv.18) until they had been ritually purified (cf. Rev.7f, 16f). All in all, the evidence pointing to the burial of Ešarra-ḫamât seems too consistent to be regarded as just accidental. See also under *LAS* 197.

Notes:

13. Cancel the restoration in Pt.I, and restore instead: *šu-ru-up-t*[*ú šá* LUG]AL "the funeral burning [(provided) by the kin]g". Cf. note on 4:17, and II Chron. 16:13-14 ("He rested with his forefathers . . . and was buried in the tomb which he had due for himself in the city of David, being laid on a bier which had been heaped with all kinds of spices, skillfully compounded; and they performed a great funeral burning (*š*^{e}*rēpāh*) on his behalf"). Judging from the continuation, it seems likely, though, that in the present context the term *šuruptu* does not refer to the actual burning ceremony but rather to the *items* (*anūtu*, K 164:32) to be burnt in the *šuruptu*; cf. note on Obv.15. This would mean that the letter was written *before* the burning ceremony.

14. Restore, possibly, [*šá* ^{URU}ŠÀ]-URU "[of Ass]ur", and cf. Discussion. Other restorations are naturally also possible (e.g., [*šá* MURUB$_4$] URU).

15. Slightly modifying the rendering of this line in Pt.I, I would now read *pa-aḫ-ḫu-ra-k*[*a*]! and translate "I have collected", taking the form as 1 Sg. Stative of *pḫr* D (with transitive meaning); the form of the restored suffix would be somewhat unusual (*-akā* for normal *-āku*/*-āk*), but does occur elsewhere (cf. *na-ka-ra-ka*, *ABL* 463:7). In any case, there cannot be any doubt that the verb refers to the items to be burnt in the *šuruptu* ceremony. Earlier translators have taken it to refer to the women participating in the rites ("In einem Hause . . . sind (die Frauen) versammelt", Behrens 1906; "In the midst of the keep the women of the city are assembled", Waterman 1930; "[The women of] the city are gathered in a single house in my charge", Pfeiffer 1935), but this is out of the question, firstly because the pronoun *ammāte* in line 16 implies that the women are there mentioned for the first time, and secondly since the question of where to lodge the women is only taken up in Obv.18 ff.

18-22. This passage simply means that the place where the women were being lodged was not the most ideal place for *decent dining* and living over the period of several days they were to be kept in separation from the outside world (cf. Discussion); there is nothing in the passage to suggest that the women were to partake in a banquet or the like. For *akālu šatû* "to dine" cf. *KAV* 197 r14 f. (*ina* É-ŠU^{2}.MEŠ *ša* ^{L}[Ú*]DAM.GÀR KÚ^{MEŠ} NAG^{MEŠ}) and 215 r6 f. (*ina* É PN . . . KÚ NAG); for the idiom "to pour oil on the head" = "to make one's toilet" cf. *EA* 34:50 f. (*ḫa ba na-at ša* Ì DÙG *ma-la-at a-na ta-pa-ki a-na* [*ka-qa*]*-di-ka*); ibid, 29:23 (Ì^{MEŠ} [*a-na k*]*a-aq-qa-ti-ša it-tab-k*[*u*]); and *KAV* 1 vi 19 f. (*šum-ma* LÚ *lu-ú* Ì×GIŠ *a-na* SAG.DU *it-bu-uk lu-u ḫu-ru-up-pa-a-te ú-bíl*).

r1. *"Because they are so many"*: Judging from the amounts of wine allotted to the king's harem in the Nimrud Wine lists (see Kinnier Wilson, *CTN* 1, nos.3, 4, 8 and 18, and cf. ibid., p. 117, for the probable daily ration by which amounts of wine listed in the text can be translated into numbers of persons), the number of women in question may have been close to 300 or even more.

r13. *MÍ+KUR* "*slave-girl*": perhaps rather "female servant" or even "queen" (KUR = É.GAL). See note on 151 r8.

196

Bibliography:
(I) Waterman, *RCAE* 1168.

Writer:
Marduk-šākin-šumi. The grounds for this assignation are as follows: (1) The reference to the apotropaic ritual to avert the "evil of cult(ic offenses)" in Rev.2 (see relevant note) as well as the wording of Rev.12 ff. (cf., e.g., 185 r1 f. and 197:10 f.) shows that the writer of the letter was an exorcist; the only exorcist writing about matters of cult in the present correspondence is Marduk-šākin-šumi. (2) Rev.3 indicates that the writer was in "speaking terms" with the king, hence most naturally the chief exorcist; as as matter of fact, the phrase *ša šarru bēlī iqbûni* "what the king, my lord, said" is attested as many as 11 times in letters by Marduk-šākin-šumi (*LAS* 139, 166bis, 173bis, 180, 181bis, 187, 190), but only 6 times in letters of all other exorcists taken together (*LAS* 125, 144bis, 171, 223bis). (3) Of all the exorcists of the *LAS* corpus, only Marduk-šākin-šumi regularly spelled the present tense of the verb *epāšu* with geminated *p* (*né-ep-pa-šú-u-ni*, Obv.14; for spellings in other letters, see note on 166: 14); all other exorcists preferred spellings with one *p* only (cf. *e-pa-áš*, 208:8.r1, 210 r11, 211 r12, by Nabû-nādin-sumi; *e-pu-šu*, 137 r12, 142 r9, and *e-pu-šú*, 159 r5', *né-e-pa-áš*, 160 r4, *né-pa-áš*, 140 r1.3, 154:11, 167 r1, all by Adad-šumu-uṣur; *né-pa-áš* 204:11 [Nabû-nādin-šumi] and 223:8.r11.19 [Urad-Gula]; the only spellings with geminated *p* are *né-ep-pa-áš* in 155:9, 157 r4, 159 r8', 219 r1, and *né-ep-pa-šú-u-ni*, 156 r2, all but 157 and 219 by Adad-šumu-uṣur, for whom cf. above); the other orthographic features of the letter also agree with Marduk-šākin-šumi's conventions (URU *Arba-ìl* Obv.4' = 186:6, 191:8 and 195:5; KUR *Aš+šur*[KI] Obv.10' = 181 r9; *šá-ka-A-ni* Obv.11' cf. *šá-ṭa-a-ri* 198 r4, *ta-ba-a-ki* 195:20, *e-pa-a-še* 172 r16; for UD *11*.KÁM in Rev.12 cf. 189:15 – in this case the standard spelling in Marduk-šākin-šumi's orthography would have been UD *11*.KÁM*). (4) By physical appearance, the tablet closely resembles *LAS* 173 (personal collation; cf. Pt.I, p.336); one palaeographic detail meriting special attention: the shape of the sign MUN in Obv.2' ( for normal ), which closely resembles the shape of TIM in 177:5 ( for usual ) but does not find parallels in any other letter of the whole corpus. Finally, (5) what remains of the blessing formula shows that it ended with a blessing addressed to a single goddess, probably Ištar; such a blessing recurs in *LAS* 195, but in no other exorcist letter of the whole *LAS* corpus.

Date:
Probably early Arahsamna = early November, 670 BC. While this date is not absolutely certain, it is rendered very likely by the following considerations. Firstly, there is the reference to the *erāb āli* ceremony at Arbela in Obv.4'f. This ceremony was not an everyday incident; it involved the king entering a religiously important city at the head of a triumphal procession, usually after significant military victories (cf. note on line 4'), and as far as the evidence available at present goes, seems to have been celebrated at Arbela only twice in the period covered by the *LAS* correspondence (ca. 680-645, cf. App.I 4): once in the reign of Assurbanipal, following two victorious campaigns to Elam and Gambulu (see commentary to *LAS* 170; ca. 653 BC), and once in the reign of Esarhaddon, subsequent to the conquest of Egypt in 671 BC (see Borger, *Ash* p.95:16-32 and, for the terminus post quem of the inscription, ibid. p.94:28). That both incidents were exceptional, and therefore of rare occurrence, is indicated by the fact that in both cases the *akītu* temple of Ištar outside Arbela, which the goddess visited prior to the triumphal procession, was completely rebuilt for the occasion; in the latter case, even the temple of the goddess in Arbela and the statue of the goddess itself were redecorated, probably by means of the rich spoils looted from Egypt. In the light of the overall chronological structure of Marduk-šākin-šumi's correspondence (cf.App. O 2), it appears a priori likeliest that the incident referred to in the present letter, if identifiable with any of these two cases, was the one which took place in Esarhaddon's reign. This conclusion is supported by the reference to the Cimmerians in Obv.8'. We know from a letter of Assurbanipal to his father (*ABL* 1026) that the Cimmerians caused serious

trouble to Assyria at some phase of the crownprincehood of Assurbanipal (672-669);[331] the nature of this trouble appears from *AGS* 23+75, an oracle query on behalf of Assurbanipal (as crown prince), where the possibility of sending armed forces to Ellipi to recapture a city lost to a coalition of Medes and Cimmerians is considered; cf. the present letter, Obv.5'f. Two other queries, *AGS* 108 and 109, also mentioning the Cimmerians, possibly date from approximately the same time; they refer to Egyptians as potential rebels against Esarhaddon, and were consequently certainly written after the conquest of Egypt, most likely after the crushing of the unsuccessful coup d'état of 670 (see under *LAS* 247).

The inscription of Esarhaddon mentioned above (*Ash* p.93 ff), after recounting the king's various building activities in Arbela, mentions a date, Ulūlu 17 (p.95:25), on which animal sacrifices were made in the *akītu* chapel. The text is fragmentary at this point, but comparison with parallel passages in Assurbanipal's inscriptions indicates that the sacrifices in question were made in the context of Ištar's sojourning in the chapel immediately before the *erāb āli* procession. Considering the extent of the construction work carried out before the event, and further the fact that the campaign to Egypt was only concluded toward the end of the month Du'ūzu (see under *LAS* 59), it seems impossible that the festival described in the inscription could have been celebrated in the same year as Egypt was taken; this would give the present letter a terminus post quem, Ululu 17, 670.[332] On the other hand, the hemerological quotation in Rev.5-10 (see note) shows that the letter was written in the month Arahsamna, and certainly before its 11th day (cf. Rev.13). Since the king to whom the letter was addressed clearly had been involved in the *erāb āli* procession, it follows (supposing that the *erāb āli* took place in Esarhaddon's reign) that this terminus ante (and *ad*) quem, Arahsamna 11, is to be placed in 670. Esarhaddon died on Arahsamna 10, 669, on his way to Egypt (see Grayson, *TCS* 5, p.86:30f); it is excluded that the present letter could have been written immediately before that event.

For further evidence supporting the dating just suggested see note on Obv.13'.

Notes:

4'. *e-rab URU ša* ^{URU}*Arba-ìl*: cf. *e-rab* URU *a-na* ^{URU}*La-ab-ba-na-at, LAS* 29:15f (transport of the statue of Marduk); *e-reb* ^{URU}*Arba-ìl e-pu-uš ina* HÚL^{MEŠ} "I performed the (triumphal) entry to Arbela with joy", *AfO* 8 184:47 (Assurbanipal after victory over Teumman, quoted more fully in commentary to *LAS* 170); [UD] *16*.KAM *e-rab* URU "on the 16th day, the (ceremonial) entry into the City (of Assur was performed)", van Driel, *CA* p.125 i 5 (referring to religious acts performed by Assurbanipal in Šabāṭu 650, presumably in preparation for important military operations against Šamaš-šumu-ukīn); *e-rab* URU *a-na ma-dak-te up-pa-áš* "(the king) mimics triumphal entry (lit. "entry into the city") into the camp", K 10209 r22' (unp. NA cultic ritual; the passage cited is preceded by acts symbolizing defeat of enemy, reflecting Marduk's victory over Tiamat and corresponding mythological battles). Note further Piepkorn, *AS* 5 72:49 ff: *šal-meš a-tu-ra a-na* ^{URU}NINA^{KI} [50] SAG.DU ^{I}*Te-um-man* LUGAL KUR NIM.MA^{KI} [51] *ina ki-šad* ^{I}*Du-na-nu a-lul* [52] *it-ti ki-šit-ti* KUR NIM.MA^{KI} [53] *šal-la-at* ^{KUR}*Gam-bu-li* [54] *šá ina qí-bit* AN.ŠÁR *ik-šu-da* ŠU^{2}*-a-a* [55] *it-ti* ^{LÚ}NAR^{MEŠ} *e-piš nin-gu-ti* [56] *a-na* ^{URU}NINA^{KI} *e-ru-ub ina* HÚL^{MEŠ} "Safely I returned to Nineveh; the head of Teumman, king of Elam, I hanged on the neck of Dunānu, and I *joyfully entered Nineveh* with the booty of Elam and spoils of Gambulu which by order of Assur I had conquered, with musicians making merry music."

5'. The beginning of this line is certainly to be restored [*e-pu-šu-u-n*]*i* on the basis of the passages quoted in the preceding note.

13'. *BAD e-ni* "opening the eyes": possibly a reference to Esarhaddon's eye troubles, cf. *LAS* 180:8

[331] Collated; at the end of line 10, read LÚ*!*g*[*i*!*-mir-a-a*]; in line 14, LÚ*!*gi*!*-mir*!*-a a* (over erasure). The tablet joins *CT* 53 226, a large fragment referring to the conquest of two cities, obviously by Medes assisted by Cimmerians (note DUMU ^{l}*ú-ak-sa-t*[*a-ar*] = Kaštaritu, Obv.4'), and therefore almost certainly associated with the events forming the subject of *AGS* 23+75.

[332] For Ulūlu as *the* month of Ištar festivals, cf. *KAV* 218 ii 19ff (Astrolabe B), explaining the name of the month. It is probable, however, that other factors were taken into consideration is setting the date of the festival, cf. *LAS* 11. [Note, incidentally, that Venus rose heliacally (as evening star) in September 4 = Ulūlu 18, 671, which would favour placing the present letter in 671 rather than 670; see App.C.]

and 183:5f, and see corresponding notes. Cf. also line 14'with 180:7, and note that the benediction in 16'ff is explicitly addressed to gods of medicine. Lines 13'-r1 are written in smaller script than the balance of the Obverse.

r2. [*dul-l*]*i ḪUL GARZA*^{MEŠ}: referring to the apotropaion for "evil of cult(ic offences resulting from) neglect of rites and purifications" (NAM.BÚR.BI ḪUL GARZA NAM.TAG.GA KI.DU.DU *u* ŠU.LUḪ.ḪA), published by Caplice, *Or*NS 39 (1970) 124 ff; see also *RA* 18 28:15 ff ([NAM.BÚR.BI ḪUL] GARZA^{MEŠ} *ki-du-de-e*) and Ebeling, *RA* 49 184. It is unclear whether the cultic offences meant here were incurred during the festival in Arbela or at some later occasion (cf. *LAS* 10+ and 72); the wording of the ritual would easily allow both possibilities.

r5-10. This sequence of auspicious days only fits the month Arahsamna, see the synopsis in Labat, *RA* 38 (1944) 20 f; no other month contained the sequence 7—13—19—24—30.

197

Bibliography:
(I) Waterman, *RCAE* 26.
(II) Behrens, *ABB* (1906) 92; Dhorme, *RHR* 113 (1936) 145; Labat, *Royauté* (1939) 152; Deller, *Or*NS 33 (1964) 95.

Addressee:
Esarhaddon.

Date and discussion:

Ca. Addāru 18, eponymy of Atar-ili = February 20, 672 BC. This date is based on the following evidence. Firstly, the letter is opened with an exceptional salutation formula (*lū šulmu A-DAN-NIŠ ana šarri bēlīja*) otherwise attested in the whole corpus only in two other letters of Marduk-šākin-šumi, *LAS* 195 and 198. The latter of these letters was certainly written immediately after the present one. Since *LAS* 195, in addition to the salutation, also displays an introductory blessing very similar to that of the present letter, it is likely that these two letters, too, are approximately contemporaneous. The date (20th day) mentioned in the present letter would make it postdate *LAS* 195 by about a week. *

Secondly,an analysis of thecontent of the letter raises its connection with *LAS* 195 beyond doubt. It was concluded in the commentary to *LAS* 195 that the letter pertains to rites following the burial of Esarhaddon's wife Ešarra-ḫamât. The present letter also clearly refers to rites following a burial, but to slightly later ones than those alluded to in *LAS* 195. Note firstly the reference to the "house of mourning" (*bēt tādirti*) in Rev.11. The verb *adāru* was in Akkadian used as a term for the mourning of the dead (see below), which, as in ancient Israel (and all comparable cultures), probably involved dressing in ashes and soiled rags, abstinence from food, and separation from the outside world for a certain period of time; the period in question may have varied (depending on the intensity of the sorrow of the mourner) but it does not seem to have generally been longer than a couple of days (cf. Grayson, *TCS* 5 p.107: "The queen mother died . . . The prince and his army were in mourning for 3 days (*3 u_4-mu šu-du-ru*) . . ."). The "house of mourning" mentioned in the present letter is hence most naturally to be understood as a building where the king had kept in isolation during his period of mourning, displaying a behaviour customary in the situation; its mentioning here might imply that the period of mourning was over or nearing its end. In any case, this is implied by the directions in Rev.4-9, which clearly represent "rites of reintegration" intended to adapt the king to normal life after the "rites of separation" and "period of liminality" he had went through in the "house of mourning" (see Arnold van Gennep, *The Rites of Passage* (London 1960), passim esp. 146 ff, for a detailed discussion of these rites from a phenomenological point of view).[333] Dressing in white (Rev.4f), an ostentuous symbol of merry life (cf. Gilg. M iii 10ff, and Eccles. 9:7 ff: "Go to it then, eat your food and enjoy it, and drink your wine with a cheerful heart; . . . Always be dressed in white (*lᵉ banîm*) and never fail to

[333] I owe this reference and many of the interpretations proposed here to my brother Asko Parpola.

anoint your head. Enjoy life . . ."), here certainly symbolizes a kind of rebirth (cf. the Christian notion of donning white garments in heaven), a necessary "rite of passage" between the period of mourning just finished and the normal life soon to be resumed; cf. *LAS* 198:10-r3 (esp.13 ff), and note the parallel function of white clothes in the mourning rites of present-day India, China and Japan. Eating food at a *polished* table likewise symbolizes resumption of normal life; it is implied that the table at which the king had previously eaten was *not* polished but of very coarse make, and the direction that the king may "ask" (or "demand") food (scil. in any quantities) seems to imply that he had eaten sparingly in the preceding days. It is important to note that both directions were clearly intended as (reintegration) *rites* and also understood as such by the king (cf. 198:6ff, "how many days should I wear . . .?"). This shows that their symbolic interpretation presented above is to be considered as primary and not as mere speculation. Their transitory nature is also evidenced by the fact that the white robes were supposed to be worn only for two days (198:10f).

Notes:

r8-9. *^{GIŠ}BANŠUR ṣu-up-pi*: cf. *4* ^{GIŠ}BANŠUR^{MEŠ} *ṣu-pat* ^{42} *2* ^{GIŠ}GÁN.GÁN-*ni ṣu-pu-ti* "4 polished tables, 2 polished potstands", ND 2460 & 2490:41 f (*Iraq* 23 pl.17), preceded by *2* ^{GIŠ}BA[N]ŠUR!^{MEŠ} KÙ+UD *lab-bu-na-te ša* NU^{MES} ^{10} *1 kan-kan-nu* KÙ+UD *ša* 3BÁN "two reinforced(?) silver(-plated) tables of (divine) statues, 1 silver potstand of 3 *sūtus* (capacity)", ibid.9-10. Silver-coated potstands were used in temple breweries (see Oppenheim, *Beer* p.45); other items listed in the text include such well-known cultic objects as libation bowls (*pāgulu*, ll. 2, 24), incense burners (NÍG.NA *ša qu-ta-ri*, ll. 4, 15, etc.), purification consers (*ša tēlissi*, 8, 29), etc.; it seems reasonable to conclude, accordingly, that the table mentioned in the present letter also was a cultic object with a specific symbolic value, such as required by the present context. For *ṣuppu* = "polished" see Deller, *Or* 33 (1964) 95. The king's table is also mentioned in *LAS* 143:15 (cf. pertinent note) and 311:20, however without reference to its material.

198

Bibliography:

(I) Waterman, *RCAE* 379 (cf. IV 249); Pfeiffer, *SLA* 266; Oppenheim, *Letters* (1967) p.165 (no.107; transl. only).
(II) Behrens, *ABB* (1906) 91f; Landsberger, *LSS* 6/1-2 (1915) 107, 122; Schott, *Quellen und Studien* (1933) 365; Dhorme, *RHR* 113 (1936) 145f; Labat, *Royauté* (1939) 319; Oppenheim, *JAOS* 61 (1941) 268, and *Or*NS 14 (1945) 239.

Date:

Ca. Addāru 19, eponymy of Atar-ili = February 21, 672 BC. See discussion under *LAS* 197.

Addressee:

Esarhaddon.

Notes:

10 ff. "*The king should wear (white clothes) on the 20th and 21st*": This direction has hitherto been associated with the injunctions of the royal hemerology *Inbu Bēl Arhi* forbidding, among other things, king's donning clean robes on "evil" days, that is, on the 7th, 14th, 19th, *21st*, and 28th of each month; cf. note on 210 r2 ff. Accordingly, there has been some confusion as to how to interpret the present passage; it has been taken either to indicate that the *Inbu* series did not have "canonical recognition" (thus Landsberger 1915, followed by others) or that the "shepherd of the great people" (SIPA UN^{MEŠ} GAL^{MEŠ}) whom the *Inbu* injunctions concerned actually was not the king but an obscure "Oberpriester" (Behrens 1906), both interpretations suggesting some sort of conflict between the present passage and the hemerology. Actually, there is no conflict at all. *White* (UD = BABBAR/*paṣiu*) robes, referred to in the present letter, are not the same thing as *clean* (UD.UD = DADAG/*ebbu*) robes, mentioned in the *Inbu* series; robes of any colour can be "clean", but "white" robes are not necessarily clean – especially if they have been used in the preceding day, as in the present case. For the symbolic meaning of the white clothes see discussion on *LAS* 197.

11. *ma-'a-ad*: lit. "much", here in the meaning "enough", as in *ABL* 100 r8 and *LAS* 318:11; cf. *ēṣe* "not enough", lit. "it/there is little", *LAS* 51:9 and 174:9.

14f. Cf. *ki-i šá* LUGAL EN-*iá* MURUB$_4$^{MEŠ}-*šú* [16] *i-rak-ka-su-ma a-na pa-an* ^{d}AMAR+UD DINGIR-*ka* [17] *te-ru-bu* "just as the king my lord dresses himself when entering into the presence of Marduk, your lord", *BBEA* p.8:15 ff. In the present context, however, changing into ordinary (not ceremonial) robes is certainly meant. On the expression *qablē rakāsu* in general see note on 171:23.

r4f. *"The writing of the king"*: almost certainly referring to a text actually *written* by the king himself, cf. note on r8f. Esarhaddon is usually, in contrast to his son Assurbanipal, portrayed as an illiterate unable to read and write (cf., e.g., Oppenheim, *Centaurus* 14 [1969] 119), but the present passage suggests that this picture is not necessarily true. Note that in one of his inscriptions, dating from the time of his crownprincehood, Esarhaddon actually claims to have acquired "knowledge of the entire scholarship" in terms very similar to those of his son ([^{I}*Aš+šur-e-tel*-DINGIR]^{MEŠ}-GIN-IBILA DUMU-MAN GAL-*u ša* É *re-du-u-ti* [2] [*ša . . . gu*]-*um-mu-ru šu-tu-ru a-na ṭè-e-mi* [3] [. . . .]x *ni šá gi-mir um-ma-nu-te lit-mu-du ka-ras-su* "(I am) [Aššur-etel-ilā]ni-mukīn-apli, the great crown prince of the Succession Palace, [whose . . .] is perfect, whose intelligence is superb, and whose mind has learned the [. . .] of the entire scholarship", Borger *Ash* p.68 § 30:1-3; cf. Streck, *Asb* p.252 i 10-19 and 25, etc.). The nature of the "writing" in question unfortunately necessarily remains a matter of speculation.

r6. ^{I}*GIN-i*: probably identical with ^{I}GIN-*i* ^{LÚ}DUB.SAR DUMU-MAN "Kēnî, the scribe of the crown prince (Assurbanipal)" mentioned in the colophon of a tablet of HARra=*hubullu* copied for "Assurbanipal, the great crown prince of the Succession Palace" (Hunger, *AOAT* 2, no.345:6). Another man with the same name is known to have functioned as public scribe in Nineveh in years 668-665 BC (cf. ^{I}GIN-*i* ^{LÚ}A.BA, *AR* 71:30 and 101:38).

The conjunction *kīma* may here have a conditional as well as a temporal nuance ("*if* K. saw it, he would 'die' of rage"); see note on 156:11 ff.

r8 f. Render "Bēl and Nabû have given (lit. "set") a beautiful hand to the king, my lord", and correct the translation in Pt.I (and elsewhere) which is impossible since the text has *a-na*, not *ina* UGU LUGAL. Note also that ŠU.2 "hand" (Sg.!) lacks a pronominal suffix, which is should have if it referred to the hands of the gods. The specific meaning of ŠU.2 required by the context ("handwriting") is well attested in colophons (see Hunger, *AOAT* 2, Glossary s.v. *qātu*); the characterization of the king's hand as "beautiful" probably has to be understood as an irony, cf. the continuation (and note to 65 r19).

r10. *te-gér-tu*: meaning obscure, possibly "negotiations" (thus Postgate, *TCAE* [1974], p. 273) or the like, certainly not "observation" (thus Oppenheim 1967, following Waterman). The word is otherwise attested in the following contexts:

(1) *ú-ma-a šu-ú i-tal-ka* [13] *ma a-ta-a* ^{LÚ*}ÌR^{MEŠ}-*ia tú-še-l[i]* [14] *ma-a ina* É.GAL *a-šá-pa-ra a-na-ku te-g[ér-t]ú* [15] *a-[sa-ka]n mu-[k]u* ^{LÚ*}ÌR^{MEŠ}-*ka a-na* ^{LÚ*}⌜ÌR^{MEŠ}⌝-[*i*]*a* [16] *i[h]-ta-sa-'u mu-ku* TA *ma-ṣi* ⌜^{LÚ*}ÌR⌝ [17] *ša* LUGAL *at-ta-ni mu-ku* A.Š[À GE]ŠTIN GIŠ.SAR [18] *ina* ^{KUR}*Ja-su-bu-qi la-di-na-ka ṣa-bat* "Now then he (= an Arab sheikh) came to see me, saying: 'Why have you removed servants of mine? I shall write to the Palace'. I set up a *tegertu*, saying: 'Your subjects have harassed my subjects. (But) as soon as you become a servant of the King, I will give you fields, vinyards, and orchards in the land of Jasubuqu; take it!' " *CT* 53 10:12ff;

(2) *a-na šú-na-šú-nu* [21] *ina lìb-bi e-gér-te*^{MEŠ} [22] *i-sa-ṭa-ru* [23] *a-na te-gér-te-šú-nu* [24] *i-sa-ak-nu* [r1] *na-ṣu-u-né a-na* LUGAL *be-lí-ia* [2] *ú-šá-áš-mu-u-ni* "they (= Šubrian authorities) wrote 'them' (= the names of Assyrian runaways) down on letters, set (them) up as their *tegertu*, brought (the tablets) here, and had me notify the king, my lord", *ABL* 252:20 ff;

(3) *ma-a* ^{I}*Ḫu-Te-šub ma-ri-ṣi ma-a an-nu-te* [15] *a-na te-gér-te it-tal-ku-u-ni* "They said: Ḫu-Tešub is ill; these came for *tegertu*", ibid. 14 f;

(4) *an-nu-te* ^{LÚ}MAḪ^{MEŠ}-*ni* [8] *ša il-lik-u-ni-ni a-na te-gér-te šú-u-tú* [9] ^{I}*Ḫu-Te-šub ma-ri-ṣi ma-a ni-il-lik* [10] *né-mur* "these emissaries who came for *tegertu*, Ḫu-Tešub being ill, said: 'Let us go and find out' ", ibid. r7 ff;

(5) [*šum*]-*ma te-gér-tú me-*[*me-ni*] "if any *tegertu* takes place", *CT* 53 76 "B" 12' *abat šarri* giving instructions as to how to deal with a "traitor" [*parriṣu*]).

Etymological considerations are not helpful in defining the meaning of the word; despite the context in (2), it has probably nothing to do with *egertu* "letter; horizontally oblong tablet", a derivate from *egēru* "to twist" (lit. "twisted tablet"). The relationship of the word to *taggirtu* "complaint" (*AHw.* p.1300), *magīrtu*/*migūrtu* "freche Herausforderung(?)" (*AHw.* p.576*b*) or *nagurtu* (meaning obscure, cf. e.g. *ABL* 544:18) remains unclear.

r13. The fact that *ú-ma-a* here is contrasted with *ina timāli* "yesterday" (r10) indicates that it here is synonymous with *ūmu anniu* "today", and strongly suggests that this NA adverb actually is a loan from Aramaic *yōmā* "today".[334] Note the alternation of *ú-ma-a* and u_4*-mu an-ni-u* in *LAS* 224:8 || r4', and cf. *LAS* 2 r1, where the translation "today" also fits better than "now", since *ú-ma-a* there contrasts with *iššiāri* "tomorrow". Cf. NB *enna* (in the expression *enna adû* corresponding to NA *ūmâ annūrig*) < *inanna*, the latter originally *ina+anni* "on this (day)".

199

Bibliography:
(I) Waterman, *RCAE* 665 (cf. IV 186).

Copy (with join):
CT 53 pl. 49, no. 152.

Discussion:

The tone of this letter recalls that of *LAS* 246-247, and it seems accordingly possible that the letter was written in response to a letter of the king blaming Marduk-šākin-šumi for an attack of illness which the chief exorcist had been either unable to cure or foresee. Other interpretations are, naturally, also possible. In any case, it is unlikely that the letter reflects the same situation as *LAS* 180 f and 246 f since it refers to a journey planned by the king (r3 ff). See below.

Notes:

7 f. Delete the rendering in Pt. I, and render instead: "Is this the [tr]uth?" (*an-ni-tu-u ši-i* / [*ket-t*]*u*), "this" perhaps referring to the diagnosis and prognosis given in *LAS* 182 (cf. pertinent commentary). In that case, the letter would be datable to 672 BC and would predate Esarhaddon's campaign to Egypt.

r3. At end, read *ù šu*[*m-ma*] "and ver[ily]", and cancel the reading D[UMU-LUGAL] given in Pt.I; the following lines accordingly refer to a trip (or campaign) planned by the king himself, not by the crown prince. The omission of the subjunctive marker in the predicates of this passage, otherwise strictly required in oaths or strong assertions introduced with *šumma*, is not paralleled elsewhere but may be due to the repetition of *šumma*.

[334] Cf. *GAG* § 119c and Ylvisaker, *LSS* 5/6 p.58.

203

Bibliography:

(I) Waterman, *RCAE* 370; Pfeiffer, *SLA* 270; Oppenheim, *Letters* (1967) 165f.

(II) Behrens, *ABB* (1906) 95f; Dhorme, *RHR* 116 (1937) 21; Labat, *Royauté* (1939) 345; Oppenheim, *JAOS* 61 (1941) 263; Laessøe, *Bīt rimki* (1955) 28.

Discussion:

The namburbi ritual paraphrased in this letter remains unidentified and its cause and purpose correspondingly obscure. None of the namburbis so far published by Ebeling (*RA* 48 [1954] 1 ff, 76 ff, 130 ff, 178 ff; 49 [1955] 32 ff, 137 ff, and 178 ff; 50 [1956] 22 ff and 86 ff) and Caplice (*Or* NS 34 [1965] 105 ff; 36 [1967] 1 ff, 273 ff; 39 [1970] 111 ff; 40 [1971] 133 ff; 42 [1973] 508 ff; *JNES* 33 [1974] 345 ff; *SANE* 1/1 [1974] 1 ff), or the ones listed by Borger, *HKL* 3 (1976) p. 87, resemble it closely enough, even though some of its distinctive features do occur in these texts (cf. notes on Obv.10, 11, r3 and 9). In fact, if it were not for Nabû-nādin-šumi's preoccupation with namburbi rituals in the rest of his correspondence, too, which makes it reasonable to believe that a namburbi indeed is in question in the present case, one would be tempted not to take the identification of the ritual as "namburbi" literally but to see in it a paraphrasis of either *bīt rimki* or (more plausibly) *bīt salā' mê*; both of these rituals involved repeated purification ceremonies (*takpirtu*), a long cycle of prayers to stars ("nocturnal gods"), king's treatment as a "sick person" and his seclusion for a period of time in a reed hut, i.e., all the characteristic features of the ritual under consideration (for *bīt rimki* see the outline of the ritual acts given by Laessøe, op.cit., p. 83 f, and cf. below, note on Rev.7f; cf. also *LAS* 167 showing that the purification ceremonies of *bīt rimki* went on for 7 days, which would agree with Obv.10 of the present letter;[335] for *bīt salā' mê* see, provisionally, Kunstmann, *LSS* NF 2 [1932], p.62[3]; the *bīt ṣibitti* structure where the king was kept "imprisoned" in this ritual also occurs in the same function in the ritual tablet of *ilī ul īdi*, Ebeling *TuL* p. 114 ff). However, while both *bīt rimki* and *bīt salā' mê* were partly apotropaic in character, they are nowhere explicitly called namburbis, and the fact that both were frequently performed at court (*bīt rimki* during every lunar eclipse concerning the king, *bīt salā' mê* every year in the month Tašrītu [cf. sub *LAS* 136:11]) would make it hard to explain why an outline of these rituals should have been presented to the king. For the time being, therefore, it seems safest to assume that an as yet unidentified namburbi, rather than either of these two rituals, is in question. Cf. discussion sub *LAS* 204.

Notes:

10. *UD 7.KÁM*: here not "the 7th day", as usual in the Sargonid correspondence, but "7 days"; cf. Rev. 5 f. This otherwise very uncommon spelling for normal 7 UD-*me*/MEŠ is relatively frequently encountered in namburbi texts, e.g. ^{NA_4}.GUG . . . UD 7.KAM *ina* GÚ-*šú* GAR-[*an*] "you place (a phylactery of) carnelian around his neck for 7 days", *LKA* 114:44 = *RA* 50 p.90.

11. Cf. ^{GI}URÌ.GAL *šá* LUGAL *ina lìb-b*[*i* . . .] "(the exorcist makes) an *urigallu* hut inside of which the king [. . .]", *BBR* 26 iii 24 (*bīt rimki*, ritual tablet, immediately before the section dealing with prayers to stars); also [. . . . . . .]È-*ma ina* ^{GI}URÌ.GAL [. . .] "the [. . .] comes out and [enters] the *urigallu* hut", ibid. iv 49. The *urigallu* was a hut made of reed bundles of standard shape, each of them separately planted in the ground; cf. *ana* IM.[TAB+TAB.BA ^{GI}URÌ.GAL] 16'[*tu*]-*za-qàp* LÚ BI *ana* ŠÀ ^{GI}[URÌ.GAL KU$_4$-*ub*] "you plant an *urigallu* hut against the four winds, that man enters the *urigallu* hut", K 6142:15'f (*Or* NS 36 p.28, namburbi for snakes); similarly *AMT* 44,4:5f; ^{GI}URÌ.GAL^{MEŠ} *šá ina* SAG ^{LÚ}GIG *zu-uq-qu-pu* ^{d}7.BI DINGIR^{MEŠ} GAL^{MEŠ} DUMU^{MEŠ}

---

335 The fact that every ki-^{d}utu-kam prayer of *bīt rimki* was supposed to be recited at sunrise also suggests that the performance of this ritual took 7 days, contra Laessøe, op.cit. p.28. Note further that the "universal namburbi" mentioned in Rev.3 of the present letter formed an integral part of *bit rimki*, cf. *BBR* 26 iii, and *LAS* 185:13f.

dIš-ḫa-ra šu-nu "the *urigallu* bundles which are planted at the head of the patient are the Seven (= the Pleiades), the great gods, the children of Išḫara", Sp. I 131: 241f (*ZA* 6 241 ff); note also the lexical equations gi-urì-gal = *ú-rì-gal-lu*, Hh IX 286, and gi-šú-a = *šu-tuk-ku* "reed hut" = GIURÌ.GAL-*lu*₄, Hg to Hh IX 376 (*MSL* 9 p.70). For a picture of an *urigallu* cf. e.g. the seal scene reproduced in Labat, *Royauté* Fig.27, which, incidentally, could well pertain to the ritual described in the present letter: the king is lying on a bed inside a reed hut, an exorcist kneeling at his head (cf. *LAS* 142 r1!), and another performing a ritual over him; the emblems of the moon, the Pleiades, Venus, Sagittarius and Lyra are depicted outside the hut. For the magic function of the *urigallu* huts cf. note to *LAS* 137:7f.

r1. *ŠU.ÍLA.KÁM-ni*: for /šu'illakāni/, Pl. of **šu'illakku*/*šu'illāku* "hand-lifting prayer", lit. "(incantation) of uplifted hand(s)" (< Sum. šu+íl+a+ak). Other spellings of the plural of this word are *šu-íl-la-ka-nu*, *LAS* 334:2. 4.r6; ŠU.ÍL.LA.KÁM-*a-nu*, *CT* 22 no.1 r2; ŠU.ÍL.LÁ.KÁMMEŠ-*ni*, *BMS* 18 r10; ŠU.ÍL.LÁ.KÁMMEŠ, *LAS* 185:5 and 233 r4; the closest parallel to the present (defective) spelling is found in the colophon of *BMS* 47, reading ŠU. ÍL.LÁ.KAM-*ni* "(the . . .th tablet) of (the series) hand-lifting prayers". On these prayers see also note on 185:21f.

r3. *NAM.BÚR.BI ḪUL.DÙ.A.BI*: cf. notes on *LAS* 67 and 185:13f. In addition to *bīt rimki*, the performance of this namburbi is also prescribed in conjunction with the namburbi for "the evil of bad forces and signs portending the scattering of one's house, etc." (NAM.BÚR.BI ḪUL ÁMEŠ ISKIMMEŠ ḪULMEŠ, etc.), *LKA* 120 (= Ebeling, *RA* 49 140 ff) || K 2777+ (= Caplice, *Or* NS 39 142 ff) || BM 59808 (= *Or* NS 42 508 f).

r6 ff. These lines probably refer to the promise made at the end of hand-lifting prayers ("I shall praise your divinity [forever]"; for examples see e.g. *CAD* D s.v. *dalīlu*). The "praise" may have taken various forms, cf. sub *LAS* 308.

r7. Cf. the ritual tablet of *bīt rimki*, *BBR* 26 v 18, mentioning the king's personal god in a context recalling the present passage.

r8. *a-ki-i*: probably for *a-ke-e* "thus"; cf. *a-ke-e ta-ri-iṣ*, *LAS* 252:13f, and corresponding note.

r9. *iq-qab-bi*: not "(perhaps the king) is told" (Oppenheim 1967) but "(perhaps the king) *says*"; the gemination of *q* does *not* indicate that the verb *qabû* is here in the N stem (cf. the innumerable other attestations of the phrase *issurri šarru iqabbi* in Neo-Assyrian letters, e.g. *LAS* 110 r4, 247 r20.27, 258 r9', 308:9; *ABL* 191:13, 252:7.11, 492:14, 573:12, 799:6, 992 r3, 1093 r21 [the verb in each case spelled *i-qab-bi*] and *ABL* 314:5, 433 r7, 546 r10, 685 r19, 984:8, 1019 r4, 1063 r1, 1348:2 [*i-qa-bi*], where the meaning of the phrase unquestionably is "perhaps the king will say", as opposed to *LAS* 279:19f, *i-su-ri . . . a-na* LUGAL EN-*já i-qa-bi-i-u* [similarly *ABL* 150 r6f and *LAS* 46:13 and 136:8] showing that the passive "perhaps the king is told" was expressed with the 3rd person plural of the G stem, not with the N stem singular); it has to be explained otherwise.

Comparable morphologically unmotivated consonantal geminations occur relatively frequently in Nabû-nādin-šumi's letters: *še-tu-UQ-QI*, 204 r4; *ú-še-tu-UQ-QU*, ibid. r6; *IB-BA-áš-ši*, 208 r5; *ID-DA-ab-bu-ub*, 204 r2. The latter spelling (for /idabbub/) is also attested in a namburbi text (*Or* NS 36 p.3:34) possibly attributable to Nabû-nādin-šumi, and paralleled by *ni-ID-DA-bu-ub*, *ABL* 997 r15, and *AD-DA-bu-ub*, *ABL* 211:7 (cf. ibid. r4 *ID-DA-gal-an-ni* for /idaggal-anni/), but otherwise corresponding forms occur very infrequently in Neo-Assyrian texts (disregarding geminations at morpheme boundaries, on which see note to 246:10, the present writer has only noticed [*I*]*Q-QA-bi*, *LAS* 298 r7'; *IQ-QAB-bu-u-ni*, *ABL* 634 r3; *AQ-QA-ba-kan-ni* = /aqbakkanni/, *4R* 61 i 14'; *li-IṬ-ṬIB-bu* = /liṭību/, *ABL* 1285:9; *an-ni-nu* = /anēnu/, *ABL* 251 r7 and ND 2495 r13; *an-nu-ku* = /anāku/, *ABL* 555 r9, plus a handful of similar forms of uncertain interpretation referred to in fn. 621). The rarity of these forms makes it tempting to brush them away as scribal mistakes; on the other hand, the fact that they occur so frequently in letters by Nabû-nādin-šumi and some other scribes (*ABL* 211 and 1285) makes one wonder whether they do not actually have some phonetic (not necessarily phonemic) relevance. Some of the forms listed above undoubtedly require different explanations.

204

Bibliography:

(I) Waterman, *RCAE* 51 (cf. IV 232); Pfeiffer, *SLA* 278; Oppenheim, *Letters* (1967), p.167 (no.112).
(II) Dhorme, *RHR* 116 (1937) 18; Labat, *Royauté* (1939), 213; Oppenheim, *JAOS* 61 (1941) 266.

Copy:

Cf. S.A. Smith, *PSBA* 10 p.61f (pl.1).

Photo:

RCAE IV pl.6 (obverse only).

Discussion:

The reference to the "universal namburbi" (Obv.6) and the spelling *ID-DA-ab-bu-ub* may imply that this letter was written soon after *LAS* 203, but this does not help identify the portent mentioned in Rev.1, not to speak of dating the letter. Tentatively, though, one may conjecture that a lunar or solar eclipse was in question, cf. *LAS* 40. This would agree with the analysis of the ritual outlined in *LAS* 203 (cf. relevant discussion) but less well with the date ("the 8th day") mentioned at the end of the letter.

Notes:

8. *a-na ši-ja-a-ri* "tomorrow": see notes on *LAS* 39 r3 and 158:6.

205

Bibliography:

(I) Waterman, *RCAE* 53 (cf. IV 233); Pfeiffer, *SLA* 262.
(II) Behrens, *ABB* (1906) 31f, 100; Dhorme, *RHR* 116 (1937) 18f; Labat, *Royauté* (1939) 326, 343, 348; Leichty, *TCS* 4 (1970) 12.

Discussion:

The identification of the rites alluded to in this letter poses a problem. While the writer refers to a ritual (to undo the evil) of a malformed birth (*šá iz-bi*) in Rev.9, and while the *izbu* namburbi (Ebeling, *RA* 50 86ff and dupls.) involved, among other things, a trip to the river bank by the man affected by the evil, as also prescribed in Obv.11f of the present letter, this namburbi does not qualify for the ritual described on the Obverse: the wording of Rev.9 ff clearly indicates that the topic of the *izbu* ritual is there introduced for the first time, and analysis of the *izbu* namburbi shows that its structure and ritual components entirely differ from the scenario outlined in the present letter.

The possibility that the *izbu* namburbi is in question thus being excluded, the letter offers very few tangible criteria for a conclusive identification of the rites. The interpretation offered below must therefore be regarded as tentative only. I would suggest, primarily on the basis of the elliptic usage of the verbs *ušābu* and *tabû* in Obv.9f, that the letter concerned the enthronement and dethronement of a substitute king (Obv.9f), and subsequent purification rites to be undergone by the king (Obv.10f). See note to *LAS* 185 r18 on *ušābu* "to ascend throne" and *šēšubu* "to enthrone", specifically referring to the substitute king when used without the object *kussû*; for *tabû* "to be dethroned" cf. *šarru ina* ^{GIŠ}GU.ZA-*šú itebbī-ma mamman uššab* (unp., quoted *CAD* K 591*b*) and the other examples of *tabû* in connection with thrones quoted in *CAD* A/2 p.396. If this interpretation is correct, the proposed reign of the substitute king would have been exceptionally short, only 7 days (15th through 22nd), the normal duration being 100 days (cf. Intr., p.59). While there is evidence that the "reign" was occasionally terminated before the full 100 days had elapsed (see under *LAS* 166 and 280), even the shortest reign so far attested lasted for 20 days (from Du'ūzu 14 to Ābu 5, 666), and that reign was explicitly characterized as exceptional in every respect (see *LAS* 298 and pertinent commentary). Considering the fact that we are relatively well informed of virtually every case of the substitute king ritual between 677 and 666 (cf. Intr., p.000), the very period in which Nabû-nādin-šumi was active as royal exorcist (cf. App. 0), is there any place then for a 7-day long mini-reign in this period? Very unlikely; it seems likelier to suppose that the present letter, if indeed referring to a case of the substitute king ritual, presented a *preliminary* plan (later to be modified in discussion with the king, cf. Rev.1 ff) for the exceptional performance of the ritual in 666 BC which eventually turned out to involve a 20-day reign of the substitute. This would date the letter to early Du'ūzu/July, 666 BC. The proposed day of enthronement, [Du'ūzu] 15, would then have been the 88th day after the lunar eclipse of Nisannu, which furnished the cause of the ritual, and the proposed dethronement would have taken place 95 days after the same eclipse. Cf. Discussion under *LAS* 298 for the reasons calling for such an arrangement.

Notes:

7. ^{I}*Ba-<la>-si-i*: possibly also ^{I}*Ba-ni!-i* (cf. *LAS* 263 and App.N, nos.18-20). The former emendation is, however, preferable[336] considering the role the man plays in the letter: he is clearly the one who determined the dates of the ritual proposed in Obv.9ff, and hence a scribe, very unlikely a physician. The fact that Balasî was the *ummânu* of Assurbanipal while the latter was crown prince (cf. *LAS* 34) would also explain why the king wanted to have his advice in the present matter.

Incidentally, the reference to Ba<la>sî lends support to the hypothesis that the letter deals with the substitute king ritual, since proposals to enthrone a substitute appear often to have been made by collegiums of scholars including a scribe and an exorcist (cf. *LAS* 28 and 31).

11 f. Clearly a reference to a purification ritual performed on the river bank (involving a bath in the river and donning of new/clean garments afterwards), the purpose of which was to wash away the ritual pollution to which the object of the rites had been subjected previously. Cf., e.g., *KAR* 141 (at end) and the namburbi passages cited in note to 160 r6, and passim in various exorcistic rituals; for river as a scene of ritual purification see also *LAS* 60 r1, 195 r7 f, and 210 r4. Note that the king was supposed to undergo a purification ritual on the day following the dethronement of the substitute king (*LAS* 166), just as implied by the present passage.

r6. *dul-lu ma-AḪ-du šu-u*: cf. *dul-lu ma-a'-du* [*šu-u*], 191 r11 f. There is no need to take *ma-AḪ-du* (hapax legomenon) as a phonetic variant of *ma'du*; the spelling can easily be explained graphically: AḪ = *a'* with two superfluous wedges. Cf. RU (written with an extra vertical) in 203:5.8, and 204:5; MA (written with an extra horizontal) in 205 r10, etc.

r7. *de'iq akī . . . išammûni*: cf. SIG$_5$ *a-dan-niš* / *ki-i ša taq-bi-ni*, *ABL* 303 r2 f; *de-e-qe* / *ša taš-pur-an-ni*, *ABL* 417 r2 f, and the other similar examples quoted in note to 144 r8. Beside the translation in Pt.I, the present passage could also be rendered simply "It is good that (the king) listens to (what we have to say)."

r9. *šá iz-bi*: an ellipsis for (*dul-lu*/NAM.BUR.BI) *šá iz-bi*, cf. Obv.6, *LAS* 167:12 (*šá ḫa-liq-ti* UZU = *dul-lu šá* . . .), etc. Translate accordingly: "And as to the *izbu* (anomaly) ritual of which the king wrote . . .", and delete the translation in Pt.I.

r10. *su-me*: interpretation uncertain; probably not "it is crippled" but rather "it is obscure", or the like. Cf. *AHw.* 1020*a*.

r11 ff. *a-ki-i šá ina* ^{GIŠ}*le-'i šá-ṭir-u-ni*: cf. the *izbu*namburbi DT 90 (*Or* NS 34, pl.18), the colophon of which reads: [*ki*]-⌜*i*⌝ KA ^{GIŠ}[*lē'i šaṭir*] "written according to a writing-board (original)". Is this tablet (found in Nineveh) the tablet meant here?

336 Leaving the name unemended is, of course, also possible theoretically but would cause difficulties of interpretation, since the man in question was clearly well-known at court and no scholar named ^{I}*Ba-si-i* is known from contemporary sources.

206

Bibliography:

(I) Waterman, *RCAE* 52 (cf. IV 232); Pfeiffer, *SLA* 280.

(II) Behrens, *ABB* (1906) 50f; Dhorme, *RHR* 116 (1937) 18; von Soden, *ZA* 44 (1938) 182; Kinnier Wilson, *NWL* (1972) p. 11.

Discussion:

The cleansing rites (*takpirtu*) reported in this letter were presumably carried out in anticipation of a visit by the king to the city of Kasappa (cf. Rev.9), and had probably been occasioned by a natural catastrophy or an ominous incident recently occurred on the route (cf. *LAS* 349 r5); it is unlikely that routes taken by the king were similarly "cleansed" every time prior to royal trips. The historical context of the letter remains obscure; there is hardly any connection between it and *LAS* 125 r9 f.

Notes:

8. *tak-pir-tu da-at-tu*: Cf. *LAS* 188 r1 ff, *kī ša šarru bēlī išpuranni ētapaš tak-pir-tu* KALAG-*tú* . . . *ussētiq* "I did exactly as the king, my lord, wrote to me and performed a powerful cleansing ritual." This parallel indicates that *da-at-tu* in our letter is not an adverb to be translated "afterwards" (thus *CAD* D p.122b), but Fem. of the adjective *dannu* "strong". Cf. *ina* IGI KÁ.GAL *da-at-ti ša* MÚRUB URU "in front of the main gate of the citadel", *ABL* 984 + K.1612:8', *a-ka-ni da-'a-tu* [12]*a-bu-tu* [13]*e-ta-ap-šú-ni-ma* "now they have made a great effort", *ABL* 420:11-13; and *a-na-ku d*]*a-'a-at-tú at-ta* [. . .] "[I am] strong, you [. . .]" 82-5-22, 527 i 13' (= Langdon, *TI* Pl. III, Ištar speaking). As can be seen from the last two examples, the original form of the word has to be posited as **da'-antu* > *da'attu*, i.e. with a glottal stop between *d* and *t*; cf. also *da-a'-nu-tú-*[*ni*] *LAS* 42:13 with note. In practice, however, it is irrelevant whether one interprets the spelling *da-at-tu* as *da'attu* or *dâttu*, for the glottal stop in Neo-Assyrian generally disappeared between two similar vowels (e.g., *iddi'in* "became strong" > *iddīn* > *i-di-i-ni, ABL* 112 r11).

In passing, it may be noted that the lemma *dattu* "afterwards" posited in *CAD* has to be stricken. The other example quoted ibid. (*iš-ši-ja-a-ri qa-ret* DINGIR[MEŠ] [9]d*Taš-me-tu*$_4$ *da-at-tú* [10]*tu-ṣa-a, ABL* 858:8 ff) is not pertinent, since there, too, the Fem. of *da'nu* "strong" clearly is in question. Cf. LUGAL *be-lí ú-da* [9]*ki-i* d*15 šá* URU*Arba-ìl* [10]*dan-na-at-u-ni* [11]*qa-re-tu ina* URU*Arba-ìl, ABL* 876:8 ff.

11 ff. *Zikkû* and *Sasiqani*: otherwise unknown, but probably on the east bank of the Tigris between Nineveh and Calah (30 km SE of Nineveh). *

r3. *dajālu* "inspector": thus following *CAD* D 28*b*; however, the present context as well as the NB references quoted in CAD, where *dajālu* is connected with temples, point rather to a meaning like "(temple) courier", which would better agree with the etymology of the word. Cf. note on *LAS* 66:15, and note NÍG.NA URUDU *ša da-aja-la-te* "bronze censer of (used in) excursions", ND.2490+2460:35 (*Iraq* 23, Pl. 17). See also von Soden, *Or*NS 37 (1968), 270.

r8. *tu-ba-la* = Prs. 2m Sg. of *wbl* + paragogic vowel indicating continuation (cf. note on 18 r8).

r9. *Kasappa*: mod. Kashaf/Kushaf on the Greater Zab (15 km SE of Calah.)

r10. *tu-ša-ba-a* has hitherto been interpreted as Prs. 2 Pl. of *wšb* "to sit", but this is unlikely in view of the long final *-a*. Since the letter deals with a purificatory ritual and one of the most common technical words used in that connection in magical texts, is *bâ'u* Š "to move (a censer) alongside (a person or object)" (e.g., *tak-pi-ra-a-te eb-bé-e-ti* LUGAL *tu-kap-pár* NÍG.NA GI.IZI.LÁ *tuš-ba-a'*), it is hardly to be doubted that this verb is in question here, even though it has not been attested elsewhere in purely NA texts. Contrary to what might be deduced from *GAG* § 104 and Parad. 28, *tu-ša-ba-a* accords with the NA paradigm of verba II infirmae; cf. *nu-šá-ra-qa, ABL* 452:17, and *ú-šá-ra-qu*, ibid. 8.17, both Š-stem Prs. of *râqu* "to be empty". The pattern *ušbīat* given in GAG applies only to Old-Assyrian and should be corrected to *ušarâq* as far as Neo-Assyrian is concerned.

207

Bibliography:
(I) Waterman, *RCAE* 55 (cf. IV 233); Pfeiffer, *SLA* 210.

Photo of Obv.:
RCAE IV pl. 6.

Notes:

7 ff. Cf. *LAS* 4:6-10 *ša šarru bēlī išpuranni ma-a a-na* ^{I}EN-PAP-*er* . . . . *šá-'a-al* "ask Bēl-nāṣer"; 125 r7 *ina* UGU *a-bé-te šá* LUGAL *be-lí* ^{8}*iq-bu-u-ni ma-a a-na* ^{Id}PA-SUM-MU *šá-al-šú* "as regards the matter on which the king, my lord, said to me: 'Ask Nabû-nādin-šumi!' (I have not been able to ask him)". The writer of our letter is also mentioned (in a similar context) in another letter of Adad-šumu-uṣur, *LAS* 122 r27; perhaps the unknown man here meant is, after all, the well-known Adad-šumu-uṣur himself?

208

Bibliography:
(I) Waterman, *RCAE* 56; Pfeiffer, *SLA* 269.
(II) Behrens, *ABB* (1906), p. 103; Dhorme, *RHR* 116 (1937) 20; Labat, *Royauté* (1939) 151; Abusch, *JNES* 33 (1974) 259 ff.

Date:
Possibly late Ābu = early August, 670 BC. See under *LAS* 286.

Notes:

7. *ma-aq-lu-u*: The only explicit mention of the anti-witchcraft ritual *Maqlû* in the present corpus. Despite the shortness of the passage, it is significant in that it not only clearly implies that the ritual was to be (periodically) performed in the month Ābu but also shows that the king took personally part in it, both facts not explicitly stated in the extant ritual instructions. The "balance of the ritual" to be performed in the following morning (Obv.9-10) comprised the ceremonies explained in the latter part of the ritual tablet (IX 150 ff), beginning with the words *i-na še-r[i . . . .]-pa šur-pu ta-šar-rap* "in the morning [. . . .] you perform the *šurpu* combustion".[337]

r2-3. Cf. *LAS* 223:6-8 also mentioning "rituals of the month Ābu", without further specifications; 219: 4' ff referring to "rituals of Ulūlu" (*né-pe-ši ša* ^{ITU}KIN), which included a ceremony performed on the 16th day for attainment of good dreams; 183 r2'-4' reading "we shall perform the rites of Ajā[ru] (*né-pe-še ša* ^{ITU}GU[D]) against fever of [. . . . .]"; and 218:10 ff listing different rituals against malaria, witchcraft, plague and pestilence, performed by the writer and his colleagues in the months Kislīmu, Kanūnu and Šabāṭu. With these passages are to be compared the monthly rituals mentioned in the *Exorcist's Manual* (*KAR* 44), Obv.5: *né-peš* ^{ITU}ŠU.^{d}INANNA ^{ITU}NE ^{ITU}KIN ^{ITU}DU$_6$ "rites of Du'ūzu, Ābu, Ulūlu and Tašrītu"; what is known about the nature of the relevant rites[338] points to a system of calendrically fixed ceremonies intended to protect the royal family from contagious diseases, witchcraft and other plagues.[339] Incidentally, the fact that the writer of the present letter had to inquire whether the rites should be performed for the queen mother, too, indicates that this lady was generally not considered a member of the royal family ("the king and his house", cf. 201 r8 and 218:14). She had her own

---

337 See in detail Abusch (1974), 256 ff.

338 The ritual of Du'ūzu (Farber, *Atti Ištar* p.68 ff) was directed against ghosts and demons; the ritual of Tašrītu, probably identifiable with *Bīt salā' mê*, seems to have been partly lustrative, partly prophylactic (cf. on LAS 136:11 and 203); the prophylactic ritual *Bīt mēsēri* was, according to its ritual tablet Sm 1939 r7' (*ZA* 36, 215 ff), to be performed regularly in Tašrītu and Araḫsamna.

339 For comparative evidence from other cultures see e.g. J.G. Frazer, *The Golden Bough* (abr. ed., New York 1927), 551 ff.

household and was presumably normally protected by her own court exorcists; the present reference to her was probably only due to a temporary visit to the royal court.[340]

r3. For the restoration of the broken date (probably 28/29th) see Abusch, loc.cit. and cf. also below.

r5. For rituals involving the use of a Gilgameš figurine see Ebeling, *TuL* no.30A (*KAR* 227 || *LKA* 89 (+) 90); W.G. Lambert, *AfO* 18 288 ff; Köcher, *BAM* 231 || 332 and *KUB* 37 no.88. The purpose of all these rituals was to cure diseases caused by ghosts and spirits of the dead, which in most cases at least had been activated by evil sorcery; the rituals thus closely resembled *Maqlû*, in which Gilgameš also plays a part (see Tablet I 38). *AfO* 18 288ff contains an explicit reference to the 2⌜8⌝th day of Ābu (cf. ibid. p.292:44), and *BAM* 231 states (i 17) that the relevant ritual was to be performed in Ābu; in the other texts a corresponding indication is lacking. A couple of similar rituals (making no mention of Gilgameš) are also known to have been regularly performed at the end of Ābu; see Gurney, *Iraq* 22 221ff (anti-witchcraft, 28 Ābu); Köcher, *AfO* 21 13ff (muššu'u, 29 Ābu); Ebeling, *TuL* no.21 (p.84f:23-32; hand of ghost, 27-29 Ābu). These were probably the other (periodical) rites of Ābu meant in our letter. On the association of Ābu with the Netherworld, Gilgameš and other infernal gods, as well as spirits of the dead, see Abusch, loc.cit.; on Gilgameš as the infernal judge, Falkenstein, *RlA* 3 359f.

⌜*ib*⌝*-ba-áš-ši*: despite the spelling with double *b*, almost certainly for *ibašši* "wirklich" (cf. Landsberger, *BBEA* 48[86]); cf. the other similar spellings listed in note to 203 r9.

r8. *le-e-pu-u-šu*: not "should *they* perform" (thus Pt.I) but "should *I* perform", despite the final *u*. In Neo-Assyrian, the peak of the interrogative pitch contour fell on the final syllable, whereby the vowel in question was always lenghened; in the case of closed final syllables, a paragogic vowel (of the same timbre as the preceding one) was regularly appended. Accordingly, *le-e-pu-u-šu* cannot be a plural form, the appended *u* indicating that *-puš*, not *-šu*, is the final syllable. For the development *lēpúš* > *lepûšu* cf. *la-as-de-e-re* (= *lásdêre* < *lásdír*) "should I maneuvre?", *ABL* 440:14 and 545 r10; *ni-iš-pu-u-ru* (< *níšpur*) "shall we send?", *ABL* 488:7, etc.; the question "should they perform?" would have been written *le-(e-)pu-šu-u*, cf. *il-la-ku-ú* "are they going?" *ABL* 1199 r4; *il-la-ku-ú-né-e* "are they coming?" 67 r3; *ú-ša-an-ṣu-u* "are they able?", *LAS* 8 r5, etc.

209

Bibliography:

(I) Waterman, *RCAE* 369 (cf. IV 249); Pfeiffer, *SLA* 238.
(II) Labat, *Royauté* (1939) 212.

Notes:

7. *rābiṣu* (MAŠKIM): one of the Seven Demons (^{d}7.BI) considered as principal causes of many diseases., often mentioned together with the others in incantations directed against the "Seven" (e.g., *Utukkī lemnūti, Asakkī marṣūti, Lamaštu, Bīt-mēsiri, Maqlû, Šurpu*); the diagnostic work *Bīt Marṣi* identifies a disease as "hand of *rābiṣu* (MAŠKIM)" (Labat, *TDP* p.192:40).[341] It is probable that a specific exorcistic ritual, such as is referred to in our letter, had been devised to drive out the demon; the relevant ritual text has not been identified to the present date, however.

210

Bibliography:

(I) Waterman, *RCAE* 553 (cf. IV 257); Pfeiffer, *SLA* 271; Oppenheim, *Letters* (1967) 167.
(II) Behrens, *ABB* (1906) 100; Ylvisaker, *LSS* 5/6 (1912) 40[3]; Landsberger, *LSS* 6/1-2 (1915) 122; Labat,

---

340 The four letters of the present corpus referring to the queen mother's health, all written by the king's exorcists (LAS 159-160, 184 and 222) were probably also exceptional: the old lady was being too sick to be left into the hands of her less competent exorcists.

341 Note also SÌG-*iṣ* MAŠKIM "blow of *r.*" ibid. p. 40:27, 42:28 etc.

Royauté (1939) 292, 319, 343f, and *RlA* 3, 179; Oppenheim, *JAOS* 61 (1941) 263; *Or*NS 11 (1942) 127; Böhl, *Opera Minora* (1953) 409ff; Deller, *AOAT* 1 (1969) 55f.

Copy:

Cf. Zeitlin, *SACA* (1903) no.17.

Writer:

The identity of the writer is more uncertain than indicated in Pt.I. Assuming that the letter was written by an exorcist, (cf. Obv.9-13 and Rev.6-11), one is led to Nabû-nādin-šumi by stylistic and orthographic considerations. One of the distinctive features of this writer is the omission of the word "my lord" after *šarru* "king" (14 examples in 10 letters certainly written by N-n-š), and while the word has been omitted *three* times in the present letter, there are only 18 corresponding cases in the letters of other exorcists: 7 in the 46 letters written by Adad-šumu-uṣur (*LAS* 119 r2.12, 133 r16', 140:10, 142 r20, 143 r20 and 146:11), 6 in the 38 letters of Marduk-šākin-šumi (173:5.12.r11, 179 r7, 195 r4 and 204 r4'), 5 in the letters of Urad-Gula (223:12, 224:4.7.13.r13'), and none in those of Nabû-nāṣer. While the orthography of the letter also generally agrees with the conventions of Nabû-nādin-šumi (cf. simply *LAS* 207-208), the same cannot be said about the other exorcists, except possibly Adad-šumu-uṣur. Marduk-šākin-šumi is certainly out of the question, for he wrote consistently *ep-pa-áš* instead of *e-pa-áš*, found in the present letter (Rev.11).

However, two tiny orthographic details render the attribution of the letter to N. uncertain. The fact is that the spelling *iš-pur-A-ni* (Obv.15, besides *iš-pur-AN-ni* Obv.8) is otherwise found in the present corpus only in letters of *Akkullānu*, where it is attested twice (298:6, 314:6, besides *iš-pur-an-ni* 309:6 and *iš-pur-an-né-ni* 312:4; cf. *áš-pur-A-ni* 312 r20' likewise attested only in letters of Akkullānu). Similarly, the syllabic value KI = *qí* (in *qí-ba-a-ni* Rev. 1.3) does not recur in letters of Nabû-nādin-šumi (cf. *še-tu-uq-QI* 204 r4) but may have been used by Akkullānu (*ú-paq-qí-du-ni* 310 r7). In addition, all features adduced above in favour of Nabû-nādin-šumi are also to be found in letters of Akkullānu: omission of "my lord" in 298 r15.18, 299:6', 302 r6'.10', 308 r7, 312 r9'.12'f, 315 r1.4.12; the spelling *e-pa-áš* in 308 r8; the introductory formula in 307:1-6. True, Akkullānu was no exorcist; but a reference to exorcistic rituals does not as such tell anything about the *profession* of the writer, as appears e.g. from the reference to *né-pe-e-še ša a-ši-pu-tú* in *LAS* 280:18f (from Mār-Ištar). From a purely orthographic point of view, the only suitable writer is, accordingly, Akkullānu; the validity of this conclusion is of course relative to the question as to whether the letter was in reality written down by the sender himself.

Notes:

9. The nature of the exorcistic ritual (for the emendation <*ša*> cf. *LAS* 280:18f, quoted above; a st. cstr.-form *dul-lu* [for *dulli*] would *per se* also be acceptable, note the spelling *dul-lu* for *dulli* (Gen. Sg.), attested in *LAS* 219 r9 and Rm.2,189 r5) referred to here cannot be established from the extent evidence.[342]

13. [*l*]*e-pu-šú*: formally 3rd Pl., but can also stand for the 3rd Sg.; see note to *LAS* 246 r1.

14. *qí-ba-a-ni*: hitherto mostly read *ki-ba-g̣-ni*, a crux interpretum (cf. Landsberger 1915 "Hunger", Waterman 1930 "overseers", Pfeiffer 1935 "flames(?)", von Soden *AHw* 470b "ein Ggst." [s.v. *kibbu*], 920b "Meldung(?)" [s.v. *qību*], Oppenheim 1941 "prescriptions", but 1967 "formulae to be pronounced", Deller 1969 "Brandblasen(?)" *CAD* K (1971) 330 "*kibbu*-objects"), but the context leaves no doubt that the correct translation is "injunctions", "commands", as the writer clearly refers to the "evil day" entries of the series *Inbu Bel Arḫi* (cf. note to *LAS* 185:21).[343] The "commands" in question were identical for all "evil days", excepting the regulation concerning food cooked on fire which is found only in the entry for the 19th day. Consequently, our letter was most probably written on the 18th, and the king's ritual on the river bank, which certainly was of purificatory character and involved donning clean garments, had to be postponed till the 20th because of the "commands" which read:

I UD *19*.KÁM *ib-bu-u šá* ᵈGU.LA (var. ᵈBA.Ú) UD ŠE
UD ḪUL.GÁL SIPA UN^MEŠ *ra-ba-a-ti*

---

342 One would be inclined to think of a *namburbi*, as such rituals often involved the river scene referred to on r7. Cf. also *LAS* 166 (substitute king ritual).

343 Cf. also Exodus 35:1-2: "These are the Lord's *commands* to you (*'lh hdbrym 'šr ṣwh yhwh*) . . . . . . : On six days you may work, but the seventh you are to keep as a sabbath of sacred rest, holy to the Lord."

mim-ma šá IZI TAG NU (var. *ul*) KÚ
TÚG *pag-ri-šú ul* KÚR-*ár eb-bu-ti ul* MU_4.MU_4
ni-qu-u ul BAL-*qí* LUGAL ^{GIŠ}GIGIR *ul* U_5
šal-ṭiš ul i-ta-me

"The 19th day (is the day) of wrath (dedicated to) Gula (var. Bābu), an auspicious day, an evil day. The shepherd of the great people does not eat anything cooked on fire; he does not change the garment of his body, put on clean ones, nor does he perform a sacrifice. The king does not ride a chariot, nor speak in an authoritative tone." (*4R*^{2} 32 ii 39-44; cf. Langdon, *Babylonian Menologies*, p. 74 ff and Landsberger, *LSS* 6/1-2, p. 136 f.)

r4. *ku-zip-pi ša ta-ri-ti*: "clothes of a nurse", probably a euphemism for "stained, polluted garments"; cf. Labat, *RlA* 3 178*b*-179*a*, but note that *tārītu* does not mean "pregnant woman" (*erītu, arītu*) but certainly "midwife, nurse, maid", cf. e.g. Craig, *ABRT* I 27 r6 f (Ištar acting as the nurse [*ta-ri-ti, ta-ri-su-ni*] of Assurbanipla; note that the word is spelt in this text too without the feminine determinative). The connotation of "dirt" attached to the expression may indicate that any contact with a woman giving birth was considered contaminating; such an interpretation actually fits very well the present passage, as it is unthinkable that the king's garment's could have been "filthy", let alone be called so by any of his inferiors on any occasion.

r6. *a-na šal-ši* "the day after tomorrow": ellipsis for *ina šalši ūmi*, lit. "on the third day" (referring both to the future and the past); cf. *ABL* 311:10, TA* ^{URU}*Ḫa-ban ú-na-ma-áš* [11]*a-na šá-al-še ina lìb-bi šu-u* "setting out from Ḫabban, he will be there on the third (day)", and *BBR* 48:3, *ana* URU E_{11}-*ma ina šal-ši* u_4-*mi ina* ÙR BÁR.SI.GA [. . .] "you go up to the city, (and) on the third day you [build] a small socle on the roof"; see also notes to 39 r3 and 158:7 for the substitution of *a-na* for *ina*.

211

Bibliography:
(I) Waterman, *RCAE* 57.
(II) Dhorme, *RHR* 116 (1937) 20.

Date:
Probably Nisannu/Ajāru, eponym year of Nabû-bēlu-uṣur (= April/May, 672 BC). Cf. *ina a-de-e at-ta-la-ka* "I left for the treaty" (Obv.12) and see commentaries to *LAS* 1 and 2. The possibility that the treaty in question was identical with the "Vassal-Treaties" of Esarhaddon is increased by the reference to Calah (14), which obviously served as the scene of the ceremony; see on *LAS* 1. Cf. also below, on r11.

Notes:

7. *IŠ-sap-ra-a-né*: for /issapar+anni/ "*he* sent me", cf. r13f and *tu-šaḫ-si-sa-a-né, LAS* 302 r13', 306 r6; *ú-sa-ni-qa-a-né, ABL* 152:11; *ú-sa-ḫi-ra-a-né* 243:10; *iq-ṭi-ba-a-na-a-ši* 342 r4; *na-i-da-a-né*, 4 *R*^{2} 61 ii 33', etc. IŠ = *ís* also in *a-bu-tú pa-ri-IŠ-tu, CT* 53 364:1', and *IŠ-ḫu-ra-an-ni, ABL* 1063:21; cf. note to *LAS* 147 r15. The subject of the sentence is doubtless simply the king, restore accordingly [LUGAL *be-lí*]-⌜*j*⌝*a* "the king, my lord" (*bēlī(j)a* standing for the nom. as in *ABL* 154:5, 486:5, 514:14, 550:5, 766:12, 885:16, 927:5, 1012 r12 etc.).

9. ^{MÍ}*KUR-i-ti*: a daughter of Sennacherib and a sister of Esarhaddon, cf. *ADD* 804 = *AR* 102:4ff (^{MÍ}KUR-*i-tú* [5]DUMU.MÍ-*su šá* ^{I}*30*-PAP^{MEŠ}-SU MAN KUR *Aš+šur* NIN-*su* [6]*ša* ^{I}*Aš+šur*-PAP-AŠ MAN KUR *Aš+šur-ma* buying a maidservant; no date). The reading of the name is unclear. On the one hand, its consistent spelling with KUR-*i* in the above examples would suggest *Ša(d)dītu*, to be compared with MA ^{MÍ}*Šadda'ītu*(Saporetti, *OMA* I 427; MA fem. nisbe -*a'īt*- > NA -*īt*-); on the other hand, the fact that the determinative MÍ is likewise consistently ligatured with KUR suggests that MÍ+KUR here stands for ^{MÍ}É.GAL "queen", as often in NA (cf. *CAD* E 61), probably to be read (with von Soden, *ZA* 45 [1939] 51) *ekallītu* not *ša-ekalli* (*CAD* l.c.; Landsberger, *Fs Baumgartner* [1967] 198ff; Millard, *UF* 4 (1972) 161-162; this = ^{MÍ}*šá* É.GAL cf. *BE* 9,28:1 and 50:4) or *sinnišat ekalli* (Weidner, *AfO* 17 [1954-6] 261[19]; Borger *Ash* p.99 and *AOATS* 6 [1971] 53). Cf. ^{MÍ}É.GAL-*tú ina lìb-bi* [. . .] *ABL* 1291 r5[344]

[344] This latter dates from ca. 670 BC and could hence well refer to Esarhaddon's sister.

[^{MÍ}É.GAL-"*la-at*" BM 12 1206 viii 52' (van Driel, *CA* p.98; see ibid. 117) is not pertinent; the passage has to be read (after photo) *ina ma-at lìb-ba-šá-ni* "whenever she desires".]

13. ^{I}*Šu-ma-a*: doubtless identical with the exorcist mentioned in 174 r7 (^{I}*Šu-ma-a* DUMU ^{Id}PA-NUMUN-[GIŠ]) and 238 r1 (^{I}*Su-ma-a-a* ditto). The spelling of the name (one final *a*) indicates that a native of Babylonia is in question. See also on Obv. 18.

14. Cancel the translation of this line given in Pt.I and translate instead (with von Soden, *Or* NS 37 [1968] 265): "Why did Š. hurriedly come from Calah (and) . . ."

18. *e-pu-sa-ak-ki*: taken as Neo-Assyrian spelling for NB /eppuš+akki/ "I shall perform for you (f)"; cf. above, note to 13. For NA <s> = /š/ see most recently my remarks in *Assur* 1/1 (1974) p.4. To the examples of NA renderings of Babylonian names, forms or loan-words with /š/, quoted ibid., add NA ^{I}*La-an-si-i* (*CT* 53 61 14. r6.11, and 102 r3) = NB ^{I}*La-an-še-e* (*ABL* 849:2 etc.); ^{I}*Su-la-a* (*LAS* 295 A 2') = NB ^{I}*Šu-la-a* (*ABL* 854 r10, etc.); ^{I}*Sa-pi-ku* (*ABL* 222: 1.r16) = NB ^{I}*Šá-pi-ku* (*RMA* 2r1, etc.); *ta-as-mu-ú-ni* (*ABL* 523:11, Bab. sender) = /tašmûni/; *a-ra-si* (*ABL* 685:11, letter from NE Babylonia) = /arāši/; *ki-ik-ki-si* (*LAS* 137:8) < Bab. *kikkišu*; *sa-kik-ke-e-šu* (*LAS* 256:12) < Bab. *šakikkû*, etc.

r11. This prophylactic ritual is also mentioned in "Exorcist's Manual" (GÌR ḪUL-*tim ina* É LÚ TAR-*is*, *KAR* 44:20) and "Exorcist's Almanac" (GÌ[R Ḫ]UL-*tim ina* É NA TAR-*si*, *STT* 300 r13; GÌR ḪUL-*tú ina* É LÚ TAR-*si*, *BRM* 4 20:24; GÌR ḪUL-*tim ina* É NA TAR-*si*, ibid.19:13, to be performed on the 28th of Addāru; cf. above, sub Date). For the ritual itself, see *KAR* 298:1 ff (= Gurney, *AAA* 22 64 ff); cf. also ibid. r30-37 and 38-40.

r15. *ú-du-lìḫ*: probably for /uddalliḫ/ (*dlḫ* D pf sg 3m), though the change *a* > *u* (= [o]) is, as far as I know, otherwise not attested in Neo-Assyrian in the environment d_l; cf. /uddabbikū/ > *ú-du-⸢bi⸣-ku* ND 2452 = *NL* 35:7 (*Iraq* 18 pl.11), /ūtalli/ > *ú-tu-li LAS* 254 r5 and *ú-tu-li-u*, *ABL* 444:17 (and similar forms of verbs I ' in *LAS* 109 r3, 276 r8, 289:7'.r1, *ABL* 621:8, 950 r5, etc.). Instead of the translation given in Pt.I, the passage may also be rendered "why did he hasten to perform . . ."; note *ur-ru-ḫu* = *ḫa-ma-ṭu* = *dul-lu-ḫu*, *LBTA* 2 no.1 v 23, and the examples of *dulluḫu* in hendiadys quoted in *CAD* D 45*b*.

r18. Thus according to *CAD* A/2 p.22; but what is the precise idea of this line?

212

Bibliography:

(I) Waterman, *RCAE* 1173.
(II) Deller, *AOAT* 1 (1969) 59.

Writer:

According to Deller (1969), Adad-šumu-uṣur; but the authorship of Nabû-nādin-šumi is assured through collation of Obv.1 and by the spelling *a-ki-i* in Obv.11 (cf. App. M 6).

Date:

Possibly the beginning of Esarhaddon's 11th year (670 BC). The references to Urad Nanâ (11, r9') might imply a connection with *LAS* 257 (q.v.), and the content of the letter would fit well the political situation in Assyria in early 670. See in more detail on *LAS* 247. However, it is by no means certain that the person meant here is identical with the *physician* Urad-Nanâ.

Notes:

9. See note to 125:7.

r4. *aḫ-šú . . . ta-ta-lak*: exact meaning obscure. The idiom is not noted in the dictionaries, though it also occurs in *ABL* 493 r22ff: *ú-ma-a* [21] *a-na ki ma-ṣi i-tur-ru* [22] *la-mu-du a-ḫa-šú-nu* [23] *ina* É.KUR *ta-la-ka* [24] AD-*ka a-ḫa-šú-nu ina* É.KUR [25] *ta-ta-lak* "They have now returned, for how long (I don't know); they are informed, (and/ but) their "arms" (still) "goes" in the temple; their "arm" (already) "went" in the temple under your father" (referring to persons accused of stealing of temple property; the context would point to a meaning like "to have free access", or the like). Cf. *qātu* + *alāku* (*LAS* 19 r8'); *ubānu* + *alāku* (39 r11f); and *aḫu* + *ubālu* "to interfere" (e.g. Á^{2}-*ka ina* ŠÀ-*šú-nu la tu-bal*, *ABL* 579:9f; *i-tal-ku-u-né i-du-ku-šú-nu* [12] *an-nu-rig 5-šú 6-šú* ^{UZU}Á^{2}-

šú-nu [13]*i-tu-bu-lu*, *CT* 53 83 r11ff; [*ma*]-⌜*a*⌝ : Á²*-ni ina* ŠÀ KUR *Aš+šur*KI [7][*ni-t*]*u-bil ma-a ú-za-'u-u-na*-⌜*ši*⌝, *CT* 53 424 r6f; KUR*I-tú-'a-aje* . . . [8]⌜Á²⌝*-šú-nu ina na-gi-e* [9]*i-ta-ba-lu* UDUMEŠ [11]*iḫ-tab-tú*, *Iraq* 28 pl.54 no.87:6ff).

213

Bibliography:

(I) Waterman, *RCAE* 58.

(II) Dhorme, *RHR* 116 (1937) 20f.

Date:

Possibly early 670 BC, supposing that the person alluded to in the reverse was involved in the conspiracy detected at that time. See commentary to *LAS* 247.

Addressee:

Esarhaddon(?).

Notes:

r1. *kīma* = *šumma* "if": see note to 156:11.

r2. Cf. *pa-ni-ka* [18]*am-mu-u-tu* SIG_5 MEŠ *la-mur* "(O king, my lord), let me (again) behold that beautiful face of yours", *ABL* 474+ r17f; *pa-ni am-mu-t*[*i ša* LUGAL *be-lí-ja*] [3]*dam-qu-ti* "that beautiful face [of the king, my lord]", *ABL* 1110+ r2'f; *a-na pa-ni am-mu-te* [SIG_5 ME]Š [10]*lik-ru-bu* "(may these gods) bless that [beautiful] face", *LAS* 241:9f; *ḫa-diš ap-pa-lis-*[*su-ma*] [48]*pa-ni-ja* SIG_5 MEŠ UGU-*šú áš-kun* "(wishing to conclude a treaty of peace and serve as my slave, he kept imploring my majesty); I looked upon him friendly and turned by beautiful face on him", Streck *Asb* 144 ix 47f; note also the saying "Beautiful is the king to behold", *ANET*² 428*a* (Ahiqar), and cf. *di-ib-bi am-mu-te* SIG_5 MEŠ [11]*ša* LUGAL EN-*ja*, *LAS* 34 r10f. Obviously, it was considered a great favour to be allowed to look at the king face to face – a favour mostly granted only to those privileged to stay in the king's entourage; this implies that the person referred to here was a courtier, possibly a eunuch (cf. *BBEA* p.12: 33ff). The adjective *damqu* ("beautiful, friendly, gracious", etc.) attached to *king's* face has of course to be understood to refer to the *image of kingship* rather than the physical features of a specific king. Cf. Ass. *mār damqi* = Bab. *mār banê* "nobleman", i.e. "beautiful" by birth. Another idea associated with the royal face was that of luminosity, cf. e.g. *ABL* 916:11ff and *BWL* p.102:90f (*būnū namrūti*; cf. the remarks of Lambert ibid. p.308:235).

r4ff. The writer is here doubtless quoting an ecstatic prophet(ess) (*raggim(t)u*), though the present passage is not included (or preserved) in the extant collections of Neo-Assyrian prophecies (Craig, *ABRT* I 22-27; Pinches, *4 R*² 61; Langdon, *TI* pl.2f; cf. also Zimmern, *ZA* 24 168ff; 83-1-18,726; Bu.91-5-9,106+; Bauer, *IWA* pl.45f, and similar smaller prophecies to be (re-)edited by K. Deller and myself). A similar prophecy is quoted in three letters bearing on the conspiracy of 670 BC (*ABL* 1217:5ff, *CT* 53 17:4ff, *CT* 53 938:5ff; see on *LAS* 247), though only Mylitta (dNIN.LÍL) is there mentioned as the oracular deity, cf. also Langdon, *TI* pl.2 iii 30'ff: *a-ki ta-ap-pa-la la ke-nu-ti* [31']*a-bat* d*15 ša* URU*Arba-ìl a-bat šar-ra-ti* dNIN.LÍL "thus (*or* how) will you (*or* she) answer the disloyal ones: a word of Ištar of Arbela, a word of queen Mylitta . . ."

r11. *šùl-mu . . . liš-'u-lu*: cf. שלם שאל in the Aramaic letters from Elephantine, and see Landsberger, MAOG 4 (1928) 302.

214

Bibliography:

(I) Waterman, *RCAE* 59.

(II) Deller, *Or* NS 34 (1965) 272.

Notes:

r1'. For the spellings [*li-i*]*s-qur* and *liš-ṭur-né* (both for pl. 3 m) see provisionally my remarks in *Iraq* 34 (1972) 24 and 27.

r3'. TA* *pa-an* LUGAL has to be connected with *i-pa-laḫ* not with *i-šam-me* (r4'), as clearly appears from parallels such as TA* *pa-an* LUGAL *pa-làḫ-ku* (*CT* 53 55:10), T[A*] *pa-an ši-ip-ṭu* . . . ⌜*ap*⌝*-ta-làḫ* (*LAS* 281 r22f), etc. Deviations from the normal word order (predicate closing the sentence) are not at all infrequent in Neo-Assyrian especially in sentences containing an adverbial expression; cf. e.g. *mé-e-tu* [19]TA* *pa-an da-ba-bi*, *LAS* 247:18f; *i-sa-pa-ru-u-né* [15]*ina muḫ-ḫi-ja*, *ABL* 310 r14f, 1049:4f; *i-tal-ku* [3]*a-na ma-ṣar-te* 381 r2f; LUGAL *lip-ru-us* [21]*ina ber-tu-un-ni*, 168 r20f; LÚ*GAL ÌR^MEŠ [2]*ša* AD-*ka* [3]*ip-qi-du-u-ni* [4]*ina muḫ-ḫi-šú-nu*, 533 r1ff. More examples in note to 247:16ff.

215

Bibliography:

(I) Waterman, *RCAE* 178 (cf. IV 237); Pfeiffer, *SLA* 185.
(II) Behrens, *ABB* (1906) 82[1].

Copy:

Esarhaddon.

Date:

670 BC. As appears from *LAS* 216 (q.v.), the designation "charge (ward) of the Queen of Cults" refers to a baby (teething) and thus probably was used only over a relatively short time span, perhaps only during the infancy of the child; *LAS* 143, on the other hand, shows that this designation was in use in Ajāru 670. There is no reason to doubt that the same child is in question: Nabû-nāṣer and Adad-šumu-uṣur had other common patients, too, e.g. Aššūr-mukīn-palū'a (cf. *LAS* 145 with nos. 157 and 218f).

Notes:

r3ff. The same benediction also in *LAS* 186 (16f) and 187 (2'f).

216

Bibliography:

(I) Waterman, *RCAE* 586 (cf. IV 185 and 257); Pfeiffer, *SLA* (1935) 284. Townend, *Iraq* 5 (1938) 82ff; Denton, *JNES* 2 (1943) 314f.
(II) Deller, *AOAT* 1 (1969) 56.

Photo:

Iraq 5 p.82.

Writer:

According to Deller (1969) Adad-šumu-uṣur, but there are more weighty facts pointing to Nabû-nāṣer: (1) The spelling ^dGAŠAN *par-ṣi* (Obv.6) occurs only in letters of Nabû-nāṣer; Adad-šumu-uṣur always wrote ^dGAŠAN.GARZA. (2) The remark *ú-ma-a šul-mu a-dan-niš* (r7f) recurs in 217 r3 but not in the letters of Adad-šumu-uṣur. (3) According to collation, only 3 lines are missing at the beginning of the letter: this implies that it did not contain the salutation formula (*lū šulmu* etc.), which is missing only in 4 letters of Adad-šumu-uṣur (*LAS* 138, 148, 156, 158) but is *regularly* omitted in the letters of Nabû-nāṣer.

Addressee:

Esarhaddon.

Date:

670 BC. See on *LAS* 215.

Discussion:

Of the two specialists in odontology who have treated this letter, Townend (1938) believed that it dealt with a case of *systemic infection* due to teeth, and took Rev.3f to indicate that the ancient physician had not only correctly diagnosed the cause of the infection but also recognized that it could be removed by *extracting* the diseased teeth; accordingly, the present letter would furnish evidence of the first known extraction operation, and in particular, one antedating any other corresponding case by several centuries. Denton, however, correctly pointed out (1943) that his interpretation is abortive since "his teeth are to come out" (r3) does not mean "his teeth must be extracted"; according to Denton, "the Assyrian physician is only indicating the condition of the teeth and not their treatment, . . . we have present, whatever else, a chronic condition – teeth so badly diseased and for so long a time that they are ready to fall out . . . Manifestations of secondary foci or an ideopathic neuralgia in the head, hands and feet often accompany such a condition . . ." Unfortunately this interpretation is as unsuccessful as that of Townend, for it can be shown *with certainty* that the letter actually refers to a *teething baby* and consequently has nothing to do with *diseased* teeth: the diagnosis given in the letter originates from the 40th tablet of *Bīt marṣi* (the diagnostic and prognostic handbook of Mesopotamian exorcists) dealing with infants' diseases. The writer's dependance on this source is so obvious that there is no reason to credit him with any particular medical insight nor with "moral and scientific courage" (Waterman, *RCAE* IV 36). Like Urad-Nanâ (cf. on *LAS* 251 and 253), Nabû-nāṣer appears to be, above all, a man "versed in the scriptures" (and, as such, naturally stands on an equal footing with his ancient and modern colleagues).

Notes:

11ff. Cf. Labat, *TDP* 218:10ff, I ^{LÚ}TUR SAG.DU-*su* KÙM *ú-kal pa-gar-šú* KÙM *la ḫa-aḫ-ḫa-aš* IR *la i-ši* ŠU^{2}-*šú u* GÌR^{2}-*šú* ṢA *em-ma* ^{11}*il-la-tu-šú* DU-*ka u ú-sar-ra-aḫ ma-la* KÚ *ina* ŠÀ-*šú la ina-aḫ-ma i-tab-ba-ka* ^{12}^{LÚ}TUR BI ZÚ^{MEŠ}-*šú* È^{MEŠ}-*ni* UD *15*.KÁM : UD *20*.KÁM ^{MÍ}KALAG.GA IGI-*ma* DIN! "If a baby's head is feverish but its body has no temperature and does not sweat, if its hands and feet are hot, its saliva runs and it cries, and if whatever it eats does not remain in its belly but pours out, that baby is teething (lit. its teeth are coming out): it will have a bad time for 15 to 20 days, but it will get well". Cf. also ibid. 230:115f (same tablet): I ^{LÚ}TUR *pa-gar-šú* KÙM *la ḫa-ḫaš* SAG.DU-*su* KÙM TUKU UBUR KÚ-*ma ma-gal ú-sar-ra-aḫ* ZÚ^{MEŠ}-*šú* È^{MEŠ}-*ni* UD *14*.KÁM UD *20*.KÁM ^{MÍ}KALAG.GA IGI-*ma* DIN ^{116}I ^{LÚ}TUR KÙM NU TUKU SAG.DU-*su* KÙM ZÚ^{MEŠ}-*šú* È^{MEŠ}-*ni* UD *21*.KÁM ^{MÍ}KALAG.GA IGI-*ma* DIN "If the body of a baby has no temperature but its heat is feverish (and if) it takes the breast and cries a lot, its teeth are coming out: it will have a bad time for 14 to 20 days, but it will get well. If a baby has no fever but its head is feverish, its teeth are coming out: il will have a bad time for 21 days but it will get well."

r7. *ú-sa-pi-il*: taken as Š-stem of *apālu*, lit. "to make (somebody or something) answer"; cf. on 294:18'. Less likely D-stem of *šapālu* (Deller, *Or* NS 34 [1965] 261 and *AOAT* 1 [1969] 56).

217

Bibliography:

(I) Waterman, *RCAE* 1347.
(II) Landsberger, *MAOG* 4 (1928) 317; Schott, *OLZ* 40 (1937) 297.

Date:

670 BC. See on *LAS* 215.

Addressee:

Esarhaddon.

Notes:

11. *Tarbiṣu*: a town near Nineveh, site of the crown prince's "rear palace" (completed 672 BC) and a temple of Nergal. Cf. notes to 126:6 and 306:8.

r1f. Cf. Oppenheim, *Dreams* 342, Excerpt I 1f, ÉN *šu-ut-ti dam-qa-at e-gir-ru-ú-a da-mi-iq* . . . ^{3}*ina qí-bit šar-ra-tú* ^{d}NIN.LÍL . . . ^{5}*aš-kun du-un-qu lu da-mi-iq-tum* "Conjuration: My dream was pleasant, my *egirrû* good. . . . Upon the command of queen Mylitta . . . , I made a good omen – may it be for the good!" (an incantation to remove evil dreams; cf. also ibid. I 17ff, and p.300); Borger *Ash* p.2:17ff, *iš-šak-na-nim-ma* ^{18}*i-da-at dum-qí* ^{19}*ina* MÁŠ.MI *u ger-re-e* "good signs were granted to me in a dream and *egerrû*"; Streck, *Asb* p.86 x 70f, *ina ma-aja-al mu-ši du-um-mu-qa* MÁŠ.MI^{MEŠ}-*u-a* ^{71}*ina ša še-e-ri ba-nu-ú e-ger-ru-u-a* "my nocturnal dreams were pleasant, my *egerrûs* were beautiful in the morning". From these (and similar) passages it is evident that good dreams and *egerrû*-utterances (cf. *CAD* E 45 and the literature there quoted; but see presently) were regarded as portents whose realization was seriously reckoned with, and the present passage quite explicitly connects the patient's recovery with such dream-omens. Perhaps these dreams had in fact been "produced" by the writer himself? Cf. *LAS* 219.

r2. "I have heard his *egerrû*": since the patient in question was a baby and therefore unable to speak, doesn't this passage imply that *egerrû* (lit. "utterance") as an ominous term refers to sounds uttered asleep (or in ecstacy) and interpreted as signs of pleasure, distress, etc.? That is, a veritable "oracle" (in the literal sense of the word)?

218 + 221[345]

Bibliography:
(I) Waterman, *RCAE* 977 (cf. IV 193; 266); Pfeiffer, *SLA* (1935) 277.
(II) Meissner, *BAW* I (1931) 59; Labat, *Royauté* (1939) 212; Böhl, *Opera Minora* (1953) 409ff; Ritter, *AS* 16 (1965) 320.

Writer:
Identified as Nabû-nāṣer on the following grounds: (1) The introductory salutation is missing (cf. on *LAS* 216). (2) The phrase *lìb-bi ša* LUGAL EN-*ja lu ṭa-ab-šú* appears in this form only in letters of Nabû-nāṣer (cf. 215:10ff, 217:9, 219:7); Adad-šumu-uṣur wrote *lì*(?)*b-bu ša šarri bēlīja lū ṭa-(a-)ba*/DÙG+GA (123:5f, 130 r5ff, 143:12f, 150:16f, 151:8f, 152 r9f, 154 r1'ff, 156 r4'f, 159 r9'f, 160 r9'f), Marduk-šākin-šumi *lìb-BU ša* LUGAL EN-*ja lu ta-ab-šu* (188:10'f), whereas the phrase does not occur at all in the letters of other exorcists. (3) The lavish use of *a-dan-niš* (Obv.4.5.7) is typical of Nabû-nāṣer (cf. 215:5.7.12, 216 r8, 217:5.6.r3, 219:5', 220:5) but does not belong to the characteristics of Marduk-šākin-šumi's letters. (4) Similarly, the gods Nabû and Marduk invoked in the introductory blessing are invariably written ^{d}*AG* *ù* ^{d}AMAR+UD in the letters of Nabû-nāṣer, whereas Marduk-šākin-šumi rather consistently wrote ^{d}PA(*u*) ^{d}AMAR+UD (^{d}AG only in *LAS* 177, 186, 195); note also UŠ$_{12}$.BÚR.RU.DA^{MEŠ} and ŠU.ÍL.KÁM^{MEŠ} (Obv.15.17) as against UŠ$_{12}$.BÚR.RU.DA-*(a-)ni* and ŠU.ÍL.LÁ.KÁM^{MEŠ} of the letters of Marduk-šākin-šumi (cf. 164:10, 173:15.r2, 177:6, 185:5.r10). (5) The spelling *né-pe-ši* (Obv.10, r2.16) is against the authorship of Adad-šumu-uṣur, Nabû-nādin-šumi and Urad-Gula, for the word is spelled *né-pe-(e-)ŠE* in their letters (cf. 159 r4, 208 r2, 223:6); Urad-Gula is out of the question also in view of the spelling UD *1*.KÁM* (r2), cf. UD *22*.KÁM in 224:8.13.r4'. (6) Finally, it is worth noting that *no* orthographical and linguistic features of the letter *hamper* its attribution to Nabû-nāṣer, a remarkable fact in view of the length of the text.

Addressee:
Esarhaddon.

Date and Discussion:

Possibly Addāru 1 (cf. r2), eponym year of Kannūnāju = February 10, 670 BC. Obv.10f shows that the rituals described in this letter were performed by order of the king: and as most (if not all) of Nabû-nāṣer's letters appear to have been written in the last years of Esarhaddon (in the present letter, notice the reference to two sons of this king), this order may very plausibly have been occasioned by the total lunar eclipse of December 29, 671, and its consequences. Cf. *LAS* 279 r13ff (NAM.BÚR.BI^{MEŠ} ÉR.ŠÀ.ḪUN.GÁ^{MEŠ} [*né-p*]*e-še ša di-ḫu mu-ta-a-ni a-na* MA[N EN-*j*]*á ù* DUMU^{MEŠ} MAN EN^{MEŠ}-*e-a* ⌈*lu*⌉-[*bal-l*]*i-ṭu le-e-pu-*[*šú*]) and see relevant note. Though *LAS* 279 was written in Kanūnu 20 (January 3) 670, it is clear from the context that the rituals mentioned were to be performed during the entire reign of the substitute king, i.e. also during the months Šabāṭu and Addāru; see on *LAS* 280.

If this interpretation is correct, then the ceremonies described in the letter were not "monthly rituals" comparable to those referred to in *LAS* 208 r2f and pertinent note. Nevertheless, they served similar purposes, viz. safeguarding the king and the royal family.

---

345 This join, discovered by me on 15.8.1976, was confirmed by C.B.F. Walker on 2.11.1976.

Notes:

11f. Probably a namburbi (cf. r1), text unidentified as yet. Cf. *Or* NS 39 (1970) 118:1f, *a-na di-i'-ḫu šip-ṭi* NAM.ÚŠ^{MEŠ} *a-na* ^{AN}[^{ŠE}KUR.RA *u*] ^{2}ERIM$^{\text{ḪI.A}}$ LUGAL NU TE-*e e-nu-ma* NAM.BÚR.BI [*te-ep-pu*]-*šú* "That headache, plague (and) pestilence may not approach the king's horses and troops, when you perform a namburbi (you do as follows)" (a ritual for the chanter, cf. on *LAS* 137). Note also *di-ḫu : šip-ṭa* NAM.ÚŠ^{MEŠ} *šu-tu-qí* "averting headache (= malaria), plague and pestilence", mentioned among exorcistic compositions in *Exorcist's Manual* (*KAR* 44), 20.[346]

14. Certainly referring to the ritual *KAR* 298 r1ff, ending GIG *di-ḫu di-lip-tú u* NAM.ÚŠ^{MEŠ} *ana* NA *u* É-*šú* MU.*1*.KÁM NU TE-*šú* "(perform this, and) disease, malaria, sleeplessness and pestilence will not approach the man and his house for one year" (r40).[346]

15. Cf. *LAS* 173:15f, *ina* ^{ITU}AB *a-na* UŠ$_{12}$.BÚR.RU.DA-*a-ni e-pa-še ṭa-*[*a-ba*] "it is good to perform the counterspells in Kanūnu", and see relevant commentary.

18. Referring to [NAM.BÚR.BI ḪUL *kiš-pi ru-ḫe-e ru-se-e up-š*]*a-še-e* ḪUL^{MEŠ} *šá* LÚ MÍ *il-pu-tu-ma* . . . ^{4}[ḪU]L Á^{MEŠ} ISKIM^{MEŠ} N[U KUR *ana* NA *u*] ⌜É⌝-*šú* NU TE-*e* "namburbi for the evil of sorcery, witchcraft, magic (and) evil spells which affect a man (or) woman, . . . that the evil of signs and portents may not affect him, that they may not approach the man and his house", *Or* NS 39 (1970) 134ff.

r1. Referring to the same ritual as obv.11f.

r2. *ni-ip-tar-ṣa*: here hardly a denominative of *parṣu* "cult, cultic service" (thus von Soden, *AHw* 832*b* after Landsberger, *AfK* 2 [1924/25] 65): note that the verb is not in the D-stem, as required by *GAG* §88g and other attestations of the den. verb; that the verb is here in the ventive, unlike any occurrences of the den. *prṣ*; and that exorcistic rituals (*nēpēšu*) were not included under the concept *parṣu*, as clearly appears from the evidence collected in *AHw* 778*b* s.v. *nēpešu*. For these reasons, I would rather think of the homophonous verb *parāṣu* I (*AHw* 832*a*), best attested in the meaning "to break", but also meaning "to burst into, to penetrate" like Hebr. *pāraṣ* (Koehler - Baumgartner, *Lexicon* 780*b*; cf. *pa-ra-ṣu* = *e-te-qu e-te-e* "to transgress a limit", Malku IV 110). Such a meaning would account for the ventive suffix, and a semantic development into a meaning like "to proceed (to do something)", implied by the context, is not unthinkable. Cf. *KAV* 113:4ff (Ebeling, *SVAT* 29 b 4ff): "As regards the chutes (? ^{GIŠ}*ra-ṭe-e-te*) of Adad and Bābu, I wrote to the palace (and) they told me as follows: 'The 1st day of Sabāṭu is a good day, let them set to the work (*li-ip-ru-ṣu-né* Á^{2}-*šú-nu ina muḫ-ḫi liš-ku-nu*) then. Let them apply themselves and perform the work quickly.'"

r3ff. To judge by the materia magica mentioned in these lines, the rituals to be performed in Addāru must have been very similar to those performed in the earlier months, if not identical with them. No doubt several different rituals were involved. The figurine of "the daughter of Anu" (r3) points to the *Lamaštu* ritual (performed for protection of infants; cf. *ina* UD 4.KÁM DUMU.MÍ ^{d}*A-nim šá* IM DÙ-*uš* "on the forth day you make a "daughter of Anu" of clay, 4 R^2 55 r26 = Myhrman, *ZA* 16 192 [Lamaštu III]; DUMU.MÍ ^{d}*A-nim šá* IM PA$_5$ DÙ-*uš* "you make a daughter of Anu of ditch clay", *ZA* 16 196 iv 2'); the statues of Namtar, Latarak and Death point to prophylactic rituals such as *KAR* 298:1ff and *BBR* II 41+ etc. (= Gurney, *AAA* 22 [1935] 31 ff; cf. (NU) ^{d}*La-ta-rak*, *BBR* II 54:27; ^{d}*La-ta-rak*, *KAR* 298 r13f; *2* NU ^{d}*La-ta-ra-ak šá* IM, *BBR* II 50 ii 6; explicit references to statues of Namtar and Death are lacking, but the two demons occur frequently together in rituals of this type, e.g. *BBR* 45 = *AAA* 22 42 i 7, ^{d}NAM.TAR . . . *mu-tu*); the different metals and bottles filled with various drinks (r10; r13f) figure prominently in the namburbi against headache, plague and pestilence, which was also performed in Kislīmu and Šabāṭu (cf. [KÙ.UD] ⌜KÙ.GI⌝ URUDU AN.NA A.BÁR AN.BAR . . . [*ana l*]*ìb-bi* ^{DUG}NÍG.TA.TAB ŠUB.ŠUB-*di* "you throw into the *kukkubu* vessels [silver], gold, copper, tin, lead, iron (etc.)", *Or* NS 39 (1970) 118:8f, and *9* ^{DUG}LA.ḪA.AN KAŠ.SAG GEŠTIN GA KAŠ.ZÍZ.ÀM . . . . DIRI-*ma* "you fill nine bottles with fine beer, wine, milk, emmer beer (etc.)", ibid.13f); and the substitute figurines mentioned in r5f could point to the namburbi against witchcraft (cf. *2* NU IM *2* NU NÍG.ŠID.GÁ *2* NU GAB.LÀL *2* NU Ì.UDU *šá* NITA *u* MÍ DÙ-*uš-ma* "you make two images of clay, two images of dough, two images of wax, two images of tallow, (each group consisting) of male and female", *Or* NS 39 135:32), though there are also other possibilities (cf. relevant note). The materials mentioned in our letter constituted only a fraction of the magical apparatus needed in the performance of the rituals just mentioned, and as it is evident that still other rituals are concealed behind the passage, the preparations for

[346] Amulet-stones of *di-ḫu* NAM.ÚŠ^{MEŠ} and GIG *di-'i* e.g. in *KAR* 213 ii 20 ff.

the ceremonies must have gone on for several days even after the dispatchment of the letter (r16). Apparently several exorcists were involved in the preparations, each of them taking care of one specific ritual.

r5. Cf. NU *pu-u-ḫi* LÚ [. . . .], *AMT* 94,1:2 (ritual against "hand of ghost" and "hand of oa[th"), and the *pūḫi amēli* -ritual (*KAR* 245, *LKA* 79 and 80) mentioned in *LAS* 140:14 and 299 r5.

r7. *5 ^{d}ILLAT^{MEŠ}*: possibly referring to Šurpu VIII 39 (^{d}KAS+KUR ^{d}KAS+KUR ^{d}KAS+KUR ^{d}KAS+KUR ^{d}KAS+KUR *a-ši-bu* KUR^{MEŠ} *e-lu-ti ri-šá-an e-la-a-ti* "Illat, Alba, Alḫa, Baliḫa, KAS+KUR, who dwell in the high mountains, the high peaks"; cf. Reiner, *Šurpu* pp.41 and 60; for the reading Illat, cf. il-lat KAS+KUR = *il-lat,* S^{b} II 77). The reference to DUMU.MÍ Ì.UDU is unclear.

r8. *15 šul-pu KÙ.UD*: A. Salonen, *HAM* I p.46, quotes only one example of *šulpu* in ritual use, viz. *RAcc.* p.72 r4, where a golden *šulpu* is used in libation ceremonies; references to exorcistic rituals are entirely lacking. Possibly drinking tubes used in libation ceremonies to infernal gods (cf. the following line) are meant in the present instance.

r10. Cf. 7 ŠE KÙ.UD "7 grains of silver", *Or* NS 34 (1965) 121:15' (scorpion-namburbi); *BBR* 45 iii 10' (prophylactic ritual); *Or* NS 40 (1971) 162:7' (unidentified namburbi); *1* ŠE KÙ.UD *1* ŠE KÙ.GI, *Or* NS 34 (1965) 126:10 (izbu-namburbi), etc.

r11. *DUMU.MÍ ÍD* ("daughter of River"): a demon otherwise known to me only from two NA exorcistic rituals, *KAR* 141 (*nāṭu* of DUMU.MÍ ÍD) and *PKTA* 17 (ritual to undo lightheartedly sworn oath).

219

Bibliography:

(I) Waterman, *RCAE* 450 (cf. III 374); Pfeiffer, *SLA* 292.
(II) Behrens, *ABB* (1906) 8, 17f, 85^{4}; Kunstmann, *LSS* NF 2 (1932) 69f; Oppenheim, *JAOS* 61 (1941) 253; Böhl, *Opera Minora* (1953) 409ff; Oppenheim, *Dreams* (1956) 233.

Copy:

Cf. Harper, *AJSL* 15 (1898/99) 130.

Writer:

Nabû-nāṣir. The criteria on which this assignation is based are the same as presented under *LAS* 218, q.v.
N.B. The letter does *not* join *LAS* 220, as kindly confirmed for me by C.B.F. Walker (in a letter dated November 2, 1976).

Discussion:

The ritual paraphrased in Obv.9-17 of the present letter is also found, in a more complete form, in two exorcistic texts, Combe *Sin* no.6 (r6 ff),[347] and Langdon, *PSBA* 40 (1918) 104 ff (r5 ff). In both cases, it is preceded by a well-known "hand-lifting" prayer to the moon-god (INIM.INIM.MA ŠU.ÍL.LÁ ^{d}EN.ZU.NA.KÁM), the closing part of which specifies the purpose of the ritual, and reads as follows:[348]

22 INIM.GAR *dum-qí u me-šá-ri* GAR-*un* UGU-[MU]
23 DINGIR-MU *u* ^{d}IŠDAR-MU *ša iš-tu* UD-*um ma-du-ti is-bu-su* [UGU-MU]
24 *ina kit-ti u* NÍG.SI.SÁ *lis-li-mu* KI-MU : *ur-hi lid-mì-iq pa-da-ni* [*li-šir*]
25 *ú-ma-'i-ir-ma* ^{d}ZA.QAR DINGIR *šá* MÁŠ.MI[^{MEŠ}]
26 *ina šat* MI $DU_6^{MEŠ}$ *ár-ni*-MU *lu-uš-me šèr-ti lu ta-a*[*b-kat? anu-ku*]
27 *ana dà-ra-ti lud-lul dà-lí-lí-*[*ka*]

"Place upon me a dream-oracle of fortune and success;
may my god and goddess, who have been angry at me since many days, become reconciled with me in (= through my) justice and righteousness; may my ways become good, may my path become straight. I have sent (for) Zaqīqu, the god of dreams; may I hear the pardoning of my sins in the course of the night, may my fault be forg[iven, and I] will praise you (Sîn) forever!"

[347] Written for Šamaš-šumu-ukīn (as king of Babylon).
[348] Here quoted from the duplicate King, *BMS* no.1.

The purpose of the ritual was, accordingly, to secure good dreams and dream-oracles (INIM.GAR/*egerrû*) for a patient, which suggests that the letter at hand might somehow be related to *LAS* 217 (q.v.). On the other hand, it would be quite unwarranted to draw from this the conclusion that the patient ("charge" of ᵈ*Šarrat parṣī*) figuring in *LAS* 217 would be identical with either of the persons mentioned in the present letter: there is no guarantee that the ritual section pertained to the cure of either patient (it *may* have pertained to the "charge") and besides, the same ritual may well have been performed for different persons at different times.

Notes:

9. The parallel texts describe the preparation of the offering table in more detail than the present letter, which only gives the most essential features of the ritual. Cf. *PSBA* 40 108 r5 ff, [ᴳᴵŠBANŠUR ᴳᴵŠŠIN]IG ⌜GAR⌝-*an 12* NINDA *ḫa-še-e 12* NINDA ŠE.GIŠ.Ì ⁶[ZÚ.LUM.MA ᶻᴵᴰA.TIR G]IN-*an* NINDA.Ì.DÉ LÀL Ì.NUN GAR-*an* ⁷[KAŠ BAL-*qi* ÉN *3-šú*]ŠID-nu "you set a(n offering) table made of tamarisk wood, place upon it 12 loaves of *ḫašû*-bread, 12 loaves of linseed bread, dates and *sašqû*-flour, set aside confections (of) honey and ghee, libate beer, and recite the (hand-lifting) incantation (to Sîn) three times" (restorations from Combe, *Sin* no.6, which runs parallel with minor variants).[349]

10. On the dream-god Zaqīqu, the Mesopotamian "sandman", see Oppenheim, *Dreams* p.233 ff.

11 f. The parallel texts mentioned insert here instructions for reciting an incantation to the dream-god.

17. ᵀᵁ́ᴳ*ši-ši-ik-ti-šú*: rendering spoken /sissikti-su/, cf. *Assur* 1/1 (1974) 4; the spelling with <š> indicates that *sissiktu* in NA was only a (late) technical loanword from Babylonian (literary and scientific texts); the proper NA word for "hem" was *qannu*. For other similar "technical" loanwords in the present correspondence cf. *pi-iš-šá-tu*, 110 r8 (= *pissatu*); É *šá-la me-e*, 280:18 (= *bīt salā' mê*); *ki-ik-ki-si*, 137:8 (= *kikkišî*); and *sa-kiq-qé-e-šú*, 246:12.

18. *re-e-ši ni-it-ti-ši*: the logical object of this expression is *né-pe-ši* in Obv.8; the long ritual section inserted between the predicate and the object served to specify the meaning of *né-pe-ši*, and has to be understood as a parenthetical clause. For a similar construction see *LAS* 173:11 ff.

r3 f. On Aššur-mukīn-palē'a see note to 17:9. The child called *lakû* "baby" (sic, not "weakling" [Pt.I]) also occurs beside Aššur-mukīn-palē'a in *LAS* 250 and 254, both letters by the physician Urad-Nanâ who in *LAS* 222 appears as an associate of Nabû-nāṣir. In both letters (and probably here, too) *lakû* evidently functions as a pet name, since it is treated as an undeclinable proper name.[350] The implication of the present passage is that the "Baby" was to be protected from potentially infectious contact with Aššur-mukīn-palē'a.[351]

r5 ff. These lines seem to imply that the "Baby" had recently passed his infancy, that is, more precisely, had *learned to speak*. Cf. *LAS* 254 r11 f, *šu-tú-ma pi-i-šú it-ti-din* "he himself gave his word (for it)", referring to the *lakû* who accordingly must have been able to speak. There is no cogent reason to take the passage to imply that the child had recently died (thus *CAD* B 175*b* following Behrens 1906, Pfeiffer 1935 and Oppenheim 1941); the idiomatic expression "to reckon among people" occurring here did *not* imply "to reckon among *the living*" but "to endow (non-Assyrians) with (Assyrian) citizenship", cf. the references listed in *AHw*. 604*b*. Translate accordingly: "Until (*adu*) Aššur etc. reckoned him among people (= gave him ability to speak) we did not . . ."

---

349 The latter text continues (after KAŠ BAL-*qí*): IGI ᵈ[ZA.QAR] ⁹*ina* SAG GIŠ.N[Á] NÍG.NA ŠEM.LI [GAR-*an*], just like the present letter (Obv.10 f), and closes with the words: ᵈZA.QAR *na-áš-par-ti* ᵈŠEŠ.KI "O Zaqīqu, the messenger of Sîn" (the incipit of the subsequent incantation to the dream-god).

350 In lexical texts, *lakû* is given as a synonym of *ṣehru* and *šerru*, both meaning "little one, child" (cf. Diri II 163 ff, IV 156 ff, etc.), and Assurbanipal himself uses the word of himself when referring to his infancy ("you were an infant [*ṣe-eh-ru*], O Assurbanipal, when they submitted you to the care of Šarrat-Nīnua; you were a babe [*la-ku-u*], O Assurbanipal, when you sat in the lap of Šarrat-Nīnua", Streck *Asb* p.342:6f, cf. commentary on *LAS* 123).

351 Note that the translation of r2-9 recently proposed in *CAD* (L 46), which would radically alter the interpretation of the passage, is not acceptable since TA*/*issu* is otherwise never used as a subjunction in NA, and since *ni-ib-ṭi-li* in r8 is not in the subjunctive, as it should be if it belonged to the *šumma* clause.

222

Bibliography:

(I) Waterman, *RCAE* 719 (cf. IV 186).

Date:

June (?), 670 BC. See under *LAS* 151.

Addressee:

Esarhaddon.

Discussion:

This letter is the only one in the present correspondence authored jointly by an exorcist (Nabû-nāṣir) and a physician (Urad-Nanâ), but the cooperation of the two crafts is well-known from other texts; see Ritter, *AS* 16 (1965) 299 ff and commentary on *LAS* 264 r7. The fact that the name of the exorcist here precedes that of the physician may indicate that the former ranked higher in the hierarchy of scholars in Sargonid times.

Additional details about the nature of the queen mother's illness (here reported as cured) may be gleaned from *AGS*101, a haruspical query referring to an illness of "Niq'a, the mother of Esarhaddon" (^{d}UTU EN GAL-*ú šá a-šal-lu-ka* [..........] ^{2}^{MÍ}*Ni-iq-a* AMA ^{Id}*Aš+šur*-ŠEŠ-SUM-*n*[*a* ......] ^{3}*šá i-na-an-na mar-ṣa-tu-ma* ŠU^{2} [.......] ^{4}*i-na* MÁŠ *iš-šá-ak-un-ši*, etc.). According to J. Aro, *RAI* XIV (1966) 116, the text, of which only the lefthand portion was edited by Knudtzon, "is now complete: BM 98987 (Ki.1904-10-9,16) gives the other half. Knudtzon's restorations have been almost completely verified, except that it is not 'the hand of Nana of Uruk' which caused the illness . . . , but the hand of ^{d}KA.BI.SIG$_{5}$." Unfortunately no symptoms associated with this god are included in the extant fragments of the diagnostic series *Enūma ana bīt marṣi* (cf. Labat, *TDP* p. XXII f). For other letters referring to Nagia's health see *LAS* 159, 160, 184 and 208; these give the impression that the queen mother may have suffered from psyche disorders, possibly paranoia.

223

Bibliography:

(I) Waterman, *RCAE* 118.

(II) Behrens, *ABB* (1906) 54; Labat, *Royauté* (1939) 212; Oppenheim, *JAOS* 64 (1944) 191; Deller, *Or*NS 33 (1964) 91.

Date:

Ca. 672-669 BC. See note on r5' ff.

Addressee:

Esarhaddon.

Notes:

6. *nē-pe-še ša* ^{ITU}*NE*. See note on *LAS* 208 r2-3.

8. Cf. 173:5 ff, 203 r10 f, 204:6 ff and 209:7 ff. These parallels and the continuation show that *a-na u*$_{4}$*-me* has here the meaning "before the set day", not "on the day" (Waterman).

9 ff. This saying, resembling those preserved in the "Words of Ahiqar" (see Ginsberg, *ANET*^{2} [1955] 427 ff with literature), was obviously widely spread in Sargonid times, for it also occurs (in elliptic or otherwise slightly modified form) in several other Kuyunjik letters. See Pt.I, Critical Note on *LAS* 199:7-8, and note also *ABL* 1107 r9, LÚ *ša a-na* LUGAL EN-*šú* ^{10}[*i-d*]*u-lu-u-ni* ^{11}[. . .]X. For the spelling EN^{MEŠ}-*šú* = *bēlīšu* (Gen. Sg.) cf. *LAS* 60 r2; EN^{MEŠ}-*šú* = Gen. Sg. also passim in NA legal texts.[352]

r5' ff. Cf. 174 r8 ff, where Nabû-lē'ûtu is also mentioned as an associate of Urad-Gula, together with [Bē]l-nāṣer (= the son of Nabû-lē'ûtu??) and other exorcists. *LAS* 174 dates from Esarhaddon's reign (Kanūnu,

[352] In the formula *kaspu ana ešrāti ana bēlīšu utāra*, e.g. *AR* 43:18, 53:22, 61:21, 66:25, 70:21, 75:17, 76:17, etc.; cf. *a-na* EN-*šú* (in the same formula), ibid. 59:18, 81:19, 82:19, 86:20, etc.

670 BC); it is likely that this general date applies in the present case, too, cf. the date of the following number and see Discussion on *LAS* 120.

r7' ff. Cf. 142 r8 f. The parallelity of the two passages does not, of course, imply any connection whatever between the two letters.

r10'. *qanni aḫē'ūš*: see note to *LAS* 184 r4 f.

r12'. *a-sa-par-ra* = /*assapara*/. The gemination of the last root consonant has to be interpreted graphemically (see *Iraq* 34 [1972] 25, note on l. 19), whereas the *a*-vowel inserted between *p* and *r* was certainly pronounced (contra Deller, *Or* NS 31 [1960] 194 ff); cf. *a-sa-pa-ra, ABL* 235 r7, 251:11.14, 463:3, 1086 r2, ND 2625 r12 and 2683:11 (*Iraq* 21 pl.49); *a-sa-par-ra, ABL* 243 r15, *as-sa-pa-ra, ABL* 85 r12; *i-sa-pa-ra, ABL* 556 r5, *CT* 53 160:15; *i-sa-par-ra*, ibid. 15:8; *is-sa-pa-ra, ABL* 868:7; *ni-sa-pa-ra, ABL* 1211:4. Corresponding forms of other verbs with ventive endings are also attested, e.g. *a-sa-ṭa-ra, ABL* 910:8 and *i-su-ḫu-ra, ABL* 515 r6, 1371 r2. With regard to the relatively high frequency of spellings of this type (the above list of examples is by no means complete), it seems legitimate to consider *assapara* (and other similar forms) an alloform of the more paradigmatic type *assapra*, which occurs about four times more frequently than the former.

r14'. *šá-al-mì*: on this alloform of the stative *šalim* see, provisionally, my remarks in *Iraq* 34 (1972)24.

r18'. For the final *a* in *a-za-za* see note to *LAS* 18 r8.

224

Bibliography:

(I) Waterman, *RCAE* 117 (cf. III 373).
(II) Meier, *Or*NS 8 (1939) 304; Oppenheim, *JAOS* 61 (1941) 256; 64 (1944) 191; Postgate, *Taxation* (1974) 48 and 254 f.

Copy:

Cf. also Lehmann, *Ššmk*, pl. 40-41.

Addressee:

Esarhaddon.

Date:

672-671 BC. The mention of Assurbanipal and Šamaš-šumu-ukīn side by side with the king (= Esarhaddon) in Obv. 4 f implies a date of composition between the promulgation of the "Vassal-Treaties" and Šamaš-šumu-ukīn's change of residence to Babylonia. Cf. sub *LAS* 173.

Notes:

3 ff. This blessing in an adaptation of a prayer formula fairly often encountered in exorcistic texts. Cf. ^{d}*É-a u* ^{d}AMAR+UD *ina u$_4$-me an-ni-e* ^{19}[*i-n*]*a di-ni-ja i-ziz-za-nim-ma* "Ea and Marduk, on this day stand by me in my trial", *Or*NS 36 14:18 (namburbi ritual); (*Girra . . .*) *ina u$_4$-mi an-ni-i ina di-ni-ja i-ziz-za-am-ma, Maqlû* II 144; (*Girra . . .*) *ina di-ni-ja i-ziz-za-am-ma ki-ma* ^{d}UTU *qu-ra-du* ^{130}*di-i-ni di-ni* EŠ.BAR-*a-a* KUD-*us*, ibid. 129 f. Cf. also the beginning of the Cassite letter *BE* 17/1 no.5 (= Waschow, MAOG 10/1 p.20): DINGIR^{MEŠ} *ma-la be-lí* ^{9}*pa-al-ḫu-šu-nu-ti* ^{10}*na-ap-šá-a-ti ša be-lí-ja li-iṣ-ṣu-ru* (Obv.9 ff).

11 ff. The translation of this passage is more uncertain than indicated in Pt. I and needs explanation. First of all, it is uncertain to whom the pronoun *šu-ú* in Obv.11 and 16 refers. Logically, the person in question should be the king, for nobody else (except the two princes) has been mentioned so far, but the continuation (where *šu-ú* clearly contrasts with LUGAL) excludes such an interpretation; my hypothesis is accordingly, that the man concerned is identical with the one reproached on the reverse, who clearly is a fellow-exorcist of the writer (cf. Rev.14). Secondly, the verb *baṣāru* occurring in line 11 (together with the hapax legomenon *ma-ga-ṭi*) does not seem to be otherwise attested in Akkadian in the G-stem (except in lexical lists), and hence the translation "cutting" given in Pt.I remains uncertain; the word GEŠTIN "wine" in line 17 suggests that the verb might have here a meaning similar to Bibl. *bṣr* G "do the vintage, gather grapes" (Koehler-Baumgartner, *Lexicon* p.142b). Thirdly, the fragmentary condition of ll. 13-17 prevents reconstructing the sense of these lines reliably, a fact not

clearly enough indicated in the translation. Notwithstanding, it seems on the whole pretty certain that the writer in these lines blames his unnamed colleague for neglecting his professional duties, and the passage may therefore be regarded as a prelude to the charges preferred against this man on the reverse.

12. Cf. *me-me-e-ni* [16]*ina muḫ-ḫi la iq-ri-ib* "nobody has gone at it", lit. "proceeded to (do) it", *LAS* 277 r15 f. The meaning "to be pertinent" attested for *qarābu* in the idiom *ina libbi* / *muḫḫi qurbu* (e.g., *LAS* 46 r5 f, 148 r7 f; 186 r14; see Meier, *OrNS* 8 [1939] 304) does not seem to apply here.

13. Cf. *a-na lìb-bi* ÌR^{MEŠ}*-ni-i-ka* [4]*ki-i tar-'u-ú-bu* "when you (= the king) were angry with your servants", *RMA* 170 r3 f, and notice *LAS* 306 r3 f (LU[GAL] *be-lí* [4]*la i-ra-ú-bu*). The spelling *er-ú-bu-u-ni* shows that the word was syllabified /ir-(') u-bū-ni/; taking the form as Pret. of **'rb* "to enter" is therefore out of the question.

15. [*m*]*u-ú-a-te*: taken as an "unorthodox" spelling of *muātu* "to die" (the sign *ú* representing the glide [*w*]pronounced between two contiguous vowels); cf. [*i*]*t-tu-ú-aḫ CT* 53 197:15'; *šu-u-a-te* = *šuāte* [suwa:ti], *ADD* 319: 12 and *tu-u-a-ru* = *tuāru* [tuwa:ru] "to return", ibid.8, and note *pa-ni-*⌈*i-ú*⌉*-*[*te*] = *pānijūti* in r3', the sign *i* standing there for the glide [j] as in the letters of Mār-Ištar and Balasî. It seems that the sign *u*/*ú* functions as a marker of the glide [w] also in spellings such as ^{I}*I-tu-u-an-dar* (= Ετεϝανδρος), Borger *Ash* p.60, 66; ^{URU}*Ni-nu-u-a* (*ABL* 633: 12, *ADD* 1116:3, *AR* 615 = *ADD* 500:19, for more common ^{URU}*Ni-nu-a*) or $^{\text{KUR/URU}}$*Qu-u/ú-e* (*AOAT* 6 p. 288 f), if the original forms of these toponyms can be reconstructed as **Nīnu(w)a* and **Qu(w)ē* as the Biblical spellings נִינְוֵה and קְוֵה suggest.

r5'. [^{TÚG}*gu*]*lēnu*: "Es dürfte sich um das bis zu den Knien reichende, k u r z ä r m e l i g e G e w a n d handeln, das an den Hüften von einem doppelten Gürtel zusammengehalten wird" (Weidner, *AfO* Bh 6 [1940] 34, n. 10); possibly = Hebr. *g^{e}lōm*, Aram. *g^{e}līmā* "wrapping, garment" (thus *CAD* G 127, *AHw* 296); cf. also Jes.3:23 גלינים, more probably referring to a garment than a "mirror" (?) גליון); context: "mantles, cloaks, flounced skirts, ———, kerchiefs of linen, turbans, flowing veils.

r.7' f. Cf. NA_4.^{MEŠ} *ša-ku-tu₄* *gab-bu ina* IGI-*šú a-na mé-mé-e-ni* [4]*is-se-e-šú la ú-kal-lam* "the jewels and the whole decoration are in his hands, he does not show them to anybody with him", *ABL* 951 r3 f (sense?); similarly ibid. r6 *mé-mé-e-ni is-se-e-šú la-a em-mar*, "nobody sees (the divine statue) with[353] him." The exact meaning of the preposition *isse* in the present context eludes me.[354] It seems, however, that all exorcists hired by the palace received – at regular intervals – a certain amount of clothes as a payment for their services, and that the distribution of these clothes was normally controlled by the chief exorcist (or one of his highranking colleagues) to prevent misuses; in the present case, the person responsible for the delivery had apparently taken the whole consignment of garments for himself and left the chief exorcist and his assistant "empty-handed".[355] At the end of the line restore [*id-din*] rather than [*ú-kal-lam*].

r10' ff. Cf. *a-na bat-qi* . . . TA* *a-ja-ka ni-na-ši-a* "whence are we supposed to levy (labour) for the reparation (of the temples so-and-so)", *ABL* 578 r2-6.

r9' and 10'. *TA*a-ḫi-in-ni ra-aq-te*: cf. *i-na qa-tim re-eq-tim* "empty-handed", *ARM* 239:20.

r12' f. Cf. *šúm-mu am-mar* KUŠE.SÍR *am-mar ig-ri* [28]*ša* ^{LÚ}TÚG.KA.KÉŠ *ma-aṣ-ṣa-ku-ni* "verily I cannot afford either (a pair of) sandals or the wages of a tailor", *ABL* 1285 r27 f. The rendering of the present passage proposed in *CAD* I/J p.45*a* is not acceptable, since *ig-re-e* does not belong to the relative clause.

225

C o p y :
CT 53, pl 40 no.123.

---

[353] Thus *CAD* A/2 (1968) 6 *b*. Or "nobody of his associates sees (the statue)", cf. note on *ša issē 'a* sub *LAS* 264 r7?

[354] Cf. *iš-ku ša-ni-tu il-te-šá-ma ta-at-ta-al-pa-at*, *KAV* 1 I 83f (MA), where *ilte* "with" = "in addition to".

[355] *LAS* 359 (below, p. 483) possibly represents the accused man's answer to the charges here presented against him.

226

Copy:
Ungnad, *PBS* VII (1915), no. 132.

Discussion:

In spite of the fact that this letter was found in Sippar, there is reason to believe that its addressee is identical with the well-known son of Adad-šumu-uṣur who wrote the preceding numbers. It is virtually certain that the addressee was Assyrian, not Babylonian, since Sargonid royal orders addressed to Babylonian officials were usually written in the mother tongue of the latter;[356] the name Urad-Gula itself was quite rare in Assyria proper (see Tallqvist, *APN* s.v. Arad-Gula), and the contents of the letter are best accounted for by supposing that the recipient was a professional exorcist (cf. *me-eli* "phylacteries", Obv. 7, and DÙ.DÙ.BI-*šu* "its ritual", ibid. 9). The stay of an Assyrian scholar in Sippar could plausibly be combined with the systematic search for rare pieces of literature (missing in the Ninevite libraries) organized by Assurbanipal, cf. *CT* 22 no.1 = Pfeiffer, *SLA* 256 = Waterman, *RCAE* IV p.212 ff, and note our letter, Obv.4 ff and Rev. 1 ff.

Notes:

7. *me-eli*: see note to *LAS* 239:3'.

10, r3'. As copied, these lines do not make much sense to me. A collation of the tablet is an obvious necessity before any definite interpretation can be suggested.

11. *miqitti šamê*: cf. Oppenheim, *Dreams* p.283 for dream-omens concerning falling stars, weeping heavens, etc.

227

Bibliography:
Waterman, *RCAE* 932.

Discussion:

The letter appears to be a petition on behalf the brother of the writer (a servant of the crown prince? Cf. 174).

228

Bibliography:
Previously unpublished.

Copy:
CT 53, pl 31 no.88.

Date:
672-669 BC. See note on 173:17.

Addressee:
Esarhaddon.

Writer;
Hand of Adad-šumu-uṣur (personal collation, March, 1968).

---

[356] An exception is constituted by two royal orders to Nabû-ušabši, *ABL* 273, 543 and 1244), which are in Assyrian; the other royal orders to Nabû-ušabši are written in Babylonian.

Discussion:

This small fragment is clearly associated with the oracle query BM 99062 (= Aro, *RAI* XIV [1966] 117) mentioning "an illness of the crown prince Assurbanipal [*šá ina*] ⌜U$_5$⌝ *u* GIN ^{KUŠ}MÚRU^{MEŠ} KÚ.KÚ-⌜*lu*⌝-*š*[*ú*] 'whose hypochondrium hurts him when he rides or walks'". Two letters of the present collection also show that the crown prince's physical condition did not always permit hard bodily exercises; see *LAS* 252:8-14 and 253:7-11, the former making reference to a treatment of the prince's chest; cf. also *LAS* 140-141 and 144. Nonetheless, the very fact that in the present letter the prince was explicitly *denied* riding and drawing a bow, indicates that Assurbanipal's proud description of his athletic exercises in his youth is not at all unrealistic. Cf. Streck, *Asb* p. 252 i 19 ff: *an-na-a šá ep-pu-š*[*á*] *gi-mir u$_4$-me-ja* [20] *ši-taḫ-ḫu-ṭa-ku mur-ni-is-qi rak-ba-ak ḫi-iš-šá-me-e šit-ma-ru-ti* [21] [*ta*]*m-ḫa-ak til-pa-nu ú-ṣu ú-šap-ra-áš si-mat qar-ra-du-ti* "this is what I was doing every day: I kept mounting on pedigreed horses, rode on fiery thorough-bread stallions, seized the bow, and let the arrow fly as befits a hero."[357]

Notes:

r4. Cf. LUGAL ^{GIŠ}BAN *ina* IGI ^{d}UTU *ú-ma-la* [13] *'ina* UGU *qaq-qa-ri* GAR-*an* "the king 'fills' (= bends, draws?) the bow and places (it) on the ground" K.3438a + 9912 Obv.12' f (|| K.9923:17), unp. cultic ritual).

229

Bibliography:
Previously unpublished.

Copy:
CT 53 pl. 40 no. 117.

Discussion:

By comparing the king to Adapa, the writer of this fragment means that the king had acted extraordinarily wisely. We meet the same comparison also in other texts of the Sargonid period, the king intended being in most cases Esarhaddon. Cf. *LAS* 57 r5, 117:8, 318 r3 and 321 r2; *CT* 53 963 r9' [LUGAL *b*]*e-lí a-ki a-da-p*[*i e-piš*] "the king, my lord, [is built] like Adapa"; also Borger, *Ash* p.34 45 ff: *ja-a-ti* ^{I}*Aš+šur*-ŠEŠ-SUM-*na* MAN KUR *Aš+šur*^{KI} NUN *na-a'-du* [46] *šun-na-at* NUN.ME *A-da-pà šá iš-ru-ku ru-bu-u* ^{d}*Nin-ši-kù* [47] *ša tam-le-e šu-a-tu ina uz-ni-ja ib-ši-ma uš-ta-bi-la ka-bat-tu*! "I, Esarhaddon, king of Assyria, a pious prince, pondered over that terrace and conceived in my mind plans as clever as those of the sage Adapa, which were a gift from the princely Niššiku."[358] In *LAS* 184, the person linkened to Adapa is exceptionally Esarhaddon's mother, Naqia (cf. *LAS* 230!). Note also *AfO* 19 p.64:72 (a prayer to Marduk), where the supplicant (a king) speaks of himself as "the wise (*a-da-pà*) servant" of the god.[359]

For the "deeds of Adapa" see Speiser, *ANET*^{2} p.101 and Jensen, *KB* 6/1 (1901), p. 92 f. On Adapa himself, see Jensen *RlA* I p.33 ff and the literature ibid.; Reiner, "The Etiological Myth of the 'Seven Sages'", *Or*NS 30 (1961) 1-11; Gurney, *JRAS* 1935, 459 ff; Borger, *JNES* 33/2 (1974) 186; Foster, *Or*NS 43 (1974) 344 ff; and de Liagre Böhl, "Die Mythe vom weisen Adapa", *WO* 2 (1959) 416-31. Adapa was identical with Berossus' Oannes, the alleged founder of the Mesopotamian civilization, see W.G. Lambert, *JCS* 16 (1962) 74.

Notes:

3' f. Cf. [^{d}EN ^{d}AG DINGIR^{MEŠ}-*kal*] [15] *lu ú-du-u šúm-ma dul-la-ti* [*ša ina tar-ṣi*] [16] LUGAL^{MEŠ}-*ni* AD^{MEŠ}-*ka ep-šá a n*[*i a na dul-la-ti*] [17] *ša ina tar-ṣi* LUGAL *be-lí-ja e*[*p-šá-a-ni*] [18] *muš-la-ni i-ba-áš-šú-u-ni* "by Bel and Nabû, your gods, there are no works done [in the time of] your royal ancestors that can be compared with

[357] This passage has an exact counterpart in the sculptures found in the NW Palace of Assurbanipal in Nineveh; see the famous hunting scene published in R.D. Barnett, *Assyrian Palace Reliefs* Pl. 93 = E. Strommenger – M. Hirmer, *The Art of Mesopotamia* Pls. 258 and 260.

[358] Cf. LUGAL *pe-et ḫa-si-si le-'i-i-ni ka-la-ma šun-na-at* NUN.ME Lyon, Sg 6:38.

[359] The semantic development from *Adapa* = personal name associated with highest learning and wisdom to the adjective "skilled, wise" is also attested lexically; cf. ù - t u - a - a b - b a = *a-da-pu* (between NUN.ME. TAG = *enqu* etc., and š u - g a l - a n - z u = *eršu* etc.) Igituḫ I 107.

[the works] d[one] in the time of the king, my lord!", *ABL* 841:14 ff (Aḫa-lurši to Sargon II.). The unusual stative-form *mušlā* (for **mašlā*; note also *mu-šu-ul*, *LAS* 35:17 231 r9, *muš-lu* 247 r17) should be compared with *pu-uḫ-ru*, *ABL* 506:14, 548 r6, 639 r11 (for **paḫrū*) and *qu-ru-ub/qur-bu* passim (for **qarub/qarbu*); *šul-mu* etc. since none of the asterisked forms are actually attested in Neo-Assyrian texts, it seems warranted to regard the pattern *purus* underlying all the attested forms as a replacement, rather than an allomorph, of the older pattern *parus* used to form verbal adjectives (side by side with the patterns *paris* and *paras*; see von Soden, *GAG* § 55 e-g); naturally, she shift *a* > *u* may have been realized through an intermediate [*o*], as suggested in *GAG* § 87 1 (cf. also *AHw* s.vv. *mašālu*, *paḫāru* and *qurbu*).

5'. Instead of *a-sa-di-ru-u-ni*, one may, naturally, also read *la-a sa-di-ru-u-ni* "(which) has not been arranged."

230

Bibliography:
Previously unpublished.

Copy:
CT 53 pl.31 no.84.

Writer:
Very probably Ištar-šumu-ēreš, in view of the spelling *be-li* in Rev.7 (see Appendix M 6.4) and the characteristic form of *ša* in lines 1 and 6 (three horizontal wedges only, cf. *LAS* 3, 10 and 11). See also *LAS* 21, addressed to the queen mother.

Addressee:
Naqia/Zakūtu.

Date:
Cf. under *LAS* 21.

Discussion:

The flatteries in this letter provide an excellent illustration of the influential position the queen mother Naqia had obtained under Esarhaddon (see Streck, *Asb* [1916] p.CXXXIXf, CCXXVIII; Schmidtke, *AOTU* 1/2 [1916] 124ff; H. Lewy, *JNES* 11 [1952] 264f; Borger, *BiOr* 29 [1972] 33f, and cf. *LAS* 21 and 184, and relevant commentaries). Elsewhere only kings are credited with godlike omnipotence and perfection (r1; cf. on 125:18f), and the same is true as regards the queen mothers alleged ability to make true her curses and blessings (r2ff). Cf. Streck, *Asb* p.22 ii 123ff, *iṣ-ba-ta* GÌR[2] LUGAL-*ti-ja um-ma* LUGAL *šá* DINGIR *i-du-u-šú at-ta* [124] AD-*u-a ta-ru-ur-ma* [MÍ]ḪUL *iš-šá-kín ina pa-ni-šú* [125] *ja-a-ti* ÌR *pa-liḫ-ka kur-ban-ni-i-ma la-šu-ṭa ab-šá-an-ka* "(Ardys the son of Gyges) grasped my royal feet, saying: 'You are the king whom the God cares for; you cursed my father, and misfortune was his share; but bless me, your obedient servant, so that I may pull the yoke of you(r chariot)". Note how the present letter contrasts with Ahiqar's words "What me[n's] l[i]ps curse, God does n[ot] curse" (*ANET*[2] p.249*b*)!

Notes:

r2. For *bēt* = *ša* "what" see on *LAS* 144:8.

r2ff. The verbs "to curse" and "to bless" are found in antithesis in other Akkadian texts, too, though mostly expressing an idea different from the present passage. Cf. *ša ta-ru-ri at-ti-ma ta-kar-ra-bi* "you (the goddess) bless him whom you have cursed", 79-7-8,50:2 (unp., quoted *CAD* A/2 235*a* and K 193*b*); KA *ša iz-zu-ru-šu i-kar!-⌈rab⌉-šú* "a mouth which has cursed him will bless him", *Babyl.* 4 104, K.3769:3' (hemerology).

231

Bibliography:
Previously unpublished, transliteration only.

Discussion:

This fragment ist quite arbitrarily placed among the letters of exorcists; it may equally well (and even better) originate from a *physician* (cf. the description of the plant in r7ff with *LAS* 247 r15ff) or from a *scribe* (cf. the omens quoted in r6(?) and the left edge, the plant just referred to may have been mentioned because it had ominous significance).

Notes:

r5. At the end of the line restore possibly ŠU[B-*ut*] on the analogy of *LAS* 239:1'f.

r6. Cf. *ina kīli me-se-ri* [È?], K.2617+ ii 10 (unp. *tamītu*, quoted *AHw* 647*a*)? In any case, the logographic spelling È suggests a literary quotation.

r7. Restore [ᴵ*Na-ṣ*]*i-ru*? In any case probably a personal name.

r9. *ú-mu-ma*: despite the spelling with *ú*, certainly for u_4*-mu-ma* "today". Cf. PAP *29* KUR[MEŠ] ² *ú-mu-um-ma* ³ *e-tar-bu-ú-né* "altogether 29 horses have entered (the *bēt māšarti*) today", *ABL* 575r1ff, for usual PAP *n* KUR[MEŠ] u_4*-mu an-ni-ú e-tar-bu-ú-né* (e.g., *ABL* 538 r8ff, 649 r7ff, etc.); cf. also u_4*-mu-ma an-ni-i* "this very day", *LAS* 127 r17. Two other unconventional spellings of *ūmu* "day" with <ú> in *LAS* 143 r3 (*ši-it-ta ú-ma-ti*) and 173 r14 (*ú-ma-a-ti* [*šá-ni-a*]*-ti*), note also [d]*ú-mu* (refs. *Tākultu* p.117).

r8. *pi-ri-i'-ti* "shoot": hapax; the following attestation of *parā'u* "to burst out" (r9) is also to be added to *AHw*.

L.E.1 This apodosis also in *LAS* 108:2'.

232

Bibliography:

(I) Waterman, *RCAE* 1004.
(II) Wiseman, *Iraq* 20 (1958) 5[39].

Date:

Late Kanūnu = early January, 670 BC. The reference to the princes (obv.7) places the letter between 672-669 BC (cf. note to *LAS* 173:17); for the exact date see on r3f.

Addressee:

Esarhaddon.

Discussion:

This letter is placed among the letters of exorcists because of its content and the reference to Adad-šumu-uṣur in obv.9'; whether its writer in fact was an exorcist remains a matter of speculation.[360] Nevertheless, it is certain that the text dealt with events preceding the enthronement of a substitute king (cf. on r3f), and has noth ing to do with the treaty ceremonies of 672 BC (thus Waterman and Wiseman).

Notes:

6. Restore *a-na* [uru][*Kal-ḫa*] "to Calah" after 185 r10ff.

9. *e tab-Á*[*Š*]: probably simply *e-t*[*a!-rab*] "entered", with a badly written *ta*; less likely *e-tab-r*[*a*] "crossed (the river)", as the verb in obv.7' is *alāku*, not *ebāru*.

r1. *Aššūr-nāṣir*: identical with ᴵ*Aš+šur*-ŠEŠ*-ir* [LÚ]GAL.SAG[MEŠ] "chief eunuch A.", *ABL* 965.14 (dated to 680 BC by Dietrich, *AOAT* 7, 28f)? Note also ᴵ*Aš+šur*-PAP*-ir*, together with ᴵ*Da-ni-i* (cf 142:12), in *CT* 53 150 r7, and K.920, unp. report signed by ᴵ*Aš+šur*-PAP*-ir*.

r2. *Sāsî*: see on 115:2. At the end of the line restore [*id-du-bu-ub*] "he spoke".

---

[360] The sign LÚ* (r 1.6) occurs in the present corpus virtually only in letters of Urad-Nanâ and Mār-Ištar.

r3f. Restore *a-du la* AN.M[I *iš-kun-u-ni*] [4]*lu-ši-ib*, and translate "let him (the substitute king) sit on the throne before the eclip[se occurs]"; both the restoration and the rendering are certain: note the point of time (middle of the month), the association of *lu-ši-ib* with the eclipse (cf. note to 185 r18) and the parallelity of the passage to 185 r14ff (the speaker there Marduk-šākin-šumi, here Adad-šumu-uṣur). As a matter of fact, the present letter pertains to the same incident as *LAS* 185. Here, as in *LAS* 185, the eclipse occurred only after the 14th day of the month, which fits the eclipse of Kanūnu 15 = December 27/8, 671, but not the other eclipses (Du'ūzu 14, 671 and Ajāru 29, 669) starting the substitute king ritual between 672 and 669 BC; see Intr. p. XXIII.

233

Bibliography:

(I) Waterman, *RCAE* 1401.

(II) Schott, *OLZ* 40 (1937) 362.

Writer:

Adad-šumu-uṣur. Obv.7'-10' and rev.1'f (q.v.) point to an exorcist (cf. r4'ff) with a scribal background, and Adad-šumu-uṣur is the only writer in the present corpus meeting this requirement (see Intr., p.28). Orthographical and linguistic features of the fragment are consistent with the attribution.[361]

Addressee:

Esarhaddon.

Date:

Mid-Addāru to mid-Nisannu (= mid-March to mid-April), 669 BC. The hand-lifting prayers to be recited before Mars, mentioned in r4', were, as appears from r1' (see pertinent note), occasioned by an extraordinary luminosity of the planet at the time concerned; consequently, the letter was written during a retrograde period of Mars, and obv.9' shows that the planet was then moving in the constellation of Virgo. Obv.10' may indicate that it was approaching Spica (see pertinent note). Such a situation prevailed only once during the period 681-655 BC (which more than sufficiently covers the attested career of Adad-šumu-uṣur and all other exorcists of the present corpus), viz. from February 15 to May 1, 669 (see App.D). If ^{MUL}AB.SÍN here means "Spica" not "Virgo", as is likely, the letter can confidently be dated to mid-Nisannu 669, or slightly later; Mars reached Spica on May 1 = Ajāru 3.[362]

Notes:

10'. Probably an allusion to *ACh* 2 Spl 81:1', [I ^{MUL}]UG$_5$.GA *ana* ^{MUL}AB.SÍN ŠU.ÚR BURU$_5$ ZI "If the crow-star (*aribu* = Mars) . . .s the furrow-star (= Spica), there will be an invasion of locusts (*eribu*)"; same omen also in *ACh* 2 Spl 80:4 (^{MUL}UGA).[363] ^{MUL}AB.SÍN here certainly = Spica (= the head of corn held by the virgin in Mesopotamian pictorial representations of Virgo). Accordingly, the present passage is probably to be restored [*ti-bu-ut*] BURU$_5$(NAM+BÍR), [. . . .] BURU$_5$ [11'][*i-tab-bi*] (cf. 120:13f), or similarly.

r1'. Certainly to be restored [*ba-('i-)il šá-ru-r*]*i na-ši* "[(Mars) is bright] (and) clothed in br[illiance]" after 45:10f, 46 r10f, *RMA* 167 r7f, and other parallels.

r2'. Problematical. One would expect [*du-un-qu š*]*a*! *SU*.BIR$_4$^{KI} (cf. on *LAS* 45), but the traces actually point to ḪU]L "bad luck".

r3'. Delete *te-ni-siḫ* (Pt.I) and read [. . . an?]-*nu-te ni-suḫ*$_4$ "we will extract (or eradicate) thes[e? . . .]". For SIḪ = *suḫ*$_4$ cf. *is-suḫ*$_4$, Labat *IE* p.220:5, etc.

361 Obv.6' cf. 142:9; *šu-tu-ni* (7') = 139:11; obv.9' cf. 120:10.13; *ka-aja-ma-nu* (r6') = 131:4; *ḫi-iṭ-ṭu* (r7') cf. *ḫi-iṭ-ṭi* (141:3'); *ḫiṭṭu laššu* = 154:8; *libbu . . . lu ṭāba* (r8'ff) = 154r1'ff, etc. By contrast, Marduk-šākin-šumi wrote consistently *ḫi-ṭu* (180:14, 182:7, 185 r13) not *ḫi-iṭ-ṭu*; note also his *laššu ḫiṭṭu* (180, 182; here *ḫiṭṭu laššu*) and the placement of [*ina* UGU] in obv.4', which is not typical of his letters (cf. on *LAS* 149). Nabû-nādin-šumi is unlikely in view of the lack of *adanniš* in the introductory formula. That the writer cannot be a scribe is indicated by the spelling *be-lí-ja* in obv.2' and r.9'; see App. M 6.

362 At that date, Mars's longitude was 166°.6 (App. C3); Spica's right ascension 669 BC = 167°.2.

363 A bad omen at the time of the harvesting! Cf. on *LAS* 38.

234

Bibliography:

(I) Waterman, *RCAE* 1080.

(II) Weidner, *OLZ* 15 (1912) 459; *AfO* 13 (1939/40) 231f.

Writer:

Balasî. This attribution seems certain, despite the small size of the fragment. First, the sender was certainly a scribe (see on r5), not an exorcist (thus Pt.I). Secondly, the phrase *ki-i an-ni-i-*[*e*] *pi-še-er-šu* (obv.3'f, cf. relevant note) occurs in this spelling only in the letters and reports of Balasî (*LAS* 326:5f, *RMA* 277F r2); Ištar-šumu-ēreš and Mār-Ištar wrote consistently *pi-šèr*(SAR)*-šú*, Nabû-aḫḫē-erība always *a-ki an-ni-e*, Akkullānu either *ki-i an-ni-i pi-šèr-šú* or *an-ni-u pi-še-er-šú*, see note on the writer of *LAS* 108.[364] Thirdly, the general appearance (disposition of signs, dividing lines, ductus) and physical characteritics of the tablet agree well with the corresponding features of the letters of Balasî, cf. e.g. *LAS* 35f (and see Pt.I, p.332 and 337). Finally, the content of the text can be matched with *LAS* 35 (cf. obv.1'ff) and 38:11ff (cf. r2ff). Thus the attribution to Balasî is not only possible but also plausible, and as the above considerations exclude all other writers of the present letter corpus, there does not seem to be any reason to assume that an otherwise unknown scribe is in question.

Addressee:

Esarhaddon.

Date:

Early Simānu = early June, 669 BC. The reference to an earthquake in the month Simānu (obv.5'f) implies that the eclipse mentioned in r2 also occurred in the same month, or possibly at the end of the preceding month, if a solar eclipse is in question. During the time span covered by the letters and reports of Balasî (674-665 BC), suitable eclipses occurred only in the year 669, viz. a solar eclipse on Ajāru 29 = May 27, and a lunar one on Simānu 14 = June 10, 669; see App.E/F. As it is known from *LAS* 137 that an earthquake had indeed occurred in the said year in early Simānu, and as one of the letters of Balasî (*LAS* 35) may well deal with that particular earthquake (in retrospect; see pertinent commentary), the date suggested above seems virtually certain. Note that no earthquake is mentioned in *RMA* 270, a report on the lunar eclipse of Simānu 14 = May 22, -677.

Notes:

3'. Contra Harper, it is possible to read here *an-ni-*⌜*i*⌝*-*[*e*] in accordance with the orthography of Balasî. "All that remains [at the end of the line] are the two bottom horizontals [of *i*]" (collation Sollberger 19.1.1976).

5' ff. A quotation from *Enūma Anu Enlil*, cf. Virolleaud, *ACh* Adad 20:38 (I KI *ina* ^{ITU}SIG$_4$ "*šu!-bat na-me-e* ŠUB^{MEŠ}[. . . . .]) and Lacheman, *RA* 34 (1937) 2:4 (I *i-na* ^{ITU}SIG$_4$ *i-ru-ub šu-bat na-me-e* ŠUB-*ti i-na* INIM ^{d}*50* <TUŠ^{MEŠ}>). The same omen, in a slightly different form (the word *nadûti* omitted) was also incorporated in the series *Iqqur īpuš*, see Labat, *IE* p.190 § 101:2, and cf. ibid. fnn. 1 and 2.

9'. This line ("at the command of Illil") was inadvertently left untranslated in Pt.I.

r5. *li-is-sa-ḫu-u-né*: the translation "let them excerpt (the relevant omens) for me" proposed in Pt.I in accordance with *AHw* p.750b (sub *nasāḫu* mng. 8d) is abortive, since the writer of the letter could, as clearly appears from the quotation in obv.3'ff, have easily looked up the pertinent interpretations himself. Translate "let them eradicate (the evil from that place)" (by means of apotropaic rituals); for this meaning of *nasāḫu* see, e.g., *LAS* 172:10 and r11.

r7. At the end of this line, restore, perhaps, [*le pu uš*] in accordance with *LAS* 30:19.

235

Bibliography:

Previously unpublished. Copy *CT* 53, pl.20 no. 50.

364 Note also the spellings *me-me-ni* and ^{URU}*Ni-nu-*[*a*] in the present letter: Akkullānu spelled these words consistently *me-me-e-ni* (*LAS* 299 r11, 312 r24', 314 r2', *RMA* 235:6.10) and URU.NINA (*LAS* 309 r8, 312 r19'); Balasî wrote *me-me-ni* (*LAS* 38:13, 41:8.12, 45 r2), Nineveh is not mentioned in his letters and reports.

Writer:
Adad-šumu-uṣur. This attribution can be regarded as certain on the following grounds: 1) Handwriting (the signs RU, RA und IN are especially distinctive); 2) Orthography (the spelling *šul-mu* [obv.9.15] is not attested in letters of any other exorcists and physicians than Adad-šumu-uṣur and Urad-Nanâ; the latter is excluded in view of the introductory formula; other spellings in the letter are in agreement with the orthography of Adad-šumu-uṣur)[365]; 3) Introductory formula (cf. above); 4) Subject matter (cf. *LAS* 137f, etc. [letters to ᴸᵁENGAR]; *LAS* 147 etc. [medical matters]; *LAS* 142 etc. [ᴸᵁMAŠ.MAŠᴹᴱŠ]); 5) Negative evidence: no other exorcist or physician meets the criteria 1) and 2) above.

Addressee:
Esarhaddon.

Date:
Perhaps Simānu to Du'ūzu (= June to July), 669 BC. The fact that the king is addressed as "farmer" *may* imply (but there is no certainty) that the substitute king in question was resident in Nineveh, a situation that actually occurred only once between 675-665; see Intr., p. XXIV. Cf. *LAS* 135f and 166. The ref. to the patient (= the "charge" of the Rear Palace?) supports this dating, see on *LAS* 152, 154 and 167.

Notes:

6. *EN-l*[*í*]: this spelling is otherwise not attested in the present corpus, while one of the letters of Adad-šumu-uṣur does have EN for *bēlī* (*LAS* 144 r6). Accordingly, cancel EN-*l*[*í* and restore instead EN *in*[*a ti-ma-li*] "(what) my lord (wrote) [yesterday]", which is also compatible with the trace following EN.

14. *né-rab* "we were about to enter": cf. *a-na pa-an* LUGAL *EN-já al-la-ka* "I was about to leave for (the audience of) the king, my lord (when PN came and said)", *BBEA* 8:3 (cf. sub date of *LAS* 286). Further examples of the present tense used in this way in *GAG* §78f.

r9. This line was by oversight left untranslated in Pt.1: "[. .] did not tremble". The verb can be restored *ig-ru-ur-*[*ru*] (cf. note to 247:10), in which case it would refer to the exorcists mentioned earlier.

r12. "*Now* [*he is well*]": cf. 216 r7f, 217 r3, and 222 r4'ff.

237

Bibliography:
Previously unpublished; cf. Deller, *AOAT* 1 (1969) 59. Copy *CT* 53, pl.94 no.357.

Writer:
Marduk-šākin-šumi? Note that the Aramaic loan-word *katāru* "to wait, hesitate" (von Soden, *Or*NS 35 [1966] 12 f; *CAD* K [1971] 304) is otherwise attested only in three Kuyunjik letters, two of which (*LAS* 166 and 180) were written by Marduk-šākin-šumi. Note, furthermore, that Šamaš-šumu-ukīn (A 4') figures among the patients of Marduk-šākin-šumi in *LAS* 172. The orthography of the fragment agrees perfectly with the proposed identification.[366]

Addressee:
Esarhaddon.

Notes:

A 6'. The verb at the end of the line probably reads, after renewed collation (17.5.74), *i-*⌜*šá-lu*⌝*-*[*p*]*u* "(let them not) snatch"; cf. *AHw* 1145*b*.

[365] *iš-pu-ra-an-ni* (obv.7) = 122:15; EN (obv.6) = 144 r6; *a-ḫi-ja* (obv.10) = 122 r29, 124 r5; *šá* (rev.1) = 119:12, and passim. For other spellings of the letter adequate points of comparison are missing.

[366] *iṣ-ṣa-bat-su* (Pf.) A 2' cf. *i-ṣa-bat-su* (Prs.), 181:14 (Pf. not attested in letters of M-š-š); *e-tap-šú-ma* A 3' = 174:11; ᴵᵈGIŠ.NU$_{11}$-MU-GI.NA (A 4') = 172:6; LUGAL *be-lí liš-pu-ra* (A 5') = 195 r11; LUGAL *be-lí ú-da* (B 4') = 185:20 etc.; *i-kàt-te-ru* (B 7') cf. *ni-kàt-ter* 166 r4; *ep-pu-šu* (B 7') = 172:10; *ṭè-e-mu liš-ku-un* (B 8') = 191 r5' (there written *liš-kun*, but cf. *ku-un-na-ta* 190:19; *ḫu-un-ṭu* (A 2') = 180:10; *a-na-ku* (B 11') = 183:7 etc.; UZU.MEŠ-*šú-nu* (B 10') = 186:18.

B 3'. For *pu-tú-ḫa* read perhaps, with K. Deller (orally), *pu-ut-ḫa*, Imp. Pl. of *patāḫu* "durchstoßen" (*AHw* 846*b*) though it is difficult to see how this verb could occur in the present context.

B 9'. *bu-ur-ba-ni*: cf. *ABL* 192 r5 *lip-šu-ḫu* [6] *bur-ba-a-ni* (unclear, referring to horses).

238

Bibliography:
Waterman, *RCAE* 873.

Sender:
Urad-Gulā. This assignation seems likely on the basis of the spellings *ŠÚM-mu* (Rev.3), which does not occur in letters of other exorcists,[367] and *be-LI* (Obv.6'.10'), which is not attested in letters of any other exorcists than Urad-Gula and Adad-šumu-usur (cf. sub *LAS* 10). In addition, the spellings *iš-pu-ra-an-ni* (Obv.6'), [Id]AG-*ga-mil* (Obv.11'), [I]*Su-ma-aju* (Rev.1), and *ma-ḫe-er* (Rev.4) clash with the orthographical conventions of Marduk-šākin-šumi[368], who was the only other contemporary exorcist writing *šum-MU* for *šum-MA*. That the writer was an exorcist is clear from his association with the persons mentioned in the letter.[369]

Date:
672-669 B.C. Cf. *LAS* 174, likewise referring to Šumâ and Nabû-gāmil in combination with the crown prince (Assurbanipal).

Addressee:
Esarhaddon.

Notes:

4'f. Cf. *LAS* 39:14 ff (referring to the same situation?).

11'. *Ninurta-aḫu-iddina* is known as the author of two letters to the king (*ABL* 334 and 335), both written in Babylonian; one is badly broken, the other deals with literature to be included in the royal libraries.

r4. *Balāssu*: probably identical with the man mentioned in 224 r16. For the other exorcists here mentioned see commentary on *LAS* 174.

239

Bibliography:
Waterman, *RCAE* 1289.

Writer:
Nabû-abu-(u)da''in. See note on r4.

Notes:

1'. *AN.TA.ŠUB.BA*: the identification of this disease as *epilepsy* can be regarded as certain on the basis of its symptoms presented in Labat, *TDP* p.80 ("If the patient keeps turning his neck to the right, (if) his hands and feet are cataleptic(?), his eyes (now) closed, (now) rolled back, (if) spittle runs from his mouth and he makes a croaking sound: AN.TA.ŠUB.BA. If, when it attacks him, he remains conscious: normal, if, when it attacks him, he loses his consciousness: abnormal", ibid. 1-3; cf. also 4-6). Cf. Labat, a.l. and p. xxvii on the distinction between "normal AN.TA.ŠUB.BA = hysteria" and "abnormal AN.TA.ŠUB.BA = epilepsy".

367 Adad-šumu-uṣur: *šum-ma* 119:14, 133 r7'.8', 135:13, 147 r12', 151 r13'.14'; Nabû-nādin-šumi: *šum₄-ma* 214 r6'; Nabû-nāṣer: *šum-ma* 219 r3; Urad-Gula: *šum-ma* 223 r14' but *šúm-mu* in *ABL* 1285 r27 (cf. commentary on *LAS* 339+). Nabû-gāmil (*LAS* 227) cannot be the writer since he is mentioned in rev.3.

368 The words in question are consistently written *be-lí, iš-pur-an-ni,* [Id]PA-*ga-mil,* [I]*Šu-ma-a, šum-mu* and *ma-ḫer* in letters of Marduk-šākin-šumi.

369 For this reason the writer can hardly be a physician, though the remains of the introductory formula recall the formulae used by Urad-Nanâ, Ikkāru, Banî and Nabû-tabni-uṣur. The spellings just discussed are, moreover, not attested in any letters of these physicians.

3'. *NA$_4$^{MEŠ}. . . AN.TA.ŠUB.BA*: referring to a string of amulet stones put in the right hand of the patient.[370] Cf. *KAR* 213 ii 6'ff (and dupl. *BAM* 356 i 1ff): *aš-pu-u* AN.KAL *saḫ-ḫu-u* ŠUBA.SIG$_7$ GIŠ.NU$_{11}$.GAL $^{7'}$DÚR.MI.NA.BÀN.DA AN.ZAḪ "BABBAR" GE$_6$ $^{8'}$KUR-*nu*-DIB PA NI.B[U] SAL.LA PEŠ$_4$.ANŠE *14*AN.TA.ŠUB "jasper, AN.KAL-stone, *saḫḫû*-stone, green vitriol, alabaster, breccia, frit, white dito, black dito, "gazelle" hematite, cowrie, *janibu*-stone, *multasḫiptu*-stone, *biṣṣirtānu*-shell: 14 (stones of) epilepsy"; ibid. 9'ff, *aš-pu-u* BABBAR.DIL BABBAR.DIL.DIL AN.KAL GIŠ.NU$_{11}$.GAL ŠUBA $^{10'}$ÁŠ.GÌ.GÌ PA SAL.LA ZA.GÌN DÚR.MI.NA *11* AN.TA.ŠUB.[371] Cf. also note to 181 r3 (*ṭurru*) and Köcher, *AfO* 20 (1963) 156ff.

^{KUŠ}*me-el*: this rare spelling[372] also in *LKA* 146:22 (*me-el an-nu-ti* "these phylacteries").[373] As illustrated by the present letter, and as it is easy to guess even a priori, the treatment of epilepsy in Assyria rested heavily on purely magical means, of which the use of apotropaic phylacteries (small leathern bags filled with *materia magica et medica* and hung around the neck of the patient, see W. Farber, *ZA* 63 [1973] 66f) was most widespread. Cf. *BAM* 311 r59' ff: *ana* A[N].TA.ŠUB ZI PA SU.TIN^{MUŠEN} PA *zi-i-bi* ^{Ú}KU$_6$ *ina* KUŠ $^{60'}$I KI+MIN *èš-me-ku* AD.BAR AN.BAR Ì.SUMUN KÁ ^{d}GIŠ.GÍN.MAŠ *ina* KUŠ $^{61'}$I KI+MIN *el-kul-la ak-tam* SÍG KA$_5$.A AN.BAR ^{NA_4}.BABBAR.DIL *ina* KUŠ "to eradicate epilepsy, (lace) (pieces of) the wing of a bat, the wing of a vulture (and) *urānu*-plant into (a shread of) leather, (and hang it around the patient's neck); dito, malachite, basalt, iron, (and) old oil from the Gilgameš gate into leather; dito, *elkulla* and *aktam*-plant, fox's hair, iron, *pappardilû*-stone into leather", etc. (altogether 12 similar prescriptions follow, whereafter the text goes on listing similar recipes for use I NA *lu* AN.TA.ŠUB.BA *lu* ^{d}LUGAL.ÙR.RA *lu* ŠU G[IDIM DIB-*su*] "in case either epilepsy, 'hand of Lugalurra' or 'hand of ghost' seizes a man", r.77'ff). Similar prescriptions also in *STT* 286 ii 2ff and 57:11 ff (cf. ibid.30, *6 me*-UGU *lat-ku-tum* G[AB].RI ER[I.DU$_{10}$ *š*]*á ṭ*[*up-pi* . . .] "6 tested phylacteries originating in Eridu, ta[blet of . . .]"). The cure of an epileptic child, which forms the subject matter of the present letter, is dealt with in *STT* 57:31' ff (= *STT* 58:2ff = *LKU* 32:1'ff). The text gives altogether 5 alternative prescriptions, one very long and detailed[374], the others shorter and more or less of the same type as those quoted above[375]; it is impossible to make out which was the one followed in the present letter. A few recipes of the same (phylactery) type, to be used against different variants of epilepsy, are also to be found in *TDP* p.192:40ff.[376]

5'. Cf. *ABL* 885:11, *qa-an-ni iš-mu-u-ni* ^{12}*ma-a* ^{LÚ}A.BA *pa-qí-id dul-lu it-ta-ṣu* ^{13}*ur-ta-am-me-u iḫ-tal-q*[*u*] "soon as they heard that a scribe had been appointed (to supervise the work), they immediately quitted the(ir) work (and) disappeared." Cf. also *LAS* 36 r15. The translation of *(ina) qanni (ša)* here adopted after *CAD* D 174*a* (*AHw* 897*a* "damit?") fits perfectly the present context, and is supported by the analogy of the temporal subjunction *(ina/issu) bēt.*

370 Cf. *STT* 273 iii 4, 7 NA$_4$^{MEŠ} AN.TA.[ŠU]B.BA *ina* ŠU^2 *15-šú* X[. . . . .] "7 epilepsy stones; [put them] in his right hand [. . . .]".

371 Another (slightly different) list of epilepsy stones is found in *STT* 273 iii 2f. Cf. also *11* AN.TA.ŠUB.BA (in broken context) *BAM* 365 i 2'.

372 Perhaps better ^{KUŠ}*me*-SIKIL(*ellu*), cf. *me*-UGU(*eli*), A(*mê*)-UGU(*eli*) (Reiner, *AfO* 19 150f) and similar "rebus" spellings of *qutāru* "fumigation" (*qut*-PA, KÙ-GUR, etc.).

373 In view of this parallel, the present passage may also refer to *several* phylacteries, not just to one.

374 Obv.31'-45': "If a child has been seized by epilepsy, lace *aštatillu*- and *ankinutu*-plant, and "male" and "female" *namiru*-plant" (wrapped) in the fleece of an unmated female kid into a shread of leather, (and then) [find] a lost child who [has no] father and mother. The exorcist goes and draws water from the stream into a [ ]bottle; having [returned], he scatters around 12 loaves of emmer and date cakes and fine floor, sets out confections of honey and ghee, and libates beer. You (yourself) strech the patient (on the bed) and recite the following incantation in front of the moon god: [An incantation of 7 lines follows].
Its ritual: Draw water from the river and wash the [ ] of the other child with water; sprinkle water around; take out the phylacteries which you have (previously) laced, and have the patient recite the said incantation thrice. (Then) hang the phylacteries round his neck, and as long as he lives, it (the disease) will not return and seize him (again)."

375 E.g. 52'-53': "If dito, lace (DU$_{11}$.DU$_{11}$ for usual DÙ.DÙ!) roots of *šūšu* and [ ] tree, *ašqulalu*-plant, black sulp[hur, ...] and *nikiptu*-plant into a shread of leather, [place] (the phylactery) [on the neck] of the child, [and he will get well]."

376 E.g., p.194:53f: "If the 'hand of Lugalurra' turns into epilepsy or 'hand of Ištar': hand of Ištar. To save him, lace the penis of a tortoise, seeds of the *urānu*-plant, and "male" and "female" *nikiptu* into (a) leather (bag), etc. (= place the phylactery on his neck and he will get well, line 42)."

r2. ^{MÍ}*a-ḫa-ti-ka*: uncertain whether a personal name (^{MÍ}*A-ḫa-ti*-DUG$_4$, cf. ^{MÍ}*A-ḫa-ti-ṭa-bat* (*APN* 14*b*) with ^{I}PAB-*qa-bi*/DÙG.GA (ibid.17*b*)) or indeed a reference to the king's sister is in question, as assumed in Pt.I.[377]

r3. [. *l*]*i ja*: possibly a personal name ("your sister [or ^{MÍ}Aḫatika] and PN placed (the stones and phylacteries) on a certain shepherd"), though I do not find any convincing restoration.

r4. Contra Pt.I, the signs X ^{d}AG *ad dan* have certainly to be read as a personal name: $^{I.d}$AG-AD-KALAG = Nabû-abu-(u)da'ʾin, a name also occurring in *ABL* 1372:24 (same person?). Should one restore [*a-na-ku*] at the beginning of the line? In that case, one would obtain the name of the writer of the letter ("[I am] Nabû-abu-da'ʾin, a dead dog . . . "). Cf. *ABL* 1216:7', [*a-na*]-*ku* $^{I.d}$EN*-*ú-še-zib* ÌR-*ka* UR.[KU]-*ka ù pa-liḫ-ka* "I am Bēl-ušēzib, your servant, your dog, sour supplicant" (letter written by the same Bēl-ušēzib).[378] It is, of course, exceptional that a sender introduces himself twice in his letter, but in a letter like the present one (and *ABL* 1216), where the writer evidently wants to convince the king of his ability and thus obtain admission to court, such an emphatic self-introduction would seem quite appropriate. Cf. also *ABL* 992 r15, *kal-bi me-e-ti a-na-ku*. For additional examples of this phrase, denoting humility, and very frequently occurring in Sargonid letters, see *CAD* K 72.

240

Bibliography:
Previously unpublished. Copy *CT* 53, pl.212 no.955.

Writer:
Nabû-nāṣer. The latter element of the name is actually preserved in Obv."3" (= 2!,[$^{I.d}$AG-P]AP-⌜*er*⌝), misread as LUGAL in Pt.I; the beginning of the letter has to be restored according to *LAS* 218(+221) and 219. Notice that the orthography of the writer has been influenced by that of Urad-Nanâ (cf. *a*]*d-dan-niš*, r2', not *a-dan-niš* as in other letters of Nabû-nāṣer), who appears as an associate of Nabû-nāṣer in *LAS* 222.

Addressee:
Esarhaddon.

Date:
672-669 BC. The reference to Aššur-mukīn-palū'a (Obv."8") indicates that the letter dates from approximately the same time as *LAS* 218 and 219 (cf. also 157 and 250); it is not excluded that the date is actually 670 as in other datable letters of Nabû-nāṣer.

Notes:

7. The dito sign (") here and in r2' certainly indicates repetition of the *preceding* word (*ad-dan-niš*) cf. 215:7, 217:6, 218:5, etc. This usage is unparalleled in other Sargonid letters, where the sign always stands *under* the word is repeats, but does occur in medical texts, e.g. *BAM* 311:14' (AN.ZAḪ " [= AN.ZAḪ] BABBAR " [= AN.ZAḪ] MI).

r3'. -*j*]*a-aḫ*: Comparison with Obv."8" suggests a name of a patient, perhaps a son of Esarhaddon. Cf. also 150:12.

242

Bibliography:
Previously unpublished. Copy *CT* 53, pl.128 no.508.

Discussion:

Is this a fragment of a royal letter? Cf. *LAS* 162 and *ABL* 1006 r5 (UGU *šu-mu a-ga-a* LUGAL *ma-a'-du lu-ú ra-ḫu-uṣ* "the king should rely much upon this prediction"); cf. also Obv.12' with *LAS* 298 r12'. The reference to the *turtānu* (^{LÚ*}*tur-ta-nu*, collated) in line 14' actually suggests that the fragment is part of the same tablet as

[377] Both Esarhaddon and Assurbanipal had sisters; see notes to 129:25f and 211:9.

[378] A similar self-identification also in *ABL* 880:16.

LAS 162 (= obverse; present fragment = reverse), but collation by C.B.F. Walker (27.1.1976) gave a negative result (see on *LAS* 162).

243

Bibliography:
(I) Waterman, *RCAE* 1140.
(II) Labat, *Royauté* (1939) pp.302 and 308; *RA* 38 (1944) 14; *MIO* 5 (1957) 311[27]; Matouš, *Sumer* 17 (1961) 31 ff; Deller, *AOAT* 1 (1969) 61.

Addressee:
Esarhaddon (?).

Discussion:

This letter is to be compared with *LAS* 145 and 332, with which it may well be contemporary;[379] note that the enumeration of the favourable days of Ajāru begins in both *LAS* 332 and the present letter only with the 10th, though the 2nd, 5th and 8th day of the month were also regarded as favourable (see below). Why the writer of the present letter also omitted in his list the 12th, 28th, 29th and 30th days, which do figure among favourable days in No. 332, remains obscure. If he wanted to mention only those days which were suitable "for undertaking an enterprise and revering the gods" (Rev.3-4), why did he omit the 28th, designated as "entirely favourable", or the 29th which had exactly the same designation as the 20th?

Date:
Ajāru 9, 669 BC, if contemporary with *LAS* 145.

Notes:

r5-11. A free quotation from the *Babylonian Almanac* (cf. Labat, *RA* 38 [1944] 13 ff); contrary to what the writer of the letter contends, the month Ajāru according to this hemerology contained altogether 15 favourable days, listed in *STT* 301 i 10ff: [I ^{I}]^{TU}GUD UD *2*.KÁM ŠE.GE

[U]D *5*.KÁM DAM ḪÉ.TUK.TUK LIBIR.RA
[U]D *8*.KÁM IDIM ŠE.GE
[U]D *10*.KÁM *in di-ni*$_6$ ŠE.GE
[U]D *12*.KÁM *in* SILA ŠE.GE
[U]D *15*.KÁM ^{ŠE}NUMUN ŠU.DU$_7$
[U]D *16*.KÁM ŠÀ.ḪÚL.LA
[U]D *18*.KÁM *za-ku-tú pu-šu-ur*
[UD] *20*.KÁM MUŠ ḪÉ.EN.GAZ SAG.KAL DU
[UD 22.K]ÁM *ina di-ni*$_6$ ŠE DÙ-*eš* ZÍZ
[UD 25.KÁ]M ŠÀ.ḪÚL.LA
[UD 2]6.KÁM *bu-sú-ra-tu*$_4$
[UD 2]8.KÁM *ka-liš ma-ger*
[UD 2]9.KÁM MUŠ ḪÉ.EN.GAZ "
[UD 30].KÁM ISKIM SA$_6$

Cf. *RA* 38 24f and the list of auspicious days ibid.20.

244

Bibliography:
Previously unpublished. Copy *CT* 53, pl.205 no.928.

---

379 Is *LAS* 332 an "appendix" to *LAS* 145?

Writer:
Marduk-šākin-šumi? Orthographical criteria as well as the manner in which the tablet is inscribed favour this attribution (cf. *LAS* 179); note especially Obv.6, where *lik-ru-bu* and *ina* UGU are placed on the same line, as in most letters of Marduk-šākin-šumi[380], whereas other writers preferably began their messages only in the line following the last word of the blessing (*likrubū*). The contents of the letter can be matched with *LAS* 163, 174, 176-177 and 187; for the sequence QUESTION + *ú-la-a* (Obv.9 f) cf. 175:6' ff and 195 r16 ff.

Addressee:
Esarhaddon (cf. note on 173:17).

Notes:

r5ff. These lines read, after collation (12.6.74), [. .]·*ina* ŠÀ ⌜X⌝[. .] ⁶[ᵈPA] *le-ru-ub*; r8 has probably to be corrected to read ⌜*e*⌝*-ru-ub-*⌜*ú-ni*⌝, but the script is here so obliterated that full certainty about the reading cannot be obtained.

245

Bibliography:
Previously unpublished. Copy *CT* 53, pl.213 no.962.

Writer:
Possibly Nabû-nādin-šumi, judging from the spelling *a-ki-i* in r2 (cf. note on the writer of *LAS* 128).

Discussion:

The obverse of this fragment probably contained titles of exorcistic compositions (incantations etc.) or quotations of them, like e.g. *LAS* 151, 160 and 161. *E-nu-ma* (Obv.4') was the characteristic incipit of tablets with ritual instructions (e.g., *Enūma nēpēšī ša maqlû/bīt-rimki/bīt-salā'-mê* etc. *teppušu, Enūma pī ili temessû, Enūma šarru šigû ana ili iqabbû*) and literary compositions (*Enūma eliš, Enūma ilū awīlum, Enūma Purattu iššâ, Enūma ana nuḫuš nišê*, etc.; also collections of omens such as *Enūma Anu Enlil* and *Enūma ana bīt marṣi*); Obv.5 may be an incipit of an incantation, cf. ÉN *at-ta* ᵈGÌR.UNUG.GAL *gaš-ri, OrNS* 40 (1971) 172:25; ÉN *at-ta* GEDIM *LKA* 89 r19; *at-tu-nu* DINGIR^{MEŠ} GAL^{MEŠ} *STT* 231:31; ÉN *at-tu-nu* ᵈ*A-nun-na-ki LKA* 90 r12, etc.

Notes:

r2. The last sign is, according to collation, *ta*[*q*.

246

Bibliography:
(I) Waterman, *RCAE* 391 (cf. IV 250); Pfeiffer, *SLA* 286, Oppenheim, *Letters* (1967) 155 (no.92, translat. only). (II) Meissner, *BuA* 2 (1925) 321f; Oppenheim, *JAOS* 64 (1944) 192 and *Or* NS 31 (1962) 32; Böhl, *Opera Minora* (1953) 409 ff; Kinnier Wilson, *Iraq* 18 (1956) 140 f; Reiner, *AfO* 19 (1959/60) 150 f, Lambert, *BWL* (1960) 294; Ritter, *AS* 16 (1965) 319, Thorwald, *Macht und Geheimnis der frühen Ärzte* (1967) 126.

Date:
Probably Ajāru (= April), 670 BC. This date is based on the affinities of the letter with *LAS* 247. The two letters are so exceptionally uniform in regard to their general appearance[381], orthography[382] and subject matter[383]

---

380 See *LAS* 173, 174, 176, 178-183, 187,189, 198-201.

381 Cf. Pt. I, p. 338.

382 *LAS* 246:1-6 is an exact duplicate of 247:1-6; in all other letters of Urad-Nanâ, the introductory formulae differ both in orthographic details and in the disposition of individual words in different lines.

383 The background situation is the same in both letters: the king is badly sick and blames his physician for inability to relieve his pains. This situation does not recur in other letters of Urad-Nanâ.

that they cannot possibly have been written a long time (say, several weeks) apart from each other; most likely their temporal distance is only a couple of days.[384] The mutual order of the two letters cannot be determined, but *LAS* 247 is datable to (mid-)Ajāru 670 BC on the basis of the historical allusions it contains. See in detail the relevant commentary. Cf. also *LAS* 181.

Addressee:
Esarhaddon.

Discussion:

The agonized outcry "Why don't you diagnose the nature of this illness of mine and cure it?" (Obv.8ff) put in the mouth of the king (Esarhaddon), as well as the medical instructions of the continuation, give occasion to assess here at some length the numerous letters and other texts referring to bodily and mental troubles of Esarhaddon, with the purpose of studying whether it is at all possible to arrive at a reasonably clear idea of what was troubling the king. In view of the great number of the relevant texts (cf. below, Sect.A), the matter has been surprisingly little studied so far, though it has of course long been recognized that Esarhaddon's health was badly failing, especially in his last years.[385] As far as I have noticed, the only scholars who have ever ascribed the king's troubles to a definite disease are Meissner[386] and (following him) Thorwald[387], who suggested that the king was suffering from *(chronic) rheumatism*. The medical background of Thorwald gives this suggestion some weight, yet it has to be borne in mind that the translations by which he could judge the evidence (Meissner, Waterman, Pfeiffer) are outdated and, above all, that Meissner operated on the mistaken idea that the word *sakikkû* "symptom"[388] occurring in the present letter (l.8) means "rheumatism". It is hoped that the following study will put the identification on a firmed footing. I shall first list the sources on which the study is based, and then gradually proceed through a discussion of the symptoms to a tentative diagnosis of the underlying disease.[389]

A. Sources

1) *Letters*: *LAS* 51 (Balasî + Nabû-aḫḫē-erība); 130, 133, 143, 159 (Adad-šumu-uṣur); 180-183 (Marduk-šākin-šumi); 246-248, 253-257, 265-267 (Urad-Nanâ); 258 (Ikkāru). 2) *Reports*: *LAS* 322 and *RMA* 257 (Ištar-šumu-ēreš). 3) *Haruspex queries*: *AGS* 99-100 (see on l. 18f). 4) *Chronicles*: Grayson, *TCS* 5 p.87, entry for Esarhaddon's 11th year (669 BC).

B. Somatic symptoms

The following list includes the most significant somatic symptoms that can be isolated from the above sources. Most of them are taken from texts dealing with acute attacks of disease; texts probably referring to other (latent) phases of the disease are indicated with asterisks.

---

384 Cf. the commentaries on *LAS* 70, 121 and 174.

385 Cf. eg., von Soden, *Herrscher im alten Orient* (1954), p. 125: "Wir erfahren aus ihnen [= Briefen an den König] auch, daß Assarhaddon schon ziemlich früh kränkelte und daß sein sonst offenbar tüchtiger und erfolgreicher Leibarzt Arad-Nanâ ihm weder mit medizinischen noch mit magischen Mitteln recht helfen konnte."

386 Cf. Meissner, *Babylonien und Assyrien* II (1925), p.321: "Asarhaddon muß öfter an Krankheiten, speziell an Rheumatismus, gelitten haben."

387 Cf. *Macht und Geheimnis* (1967) p.126: "Arad-Nana befand sich in der unglücklichen . . . Lage, mit dem vielgesichtigen Ungeheuer des chronischen Rheumatismus ringen zu müssen."

388 On this meaning see Oppenheim, *Or* NS 31 (1962) 32 and Kinnier Wilson, art.cit.

389 It is a pleasant duty for me to acknowledge here my indebtness to Dr. J. Rantasalo (Helsinki) for medical assistance received in the study of the problem. While the diagnosis proposed below is the result of our collaboration, the responsibility for the views presented and errors committed remains entirely mine.

Symptom	*Attestation*
("Unbalanced") fever (*ḫunṭu* [*lā mitḫar*])	*LAS* 180, 181, *183, 246, *258
Feebleness (*lā emūqā*)	*LAS* 180, 247: 12f
Lack of appetite (*lā akālu*)	*LAS* 51, 143
Articular stiffness (*šimmatu*)	*LAS* 180, *265-267
Eye affection (*ḫunṭu ša ēnāti*)	*LAS* 180, *183, *258(?)
Cutaneous eruption, blisters (*undī, pi'āru, muggu*)	*LAS* *255, 246, *257, *265-267, *322
Chills (*kuṣṣu*)	*LAS* 181, 182
Earache (*šugummê uzni*, etc.)	*LAS* *248, *253, *265-267

The psychic symptoms are discussed below, sub G.

C. Course of the disease

The texts make it clear that the disease in question must have been *chronic*, with *acute* fits at irregular intervals; it also must have remained more or less *latent* between its acute periods, otherwise the patient scarcely would have ventured partaking in two military campaigns personally in 671 and 669. The chronic nature of the disease is borne out by *RMA* 257 r7 (*im-da-na-ra-aṣ* "he is sickly"; year 672 BC) and the present letter ("the king *keeps* saying: 'Why . . .' ") on the one hand, and on the other hand by *LAS* 258:15ff showing that the "fever of [ey]es (or [ea]rs)" harassing Esarhaddon in his last years (cf. *LAS* 180, 183, 246) had already troubled him before 681 BC. At that time Esarhaddon must already have passed his 30th year of life, but can hardly have been older than 35.[390] There are indications that the acute periods of the disease turned more frequent and increased in intensity, the older the king grew. *RMA* 257 and the query *AGS* 99 (dated in the eponym year of [Nab]û-bēlu-uṣur) shows that the king was seriously ill in 672 BC; most of the letters of the present corpus referring to bad health of the king are datable to 670 – to judge from *LAS* 133 and 159, he must have been on the brink of death at that time. The last fit occurred a year later, in Arahsamna 669, when the king fell ill and died in the course of his campaign to Egypt (Grayson, *TCS* 5 87). Exposure to heat (cf. *LAS* 181:14 f, 255 r6 ff, 258 r10; *RMA* 257, written in the month Ābu [= July/August]; *LAS* 51, 143, 181 and 246f, written in Ajāru [= May]), drafts (*LAS* 255) and excessive strain (the military expedition of 669) seem to have worsened the king's condition; on the other hand, they did not necessarily cause any inconveniences in the latent periods of the disease, as is indicated by the fact that the king got luckily through the strains of the campaign to Egypt in 671.[391]

D. Treatment

Lotions and poultices (? *ṣilbānu*) to relieve fever (*LAS* 181, 246); salves, to protect diseased skin (*LAS* 246, 255); rest and appropriate diet (*LAS* 143, 180). The other remedies mentioned are of magical nature.

E. Tentative diagnosis

An evaluation of the data presented above is of necessity a thankless enterprise: there is no chance to arrive at an absolutely certain diagnosis, as one does not have at one's disposal *exact* information such as can be acquired nowadays in clinical examination. All that can be done is to play with probabilities, trying first to determine the *general* nature of the disease and then to find a *specific* disease whose clinic picture would satisfactorily agree with the picture conveyed by the texts. Methodically, one has to proceed from two basic assumptions: (1) that the bulk of the symptoms listed under B are manifestations of the same disease, and (2) that the sources available suffice to convey a reasonably balanced idea of its form of manifestation, i.e. that no significant symptoms re-

390 If it is accepted that Assyrian princes must have been at least 20 years old before they could be introduced into the Succession Palace, and that they married at approximately the same age (cf. *ABL* 308), it follows that Esarhaddon was born in the year 713 at the latest (Assurbanipal and Šamaš-šumu-ukīn were nominated crown-princes in 672, hence the older brother must have been born in 693 at the latest). A much earlier year of birth cannot be considered seriously, since the birth years of Sargon II and Sennacherib (approximately *770 and *745) would then be pushed too far back in time. Borger, *Studiën* (1954) p. 56 reckons with a date of birth ± 710 at the latest.

391 *LAS* 159 ("when Bēl took off the king's illness") may refer to a sudden "miraculous" bettering of the condition of the king – i.e., to a spontaneous remission of a chronic disease.

main beyond our knowledge and that no insignificant ones are excessively stressed. Both assumptions seem fairly justified taking into consideration the number of the texts at our disposal (see under A), the medical experience of their authors (including a chief physician and a chief exorcist), and the fact that many of the symptoms are attested more than once, some texts even listing several symptoms at a time (*LAS* 180 and the present letter),

On these premises, then, one has to look for an extremely chronic disease affecting the entire body of the patient, and characterized by intermittent fever, lassitude, muscular troubles and cutaneous eruption. One can exclude epidemic diseases, such as pestilence, and one can also take it for granted that no well-known, easily identifiable disease (malaria etc.) is in question, as the ancient doctors would then certainly not have had any difficulties in diagnosing it (cf. present letter, 8ff). The picture of the disease thus emerging is admittedly, still rather vague but can, as far as I can see, best be reconciled with the general appearance of the r h e u m a t o i d diseases, as already conjectured previously (cf. p. 230). Granting this general identification, one has still to choose between a great number of independent diseases and their variants. The choice has to be made with an eye to the assumption (2) above. Accordingly, at least rheumatoid arthritis and rheumatic fever seem to be out of the question, the former since our sources do not contain any reference to severe articular pains or deformations, the latter since cardiac inflammation/pains play no role among the symptoms collected under B. Besides, cutaneous eruption does not belong to the distinctive features of these diseases. By contrast, it is precisely *the* criterion which has suggested the diagnosis proposed here. In identifying the illness of Esarhaddon as *systemic lupus erythematosus* (= lupus erythematosus disseminatus, abbr. LED) for reasons to be given in detail below, I do not contend that other interpretations are not possible; I simply wish to point out a disease which not only fully fits the facts known about the king's disease in particular, but also explains certain disputed features in his personality and life. See below, under G.

F. A brief description of systemic lupus erythematosus[392]

LED is a clinic syndrome belonging to the group of so-called diffuse connective-tissue diseases, with an unknown etiology. Its clinical picture can vary considerably. The course of the disease can be acute, even fulminant, but also extremely chronical. It may begin very "typically", but also with a single manifestation which only in the course of several years is joined by others. The number of different symptoms and findings is great (see Table 3) and their possibilities of combination almost infinite.

TABLE 3. *The frequencies of occurrence of the general manifestations and findings of LED*

Symptom or finding	Appr. frequency (in %)
A r t i c u l a r i n f l a m m a t i o n o r p a i n s	90
F e v e r	80
LE cell phenomenon	80
C u t a n e o u s e r u p t i o n	80
Alterations in blood albumin	70
Renal lesions	60
Enlargement of lymph nodes	50
Anaemia	50
I n d i s p o s i t i o n , v o m i t i n g	50
M u s c u l a r p a i n s	50
Pleurisy	50
Leucopenia	40
Pericarditis	30
C e n t r a l n e r v o u s s y s t e m s y m p t o m s	20

392 This section is an adaptation of E.J. Jokinen, "Lupus erythematosus disseminatus", *Duodecim* 85 (Helsinki, 1969), 11-39. The wording of the article has not been changed (excepted for adjustments necessary in translating from Finnish into English), but many unnecessary details have been omitted, e.g. the chapters dealing with the etiology, pathology and immunology of the disease, which are of no relevance to the present case. For a thorough and up-to-date account of LED see E.L. Dubois (ed.), *Lupus erythematosus*, McGraw-Hill Book Company, New York, 1966. The article of Jokinen just mentioned contains a good bibliography, which can be consulted for literature postdating 1966.

The general condition of the patients varies considerably depending on the activity of the disease. In acute cases, the condition deteriorates rapidly and the patient loses much in weight, which is also partly due to impaired appetite. The more chronic the disease is, the longer the general condition keeps good. Even an unattended patient may then fell quite healthy and symptomless, at least during the spontaneous remissions of the disease.

Most of the patients have fever, at least in some phase of the disease. It can be of any kind whatsoever.

Articular symptoms are the most common manifestation of LED in practically all major patient samples; they occur in about 90 % of the cases, and can be divided into three groups as follows: 1) mere pains, 2) inflammation jumping from one joint to another, and 3) chronic deforming polyarthritis. Typical of the patients belonging to group one is that despite the pains, which may be severe and continue for years, no deformations are to be observed in their joints in physical examination. In examining patients belonging to group two it is repeatedly observed that inflammated joints have become symptomless, and contrariwise, that previously symptomless joints have turned swollen and aching. The picture of the disease thus resembles rheumatic fever. Typical is that even after the pains have continued for years, the functioning of the joints is good and nothing morbid is to be observed in them in radio diagnosis. Only a small number of patients develop progressive deforming arthritis, which clinically entirely resembles that occurring in rheumatoid arthritis.

Muscular pains are a very common manifestation. They can be severe and jump from a place to another like the pains in the joints. A true polymyosite seldom develops. The patient then experiences muscular feebleness, electromyography gives a myosite result, and the number of muscular enzymes in the blood may be increased.

Vasculite is a very important cause of tissue damage. It may occur in any part of the organism, a fact that largely explains the extraordinarily variagated symptom complex of LED. The most usual group is formed by cutaneous symptoms, which occur almost as frequently as articular pains, and often are the first indication of LED. It is just the combination of the cutaneous and articular symptoms that frequently leads the clinician to the correct diagnosis. The changes in the skin can be of many kinds. The socalled 'butterfly figure' results from the location of the lesion in the middle of the nose or on the cheeks. Location in the front of the neck, in the middle of the chest and on the palm of the hand as well as on the soles is also very common. The most usual change in the areas mentioned is mere redness; in addition, papules and blisters occur in the 'butterfly figure' area and on the neck and the breast. If the eruption has endured long enough and been cured either spontaneously or by treatment, the skin affected may atrophy. The sensitiveness of a LED-patient to ultra-violet radiation is best seen in the eruption, which appears or gets worse after baths in the sun.

Clinically important is also the impairment of the nervous system. It is attested in about half of the patients and represents the most usual cause of death after renal lesions. The three most common forms of its manifestation are different kinds of paralyses, epileptic attacks and psychoses. Slight alterations of the psyche are common, and the patients are easily regarded as neurotics.

In alimentary canals, vasculite brings about infarcts which may cause the patient severe pains. Vomiting and diarrhea are a not unusual consequence.

Deformations in the bottom of the eye are observed in a good number of the patients. Typical are light inundate blotches as well as small bleedings in the retina. In addition, inflammations of the conjunctiva etc. may occur. Normochromic anaemia is very common and mostly lenient.

LED begins at any age. Every manifestation can be the first, and each of them can likewise later develop into the "leading" symptom. The most important primary manifestations are presented in Table 4.

TABLE 4. *The order of frequency of the most common primary manifestations of LED*

Primary manifestation or finding	Percent of the total number of the cases
Articular inflammation or pains	50
Cutaneous eruption	20
Fever	4
Lassitude, sense of illness	4
Renal affection	4
Pleurisy	3
Wrongly positive syphilis-reactions	3

Oedemas	2
Enlargement of lymph nodes	2
Anaemia	2

Typical of LED is the wavelike alternation of its activity. The length of the wave hinges upon the acuteness of the case. Thus the fever curve can in fulminant cases fluctuate in periods of 2-3 weeks, whereas spontaneous remission can in the most chronic cases last as long as twenty years. During that time, the patient may remain almost symptomless. A significant feature noticed in about a half of the patients is their sensitiveness to ultra-violet radiation, which most often manifests itself in the aggravation of the symptoms after sun-bathing. During the spontaneous remissions of the disease the patients however can often linger in the sunshine without any harmful consequences.

All patients have a great liability to infections. Before the era of antibiotics, these constituted the most common cause of death, but nowadays most patients succumb to active glomerulone frit, apoplexy, or lesions of the central nervous system.

So far no causal treatment of LED is known. The symptoms and pains of the patients can however be significantly relieved and their lifetime extended by modern means. In most cases, the need of rest of the patients is obvious. In active cases of the disease, not to speak of the acute ones, all kinds of exertion should be avoided. Elimination of the factors activating the disease has also to be borne in mind. Patients sensitive to sunlight must be protected of it and, if necessary, appropriate skin ointments have to be used.

(A survey of the medications used in the treatment of LED appears superfluous in this context. Suffice it to mention that salicylates, malaria drugs and corticosteroids are most commonly used.)

Elaboration of an exact prognosis is difficult in the case of disease like LED. Diagnostics has often proved unreliable, especially before the recognition of the LE cell phenomenon, and it is often impossible to deduce the exact moment in which the disease has begun. If all the patients are regarded as a single group, about 10% of them seem to die yearly after diagnosis. The prognosis of single patients varies considerably, depending, among other things, on the activity and localization of the disease.

G. Implications

Whatever modifications to the above diagnosis may ultimately prove necessary, the very possibility that Esarhaddon may have suffered from a disease like LED is startling and may well provide a clue explaining many features in the personality, life and actions of this curious ruler. Just consider the following. If the LED hypothesis is accepted, it follows that the king was suffering from a *lethal* disease, which is *incurable* today and certainly could not be cured (nor diagnosed) by any methods known in ancient Assyria; despite the efforts of his most qualified doctors, the king's condition deteriorated continuously. A particularly significant fact is that the king was *perpetually* harassed by muscular pain, articular stiffness, fever, eye affection and buzzing ears; and not enough with that, his *looks* were apparently seriously disfigured by cutaneous eruption, papules and blisters in hands, feet and probably even on the face. All this, especially the effect of the disease on the central nervous system, must have considerable affected the king's psyche, and therefore very likely had wider consequences, too.[393]

---

393 Psychiatric studies have established beyond doubt that grave somatic illnesses markedly alter the psychic structures of most patients. Alterations in the psyche are particularly clear in the case of rheumatoid arthritis, a close "relative" of LED. See G.C. Booth, "Personality and chronic arthritis", *Journal of Nervous and Mental Disorders* 85 (1937) 637; M.B. Cornier, *et al.*, "Psychological Aspects of rheumatoid arthritis", *Journal of the Canadian Medical Association* 77 (1957) 533; R.H. Moos, "Personality factors associated with rheumatoid arthritis: A review", *Journal of Chronical Diseases* 17 (1964) 41 ff; H. Geist, *The Psychological Aspects of Rheumatoid Arthritis* (Chicago 1966); J.K. Rekola, *Rheumatoid Arthritis and the Family* (= *Scandinavian Journal of Rheumatology*, Suppl. 3, Helsinki 1973), 26 ff and 105 ff. Of special interest to the present case is the observed prominence of *depressive neuroses* among the psychic disturbances of the rheumatoid arthritic patients: "About a third of the patients in Rimón's (1969) series were depressive, and considerably higher percentages have also been reported. As already stated, the percentage was as high as 50 in the present study, as 15 out of the 30 patients were found to exhibit depressive features in examination ...... The depressive effect – and features such as helplessness and hopelessness associated with it

Take for example Esarhaddon's attitude toward astrology and magic. It was pointed out in my dissertation (p.47) that the notious of "superstitiousness" and "susceptability to magic" usually attached to Esarhaddon's person are anachronistic and misleading insofar as belief in the supernatural was so firmly rooted in the culture and way of thinking of the Sargonid Era that *any* contemporary of Esarhaddon would have been deemed extremely superstitious by the standards of the present time. Nevertheless, the fact remains that far more letters and reports dealing with astrology and magic are extant from the reign of Esarhaddon *alone* than from the time of all his successors and predecessors *together* (see App. 2A), a fact that cannot be accounted for easily even assuming that the extant Sargonid letter corpus represents only a fraction of the original correspondence. An understanding of the situation of Esarhaddon puts the matter into a new perspective. Is it not, after all, entirely understandable that a *deadly sick* man "cares" more about the gods than a healthy one? In Ancient Mesopotamia, religious-minded people simply could not ignore astrology (providing the means of interpreting "signs" sent by the gods) and magic (providing a chance to alter the course of destiny). There is evidence that Esarhaddon was generally considered a God-fearing man.[394] But what about, for instance, Sargon II? Leaving aside the tradition-bound pious formulae met in his inscriptions, there is nothing in the life of that man suggesting any particular interest in transcendental matters. And why should he have been particularly interested in them? Come to power on the brink of his 50th birthday[395], he was – as clearly appears from his correspondence – all his reign occupied with military and administrative matters, which he pursued up to the point of hubris (letting construct a new capital out of nothing); above all, *he appears to have been in excellent health*, as indicated by the fact that medical matters are not even touched in his correspondence[396] or that he, though already elderly, personally conducted several strenuous military campaigns[397], being ultimately killed in a battle against the Medes.[398] What has been said above should not be taken to imply that grave illness (and its psychic consequences, despair and morbid wishful thinking) *alone* would explain Esarhaddon's (or any other individual's) interest in astrology and magic. It is only one factor among others, but certainly a factor that should not be left out of consideration.

Other examples: Neuroses such as evidenced e.g. by *LAS* 38 become more understandable if viewed against the background provided by Table 3 above. The sudden and unexpected death of the king on his way to Egypt could be due to the great liability of all LED patients to infections (see above, sect. F). The "evil rumors, calumnies and lies" (EME ḪUL-*tì kar-ṣi taš-qir-ti*) put in circulation against Esarhaddon by his brothers after the former had been nominated the crown prince of Assyria (Borger, *Ash* p.41; cf. *ABL* 1216:8 ff) may have been malevolent references to the physical "debility" of the prince. One of the reasons prompting Esarhaddon to settle his succession already in 672 – only 8 years after his own accession (cf. discussion of *LAS* 1) – almost certainly was his growing worry about his health, a painful feeling that he was "running out of time".[399] And finally, the king's failing health also accounts for the curious reference to the "(joint) rule of the king and the (crown) prince" in *LAS* 247 r13 (also evidenced by several haruspex queries [*AGS* 116-120, 122, 126; *PRT* 44, 46-46; BM 98975 = Ki.1904-10-9,4] on behalf of *both* Esarhaddon and Assurbanipal), which at times appears to have turned into a "rule of the crown prince" alone (cf. the queries *AGS* 66, 67, 75, 114, 143 and 144, prepared in the name of the crown prince alone, and *ABL* 817 and *LAS* 94, astrological reports to the crown prince from persons who otherwise reported to the king only): Esarhaddon was at times so ill that he could and would not take care of his administrative responsibil-

---

and often also met in the RA patients – are far from uncommon in bodily ill persons in general . . . . . ." This fact can hardly be separated from the observation that "those with RA are grateful and faithful patients who greatly appreciate a personal therapeutic interest accorded to them" (Rekola, art.cit. 32, 106 and 113).

394 Cf. *LAS* 247 r9 f and *RMA* 257.11 ff (translated in Discussion of *LAS* 182).

395 See provisionally above, fn. 390.

396 True, in one of his letters to Sargon, the governor of Arrapḫa, Ištar-dūrī, mentions that he has sent two physicians to the king (*ABL* 157:4 ff). These were, however, not meant for the king himself, but intended to be sent further to an unknown destination (ibid. 15 ff).

397 See von Soden, *Herrscher* (1955), p.102 f.

398 See *RlA* II, p.435, entry for year 705. The city-lord Ešpai (cf. Med. *aspa* "horse") LÚ*Ku-lum-ma-a-a* against whom the king had marched almost certainly ruled over the city of Kuluman repeatedly mentioned in letters to Sargon (e.g. *ABL* 1046 and 129).

399 Cf. *VTE* 83f, "If Esarhaddon, king of Assyria, goes to his fate while his sons are young", and similar provisions in the Vassal-Treaty.

ities but deferred them temporarily to his son.[400] No doubt other historical features of the last regnal years of Esarhaddon will also be seen in a new light, once the relevant evidence has been systematically restudied, giving the sickness of the king the consideration it deserves.

Notes:

12. *ú-šaḫ-ki-mì*: this form has been interpreted varyingly as 1st or 3rd person singular (+ ventive suffix), depending on the way in which the translators have understood the context; cf. "(Ich habe bereits früher vor dem Könige gesprochen: seinen Reumatismus) soll ich nicht erkannt haben?" Meissner 1925; "I did not recognize (these symptoms)" Ritter 1965, similarly Waterman 1930 and Pfeiffer 1935; against this, "he (the king) did not inform me (about his symptoms)" Oppenheim 1967; similarly *CAD* Ḫ (1956) 33a, Kinnier Wilson 1956, and Lambert 1960. Absolute preference should be given to the former rendering (Ritter *et al.*) for several reasons.

First, quite apart from the improbability of the idea that the king *would not have let* the chief physician know the symptoms of his disease, translations like "he did not inform *me*" are out of the question since the verb ends in *-i* not *-anni*, as the translation would require (cf. *a-ta-a . . . la tu-šaḫ-kim-a-ni* "why did you not inform me", *LAS* 298 r20'). This final *-i* is, moreover, not a progressively assimilated ventive suffix (**ušaḫkima > ušaḫkimi*) but something else, as is quite evident from the fact that ventive forms of *šaḫkumu* are otherwise attested only in combination with pronominal suffixes (cf. simply *lu-saḫ-ki-mu*, l.16).[401] The true nature of the final vowel becomes evident e.g. from a comparison of passages such as *ABL* 135 r3 and 166:8f: two identical sentences, the former ending in *lil-lik*, the latter in *[lil-l]i-ki*. The paragogic *-i* is in the latter case clearly due to sentence intonation[402], and the same explanation also holds for the present case. Cf. the following parallel passages:

[iš]šaššūme . . . la a-⌈ka-ṣur⌉ (<akṣūr) ú-ma-a . . .	*ABL* 99 r5' (coll. Postgate)
iššaddaqdiš . . . . ina pāni a-ti-ti-zi ú-ma-a	*ABL* 1174 r11
ina šaddaqdiš . . . . ap-ti-qi-di ú-ma-a	*ABL* 724 r9
šaddaqdiš issēʾa . . . la i-li-ki . . . ú-ma-a . . .	*ABL* 312 r6
šaddaqdiš ina ^{ITU}*Nisanni ni-ti-din-ni <ú-ma-a> šarru bēlī iqṭibi mā ina* ^{ITU}*Tašrīti dinnā*	*ABL* 241 r7
ittimāli iššaššūme . . . la ú-na-ri-ṭi ú-ma-a . . .	*ABL* 605 r1
[ ] *memmēni lā iq-ri-bi ú-ma-a . . .*	*ABL* 593:4'
14 šanāti issēʾa la id-di-bu-ub (< idbūb) ú-ma-a . . .	*LAS* 114:11

All these passages, like the one under consideration, consist of two adversative sentences, both beginning with a temporal adverb (the second always with *ú-ma-a* "now"); all verbs immediately preceding the word *ú-ma-a* bear marks of a rising intonation contour manifesting itself in the form of paragogic or anaptyctic vowels;[403] the intonation in question clearly had a disjunctive function, and most probably corresponded to the particle *u* "but", which in the above contexts had become obsolete in Neo-Assyrian (cf. NB *šaddaqad* PN ^{LÚ}ŠEŠ.UNU^{KI}*-a-a kī idūku . . . mammāma ul iqbi ù en-na* ^{LÚ}UNUG^{KI}*-a-a id-du-uk*, *ABL* 753 r6ff).

Secondly, *šaḫkumu* cannot here be translated "to inform". This translation is only permissible in contexts where the verb appears with pronominal suffixes (meaning, basically, "to make [something] clear to [somebody]", "to make [someone] understand [something]"); in all other cases one has to stick to the "basic" meaning of the verb in the causative stem, "to explain, clarify"; cf. the examples in *CAD* Ḫ 33.

400 Cf. Streck, *Asb* 258 i 27f, "I stood before my royal father, giving orders to the magnates (of the empire); without my consent no governors were appointed . . ." This passage, like most letters to and from the crown prince, certainly partly refers to normal "practicing of kingship", which however does not explain the "joint rule" evidence just discussed.

401 See also *Iraq* 34 (1972) 24, note to l. 17, on "ventives" of the type *dubbu*. The identity of the paragogic vowels and the ventive suffix is also denied by K. Deller in his unpublished dissertation *Lautlehre des Neuassyrischen* (Wien 1959).

402 Cf. note to *LAS* 18 r8. The orthographical interpretation forwarded by K. Deller (*Or* NS 31 [1962] 7 ff and 186 ff) does not stand closer study.

403 The heightened pitch affected the final syllable of the word, which was consequently lengthened; if the final syllable was closed, it was often opened by means of a paragogic vowel. This was not obligatory, as appears e.g. from the writing *id-di-bu-ub* in *LAS* 114:11 (the pitch being is in this case reflected by an anaptyptic vowel, cf. note to *LAS* 39:11).

Accordingly, the grammatically correct translation of the passage can be only "I did/could not clarify his symptoms" or "he did/could not clarify his symptoms".[404] The latter alternative is ruled out by its senselessness and by the continuation (Obv. 15 f), which shows that it was Urad-Nanâ who was supposed to explain the symptoms to the king, not vice versa (*lissijū* . . . *lūšaḫkimū* is virtually equivalent to *aqṭibi* . . . *lā ušaḫkim*; cf. also *lēruba lūšaḫkim* in Rev.13). Note also *Ludlul* II 110: *ul ušāpi āšipu šikin murṣīja* "the exorcist was not able to clarify the nature of my illness" (Lambert, *BWL* p.44), where *ul ušāpi* exactly corresponds to *lā ušaḫkim* of our text.

18 f. A number of oracle queries of the type here meant have actually been preserved: see *AGS* 99-100, 101 (+ BM 98987), 102-103, 147 and BM 99062 (unp., cf. note to *LAS* 228). Most of them are very fragmentary, and it is not always possible to reconstruct the original wordings of the individual queries; the best preserved pieces *AGS* 101 and 147 however doubtless render a fairly accurate idea of the whole genre.[405] The former reads: "O Šamaš, give a positive answer to the question which I am asking you: Niq'a, the mother of Esarhaddon king of Assyria, who is now ill and on whom the hand of the god KA.BI.SIG$_5$ was "placed" in extispicy (i.e. who was [found to be] ill with the 'hand' of the said god), if this illness will leave her, is that prescribed in the command of your august divinity, O Šamaš, great lord? Will he who has got eyes see it, will he who has got ears hear it?", etc. The latter is formulated as follows: "O Šamaš, etc., will Assurbanipal king of Assyria recover safely and alive from this illness which has fallen upon him, will he escape it and get out of it? Does your august divinity know (this)? Is the recovery and rescue of Assurbanipal . . . prescribed in the command of your mighty divinity?", etc.

Two of these queries pertain to Esarhaddon (*AGS* 99 and 100). They are poorly preserved, but resemble *AGS* 101. In all probability, both represent attempts to find about the nature of the king's illness, the particular "hand" with which he was "afflicted". The inquiry here referred to seems to have served similar purposes, and it is not excluded that *AGS* 100 in fact is the query in question. The other query dates from 672 BC.[406] and must consequently be associated with some other occasion.

r1. *LUGAL le-pu-šú*: As in obv.12, the paragogic vowel (*-u*) appended to the verb was certainly due to sentence intonation (*lḗpuš* + pitch > *lḗpûšu*), and in this case corresponded to the enclitic (coordinative or iterative-connotative) particle *-ma* which in verbal phrases had become obsolete in NA. The context does not make the *precise* meaning of the vowel immediately apparent, though. As the verb in question is immediately preceded by another (virtually homophonous) form of the same verb (*le-pu-*[*šú*] in obv.19), it is quite possible that the vowel (and the intonation) is simply due to the repetition of the word (cf. *kī ša anāku ina raminīja* . . . *amattaḫūni, šū ana raminīšu li-in-tu-ḫu, ABL* 231 r9ff). It is also possible that the intonation indicated connection with the following clause, in which case one should translate "let the king apply this lotion, *and* perhaps this fever will leave the king" = "*should* the king apply this lotion, the fever *would* perhaps leave the king." The former alternative seems more probable in light of 248:13.r4.

r12. *pa-ri-ik-tú lip-ri-ku*: the translations of this phrase previously proposed include "man soll Gewalt anwenden(?)" by Meissner 1925, p.322; cf. "they should massage him vigorously" Pfeiffer 1935, similarly Waterman 1930; "let them put (them on crosswise)" *CAD* Ṣ (1962); similarly Ritter 1965 and Oppenheim 1967. While all these renderings are compatible with the range of meaning of *parāku* (cf. *AHw* p.828 f), they ignore the object of the verb, *pariktu*, which cannot be rendered as "Gewalt", "vigorously" or "crosswise" since these notions are already included in the verb itself. The other attestations of the phrase (*LAS* 188 r4 and K 3455+ i 16', see below) as well as the analogy of related expressions (*šuruptu šarāpu, maqalūtu qalû, taklimtu kallumu, tašlimtu šallumu*, etc.) show that *pariktu* was not just a redundant adverbial accusative added to the verb to reinforce its meaning, but a concrete *object placed* or to be placed *in an obstructing position* (*pariktu* = lit. "Quergelegtes", *AHw* l.c.). The exact meaning of the word in the present context is, of course, a matter of speculation, since the nature of the treatment carried out by means of the *ṣilbāni* remains obscure (see note to *LAS* 181:6). The translation "bolt"

404 Formally, the passage could also be understood as a question and translated "Formerly, (when) I spoke . . . , *did* I not clarify . . . ?" (Thus Meissner 1925); cf. note to *LAS* 208 r8. Such a translation is however unlikely in view of the continuation.

405 For the structural affinities of *AGS* 99-103 see Knudtzon, *AGS* p.207f.

406 On the analogy of the other texts of this genre, the name [^{Id}D]N-EN-PAB found on the left edge of the tablet represents the end of a *limmu* and can consequently be restored as [Na]bû-bēlu-uṣur, the eponym of 672 BC (cf. *AGS* 51 and 149).

(German "Querriegel") suggested in Pt.1 was based on *LAS* 188 r4, where *pa-rik-tú par-kàt* could plausibly refer to the shutting of a magically purified house; cf. *ba-ba-am ip-ta-ri-ik* "he blocked the door (with his feet)" *Gilg.* Pvi 12, *iš-tù pa-ri-ik-tim ša* KÁ [d]DN, *JCS* 8 32 iii 2, and cf. *napraku* "Riegel" and *parku* "ein Teil des Schlosses", Salonen, *Türen* p.82. A further attestation of *pariktu* in K.3455+ (unp. cultic ritual, known to me from a photo kindly made available by Deller) makes it likelier, however, that the word actually meant "curtain", as already suggested by K. Müller, MVAeG 41/3 (1937) 41[1]; cf. *mar-du-tú ni-pa-ri-ik* "we draw the curtain (before stripping Ištar of her jewellery)", *ABL* 1094:9. The function of the curtain in the present case was perhaps to give the king privacy during the *ṣil(li)bānu* treatment; in K 3455+ it was hung in front of a room containing a sacred phallos? (É *e-qi*).

r15. *ina lib-bi*: not "therefore" (thus Pt.I on the basis of 180:13) but "by means of it", cf. 181:12 (for the word order see on 214 r3). *ina lub-bi* "in a wrapping" (Ritter 1965) is also possible, and perhaps even more probable in view of the fact that *libbu* is written differently (*lìb-bi*) in Obv.5. Note, however, the occurrence of *lib-bi* in *LAS* 254:6 together with *lìb-bi* ibid. r2.

r20. *edannu*: here in the meaning "(acute) period (of a chronic disease)"; cf. *CAD* A/1, p.101a, also for other examples of *adannu* in medical texts. The present passage certainly pertained to the treatment of the cutaneous eruption of the king, see on *LAS* 255.

247

Bibliography:

(I) Waterman, *RCAE* 584 (cf. IV 184) and 1370 (cf. IV 205, 250); Pfeiffer, *SLA* 214 and 288.
(II) von Soden, *ZA* 44 (1938) 182 f; Deller, *Or*NS 30 (1961) 251; Ritter, *AS* 16 (1965) 319.*

Addressee:

Esarhaddon.

Date:

Late Ajāru, eponymy of Šulmu-Bēl-lašme = early May, 670 BC. This date can be established from the wording of Obv.20 ff, considered in the light of Rev.13. There can hardly be any doubt that Obv.20 ff refers to a rebellion or conspiracy directed against the king, and quelled only relatively slightly before the letter was written (note Obv. 19!); Rev.13 shows that the incident took place in the "joint rule" of Esarhaddon and Assurbanipal, i.e. during the years 672-669 BC (see Discussion on No.247, section G). Since, furthermore, some of the king's closest men seem to have been involved in the plot (cf. especially Rev.7 f and relevant comments), our letter is obviously to be associated with the following chronicle entry for the year 670:

MU *11*.KÁM LUGAL (*ina*) KUR *Aš+šur* [LÚ]GAL[MEŠ]*-šú ma-du-tú ina* [GIŠ]TUKUL *id-duk* "In the 11th year, the king of (var. in) Assyria executed many of his magnates."[407]

As pointed out by Larsen, *RA* 68 (1974) 22, this incident is firmly placed in Nisannu 670 by a legal document (*ADD* 499 = *AR* 563) containing an eponym date of a type used only in times of political turbulance. This date is confirmed by the present letter showing that the attempted coup more or less coincided with a severe fit of disease which Esarhaddon suffered in the early part of his 11th regnal year (for the dating of this fit cf. also the notes on *LAS* 51, written at the end of Ajāru, 670); besides the present letter, the conspiracy and the king's illness are also linked in *LAS* 133, though admittedly in rather vague terms. Less tangible chronological evidence but all the more important detail information on the coup can be elicited from 3 letters from a certain Nabû-reḫtu-uṣur[408],

[407] Grayson, *TCS* 5 (1975), Chron.1 iv 29 (p.86) and Chron.14:27 (p.127). Cf. Borger, *Ash* p. 124. Corresponding chronicle entries are elsewhere explicitly associated with rebellions; e.g., Wiseman, *CCK* p.72:21, [MU] *10*.KÁM [LUGAL U]RI.KI *ina* KUR-*šú* TA ITU.KAN EN ITU.AB *bar-tu ina* KUR URI.KI [X X] [22] [LUGAL LÚ.ER]IM.ME-*šú ma-du-tú* ina GIŠ.TUKUL *id-duk*. The omission of the word *bārtu* in the present instance may be due to the fact that the chronicler was Babylonian, not Assyrian.

[408] Otherwise known only from *ADD* 448 = *AR* 443:50, where appears as a witness together with Adad-šumu-uṣur, Ištar-šumu-ēreš, Marduk-šākin-šumi, Sāsî(!), etc. (the document in question probably dates from 665 BC, see Appendix N, no.17; note also *ADD* 532 = *AR* 628:8 (date uncertain). Probably not identical with Nabû-rēḫtu-uṣur the scribe (*AR* 268:16 and 379:12', the former dated in year 646, and by no means to be confused with the instigator of rebellion against Aššur-etelli-ilāni (*NARGD* 13:14 and 14:10) or the bodyguard with the same name, mentioned in *AR* 340:37 (year 623) and 37:1.9.18 (year 624).

ABL 1031+[409], *ABL* 1217(+)K.13737 and *CT* 53 938[410], hitherto dated either to 672 or 669 BC[411], but more plausibly to be connected with the conspiracy under consideration.[412] These letters were written with the definite purpose of supplying the king with information on the plot (conspired by or on behalf of a certain Sāsî[413]), which according to the writer was in such an advanced stage of preparation that it was necessary for the king to act quickly if he wanted to "save his life".[414] Taking into consideration the mass of detailed evidence presented in the letters against the persons denounced,[415] I think it can be safely assumed that the king took a hand in the course of the events soon after the last of the letters was in his hands. Unfortunately all of them are so badly broken that only the date of *CT* 53 938 (Kislīmu[?], 671)[416] can be established with some precision. *ABL* 1031+ was probably written not much after or before *CT* 53 938, since it is a virtual duplicate of what is left of the latter; *ABL* 1217 refers to incidents taken place in the month Simānu (of 671), obviously months before the writing of the letter,[417] but is otherwise void of any useful dating criteria; it is not excluded that it is the last letter of the series. In any case, even these meagre chronological data agree well with the general dating of the rebellion proposed above. Since the base of the conspiracy obviously was in Ḫarrān[418], or in adjacent regions,[419] it is clear that the king could not take immediate action but had to make his preparations;[420] and considering the graveness

409 The five fragments (K.1034, K.9204, K.9821, K.10541 and K.11021) recently joined to, or connected with (K.9821 does not make a "physical" join), the piece published by Harper indicate that this tablet was at least as large as *ABL* 1217 and originally contained at least 80 lines with ca. 17 characters in each.

410 Unpublished; virtual duplicate of *ABL* 1031+ Obv.5-12.

411 Cf. Waterman, *RCAE* III p.322 (under No.1217) and 332 (under No.1257); Dietrich, *AOAT* 7 (1970), 50ff, Fales, *CCENA* (1973), 101 ff.

412 The king to whom the letters were addressed was certainly Esarhaddon (note especially *ABL* 1217 r4' f *a-bat* dPA+KU *ši-i ma-a* LUGAL *u tu a na* I*Sa-si-i* 5 *ma-a* MU NUMUN *šá* I.d*30*-PAP.MEŠ-SU *u-ḫal-la-qa* "This is the word of Nusku: 'The kingship belongs to Sāsî, I (or he) will destroy the name and seed of Sennacherib'", and cf. *ABL* 442 r1 f *at-ta* NUMUN.MEŠ GIN *ša* I.d*30*-PAP.MEŠ-SU "you are the true seed of Sennacherib", referring to Esarhaddon), and the letters certainly postdate the oath of allegiance of Ajāru 672 (cf. *ABL* 1217:5.6.r9' and 1034+:5 f with *VTE* 140 ff, 161 and 254, and note the repeated reference to the crown prince in K.9821:1' f; note also *ABL* 445, addressed to the crown prince). Nothing in the letters points to 672 or 669 specifically, and contemporary sources do not give the slightest hint that a conspiracy would have been suppressed in these years in Assyria.

413 It is not certain that Sāsî was spontaneously involved in the plot, in spite of the fact that he was thus blamed by Nabû-rēḫtu-uṣur. Other sources indicate that he kept finding favour with the king and was not executed along with the other conspirators.

414 Cf. *ABL* 1031+ r14' ff: *la ta-pa-làḫ* 15 dEN dPA dNIN.LÍL [*is-se-ka*] *iz-za-zu ár-ḫiš* UN.MEŠ 16 *li-mu-tú* ZI.MEŠ [*še-zib*] . . . 17 UN.MEŠ *li-mu-tú* 18 *a-du la i-ḫa-ru-*[*pu-ni*] . . . "Don't be afraid; Bēl, Nabû and Mylitta are with you. (These) people should die quickly; save your life! . . . These people should die before they find time to . . ."; similarly *ABL* 1217:8 ff.

415 The writer denounces by name several persons, exposes secret meetings, gives detailed information on acts on specific days, and quotes from letters dealing with preparations for the coup.

416 The text reads as follows (restorations from *ABL* 1031+): [*a-na* LUGAL EN-*ia*] 2 [ÌR-*ka* IdPA-*re-eḫ-tú*-PAP dEN dGAŠAN dPA d*Taš-me-tum*] 3 [d*15 šá* URU]NINA d*15 šá* U[RU*Arba-ìl* DINGIRMEŠ-*ka šá* MU-ka] 4 [*a-na* LUGAL]-*ti iz kur-u-ni šu-n*[*u lu-bal-li-ṭu-u-ku*] 5 [LÚKÚRMEŠ-*ka*] *šá* AD-*ka* (referring to Sennacherib) *ina* ŠÀ *a-de-e* [*ú-še-ri-bu-u-ni šá ina* ŠÀ *a-de-ka*] 6 [*i-ḫa-ṭu-u-ni*] *šá ina* UGU ZIMEŠ-*ka i-*[*da-ba-bu-u-ni*] 7 [*šu-nu ina* ŠU2]-*ka i-šá-ka-nu-šu-nu* M[U-*šú-nu* TA* ŠÀ KUR *Aš+šur*KI] 8 [TA* ŠÀ É.GA]L-*ka tu-ḫal-la-qa da-ba-bú* [*an-ni-ú*] 9 [*šá* dNIN.LÍ]L *šu-ú* LUGAL *be-li ina lìb-bi lu l*[*a i-ši-aṭ*] 10 [*ina* UD *n*.KÁM *š*]*á* ITUAPIN *di-ig-lu a-da-gal ma-a* [. . .]. 11 [*ma-a ina* ŠÀ . . .] *kaš-da* EN *a-de-e šá* LUG[AL . . . . .] 12 [*la-mu-qa-a-ja la ú-pa-z*]*a-ar di-ib-*[*bi* . . . . . .]; remainder lost. It seems certain that the letter was *not* written in Araḫsamna (Obv.10) but in a later month, otherwise the writer should have used in l. 10 the expression ITU *an-ni-i* "(of) this month".

417 Cf. GEMÉ *šá* IEN-PAP-PAP . . . TA* ŠÀ ITUSIG$_4$ *sa-ar-ḫa-at* "the slave-girl of PN has been (or is) . . . since Simānu", *ABL* 1217 r2'f, and note the dates UD *27*.KÁM, UD *28*.KÁM and *a!-na! 2-e u$_4$-me*, ibid. r11'-16'.

418 Cf. IEN-PAP-PAP TA* URUKASKAL *lu-bi-lu-né* dPA+KU [. . .] "let PN be brought here from Ḫarrān, Nusku [. . . .]", *ABL* 1217 r8'.

419 Note that the legal document referred to above (*ADD* 499) pertained to affairs in Šadikanni (Tell 'Ağāğa) on the Ḫabur.

420 The crushing of the rebellion of Sallāju took place only 4 months after the disclosure of his plans; see under *LAS* 30.

of the crime and the severity with which it was punished, it seems certain that the conspirators did not capitulate instantly but offered strong resistance; accordingly, the fighting in the area may well have gone on for months and not only for the month Nisannu of which we happen to have direct evidence.

In addition to the letters already mentioned, see also *ABL* 445[421], 1257[422], *LAS* 213[423], 248, 272, 284 and Landsberger, *BBEA* p.8ff[424]; cf. also the oracle queries referred to above (p.235).[425]

Notes:

10. *im-ra-aṣ-ṣu-ni* = /imruṣūni/. For the change *u* > *a* (occasioned by the following stressed *u*) see note to 166:14; the curious gemination of *ṣ* is only graphic and finds its explanation in the fact that the morpheme boundary /imraṣ+ūni/ did not coincide with the adjacent syllable boundaries (/im-ra-ṣu-ni/). Since cuneiform words were as a rule written down *syllable by syllable*, except that lexemes (on the analogy of logographic spellings) were often graphically separated from inflectional morphemes, hybrid spellings like the present one sometimes resulted in junctures where the two principles clashed, especially before suffixes of the subjunctive, ventive, and 2nd/3rd p. pl. Cf. *e-pa-áš-šú-u-ni*, *ABL* 253:12, *ip-qid-du-ni CT* 53 235:8, *id-din-nu-ni*, *ABL* 212 r1, *i-lik-ku-u-ni*, 556:16, *iḫ-liq-qu-u-ni* ib. r23, and often; *a-ḫa-ra-aṣ-ṣa*, *ABL* 198:19, *ni-iḫ-ru-uṣ-ṣa*, 1310 r8; *ip-tu-ag-ga*, 415:15, *a-du-al-la*, 382:6, *a-da-an-na*, 382:6, and often in writings such as *liš-pur-ra*, *lal-lik-ka* (*ABL* 242 r24, 729:5, etc.); *ip-qid-dan-ni*, 649:10 (cf. *KAV* 133 r5, *ABL* 84 r5), *iš-pur-ra-a[n-ni]*, *CT* 53 645:2 (cf. ibid. 533:3 *iš-pur-ra-né-ni*), *ú-ḫal-laq-qa-ni*, *KAV* 199 r9, etc.; *tu-dam-mì-iq-qa* "you have made (your name) pleasing", *ABL* 561:15, *tu-šá-aṣ-bat-ta*, *VTE* 85 (var. *-ba-ta*, *-bat-a*), *ta-na-ṣar-ra-ni*, ib. 66 (var. *-ṣar-a-ni*), etc.; for examples of forms of 3rd p. pl. see *Iraq* 34 (1972) 25.

15. As translated in Pt.I, this line does not really make sense, and it seems therefore more reasonable to turn the sentence into a question, reading *da-ba-bu ša* ERIM^{MEŠ}*-šu-ú* . . . *i-du-bu-ub* and translating: "Did the king, my lord, (really) speak of his (own) men?" Cf. the continuation.

16. The signs at the break are almost totally obliterated but hardly permit any other meaningful restoration than *un-z[a]-a[r-ḫi ḫ]a[r-d]u-te* (cf. Pt.I, p.298; the sign following *z[a]* is considerably more defaced than indicated ibid.), to be translated approximately "watchful servants". For *ḫardu* "watchful" see *AHw* 325a (cf. *CAD* Ḫ 99a); the translation "servant" for *unzarḫu* was first suggested by Ebeling, *MAOG* 7/1-2 (1933) 71^{e}.[426]

---

421 Anonymous, addressed to the crown prince; certainly from the same person who wrote *LAS* 104 (written May 27, 669).

422 From Assurbanipal to Esarhaddon, possibly connected with the crushing of the rebellion; written in a remarkably unsteady hand. The copy of Harper has to be corrected in several points (Obv.6 read ^{I}*Ku-na-a-a* without question marks; Obv.8 *šu!-pur liš!-ú-lu!*; Obv.10 *ma-a šu-tú* [*ṭè*]*-en!-šú-*[*nu*]*!*; Obv.12 *is!-sap!-*[*ru-u-né*]; Rev.3 LÚ*! *kal!-dà!-a!-a!* ^{4}*a-bat!* LUGAL; Rev.6 *ma-a* MÍ [*ár!*]*-mì-ti*; Rev.11 TA* $^{\text{I!}}$*Ab!-di-mil-ki ni-sa-al!-lim!* ^{12}*an-ni-u! šú!-tú*; Rev.13 *e-gér-tú šá ṭè!-*[*me*]).

423 Void of any dating criteria. The reverse of this letter is to be compared with the beginnings of the letters of Nabû-rēḫtu-uṣur.

424 See discussion under *LAS* 284.

425 Note especially *AGS* 108, dated Addāru 6 [= February 15, 670?] and mentioning Esarhaddon only, and *PRT* 44, dated Ajāru 1 [= April 11, 670?] and mentioning *both* Esarhaddon and Assurbanipal. A late reference to the case (from Assurbanipal's time) is perhaps found in *ABL* 1364 r 1 ff (3 PNN *ša* TA* *pa-ni du-a-ku* TA* *pa-ni* AD*-ka iḫ-liq-u-ni*).

426 Two entirely different translations of *unzarḫu* have recently been advanced in the *CAD*, viz. "free man" (Vol. K [1971], 108*b* s.v. *kalzu*) and "foreigner" (Vol. L [1973], 214*b* s.v. *lišānu*), but these are not supported by the contexts in which the word occurs. For the sake of clarity I give in the following all the attestations of the word known to me; three of the examples are Middle-Assyrian,(nos. 1-3), the rest are from the Sargonid period.

[1] $^{\text{MI.d}}$EŠDAR*-um-mi* ^{3}*um-za-ar-ḫu* ^{4}*ša* ^{MÍ}*Da-am-qa-at-*^{d}*Taš-me-te* . . . . ^{15}$^{\text{MÍ.d}}$EŠDAR*-um-mi* GEMÉ*-sa* ^{16}*a-na* $^{\text{I.d}}$*A-šur-*ŠEŠ-SUM*-na* . . . ^{18}*a-na šul-ma-ni* ^{19}*ta-ti-din* ^{20}*pu-ḫa-at* ^{21}GEMÉ *za-ku-e* ^{22}^{MÍ}*Da-am-qa-at-*^{d}*Taš-me-tum* ^{23}*na-ṣa-at* "Ištar-ummī, the *umzarḫu* of Damqat-Tašmētu, . . . she (= Damqat-Tašmētu) gave (this) Ištar-ummī, her slave-girl, to Aššur-aḫa-iddina as a gift; Damqat-Tašmētu guarantees the purity of the slave-girl", *KAJ* 100:2 ff, cf. Ebeling, *loc.cit.* p.85 f;

[2] ^{I}*Ṣíl-lí-*^{d}EŠDAR *um-za-ḫu* ^{3}EME *Áš-šu-ra-i-t*[*u*] "Ṣillī-Ištar, an *umzaḫḫu*, of nationality Assyrian", VAT 8722:2-3 (Weidner, *AfO* 13 pl.7; legal comment concerning sale of the person in question);

[3] ⌈*um*⌉*-za-ar-ḫi*, *KAJ* 175:12 (in broken context);

16 ff. The following passage undoubtedly represents the writer's response to the reproachful speech of the king quoted above, and no doubt he included himself among the "watchful servants who had performed their duty and were frightened to death" (on this translation see in greater detail below); logically, then, the subsequent remark: "because of this talk of the king" (Obv.19f) should be connected with this sentence, as already done by Pfeiffer, *SLA* (1935) p.156[427], and not with the following one, as in Pt. I. This is indeed possible, for adverbial expressions could in NA follow the predicate and thus conclude the sentence. Cf. *LAS* 214 r3', *i-pa-laḫ* TA* *pa-an* LUGAL "he will get frightened because of the king"; also *šum-ma ma-ḫi-ir pa-an* LUGAL, *ABL* 414:17; *lal-li-ka ina pa-an* LUGAL ^{6}EN-*ia*, 787 r5 f; *a-da-gal* ^{r1} [*ina* I]GI-*šú-nu*, 563:6' f; *ina* ^{KUR}*Zi-ki-ti-a* ^{r1} *šu-tú a-di* ^{2} *e-mu-qi-šú*, 515:15 ff; *la-as-de-e-re* ^{r1} *ina ši-a-ri*, 440:14 f, etc. Additional examples in note to 214 r3'.

The reference to the conspirators (19-r8) is nevertheless tightly linked with the foregoing also. The writer contends that the rebels had turned Esarhaddon into a misanthropist, and interprets the king's complaints as a manifestation of the general loathing the monarch now justifiedly felt for the whole mankind. Implied is of course that the writer had been reproached without any reason, and the passage is thus basically equivalent in meaning to the preceding one.

17. This line has hitherto been mistranslated as if *ṭè-en-šú-nu* were the s u b j e c t of the relative clause in question, cf. Waterman, *RCAE* I (1930), p.415: "(The men . . .) so much of their report is clear"; Pfeiffer, *SLA* (1935), p.156: "All those whose understanding was clear"; *CAD* Ḫ (1956), p.124*b*: "In so far as their report is intelligible". This is impossible since *ḫa-as-su-u-ni* is unambiguously a plural form (the corresponding singular is *ḫa-si-is-u-ni* [e.g. *LAS* 238:5'])[428] and hence naturally requires a plural subject, to wit *un-z*[*a*]*-a*[*r-ḫi*] in the preceding line. Consequently, *ṭēnšunu* is the object of the sentence, which implies that the stative *ḫassūni* is here – as often in NA – used actively and has to be translated "they remembered". This fact puts also the earlier renderings of *ṭēnšunu* into doubt: what sense would "they have not remembered their report/understanding" make in this

---

[4] *la-a* DUMU $^{\text{LÚ*}}$EN.URU *ša* ^{UR}[^{U}GN] ^{5}*a-na-ku* $^{\text{LÚ*}}$*un-za-ar-ḫ*[*u*] ^{6}$^{\text{LÚ*}}$ÌR *ša* LUGAL EN-*ja a-na-ku* ^{7}LUGAL *be-li ina* ^{URU}*Qu-un-bu-na* ^{8}*ip-taq-da-ni mi-i-nu* ^{9}*ša a-ma-ru-ni ša a-šam-mu-ni* ^{10}*ina pa-an* LUGAL EN-*ja a-qab-bi* ^{11}*me-me-ni* TA IGI LUGAL *la ú-p*[*a-za-ar*] "I am not the son of the city lord of GN, I am an *unzarḫu* and a servant of the king, my lord. The king, my lord, appointed me in Qunbuna; I shall tell the king, my lord, all I see and hear, I shall conceal nothing from the king, my lord", *ABL* 317:4 ff;

[5] LUGAL *be-lí a-mat i-par-ra-as-ma* ^{18}[. . . ^{LÚ}]ÌR ^{LÚ}*un-za-ra-aḫ šá* LUGAL ^{19}[. . . . .]-*šú-nu a-na* LUGAL *be-lí-já a-qab-bu-u* "The king, my lord, will decide about the matter and [. . . ; I am] (but) a servant and *unzaraḫ* of the king, [my lord, who] tells their [ ] to the king, my lord", *ABL* 1074 r17 ff (NB);

[6] *ina* UGU *un-zar*$_4$ (NUMUN)-*ḫi ša kal-za-ni* ^{7}*ša 3* MU.AN.NA^{MEŠ} "as regards the 3-year(-old?) *unzarhus* of the *kalzus*" *ADD* 1041:6 f (between ^{3}*ina* UGU ^{I}PN ^{4}$^{\text{LÚ*}}$GAL *ki-ṣir* and ^{10} *ina* UGU *ú-rat* BAD.ḪAL); cf. [n+] ^{6}KUR^{MEŠ} *un-zar*$_4$-*ḫi*, ND 2482:3;

[7] A.ŠÀ *un-zar*$_4$-*ḫi* ^{I}*Na-ni-i* ^{LÚ}[ ] ^{21}A.ŠÀ *un-zar*$_4$-*ḫi* ^{URU}ŠE *Kal-du* [. . .], *ADD* 425 = *AR* 413:21 f;

[8] ^{I}*Un-za-ar-ḫi-15* ^{LÚ}GAL *ki-ṣir*, *AR* 322:7; ^{I}*Un-za-ar-ḫu-15*, 673:4;

[9] ^{I}*Un-zar*$_4$-*ḫu-Aš+šur*, *AR* 118:30, 358:24, 377:25;
^{I}*Un-za-ḫu-Aš+šur*, 467:20;

[10] ^{I}*Un-zar*$_4$-*ḫu* ^{LÚ}SANGA, *AR* 50:17.

I believe these examples suffice to show that *unzarḫu/unzaḫḫu* (< MA *umzarḫu/umzaḫḫu*) most probably was simply a synonym of *urdu* "servant, slave": note that the two words occur twice side by side with each other [4, 5]; that in one example [1], *umzarḫu* alternates with *amtu* "slave girl"; and that it is once [2] used as a designation of a sold slave. Of importance is also the fact that the personal names in which the word occurs [8-10] are exactly paralleled by names composed with the element *urdu* (cf. ^{I}ÌR-*15*, *AR* 22:14, 44:34, 53:37, etc.; ^{I}ÌR-*Aš+šur*, 41:21, 119:1, 143:21, etc.; ^{I}*Ur-du*, 45:34, 86:9.16, 111:16, and often) and the WSem. *Abdi*-names (cf. ^{I}*Ab-di-*^{d}*Sam-si AR* 287:3, ^{I}*Ab-di-Mil-ki* 70:25, ^{I}*Ab-di-10*-U 171:25, ^{I}*Ab-da-a'* 201:32, ^{I}*Ab-di-i* 24:2, etc.); note also the names ^{I}SANGA-^{d}*15* and ^{I}*Sa-an-gi-i* (*APN* 192*b* and 215*b*), if *šangû* originally = "servant". As for the etymology of the word, the fact that it is first attested in Middle-Assyrian texts and could be used as a designation of both male and female persons suggests that it is a loan word from Hurrian.

[427] All those whose understanding was clear (nearly) died of fright on account of this word of the king.

[428] The situation is different in MA where there is no formal distinction between the corresponding singular and plural forms, in other words, Stat. 3 m Sg. Subj. = St. 3 m Pl. Subj. Cf. e.g. *us-bu-(ú-)ni* (Sg.) *KAV* 1 ii 27, 6:9.10.23 etc., and *us-bu-ni* (Pl.) VAT 16375:9 (Mayer, *AOATS* 2 p.76 f). In NA the opposition *parisūni* (Sg.): *parsūni* (Pl.) holds throughout, contrary to what is suggested by *GAG* Parad. 6 (cf. § 83 d!).

context? Isn't it much more natural that *ṭēmu* here means "order" as usual? If so, what order? This appears from Obv.11 ff where the king explicitly demands from his servants more efficient caretaking, concluding his speech with the exclamation *maṣṣartašunu akê inaṣṣurū* "how (well) did they guard them (= the earlier kings)!" Compare this with *ABL* 1006 r12, LUGAL *ṭè-e-mu il-tak-na-an-ni um-ma* EN.NUN-*a ú-ṣur* "the king gave me the following o r d e r : 'Keep my watch!'" (a letter from the Babylonian astrologer Munnabitu); see also my remarks in *Iraq* 34 (1972) 31 f. It was the duty of the Assyrian scholars to attend to the well-being (= "to keep the watch") of the king, and in this line the writer simply asserts that he had not neglected that duty.[429]

18. *ti-ri-ik lìb-bi*: cf. *pal-ḫiš ul-ta-nap-šá-qu lìb-ba-šú-nu i-tar-rak-ma i-ma-'u(-ú) mar-tú* "they were overcome by fear, their hearts throbbed and they ejected gall", Borger *Ash* p.57:85. In the present context, too, "throbbing heart" (*sic*, not "broken heart" as translated in Pt.I following *CAD* Ḫ 124b) has to be understood as an expression denoting *fear* rather than sorrow; whoever failed to "keep the king's watch" adequately, had full reason to be afraid of the consequences, as clearly demonstrated e.g. by *LAS* 41 and 264 (note especially Rev.11 ff, "I have been treated as if I did not keep the watch of the king, my lord"). It is hardly necessary to point out that the word *mé-e-tu* must not be taken literally in this context; "they died of a throbbing heart" is certainly idiomatic for "they were frightened to death".

19. *"Who plotted against the good (will)"*: cf. *KAI* No.222 C 19, *'w 'hpk ṭbt' w'šm* [20] *[l]lḥjt* "(he who does not keep the words of the inscription written on this stele but says: 'I shall erase its words') or 'I shall overthrow the good and return [to] the evil'" (from the treaty of Matī'-El [king of Arpad] with "Bir-ga'yah" of "KTK" (= Aššur-nirari V, ca. 750 BC). As this parallel clearly shows, *ṭābtu* was a terminus technicus for the contents ("spirit") of the royal treaties, and was often used as a synonym of *adê* itself; cf. W.L. Moran, *CBQ* 25 (1963) 77 ff, M. Weinfeld, *JAOS* 93 (1973), 190 ff, and see also below, on r.4. For *dabābu* + *ina muḫḫi* "to plot against" see *CAD* D 11 and 13*b*, and cf. note to *LAS* 185 r21-25.

22 f. With this passage, cf. the beginning of the Vassal-Treaties of Esarhaddon (ND 4327, ll.1-22) reading as follows: *a-de-e ša* ^{I}*Aš+šur*-PAP-AŠ MAN ŠÚ MAN KUR *Aš+šur* . . . TA* ^{I}*Ra-ma-ta-aja* EN URU *Ú-ra-ka-za-ba-nu* . . . *šá ina* UGU ^{I}*Aš+šur*-DÙ-A DUMU.MAN GAL *šá* É.UŠ-*ti* . . . *ina* IGI ^{d}SAG.ME.GAR ^{d}*Dil-bat* ^{MUL}UDU.IDIM.GU$_4$.UD . . . *ina* IGI *Aš+šur* ^{d}*A-nù* ^{d}BE ^{d}*É-a* ^{d}*30* ^{d}UTU ^{d}IM "Treaty of Esarhaddon, king of the world, king of Assyria (. . .) with Ramataja, the city ruler of Urakazabanu (. . . .) concerning Assurbanipal, the crown prince of the Succession Palace (. . . .). Before Jupiter, Venus, Saturn (etc.); before Aššur, Anu, Ellil, Ea, Sîn, Šamaš, Adad . . .". The document is here expressly designated as the *treaty of Esarhaddon*, just as *ABL* 1239+ is introduced as "the treaty of Zakūtu" (*a-de-e šá* ^{MI}*Za-ku-u-te*, Obv.1) and *KAI* No.222 as "the treaty of Bir-ga'yah" (*'dj brg'jh*, A 1); consequently, *a-de-e ša* LUGAL can here, without difficulties, be translated "the treaty of the king", as required by the context, and there is no need to interpret LUGAL as the subject of a relative clause, a proposed in *CAD* A/1 (1964) p.132 and A/2 (1968) p.249*a*. Of course, the latter rendering is also perfectly acceptable *per se* and actually paralleled by *VTE* 41 f, *a-de-e ša* ^{I}*Aš+šur*-PAP-AŠ MAN KUR *Aš+šur ina* IGI DINGIR^{MEŠ} [42] *ša* AN-*e* KI-*tim is-se-ku-nu is-ku-nu-u-ni*. For *adê šakānu* referring to the king's subject, see *LAS* 1 r19, 2 r3 and 3:11 r6.

r4. Contrary to what the wording of this line might suggest, the idea here is *not* that the traitors were pardoned *but* that they were called to account for their crimes. Cf. *ABL* 350 r4', *ù a-de-e šá* LUGAL *be-lí-já* [5] *ki-i ik-šu-du-šú-nu-ti* [6] *ša la-pa-an* GÍR AN.BAR *ú-še-zi-bu* [7] *ina bu-bu-tu i-ma-ti* "since they have been caught up by the treaty of the king, my lord, those (lit. he) who escaped the iron sword will die of hunger"; *ma-mit* DINGIR^{MEŠ} GAL^{MEŠ} *šá e-ti-qu a-mat* LUGAL-*ti-ka šá a-me-šú ik-šu-dan-ni* "the oath of the great gods, which I transgressed, and the royal order of yours which I despised, have caught up with me", Borger *Ash* p.103:23; *ma-mit* AN.ŠÁR LUGAL DINGIR^{MEŠ} *ik-šu-us-su-nu-ti-ma šá iḫ-ṭu-u ina a-de-e* [133] DINGIR^{MEŠ} GAL^{MEŠ} MUN ŠU^{2}-*šú-un ú-ba-'i-i-ma šá e-pu-us-su-nu-ti* [134] *du-un-qu* "the oath (sworn in the name) of Aššur, king of the gods, seized those who had violated the treaty of the great gods and I called them to account for the kindness and favours I had shown them", Streck *Asb* p.12 i 132 ff. In the present passage, *ṭābtu* is equivalent to *adê* and denotes the personified "spirit" and curses of the royal treaty.

r5 f. The writer may here indirectly refer to the treaty which the traitors had broken; cf. *VTE* 1. 327, *a-na zi-a-ri ina* IGI *a-ḫe-iš ta-šak-kan-a-šá-nu-u-ni* "(you swear that) you will not stir up mutual hatred in them (= Esarhaddon and Assurbanipal)".

[429] Cf. *LAS* 114:20-r4.

r9 ff. The passage comprising the next few lines is probably in no way linked with the section immediately preceding, but is rather to be combined with the beginning of the letter and understood as a kind of consolation evoked by the poor condition of the king. Cf. the similar passage in the report *RMA* 257, translated in commentary on *LAS* 182.

r16. The herbs mentioned in this line are both unidentified, and the writer's remark that one of them was very precious is certainly to the point, for ÚPA.TI is altogether not to be traced in the published portions of the series *Uruanna*, *Ḫḫ* and *Šammu šikinšu*. ÚBU (or ÚGÍD) is equated with the plant *imḫur-ešrā* in Köcher, *KADP* 1 iii 14'(!) and 11 r iii 45 (context: Ú*nap-ḫu*, Ú*šúm-'i-du*, Ú*bu-ṣi-lí-bu*, Ú*si-ju-ú*, ÚKUR.KUR[kur.kur].TI[la], ÚBU, ÚIGI.KU, ÚŠIŠ.KUR, Ú*ir-ri* *nu-ni*ḪA, Ú*šu-nu-qu*, ÚNIGIN.UR$_4$.UR$_4$, ÚKUD.UZU-*la-nu* = ÚIGI.NIŠ), and hence probably was a climbing plant, as the logogram used also indicates.[430]

r17. Cf. *ša-am-mi . . . ša a-na a-ḫa-mi-iš ma-aš-lu*, *EA* 11 r11.

r18. *il-du* = *išdu* "base": the occurrence of a Bab./MA form here (note also the faulty genitive suffix) is probably due to the fact that the writer drew his description of the plant from a literary source, to wit *Šammu šikinšu* (cf. below).[431] For pictorial representations of Assyrian earrings in sculptures, see B. Hrouda, *Flachbild* (1965), Pl. 8.

321 f. The wording of this passage suggests a(n in)direct quotation from the pharmaceutical compendium *Šammu šikinšu*. Cf., e.g., Ú GAR-*šú* GIM GI ZÚ.LUM.MA PA[MEŠ]-*šú* GIM PA[MEŠ] ÚGIŠ.ḪAŠḪUR!(copy MA) GIŠ.GI . . .[44]⌜Ú⌝[. . .] MU.NI [45]*ana* UŠ$_{12}$.BÚRU.DA SIG$_5$ *ina* UD.GIG.ÀM-*šú* [XX] *na* [. . .] *lum* [.] "The plant whose appearance is like that of a date reed, whose twigs are like the twigs of an "apple of the swamp" —— the name of [that] plant is [ ]; it is fit for 'counter-spells'. On the day when he is sick [. . . . .]", *STT* 93:43' ff. Similar statements were, it is true, also found in other pharmacological compendia, cf. only the following passage from the series Uruanna: *šam-mu ina* UGU-*ḫi-šú* MUŠ.DÍM.GURUN.NA [41]*ra-ab-ṣu* ÚNÍG.PA EME UR.KU MU-⌜*šú*⌝ [42]*a-na* ŠÀ.ZI.GA SIG SÚD *ina* Ì ŠÉŠ-*šú* "The plant on which geckoes lie: it is called 'shepherd's staff' (or) 'dog's tongue'; it is good for potency; to be crushed and rubbed on him (the patient) with oil", *KADP* 2 v 40 ff (cf. Biggs, *TCS* 2 p.3 f).

r26. This line remains unclear. Cf. Pt. I, p.298; all signs are slightly defaced, but the reading of the signs *ša*, *i* and *ku* appears to be certain.

248

Bibliography:

(I) Waterman, *RCAE* 465 (cf. IV 183).
(II) Oppenheim, *JAOS* 64 (1944) 163; Böhl, *Opera Minora* (1953) 409 ff; Deller, *Or*NS 33 (1964) 90; Ritter, *AS* 16 (1965) 319; Postgate, *TCAE* (1974) 66.

Addressee:

Esarhaddon.

Discussion:

This letter is to be compared with *LAS* 253, also concerning the cure of (the king's) ears and to be placed roughly in the years 672-669 (see ibid.). It is not at all impossible that both letters actually refer to the same kind of ear trouble, particularly if it is remembered that such troubles may simply have been manifestations of the systemic disease the king suffered from (see above, on *LAS* 246; on the possible nature of the ear trouble in question, see notes to *LAS* 253). On the other hand, it is hardly possible that the two letters are *chronologically* related (i.e. written approximately at the same time), for they differ considerably from each other in the writing of certain

[430] The translation "chaff" given in Pt.I should be cancelled. It was based on the writing Ú.BU-*e* standing for *pê* "chaff" in certain NA letters and inscriptions (*ABL* 757:11; *Sg*.8:186.275), from which it was inferred that *pû* was in general written Ú.BU in NA texts. However, in scholarly texts the word was always written logographically IN.BUL+BUL, and this writing should be expected in the present letter, too.

[431] The form *ildu* also occurs in the NA *naptunu* ritual *MVAeG* 41/3 p.64:40 (*il-da-a-te*) where its presence probably is due to the fact that the scribe was copying from a MA original.

characteristic words (*ṭu-ub* 248:5f [thus also 246:5, 247:5, 256:7'] against DÙG-*ub* 253:5; UZU 248:6 [thus also 246:5, 247:5, 255:6] against UZU.MEŠ 253:5; and UZU.PIX2 (248:9.r2) against *uz-ni* 253 r8). It would seem more likely that the present letter dates approximately from the same time as Nos. 246-247 and 256, i.e. from early 670.

Notes:

13. *le-pu-šú*: possibly to be interpreted as 3rd p. Masc. *Sg.*, the final vowel being due to expressive intonation (having the same function as the enclitic particle *-ma* in Babylonian); cf. *LAS* 246 r1 and corresponding note. The interpretation of *le-pu-šú* in r.4 should then also be modified accordingly.

r5 f. On the ground of this passage it would seem that even the physicians had to perform on certain fixed days the kind of public service called *ilku*; no doubt the services rendered were of medical nature, but for which authority they were performed remains unclear.[432] Cf. *LAS* 85 r3 ff (scribes under *ilku*-duty) and Falkenstein, *LKU* 51:12, [. . . . U]D *15*.KÁM *il-ki šá* ^{LÚ}MAŠ ^{LÚ}UŠ.KU *u* ^{LÚ}N[AR] "[On the . . .] 15th day; *ilku*-service of the exorcists, chanters and sin[gers]" (entry in a list of services performed in the temples of Uruk; cf. ll. 21, 32, 33, r3, r12, r19, r24 and r28, according to which a corresponding service had to be performed on the 1st, 2nd, 6th, 7th, 14th and 15th day of *each* month excepting Tašrītu and Du'ūzu).

r10. Cf. *ABL* 203 r5, *pa-al-ḫa-ak* [6]*šá la* LUGAL *la e-pa-áš*; *ABL* 992 r5 *pal-ḫa-ak ša la*! LUGAL [6]EN-*ja la a-ṣab-bat-si* (coll. Postgate); and 471:21, *la-áš-šú ša la pi-i ša* LUGAL [22]*la al-lak*. If the present letter was approximately contemporary with Nos. 246 and 247, as suggested above, the timidity of the writer could be taken to indicate that a certain feeling of insecurity prevailed in Nineveh after the attempted "coup" had been detected, but other interpretations (e.g. servile "fear" of the king) are, of course, also possible.

L.E.1. As indicated in Pt.I, the traces at the end of this line really point to ⸢*šá*⸣ rather than ⸢*ṣa*⸣, but it is nevertheless better to adopt the latter reading since no stone beginning with ^{NA_4} *mu*-⸢*šá*?⸣[appears to be known. By contrast, the *mūṣu*-stone (often written ^{NA_4} *mu-ṣa*, cf. Thompson, *DACG* p.113) is a well-known ingredient of medical preparations (cf. *AMT* 19,6:12, 29,1:5.6, 30,12:4, 33,3:6, 34,6:8), even in drugs used to relieve earache (*AMT* 33,1:33).

249

Bibliography:

(I) Waterman, *RCAE* 594 (cf. IV 258); Pfeiffer, *SLA* 338.
(II) Behrens, *ABB* (1906) 25; Labat, *Royauté* (1939) 358f and *RA* 40 (1946) 130; Böhl, *Opera Minora* (1953) 417; von Soden, *Fs Christian* (1956) 104; Landsberger, *BBEA* (1965) 50 f; Kümmel, *StBoT* 3 (1967) 173f, 176f, 179f.

Copy:

Cf. Lehmann, *Ššmk* (1892) pl.46 and Winckler, *SKT* II (1894) 19.

Writer:

While students of this letter have generally refrained from assigning it to a definite author, Landsberger has in passing (1965) suggested that the writer was Akkullānu.[433] This identification cannot be accepted, however, since the information given on the health of a (royal) patient in Obv.1' ff implies that the letter was written either by an exorcist or a physician; a priest or astrologer like Akkullānu is out of the question. Detailed orthographical analysis of the letter narrows down the number of possible authors even more effectively. The spelling *šúm-ma* occurring in r.5 is otherwise attested, within the present corpus, o n l y in letters of Mār-Ištar (11 times) and Urad-Nanâ

432 Since physicians working for the king received their livelihood from tax-exempted estates granted to them by the king himself (cf. *RMA* 240:7 ff and Oppenheim, *Centaurus* 14 (1969), 115 ff), and thus were not economically dependent on any other authority, it seems logical to assume that they had to render their *ilku*-services to the palace, perhaps by giving free medical care to the palace personnel on the days concerned. Does the present passage explain Herodotus I 197?

433 "[*ABL*] 594 . . . , vermutlich von Aqqulānu", *BBEA* p.50; cf. p. 38[56], which indicates that this identification was based on the occurrence of the city-name URU.*Ak-ka-di* in r.2 – a totally unreliable criterion in light of the evidence discussed below, under *LAS* 275.

(twice, in 252 r18 and 254 r9); Adad-šumu-uṣur, Ikkāru, Nabû-nāṣer and Urad-Gula wrote regularly *šum-ma*, Marduk-šākin-šumi both *šum-ma* and *šum-mu*, and Nabû-nādin-šumi *šum₄-ma*. Since Mār-Ištar was no physician/exorcist, the obvious conclusion is that Urad-Nanâ is the author. This conclusion is supported by the occurrence of the division-mark (:) in Obv.6, 8 and Rev.7; cf. 247 r11, 248:10.r5, 252 r11.12 and 255 r1.3. There are no attestations of this mark in the letters of Bānî, Ikkāru, Nabû-nādin-šumi, Nabû-nāṣer and Nabû-tabni-uṣur, and only four in the letters of Adad-šumu-uṣur (145 r12), Marduk-šākin-šumi (188:8'.r7'f), Nabû-gāmil (227 r6') and Urad-Gula (223 r7').

Since Urad-Nanâ as a rule wrote *šul-mu, lib-bu* and *ṭa-a-ba*, the spellings *šùl-mu* (Obv.1'), *lìb-bu* (2') and DÙG.GA (3') would at the first sight seem to speak against his authorship. However, this is only a seeming obstacle since the latter type of spelling is also attested in some letters of Urad-Nanâ: note *šùl-mu* 246:3, 247:3 and 256:3'; *lìb-bu* 247:18.24 and 256:7'; DÙG+GA 256:4'. In compensation, all other orthographic and linguistic features of the letter perfectly harmonize with the conventions of Urad-Nanâ; e.g., *a-du* (Rev.7) = 250 r12 and 254 r16 (not *a-di* as in the letters of Marduk-šākin-šumi); *me-me-ni* (Obv.11') = 250 r17 and 254 r9; UD^{MEŠ} (Rev.7) = 254 r16; DUMU.MAN (Obv.7') = 250:14 (against DUMU.LUGAL 247:12, 252:8 and 253:8), etc. Note also the omission of *bēlī* "my lord" in Obv.3' and Rev.4', as in 246:11.15.r1.7.10.14.17.21, 247:20.22.r2.4.12.13.27, 248:11.14, 250 r3.14, etc.

Addressee:
Esarhaddon.

Date:
Ulūlu/Tašrītu = September/October, 671 BC; see on *LAS* 26. A terminus *ante ante quem*, Tašrītu 22, is furnished by Obv.8'; a terminus *post quem*, Du'ūzu 14, is obtained by subtracting from this the hundred days which the substitute king had to "complete" before the two crown princes could risk going outdoors (Obv.7'ff and Rev.7 ff, cf. note on 135 r6). Since all "reigns" of substitute kings were started by eclipses, and those lasting a hundred days specifically by lunar ones, it is certain that a lunar eclipse had occurred at the latter date, Du'ūzu 14. The identification of the eclipse in question, and consequently the dating of the letter in a specific year, is made possible by the reference to the crown prince [Assurbanipal] and his brother Šamaš-šumu-ukīn (in Obv.7'), which shows that the event took place between the years 672 and 669 (cf. note on 173:17); a appears from App. F1, the only suitable eclipse visible in Mesopotamia within that span of time was that of July 2, -670. This date agrees exactly with the Babylonian date Du'ūzu 14 mentioned above, see App. A3.

Discussion:

See commentary on *LAS* 26. For another letter of Urad-Nanâ associated with the substitute king ritual, see *LAS* 257.

250

Bibliography:
(I) Waterman, *RCAE* 109 (cf. IV 174, 238); Pfeiffer, *SLA* 291.
(II) Behrens, *ABB* (1906), 85; Landsberger, *ZA* 41 (1933) 221; Böhl, *Opera Minora* (1953) 409 ff.; Deller, *Or* NS 30 (1961) 349; Ritter, *AS* 16 (1965) 319.

Date:
672-669 B.C. Notice the ref. to the crown prince in Obv.14, and see note on 173:17.

Notes:

13. *lakû*: see note on 219 r3. The present passage shows unambiguously that the child in question was not identical with Aššur-mukīn-palū'a, as presumed in *CAD* L (1973), p. 46.

r1 ff. Whether this passage means that the writer was making preparations to cure an aching tooth (cf. *LAS* 248) or collecting relevant recipes for the royal library remains uncertain. As a medical terminus technicus, *bulṭu* could mean both "healing (prescription), recipe" (thus in *LAS* 153:3 and in the present letter, Rev.5) and "(act of) healing, cure" (thus in *LAS* 246:10 and 248:8). For texts containing prescriptions for teeth see Thompson, *AMT* 21,2, 27,5, 28,1+, 30,13, 31,6+, and Köcher, *BAM* I 26-30.

r8. Against Deller (1961), there is no need to interpret *ta-di-li-bi* as Pret. of the N-stem; the form is quite simply Pf. of the G-stem with an paragogic vowel owing its existence to interrogative intonation (cf. note to *LAS* 208 r8). For other examples of the perfect in echo questions, see note to *LAS* 148:8.

251

Bibliography:

(I) Waterman, *RCAE* 111.

(II) Oppenheim, *JAOS* 64 (1944) 191; Ritter, *AS* 16 (1965) 319.

Addressee:

Esarhaddon.

Discussion:

This letter has clear affinities with the reverse of No.252, and there is actually no reason to doubt that both texts pertain to the cure of the *same* bleeding nose, especially since the wording of 252 r7 ff virtually requires the existence of a letter like the present one; cf. Ritter (1965), and note that the fragment K.7553 now joined to *ABL* 111 confirms that the prescriptions of the letter really were intended for treatment of nosebleed (*a-n*]*a* MÚD KIR_4 *pa-*⌜*ra*⌝*-si*, cf. note to Obv.11). As in No.252, this treatment consisted of inserting medicated tampons into the nostrils of the patient; the writer quotes altogether four different methods of preparing such tampons (*1* = Obv. 13-17; *2* = Obv.18-r5; *3* = r6-10; *4* = r11-15), probably *not* implying that *all* of them should necessarily be employed. The source on which the prescriptions were based has not been preserved, though we do have certain medical recipe texts dealing with nasal hemorrhage (see note to Obv.11). Note that the prescriptions cannot be verbatim quotations, but rather adaptations of the originals, since they are given in Neo-Assyrian.

Notes:

8 f. The restoration of these lines proposed in Pt.I is obviously not correct: the traces of the last sign in line 8, correctly reproduced as A]Š in "copy" Harper, hardly permit the reading B]A; moreover, the restored formula *libbu* --- *lu ṭāba* is missing in corresponding positions in *LAS* 250, 252 and 253 (though not in Nos. 249 and 256). Consequently, the writer probably began his actual message already in line 8, and it is only logical to assume that he used in this connection the word "tampons" (*li-ip-pi*) leading more directly to the following prescriptions than the "seed of martakal" mentioned in line 9. The traces as well as the width of the break in l.8 are fully compatible with this assumption. We may accordingly restore: ^{8}[*ina* UGU *li-ip-p*]*i* ^{9}[*ša*! NUMUN] ^{Ú}[*mar*]-*ta-kal* "[as to the tampo]ns [(made) of seed] of the *martakal*-plant (concerning which the king wrote to me)". This restoration also affects the rendering of the continuation, cf. below.

9. ^{Ú}*mar-ta-kal*: a soapwort, possibly = *Struthium*, *Saponaria*; see Thompson, *DAB* (1949) p.39 ff.

11. The reading of this line suggested in Pt. I should be cancelled; instead, read [*ša a-n*]*a* MÚD KIR_4 *pa-*⌜*ra*⌝*-si* "which are (intended) to stop nasal hemorrhage". This remark naturally pertains to the tampons mentioned previously. For a discussion of the *ša ana* construction occurring here see J. Aro, *Or* NS 32 (1963) 402 ff; on the infinitive construction *ana* + object + infinitive, see idem, *StOr* 26 (1961) 171. Cf. NAGAR-*nu* MÚD TAR-*si* "suppository to stop bleeding" *AMT* 53,9 r4.

Several medical texts dealing with nosebleed are known, but the relevant prescriptions do not resemble the one given in our letter, as far as it is possible to ascertain. Cf. ND. 4368:10 ff (Kinnier Wilson, *Iraq* 19 [1957] 40; pl.25): I NA *si-mat* $IGI^{\text{MEŠ}}$-*šú* KÚR.KÚR-*ir* IGI^{2}-*šú it-ta-nab-ra-ra* ^{11}NUNDUN-*šú zu-qat-su ú-lap-pat* u MÚD *ina* KIR_4-*šú* DU-*ku* ^{12}*la* ⌜*i*⌝*-kal-lu-u* NA BI ḪUL DIB-*su* ^{13}^{Ú}*an-ki-nu-te* ^{Ú}LAL SÚD ^{14}[K]I MÚ[D U_5?].GIŠ MUŠEN ḪI.ḪI ŠÉŠ-*su-ma* TI-*uṭ* "If the colour of a man's face constantly changes, (if) his eyes wander, (if) he keeps touching his lip and chin, and blood flows from his nose, that man has been gripped by an evil *gallû*. (To cure him,) pound *ankinutu* and *ašqulālu* (plants), mix them with blood of an [o]wl(?), smear him (with the ointment) and he will get well";[434] [I *ina* GÚ]-*šú* SÌG-*iṣ-ma e-li-a-at* ^{15}IGI^{2}-*šú* $KÚ^{\text{MEŠ}}$-*šú* LUGUD : MÚD *ina* KIR_4-*šú* ŠUB.ŠUB ... ^{19}NA BI ḪUL DIB-[*su*] *ana* KAR-*šú* "If he is affected in his neck, (if) the upper part of his eyes hurt him,

[434] Duplicated (until line 13) by Labat, *TDP* 190:14 f.

and gore or blood keeps dripping from his nose . . . that man has been seized by an evil *gallû*-demon. To release him . . . " ibid. 14 ff (prescriptions for making a salve and a leathern phylactery follow);[435] [. . .]⌜X⌝ *3* ⌜X⌝ I NA MÚD *ina* KA-*šú* DU-*ku* "[. . . . .] . . . if blood flows from the nose of a man" *AMT* 27,9:3' (a fragmentary incantation follows); [. . . . .]-*šú lu* MÚD *ina* KIR$_4$-*šú* DUB *ina* A GAZI^{SAR} [30][. . . .] LAL *pa-ni-ta-am-ma* LÁL-*su* "[If the . . . of a man . . .s] him or blood accumulates in his nose, [you . . . .] in extract of *kasû*(mustard?)-plant, [. . . . . .] and bandage him with the first bandage", *AMT* 83,1 r29 f; cf. also I SAG.KI-*šú* DIB-*su-ma* GÙ.GÙ-*si* MÚD *ina* KIR$_4$-*šú* DU-*ku* ŠU GIDIM "If his temples continuously hurt him, making him cry, (and if) blood flows from his nose: seizure of a ghost" *TDP* 32:7; I *ina* KIR$_4$-*šú* MÚD DU-*ku* [. . . . . . .] *1-niš* DU-*ku* "If his nose bleeds (and) at the same time [his . . . . .] flows" ibid. 56:19[436].

12. The beginning of this line is probably to be restored [*a-ki an-ni-(je)*]-*e*; cf. *LAS* 153:4'.[437] There is hardly place for *je* in the break, but the orthography of Urad-Nanâ also allows the "shorter" spelling, cf. *an-ni-u* 250:9 and 257r4' besides *an-ni-ju-u* 246:9.20.r2, 247:19, 248:12 and r.3.

13. Cancel the reading [NU]MUN *Dil+bat* "Venus-flower" suggested in Pt.I, and read instead]X *ina* MÚD ^{GIŠ}EREN "with cedar balsam/resin". The name of the herb(?) to be mixed with this substance was certainly mentioned in the break but remains unclear.

14. The beginning of this line can be restored by means of parallel medical texts, where MÚD ^{GIŠ}EREN "cedar resin" is almost invariably followed by the logogram ḪI.ḪI "to mix". Cf., e.g., *AMT* 2,1:19; 33,1:21; 37,2 r14; also, with Ì(×GIŠ) instead of MÚD, *AMT* 18,6:8, 19,1:26, 33,1:25.27; 36,1:3, 42,3:7.9.10, etc. In medical texts, ḪI.ḪI stands for *balālu* G or D (see *CAD* s.v.). This verb was obsolete in Neo-Assyrian, but may have been used in the present context as a technical term (cf. on 292:11ff); more probably however, a form of *ḫiāqu*, e.g. *i-ḫi-qu*, is in question, cf. *LAS* 337 r3.

^{SÍG}*tab-re-e-bi*: the NA reading of the logogram ^{SÍG}ḪÉ.ME.DA "red wool",[438] otherwise = *nabāsu* or *tabarru* (cf. Ḫh XIX 78[a] and Ḫg C II 3-4, *MSL* 10 p.129 and 139); note ŠEM.ḪÁ ^{ŠEM}[LI *ni-ip-šu* ^{SÍ}]^{G}*tab-ri-bu ina muḫ-ḫi* [ŠUB-*di*] *BBR* 66:4 with ŠEM.ḪÁ^{MEŠ} ^{ŠEM}LI *ni-ip-šu* ^{SÍG}ḪÉ.ME.D[A] ŠUB-*di* ibid. 67:4, and see Landsberger, *JCS* 21 (1967) 168. Not to be confused with ^{SÍG}*tab-ri-mu* (e.g., *PKTA* 9:6.9.11), which probably meant "multicoloured wool" judging from its obvious derivation from the root **brm* "to be multicoloured, speckled, pied, variegated" (*CAD* B 103). Cf. Köcher, *BAM* 3 (1964) p.XXIII *ad* no. 304:19' (*tab-ri-mu tab-ri-bu*): "Das Nebeneinander von *tab-ri-mu* und *tab-ri-bu* (ebenso in dem obenerwähnten Text A 265 Rs.14' and 15') entscheidet die von W. von SODEN, *ZA* NF 17 p.143 gestellte Frage, ob *tabrīmu* lediglich eine Spielform von *tabribu* ist"; note also the occurrence of ^{SÍG}*tab-ri-bu* beside ^{SÍG}*bar-ru-mu* (probably = *tabrīmu*, cf. ^{SÍG}GÙN.NU = *bar-ma-a-tum*, Ḫh XIX 26) in *BBR* 66:4.10.11. In medical texts, ^{SÍG} ḪÉ.ME.DA seems to alternate freely with ^{SÍG}ÀKA = *itqu* "fliece" (examples *CAD* I/J s.v.).

17. The doubts as to the restoration of this line expressed in Pt. I are groundless, since the whole letter deals with tampons intended to stop *nosebleed* (cf. above). Accordingly, restore at the beginning of the line [*ina (pi-i) na-ḫi-ri*] "in(to) (the openings of) the nostril(s)" in accordance with r9.15 and 252 r14; thus probably also in Rev.5.

r1. This line could be restored either [. . . SAG.KI].DIB.BA "migraine" or [^{NA_4}.KA.GI.NA].DIB.BA "magnetic iron", with the reservations that Mesopotamian textual evidence linking migraine with epistaxis is extremely slight and that the use of magnetic iron as a remedy against nosebleed also isn't entirely beyond doubt. For the former restoration, cf. *AMT* 32:7,I SAG. KI-*šú* DIB-*su-ma* GÙ.GÙ-*si* MÚD *ina* KIR$_4$-*šú* DU-*ku* (for translation see above, note to obv.11); for the latter, cf. passages such as *AMT* 30,3 ii 6 and 102:17 34, as well as *Iraq* 19 (1957) 40:21 f.

r4. ^{UZU} BAL: *sic* on the tablet, interpretation unclear. An emendation to ŠEM!.BAL "styrax" seems warranted, see *AMT* 27,2:18, 35,1:7, 37,2:9, 41,1:2, 64,1:20, etc. Hardly = ^{UZU}TI! "ribble".

435 This text is duplicated (up to line 19) by *TDP* 82:21.

436 In *AMT* 42,5:3 and *TDP* 149:34' ff the logogram KA more probably denotes "mouth" than "nose".

437 From Urad-Nanâ, not from Adad-šumu-uṣur; see pertinent notes.

438 Cf. ^{SÍG}ḪÉ.ME.DA = *tab-ri-bu*, *PVA* 206 (*AfO* 18 33). The word is a loan from Hurrian, see Landsberger, *JCS* 21 (1967) 168*b*.

r6. This line, unresolved in Pt.I, probably reads [. . . SAḪAR] *šá* ⸢*su-qi*⸣ *er-bet-te* "dust from a crossroads". Cf. *LKU* 32 r10, SAḪAR SILA.LÍMMU SAḪAR KÁ ᵈME.ME ᴜ́AŠ . [. . . .]; ibid. 33 r30, SAḪAR SILA.LÍMMU. BA BE NA_4 [. . .] (both *Lamaštu*-texts); *AMT* 76,5:5 *ina* A TÚL *šá* É ᵈAMAR+UD SÚD SAḪAR SILA.LÍM *ana* IGI *ta-šap-*[*pak* . . . . .] (text dealing with paralysis); *TU* 34 iii9, SAḪAR RI.ḪA.MUN SAḪAR SILA.LÍMMU.BA ᴜ́LÚ.U_x.LU (salves to be applied against the *kīs-libbi* disease); cf. also *AHw* p.1062a. The medical function of the substance in the present case remains undetermined.

r11. The verb *marāqu* is well attested in medical texts in the meaning "to crush", "to chop fine" (said of drugs); see the references gathered in *AHw* 608*b* s.v. It is quite unnecessary to emend the text into *i-ba!-šal-u-ni* (thus Oppenheim, *JAOS* 64 [1944] 191).

r14. Restore [*ina ni*]*-ip-šú* "(they wrap it) in a tuft of word" (for parallels cf. *AHw* 792*a*).

r15. Cf. *LAS* 252 r14f.

r16. *mal-ṭi-ri*: Cf. *mal-ṭa-rat a-su-ti* "medical prescriptions" *AfO* 18 (1957/8) 44 r8 (Epic of Tukulti-Ninurta); note that in *LAS* 286 r2' *ma-al-ṭu-ru* means "(royal) inscription. It is not clear whether the author refers to prescriptions given in this letter or in a separate message.

252

Bibliography:

(I) Waterman, *RCAE* 108 (cf. IV 234); Pfeiffer, *SLA* 290.
(II) von Soden, *ZA* 45 (1939) 59; Böhl, *Opera Minora* (1953) 405 ff; Ritter, *Studies Landsberger* (1965) 319.

Addressee:

Esarhaddon.

Discussion:

See under *LAS* 251. The nature of the medical treatment described on the obverse remains obscure, largely because one is left in uncertainty about the kind of the trouble in question. The writer refers broadly to the chest of the patient, leaving unspecified whether the trouble was located inside or outside of it; as a result of the treatment, evidently, the patient was able to sit up (Obv.12f), but again one is left in uncertainty as to whether he had earlier remained in lying position because of excessive pains, bodily injury or simply unconsciousness, although the first alternative would seem most probable in the light of external evidence. Thus the haruspical query BM 99062 (quoted in the commentary on *LAS* 228) states that the crown prince felt pains in his hypochondrium while walking and riding, and in *LAS* 228 the crown prince is expressly denied riding and drawing a bow, probably because of those very pains. If the present letter and the two texts just mentioned all pertain to the same illness, which is not unlikely in view of the fact that they all date from a relatively limited time span (672-669), their combined evidence would point to muscular pains in the thorax and epigastric region. Cf. note to Obv.12. Cf. also *LAS* 140:14f, 141:2' and 144!

Notes:

10. *ni-din-u-ni*: the occurrence of this verb here is surprising and probably pleonastic. True, *dullu epāšu* is elsewhere often accompanied by *tadānu*, but the intended meaning is then regularly "to bestow" or "to deliver", which does not suit here. Cf. *ABL* 885:17 ff: *a-na-ku dul-lu* [18]*ša ina* ᵁᴿᵁ*Kal-ḫa* . . . [19]*le-e-pu-uš a-na* DUMU. LUGAL *la-ad-din* "I will perform the work to be done in Calaḫ . . . and bestow it upon the crown prince"; *dul-lu le-pu-šú a-na* LUGAL *be-lí-já la-*[*ad-din*] "I will carry out the work and deliver it to the king, my lord" *CT* 53 61 L.E.1; *dul-la ra-bu-ú* [20]*lu-ú e-pu-uš-ma a-na* EN LUGALᴹᴱŠ *be-lí-ja* [21]*lu-ú ad-din* "I should have performed a great deed and bestowed it upon the lord of the kings, my lord" *ABL* 462 r19 ff (NB); *dul-la-ni ša* DUMU.LUGAL *ep-pa-áš* [25]*a-na* DUMU.LUGAL EN-*ja ad-dan*, 885:24 f.

10 ff. The ambiguity of the forms *aḫ/iḫ-ti-ri-di* and *uk-ti-il* (both formally either 1st or 3rd p. Sg.) makes the interpretation of the following passage difficult, as reflected by the fact that all hitherto proposed translations differ wildly from each other. Cf. Waterman, *RCAE* I (1930) 73, "(The ritual which we performed for restoring

him), we gave for five-sixths of a double hour. The day he came, he tarried. He gained strength. He remained until he had completed the month"; Pfeiffer, *SLA* (1935) p.202: "(The rites which we prepared for him), we have performed at intervals of an hour and forty minutes all through the day: he walks, he is well, he gains strength, but he stays (indoors)"; *CAD* Ḫ (1956) 88*a*, "when 5/6 of the first double hour of the day had passed (7.30 a.m.) (the patient) woke up (and) remained (awake)", similarly ibid. A/2 (1968) 388*a*, "(the patient) woke up, stayed (awake) and afterwards (even) sat up". It is not necessary to defend the translation given in Pt.I against the renderings of Waterman and Pfeiffer, since these are grammatically impossible, but the rendering of *CAD* (which is grammatically sound), calls for two critical remarks. First, *a/iḫtirid* can hardly be translated here "he awoke" because everywhere else *ḫarādu* means only "to watch (over), to be alert" (see the dictionaries); by virtue of this meaning, it is also natural to assume that the verb here refers to the writer (a physician) rather than to the patient. Second the rendering of 5/6 DANNA *u_4-mu it-ta-lak*, "7.30 a.m.", which is clearly influenced by the above interpretation of *a/iḫtirid* (or vice versa?), cannot be accepted since the verb used in idioms indicating morning time was *šaqû* G/ *matāḫu* N not *alāku* (cf. *LAS* 4:12.15, 109:6' f, 139 r1 f, and the passages mentioned in note to *LAS* 4:12); *alāku* lacked reference to any particular part of the day, cf. *CAD* A/1 311 f, and hence probably indicated here only the duration of the treatment performed.

11. *aḫ/iḫ-ti-ri-di*: for the final *-i*, corresponding to the enclitic particle *-ma* "and (thus)", cf. notes to 246:12 and r1, 248:13, etc.

12. *uk-ti-il*: cf. *AMT* 16,1:5, [*k*]*a-la u_4-me 3-šú* KEŠDA *ú-kal-ma* ZI "you put it on three times a day, he keeps it on and gets up" (referring to poultice for sore eyes); cf. also *AMT* 98,3:7, referring to poultices applied to sore arms and feet.

13. *a-ke-e*: here obviously in the meaning "so, thus", as in *ABL* 726 r5 ([DUMU[MEŠ]] KUR KÚR *a-ke-e* [6][*a-na*] LUGAL EN-*ja i-lu-ku*) and *TI* pl.2 iii 30' (*a-ke-*<*e*> *tap-pa-la la ke-pu-ti*); < MA *a-ki-a* "so, folgendermaßen" (W. Mayer, *AOATS* 2, §85.1; e.g. *a-ki-a iq-ṭi-bi ma-a*, *KAV* 217:13; *a-ki-a i-*[*q*]*a-bi*, *KAR* 135+ i 28, ii 29, etc.) cf. also *ke-e ke-e lu-pu-uš* É "so, so, I will make a home", *BWL* p.146:37.

14. *tarṣu* was in NA more or less synonymous with *ṭābu* "good" and *damqu* "fine"; cf. *VTE* 73 ff, *šumma at-tu-nu a-bu-tú la* SIG_5*-tú* (var. *la* DÙG.GA-*tu*) *la ba-ni-tú* [74]*la ta-ri-su ša e-peš* LUGAL-*ti šá ina* UGU [I]*Aš+šur*-DÙ-A [75]DUMU.MAN GAL *ša* É.UŠ-*ti la tar-ṣa-tu-u-ni la ṭa-bat-u-ni*, etc.*

r3. [LÚ]*GAL mu-gi*: possibly referring to Nabû-šarru-uṣur [LÚ]GAL *mu-gi* mentioned in *AGS* 66f (ca. 671-669 BC).[439] The rendering of *rab-mugi* in Pt.I (cf. *AHw* 667b) is based on the equation *rab-māg* = στρατηγος in the Aram.-Greek bilingual Benveniste, *RÉJ* 82, 55 ff, cited in Koehler – Baumgartner, *Lexicon*, p.492*a*. Note that *rab-māg* of *Jer.* 39:3.13 is now rendered "commander of the (frontier) troops" in the *New English Bible* (Oxford and Cambridge 1970).*

r10. *na-aḫ-na-ḫe-e-te* = /naḫnaḫḗte/, for usual /naḫnā́ḫiti/. The shift of stress (and the concomitant vowel change) certainly served to lend the word additional emphasis. Cf. *pil-ka-šú-u-nu*, "their portion of work", *ABL* 503 r7; /árḫiš/ "quickly" > *ar-ḫi-ši ar-ḫi-ši* /arḫíši arḫíši/ "most quickly", *KAV* 214:12, etc.

253

Bibliography:

(I) Waterman, *RCAE* 570 (cf. IV 184).

(II) Oppenheim, *JAOS* 64 (1944) 193; Labat, *RA* 55 (1961) 152 f.

Addressee:

Esarhaddon.

Date:

672-669 B.C. Note the reference to the crown prince (Obv.8 ff) and see commentary on 173. Cf. also note to Obv.8 ff.

---

439 Identification certain if there was only one *r.m.* at a time.

Discussion:

Despite considerable effort, I have not been able to identify the source of the prescriptions given on the reverse, and there is in fact reason to believe that no direct quotation from a remedy-text is in question; cf. above, sub *LAS* 251. Though both *kanaktu-* and *nikiptu*-oil was used for curing diseased ears in the various ways mentioned in our letter (cf. *BAM* 3 iv 24 [dropping *nikiptu*-oil into the ear], *AMT* 35,4:6' [inserting tampons sprinkled with *kanaktu*-oil into ears], *AMT* 38,2 iv 2f [fumigating *nikiptu* into ears]), these plants never formed the medication by themselves but only in connection with other substances (e.g., root of cornel-wood + *nikiptu* + soiled rags, fumigated, *AMT* 33,1:30; pulverized *ašgikû* + *nikiptu*, inserted into ear in a tampon, *AMT* 37,2 r9; *kanaktu*-oil + oil of "sweet reed" (=Cymbopogon?) + juniper oil + salt of "fine taste", tamponed into ear, *AMT* 35,2:31 ff). Moreover, even if it were possible to restore the name of an additional medical substance in Rev.2 f or 6 – a possibility hardly to be taken seriously –, the prescription to use the *same* substances both for fumigation *and* tamponing remains without parallels in the remedy-texts. In complicated treatments (e.g., *AMT* 36,1:1 ff and 12 ff), fumigating, tamponing and dripping alternatingly served as means of introducing medicaments into the ear, but the medicaments in question naturally varied accordingly. It may furthermore be noted that the use of the verb *nattuku* "to drop" in our letter differs from that habitual in medical texts, where it always refers to dripping a liquid medicine on the part of the body requiring treatment; with reference to ears, the stereotype formula *ana* ŠÀ PI^2-*šú* BI+IZ/*tu-na-tak* "you drop it into his ears" was always used. Such a formula can hardly be restored in our letter, because the verb is in Rev.4 followed by *lu-qa-at-t*[*i-ru*] "they should fumigate". The latter operation was always performed by placing the drugs to be fumigated upon glowing embers[440], gumlike substances like the oil of *nikiptu* and *kanaktu* being naturally d r i p p e d on the coals from the bottles in which they were kept.[441]

It follows, then, that the present prescription not only is a rather free adaption of the original remedy-text entry, but that it lacks many details essential for the identification of the source text but of no relevance to the recipient of the letter. In particular, it is clear that the "oil of *kanaktu*" and the "oil of *nikiptu*" mentioned in obv.15f have nothing to do with the fumigations referred to in obv.13, which probably had been dispatched to the king earlier, though both medications obviously t o g e t h e r constituted the ear therapy recommended in the letter. An identification of the source prescription, and accordingly the exact nature of the ear trouble in question, is unfortunately not possible even on these premises. It can only be stated that in ear therapy, *nikiptu* was used in remedies for "buzzing ears" (see *AMT* 33,1:28 ff with the rubric I NA *ina* DIB-*it* ŠU.GIDIM.MA PI^2-*šú i-šag-gu-ma*; AMT 34,1:5 f, 35,4:6, 37,2 r8 and 38,2 iv 1-2, with the rubric I NA PI^2-*šú i-šag-gu-ma*) and aural hemorrhage (see *BAM* 3 iv 23 f, with the rubric I NA *ana* ŠÀ PI^2-*šú* MÚD DU-*ak*; also *AMT* 36,1:1 ff), whereas (oil of) *kanaktu* was used to remove earwax (see AMT 35,4:1 ff and 37,2:8' ff, with the rubric [I NA *ina* PI^2] KAB-*šú* IR *ana qer-bi-nu ip-ḫur*) or to cure aching ears (see *AMT* 35,2:11' ff and *BAM* 3 v 12 ff, with the rubric I NA (*ina* ŠÀ) PI^2-*šú* GIM (*šá*) ŠU.GIDIM.MA KÚ(.MEŠ)-*šú* u SÌG.SÌG-*su*; also *BAM* 3 iv 28 ff, with the rubric I NA PI^2-*šú* DUGUD).

Notes:

8 ff. Cf. *LAS* 252:7 ff, and see relevant notes and discussion. The orthography of the two letters is identical, which makes it legitimate to assume that they are approximately contemporary, the present letter perhaps slightly postdating no. 252.

13. *qutāru* "fumigation, (drug for) smoke therapy": cf. 193:8', 258:8, and see E. Reiner, *AfO* 18 (1957/8) 394 and 19 (1959/60) 150; E. Ritter, *Studies Landsberger* (1965) 314*b*. Cf. *AMT* 33,1:31 f, ^{ŠEM}GÚR.GÚR ^{ŠEM}LI ^{ŠEM}ŠEŠ ^{GIŠ}EREN GI.DÙG.GA ^{ŠEM}MUG GAZI^{SAR} IM.KAL.GUG ^{32}*8* Ú.ḪI.A KÙ.GUR *ša* PI^2 *ina* DÈ ŠÀ PI^2-*šú* SAR "terebinth(?), Juniper, myrrh, cedar, "sweet reed", styrax(?), mustard, red clay, (altogether) 8 drugs for fumigating ears, you fumigate the inside of his ears (by throwing these drugs) on glowing embers)"; similarly *BAM* 3 iv 33 f, [^{ŠE}]^{M}GÚR.GÚR ^{ŠEM}LI ^{ŠEM}ŠEŠ ^{ŠEM}MUG ^{GIŠ}EREN GI.<DÙG>.GA ^{34}^{ŠEM}MAN.DU GAZI^{SAR} ^{IM}KAL.GUG *9* KÙ.GI PI^2 *i*[*na* DÈ ^{GIŠ}]⌈Ú⌉.GÍR SAR-*šú*. Note that neither the *nikiptu* nor the *kanaktu* plant is included in either passage, and cf. discussion above and below.

---

440 Cf. note to Obv.13.

441 See, however, note to Rev.2 f.

15. $^{\check{S}EM}$GIG = *kanaktu* ([Ì] $^{\check{S}EM}$GIG = [MIN] *ka-na-ak-*[*ti*], Ḫḫ XXIV 31): a gum-yielding plant or tree growing in mountains, perhaps *Boswellia* sp. or *Olibanum*; see Thompson, *DAB* p.344 ff, but note the reservations made in *CAD* K 136. As far as I know, there are no medical texts attesting to the use of this plant in the fumigation of the ears.

16. ŠEM.^{d}MAŠ = *nikiptu* (cf. l i - g i - i d - d a = ŠEM ^{d}NIN.URTA = še-em nin-nu-ur-ta-ku = *ni-kip-tum*, Diri VI E 64): a gum-yielding shrub, possibly *Euphorbia Antiquorum* L., or the like, see Thompson, *DAB* p.346 ff. For remedy-texts attesting to the use of this plant in smoke therapy of the ear, see *AMT* 33,1:28-29, ibid. 30, 35, 1:5, and 38,2 iv 1-2.

r5. The restoration *uq-ṭa-nat-*[*ti-ru*] suggested in Pt. I should be cancelled, since in NA the Pret was obsolete in positive *kīma*-clauses; the correct reading is, of course, *uq-ṭa-t*[*e!-ru*].[442]

r2 f. The restoration of these lines is rather problematical (actually, almost impossible) unless one accepts the hypothesis that the *nikiptu-* and *kanaktu* oil did not constitute (and were not included in) the fumigations described in the following lines; see in detail the above discussion. On this premise, the likeliest restoration of r2f would be *li-iḫ-ru-p*[*u ina* ŠÀ *uz-ni*] [3]*lu-na-ti-k*[*u*] "they should first drip (the oil-medicaments) into the ears" (cf. p.303); r3f could then be restored [*i-da-te*] [4]*lu-qa-at-t*[*i-ru*] "thereafter they should fumigate (him)"; cf. *ta-ḫar-ru-pu pa-an* LUGAL *te-e-rab* [4]*i-da-a-ti* LUGAL *e-rab* "(Ištar) will set out earlier and enter (the city) before the king, thereafter the king will enter (into the presence of the goddess)", *ABL* 1164:3 f.

r6. Restore, perhaps, *lu-sa-ḫi-ru* [*re-eḫ-ti* Ì×GIŠ] [7]*lu-na-ti-ku* and translate "they should repeat[443] (the procedure) (and) drip the rest of the oil (out of the bottles)"; cf. below.

r7. Tampons for the ears, like those for the nose (see note to 251:14), were prepared of fliece (^{SÍG}AKA = *itqu*)[444] or red wool (^{SÍG}ḪÉ.ME.DA = *nabāsu/tabarru*)[445], so both restorations are possible here. It is also possible to restore *in*[*a* ^{SÍG}*tab-re-e-bi*] "in red wool" in accordance with *LAS* 251:14.

r10. ^{NA_4}*.bu-ra-al-li*: identified as "beryl" (= Aram. *bērullīn, burlā* etc.) by H. Zimmern, *Akkadische Fremdwörter* (1917), p.60, and Thompson, *DACG* p.174; the doubts as to this rendering expressed in *CAD* B (1965) 326*b* are groundless since in ND 2307:37 NA$_4$ *bu-ra-a-li* does *not* represent a stone object as such but denotes the *material* of which a spoon was made (as opposed to two spoons made of *haltu*-stone).

r11. On the cooking of drugs (an essential step in the process of their preparation) see, in general, Ritter, *loc.cit.* p.213; for more references, see the dictionaries.

254

Bibliography:

(I) Waterman, *RCAE* 392 (cf. IV 250); Pfeiffer, *SLA* 289.
(II) Oppenheim, *JAOS* 61 (1941) 261; Meissner, *BuA* II (1925) 323.

Photograph:

Obverse: F. von Oefele, *Keilschriftmedicin* (Breslau 1902), pl.3; Reverse: *RCAE* IV pl.10.

Copy:

Cf. also S.A. Smith, *Keilschrifttexte Assurbanipals* II (Leipzig 1888), pl.22.

Notes:

10. *sikru*: literally "blocking", here probably referring to an abscess or tumour; not otherwise attested as a medical term. Cf. *AHw* 1043*a* and note to line 13.

11. Instead of *ku-tal* IGI^{2}-*šú* (Pt.I), read, with *CAD* K 604*a*, *ku-tal* PI!^{2}-*šú* "the back of his ear"[446] (col-

442 Confirmed by collation (E. Sollberger 19.1.1976).
443 For this meaning of *saḫḫuru* cf. *AHw* 1006a, *saḫāru* D mng. 5.
444 Cf. *BAM* 3 iv 28.
445 Cf. *AMT* 35,4:6.
446 *Sic*, not "ears" (*CAD*). The spelling PI^{2} pertains to the singular as well as to the plural, cf. e.g. [IG]I^{2}-*šú* . . . [*t*]*a-tu-qut*, *LAS* 53 r5 f and IGI^{2}-*šú nam-rat*, 14r8. Note also uzu[.PI.2] = *uz-nu*, Ḫḫ XV 39 (*MSL* 9 p.7).

lation confirmed by E. Sollberger, 19.1.1976, and cf. egir-giš-tu$_9$-PI-mu "back of my ear" (between šà-giš-tu$_9$-PI-mu, še$_{10}$-giš-tu$_9$-PI-mu, la-ga-giš-tu$_9$-PI-mu and gal$_4$-la-giš-tu$_9$-PI-mu "the inside, excrement, . . . and vagina of my ear"), *Ugumu* [unilingual version] 144, corresponding to ⌜egir⌝.geštu.mu = *w[a-ar-ka-at] uz-[ni-ja]* of the bilingual version (cf. *MSL* 9 p.72 ad C 19).[447] The reading *ku-tal* IGI^2-*šú* presented two kinds of difficulties which are now removed. First, the term "back of the eye" does not occur among the 25 different "parts" of the eye enumerated in the series *Ugumu* (*MSL* 9, p.53 f), nor does it seem to be attested anywhere else (cf. *CAD* I/J 156*b*, lex. section). Secondly, it is difficult to see how a plaster could have been fastened upon the "*back*" of one's eye and why the patient's *nose* (Obv.13) should have been mentioned in that connection. The translation "back of the eye" = "eye socket" suggested in Pt.I was only an attempt to obviate these difficulties, and has no reason to be maintained.

12. *tal'ītu*: rendered "plaster" after *CAD* E (1958) 127*a*, Ṣ (1962) 181*a*, and A/2 (1968) 185*b* ("bandage"); cf. *AHw* Lfg.11 (1972) 953*b* ("Verband"). The word seems to be a *taprīs(t)*-formation from *la'ātu* "to swallow" (cf. *GAG* § 56 1), so a translation like "absorptive dressing" would perhaps be more to the point.

13. *ina ap-pi-šú*: cancel the translation "in his nose" given in Pt.I; it is unthinkable that a dressing applied to the back of the ear would have had anything to do with the nose of the patient. Translate instead, "it (= the plaster) remained loose (*er-tu-mu*, cf. *AHw* 953*b*) at its (referring to the *sikru*) tip", and see *CAD* A/2 187 ff for other examples of *appu* = "tip"; cf. also *LAS* 231:10'. That a *sikru* could have a "tip" fits well its interpretation as a kind of abscess, cf. note to Obv.10. See also below.

r5. *šarku*: in Pt.I, this word was, under the influence of *CAD* D (1959), 75*b* and Ṣ (1962) 181*a*, translated "clotted blood", but it now seems to me better to revert to the translation "pus" given in the earlier editions (*RCAE* I p.273, *SLA* p.202). For one thing, the logographic writing of *šarku* (ÚŠ.UD) means literally "white blood"; cf. lu-gu-ud ÚŠ.UD = *šar-ku* (followed by a-da-ma ÚŠ.MI = *a-da-ma-tum* "black blood"), Diri VI B 22'; UZU.$^{lu-gu-ud}$ÚŠ.UD = *šar-[ku]*, Ḫḫ XV a$_2$ 4 (*MSL* 9 p.11); ÚŠ.UD = *šar-ku*, *MSL* 9 p.79:114 and 95:158 (OB list of diseases); it seems that the proper word for "gore, clotted blood" was *adāmatu*, which incidentally is equated with *šarku* in the Ḫg to the Ḫḫ-passage just cited (UZU.$^{a-da-mu}$ÚŠ.MI = *a-da-ma-tum* = *šar-ku*, *MSL* 9 p.35:34).[448] Secondly, the translation "pus" fits the proposed interpretation of *sikru* as a kind of abscess much better than "clotted blood". The appearance of *šarku* on the dressing was clearly interpreted as a favourable sign (cf. Rev.13 ff), which would be rather odd in the case of a injury bleeding by itself (cf. Rev.9 ff), but entirely understandable in the case of a boil beginning to run without external interference.

r9-11. Cf. note to *LAS* 13:9 ff. The translations of this passage suggested in *RCAE* and *SLA* ignore the fact that *šumma* here introduces an *assertory oath*, as indicated by the preceding elliptic DINGIR^{MEŠ}-*ka* and the following subjunctive (*ú-mì-du-u-ni*).

r12. *pi-i-šú it-ti-din*: cf. OA *ma-la pa-i a-dí-nu-šu-ni* "for which I gave my word to him", *CCT* 5 4a:21.

r16. This prognosis is quite in keeping with the standard phraseology of medical texts, cf. e.g. Labat *TDP* p.158:13, NA BI *ana* UD 5.KÁM *ana* UD 7.KÁM TI "that man will recover within 5 (or) 7 days" (Tablet XVII of the diagnostic and prognostic series *Sakikkû*). Whether, however, the writer is here quoting a medical text or giving a subjective prognosis remains uncertain for lack of positive evidence. The latter alternative is also entirely possible, cf. simply the 'prognosis' *a-du* UD^{MEŠ} *5 6* ^{MUL}AL.LUL *i-kaš-šá-ad* "he (= Venus) will reach Cancer in 5 (or) 6 days", *RMA* 207:6.

255

Bibliography:

(I) Waterman, *RCAE* 110 (cf. IV 174, 235); Pfeiffer, *SLA* 287.
(II) Behrens, *ABB* (1906) 17; Meissner, *BuA* II (1925) 321; Böhl, *Opera Minora* (1953) 409 ff.

Addressee:

Esarhaddon.

447 This expression is an exact equivalent of the *kutal uzni* of the present letter, the word *warkatu* having been replaced by *kutallu* in Neo-Assyrian.

448 In this context, *šarku* is translated "pus" even in *CAD*; see Vol. A/1 (1964) 94*b*.

Notes:

8. *un-di* (sic after collation, not *iṣ-ṣa-di* [Behrens, Waterman, Pfeiffer] or *pa!-ṣa-di* [*CAD* B 133*b*]): hapax legomenon, taken as Pl. of **umdu* (cf. *imdu* > NA *indu*), derived from *emēdu* "to lean (upon), to inflict" after the pattern *purs* (GAG § 55d; cf. *ḫumṭu* "fever", *kuṣṣu* "cold", *lu'tu* "debility", *muggu* "paralysis", *murṣu* "illness", *ṣurḫu* and *ummu* "fever", *zūtu* "perspiration", etc.)[449]. The translation "rash" (thus also Meissner [1925] and Johns, *Babylonian and Assyrian Laws, Contracts and Letters* [Edinburgh 1904], 375) has been inferred from the context, and seems pretty certain: some easily irritable (cf. Rev.2-3, 5-6 and 11) cutaneous disease (Rev.3-4) must be in question, and the fact that it is referred to by a word in the plural suggests that it was manifested in the form of blotches, papules, blisters, or corresponding lesions. According to Rev.8, the rash was principally located in the hands. Note that this agrees well with the cutaneous symptoms of LED described in the discussion of *LAS* 246 (above,p. 232ff).See also note to *LAS* 257:7.

r2. u_4-*mu-šú-nu*: in the orthography of Urad-Nanâ, the sign *šú* never begins a word[450]; hence *šú-nu* is a suffix attached to u_4-*mu*, not an independent personal pronoun (thus Pfeiffer and Waterman). Cf. ^{LÚ}MU *an-ni-u a-na ḫa-an-ši* u_4-*me-šú* ^{7}*ḫa-si*, *ABL* 1372 r6 f, and *an-na-a šá ep-pu-š[á] gi-mir* u_4-*me-ja*, Streck *Asb*, p.25 i 19.[451] For the spelling u_4-*mu* (for *u_4-*me*) cf. Deller and Parpola, *Or* NS 26 (1967) 337 f, but note that the sign *mu* may also serve here as a phonetic complement of the kind discussed by Leichty, *TCS* 4 (1970) 27 f.[452]

r3. Ì MUŠEN: sic, not *né-ḫu* (*RCAE, SLA*). This line and the following one represent the writer's answer to the question presented in Obv.10 f and consequently must contain the name of the substance with which the king was to be anointed. The use of *bird*'s fat as an ointment is in no way surprising (considering the variety of animal "drugs" used by the Mesopotamian physicians; cf. Meissner, *BuA* II [1925] 307 ff and Ritter, *Studies Landsberger* [1965] 308 f), though I have not come across any medical text attesting to this particular usage. That bird's fat *was* used in Assyria for various purposes cannot be doubted. Cf. *PVA* 133 ff:

133 Ì^{MEŠ} ^{d}MAŠ *ni-ki-[ip-tú]* "*nikiptu*-gum"
134 Ì^{MEŠ} *sad-ru* "regular(?) oil"
135 Ì^{MEŠ} GUD^{MEŠ} "bull's fat"
136 Ì^{MEŠ} UDU^{MEŠ} "tallow"
137 Ì^{MEŠ} ŠAḪ^{MEŠ} "lard"
138 Ì^{MEŠ} UR.MAḪ^{MEŠ} "fat of lion"
139 Ì^{MEŠ} KU_6^{MEŠ} "train oil"
140 Ì^{MEŠ} MUŠEN^{MEŠ} "bird's fat".

Waterman's attempt to explain **né-ḫu* as a variant of *nāḫu* "lard" [occurring as a vehicle for drugs in medical texts] is to be rejected since phonemically long, stressed *a* was never changed into *e* in Neo-Assyrian. Moreover, syllabic spellings of *nāḫu* are extremely rare [cf. *AHw* s.v.] and in medical texts the logographic spelling Ì. ŠAḪ is utilized throughout.

r5 f. Cf. ^{MUL}SAG.ME.GAR *ina* ŠÀ ^{MUL}GUD.AN.NA *e-ta-rab* ^{3}LUGAL *be-lí* TA* IGI *zi-i-qi lu e-ti-ik* "Jupiter has (just) entered Taurus: the king, my lord, should be on his guard against draughts", *RMA* 103 r2 f.

256

Bibliography:

Previously unpublished. Copy *CT* 53, pl.51 no.157.

---

[449] This interpretation entails, however, two difficulties which cannot be overlooked: first, most deverbal *purs*-words are derived from *intransitive* verbs (exceptions: *bulṭu, šurpu*), whereas *emēdu* is transitive; second, only primary *purs*-words are attested in the plural (exception: *bulṭu*). Is **umdu* perhaps an alloform of *um-me-di* (*AMT* 31,7 ii 8, cf. Labat, *RlA* 3 231*b*)?

[450] Statistics: *šú* occurs 0 times in initial position, 9 times in medial position, 29 times in final position and 0 times alone. Corresponding figures for the sign *šu* are 13 (init.), 5 (med.), 0 (fin.) and 0 (al.).

[451] Pronominal suffixes (referring to the subject) are also appended to other time indications, cf. e.g. *i-na ša-a-at mu-ši-ti-ja ša-am-ḫa-ku-ma*, *Gilg.* Pennsylvania I 3 f, MÁŠ.GE_6 *aṭ-ṭu-la mu-ši-ti-ja*, *Gilg.* I v 26.

[452] Cf. *am-mar* u_4-*mu*^{MEŠ}, *ABL* 342 r6; *6* U_4-*mu* ^{MEŠ} *CT* 53 716:2'; u_4-*mu*^{MEŠ} *ša* LUGAL, *ABL* 438:14.

Date:
Probably late 671/early 670 BC. Note the orthographical affinities of the letter with *LAS* 246-249 (discussed in the commentary to *LAS* 249) and the similarity in content to *LAS* 246.

Addressee:
Esarhaddon.

Discussion:

Note that the introductory formula of this letter is not placed in the beginning but only in the middle of Obverse.[453] The reasons for this are entirely obscure; corresponding misplacements do not occur in other Neo-Assyrian letters. True, a unique private letter (BM 103016 = *CT* 53 974 contains two introductory formulae, one at the beginning of Obverse (*a-na* ^{MÍ}*Me-ja* ^{2}NIN-*ja* ^{3}PAP-*ki* $^{\text{I.d}}$ME.<ME>-KAR-*ir*), the other at the beginning of Reverse (IM $^{\text{I.d}}$ME.ME-K[AR-*ir*] ^{2}*a-na* ^{I}SU-*aja* PAP-*ja* ^{3}*ak-tar-rab-ka* ^{4}*ina* IGI ^{d}NIN.LÍL), but this case may not be comparable since the letter consists of two different messages addressed to two different persons (the brother and sister of the writer).[454]

Notes:

3'. *ta-ba-laṭ* "she will recover": cf. *LAS* 254:16 and 222 r4' ff. A translation "you (= the king) will recover" is also thinkable, cf. note to 121.24.

257

Bibliography:
Previously unpublished. Cf. Deller, *AOAT* 1 (1969) 58. Copy *CT* 53, pl.20 no.58.

Writer:
The spelling *i-su-ur-ri* (Rev.3') occurs in the present corpus only in the letters of Urad-Nanâ (see 246 r1.14 and 247 r20.27). The remains of the introductory formula as well as the medical content of the Obverse likewise point to Urad-Nanâ.

Addressee:
Esarhaddon.

Date and Discussion:

Simānu 14, eponym year of Šamaš-kāšid-ajābi = June 10, 669. As appears from the omission of the word "king" in r.3' and from the traces preceding EN-*ja* in Obv.6, the king was in this letter addressed as the "farmer", and consequently a substitute king must have occupied the throne while the letter was written. It is very likely that the reign of the substitute had been occasioned by a solar eclipse, to judge from the indirect reference to a subsequent *lunar* eclipse (cf. u_4*-mu šá ta-de-er-ti* ^{6}*šu-ú*, *LAS* 61:5 f, pertaining to a lunar eclipse) in Rev.4 f. This would place the letter with certainty in Simānu 14,669, see notes on *LAS* 77. For another letter of Urad-Nanâ associated with the substitute king ritual, see *LAS* 249.

Notes:

7. *pi-'a-ri*: hapax legomenon (cf. *AHw* p.836*b* and 861 ff); possibly a scribal mistake (for *ši-'a-ri*)[455], but rather an alloform of *bi'āru* (*CAD* B 217*b*, *AHw* 124*a*) = Hebr. *bahärät* (Koehler – Baumgartner, *Lexicon* p. 111) "spot, blotch on the skin (as sympton of a disease)". The word is attested only twice, in *CT* 23 3:10 (*tal-a-šú bi-'a-a-ra ù bu-u'-šá-nu*), an incantation against the *sagallu* disease,[456] and in *AMT* 31,2: 14 (copy *b*]*u?-'a-a-ru*, read [*p*]*i!-'a-a-ru?*), there also in connection with *bu'šānu* (a type of leprosy). Should this word really be in question

[453] The identity of the obverse can be established from the direction in which the script runs on the left edge of the tablet.

[454] *LAS* 36, where the blessing formula is repeated in r4-5, presents an analogous case: the letter actually consists of two separate messages, an omen report and a petition.

[455] Thus K. Deller (orally). The passage has been collated carefully and there is no doubt as to the reading of the questionable sign as PI.

[456] A muscular disease associated with feet.

here, the text would provide a welcome support for the interpretation of the word *undu* occurring in *LAS* 255 as a kind of rash, for naturally it is the king himself to whom the present passage pertains. Indeed, a word like "blotch" fits excellently to the picture of Esarhaddon's chronic disease as reconstructed in the commentary to *LAS* 246.

Accepting tentatively the interpretation *pi'āru* = *bi'āru*,[457] the preceding gap can be restored [*ina* UGU *bu-ul-ṭi*] [7]*ša pi-'a-ri* and the whole passage translated "[as regards the cure] of the blotches . . . " Cf. *LAS* 248:8 and 250 r1.

9. SILÁ (= GAZI)[458].SAR = "mustard, Sinapis nigra" according to Landsberger, *AfO* 18 (1957/8) 337 f. It was widely used as a medical substance, cf. *CAD* s.v. *kasû* and, for additional examples, Thompson, *DAB* (1949) p.195 ff.

258

Bibliography:
(I) Waterman, *RCAE* 740.
(II) Meier, *ZA* 45 (1939) 215; Reiner, *AfO* 19 (1959/60) 150 f; Deller, *Or* NS 31 (1962) 230.

Addressee:
Esarhaddon.

Date:
Latter half of the reign of Esarhaddon. The background situation of the letter greatly resembles that of *LAS* 143, 180, 246-247 etc., dated to 670 BC; note especially the reference to the king's youth in Obv.15 ff linked with allusion to a [successful?] treatment of his rheumatism, which strongly suggests that the king was ill while the letter was written; the same is suggested by the mention of several medicaments sent to the king [Obv.8 ff] and by the fact that the writer of the letter had not heard of the king for some time [Obv.12-14; cf. *LAS* 51 and 143], note also Rev.7-8 and the end of the letter suggesting that the writer was really worried about the king's health. However, there are no tangible dating criteria in the letter allowing to place it in a definite year and, as indicated in the note on *LAS* 246:18 f, Esarhaddon seems to have been badly ill also in 672 BC and perhaps in other years, too, of which we have no knowledge. The reference to Šamaš-šumu-ukīn (Rev.12 ff) is not specific enough for dating purposes, though it does point to the latter half of Esarhaddon's reign. Cf. *LAS* 140 and 237, the former perhaps associated with the substitute king ritual.

Notes:

9-11. Cf. Köcher, *KADP* 36 r. vi 14 ff, ${}^{\text{Ú}}$*qúl-qúl-la-nu* [15]*maš-qi-a-te* [16]KÙ.GI(= *tāri*)${}^{\text{MEŠ}}$ [17]*te-qi-a-te* [18]*nap-šal-a-te* [19]NAGAR-*nu*${}^{\text{MEŠ}}$ [20]*mar-ḫaṣ*${}^{\text{MEŠ}}$ "cassia, potions, fumigations, salves, ointments, suppositories, lotions" (etc.; last section of an inventory of a drugstore); cf. also *LAS* 193:8f. Note that potions, salves, fumigations and phylacterics also figure among the medications mentioned in the letters of Urad-Nanâ and evidently belonged to the remedies considered most appropriate for the cure of Esarhaddon (cf. above, Discussion of 246, Section D); on the other hand, note also that *LAS* 246 puts much emphasis on the use use of *lotions*, which are not mentioned in the present letter.

16. A geographical name (a country or a city; cf. *LAS* 277:9 f) is expected here, but the traces remaining do not seem to fit any toponym known from NA sources; cf. *AOAT* 6, Reverse Index. As Esarhaddon was at the time of the murder of Sennacherib campaigning in a country west of Ḫanigalbat (Mitanni), one would be tempted to read the name(?) as [${}^{\text{KUR}}$*Qu*]-⸢*ú*⸣-*u-u*, but this is not actually warranted by the traces.

[457] For other NA instances of *p* in lieu of *b*, cf. *a-pi-ik-te* (*ABL* 158:22), *li-pe-lu* (*LAS* 125 r2), *a-pi-al* (*TI* pl. III i 21'), *ú-sa-ar-ki-pi* (*ABL* 420:8), *iq-ṭi-pi* (*LAS* 339:12'.r2), *i-pa-tu-qu* (*KAV* 197 r24), *ni-i-pi* (*ABL* 92 r10) and *ni-pa-ni* (ibid. obv.11). Examples of *b* for *p* are much more numerous, e.g. *e-bi-šú-ni* (*KAV* 115:11), *a/i-sa-bar* (*ABL* 138:10.r5; 704+:7, *CT* 53 101:19.r5, etc.), many forms of the verbs *da'āpu, dalāpu, ḫarāpu, radāpu* and *raṣāpu* (see the dictionaries), GIŠ.*bi-sa-na-te* (ND.2666 r2 = Iraq 25 pl.12 no.67), *za-qi-ba-a-ni* (*ABRT* 1 25 r. ii 29), *e-ber-tú* (*LAS* 291:14', 283 r6').

[458] The tablet has MAL×PA = SILÁ, but no doubt MAL×ÁŠ = GAZI was intended.

18. The emendation *eṣ*]-*ma!-a-te* suggested in Pt.I on the ground of 180:11 is not permissible after collation (Sollberger 19.1.1976); read (with Harper) [*e*]-*na-a-te* and see on 183:6.

19. ᴵ*Kab-ti-i*: in view of the context, plausibly identical with ᴵDUGUD-*i* LÚ*A.BA "Kabti the scribe" mentioned in *ADD* 161 = *AR* 51:22 (dated 679 BC). The same man possibly also in *ABL* 733:2-4 (ᴵ*Kab-ti-i* LÚ=DUB.SAR ³*ša* LUGAL *be-lí*⁴ *ina* É LÚ*šá* IGI É.GAL *ip-qi-da-ni* "[from] Kabtî, the scribe whom the king, my lord, installed in the house of the palace-overseer") and *ABL* 872:8-9 (ᴵ*Kab-ti-i* LÚA.BA ⁹ÌR *ša* ᴵ*Aš+šur-da-in*-IBILA DUMU ᴵ*Šùl-ma-nu*-MAŠ "Kabtî the scribe, a servant of Aššur-da' 'in-aplu son of Shalmaneser [V?]").

r1: [*I.dAMAR+U*]*D-SILIM-PAP*MEŠ: The reading of the broken sign as [U]D is, according to collation, not absolutely binding (only the upper part of the vertical is preserved), but in any case it is certain that the sign is neither [P]A nor [DING]IR (as suggested by the "copy" of Harper). The only gods attested in names with *-šallim-aḫḫē* as predicative elements being Aššur, Ilu, Marduk, and Nabû (cf. *APN* 308 s.v. *šlm* and Saporetti, *OMA* I p.157f), it follows that the only thinkable restorations are Aš+šu]r, ᵈAMAR+U]D, ᵈME]S, and (if necessary) ᵈŠ]Ú. Epigraphically, all four are equally possible, and the same can be said judging the matter on prosopographical criteria. There is no evidence showing for certain that persons named Aššur-šallim-aḫḫē or Marduk-šallim-aḫḫē were *strictly* taken contemporaries of the Kabtî just mentioned, but both are known to have been active in the early part of Assurbanipal's reign: an ᴵ⁽ᵈ⁾*Aš+šur-šal-lim*-PAPMEŠ is mentioned in *ABL* 1219:8' (a letter dealing with the rebuilding of Esangil and in all probability dating from 668 BC) and in *ADD* 270 = *AR* 67:2 (a legal document drawn up for Rēmanni-Adad, the chariot driver of Assurbanipal, date broken away); Marduk-šallim-aḫḫē is well known from his many letters (*ABL* 840, 979, [1023], 1092, [1143], [1160], 1171!, 1218!, 1384 and [K. 14244]) showing him to be a contemporary of Akkullānu (cf. *ABL* 840 and Appendix M); other texts indicate that he functioned as scribe of the Aššur temple (of the city of Assur).[459] Since the above-mentioned Kabtî also was a scribe associated with the temple of Aššur (cf. the introductory formula of *ABL* 733), the reading [Mardu]k-šallim-aḫḫē has been given provisional preference here.[460]

r7 f. *ana kinniš alāku* is evidently the opposite of the technical expression *ana pāni alāku* "to make progress" (*LAS* 259 r3) and consequently means here "to make regress" (in the medical sense; cf. *AHw* p.480*b* and correct the interpretation of *di-il-pe-e* given ibid., p. 170 s.v. *dīlu*).

r10. *UD*MEŠ *ṣar-ḫu* "the weather is hot": cf. UD-*mu em-*[*mu*] (same meaning) *EA* 7:54. The implications of the passage remain unclear owing to the preceding break. Cf. Discussion of *LAS* 246, Section F, on the harmful effect of extremes (heat etc.) to the condition of LED-patients.

r13. The phrase *PN šulmu* occurring here is equivalent to the more common *šulmu ana PN* "PN is well"; cf. GIŠMÁMEŠ *šùl-mu*, *ABL* 430:6 and ÌRMEŠ-*ni* . . . *šùl-mu*, *Iraq* 7, 99:10; also *ú-ma-a šul-mu* ⁹*a-dan-niš*, *LAS* 216 r7f.

r15. Blood (animal and human) is well attested as a remedy in medical texts (cf. simply the references given in *CAD* D p.77 f) though most of the relevant passages are so fragmentary that it is difficult to ascertain whether it was an accepted medical practice to have the patient take it orally, as done in our letter. In any case, *AMT* 73,2:5 f provides an example of a blood remedy swallowed by means of a snack of beer.

Note that it is quite unnecessary (and even impossible) to emend *da-mu* into *ša!-mu* "drug", as proposed by Deller, *Or* NS 31 (1962) 230 (followed by *CAD* B [1965] 274*b*). According to collation, the text has a clear DA; moreover, the sign ŠA was used by Ikkāru only for writing the "determinative" pronoun *ša*, which means that a spelling like *ša-mu* is not even theoretically likely in his letters.

r20. ⌜*ú*⌝-*ṭi-ib-bi*: a surprising form in view of the plurality of the subject (3 DNN in l.18), perhaps due to progressive assimilation (uṭṭibbū > *uṭṭibbu* [*Iraq* 34 23 *ad* 15] > *uṭṭibbi* [*Or*NS 36 337]); cf. *kettu* > *ket-ti*, *ABL* 212 r2; *libbu* > *lìb-bi*, *LAS* 215:10, *ABL* 157 r11, 208:14, etc; *dulli* > *dul-lu*, *LAS* 219 r9; *šumma* > *šum-mu* 173:14, 174:9, 175 r6, etc. Reading ⌜*iṭ!*⌝-*ṭi-ib-bi* "he got well" is excluded after collation. Cf. also *LAS* 263 r1 ff.

---

459 All attestations of the name quoted in *APN* p.132*a* pertain to the same individual. Note Hunger, *AOAT* 2, Nos. 508:2 and 519:4.

460 Note, however, that *ADD* 266 = *AR* 538:1 ff (dated 671) mentions three sons of one Aššūr-šallim-aḫḫē, who would thus perhaps be a more suitable alternative on chronological grounds.

259

Bibliography:

(I) Waterman, *RCAE* 248 (cf. IV 178, 242); Pfeiffer, *SLA* 282.

(II) Oppenheim, *JAOS* 64 (1944) 192; von Soden, *OLZ* 55 (1960) 489.

Copy:

See also S.A. Smith, *PSBA* 10 (1888) 166 f, pl. 6.

Notes:

r8. Cf. *LAS* 246 r4 ff. Lotions (*marḫuṣu*) prepared of an oil mixture (as in *LAS* 246) or, more often, of various drugs, were used for the treatment of several kinds of diseases, not only of muscular troubles (as in *AMT* 98,3:13 ff), and it is consequently impossible to conjecture about the nature of disease concerned here. The expression "two or three times" has of course not to be taken literally, no more than in *LAS* 246 or elsewhere in letters of the present corpus.

r9 f. *ṭūb(u) libbi emmar* is obviously the (NA) equivalent of the phrase *ṭūbu amāru* occurring in medical texts in the sense "to show signs of recovery". Cf. BE-*ma* DÙG NU IGI.DU_8 . . . , *AMT* 31,5:4', DÙG+GA IGI-*mar*, *AMT* 26,3:7', etc. The final *u* in *ṭu-bu lìb-bi* (cf. *ṭu-ub lìb-bi* in obv.6) is certainly due to the emphasis laid on the word r e c o v e r y in this context; in Neo-Assyrian monosyllables of the structure (C)$\bar{V}$C regularly received a paragogic vowel in s t r e s s e d position. Cf. (unstressed) *iḫḫur/aḫḫur* > *a-na ḫu-ru* in *ABL* 1432 r2 (context: emphatic request, "[let] nobody any m o r e [neglect] the work"); *šūt* (always) > *šūtu*, since never unstressed; *ṭāb* > *ṭāba*, etc.

263

Bibliography:

(I) Waterman, *RCAE* 204 (cf. IV 240); Pfeiffer, *SLA* 296.

Copy:

See also Pinches, 5 *R* (1884) pl.53 no.4.

Photograph:

RCAE IV pl.7 (Obverse only).

Notes:

8. *Nabû-nādin-šumi*: probably identical with the writer of *LAS* 203-214. Excepting *ABL* 54 (letter to a princess [*mar'at šarri*] from a Nabû-nādin-šumi writing in *Babylonian*), all references to N. in Sargonid texts pertain to the exorcist concerned (cf. *APN* 155*a*); note also that Bānî and the exorcist N. were contemporaries (see Intr., pp. 30 and 39), had mutually complementary professions (see on 265 r7), and thus certainly came repeatedly into contact with one another.

r1ff. *Bēl, Nabû and Bēlet balāṭi*[461] (in this order) are also "humbly" given the credit of reviving a patient (Šamaš-šumu-ukīn) in another letter of a physician (258 r18ff; cf. obv.6f) instead of the true gods of medicine, Ninurta and Gula. All three gods are otherwise too known as "revivers" and "prolongers of life" (see Tallqvist, *Götterepitheta* s.vv. and Hirsch, *AfO* 22 [1968/69] 55ff), Bēl even as a physician (*asû*; *BA* 5 391:8). Cf. *LAS* 180, 182, 183.

r2. *ša ú-tak-kil-<u>-ka-ni*: cf. *áš-pur-ka-a-ni*, *CT* 53 974:6; *áš-pur-[ke]-e-ni* ibid.r5; *a-šap-par-kan-ni*, *ABL* 424:20; *il-lik-ni-ni* 1063 r6; *tu šc-bal-ni*, *AfO* 8 24 iii 14; *e-pal-ka-ni*, *ABL* 579 r3; *i-ša-kun-šú*, *CT* 53 136 r5; *iḫ-bíl-šú-ni*, *ABL* 916:8; *ú-šá-gal-na-ši-ni*, *ABL* 131 r6; for additional parallels and a discussion of the unmarked subjunctive morpheme, see Parpola, *Iraq* 34 (1972) 24.

---

[461] = dNin-ti, a manifestation of Damkina (cf. *CT* 24 15:58). Not to be confused with dNin-tin-ug_5-ga (= *bēltu muballiṭat mēti*), a manifestation of Gula.

264

Bibliography:

Waterman, *RCAE* 525.

Addressee:

Esarhaddon.

Date:

672-669 B.C. Note the reference to the crown prince and Nabû-rība-aḫu, also mentioned together in *LAS* 174 (q.v.).

Notes:

r7. *ša is-si-ja*: lit. "the one with me" = my assistant, associate. See Deller, *Or* NS 30 (1961) 251. The fact that the *exorcist* Nabû-rība-aḫu (see on 174 r2 ff) here appears as an associate of the writer illustrates the close co-operation of physicians and exorcists already discussed in commentary to *LAS* 222.

r14. *is-su-gu*: connected by von Soden, *AHw* 1003*a* (s.v. *sagû* III), with Arab. *šağiya* "betrübt sein"; rather = Hebr. *swg*/*šwg* "to turn back, be displaced", cf. Bibl. *sūg lēb* "backsliding in heart" (Koehler – Baumgartner, *Lexicon* p.650*b*).[462] The infinite of the verb should then be posited as **suāgu*, cf. *id-du-lu* (3 Sg. Pf. of *duālu*), *ABL* 561:7, *ir-tu-bu*(3 Sg. Pf. of *ruābu*), *Iraq* 4 186:7, etc.

r17. See note to *LAS* 184 r4.

265(+)266(+)267

Bibliography:

No.266: Waterman, *RCAE* 1157 (cf. IV 200). The other two fragments are previously unpublished. Copy of No. 265 in *CT* 53, pl.80 no.290, of No.267 ibid. pl.312 no.956.

General remarks:

The three fragments do not join, but they are unquestionably parts of the same tablet (personal collation, 13.6.1974). While the text clearly is no letter (267 "Rev." 1, which, according to collation, is the first line of the whole tablet, reads: [*nap-šal-tú*? *ša* SA]ḪAR.ŠUB.B[A], cf. 266:9'), it may well be a list of remedies pertaining to the cure of the king, sent to the palace along with a letter; note the affinities of the text with *LAS* 248 and 253.*

Writer:

Urad-Nanâ (judging from the handwriting).

Notes:

1) *LAS 265*

2'. *TUK.TU*[*K-ši*]: possibly (in view of r4') quoting *BAM* 228:23ff = 229:17'ff = 323:33ff (Ebeling, *TuL* 85ff), I NA SAG.KI.DIB.BA TUK.TUK-*ši* PI^2-*šú i-ša-gu-ma* "If a man is sick with the *sankidibbû* disease and his ears buzz (etc.)"; cf. also (in view of L.E.1-2), [I N]A KA.DIB.BI.DA TUK.TUK-*ši* "If a man suffers from aphasia", *AMT* 23,2.6, I KA.DIB.BI.DA TUK.TUK, ibid. 78,1:28; [I NA KA-*šú* DIB-*i*]*t-ma* KA.DIB.BI.DA TUK^{MEŠ}-*ši*, ibid. 28,2:1, etc.

r2'. *i-ma-ta*: possibly end of an unfavourable prognosis (cf. Labat, *TDP* passim for prognoses ending with *imât*), though it is unclear why such a prognosis would have been quoted here.

r4'. *šu-gu-mi*-[*e*? (PI^2)]: probably a *puruss(ā')* formation from *šagāmu* "to buzz" (said of ears), cf. *rugum=mû* "complaint" from *ragāmu* "to complain", and see *GAG* §§55q and 56 o. Note that buzzing ears were treated by fumigation (*LAS* 253; cf. r3') and that *LAS* 248 refers to potions in discussing treatment of Esarhaddons ears (cf. r3'; 267:2.4).

L.E. Restore (with the help of *LAS* 266):

---

[462] If this etymology is accepted, the literal meaning of the present expression would be "my heart was displaced", i.e. I got startled.

1 *ka-par pi-i nap-šal-*[*tú ša*] KA.DIB.[BI.DA *ù né-pe-še*]
2 *ša* KA.[DIB.BI].DA

kapār pî ("wiping of the mouth", scil. with drugs prepared of botanical and/or mineral substances) was a measure carried out in the treatment of oral diseases such as dyspnoea and stinking breath (cf. *CAD* K 178*b*); as the term occurs here in connection with ***kadibbidû*** "aphasia", it is, however, also possible that "wiping" in the magical sense is meant.

2) *LAS 266:*

9'. Restore *nap-šal-tú ša* SAḪAR.[ŠUB.BA] "salve of le[prosy]" and cf. 267 "Rev." 1.

r4'f. Cf. I NA Á *2,30-šú* ⸢*i*⸣-[. . . .], *BAM* I 40 r10; I Á-*šú ša* KAB [. . . . .], *TDP* p.86 r1'; [INIM.INIM.MA *šum-ma* LÚ Á] ZAG-*šú i-šam-m*[*a-am-šú*] "if a man's right hand is paralysed", *AMT* 88,1:11; INIM.INIM.MA *šum-ma* LÚ Á KAB-*šú i-šam-ma-am-šú*, ibid. 93,3:12 (Series *Muššu'u*, see Köcher, *BAM* 3 [1964] p.VIII). Is *LAS* 180:6f relevant in this context?

r6'. Read, perhaps, *ša kal-la* UZ[U!], cf. *ka-la šērēšu šimmatu* TUK^{MEŠ}-*ú*, *KAR* 26:8 (not collated).

3) *LAS 267:*

"r"1. See sub general remarks.

"r"3. Instead of ^{ŠEM}KUR, read *šim-mat* "paralysis", and cf. e.g. *nap-šal-ti šim-ma-ti* "salves against paralysis", *AMT* 92,5:4'; *né-pi-ši* (scil. of *šimmatu*) ibid.3; I NA *šim-mat* GIG, ibid.91,1:13,91,3:4; I NA *šim-mat* UZU GIG, ibid. 94,2 r10.12, etc. Does *šimmatu* in this context refer to articular stiffness? Cf. discussion of *LAS* 246.

"r"5. Perhaps ŠE].SA.A (= *laptu*), "roasted barley", cf. *AMT* 36,1:7' and 38,4 ii 3.

268

Bibliography:

(I) Waterman, *RCAE* 625; Pfeiffer, *SLA* 236.
(II) Behrens, *ABB* (1906) 13 and 103. *Copy* also Zeitlin, *SACA* (1903) no. 21.

Writer:

Certainly Urad-Ea. Cf. the following numbers, and note 1) that the introductory formula of these letters does not recur in any other NA letters and 2) that Urad-Ea is the only Assyrian chanter who is known to have corresponded with the king.

Notes:

8. [*l*]*i-li-si*: a kettledrum made of bronze (cf. note to 270:9) and covered with the hide of a black bull (symbolizing the bull of heaven slain by Gilgameš and Enkidu, i.e. the constellation of Taurus), exclusively used to accompany chants of the ***kalûs***. Before use, the drum had to be consecrated, much in the same way as divine statues (cf. note to 188 r6), to endow it with divine potencies, see Thureau-Dangin, *RAcc.* p.10 ff and *RA* 16 (1913) 154 ff; cf. also Contenau *Magie* p.111 ff; for a drawing representing a *lilissu* (with the subscript ^{d}LID×DÚB) see *RA* 16 145. It is not quite clear whether the kettledrum was set up on every occasion the *kalû* officiated or whether its use was restricted to the performance of certain types of chants only. It would *seem* that chants of the genres ***balaggu*** and ***šuilakku*** were accompanied by harps, those called ***eršemmakku*** by ***ḫalḫallatu*** drums, and only the ***eršaḫunga***-chants by kettledrums. Cf. [^{L}]Ú*GALA GUB-*az-ma* (. . .) ŠU.ÍL.LÁ.KÁM *ina muḫ-ḫi pa-la-ag-g*[*i izammur*] "the chanter takes his stand and sings the *šu'illakku* chant to the accompaniment of the harp", *TCL* 6 43 r19-20; EGER-*šú* D i l m u n^{ki} n i g i n - n a ^{d}U t u l u g a l - à m é - š à - a b - ḫ u n - g á - t a *ina ḫal-ḫal-la-tú* . . . ŠÈR "thereafter you sing *Dilmun nigina* (an *eršemmakku* chant according to 4 R^2 53 iii 22), *Utu lugalam* and *E-šab-ḫungata* (cf. 4 R^2 53 iii 11) to the accompaniment of the *ḫalḫallatu* drum", *TCL* 6 45:13-14; ÉR.[ŠÀ.ḪUN.GÁ] ^{36}[*ina*] LID×DÚB UD.KA.BAR *a-na* LUGAL *tu-*[*šad-bab*] "you have the king recite the *eršaḫunga* lamentation to the accompaniment of the bronze kettledrum", *AJSL* 42 117:36; and see Krecher, *Sumerische Kultlyrik* p. 25. One could consequently hypothesize that the situation of the letter entailed a recital of some of the 27 *eršaḫunga*-chants to Marduk mentioned in Rm.2,220 (Langdon, *RA* 22 [1925] 123; cf. 119 and 120). On the other hand, it is known that the kettledrum was used (along with other instruments) in the performance of the chants sung on the occasion

of lunar eclipses, which at least partially consisted of *eršemmakkus* (see Krecher, *op. cit.* p. 24[31] and cf. note to 278:9 f). This would indicate that the above picture is too simplified and that chants other than the *eršaḫunga* could also have been sung in the present case (cf. *LAS* 167:12ff, 185:19f and 333:6f referring to *šu'illakku* chants).[463] In any case, the nature of the *eršaḫunga* lamentations would well fit the hypothetical context of the letter (cf. the following note). – For the final *i* of [*l*]*i-li-si* (Nom. Sg.) see note to *LAS* 258 r20.

12. "*tonight*": In the ritual instructions for the *kalû* published by Thureau-Dangin, *RAcc.* pp. 1-59, pertaining to cases such as aversion of evil portents (earthquake, dog in temple, etc.), reconstruction of a temple and covering of the *lilissu* drum, the chanter was generally supposed to officiate in the morning (if any time was specified), whereas here as well as in the letters 185, 269-270, 278 and 333, the ceremonies took place in the nighttime (*ina nubatti* or *ina muši*). This circumstance is clearly associated with the fact that in all the letters in question, the object of the chanter's activity was an astral deity (Saturn and [Mars] in 269; Venus in 270; Venus and Sirius in 333; the moon, in 278; different stars and planets in 185; cf. also 334, pertaining to Mars). Analogously, it is probable that in the present text, too, the god Marduk was actually approached in his astral embodiment (the planet Jupiter) visible in the sky while the ceremonies took place; for the expression "before the star/god DN" cf. note to *LAS* 187:11'. It can be safely assumed, furthermore, that in all the instances mentioned the purpose was to soothe the "wrath" of the angered celestial bodies; cf. notes to *LAS* 61:5 ff and 278:9, on the interpretation of eclipse as manifestations of divine anger, and see Introduction, p. 15 (cf. NAM.GALA *ni-ṣir-ti* NUN.ME *ša a-na nu-uḫ lib-bi* DIN=GIR^{MEŠ} GAL^{MEŠ} *šu-lu-ku* "the chanters' text corpus, secret lore of the sages, which is suited to appease the heart of the great gods", Streck *Asb* p.366:13); as already intimated in the preceding note, the chants most appropriate for this purpose were of the type *eršaḫunga*, lit. "lamentation of placate the heart (of . . .)"; cf. *LAS* 279 r14, 280: 19, 334:2 and note to 271 r3. The exact nature of the portent here counteracted remains unclear, of course; thinkable would be, e.g., the occultation of Jupiter referred to in *LAS* 14 or the retrograde movement of the planet in Leo mentioned in *LAS* 13. Cf. the pertinent comments.

r2 f. "*He will bless the king*": see note to 269 r3 ff.

269

Bibliography:

(I) Waterman, *RCAE* 612, Pfeiffer, *SLA* 235.

(II) Behrens, *ABB* (1906) 13 and 103; Dhorme, *RHR* 116 (1937) 10; Labat, *Royauté* (1939) 153, 353.

Writer:

See on *LAS* 268.

Addressee:

Esarhaddon.

Date:

Possibly Kanūnu 23, eponymy of Šulmu-Bēl-lašme = January 23, 669 BC. For reasons stated in note to *LAS* 268: 12, there is ground for assuming that the ceremonies described in the present letter were occasioned by a conjunction of Saturn with another planet (cf. Obv.10), and as the nature of the ceremonies implies that the conjunction was considered ill-boding, the other planet in all likelihood was Mars (see under *LAS* 54; for the floruit of Urad-Ea [*680-667 BC], see Appendix 0). One of the few extant astrological reports from Urad-Ea actually refers to a simultaneous appearance of Saturn and Mars in a lunar halo; the report (*RMA* 100) is datable to 674/673 (Schaumberger, *ZA* 44 [1938] 287[23]), but it is very questionable whether the present letter dates from the same time: as appears from the omens quoted in the report, the appearance of Saturn in the halo was not considered ill-portending, and the planets themselves were not in conjunction at the time concerned. The well-known conjunction of Saturn and Mars in March 669 reported in *LAS* 54, *RMA* 88, etc. is likewise out of the question since the writer here states that the kettledrum was to be played on the *25th*, whereas the conjunction of March 669 was already over by the *16th*. Fortunately, the possibilities of identifying the event are not exhausted at that, for Mars had already previously in

---

463 The *šu'illakku*-chants being closely related to the *erša ḫungas*, it is not excluded that the former are meant in the present letter, too.

669 been in conjunction with Saturn (MUL*Ṣal-bat-a-nu* MULUDU.IDIM *is-sa-na-aḫ-ḫur*, *RMA* 88:2), to wit on January 23, 669.[464] According to App. A3, this corresponds to Kanūnu 23 and can thus be easily reconciled with the date mentioned in our letter. There are hardly better alternatives left, for the date June 6 on which Mars the next time approached Saturn corresponds to Simānu *10* and cannot hence be taken into consideration.

It seems worth adding that, according to BM 121206 vii 13'ff (van Driel, *CA* (1969), p. 90), no regular kettledrum-performances were prescribed for the 25th day of *any* month, so the date mentioned in the letter was in all probability dictated by the celestial event to be "pacified" and none else; cf. also Langdon, *AJSL* 42 (1925/6) 110 ff and Thureau-Dangin, *TCL* 6 48.

Notes:

10. At the end of the line restore d[U]GU[R] in accordance with the above discussion.

11 f. As appears from the instructions for the *kalû* published in *RAcc.* pp. 34-59, it was essential that the king himself participated in the expiatory ceremonies performed on his behalf, and it seems therefore certain that the clothes mentioned here (as well as in *LAS* 271 and 272) functioned as full representatives of the monarch who for some reason could not be present in the flesh. Similarly, in *LAS* 175 and 187, clothes function as representatives of various members of the royal family. For the magical doctrine underlying such usage, see J. Frazer, *The Golden Bough* (abridged ed.), p. 43, and cf. the analogous examples quoted ibid. p. 43 f; cf. also Introduction, p. XXIV, on the role of royal clothes in the substitute king ritual.

r3 ff. Almost all chants of the *kalû* began with a long litanylike praise of the divinity approached; it can be perhaps be inferred from the present passage that this praise was the primary "instrument" by which the goal of the chant (i.e., softening the heart of the god) was thought to be reached. Cf. note to *LAS* 126 r1-12.

270

Bibliography:

(I) Waterman, *RCAE* 669.

Notes:

9. Cf. LI.LI.ÌZ UD.KA.BAR *RAcc.* 10 ff i 1, ii 25.29, iii 15.25, and passim in the technical literature of the chanters. On the other hand, in *ABL* 1092 r13 and *LAS* 278:9 we find *li-li-su* / ⌜LI⌝.[LI.ÌZ] URUDU. The interchange UD.KA.BAR ~URUDU does not imply that the drums were made of different materials (bronze : copper) but has to be explained with reference to the different professional backgrounds of the relevant scribes (chanter : non-chanter). In NA non-literary texts, URUDU no more meant "copper" alone but was widely used as a logogram for "bronze", while the use of UD.KA.BAR was predominantly limited to literary contexts. A clear illustration of this usage is furnished by the different spelling of the toponym Kār-Siparri (*AOAT* 6 p.198).[465]

11 ff. The implications of this passage as well as the exact meaning of [*š*]*a ma-se-e kaq-qa-da-*[*te*] (a profession? Cf. LÚIGI *ma-né-e*, *ABL* 885 r2) remain unclear. Cf. Oppenheim, *Ancient Mesopotamia*, p.186 ff.

271

Bibliography:

(I) Waterman, *RCAE* 29

(II) Behrens, *ABB* (1906) 34 f; Dhorme, *RHR* 116 (1937) 10; Labat, *Royauté* (1939) 353.

Notes:

9. For a list of the gods worshipped in Kurba'il see Frankena, *Tākultu* p.5 ff, Rev. i 2'-14'. The most important ones were naturally Adad and his consort Šala; cf. Ebeling, *PKTA* pl. 11:13-14, and note BM 79099:1 ff

[464] See Schaumberger, *art. cit.* p.284. The distance of the two planets was at that time as small as two months later, i.e. 0.4° = 5 fingers.

[465] See in more detail C. Zaccagnini, "La terminologia accadica del rame e del bronzo", *OrAnt* 10 (1971) 123-144.

(unp. NA letter): *a-na* LUGAL EN LUGAL^{MEŠ} [EN-*ja*] ^{2} ÌR-*ka* ^{I}IBILA-*aja* ^{3} LÚ*SANGA ⌜*ša*⌝ ^{URU}*Kur-ba-ìl* ^{4} *lu-u* SILIM *a-na* LUGAL EN-*ja* ^{5} ^{d}IM ^{d}*Ša-la* ^{6} ^{d}GAŠAN-*rat na-kan-ti* ^{7} DINGIR^{MEŠ} *a-ši-bu-tu* É.DÚR.ḪE.NUN.NA ^{8} *a-na* LUGAL EN-*ja lik-ru-bu* (courtesy A. Millard).

11. Cf. 272:9 f. The verb *tabû* is used here in the technical sense "to set out (in procession)", as e.g. in *ABL* 1092:20 ff, [UD *11*.KÁ]M *ša* ^{ITU}SIG$_4$ ^{21} ⌜^{d}⌝[NIN].⌜LÍL⌝! *lu ta-at-bi*! ^{22} [*ina* BAR]AG!-*ki-šá lu*! *tu!-šib* (collated). Processions of gods apparently always required the presence of a chanter (cf., in addition to the present text, Borger *Ash* p.89, Streck *Asb* p.264, and the letter to be quoted presently); it is interesting to note that the king, too, was supposed to participate (even if only in the form of his clothes) in the yearly procession of Kurba'il, and no doubt of other major Assyrian cities as well. Cf. *ABL* 1197:2' É!.[DINGIR^{MEŠ}] $^{3'}$*ša* ^{URU}*Kàl-zi*! [. ^{M}]EŠ! $^{4'}$*šak-n*[*a*] ^{5} ^{ITU}GUD UD *6*.KAM ^{6} ^{d}IM *i-te-bi* ^{7} *ina* ŠÀ *a-ki-te* ^{8} *ú-ša-ab* ^{9}LÚ*MAŠ!.MAŠ! ^{LÚ}GALA $^{\text{r.1}}$ [L]UGAL *be-lí* ^{2} [T]A* : ^{d}IM ^{3} [. .]X *ina* É-*šu* ^{4} [*er-r*]*u-bu* (text collated).

r3: *ÉR.ŠÀ.ḪUN.GÁ*: on this type of chant see Krecher, *Sumerische Kultlyrik* (1966), p. 25; for samples of pertinent texts, see Langdon, *Babylonian Liturgies* (1913), passim, and cf. idem, "A list of the known titles of Sumerian penitential psalms (eršaḫunga), arranged in alphabetical order", *RA* 22 (1925) 119 ff. Cf. also note to 268:8.

272

Bibliography:

(I) Behrens, *ABB* (1906) no. 1 (p.21 ff); Waterman, *RCAE* 667 (cf. IV 186); Pfeiffer, *SLA* 220.

(II) Dhorme, *RHR* 116 (1937) 10; Labat, *Royauté* (1939) 211, 317 and 353; Lewy, *Goldziher Memorial Volume* I (1948) 317.

Addressee:

Esarhaddon.

Date:

Ca. Ajāru 10, eponymy of Šulmu-Bēl-lašme = April 20, 670 BC? For the day and month see Obv. 9; the year is uncertain but is suggested by the curious postscript of the letter (r3-7); note that 1) the month in which the rebellion discussed under *LAS* 247 was crushed, was Nisannu or Ajāru; 2) that some of the conspirators has escaped punishment (cf. *LAS* 284:25 and relevant commentary); and 3) that the geographical centre of the rebellion was Harran. *LAS* 273, which may have followed the present letter, would lend support to this dating, as the king was evidently ill while it was written (note 273 r 6 ff and cf. on *LAS* 247).

275

Bibliography:

(I) Waterman, *RCAE* 746.

(II) Landsberger, *BBEA* (1965) 39 f.

Addressee:

Esarhaddon.

Date:

Probably late 670 BC, and in any case between Ābu (July) 671 and Araḫsamna (November) 669. These time brackets follow from the affinity of the letter with the following chronicle entry for the 7th year of Esarhaddon:

16 MU *7*.KÁM ^{ITU}ŠE UD *5*.KÁM ERIM KUR *Aš+šur ina* ^{KUR}*Mi-ṣir* GAZ^{MEŠ}
17 *ina* ^{ITU}ŠE ^{d}INANNA ⌜A⌝.GA.DÈ^{KI} *u* DINGIR^{MEŠ} *šá* A.GA.DÈ^{KI}
18 TA KUR NIM DU^{MEŠ}-*nim-ma ina* ^{ITU}ŠE UD *10*.KÁM *ana* A.GA.DÈ^{KI} TU^{MEŠ}

"In the 7th year, on Addāru 5, the troops of Assyria were defeated in Egypt. In Addāru, Ištar of Akkad and the gods of Akkad returned from Elam and entered Akkad on Addāru 10." (*CT* 34 iv 16ff = Grayson, *TCS* 5 [1974] p.84).

There is no doubt about the identity of the "Lady of Akkad" of the present letter with the "Ištar of Akkad" of the chronicle (cf. below on Obv.7). The order to repopulate the town of Akkad (Obv.7f) can only have been given after the returnal of the goddess, hence after Addāru 10 = February 11, 673 (cf. App. A2). According to Obv.11, our letter was written *at least* 2 years ([ ] MU.AN.NA^{MEŠ}) after this date, hence in late February 671 at the earliest. A considerably later terminus post quem is required, however, since the wording of Obv.11ff implies that the deliveries of regular offerings for the goddess had been interrupted at least for a period of some weeks. This places the letter after Esarhaddon's Egyptian campaign (late March to June 671). On the other hand, the letter must have been written before Esarhaddon's death (Araḫsamna 669) because the writer states that the king to whom the letter was addressed had himself given the order to repopulate Akkad and to reorganize the cult of the goddess (Obv.9). A more exact dating of the letter is hardly possible. One might infer from Obv. 12f that the writer had only relatively recently been charged with the supervision of the matters in Akkad, and the economic situation of the temple appears to have been still rather chaotic at the time concerned. It is very unlikely that such a situation could have prevailed for a long time without the writer losing the favour of the king. In *LAS* 280 (written in the beginning of the year 670) the cult of the goddess already seems to have stabilized in every respect. It would accordingly seem that our letter predates *LAS* 280 (and the closely related 278 and 279), in other words, was written before Kanūnu = December, 671. However, this is very uncertain in view of the spelling *ÁR-ku-te* in Obv.3, since the word is spelled *AR-ku-te* in all letters of Mār-Ištar certainly datable between Ābu and Sabāṭu, 671 (nos. 276-278). The spelling *ÁR-ku-te/i* occurs otherwise in *LAS* 286f (August 670) and 293.

Notes:

7. ^{URU}*Ak-kad*: In *BBEA* p.38 ff, Landsberger rather categorically argued that the city of Akkad frequently mentioned in the letters of Mār-Ištar actually was only a *cover name for Babylon*. Attractive as this interpretation is, especially since it would explain why several substitute kings were enthroned in Akkad (cf. Introduction, p. XXV)[466], I don't think it is actually warranted by the data in our disposal. First, if a "Deckname" were in question, one would expect a certain consistency in its use; yet Mār-Ištar quite frequently also uses the name Babylon (^{LÚ*}=GAR.NÁM KÁ.DINGIR^{KI} 276:23, DUMU^{MEŠ} KÁ.DINGIR(.RA)^{KI} 276 r2.6f.9, 297:2; KÁ.DINGIR^{KI} 280:7, 281 r15.30, 287:13, 295:6.8, 297:5'), twice even side by side with Akkad (see 280 and 281). Second, the city of Akkad also occurs in several other documents from the same period and even in inscriptions of Assurbanipal (cf. *LAS* 134:7, 249 r2 and 298:8; *CT* 53 206:5' (^{URU}URI); *ABL* 1123:1'. r6.8.16 [mentions Babylon *and* Akkad + the Lady of Akkad]; *ADD* 930 ii 2.6, iii 7, iii 14; *VAB* 7 266:12; *IWA* 37 Rm. 589 iii 8). Third, and most important, the city of Akkad is both in the present letter and in the chronicle entry quoted above explicitly associated with the returnal of the Ištar of Akkad from Elam. Landsberger tried to obviate this difficulty by equating Ištar of Akkad with the "Lady of Babylon" (Zarpānītu), but had to admit (p.40) that this solution is not entirely satisfactory, since the "Lady of Babylon" resided in a temple called Eturkalamma, whereas the residence of the "Lady of Akkad" was called Eulmaš (see *RlA* 2 484b). Now, we know for certain that Esarhaddon restored Eulmaš at some phase of his reign. The original building inscription has not been preserved (or found), but the matter is referred to in an inscription of Nabonidus (Langdon, *VAB* 4 246 ii 36 ff). who himself restored the temple a century later. There was no temple called Eulmaš in Babylon, and none of the numerous building inscriptions of Esarhaddon pertaining to Babylon mention Eulmaš. As far as I can see, this can only mean that there really existed in Esarhaddon's time a city called Akkad, different from Babylon.[467] At the same time, our letter makes it clear that the city had been in a state of decay for centuries owing to the disintegration of the cult of its patron goddess, so that the reconstruction of Eulmaš in a way also entailed a rebuilding of the whole city. I think it is a mere historical coincidence that the work of reconstruction was commenced almost simultaneously in Babylon and Akkad; the realization of both projects had become increasingly urgent towards the end of Esarhaddon's reign and could be finally undertaken in 671 thanks to the rich spoils obtained from Egypt.[468] Accordingly, the fact that works carried out in Babylon and Akkad are referred to in the same letter (*LAS* 283) cannot be taken as evidence that the two cities were identical. One cannot argue, either, that Mār-Ištar was far too important a person to have been stationed in an insignificant town such as Akkad, and that it is for this reason necessary to identify Akkad with Babylon. It has to be remembered that rebuilding an entire city, however small, is by no means a trivial matter, and besides, the letters of Mār-

466 Cf. also Brinkman, *AnOr* 43 (1968), note 874.

467 Note that it is explicitly stated in the chronicle passage quoted above that the goddess was returned to *Akkad*, not Babylon. Why should any chronicler use cover names?

468 Cf. Borger, *Ash* p.94:28-29.

Ištar clearly indicate that he did not by any means pass all his time in Akkad but was constantly on the move supervising *all* the reconstruction work carried out in Babylonia during the time of his appointment.

The location of Akkad has remained an enigma up to the present time, but recent archaeological surface surveys favour identification with *Ishan Mizyad*, an oblong, relatively low tell about 15 km E-NE of Babylon and 5 km N-NW of Uḥaimir. See H. Weiss, "Kish, Akkad and Agade", *JAOS* 95 (1975) 434ff, esp. 442ff. *

8. The deputy of the majordomo of Laḫīru also appears in *LAS* 291 r5 as a person responsible for carrying out royal orders in northern Babylonia (within the circle Ābu Ḥabba [Sippar] – Imām Ibrāhīm [Cutha] – Inġarra [Ḫursagkalama] – Dulaim [Dilbat]). This supports the thesis of H. Lewy (*JNES* 11 [1952] 276) that "Laḫiru was [in Esarhaddon's reign] the administrative center of Babylonia". Cf. note to 280:11. On the geographical location of Laḫīru (in the region where the Diyāla cuts through the Ǧebel Ḥamrīn?) see Brinkman, *AnOr* 43 (1968) fn. 1093.

276

Bibliography:

(I) Waterman, *RCAE* 340.

(II) Weidner, *AfO* 13 (1939-40) 55; Landsberger, *BBEA* (1965) 53 f.

Addressee:

Esarhaddon.

Date:

Ābu 2, eponym year of *Kanūnāju* = July 22, 671 B.C. This letter must be studied in the light of *LAS* 57f and 281, all of which likewise concern the fashioning of a tiara belonging to the ceremonial dress of the god Nabû [of Borsippa] (cf. discussion of *LAS* 58 and below, note to Obv.16f). The fact that *LAS* 58 also refers to the crown prince (Assurbanipal?) and *LAS* 281 to the crown prince [of Babylon] (Šamaš-šumu-ukīn) makes it possible to place all letters with certainty between 669 and 672 (see note on *LAS* 173:17, and cf. present letter 1.18f). *LAS* 281 was certainly written either in 670 or 669, since it contains (Obv.13f) a reference to spoils taken from Egypt [in June-July 671], and was according to Rev.24f, written before the procession of the Lady of Akkad to the *akītu*-chapel (taking place in Ajāru). Our letter, on the other hand, was certainly written during the year *preceding* the dispatchment of *LAS* 281: Obv.5ff shows that the jewellery to be used for the tiara was sent to Mār-Ištar in the *middle* of the year (5th month), whereas *LAS* 281 indicates that the tiara was completed in *Nisannu* (1st month); this means that the making of the crown had lasted for $8 + n{\cdot}12$ months, and even though there is no reason to underestimate the difficulty of the job, it can hardly be denied that the formula makes sense only if $n = 0$. Consequently, our letter must be placed either in Ābu 671 or 670. Which of these years is to be preferred depends on the implications of Rev. 4ff. Can it be supposed that Esarhaddon ordered the commandants of the Babylonian cities mentioned to check (= to compensate for) the (losses of their) war-chariots in the middle of the summer, more than a year after the termination of the Egyptian campaign in which they had partaken? To me, it seems more likely that the writer refers to a royal order *immediately following* or preceding the said campaign, particularly since no major campaigns were (because of the king's illness?) undertaken in 670 B.C. This would make the year 671 the only acceptable alternative.

Notes:

11. ^{NA_4}IGI × 2^{MEŠ}: see note to 58:8. If our passage really refers to the same "eye-stones", as is probable (cf. ibid.),[469] a combination of the two passages would give a clue to the function of these objects: *they were mounted on divine tiaras*, perhaps to symbolize the all-pervasive power of sight of the gods.

---

[469] The material of the "eye-stones" mentioned in *LAS* 58:8 is not specified (the obsidian beads mentioned ibid. 17 ff belonged to a different set), so they may well have been made of serpentine as those mentioned in the present letter.

23. The name of the commandant of Babylon here meant was Ubāru; see Landsberger, *BBEA* p.29f and note on *LAS* 295 A 9'. On the office and function of the (purely Babylonian) official ^{LÚ}GAR.NÁM see Brinkman, *AnOr* 43 (1968) 307ff; note the syllabic spelling $^{\text{LÚ*}}$*ši-kín ṭè-m*[*e*] in *ABL* 1433:7'.

r4. *te-ki-i-ti*: unclear, translated *ad sensum*; hardly = *tēqītu* "blasphemy, sulky words, complaint" (see, most recently, Sjöberg *ZA* 64 [1975] 167).

r8. *ú-tu-UŠ-si-ku*: for this spelling cf. notes to 147 r15' and 211:7; cf. also *SA-ṭir-*[*u-ni*] 278 r4 (for normal *šá-ṭir-u-ni*) and *ba-la-tu-US-šú-nu* 277 r1. It is possible that graphemic oddities like these are due to the influence of the Neo-Babylonian writing, where graphemic <s> stands for phonemic /š/ (and graphemic <s> for phonemic /s/), whereas in Neo-Assyrian the matter is just the other way round, i.e. <š> = /s/ and <s> = /š/, see S. Parpola, *Assur* 1/1 (1974) 4.

r16. *Ṭābî* the judge: not otherwise known. Hardly identical with ^{I}*Ṭa-bi-ja*, a writer of astrological reports to king (*RMA* 12, 71, 73, 193, 222 and 260).

277

Bibliography:

(I) Waterman, *RCAE* 476 (cf. III 374).
(II) Meier, *Or* NS 8 (1939) 304; Oppenheim, *JAOS* 61 (1941) 253, 257; Deller, *Or* NS 31 (1962) 230; Deller + Parpola, *RA* 60 (1966) 67f; Postgate, *TCAE* (1974) 48f.

Writer:

The attribution of this letter to Mār-Ištar is certain on the ground of the introductory formula, which is used by no other writer in the whole Sargonid royal correspondence.

Addressee:

Esarhaddon.

Date:

September 27, 671 BC. = Tašrītu 12, eponymy of Kanūnāju. This date follows from the astronomical observation communicated in Rev.30f (Mars emerging from Scorpio and heading towards Sagittarius), which can be identified with the help of *LAS* 292 and the other data found in the present letter. First of all, the reference to the returnal of Uṣur-amatsa to Uruk (Obv.19) places the letter firmly in the reign of Esarhaddon (cf. note on Obv.12 ff). In this reign, Mars emerged from Scorpio (moving onwards) approximately on the following dates:[470]

Year	Date (Julian : Assyrian)			Visibility
679	December 18	=	Kanūnu 7	+
677	November 27	=	Kislīmu 8	–
675	November 7	=	Araḫsamna 9	–
673	October 17	=	Araḫsamna 11	+
671	September 27	=	Tašrītu 12	+
669	September 1	=	Ulūlu 8	+

Of the four years in which the phenomenon could be sighted, year 679 can be ruled out since Uṣur-amatsa's return to Uruk is not recorded in any inscriptions of Esarhaddon predating 671 BC. Year 673 is unlikely for the same reason; moreover, the date on which Mars emerged from Scorpio in 673 (October 17 = *Araḫsamna* 11) cannot be reconciled with the statement of the letter (Obv.28f) that the "bishop", *qēpu* and temple scribe of Uruk were on a visit to Nineveh, which definitely points to early *Nisannu* or *Tašrītu*, the times of the New Year reception of the Assyrian king.[471] Of the remaining two alternatives, Tašrītu 12, 671, and Ulūlu 8, 669, the former fits perfectly,

---

[470] Cf. App. D and Stahlman-Gingerich, *Solar and Planetary Longitudes* . . . (1963), p.224ff.

[471] Cf. Postgate, *TCAE* (1974) 121 and 125ff; for the *Tašrītu*-reception, see e.g. *ABL* 971:8ff. Cf. also the "Ist.-Brief" of Šum-iddin discussed under Nos. 284 and 286.

whereas the latter would be a bit too early from the viewpoint of the visit just mentioned. That the year in question really was 671 is raised beyond doubt by *LAS* 292 written on Tašrītu 22, 671, and containing (in its lines 11'f) a reference to the present letter. See, in detail, discussion of the date of no. 292.

Notes:

6. *"Itti-Marduk-balāṭu of Uruk has written to me"*: A letter from this man has actually been preserved (*ABL* 831), but this can hardly be the letter meant here, though it was obviously written to Esarhaddon[472] either in Nisannu or Tašrītu[473] between 672 and 669[472], and contains a break in which the present quotation might well have been included (Obv.13ff, preceded by *šul-mu* ^{11} *a-na ma-aṣ-ṣar-ti* ^{12} *šá* É.KUR *i-na* [. . . .). *ABL* 831 r5ff ("the sheikhs have come here . . .") indicates that this letter was sent from Uruk, whereas Obv.28f (cf. Rev.8f) of the present letter shows that Itti-Marduk-balāṭu was in Nineveh while the letter referred to here (a request for an audience?) was written.

7. *Surmarrāte*: modern Sāmarrā' on the Tigris ca. 100 km NW of Baghdad and 150 km S of Assur. See Grayson, *AfO* 20 (1963) 88 and the earlier literature quoted there.

12ff. Cf. Borger, *Ash* p.84:43ff, ^{d}*Ú-ṣur-a-mat-sa ma-li-kàt mil-ki ṣa-bi-ta-at ab-bu-ut-ti a-na* UNUG^{KI} URU-*šá ú-tir* "I returned Uṣur-amatsa, the councilor who invervenes (for me), to Uruk, her city". The titulary of Esarhaddon in the obverse of this inscription places it after the king's Egyptian campaign (i.e. July, 671). The inscription (AsBb A) does not mention Nanâ, perhaps because the statue of this goddess was not yet completed (cf. Obv. 12f, 26 of our letter), but cf. the inscription Uruk C (ibid. p.77) 11ff: *É-ḫi-li-an-na* É *pa-pa-ḫi* ^{d}*Na-na-a* GAŠAN-*ja ša qé-reb É-an-na* ^{12} *ša* MAN *maḫ-ri i-pu-šu la-ba-riš il-lik-ma mi-qit-ti ir-ši* ^{13} *áš-ra-ti-šú áš-te-'i-i ina a-gur-ri* UDUN KÙ-*ti ma-qit-ta-šú ak-še-er* ^{14} ŠU^{2} ^{d}*Na-na-a* GAŠAN GAL-*ti aṣ-bat-ma a-na qé-reb-šú ú-še-rib šu-bat da-ra-a-te ú-šar-me* "I restored Eḫilianna, the chapel of Nanâ, my Lady, which is situated in the middle of Eanna . . . took the hand of the great lady Nanâ, guided her into it and let her settle down in the seat of eternity". In any case, it is certain that the work on the statues of both Uṣur-amatsa and Nanâ was completed during the reign of Esarhaddon, for both goddesses appear among the gods of Akkad who welcomed Marduk to Babylon at the beginning of the first year of Assurbanipal (cf. ^{d}GAŠAN *šá* A.GA.DÈ^{KI} ^{d}*Na-na-a* ^{d}*Ú-ṣur-a-mat-sa* ^{d}*Ḫa-ni-bi-ia* ^{d}*A-da-nis?-si?* ^{13} [*ina*] *kib-ri* ÍD *šub-tu šit-ku-na-ma ú-qa-'u-ú* LUGAL DINGIR^{MEŠ} EN EN.EN, Streck *Asb* p.266:12f).[474]

16. At the end of the line restore probably [*šu-un-gal-l*]*i* "dragons"; cf. *ABL* 951:12f (*šu-un-gal-li* ^{13} *ša* ^{d}PA *ina muḫ-ḫi iz-za-zu-u-ni* "the dragons on which Nabû is standing") and Diodorus Siculus Book II 9:5 (". . . at the knees of the goddess Rhea [of Babylon] stood two lions, while near by were huge *serpents* of silver, each one weighing thirty talents . . .").

19f. The goddess Arkājītu (cf. Streck, *Asb* p.186^{6} and König, *RlA* I 151) is not mentioned in the inscriptions of Esarhaddon, which may indicate that the statue referred to here was not completed before the reign of Assurbanipal; in the inscriptions of Assurbanipal the goddess appears only in passage bearing on the returnal of the statue of Nana from Susa to Eanna (cf. Steck, *Asb* p.220:29ff, ŠU^{2} ^{d}*Na-na-a* ^{d}ŠEŠ-INIM-*sa* ^{30} ^{d}UNUG^{KI}-*a-a-i-tu* [var. ^{d}*Ar-ka-a-a-i-tú*] *at-mu-uḫ-ma* . . . ^{33} *ina qé-reb* UNUG^{KI} *ú-še-rib-ši-ma* "I took the hands of Nanâ, Uṣur-amatsa, and Arkājītu . . . and introduced her(!) into Uruk"; similarly ibid. p.186:16; Bauer, *IWA* pp.58 and 71). The other gods mentioned here do not figure in the inscriptions of either Esarhaddon or Assurbanipal; Palil (written ^{d}IGI.DU) is mentioned among the gods of Uruk in an inscription of Sennacherib (*1 R* 43:32 = Luckenbill, *OIP* 2 p. 85 ff).

r1. *ba-la-tu-US-šú-nu*: cf. note on 276 r8.

r19f. "The crown prince of Elam has become troublesome": sic, contra Waterman, *RCAE* I p.337 ("the son of the king of Elam is sick") and Deller + Parpola, *RA* 60 (1966) 67 (". . . ist 'erkrankt'"). The correct meaning of the passage appears from the reference to the strategic position of Dēr on the borderland of Elam and Assyria (r21f). The writer implies that by sending Elamite workmen to assist in a building enterprise long neglected by the

---

[472] *ABL* 831 r1'ff is a reference to the Vassal-Treaties of Esarhaddon. See Parpola, *Iraq* 34 (1972) 31.

[473] Note the reference to a "festival of the king's gods" involving a procession of gods (831:8ff). Cf. Thureau-Dangin, *RAcc* 89ff and 99ff and see commentary on *LAS* 195.

[474] The statue of Nanâ referred to in the present letter has naturally nothing to do with the statue of Nanâ returned by Assurbanipal from Susa (Streck, *Asb* p.58:107; cf. ibid. p.757).

Assyrians, the Elamite crown prince[475] was seeking to lower the prestige of Assyria in Dēr in favour of Elam, perhaps with an eye to a subsequent annexation of the city. For another example of *marāṣu* in the meaning "to be(-come) troublesome" see *LAS* 213 r1; cf. also *AHw* 610*a*.

r20. $^{\text{LÚ}*}$*ú-ra-si*: an occupational term mostly found in contexts dealing with masonry (cf. *ABL* 91, 119, 209, 464, 580, 1310, etc.), exact meaning unknown; probably "(mud-)brick mason", see K. Deller, *OrNS* 35 (1966) 194, and J.N. Postgate, *CTN* 2 (1974) 192 n.4, but note that the Akkadian etymology (< *warrāsu*) proposed by Postgate is subject to doubt since the word probably is of Hurrian origin (K. Deller, orally). The word occurs in LB texts in the form *urāšu* denoting a type of worker "employed in maintenance of canals, levees, and other similar public works"; see Stolper, *Bibliotheca Mesopotamica* 7 (1977), 256.

r26ff. Cancel the restorations given in Pt.I and restore instead: [*le*]-*e-pu-š*[*u šu-mu ša* MAN EN-*já*][27] *a-na da-ra-*[*a-ti liš-ku-nu*][28] *a-na ma-ṣar-ti š*[*a* É.DINGIR^{MEŠ}] "let them finish the building (of the temple) and [establish the name of the king, my lord,] for ever; let the king, my lord, not neglect the guard of the [temple]." Cf. LUGAL EN *šu-un-šú a-*[*n*]*a* [*d*]*a-ra-a-ti*[10] *liš-k*[*u*]*n*, ND 2673:9f (= *Iraq* 20 pl.41, NL 45), and *šul-mu*[11] *a-na ma-aṣ-ṣar-ti*[12] *šá* É.KUR, *ABL* 831:10ff; for other similar examples see the dictionaries s.vv. *dārâtu* and *maṣṣartu*.[476]

The restorations proposed in Pt.I are out of the question despite the fact that the year in which the letter was written (671) was a potential leap year (see on *LAS* 190) and contained two total eclipses of the moon (July 2 = Du'ūzu 13, and December 27/28 = Kanūnu 15): a letter written in the middle of Tašrītu (the 7th month) cannot have contained a request for intercalation, and since a lunar eclipse had occurred only 3 months before the writing of the letter, there was no reason to expect an eclipse either to occur in the near future.

278

Bibliography:

(I) Waterman, *RCAE* 337 (cf. IV 180, 246); Pfeiffer, *SLA* 309.

(II) Schott, *OLZ* 40 (1937) 361; Labat, *Royauté* (1939) 329; Oppenheim, *JAOS* 61 (1941) 264; Schott, *ZA* 47 (1941) 89f; Böhl, *Opera Minora* (1953) 411; Landsberger, *BBEA* (1965) 44[67]; Kümmel, *StBoT* 3 (1967) 175.

Addressee:

Esarhaddon.

Date:

Appr. Du'ūzu 17, eponym year of Kanūnāju = July 6, 671 BC. The resemblance of Rev.11'ff to *LAS* 279:15ff certainly strongly suggests, at first sight, that the present letter refers to the same eclipse as *LAS* 279 and should hence be dated to late Kanūnu (December), 671; but on second thought, two difficulties with this dating become evident. Firstly, why should Mār-Ištar have written two letters of almost the same content within a span of only a few days? Secondly, the (language and) orthography of *LAS* 279 differs noticeably from that of the present letter[477], which would be strange if the latter were written only a few days before the former.[478] In fact, the summary description of the eclipse given here also fits the eclipse of July 2, -670,[479] and the orthography of the letter is fully consistent with that of *LAS* 276, written approximately on July 22, 671.[480] Since the writer refers to a royal letter dealing with the eclipse (Obv.6), the present letter must have been written at least 3 days after the occurrence of the eclipse, hence on Du'ūzu 17 at the earliest; and since the solar eclipse potentially following the eclipse had not yet occurred (Rev.8'f), the letter was certainly written before the end of the month Du'ūzu. The only difficulty with this dating

475 The identity of the prince is obscure owing to the complicated order of succession in Elam; possibly Ummanigaš (Humban-nikaš) II or Tammaritu I, cf. Hinz, *Das Reich Elam* (1964) p.129, and note *ABL* 1385:13f, where ^{I}*Um-man-i-gaš* (II) is entitled "crown prince" (DUMU.MAN).

476 That the king did heed the plea of Mār-Ištar and send workmen to Dēr to quickly complete the temple is made likely by *LAS* 190. Cf. note on 190 r8.

477 Note UZU *ù ḫu-ud* (line 4) as against UZU *u ḫu-*[*ud* of 279:4, *an-ni-i* (nom.) of 278 r11' against *an-ni-i-u* of 279:15, *šá-ni-iš* (278 r15') against *šá-niš* (279:18), KUR *Kal-du* (278 r15') against KUR *Kal-di* (nom.), 279: 23.

478 Cf., e.g., *LAS* 1-2 and 246-247.

479 See App. F2.

480 Cf. UZU *ù ḫu-ud* 276:4, *an-ni-i* ibid. r22.

is that it is unclear whether Esarhaddon had already returned from his campaign to Egypt by Du'ūzu 14, the date of the eclipse. The Assyrians conquered Memphis on Du'ūzu 22 (cf. on *LAS* 59) and inflicted a defeat upon the Egyptian army as late as on Du'ūzu 28 (ibid.), but the wording of *LAS* 59 r3ff and the content of *LAS* 276 in fact make it likely that Esarhaddon had returned to Assyria before the campaign was completely over.

Discussion:

As stated in Rev.13'ff of the present letter, the lunar eclipse of July 2, -670, portended calamity to the "Westland" (Amurru), under which concept also Egypt was included (cf. 279 r6). One cannot help speculating that the occurrence of this eclipse might have affected the timing (and perhaps also the outcome?) of the decisive battles of Esarhaddon's Egyptian campaign of 671, which were fought on Du'ūzu 16, 22 and 28, i.e. respectively only 2 days, 8 days and 2 weeks after the eclipse.

Notes:

6ff. While Babylon, Borsippa and Nippur are well attested as seats of astronomical schools and sites from where astrological reports were regularly sent to Sargonid kings,[481] Akkad is not; and since Akkad is here found in a position where one would actually rather expect to find Babylon,[482] it might seem that the present passage supports the thesis of Landsberger, refuted above (sub *LAS* 275), according to which Akkad in Mār-Ištar's usage was just a cover name for Babylon. Such a conclusion would be premature, though; there is nothing in the passage suggesting that Akkad served as a place of *regular* astronomical observations, and Obv.8f in fact suggests that the town was mentioned here simply because it was the place where Mār-Ištar *himself* had been watching the eclipse. On the reasons of Mār-Ištar's stay in Akkad see commentary to 275.

9f. "*They set up a bronze kettledrum*": referring to a ritual lamentation performed in order to appease the "angered" moon. Cf. the "Gebet an einen verfinsterten Gott" published by Ebeling, *Or* NS 17 (1948) 416ff, and the *kalû*-ritual against lunar eclipses, *BRM* 4 no.6 (edited by Ebeling, *TuL* p.91ff). Note also Layard, *Nineveh and Babylon* (abr. ed., 1867), p.314f: "I gained . . . some credit for wisdom and superhuman knowledge by predicting, through the aid of an almanack, a partial eclipse of the moon. It duly took place to the great dismay of my guests, who well nigh knocked out the bottoms of all my kitchen utensils in their endeavour to frighten away the Jins who had thus laid hold of the planet. The common notion amongst ignorant Mohammedans is, that an eclipse is caused by some evil spirit catching hold of the sun or moon. On such occasions, in Eastern towns, the whole population assembles with pots, pans, and other equally rude instruments of music, and, with the aid of their lungs, make a din and turmoil which might suffice to drive away a whole army of evil spirits, even at so great a distance."

r4'. *sa-ṭir-*[*u-ni*]: taken as a "Babylonian" spelling for Assyrian <šá-ṭir-u-ni> = /satirūni/; cf. note to 276 r8. Reading *sa-dir-*[*u-ni*] (Ylvisaker, *LSS* 5/6 [1912] 10[1]; Schott, *ZA* 47 [1941] 104; von Soden, *AHw* 1000*b*) is of course also possible, but lacks parallels; it also makes less sense than the phrase *ina ṭuppi šaṭir* which repeatedly occurs in the present corpus (cf. the parallel passage *LAS* 289 r11f and 205 r11; 1 r11ff; 12 r13ff; 13r15; 110+300 r6ff; 166 r7).

r12'. *KUR.KUR ul-tap-pi-it*: cf. *a-na* KUR MAR.TU^{KI} *il-ta-pat*, 279:16f. *Lapātu* is here in the D-stem because of the plurality of the object, see note on 142 r8.

r18'. *nam-búr-bé-e-šú*: here possibly referring to the substitute king ritual (the ritual tablet of which resembles namburbi texts and may originally have contained a customary namburbi "rubric"); yet it is also possible, in view of 280:17, that the word here simply refers to apotropaic rituals in general, as in 279 r13.

---

481 Reports were sent from Babylon, Barsip, Cutha, Dilbat and Uruk (cf. App.Q5); Pliny and Strabo mention Babylon, Borsippa, Sippar and Uruk as seats of astrological schools; *RMA* 274 refers to observatories in Babylon, Nippur, Uruk and Barsip (in this order).

482 Cf. the prededing note.

279

Bibliography:

(I) Waterman, *RCAE* 629 (cf. IV 185, 258); Pfeiffer, *SLA* 323.
(II) Behrens, *ABB* (1906) 14^{4}, 98^{1}; Schott, *ZA* 47 (1941) 90ff; Labat, *Royauté* (1939) 355, 358, and *RA* 40 (1946) 131, 133ff; Böhl, *Opera Minora* (1953) 411, 417; von Soden, *FS Christian* (1956) 104; Landsberger, *BBEA* (1965) 43^{65}, 45f; Kümmel, *StBoT* 3 (1967) 172f, 175, 179f; Oppenheim, *Centaurus* 14 (1969) 118.

Writer:

The attribution of this letter to Mār-Ištar is certain on the grounds of the introductory formula alone. Additional confirmation is provided by the criteria put together in Appendix M 6.

Addressee:

Esarhaddon.

Date:

Kanūnu 20, eponymy of Kanūnāju = January 1, 670 BC, or slightly later. The day follows from Obv.9; the year and month from the reference to the lunar eclipse (Obv.15ff), which can be only identified with that of December 27/8, -670. This was the only lunar eclipse between 680 and 660 BC to occur in the month Kanūnu/Ṭebētu (cf. App.F1), and its properties perfectly agree with the summary description given in the present letter.[483] The date on which the eclipse is said to have taken place (Kanūnu 15) is also consistent with the identification, since it is known for certain that the eclipse of December 27/8, -670, indeed occurred on Kanūnu 15. Cf. *ABL* 137:6ff:

UD *15*.KÁM* *šá* ^{ITU}AB ^{7}*ina* EN.NUN MU[R]UB$_4$ [^{d}]*30* AN.MI *iš-ta-kan* ^{8}*ina* ^{ITU}KUR *ul-tar-*[*ru*] *ù* UGU ^{9} ^{IM}MAR *il-t*[*a-ḫ*]*a-aṭ* ^{10}*lum-nu*! : *par-su šá* ⸢LUGAL⸣! MAR^{KI} ^{11}*ù* KUR-*šú lu-*[*mun*]-*šú par-su* ^{12}*lu-mun-šú ana* LUGAL MAR^{KI} *u* KUR-*šú* ^{13}*na-din ki-i* LÚ*EN.ÚŠ *ša* LUGAL EN-*já* ^{14}*ina* KUR MAR^{KI} *i-ba-áš-šú-ú* ^{15}LUGAL EN *ki-i šá i-le-'u-ú* ^{16}*le-pu-uš* ŠU^{2} LUGAL EN-*já* ^{17}*i-kaš-šad a-bi-ik-ta-šú* ^{18}LUGAL *i-š*[*a*]*k-kan* "The moon was eclipsed in the middle watch of the 15th of Kinūnu, (the eclipse) beginning in the east and moving westward. This is definitely to the disadvantage of the king of the Westland and his country. There is no doubt about the evil in question: it will befall the king of the Westland and his country. If the king, my lord, has an enemy in the West, the king, my lord, can do as he pleases: the king, my lord, will capture (him) and inflict a defeat upon him." Note the similarity of this prediction with that given in the present letter. The identification of the eclipse as that of December 27/8 -670 is beyond doubt, since the writer of *ABL* 137, Zākir, was a contemporary of Esarhaddon.[484]

The (mainly historical) objections raised against the identification of the eclipse by Landsberger (*BBEA* [1965] 43f)[485] are quite groundless. The fact that the eclipse was interpreted to the disadvantage of Amurru doesn't by any means imply that it was not total (cf. simply 278 r12'f and *ABL* 1006:4, quoted in Appendix F4); and why should the predictions of Rev.6ff necessarily refer to time preceding the conquest of Egypt, as all the kings mentioned were alive and constituted a potential threat to Assyria even after the death of Esarhaddon?

11. *na-qa-bi-ja-te ša DUB.SAR-u-te*: also in 280:12 (*na-qa-ba-a-te sa ṭup-šar-ru-tú*);[486] cf. LÚ *si-i-ru naq-bi-tú ina* IGI ^{d}*15* [*i-qab-bi*] "the painted man utters a *naqbitu* in front of Ištar", K.3455:19' (unp. NA cultic ritual); ^{LÚ}SANGA^{MEŠ} *šá* É^{MEŠ} DINGIR^{MEŠ} TIR.AN.NA^{KI} ... ^{17} ^{d}*60 uš-tu-pu-u ina nap-ḫar* KUR.KUR *ù it-ta-ṣa-a ṣa-lam ba-nu-ú naq-bit i-qab-bu-ú* "the priests of the temples of Uruk ... utter (the hymns) 'Anu appears in splendour in all the countries' and 'The beautiful statue has emerged' in the *naqbītu* manner", *RAcc* p.120:14ff (similarly ibid. 77:45.47, 78:9, 119:32, etc.). These parallels show quite clearly that *naqbītu* was a term referring to solemn-

---

483 Cf. App. F2 and Schaumberger, *ZA* 47 (1941) 125ff; note, however, that *LAS* 278 quoted by Schaumberger as evidence of the totality of the eclipse probably refers to another eclipse.

484 Cf. *ABL* 416 and 702, both written in the early part of the reign of Esarhaddon (Dietrich, *AOAT* 7 p.40). The astrological reports of Zākir (App.05) cannot be dated reliably.

485 "... die Finsternis war gewiß nicht total, da nur Amurru von ihr betroffen wird. Auch passen die ... Voraussagen ... schlecht zu diesem Jahre, in welchem der König von Tyrus (so mit großer Wahrscheinlichkeit Rs.6 zu ergänzen) und von Aethiopien schon besiegt waren. Wir müssen diese Finsternis früher legen."

486 For the anaptyptic vowel between *q* and *b* see note to 39:11.

ly recited litanies; on the other hand, the specification *ša ṭupšarrūti* shows that the litanies meant here consisted of o m e n s, not of prayers (thus Landsberger, *BBEA* p.47). A comparison with *LAS* 26 r1'ff and 30:6ff suggests that the omens in question were those which the substitute king had to "take upon himself" at the moment of his coronation.

19. $^{\text{LÚ*}}$*um-ma-ni*: referring to the court astrologers of Esarhaddon (Ištar-šumu-ēreš, Balasî, Nabû-aḫḫē-erība). Evidently Mār-Ištar did not consider himself an *ummânu*, despite his obvious scribal background. This supports the view taken in my dissertation, p.6f, that the men designated as *ummânu* were basically "masters", or highly trained experts of specific crafts.

r6. *"The king of Kush"*: referring to Pharaoh Taharqa, defeated by Esarhaddon but still holding Upper Egypt in 671 and due to regain control of the Delta region soon after the death of Esarhaddon. See Streck, *Asb* p.7 ff and Labat, *Fischer Weltgeschichte* 4 (1967) 84f.

The king of Tyre here referred to is Ba'al, who was forced to conclude a disadvantageous treaty with Esarhaddon (Borger, *Ash* p. 107ff; cf. recently Spaliger, *Or* NS 43 [1974] 299f) but was nevertheless able to maintain the independence of the city, even under continuous siege, down to the first year of Assurbanipal. See Streck, *Asb* p.CCCLXVIIIf and cf. Borger, *Ash* p.112:12ff.

r7. *Mu-gal-lu*$_4$: the king of Tabal who conquered Melidi (Melitene) in 675 and ever since remained a thorn in the flesh of Esarhaddon (cf. Aro, *RAI* 14 [1966] 113), submitting to Assyria only under Assurbanipal (Streck, *Asb* p.CCCLI; Fales, *Assur* 1/3 [1974] 14f).

r10. Esarhaddon had captured the harem of Taharqa in Du'ūzu 671 (cf. Borger, *Ash* p.99:43, ^{MÍ}E.GAL-*šú* MÍ+ERIM.É.GAL^{MEŠ}-*šú* . . . ^{45} *áš-lu-la a-na* KUR *Aš+šur*^{KI}), but of course the present passage need not necessarily pertain to the king of Kush alone but to any one of the kings just mentioned.

r14f. Cf. *LAS* 218:10ff; was this letter written in response to a royal order issued on the ground of the present passage?

280

B i b l i o g r a p h y :

(I) Waterman, *RCAE* 437 (cf. III 374).

(II) Behrens, *ABB* (1906) 97f; Ebeling, *TuL* (1931) 59f; Labat, *Royauté* (1939) 86, 119f, 127f, 257, 349, 351, 359; Oppenheim, *Or* NS 9 (1940) 221; Dhorme, *RA* 38 (1941) 59ff; Labat, *RA* 40 (1946) 131f, 135ff; von Soden, *ZA* 43 (1936) 255ff; *ZA* 45 (1939) 64; Böhl, *Opera Minora* (1953) 406ff, 417ff; *Fs Christian* (1956) 103f; Landsberger, *BBEA* (1965); Kümmel, *StBoT* 3 (1967) 172, 174, 176ff, 182; Biggs, *ANET*^{3} (1969) 625f; Caplice, *Or* NS 42 (1973) 510.

C o p y :

Cf. also Winckler, *SKT* II (1893-94) 28f and Lehmann, *Ššmk* II (1892) pl.45f.

W r i t e r :

The attribution of this letter to Mār-Ištar hardly needs any justification. Cf. on the previous number.

A d d r e s s e e :

Esarhaddon.

D a t e :

Šabāṭu/Addāru, eponymy of Kanūnāju = January/February, 670 BC. Though the letter does not contain any *concrete* chronological data (save the reference to Šamaš-šumu-ukīn in Obv.11, cf. the relevant note), its connection with the preceding number is beyond doubt both in view of Obv.8 and 16ff (cf. 279:12ff and r13ff) and the content of the letter in general; and as the elaborate burial ceremonies and the other incidents described cannot possibly have taken place within a time shorter than a week, the terminus post quem of the letter is certainly Šabāṭu 1 = January 12, 670. A terminus ante quem (Addāru 28 = March 10, 670) is obtained from Rev. 11f indicating that the 100 day period usually covered by the substitute king ritual (cf. Introduction, p. XXVf) was not yet over and that at least one conjunction of the "gods" (i.e. the moon and sun) was yet to take place before those 100 days were completed. Kanūnu 15 + 100 days gives Nisannu 25 ± 1; consequently, the letter must have been written before the preceding new moon, i.e. before the end of Addāru.

Notes:

9. "*. . . died on the night of* [. . .]": does this remark imply that the death of the substitute king and his queen was arranged through an "overdosed soporific", i.e. poisoned food or drink? This would certainly have been the most convenient way of getting rid of the two and, at the same time, of creating for the public the impression of a natural death, which doubtless lay in the interests of both the king and his aides.[487] On the use of poison as a means of getting rid of "troublesome" persons in Sargonid Assyria see *LAS* 144 and pertinent commentary.

10f. From the viewpoint of the dating of the letter, it is important to notice the clear distinction made here between the ruling king and Šamaš-šumu-ukīn as regards the purpose of the substitute king ritual; Damqî had "went to his fate" as *substitute* for the former, but merely *for the life* of the latter. Keeping in mind that the substitute took over all the dominions of the ruling king (cf. 279:13f), it follows that the king in question had ruled over "Assyria, Babylon and all the countries" (Obv.7f) and consequently can be only Esarhaddon, not Assurbanipal (thus Waterman, *RCAE* III 162). Šamaš-šumu-ukīn is mentioned here because of his position as the crown prince of Babylon, which gave him a share of royal power (cf. on *LAS* 247 and 281:5) but also entangled him, in cases like this (total eclipse of the moon), in dangers threatening the king himself. The fact that Šamaš-šumu-ukīn alone is mentioned with his father (omitting Assurbanipal) implies that the prince was resident in Babylonia while the letter was written, hence in January/February 670 BC (cf. above). Curiously enough, though Šamaš-šumu-ukīn probably began "practicing kingship" soon after his official nomination as heir apparent (cf. commentary to *LAS* 246), the present passage actually furnishes the *earliest* reference to the prince's stay in his princedom.[488] Slightly later is *ADD* 625 = *AR* 116, a deed concluded between Nergal-ilāja, the governor (^{LÚ}EN.NAM) of Laḫīru, and Atar-ilī, "eunuch of the crown prince of Babylon" (formerly, the governor of Laḫīru, eponym 672),[489] which indicates that the prince was resident in Laḫīru on Ajāru 1 = April 11, 670, i.e. about two months after the writing of the present letter, *LAS* 281, referring to Šamaš-šumu-ukīn in a manner similar to the present passage, dates from approximately the same time (Ajāru, 670). Further datable references to Šamaš-šumu-ukīn residing in Babylonia as crown prince are *LAS* 70 r8ff (Addāru 30 = March 29, 669) and 29:11 (Ajāru 18 = May 15, 669); cf. also *LAS* 295: 8 and *Iraq* 34 21ff, of unclear date.

12. Cf. [*ana pu-ḫ*]*i-ja ad-din-ka ana pi-di-ja ad-din-ka ana an-du-na-ni-ja* [*ad-din-ka*] in the namburbi ritual BM 59808:25' (Caplice, *Or* NS 42 (1973) 508ff) showing that the word *pīdu* is a synonym of *pūḫu* and has therefore to be rendered "surrogate" or "ransom" rather than "rescue" (Pt.I).

14ff. On the terms *taklittu* and *šuruptu* see notes to *LAS* 4:13 and 17; on the Assyrian funeral ceremonies in general, see commentary to *LAS* 195; on the *Bīt rimki* and *Bīt salā' mê* rituals, notes to 136:11, 185 (discussion), 203 (discussion) and 208 r8. The spellings É *šá* (for *sa*)-*la me-e* and *pa-áš-šá* (17, for *pa-as-sa*) are to be understood as Neo-Assyrian spellings of literary loan-words, cf. notes to 219:17, 276 r8, 278 r4 and 300+ r8. On the long *e* in *né-pe-e-še* (18) and the assimilated genitive suffix in *a-ši-pu-tú* (19) see note to 126 r13.

23. [^{M}]^{Í}*ra-gi-in-ti*: cf. ^{KUR}*Kal-di* (nom.) 279:23, *lìb-bi* (nom.) 284 r14, *šùl-mu* (gen.) 279:9, *ni-ib-zu* (gen.) 288 A 12', ^{GUD}*šak-lu-lu* (gen.) 281 r1, *ka-a-ri* (st.cstr.) 291:15' and *la-ba-ri* (st.cstr.) u_4-*mu* (gen.) 276:20, all exemples of the influence of Neo-Babylonian on Mār-Ištar's idiolect. Taking the final *-i* as the possessive suffix of 1 sg (my prophetess) is out of the question considering the social background of Assyrian ecstatic prophets (mostly oblates of Ištar, and in any case never professionally serving private persons).

The final *-u* in *tar-tu-gu-mu* is due to raised pitch indicating continuation. See notes to 18 r8 and 246 r1. Other similar cases in the present letter are *lu-u pa-qi di . . . lu-qar-rib* (r16), *lis-ru-qu . . . lil-*[*lik*] r18ff) and *li-zi-zi . . . liš-li-m*[*u*], the spellings *lip-qi-d*[*i*] (r27), *ú-sa-za-an-zi* (286 r6) and *lu-ṣi-ṣi* (293 r12) are examples of the same intonation contour with a different (emphasizing-iterative) function, expressed in corresponding NB utterances by means of the enclitic particle *-ma*.

[487] Cf. simply the euphemism *ana šimti alāku* used in referring to the execution of the substitute king in Obv.12 and elsewhere in the present corpus.

[488] Note that according to *LAS* 185 r10ff and 232:7, Šamaš-šumu-ukīn was sojourning in Calah as late as on December 26, 671. Had he not yet permanently stayed in Babylonia before that date?

[489] Cf. *lim-mu* ^{I}*A-tar*-DINGIR [8] ^{LÚ}EN.NAM ^{URU}*La-ḫi-ra*, *ADD* 8 = *AR* 257:7f; ^{I}*A-tar*-[DINGIR] GAR *La-ḫi-r*[*i*], *RlA* 2 p.429; [^{I}*I*]*t-ri*-DINGIR [19] L[ÚGAR.K]UR ^{URU}*La-ḫ*[*i-ri*], *AR* 98:18f. Cf. also Borger, *BiOr* 29 (1972) 34*a*.

r11-13. The rendering of this difficult passage (cf. Landsberger, *BBEA* [1965] 48f with fnn. 85 and 87) suggested in Pt.I is based on the following parallels:

(1) ^{MUL}*Ṣal-bat-a-nu* [16] *ki-ma ba-'i-il . . .* [20] *a-na ka-aq-qí-*⌜*ri*⌝ [21] *šá* ^{KUR}*Su-bar-ti* [22] *la i-tu-a-ra* "When Mars is bright . . . he will not return to the area of Subartu", *LAS* 45:15 ff.

(2) LUGAL *lu i-di lu la-ti-ik* [r1] *ma-ṣar-ti šá ra-ma-ni-šú* [2] *li-iṣ-ṣur ina* UD⌜*la*⌝ *ṭa-a-bi* [3] LUGAL *a-na su-ú-qu la uṣ-ṣa-a* [4] *a-di a-dan-šú* [5] *it-ti-qu* [6] *it-ti šá* MUL *a-di* ITU UD^{MEŠ} "the king should know (this) and be on the alert, guarding himself; let the king not go out to the street on an inauspicious day until its time has passed. The sign of a star is (valid) for a full month", *RMA* 245:6 ff (cf. *RMA* 247A and the passages cited in the note to *LAS* 135 r6).

(3) *ma-a* DUMU.MAN TA* $^{\text{I.d}}$GIŠ.NU$_{11}$-MU-GI.NA [8'] *ma-a : a-du* UD *22*.KÁM *ša* ^{ITU}DU$_6$ [9'] *a-na qa-an-ni la ú-ṣu-u . . .* [r7] *ma-a : a-du 1 me* UD^{MEŠ} [8] *ú-mal-lu-ú-ni* "the crown prince and Šamaš-šumu-ukīn should not go outdoors before Tašrītu 22 . . . until he (= the substitute king) has completed the 100 days . . .", *LAS* 249:7' ff.

(4) *áš-šú šá* ITU [6] EN.NU *šá* ^{d}UTU [7] *šu-ú* LUGAL *ina* EDEN *šu-u* [8] *a-na muḫ-ḫi ana* LUGAL [9] *áš-pu-ra um-ma* [10] LUGAL PI^2 [11] *liš-kun-ma* [12] *ki-i i-ba-áš-ši* [13] *u ki-i ja-a'-nu* "since it is (now) a month in which a solar eclipse is liable to occur and since the king is (at present) in the open country, I have written to the king: 'Let the king be attentive, whether it occurs or not'", *ABL* 477 r5 ff.

All these passages, though differently formulated, have one feature in common: they all imply that it is risky for the king or his son to move outside the palace precincts during a period of time marked as unlucky by a celestial portent. This idea seems also to underlie the present passage, assuming that *dūru ša attalê* "duration (German "Dauer", *AHw* 178*a*) of eclipse" here corresponds to what is normally expressed by *adannu* ("term") *ša attalê*; for *kaqquru* = "ground, open country" see above, example [1].

Warnings like these were of course not given in the naive belief that something unpleasant would automatically happen to the king if he ventured outside his palace. However, it is evident that "terms" of portents were generally considered risky for the persons they pertained to, even after the predicted calamities had actually been "averted", as in the present letter.

The present passage should accordingly be understood as a *recommendation* for the king not to *seek* trouble in a time considered risky from the astrological point of view, not as an absolute prohibition to keep off the streets. Such a recommendation is quite understandable considering that journeys in open country were potentially dangerous in Sargonid Assyria even under normal conditions. Cf. *LAS* 72 r8 ff: *ina* UGU ^{I}*Aš+šur-mu-kin-*BAL*-ja . . .* [10] *lil-li-ka ṭa-ba* [11] *a-na a-la-ki . . .* [16] *ina ši-id-di* KASKAL . . . [18] *lu et-ku li-iṣ-ṣu-ru-uš* "As regards (the prince) Aššūr-mukīn-palēja . . . let him come; it is favourable to travel (now); . . . (however), let them be alterted in the course of the journey and let then guard him (well)"; *LAS* 145:5 *ša* LUGAL *be-lí* [6] [*iš*]*-pur-an-ni ma ṭa-ba-a* [7] [*ma*] ^{I}*Aš+šur*-GIN-BAL^{MEŠ}*-ja* [8] [*a-n*]*a pa-n*[*i-j*]*a le-li-ja* "As to the king's writing to me: 'Is it safe? Aššūr-mukīn-palēja should come up to see me'", and cf. the similar passages in letters listed in the note to *LAS* 17:9. Further, *LAS* 272:13 ff, [^{TÚ}]^{G}*gu-zip-pi . . .* [14] [*iṣ*]*-ṣi-ja lu-*[*bi-la*] . . . [r3] $^{\text{LÚ*}}$*qur-bu-te* [4] [*iṣ*]*-ṣi-ja* [5] [*liš*]*-pu-ru* [6] [TA*] *pa-an* [7] [*par-r*]*i-ṣu-te* "I shall take the (royal) clothes . . . with me (scil. to Harrān); . . . Let them send a bodyguard with me – because of the traitors", and cf. 29 r15f. A telling passage is also *VTE* 198ff: "(You swear) that if anyone makes an insurrection, whether by day or by night, whether on the open highway or within the palace, against Esarhaddon, king of Assyria, and you have heard about it, and if by day or night a messenger (then) comes from the palace to the crown prince, saying: 'Your father has summoned you, let my lord come', you will not let him go but will strengthen his guard until one of you, who loves his lord and is loyal to the house of his lords, goes and ascertains in the palace the command of the king, your lord. Only thereafter will you go to the palace with the crown prince, your lord." Note lastly the specification "safely" (*ina šulme, ina šalinti*) frequently found in letters reporting on completed trips, e.g. *ina šùl-mu* [10] *a-na* ^{URU}*Ak-kad e-ta-rab* "(the substitute king) arrived safely in Akkad", *LAS* 279:9f; *Aš+šur* ^{d}NIN.LÍL *ina šul-me* [8] *it-tu-ṣi-ú ina šá-li-in-ti* [9] *e-tar-bu-u-né* "Aššūr and Mylitta set out safely and entered (their cellas) in safety", 311:7ff; ^{d}EN*:ZU *i-su-*[*ḫur*] [2] *ina* É*-šu e-ta-rab* [3] *i-na ša-lim-ti i-na šub-ti-šu* [5] *it-tu-ši-ib* "Sîn returned, entered his temple and took his seat in safety", *ABL* 134 r1ff; [*ina šá*]*-li-im-te ni-is-su-ḫu-ra* "we returned in safety", 126:9; [*i-sin-n*]*u e-pi-*[*iš*] [5] ^{d}[DN *ina š*]*ul-me* ⌜*it-tu-ṣi*⌝*-*[*a*] [6] *e-ta-rab* "the festival is over; the god [DN] has gone out and entered (his holy chamber) safely", ND 2765:4ff (*Iraq* 17 pl.33).

281

Bibliography:

(I) Waterman, *RCAE* 1202 (cf. IV 203, 269); Pfeiffer, *SLA* 350.
(II) Oppenheim, *JAOS* 61 (1941) 258; Holma, *Or* NS 13 (1944) 110; Landsberger, *BBEA* (1965) 53ff.

Writer:

The attribution of this letter to Mār-Ištar is certain on the ground of the introductory blessing alone, which was not used by any other writer, and can be easily confirmed by the criteria presented in App. M 6.

Addressee:

Esarhaddon.

Date:

Late Nisannu (or early Ajāru), eponymy of Šulmu-Bēl-lašme = early April, 670 BC. For the month cf. Obv.23 and Rev.24; the grounds for placing the letter in 670 BC are presented in the commentary to *LAS* 276.

General discussion:

Apart from a fragmentary building inscription pertaining to the restoration of the Gula temple of Borsippa (Borger, *Ash* p.32) and a short reference to the restoration of Ezida (ibid., p.95:10ff), the only mention of Borsippa in the inscriptions of Esarhaddon is the king's statement (ibid. p.52:62ff; p.32) that he had returned to the citizens of Babylon and Borsippa the fields which the head of Bīt-Dakūri, Šamaš-ibni, had appropriated during the "kingless years" of Babylonia at the end of Sennacherib's reign.[490] The present letter shows why this measure was considered significant enough to be recorded in the royal inscriptions. The moment the fields passed under foreign possession, regular deliveries of sacrificial victims to the temple of Nabû ceased (cf. *LAS* 275:5ff), and it was only by returning the fields to their old owners that the cultic services in the temple could be properly resumed. For this purpose, an account of the bulls and sheep consumed daily by Nabû had to be made and their delivery arranged on the ancient basis, i.e. the animals were to be collected as tax from local shepherds and cattle-owners (Obv.17ff). The quantities of bulls and sheep collected in "olden times" must have been large indeed (cf. 292 L.E.1, "[daily 2 ox]en, 4 sheep, 2 ducks, 2. . ."), for it appears that the shepherds were not at all willing to return to the old order but tried to keep their herds intact by briding the local officials responsible for the tax collection. The fact that they obviously had succeeded in their aspirations, being able to obstruct a direct order of the king (cf. Obv. 14 ff), is a further testimony of the state of anarchy and corruption prevalent in Babylonia at the end of Esarhaddon's reign (cf. Landsberger, *BBEA* p.28ff, and below, note to 284 r4).

Notes:

5. *a-gu-u ša* [^{d}]PA: see comments on *LAS* 57-58 and 276. Note the reference to a dedicatory inscription written in the names of *both* Esarhaddon *and* Šamaš-šumu-ukīn. This implies that the latter was residing in Babylonia in the capacity of crown prince at the time the letter was written. Cf. note to 280:11.

17. *ki-i ša* [*ina la*]-*bi-ri* "in olden times": possibly not referring to a more distant past than the time predating the destruction of Babylon (689 BC), to judge from *LAS* 309 r27: *ina la-bi-ri a-du* ŠÀ ^{I}MAN-GIN ^{I}*30*-PAP^{MEŠ}-SU "in olden times up to the reigns of Sargon and Sennacherib" (a letter written between 665 and 660 BC). Cf. however r10ff and corresponding note.

23, 25 and r1. ^{GUD}*šak-la-lu-te* and ^{GUD}*šak-lu-lu*: compare with these spellings NB writings such as ^{GUD}*šuk-lu-lu*^{MEŠ} (*CT* 22 46:7) and ^{GUD}*šuk-*<*lu*>*-la-nu*^{MEŠ} (*VAB* 4 114:2). The fact that GUD is here not followed by the plural sign and that *šuklulu* in NB could receive the plural morpheme *-ānu* of masculine nouns indicates that (the adjective) *šuklulu* was here used as a noun and the sign GUD could occasionally serve as a determinative, as in Urartian script (cf. ^{GUD}*paḫini* "bull", Melikišvili, *StPohl* 7 [1971] 85).[491] For additional

[490] The episode is datable to 678 BC on the ground of a chronicle entry referring to the deportation of Šamaš-ibni to Assyria in the third year of Esarhaddon (Borger, op.cit. p.122; Grayson, *TCS* 5 (1975) 83).

[491] This interpretation seems inevitable despite cases where *šuklulu* is clear used as an adjective, e.g. *gu*$_4$*-maḫ-ḫi šuk-lu-lu-ti* (var. *šuk-lul-ú-te*), Borger, *Ash* p.53:76. Cf. also the Nebuchadnezzar passage quoted below. – ^{GUD}*mu-u-ru*, *AnSt* 323:6 and ^{GUD}ÁB (var. ÁB, see note on 161:11) are further clear examples of the use of GUD as determinative of bovines in Akkadian.

references to $^{\text{(GUD)}}$*šaklulu* (= ^{GUD}ŠU.DU$_{7}$) in texts dealing with sacrifices, as well as for the rendering "bull without blemish; not castrated, ungelded bull", see Landsberger, *MSL* 8/1 (1960), p. 71 ff; the evidence at hand suggests that ungelded bulls were offered to major gods only, whereas minor gods had to content themselves with castrated ones (ibid.). With the present passage in general cf. Langdon, *VAB* 4, p.158f: *šá u$_{4}$-mu 1-en* GUD.MAḪ *ma-ra-a šuk-lu-lu* ^{4} *ša mi-na-a-tu-šu* [*šu*]*-uk-lu-la-a-at* ^{5} [*ša zu-mur*]*-šu pu-ṣa-am* ^{6} *16* UDU.NIṬÁ *mi-ri sú-lu-ḫe-e da-am-qu-tim* ^{7} *qá-du ša* DINGIR^{MEŠ} BÁR.SIPA^{KI} . . . ^{18} *pa-áš-šur* ^{d}AG *ù* ^{19}*Na-na-a* EN^{MEŠ}*-e-a* ^{20} *el šá pa-nu ú-da-áš-*[*ši*] "each day one fattened, choice bull without blemish, with perfect limbs and spot<less> skin, (as well as) 16 fattened sheep, excellent sacrificial lambs befitting? the gods of Borsippa . . . (Thus) I provided the sacrificial table of Nabû and Nanâ, my lords, with more (offerings) than ever before" (Nbk. No.19 A vii 3 ff).

25. *kāribu* "blesser": according to *CAD* K 216, a kind of priest; according to *AHw* 449*a*, "ein Fürbitt-priester". Personally, I would prefer Landsberger's more neutral rendering "frommer Stifter" (*BBEA* p.55) for a number of reasons. First, the word can hardly be separated from a well-attested meaning of *karābu*, "to dedicate an offering by pronouncing the relevant [blessing] formulae" (*CAD* K 197*b*), which is used of private individuals as well as of priests. Secondly, lexical evidence (nam-šita = *ka-ri-bu*, lú-šu$_{12}$-dè = KI.MIN, Lu IV 96f; context: *bēl parṣi* "performer of a religious ceremony" and *lābiš kitê* "person dressed in linen clothes"; si-is-kur AMAR×ŠE.AMAR×ŠE *ka-ri-bu*, Diri IV 4, context: *ikribu* "prayer" and *karābu* "to pray"), quoted in support of the dictionary renderings, does not in the least point to a specific clerical class; and thirdly, the present letter shows that the *k.* offerings did not form part of regular temple offerings, but were brought to the temple gate voluntarily and apparently on the *k.*'s own initiative. Accordingly, it seems more natural to see in *kāribu* a designation of any person wealthy enough to bless the king (cf. *CAD* K 195 sub *karābu* 2b) by dedicating to a temple a royal offering, viz. a blemishless bull (whose exta, judging from r1ff, were subsequently inspected in order to establish the divine response to the good deed done; cf. note on *LAS* 126 r1ff). In any case, it is clear that the offerings of the *kāribu* referred to in this letter were *not* "durch königliche Stiftungen gesicherte Institutionen der babylonischen Tempel" (thus Landsberger, l.c., fn.102), since they kept coming to the temple even though the responsible *šatammu* and the *šākin ṭēmi* had been brided to *obstruct* the royal order by which the regular offerings to the Nabû temple were supposed to be levied.

27. Cancel the translation of this line given in Pt. I (based on Landsberger, l.c.), and translate instead: "(The bulls) have been served on the table of Nabû." The passage of course does n o t mean that the magistrates brided by the shephers would have turned back all bulls of the "blessers" (how could *that* possibly have profited the shepherds?), but that they were c o n c e a l i n g their abuses by using the *kāribu* offerings instead of the institutional ones in setting the sacrificial table of Nabû. Cf. the many examples of *šēlû* in the meaning "to offer or dedicate something to a deity" in *CAD* E p.130*a*, and note especially *a-na* ^{GIŠ}BANŠUR *šu-ú-li* "serve (the sheep) on the sacrificial table!", *YOS* 6 156:20; similarly ibid.22 and *VAS* 15 37:5 (all NB).

r1-5. Though apparently introducting a new topic, this passage combines organically with the foregoing, giving additional evidence of corruption in the Nabû temple and thus supporting the interpretation of Obv.25ff suggested above. Referring to an inspection of exta in the *Nanâ* temple, of which he *had* "heard", Mār-Ištar goes on to point out that nothing was heard of such inspections carried out in the *Nabû* temple (r4f) – clearly implying that nothing *could* be heard since the bulls of the *kāribu* were exclusively used for the meals of the god. The translation given in Pt. I has to be modified accordingly; insert "(But)" before "All the citizens . . . ", and add quotation marks after ". . . from the country". The following question ("Why do they . . .") does not belong to the quotation, as indicated by the absence of the particle *ma-a* in Rev.5.

According to J. Aro (orally), no omens derived from *missing* kidneys are to be traced in Mesopotamian extispical literature. The omen referred to here was therefore perhaps included in the series *Šumma Izbu*, whose Tablet XIX (*TCS* 4 177ff)dealt with anomalies of bulls and cows (cf. also Tablet XVI 47'f, 79' and 83'). Though the interpretation of the omen was obviously a matter of no importance to the writer, it may be pointed out that since an abnormally large number of kidneys is interpreted as a lucky sign in r30f, the present case most probably was considered an unlucky one.

r10 ff. Contra copy Harper (and my transliteration in Pt. I) the left-hand portions of the fragmentary lines here have to be systematically moved one line upwards, so that the beginning of "r11" actually combines with the end of r10, and so on. This adjustment of course considerably affects the transliteration and translation of the passage given in Pt.I, which should be modified as follows:

10 [*lu-u*] *ú-di i-*[*su-ri a-n*]*a* MAN EN-*já i-qab-bi-i-u*
11 *ma-a* TA* *la-bi-r*[*i* NÍG.ŠID^{MEŠ}] ⌜*la*⌝ *ú-pu-šú*
12 *i-sa-na-li-i-*[*u ina* (ŠÀ) *ti*]*-il-ti*
13 *ša ḫur-sa-an š*[*a* ^{I}Bur-na-bu-*r*]*i-ja-áš*
14 MAN K[Á.DI]NGIR!^{KI} *q*[*a-bi ma-a ḫ*]*ur-sa-an*
15 L[Ú*]SI[PA^{MEŠ} NÍG.ŠID *ṭup-pa-šú a-na* MAN] EN-*já ú-se-bi-la*

"(The king, my lord,) should know this. [Perh]aps they tell the king, my lord: 'In olden times, [no accounts] were made.' (If so), they are cheating. [In] an ordeal proverb attributed to [Burnabur]ijaš, king of B[aby]lon, it is s[aid: 'The (time of) accounting is] the ordeal of sheph[erds].' I have dispatched [the relevant document to the king], my lord."

[The misplacement of the lines in Harper's copy is due to the fact that the two separate pieces of which this letter consists have been fitted together incorrectly; the gap separating the two fragments is slightly smaller than assumed by the maker of the join. Harper's copy renders the present form of the tablet accurately and is not to be blamed for the confusion.]

r13f. Besides [Burnabur]ijaš (for the various spellings of the name cf. *APN* p.66), one could of course also restore [Ulambur]ijaš or [Šagarakti-Šur]ijaš. The fame of Burnaburijaš II (1375-1347)[492], however, makes him the most likely alternative.[493] As far as I know, the proverb here quoted does not occur elsewhere.

r24 ff. Cf. *LAS* 282 r2' ff; referring to the same event?

r27. [*k*]*i-ip-su*: reading and interpretation uncertain; read perhaps rather [*k*]*i-ib-su* "steps".[494] Note the plural *il-lak-u-ni* in r28.

r30f. Cf. above, note to r1-5.

282

Bibliography:
Previously unpublished. Copy *CT* 53, pl.14 no.34.

Writer:
Certainly Mār-Ištar (note introductory formula, subject matter, orthography, and see App. M 6.

Addressee:
Esarhaddon.

Date:
Mid-Ajāru, eponymy of Šulmu-Bēl-lašme = early May 670 BC(?).Rev.2'ff looks like a reference to 281 r24ff, hence the date: but note that the letter seems otherwise to deal with affairs of Uruk only.

Notes:

6. Cf. No. 277. The present letter perhaps gave further details on the (incompleted) reconstruction work carried out in the temple of Mummu (277:24f).

7. *i-šáḫ-ḫu-*[*ṭu*]: Cf. 283 r7' and relevant note.

r12'. The interpretation of *ba-nu-a-ni* is uncertain; formally either Stat. 1st p. Pl. or 3rd p. Pl (+ Subj.) of **bnû* "to be beautiful" (*CAD* B 90ff, *AHw* 102f), but this verb is otherwise not attested in Neo-Assyrian. A Babylonianism?

r14'. Why is the king of Elam mentioned in this context? Cf. No.297; note also the reference to Na'id-Marduk, the deposed governor of the Sealand, on the left edge.

---

492 Cf. Brinkman, in Oppenheim, *Ancient Mesopotamia* (1964), p.338.
493 Cf. Weissbach, *RlA* 1 p.80 ff.
494 Cf. *ABL* 1349 r10, *kib-su an-ni-i ma-a'-du*.

L.E.1. *ki-i la ut ṭu a nu*: sic according to collation (C.B.E. Walker, 27.1.1976). One would expect *ki-i ba!-la!-ṭu-ni!* or *bal!-ṭu-ni!* "when [PN (and?)] Na'id-Marduk were alive".

283

Bibliography:
Previously unpublished. Copy *CT* 53, pl.37 no.106.

Writer:
Cf. corresponding note on the previous number.

Date:
Uncertain. A comparison of the letter with Nos.275, 284 and 291 would suggest a date of writing in the latter half of 671 or in 670 BC, but Rev.10'f calls for caution: if the king to whom the letter was sent was Esarhaddon, the "father of the king" said to have appointed a canal inspector in Akkad should be Sennacherib, and how can that be combined with *LAS* 275 telling that it was only Esarhaddon who repopulated Akkad? Consequently, the letter is perhaps to be placed in the beginning of the reign of Assurbanipal, like No.286 (q.v.; note also, though this certainly is a pure coincidence, that Gabbāru, mentioned in Rev.12', was eponym in 667). On the other hand, the "father of the king" referred to in *LAS* 291:4' was certainly Sennacherib; and, as a matter of fact, nothing really *prevents* this being the case here, too, since there is no *concrete* proof that the city of Akkad was totally uninhabited in the reign of Sennacherib and next to nothing is known about Sennacherib's administrative measures in Babylonia on the whole.[495]

Discussion:

While the obverse of this letter deals with the fashioning of divine statues for various temples of B a b y l o n (Esangil is mentioned in Obv.12, but other temples were also involved, cf. the notes below), the reverse deals with reconstruction work carried out in A k k a d. This does not imply that Mār-Ištar used Akkad as a "cover name" for Babylon, as suggested by Landsberger (*BBEA* [1965] p.38 ff), but rather that both cities were being restored at the same time. See in detail the commentary to No. 275.

Notes:

6. ^{d}⸢X⸣.⸢IB⸣?.KÀD.AN.NÉ.SI: sic according to collation, except that the last sign is not SI but clear E (Sollberger, 19.1.1976). Possibly a scribal mistake for ^{d}AMA.GÙ/GÚ.AN.NÉ.SI or ^{d}AMA.TU.GÙ.AN.(NÉ.)SI.[496] Cf. [.......] ^{d}AMA.TUR : ŠU ^{22} [.......] ^{d}AMA.TU.GÙ.AN.SI ^{23} [......] ^{d}GU.LA.KE$_4$ (*CT* 24 47:21 ff = An-Anum, Tablet V, section dealing with the court of Gula) and ^{9} ⸢^{d}⸣AMA.TUR ŠU ^{10}⸢^{d}⸣AMA.Ù.TU ŠU ^{11} ⸢^{d}⸣AMA.GÙ.AN.NÉ.SI ŠU (*KAV* 69:9ff, list of gods); note also ^{d}KÙ!.AN.NÉ.SI = DAM.BI MÍ (*CT* 25 6:17, referring to the spouse of Lugalgirra), ^{d}GÙ^{gu}.A.NU.SI = ditto (= Allatum, *CT* 25 4:25) and ^{d}GÚ.AN.NÉ.SI.I[L] = ^{d}NIN.URTA (*CT* 25 13:35; also ^{d}GÚ.AN.NÉ.SI.ÍL$^{gu-an-né-si-il-la-ku}$ = ditto, ibid. 1:12). If the suggested emendation is accepted, the present passage could be taken as evidence of the restoration of a Gula-temple in Babylon, carried out simultaneously with the restoration of Esangil; which of the t h r e e Gula-temples of Babylon (see Unger, *RlA* I p.351) is in question remains unclear.

7. ^{d}*Šar-ra-ḫi-i-ti*: A goddess worshiped in Esangil.[497] Cf. ^{d}*Šar-ra-ḫi-tum* = ^{d}*Aš-rat ša É-sag-íl* = ^{d}*Šá-ra-ḫi-i-tú* = ^{d}*Aš-rat a-ḫi-i-tum* "Š. = Ašrat of Esangil; Š. = foreign Ašrat", *ZA* 6 (1891) 241, 11; for ^{d}Ašrat (consort of Amurru) see Ebeling, *RlA* 1 p.169, and cf. [^{d}*Aš-ra*]-*tum* = DAM.BI MÍ (scil. Amurru), *CT* 25 23:20*b*. In *BRM* 2 55:5 Šarraḫītu is equated with Bēlet-ṣēri, a goddess also regarded as the consort of Amurru (^{d}GAŠAN.GÚ.EDIN.NA | ^{d}NIN.GÚ.EDIN.NA | DAM.BI MÍ [scil. Amurru], *2 R* 53, 43*a*). Note, however, that Šarraḫītu and Bēlet-ṣeri are kept clearly apart in *TuL* No.2 I 16f (^{d}*Be-lit* EDEN = LUGAL *ša Du-ni-sa-i-di*^{KI} ^{17} ^{d}*Šár-ra-i-tum* = *šar-rat Šu-*^{d}EN.ZU^{KI}), if ^{d}*Šár-ra-i-tum* = Šarraḫītu, as suggested by Ebeling, ibid. p.10.

---

495 Note that in *ABL* 327,, a letter addressed to Esarhaddon, Sennacherib is said to have safeguarded the water-supply of Nippur (granting the Nippurians the permission to use water of the *Banītu* canal).

496 The last signs can hardly be read *an-ni-e* "this"; the gen. of *anniu* is otherwise consistently spelled *an-ni-i* in letters of Mār-Ištar.

497 and in Uruk. Cf. *RAcc.* 114:17 (wr. ^{d}*Ša-ra-ḫi-i-tum*).

8. ^{d}*NIN.É.GAL*: Consort of Uraš (cf. on obv.10), worshiped in Dilbat (mod. Dulaim, ca. 25 km south of Babylon); cf. ^{d}IB *u* ^{d}NIN.É.[GAL] *KAV* 154:7 (a list of god-pairs, cf. Schroeder, *StOr* 1 [1925] 259 ff); *pa-pa-ḫu* ^{d}IB *u* ^{d}NIN.É.GAL, *VS* 5 35:9; ^{d}IB *ù* ^{d}NIN.É.GAL *a-na* DIN ZI^{MEŠ} . . *šá* LUGAL *kiš-šat* . . *ú-ṣal-la* "I am praying to Uraš and Ninegal for the sake of life of the king of the world", *ABL* 326:2-4 (a letter from Dilbat); similarly *ABL* 994:4.

9. ^{d}*ZA.BA$_4$.BA$_4$*: The city-god of Kiš, see Tallqvist, *Götterepitheta* (1938), p.483. There was possibly a Zabāba temple in Babylon, too, Unger, *RlA* 1 p.363.[498] The reading of the god's name as Zabāba (not Zamama) is assured by Ea IV 220, ba-a GÁ *šá* ^{d}*Za*-GÁ.GÁ, and by the spelling ${}^{I.d}$*Za*-KÁ (= *bābu*)-SU (*ADD* 46 = AR 302:7. 10, ND 2323 and 2326 [*Iraq* 16 42]) for normal ${}^{I.d}$ZA.BA$_4$.BA$_4$ SU (passim). Note also the spelling ^{d}*Za-ba-ba* in BM 121206 v 2' (van Driel, *CA* 80, coll. W. Farber in *BiOr* 30 (1973) 435) besides ^{d}ZA.BA$_4$.BA$_4$ ibid. 14'.

10. ^{d}*IB*: This god was primarily worshiped in Dilbat (see Tallqvist, *Götterepitheta* [1938] p.480 and Deimel, *Pantheon Babylonicum* [1914] p.143), but had also a shrine in Babylon, probably in the neighbourhood of the Uraš gate; see Unger, *RlA* 1 p.363, and cf. p.342. The name Uraš (cf. ${}^{d.}$${}^{ú-ra-aš}$IB, *CT* 24 19:2, 49:2 etc.) is probably a derivative from the root '$_3$*rš* "to cultivate", as indicated by the god's late title "Marduk of cultivation" ([^{d}]IB ^{d}AMAR+UD *šá e-re-šú*, *CT* 24 50 No.47408:1).

^{d}*È[R.R]A.GAL*: restoration uncertain; traces fit, but this god (a manifestation of Nergal, cf. *CT* 24 36: 52ff) did not, as far as is known, have a shrine of his own in Babylon. On the other hand, there were as many as three different temples of *Nergal* in Babylon, see Unger, *RlA* 1 p.359.

^{d}*LUGAL.[MARAD.DA]*: This city god of Marad (mod. Wannah wa-ṣ-Ṣadūm, ca. 50 km SE of Babylon) also had a shrine of his own in Babylon, see Unger, *RlA* 1 p.352. Besides the suggested restoration, there are several alternative ones: ^{d}LUGAL.[GÌR.RA] (cf. *ABL* 877:11), ^{d}LUGAL.[BÀN.DA] and ^{d}LUGAL.[GIŠ.ASAL] (for the two latter cf. Unger, *loc. cit.*).

r4' (ff). Cf. Herodotus' account of the building of the outer walls of Babylon: "As they dug the fosse, they made bricks of the earth which was carried out of the place they dug, and when they had moulded bricks enough they baked them in ovens; then using hot bitumen for cement and interposing layers of wattled reeds at every thirtieth course of bricks, they built the border of the fosse and then the wall itself in the same fashion. –– There is another city called Is, eight days' journey from Babylon, where is a little river, also named Is, a tributary stream of the river Euphrates; from the source of this river Is rise with the water many gouts of bitumen, and from thence the bitumen was brought for the wall of Babylon." (Book I 179, translat. of A.D. Godley, Loeb Classical Library, 1920). The city of Is referred to is identical with modern Hît, which is even today noted for its bitumen resources (A. Salonen, *Ziegeleien* p. 54) and occurs in Assyrian sources as ^{URU}ÍD or ^{URU}*I-tu* (see *AOAT* 6 p.179 and cf. *ina pu-ut* ^{URU}ÍD *ina* SAG *e-ni šá ku-up-ri*, Schramm, "Die Annalen des assyrischen Königs Tukulti-Ninurta II (890-884 v.Chr.)", *BiOr* 27 [1970], 150:59). Unfortunately it does not seem possible, because of the determinative KUR, to restore ⌜*I*⌝-[*te*] in the present context: moreover, there is no evidence that the city of It had a governor (^{LÚ*}EN.NAM, r8) of its own, though this is of course possible taking into consideration the economic importance of the region. On the other hand, the restoration ^{KUR}⌜*I*⌝ [*sa na*] made in Pt.I seems also abortive since Isana most probably was located north of Ḫindāna (on the Euphrates ca. 34°30' N.lat.; cf. note to 309:15, *AOAT* 6 p.176 and see Forrer, *Provinzeinteilung* p.12) and would thus be too far from it to be the capital of the province to which the latter city belonged.[499] A more plausible restoration would perhaps be ^{KUR}⌜*I*⌝-[*tu-'i*], considering that the city of It obviously was situated in the immediate vicinity of the homeland of the Itu'eans.[500] However, this restoration also suffers from the lack of references to a governor of the Itu'aeans in other texts.

r6'f. For *ebertu šaḫāṭu* "to glaze (kiln-fired) bricks" see now A. Salonen, *BiOr* 28 (1971) and *Ziegeleien* (1972) 67ff; correct the translation of the passage given in Pt.I.[501] The proposed interpretation of *šaḫāṭu* as a

498 Note also the courtyard of Ištar and Zabāba (*kisal Ištar u Zabāba*) in Esagil, ibid. p. 354.

499 Note that Ḫindāna had a governor of its own (*AOAT* 6 l.c.).

500 Cf. *AOAT* 6 180 and the Tukulti-Ninurta passage cited above.

501 Postgate, *JRAS* 1974 p. 52f, has criticized Salonen's interpretation of *šaḫāṭu* and would revert to the old rendering "to mould (bricks)". This is not possible, however, since in most cases the object of *šaḫāṭu* is *epertu* "burnt brick" (for gilded and glazed sundried bricks see presently). In *ABL* 1180 the straw may have served as fuel.

terminus technicus for brick glazing is supported by the present passage (overlooked by Salonen), where *i-šaḫ-ḫu-ṭu* is followed by the verb *sakāru* "to gild (bricks)."[502] For the use of glazed and gilded bricks in the building of monumental (especially sacral) edifices see Langdon, *VAB* 4, passim; cf. also *LAS* 291:14f, *ABL* 119:9-15, and *ADD* 932:4 (*108* SIG$_4$^{MEŠ}KÙ.UD "108 silver-coated bricks"), and note that sun-dried bricks, with the remains of gilding, have been discovered together with enamelled bricks in Nimrud[503] and other Mesopotamian cities of the Neo-Assyrian/Neo-Babylonian periods (see, e.g., Unger, *RlA* 3 29f).

r9'. ^{LÚ}*ú-ra-si*: see note to 277 r20.

r12'. On *Gabbāru* and the passage in general see above, sub Date.

284

Bibliography:

Previously unpublished. Copy *CT* 53, pl.28 no.75.

Writer:

Certainly Mār-Ištar. The correctness of this attribution can be easily tested by means of the criteria listed in App. M 6.

Addressee:

Esarhaddon.

Date:

Between Ajāru and Tašrītu (= April to September), 670 BC, approximately. The terminus post quem is obtained from the treaty stipulation of Obv.24ff concerning the extradition and returnal of [Assyrian] refugees to their home country. Such a stipulation is not found in the Vassal Treaties of Esarhaddon, though it does occur elsewhere (see note on Obv.24ff), and it is therefore extremely likely that it had been included in the treaty because of the complot against Esarhaddon crushed in Nisannu 670 (see commentary to 247). That Assyrians involved in the complot had fled to Babylonia is established with certainty by TKSM 21/676, the so-called "Ist.-Brief" edited by Landsberger, *BBEA*, which at the same time gives the approximate terminus ad quem (lines 33 ff): *2* ^{LÚ}SAG^{MEŠ} ^{34} *ul-tu* KUR ^{d}*Aš+šur ki-i iḫ-li-qu-ni* ^{35} ^{LÚ}*qí-i-pi ina* É-*šú ip-te-sím-šú-nu-ti* ^{36} *ù en-na a-na* BÁR.SIPA^{KI} ^{37} *il-ta-par-šú-nu-ti a-na-ku* ^{38} *ul a-šal-laṭ-ma ul-tu* BÁR.SIPA ^{39} *ul ú-še-ṣa-a ki-i pa-an* LUGAL EN-*já* ^{40} *maḫ-ru* ^{LÚ}DUMU-*šip-ri šá* LUGAL ^{41} *it-ti-šú-nu lil-li-kam-ma* ^{42} *a-šar áš-bu li-bu-ku-ni* . . . ^{45} ^{LÚ}SAG *šá* LUGAL EN-*a iš-pu-ra* ^{46} *aṣ-ṣa-bat-su a-du-u ina* ŠU ^{I}DUMU-^{d}*15* ^{47} *ú-šu-uz-za-ku ki-i šá dul-la-ni* ^{48} *nu-uq-ta-at-tu-ú it-ti-já* ^{49} *ab-ba-kaš-šú* "The two eunuchs had, after their flight from Assyria, been hidden by the royal delegate (cf. Obv.12 of the present text!) in his house, but now he has sent them to Borsippa . . . If it is acceptable to the king, my lord, let a royal messenger come with them and pick up the eunuchs (before they get informed and go elsewhere). I have arrested the eunuch about whom the king, my lord, wrote to me. I am at the moment at the disposal of Mār-Ištar, but after we have finisched our task, I shall take the eunuch with me (to Nineveh)." For reasons stated in commentary to *LAS* 286, this letter was certainly written in the last year of Esarhaddon, and the reference to the eunuchs places it most naturally in 670. The fact that the writer was expected to pay a visit to the king very strongly points to the beginning of the month Tašrītu, cf. on the date of *LAS* 277, and the same is suggested by the affinity of the letter with *LAS* 286. It would seem that the "Ist.-Brief" postdates the present letter, supposing that the action of the royal delegate mentioned in lines 36f was occasioned by the treaty quoted in the present letter.

Notes:

6ff. It is uncertain whether the writer here refers to the Ezida of Borsippa or Babylon. The former is however the more probable alternative. Cf. *du-ú* BARAG^{MEŠ} *qe-er-bi-šú* ^{58} *pi-ti-iq ka-as-pa* . . . ^{61} *ú-ba-an-nim* "I a-

---

[502] Missing in *AHw*, but note, in addition to the present passage, *ABL* 1194:7 *i-sa-ki-ru-šú* "they will use it for gilding." The adjective *sakru* (*sakiru/sagēru*, Bibl. *sāgūr*), "(gold) hammered to thin foils", "pure (gold)" also belongs here. Note *ABL* 114:18f.

[503] See Layard, *Nineveh and Its Remains* II, p.264; cf. ibid. 312.

dorned its platforms and daises with cast silver", *VAB* 4 128:57ff (referring to the Ezida of Barsip); and [BARAG NAM]^{MEŠ} *šu-bat ši-tul-ti ša* ^{d}AG . . . ^{14} [*ina* KI].SAG *eb-bi nak-liš ap-ti-iq-ma* "I artistically coated the shrine of destiny, the habitation of Nabû (of Barsip) with pure silver", Borger, *Ash* p.95:13f.

8f. In spite of the traces in line 9, one should probably read here *a-na man-za-al-ti* MAN EN-*já* ^{9} ⌜*ša*⌝! *É-sag-gíl* and translate: "(Limestone) for the 'stand' of the kind, my lord, *in* Esagil." The stand in question almost certainly refers to (an) inscribed slab(s) on which the king was to perform ritual acts of worship before Marduk in the god's holy chamber É-tuš-a. Cf. "Ist.-Brief", obv.10ff.[504]

10. *is-qa-a-te*: to judge from the context, the term here refers to "shares of booty" (scil. from Egypt) or other "income assigned by a ruler to cities, temples and individuals" (*CAD* I/J 199f) rather than to "income derived form temples (prebends) assigned to officials of the sanctuaries" (ibid. 200*b*). No doubt the "shares" were meant to cover at least partially the expenses of the work of restoration being carried out all over Babylonia. Note that the "shares" were *not* assigned to the officials providing the labour power (*šatammu*, *šākin ṭēmi*) nor to the supervisors (*bēl piqitti*) but to the royal "delegates" (*qēpu*); this seems to validate Landsberger's definition of this official as "einen direkt dem König unterstellten Aufsichtsführer über den *šatammu* und Garnisonskommandanten" (*BBEA* p.30).

11. ^{I}*Id-ri-a-ḫa-a-ú*: possibly identical with ^{I}*Ad-ra-a-ḫa-ú/u* of *ABL* 775:7.r18 (a letter from Dēr to Esarhaddon; brings [for the Assyrian garrison at Dēr?] a dispatchment of sandals and then leaves for Nineveh); note also ^{I}*Id-ri-a-ḫa-ú*, *ABL* 593 r2 (fragmentary context). The name is to be analysed, according to Dr. Klaus Bayer (Heidelberg) as /ʿidrī-aḫā-hū/ "my brother is my help"; for the interchange <i ~a> in the first syllable cf. note to 39 r3.

15-19. These lines certainly deal with foundation ceremonies, the object of which however unfortunately remains obscure. A number of points suggest, nevertheless, that a building of considerable importance was in question. Note, firstly, that the adjuration of the delegates of (all) Babylonia was obviously deliberately synchronized with the laying of the foundation stones, as if the latter would have been an incident worthy of the greatest possible publicity. Secondly, it is worth noticing that as many as *seven* foundation stones were involved in the ceremonies, not just one as usual in ancient Assyrian[505] as well as modern foundation rituals. The religious implications of the number 7 should not be overlooked, either, and the solemn expression *a-na ṣa-a-ti* u_4*-me* (Obv.18) was certainly not used when laying the foundations of minor chapels (cf. "as the bricks of Etemenanki are established forever, so . . ." *VAB* 4 64 iii 46, and similar passages). Perhaps, then, the delegates were witnessing an occasion as important as the laying of the foundations of Marduk's private sanctuary (É-tuš-a) or the ziqqurrat of Esangil. Was the edifice under construction identical with the "dais" (i.e., sanctuary) mentioned in Obv.21, and if not, why was the dais mentioned at all?[506] Cf. also the following note (at end).

16f. The ceremony described here (slaughtering a ram and smearing the stones with its blood) markedly deviates from the accounts of foundation ceremonies found in royal inscriptions, and may therefore have had a special significance. Cf., e.g., Esarhaddon's account of the laying of the foundations of Esangil (Borger, *Ash* p.22, Ep.27:21f): [DINGIR^{MEŠ}] GAL^{MEŠ} *ù* ^{d}SIG$_4$ EN *uš-ši* SIG$_4$ ^{UDU}SISKUR^{MEŠ} KÙ^{MEŠ} B[AL-*qí*] ^{22} [. . .] A GEŠTIN *ku-ru-un-ni uš-ši-šú-un ad-di-ma ú-kin te-me-en-*[*šun*] "I performed pure sacrifices to the great gods and Kulla, the lord of the fundament and the brickwork, I laid their foundations [upon a . . . mixed with] wine and choice beer, and made their superstructure durable": though animal sacrifices are mentioned here, the *blood* of the victims is not, and the emphasis is put on the beverages poured into the foundations. Cf. further *ABL* 471 r7ff: *ina* UGU ŠEM.ḪI.A ^{8} Ì DÙG.GA ^{IM}SIG$_7$ SIG$_7$ *ù* NA$_4$^{MEŠ} ^{9} [*ša ina* Š]À URU$_4$ *ni-kur-ru-ru-u-ni* "as to the

---

504 Cf. also K 4732+Sm 1081 (unp., courtesy W.G. Lambert), rev.1ff: *ši-ik-nu ša* UGU [^{N}]A$_4$ I.DIB^{MEŠ} ^{2}*ša* NA$_4$*a-lal-lum ša* É ^{d}*aš+šur* ^{3}*ša* LUGAL *ina muḫ-ḫi i-za-zu-ni* ^{4}*'kaq-qu-ru i-na-áš-ši-qu-ni* "the arrangement (of script) on the *alallu*-slabs of the temple of Aššur on which the king stands and kisses the ground."

505 Cf. the passages quoted in Deller + Parpola, *RA* 60 (1966) 63.

506 As the daises of major Mesopotamian gods were built of massive limestone slabs (cf. e.g. the pedestal of Nabû in Ezida of Calah, Mallowan *Nimrud* I 262f), it is thinkable that the *pūlāni* mentioned here refer to the slabs forming the dais of Marduk and accordingly should not be translated "foundation stones" but "limestone slabs".

parfumes, sweet oil, *da'matu*-paste and (precious) stones which we shall place [in] the foundations (of Etemenanki)".[507] While similar examples exist in abundance, evidence of the use of blood in foundation ceremonies is much harder to find, yet the present letter is by no means unique in this respect. A text from Assur refers to "2 rams sacrificed upon the foundations of new 'houses'" (*2* <UDU.NITÁ^{MEŠ}> *a-na* UGU *uš-še* 7 *ša* É^{MEŠ} 8 *ep-šú*, VAT 9375 = *AfO* 10 32:6ff); Layard, *Nineveh and Its Remains* II 256, tells he found "on all the slabs forming entrances in the oldest palace of Nimroud . . . marks of black fluid, resembling blood, which appeared to have been daubed on the stone", and adds: "I have not been able to ascertain the nature of this fluid, but its appearance cannot fail to call to mind the Jewish ceremonies, of placing the blood of the sacrifice on the lintel of the doorway" (ibid.). The most important parallel to the present passage, however, is provided by the Tempelbau-Ritual edited by R. Borger in *ZA* 61 (1971) 72ff and *Symbolae Böhl* (1973) 50ff, the relevant part of which reads as follows (*Symbolae Böhl* 51, Si. 12 r4'ff): [*e-nu-m*]*a* URU$_4$ É LÚ BAD-*ú ina* 1[T]U DÙG.GA *ina u$_4$-mu šal-mu* GIM URU$_4$ BAD-*ú* SIG$_4$ Š[U]B-*ú* . . . 7' *a-na* ^{d}SIG$_4$ EN URU$_4$ *u* SIG$_4$.HI.A KEŠDA *tar-káš* NÍG.NA ŠEM^{LI} GAR-*an* KAŠ.SAG 8' BAL-*qí* Ì.GIŠ *hal-ṣa* Ì ^{GIŠ}ERIN Ì ^{GIŠ}ŠUR.MÌN LÀL GA GEŠTIN NA$_4$ ^{MEŠ} DÙ.A.BI KÙ.UD KÙ.GI 9' ŠEM.HI.A DÙ.A.BI *a-na* ŠÀ ^{d}ÍD *ta-za-ar-ru* UDU.NITÁ KUD-*ma* ÚŠ^{MEŠ}-*šú ana* ŠÀ URU$_4$ 10' [*ta-tab*]-*bak*

"[I]f one has to open the foundations of a house, in a propitious month, on a favourable day, when he opens the foundations and lays the brick . . . you set up an offering arrangement to Kulla, the lord of foundations and brickwork, set out a censer of juniper, libate fine beer, scatter pressed-out sesame, cedar resin, cypress oil, honey, milk, wine, all kinds of stone, silver, gold and all kinds of aromatics into the River god, *sacrifice a ram and pour its blood into the foundations*."

After an incantation, the prescription to sacrifice a ram and pour its blood into the foundations is repeated again (r.15').

While the use of blood in foundation ceremonies thus certainly was an established custom, the emphasis given to this particular detail in the present letter is nevertheless worth attention. Did the ram perhaps function as a scapegoat, and was its blood used for washing away the sacrilege committed in the destruction of Babylon and its temples, in a way so well known from the Old Testament? Such an interpretation would seem justified, supposing that ceremonies pertaining to the cella of Marduk were in question, for blood was used for cathartic purposes in Mesopotamia too. Cf. ^{LÚ}MAŠ.MAŠ *ina* KÁ AN.AŠ.ÀM È-*ma* UDU.NITÁ [. . .] 20 *ina* KÁ É.GAL BAL-*qí ina* ÚŠ MÁŠ-*zi šu-a-tum* I.[DIB^{MEŠ}] 21 LU.BAR^{MEŠ} *u sip-pé-e 15 u 2,30 šá* KÁ É.GA[L . .] "The exorcist goes to the outer gate and sacrifices a ram [. . .] at the gate of the palace; with the blood of the (scape)goat he [smears] the thre[sholds] . . . and lintels on the right and left sides of the palace gate", *BBR* 26 iii 19ff (in a context dealing with purificatory rites); note also *CT* 4 5:27, 17 5:50ff and the "Yom Kippur" passage *RAcc* 141. 350ff prescribing the purification of Esaggil with the carcass of a slaughtered ram (*ina pag-ri* UDU.NITÁ ^{LÚ}MAŠ.MAŠ É *ú-kap-par*, l. 354).

18. Restore perhaps [*ina* (ŠÀ) *uš-še i-š*]*ak-ku-nu*, cf. *ABL* 628:6f.

19-22. For the structure of this sentence cf. *VTE* 41f (*a-de-e ša* RN *ina* IGI DINGIR^{MEŠ} . . . *is-se-ku-nu iš-ku-nu-u-ni*), 153ff and 351f; *Iraq* 34 22:28ff (*a-de-e is-se-šú-nu is-sa-kan . . . ut-ta-me-šú-nu*) *LAS* 247:22 etc. The inserted line 20 is in view of its position, perhaps to be compared with the heading of the "Vassal-Treaties", NA$_4$KIŠIB ^{d}*A-šur$_4$* LUGAL DINGIR^{MEŠ} EN KUR.KUR *ša la šu-un-né-e* "seal of the god Aššur, king of the gods, lord of the lands, not to be altered" (Wiseman, *VTE* p.30). For other NA treaties (*adê*), see the commentaries on *LAS* 1 and 247; on the relationship of the present treaty to the "Vassal-Treaties", see above, note on the date of the letter.

24 ff. A similar provision pertaining to the extradition of political refugees is also found in the Sfire-treaty (Donner – Röllig, *KAI*, No.224:19 ff: *wyqrq qrqy ʾl ḥdhm wyqrq qr* 20 *qhm wyʾth ʾly hn hšb zy ly ʾhšb [zy lh wʾ]l tʿšqny ʾt whn lhn šqrt bʿdyʾ* 21 *ln* "Wenn mein Flüchtling zu einem von ihnen flieht, und wenn ihr Flüchtling flieht und zu mir kommt – wenn er (mir) zurückgibt, was mir gehört, (dann) werde ich (ihm) zurückgeben, [was ihm gehört. Und] du selbst sollst mir [ni]cht mit Gewalt dazwischentreten! Wenn (du) das jedoch nicht (tust), (dann) hast du diese Vereinbarungen gebrochen") and the treaty of Šamši-Adad V with Marduk-zākir-šumi I (Weidner, *AfO* 8 28:12'-14'). Cf. also Borger, *Ash* p.103 i 15, *šar-ra-qa-ku-ma ina hi-ṭi ah-ṭu-u 50.*ÀM *im-bé-e*

[507] Cf. *VAB* 4 62 ii 45ff (Nabopolassar), etc.!

lu-ma-li [16] *áš-šú 1-en ḫal-qu mun-nab-tú* DUMU KUR *Aš+šur 1 me-a-a ri-bi-šú lu-ri-ib* "I have been a thief; for what I have done wrong I will compensate the losses fifty-fold, and for every Assyrian deserter and runaway I will give a compensation hundredfold" (king of Šubria speaking), and ibid. p.106 iii 32 *[áš]-šú a-de-e na-ṣa-rim-ma* . . . [34] *[ḫal-qu] mun-nab-tú* KURURI-*aju 1-en ul ak-la e-du ul e-zib ana* KUR-*šú-nu ú-tir-šú-nu-ti* "to execute the terms of the treaty . . . I did not retain or leave behind one single Urartean deserter or runaway but had them returned to their country." LU***ḫu-u[b]-tu* in line 24 has probably to be understood as a collective designation of people deported from Babylonia; cf. *CAD* Ḫ p.216.

r4. *Ru'ūa*: one of the several Aramean tribes living in Babylonia in Sargonid times.[508] The name occurs frequently in historical sources from the reigns of Tiglatpileser III, Sargon, Sennacherib and Assurbanipal, but the present occurrence seems to be the only one from the time of Esarhaddon (cf. *AOAT* 6 p.295). This is certainly due to the anarchy prevailing in Babylonia under Esarhaddon.[509] Sennacherib had designated Ru'ūans as "not submissive" (LÚ*Ru-'u-u-a* LÚ*A-ra-mu la kan-šu*, *OIP* 2 p.57:15), and it is more than likely that this designation fully applied to the tribe in the reign of Esarhaddon, too. It is not likely, however, that this tribe alone was responsible for the troubles reported in the present letter, though the data on its whereabouts (in the reign of Sennacherib, around the Uqnû/Kerḫa River[510]; in the reign of Assurbanipal, in the vicinity of Ur and Uruk[511]) would in itself allow such an interpretation: The fact that the son of Nikkal-iddina (cf. on r14) could consider interfering with the affairs of the rivaling tribes indicates that the base of the troubles was in the vicinity of Ur, and the reference to the Canal of Merodach-Baladan (r16) points decisively to the surroundings of Uruk.

r11f. *i-sa-a-ḫe-iš id-du-ub-bu*: in lieu of the translation given in Pt.I, render rather: ". . . have conspired with each other" (cf. *CAD* D 8). Does the writer refer to a tribal agreement made with or against the Ru'uans? In any case, many tribes must have been involved in it, as it is unthinkable that a single tribe could have had as many as 80 sheikhs (cf. Brinkman, *AnOr* 43 274f). Some of the tribes probably were under Assyrian control, cf. r14.

r12. *ṭè-en-šú-nu la iš-še-me*: interpretation uncertain, as *ṭēmu* can mean either "order" or "report/news", and *šamû* both "hear" and "listen to, obey". The likeliest translation is, however, judging from the context, "no news of them has been heard" (cf. Pt.I).

r13. *pa-ḫu-te*: probably for /palḫūti/, note *libbu šakānu* "to encourage" in the following line and cf. *ip-tal-ḫu* ŠÀ *nu-sa-áš-kin-šú-nu*, 280 r7f. It is not excluded, however, that a Babylonianism in the idiolect of Mār-Ištar is in question: cf. *peḫû* "verschlossen, dumm" (*AHw*. 852f, O/NB examples only), especially *pe-ḫu-ú-te* "dumm, unfähig" in an inscription of Assurbanipal (Bauer, *IWA* p.77 r13).

r14. *"The son of Nikkal-iddina"*: almost certainly referring to Sîn-balāssu-iqbi, who succeeded his father as governor of Ur approximately in the middle of the reign of Esarhaddon (cf. Brinkman, *Or* NS 34 [1965] 248; Dietrich, *AOAT* 7 [1970] 38f).[512] Nikkal-iddina also had two other sons, Sîn-tabni-uṣur and Sîn-šarra-uṣur, but these gained political significance only 20 years later under Assurbanipal and Šamaš-šumu-ukīn (cf. Brinkman, l.c. 253f and Dietrich, o.c. 110f).

r16. *ḫar-ru ša* I.d*AMAR+UD-IBILA-AŠ*: a canal supplying Uruk with water (from the Euphrates?), dug by Merodach-Baladan in 718 BC; also mentioned in *ABL* 747:8f, 942 r13, 1293+, *YOS* 3 74, and *AnOr* 9 no.1; cf. Brinkman, *Studies Oppenheim* (1964) 17[89] and Dietrich, o.c. 177. On the blocking of the canal as a device to force submission, see Brinkman, *AnOr* 43 (1968) 43, and Kraus, *Symbolae M. David* II (1968) 9-40; cf. also Layard, *Nineveh and Babylon* (abr. edition), 269: ". . . This busy throng was building up the dam which was to shut

508 See Brinkman, *AnOr* 43 (1968) p. 270 ff.

509 The general situation appears to have been closely parallel to that prevalent in southern Iraq towards the end of the Turkish domination; cf. Layard, *Nineveh and Babylon* (abridged ed.), p.266 f: "During my residence in Baghdad no one could go far beyond the gates without the risk of falling into the hands of wandering Arabs, who prowled unchecked over the plains, keeping the city itself almost in a continual state of siege", and other similar passages ibid.

510 Cf. Luckenbill, *OIP* 2 49:13.

511 Cf. Dietrich, *AOAT* 7 101f and Parpola, *AOAT* 6 s.v.

512 Note than in *ABL* 445, a letter to the crown prince (Assurbanipal), Sîn-balassu-iqbi, already governor, is likewise *explicitly* referred to as "the son of Nikkal-iddina".

out the waters of the Euphrates from the canal, dry the marshes, and bring the rebellious tribes to obedience. . ."

r21. The restoration [*ša*] ⌜É⌝.DINGIR suggested for the beginning of this line in Pt.I has to be given up since "temple" is elsewhere in the letters of Mār-Ištar always written É.DINGIR^{MEŠ}.[513] Restore instead [TA* *p*]*a!-an* ^{LÚ*}GÚ.DU$_8$.A^{KI}*-a-a*[514] and translate: "(the commandant . . . has taken) from the Cuthaeans (so-and-so many sheep and oxen)".[515] The commandant denounced was possibly named Ašarēdu; cf. Dietrich, *WO* 4 (1967/8) 220ff and *AOAT* 7 162ff.

r22f. *ma-'a-áš-šú* and *m*]*a-'i-i-šú*: sic. Certainly not mistakes for *ma-a'-da* and *ma-'a-ad.*

285

Bibliography:

Previously unpublished. Copy *CT* 53, pl.39 no.116.

Writer:

Attribution to Mār-Ištar is certain on the grounds of the spelling *li-diri-i-u* (A 4'), the format of the tablet, the handwriting and the orthographical conventions on the whole; cf. Appendix M 6. Note also the affinities of Side A with *LAS* 279:15ff and 287.

Addressee:

Esarhaddon.

Date:

Late Ābu, eponymy of Šulmu-Bēl-lašme = early August, 670 BC. Cf. Obv.3'-7' and see commentary on *LAS* 190.

Notes:

A 1'f. Part of a quotation? Cf. *LAS* 288 and 294 (the fragments do not join).

A 7'. *pe-te* K[Á] = /pēt bābi/ (cf. *AHw* 871*a* s.v. *pītu*). For the paragogic *-e* see note to 259 r9f, for the ceremony itself, commentary to 190.

B 6'. This is probably a reference to the destruction of Babylon by Sennacherib in 689 BC. Since full 20 years had not yet passed from this incident by the middle of 670 BC, one should perhaps read 20 MU.A[N.NA "the 20th year" rather than MU.A[N.NA^{MEŠ}].

286

Bibliography:

(I) Waterman, *RCAE* 257.
(II) Behrens, *ABB* (1906) 50; Schott, *OLZ* 40 (1937) 296; Poebel, *AS* 9 (1939) 88; Deller, *Or* NS 31 (1962) 229; Landsberger, *BBEA* (1965) 52.

Addressee:

Assurbanipal(?).

Date:

Probably Ulūlu 3, eponymy of Gabbāru = September 4, 667 BC, less likely Ulūlu 3, eponymy of Sulmu-Bēl-lašme = August 9, 670 BC. The month and day are obtained from r10' (cf. note); r8' shows that the letter was written in a leap year containing an intercalary Ulūlu, hence either in 670 or 667 (cf. App.A1). Which of these years has to be preferred depends on the relevance of the eclipse prediction communicated in r8'ff. No lunar eclipse occurred (nor was liable to occur) in Tašrītu 670, whereas a lunar eclipse *did* take place in Tašrītu 667, just as predicted here (cf. App. F1). Accordingly, supposing that Mār-Ištar's astronomical informants were even moderately com-

513 Collated by Sollberger (19.1.1976): "p]a-an damaged but possible!"
514 In view of 277 r11 and 291 r7, one would also expect the writer to speak of the temple of *Cutha* (GÚ.DU$_8$.A^{KI}) rather than Cuthaeans.
515 Cf. *mi-i-nu* PN TA* *pa-ni-šú-nu iš-šu-u-ni, ABL* 131:12f, etc.

petent (which can hardly be doubted in view of *LAS* 289-291) and that their words are correctly repeated, year 667 seems the only acceptable solution. In support of this date one may also note that the writer evidently knew already on the 3rd of Ulūlu that the following month was to be intercalary; in 670, the royal order announcing this arrived in Babylon only on the 6th of Ulūlu (cf. *LAS* 287:8-14).[516]

However, supposing that the prediction was faulty, certain indications rather strongly favour placing the letter in 670 BC. Firstly, save for *LAS* 283, which is of uncertain date, there is no evidence that Mār-Ištar's activity in Babylonia was continued in the reign of Assurbanipal; on the contrary, it seems that his place was later taken by a man named Urad-aḫḫēšu, who wrote a number of letters dealing with the reconstruction of the sacred precincts of Babylon in the first years of Assurbanipal and never mentions Mār-Ištar (see ABL 119-120, 464, 471, 1219, and *CT* 53 60, 635, 759 and 959). Secondly, the matters dealt with in the present letter would seem to fit best in the historical context of year 670. The pedestal of Tašmētu referred to in r4'f certainly had its place either in Ezida of Borsippa[517] or more likely in the É-tuš-a chapel of Esangil[518], both of which were under restoration in 670. Cf. Borger, *Ash* p.84:39f, KI.TUŠ GIŠMES.MÁ.GAN.NA *iṣ-ṣi da-re-e . . . a-na* dKURNUN (var. d*Taš-me-tum*) GAŠAN GAL-*ti a-ši-bat* É.TUŠ.A *pa-paḫ* dAMAR+UD *šá qé-reb* TIN.TIRKI [40] *eš-šiš* DÙ-*uš*,[519] and *É-zi-da* É dAG *šá qé-reb* BÁR.SIPA . . . *nak-liš ú-ban-ni-ma*, ibid. p.95:10ff.[520] It is certain that both projects were continued in Assurbanipal's reign[521], but there is reason to believe that at least the building of Esangil was completed already by the end of the accession year of Assurbanipal, i.e. early 668 BC. Cf. *ABL* 119:12ff: *É-sag-íl ki-sal-lu e-le-nu-u* [13] *ina* É dEN dGAŠAN-*ja uš-ša-bu-ni* [14] *a-di* É.KURMEŠ-*šú* É *pa-paḫ* d*Taš-me-tum* [15] *ki-sal-lu šap-li-ú a-di* É.[KURMEŠ]-*šú* [16] PAP *an-ni-ú gab-bu e-piš* "Esangil, the upper countyard in which Bēl and Bēltīa live, including its shrines, the sanctuary of Tašmētu, the lower courtyard including its s[hrin]es, all this has been completed."[522] Thirdly, the letter has remarkable affinities to a letter sent to Esarhaddon very probably in early Tašrītu 670,[523] as will become readily apparent from the following extract (Obv.3ff): "I was about to (leave for Nineveh to) visit the king, my lord, when Mār-Ištar came and declared: *'I shall inscribe the pedestals.'* He was pleased with nothing, so I had to delay my visit because of him. Soon as he is through with me, I shall come and kiss the feet of the king, my lord. (As to) *the royal statues* which Mār-Ištar brought, saying: 'Have a look; let the one which is best stand', I have studied them with the artists, and found that the statue which I am herewith sending to the king, my lord, is the best. Just as the king, my lord, prepares himself when he is to enter into the presence of Marduk, your god, so does the statue which I am sending to the king, my lord, represent the ceremonial make-up of the king, my lord. Just as they have set up (the king's statue) upon the seat of Bēl in Assur, so have I now set (it) up in Esangil and other temples of Babylon. Let the king look (at the statue), and if it pleases the king, my lord, its kind may stand (in the temples). Yet if it does not please the king, the kind of statue which the king, my lord, chooses to send will stand (in its stead)" (*a-na pa-an* LUGAL EN-*já al-la-ka* [4] IDUMU-d*15 ki-i il-li-ka* [5] *um-*

516 Note, however, that Mār-Ištar himself may have directed the king's attention to the fact that a second Ulūlu had to be intercalated (*LAS* 285); accordingly, he may have reckoned with an intercalary Ulūlu even before the matter had been officially confirmed.

517 See Unger, *RlA* 1 420f.

518 Ibid., p.355*a*.

519 The titulary of Esarhaddon at the beginning of this inscription (AsBbA; ll. 28ff) establishes its terminus post quem 671.

520 The explicit reference to spoils from Egypt at the beginning of this inscription (ll. 28ff) gives it a terminus post quem 671. Most probably the text was written towards the end og 670 BC, or later, cf. note to 196:4'.

521 See Streck, *Asb* p. CCCLXXXV and the texts mentioned ibid.

522 This letter of Urad-aḫḫēšu can have been written in Nisannu 668 at the earliest, because it refers to Šamaš-šumu ukin as "king of Babylon" (r8ff; cf. Streck, op.cit. CCLVI). On the other hand, r6f of the same letter (*ina* IGI GAR[ZA].MEŠ *ni-dag-gal* "we are waiting for the ceremonies") suggest a date of composition before Ajāru 24/25 of the same year, as the meaning of the remark clearly is, taking into consideration the context, "the stage has been set and we are ready for the returnal of Marduk to Babylon" (arranged on the said date). Another letter of Urad-aḫḫēšu (*CT* 53 60) deals with the roofing of the sanctuaries of [Bēl] and Bēltīa, and hence certainly predates *ABL* 119; on its left edge mention is made of citizens of Barsip (context fragmentary), which might indicate that reconstruction work in Borsippa was also discussed in this letter.

523 The "Ist.-Brief" edited by Landsberger, *BBEA*. On the exact date of the letter see commentary to *LAS* 284; the letter was certainly addressed to Esarhaddon since, according to the writer, Bēl was still resident in Assur and the king who intended to "take the hand of Bēl" had his court in Nineveh.

ma ^{GIŠ}*ki-gal-la-a-nu a-šaṭ-ṭar* [6] *mìm-ma šá it-ti-šú a-na a-ma-ru ṭa-a-bu ja-a'-nu* [7] *ina pa-ni-šú at-te-mir-ka* [8] *a-di ina pa-ni-já ú-qat-tu-ú* [9] *al-la-kam-ma* GÌR[2] *šá* LUGAL EN-*já a-né-šiq* [10] ALAM^{MEŠ} *šá* LUGAL *šá* ^{I}DUMU-^{d}*15 iš-šá-a* [11] *um-ma a-mur-ra-ma šá šá-lam li-iz-zi* [12] *a-na-ku u* ^{LÚ}*um-ma-nu* ÌR^{MEŠ} *šá* LUGAL [13] *a-ḫa-meš ki-i nu-kal-li-mu* [14] *lib-bu-ú* ALAM *šá a-na* LUGAL EN-*já ú-še-bi-la* [15] *šá-lim ki-i šá* LUGAL EN-*já* MURUB$_4$^{MEŠ}-*šú* [16] *i-rak-ka-su-ma a-na pa-an* ^{d}AMAR+UD DINGIR-*ka* [17] *te-ru-bu lìb-bu-u* ALAM *šá a-na* LUGAL EN-*já* [18] *ú-še-bi-la ri-ik-su šá* LUGAL EN-*já* [19] *lìb-bu-ú šá ina* BAL.TIL^{KI} *ina* UGU ^{GIŠ}*šub-ti šá* ^{d}EN [20] *ú-šá-az-zi-zu ina É-sag-gíl* u É.KUR^{MEŠ} [21] *šá* TIN.TIR^{KI} *ul-ta-az-zi* LUGAL *le-m[u]r-ma* [22] *ki-i pa-an* LUGAL EN-*já maḫ-ru* [23] *lìb-bu-šú li-iz-zi u ki-i pa-an* LUGAL [24] *la maḫ-ru lìb-bu-ú*ALAM *šá* LUGAL EN-*já* [25] *ú-še-bi-la li-iz-zi*). It would indeed be a remarkable coincidence if Mār-Ištar had twice, at the same time of the year, but in different years, been engaged in virtually identical activities.

So it must be stressed that the evidence is controversial, and neither of the possible dates can be given *absolute* preference nor be excluded with *certainty*. However, the facts mentioned above as well as the orthographical differences of the present letter from *LAS* 287 (written on Ulūlu 6, 670) make year 667 the likelier alternative.*

Notes:

r1'-3'. *Sic* according to personal collation (28.3.1968); the passage is rendered by Landsberger (*BBEA* p.52) "[(Antwort auf) was mir der König schr]ieb: 'Wie lautet die Inschrift?' Wie ich es früher meinem Herrn vorlas . . . "), but this is impossible since the text should read *a-na* (= nota accusativi) MAN EN-*já*, if the king were the object of the verb *šašmû*; cf. *a-na* MAN EN-*já ú-sa-áš-me*, *LAS* 277:12.

r5'f. See commentary to *LAS* 7.

r8'f. *ú-še-taq*: an ellipsis for *Sîn attalû ušētaq* "the moon will skip the eclipse"; also attested in *LAS* 42. For the construction *pān* + infinitive + *šakin* see note to *LAS* 173 r16f.

r10'. *UD 3.KÁM* šá* ^{ITU}*KIN*: the purpose of this date (the only one found in the letters of Mār-Ištar) was to confirm that the eclipse precition communicated in the letter was indeed made before the eclipse actually took place; successful prognosticators could be sure of royal favour (cf. on 65 r19). Similar datings are found also in other reports dealing with eclipses, e.g. *RMA* 271A r2'ff: ^{d}*30* . . . [AN.MI] *ú-še-taq la i-šá-kan* [3] *šá* $^{I.d}$PA-PAP=MEŠ-SU [4] UD *13*.KÁM "The moon will skip [the eclipse], it will not make it. (Predicted) by Nabû-aḫḫē-erība on the 13th."

287

Bibliography:

(I) Waterman, *RCAE* 338 (cf. IV 180, 246); Pfeiffer, *SLA* 218.
(II) Behrens, *ABB* (1906) 63f, Labat, *Royauté* (1939) 215; Landsberger, *BBEA* (1965) 41 and 52; Oppenheim, *Letters* (1967) 165 (no. 106).

Photograph:

RCAE IV pl.8 (Obv. only).

Addressee:

Esarhaddon.

Date and discussion:

Ulūlu 6, eponymy of Šulmu-Bēl-lašme = August 12, 670 BC. Cf. Obv.6-12 and r6ff, and see in more detail under *LAS* 190;[524] note that r9 ("ceremonies of *Ulūlu*") proves for certain that the festival described in the letter was *not* celebrated in *Tašrītu* like the one referred to in *LAS* 190. While the intercalation of a second Ulūlu did not alter the name of the month in which the festival took place, it was necessary to postpone part of the ce-

[524] That the present letter was not addressed to Assurbanipal is shown by the fact that the order to intercalate came from Assyria. The Ulūlu intercalated in 667 BC (*LAS* 286) was ordered by Šamaš-šumu-ukīn; Assurbanipal had intercalated Addūru (*LAS* 325).

remonies till the following month since the festival of Ulūlu was organically connected with the New Year's festival of Tašrītu, and it would have been unthinkable to break the sequence of cultic events leading from one festival to the other by a hiatus of a month or more. Cf. the royal order *YOS* 3 152 r1 ff (App. Q6).

9ff and r9ff. Two Sargonid royal orders announcing intercalary months have actually been preserved (*ABL* 401 and 1258); a comparison of these quite stereotype announcements with the present letter indicates that Mār-Ištar did not quote the king's words verbatim, though he accurately rendered the content of the message; the same presumably applies to the other quotations in his letters, too. Of the two orders in question, the better preserved (*ABL* 401) reads as follows: ^{1} *a-mat* LU[GAL] ^{2} *a-na* ^{I}NUMUN-*ú-[tú]* ^{3} *ù a-na* $^{\text{LÚ*}}$TU^{MEŠ} É ^{4} *šá* BÀD.DINGIR^{KI} ^{5} *šùl-mu ja-a-ši* ^{6} *lìb-ba-ku-nu* ^{7} *lu ṭa-ab-ku-nu-šú* ^{8} ^{ITU}ŠE *di-ri* ^{9} *lu me-dak-ku-ú-šu* ^{10} EZEN UD GARZA^{MEŠ} ^{11} *ša* DINGIR^{MEŠ}*-e-a* ^{12} *ina* ITU *šal-me* ^{13} *ep-šá-a'* "An order of the king to Zērūtu and the 'enterers' of the temple of Dēr: I am well, you can be happy. This is to inform you that the month Addāru is intercalary; perform the festival and the ceremonies of my gods (referring to the New Year's festival) in the correct (lit. "intact") month." *ABL* 1258, addressed to Nabû-iddina and other priests of Cutha, runs quite parallel.[525] Both texts bear indistincts traces of a date on the reverse. For corresponding Neo-Babylonian royal orders see Clay, *YOS* 3 no.115 and 152; cf. also ibid. 15 and 196.

288

Bibliography:

(I) Waterman, *RCAE* 1336 (cf. IV 205).
(II) Deller, *Or* NS 33 (1964) 103.

Writer:

The handwriting, the shape of the tablet, the spellings MAN *be-lí* Obv.5' (compared with EN-*já* [gen.] Rev.1') and [*l*]*u-u ú-di-i-u* Rev. 6, and lastly the subject matter of the letter (cf. Rev.10 with the preceding three texts) show that this tiny fragment too was written by Mār-Ištar. Cf. App. M 6.

Addressee:

Esarhaddon?.

Date:

The quotation from *Enūma Eliš* in Obv.11' as well as the reference to the "opening of the gate" (of Esaggil?) in Rev.10 indicate that the letter dealt with matters associated with the New Year's festival of Babylon, and was hence probably written either in the month Addāru or Nisannu (= March to April). There is no way of telling what year was in question, except that the last years of Esarhaddon (671-669) suggest themselves as the most likely time brackets (cf. dating of No.286).

Notes:

5'. [*MÁŠ*].*MI-ja* "in my dream": this restoration rests mainly on orthographical grounds: the sign MI was used by Mār-Ištar in f i n a l position only in the i d e o g r a m s AN.MI (10 times), MÁŠ.MI (twice) and MI (6 times), and otherwise only in initial position (*mi-i-nu* 4 X, *mi-iḫ-ṣu* 1 X, *mi-qit-ti* 1 X, *mi-il-u* 1 X); in all other cases the sign ME was used (init. 5 X, med. 10 X, fin. 25 X). Obviously neither AN.MI "eclipse" nor MI "night" fit the context, whereas MÁŠ.MI "dream" would explain why the writer cared to describe in detail doings of the king *in a letter sent to the king himself*. Cf. also *LAS* 294. The dream evidently concerned the ceremonies of the impending New Year's festival, in which the king was to participate personally. Note that the passage cannot be interpreted as containing instructions or suggestions as to the ceremonies the king had to perform: were this the case, the writer would have used the present tense instead of the stative (Obv.6'f *kam-mu-su, ma-gi-gi*), cf. 291:11'.

---

525 Note also *ABL* 866:5ff, ^{I}ÌR-^{d}*Na-na-a* ^{6} $^{\text{LÚ*}}$*qur-bu-tu šá un-qu* ^{7}*a-na* UGU *di-ri* LUGAL *BE-LÍ-a* ^{8}*ina* šu.2-*šú ú-še-bi-la* (refering to an intercalation order).

7': *ma-gi-gi*: cancel the translation "sprinkled" given in Pt.I (following *AHw* 574*b*) and render instead: "[ ] was swelling upon it". For *magāgu* "to be swollen, tumescent, stiff" see Biggs, *TCS* 2 (1967) 8. The paragogic vowel appended to the stative indicates continuation (cf. note to 246:10).

8': *nibzu*: this word (< Aram. *nbz* "receipt", see Kaufman, *AS* 19 (1974) 77, and von Soden, *Or*NS 37 [1968] 261 and *AHw* [1969] 786*a*) appears to have been in Neo-Assyrian simply a synonym of *ṭuppu* "tablet", covering various kinds and uses of clay tablets; the translation "Document, Urkunde" suggested by von Soden (*loc. cit.*) is unnecessarily narrow. Cf. [*u*$_4$*-mu*] *šá ni-ib-zu* [8] *an-ni-u ta-mar-u-ni* "the day you see this *nibzu*", VAT 8650:7f (unp.), referring to a private clay letter of the usual vertically oblong type (note IM [I⌜ X X⌝]-*Aš+šur* [2] *a-na* [I]*Aš+šur-re-ṣu-u-a* "A tablet of PN$_1$ to PN$_2$" in the address of the letter, yielding the reading IM = *nibzu* for the usual IM = *ṭuppu*). Cf. also [LÚ] *šá* MU-*šú ina* ŠÀ [IM]*ni-ib-zi* [N]E/*an-n*[*é*]-⌜*e*⌝ *šaṭ-ru-ú-ma* / MU-*ma* "the man whose name is written on this *nibzu*", *PRT* 124:9f and 139 r6f, referring to haruspical reports of the late (Assurbanipal) type; *ni-ib-zu* TA* ŠÀ É.GAL [5] [*it*]*-ta-nu-ú-né* [6] [*ma-a*] UDU[MEŠ] TA* [KUR]*Lab-du-di* [7] [*šu-du-ud*] "a *nibzu* was given to me from the Palace, (with the order) '[Extract] the sheep from GN!'", *ABL* 798:4ff; AD-*šú ša* MAN [13] EN-*já* KÙ.UD ÉŠ.GÀR *ša* [LÚ*]SIPA[MEŠ] *ina lìb-bi ni-ib-zi Aš+šur-aje* [14] *ina lìb-bi ni-ib-zi Ár-ma-aje i-sa-ka-nu* "(in the days of) the father of the king, my lord, they specified the silver (equivalent) of the shepherds' *iškāru*-dues in *nibzus* written in Assyrian and Aramaic", *ABL* 633+ Obv.(!) 12ff.

11': For *iqṭibi* "said" referring to tablets cf. *LAS* 298 r8f. and pertinent commentary. The subsequent quotation is from Tablet IV of *Enūma Eliš*: *Be-lum šá tak-lu-ka na-piš-ta-šu gi-mil-ma*, "O Lord, save the life of the one who puts his trust in you" (line 17); line 12' in the present letter can accordingly be restored [*na-piš-ta-šu gi-mi*]*l-ma*. It is noteworthy that Mār-Ištar has not quoted the standard version of the epic bit its Assyrian "forgery" (D.D. Luckenbill, "The Ashur Version of the Seven Tablets of Creation", *AJSL* 38 [1921] 12 ff) in which Marduk's name had been systematically replaced by that of Aššur; this proves that this version, composed under Sennacherib, was still recognized at the end of Esarhaddon's reign and was perhaps even (scheduled to be) recited in Babylon. Another quotation from the same epic (and even the same tablet), but from its standard version, occurs in a Neo-Babylonian letter (*CT* 54 22 = Dietrich, *WO* 4 [1968] 234ff) also addressed to Esarhaddon: DINGIR[MEŠ] GAL[MEŠ] [30] *a-na* [d]EN *iq-ta-bu-ú um-ma šu-uš-qu-ú u šu-uš-pu-lu* [31] [*ši-i lu qa*]-⌜*tu-uk*⌝*-ka* [d]AMAR+UD *ša* UN[ME] *at-ta* "the great gods said to Lord: 'Be it in your power to exalt and to humble' – you (= king) are Marduk of the people" (Rev.29 ff; cf.En.el. IV 8).

Note the presence of the vertical wedge (I, not to be read!) after *ma-a*, indicating that a literary quotation is in question.

r3'ff: These lines must have contained an assertive oath with a long list of gods invoked as witnesses, cf. note to 13:9ff.

289

Bibliography:

(I) Schott and Schaumberger, *ZA* 47 (1941/2) 92 ff and 115 ff.
(II) Weidner, *OLZ* 16 (1913) 204; *BA* 8/4 (1911) 16 ff.

Copies:

Craig, *AAT* (1899) p.39; Virolleaud, *ACh* 2 Spl. (1912) no. 62.

Writer:

This letter was already attributed to Mār-Ištar by Schott (1941) on the ground of its evident coherence with *LAS* 290; for safety, here some additional criteria confirming the assignation: 1) Orthography: especially *nam-búr-bé-e-šú le-e-pu-šu* and *e-da-ni-i-šú* (Obv.18' ff; cf. Appendix M 6), *šúm-ma* (Obv.6'; cf. 275 r3', 277 r23, 278 r9', 280 r13, 291:14'), MAN (Rev. 12; App. M 6), *ki-i an-ni-i* (Obv.10', Rev.2; cf. 276 r21, 284:14) *pi-šìr-šú* (cf. 291 r11), etc.; 2) Physical features of the tablet: see Pt.I, p.339; 3) Phraseology: especially *ana maṣṣarti namburbēšu lēpušū* (Obv.18'f; cf. 278 r17'ff, 279 r13ff) and *kī ša ina ṭuppi šaṭirūni pišaršu attasḫa* (Rev.11f; cf.278 r3'f).

Addressee:

Esarhaddon.

Date:

Simānu 11, eponymy of Šamaš-kāšid-ajābi = June 8, 669 BC. The month and day are obtained from Obv.8'ff coupled with Obv.19'ff (Simānu 6 + 5 days); a slightly later (say, by 1-2 days) date may perhaps be permitted, but the terminus ante quem is absolutely Simānu 14, since the letter does not contain a word about the lunar eclipse which took place on that date. The year in question is established with absolute certainty by the heliacal rising of Jupiter reported in the letter (Simānu 6 = June 3, 669); see App. C4 and in detail, Schaumberger, *ZA* 47 127 ff. Further confirmation is provided by *LAS* 290, q.v.

Notes:

3'. As already pointed out by Schaumberger, *ZA* 47 129, the date of the heliacal rising of Jupiter [at Babylon] in 670 mentioned here (Ajāru 22 = May 3) is of considerable chronological importance since it shows that the year 670 must have been intercalary (cf. under *LAS* 190). The longitude of Jupiter at the time concerned (15°) implies that the constellation in which the planet was sighted was Perseus (sic; cancel the restoration [*Aries*] in Pt.I).

5'ff. Jupiter's period of invisibility at conjunction between evening last and morning first is, according to Schoch (*Venus Tablets* p.108), for Babylon 28 to 34 days; P.V. Neugebauer (*Astronomische Nachrichten* 264 [1937], 6331) gives as extreme values 26 ($\frac{1}{2}$) and 35 ($\frac{1}{2}$) days. Even though Mār-Ištar's corresponding lower value (20 days) thus is "inaccurate", he is correct in defining the mean duration or "term" (*edannu*) of Jupiter's period of invisibility as ca. 30 days and in saying that after 35 days of absence Jupiter had exceeded this term by 5 days.[526] From the astrological point of view, such a delay was significant, and more than justified the prediction communicated on Rev.3 ff. Schaumberger's conclusion that "Mār-Ištars Aufregung war unbegründet" just because "Jupiter hatte . . . das Höchstmaß seiner Unsichtbarkeit nicht überschritten" (*loc.cit.* p.124) is hence not quite to the point.

8'f. This note on Jupiter's position at its appearance is erroneous. Actually the planet stood at the date concerned exactly above ζ Tauri, on the way of the Enlil stars; see in more detail the commentary on the following number. The predictions quoted in the sequel were accordingly also irrelevant.

10'ff. Quoted from *ACh* Ištar 16:3 (series *Enūma Anu Enlil*): I ^{MUL}SAG.ME.GAR *ina* ^{ITU}SIG$_4$ IGI-*ir šal-pu-ut-ti* KUR *iš-šak-kan* ŠE.IM *iq-qir.*

12'f. This omen does not seem to be attested elsewhere.

13'f. Cf. *LKU* 109:5-9 (series *Enūma Anu Enlil*): I ^{MUL}SAG.ME.GAR *ana* IGI ^{MUL}SIPA.ZI.[AN.NA . . . .] [6] I ^{MUL}SAG.ME.GAR *ana* EGER ^{MUL}[SIPA].Z[I.AN.NA . . . .] [7] I ^{MUL}SAG.ME.GAR *ana* ZAG ^{MU}[^{L}SIPA. ZI.AN.NA . . . .] [8] I ^{MUL}SAG.ME.GAR *ana* KAB ^{M}[^{UL}SIPA.ZI.AN.NA . . . .] [9] I ^{MUL}SAG.ME.GAR *ana* [ŠÀ ^{MUL}SIPA.ZI.AN.NA TU . . . .].

14'ff. This omen is not otherwise known. Note, however, *ACh* Ištar 16:13, I ^{MUL}SAG.ME.GAR *ina* KASKAL *šu-ut* ^{d}*A-nù* IGI A.KAL GÁL-*ma* EBUR KUR SI.SÁ "If Jupiter appears on the way of the Anu stars, there will be flood and the crops of the land will prosper." It is unclear why Mār-Ištar, unlike the authors of RMA 185 and 196, did not quote this favourable prediction but chose the other alternative instead. Did his informants follow another tradition, or were political speculations influencing the choice?

17'. *a-na . . . id-da-gi-il*: for *dagālu* N "to be intended, destined for" = "pertain to" cf. *ADD* 640 = *AR* 45:10 ff, (PN . . .) *a-na* ^{d}NIN.URTA EN-*šú-nu* [11] *a-na ši-rik-ti is-sa-ar-ku* [12] *a-na il-ki tup-šik-ki ina* É ^{d}NIN.URTA *id-da-gal* "they have presented PN to Ninurta, their lord; he is destined to (perform) *ilku-* and *tupšikku*-work in the temple of Ninurta"; cf. also A.ŠÀ DIRI *u* LAL-*ṭi pa-an* PN *id-dag-gal, BRM* 1 34:34 (cf. *CAD* A/2 489*a*) and the examples quoted in *AHw* p.150*a* sub *dagālu* Gt.

---

[526] The limits "20 to 30 days" given here for Jupiter's period of invisibility were obtained from the compendium Mul Apin. Cf. VAT 9412 (unp., courtesy H. Hunger) i 49-50, I MUL ^{d}SAG.ME.GAR *ina* ^{d}UTU.ŠÚ.A TÙM-*ma 20* UD-*me ina* AN-*e uḫ-ḫa-ra* / KI.MIN ITU *uḫ-ḫa-ram-ma ina* ^{d}UTU.È *ina* KASKAL ^{d}UTU SAR-*ḫa* IGI. LAL "Jupiter disappears in the West and stays invisible in the sky for 20 days; ditto, stays invisible for a month and then lights up and becomes visible in the East on the path of the Sun" (Mul Apin, Tablet II).

18'f. Schott (p.93) renders *ana maṣṣarti namburbēšu lēpušū* "wegen der Wache möge man die ihrethalben (vorgesehenen) Sühnriten vollziehen", and explains (on p.101f and 115) *maṣṣartu* as "Fachausdruck" referring to the observation of eclipses; the eclipse concerned would be the lunar one of June 10, -668. Such an interpretation is rendered extremely unlikely by *LAS* 278 r 6'ff and 279 r12ff, as well as the parallels quoted in the note on 280 r11-13, which show that the word *maṣṣartu* rather referred to the *guard of the king* (cf. *RMA* 245 r1: (LUGAL . . .) *ma-ṣar-ti šá ra-ma-ni-šú* [2] *li-iṣ-ṣur*).[527] Accordingly, *a-na* is rather to be taken as a nota accusativi and the whole phrase as an abbreviation of the more explicit one in *LAS* 278.

r1. *ú-tu-uk-kiš*: contra Schott (p.115), this form cannot be derived from *utukku* "demon/ghost" (in purely Neo-Assyrian contexts, like the present one, adverbial *-iš* could be appended only to a limited number of *adjectives*) but must be taken as Pf. of the verb *ukkušu* (cf. *ú-tu-ḫe-er* Obv.7' and similar forms listed in note to 211 r15). *Ukkušu* occurs as astronomical term also in *LAS* 109 r3 (MUL*Ṣal-bat-a-nu ina lìb-bi* MULSUḪUR.MÁŠ KU_6 [3] *ú-tu-uk-kiš it-ti-it-zi*) and is rendered in both instances "to staff off (one's path)" in *CAD* A/1 (1964) p.265*a*.

This is unacceptable since only in the case of *LAS* 109 the verb *might* refer to the "loop" the outer planets perform when retrograding, whereas in the present context (heliacal rising) such an interpretation is out of the question.

Accordingly, it seems that no "technical" rendering of *ukkušu* is needed here but that the verb is to be translated simply "to move on, to progress", as elsewhere in Neo-Assyrian texts. A very clear example is found in *CT* 53 5, Rev.9ff: *ṭè-e-mu ša* LUGAL *be-lí-já* [10] *a-se-me ma-a* LUGAL *ka-ri-im* [11] *il-lak* TA* I*Aš+šur*-EN-LAL-*in* [12] *a-di lìb-bi* URU*Da-ar*-⌜X⌝ [13] *at-tal-ka ina lìb-bi a-se-me* ⌜*ma-a*⌝ [14] LUGAL *be-lí uk-ku-uš* [15] *a-su-ḫur a-na* ⌜X X⌝ [ ] [16] *at-ta-lak* "I received news of the king my lord, telling "the king has been detained (and) is going away",[528] so I retreated with PN until the town of GN_1. Having heard there that the king my lord is *moving on*, I turned back and went to [GN_2]." This NA (itr.) usage of *ukkušu* corresponds to Babylonian forms of *ukkušu* with *ta*-infix, which were obsolete in Neo-Assyrian, and probably is an ellipsis for *ramanša ukkušu*; cf. notes to 13 r26 and 51 r1, and note the similar elliptic (intransitive) usage of *nammušu* "to set out" in NA (*AHw* 726*b*).

r2. "It completed 40 days": This statement is interpreted by Schaumberger (p.124) simply as a repetition of Obv.7', the 40 days being a "rounding" of the exact term of 35 days; "solche Aufrundungen waren den Semiten ja gerade bei der Zahl 40 geläufig" (ibid.). I do not think it is methodically right to assume such inexactitudes in a text dealing with astronomical observations; moreover, the verb *ukkušu* makes such an interpretation actually impossible, since it implies that the planet had been concretely o b s e r v e d moving on. Hence the passage can only mean that 5 days had passed *since* the sighting of Jupiter, and the figure 40 must have a special significance of its own. There is reason to believe that it was occasioned by the immediately following prediction. Jupiter is there called *Nēberu*, which was a designation usually applied to the planet only when it stood near the meridian ([MU]L dAMAR+UD . . . *ina* MÚRUB AN-*e* GUB-*ma* d*Né-bi-ru*, *RMA* 94:7-r1);[529] the number of days which had to pass after the heliacal rising of the planet until this altitude was reached was, according to Schott (art.cit., p.116), the same 40 as in our passage. Taking into consideration the prominent part played by number symbolism in astrology, it seems thinkable that even at its heliacal rising, Jupiter had to "complete" those 40 days (counted from the moment of its disappearance) before this particular *Nēberu*-omen could be quoted.

r3 ff. This omen is not preserved elsewhere. Cf. *RMA* 186 r2 ff, pertaining to the exactly opposite case: [I] MUL*Né-bi-ru* KUR-*ḫa-ma* DINGIRMEŠ SILIM.MA[MEŠ] [3] *e-šá-a-tu*$_4$ IGIMEŠ*dal-ḫa-a-tu*$_4$ *i-zak-*[*ku-u*] [4] ŠÈG=MEŠ *ù* ILLUMEŠ DUMEŠ-*ni* "If Nēberu 'lights up' (= appears at normal time), the gods will be friendly; dull things will become bright, confused things clear; rain and floods will come", etc. Same omen also in *RMA* 187:7 ff.

r4. *me-še-er ib-ba-áš-ši*: hardly " 'Gerechtigkeit' (= ein allgemeiner Steuer- und Schuldenerlaß) wird (verkündet) werden" (Schott, ibid. 93; cf. 117: ". . . ähnliche Maßnahmen setzen immer völlige Zerrüttung der Wirt-

---

527 Similarly *RMA* 33 r5f.

528 Cf. note to 290 r11.

529 Cf. also I MUL GAL UD.DA-*su da-a'-mat* AN-*e* MAŠ-*ma* GUB-*zu* dAMAR+UD *né-bi-ri*, *CT* 33 pl.2 i 37 (Mul Apin, Tablet I).

schaft des Landes voraus; also eine schlimme Vorhersage"). More probably "justice will be put to shame", *ib-ba-aš-ši* standing for /i(b)bâš/ "is put to shame", cf. the PN [I]*La(-a)ba-a-ši* and the opposite omen, *RMA* 187:8.

290

Bibliography:

(I) Waterman, *RCAE* 744 (cf. IV 187,260); Pfeiffer, *SLA* 319; Schott and Schaumberger, *ZA* 47 (1941/2) 94 ff and 117 ff.
(II) Behrens, *ABB* (1906) 85f; Weidner, *BA* 8/4 (1911) 2ff; *HBA* (1915) 47f; Schaumberger, *SSB* Erg. (1935) 315ff; Schott, *OLZ* 40 (1937) 361.

Copy:

Cf. also G. Smith, *3 R* 51, 9 (1870).

Photo:

RCAE IV pl.13 (Obv. only).

Addressee:

Esarhaddon.

Date:

Du'ūzu 1, eponymy of Šamaš-kāšid-ajābi = June 27, 669 BC. For the month and day cf. Obv.12; the year is obtained by comparison with the preceding number (cf. Obv.14ff with 289:8'ff). The correctness of the dating is raised beyond question by the beginning of the letter reporting on the watch for a solar eclipse which after all did not occur. Solar eclipses were watched for only at the time of the moon's disappearance immediately before and after (potential) lunar eclipses (see on *LAS* 41 r1ff and *LAS* 42); hence a lunar eclipse must have occurred, or been liable to occur, two weeks before or after our letter was written. As a matter of fact, there was a lunar eclipse on June 10, 669 (see App. F1 and cf. *LAS* 25, 105(?) and 234), and in accordance with the letter, no solar eclipse took place during the subsequent conjunction (June 26, 6:30 p.m.).

Notes:

14 ff. For the factors causing the faulty Jupiter observation communicated in the "previous letter" (*LAS* 289) and here corrected, see Fig.2 on p.290, and cf. the situation prevalent during the writing of the present letter, shown in the same figure. Cf. further Schaumberger (1941/2), p.124: "Tatsächlich stand Jupiter schon am Morgen des 3. Juni = 6. Siwannu mit 47.7 Grad Länge und -0.6 Grad Breite genau über ζ Tauri [λ 45°2] und mit 16.7 Grad Deklination im Wege Enlils, hart an der Grenze zum Wege Anus (16.6 Grad). Der Irrtum der ersten Beobachtung ist entschuldbar. Jupiter ging ungeführ 50 Minuten vor Sonnenaufgang durch den Horizont. Sein kleiner Nachbar ζ Tauri konnte wegen der Horizontnähe und des Dämmerlichtes nicht erkannt werden. Der Beobachter war also auf Distanzschätzung von größeren Fixsternen, etwa Aldebaran oder Capella, aus angewiesen und konnte darum leicht den Ort des Planeten etwas zu weit gegen Südost rücken. Damit war aber der Weg des Anu und das Sternbild des Orion erreicht. Orion reicht in seiner heutigen Ausdehnung zwischen ζ Tauri und η Geminorum bis an die Ekliptik heran und sogar um ein Weniges nach Norden über sie hinaus. Heute is das beinahe der höchste Punkt der Ekliptik. Damals war es ungefähr die Mitte ihres nördlichen Teils, d.h. die Grenze zwischen den Wegen Anus und Enlils."

r11. *a-na* [MUL.GIŠ]*GIGIR lu-u ik-ri-im*: probably an ellipsis for "even if it(s way) to the Chariot became blocked" = even if it did keep off the C." The renderings suggested in *CAD* K (1971) 201*a* ("he is indeed slow in coming" . . . "The ref. should rather be connected with *qarāmu* (or *garāmu*) said of the planet Venus" [cf. *AHw* 282*a*]) and Schott, p.95 ("Zum Streitwagen-Sternbild (= Perseus + A, U, κ, ϕ, ψ Tauri) sogar(?) 'nahm'(?) er"; cf. the discussion ibid. 119ff) are out of the question, since Jupiter was not approaching but actually *distancing* itself from the constellation in question. [In fact, something like "it is distancing itself from the Chariot" would be expected, but that would most likely have been expressed otherwise (cf. *RMA* 88:8, SN_1 TA* IGI SN_2 *pa-a-te la iṭ-ḫi*; ibid. r10, SN_1 TA* ŠÀ *an-ni-i-e i-pat-ti il-lak*; 112 r6, *la i-ṭa-aḫ-ḫi i-pa-at-ti*, and ibid. r11, [TA*] ŠÀ *pa-ni-šú ip-ti-e-ti*).] The astral situation and other attestations of *karāmu* (in addition to the examples quoted in *CAD* and *AHw*, note also *KAV* 214:6, *an-nu-ri ka-rim*; *CT* 53 5 r10, LUGAL *ka-ri-im*, quoted in note on 289 r1; *ABL* 302:11, *ki-i* [LÚ]GÌR+AD_4 [12] *ik-rim-u-ni*; and cf. *tak-ri-ma*⌈*a*-⌉[*te*], *CT* 53 150 r3) imply that *karāmu* is here not

FIGURE 2

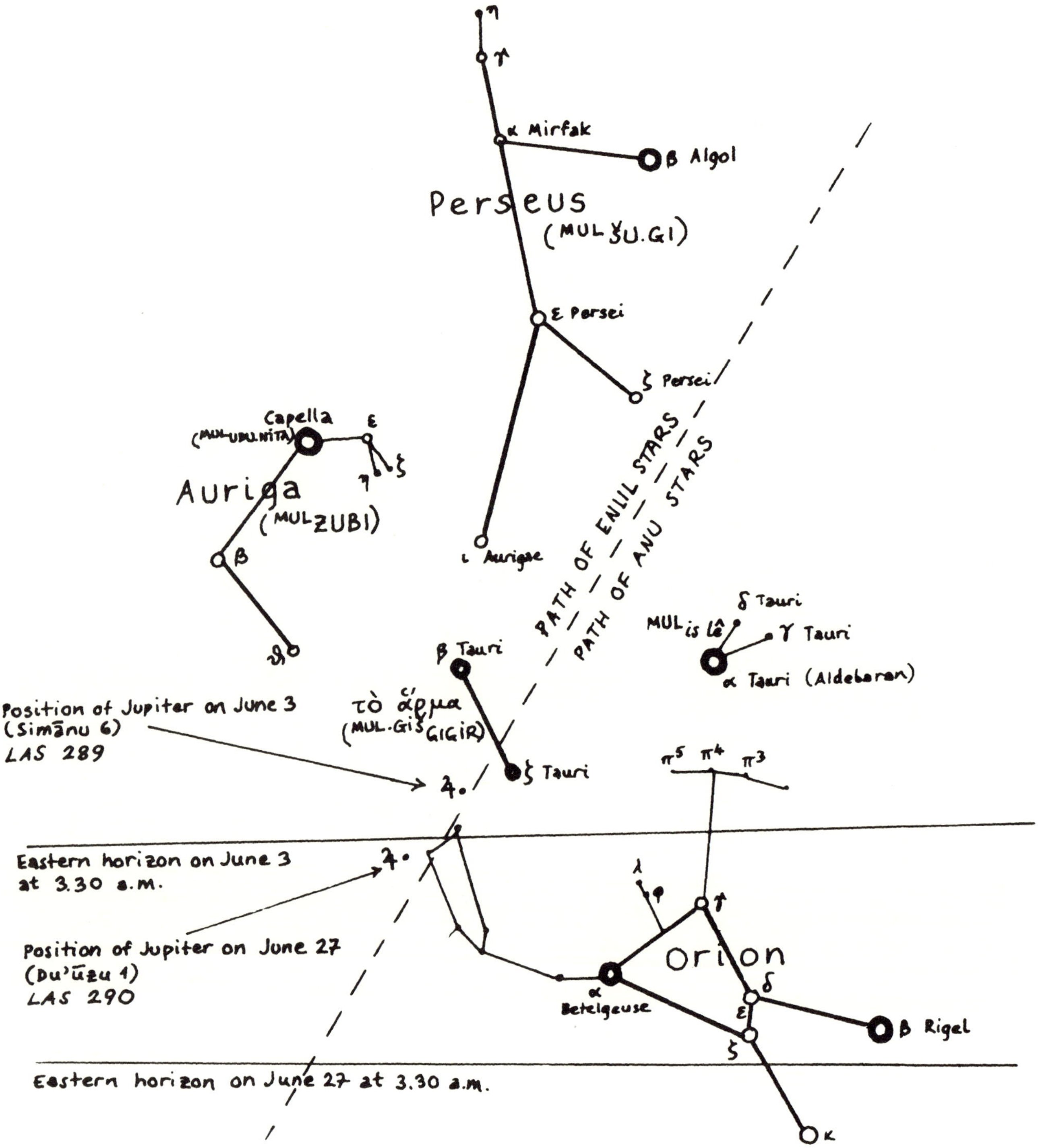

Heliacal rising of Jupiter in June 669 BC (Babylon)

Positions of fixed stars according to P.V. Neugebauer, Sterntafeln (1912). Positions of Jupiter after J. Schaumberger, ZA 47 (1941/2) 124.

used transitively but *intransitively*, and means "to be detained" or "blocked, hindered", as often in contexts dealing with travels and journeys;[530] note that in *CT* 53 5 *karim* is clearly the opposite of *ukkuš* "moving (on)". Assigning to *karāmu* a *transitive* meaning ("to hinder" etc.), taking *a-na* as nota accusativi and translating "even though it has blocked the Chariot" is clearly nonsensical, and the reading *ig-ri-im* pondered in *CAD* loc.cit. (from *garāmu* "to move") is absolutely out of consideration for reasons already stated above (cf. also the adjoining figure). In view of the frequent occurrence of *karāmu* with *ḫūlu* "road", it seems legitimate to take the passage as an ellipsis for (*ḫūlšu*) *ana SN lu ikrim*, which would plausibly account for the troublesome *a-na*.

For *lū* = "even though" cf. *GAG* § 153c, and note that it is not possible to translate *lu-u ik-ri-im* "it should have . . ." or "should it have . . . ", since the particle *lū* is not repeated in the following main clause; cf. *lu-u e-pu-šu* . . . *lu-u iš-ši* in *LAS* 298:12, *lu iḫ-ḫur* TA* *a-ḫa-aji-iš lu ni-id-bu-ub* "had he appealed (to the king while I was there), we could have talked with each other", *ABL* 168 r8 f, etc. Schott's and *CAD*'s "sogar/indeed" is of course out of the question, since this meaning of *lū* was in Neo-Assyrian covered by *ibašši*.

As appears from Fig. 2, the present letter fully confirms the identification of MUL.GIŠGIGIR as β + ζ Tauri (= τὸ ἅρμα of the *Sphaera Barbarica* of Teukros "the Babylonian") first proposed by Kugler, *SSB* I (1907) p. 29. Schott's "Perseus + A, υ, K, φ, ψ Tauri"[531] lies too far to the west. See in general Gössmann, *Planetarium* p. 29.

291

Bibliography:

(I) Waterman, *RCAE* 1214 (cf. IV 203); Pfeiffer, *SLA* 122.
(II) Oppenheim, *JAOS* 64 (1944) 196.

Writer:

Though the address formula of this letter has not been preserved, its attribution to Mār-Ištar is absolutely certain. Note the following distinctive features (and cf. Appendix M 6): (1) *Orthography*: MAN EN-*já* (Obv.7', 14' etc.)/MAN *be-lí* (10'f, etc.), *šúm-ma* (14', cf. on *LAS* 289), LÚ**qe-e-pa-a-ni* (r6), *up-ta-at-ti-i-u*, *šá-ni-i-u-te* (r8); (2) *phraseology*: *šumma pān šarri bēlīja maḫir* (14', cf. 277 r23, 280 r13), *šarru bēlī lū ūdi* (r9); (3) *measurements of the tablet*: see Pt.I, p. 339. Note, furthermore, the geographical setting, subject matter, and date of the letter, and cf. Obv. 14'f with 282:7 and 283 r6'f, and Rev. 5 with 275:8f.

Addressee:

Esarhaddon (cf. note on Obv. 4').

Date:

Du'ūzu 10, eponymy of Šamaš-kāšid-ajābi = July 6, 669 BC. This date can be established with absolute certainty from the astronomical observations communicated in the letter, viz. the "appearance" of the moon in the vicinity (to the left) of Scorpio on the night of Du'ūzu 10 (r9ff) and the simultaneous sighting of Venus in the middle of Leo (r17f). Both are, of course, rather frequently recurrent events, but their identification is helped by the fact that the letter certainly dates from the reign of Esarhaddon (see on Obv.4'). As appears from App.D, in this reign Venus was seen in four different years in Leo around Du'ūzu 10: in 680, 677, 675 and 669. Since no other letter of Mār-Ištar predates 672 BC, the only a priori likely alternative is the year 669. App.A1 gives Du'ūzu 10, 669 = July 6. A computation carried out by means of P.V. Neugebauer's *Tafeln für Sonne, Planeten und Mond* (1914) gives as the coordinates of Venus at the date concerned $\alpha = 131^\circ\!.5$; $\delta = +27^\circ\!.4$, which indeed locates the planet in the centre of Leo (see Fig. 3). The lunar position on the same day, 45 minutes after sunset (cf. Rev.11!), i.e. at 8^h p.m., was according to the same tables $\alpha = 223^\circ\!.7$; $\delta = -18^\circ\!.28$, which again pretty well agrees with the data of our text, the moon being situated to the

---

530 This intransitive usage may indeed derive from phrases where *karāmu* appears in the stative (*karim*, *šarru karim*, *ḫūlu karim*, *ḫūlu karmaššu adanniš*); cf. *mariṣ* "it is difficult", *šarru mariṣ* "the king is ill", *kaqquru mariṣ* "the terrain is difficult", *urdu ša marṣaššūni* "the servant who is doing badly", and similar usages of *ṭāb*. Note also the existence of intransitive and transitive *kašādu*.

531 Cf. Weidner, *StOr* 1 (1925) 350: "*mul* ^iš^*narkabtu* . . . [=] κ, τ, υ, φ, χ, ψ, A Tauri"; in *HBA* (1915) 48, however, correctly "β+ξ Tauri".

FIGURE 3

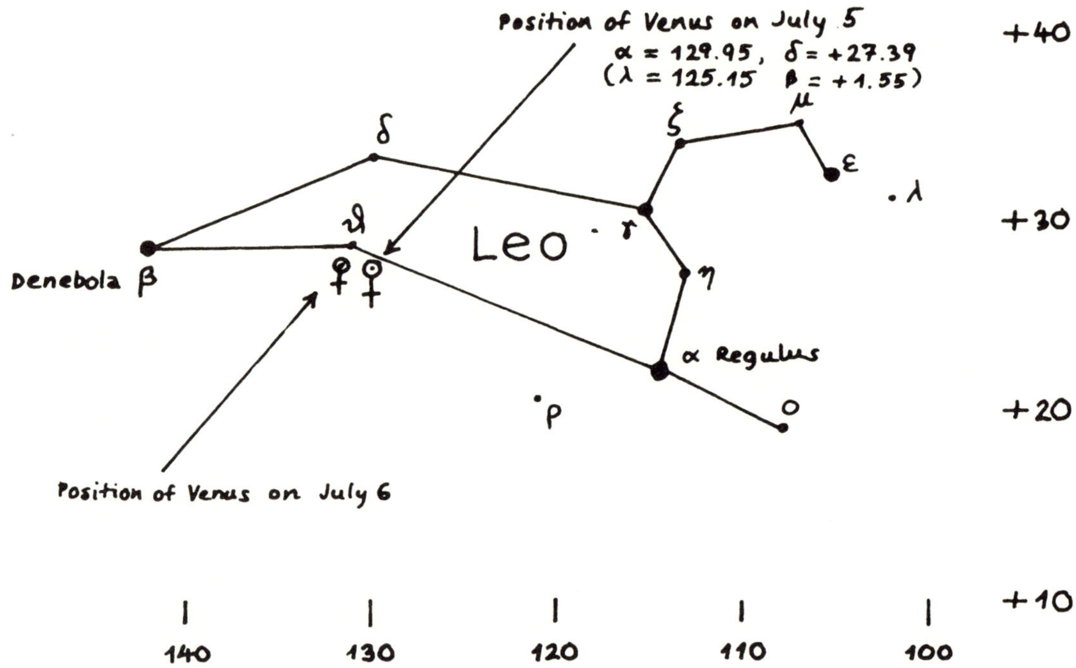

Position of *Venus* -668 July 5 8^h p.m. Babylon

Computed with P.V. Neugebauer, Tafeln für Sonne, Planeten und Mond (1914). Positions of fixed stars according to idem, Sterntafeln (1912).

FIGURE 4

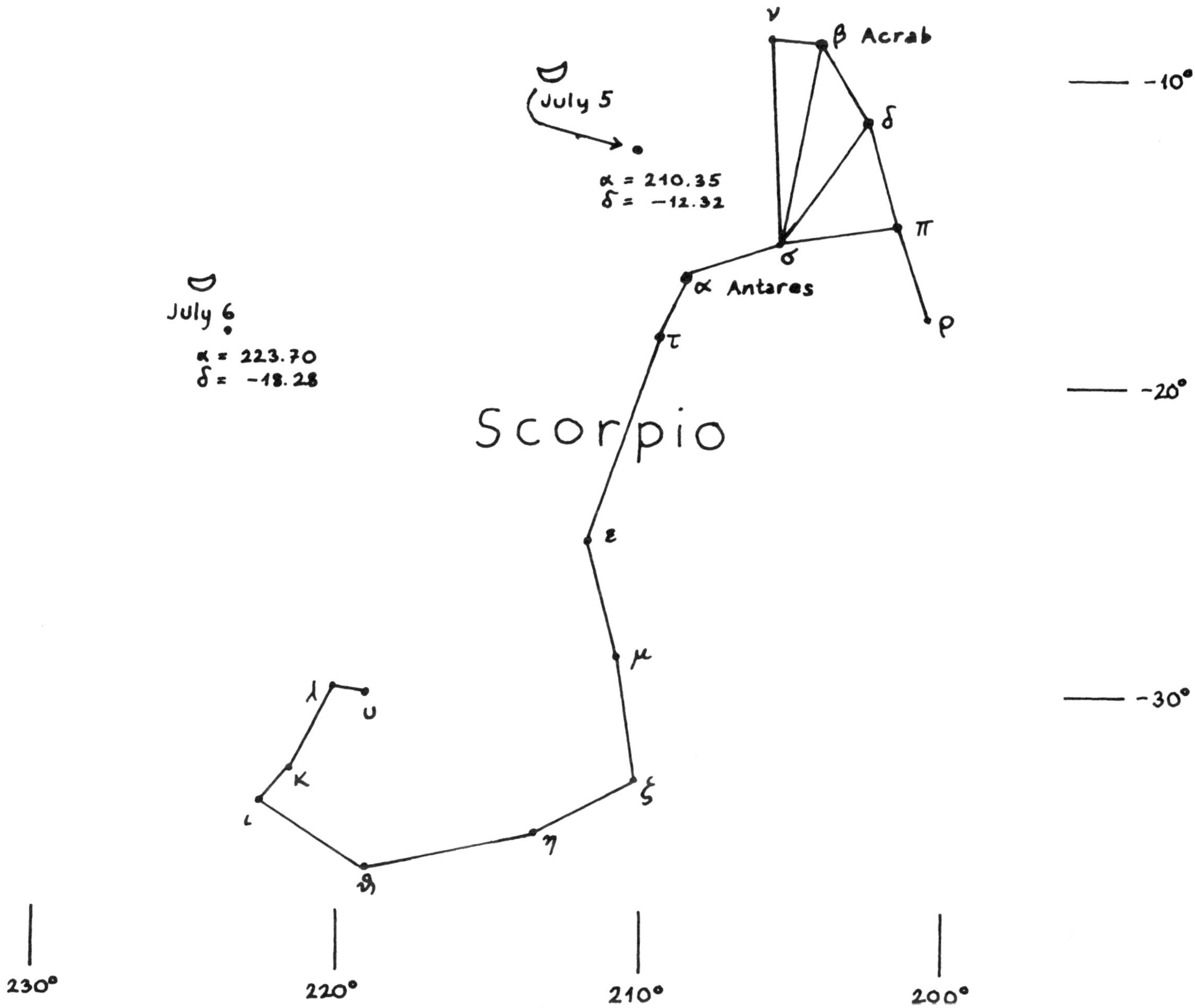

Lunar position -668 July 5 8^h p.m. Babylon (LAS 291 r9f)

Computed with P.V. Neugebauer, Tafeln für Sonne, Planeten und Mond (1914). Positions of fixed stars according to idem, Sterntafeln (1912).

left of Scorpio, at a distance of about 15° from Antares and about 12° from λ Scorpii (the "sting" of the constellation, see Fig. 4). However, on the preceding day (July 5), the agreement with the text was still better. the moon was then at a distance of only about 5° from the two brightest stars of Scorpio, Acrab and Antares, which were both visible near the right "horn" of the moon, just as the text states (Rev. 12; cf. Fig. 4). Venus, too, was on July 5 nearer the centre of Leo than on July 6, her position being α = 129°.95, δ = +27°.39; cf. Fig. 3. Accordingly, it can be concluded that the Julian date of the observations communicated in the letter was July 5, 669, and as a matter of fact, this date indeed agrees with the Assyrian date Du'ūzu 10 given in the letter, since the Mesopotamian day already began at sunset. However, the actual date of the letter must be given as July 6, since the letter was certainly written down only in the following morning at the earliest.

Discussion:

The possibility to date the present letter exactly considerably adds to its historical significance. Firstly, it appears that hardly 4 months before his death, in the middle of 669 BC, Esarhaddon was preparing for a journey to Borsippa (and Babylon?) – a fact not known previously. Secondly, it seems extremely likely that the king had never before personally visited Borsippa (or Babylon): otherwise it would not have been necessary to explain in detail on what kind of bridge the kind was supposed to cross the River of Borsippa, as the bridge had been there from the times of the king's father and even grandfather (Obv. 3'ff).[532] Obviously, then, the king had exceptionally good reasons for the trip this time, but what reasons exactly? My guess is that he intended to be present at the ceremonial reintroduction of Marduk's statue in Babylon, which had already been unsuccessfully attempted earlier in the same year (*LAS* 29), and for which the next suitable occasion presented itself at the time of the New Year's festival of the month Tašrītu (cf. on *LAS* 190). The existence of *three* different haruspical queries concerning Marduk's journey from Assur to Babylon from the time of Esarhaddon (*AGS* 104-106) indicates that the king considered sending the statue off more than once, and *AGS* 149 implies that the king's presence on the journey was (at least theoretically) obligatory. Of course, it is also possible that the king simply wanted to inspect the restored temples of Borsippa and Babylon on the spot, with an eye to another visit next year.

Notes:

3'. *"The River of Borsippa"*: a canal connecting Borsippa with the Euphrates, ending at Babylon. See in more detail Unger, *RlA* 1 p. 408.

4'. *"Under Sargon (and) the king's father"*: This remark shows unequivocally that the present letter was addressed to Esarhaddon. In Neo-Assyrian letters, the father of the ruling king was *never* referred to by name (cf. *LAS* 60:11.r3, 114:6, 125:18, 224 r16', 283 r10', *ABL* 474+659:18.20, 493:11.16f, 633+K.11448:12, 951: 19, 1160:9', also *CT* 53 44 r3 and 139:5, all referring to AD-*šú ša* LUGAL EN-*ja*, and *LAS* 198:11.15, 309 r15, *ABL* 166:5, 493 r24, 533 r2, 885:10, 948 r7, 1078 r7, 1103 r1, 1250 r8 and 1377:5 referring to AD-*ka* "your father"); hence the passage cannot be translated "Sargon, the father of the king" (thus *SLA* and *RCAE*), and the addressee cannot be identified as Sennacherib. On the other hand, the addressee cannot be Assurbanipal either, since if the ref. to the king's father is taken to pertain to Esarhaddon [who, as far as it is known, actually *never* visited Babylonia], one would be in trouble trying to explain why the writer had omitted Sennacherib who repeatedly campaigned in Babylonia. See also note on the date of the letter.

5'. *sa-qu-u-ni*: cancel the translation "was high" given in Pt. I and translate instead (with *RCAE*, *SLA* and *AHw* 1039*a*) "was narrow"; the context (Obv.7' and 12') shows unequivocally that the former rendering (based on the assumption that *SA-qu-u-ni* stands for /saqûni/; cf. note on 278 r4') is unacceptable. The stat. of *siāqu* is otherwise *sīq*, but one may reckon with Neo-Assyrian *sāq* on the analogy of *riāqu* "be empty", Stat. Bab. *rīq*, Ass. *rāq* (*AHw* 979*a*).

ti-[*tur-ru*] "bridge, ramp" (= Aram. *t(y)twr'* "bridge", see Kaufman, *AS* 19 p. 108): cf. Luckenbill, *OIP* 2 p. 802:90, *ina meḫ-rat* KÁ.GAL MÚRUB URU *ina a-gur-ri* ^{NA_4}*pi-i-li pe-ṣe-e a-na me-ti-iq be-lu-ti-ja ú-šak-bi-is ti-tur-ru* "at the access to the gate of the citadel, I had a ramp made with kiln-fired bricks and white limestone for

[532] *LAS* 277:9 shows that Esarhaddon had once visited Samarra (between Assur and Baghdad). But there is no corresponding evidence suggesting that he had ever visited Babylonia proper.

my lordly processions", and note *OIP* 24 pl. 18:8 *ša pi-i-li pe-ṣi-i ú-šak-bi-is ti-tur-ru* "I had a ramp of white limestone made" referring to the Jerwan aqueduct of Sennacherib. In the Kuyunjik letters, *titurru* also occurs in *ABL* 198 r6 (KASKAL^MEŠ^*-ni ša muḫ-ḫi* [. . .] [6]*ú-ṭa-a-bu ti-tur-ra-a-te ú-k*[*ab-bu-su*]), 503 r9 (*ti-tur-ru-šú e-piš* [10] *gamir*) and 1463 r2 (fragmentary context); note also *ADD* 364:4, (garden) *ina* IGI *ti-tu-ri* SUMUN "by the old causeway"; it seems that the word could denote any paved or raised road leading across wet ground (river, fosse, marsh etc.). For the present context specifically cf. note on Obv. 8'ff.

8'ff. *gi-iš-r*[*u*] *ša* [^GIŠ^]MÁ^MEŠ^: As far as I am aware, the present passage is the only Akkadian text giving a fairly detailed account of the structure and construction of a bridge of ships; in fact, there is hardly any other cuneiform evidence that such bridges were ever used in ancient Mesopotamia, if one may judge from the data presented in *CAD* G 107f (s.v. *gišru*) and *RlA* 2 p. 72. A bridge in Borsippa is also mentioned in a document dating from the reign of Darius (Strassmeier, *Dar.* 64:1 É *šá* SAG.DU *gi-iš-ri*; cf. Unger, *RlA* 1 p. 424, according to whom "es ist möglich, daß die Brücke das 'Jenseitige Viertel' mit der Altstadt verband"); but the nature of the bridge is not further specified in the text. The bronze gates of Balawat (bands 17 and 18) include two scenes in which a bridge is depicted (see e.g. Y. Yadin, *The Art of Warfare in Biblical Lands* [London 1963], p. 403, or E. Strommenger – M. Hirmer, *The Art of Mesopotamia* [London 1964], pl. 213); they seem to represent "a pontoon-bridge, made by running a plank over round-bottomed boats tied together" (Yadin, *loc.cit.*), and similar to those used even today in Iraq (cf. A. Salonen, *Wasserfahrzeuge*, Tf. 39,1). However, this cannot be the type of bridge described in the present letter, since it is unthinkable that the word ^GIŠ^MÁ "boat, ship" could refer to the round-bottomed *guffas* (= Akk. *quppu*, see Salonen, *op.cit.* p. 71 ff) of the gates.[533] A better point of comparison is provided by the bridge built by Xerxes across the Hellespont, whose construction Herodotus describes in the seventh book of his *Historiae* (cap. 34 ff). Cf. especially VII 36:7, "Having done this, they brought planks upon the beams, and having put these too in order, they brought earth upon the planks; having then trodden the earth hard (cf. *titurru iktabsū* in the present letter), they sheltered the edges on both sides so that the draught animals and horses would not get frightened at seeing the sea underneath." On the whole, it seems to me that the Persian bridge must have been essentially identical with the Babylonian one described here, and it is hardly necessary to point out that the former may well have been an adaptation of the latter.

That bridges of ships were later used in Iraq is of course well known. Nevertheless, our passage is so strikingly similar to the description of the bridge of Mosul given by Layard, *Nineveh and its Remains* II p. 76, that I think it is worth while quoting the pertinent passage in full: "The bridge of Mosul consists of a number of rude boats bound together by iron chains. Planks are laid from boat to boat, and the whole is covered with earth. During the time of the floods this frail bridge would be unable to resist the force of the stream; the chains holding it on one side of the river are then loosened, and it swings round . . ."[534] It would seem that a corresponding situation prevailed while our letter was written (cf. Obv.12'), probably owing to an excessive flood in the beginning of the year (cf. Borger, *Ash* p. 7 III 8, referring to the flood of the Tigris in Ajāru = May, 669, and note also *LAS* 294 r14f).

10'. *tam-li-ti*: for *tamlītu* (cf. note to 126 r13). Probably referring to the earthern filling trod upon the planks (= *titurru*?). Cf. above.

11'. *ú ṭa ab-bu*: cf. *ú-ṭi-ib-bu ger-ru* "they improved the (mountain) path" *Sg 8* 24 and KASKAL^MEŠ^*-ni* . . . *ú-ṭa-a-bu* "they'll improve the roads", *ABL* 198 r5 f. For the rest of the line cf. *ABL* 100 r14 ff, *i-su-ri gi-iš-ru* [15]*nu-ga-mar* LUGAL *ina* UGU [16]*gi-iš-ru e-bir* "perhaps we shall (be able to) complete the bridge so that the king may pass over it" (most likely pertaining to a pontoon bridge).

13'. ^d^*ALÀD* = ^d^*I-šum*, *2 R* 50, 11c. Išum ("fire") was a manifestation ("counselor") of Nergal, cf. ^d^*I-šum ma-lik-šú* "Išum, his (sc. Nergal's) counselor", *ZA* 43 (1936) 17:56; note also *ta-nit-ti* EN GAL-*i* ^d^U+GUR *u qu ra du* ^d^*I-šum* "praise to the great lord Nergal and the valiant Išum", Cagni *Erra* V 39 (ibid. 41 ^d^*I-šum ma-lik-šú*, scil. of Erra, another "aspect" of Nergal). Since there apparently was no temple of Išum or Nergal in Borsippa (see Unger, *RlA* 1 p. 414 ff), it seems likely that the oblates mentioned here were procured from the Nergal temple of Cutha (= mod. Tell Ibrāhīm, 50 km N of Borsippa), which is mentioned (as object of building activities?) in the immediate sequel (Obv. 17').

---

533 Incidentally, the identification of the supporters of the bridge as *guffas* is not at all certain; one could equally well think of pontoons or inflated skins (*maškuru*), cf. Xenophon, *Anabasis* III 5:8 ff.

534 Cf. also *Nineveh and its Remains* (abridged edition), pp. 266, 268 and 270.

15'ff. *ka-a-ri É-zi-da*: This structure does not seem to be referred to elsewhere; however, it can hardly be doubted that the place was situated near the "lapis lazuli gate" (KÁ.GAL ^{NA_4}.ZA.GÌN) located by Unger (*RlA* 1 p. 409f; cf. Tf. 59) in the middle of the NE side of the circuit wall of Ezida, at the point were the procession street of Nabû and the Borsippa river meet the fosse surrounding the temple. The suggestion of Mār-Ištar that glazed (kiln-fired) bricks should be used for the structure (cf. note on *epertu šaḫāṭu* sub *LAS* 283 r6f) specifically speaks for this interpretation. The remark "they should cut the waters off" probably means quite simply that the former quay-wall had been completely inundated by the spring flood and that its level was now to be raised above the water line. – For the final vowel in *ka-a-ri* cf. note to 280:23.

17'ff. No building operations in Cutha – if, as it is likely, the present passage refers to such – are recorded in the extant building inscriptions of Esarhaddon. This must be simply due to the fact that the king died only four months after the present letter was despatched.

r4. *Nergal-šarru-uṣur*: A bodyguard of this name is otherwise not known, but it does not seem excluded that the man meant is in fact identical with the "third man" (*tašlīšu*) N. frequently met as witness in contemporary contracts from Nineveh (particularly those of Rēmanni-Adad, the royal charioteer). Cf. *ABL* 580 r1-3, where mentioned together with Ištar-šumu-ēreš and the *bodyguard* Marduk-šarru-uṣur (see on 190 r12).

r5. LÚ**2-i ša* LÚ*.URU*La-ḫi-ra-aje*: See note on 275:9.

r6ff. Was the dismissal of these magistrates occasioned by the evil portents (delayed heliacal rising of Jupiter, solar and lunar eclipses, earthquake) received during the preceding month? Cf. *RMA* 272 r13 ff: "The noblemen which your royal father had installed in Akkad destroyed Babylon and carried away the valuables of Babylon; that is why these evil signs have appeared. Let the king's troops come and seize them, and place others in their stead . . ."

r11'-14'. Quoted from *Enūma Anu Enlil*, Tablet VI; cf. *ACh* Sîn 18:10, [I *ina* SI ZAG-*šú* GUB *ina*] MU BI BUR_5 TE-*ma* EBUR KÚ ù LUGAL NIM.[MA^{KI} . . . .].

r15'f. Free rendering of the following omen, quoted in *RMA* 213 and 214: I ^{MUL}GÍR.TAB *ana* IGI *30* TE-*ma* GUB-*iz* BAL LUGAL GÍD.DA-*ik* ^{LÚ}KÚR TE-*am-ma* ŠUB-*ta-šú* GAR-*an* "If Scorpio approaches and stands before the Moon, the king's reign will become long; an enemy will rise, but he will defeat him."

292

Bibliography:

(I) Waterman, *RCAE* 1014.

(II) Labat, *Royauté* (1939) 358; *RA* 40 (1946) 130f; von Soden, *Fs Christian* (1956) 105; Landsberger, *BBEA* (1965) 50f, 56; Kümmel, *StBoT* 3 (1967) 173, 176ff.

Writer:

The attribution of this letter to Mār-Ištar is certain on the grounds of the subject matter (substitute king ritual, affairs of Borsippa; cf. *LAS* 279ff and 291), orthography (MAN *be-lí* thrice, *le-e-pu-šú* [r.17']; cf. Appendix M 6) and the phrase MAN *be-lí lu-u ú-*[*di* (Obv.5'; cf. ibid., p. 445; note also Obv.4' [*ki*]-*i ša* MAN *be-lí iš-pur-*[*an-ni*] matching *LAS* 276:15f, 278 r7', 287 r11, etc.). See already Landsberger (1965), 50.

Addressee:

Esarhaddon.

Date:

Tašrītu 22, eponymy of Kanūnāju = October 7, 671 BC. This date can be fixed with certainty on the following evidence. The substitute king ritual was performed only thrice during the entire time span Mār-Ištar is known to have been stationed in Babylonia, viz. twice in 671 (following the lunar eclipses of Du'ūzu 14 = July 2 and Kanūnu 15 = December 27/8) and once in 669 (following the eclipses of Ajāru 29 = May 27 [sun] and Simānu 14 = June 10 [moon]); cf. commentary on *LAS* 26. The case of 669 is out of the question, since the substitute king was then resident in Nineveh and was consequently of no concern to Mār-Ištar.[535] By contrast, it is known with certainty that in 671 the scene of the ritual was in both cases Akkad,[536] and it is hence a priori probable that Mār-Ištar was in both cases directly involved in the supervision of the ceremonies.[537] The question as to which one of the two alternatives has to be chosen is settled by Obv.2'f (stating that the substitute king had completed his 100 day reign; cf. relevant note) and Obv.11'f (referring to a celestial observation). We know that the substitute king enthroned on account of the Du'ūzu-eclipse of 671 was due to "sit" full hundred days (cf. *LAS* 249 and relevant commentary) whereas it is very likely that the ritual following the Kanūnu-eclipse was terminated before the 100 day period was over (cf. *LAS* 280 r11 and notes on the date of the letter). The present letter would thus have been written 100 days after the occurrence of the lunar eclipse of Du'ūzu = July 2, 671, i.e. on Tašrītu 22 = October 7, 671.[538] This conclusion is confirmed by the astronomical observation reported on Obv.11'ff. The star name partially preserved in the beginning of line 11' can be only restored as [MUL*Ṣal-b*]*at-a-ni*; the subsequent remark *ina pānīti* implies that the writer had earlier too reported a Mars observation to the king, and the verb *iṭ-ḫu-u-n*[*i*] in the next line suggests that the planet had then been approaching another star or constellation. Now in *LAS* 277 (r30f), written on Tašrītu 12 = September 27, 671, i.e. only 10 days before the suggested date of the present letter, Mār-Ištar indeed reports that Mars had emerged from Scorpio and was approaching Sagittarius. By October 8 the situation had altered; Mars had then reached the bright stars in the "bow" of Sagittarius (its longitude being, according to the tables of Stahlman and Gingerich, 232°.7; the *Sterntafeln* of Neugebauer give as the right ascensions of $\gamma, \eta, \epsilon, \delta$ and μ Sagittarii (for -670) 230°.0, 230°.8, 233°.0, 233°.6 and 234°.0, respectively). This would have constituted a sufficient motivation for another report (cf. *RMA* 236G), whereas no corresponding explanation can be found for the alternative date (January 26, -670 = Kanūnu 15, 671 + 100 days), Mars staying at that time already for the 12th day in Pisces (longitude 319°.0) and having just disappeared in the rays of the sun.

Notes:

2'ff. The rendering of these lines suggested in Pt.I must be corrected according to von Soden (1956), 105. The traces in line 3' do not warrant the restoration ⌜*a*⌝-[*na*]/*in*[*a šim-ti lillik*] considered by me earlier, and as a matter of fact the suggested translation would have rendered the line 3' entirely superfluous; moreover, there is place at the end of line 2' for many more signs than the translation presumes ("only after . . ." would only account for a missing [*ki-ma*]). But if the restoration [*ki-ma*] in line 2' is thus out of the question, *un-tal-li* in line 3' cannot refer to the future, and one is hence forced to conclude that the substitute king had actually completed his reign just before the letter was written. Restore, accordingly: [*ú-ma-a an-nu-rig*] 3' [*1*] *me u$_4$-me un-tal-li* LU[GAL[539]*-us-su ga-am-rat*], and translate: "Now then he has completed the 100 days, his reign is finished." Cf. also above, note on the date of the letter.

6'. *mi-iḫ-ṣu*: the context (cf. Obv.9' *pa-áš-šú* "cancelled" [scil. *lumnu* "evil"] with 280:17) suggests that this word somehow pertains to the final phase of the substitute king ritual, hence perhaps = "a blow (of mercy)"; cf. *KAV* 1 VII 89f, *mi-iḫ-ṣi ki-i mi-iḫ-ṣi* 90 *i-ša-ak-ku-ú-nu-uš* 91 *nap-šá-a-te ú-mal-al-la*, "they shall inflict blow for blow upon him, (and) he shall compensate with a life." For other possible translations ("sting [of a scorpion, or a snake]", etc.) see *AHw* p.641f. Cf. note to *LAS* 280:9.

---

535 In the lunar eclipse of June 10, 669, only the southern quadrant of the moon (pertaining to Assyria) was touched by the earth's shadow; there was consequently no reason to have a substitute king rule in Babylonia. The solar eclipse of May 27, 669, likewise portended death for the king of *Assyria*, but not for the king of Babylonia; cf. *RMA* 269 r9. Cf. also *LAS* 25, 28, 136-138, 234-235 and 257, associated with the ritual, and note that Mār-Ištar's letters written during the ritual (*LAS* 289-291 = Simānu Du'ūzu 669) contain no word about the substitute king.

536 See *LAS* 26-27, 134-135, 166 and 249 (pertaining to the ritual occasioned by the Du'ūzu-eclipse) and 180 and 278-280 (Kanūnu-ecl.).

537 Mār-Ištar's involvement in the latter case is certain on the ground of *LAS* 279-280. Cf. *LAS* 276-277 showing that he was stationed in Babylonia in the early part of year 671 also.

538 Cf. *LAS* 249:81f.

539 Collation E. Sollberger 19.1.76 ("all that's left are the heads of two parallel horizontals").

7'. *ša 2,30* ^{I}*Aš+šur*-⌜PAP⌝-[AŠ]: the reading of the preserved signs is certain, but the restoration is in doubt. It is obscure why (a statue of?) Esarhaddon should be referred to in this context, and it is even more surprising that the king to whom the letter was addressed should be referred to by his proper name here. I am consequently at present more inclined to restore the personal name as *Aš+šur*-PAP[$^{\mathrm{(MEŠ)}}$-PAP] (*APN* p. 33f), or the like, and to connect *ša 2,30* "left-hand" with the word broken away in the beginning of the line.

8'. [*š*]*a ma-ka*: possibly]x-*ma-ka* "your . . .". For *maka* <*ammaka* "there" cf. TA* *ma-ka*, *ABL* 146:11, and TA* *ma-ak-ka*, *TCL* 9 67:24.

9'. For *pa-áš-šú* see note on Obv.6'; I cannot suggest any convincing restoration for *i-sa-*[ ] at the line end.

10'. *10* UD^{MEŠ} *a-še-er*: perhaps "[waiting] 10 days is in order (= appropriate)", *ašer* being taken as Stat. of *ešāru* "to be(come) all right", cf. *LAS* 121:20f, *ta-lit-tu áš-rat*. This remark may be an allusion to Obv. 4'f, the preceding line (*kīma issa*[. . .]) stating the condition under which Mār-Ištar considered it appropriate to wait for 10 days (only?) before proceeding to [the burial? of the substitute king?]. For *kīma* = "if" see 213 r1 and corresponding note.

11'ff. This passage contained an astronomical observation, as unequivocally appears from the verb *iṭ-ḫu-u-ni* in line 12'; *ṭeḫû* "to approach" was obsolete in Neo-Assyrian, and was only used as an astronomical and exorcistic terminus technicus in scientific contexts (cf. *LAS* 110+300:9.16, 218:14, 280 r12, 291 r10, *ABL* 1113 r1, and *RMA* passim). Consequently, one has to restore two *star names* in the initial breaks of Obv.11' and 12'. The only possible restoration in line 11' is [^{MUL}*Ṣal-b*]*at-a-ni* "Mars" (cf. the list of star names in Gössmann, *Planetarium* p. 217 ff; for the ungrammatical nominative *-āni* (pro *-ānu*) see note on *LAS* 280:23; there is hardly space for *ina* UGU in the beginning of the line, even if one were to restore ^{d}*Ṣal-* instead of ^{MUL}*Ṣal-*); in line 12', one has to restore [^{MUL}PA.BIL.SA]G$^{!}$ in accordance with the discussion above (sub Dating).[540] At the end of line 12' one could restore *a-na e-r*[*a-(a-)bi*] "to enter",[541] and in line 13' one would expect a verb in the subjunctive, belonging to the relative clause begun in line 11'. In Obv.13'f restore *ú-m*[*a-a*]$^{14'}$[*ina lìb-bi-šú e-ta-rab*] "he (= Mars) has now entered into it (= Sagittarius)", or the like, in accordance with the discussion above.

r2'. The first sign preserved in this line is (according to collation 1.12.1966) probably [*l*]*u*.

r3'. Cancel the restoration $^{\mathrm{LÚ*}}$*sa-a*[*k-lu*] given in Pt.I. In *LAS* 280 r15, on which the restoration was based, one has to read *amēlu sa-ak-lu* (the sign LÚ standing in the orthography of Mār-Ištar without exception for the substantive "man"), and the case is therefore not parallel to the present passage where LÚ* functions as a determinative. In fact, only part of a horizontal wedge is visible after *sa*, and it is not even certain that the broken sign began with one horizontal only. No obvious restoration suggests itself.

r4'. [^{I}*Aḫ-ḫi-šá-aj*]*a* $^{\mathrm{LÚ*}}$SANGA: restored from Rev. 10. In view of the context it is hardly possible that Aḫḫēšâ of Uruk, priest of Eanna and sender of astrological reports to Esarhaddon and Assubanipal (cf. Dietrich, *AOAT* 7 p. 65f and 61f; for letters of A., see *ABL* 1062 and K.4670+ [*WO* 4 227f], and for reports signed by ^{I}ŠEŠ^{MEŠ}-*šá-a* ^{LÚ}UNUG^{KI}-*aja*, *RMA* 13, 125, 203, 236G and 252), is in question here. A more likely alternative is another Aḫḫēšâ mentioned in *ABL* 336:3, a letter addressed to Esarhaddon; this man is designated as "temple [enterer]" ([^{LÚ}TU].É) and occurs in a context definitely pointing to Borsippa as his sphere of activity (cf. Dietrich, *WO* 4 [1968] 227[88] and *AOAT* 7 [1970] 61[2]). This tallies with the traces of the divine name in the present line, which hardly allow any other restoration than ^{d}P[A], making Aḫḫēšâ the priest of Nabû (of Borsippa) and hence naturally also an enterer of the temple (Ezida).

r7'. ^{I}*Si-i-li*: contracted form of ^{I}*Sa-i-lu* (*APN* p.190*b*), cf. *lim-mu* ^{I}*Si-i-li* ^{36} ^{LÚ}GAL.MU, *AR* 180:35f etc., with [*lim*]-*mu* ^{I}*Sa-i-lu* ^{LÚ}GAL.MU, *AR* 447:29 etc.(618? B.C.); West Semitic, possibly Aramaic, cf. Palm. שילא Phoen. שאל (*KAI* 24:4), Bibl. Σίλας. Cancel the interpretation Sī'-li (<Sī'-ilī) in Pt. I. After the PN, the traces read either ⌜KUR⌝*Gam-*[*bu-la-aju*] or ⌜KUR⌝*P*[*u-qu-da-aju*] both being acceptable geographically but the former more likely according to collation.

---

540 Restoration confirmed by E. Sollberger (19.1.1976): "SA]G possible although only tail of upper horizontal of PA remains with faint trace of upright."

541 Sollberger 19.1.76: "*-n*[*a* possible though only beginning of parallel horizontals remain".

r8'. É *TAK-ba-a*[*ju*]: otherwise unknown. Probably to be emended into É *I!-ba-a*[*ju*]; cf. É ^{I}*I-ba-a*, *ABL* 454:8 and *YOS* 7 84:9, and see *RlA* 2 44*b*; cf. also ^{Id}EN-KAR DUMU ^{I}*I-ba-a* mentioned in *ABL* 1007 r15, K. 1351:1 (unp.) and K.2998+ r.8 (Dietrich, *AOAT* 7 p.32[1]).

r9'. *Dūr-Šarruku*: A town in northern Babylonia, probably in the vicinity of Upî/Opis (=? Seleucia/Tell 'Umar; cf. Brinkman, *AnOr* 43 p. 111[608]); see Unger, *RlA* 2 249*b* and Landsberger, *BBEA* p. 55[542]. Also called Sippar-Arūru, cf. [UD.KI]B.NUN-^{d}*A-ru-ru*^{KI} = BÀD-LUGAL-GI.NA, 2 *R* 50, 64a; cf. also note on *LAS* 293:10f.*

r10'. *ug-da-*[*lib-šú-nu*]: in spite of Aḫḫēšâ's priestly status, *gallubu* "to shave" can hardly have here its usual connotation "to consecrate" (scil. a person as a priest by shaving his head and body, see *CAD* G 130*b*), since *šangûs* were not responsible for this operation (which was normally carried out by kings or *šatammus*, see *CAD* ibid.) and since the persons in question were subsequently impaled (cf. next line). More likely, the shaving was meant as an act of humiliation (the beards of the men being cut off so as to deprive them of their virility); cf. *CAD* G 130*a*. Alternative renderings: *uq-ṭa-*[*lip-šú-nu*] "he has flayed them" (hardly acceptable, since only inanimate objects and animals are elsewhere attested as objects of *qalāpu*/*qullupu*, see *AHw* p. 893f)[543]; *ug-da-*[*mir-šú-nu*] "he has annihilated them" (cf. *CAD* G 25 ff; hardly possible, since it seems that people were usually impaled alive, to judge from the evidence quoted in *CAD* Z 58*a*). Cf. also ^{LÚ}SANGA *uq-ṭa-ri-da-áš-šú* in *ABL* 633 + K. 11448 obv.(!)26 (in obscure context).

r11'. For pictorial representations of impalement in sculptures see e.g. Botta and Flandin, *Monuments de Nineveh* I (Paris 1849), pl.55 = Yadin, *Warfare* (London 1963) p. 424-425 bottom (time of Sg II): the impaled hang from stakes of the height of a man driven perpendicularly into the ground, their bodies transfixed just below the throat.

r14'. *su-qa-a-te*: the NA word for "street" was *suqāqu*, pl. *suqāqāte* (> Aram. *š(ū)qāqā*), see Kaufman, *AS* 19 p. 94f and *AHw* p. 1061 s.vv. *suqāqû* and *sūqu* and note, in addition to the examples quoted there, *su-qa-qu CT* 53 675:3' beside *su-qa-qa-a-te* ibid. r4', and ND 2438 (*Iraq* 21 pl.44 no. 54) Obv. 12 URU *ḫi-ir-da su-qa!-qa-a-te* ^{13}*ṣab-bi-ta* "watch over the city, seize the streets". The present instance cannot be taken as evidence that "street" could also be *sūqu* in standard Neo-Assyrian, but has to be evaluated as a further example of Babylonian influence on Mār-Ištar's idiolect (cf. on 280:23; note, however, *su-qi* ADD 338:5). On royal statues set up in temples cf. discussion of *LAS* 7; another reference to such statues standing in streets of a city is found in *CT* 53 921 (a letter addressed to Ash), Rev. 17: [AL]AM *ša* AMA.L[UGA]L *ina* UGU [. . . M]EŠ ^{18}⌜*ša* X X SILA⌝MEŠ URU*Ga-di-*⌜*se-e*⌝ ^{19}*ú-se-piš* "I had a statue of the queen mother made upon the [. . . .]s in the streets of the town of Gadisê".

r15'. *li-ba-a-ni* is well attested in NA in the meaning "neck" (see *AHw* p.524*b* and cf. e.g. *ki-i* ^{NA_4}.KIŠIB *ina li-ba-ni-ka* "you have hung him around your neck like a seal (string)", *ABL* 1042:6), and this meaning is most naturally to be assumed here too, despite the broken context.[544] It would seem that the royal statues referred to above had been deprived of their apparel and these had then been set on divine statues. At the end of the line restore ^{d}*Ta*[*š-me-tu*$_4$] (coll. of 1.12.1966).

L.E. 1. This line evidently lists daily offerings to a god, most probably Nabû, cf. *1* GUD *10* UDU *1* MUŠEN.GAL KÁ *suk-ki dan-nu* ^{2}*1* GUD *10* UDU *1* MUŠEN.GAL KA *suk-ki*$_4$ *qàl-li* ^{3}*2* GUD *1 si-sal ḫu 30* UDU *2* MUŠEN.GAL IGI ^{d}*15* É.DINGIR ^{4}PAB *4* GUD 1 *si-sal-ḫu 50* UDU^{MEŠ} *4* MUŠEN.GAL ^{5}SISKUR^{MEŠ} ITUNE UD *11*.KÁM "1 bull, 10 sheep, 1 duck (at) the gate of the major sanctuary; 1 bull, 10 sheep, 1 duck (at) the gate of the minor sanctuary; 2 bulls, 1 *sisalḫu*, 30 *sheep*, 2 ducks before Ištar, (in) the temple: a total of 4 oxen, 1 *sisalḫu*, 50 sheep, 4 ducks, offerings of the 11th of Ābu", *ADD* 1014:1-5; similar lists passim in *ADD*, nos. 1000 ff. Cf. also *1-en* GUD

---

542 Additional references in *AOAT* 6 p.112 ff. *ADD* 899 II 18; *ABL* 960 r3; *AR* 413:46; Borger *Ash* 35:63, 72:40; *VTE* 670; *Iraq* 24 116:63.

543 For examples of simultaneous flaying and impalement see e.g. Streck *Asb* p. 14 ii 3, ^{LÚ}ÚŠ^{MEŠ}-*šú-nu i-lu-lu ina* ^{GIŠ}*ga-ši-ši* ^{4}KUŠ^{MEŠ}-*šú-nu iš-ḫu-ṭu ú-ḫal-li-pu* BÀD URU "they hung their bodies on stakes, flayed off their skins and covered (with them) the wall of the city."

544 In addition to the dictionary references, note also ^{GIŠ}*lab-bu-na-te* ^{14}[. . . *l*]*i-ba-a-ni gab-bu* (referring to divine statues), *ABL* 120 r13f.

12 UDU^{MEŠ} ^{5}MUŠEN.GAL-*i* "1 bull, 12 sheep, a duck", *ABL* 368 r4f and GUD.NITÁ *12* UDU^{MEŠ} ^{2}MUŠEN. GAL "a bull, 12 sheep, a duck", *ABL* 569r1f, both texts referring to offerings to Tašmētu. The present passage may further be compared with *VAB* 4 158 VII 3 ff, an inscription of Nebuchadnezzar recording the daily offerings to Nabû of Barsip established by the king: *šá* UD-*mu 1-en* GUD.MAH̬ *ma-ra-a šuk-lu-lu* . . . ^{6}*16* UDU.NITÁ *mi-ri* . . . ^{8}*2* UZ.TUR^{MUŠEN} *3* TU.GUR$_4$^{MUŠEN} "daily 1 fat uncastrated bull, . . . 16 fattened sheep, 2 ducks, 3 doves" (etc.); cf. also ibid. 154:34 ff and 168:17 ff. It is strange that the number of bulls mentioned in the present letter exceeds the corresponding figure in the Nebuchadnezzar passage (considering that the offerings of Nabû were there explicitly characterized as larger than ever), while the number of sheep is considerably lower. Does this indicate that the offerings mentioned were not yet institutionalized? Cf. *LAS* 281.

293

Bibliography:

(I) Waterman, *RCAE* 339 (cf. IV 246f); Pfeiffer, *SLA* 353.

(II) Ylvisaker, *LSS* 5/6 (1912) 20; Landsberger, *BBEA* (1965) 56f.

Notes:

7'. ^{LÚ*}*EN.NAM*: probably referring to Nabû-bēlu-uṣur, governor of Dūr-Šarruku and eponym in 673 BC.

10f. [^{d}*Ši*]-⌜*i*⌝-*ma-lu-u-a* and ^{d}*H̬um-h̬um*: gods of Dūr-Šarruku. The former, a female goddess equated with Nanâ[545] (also written ^{d}*Šu-ma-li-ja* [passim] and ^{d}*Ši-i-ma-li-ja* [5R 44,4:36, Borger, *Ash* p. 84 r44][546] was worshiped, together with Šuqamuna, as a kind of personal god of the Kassite dynasty (cf. ^{d}*Šu-qa-mu-na u* ^{d}*Šu-ma-li-ja* DINGIR^{MEŠ} *mûr-ta-mu* "Š. and Š., gods who love each other", *MDP* 2 91:22, and see K. Balkan, *Kassitenstudien* 1 (New Haven 1954), 118); the only hint as to the nature of the goddess is provided by *BBSt* no.6 II 47f, ^{d}*Šu-ma-li-ja be-lit* KUR^{MEŠ} *el-lu-ti* ^{47}*a-ši-bat re-še-e-ti ka-bi-sa-at kup-pa-a-ti* "Š., the goddess of pure mountains, who dwells on heights and frequents springs". H̬umh̬um was a kind of vegetation-god, cf. [^{d}]*H̬um-h̬um* = ^{d}DUMU.ZI, H. Zimmern, *Der babylonische Gott Tamūz* (Leipzig 1909) p. 708, 25. Both gods, carried away to Assyria by Šamšī-Adad V in 811 B.C. (see Brinkman, *AnOr* 43 p. 212), were returned to Dūr-Šarruku by Esarhaddon in 680 B.C.; cf. *Babylonian Chronicle*, *CT* 34 50 III 39ff (Grayson, *TCS* 5 p.82), MU *1*.KAM.AN.ŠÁR-ŠEŠ-MU . . . ^{44} *ina* ^{ITU}KIN ^{d}KA.DI *u* DINGIR^{MEŠ} [*ša* BÀD.DINGIR^{KI}] ^{45}*ana* BÀD.DINGIR^{KI} DU^{MEŠ} [*u* DINGIR^{MEŠ} *ša* BÀD.LUGAL-GIN] ^{46}*ana* BÀD-LUGAL-GIN DU^{MEŠ}, "In the first year of Esarhaddon . . . in the month Tašrītu, Ištarān and the gods of Dēr went (back) to Dēr, and the gods of Dūr-Šarruku went (back) to Dūr-Šarruku", var. *BHT* pl.1:14, ^{d}*H̬um-h̬um-ja u* ^{d}*Ši-ma-li-*[*ja ana* BÀD-LUGAL-GIN DU^{MEŠ}] "H̬umh̬um and Šīmalīja went (back) to Dūr-Šarruku". Cf. Borger, *Ash* p. 84 r44, ^{d}*H̬um-h̬um*-MU ^{d}*Šu-qa-mu-na* ^{d}*Ši-i-ma-li-j*[*a a-na*] UD.KIB.NUN^{KI}.^{d}*A-ru-ru ú-tir* "I returned H̬umh̬um, Šuqamuna and Šīmalīja to Sippar-Arūru".[547]

r5. ^{LÚ*}*GAR.KUR "prefect"*: in NA texts often referring (without any further specification) to the prefect of Assur, e.g. in *ABL* 473 Obv.! 8.14.19,r1.4.13 (cf. Rev.3); the full form in *RlA* 2 438*b* no.73, *ša-kín* KUR ^{URU}*Aš+šur*. For the reading GAR.KUR = *šakin māti* see Borger, *AfO* 23 (1973) 9f.[548]

r8f. According to the Code of Hammurapi (§6), stealing god's and king's property was a crime calling for capital punishment. Was this also the punishment alluded to by Mār-Ištar in r14?

r17. For [^{LÚ*}NA]M^{MEŠ} vs. ^{LÚ*}EN.NAM (Obv.7, Rev.5.13) see note on 309:13-16.

---

545 See Reiner, *JNES* 33 (1974) 230.

546 For the present spelling with a final *-ū'a* instead of *-īja* cf. similar alternation in the personal names ^{I}*Aš+šur-h̬a-mat-u-a* (*CT* 53 18:2) vs. *-h̬a-mat-ja* (*ABL* 1249 r6 and 1389:2) and *Aššūr-mukīn-palū'a* vs. *palīja* (examples sub *LAS* 129:25f).

547 For Sippar-Arūru = Dūr-Šarruku see note on 292 r9'.

548 Note, however, that the reading GAR.KUR = *šaknu* is legitimated by the lexical entry LÚ.GAR.KUR | LÚ. GAR-*nu* (*MSL* 12 240 vi 30, cf. e.g. ibid. v 7.8.10) and by the spelling MÍ.GAR.KUR-*tú* for usual MÍ *šá-kín-tú*/*šá-ki-in-tú*) occurring in *ADD* 209:6.

294

Bibliography:

(I) Waterman, *RCAE* 1021 (cf. IV 194).
(II) Oppenheim, *Dreams* (1956) p. 192.

Copy:

See also Winckler, *SKT* 2 (1893-4) 50.

Writer:

The attribution of this letter to Mār-Ištar is certain on the ground of the date (cf. below), geographical setting (URU= *Akkad* Rev. 13; cf. 275:5.7.10.13, 278:6.8, 279:10. 281 r25.28, 283 r5f.11', and note that the city is otherwise mentioned only in letters of Adad-šumu-uṣur, Akkullānu and Urad-Nanâ), subject matter (supervision of temples, Obv. 11'f), orthography (MAN r12, *be-lí* Obv.4 v. EN-*já* r6 18, *ša* 10'.11'.12'.14' etc. v. *ep-šá-ku-u-ni, an-ni-i-u* and *am-mì-i-u* r.2 and 11 [cf. 279:15], *i-sa-kan** r1 [cf. 280r19]) and phraseology (*ša ina pānīti ana sarri bēlīja ašpuranni* r12f [cf. 277:9, 282 r3', 286:6, 290 r15, 292:11'] and *šumma pān šarri bēlīja maḫer* r18 [cf. 277 r23, 280 r6'f, 291:14']). See already Landsberger, *BBEA* (1965) p. 38 (without detailed argumentation).

Addressee:

Esarhaddon.

Date:

Probably Ajāru, eponymy of Šamaš-kāšid-ajābī = May, 669 B.C. This is just a conjecture, but a rather probable one considering that all letters of Mār-Ištar (with only two uncertain exceptions, *LAS* 283 and 286, q.v.) date from the last years of Esarhaddon, 671-669 B.C. The reference to the flood in Rev.14 places the letter in late April or early May, i.e. approximately in the month Ajāru; cf. Ebeling, *RlA* 3 p. 96: "Im April erreichen beide Flüsse ihre größte Wassermenge, der E[ufrat] bei Hit 2750 cbm, der T[igris] bei Baghdad 3000 cbm Wasser in der Sekunde"; Salonen, *Fischerei* p. 11; "Der Tigris führt Wasser . . . bei Kut im Mai etwa 4500 m^3/Sek" [quoting M.I. Al-Hamed, *Limnological Studies on the Inland Waters of Iraq* [1966]); Layard, *Nineveh and Babylon* (abridged edition, London 1867), p. 70: "It was not until the month of April . . . that the floods caused by the melting of the snows in the mountains of Kurdistan enabled me to send these sculptures by rafts to Baghdad . . . The waters of the Tigris throughout its course had risen far above their usual level . . . " Since Esarhaddon was absent from Assyria during the first four months of 671 (see commentary to *LAS* 59), that year is out of the question. The fact that the flood is characterized as "strong" (*dannu*) points distinctly to 669, since it is known that the floods in that year were exceptionally powerful. Cf. *LAS* 291:12' *šat-tu an-ni-tú* A^MEŠ *id-dan-nu*, referring to the flood of 669 B.C.; Esarhaddon's inscription Assur C (Borger *Ash* p. 7) shows that this flood was added to by heavy reigns and explicitly places it in the month Ajāru.[549] See also note on Rev.6 ff.

Discussion:

On the fragmentary obverse Mār-Ištar seems to communicate to the king, beginning in line 7', complaints of an unidentifiable but obviously important Babylonian who has taken the side of the Assyrians but considers himself poorly rewarded for his services. The dream quoted in Obv.15'ff served to bring home the point.

Notes:

6'. In view of its vocalization, *-t]a-ta-ap* could be taken as Dtt present of a verb having as its 2nd and 3rd radicals *tp*, but the 1st radical of this hypothetical verb presents difficulties; *ḫtp* (*AHw* 336*a*) and *qtp* (ibid. 907*a*) are not attested in the Dtt stem and would hardly make sense in the context. But is a verb in question after all? Cf. ^ÍD*Tak-ka-tap*, *ABL* 520:9.

12'. *nap-tu-nu*: here naturally referring to meals served daily to gods in temples. Cf. *TU* 38 = *RAcc* p. 76: 21 ff, u_4*-mi-šam kal* MU.AN.NA *IX en* BUR *3* GUR *3* PI ŠE+BAR ⌜ù⌝ [^ŠEZÍZ.ÀM] . . . ²³*šá* LÚUR$_5$^MEŠ *ina* É LÚMU^MEŠ *a-na 1X en* u_4*-mu a-na 4 nap-tan šá* ^d[*60*] *An-tum* ²⁴^dINNIN ^d*Na-na-a ù* DINGIR^MEŠ *a-šá-bu-tu šá* UNUG^KI *a-na* LÚMU^MEŠ *i-na*[*m*]*-di-in* "every day, the whole year, the millers deliver to the bakers in the bakers' house a bowl (containing) 3 kor 3 ephas of barley and wheat for 4 daily meals of Anu, Antu, Ištar, Nanâ and the gods dwelling in Uruk", and see van Driel, *The Cult of Aššur* (1969), p. 159f.

[549] For the date of this inscription see commentary to *LAS* 29.

The restoration *ú-k*]*al-la* at the beginning of the line should be replaced by *a-k*]*al-la*; there are no NA attestations of *kalû* in the D stem, see *CAD* K 102f.

13'. The passage beginning in this line links up so well with the preceding one (cf. Discussion) that one would expect the speaker to be the same as above; the word *i-qab-bi* is hence a bit surprising in the context. Instead of a personal name, restore perhaps [*ú-m*]*a!-a* in the beginning of the line (not collated) and translate "he is now saying"?

18'. *ú-sa-pil-šú*: either *špl* D ("I humiliated him", implying that the question "who will give (this)" was considered by the speaker a slip humiliating the god as if putting his omnipotence in doubt) or, much more plausibly, *'pl* Š "I begged him to answer"; cf. *LAS* 216 r7 and the dictionaries, where however only OB examples are quoted. Note also *Isaiah* 6:1 ff: "In the year of King Uzziah's death I saw [in a dream] the Lord seated on a throne, high and exalted, and the skirt of his robe filled the temple. ––– [8]Then I heard the Lord saying, "Whom shall I send? Who will go for me?" And I answered, "Here am I; send me." He said: "Go and tell this people: 'You may listen and listen, but you will not understand. –––'" *Then I asked*, "How long, O Lord?" *And he answered*, Until cities fall in ruins . . .", etc.

r3. *ši-id-di-im-ma*: taken as an abbreviation of *ina šiddi ḫūli* (*LAS* 72 r16ff; *ABL* 1133:14; ND 2672:21 = Postgate, *Taxation* p. 388, etc.), cf. *ina šid-di-i*[*m-ma*], *CT* 53 639:5', referring to the course of a river. Note that the word cannot pertain to *e-gér-a-te-e-a* in the next line, as appears clearly from the parallel sentence Rev. 9f.

r4. *šá* É *mar-di-a-te*: these words constitute the subject of *i-pa-qi-du* in Rev. 5 and hence probably stand for the plural of LÚ**šá* É *mar-di-te* "personnel of a post station"; for *bēt mardītu* "post station" see provisionally K. Deller, *Or* NS 27 (1958) 312 and J.V. Kinnier Wilson, *CTN* 1 (1972) 57; for names of professions of the type (LÚ)*ša* É x, cf. (LÚ)*ša* É *2-i/e* (*CAD* B 296*b*), (LÚ)*ša* É *ku-din(-ni)* (*CAD* K 492*b*) and (LÚ)*ša* É (1)*qi-qi-i* (Kinnier Wilson, op.cit. p. 73f); and for plurals of nouns formed with a prefixed *ša*, cf. note on *LAS* 174 r12. – The present passage, which gives a good illustration of the Assyrian postal service, should be compared with Herodotus' account of the postal system of the Persians, *Historiae* VIII 98; cf. also Weidner, *AfO Beiheft* 6, p. 11.

r6ff. "*Two and three times (already) they have returned my letters*": this remark would account for the fact that no letters of Mār-Ištar are datable to the end of Esarhaddon's 11th year and the first month of his 12th year, and can be taken as an indirect corroboration of the dating of the letter suggested above.

r7. URU*Ka-ma-na-te*: a town otherwise known only from the geographical list 3 *R* 53,1 (URU*Ka-ma-na-a-te*, rev. I 20) and situated, to judge from the context there, on the west bank of the Tigris.[550] The town of *Ampiḫābi* has to be located, on the ground of *ABL* 802, near the point where the 'Aḏaim (= ancient Radānu) meets the Tigris: the writer of this letter, who was a governor of Arzuḫina, states that he was to supply Ampiḫābi (written KUR*Am-pi-ḫa-a-bi*, Obv.6) with straw and fodder and specificly adds that the transport was to take place by ship, hence downstream the Radānu. It would thus seem that the post route referred to by Mār-Ištar was more or less identical with the modern road leading from Mosul to Baghdad through Assur and Sāmarrā' on the western bank of the Tigris (cf. e.g. *The Archeological Map of Iraq* [Directorate General of Antiquities, Baghdad 1967] and the National Geographic Society map *Lands of the Bible Today* [The National Geographic Magazine, Vol. 132, No. 6, December 1967]). This is of course natural in view of the geography of the region, the east bank of the Tigris being cut by many more rivers than the western one.

r8. [ ]*-ga-re-e-šú*: a town not otherwise known. Cf. URU*Mag(a)rīsu* (in the Ǧaǧǧaǧ depression, see Fales, *Consimenti* p. 97) and URU*Šabirišu* (*AOAT* 6 329, between Nisibis and Nineveh; written URU*Šá-bi-re-e-šú* in *AR* 657:3).[551]

r16. GIŠ*a-mur-din-nu*: sic according to collation (beside *-din-* also *-ti-* possible), but it is difficult to see why a bramble (cf. *CAD* A/2 90f) should have been mentioned here. Was the shrub perhaps blossoming unusually early (cf. *in-na-mer* r17) and was the incident accordingly considered ominous, having a bearing on the transport of the beam?

550 Cities listed immediately before K. include Raṣappa, Tamnūnu, Tillê, Apku, Isāna, Šabirišu, Šūdu, Tušḫan, Guzāna, Naṣībina, Ḫamedê, Sūru-Nūrāni, all W of the Tigris. It seems too bold to equate Kamanāte with Gananāte (*RlA* 3 139f), even though the latter is not mentioned in the list.

551 Though Šabirēšu is known to have maintained a post station (see Nimrud Letter 62, *Iraq* 21 172f), the present place-name cannot be emended into [URU*Ša*]*-bi!-re-e-šú* since this town was not situated along the road connecting Nineveh and Babylon.

295

Bibliography:

Previously unpublished. Copy *CT* 53, pl. 46 no. 143.

Writer:

This fragment is assignable to Mār-Ištar on the ground of the handwriting, the shape of the tablet, the orthography (*muḫ-ḫi-i-ni* A 4', KÁ.DINGIR[KI] 6'.8' and the determinative LÚ* instead of LÚ), as well as the subject matter of the letter (affairs in Babylon).

Addressee:

Esarhaddon.

Date and discussion:

670? The text has remarkable points of contact with a letter of Šamaš-šumu-ukīn to Esarhaddon (BM 135588), published by myself in *Iraq* 34 (1972) 21ff and dated there tentatively to 670; note the references to Sulāḫju] (A 2', cf. BM 135588:37), Barsip and Babylon (6' and 9', cf. BM 135588:6.7.17) and last but not least to the crown prince of Babylon = Šamaš-šumu-ukīn (Obv.8'). In view of the small size of the fragment such coincidences seem more than accidental. The plural forms in A 1' and 2' show that Mār-Ištar is quoting a letter or speech of other persons, and it does not seem farfetched to assume that the information in question was denunciatory in character and perhaps pertained to the same persons as the ones denounced in BM 135588. It may further be hypothesized that the informers had also turned to the commandant and the crown prince of Babylon, as in BM 135588, and were only applying to Mār-Ištar after having received, for some reason or other, not sufficient attention from the administrative authorities.

Notes:

2'. [I]*Su-la-a*: better [I]*Su-la-a[ju]*. Cf. *Iraq* 34 33 where it was hypothesized that the man with this name mentioned in BM 135588, a Babylonian hostage schooled in the *ekal māšarte* of Nineveh, was later appointed by Šamaš-šumu-ukīn the commandant of Dilbat.

6'. "*The other Babylon*": a roundabout expression for Barsip. Cf. DIN.TIR.*2*.KÁM[KI] = BÀD.SI.A.AB. BA[[KI]] "the other Babylon (is) Barsip", *Antagal* N ii 25' (*CT* 19 25). Cf. also Unger, *RlA* p. 405 for discussion of the expression.

9'. [I]*Ú-bar*: commandant of Babylon under Esarhaddon. Cf. the legal document Amh. 224 (= AfO 13 Tf. 3-4), dated *lim-mu* [I]*Ú-bar* LÚ*GAR.NÁM DIN.TIR[KI] (probably 680 B.C.), and *ABL* 418, signed by [I]*Ú-ba-ru* LÚ*GAR.NÁM DIN.TIR[KI] (Obv. 2f) and obviously written immediately after Ubāru's appointment in Babylon (see Pinches and Ungnad, *AfO* 13 (1939-41) 50 ff and Landsberger, *BBEA* 28f). Cf. also *ABL* 327 r11 ([I]*Ú-bar* LÚ*GAR.NÁM *šá* DIN.TIR[KI])and 702:5 ([I]*Ú-ba-ru* LÚ*!GAR!.NÁM), both letters addressed to Esarhaddon and most probably dating from approximately 673 BC (note the references to Ṣillâ, and see on *LAS* 30).

296

Bibliography:

(I) Waterman, *RCAE* 745.
(II) Schott, *ZA* 47 (1942) 95.

Writer:

Assignation to Mār-Ištar certain on the grounds of the geographical setting ([URU]*Si-pur*), orthography (MAN *be-lí*), phraseology (*šarru bēlī lū ūdi*) and idiolect (*pa-ni-i* nom. sig.) combined with the rests of the introductory blessings and the first half of the name preserved in Obv. 2. Cf. App. M 6.

297

Bibliography:
previously unpublished. Copy *CT* 53, pl. 40 no. 121.

Writer:
Assigned to Mār-Ištar primarily on the grounds of the handwriting, which is unmistakably Mār-Ištar's. Additional corroboration is provided by the geographical setting (Babylon), orthography (*šúm-ma*) and the subject matter (appointment of a *šatammu*; cf. *LAS* 280).

Discussion:

The significance of this tiny fragment lies in the surprising piece of information furnished by line 4'f, viz. that the king of Elam intended to visit Babylon [in the last years of Esarhaddon]. Was this to honour the reintroduction of Bēl into Esangil? – For further contact of Elam and Babylonia as evidenced by the letters of Mār-Ištar see *LAS* 276 and 282.

298

Bibliography:
(I) Waterman, *RCAE* 46 (cf. III 373 and IV 173).
(II) Behrens, *ABB* (1906) 14[11], 96; Dhorme, *RHR* 113 (1936) 136, and 116 (1937) 15 f; Schott, *OLZ* 40 (1937) 295; Labat, *Royauté* (1939) 337f, 354, 356 amd 358; Oppenheim, *JAOS* 61 (1941) 263; Labat, *RA* 40 (1944) 134f and 141; Böhl, *Opera Minora* (1953) 406, 415f; von Soden, *Fs Christian* (1956) 101f and 105f; Landsberger, *BBEA* (1965) 42; Kümmel, *StBoT* 3 (1967) 172, 174f, 178ff.

Addressee:
Assurbanipal.

Date:
Ābu 8, eponym year of Kanūnāju of the new palace = July 30, 666 BC. The month and day are obtained from Rev. 28'; it is very probable, to judge from the general tone of the letter, that the present letter was written immediately after Akkullānu had received the king's answer referred to in the said lines. The year follows from the reference to the eclipse in Rev. 8'ff combined with other historical particulars mentioned in the letter. It is certain that the eclipse in question was a lunar one, since the omen quoted in Rev. 10'f occurs in *Enūma Anu Enlil* in a context specifically pertaining to lunar eclipses;[552] moreover, all other letters and reports in which it is cited, explicitly deal with lunar eclipses.[553] Akkullānu is known to have served both Esarhaddon and Assurbanipal (see Appendix 0); it is theoretically possible – though we have no relevant positive evidence – that he was active already under Sennacherib, but the possibility that the present letter could have been *written* to Sennacherib is ruled out by Rev.19': it is simply impossible that the writer could already have served Sargon II! Now it is certain that the king addressed cannot be Esarhaddon either, since no lunar eclipses occurred in the month Nisannu during the reign of this king (cf. App. F1). Thus only eclipses taken place in the reign of Assurbanipal can be in question, and one can, moreover, safely leave out of consideration those eclipses which occurred after 650 (it is unthinkable that the king's father could have been repeatedly mentioned in a letter written 20 years after his death). Between 669 and 650, only two lunar eclipses occurred in the month Nisannu: one on April 21, 667, another on April 10, 666 (see App. F1 and Kudlek-Mickler, *AOATS* 1, p. 146f).[554] The former was total, whereas in the latter, only the southern half of the moon's disk was eclipsed, including the whole of the southern quadrant and about half of the eastern and western ones (see App. F2); of the guardian planets, both Venus and Jupiter could be seen during

---

552 See *ACh* 2 Spl. 29:14. Jupiter's visibility during a *solar eclipse* mostly implied a simultaneous visibility of Venus, owing to the short elongation of the latter planet from the sun. Cf. *ACh* Šamaš 8:39, I AN.MI GAR-*ma* d*Dil-bat u* dSAG.ME.GAR IGI.LAL^{MEŠ} *ana* LUGAL *šùl-mu ana* K[UR ÚŠ^{MEŠ}]; similarly, with slightly different apodoses, ibid. 6.22.56, 9:21.39, 10:35.48.80.99, 11:15.42.53.75, for each month of the year.

553 See *ABL* 1006 and *RMA* 272.

554 The eclipse of March 20, 656 has to be placed in the month Addāru, cf. App. F1.

the former eclipse, whereas in the course of the latter Jupiter alone was to be seen (see App. F3). These differences suffice to show that only the latter alternative can be in question: the omen quoted in Rev. 10'f implies that *only* Jupiter was visible during the eclipse, and the remark that the eclipse portended evil to Subartu (Rev. 24'f), not to Akkad (Obv. 13), shows that the quadrant of Subartu was worst "afflicted" by the earth's shadow, which fits only the eclipse of June 666; had the eclipse been total, the area worst afflicted would have been Amurru, whose quadrant was last touched by the earth's shadow (cf. App. F2 and *LAS* 61 and 279).

Discussion:

This letter is important in that it shows that the substitute king ritual was in the Sargonid period by no means confined to the reign of Esarhaddon only (as frequently centended in the past, cf. Introduction, p. XXIII), but was also performed in the reign of Assurbanipal, though in a somewhat exceptional way – at least as far as the present case is concerned![555] The substitute king in question was not enthroned immediately after the eclipse, as usual, but only at the last moment, viz. when already 87 days of the 100-day eclipse period (Introduction, p. 59) had passed (Du'ūzu 14 [Obv. 6] = Nisannu 15 + 87 days, supposing that two of the intervening months had 30 days). Why so? The answer is given by *LAS* 299, which doubtless is the "previous letter" Akkullānu in Rev. 27' claims to have sent to the king on the 12th of Du'ūzu, i.e. *two days before* the substitute began his 20-day reign in Akkad. In that letter Akkullānu draws the king's attention to the fact that nothing had been done for months to counteract the evil portents of a recent eclipse of the moon (Rev.9f; cf. Obv.2') and warns that unpleasant consequences may follow from such negligence (Rev.10'ff). As an appropriate counter measure he suggests that one should, among other things, perform an exorcistic ritual called "giving a man's substitute to Ereškigal", and adds that the king should stay in his palace while the ritual was being performed in "another region" (Rev. 5'ff). There can't be any doubt that it was exactly because of this letter that the substitute king was hurriedly enthroned in the city of Akkad, and it would seem that the king himself had given the pertinent order, to judge from the manner in which he informs his servant on the fait accompli (present letter, Obv.6ff). No doubt the king had believed to have followed the instructions of his adviser exactly but, unfortunately, as Akkullānu's indignant reaction shows, he had utterly misunderstood these. He had evidently taken it for granted that "giving a man's substitute to Ereškigal" meant the substitute king ritual which had been repeatedly performed under his father, and had consequently taken Akkullānu's "other region" to mean Babylonia and specifically the city of Akkad, which had served as the scene of the ritual every time it had not been performed in Nineveh. From the "scientific" point of view, the performance of the ritual in this case was an obvious mistake. First, no substitute king at all would have been needed, since Jupiter had been "present" in the eclipse (cf. Rev. 8ff), as Akkullānu had already pointed out in his earlier letter (*LAS* 299:6'f). Second, there was absolutely no reason to enthrone a substitute in A k k a d, since the eclipse concerned Assyria, not Babylonia (cf. Obv.10'ff). By having a substitute "sit" in Akkad the king had only been able to assure the safety of the king of Akkad (Obv. 22), i.e. Šamaš-šumu-ukīn, but had done nothing whatsoever for his own welfare (Rev. 15'f). Little wonder that Akkullānu was so upset. It is hard to believe that any of the king's other scientific advisers, whom Akkullānu seems to accuse for the happened, could have acted so ignorantly; it is more likely – as already pointed out above – that the king had acted on his own, perhaps believing that on the ground of his careful education he was able to handle the seemingly straight-forward case properly, and the present letter would thus provide an illustration of how profound the king's schooling actually was (cf. commentaries on *LAS* 34 and 331). A further detail in the letter bearing on the early history of Assurbanipal is also worth noticing: in spite of the unjust split of the empire between Assurbanipal and Šamaš-šumu-ukīn (cf. *LAS* 129 with notes), the two brothers were in 666 obviously still in perfectly brotherly terms, for it is unconceivable that Assurbanipal could otherwise have so quickly enthroned a substitute in Akkad, which lay within the confines of the kingdom of his brother – even granting that the action was to the advantage of the latter.

Notes:

5. *ṣa-lam pu-u-ḫi*: even though this expression literally means "substitute *statue*", the verb *it-tu-šib* in line 8 seems to imply that a living person is meant. Note that King Erra-Imitti's substitute Ellil-bāni (King, *Chron-*

555 See also *LAS* 334.

icles II, p. 12) was also called NU NÍG.SAG.GIL-*e* "substitute statue", a term referring in exorcistic texts to inanimate figurines (e.g. NU NÍG.SAG.ÍL-*e*, *Maqlû* VII 137 and IX 164), even though he was so fully alive as to manage becoming a real king after Erra-Imitti's accidental death. It is naturally entirely possible *in itself* that the present passage refers to a statue, since each substitute king had such one given as substitute to the Nether World. See Introduction, p. XXIV and cf. *LAS* 134:10f and note on 140:14.

7. The date Ābu 5 is 107±1 days distant from Nisannu 15. The reign of the substitute king had thus exceeded the 100-day "period" of the eclipse by a week, the delay probably only representing a "margin of safety". Cf. *LAS* 292:4'f and 10', and the note on the latter.

13. *a-ta-a at-ta*: probably an elliptic exclamation comparable to Rev. 29' *a-ta-*⸢*a*⸣ LUGAL *be-lí* "why, O king, my lord!" The rest of the line can be interpreted similarly (sense: "Why [did] you [act like this] and why [for heaven's sake this fuss about] the evil of Akkad!").

r19ff. Restored according to the context; see also discussion. Cf. "Diviner's Manual" (Oppenheim, *JNES* 33 197ff.), line 39 ff: AN-*e* KI-*tim* UR.BI GIŠ.GIM.MA *ub-ba-lu-ni* ^{40}*a-ḫe-en-na-a ul* BAR^{MEŠ} AN *u* KI *it-ḫu-zu* ^{41}*it-tum šá ina* AN-*e lem-né-tu*$_4$ *ina* KI-*tim lem-né-et* ^{42}*ša ina* KI-*tim lem-né-tu*$_4$ *ina* AN-*e lem-né-et* "Sky and earth both produce portents; though appearing separately, they are not separate (because) sky and earth are related. A sign that portends evil in the sky is (also) evil on earth, one that portends evil on earth is evil in the sky." (An exactly opposite case, but structurally an exact parallel to the present passage). Cf. also *RMA* 199:1f, ISKIM *šá a-na* LUGAL *lem-ni-ti a-na* KUR *dam-qat*! ^{2}ISKIM *šá a-na* KUR *dam-qa-ti a-na* LUGAL *lem-n*[*i-ti*].

23. *at-ta-aḫ-ḫar*: perhaps better *at-ta aḫ-ḫur* "you are still [. . . . . .]", in view of the unmotivated gemination of the second radical.

r7'. [*i*]*q-qa-bi*: for the geminated first radical see note on 203 r9.

r8'f. *ÉŠ.GÀR . . . iq-ṭi-bi* "the series . . . has said":[556] cf. [^{GIŠ}]DA . . . *iq-ṭ*]*i-bi*, 43:5'ff; (text) *iq-ṭi-bi*, 109:14'; *iq-ta-bi* in an esoteric commentary from Cutha published by Biggs, *RA* 62 (1968) 53ff, and *ina* ŠÀ *e-nu-ma e-liš iq-ṭi-bi*, *KAR* 143 || 219:54 (*ZA* 51,130ff.).

r10'f. Quoted from Tablet XX of *Enūma Anu Enlil* = *ACh* 2 Spl 29:14, [I *30* A]N.MI GAR-*ma ina* AN.MI BI ^{MUL}SAG.ME.GAR GUB *ana* LUGAL *šùl-mu ki-mu-šú* IDIM SIG ÚŠ "If the Moon makes an eclipse and Jupiter is present in that eclipse, the king will be well; a noted dignitary will die in his stead."

r13'. The paragogic vowel in *il-la-ka* (no ventive!) indicates continuation. Cf. notes on 18 r8, 246:12 and r1, 288:7, etc.

r14'. ^{LÚ}*sar-tin-nu-šú mé-e-te*: judging by the continuation, a reference to a servant of *Šamaš-šumu-ukīn* not Assurbanipal. For *sartinnu* cf. Deller, *Studi Volterra* 6 (1973), 652: "Ohne auf die neu- und spätbabylonischen Belege für *sartinnu* einzugehen, kann wenigstens von den neuassyrischen Stellen nicht ausgesagt werden, daß sie dazu zwängen, für *sartinnu* eine der Bedeutungen "Oberrichter", "Gerichtspräsident", "Oberstaatsanwalt" anzunehmen. Es scheint vielmehr, daß der *sartinnu* wie der *sukkallu* ein hoher Verwaltungsbeamter ist, der gelegentlich auch das Richteramt ausübt. Die Beziehung zu *sartu* ist zu wenig ausgeprägt . . ."

r21'. This usage of *šūtu* is surprising; cf. perhaps *ABL* 252 r7ff *an-nu-te* ^{LÚ}MAḪ^{MEŠ} ^{8}*ša il-lik-u-né-ni a-na te-gér-te šu-u-tú* ^{9}^{I}*Ḫu-Te-šub ma-ri-ṣi* and *1 Chron.* 11:4 ירושלים היא יבוס "Jerusalem that is Jebus", and similar Biblical passages.

r22'. *ú-ta-s*[*i-iq*]: cf. *at-mu-šu nu-us-su-uq* "his utterance is choise", *AfO* 19 p. 57:112: *nu-us-su-qa a-mat-ú-a* "my words are well chosen", *VAB* 4 292 ii 32, etc. Von Soden, *AHw*. p. 751*b* restores *ú-ta-s*[*i-iḫ?*].

299

Bibliography:

(I) Waterman, *RCAE* 1397.

(II) Oppenheim, *JAOS* 61 (1941) 263.

---

[556] The perfect seems to have here an aoristic nuance not otherwise attested in Neo-Assyrian.

Addressee:
Assurbanipal.

Writer:
This letter can be attributed to Akkullānu without the slightest doubt on the ground of its internal coherence with the preceding letter. The handwriting and the shape of the tablet are also distinctly Akkullānu's. Note also the orthographic and stylistic points of contact with the previous number.

Date:
Du'ūzu 12, eponym year of Kanūnāju of the new palace = July 5, 666 BC. See commentary to the preceding number.

Notes:

3'f. "Oxen and horses": unclear; perhaps some casualty portended by the eclipse. Line 3' read [*mì-qi*]*t!-ti*? Cf. *RMA* 260:3, I *ina* ITUDU$_6$ AN-*ú* ŠUR-*nun* [4]ŠUB-*tim* GIG^MEŠ^ [5]*u* GUD^MEŠ^.

5'. After *pu-ud-de-e* read perhaps *ta-n*[*iš-t*]*i*, cf. *tāništum ina libbim i-ti-ṣí-i* "the worry(?) has left (my) heart", *CCT* 4 25b:27 (OA), cf. *CAD* A/2 p. 359*a*. In view of *LAS* 280:12, I am inclined to see in *pu-ud-de-e* a D-stem Inf. of *padû* (*AHw* p. 808*b*, cf. Hebr. Arab. *pdī* "ransom"), in spite of the fact that no D-stem forms are listed in the dictionaries. Hardly = BU-*de-e* *ADD* 1022 r3, 1018 r5f, etc.

8'ff. See note on *LAS* 14:14f, and modify the translation in Pt. I accordingly.

10'f. These lines are quite unclear to me. The tentative rendering in Pt.I is based on the idiom *īṣu u ma'du* "much and little" = "everything", on which see *CAD* I/J 221f and *AHw* 391*b*.[557]

r5f. Cf. *LAS* 140:14 and corresponding note.

300 + 110

Bibliography:
300: (I) Waterman, *RCAE* 679.
(II) Kugler, *SSB* II (1909-10) 75; Oppenheim, *JAOS* 64 (1944) 194.
110: (I) Waterman, *RCAE* 1391 (cf. IV 207); Hartman, *JNES* 21 (1962) 25-37.
(II) Landsberger, *AfO* (1935/6) 150[48]; Schott, *OLZ* 40 (1937) 297; Dhorme, *RHR* 116 (1937) 17.
Join by myself, 10.1.1973. *Collated* by E. Sollberger, 5.2.1973.

Photograph:
L.W. King, *Cat.* Spl. pl. 3.

Copy:
See also King, *CT* 34 (1914) pl. 10f.

Addressee:
Assurbanipal.

Date:
Simānu 1, eponym year of Lābāši = May 15, 657 B.C. The month and day are obtained from Rev. 12; the year follows from the reference to the solar eclipse in Obv. 28 coupled with the heliacal rising of Mars reported in Obv. 5ff. See in detail Hartman (1962), p. 34ff, and relevant notes below.

Discussion:

The historical yield of this exceptionally long letter, which can dated with exceptional accuracy, is restricted to the short sections of Obv. 13-15 and Rev. 2-3, the former containing a rather vague reference to Cimmerians and the latter showing that Assyria experienced a serious economic setback in 657, the first harvest of the year being totally lost. To Hartman, who worked on the letter without the piece recently joined to it, such information seemed "of no great historical significance" (p. 26); "it is a pity that our astrologer did not give us more de-

[557] Note also [*ša*]^MEŠ^ *u i-ṣa-a-ti a-na mu-u'-de-e* ⌜*ú*⌝*-tar-ru*, Bu.91-5-9,142:12 (unp.).

tails about the events he refers to . . . For there are very few documents in antiquity which can dated with such absolute certainty to within a day or two of their composition" (p. 37). True; but luckily, now that the text is complete, its historical significance has quite substantially increased. The complete version of Obv. 13-15 discloses the fact that in 657 the "land of Amurru" (= Syria) was not under the control of Assyria but had switched under the "hegemony" of the Cimmerians![558] Nothing of the kind was to be expected on the ground of the inscriptions of Assurbanipal, where the Cimmerians, though designated as "troblemakers" and "unsubmissive" (LÚ*Gi-mir-ra-aje mu-dal-li-pu* UNMEŠ KUR-*šú* [105]*šá la ip-lu-ḫu* ADMEŠ-*ja ù at-tu-u-a la iṣ-ba-tú* [106]GÌR+2 LUGAL-*ti-ja* "the Cimmerians, who harass the inhabitants of his [scil. Gyges'] country, who did not fear my fathers and had not embraced my royal feet", Streck *Asb* 20 ii 104, cf. ibid. 119f), only figure as a power of marginal significance in comparison with Assyria. The true situation, as revealed by the present letter, would seem to correspond closer to the historical tradition preserved by Herodotus according to which Assyria experienced a period of weakness around 640 B.C. while the Scythians "made themselves masters of all Asia" for 28 years (Book I 103-106). True, the Scythian rule was, as Herodotus explicitly points out, expressed in the form of violence and raids rather than consolidated administration, but the important thing is that Assyrian historical sources pass over it in silence, as in the present case. Since Herodotus further tells that the Scythians "invaded Asia *after they had driven out the Cimmerians*" (I 103), it can very plausibly be conjectured that they owed their position of power at least partly to the latter, and consequently, that the Cimmerian hegemony referred to in the present letter had been pretty similar in nature to the Scythian one described by Herodotus.

Notes:

5ff. Viewed in isolation from the rest of the letter, the description of the heliacal rising of Mars given here would fit equally well to two different years: 672 and 657 B.C. Computation based on the *Astronomical and Calendrical Tables* of Schoch (1928) indicates that in 672, Mars had its "morning first" (in Babylon) on May 31, a date which, as appears from App. A2, could roughly agree with the date Ajāru 26 given in the letter. The longitude of the planet at that time was 28°7, i.e. halfway between the constellation of Perseus and the Chariot (cf. note on 290 r11), which would plausibly locate it at the "feet" of Perseus (cf. below) and close to the borderline of the path of the Enlil stars (*c.* +16°); its relatively great luminosity (+1.5) at the time concerned would pose a problem, but could also be accounted for (cf. below). However, the possibility that year 672 could be in question is ruled out by the reference to the solar eclipse in Obv. 29f (see relevant note): no such eclipse took place in that year and, for that matter, not even in the whole reign of Esarhaddon. Therefore the writer must refer to the heliacal rising of Mars in 657, which likewise happened at a suitable time of the year and was preceded by a suitable eclipse. In that year the planet was, according to the tables of Schoch, first visible on May 2 = Ajāru 17 (the year in question beginning on March 18, cf. Hartman p. 37f), its longitude being 10°4 and magnitude +1.5. At first sight this would seem to contradict the present description, for Mars is often at its first appearance considerably dimmer than +1.5,[559] and the longitude 10°4 does not locate it at the "feet" of Perseus but at the "hind leg" of Aries.[560] However, it has to be noted that the present passage actually is not a report on the first sighting of the planet, but simply states the situation prevailing while the letter was written ("I saw it on the 26th while it had (already) gained altitude . . ."). By Simānu 1 = Ajāru 30 = May 15, the latest date referred to in the letter (Rev. 12), the position of Mars had changed to λ = 18°10, β = -0°58 (α = 16°99, δ = +6°61),[561] and the planet was, accordingly, then staying within the "area" of Perseus, more exactly below the right foot of the constellation (cf. Fig. 2 on p. 290; according to the *Sterntafeln* of Neugebauer, right ascension of α Persei in 660 B.C. was 10°87, its declination = +37°16; for o Persei, α = 17°60, δ = +20°50; ϵ Persei, α = 19°00, δ = +28°58; ζ Persei, α = 19°87, δ = +20°47). The paleness of the planet, as reported by Akkullānu, was possibly due to atmospheric conditions (cf. Hartman,

558 "This (omen) means bad to Amurru. By your gods, verily your god Assur will take away the hegemony (*kiššūtu*) which the Cimmerians have exercised and give it to the king, my lord." This interpretation reflects clearly the last line of the omen quoted, and one is hence almot tempted to conclude that it was no more Assurbanipal but the king of the Cimmerians who was considered the "king of the world" (*šar kiššati*) of the period!.

559 E.g. +1.9 on Aug.24, 666, and Sept. 13, 664.

560 Cf. also *LAS* 334 and relevant commentary.

561 computed by means of P.V. Neugebauer, *Tafeln für Sonne, Planeten und Mond* (1914).

p. 36). From the astrological viewpoint, it was irrelevant whether the paleness was of transitory or permanent nature, both cases yielding the omens quoted in Obv. 18ff.

On the other hand, the statement that Mars was seen on the path of the Enlil stars, i.e. 16° or more to the north of the equator, is clearly erroneous and is best taken as a lapsus occasioned by the fact that Perseus, as well as its "feet" (= Enmešarra), belonged to the stars of Enlil (cf. [I ^{MUL}ŠU].GI ^{d}EN.ME.ŠÁR.RA . . . ^{39} MUL^{MEŠ} *šu-ut* ^{d}EN.LÍL, Mul Apin I i 3ff [*CT* 33 pl. 1]). As we have seen, the declination of Mars even on May 15 was only +6°61, and never could exceed +16° at the planet's heliacal rising near Perseus, since the ecliptic (in the period concerned) intersected the borderline of the "Enlil path" only at longitude 44° (near the constellation of the Chariot; cf. *LAS* 290).

7. *a-du iš-qa-an-ni* "when it had (already) risen high": Sic, cancel the translation given in Pt. I. On Ajāru 26 = May 11, nine days after his first appearance, Mars already was at the distance of 28° from the sun, and there would have been no reason to "keep observing until it had risen higher". *Adu* accordingly has here the connotation of Latin (historical) *dum* "while, when", or German "erst als"; cf. *AHw* p. 12*b*, *adi* B2b.

9ff. Quoted from *Enūma Anu Enlil*, Tablet LVI; cf. I ^{MUL}*Ṣal-bat-a-nu ana* ^{M}[^{UL}Š]U.GI! TE! *ina* ^{KUR}= MAR.TU^{KI} BAL-*tu*$_4$ GÁL-*ma* ŠEŠ ŠEŠ-*šú* GAZ É.GAL NUN *iš-šal-lal* ^{93}*ni-ṣir-ti* KUR *ana* KUR *šá-ni-tim* È-*ma* ŠU.NIR KUR ḪUL^{MEŠ} ^{94}LUGAL ŠÚ DINGIR^{MEŠ}-*šú ana* ^{LÚ}KÚR-*šú ú-saḫ-ḫa-ru-šú* ŠÈG^{MEŠ} *u* ILLU^{MEŠ} KUD= MEŠ, *ACh* Ištar 20:92ff; Largement, *ZA* 52 (1957) 254f.

16. Quoted from *Enūma Anu Enlil*, Tablet LII. Cf. I ^{MUL}MAN-*ma ana* EN.ME.ŠÁR.RA [TE] ^{20}[ŠÀ KUR] DÙG-*ab* UN^{MEŠ} DAGAL^{MEŠ}, AO 6486 + VAT 7850 r19f (Weidner, *StOr* 1 354); I ^{MUL}MAN-*ma ana* ^{d}EN.ME.ŠÁR.RA TE ŠÀ KUR DÙG-*ab* [UN^{MEŠ} DAGAL^{MEŠ}], *ACh* Ištar 24:15 and 2 Spl 85 r8; cf. also *RMA* 184:6ff, I ^{MUL}MAN-*ma ana* ^{MUL}EN.ME.ŠÁR.RA TE ^{7}UN^{MEŠ} DAGAL^{MEŠ} ŠÀ KUR DÙG-*ab*, where however the omen pertains to Mercury, not to Mars. For ^{MUL}MAN-*ma* = Mars cf. also ^{MUL}MAN-*ma* = ^{d}U+GUR, *CT* 26 40 ii 10', and note that the reading MAN-*ma* = *šanumma*, doubted by Hartman (p. 30), is certain on the ground of Ḫg B VI 36 (cf. *CAD* A/1 p. 210*a* and 213*a*). The constellation of Enmešarra is defined in a commentary to the above-mentioned tablet of *Enūma Anu Enlil* as the lower part of "Perseus, from his knees to his heels" ([^{MUL}ŠU].GI TA *kin-ṣi-šú* EN *a-si-di-šú*: EN.ME.ŠÁR.RA MU-[*šú*], *TU* 18 r15' = *StOr* 1 352; cf. [TA *kin-ṣi* ^{MUL}]ŠU.GI EN *a-si-di* [^{d}E]N.ME.ŠÁR.RA, *ACh* 2 Spl 53 r15), which agrees with the implications of the present passage according to which Enmešarra was identical with the *feet* of Perseus.

18f. Cf. *RMA* 232:6, [I] ⸢^{d}⸣*Ṣal-bat-a-nu um-mu-liš* KUR-*ma* ŠE.ER.ZI^{MEŠ}-*šú* SIG$_7$ ^{7}LUGAL NIM.MA= KI ÚŠ, pertaining to the "morning first" of Mars in Du'ūzu (670). The corresponding passage in the series itself does not seem to have been preserved.

20ff. Quoted from *ACh* 2 Spl 70:16ff. Cf. *RMA* 232:8 ff, I ^{d}U+GUR *ina* IGI.DU$_8$.A-*šú ṣú-ḫur u* BABBAR GAR-*in* ^{9}*ki-ma* MUL^{MEŠ} AN-*e ma-a'-diš um-mul* ^{10}*a-na* KUR URI^{KI} ARḪUŠ TUK-*ši* ^{11}Á ERIM-*ja* GUB-*ma* ERIM ^{LÚ}KÚR GAZ ^{12}KUR *ú-ṣar-ra-mu* KUR-*á*[*d*] ^{13}ERIM-*ni* ^{LÚ}KÚR *ina* IGI ERIM-*ni-ja* NU GUB.GUB ^{14}MÁŠ.ANŠE KUR URI^{KI} *ina* EDIN *par-ga-niš* NÁ^{MEŠ} ^{15}ŠE^{GIŠ}.Ì ZÚ.LUM.MA SI.SÁ^{MEŠ}. On the discrepancies of the two quotations cf. note on *LAS* 108:6'.

25f. This omen is not otherwise known, but it was probably included in the commentary series to *Enūma Anu Enlil*, to judge from the gloss *šalputti umman-manda* specifying the general term ^{MÍ}KÚR^{MEŠ} ("hostilities"). Cf. Hartman, p. 31f, but note that the writer certainly meant that the Cimmerians were to suffer the "destruction", not to cause it.

28ff. This section places the letter with absolute certainty in 657 B.C.: during the reigns of Esarhaddon and Assurbanipal only two solar eclipses (those of 15.4.-656 and 6.4.-647) were visible in Nineveh within 60 days after the spring equinox (cf. App. F), and the latter of those is out of the question since Mars was then well visible through the entire year[562]. In addition, the data of the present letter fit perfectly the eclipse of 657 B.C. "The day of this eclipse, April 15, was Nisan 28 in the Babylonian calendar. Though this eclipse was total in the lands farther to the west, it was partial at Nineveh,[563] the northern or 'Subartu' portion of the sun not being darkened for an

[562] Cf. Stahlman and Gingerich, *Solar and Planetary Longitudes* (1962), p. 228, according to which Mars had its heliacal rising in October 649 and was in opposition with the sun in August 648.

[563] According to Kudlek and Mickler, *Solar and Lunar Eclipses* (1971), the maximal magnitude of the eclipse at Nineveh [at 11^{h}6^{m} a.m.] was 0.84 solar diameter.

observer there, as our text says" (Hartman, p. 35). Moreover, Jupiter was at the time concerned only 22° distant from the sun and was therefore certainly visible (= "present") during the eclipse, as our text implies. According to the tables of Schoch (1928), the heliacal setting of Jupiter for Babylon occurred in this year on May 4 = Ajāru 18, i.e. 18 days after the solar eclipse. However, in the latitude of Nineveh the phenomenon was observable already (at least) two days earlier, cf. Schaumberger, *ZA* 47 (1941/2) 122f. Therefore the agreement with our text (stating that Jupiter stayed visible 15 days after the eclipse) is again perfect.

32. Despite its formulation, this omen did not pertain to a mere atmopsheric phenomenon (thus Hartman, p. 32), but to the heliacal setting of Jupiter just discussed. The same omen is namely also cited in three astrological reports from the same period[564] and it is there explicitly derived from Jupiter's prolonged stay in the sky and associated with its heliacal setting. Cf. *RMA* 183:3, I ^{d}UTU *ina ni-di* KUR-*ḫa 3,20 iz-ziz-ma* ^{GIŠ}TUKUL ^{4}ÍL-*ši: 3,20 : šar-ri* $^{5 MUL}$SAG.ME.GAR *ana* UGU *a-dan-ni-šú* ITU GUB-*ma* ^{6}I ^{MUL}SAG.ME.GAR *ana* ^{d}UTU.ŠÚ.A DIB-*iq* KU[R KI.TUŠ] ^{7}*ni-iḫ-ti* TUŠ-*ab* $^{8 MUL}$SAG.ME.GAR *ana* UGU *a-dan-ni-šú* ITU GUB-*ma* "'If the sun lights up in a *nīdu*, the *eššana* will become angry and raise his weapons.' *Eššana* = king, Jupiter was present a month over its (mean) period (of visibility). 'If Jupiter passes away in the west, the land will live a quiet life': Jupiter was present a month over its period"; [I] ^{MUL}SAG.ME.GAR *a-na* ^{d}UTU.ŠÚ.A DIB-*iq* ^{3}KI.TUŠ *ni-iḫ-ti* DI-*mu ana* KUR ^{4}[I ^{d}U]TU *ina ni-du* KUR-*ḫa 3,20* ŠÚR-*ma* ^{GIŠ}TUKUL GÁL-*ši* ^{5}[^{MU}]^{L}SAG.ME.GAR UD-*me* DIRIG^{MEŠ} *ina* AN-*e* ^{6}GUB-*az-ma* "(the two omens quoted in *RMA* 183, then:) Jupiter is staying overtime in the sky", *RMA* 29 r2ff; I *20 ina ni-du* KUR-*ḫa 3,20* [ŠÚR-*ma*] $^{4 GIŠ}$TUKUL ÍL-*ši* ^{5}[^{d}]SAG.ME.GAR ITU *ut-*[*ru*] ^{6}[*ina* AN]-*e ik-tu-*[*un*] ^{7}[LUGAL] KUR.KUR *lu da-*[*ri*] "'If the sun lights up etc.'; (this pertains to) Jupiter's being established an extra month in the sky, may the king of the world live forever!", *RMA* 181B r3ff. It would thus seem that the traditional interpretation of *nīdu* as a kind of cloud (Weidner, *Babyl.* 4 [1911] 162; *AHw* 786*b*) is not in order, not at least in the present omen referring to the moment Jupiter is for the last time seen in sunset glow before being swallowed by the rays of the sun. I cannot, however, offer any better suggestion as to the exact meaning of the word; quite specifically, it eludes my why the omen is always linked with Jupiter's *belated* heliacal setting; what has that got to do with *sunrise*?

r7. *Marduk-nādin-aḫḫē*: King of Babylon 1098-1081 B.C.; see Brinkman, *AnOr* 43 (1968) 119ff. His astrologer Ea-mušallim is not otherwise known. For the passage in general cf. Brinkman, *op. cit.* p. 123.

r8. Cf. "Diviner's Manual" (Oppenheim, *JNES* 33 197ff), 45, BE-*ma* ISKIM *mi-ḫir* ISKIM *la it-tab-ši-ma pi-is-sà-tu la ir-ta-ši* "Should no sign have occurred to counteract (that) sign, should no annulment have taken place." *Pi-iš-šá-tu* in the present letter is simply a genuinely Assyrian spelling of Babylonian *pissatu* "cancellation", which was only a learned loan-word in Neo-Assyrian; cf. *pa-áš-šá LAS* 280:17 and *pa-áš-šú* 290:9'. For Assyrian <š> = /s/ see note to 276 r8.

r9. *ib-ši-ka*: Pret. of *bašû* "to happen" with a dative pronominal suffix referring to the astrologer to whom the instructions were addressed and to whom also the imperative *šu-uṣ-bit* in Rev. 10 pertains. Cf. *ib-šá-ki* PI^{2}-*ja* "I heed you (alone)", *STC* 2 pl. 81:79, similarly *ib-šá-ku* PI^{2}-*ja*, *BMS* 21:62, cf. *AGH* 22:21. Note also BE-*ma* ISKIM . . . *it-tab-šá-ak-ku* . . . *a-dan-šá ḫi-iṭ-ma* "should an omen occur to you, examine its term" in the Diviner's Manuel just referred to, line 43f.[565]

r12. Cf. *ACh* 2 Spl 13a:13, I *ina* ^{ITU}SIG$_{4}$ UD *30*.KÁM IGI.LAL *ṭuḫ-da* MAR.TU^{KI} *Aḫ-la-mu-ú* KÚ. This omen naturally does not imply that our letter was written on the 30th of Simānu but that the 30th (of Ajāru) coincided with the beginning (= 1st) of Simānu; in other words, the lunar crescent had appeared about an hour after the commencement of the 30th day, thereby "repudiating" this day and showing that a new month was to begin. Cf. notes on *LAS* 100. By combining the present passage with data on the appearances of the lunar crescent

---

564 *RMA* 29, 181B and 183. It does not seem to be extant in the presented framents of the series *Enūma Anu Enlil* itself.

565 Oppenheim, *JNES* 33 (1974) 209 is inclined to date this manual on internal evidence to the Sargonid period, but in view of its remarkable points of contact with the present quotation I would rather favour a date of composition in the second dynasty of Isin. On the literary activity in this period see Brinkman, *op.cit.* p. 114f; Lambert, *Symbolae Liagre Böhl* (1973) 276, etc.

in 657, computed by means of the tables of Schoch, the chronology of the beginning of Assurbanipal's 12th year can be reconstructed as follows:

Nisannu 1	=	March 18
Ajāru 1	=	April 16
Simānu 1	=	May 15.

Cf. Hartman, p. 36f.

301

Bibliography:
Waterman, *RCAE* 44; Pfeiffer, *SLA* 165.

Photograph:
RCAE IV pl. 6 (Obv. only).

Addressee:
Assurbanipal.

Date:
Approximately 666 B.C. This letter shares so many orthographic, phraseologic and stylistic features with *LAS* 298 (r29f) that it seems justified to assume that the two were not separated by a long time interval. Cf. also below.

302

Bibliography:
(I) Waterman, *RCAE* 50.
(II) Behrens, *ABB* (1906) 92^3; Dhorme, *RHR* 116 (1937) 16f; Labat, *Royauté* (1939) 217; Meier, *Or* NS 8 (1939) 306; Oppenheim, *JAOS* 61 (1941) 258.

Addressee:
Assurbanipal.

Date:
Kanūnu 15, eponymy of Kanūnāju of the new palace = January 1, 665 B.C.(?). This date is based on the hypothesis that the orthographic, phraseological and stylistic affinities of the present letter with No. 298 are not accidental but can be taken as indications of an approximate temporal coherence of the two letters; more specifically, it is hypothesized that the temporal distance of the two letters cannot be more than a year. Among the features warranting such a hypothesis note (1) the request for a reply letter (Obv. 6ff), otherwise attested (in almost identical form) only in Nos. *298* and *301*; (2) the apology for reminding the king unasked (Rev. 11ff), closely resembling *298* r17'ff (and 305 r5'ff, *306* r1ff, *308* r3ff, which may also be roughly contemporary); (3) the *consistent* spelling of /bēlīja/ as EN-*iá* (Obv. 3.5.6), agreeing with the orthography of *298*, *299*, *301*, *306*, *308* and *313*; (4) and, (as a somewhat weaker argument,) the spellings *šul-mu* and ᵈAG (Obv. 3f, etc.) predominantly occurring in letters datable to the reign of Assurbanipal (298, 299, 300, 309, and many other less certain cases), as against the spellings *šùl-mu* and ᵈPA occurring in letters broadly datable to Esarhaddon's reign (303, 307, 312, 314, 315 and 316). Granting this initial premise, two alternative dates remain: Kanūnu 15, (cf. Obv. 12) = January 12, 666, or January 1, 665 (cf. App. A2). The former of these can be eliminated on the ground of the omens quoted in the letter. If the letter had been written in January 666, it would certain have contained some reference to Jupiter, which was at that time retrograding in Leo towards Regulus: this was an evil omen predicting the king's death (cf. 13 r12ff) and accordingly one which under no circumstances could be left unnoticed in a letter dealing with astrological matters. However, the present letter only contains omens derived from the opposition of the sun and the moon, and foggy weather. This is true even allowing for the possibility that some omen(s) may have been lost in the break following Obv. 14. The length of the break is namely only 5 or 6 lines,[566] and since the omen ending in Rev. 1' was a lengthy one

[566] The tablet in its present condition measures 35 × 60 mm. This means that a fragment measuring 1 cm in height has been broken away at its bottom, the ratio between the short and long axis being 1 : 2. The preserved portion of Obv. has a script density of 14 lines to 60 mm, i.e. line to 4,3 mm; consequently only two lines have been lost on the obverse, the same amount on the reverse and 1 or possibly 2 on the bottom edge.

(cf. 108:6'-10', and relevant note), it must have filled the gap almost entirely, leaving room for a very short omen at the most, and under no circumstances for the Jupiter-omen in question requiring at least 3 compactly written lines.

The date January 1 thus obtained was only 5 days distant from the winter solstice (in the 7th century B.C. = December 26), and would thus plausibly account for the reference to the *kanūnu*-festival in Rev. 6'ff, supposing that this festival was movable and celebrated at the time of the winter solstice, as hypothesized in the commentary on *LAS* 312.

Notes:

12ff. Cf. *ACh* 2 Spl 13a 6, [I *ina* ^{ITU}AB :] ÚŠ^{MEŠ} GAR^{MEŠ} DINGIR KÚ.

r1'. Cf. note on 108:6'ff.

r2'f. Cf. *ACh* Sin 4:1', [I *30* UD *15*.KÁM IGI.LAL-*ma*] SIG$_5$ KUR URI[^{KI} ḪUL . . .].

r4'f. Cf. *ACh* 2 Spl 103a 26, I *ina* ^{ITU}AB IM.DUGUD *iq-tur* [AN.MI KUR.KUR]; ibid. 103b vs.10, I *ina* ^{ITU}AB AN.MI [KUR.KUR]; ibid. 103c, 9, [I *ina* ^{ITU}AB] AN.MI KUR.KUR.

Note that the omens quoted in Obv. 12ff and Rev. 4'f were also incorporated into the series *Iqqur īpuš*, see Labat, §§ 67:4 and 98:10. The writer of the present letter, however, was probably quoting *Enūma Anu Enlil.*

r6'ff. See commentary to *LAS* 312.

303

Bibliography:

Waterman, *RCAE* 1390.

Addressee:

Probably Esarhaddon. Note the spellings ^{I}*A-[kul-la-nu]*, *šùl-mu*, and ^{d}PA, as against ^{I}*Ak-kul-la-nu*, *šul-mu* and ^{d}AG found in letters written to Assurbanipal (cf. above, note on the date of *LAS* 302). Note also that most (if not all) of the other letters dealing with journeys (of princes) were certainly addressed to Esarhaddon (cf. *LAS* 17, 45-48, 52, 69-72, 107, 145-146, 148, 157(?) and 199).

Notes:

6. Cf. *LAS* 10:3', *ina* UGU *a-la-k[i]* ^{4}*ša* LUGAL *be-l[i-ni]* $^{5'}$*iš-pur-an-n[a-ši-ni]*. . . $^{7'}$*ina* ^{ITU}DU$_6$ *ṭ[a-a-ba]* $^{8'}$*a-na a-la-[ki]* (referring to a journey of the king), and *LAS* 72 r8 ff, *ina* UGU ^{I}*Aš+šur-mu-kin*-BAL-*ja* ^{9}*ša* LUGAL *be-lí iš-pur-an-ni* ^{10}*lil-li-ka ṭa-ba* ^{11}*a-na a-la-ki.*

304

Bibliography:

(I) Waterman, *RCAE* 680.

(II) Behrens, *ABB* (1906) 92; Dhorme, *RHR* 116 (1937) 16.

Addressee:

Esarhaddon? This is just a guess based on the reference to the chieftains of *Bēt-Kāri* in Obv.9, a place in Media becoming strategically and economically important to Assyria toward the end of Esarhaddon's reign (cf. the note below). The spelling of the writer's name (^{I}*A-kul-la-nu*) is indeed best attested in letters from this reign (cf. above, on 303); the spellings *šul-mu* and ^{d}AG (characteristic of letters of A. sent to Assurbanipal) could perhaps be taken as evidence pointing to the *last year(s)* of Esarhaddon.

Notes:

9. *Bēt-Kāri*: An Assyrian outpost on the border of Media. Cf. 1) Knudtzon, *AGS* 30:3ff, [^{LÚ}GAL^{MEŠ} ^{LÚ}EN.NAM^{MEŠ}] ^{4}*ša* KUR*É-Ka-a-ri [u]* KUR*S[a-par-da a-na e-se-er man-da-at-ti]* ^{5}*ša* ANŠE$^{\text{KUR.RA}}$^{MEŠ} *a-na [n]a-g[i]-i ša* KUR*[Ma-da-a-a (a-di* ERIM^{MEŠ} ANŠE$^{\text{KUR.RA}}$^{MEŠ} *e-mu-qu mal* ŠÀ-*šú-un ub-lam)]* ^{6}*[lil-l]i-ku* UGU DINGIR-*ti-ka* GAL-*ti* DÙG-*ab* "should the magnates and governors of Bēt-Kāri and Saparda go to the territory of Media to collect horses as tribute, (together with as large troops of men and horses as they desire), is it agreeable

to your august divinity?" (restorations from Rev. 1ff; cf. also *AGS* 31-35 and *PRT* 20-22, likewise dealing with collection of horses as tribute from Media). The name of the king for whom the inquiry was prepared has been broken away, but the mention of Scythians in Rev. 3 points to the reign of Esarhaddon, "besonders da ein gegen Assyrien auftretender Asguzäer zu Asarhaddons Zeit sonst bekannt ist [cf. *AGS* 35]. Außerdem scheint Asarhaddon in diesem nordöstlichen Teil des Reiches mehr zu thun gehabt zu haben als Assurbanipal" (Knudtzon, p. 123); 2) *ABL* 67 r1'ff, [ANŠEKUR.RAMEŠ] 1'*ša* LÚ*GALMEŠ *ša* É *Ka-a-r*[*i*] 2'*il-la-ku-ú-né-e* 3'*mi-i-nu ša* LUGAL *be-lí* 4'*i-šap-par-an-ni* 5'*ša* KUR!*E-ber* ÍD *la il-lak-u-ni* "will [the horses] of the magnates of Bēt-Kāri come here (i.e. the *bēt mašarti* of Calah)? What will the king, my lord, write me? Those of *Abar Nahara* have not (yet) arrived" (Nabû-šumu-iddina to king, probably Esarhaddon, to judge from *ABL* 65, 66, and 545; Bēt-Kāri here certainly a toponym, cf. *AGS* 30 and note the parallelism with KUR*E-ber* ÍD), 3) *ABL* 242 r7ff, ANŠE*ku-din*MEŠ *an-nu-te* 8'*ša* LUGAL *ina muḫ-ḫi-ja iš-ku-nu-u-ni* 9'*ina* É *Ka-ri a-šap-pa-ra* 10'*ú-ba-ú la-šú* "(as to) these mules which the king imposed on me, I write to Bēt-Kāri, they search (for them), but there are none" (time of Sargon II; the provenance of the letter suggests that Bēt-Kāri here refers to the same place as the former texts, though it is not, of course, excluded that at the same time it retained its original meaning "trading station"). In all these three texts, Bēt-Kāri functions as an outpost channeling Median horses to Assyria, and it is hence possible, though of course not obligatory, that the visit of the chieftains to Nineveh was connected with Assyria's growing difficulties to obtain horses from the East.

r2'f. *ku-zip-*[*pi*] *ša SÍG*: cf. *2* TÚG*ku-zip-pi ša* SÍG SA_5 *ka-a-ri* "2 *kuzippu*-garments of red wool of ordinary quality", ND 2307:14 (*Iraq* 16 37). At the end of line 3' read probably KUŠE.[SÍRMEŠ] "sandals". This reading was rejected in Pt. I since it leaves no space for a verb at the end of line 3'; however, it is possible to obviate this difficulty by taking the verb at the beginning of line 2' as the predicate of the sentence, and rendering the passage as follows: [*lu-bi*]*l-u-né ku-zip-*[*pi*] 3'*ša* SÍG KUŠE.[SÍRMEŠ] "[let] them bring me woolen garments and sa[ndals]." True, the word order predicate + object is extremely rare in (non-poetic) Neo-Assyrian, but it *is* attested at least in *LAS* 300+110:8 (*as-sap-ra pi-še-er-su*), ND 2416+ = *Iraq* 20 pl. 38 No. 41:32f (*u-ta-ta-ḫa* 33IGI2.MEŠ-*ja* URUŠE *a-ta-mar* "I lifted my eyes and saw the village") and ND 2759 = *Iraq* 35 p. 24:64 (*ba-si a-šap-pa-ra* UNMEŠ-*šú* 65*ša ḫa-na-ka ú-sa-ḫar-u-ni* "I shall soon send his people whom he left back here"); cf. also *ABL* 192 r5f.

r6'. *ú-ka-la*: taken as 1st *not* 3rd person singular on the ground of the parallel question *LAS* 302 r8'ff. On the white garments see commentaries to *LAS* 197 and 198.

305

Bibliography:

Previously unpublished. Copy *CT* 53, pl. 197 no. 900.

Writer:

The assignment of this fragment to Akkullānu (mainly on the grounds of Rev. 5'ff) is rendered uncertain by the spelling *lu-ra-ad-di-i-u* (Rev. 4') which, as far as the present corpus of letters is concerned, is in agreement only with the orthography of Mār-Ištar (cf. Appendix M 6). However, Mār-Ištar cannot be the writer because of the spelling *be-lí-ja* (Obv. 4) and the introductory blessing differing (from Obv. 7 on) from that regularly found in his letters.

Discussion:

Cf. discussion of *LAS* 331.

Notes:

r3'. *ra-ad-du-u*. contracted from **raddui* (Inf. Gen. *rdī* D), cf. *šá ma-lu-u* <**mallui*, *4* R^2 61 iv 12; *ša tu-bu!-u!* DINGIRME *gab bu*, van Driel, *CA* p. 100 ix 57!

306

Bibliography:

(I) Waterman, *RCAE* 47 (cf. IV 232); Pfeiffer, *SLA* 233.

(II) Behrens, *ABB* (1906) 24[4].

Addressee:

Probably Assurbanipal. Cf. discussion of the date of *LAS* 302.

Notes:

8. *ri-in-ku* "bath": here naturally not referring to the ablutions performed in the course of the *bīt rimki* ritual (cf. *LAS* 167 and 185) but, as appears from the reference to the king's sacrifices (9f) and the time of the ceremony (evening)[567], to a more or less established cultic event. Cf. (LUGAL . . .) 2'[. . .]-*bu* 3'⌈*ú*⌉!-*še*!-*rab*! 4'*ri-in-ku* 5'*i-šá-kan* 6'TA* UGU *ri-in*-⌈*ki*⌉! 7'*ú-ṣa-a* 8' UDUSISKURMEŠ 9'*i-na-sah̬* 10'LUGAL *ina* É.GAL 11'*i-še-er* "(the king . . .) introduces [. . .], sets up the "bath"; leaves the "bath", performs the sacrifices; the king (then) goes straight to the palace", *ABL* 864:2'ff (extract from a cultic ritual; cf. e.g. *KAR* 146 [= Ebeling, *Or* NS 21 142ff] ii 12ff, *ki-i na-a-ṭu šá* dKu-li-[*tum*] 13LUGAL *ep-pa-šu-ú*-[*ni*] 14LUGAL *ú-ṣa-a* dINANNA *ú-še-ra*[*b*] 15UDUSISKUR *pa-an Aš+šur i-na*-[*sah̬*] . . . rev.ii 30LUGAL *a-na* É.GAL *i-še-er*). Furthermore, though every royal sacrifice was by necessity preceded by a ceremonial bath,[568] the formulation of the present passage implies that in this case the emphasis was on the "bath", not on the sacrifices, in other words, the "bath" in question probably was a *cyclically* (yearly?) *recurrent cultic event* (accompanied by royal sacrifices).[569] There is evidence that at least one cultic bath was performed yearly in the month Ajāru, cf. *ina* ITUGUD 5[*a*]-*na ri-im-ki a-na* IGI LUGAL 6⌈*a*⌉-*da-gal* "I am waiting for the king (to participate) in the "bath" in Ajāru", *CT* 53 193:4'ff.[570] Whether or not the present letter pertained to this occasion cannot be made out with certainty.[571]

URU*Tar-bi-ṣi*: modern Šarīf H̬ān, 5 km NW of Nineveh on the Tigris; centre of the cult of Nergal in Assyria. Cf. von Weiher, *AOAT* 11 (1971) 99.

307

Bibliography:

(I) Waterman, *RCAE* 681; Pfeiffer, *SLA* 250.

(II) Dhorme, *RHR* 116 (1937) 16.

Addressee:

Possibly Esarhaddon. Cf. under Date of *LAS* 303.

Notes:

r1'ff. This passage is perhaps to be understood as an apology for a (outspoken) question asked in the preceding break. Cf. *ša a-na* LUGAL EN-*ja la a-šam*-[*mu-u*]-*ni* 9*a-na man-ni-ma ah̬-h̬ur la-áš-me* "if I did not listen to the king, my lord, to whom else then would I listen?", *ABL* 455:8f; *a-ke-e ina pu-ut* 15LUGAL EN-*ja* 16*la az-za-az* 17TA* *man-ni-im-ma* 18*ah̬-h̬ur* r1 *e-ni-in-ni* 2*šá-ak-na* "how should I not remain in the service of the king, my lord? To whom else could we feel devoted?", *LAS* 59:14ff, etc. Rev. 2' is perhaps an ellipsis for "why did he (= Akkullānu) ask *me*", and Rev. 5' could be taken to mean "whom (else) would I (= Akkullānu) ask (if not the king)."

---

567 The *bīt rimki* washing ceremonies as well as baths in other magical ceremonies were usually performed in early morning hours. See Laessøe, *bīt rimki* p. 11.

568 Cf. Borger, *Ash* p.105 ii 29, *ki-ma li*[*l-li* . . .]X-*a* EGER UDUSISKURMEŠ-*ka ta-ra-muk* AMEŠ 30 *ki*-X[. . .]-*šú ar-ki za-na-an* AN-*e ta-šá-kan na-an-ṣa-bu* "like a fool you take the purifying bath after your offering, like a [. . .] you put in a drain after the rainfall"; *BBR* 11 r16, *e-nu-ma* LÚH̬AL *bi-ra i-bar-ru-u* A.GÚB.BA *li-ir-muk* "when a haruspex is to perform an extispicy, he should (first) wash himself in the holy water basin"; etc.

569 That a cyclically recurrent event was in question is also implied by Rev.2ff "if I had not *reminded* . . ."

570 Cf. also Laessøe, *Bīt rimki* p. 97 with a reference to a Neo-Babylonian economic text dated on Ajāru 27, 8th year of Nabû-na'id.

571 It is certain that there were several cultic baths yearly in different temples. Cf. *ABL* 1094:6 ff, UD *28*.KÁM É *nu-pa-sa-ak* 7 GIŠ*me-li-ja-a-ni* 8*nu-qar-ra-ab* 9UD *29*.KÁM *mar-du-tú ni-pa-ri-ik* 10*šu*!-*ku-ut-tu ša* d*15* 11*gab-bu nu-še-ra-da* 12d*15* [T]A* UGU UR.MAH̬ 13[*nu-na*]-*ka-ra* 14[. .] LUGAL [. .] r1 [UD 2]9.KAM ⌈*šum*⌉!-*ma* DINGIR 2*it-ta-mar* 3 AMEŠ *ša rim-ki* 4*nu-ma-al-la*, probably pertaining to the ritual wash of Tammuz at the end of Du'ūzu. Cf. also *CT* 53 254:1'ff, *ina* UGU *ri-in-ki* 2'*mi-i-nu* r1*ša* LUGAL *be-lí* 2[*i-q*]*ab-bu-u-ni* 3[. .] *ú-ma-a* (remainder broken away). See also note to *LAS* 310:6'.

r3'. *i-lu-um-ma*: cf. *LAS* 111 L.E. 2 with note.

r3'. *ēnē šakānu* "to set eyes on": an idiom with several nuances of meaning; see Oppenheim, *JAOS* 61 (1941) 259, and cf. *LAS* 34 r2f (with note), 59:17ff, 227 r5'f and 336:8f, all in the meaning "to be devoted to". In the present context a meaning like "to have in mind" seems to fit best.

308

Bibliography:

(I) Waterman, *RCAE* 45; Pfeiffer, *SLA* 234.
(II) Ylvisaker, *LSS* 5/6 (1912) 59f; Dhorme, *RHR* 116 (1937) 15; Böhl, *Opera Minora* (1953) 402.

Addressee:

Judging from the orthography, Assurbanipal (666-665 B.C.?). Cf. sub Date of *LAS* 302.

Discussion:

This, at first sight, rather enigmatic letter becomes understandable once it is realized that "wearing the spindle for Venus" (11 f) actually means "partaking in orgiastic ceremonies of the Ištar cult". The letter is simply a note in which the writer informs the king that he will be absorbed in the worship of Venus (and, therefore, out of the king's reach) for the next three days. Was it the licentious nature of the ceremonies concerned that induced the writer to inform the king of his "disappearance" in advance (and to ground his participation in the ceremonies with "theological" arguments)?

Notes:

6. *di-lil-šu-nu ina muḫ-ḫi-já*: lit. "their praise is upon me", i.e. "I have to praise them" (cf. the following line). Purely formally, the gods to be praised should be Nabû and Marduk, the only gods mentioned thus far, but this is not compatible with the fact that the rest of the letter pertains solely to the worship of *Dilbat* (Venus).[572] Consequently, the writer probably only wanted to say that he regarded it as his duty to partake in religious ceremonies promoting the health of the king, the suffix *-šunu* referring to gods collectively.

Cf. *ABL* 514 r10ff, [LUGA]L *be-li re-e-mu* [11] *[a]-na* ÌR*-šú is-sa-kan* [12] *ma-a a-na* d*30 du!-ul-lu* [13] *šá-ni-ú ina u*$_4$*-me an-ni-e a-da-lal* [14] *iš-ši-a-ri ug-ga-mar* [15] UDUSISKUR *šá šul-me ina* IGI d*30* [16] *ep-pa-áš a-na* LUGAL EN-*ja* [17] *a-kar-rab* "the king, my lord, had mercy on his servant, saying "Praise Sîn (for your salvation)." This is already the second day I am praising (him); I shall be finished (with the praise) tomorrow. I shall perform a sacrifice of wellfare in front of Sîn (and) bless the king, my lord." Is it a mere coincidence that the worship was in both cases due to last for three days? Cf. *LAS* 287 r3ff, according to which the main gate of Esangil was kept open for *three* days during the Tašrītu-festival of Babylon (to let the devotees perform their sacrifices before Bēl and Nabû). The same practice may have been followed also during other major religious festivals.

7. Cf. *ABL* 65 r10ff, *pa-ar-ṣi ša* DINGIR^{MEŠ}*-šú-nu* [11] *a-na bu-luṭ nap-šá-a-te* [12] *ša* DUMU.LUGAL *be-lí-ja* [13] *lu-šal-li-mu le-pu-šú* "let them complete the ceremonies of their gods for the well-being and life of the (crown) prince, my lord"; similarly *ABL* 1384 r3ff, *a-na ba-la-aṭ nu-up-[šá-a-te]* [4] *ša* LUGAL *be-lí-ja* . . . [6] UDUSISKUR^{MEŠ} *ina* IGI d*Aš+šur* . . . [9] *e-tu-pu-úš* "I performed the sacrifices before Assur for the well-being and life of the king, my lord" (cf. 1023 r2ff, 1160 r2'ff and 1171 r2ff); *LAS* 272:15ff, [É]R.ŠÀ.ḪUN.GÁ *ina [muḫ-ḫi]* [16] *[in-né]-pa-áš* . . . [18] *ba-laṭ na-p[iš-ti]* [19] *[šá u]*$_4$*-me ru-q[u-ú-ti]* r1 *a-na* LUGAL *be-lí-[já]* [2] *i-da-an* "an *eršaḫunga*-lamentation will be chanted on (the garments), he (Sîn) will grant a life of 'distant days' to the king, my lord", etc. These parallels do not, of course, imply that the "praise" which Akkullānu had in mind necessarily involved sacrifices and prayers (though this is well possible, cf. *CAD* D 50 s.v. *dalīlu*), but they do indicate that a religious act performed in public cult, not just private devotional exercise, was in question.

11. *pi-laq-qu*: a sacred emblem of Ištar. Cf. *ku-za-zu*^{MUŠEN} = *ḫa-an-zi-zi-tú* = *pi-laq-qi* d*15*, Hg B IV 306 (*MSL* 8/2 p. 170; also Hg C I 41, ibid. p. 173); NIM*ḫa-[zi]-ze-e-tu* = GIŠBAL [d]*15*, var. *pi-laq* d*15*, Uruanna III 225a (ibid. p. 61); *ḫa-an-zi-zi-tu* = GIŠBAL d*15*, Pract. Voc. 422a, *ku-za-zu* = *ḫa-an-zi-zi-tú* = *pi-laq* d*15*, VAT

[572] Note the PN *Dilil-Ištar* "Praise of Ištar" (*APN* p. 70).

13766+ r26 (quoted CAD Ḫ 83*b*). *Pilaqqu* meant actually a spindle or stiletto (see A. Salonen, *Hausgeräte* I p. 152ff (and *AHw* p. 863a), but as an emblem of Ištar it was – as appears from the lexical passages just quoted – closely associated with the fly(-shaped beads) worn by the mother goddess in her necklace as a remembrance of the Deluge.[573] In cult, devotees of Ištar probably stung themselves with such fly-shaped spindles to show their affection to the (mourning) goddess; cf. lú-gišbal-šu-du$_7$ = *na-áš pi-laq-qi* "carrier of a spindle" listed in group with lú-gub-ba = *maḫ-ḫu-ú* "ecstatic", lú-ní-zu-ub = *za-ab-bu*, kur-gar-ra = ŠU-*u*, ur-SAL = *as-sin-nu* and other servants of Ištar in Lú I 215-217 (*MSL* 12 p. 103), and note the following passage in a Neo-Assyrian battle ritual (K.3438a+ K.9912:8'ff and dupl. K.9923:15ff): *ú-ḫab-bu-bu i-raq-qu-du* 9' LÚGAR.KUR.RAMEŠ [sic] *mi-lu-li qab-lu-ú* 10' *i-za-mu-ru* LÚUR.SALMEŠ *ja-ru-ru-tú* 11' *ú-saḫ-ḫu-ru mi-il-ḫu i-ma-al-lu-ḫu* . . . r3 LUGAL GIŠ*pi-lag-gu ina* MAŠ.QA-*šú* ⸢*e-lal*⸣ "they give shrill cries and dance; the *kurgarrû*s sing 'my game is the fight", the hermaphrodites (*assinnu*) respond with war-cries and . . . the king hangs the spindle in his waist . . .".[574] Cf. also Oppenheim, *Dreams* p. 332 C ii 2; I GIŠBAL *na-ši-ma ú*-X [. . . . .] "If (a man in his dream) carries a spindle and does [ ]" (in a section preceded by dreams dealing with theophanies and therefore perhaps also pertaining to the worship of Ištar).*

12. *a-na* d*Dil-bat a-na-áš-ši*: the fact that Ištar is here referred to by her astral name is worth noticing and suggests that the ceremonies in which Akkullānu was to pertake were occasioned by some phase of the planet Venus, perhaps its heliacal rising after superior conjunction. Cf. *LAS* 11.

13. *3 UD*MEŠ-*ti*: cf. above, note on line 6.

r5. For this construction cf. *ki-i* É.DINGIR *š*[*a*] ⸢NINA⸣KI *a-na a-ba-li-ka* 10 MUN *a-na ka-ra-*[*ri*]*-ka-ni* VAT 8005 = *PKTA* 10:9f (= *Or* NS 21 129ff); *ki-i šar-pu . . . ana šá-ka-ni-ka-ni* ibid. 7.15; [*k*]*i-i šá te-li-si . . . ana še-tu-qi-ka-ni*, ibid. 9; *ki-i pa-gu-lu a-na ga-mu-ri-ka-ni*, ibid. 24, and passim in rubrics of Neo-Assyrian cultic rituals of the type "when you have to do this or that".

309

Bibliography:

(I) Waterman, *RCAE* 43 (cf. IV 173); Pfeiffer, *SLA* 355.

(II) San Nicolo, *ArOr* 6 (1934) 196f; Dhorme, *RHR* 116 (1937) 12f; Labat, *Royauté* (1939) 206; Oppenheim, *JAOS* 61 (1941) 266; J. Lewy, *HUCA* 27 (1956) 39 and 42; Deller, *Or* NS 36 (1967) 206; van Driel, *CA* (1969) 178 and 190; Kinnier Wilson, *NWL* (1972) 17, 72; Millard, *AfO* 24 (1973) 72; Postgate, *TCAE* (1974) 214 and 247f.

---

573 The grounds of this association are unclear – perhaps the sharp point of the Mesopotamian spindle recalled the bite of the insect – but its existence cannot be doubted. Note, on the one hand, the equations nim-sig$_7$-sig$_7$ "green fly" = *ku-za-zu* = *ḫa-an-zi-zi-tú* (Ḫg A II 291)and nim-zu-ra-aḫ "biting fly" = *ku-za-zu* = *ḫ*[*a-an-zi-zi-tú*] (Ḫg B III 187), and on the other hand, the Deluge passages in Gilgameš (XI 160-169) and Atraḫasīs (III iv 46- v 4) telling how Ištar/Nintu/Belet-ilī came to wear "big flies" (NIMMEŠ GALMEŠ / *su-bé-e ra-bu-ti*) as part of her jewellery. For a discussion of the passages see W.G. Lambert, *Atra-ḫasīs* p.163f, with references to actually found lapis beads in fly-shape and Ḫh XVI 89 (RS Recension, *MSL* 10 p.89), na$_4$-nim-za-gìn = *zu-bu* "fly (of lapis lazuli)."

574 Cf. [LÚ]KUR.GAR.RAMEŠ *ša tu-ša-ri i-ma-li-lu mì-il-ḫu i-m*[*a-al-lu-ḫu*] 29 [*kiš-k*]*i-la-te i-maḫ-ḫu-ṣu ja-ru-ra-te* Š[UBMEŠ-*u*] . . . 34 [d]*sa-ra-nu sa* IGI d*Is-tar* [ ]LUGAL[. . .] "the *kurgarrus* who play a war game in the arena, beat *kiškilatu*-instruments shout their cries, are [. . . .]; . . . the *sārānu*-emblems placed before Ištar, [which?] the king [. . . .]" K.3476:28ff (*CT* 15 43 = Pallis, *Akītu* pl.5). For other passages indicative of the nature of the Ištar cult cf. e.g. *ABRT* I 55:6 ff ("the expert singers sit before her on the ground, the . . . players of the flute, of the *ṣinnatu*-instruments and of the long pipes, the *kurgarrû*s of the temple, who . . . the whip, ease her mind with (incense of) sweet reeds") and *Erra* IV 52ff (Cagni p.110) "Uruk, the abode of Anu and Ištar, the city of . . . prostitutes whom Ištar has deprived of their men and taken to herself(!), male and female Sutians, who shout frantic cries, (the city of) *kurgarrû*s and *assinnus*, whom Ištar has turned from men into women to teach the people religious fear; carriers of daggers, carriers of razors, stilettos and flint blades, who have the licence of tasting the forbidden to delight the mind of Ištar." In view of these and similar passages, I do not hesitate equating *kurgarrû*s with Greek *galloi*, Lat. *gallī* (cf. Driver, *Iraq* 6 [1939] 69), and cannot subscribe the view expressed in CAD A/2 341f.

Date:

Reign of Assurbanipal, probably between 665 and 660 B.C. The assignation to Assurbanipal's reign is clear on the ground of the historical allusions of the reverse distinguishing between "the king's father" (= Esarhaddon), *not* referred to by name (cf. note on 291:4'), and his more distant predecessors (Sennacherib and Sargon) mentioned by name. The orthography of the letter is in agreement with this broad assignation, see on *LAS* 302. A more exact dating can perhaps be obtained from Rev. 22f, where it is stated that a priest of the Aššur temple consecrated by Sennacherib had died about 7 years before the writing of the letter. This could indicate that the death of the priest had occurred after the ascension of Assurbanipal or toward the end of the reign of Esarhaddon (cf. Rev. 15),[575] and furnish an approximate terminus post quem, 665-663. On the other hand, since the letter shows that another priest consecrated by Sennacherib was still in his office while the letter was written (cf. Rev. 6-11), a date of composition much later than 660 – 22 years after the murder of Sennacherib – can hardly be seriously considered. Of course, the time brackets 665-660 thus obtained must, in the lack of tangible evidence, remain entirely hypothetical, and the possibility of a slightly earlier (or later) date cannot be excluded.

Discussion:

The present letter evidently pertained in its *entirety* to affairs in *a temple of Aššur* (note the internal connection of the section referring to bakers etc. with the preceding section dealing with delivery of foodstuffs; and the fact that the temple to which the various priests belonged is not identified by name [as in *LAS* 310, 312, 314 and 315], which implies that a sufficient identification had already been given in Obv. 5; cf. also Rev. 13), and therefore constitutes an important source for the study of the organization of the cult of Aššur in the Sargonid period, as already pointed out by van Driel (1969), p. 190. However, which Aššur temple was in question? Aššur was worshipped in many cities of Assyria (besides Assur, also in Nineveh [cf. K.252 v 8 = Frankena, *Takūltu* p. 6], Kār-Tukulti-Ninurta [cf. KAḪ II no. 60:120], Arbela [cf. VAT 8005 r9 = *PKTA* pl. 11], Dūr-Šarrukīn [cf. *ABL* 433 r9] and Calah [cf. K.252 vi 11, where Aššur is mentioned at the head of the gods of the Ninurta temple]); *none* of these cities can a priori be left out of consideration, since in his other letters Akkullānu deals with the matters of temples in three different cities, Nineveh (*LAS* 312), Calah (314) and Assur (311, 315-316, probably also 310). Van Driel seems to have taken it for granted that the present letter refers to the Aššur temple of Assur, and though this undoubtedly is the correct interpretation, the importance of the letter demands that the relevant grounds be more clearly specified. Actually, I can find only two indications specifically pointing to the city of Assur: (1) The great number of provincial governors obliged to supply the temple with sacrificial sheep and foodstuffs: in addition to those mentioned in the present letter, many more must have been under the same obligation, a situation implying that the sanctuary concerned was of primary national importance (cf. van Driel, p. 185ff and Postgate, *TCAE*, p. 215); (2) the reference to the "priest of Nineveh" in Rev. 8: had the temple under consideration also been situated in Nineveh, the said priest should certainly have been identified with reference to his *god* rather than his *domicile*; hence the passage implies that the priest concerned was the head of the Aššur temple of Nineveh, which rules out the second largest cult centre of the god; for a further, somewhat weaker argument see note on Rev. 1.

Notes:

5. ^{UDU}*da-ri-e*: sheep-offering performed in each temple on certain fixed days (perhaps each week, or at the time of the four principal lunar phases) throughout the year. Cf. ^{UDU}*d[a-ri]-ú ša* U[D 1].KAM UD 7.KAM UD *15*.KAM ⌜*ina* IGI⌝ ^{d}GAŠAN KUR-*ḫa* ^{10}*in-[né]-pa-šu-u-ni*, *PKTA* 32:9' (= Ebeling, *SVAT* 12); [^{UD}]^{U}*da-ri-ú ša* UD *13*. KAM* ^{8}*ina pa-an* ^{d}AG *ša-kin-u-ni*, *ABL* 975:7f (cf. 634:6f); ^{UDU}*da-ri-ú ša ina* É ^{d}AMAR.UD ^{12}*in-né-[pa]-šú-u-ni* . . . *2* ITU^{MEŠ}-⌜*ni*?⌝ *ba-ṭi-il* "the sheep-offerings (regularly) performed in the Marduk temple have come to a standstill during the (past) 2 months", *ABL* 951 r11f. The offerings were extracted from the local population (cf. UDU^{MEŠ} *dà-ri-[a-te]* ^{4}*ša* MAN *be-lí a-na* É ^{d}[PA] ^{5}*[i]k-ṣur-u-ni ina ki-iṣ-ri* [. . .] ^{6}*[š]a* URU-*ia šaṭ-ru* "the sheep-offerings which the king, my lord, fixed for the temple of [Nabû] were written down as the obligation [. . .] of my city", *ABL* 1087:3ff, a letter from Dūr-Šarrukīn) or, in the case of large establishments (such as the temple of Aššur), from provincial governors.

[575] Note that according to this passage, Esarhaddon had appointed a son of a priest of the Aššur temple to take care of the duties of his father, who had been *killed* in unclear circumstances, perhaps in the purge of 670 (see on *LAS* 247). As it is unthinkable that while filling one post the king would have left another (in the same temple) vacant, the death referred to in Rev.22f must have occurred *after* the one mentioned in Rev.15.

gi-né-e: "permanent" offerings consisting of sheep, specific pieces of meat, and loaves of bread of three different types; these offerings constituted the daily meals of the gods and, as appears from the present text, were extracted much in the same way as the *dariu*-offerings. See in more detail van Driel, p. 209ff, and cf. the relevant *ADD*-texts discussed ibid.

9. *la ú-si-ik*: ellipsis for (*a-na* LÚGAL.MEŠ) *la ú-si-ik* "I could not ascribe (the missing deliveries) to individual magnates"; for parallels see the dictionaries. Cf. *LAS* 45 r2 and 298:13.

13-16. All the cities enumerated here are elsewhere explicitly attested as seats of provincial governors (*bēl pāḫiti* or, in the case of Kullania, *šakin māti*; for evidence see *AOAT* 6 s.vv.), and it is hence legitimate to infer that the word LÚEN.NAM in line 13 pertains to all the following toponyms, not just to Barhalza, as might be suggested by the omission of the plural sign MEŠ after NAM (cf. LÚ*EN.NAM.MEŠ *gab-bu ABL* 381 r 7; LÚ*EN.NAM.MEŠ *ša* KURURI, 444:4; LÚ*EN.NAM.MEŠ *ša pu-ut* GN, 646:12, LÚ*EN.NAM.MEŠ-*šú* 197:11 and 646:12; LÚ*EN.NAM.MEŠ-*te*, 197:13 and 198:14). The word "governor" has simply been omitted to avoid repetition, as e.g. in *LAS* 293 r5 LÚ*EN.NAM [6]*ša* URUNINA *u* URU*Arba-ìl* "the governors of Nineveh and Arbela" (there also LÚ*EN.NAM without MEŠ!) or *ABL* 444:6ff, I*Se-ti-nu* LÚ*EN.NAM *ša p[u!-t]u!-ni* [7] I*Qaq-qa-da-nu ša pu-tu* [8] KUR*Ú-ka-a-a* I*Sa-ku-a-ta-a*[9] *ša* KUR*Qa-ni-un*, etc. (cf. *ABL* 646:6ff, where the LÚ*EN.NAM is repeated before each geographical designation). It may be noted in passing that despite the 7 contrary examples quoted above, the plural of LÚ(*)EN.NAM was in Neo-Assyrian mostly written LÚ(*)NAM.MEŠ, i.e. *omitting* EN; cf. (Sg.) LÚ(*)EN.NAM *vs.* (Pl.) LÚ(*)NAM.MEŠ in *LAS* 293:7.r5.13.17, *ABL* 409:5.9, 415:9.11, 543:12.r5f, 1108:4.10.r5.6, and LÚ*NAM.MEŠ 148 r1, 464 r3, 508:7, 1239:6, 1250 r6 and passim in non-epistolary texts. The relative consistency of the usage seems to reflect linguistic reality (cf. *AHw* 862*b* mng. 5).

13. KUR*Bar-ḫal-za*: in the vicinity of Nineveh, to the (N)W of it; cf. note on 114:13.

14. KUR*Ra-ṣap-pa* = mod. Riṣāfa SW of the confluence of the Balīḫ and the Euphrates; Bibl. Rezeph, class. Ρησαφα / Sergiopolis.[576] URU*Kàl-zi* = Qasr Šamāmōk 20 km SW of Arbela, cf. on *LAS* 86.

15. URU*I-sa-na*: cf. note to *LAS* 283 r4' and Postgate, *RlA* s.v. perhaps = mod. Tell Isān, Isan Köi, cf. *BA* 2 p. 49. URU*Til-e*: exact location unknown, according to Forrer (*Provinzeinteilung* p. 18) between Nisibis and the Tigris; [577] cf. *AOAT* 6 356f. URU*Kul-la-ni-a* = Bibl. Calneh/Calno, near Aleppo.*

16. URU*Ar-pad-da* = Bibl. Arpad, mod. Tell Arfād/Rifa'at, 35 km N of Aleppo.

18. URU*Di-qu-ki-na*: location unknown, probably however in the Ḫābūr region not far from Nisibis. Cf. *AOAT* 6 p. 105. For LÚGAL-*kar-man* cf. URUGAL.KAR *ADD* 919 ii 9, in the vicinity of Ṣimirra / Simyra; in view of this parallel and the general context, the present instance has to be understood (despite the spelling) as a toponym, perhaps named after the official residing there (cf. LÚGAL *kar-ma-ni* following LÚGAL *ka-a-ri* in the professions list K.4395 = *MSL* 12 p. 239 iii 24f). IDI.KUD-dIM stands for URUDI.KUD-dIM (*AR* 144 = *ADD* 628: 5), written syllabically URU*Da-aja-nu*-dIM in *AR* 400 = *ADD* 373:3. It is of course possible that the town of Dajān-Adad had grown out of an estate possessed by a magnate with this name, and this magnate could actually have lived while the present letter was written and thereofre be meant here; such an interpretation seems favoured by the fact that both *AR* 400 and 144 date from the last years of Assurbanipal.[578]

19. KUR*ḪAL-zi-AD.BAR*: a province to the north of Nineveh, probably approximately identical with the present district of Dohuk. See Postgate, *Sumer* 29 (1973) 55 correcting id., *RlA* 4 p. 64.

20. URU*Bir-tu*$_4$: a town with this name, and designated as a provincial capital, appears to have been situated in NE Assyria not very far from Nineveh, and could hence (in view of the context) plausibly be identified with the city meant here. Cf. *ADB* 5 = Fales *CCENA* no.21 i 20.24 (NAM ḪAL.ṢU; in the context NAM NINAKI and NAM URURI-*mu-si*); *ADD* 516 = *AR* 410:4 (EN.NAM URU*Bir-ta-aju*); *ADD* 1141 = *AR* 113:53 (LÚEN.NAM *ša* URUḪAL.ṢU); and *Billa* 72:36 (*ša* URU*Bir-te*, beside URU*Ka-ru-ḫa*/Tell Fikhar). Note also Eponym Canon Cb 1 (*RlA* 2 431) Obv. 35, *a-na* KUR*Ul-lu-ba* URU*Bir-tu ṣab-ta-at*, suggesting that Birtu is an Assyrianized form of Biturra, the capital of Ulluba/Ḫabḫu ša bētāni (= mod. Amadiya/Berwari, see Postgate, *art. cit.* 57f).

576 Sic, despite the objections of Forrer, *Provinzeinteilung* p. 12.

577 For further discussion see Falkner, *AfO* 18 (1957/8) 2.

578 Note also the occurrence of the personal name IDI.KUD-dIM (in broken context) in *ADD* 907:2 and (as a patronym) in *ADD* 631:4 (680 B.C.).

URU*Ar-zu-ḫi-na*: a provincial capital to the east of Yorghan Tepe (Nuzi) and south-east of Kirkūk (Arrapḫa). See H. Lewy, *JAOS* 88 (1968) 160ff and Zaccagnini, *OrAnt* 13 (1974) 33.

22. Instead of URU*Šá-riš*, read possibly with Postgate (*TCAE*, p. 248) URU*Šá-ḫu!-pa!*, the capital city of Katmuḫi in NW Assyria (Millard, *AfO* 24, 72). URU*Par-nu-na*: location unknown, placed by Forrer (*Provinzeinteilung* p. 38) tentatively between the Tigris and Jebel el-Abiadh. Attested as seat of a provincial governor in *ADB* 5 = Fales *CCENA* no.21 ii 23 (NAM *Par-nun*). *

URU*Ri-mu-su* = mod. Jera(h)īya a couple of miles north of Dūr-Šarrukīn (Ḫorsābād), see Jacobsen, *OIP* 24 (1935) 39; attested as seat of a provincial governor in *ABL* 102:10 and ADD 59 = *AR* 123:2.11. The name is possibly to be read Talmusu in view of *Ta-al-mu-ú*šKI, *ARM* 43 6, see Goetze, *JCS* 7 (1953) 62[78].[579] *

24. *ŠEPADMEŠ*: the NA logogram for "barley" (Bab. ŠE+BAR).[580] Cf. Aram. *š'rn zj br mlk' 'l Ḫmṭṭ mn Ḫdwh* rendering Ass. ŠEPADMEŠ [2]*ša* DUMU.LUGAL . . . [4]*ina* IGI I*Ḫa-ma-ṭu-ṭu*[5]*ša* URU*Ḫa-an-du-a-te* in *ADD* 129 = *AR* 313 (similarly *ADD* 130 = *AR* 327+ ŠEPADMEŠ = *š'rj'* in *ADD* 128 = *AR* 322) and see Borger, *RlA* 3 p. 310; note also that despite its spelling, ŠEPADMEŠ is sg. fem., not pl. (cf. ŠEPADMEŠ *an-ni-ti*, *ABL* 1385:17 and ŠEPAD=MEŠ . . . *pa-ti-a-at*, ND 2452:10f and 15f, *Iraq* 18 pl.11 no. 35), which supports Borger's suggestion that also ŠEPAD=MEŠ is to be read *uṭṭetu*.

r1. *LÚSANGA É LÚMU* "priest of the cookhouse": *sic*, not "*scribe* of the cookhouse" (Waterman 1930; Pfeiffer 1935; Oppenheim 1941; *CAD* G [1956] 130*b*, Ṣ [1962] 182*b*; von Soden, *AHw* p. 297*b*; etc.). Though LÚŠID (= SANGA) can admittedly in certain texts be read LÚUMBISAG "scribe" (cf. [s]ag-gá ŠID = *ša-an-gu-u* followed by [um-bi-s]ag ŠID = DUB.SAR in *Ea* VII 202f;[581] UMBISAG = [*ṭup-šar-ru*], *Lu* I 139b (*MSL* 12 p. 98) û-bi-sag ŠID = *tu-up-ša-rum* Proto-Izi I 255a, preceded by sa-ág-gá ŠID = *ša-an-gu-um* ibid. 247 (*MSL* 13 p. 25); and the alternation of LÚA.BA (É.DINGIR) and LÚŠID (É.DINGIR) in Neo-Babylonian texts[582] and Assyrian colophons[583]), this reading is in the present case definitely out of the question; note that

1) the title LÚSANGA É (LÚ)MU recurs in *PKTA* pl. 39 i 13 side by side with LÚSANGA dEN.TÙR (i 12), LÚSANGA d*Še-ru-u-a* (i 9) and other priests (LÚSANGA) of the Aššur temple; it is unthinkable that the sign ŠID could have had a double function (priest/scribe) in this text, since in i 7 "temple scribe" is explicitly written LÚA.BA É.DINGIR;

2) in other letters of Akkullānu, LÚŠID means unequivocally "priest"; cf. LÚSANGA *ina* É dIB (310 r4), LÚSANGA *ša* É d7.BI (311 r18'), LÚSANGA *ša* É dUTU (ibid. 25'), LÚSANGA *ša* URUNINA (309 r8) and LÚ=SANGAMEŠ *ša* URU*Kal-[ḫa]* (314:5). By contrast, "scribe" is elsewhere in his letters quite regularly written either LÚDUB.SAR (311 r12) or LÚA.BA (315:12). It is highly unlikely that Akkullānu in just one of his letters would have deviated from this norm, especially considering that, excepting the present passage,

3) there is not a single Neo-Assyrian non-literary text where the reading LÚŠID = LÚUMBISAG would be called for by the context; everywhere else LÚŠID is most satisfactorily taken to stand for LÚSANGA, "scribe" being (as in the letters of Akkullānu) written either LÚDUB.SAR or LÚA.BA. Cf. e.g. *ABL* 493:3, 555:9, 710:3, 724 r4, 1221 r2, *ADD* 255 = *AR* 50:17ff, and note especially the co-occurrence of LÚSANGA and LÚA.BA (meaning "priest" and "scribe", respectively) in *ABL* 633 Obv.(!) 2f, 724 r4ff, *ADD* 640 = *AR* 45:18ff, *ADD* 642 = *AR* 464: 24ff, *ADD* 575+ = *AR* 161:7'ff, etc. This is in accord with the implications of the Neo-Assyrian professions lists *STT* 382-385 (= *MSL* 12 233ff) and K.4395 (= ibid. 238ff) listing LÚŠID only in the section "priest" and quoting for "scribe" only the logogram LÚA.BA.[584]

---

579 Cf. also URU*Ta-la-mu-sa*, *ADD* 877':7'. It seems to me, however, that the identity of this city with URU*Ri-mu-uš/sa* is not at all assured.

580 ŠE.BAR also occurs in Neo-Assyrian but only in the broad meaning "corn". Cf. e.g. *ADD* 128 and 148, and see Borger, *RlA* 4 p.310*b*.

581 Note that SbB differentiates between sa-an-gu ŠID *šá-an-gu-u* and um-bi-sag ŠIDxA *ṭup-šar-ru* (*MSL* 3 144f, lines 236 and 241).

582 Examples in Ungnad, *NRV Glossar* s.v. *ṭupšarru*.

583 See Hunger, *AOAT* 2 p.179f.

584 The fact that in the section "priest" of *STT* 383 LÚSANGA is preceded by LÚÉ.MAŠ*šá-an-gu-u* does not, of course, imply that the former was read *ṭupšarru*; the text simply lists two variant spellings of *šangû* comparable to the variant spellings of *āšipu*, *bārû*, *šāqiu* etc. listed in the preceding sections.

The undeniable clumsiness of the translation "priest of the cookhouse" illustrates the difficulties encountered in any attempt to set up a one-to-one correspondence between ancient and modern terminology. Though temple cooks definitely formed part of the clergy (cf. *ADD* 640:27ff listing a cook of the [Ninurta] temple in a group of witnesses defined as "temple [enterers]"[585] and including as other members "the priest of Ištar", "the priest of Adad", "the (priest) responsible for the incensation" and "the chief cupbearer of Ninurta") and were, as appears from the present letter, consecrated like the rest of the clergy, a "cookhouse" (i.e. the building where the sacrificial meals of the gods were prepared, see *RAcc.* p. 77ff) hardly formed the scene of strictly "priestly" activities in the modern sense of the word. On the other hand, a survey of the functions of the *šangû* (as compared with those of the other clergymen) bears out without any doubt whatever that this functionary was the closest equivalent of our "priest" (in the sense of "a person whose function is to make sacrificial offerings and perform other religious rites", as the term is defined in Webster's *New World Dictionary*). See in particular the letters of the priest Urad-Nabû (*ABL* 113-116, 427, 494-495, [6]06, 668, 971!. 1094, 1133!, 1147! and *CT* 53 349; cf. IÌR-dPA LÚSANGA, *ABL* 177 r7) dealing almost exclusively with sacrifices and other religious ceremonies, and cf. van Driel's survey of the Assyrian data on the *šangû* in *The Cult of Aššur*, p. 175ff. However, the point is that while cultic activity thus formed an essential part of the tasks of the *šangû*, his *primary* function appears to have been that of the *head of a sanctuary*, a kind of supervisor of the economy and (administrative) affairs of the particular "household" under his responsibility. See *ABL* 114-115 and 494 (from the aforementioned Urad-Nabû), *ABL* 419 (from Mutakkil-Aššūr, assistant priest of Ešarra), *ABL* 493 (from Aššūr-rēṣū'a, priest of Ninurta), *ABL* 498 (from Rāši-ili, priest of Marduk), *ABL* 1389 (from Aššūr-ḫamātūa, referring to a priest of Ea), BM 79099 (unp., from Aplāju, priest of Kurba'il), and cf., for Sumerian and Old Babylonian evidence, N. Schneider, "Der sangu als Verwaltungsbehörde und Opfergabenspender im Reiche der dritten Dynastie von Ur", *JCS* 1 (1947) 122-142, and J. Renger, "Untersuchungen zum Priestertum der altbabylonischen Zeit, 2. Teil", *ZA* 59 (1969) 104-230. In principle, each sanctuary had, accordingly, only one *šangû*, possibly assisted by a *šangû šaniu* "assistant priest" (cf. LÚSANGA *2-u/ú ABL* 419:3, 577 r2, 951 r6, *ADD* 485 = *AR* 177:15', and *MSL* 12 236 vi 8, where [LÚSANGA] ⌜2⌝-*u* follows LÚSANGA and [LÚSAN]GA GAL-*u*; see also Landsberger, *BBEA* p. 15[8] and van Driel, *op. cit.* p. 177f), but large establishments such as the Aššur temple could, as appears from the present letter, have several šangûs each presiding over one particular building within the temple complex. The heads of such large establishments were called *šangû rabiu* "high priest" (cf. LÚ*SANGA GAL-*u CT* 53 980:5', LÚ=SANGA GAL-*e AR* 23:6, LÚSANGA GAL *AR* 676:3.6, *KAR* 135+ iii 7, 215 vi 6').

It is worth noting that *šangû* is not to be viewed as an actual *profession* but rather as an honorary title. This is evident not only from the fact that the king himself bore the title, but also from *ABL* 1389, where Nabû-ēpuš, a priest of Ea (I.dPA-DÙ-*uš* LÚSANGA! *šá* dÉ-*a* Obv.6 [collated]), is in another connection referred to as *kalû*-chanter (I.dPA-DÙ-*uš* . . . LÚGALA *šu-u*, Rev. 15ff). Accordingly, it seems likely that the "priest of the cookhouse" mentioned in our letter actually was but the foreman of the temple cooks officiating in the É LÚMU, comparable to the chief baker (LÚGAL.NINDAMEŠ) mentioned in the next line, who probably had no separate building under his supervision and therefore was not called *šangû*.

r2. *LÚSANGA SUM.NINDA*: abbreviation for LÚSANGA *ša* É LÚSUM.NINDA "priest of the confectionery" (Rev. 12). Cf., in general, note on the preceding line. The Neo-Assyrian reading of LÚSUM.NINDA (*karkadinnu*) is established by *STT* 382+ iii 23ff (*MSL* 12 p. 235); note also the alternation of LÚSUM.NINDAMEŠ with LÚ*kar-ka-di(n)-na-te* in the Nimrud Wine Lists (Kinnier Wilson, *CTN* 1, nos. 8, 9 and 15 against nos. 1, 6, 11, 19 and 33). The rendering "butler" given in Pt.I must be stricken; translate instead "confectioner", and see the evidence presented in *CAD* K 42f and Kinnier Wilson, *op. cit.* p. 81f.

The translation of LÚGAL.NINDAMEŠ in Pt.I ("chief miller") is probably also to be corrected into "chief baker". As pointed out to me by K. Deller, the equation LÚNINDA = *laḫḫinu* suggested in *CAD* A/1 p. 296 is unacceptable, since "(1) there is a LÚGAL.NINDA(MEŠ) but not a LÚGAL *laḫḫini*; (2) there is always only *one* laḫ=ḫinu at a given temple but several LÚNINDAMEŠ". Moreover, both LÚ*láḫ-ḫi-nu* and LÚGAL.NINDA are mentioned in the decree PKTA pl. 36-38 specifying the responsibilities of the clergy of the Assur temple, and the relevant stipulations show that the tasks of the two functionaries were entirely different: the *laḫḫinu* had to open the doors, to look after the clothes and decoration of the divine statues, and to guard the temple utensils (ii 8-13), whereas the LÚGAL.NINDAMEŠ was simply obliged to provide "the temple of Aššur and all the temples with bread and

585 PAB 5 [LÚTUMEŠ] É *ša* DINGIR (line 32).

[ ]" (NINDA[MEŠ]-*a šá* É AN.ŠÁR 3' *šá*⌜E⌝.[KUR]MEŠ *gab-bu* 4' LÚGAL.NINDA *ša* É AN.ŠÁR *pu-tu-ḫu na-ši*, iii 2'ff). A comparison with the immediately following paragraph[586] makes it virtually certain that the bread in question was produced by the LÚGAL.NINDA and his subordinates, hence LÚNINDA = "baker", a rendering that, after all, is best in agreement with the meaning of the logogram NINDA. The rendering "baker" also tallies with the position of the section LÚNINDA in the profession list *STT* 382+, where it is preceded by LÚMU "cook" and LÚGÍR.LÁ "butcher", and followed by LÚŠIMxA "brewer", LÚKAŠ.LUL "cupbearer", LÚ*ša* UGU *kan-ni* "winekeeper" and LÚSUM.NINDA "confectioner". Note also *NARGD* no. 42:10ff, 20ff and 28, where LÚNINDAMEŠ are explicitly mentioned as recipients of barley and wheat for making breads (*a-na* NINDAMEŠ ... LÚNINDAMEŠ *i-na-ši-ú*). The reading of the logogram remains unclear, though. "Baker" was in Babylonian *ēpû* (see *CAD* E 248) but as far as I am aware, the verb *ēpû* is not attested in Assyrian. The reading LÚ*hundurāju* considered by Deller, *Or* NS 33 (1964) 95 (on prosopographical grounds), seems to be out of the question in view of the spelling LÚNINDAMEŠ-*ni* occurring in ND 2489 ii 6.20 (*Iraq* 23 pl. 16).

r8. I*Aš+šur*-NUMUN-AŠ: otherwise unknown; possibly head of the Aššur temple of Nineveh, see above, under Discussion.

r9. *mar-šá-a-ni*: taken as Pl. of **maršu* "harassment", a *pars*[587]-formation from Aram. *mrs* (Jud.-Aram. *mrṯ*, *mrs*, *mrš* maceravit, subegit, Eth. *marasa* putrivit) 1. pressit, 2. contudit (Brockelmann, *Lex. Syr.*^{2} p. 405a), attested as a loan-word in Neo-Assyrian in Wiseman, *VTE* l. 602 (LÚKÚR-*ku-nu lim/li-im-ri-is-ku-nu*, cf. von Soden, *Or* NS 35 [1966] 18 and *AHw* 609*a*).[588] Cf. Syr. *mirsōtā* "maceratio" (ibid.). Hardly = *maršu* "1. Sänfte(?), 2. Geldbeutel(?)", *AHw* 614*a*.[589]

The present passage as a whole may be compared with *ABL* 1372 r5 ff, IdPA-AD-KALAG 6 LÚ*MU *an-ni-ú u-nu ḫu-an-ši u*$_4$*-me-šú* 7 *ḫa-si ina ḫi-si-'a-a-ti* 8 *mē-e-te* "this cook Nabû-abu-(u)dannin was mistreated on his fifth day, and (later) died of the mistreatment." The circumstance that the mistreated person here too happened to be a cook is of course purely accidental.

r10. *TÚGU.SAG*: a tall cone-shaped hat serving (together with shaven head) as distinctive mark of priesthoos in Assyria. For pictorial representations of such headgears see Hrouda, *Flachbild* pl. 50:5 and 52:4 (upper band); Meissner, *BuA* II Abb. 16 on p. 56; Mallowan, *Nimrud* I fig. 251, and cf. Hrouda, *op. cit.* p. 45f and Reade, *Iraq* 34 (1972) 96. The caps worn by Assyrian kings as a token of their priestly status were also called *kubšu* (cf. LUGALMEŠ *šu-ut* TÚGU.SAG, *AKA* 35 i 55, and LUGALMEŠ *ša ina ku-ub-še*, *KAR* 98:3) but differed in details from those of the priests, being considerably lower than these (on the average); the fezlike cap of the *alaḫḫinu* Sibitti-rēmanni (*KAH* II 138) shown in *BuA* II fig. 15 cannot be taken as evidence that priestly headgears occasionally resembled the royal ones, for the cap in question may actually have been much higher (see Reade, *loc. cit.*).

r12. Can one generalize from this passage that it was usually the (chief) *kardadinnu* who (by custom) set the sacrificial tables of the gods? The relevant paragraph in the aforementioned decree (*PKTA* 36-38) has not been preserved, but it may be noted that the *karkadinnu* appears in this function at least in one further ritual text (ND 1120 r5 LÚ*kar-ka-di-nu nap-ta-an-šu i-šak-*⌜*kan*⌝ "the confectioner places his meal (on the table)", cf. van Driel, *The Cult of Aššur* p. 203). In *ABL* 611 a temple charioteer is said to have (once) set the sacrificial table of Šamaš, but the wording of the letter makes it apparent that this was an exception rather than a rule.

r14. *de-e-ke* "was killed": sic, not *de-e-qí* "pious act" (*CAD* K [1971] 208*a* following Waterman).[590] Reading *de-e-qé* instead of *-ke* is, of course, not excluded if the form is taken as *stative* of *damāqu* (cf. *de-e-qe ABL* 157

---

586 Col. iii 5'-8': KAŠMEŠ KAŠ *ḫa-ḫur-tu šá* AN.ŠÁR 6' *ša* É.KURMEŠ *gab-bu* 7' LÚGAL.ŠIM×AMEŠ *šá* É AN.ŠÁR 8' *pu tu-ḫu na-ši* "the chief brewer of the temple of Aššur is responsible for the beer and the *ḫaḫurtu*-beer of Aššur and all the temples".

587 Possibly also *pirs*, cf. notes on *LAS* 35 r1 and 39 r3.

588 The different sibilant in *VTE* 602 can be accounted for on the Judaeo-Aramaic evidence. Actually the writing with <S> renders more accurately Aram. *mrs*, see note on *LAS* 276 r8.

589 One could also think of a meaning like "whip", cf. ŠÀ KUŠ*mar-šá-ni* ... *li-ṭu-ša* "let them strike him with whips(?)", *CT* 53 840 r7f.

590 "Pious act" could be (*epšitu*) *de'iqtu* (cf. *LAS* 122:18f.r1.4) but never **dêqu* (< *damqu*); the change *m* > ' > Ø occurred in Assyrian only in intervocalic position.

r10 and 417 r2, *da-ií-qi* 129 r14, *de-ií-qi* 971:14 and *de-e-i-qi RMA* 257 r4, besides *de-'i-iq ABL* 348 = *LAS* 180 r7 etc. and *de-eq/iq ABL* 358 = *LAS* 122 r22, etc.), in which case the passage could be translated "he was efficient in this (office)", or similarly, but this is rather unlikely in view of the fact that /qi/ is elsewhere in the same letter written with the sign *qi*, not *qí* (cf. *ip-ti-qi-su* r16). Note also the parallel passage 310:7'ff. The fact that the text reads "was killed" not "died" (*mēte*) is worth noticing (see above on the dating of the letter and cf. *LAS* 314).

r19f. This passage probably corresponded roughly to *PKTA* 38 iii 2'-4' (quoted above, note on r2), and one is accordingly tempted to emend the beginning of line 20 into *i[p-ti-q]i(d)-su*!? and translate "(Sennacherib) ma[de] him(!) [responsible] for their (= the gods') bread"; for *paqādu* + *ina muḫḫi* cf. *ABL* 471:19, 573:11, 885:11, etc.[591]

r22. For the rendering "the eigh*th* year since" instead of "eight years since" (Waterman, Pfeiffer, *et al.*) see note on *LAS* 34:15f.

310

Bibliography:

Previously unpublished. Copy *CT* 53, pl. 48 no. 149.

Writer:

The subject matter of the letter (cf. *LAS* 309, 312 and 314) as well as stylistic considerations (e.g. r1-3) make the attribution of this letter to Akkullānu seem warranted, even though its introductory blessings do not recur in any other letter of Akkullānu[592] and the orthography of the letter is not in accordance with the conventions of Akkullanu[593]. The handwriting and general appearance of the tablet, however, resemble very closely those of No. 316.

Notes:

1'. Cf. ᵈ*15 ša* ᵁᴿᵁ*Arba-ìl am-mar* ᴸᵁ́KÚRᴹᴱŠ*-ni* ⁹[*ina* IGI LUGAL EN-*ja l*]*u-u tu-sa-ḫi-ip* "may Ištar of Arbela make all the enemies succumb before the king, my lord" *CT* 53 111:8f (letter from Nabû-zēru-iddina). The damaged signs in the beginning of the present line are, unfortunately, not clarified by this parallel.

3'f. A blessing recalling the poetical language of the royal inscriptions but otherwise not attested in Neo-assyrian letters. Cf. *ina e-le-li ul-ṣi ḫu-ud lìb-bi* ⁴⁰*nu-um-mur pa-ni ub-ba-lu*₄ *u*₄*-um-šú-un* ⁴¹*ši-pir-šá ina ḫi-da-a-ti ri-šá-a-ti za-ma-ri tak-ni-i* ⁴²*ag-mu-ur-ma* Borger *Ash* p. 62 vi 39ff, and *ina ṭu-ub* UZUᴹᴱŠ *ḫu-ud lìb-bi nu-um-mur ka-bat-ti* ⁵⁶*še-bé-e lit-tu-ti* ibid. p. 64 vi 55f.

5'. ᴸᵁ́*šá (or NÍG.)U.U*: a craftsman probably working in metal and/or stone, Akkadian reading unknown. Cf. [ᴸ]ᵁ́NÍG(text A).U.U ¹⁴[ᴸ]ᵁ́URUDU.NAGAR ¹⁵[ᴸ]ᵁ́BUR.GUL ¹⁶[ᴸ]ᵁ́KAB.SAR "..., bronze-worker, lapidary, engraver" listed as a separate group between "carpenter" and "smith" on the one hand and "leather-worker" and "jeweller" on the other in *STT* 382+ ii B 13-16 (*MSL* 12 p.234). The fact that the craftsman in question had access to the ablution chamber of a temple (Obv.6') suggests that he was responsible for the proper functioning of the temple drainage, and his association with (divine) statues (Obv.7') also agrees with the lexical evidence just quoted. That the particular functionary referred to in the present letter had been subjected to shaving only shows that he had been permanently attached to the temple, and of course does not indicate that he had any specifically priestly functions to fulfill; cf. *LAS* 309 and the Neo-Babylonian passages quoted in *CAD* G 130*b*. The identity of the temple in question remains uncertain, but the odds are that the writer here too refers to the Aššur temple of Assur, as in *LAS* 309, 311 and 315.[594]

591 The emendation is not warranted; the questionable signs read, according to collation (Sollberger 19.1.1976), *ki*]*t-tu*, as given by Harper.

592 All other letters of Akkullānu begin simply with the "Reichsgruß" *lu šulmu ana šarri bēlīja Nabû u Marduk ana šarri bēlīja likrubū*. However, this is not a binding argument since corresponding deviation from the normal usage also occurs in letters of other writers (e.g. Balasî, Nabû-aḫḫē-erība, Nabû-nādin-šumi).

593 Orthographical features agreeing with the conventions of Akkullānu are the spellings with LÚ, not LÚ**šum-ma* 12'.r7, cf. 300:13, 312:9) and *ma-ḫer* (12', cf. 309 r21); against are *rin-ki* (Obv.6', cf. *ri-in-ku* 306:8), *iz-za-az* (11', cf. *i-za-az* 309 r25), *us-saḫ-ki-im* (r3, cf. *ú-sa-aḫ-si-is* 304 r10'), *pe-er-te* (cf. *pe-er-ti* 309 r25). However, this does not exclude the authorship of Akkullānu since the letter may have been written down by a public scribe according to dictation.

594 Note Akkullānu's personal attachment to the Aššur temple (Appendix M) coupled with the fact that the writer obviously took it for granted that the king knew what temple he was speaking about, and the reference to the Uraš temple of Assur in the continuation.

For other attestations of the profession in Neo-Assyrian texts see Postgate, *CTN* 2 p. 69; add LÚ*šá* U.U!, *ABL* 611 r11 (collated), mentioned in a context involving, among other things, reparation of a sacrificial table and a divine statue.[595]

6'. The ablution chamber (É *rin-ki*) here mentioned has, despite its name, nothing to do with the wooden structure which served as the scene of the *bīt rimki* ritual (cf. Laessøe, *Bît rimki* p. 83ff), but was without any doubt a special room within the temple itself. Cf. [I]G?ME *ka-ma-a-te gab-bu* ³¹*ina* IGI⌜-*šú*⌝! *šu-ú* ⌜*i*⌝!*-pat-te i-ka!-nak* r¹*ina* É *rin-ki ša* dEN *ù* dPA! *er-rab* ²*2-šú ina* ŠÀ MU.AN.NA *qab-li ša* dŠÚ *ip-pa-ṭa-ra* "all outer [doo]rs are under his supervision; he opens and seals them; he enters the ablution chamber of Bēl and Nabû. Twice a year the loins of Marduk are ungirded . . .", *ABL* 951:30ff (collated). The place doubtless resembled the bathrooms excavated in Assyrian palaces and private houses, which almost invariably had the same simple structure: walls with one or several niches (and possibly covered with mural paintings), burnt-brick floor overlaid with a bitumen coat to make it waterproof, a (terra cotta) drain carrying the water out, and smoothed stone-slabs serving as bases for the bathers to stand on while water was poured over them. See Müller, *RlA* 1 p. 388f; Mallowan, *Nimrud* I p. 40f (with two photographs) and II pp. 424 and 450; Andrae, *WVDOG* 10 p. 89f,[596] and Reuther, *WVDOG* 47, pp. 53, 58, 89ff. Such non-cultic bathrooms were, it is true, not called *bēt rinki* but *bēt ramāki*, cf. [K]Á *ša* É *ra-m[a-ki]* ⁵[*ša*] É *ḫi-la-ni dan-nu* "the gate of the bathroom of the great portico-house", *ABL* 487:4f; É *tu-'i-in-te* ⁵[*ša ki*]*-sa-al-li* É *ra-ma-ki* "the gate-house(?) of the courtyard of the (public) bath", ND 1113 = *GPA* 241:4f; *ap-tu šá* É *ra-ma-ki* "the window of the bath", VAT 13846:4 (= Meier, *AfO* 12 p. 241); É *ra-ma-ki* ⌜KALAG⌝ "large bath-house", *CT* 53 505:9'; the logogram É.TU$_5$ referring to baths of private houses (*ADD* 326:5, 340:9, 341:3, 964:9.11) is probably also to be read *bēt ramāki* (against *AHw* 134*a*). However, this does not mean that *all* bathrooms of the said type would have been called similarly; on the contrary, it seems certain that the designations of the rooms depended on the kind of bath performed in them, those serving purely p r a c t i c a l purposes being called *bēt ramāki* and those having a c u l t i c function, *bēt rimki*. Conversely, externally different bathrooms could be called similarly if their basic functions coincided (as in the case of two kinds of *bēt rimki*, one functioning as the scene of magical purification, the other being used in religious ceremonies called *rimku*; no doubt there also were different types of *bēt ramāki*).

The exact purpose of the wash-rituals performed in the ablution rooms of the temples is unknown. It is certain, however, that the object of the ablutions were the (divine) statues kept in the temples. Cf. the *ABL* 951 passage quoted above, where a *bēt rimki* is explicitly specified as one of *Bēl and Nabû*, and VAT 13596 rev. iv 17'. 21'. 24' (= *PKTA* pl. 15 = Ebeling, *Or* NS 22 27ff) as well as BM 121206 vii 7' and 10' (= van Driel, *The Cult of Assur* p. 90f) referring to ablutions (*rim-ka-a-ni*) of Aššūr, Anu, Adad, Sîn and Šamaš on specific days.[597] Cf. also note on *LAS* 306:8.

r1f. "*The days of the ritual*": in view of the foregoing, the writer here very probably refers to the 16th of Ulūlu, on which date there were "new ablutions of Aššūr (and Adad)" according to VAT 13596 iv 17'ff.

r4. *É dIB*: probably the temple of Uraš in Assur (not excavated, but cf. DINGIRMEŠ *šá* É dIB ⁹*ša* URUŠÀ.URU, K.252 = 3 *R* 66 iii 8f [Frankena, *Tākultu* p. 5ff]). As far as I know, there is no evidence that Uraš had a temple of his own in other Assyrian cities.

r7ff. The rendering of these lines given in Pt. I can be slightly improved after collation: *šum-ma* ŠEŠ M[EŠ-*šú* . . (.)] ⁸*ina* É dIB *is-se-e-šú i-ta*[*l!-ku* (. .)] ⁹⌜LÚSANGA *2!-ú*⌝! LÚx[. . . .] "if [his] brothers had go[ne] to the temple of Uraš with him . . ."

311

Bibliography:

(I) Waterman, *RCAE* 42 (cf. IV 232); Pfeiffer, *SLA* 354.

(II) Dhorme, *RHR* 116 (1937); Oppenheim, *JAOS* 61 (1941) 271; Kinnier Wilson, *NWL* (1972) 72.

---

595 Note also *ADD* 827:5' (MÍ*šá*-U.UMEŠ beside [MÍ]SIMUGMEŠ "female smiths").

596 The bathroom described by Andrae was found in the Anu-Adad temple of Assur, but it is doubtful whether it ever was in cultic use.

597 The ablution of Aššur is also referred to in *KAV* 74:15 (*šá rim-ki* AN.ŠÁR *at-ta-*[*di* . . . .]).

Copy:

Cf. also Pinches, *PSBA* 6 (1878) 219.

Notes:

6ff. This passage certainly refers to Aššur's procession to the *akītu*-chapel of Assur (on the Tigris about 200 m to the west of the city-wall, at a distance of c. 1 km from the Aššur-temple; cf. the folding map in W. Andrae, *Das wiedererstandene Assur* [Leipzig 1938] and see the description of the chapel ibid. p. 151ff) but, contrary to the translation in Pt. I, the text does not imply that the gods were still staying in the chapel while the letter was written but that they had already returned to the main temple. Cf. the parallel passages in *ABL* 134:7ff (UD *1*7.KAM [8] [dEN.ZU *i*]*t*!*tu-ṣi-a* [9] [*ina* É *á*]-*ki-it* [10] [*e-t*]*a-rab* . . . r[1] *i-su-*[*ḫur*] [2] *ina* É-*šu e-ta-rab* [3] *i-na ša-lim-ti* [4] *i-na šub-ti-šu* [5] *it-tu-ši-ib* "On the 17th [Sîn] set out (and) entered the *akītu*-[chapel] . . . turned back, entered his temple and took his seat in safety"), 366:6ff (esp. r5) and 858:8ff where the phrase *ina šubti ušābu* "to take one's seat" without exception refers to the gods' returnal to their original posts in the temple; note also the ventive suffix in *e-tar-bu-u-né* indicating movement *towards* the place from where the letter was sent, hence more naturally the Aššur temple than the *akītu*-chapel. The passage has accordingly to be translated, "Aššur and Mylitta[598] went out . . . and (re-)entered (the Aššur temple) in safety." For additional examples of *erābu* – *uṣû* indicating coming out and returning of gods in procession seen *CAD* A/2 362*a* and E 268.

The procession itself was probably only part of a lengthy festival celebrated at the beginning of Tašrītu on account of the beginning of the second part of the Mesopotamian year and probably greatly resembling the New Year's festival celebrated in Nisannu. Cf. *LAS* 190 and relevant commentary.[599] In the Nisannu-festival, the gods left for the *akītu* on the 2nd and returned on the 3rd at the latest, possibly already on the evening of the second; see van Driel, *The Cult of Aššur* p. 145. The ceremonies involved in the journey are described in detail in VAT 13596 (= *PKTA* 14f) i 16'ff; unfortunately the text is only fragmentarily preserved, especially as regards the stay in the *akītu* chapel. That much seems to be certain, however, that the journey to the chapel took place by land (on chariots drawn by white horses), whereas the return happened by boat.[600]

10. The gods escorting Aššur during the visit to the *akītu*-chapel are listed in VAT 13596 i 1'-14' (*PKTA* 14 = *Or* NS 22 27ff)[601] and *KAV* 49 ii 11'ff[602]; the same gods are enumerated, with minor variations (including additions and omissions), also in BM 121206 v 1'ff (van Driel, *CA* p. 86f; significantly improved text in Farber, *BiOr* 30 [1973] 435) and Luckenbill, *OIP* 2 p. 142:11ff. In the latter text – a description of the sculptured gates of the *akītu*-chapel – the gods are said to follow Aššur "advancing to battle against Tiamat" (*ṣa-lam* AN.ŠÁR *u ṣa-lam* DIN=GIR.DINGIR GAL^MEŠ [7] *ma-la it-ti-šú a-na* ŠÀ *Ti-amat ṣal-ti il-la-ku* p. 141:6f); quite obviously, the journey to the *akītu* symbolized this mythological event (which also took place by chariot). See in detail Pallis, *Akîtu* (1926), 264f.*

17f. How these lines are to be restored remains uncertain. The traces in l. 18 would permit reading ⸢*ša*⸣ *ina* ⸢É⸣ [*á-ki-i*]*t*, "in the [*akī*]*tu*-chapel", in which case the most natural restoration of l. 17 would be [*š*]*a ina* ⸢É⸣! [*Aš+šur*] (or ⸢É⸣.[ŠÁR.RA]), but unfortunately the third sign in this line is definitely not ⸢É⸣ but most likely I[GI] or U[GU]. Perhaps therefore one should, with an eye to *LAS* 300+310 r1, 309 r1.18 and 312 r18', simply read ⸢*ù*⸣! *ina* U[GU LÚ.MEŠ] ("furthermore, as regards the [. . . officials] (who fill the vats etc.)"), even though there does not seem to be enough space for a normally drawn *ù* in the beginning of the line. This would imply that the *akītu*-chapel had its own wine-department (cf. r11f), for which there is otherwise no evidence;[603] alternatively one should refrain from reading [*á-ki-i*]*t* in l. 18 and read [*Aš+šu*]*r*! or ⸢É⸣.[ŠÁR.R]A! instead, which is not permitted by the traces. Non liquet.

---

598 For this reading of the logogram dNIN.LÍL see provisionally Reiner, *JNES* 26 (1967) 198; Postgate, *BSOAS* 34 (1971) 390 and Parpola, *Assur* 1/1 (1974) 4 fn.13.*

599 For other ceremonies performed during the Tašrītu-festival see van Driel, *CA* p.146f. It is strange that van Driel makes no reference to the present letter in the discussion of the festival.

600 VAT 13596 iv 8'ff; cf. also Andrae, *op. cit.* p.154.

601 Note the rubric [DINGIR^MEŠ *šá* (*ina*)] *a-ki-ti ša* ZAG KAB *šá Aš+šur* ibid. i 6'.

602 Cf. PAB DINGIR^MEŠ *ša ina pa-na-*[*at Aš+šur*] [17'] *a-na* É *á-ki-it* [*il-la-ku*(-*ni*)] ibid. ii 16'f.

603 The ground-plan of the chapel does not allow for a wine-cellar, nor were any traces of storage-jars found in excavation.

19. ^{DUG}*ḫa-ri-a-te*: Spacious containers (with a capacity of up to 2 homers = about 360 litres, cf. *ADD* 964:5f) having probably the shape of a vat or tub (see Salonen, *Hausgeräte* II p. 199) and used in temples to store the wine (or beer) libated during sacrifices. Cf. Thureau-Dangin, *Sg 8* 1.397, *1 ḫa-ri-ú* URUDU GAL-*tu ša 1,20 i-na mìn-da-at* A^{MEŠ} *lìb-ba-šá ṣab-tu a-di kan-ni-šá* GAL-*i* URUDU ^{398}*ša* LUGAL^{MEŠ}-*ni ša* ^{KUR}*Ur-ar-ṭi a-na e-peš* ^{UDU}SIS= KUR^{MEŠ} *ma-ḫar* ^{d}*Ḫal-di-a ú-mal-lu-ú* GEŠTIN^{MEŠ} *ma-qi-te* "one large bronze vat with a capacity of 80 measures of water together with its large bronze stand, which the kings of Urarṭu had used to fill with libation wine for the performance of sacrifices to the god Ḫaldia." For NA cultic texts referring to *ḫariu* in connection with sacrifices see *BBR* 60 and 68; *KAR* 141and 146; and *CT* 15 pl. 44:17 (the phrase *ḫariu ipatti* "he opens the vat" occurring in these texts suggests that the containers were covered with lids).

r8. ṣu-ra-ri: libation-offering performed by dripping (cf. *ṣarāru* "to drip, flow" and [*ina* S]À *gi-di-ma-a-ti* . . . *ṣu-ra-a-ri ú-ṣar-ra-*[*ru-ni*] "they make libations by means of ladles", *ZA* 52 p. 226:9) in contrast to libations made by pouring (*maqqû*), the latter being usually associated with the *ḫariu*-vats (cf. *ma-qe-e ša ḫa-re-e ú-*[*ga-mar*], *KAR* 146 Rev. ii 2). The latter type of libation seems always to accompany animal sacrifices, whereas the former probably consituted a sacrifice in itself; cf. the dictionaries s.vv. *maqqû* and *ṣarāru/ṣurāru*, and note the new examples of *ṣurāru*/SUR in Kinnier Wilson, *Wine Lists* no. 3:6, 4:3(!), 5:7(!), 6:3, 11 r26', 14:5 and 18 r21. The wording of the present passage clearly implies that *two* kinds of libations had been affected by the strike; it is not possible to render the passage as "there is no libation wine (since) they have not filled the vats" (so Waterman and Pfeiffer): this would require a wording like *karān ṣurāri laššu ḫariāte lā umalliū*, i.e. placing the negation *after* the subject, whereas its present position unambiguously shows that *la-a* . . . *la-a* here (as in Rev. 11f) means "neither – nor" and that consequently both GEŠTIN *ṣu-ra-ri* and *ḫa-ri-a-te* are objects of *ú-ma-al-li-ú*. – Cf. also *BBR* 68:8, *ṣu*]-*ra-ra-ni 2* ^{DUG}*pa-gi-li* [. . . . .] (as opposed to) ^{9}[. . . .] *ša* GEŠTIN^{MEŠ} ^{DUG}*ḫa-ri-u* x[. . . . .].

312

Bibliography:

(I) Waterman, *RCAE* 49 (cf. IV 174).

(II) Behrens, *ABB* (1906) 87 and 101f; von Soden, *ZA* 41 (1933) 114; Dhorme, *RHR* 116 (1937) 13f; Oppenheim, *JAOS* 61 (1941) 258 and 266, and 64 (1944) 191.

Addressee:

Possibly (but very uncertainly) Esarhaddon. See note on the date of *LAS* 303.

Notes:

5. For the rendering of the expression *3-šú ina* u_4*-me an-ni-i* (hitherto wrongly "for the third time today") see note to *LAS* 34:15f.

7f. *mi-i-nu an-ni-u li-iḫ-ḫi-kim*: the translation of this passage proposed in *CAD* Ḫ 33*b* ("how may this be understood") has to be rejected since *mīnu* ("what") is otherwise not attested in the sense "why" in Neo-Assyrian. It seems more natural to split the passage into two independent sentences and to interpret the first of these as a rhetorical question similar to *mīnu ḫīṭu* "what is the fault?" (185 r13, etc.); *le-eḫ-ḫi-kim* can be taken either as N-stem precative ("let it be clarified") or as *lā+iḫḫikim* "it has not been clarified", cf. *le-ma-gúr-ru* <*lā+immaggur CT* 53 108:8 and *le-ma-tú-ḫu* <*lā+imattuḫū*, *ABL* 544 r7.

8. Cancel the translation of *re-eḫ-tu-šú* given in Pt.I and translate instead "(if there is anything) left of it"; cf. *AHw* p. 968*b*. The rendering "leftovers (from the sacrificial table of the gods)" (see on 316 r9') does not apply here since *rēḫtu* has this meaning only in the plural (e.g. *ABL* 187 r1, 1285:16!).

10. *lu-ta-im*: unclear. Cf. ^{GIŠ}IG^{MEŠ} *ta-'u-ma-a-te* "double doors", *ABL* 457:5 (= ^{GIŠ}IG.MAŠ.MAŠ = *tu-'a-ma-tu*, *Ḫḫ* V 217 [*MSL* 6 p. 23], see Salonen, *Türen* pp. 25 and 43) and É *tu-'i-in-te*, ND 1113 = *GPA* 241:4. Perhaps "I will make it double."

15. É *gi-ṣe-te*: a container for firewood, or a kind of lamp? Otherwise attested only in *CT* 53 1 (a letter listing spoils sent to Sargon II) in the following context:

Obv.	4	*1* ^{GIŠ}*tup-né-nu* KALAG KÙ.GI	"1 large golden chest;
	5	*1* ZU KÙ.GI *3 ṣip-rat* KÙ.UD UD-*u*	1 golden plate; 3 crests of

6	*1* ^{GIŠ}*tup-né-nu ḫu-še-e* KÙ.⌜GI⌝	white gold; 1 chest with
7	2 GÚ.ZI KÙ.GI	scraps of gold, 2 gold cups;
8	*4* ^{GIŠ}É *gi-ṣe-te*	4 *bēt gissetes* (with?)
9	NA$_4$ ^{MEŠ} KÙ.GI	stones of gold;
10	*1 ḫu-u[p-p]u*? KÙ.GI *aḫ-ḫu-zu*	1 *ḫuppu* mounted in gold;
11	*1 nar-ma-ak-tú* URUDU	1 bronze washbowl containing
12	*ú-de-e* KÙ.UD ⌜*ina* ŠÀ⌝?	silver utensils;
13	*1 tup-né-nu*	1 chest containing
14	*1 me 53 kap-pi* KÙ.UD *ina lìb-bi*	153 silver bowls . . .".

**gissutu* is probably a variant of *gassutu* "firewood" (*AHw* 282*b*, *CAD* G 53*b*; cf. ^{LÚ}*gi-ṣi-ṣi-ka ABRT* I 25 r22, a variant of *gassiṣu/gāṣiṣu* [*CAD* G 54], and see note to *LAS* 39 r3). The compound *bēt g.* may be compared with *bēt* (^{GIŠ})*buṣinni* "lamp" (lit. "house of lamp wick"; see the discussion in *CAD* B 348*b*).

r14. *ka-nu-ni*: a (massive) metal brazier or furnace (sic; the translation "hearth" given in Pt. I is misleading, see the evidence presented in Salonen, *Öfen* p. 108ff and *CAD* K 393ff) used in temples for the burning of animal offerings (*maq(a)lūtu*, cf. note on 167 r7)[604] and probably also for the heating of rooms during the cold season (cf. Falkenstein, *LKU* p.19[7]). There is evidence that each god generally had a brazier of his own;[605] the present passage doubtless refers to the brazier of Aššur kept in a courtyard of Ešarra (cf. *KAV* 74:13, *i-na* MURUB$_4$ KISAL *šá-a-šú* KI.NE UD.KA.BAR *mut-tal-l[i-ku]* [14]*a-na na-pa-aḫ* ^{d}GIŠ.BAR *ma-ḫar* AN.ŠÁR EN-*ia ú-[kin]* "in the middle of that courtyard I (Sennacherib) placed a movable bronze brazier in order to have fire burn before my lord Aššur").

"*The days of the kanūnu*": probably refering to a cyclically recurrent festival in which the kindling and burning of the brazier played a prominent part; cf. UD^{MEŠ}-*te ša dul-li* "days of the ritual" (*LAS* 310 r1f) referring to the ritual ablution (*rimku*) of the god Aššur.[606] In Babylonia, such festivals are known to have been celebrated in each of the three cold (and dark) months Araḫsamna, Kislīmu and Kinūru/Ṭebētu;[607] in Assyria, however, there is evidence for only one such festival each year, and the available indications are that this festival was predominantly celebrated in the 10th month (December-January) likewise named *Kanūnu.*[608] Cf. *LAS* 302:6'ff (dated to the month Kanūnu by the omens listed Obv.12ff) and K.8669 (Müller, *MVAeG* 41/3 p. 59ff) ii 7, where the writing ^{ITU}AB for normal KI.NE indicates a close association of the brazier with the said month. Though no month is mentioned in the present letter, there is no reason to doubt that the festival in question was the same as in *LAS* 302. True, the days of the festival mentioned in the letter (10th-11th-12th) are not identical with those mentioned in *LAS* 302 (Kanūnu 15ff). This discrepancy can, however, be accounted for by assuming that the nature of the festival required keeping it as close to the winter solstice as possible. It can hardly be doubted that the ultimate purpose of the festival was to celebrate the moment the days began to grow longer again and that the kindling of the brazier symbolized the victory of light over darkness; cf. the timing of Roman Saturnalia and our Christmas, and the symbolic meaning of our Christmas candles. The moment of the solstice could have been determined accurately enough by means of the gnomon (see commentary to *LAS* 344).

---

604 Besides the more or less irregular cases mentioned there burnt-offerings were of course also performed in the course of regular cultic services, e.g. the New Year's festival; cf. UDU.NITA <*šá*> *ina* UGU KI.NE ŠUB-*ú* [9]^{d}BIL.GI *i-qa-mu-šú* ^{d}*Qin-gu šu-ú* "the ram which is cast upon the brazier and which is burnt by the fire is Qingu", *CT* 15 43:8f (a commentary explaining the meaning of the cultic ceremonies performed in the New Year's festival). Note also van Driel, *CA* p.92:47f.

605 Cf. e.g. KI.NE^{MEŠ} *šá* DINGIR^{MEŠ} *ka-la-[šu-nu]* "the braziers of all the gods", *LKU* 51 r18.

606 For a fragmentary ritual text possibly pertaining to this festival see Bu 91-5-9,104 (Zimmern, *Neujahrsfest* I 131[1]).

607 See Reisner, *SBH* 144 and (dupl.) *BRM* 4 25; *LKU* 51; *RMA* 151 (the latter two texts referring to the month Kislīmu).

608 It is uncertain whether the month was named after the festival or simply because the cold weather made the use of braziers necessary, the latter alternative is perhaps more likely in view of the fact that January has a similar name in Turkish too (*ocak* "hearth", cf. Eilers, *Gedenkschrift Güntert* [= Innsbrucker Beiträge zur Sprachwissenschaft 12: 1974], 335). Note however the obvious connection between the name of the fourth month (Du'ūzu) and the festival of Tammuz.

r15'. Supposing that the date [Kanūnu?] 10 mentioned here corresponded to the day of the winter solstice (December 26), the year in question would have begun approximately on March 27, and the letter could accordingly be dated either to 674 or 669 BC (cf. App.A2; year 666 is out of consideration because of *LAS* 302). However, the identity of the month remains uncertain (cf. preceding note), and other years are therefore also possible and perhaps even more probable (cf. above, on the date of the letter, and note that no other letters of the present corpus predate 673 BC).

r25'f. Cf. ND 2773:4ff, ^{LÚ}A.KIN *ša* ^{I}DINGIR-*a-a-nu-ri* ^{5}KUR*Ṭa-ab-i-la-a-a* ^{6} ^{I}*E-za-zu* MU-*šú ka-ni-ku* . . . ^{8}*ú-ba-la* "a messenger of Ilāja-nūrī of the land of Ṭāb-ilu, named (lit. his name is) Ezazu, will bring a sealed letter" (*NL* 14, *Iraq* 17 pl. 32).[609] The present passage is obviously a "postscript" specifying the identity of the DUMU LÚ*SANGA mentioned in Obv.17; translate, accordingly, "(As to) the son of the priest of the Šamaš temple, his name is . . ." rather than "Of the priest . . ." (Pt. I). The youth in question was doubtless scheduled to be consecrated to the office of his deceased father, like the Priestersöhne mentioned in *LAS* 310 and 311 (cf. *ABL* 577).

314

Bibliography:

Waterman, *RCAE* 48.

Addressee:

Possibly Esarhaddon, judging by the orthography. See note on the date of *LAS* 303.

Discussion:

For another letter of Akkullānu referring to murdered(?) priest(s) see *LAS* 310. Were these murders(?) somehow connected with the purge of early 670 BC?

315

Bibliography:

(I) Waterman, *RCAE* 429 (cf. IV 253); Pfeiffer, *SLA* 245.
(II) Dhorme, *RHR* 116 (1937) 11f.

Photograph:

RCAE IV pl.11 (Rev. only).

Discussion:

A golden plate (cf. below on Obv.6) is reported disappeared from the Aššur temple also in two letters from Sîn-na'id, a contemporary of Akkullānu: *ABL* 150 and 551. These letters may have nothing to do with the present one, but it is nevertheless striking that a functionary named Ṭāb-šār-Sîn, who in the present letter appears among the men potentially responsible for the investigation of the matter, also figures in this capacity in *ABL* 150.[610] Still

---

[609] Cf. also ND 2645:30 ^{I}⌜*A*⌝-x[.]x:MU-*šú* "his name is [. . .]" (*Iraq* 17 pl.31 no.18).

[610] Rev.4 (collated). Since both *ABL* 150 and 551 have been inadequately edited hitherto, it seems worth while to give here a full (collated) transliteration and translation of both. *ABL* 551:
Obv. ^{1}*a-na* LUGAL [EN-*ja*] ^{2}ÌR-*ka* ^{I}[^{d}*30*-I] ^{3}^{LÚ}*ḫa-za-*[*nu ša* ^{URU}ŠÀ.URU] ^{4}^{d}*Aš+šur* ⌜É⌝.ŠÁR!.R[A] ^{5}*a-na* LUGAL EN-*ja* ^{6}*lik-ru-bu* ^{7}*a-na-ku an-na-ka* ^{8}*a-na šùl-mu ša* LUGAL ^{9}*be-lí-ja u-tal-ka* ^{10}*i-da-tu-u-a* ^{11}*le-'u šá* KÙ.GI ^{12}*ša* É ^{d}*Aš+š*[*ur*]! ^{13} *šá* ⌜*il*⌝!-*q*[*u-u-ni*] ^{r1} *ma-*[. . . . .] ^{2}LÚ×[. . .] ^{3}^{LÚ}*sa-r*[*u!-te*] ^{4}*ṣab-bu-tú* ^{L}[Ú! . .] ^{5}*šá* KÙ.GI *il-qu-u-ni* ^{6}*ṣa-bit* ^{I}*Ba sa li* ^{LÚ}SIMUG.KÙ.GI ^{7}*it-tal-ka* [. .]× ^{8}*is-sa-kan* ^{9}*a-n*[*a-ku*] ^{9}*a-se-me a-na* LUGAL] ^{10}EN-*ja a-sa-*[*ap-ra*] "To the king [my lord], (from) your servant [Sîn-na'id], a major(?) [of Assur]. May Aššur and Ešarra bless the king, my lord. I came here (= Nineveh) to greet the king, my lord; after my departure (from Assur) the golden plate which had been taken from the Aššur temple has been re[covered]. The [. . .] and the culprits have been arrested, and they have (also) arrested the [. . .]who took the gold. A goldsmith named Basali came and placed [. . . .]. Having heard (about the matter) I (immediately) reported it to the king, my lord."
ABL 150: ^{1}*a-na* LUGAL EN-*ja* ^{2}ÌR-*ka* ^{Id}*30*-I ^{3}^{LÚ}*ḫa-za-nu ša* ^{URU}ŠÀ.URU ^{4}*ša* LUGAL *be-lí ip-qid-u-ni* ^{5}⌜*Aš+šur*! É!.ŠÁR!.RA!⌝ *a-na* LUGAL ^{6}EN-[*ja lik*]-*ru-*[*b*]*u* ^{7} UD ×[. . . .]× *me* ^{8}GIŠ ⌜× × × × × *t*]*ú* ^{9}⌜*Aš+*

other thefts from temples are reported in *ABL* 1389 and 493 (priests of Ea and Ninurta illegally removing golden ornaments from a sacrificial table and a divine statue); cf. also *ABL* 951. Whether or not these and similar examples can be evaluated as evidence of widespread corruption in Sargonid temples is another matter; it is quite possible that the cases reported in the letters were rather exceptional, though one cannot help thinking that the increased wealth of temples in Sargonid times may well have had degrading effects on the moral of the priesthood.

Notes:

6. *le-'u-u* "plate": here probably referring to a sheet of (engraved) metal used for decorating woodwork. Cf. UD *3*.KAM *ša* ITUBA[RAG] 6 *'le-'u-u* KÙ.GI *ša bur-k*[*i* DN?] 7 *'ina* UGU *e-ṣi ni-ik-ta-r*[*a-ar*] r1 ZU *ša né-me-di* [. .] 2 *6 ina+1* KÙŠ *i-ta-lak* [. .] "On the 3rd of Ni[sannu] we fitted the golden plate covering the la[p? of DN?] on the woodwork; the plating of the couch measured 6 cubits [. .]", *ABL* 592:5'ff; for additional examples see *CAD* L 159*b*.

10f. *KÙ.GI a-na IGIx2MEŠ-šú*: precise meaning obscure. If *a-na* is taken to stand for *ina* (cf. 39 r3 with note), the passage is translatable (literally) "at the moment, the gold is in his sight[611]" or "there is gold in his sight", but neither rendering makes satisfactory sense. The expression itself is without parallels; has perhaps a verb been (unintentionally) omitted at the end of line 11?

r3. *IDÙG-IM-d30*: a high official of the Aššur temple, exact administrative position unknown. Cf. *ABL* 150 (quoted in the preceding footnote) and *ABL* 840, signed by Ṭāb-šār-Sîn, [Ak]kullānu and Marduk-šallim-aḫḫē (in this order). The last-mentioned man is elsewhere entitled scribe of the (Aššur) temple (IdAMAR.UD-*šal-lim*-PAPMEŠ LÚA.BA É.DINGIR, *ADD* 805:7; cf. also the letters of M. listed in note to *LAS* 258 r1) and could hence well be identical with the scribe mentioned in Obv. 12.[612]

r10f. Cf. OA *kaspam kabāsum* "to remit a payment, to drop a claim (on payment)" *or* "to put, pressure (upon a person) for a payment" (*CAD* K 9, mngs. b and c).

316

Bibliography:

Previously unpublished. Copy *CT* 53, pl. 52 no. 159.

Notes:

r6'. The last word in this line is, according to my copy of 1964, most likely to be read ⌜*tu-ra*⌝-*ma* (2m Sg. Prs. of *rammû* "to leave", or *tūra* "again" + enclitic -*ma*). Not collated.

r7'. EN *pi-qit-ti* "overseer": the exact connotation of the word here cannot be determined owing to the fragmentariness of the context. Possibly generally "appointee" (lit. "holder of an appointment") in the sense of a

---

šur!⌝ X[. . *ina* U]GU 10 KÙ.GI X[. . .] ZU 11 *as-sa-'a*-⌞*al*⌝! KÙ! ½! MA.NA 12 *us-se-ṣi-a* 13 [*u*]$_4$-*mu ša* ⌜*ú*⌝!-[*še ṣ*]*u*!-*ni* 14 *a-na* LUGAL EN-*ja a-sap-ra* r1 *an-nu-rig sa*-⌜*a*⌝-[*ru*] 2 *šá-ni-ju*!-⌜*um*⌝-*ma* 3 UD 21.⌜KÁM⌝! *a-ṣab-ta* 4 *a-na-ku*! I!⌜DÙG!+GA⌝-IM-d*30* 5 ⌜*ni*!-*sa*!-*'a*!-*al*!⌝ KÙ.GI 6 *nu-*[*s*]*e-ṣi-a* ⌜*is*!-*su*!⌝-*ri* 7 *a-na* LUGAL EN-*ja* [*i-qab-b*]*i*!-*u* 8 *ma-a ša is ḫu* X[. . . .] 9 *sa-ru-te ša*⌜É.⌝[DINGIRM]EŠ! 10 *ina pa-ni-ja* IdPA-PAPMEŠ-DI 11 *ú-ṣab-bit an-ni-u* 12 *šá-ni-um-ma šu-ú* 13 IdPA-PAPMEŠ-DI 14 *lil-li-ka* 15 *li-iš-al* (L.E.) 16 ZU(sic) *ina tuk-ka-ni lu la i-ḫap-pi-u* 17 LÚ**šá* UGU URU LUGAL *be-lí lip-qid*

"To the king, my lord, (from) your servant Sîn-na'id, the mayor of Assur appointed by the king, my lord. May Aššur and Ešarra bless the king, my lord. [3 lines broken] I inquired about the gold [. . . . .]and got back half a pound of it. On the very day I got it back, I wrote to the king, my lord. Now I have arrested another thief on the 21st. We – Ṭāb-šār-Sîn and myself – interrogated (him) and got the gold back. Perhaps the king is (now) told: "Those who [. . . . .]." Before m(y tim)e, it was Nabû-aḫḫē-šallim who arrested the temple thieves; this is another case. Let Nabû-aḫḫē-šallim come and investigate (the matter); let them not break the plate by force(?); let the king, my lord, appoint the city prefect (to take care of the case)."

611 For "eyes" = sight cf. *CAD* I/J 156 usage b). Pfeiffer and Waterman translate *a-na* IGIX2.MEŠ-*šú* "with him" and "in his hands", respectively; such renderings of course make sense, but are not warranted by the text which does *not* read *ina pānīšu* nor *ina qātēšu*.

612 Another possibility is INabû-mušēṣi LÚA.BA É d*Aš+šur* mentioned in K.11908 (unp.).

person entrusted with the bringing of the "leftovers". For *bēl piqitti* referring to temple functionaries (appointed by the king) see *ABL* 951:16' and r7; cf. also Kaufman, *AS* 19 (1974) p. 43 on (Imperial) Aramaic *b'l pqt* "commissioner".

r9'. For inventories of foodstuffs specified as *rēḫāti* ("leftovers") see *ADD* 1004ff, and cf. van Driel, *CA* p. 206ff. For the translation "leftovers (from the sacrificial meals of gods)" see Oppenheim, *Ancient Mesopotamia* (1964), p. 189; von Soden's "Geschenke" (*AHw* [1972] 983*a* s.v. *riḫītu*) is, in my opinion, not justified by the etymology of the word nor by the nature of the goods designated as *rēḫāti*. Note that in the present instance the "leftovers" were to be delivered directly to the king (r7'), probably on the occasion of one of his visits to Assur (r12'). It is remarkable that the goods came from a town as distant as Arrapḫa (= Kerkūk, 100 km from Assur).

317

Bibliography:

(I) Waterman, *RCAE* 149.

(II) Labat, *Royauté* (1939) 353; von Soden, *Fs Christian* (1956) 102; Landsberger, *BBEA* (1965) 49.

Date and discussion:

As pointed out by von Soden (1956), the prophetess mentioned in this letter may well be identical with the one appearing in *LAS* 280, though there are too few particulars available to make this *absolutely* certain. This would date the letter to the beginning of 670 B.C., cf. on *LAS* 279 and 280. Note that the date is not so speculative as it would appear to be at the first sight, for there is otherwise no evidence that prophetesses were active during the performances of the subsitute king ceremonies.[613]

Notes:

11. For a detailed description of an Assyrian temple throne-room (and a discussion of its function) see Mallowan, *Nimrud* I 239ff. The present letter probably referred to the Aššur temple (of Assur), cf. the introductory blessing formula.

318

Bibliography:

(I) Waterman, *RCAE* 1277 (cf. IV 205).

(II) Oppenheim, *JAOS* 61 (1941) 267; 64 (1944) 196.

Writer:

Almost certainly Ištar-šumu-ēreš. Note the subject matter of the letter (writing of new tablets), the spelling LUGAL *be-li* (characteristic of I. but not met with in letters of other scribes [except Nabû-zēru-lišer]),[614] and the high rank of the writer, which is quite evident from the tenor of the letter; cf. also Nos. 319, 321, 322 and 323.

Addressee:

Assurbanipal.

Date:

Probably the early years of the reign of Assurbanipal. Cf. *LAS* 321, which is firmly dated to the beginning of Assurbanipal's reign by the quotations in Rev. 8ff, and note that Obv. 8ff of the present letter imply that the king in question took considerable interest in literature, which fits Asb much better than Ash.[615]

---

[613] Note also that the scene (Akkad) fits only the substitute king rituals of 673, 671-670, and 666.

[614] Other orthographical features pointing to Ištar-šumu-ēreš are the spellings *lu-u-na-'i-id* (Obv.2) and *a-ḫe-iš* (Rev.7), cf. Appendix M 6. Otherwise, too, the orthography is in agreement with that of Ištar-šumu-ēreš, except for the spelling MAN in Obv.14, which is not found in *LAS* 1-29; cf. however 321:5.

[615] For the reference to the prince (Obv.4) see relevant note.

Discussion:

The writer has evidently striven for a sophisticated manner of exposition (cf. the composition of the text, the disposition of signs on the tablet, the language cloured with Babylonianisms [*an-nu-u* r9, *uš-ta-pal-u-ni* r10], the rhetorical questions on the reverse, and the development of the theme "cross" on the obverse), perhaps in order to provide the king with an example of the "perfect speech" described in Rev. 5ff, and it is probably because of this tendency that more points than usual remain obscure in this letter. In any case, it seems certain that the letter is an answer to a royal letter (*abat šarri*, lit. "king's word", cf. Obv. 1) recently received by the writer. The key to the understanding of the letter obviously lies in the contents of this royal letter, which is quoted in Obv. 15 – Rev. 2 (and indirectly in Obv. 5), and seems to have mainly dealt with a "cross" (*ispillurtu*) associated with Nabû and supposed to have ominous and/or magical significance. Unfortunately it remains uncertain what kind of cross actually is in question (cf. notes on Obv. 4 and Rev. 1).[616]

Notes:

1f. Taken as a rhetorical question (with an implicit positive answer) intended to show that the writer quite emphatically approved the contents of the king's letter; perhaps the latter had even ended with a similar question. Cf., in general, note to *LAS* 181:9ff.

3. *ki-ze-er-tú*: otherwise attested only in the Ištar-oracle *4 R* 61 (iv 26, *ina ki-zer-ti-k[a]*[617] [27]*ina* AN-*e* GAL⸢MEŠ⸣ [28]*ú-kal-ka* "I (Ištar) am holding you (Esarhaddon) by y[our][617] *k.* in the wide heavens"), where the meaning "curl, lock of hair" proposed in the dictionaries (*CAD* K 477, *AHw* 496) on etymological grounds seems acceptable in view of the context (the king being addressed as a child tended by the goddess) and parallel passages (cf. *CAD* A/1 s.v. *abūsātu* "forelock"). In the present context, however, this meaning fits less well; a curl can hardly be cross-shaped, and the fact that *kizertu* is construed as a masculine noun (Obv. 6 and 7) virtually refutes the suggested derivation from *kezēru* "to curl the hair", the final *-t* obviously being not the feminine marker but part of the stem. My guess is, therefore, that the word is a loan word having nothing to do with *kezēru* and its derivates, but referring to an ornament or insigne of variable shape, perhaps a pendant or an earring (cf. Hrouda, *Flachbild* Tf. 8); the translation "emblem" given in Pt. I is naturally only an attempt to satisfy the requirements of the context.

I do not think the suggested interpretation is weakened by the fact that the best-attested symbolic representation of Nabû was the *stylus* (+ tablet or di/triptych; see Seidl, *RlA* 3 486*a*). Whatever the precise meaning of *kizertu*, the cross was evidently closely enough associated with Nabû to be called an emblem of the god (cf. Rev. 1f, and the definition of "emblem" in Webster's *New World Dictionary*), and it should be borne in mind that some gods (e.g. Aššur) had more than one symbols; for examples see Seidl, loc. cit. In fact, it does not seem excluded that the cross-shaped pendant () occurring, together with other divine symbols (star, crescent moon, horned cap, etc.), in the neck-torcs and collars of Assyrian kings, actually is the cross meant in our text: note that such a cross is the o n l y pendant hanging from the collar of Šamši-Adad V in a statue of this king found in the temple of N a b û at Calah (Delaporte, *Assyrian Sculptures in the British Museum* II (1938), pl. 2). This cross undoubtedly symbolized the four points of compass, and could thus well have served as an emblem of Nabû, who was often addressed as "the supervisor of the world" (*pāqid kiššati*; see Tallqvist, *Götterepitheta* p. 382) and held a very prominent position in the 1st millennium pantheon (cf. 1 *R* 35 no. 2 (12) = Luckenbill, *ARAB* 744f, and Lambert, *ZRG* 26 [1974] 6).

4. Cancel the translation of this line given in Pt. I and translate instead: "The king my lord knows that on the ground of this (association) the cross (serves as) the badge of the crown prince"; the spelling *muḫ-ḫi* (instead of UGU) indicates that *ina muḫḫi* is here an adverbial expression, not a preposition, and the same is implied by the fact that the following *is-pil-ur-tú* is in the nominative, not in the genitive case. The present rendering also makes much better sense than the one in Pt. I. Nabû as the first-born son of Marduk was regarded as the crown prince of the "celestial kingdom" (cf. note on *LAS* 46 r9), and in this sense he naturally was the deity most closely linked in religious speculation to his mundame "colleagues": hence the "fitness" of the god's emblem to the use of the crown prince. That the association of Nabû and the crown prince was not confined to the realm of religious speculation only but

616 Or is the letter somehow associated with the Dialogue Between Assurbanipal and Nabû (K 1285 = *ABRT* I 5 = Streck *Asb* 342ff), beginning [*ad-da-na-ab-b*]*u-ub ta-na-at-ta-ka* dPA??

617 According to collation (from photograph), also ⸢*j*⸣[*a*] "my" possible.

had also practical consequences is evident from *ABL* 434 showing that documents issued by the crown prince were sealed with a cross-shaped stamp seal (Obv. 18ff: "should a refugee come to your posts from the land of the Manneans, . . . hand him over immediately to a messenger of yours and send him on to the crown prince. And if it should happen that he has some information . . . a scribe should write down what he has to say, they should seal (the report) with the cross-shaped stamp seal (*ina* ŠÀ ^{NA_4}*is-pi-lu-ur-te* ^{14}*li-ik-nu-ku*) and Aḫī-dūr-qalli, the commander of the troops of the crown prince, should send it to me at once by a swift messenger"[618].[619]

The present reference to the crown prince could at first sight be taken as evidence for placing the letter in the last years of Esarhaddon (672-669), which is the approximate date of *ABL* 434. It could even be speculated that the present letter was actually written shortly after Assurbanipal had received the cross-shaped seal from his father as a concrete token of his crown-princehood (cf. the next line). However, closer study shows that such conclusions are overhasty. The reference to the crown prince is too general to be used for purposes of dating, and more tangible evidence in the letter actually calls for its placing in the first year(s) of Assurbanipal. Moreover, the second hypothesis is plainly contradicted by Obv. 6f, unless "the house of Išnunak" is taken as a cover name for *Bēt rēdûti* or *Bēt kutalli*, for which there is no concrete evidence whatsoever. Consequently, the inevitable conclusion is that the writer here actually refers to the crownprincehood of the *ruling* king, and that the letter had actually been written on the occasion Assurbanipal officially *gave away* the cross. This would account for the wording of Obv. 5 (since no longer a crown prince, it was "fitting" that the king gave up the visible token of his former rank).and perhaps also for Rev. 1ff, if it is hypothesized that the cross was given away as a specific act of devotion to Nabû.

6. ^{URU}*Iš-nu-na-ak*: ancient Ešnunna, mod. Tell Asmar ca. 60 km NE of Baghdad. For the spelling of the name (attested only here) cf. ^{URU}*Iš-nu-nak*, *1 R* 66,2 ii 3; ^{KUR}*Èš-nu-nak*, *5 R* 35:31; *eš-*[*n*]*un-*[*n*]*a-ak*, *ARM* 14 82: 19, and note that the vowel *i* in the first syllable is already attested in 3rd millennium texts (*Áš-nun-na*^{ki}, *Iš-nun*^{ki}, *Èš-nun(-na)*^{ki}; references in *RépG* 2 p. 18f). What exactly the writer means by "the house of Išnunak (Ešnunna)" remains unclear, though. Ešnunna was devastated by Hammurapi in the Old Babylonian period, and is thereafter only seldom mentioned in written sources (for some references see Boudou, *Or* 36-38, pp. 26 and 58); the excavations carried out at the site have also confirmed that the city was practically uninhabited between the Kassite and Sassanian periods. It seems hence possible that the "house" referred to here (a shrine?) was not necessarily situated in Ešnunna itself but somewhere else, perhaps in Nineveh, the building being simply *named* after Ešnunna for some religious or historical reasons which remain beyond our ken.[620] [Should the line perhaps be restored [^{d}A].É and rendered (the god) [Mār]-bīti of Ešnunna? Cf. Tallquist, *Götterepitheta*, p. 361f, according to which Mār-bīti = Nabû].

9. The restoration of this line is based on the verbal forms in line 13 (cf. also l. 14) implying that the preceding lines contained a quotation from the king's speech: there is hardly room for an appropriate introductory clause in ll. 10-12. Otherwise the line could, of course, also be rendered [*a-ni-nu ki-i*] *an-ni-i ina muḫ-ḫi ni-id-d*[*u-bu-ub*] "we have discussed the matter as follows."

10. *a-na an-ni-i SIG*$_5$ "better than this": cf. note on *LAS* 143:17ff. Waterman's translation "suitable for this (purpose)" is also possible, cf. 247 r20ff.

11. *kaq-qu-ru ma-'a-ad*: cf. *CT* 24 46 xii 4f, *kaq-qu-ru im-ti-i*[*d*] ^{5}*il-te-niš al ta-ṭ*[*ar*] "there was so much space that I wrote (both lists) on the same (tablet)" (remark in the colophon of a large 12-column tablet containing the text of two god-lists, An = *Anum* and AN = *Anu* = *ša amēli*), and 2 ŠU.SI *qaq-qar ina muḫ-ḫi* ^{GIŠ}DA *muš-šu-ru* "2 fingerbreaths surface left free on the writing board (used as the source of the copy)", *JCS* 6 p. 66:26, similarly ibid. 11. 5 and 21 (see the commentary ibid. p. 70f ad line 5). Accordingly, the present passage probably simply states

618 Translation by Oppenheim, *LfM* (1967) p.171.

619 Note also *ABL* 4ff, [*ki-i* LUGAL *be*]-*lí* ^{3}DUMU LUGAL *šu-*⌈*tu*⌉*-u-ni* ^{7d}PA-MAN-*a-ni* ^{6}*ina* É *ku-tal-li ina pa-an* LUGAL ^{7}*us-se-rib-šú-nu is-pi-lu-rat* ^{8}*is-sak-nu šú nu* "[when the king, my lo]rd, was (still) crown prince, Nabû-šarrāni brought them to (the crown prince's) Rear Palace into the presence of the king, and they gave them cross(-shaped badg)es."

620 Comparison with Rev.1 would suggest that "the house of Išnunak" is just a roundaway expression for the royal palace in Nineveh, but it should be noted that there are also other ways to restore the beginning of the line. Still, keeping in mind this possibility, ^{URU}*Iš-nu-na-ak* could perhaps be explained as a cryptographic spelling for Nineveh (NINA = ÈŠ×KU$_6$ i.e., *èš-nunu*, since KU$_6$ = *nūnu*; cf. ^{URU}*Tam*-KU$_6$ = *Tamnūna*, *GPA* 95:6, and NINA.KI = *šá eš-še-ku ku-u-a i-gub ki-ki*, Diri 241).

that there was enough space for a certain text on a certain writing board, and does not refer to space left between individual w o r d s (as on the reverse ofthe present letter).

12. *MU^{MEŠ} "sentences"*: referring to lines of text (*šumu*), cf. Hunger, *AOAT* 2 p. 177. Not = *šattu* "year" (*AHw* 253*b*), which is almost without exceptions spelt MU.AN.NA in Neo-Assyrian. The rendering of *a-ki* with "some" is conjectural: I know of no other cases where the preposition would have this meaning in NA. Cf. OA *ke-e* "ungefähr" (Kienast, *ATHE* p. 86:23) and Bibl. כעשר "about 10".

14. At the beginning of the line, restore perhaps [*an-nu-rig*] "at the moment". KIN-*an-ni* = *išpuranni* "has written", hardly = *išaparanni* "will write": the latter reading would imply that the writer hoped for the king's comments on ll. 10-13, which accordingly would not represent quotation from the king's speech but a proposal made to the king, but this is unlikely since the king was in Sargonid letters seldom addressed in the imperative. Cf. note to 338 r3.

r1f. For an attempt to account for this passage see above, note on Obv. 4 (at the end). The meaning of the passage naturally depends on the rendering of Rev. 1, where [*ina*] ⌜É⌝-*a* conceivably is not the only possible restoration. [E.g., if the line is restored to read [^{d}]⌜*É*⌝-*a is-pîl-ur-tú iš-kun-*[*u*/*an-ni*] "(since) Ea set up the cross [(for me)]", the passage is turned into a reference to an astrological omen (cf. the protases quoted in *CAD* I/J 253*a* sub mng. 1b, esp. *TU* no. 16 = Largement, *ZA* 52 250:89, I ^{MUL}UDU.IDIM *iš-pa-lu-ur-ta* GAR "If the planet (Mercury) has got a cross(-shaped halo)" [*Enūma Anu Enlil*, Tablet LVI]; for the underlying astronomical phenomenon, see Largement, *art. cit.* 263); however, all the omens in question seem to have been unlucky and as such hardly in accordance with the implications of the present passage.]

r2. *a-bi-ti-e* = *abitī* (*abat* + *ī*) "my word", the lengthening of the final vowel perhaps indicating uncertainty (cf. Obv. 15); *ī* > *ê* in syllables with high pitch (cf. *akī* "as" : akê "how?"). *le-'i-i-ti* = *lē'īt* (Stat. Fem. of *lē'û* "skilled") + a paragogic vowel called forth by the structure of the final syllable. Cf. note on 208 r8.

r4. *ta-qa-ṭab-bi*: *sic* according to collation, interpretation uncertain. Hardly a scribal error for *ta-qa-ab-bi*, since /qab/ is in other letters and reports of Ištar-šumu-ēreš consistently written with the sign GAB (cf. *ta-qab-bi-a* 13:8, *ta-qab-bi-ja* 12 r12, *i-qab-bi* 1 r2 and 15:1[1], *i-qab-bu-u-ni* 3 r4, 19 r13' and 29 r1[8]). Very unlikely also an attempt to render Babylonian *taqtabi* (2m Pf.): the epenthetic *-a-* and the geminated *-b-* could be explained phonetically by assuming a shift of stress to the paenultima, but there is no recognizable reason for such a shift of stress in the context. From the morphological point of view, the only acceptable interpretation would be to take the form as Prt. Gtn (**taqṭabbi*), with an epenthetic *-a-* inserted between *q* and *t* according to the rule formulated in note to *LAS* 39:11, but this is out of the question since in NA Pret. was obsolete in positive declarative main clauses. The only remaining alternative is, accordingly, to take the form as the *present* tense of the same stem (Gtn), which is admittedly difficult, but does not seem to be entirely excluded.[621] There is evidence that besides regularly built forms (e.g. *as-sa-nam-me* Obv. 14 and *it-ta-na-al-la-ak* 38 r8), Gtn Prs. was in NA also formed after the pattern **iptanras*, i.e. inserting the *-tan-* infex directly between the 1st and the 2nd radicals of the verb without any auxiliary vowels; Cf. *la it-tal-la-k*[*u-u-ni*] 208 r8' (<**i'tanlak-ūni*), and see in detail Deller, *Or* NS 34 (1965) 271ff.[622] A form like *ta-qa-ṭab-bi* could have developed from **taqtanbi* through intermediary **taqṭabbi*[623]. It is true that such an interpretation would make the present and preterite forms of this particular verb exactly homophonous, while no confusion was possible in the case of the corresponding forms of *alāku*, for example (*ittallak* : **ittallik*), but in practice contexts will in most cases have sufficed to tell which form was in question.

r6. *né-ra-ki-šá*: *sic* according to personal collation (cf. Waterman, *RCAE* III p. 336). Obscure; cancel the translation "length" (= *mūraku*) given in Pt. I.

---

621 Cf. ^{d}PA *iq-ṭa-nab-bi* in the dialogue of Nabû and Assurbanipal (Streck, *Asb* p.342:13).

622 Gtn-forms of this type seem to occur frequently in *ABL* 1285, cf. *at-ta-aṣ-ṣar* ib. 19.20.26, *ag-du-uṣ-ṣu-uṣ* ib. 24, *as-sa-ad-da-ad* ib. 27, *is-sa*[*k*]*-kan* ib. 23 and *id-dáb-bu-ub* ibid. r.12; note further *a-tam-mar CT* 53 526:6 and *id-da-gal-an-ni ABL* 211 r4; also *at-te-'i-i-la ABRT* I 5:5, if from **antan'ila.*

623 The insertion of (a secondary) *-a-* between *q* and *ṭ* did not affect the emphatic pronunciation of latter phoneme, and one has consequently to transliterate *ta-qa-ṭab-bi*, not *ta-qa-tab-bi*; cf. *i-qi-ṭí-bu-né-šú ABL* 515:9.

r8. The final *-a* in *šak-na-ta* is due to interrogative intonation; cf. note on *LAS* 208 r8.

r10. For other examples of *šutābulu* "to argue, discuss" see *CAD* A/1 p. 27f. The verb has a literary flavour and probably here serves as a stylistic device to garnish the diction of the letter; note the preservation of the *št* cluster (normally > *ss*) and the fact that the Št-Stem was otherwise unproductive in Neo-Assyrian (cf. notes on *LAS* 39 r12 and 51 r1).

319

Bibliography:

(I) Thompson, *RMA* 152.
(II) Schott, *ZDMG* 88 (1934) 311; Weidner, *AfO* 14 (1941-44) 179f; San Nicolò, *Or* NS 17 (1948) 64.

Copy:

See also Bezold, *ZA* 5 (1890) 109.

Writer:

Judging from the orthography (*be-li*, LÚ not LÚ*) and the contents (supervision of literary activities; astrological omens), almost certainly Ištar-šumu-ēreš. Cf. App. M 6.

Notes:

1ff. Cf. *ACh* 2 Spl 18:12f, I UD *14*.KÁM 30 *u 20* KI *aḫ-meš* IGI^{MEŠ} KA GI.NA ŠÀ KUR DÙG.GA DIN=GIR^{MEŠ} KUR URI^{KI} *ana* ^{MÍ}SI[G$_5$ *iḫassasū*] ^{13}*ḫu-ud lìb-bi* UN^{MEŠ} MÁŠ.ANŠE KUR URI^{KI} *pár-ga-niš ina* EDEN N[Á-*iṣ*], and Sîn 4:15f, I UD *14*.KÁM KI+MIN KA GI.NA *lìb-bi* KUR DÙG-*ab* DINGIR^{MEŠ} KUR URI^{KI} *ana* MÍ=SIG$_5$ *i-ḫus-su-su* ^{16}*ḫu-ud lìb-bi* UN^{MEŠ} GAR-*an* MÁŠ.ANŠE KUR URI^{KI} *pár-ga-niš ina* EDEN NA-*iṣ*. The present version of the omen is more closely paralleled by *RMA* 127:4-8 (from an Assyrian writer named Bamāju, and, with minor variants, by *RMA* 128:6ff (from Ištar-šumu-ēreš himself), 129:1-6, 131:7-r3, 133:1-7, etc.

6ff. Cf. *ACh* Sîn 3:61, I *30 u 20 ši*[*t-qu-lu* . . . .] (Tablet I of *Šumma Sîn ina tāmartišu*, the commentary to *Enūma Anu Enlil*; the relevant passage in the Series itself does not seem to have been preserved). For astrological reports quoting the omen see *RMA* 127-129, 131, 136-139, etc.

r1f. *^{GIŠ}LE.U$_5$.UM . . . ša UD AN ^{d}EN*.LÍL*: literally, "a writing-board (inscribed with omens) of (the series) *Enūma Anu Enlil*", but the writer porbably did not mean a *single* board but a whole set of such, joined together to form a polyptych and containing the *entire* text of the said omen-series. A specimen of such a "luxury edition" of the series, consisting of 16 boards measuring ca. 45 × 28 × 1.7 cm each and inscribed on both sides with two columns of minutely written text, has actually been found: see D.J. Wiseman, "Assyrian Writing-Boards", *Iraq* 17 (1955) 3-13, and M. Howard, "Technical Description of the Ivory Writing-Boards from Nimrud", ibid. 14-20; cf. also Mallowan, *Nimrud* I p. 152ff. Significantly, from the viewpoint of the interpretation of the present passage, this polyptych, too, was called simply ^{GIŠ}LE.U$_5$.UM "writing-board" in the inscription carved on its cover-board, reading: É.GAL ^{I}MAN-GI.NA MAN *kiš-šá-ti* ^{2}MAN KUR *Aš+šur*^{KI} I UD AN ^{d}EN*.LÍL.LÁ ÉŠ.GÀR ^{3}*ina* ^{GIŠ}LE.U$_5$.UM ZÚ AM.SI *ú-šá-áš-ṭir-ma* ^{4}*ina qé-reb* É.GAL-*šú ina* ^{URU}BÀD-MAN-GIN *ú-kin* "Palace of Sargon, king of the world, king of Assyria: he had the series *Enūma Anu Enlil* inscribed on an ivory writing-board and deposited it in his palace in Dūr-Šarrukēn."

r4. To judge from the context the "Akkadian (= Babylonian) writing-board" here mentioned was just another luxury edition of *Enūma Anu Enlil*, of the same type as that mentioned earlier; since it would have been little point in preparing just a duplicate copy of the text, the other copy (probably also intended for royal use) was most likely written in *Assyrian* characters. Cf. 331 r8-9. It is perhaps worth mentioning in this connection that a few fragments of wax with traces of cuneiform signs still remain extant on the Nimrud writing boards, and these show that this "edition" of the series at least was Assyrian, not "Akkadian".

r6. *MUL^{MEŠ} 3.TA.ÀM*: the title of an astrological text associating each month of the year with three stars (one situated on the "path of the Enlil stars", one on the "path of the Anu stars", and one on the "path of the Ea stars"), whose heliacal risings signified the (beginnings of the) relevant months.[624] The pertinent text was available

[624] Cf. En. el. V 3f: "He (Marduk) assigned the year, established (its) boundaries, set (for) the 12 months 3 stars each" (*12* ITU.MEŠ MUL.MEŠ *3*.TA.ÀM *uš-zi-iz*).

both in the conventional list form (*KAV* 218; *LBAT* 1499f; *ZA* 32 72) and in the form of a circular design divided into twelve sectors (= months) and 3 concentric zones (= the paths of Anu, Enlil and Ea), each of the 36 sections thus obtained containing the picture of a star, its name, and a number relating to the length of the daylight in the pertinent month (see *CT* 33 pl. 11f and Schott's reconstruction of the design in *ZDMG* 88 32, also reproduced in van der Waerden, *Die Anfänge der Astronomie* p. 59). This latter form of the star-list is quite evidently meant here, cf. Rev. 7 and 9. It is noteworthy that the list formed, at least in the eyes of the writer of the present letter, an essential appendix to the series *Enūma Anu Enlil*; was it perhaps also incorporated in to the standard reconsion of the series?

320

Bibliography:

Previously unpublished. Copy *CT* 53, pl. 50 no. 154.

Note:

The addressee of this fragment remains unclear. It is *possible*, in view of Obv. 3' and the absence of any explicit reference to the king, that the letter was not addressed to the king but to a scholar; on the other hand, the verbal form in Obv. 3 has not necessarily to be interpreted as 2nd Masc. Sg. but can also be taken as 3rd Fem. Sg., in which case the letter would lose its apparent "collegial" tone, and the introductory lines could well be restored to contain the usual formula *Nabû* (*u*) *Marduk ana šarri bēlīja likrubū* (cf. *LAS* 104-105, 267, 331 and 334-335).

4. *a-ḫu-lam-ma*: see note on *LAS* 15 r11.

5. *GU.SUM*^{MEŠ}: cf. Streck, *Asb* p. 256:18, *ḫi-ṭa-ku* GÙ.SUM *ab-ni šá la-am a-bu-bi šá kak-ku sa-ak-ku bal-lu* "I have studied (archaic) inscriptions on stone from the time before the Deluge, which are "sealed", obscure and intricate",[625] and see, for GÚ(?)/GÙ.SUM = *miḫiṣtu* "Schrift(zeichen)", most recently Sjöberg, *ZA* 64 (1975) 160 (with literature). Here the term quite obviously means "sign(-form)" as also in *CT* 16 38 iv 4, *sa-niq* [*ba*]-*ri* KA GÚ. SUM *up-pu-uš* "checked, collated, and worked up according to (original) sign(-form)s" (referring to a copy of *Utukkī lemnutī* prepared after a Babylonian writingboard exemplar); a clear example of *miḫiṣtu* in the meaning "inscription" (on a clay tablet) is *JAOS* 88 (1969) 130:12f, *re-eš mi-ḫi-il-ti ù* ³ *ù qí-it mi-ḫi-il-ti a-na 2-šú i-šá-as-su-ú*.

r1ff. Cf. *LAS* 116:15ff. [*li-b*]*i-ru* in Rev. 2 is of course to be derived from *biāru*, not from *barû*, but appears to be used here more or less in the same meaning as *li-ib-*[*ru-u*] in 116:16; cf. *AHw* 122*b*, *bêru* usage 2d and 3.

321

Bibliography:

Previously unpublished. Copy *CT* 53, pl. 50 no. 155.

Writer:

Ištar-šumu-ēreš. The grounds for the attribution are essentially the same as those presented under no. 318.

Date:

Probably beginning of the reign of Assurbanipal. Rev. 8-11 (cf. corresponding note) is so clear a reference to a blessing recited at the coronation of Assurbanipal that it seems legitimate to infer that the letter was written relatively shortly after the accession of this king; compare the content of *LAS* 318. It could, of course, be speculated that similarly worded blessings were also said at the coronations of other Assyrian kings, in which case the letter could also be placed at the beginning of the reigns of Esarhaddon or Sîn-šarru-iškun. However, the attribution of the letter to Ištar-šumu-ēreš makes such speculation pointless: no datable letter of Ištar-šumu-ēreš predates 672 BC, and it is extremely unlikely that he ever saw the accession of Sîn-šarru-iškun (which happened almost 50 years after his promotion to the position of the chief scribe, cf. Appendices N and O).

---

625 Could the present passage also be a reference to the crown prince studying (archaic) inscriptions? This does not seem excluded, considering that this is the only occurrence of the term *miḫiṣtu* in NA texts.

Notes:

1f. Though not overtly marked as such, this passage is most likely to be taken as a *question*, both in view of the continuation (cf. e.g. *LAS* 13:6ff; note also present letter Rev. 4ff) and the analogy of other quotations from royal letters: with a few exceptions (*LAS* 38:6ff, 41:8f, 45:8f, 66:8f, 125:15ff, 152:10ff, 180:6ff, 181:7f and 298:6ff), these were exclusively questions and commands. Since each question necessarily had to be marked as such either by an interrogative word or interrogative intonation, it has to be assumed that the relevant information (i.e. word with lengthened vowel in the ultima), was included in the portion now broken away at the beginning of line 2;[626] for interrogative sentences of a similar type see e.g. *LAS* 199 r11ff and 298:14. Unfortunately there is no way of determining what word should be restored in the break; perhaps simply [UN^MEŠ^-*e*] "(these) people".

For *zakû* + *isse* "to become cleansed through somebody" cf. Schollmeyer, *HGŠ* no. 28 r10, *ar-ni ḫi-ṭi u gi-il-la-ti* TA ^d^AMAR+UD *i-za-ak-ku-ú* "my crime, my sin and my misdeed will become cleansed through Marduk", and cf. ibid. 5f, *ḫi-iṭ-ṭa-šú gi-il-la-tu-šú* ^6^[. . . .] TA DINGIR-*šú ù* ^d^*15-šú ip-pa-ṭa-ra* "his sin and misdeed [. . . .] will be absolved by his (personal) god and goddess"; the text in question is a *tāmītu*-query to Šamaš and Adad re a sickness conceived as a divine punishmnt, and it is not excluded that a similar situation may have been behind the present letter as well. Note that this would well fit Urad-Ea's role as an "appeaser" of angered gods. Cf. on r4.

5. The god invoked in this line probably was Marduk, Šamaš or Sîn; cf. Tallqvist, *Götterepitheta* pp. 133f, 139f. The epithets listed by Tallqvist do not suffice for a reliable restoration of the passage.

r3. Possibly [*mi*]*l-ka-ni-šá* or [*mi-i*]*l-ka-ni-šá* "her [c]ounsels" (referring to the queen mother Naqia), cf. *mi-lik ša an-za-nun-ze-e i-ḫa-ak-kim man-nu* "who comprehends the counsel of the abyss?", *BWL* 40:37, and *is-sa-ḫe-'i-iš* ^6^[*n*]*i-im-ma-al-lik* "we shall take counsel together" *LAS* 184 r5f, referring to the queen mother. Note also the continuation (r7).

r4. Possibly [*ḫi-ṭa*]*-ti-šú i-du-bu-ub* "he has spoken out (= confessed) his [s]ins"; cf. the *tāmītu*-passage quoted above (1f) and see *CAD* D 7f and 13 for *dabābu* in the meaning "to speak aloud, recite"; cf. also *ḫi-ṭu-šú-nu* LUGAL AD-*ka uz-zak-ki-šú-nu-ti* "the king, your father, purged them of their crime", *ABL* 793:17f. Possibly also [*it-ta*]*-ti-šú* "his signs" or [*ina ket*]*-ti-šú* "honestly", cf. *LAS* 30:6ff and 216:8ff. Whatever the correct restoration, the passage clearly implies that the purification of the king (scil. of his sins) was effected through a kind of confession, viz. recitation of a penitential formula under the assistance of a chanter-"priest". Cf. ÉR.ŠÈM.ŠÀ.ḪUN.GÁ^MEŠ^-*šú-bu a-na* LUGAL *tu-šad-bab* "you (scil the chanter) make the king recite their (scil. the gods') lamentations", *RAcc.* 7:19, and similar examples passim in this text.[627] The presence of the chanter was necessary since the penitent approached his god like a criminal pleading his case before a just judge, who was sure to pass a judgement exactly as severe as the deeds of the sinner called for, unless his heart was "softened" by a mediator, i.e. the chanter. It is interesting to note that the relevant religious terminology was a direct adaptation from judicial language: *ḫīṭu* "crime" = "sin", *dabābu* "plead" = "confess", *zakkû* "to free, release" = "to cleanse, absolve". Cf. *ABL* 793:17f (quoted above) and, for an even more explicit legal example, *KAV* 2 iii 18, *li-id-bu-bu lu-zak-*⌜*ki*⌝*-ú-ma* ^19^*li-il-*⌜*qí*⌝*-ú* "let (those who have a claim bring their tablets and present them ot the magistrates), plead their case, obtain clearance and take (what they have claimed)." Cf. also *LAS* 69+71:22ff, *a-na* ^d^AMAR+UD *liš-ken* ^23^ISKIM.BI *li-še-di* — — — r^1^ ISKIM.BI *li-še-di* ^3^*ma-a de-en-šú ina* IGI DINGIR ^4^*lid-bu ub* "He should prostrate himself before Marduk and make his sign known — — — 'make his sign known', that is to say, he should plead his case before the god."

r7. ^d^*UTU-šú*: perhaps simply for /šamši/ "*the* sun", the final *-šú* being a phonetic indicator rather than a possessive suffix ("*his* sun"); cf. UD-*mu* = /ūmi/ *LAS* 255 r2 and 276:23. The reference to the sun naturally directly pertained to the king also. See note on 143 r4f.

r8-11. These lines are a direct adaptation of the concluding part of the blessing recited in the course of Assurbanipal's coronation ceremonies at Assur, edited by Weidner, *AfO* 13 (1939-41) 210ff. The original wording has been abbreviated (like the quotation from Theodicy 143-147 in *LAS* 132 r9f), but there is no doubt as to the source of the quotation. Cf. *AfO* 13 211:31ff:

---

626 *az-zu-ku* at the end of line 2 is naturally not an interrogative form since the final *u* belongs to the root; with interrogative intonation, the form should be *az-zu-ku-u*, cf. *an-ti-ši-i* 34 r11, etc.

627 See also W.G. Lambert, *JCS* 33 (1974) 270.

31 *šá it-ti* LUGAL *i-da-bu-bu su-le-e u sur-ra-a-ti*
32 *šum-ma kab-tu ina* GIŠTUKUL GAZ *šum-ma* LÚ⌜*a-ḫu-ú*⌝ *a* ⌜xxx⌝
33 *šá a-na* LUGAL *ina lìb-bi-šú i-kap-[p]u-du* MÍḪU[L]
34 dÈR.RA *ina šip-ṭi šag-gaš-ti ú-qa-'a-a* SAG-*su*
35 *šá a-na* LUGAL *ina lìb-bi-šú i-ta-mu-ú nu-ul-la-a-ti*
36 *i-šid-su me-ḫu-ú pa*!(SI)-⌜x x⌝-*šú šá*!(ḪA)-*a*-⌜*ru*⌝[628]

"He who talks to the king lies and rubbish – should he be an important person, he will be killed with a weapon; should he be a stranger(?), ...;
He who in his heart plans evil for the king – Erra will haunt him with plague and killing;
He who in his heart speaks slightingly about the king.
– his stance is (but) whirl and his front is (but) wind."

322

Bibliography:
Previously unpublished. Copy *CT* 53, pl. 57 no. 177.

Writer:
Ištar-šumu-ēreš. Note LUGAL *be-li* (not *-lí*) r3, *lu-u(-)pa-ḫa-áš-šú* (not *lu-pa-*) r6, *an-ni-i* Obv.4' (thus also *LAS* 5 r3, 7:15, 12 r13, 13 r23, 318:9.r10, against *an-ni-e* 4:11.r1'), and see App. M 6.

Addressee:
Esarhaddon, to judge from the reference to "your (= the king's) *mangu* skin disease" in Rev. 1 and 7. Cf. Discussion sub *LAS* 246.

N.B.
Since the appearance of Pt.I, I have recopied the letter and thereby been able to improve the readings given in Pt. I in some points. In line 2', read] *ù áš-šú ke-e-na-ti-ka*; 5', K]UR *Šu-me-ru*; r1, *ma*]*n-gu-u šu-u tu-mu-lu i-ba-ši*; and r7,]⌜*man*⌝*-gi-ka* (cancel *nu* at the end of the line).

Notes:

2'. *áš-šú ke-e-na-ti-ka* "because of your justice": cf. *ina ke-nu-ti-šá*, *LAS* 132 r3. The preposition *aššu*, which was obsolete in NA, indicates that a literary quotation (from a proverb? Cf. 4') is in question, but I have not been able to identify the source.

3'. *ta-qip-u-ni*: cf. *it-ta-qip* 5', and *ta-qip-u-ni* 6'. Theoretically, all these forms could equally well be derived from *nakāpu* "to butt, push" (*AHw* 718), but their association with *kēnāti* (1') and *gum libbi* (7') makes a derivation from *qiāpu* "to believe" more likely.

5'. Probably part of a (otherwise unknown) proverb. [K]UR*Šu-me-ru* = "the land of Sumer".

7'. *gu-um* ŠÀ: an abbreviation (or better, a variant) of *gummurti libbi* "wholeheartedness, loyalty" (*CAD* G 133*b*, *AHw* 298*a*); also attested in Craig, *ABRT* I 9:11 (d*Na-na-a ina gu-um lìb-bi-š*[*á*]) and *STT* 360:22 (*a-ni-nu ina gu-um lìb-bi-ni*).[629]

r1'. [*ma*]*n-gu*: a disease; according to *AHw* 602*b* "eine Hautkrankheit", according to *CAD* L 257*a*, "stiffness".[630] Both translations fit to the clinic picture of Esarhaddon's illness (cf. Discussion of *LAS* 246, sect. B), and it is hence most natural to assume that the suffix *-ka* in r7 refers to this king, especially since there is no evidence

628 Possibly *pa!*⌞*na!-as!-su!*⌝ as in our text, collation necessary. Weidner reads *me-ḫu-ú si-*⌜*kil*⌝*-ta-šu* ḪA.A(uḫal=laq)⌞*aq*⌝, but his copy (Pl.XIII) indicates that all traces in the latter part of the line are indistinctly preserved and hence uncertain.

629 Both examples to be added to the dictionaries.

630 The rendering of *CAD* is based on etymological considerations (cf. note on *LAS* 288:7' for *magāgu* "to be tumescent, stiff"), that of *AHw* on the co-occurrence of the word with *lu'tu* "uncleanliness; a disease". For the latter *CAD* L 256f proposes the translation "debility", but in this case etymology as well as contextual evidence seem to favour *AHw*'s rendering "ein Hautkrankheit".

that Assurbanipal suffered from similar troubles. The lengthened final vowel (*ma*]*n-gu-u*) indicates question ("Is this stiffness/skin disease . . . . ?").

tu-mu-lu: unclear, cf. *ina lìb-bi tu-mu-lu-ka, ABL* 1237 r14. *ka*!*-mu-lu* "angered" (referring to demon as cause of illness) would make sense in this context, but is excluded after collation.

r4. *us-sa-na-lam*: if one may trust *AHw*. (1014*a* and 1144f), this is the only Dtn form of *šlm* (or *slm*) attested so far.

r6. *lu-u(-)pa-ḫa-áš-šú*: either Stat. of **pūḫ* D (*AHw*. 876*a* "(ein)tauschen") + pron. suff. in dative, in which case the translation would be "let [ ] be substituted for him", or Stat./Prt. of **pḫī* (*AHw*. 853*a* "verschließen, einschließen"), in which case one could translate "let his [mouth?] be shut up" or "let me shut up his [ ]". For lack of context one cannot exclude either alternative; both verbs are otherwise hardly attested in NA (for **pūḫ* D cf. *lu-pi-ḫu RA* 60 66:17, for **pḫī pa-ḫu-te LAS* 284 r13).

323

Bibliography:

Previously unpublished. Copy *CT* pl. 201, no. 915.

Writer:

Probably the same as in *LAS* 329, note the occurrence of the relatively rare spelling LÚDUMU *šip-ri* (mostly LÚ(*)A. KIN) in both letters. The spelling *be-li* (4') points to Ištar-šumu-ēreš (cf. Appendix M 6), and though both the present letter and *LAS* 329 are but small fragments, their orthography is consistent with this assignation. Note LÚ not LÚ*, as in the letters of Ištar-šumu-ēreš; *né-e-mur* (329 r4), to be compared with *le-e-mur* 14 r13; EN-*já* (323 r3), as in 2:3, 4:3, 12:3, 14:3.5.18, 19:4, 26:3.5; *30* = *Sîn* (323:3'), as in 14:9; *pu-un* not IGI (323:2'), as in 18 r12, UD *29*.KÁM not KAM*/KAM (329:2), as in 1 r6.14.16, 2:12, 3:8ff, etc.; *is-su-ri* 323:2', as in 13 r23, 14 r6, 15:16, and 22 r5!, not *i-su(-ur)-ri*. Note also that all other "scribes" from whom we have letters (Balasî, Nabû-aḫḫē-erība, Nabû'a, Ištar-nādin-apli, Bābu-šumu-iddina, Nabû-šumu-iddina), with the exception of Nabû-zēru-līšer, are out of the question, since the spelling *be-li* is not attested in their letters.

Notes:

5'. After URU*Arba-ìl*, there is space for one more city name, e.g. Kalizi (cf. *LAS* 85f) or Calah (cf. *LAS* 80f). For the passage on the whole cf. *RMA* 274 = *ABL* 895:5ff, *en-na* IM.DIRMEŠ *ka-la-a-ma* [6]*ki-i* AN.MI *iš-ku-nu ù la iš-ku-nu* [7]*ul ni-di* EN LUGALMEŠ *a-na* BAL.TILKI *a-na* URU *ka-la-ma* [8]*a-na* DIN.TIRKI *a-na* EN.LÍLKI *a-na* UNUGKI [9]*ù* BÁR.SIPAKI *liš-pur mìn-de-e-ma* [10]*ina lìb-bi* URUME *an-nu-ti i-ta-mar* "Now there were clouds everywhere; we do not know whether the eclipse took place or not. Let the lord of kings write to Assur and all the cities, to Babylon, Nippur, Uruk and Barsip; perhaps it was observed in those cities." One should note that only Assyrian cities are mentioned in the present letter; this is certainly due to the fact that the lunar calendars of Assyria and Babylonia were for practical reasons kept separate from one another, the crescent of the moon becoming visible at the latitude of Babylon 5 minutes later than in Nineveh.[631]

r1. The signs following *liš-pur* are not DUMEŠ, as given in Pt. I, but, according to collation (11.6.1974), IŠ NUMUN. What they stand for remains completely obscure. A verbal form like *iš-k/qul* is out of the question because of the context, and no noun like **išk/qūlu* appears to be known (cf. the dictionaries). Accordingly, though the signs are quite regularly drawn and perfectly clear, a scribal error seems possible.

324

Bibliography:

(I) Thompson, *RMA* (1900) no. 188.
(II) Oppenheim, *Centaurus* 14 (1969) 127[8].

---

[631] Cf. Schoch, *Astronomical and Calendrical Tables* (1928), p.VIII, Table E.

Writer:

Purely orthographically, this letter could have been written both by Balasî *and* Nabû-aḫḫē-erība: the orthographical conventions of these scribes were largely identical (cf. respective columns in App. M 6, and the note on the writer of *LAS* 67), and the letter lacks distinctive features which usually make it possible to differentiate between the two; thus e.g. the spellings *a-du* (9; not *a-di*), *i-da-a-ti* (r2; not *i(d)-da-(a)-te*), and EN-*já* etc.) consistently occur in letters of both B. and N. (see *LAS* 45:10 and *RMA* 70 r7, ABL 993 r1 and *RMA* 236G r2 respectively), while other less well attested spellings do not allow a clear distinction (cf. *as-sa-*[*ap-ra*] *RMA* 274O:6 (Balasî) v. [*as*]*-sap-ra LAS* 73 r2' (Nabû-aḫḫē-erība); [*ú-ìl*]*-tú LAS* 40 r3' (B) v. *ú-il-tú* 61 r4 and *ú-ìl-ti* 60:7 (N); *iq-ṭi-ri-ib* 326:3 (B?) and *RMA* 112 r5 (N); *it-tan-ta-ḫa RMA* 84:6 (N), not attested in letters of Balasî). However, it is likeliest that the writer is Balasî, since the text lacks *explanatory glosses* which occur in every letter and report signed by Nabû-aḫḫē-erība, excepting *LAS* 60-61, 65, 70 and the very short or fragmentary texts *LAS* 73-76 and *RMA* 51, 54, 254D, 271A, 274G and 274H.

Addressee:

Assurbanipal.

Date:

July 4, 668 BC = Du'ūzu 20, eponym year of Mar-larim or a bit later. This date is based on the Jupiter-omens quoted in the letter, pertaining to a heliacal rising of the planet in Du'ūzu (the 4th month) "behind" the constellation of [Gemini], i.e. a few degrees to the east of it. Within the time brackets 681-646 holding for virtually all the *LAS* correspondence and certainly for all reports and letters by Balasî and Nabû-aḫḫē-erība, such a situation occurred only once: in July, 668.[632] According to the tables of Schoch (1928), Jupiter then became observable in Babylon in the evening of the 1st day (= Du'uzu 17, cf. App. C4), in Nineveh a few days later (cf. Schaumberger, *ZA* 47 [1941/2] 122f); at the time of its appearance, its longitude was about 80°, which means that it was about 2 degrees "behind" Gemini and due to reach Cancer in about two week's time (cf. r2ff). The agreement with the data of the letter is accordingly perfect. Moreover, the statement (Obv. 3) that the planet was sighted on the path of the Enlil stars also agrees with the situation on July 4, 668, Jupiter's declination being then about +22°, i.e. about 6° above the upper borderline of the Enlil zone (approximately +16°, cf. Schaumberger, art. cit. p. 124). Historically, the year 668 of course fits excellently, since all other datable letters and reports of Balasî and Nabu-Aḫḫē-erība belong between years 674 and 666 BC. Cf. App. O.

Notes:

1f. This omen is also attested in *ACh* Ištar 16:4 (I ^{MUL}SAG.ME.GAR *ina* ^{ITU}ŠU IGI-*ir* KUR *šu-ub-tu*$_4$ *né-eḫ-tu*$_4$ TUŠ).

3f. Cancel the restoration of this omen given in Pt. I and restore instead, according to *RMA* 191:3-5, [I ^{MU}]^{L}SAG.ME.GAR *ina* KASKAL [*šu-ut* ^{d}EN*.LÍL IGI] ^{4}LUGAL URI^{KI} *i-dan-nin-ma* [*ina* KUR.KUR *na-ki-ri-šú ina* ^{GIŠ}TUKUL *ú-šam-qat*] "If Jupiter appears on the path of the Enlil stars, the king of Akkad will become powerful and smite his enemies with weapon in all countries." The same omen is also quoted in *RMA* 191A:3f, but the relevant entry in the astrological omen series itself does not seem to be extant.

5ff. This omen does not recur elsewhere, as far as I have been able to ascertain. Nevertheless, in Obv. 5 one certainly has to restore, instead of ^{MUL}AL.LUL (Pt. I), ^{MUL}MAŠ.TAB.BA (GAL.GAL) "Gemini". Rev. 2ff indicates that when the letter was written Jupiter had not yet reached Cancer, whereas the expression *ana* EGER (Obv. 5) means that it had left "behind" another constellation (cf. Largement, *ZA* 52 [1957] 259); since the motion of outer planets at conjunction always is eastward, this constellation can only be Gemini. For the underlying astronomical situation cf. above, note on the date of the letter. For another report on the heliacal rising of Jupiter in 668 BC see *RMA* 187; the planet is there said to have appeared "in front of" Cancer (*i-na pa-an* ^{MUL}AL.LUL *in-nam-mar-ma*, Obv. 3), i.e. to the west of this constellation, and the event is explicitly placed in the first regnal year [of Assurbanipal] (*re-eš* LUGAL-*ti-ka*) in Rev. 8.

---

[632] 12 years earlier, in June 680, Jupiter rose in Gemini (longitude 75°.2), 12 years later (July 656), in Cancer (84°.5). None of the other heliacal risings took place in or near these two constellations.

FIGURE 5

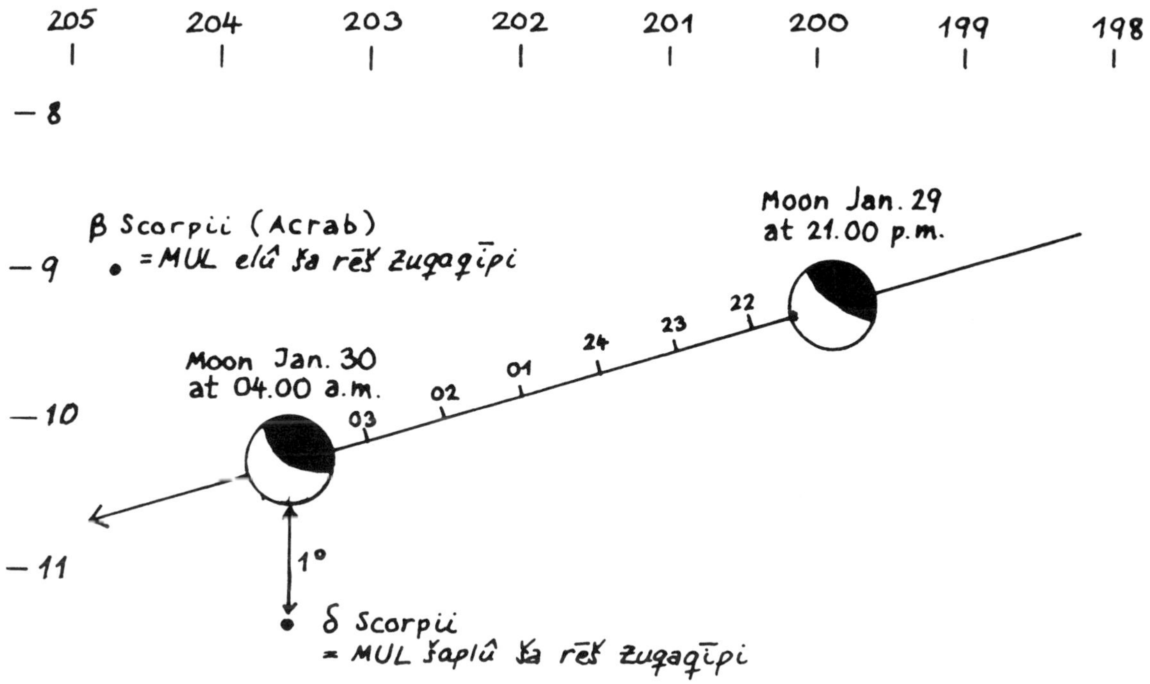

The lunar observation of LAS 325 (Šabāṭu 21 = January 30, 667 BC) Lunar positions computed with P.V. Neugebauer. *Tafeln für Sonne, Planeten und Mond* (1914). Fixed star positions after idem, Sterntafeln (1912).

8. In accordance with the previous note, cancel the restoration of this line given in Pt. I and restore instead, MULSAG.ME.GAR [*ina* EGER MULMAŠ.TAB.BA(.GAL.GAL) IGI(.LAL) / *in-na-mar-ma*] "Jupiter [is visible "behing" Gemini]".

r2ff. Though formally possible, the translation of this passage given in Pt. is illogical and therefore abortive: should Jupiter have *already* approached Cancer, the writer would naturally have communicated the relevant omens at once, not at a later occasion. It is therefore better to regard *iq-ṭi-ri-ib* (r3) as part of the temporal clause and translate: "Later, after it *has* risen (higher) *and* approached Cancer, I shall extract . . ." Cf. *it-tan-ta-ḫa it-taḫ-kim* "it has risen *and* become clearly visible", *LAS* 290 r8.

325

Bibliography:

(I) Thompson, *RMA* 251.

(II) Oppenheim, *Centaurus* 14 (1969) 133[52] and 134[54]; Weidner, *AfO* 14 (1941/4) 340. The museum number of this tablet is K. 760, not K. 670 as given in Pt. I.

Writer:

Balasî. This assignation is certain in view of the astrological contents of the text and the spelling *an-ni-i-e* (Obv. 7, for normal *an-ni-i/e*) which, within the present corpus, occurs only in letters and reports of Balasî. Cf. Appendix M 6, and note on the writer of *LAS* 34.

Addressee:

Assurbanipal.

Date:

Šabāṭu 21, eponymy of Mar-larim = January 30, 667 BC. The Assyrian month and day in question can be determined on the basis of the omens quoted on the Obverse. The first of these show that the month was Šabāṭu, the last refers to foggy weather on the "day of the city god", a monthly festival; this festival was celebrated in Šabāṭu on the 20th or 22nd day (cf. note on *LAS* 176:12 and Weidner, *AfO* 14 342). Rev. 8ff indicates that the year in question was intercalary, and specifically one containing an intercalary Addāru. In the period covered by the letters and reports of Balasî (ca. 675-665, cf. Appendix O), there were only two such leap years: the 8th regnal year of Esarhaddon (673/2 BC) and the first year of Assurbanipal (668/7 BC).[633] Šabāṭu 20, Ash 8, equals January 23, 672; Šabāṭu 20, Asb 1 equals January 28, 667 (see App. A 2). Preliminary computation reveals that in both years the moon reached the position described in the letter ("tonight a star at the head of Scorpio stood before the moon", Obv. 7ff) approximately a day later, on January 24 (= Šabāṭu 21) 9 p.m. and January 30 (= Šabāṭu 21) 4 am. respectively; that is to say, at the said moments the right ascension of the moon was approximately identical with that of the stars at the head of Scorpio, β and δ Scorpii (204°.7 and 203°.02 respectively, see note on Obv. 7f). Both years are accordingly acceptable in this respect, and more accurate computation is necessary to establish which year is actually in question. The declinations of β and δ Scorpii ca. 670 BC were respectively -9°.0 and -11°.54, and the lunar declination, which depends on its latitude, must accordingly at either moment agree with either of these two values. Computation with the help of Neugebauer's *Tafeln für Sonne, Planeten und Mond* (1914) gives the following result:

(a) Position of the moon, Nineveh, January 24 -671, 9 p.m.:
a = 205°.11, δ = -16°.28;

(b) Position of the moon, Nineveh, January 29 -666, 9 p.m.:
a = 199°.89, δ = - 9°.19,
and 7 hours later, on January 30 -666, 4 a.m.:
a = 203°.57, δ = -10°.26.

It can be seen that (a) is out of this question, since the moon was then at a distance of more than 7° from β Scorpii and almost 5° from δ Scorpii. By contrast, the situation (b), which is plotted in Fig. 5, fits perfectly. On January 30

633 See App. A1. Year 665/4 probably also contained an intercalary Addāru, but since no other letters of the present edition can be placed in this year, the odds are against its being in question here. The same naturally applies, only more emphatically, to the year 676/5.

(=Šabāṭu 21), 667 BC, at 4 am., the moon stood before *both* β and δ Scorpii, at a distance of only about 1° from both stars; the agreement with the text could not be better. Consequently, there is no need to study the situation in any other leap year with an intercalary Addāru, earlier or later: even if an equally good agreement with the data of the letter could be found in another year, which is very unlikely, 667 BC will remain the only acceptable year until it is possible to prove, on firm evidence, that Balasi wrote astrological letters and reports to king before or after 675-665.

Notes:

1f: An omen included both in the series *Enūma Anu Enlil* and *Iqqur Īpuš*. Cf. Virolleaud, *ACh* 2 Spl 103: 27 amd Labat, *IE* § 98:11. The omen is also quoted in *RMA* 249A:1-2, 250:5f, 250A:1f and 251A:1. Note that *ACh* 2 Spl 103c:10 has AN.MI LUGAL *Kaš-ši-i* "eclipse of the Kassite king", and RMA 249A, 250 and 250A simply AN.MI *Kaš-ši-i* "eclipse of the Kassite(s)", against AN.MI KUR *Kaš-ši-i* "eclipse of the Kassite country" of our text.

3. Cf. *ACh* 2 Spl 103b r13, [I *ina* KUR IM.DUGUD GÁL]-*ši nu-ḫuš ni-ši*, and ibid. 103c:13, [I *ina* KUR IM.DUGUD GÁL-*š*]*i nu-ḫuš* UN^{MEŠ}. The same omen is also quoted in *RMA* 111 r1, 251A:2, 252B:1 and, with different apodosis (EBUR *ina-pu-uš* KI.LAM GI.NA), in *RMA* 250:1f.

4. Cf. *ACh* 2 Spl 103:31, I *ina* KUR IM.DUGUD *sa-dir* BAL KUR *kiš-šú-tú* EN-*el*. Also quoted in *RMA* 111 r2f (*pa-le-e* KUR ³*kiš-šú-tú i-bé-el*), 250:3f (BAL KUR ŠÚ-*tú* EN-el), 251A:3 (BAL KUR *kiš-šú-tú i-kaš-šad*, a corruption from *i-bé-el*), 252B:2f (BAL-*e* KUR), 252D:1f and 252E:1f (BAL LUGAL KUR ŠÚ [. .]).

5. This omen is indeed not included in the section of *Šumma Ālu* dealing with omens pertaining to the "day of the city god" (Thureau-Dangin, *TU* no. 9; Nötscher, *Šumma alu* III 29). Cf. Weidner, *AfO* 14 340.

6. It is unclear on what grounds this statement rests. Foggy weather was not always interpreted as a favourable omen (cf. e.g. *ACh* 2 Spl 53:28, "If there is fog in the month Addāru, the land (of Akkad) will go to ruin", or ibid. 26, "If there is fog in the month Ṭebētu, an eclipse affecting all countries (will occur)"), and omens pertaining to the "day of the city god" were for the most part unfavourable (cf. *TU* no.9:20ff). However, since *most* of the fog omens *were* favourable (the proportion is about 9:5 in favour of good omens), the writer perhaps intended something like "fog (in general) is a good omen, it is not (usually) regarded as a bad (sign)". The translation in Pt. I could without difficulty be modified accordingly.

7f. The star mentioned here was either β Scorpii (Acrab) or δ Scorpii; cf. MUL *e* (abbr. for *elû*) *ša* SAG GÍR.TAB "the upper star of the head of Scorpio' (= β Scorpii) and MUL MURUB₄ *ša* SAG GÍR.TAB "the middlemost star of the head of Scorpio" (= δ Scorpii), Kugler *SSB* I 29 and II 551. The co-ordinates of these stars about 670 BC were, according to the *Sterntafeln* of Neugebauer (1912), a = 204°.70; δ = -9°.00 and a = 203°.02; δ = -11°.54 respectively.

r2. *ISKIM-šú la i-lap-pa-[at]*: cf. *ḫa-an-ni-i i-la-pat* "this is evil-boding", *LAS* 13 r14. Note that ISKIM is here, as also in r7, masculine, and should therefore perhaps be read *(g)iskimmu* not *ittu*. Note, however, ISKIM-*šú la-ap-ta-at* 109:17'f beside ISKIM *la-ap-tu* (not *la* <*ta*>-*ab-tu*) 30:15 and *it-ti* NIM.MA^{KI} *la-pi-it RMA* 274Fr5, and see note on *LAS* 30:15. Was *ittu* perhaps both masculine and feminine in Neo-Assyrian, like *ṭuppu*? Cf. also on 152:13ff.

lapātu is here only secondarily intransitive; the expression is an ellipsis for *memmēni lā ilappat* "it does not affect anybody (or anything)", cf. *mim+ma ul i-lap-pat, RMA* 215:6. The reason why the omen was not considered ill-bodying is given below (r7): it was not connected with the moon's appearance or disappearance, nor with any other lunar phenomenon of ominous nature, such as lunar halo, but was a more or less "normal" (*kajamānu*) event repeating itself several times each year (though not every month). The idea expressed by *lā ilappat* here clearly corresponds to that of *kajamānu*, and hence the passage is perhaps most suitably rendered "its sign is not anomalous/ abnormal"; for this meaning of *lapātu* see *CAD* L 88b, 91a and 95f. Cancel the translation in Pt. I.

r3. *la in-na-sa-[ḫ]*: an ellipsis for *piširšu lā innassaḫ* "its interpretation is not (to be) extracted", cf. *LAS* 147:11 and 278 r3'ff. The same elliptic usage also in *LAS* 25 r9', 289 r12, *RMA* 88:9, 112 r4, 244D:6 and 264:10.

r4. ^{MUL}*Ṣur-ru*: clearly the name of either β or δ Scorpii (cf. above on 7f), but occurring only here. If *ṣurru* here means "obsidian" not "insides", as seems likely, the name may possibly derive from the colour of the star: there were green (yellow) and white varieties of ^{NA_4}*ṣurru*, see *CAD* Ṣ 258b.

^{MUL}*LI₉.SI₄* = a Scorpii (Antares), see Gössmann, *Planetarium* p. 94 and Weidner, *AfO* 20 (1963) 121 (read there ^{d}NE-si₄ $^{li-si!}$). Since this star was situated not at the head but at the "breast" of Scorpio (cf. ^{MUL}GABA.GÍR.

TAB ^{d}LI$_{9}$.SI$_{4}$ ^{d}AG "the breast of Scorpio = Lisi = Nabû", *CT* 33 pl. 3 ii 30), it is possible that the sign at the end of the line is not SA[G] but GA[B]; cf. copy Thompson, *RMA* 251 (not collated). The coordinates of Antares about 670 BC were $\alpha = 208^{\circ}.96$; $\delta = -16^{\circ}.57$, which means that it was more than 4° distant from the stars at the head of Scorpio and could not have been reached by the moon during the same night as the other stars; it is accordingly unclear why it is mentioned here at all; perhaps because it was mentioned in the literary source (unidentified, hardly *Enūma Anu Enlil*) which the writer utilized.

r5. For the restoration cf. *2* MUL^{MEŠ} *ša ina zi-qit* ^{MUL}GÍR.TAB GUB^{MEŠ}*-zu*, *CT* 33 pl. 3 ii 31, and similar examples passim in the same text.

r7. See note on r2.

r8f. *"All the (fixed) stars have become tardy"*: this remark does not, of course, mean that the stars would have been retarded in motion but simply that the lunar calendar had gone too much ahead of the sideral one, so that stars whose heliacal risings were fixed (in the compendia Mul Apin and MUL^{MEŠ} *12*.TA.ÀM) in the month Ṭebētu, were appearing "only" in the month Šabāṭu, etc. Intercalating a month was the only way of amending the situation.

Yet the immediate impulse to the request of intercalation was doubtless given by the lunar observation discussed in the preceding lines. In a "normal" year, the moon would by Šabāṭu 20/22 already have been in conjunction with the stellar cluster of Sagittarius, and since the date in question was a festival one, it is certain that the "delay" attracted the attention of scholars: note the analogy with the rule by which it was decided whether a given year was intercalary or not ("If the Moon and the Pleiades have the same longitude on the 1st of Nisannu, that year is normal; if only on the 3rd, that year is intercalary", *Babyl.* 7 p. 13:8ff, cf. Schaumberger, *SSB* 3 Erg. 340).[634]

r9. *ITU.KÁM**: read ^{ITU}ŠE![635] "the month Addāru", and cancel the translation "every month" given in Pt. I. The remark "Addāru must not pass unluckily" seems to imply that it was considered inauspicious to let the year end (and at the same time, the new year begin) at a "wrong" time, viz. so much before the spring equinox that the equinox would not occur in the month Nisannu at all. Cf. *LAS* 344-345 and relevant commentary.

326

Bibliography:

Thompson, *RMA* 176.

Writer:

Balasî. Note the spellings *an-ni-i-ú* and *an-ni-i-e* (r1.5), and *pi-še-er-šú*, and see Introduction, p. 30. For the superscript gloss $^{\textit{mu-šú}}$MI (Rev. 1) cf. *RMA* 88:5 ($^{\textit{ma-ḫi-ru}}$GÁN.BA), and for the colon separating MUL and ^{d}UTU in Rev. 4, *RMA* 88 r5 and 91:3.4.7.

Discussion:

This text is probably contemporaneous with *RMA* 144 (from [Akkullā]nu; cf. also *RMA* 144E and 177, both from Nabû-iqbi, and 215A, from Nabû-iqīša, which contain a similar enumeration of omens as is found here. Unfortunately, the parallel texts contain no additional astronomical or chronological data and thus offer no help to the dating of the letter.

Notes:

[N.B.: The obverse and reverse of this text – correctly determined in the edition of Thompson – were incorrectly inverted in Pt. I: all texts of the "report" type begin with omens. For the sake of convenience, however, lines of the text are below referred to in the side order of Pt. I.]

3f. *"Saturn is the star of the sun"*: a well-known dogma, cf. ^{d}UDU.IDIM.SAG.UŠ : MUL ^{d}UTU, *CT* 41 pl. 39 r6 (Labat, *Commentaires* p.100 [comm. to *Iqqur Īpuš*]); ^{MUL}SAG.UŠ! MUL *šá* ^{d}UTU, BM 121206 viii 60' (van

---

634 Cf. also H. Hunger and E. Reiner, "A scheme for intercalary months from Babylonia", *WZKM* 67 (1975) 21ff.

635 Reading confirmed by E. Sollberger, collation of 19.1.1976.

Driel, *CA* p. 96); dSAG.UŠ : MUL GE$_6$: dUTU "Saturn = the black star = the Sun", 2 *R* 49,3:42 (Weidner, *HBA* p. 29); MUL GE$_6$ = AN*ṣa-al-me*DÙL = dSAG.UŠ dUTU "black (*ṣalmu*) star = statue (*ṣalmu*) = Saturn (as) the Sun", Ḫg B VI 40, cf. AN*ṣa-lam*DÙL = dUTU, *CT* 25 pl. 25:13; mul-gi-gi = MUL *kit-tú u me-šar* = dSAG.UŠ dUTU "*mul-gi-gi* = the star of truth and justice = Saturn (as) the Sun", Ḫg B VI 38. Saturn's association with the sun naturally had its basis in the planet's slow and steady motion, but it was also forcefully backed by linguistic and mythological speculation. Cf. simply the examples cited above, where the association of the two heavenly bodies is "explained" by two puns, one based on the homophony of *ṣalmu* "black" and *ṣalmu* "statue", the other on a play with the meanings of the verb *kūn* "to be steady".[636] A further link between Saturn and the sun was provided by the fact that Saturn had its hypsoma or "house" in the constellation Libra, the cosmic scales of life and death where the sun stayed during the autumnal equinox; cf. Gössmann, *Planetarium* p. 72, and equations such as [MUL*bi*]-*ib-bu* = d*Zi-b*[*a-ni-tum*], *CT* 26 pl. 41 K. 11283+:3'; MULUDU.IDIM d*Zi-ba-ni-tum*, *KAV* 218 ii 10; MUL GE$_6$ = d*Zi-*[*ba-ni-tum*], *CT* 26 pl. 41 K. 11283+ r4'; MUL*Zi-ba-ni-tum* = dUTU, ibid. 5'; and MULZI.BA.AN.NA = *zi-ba-ni-tum* = dSAG.UŠ dUTU, Ḫg B VI 41.

7. "Sun [sic] is the star of the king": on this dogma see, in detail, note on *LAS* 143 r4f.

r1f. Cf. *ACh* 2 Spl 52:6, I *20 ina* KI.GU[B *30* GUB . . . .]. Also quoted in *RMA* 144 r4f and 215A r1f.

r3ff. Cf. *ACh* Sîn 3:64, I AŠ+ME UGU *30 u* KI.TA *30* GUB-*iz* LUGAL KUR SUḪUŠ GIŠGU.ZA-*šú* GIN-*an* KIMIN LUGAL *ina ket-ti-šú* GUB-*az* [65]MULUDU.IDIM.SAG.UŠ UD *14*.KÁM KI *30* GUB-*ma* "If the sun stands above or below the moon, the foundation of the throne of the king of the land will be secure, variant, the king will stand in his justice: (this omen is quoted when) Saturn stands with the moon on the 14th day" (Tablet I of *šumma sîn ina tāmartišu*, the commentary series to *Enūma Anu Enlil*). The omen is also quoted (with minor variants and without the commentary item) in *RMA* 144E:6f, 215A:3ff and 177:1ff.

r6f. Cf. *ACh* Sîn 3:62, I *30 u 20 šu-ta-tu-ú* LUGAL KUR *uz-nu* DAGAL-*aš* ITU-*us-su* DINGIR KI DINGIR IGI.LAL *šá 20* [63] (*u*) MULUDU.IDIM.SAG.UŠ UD *14*.KÁM KI *30* GUB-*ma* "If the moon and the sun are looking at each other, the king of the land will increase wisdom: (this means that) the god is seen every month with the god, i.e. the sun; also (that) Saturn is standing on the 14th day with the moon" (Tablet I of *Šumma Sîn ina tāmartišu*). A variant of the same omen, together with the commentary, occurs in *RMA* 144:7-10 ([9]*ša* UD *14*.KÁM* DINGIR KI DINGIR IGIMEŠ KIMIN dUDU.IDIM.SAG.UŠ [10]UD *15*.KÁM *it-ti* d30 GUB-*az-ma*); without the commentary, in *RMA* 127 r4, 128:4f, 131:5f, 135 r1f, etc.

327

Bibliography:

Thompson, *RMA* 276. Leichty, *TCS* 4 (1970) p.8.

Copy:

Thompson, *RMA* 276. Handcock, *CT* 28 (1910) pl.6.

Discussion:

Is this the "tablet" referred to in *LAS* 39 r5ff? The two omens quoted in the text do not recur elsewhere (cf. Leichty *a.l.*).

---

636 Saturn was a "black" star through his identification with Ninurta; Šamaš (the sun) was called *ṣalmu* (statue) because Sum. an-dùl meant both "statue" and "protection": as a judge, the sun of course was looked upon as "the protection" of god and man alike. Similarly, Saturn's name *kajamānu* "the steady one", derived from the root *kūn*, provided an etymological connection with *kittu* "truth, justice" and hence an association with Šamaš, the protector of justice in heaven and earth. Note also *i-šá-ru ina* AN-*e ka-aja-ma-nu at-ta* "O Just One, you are everlasting in the sky", 4 *R* 28,1:8, where *kajamānu* occurs as an epithet of Šamaš.

328

Bibliography:

(I) Thompson, *RMA* 178.

(II) Oppenheim, *Centaurus* 14 (1969) 128[9].

Writer:

Nabû-aḫḫē-erība. This attribution can be regarded as certain on the ground of the infralinear glosses *ip-pu-ḫa-ma* and *pa-ni-šú* in Obv. 2 and the occurrence of the spelling dŠá-maš in Obv. 4; see Appendix M 6. Note also *re-eḫ-ti di-ib-bi* (r1), to be compared with *LAS* 64 r5 and *RMA* 139:5.

Date:

Probably mid-Addāru, eponym year of Atar-ilī = mid-February, 672 BC. The month is obtained from Obv. 4, the year from the reference to the Jupiter-omen in Obv. 7. It is quite evident that a recently occurred (and reported) event is in question (cf. below), and since it was specifically the *heliacal rising* of Jupiter that portended increase of royal might as well as rains and floods (see Gössmann, *Planetarium* p. 126ff for a representative survey of all Jupiter-omens, and cf. below, note on r3), the "sign" in question almost certainly was the "morning first" of the planet in Addāru (or possibly Šabāṭu).[637] Between years 681-663, only one such rising took place: that of February 12 [= Addāru 10], 672 BC. See App. C4. Since all phases of Jupiter are repeated nearly identically (only 5 days later) every 12th year, it can of course be theoretically argued that the letter could equally well be placed in years 684 or 660 BC. However, these years are virtually out of the question, since all other datable letters and reports of Nabû-aḫḫē-erība were written in 674-666 BC (cf. App. O) and *no* epistolary texts found in Nineveh are yet datable on *any* grounds (historical or astronomical) to the years 700-681 and 664-658 BC (see Introduction, p. XIII f).

Notes:

1ff. This omen is also quoted in *RMA* 183A (Assyrian writer, name lost), which however pertains to another incident: I dUTU KUR-*ma a-na* [. . .] [2'] LUGAL *kiš-šá-tú* [3'] *pa-lu-ú* [*ur-rak*] [4'] *ina* ITUBÁR *ina* SAG [MU.AN.NA] [5'] dUTU *a-ra-ak* [BAL-*e*] [6'] *ša* LUGAL EN-*ja iq-ṭi-bi* "If the sun lights and [. . .] to [. . .], the king of the world [will prolong] (his) reign. In Nisannu, at the beginning of [the year], the Sun has (thus) promised a long reign to the king, my lord." The corresponding entry in *Enūma Anu Enlil* does not appear to be extant.

4ff. Cf. *ACh* Šamaš 14:14, I *ina* ITU*A-da-ri 20 ina še-rì* TÙR NIGIN A.KAL *ku-li-li* DU-*ak* "If a halo surrounds the sun in the morning in Addāru, there will be a flood carrying dragonflies." The same apodosis also occurs in an omen pertaining to Venus (*ACh* Ištar 2:51), and is quoted and explained in *RMA* 243:3f as follows: [I] d*Iš-tar* AGA KÙ.UD *ap-rat* ⸢A⸣.[KAL] *ku-li-li* D[U-*ak*] [4] [A.KAL] *ku-li-li* A.KAL *gap*-[*šu*] "If Ištar is wearing a crown of silver, there will be a flood carrying dragonflies: a *flood c. d.* (means) strong flood." It is strange that the writer of the present report omitted the word "dragonflies" which would only have added to the propitiousness of the prediction.

7f. *"This was (also) in the sign of Jupiter"*: sic, correct the translation in Pt. I. The writer refers to a (recently occurred) "sign of Jupiter" predicting exactly the same things as the "sign of the Sun" interpreted in the present report (and thus "corroborating" these interpretations). It is excluded that a mere "line" in the astrological omen series, with no connection to a real event and only mentioned for the sake of curiosity (same apodosis!), could be meant. First, "line" is *šumu*, whereas the text has *ittu* "sign" (cf. note on 35:6). Second, there is no Jupiter-omen with an exactly similar apodosis, whereas there are several similar apodoses pertaining to other stars (cf. simply the previous note and *RMA* 184 r4f, 217:2f etc.). Third, there are no other indications whatever that Esarhaddon (or any other Assyrian king) was interested in "comparative apodosiology" except for purely practical purposes. Cf. also above (sub Date), and see note on r3 for the omens derived from the "sign" in question.

r1. *re-eḫ-ti di-ib-bi*: either referring to the omen quoted in Obv. 4ff, or to the present report as a whole, which accordingly would have been conceived as a postscript to the earlier report (dealing with Jupiter). For the former interpretation would speak *RMA* 139:5f, where *re-eḫ-ti di-ib-bi du-un-qu* [6] *šá* LUGAL EN-*ja* "the rest of the

[637] The latter alternative is improbable since the flood prediction was essentially linked with Jupiter's appearance on the path of the Anu stars (i.e. in Addāru-Nisannu-Ajāru). Months earlier than Šabāṭu are out of the question, since planetary omens were only valid for the time of one month (cf. *RMA* 245 r6).

'words' (= omens) are (likewise) favourable to the king, my lord" refers to two omens subsequently quoted,[638] as well as the fact that only the latter of the present omens portended rain and flood; the latter interpretation could be supported by *LAS* 64 r5 and 124:1, where *re-eḫ-ti di-ib-bi/da-ba-a-bi* pertains to a message (to be) sent after another message.

r3. Cf. I MULGÍR.TAB *ina* TÙR *30* [8]*it-ta-ši-iz ana* ŠÈG *u* A.KAL "Scorpio stood in the halo of the moon: (that points) to rain and flood", *RMA* 215:7f, and TÙR *šá* MULAB.SÍN [5]*a-na* ŠÈG *u* A.KAL "a halo surrounding Virgo (points) to rain and flood", *RMA* 230:4f. The sign of Jupiter meant in the present letter (= the planet's heliacal rising in Addāru/February 672 BC) portended rain and flood as follows:

I MUL*Né-bi-ru* KUR-*ḫa-ma* DINGIRMEŠ SILIM.MA TUKUMEŠ [*me*]-*šèr-tu* GÁL-*ši e-šá-a-ti i-nam-mi-ra dal-ḫa-a-ti i-zak-ka-a* ŠÈG *u* A.KAL DUMEŠ-*ni* "If *Nēberu* lights up, the gods will be peaceful, there will be justice; dull things will become bright, confused things clear; rain and flood will come . . ." (cf. *RMA* 186 r22ff and 187: 7ff);[639]

I MULEN.GÀL.AN.NA *i-ba-'i-il* A.KALMEŠ u ŠÈGMEŠ [DUMEŠ] "If *Engalanna* (= Jupiter) is bright, there will be floods and rains" (cf. *RMA* 186:7f);

I MULSAG.ME.GAR *ina* KASKAL *šu-ut* dA-*nu* IGI-*ir* [6]A.KAL GÁL-*ma* EBUR KUR SI.SÁ "If Jupiter appears on the path of the Anu stars, there will be a flood and the crops of the country will prosper" (cf. *RMA* 185 r5f and 196 r5f).

The first omen of the present report had the following coutnerparts in the "sign" of Jupiter:

I MULSAG.ME.GAR *ba-'i-il* LUGAL URIKI *a-šá-re-du-tú il-lak* "If Jupiter is bright, the king of Akkad will attain the first rank" (cf. *RMA* 186:5, 196 r2);

I MULLUGAL ŠE.ER.ZI *na-ši* LUGAL URIKI *ga-me-ru-tú* DÙ-*uš* "If Regulus (= Jupiter) is luminous, the king of Akkad will accomplish something perfect" (cf. *RMA* 185 r1f);

I MULZUBI ŠE.ER.ZI *na-ši* SUḪUŠ AŠ.TE DU-*an* "If Auriga (= Jupiter) is luminous, the foundation of the throne will be secure" (cf. *RMA* 185 r1f);

I MULSAG.ME.GAR ŠE.ER.ZI *na-ši* LUGAL *šá-lim* ŠÀ KUR DÙG-*ab* "If Jupiter is luminous, the king will be well and the land happy" (cf. *RMA* 271:16, 186:3f, 196:13f).

Finally, the omen derived from the month in which the "sign" (probably) occurred:

I MULSAG.ME.GAR *ina* ITUŠE IGI-*ir* KUR *ana* KUR [. . .] "If Jupiter appears in the month Addāru, land to land [. . . . .]" (*ACh* Ištar 16:12).

329

Bibliography:
Thompson, *RMA* 274B.

Writer:
Probably Ištar-šumu-ēreš; see note on the writer of *LAS* 323. The spelling d*Šá-maš* (Obv. 2) is not typical of Ištar-šumu-ēreš, but does occur in *LAS* 29:12.

Date:
Most probably Nisannu 30 = April 16, 657 BC. See discussion.

---

[638] or to a frequently quoted omen (e.g. *RMA* 138:1-5) left out as self-evident and therefore superfluous?

[639] In the case of *RMA* 186, this omen was quoted even though Jupiter had remained invisible for a minimum of 34 days (cf. App.3A and notes on *LAS* 289); in the case of *RMA* 187, the interval of invisibility had been only 28 days. Though the omen (to judge from its formulation) probably pertained only to Jupiter's appearance after a "normal" interval of invisibility (= ca. 30 days), these two cases show that it could well have been cited in the instance of Addāru, 672, too (interval: 31 days).

Discussion:

The general idea of this text seems clear, despite the breaks. A solar eclipse, followed by cloudy weather, had occurred on the 29th of the current month, and the question is now whether the next month should begin at the close of the 29th day or only in the evening of the 30th day. This suggests that the eclipse had taken place in the morning, for it takes a minimum of 15 hours for the lunar crescent to appear after the conjunction; had the eclipse occurred in the afternoon, any experienced astrologer would have known that the crescent could not possibly be sighted in the same evening, and the whole issue of the letter would not have become actual. A survey of the list of solar eclipses visible at Nineveh (Kudlek-Mickler, *AOATS* 1 p. 40) shows that during the attested career of Ištar-šumu-ēreš (678-650 BC), suitable eclipses occurred in 4 different years: 669, 664, 657 and 655 BC. The second and fourth of these are improbable, since no epistolary texts from Nineveh are yet datable with certainty to the years 665-659 and 656-653 BC (cf. Introduction, p. XIIIf), and the eclipse of 669, taken place at 5 a.m., is theoretically much more likely than that of 657, which occurred only towards the noon (at 10 a.m. – 0.30 p.m.).

The communicator of the eclipse observation seems to have favoured a month of 29 days (cf. Obv. 5, "we reject this day (= the 30th)"), whereas the writer himself (probably quite correctly) accepted 30 days as the length of the month (Rev. 5).[640] This decision need not, of course, be based on anything else but the failure to observe the crescent (because of the clouds). The king had to be informed because of his position as the official regulator of the lunar calendar (see Commentary to *LAS* 119).

Notes:

1. [ᴵ*Man-n*]*u*^!-⌜*ki*⌝^!-*i*-ᵁᴿᵁ*KASKAL*: a person with this name appears as witness in Ninevite contracts dating from 670 to 663 BC, see Tallqvist, *APN* p. 126*a*. The reading of the PN was confirmed by C.B.F. Walker (collation 1976).

r3. ᵈ*UTU*: according to collation by Walker, "ᵈ*20* seems preferable but is rather damaged"; probably a lapsus or scribal error for ᵈ*30* "the moon", which is expected.

330

Bibliography:

Previously unpublished. Copy *CT* 53, pl. 143 no. 603.

Writer:

Balasî (judging from the scribal hand).

Discussion:

This fragment is clearly a report on the sighting of two planets (ll. 5f) in the west (1.2). Theoretically, it thus could, but of course need not, be contemporaneous with *RMA* 209 (from Nabû-aḫḫē-erība) reporting on successive acronychal risings of Mercury (= the star of Nabû, see note on *LAS* 46 r9) and Venus on November 20 [= Kislīmu 10], 668 BC.

Notes:

1'. This is the first line of Side A, according to personal collation (1.6.1974).

2'. This line reads, after collation, [*ina*] ᵈUTU.ŠÚ.A *né*-⌜*ta*⌝-*ma*[*r*] "we have observed in the west". To judge from the curvatures of the tablet, nothing is missing beyond the restored signs here, nor in the following lines.

5'f. Restore [*ma-a*] "saying" at beginning.

7'. Traces of two signs, perhaps [. . .] ⌜TA* LU⌝ [GAL EN-*ja*] "with the ki[ng, my lord". It seems that only one line has been lost at the bottom of Side A.

---

640 Even if the date of the eclipse was May 27, 669, 5 a.m., full 24 hours had to lapse (according to the tables of Schoch [1928]) before the crescent could even theoretically be sighted, and it could accordingly not appear until the evening of the 30th Ajāru (= May 28).

331

Bibliography:

Previously unpublished. Copy *CT* 53, pl. 59, no. 187. [NB. The following comments pertain to a revised rendering of this text given on p. 513 of the present volume.]

Writer:

Akkullānu. Among the distinctive features definitely pointing to this writer note especially the following: (1) *Handwriting*: The forms of LUGAL (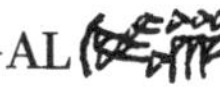), ŠA (), MEŠ () and TI (), cf. photo of *LAS* 301 (*RCAE* IV pl. 6); (2) *Orthography*: EN-*já* (cf. App. M. 6), *le-e-mur* (cf. *ta-a-mur LAS* 110+300r5, *le-e-pu-šú* 299 r9), *ma-ḫe-er* (cf. 309 r10); for the colon (:) separating literary quotations in r9f cf. *RMA* 36 r1, 87A r1, 89 r7, 144:7, *LAS* 110+300:17, and for the division-line, *LAS* 110+300:9.13 etc., 302 r4'.6', 312 r25'; (3) *Idiolect*: *ḫa-ra-me-ma* not *ḫa-ra-ma-ma* (cf. 110+300:8), and cf. r7 with *RMA* 87A:1. All remaining (ortho)graphic and linguistic features of the text likewise agree with the conventions of Akkullānu.

Addressee:

Assurbanipal.

Date:

Ca. 655 BC? Note the affinities of the text with *LAS* 108- 110+, all three dating from the 650's, the subject matter (cf. *LAS* 318-319), and the fact that the king to whom the text was addressed evidently was able to read (r8ff; see following discussion).

Discussion:

Despite its fragmentariness, this text is of considerable interest in several respects. First, the section beginning with Obv. 2 and ending in the division line (Rev. 6) gives evidence of the way in which the Assurbanipal library editions of Mesopotamian literary texts were created. Even though the passage as such hardly adds anything to what was already known from other sources (cf. Oppenheim, *Anc.Mes.* 244), it is still of importance in showing that while the physical act of editing and inscribing the texts naturally was done by expert scribes (in this case, Akkullānu), nothing was supposed to happen without the explicit endorsement of the king himself. Secondly, however the damaged portions of Rev. 7ff are to be restored, this section clearly implies that the king in question possessed a copy of *Enūma Anu Enlil* which he would (and *could*) *consult personally* whenever necessary. This not only proves that the letter was addressed to Assurbanipal (no other Sargonid even pretended to be able to write and read) but also provides a welcome illustration of the actual literary knowledge of the king. We know, of course, from *LAS* 34 that Assurbanipal had been taught by an expert astrologer, but apart from his own (a bit boastful) words we have little evidence as to how far he had actually got in his studies. The present text suggests that, somewhat exaggerated as they may be, the "autobiographical" statements of Assurbanipal's inscriptions and colophons can well have more truth in them than a critical modern reader would a priori be inclined to think (cf. also Discussions of *LAS* 129 [at the end] and 228; two other letters of Akkullānu [*LAS* 110+300 and 298] also suggest that Assurbanipal was not by any means totally ignorant in matters of astrology and magic).

Notes:

2. The break at the end of this line probably contained the name of the series to which the tablets in question belonged; the identity of the series remains unclear (despite Akkulānu's pre-occupation with astrological omens it is by no means certain that *Enūma Anu Enlil* is in question; many other compositions had an "apocryphal" counterpart, cf. simply *CAD* A/1 s.v. *aḫû*).

8ff. The lacunae here leave it uncertain whether the writing-boards mentioned were to serve as models for new tablets or whether they were to be inscribed after the model of the tablets referred to in Obv. 2f. The analogy of *LAS* 318f would make the latter alternative seem more probable, but how then to explain the fact that also "Akkadian" writing-boards are mentioned? Was Akkullānu perhaps expected to prepare two different copies of the same composition, one in Assyrian and another in Babylonian script? This seems unlikely. Accordingly, the correct interpretation probably is that the two sets of writing-boards were to *supplement* the aforementioned set of clay tablets as source materials for a new (standardized) edition of a tablet-series, which, as already pointed out, was to be prepared by Akkullānu himself. That several different manuscripts (both Babylonian and Assyrian) were utilized in the preparation of the Assurbanipal library editions of literary texts is known with certainty from the colophons of such editions, cf. e.g. Hunger, *AOAT* 2 no. 328 and see ibid. p. 6f.

r3ff. Cf. *ACh* Ištar 23:31, [PAB] 39 MU^{MEŠ} *a-ḫu-ti šá ina lìb-bi ṭup-pí šá-nim-ma in-nam-ru-ma* [. . .] "[Altogether] 39 apocryphal omens which are found in a secondary(?) tablet and [. . .]"; *18*.ÀM MU^{MEŠ} *šá lìb-bi ṭup-pi šá-nim-ma* "18 omens contained in a secondary(?) tablet", *Babyl.* 4 125 r18; *12* MU^{MEŠ} BAR.BAR *šá* KA DUB *2-ma* "12 apocryphal omens according to the diction of a secondary(?) tablet", *ACh* 2 Spl 68 r16; see also Weidner, *AfO* 14 (1941-44) 183, for more similar examples and a discussion of the term *ṭuppu šanûmma*.[641] The present passage indicates that the writer was in doubt whether apocryphal omens should be incorporated into the new tablet edition together with canonical ones, or written down in a *ṭuppu šanûmma*; does this mean that there really was in this period a desire to amalgamate the canonical and apocryphal omen collections?

r7. Cf. [d]*30 ša in-na-mir-u-ni* ²[KI.GUB]*-su ke-e-né ina* ŠÀ IM.DIR GI$_6$ *it-ta-mar*, *RMA* 87A:1f (from Akkullānu). At the end of the line, one can optionally read either *du*[*n-qi* or *šu*[*l-me*; the latter reading is perhaps more acceptable in the lack of other examples of *dunqu* spelled with the sign ŠUL (cf. *AHw* 176 and *CAD* D 180ff).

r8. Cf. *i-na* ^{GIŠ}LI.U$_5$.UM *lu-mu-ur* "let me look it up in the writing board", *PBS* 1/2 77:3f, and similar examples quoted in *CAD* A/2 p. 18*a*. The restoration [LUGAL *be*]*-lí* at the beginning of the line seems inevitable in view of Rev. 12 (and the continuation: cf. the following note).

r9ff. While all the omens quoted here are well known (cf. below), the passage is unique in one respect: all the omens seem to lack apodoses. It seems as if Akkullānu had intentionally omitted these since he knew (or gave to understand, by way of flattery) that *the king was well capable of looking up the "interpretations" himself*. If this really be so (there can be no absolute certainty because of the breaks), then we should have the first tangible evidence of Assurbanipal's ability to read scholarly texts (cf. Discussion). But what is the meaning of Rev. 9 "I shall see [. . . .]?"

r9f. The last sign of r9 is, according to collation, unquestionably ŠID [+]; however, this is probably an error for AG[A! "earthshine" (lit. "crown"), for the traces in question cannot be reconciled with any known omen derived from the moon's first appearance. By contrast, omens referring to earthshine are more than once quoted together with the second omen of the present passage; cf. *RMA* 37:5f, I *30 ina* IGI.LAL*-šú* AGA *a-pir* ⁶LUGAL SAG.KAL*-tú* DU*-ak* "If the moon at its appearance wears a crown, the king will attain first rank", cited together with I *30* UD *1*.KÁM IGI KA GI.NA ²ŠÀ KUR DÙG*-ab* ³I *30* KI.GUB*-su* GI.NA GUB*-iz* ⁴*uk-ku-u šá* ŠÈG "If the moon appears on the 1st, the country will be happy; if the moon (at its appearance) stands in its normal place, there will be want(?) of rain", ibid. r1ff; I *30 ina* IGI.LAL*-šú man-za-za* GI.NA GUB*-iz* ² *uk-ku-u šá* ŠÈG ³I AGA UD ŠÚ.ŠÚ.RU *a-pir* ⁴*30* LÚ*KÚR *i-maḫ-ḫa-aṣ* "If the moon at its appearance stands in (its) normal place, there will be want(?) or rain; if it wears a crown on a dark day, the moon god will slay (your) enemy", *RMA* 87:1ff. For other omens referring to the moon with earthshine see *ACh* Spl 1:9ff, 2 r27ff, 3:3ff, *RMA* 23A:4ff, etc., and note especially *ACh* Spl 1:9, I *30 ina* IGI.LAL*-šú* AGA *a-pir* SAG.UŠ*-ma* EBUR KUR SI.SÁ KUR *a-bur-riš* TUŠ*-ab* LUGAL DUGUD*-it* "If the moon at its appearance wears a crown and holds on (like this), the crops of the land will prosper, the land will dwell in security, and the king will become important" (also quoted, in slightly variant form, in *RMA* 9:4f, 10:5f, 11:6ff, 11A:3ff, etc.).

r10. This omen occurs with two different apodoses: cf. *RMA* 45:3f, I *30 ina* IGI.LAL*-šú* KI.GUB*-su* GI.[NA] ⁴DINGIR^{MEŠ} GALGA KUR *ana* ^{MÍ}SIG$_5$ GALGA[^{MEŠ}] "If at the appearance of the moon its stand is normal, the gods will counsel favourably about the country", and see the preceding note. There is space for only 4 or 5 signs in the break at the end of the line; this means that only the protasis was quoted by Akkullānu, since the next omen certainly began at the beginning of the next line (r11). For the implications of this curious fact see above, note on r9ff.

---

641 Sic, rather than *ṭuppu šanû* (Weidner); the presence of the enclitic *-ma* in all the above examples (as well as in the present letter) does not seem accidental in view of its association with the adjective *aḫû*, cf. MUL MAN*-ma* (= *šanûmma*) followed by MUL *a-ḫu-u*, *CT* 26 40 ii 10'f. The translation "eine andere Tafel" proposed by Weidner (ibid.) is likewise hardly to the point, since *ṭuppu šanûmma* evidently was a technical term for tables containing "extraneous" or non-canonical omens.

r11. This omen has been preserved completely in *RMA* 255 (3f), reading I *ina* UD NÁ.ÀM ŠÈG ŠUR-*nun* [4]*nu*-[*ḫuš*] UNMEŠ "If it rains on the day of the moon's absence, prosperity of the people". Cf. I *ina* UD NÁ.ÀM AN ŠUR-*nun* [4]EBUR *i-na-áš-šá-ma* [5]KI.LAM GI.NA "If the heaven rains on the day of the moon's absence, crops will thrive and there will be a stable rate of exchange", *RMA* 253B:3ff (quoted from *ACh* 2 Spl 104 r20; also quoted, with minor variants, in *RMA* 253:3f, 253C:5ff (ŠÈG for AN), 254:3f, etc.).

332

Bibliography:

Previously unpublished.

Discussion:

See sub *LAS* 243. Considering the scarcity of reports on auspicious days (cf. Oppenheim, *Centaurus* 14 [1969] 99[14]),[642] it is very likely that the present text is an "appendix" to *LAS* 145, addressed to Esarhaddon (and very probably dating from 669 BC).

333

Bibliography:

Thompson, *RMA* (1900) no. 256. Weidner, *Babyl.* 6 (1912) p. 34. Waterman, *RCAE* (1930f) no. 1426.

Writer:

Adad-šumu-uṣur. The writer is clearly an exorcist, note Obv. 6 as contrasted with Obv. 7, and note to *LAS* 172 r20 on the co-operation of exorcists and chanters. Of all the exorcists of the present corpus, Adad-šumu-uṣur alone wrote reports containing astrological omens (*RMA* 135 and 136F) or letters dealing with astrological matters (see *LAS* 119f and cf. Introduction, p. XV). The orthography of the text agrees perfectly with the assignation. Cf. *iq-bu-ú-ni LAS* 144:9, *an-ni-ú* 122 r4, 124:1, 142 r3, 146:7 and often in letters of A., against only one instance of *an-ni-u* (125:10), UD 22.KÁM 332:7 etc., *ina pa-an* 124 r2, 133 r12, 145:17.r7 and 146 r3, *a-ni-in-nu* 163 r8, and *né-ep-pa-áš* 155:10, 156:9, 159 r8'.

Discussion:

Though Obv. 4ff certainly refers to the recitation of "hand-lifting" prayers (*šu'illakku*) to Venus and Sirius (cf. commentaries on *LAS* 167, 185, 203 and 268ff), this does not concretely help to determine the exact nature and purpose of the ritual mentioned in Obv. 1. Venus and Sirius (the brightest planet and the brightest fixed star) were addressed, along with other astral deities, in apotropaic and prophylactic rituals such as *Bīt rimki* and *Bīt salā' mê*,[643] but I have not come upon any ritual with prayers addressed to these two stars only. It is excluded that a conjunction of the two stars could have necessitated the ritual, since Sirius is more than 40° distant from the ecliptic and hence never comes closer than 37°.5 to Venus.

Notes:

r1ff. This omen is, as far as I can see, not otherwise known. MUL*is le-e*, lit. "the jaw of the Bull", = Hyades + Aldebaran (α Tauri), see Gössmann, *Planetarium* p. 80. The expression "in the middle of *is lê*" probably refers to time closely following the heliacal rising of Aldebaran (= ca. May 28, cf. App. H); cf. I dIM *ina* MÚRU dUTU GÙ-[*šú* ŠUB-*di*] . . . [7]*ina* MÚRU dUTU *šá iq-bu-u* r[1] dUTU *ina na-pa-ḫi-šú* dIM [2]*ina pu-ut* dUTU *na-pa-ḫi* ig rib? x[. . .] [3]*ina še-e-ri* ⌈x⌉ *iq-ṭi-bi* "If Adad thunders in the midst of the Sun (. . . .); 'in the midst of the Sun', that is to say, the Sun is rising and Adad .[. .] opposite the rising Sun; [. .] means 'in the morning' ", *RMA* 254:5ff; I dIM *ina* MÚRU d*Dil-bat* GÙ-*šú* ŠUB-*ma* d*Dil-bat ina* IGI-*šú iḫ-mu-uṭ-ma* [. . .] "Adad thunders in the midst of Venus. (this is the case

[642] The only extant texts are K.848 (unp., no name), K.920 (unp., Aššūr-ēṭir-[ ]), K.1599 (unp., name destroyed), 82-5-22,80 (Ass. script, no name), (= *LAS* 362), 83-1-18,206 (Ass. script, no name), 1904-10-9, 142 (unp., name destroyed), *RMA* 277AD (Bab. script, Nabû-šuma-iškun) and the present number.

[643] For "hand-lifting" prayers to Sirius see *PBS* 1/2 no.110 and King, *BMS* 56 (= Ebeling, *AGH* p.150ff); for one to Venus, *BMS* 39 (= *AGH* p.126ff). See also on *LAS* 185 and 203.

when) Venus hastens to [. . .] before him (= Adad)", *ACh* Adad 14:13 and Spl 40:7; I dIM *ina* KÁ.GAL *30* GÙ-*šú* ŠUB-*di* . . . [8]*an-ni-ú šá ki-i 30 in-na-mar-u-ni* dIM GÙ-*šú i-na-du-u-ni* "If Adad thunders at the gate of the Moon (. . . . .); this is when the Moon appears and Adad thunders", *RMA* 256A:5ff.

334

Bibliography:
Previously unpublished; cf. Oppenheim, *Centaurus* 14 (1969) 134[54]. Copy *CT* 53 pl. 3, no. 8.

Date:
May 2, 657 BC = Ajāru 17, eponymy of Lābâši, or a couple of days later. This date follows from a consideration of the background situation of the text as reflected by Obv. 6f (Mars rising heliacally in the constellation of Aries after an exceptionally long interval of invisibility) and Obv. 1 (a substitute king occupying the throne; cf. Introduction, p. XXIX). During the entire Sargonid period (721-609 BC), Mars rose heliacally in Aries only twice, in mid-April 689 (at the "head" of the constellation, $\lambda = 354^{\circ}.3$) and at the beginning of May 657 (at the "hind leg" of the constellation, $\lambda = 10^{\circ}.4$; see App. C3 and cf. commentary to *LAS* 300+:5ff). In the former case, the preceding period of invisibility had lasted (according to the tables of Schoch) 209 days, in the latter case 210 days, both maximal figures for the latitudes of Nineveh and Babylon. The question as to which of these two alternatives is in question has accordingly to be settled by the reference to the substitute king ritual. As is now well known (cf. Introduction, p. XXV), the ritual could only be started by eclipses predicting death of the king; the theoretical length of the substitute king's "reign" was in the case of a lunar eclipse 100 days, and certainly not more in the case of a solar one.[644] This implies that a solar or lunar eclipse had occurred not more than a hundred days before the dispatchment of the present text. Now, there were no lunar eclipses visible in Mesopotamia in either year (see Kudlek-Mickler, *AOATS* 1 p. 146), but both years contained a solar eclipse visible at Nineveh. The former of these occurred on January 11, -688, 98 days before the "morning first" of Mars at Nineveh (April 18), the latter on April 15, -656, 19 days before the appearance of Mars (May 4).[645] While the heliacal rising of Mars could thus in both cases theoretically have been observed during the reign of the substitute king, the fact that in the former case only two days were left of the (theoretically maximum length of the) substitute's reign virtually rules out this alternatively: it is by no means certain (in fact, it is rather unlikely) that the planet was *actually* observed already on the day computed; moreover, there is no guarantee that substitute kings enthroned on account of solar eclipses actually had to "sit" a hundred days, since their "reigns" were in practice sometimes shortened even in the case of lunar eclipses.[646] By contrast, there are no difficulties whatever with the latter alternative. Note also that the eclipse of 657, which according to the Mesopotamian calendar occurred in the month Nisannu, indeed predicted death of the king (I *ina* ITUBARAG AN.MI *20* GAR-*un ina* MU BI LUGAL ÚŠ . . .] "If the sun is eclipsed in Nisannu, in that year the king will di[e (and) . . .]", *ACh* Sîn 15:12), whereas this is unlikely in the case of the eclipse of 689 BC, which occurred in the month Kanūnu (cf. I *ina* ITUAB KAxMI *bi-ib-lu ub-bal* MAL [. . . . .] "If (the sun) is eclipsed in Kanūnu, a flood will devastate [. . . . .]", *ACh* Šamaš 11:44).[647]

Addressee:
Assurbanipal.

Writer:
Nabû-nādin-šumi? This is just a guess without real evidence, based on N's preoccupation with namburbi rituals (cf. especially *LAS* 203 and 204).[648] The orthography of the text is in general agreement with the conventions of N. (for

644 See Introduction, p. XXV, and cf. commentary to *LAS* 136.

645 The date May 2 given in App.C3 pertains to the latitude of Babylon. Both eclipses were practically identical, cf. *AOATS* 1 p.40 and the maps p.190f.

646 Cf. Introduction, p.59.

647 Solar eclipse on Kanūnu 30 portended death of the king (cf. *ACh* Šamaš 11:40) while both the 28th and 29th were harmless in this respect. Unfortunately, the Mesopotamian date of this particular eclipse is not known, nor can it be established by computation owing to the uncertainty factors discussed in App. A.

648 If the sender of this letter was Babylonian, as suggested by Obv.5 (see pertinent note), the whole argumentation here is of course groundless.

ki-i cf. 203:14, 205 r3, 213 r4, for LÚ 207 r1.4, 209:13, 212 r5, 214:7, for *šá* [Obv. 2f] 213 r5.6.11); note the omission of *bēlī* "my lord" after [LÚ]ENGAR and cf. discussion on the writer of *LAS* 210. Obv. 1 may be compared with 205:11.

Notes:

2. For an *eršaḫunga* to Nergal (ur-sag a-má-uru$_5$ šúr-àm ki-bal-a sù-sù) see 4 R^2 26 no. 1 = Böllenrücher *LAS* 1/6 (1904) p. 21ff and Langdon, *OECT* 6 (1927) p. 65f. Another text of this kind is known by its initial line (umun šà-zu a-má-uru$_5$ ḫu-luḫ-ḫa-gim e-ri-zu-šè dè-en-te-en-[te-en], "O lord, may your heart like the terrifying Deluge be calmed toward your servant"), see *4* R^2 p. 5 (K 5137). For "hand-lifting" prayers (*šu'illakku*; cf. on 203 r1) to Nergal see Ebeling, *AGH* pp. 8ff and 112ff; cf. also von Weiher, *AOAT* 11 p. 57f (listing 11 different prayers of this type).

The fact that the "universal namburbi" (purporting to ward off the evil predicted by the delayed appearance of Mars) was to be accompanied by the "performance" of all the pertinent *eršaḫunga*s (intented to soothe the "anger" of the god) and *šu'illakku*s (exorcising the god to give up his wrath) underlines the malignant character of the omen in question. Cf. *LAS* 279r13ff (referring to a total eclipse of the moon) and 289:18'ff (referring to a delayed appearance of Jupiter, evidently not so sinister an omen). It is interesting that these measures were considered necessary even though a substitute king was occupying the throne, and even more interesting that the suggested interpolations to the prayer formulae (see below) were worded not from the viewpoint of a humble "farmer" but from that of the royal palace. How can this be reconciled with the doctrine of "Rollentausch"? Cf. also *LAS* 137-138 (earthquake namburbi for "Farmer").

3ff. On this passage in general see Appendix M, and cf. also commentaries to *LAS* 67 and 185. Though the texts whose composition is prescribed here have themselves not come down to us, they can easily be reconstructed on the ground of parallel texts with corresponding interpolations. See, e.g., Lutz, *PBS* 1/2 no. 119, a *šu'illakku*-prayer to Nergal(!) written in behalf of Šamaš-šumu-ukīn[649], showing that the passage in question had to be inserted into the standard wording of the text (*BMS* 27+28) immediately after the identification of the god and the supplicant (the corresponding passage in this text reads [14]'[*ina* ḪUL ÁMEŠ] ISKIMMEŠ ḪULMEŠ NU DÙG. GAMEŠ [15]'[*šá ina* É.GAL-*ja u* KUR]-*ja ib-šá-a-ma* [16]'[*pal-ḫa-ku ad*]-*ra-ku u šu-ta-du-ra-ku* [17]'[ḪUL BI *ja-ši a-na* É]. GAL-*ja a-na* KUR-*ja* [18]'[*a-a* TE-*a a-a iq-ri*]-*ba a-a* DIM$_4$ *a-a* KUR-*an-ni* "I am afraid, frightened and worried on account of the evil and untoward forces and signs which have occurred in my palace and my country; may this (or its) evil not approach me, my palace and my country, may it not draw near, may it not press, may it not affect me!"); for similar insertions in *šu'illakkus* see ibid. no. 108:4'-8' ([7]'[ḪUL] BI *ja-ši* [É].GAL-[*ja*] *u* KUR-*ja* [8]'[*a*]-*a* TE!-*a a*-[*a*] KU!.[NU] *a-a*! DIM$_4$ *a-a* [KUR]!-[*a*]*n-n*[*i*]), *KAR* 58:33ff (prayer to Nusku for a certain Aššur-mudammiq), and *RA* 16 67:8ff (to Nisaba, on behalf of Šamaš-šumu-ukīn). For examples of "universal namburbis" with interpolations see commentary to *LAS* 67 and Ebeling, *RA* 48 (1954) 7ff; here, too, the passage was to be inserted in the prayer to Ea, Šamaš and Asalluḫi immediately after the invocation of the gods. Cf. also Caplice, *Or* NS 34 (1965) 116:5ff (ḪUL . . . [6]*a-a* TE-*a a-a* KU.NU *a-a* D[IM$_4$] [7]*a-a* KUR-*an-ni*), 130r4ff (*ina* ḪUL *iz-bi an-ni-i* [*šu-ti-qa-an-ni*] [5]ḪUL BI *ja-ši u* É.MU *a*-[*a* TE *a-a* KU.NU] [6]*a-a* DIM$_4$ [*a-a* KUR-*an-ni*]); 36 (1967) 4:11f (ḪUL-*šú a-a* TE-*a* [*a-a* K]U.NU *a-a* DIM$_4$-*qa*$_x$ (GÁ) [12]*a-a* KUR-[*an*]-*ni*); 39 (1970) 135:24 (ḪUL *šá-a-šú ja-a-ši u* É.MU *la i-qar-ra-bu* NU DIM$_4$ NU KUR-*an-ni*), etc.

5. *um-ma*: a Babylonianism for Assyrian *ma-a* (cf. discussion of *LAS* 124)? Or was the whole text actually dictated in Neo-Babylonian? It is difficult to account for a Babylonianism in the present context, where no stylistic effect certainly was striven for; and it should be noted that, excepting the script, the text does not contain any features distinctively pointing to an Assyrian author. By contrast, notice the ungrammatical plural suffix in *šu-īl-la-ka-nu* (for *-ni*), which, though sporadically attested in purely Neo-Assyrian contexts, is much more typical of Neo-Babylonian. As a matter of fact, letters dictated in Neo-Babylonian but written down in Neo-Assyrian script are by no means rarities; in addition to the Sargonid royal orders of this type published by Harper (*ABL* 289 etc.; unpub-

---

649 The name of the king appears in Obv.12' ([$^{1.d}$GI]Š.[N]U$_{11}$-MU-GI.NA). Despite its contents, this tablet had probably nothing to do with the present case but belonged to a set of *Bīt rimki*-tablets prepared for Šamaš-šumu-ukīn on account of a lunar eclipse, probably in 661 or 660 BC. For other tablets belonging to that set see Myhrman, *PBS* 1/1 nos. 12-18; Lutz, *PBS* 1/2 nos. 108, 110, 119-121, 124 and 129; Langdon, *RA* 16 67f; Scheil, *SFS* no.6, and cf. Ungnad, *Or* NS 12 (1943) 293ff and Laessøe, *Bīt rimki* p. 93 ff.

lished e.g. K.995, K.2931, K.7980(+?) 14676, 83-1-18, 129 and 83-1-18, 511), we have at least 7 letters of this type addressed (like the present text) *to* the king, viz. K.6609 + K.9899, K.9774, K.11875, Sm.2116, Sm.1871, 81-7-27, 253 and 82-5-22,88 (all unp.). For a reverse case (i.e. Assyrian letters written in Neo-Babylonian script) see *LAS* 340.

7. The end of this line has naturally to be restored *i*[*n-na-mer-u-ni*] "(which) appeared (in Aries)", cf. above, on the date of the letter, and 289:3'f; IN written with three initial horizontal wedges e.g. in *LAS* 43:4' and 106:1'. r1.4.

335

Bibliography:

Previously unpublished. Copy *CT* 53, pl. 205 no. 929.

Writer:

Nabû-nādin-šumi. Grounds: 1) Introductory formula, occurring (as far as the present edition is concerned) only in the letters of Nabû-nādin-šumi and Nabû-nāṣer; 2) orthography and language, agreeing with those of Nabû-nādin-šumi (*ki-i* [Obv. 3] cf. 203:14, 205 r3, 213 r4; *ṭè-e-mu šak-na-ku-ni* [3f] cf. 206:7; *aq*!-*ṭi-bi* [5] cf. 205:8.13; UD 11. KÁM [r4'.6'] cf. 203:10.r11, 204:10f, 209:9; EN-*já* [r7'] cf. 203:3.4 etc.) but not with those of Nabû-naṣer (cf. *a-ki* 217:10, 218 r17; UD 1.KÁM* 213 r2, 219:8; EN-*já* not attested in letters of N.); 3) handwriting, the signs RU [Obv. 2], KUN [Rev. 5] and TA* ŠÀ [Rev. 6] written with 4 vertical wedges as in *LAS* 203, 204 and 205; corresponding forms do not occur in the letters of Nabû-nāṣer.

Notes:

5. The first sign in this line is *aq* not *iq* (thus Pt. I), and the following line reads [T]A* ⌈TÚG*lu*⌉-[*bu-si* . . . .] collation 12.6.1974). Accordingly, cancel the translation given in Pt. I and translate instead: "(When . . . in Arbela,) I spoke about the [king's] cloth[es]; Urad-Ea (then) [came?] with the clo[thes . . . " Cf., on the whole, *LAS* 270-271.

r4'. This line reads, according to collation, UD *11*.KÁ[M] ⌈*pa-an* ᵈx x x⌉ [. . .] "On the 11th before the god [. . . . . . .]".

r5'. *GI.DU*$_8$: A kind of reed altar used especially in apotropaic *namburbi*-rituals, cf. *Or* NS 34 126:7, 36 2: 17, 14:8, 21:10, 25:13' (etc.) and the texts referred to in *AHw* 851*b* s.v. *paṭīru*; its function in the present text cannot be more precisely determined. At the end of the line read (after collation) *ep-pa*-[*áš*?] "I(?) shall perf[orm(?)]".

336

Bibliography:

Waterman, *RCAE* 1179. Cf. Oppenheim, *JAOS* 61 (1941) 261; Deller, *AOAT* 1 (1969) 59.

Writer:

Nabû-nāṣer? Deller (1969) attributed the letter to Adad-šumu-uṣur, but this is rather unlikely in view of the formula *lìb-bi ša* LUGAL *be-lí*-[*ja lu ṭa-ab-šú*] (Obv. 4), see note on the writer of *LAS* 218.

Discussion:

This text is clearly a petition comparable to e.g. *LAS* 227; it is hence strange that the writer has left it unsigned. Perhaps the name of the patient mentioned in Obv. 3 was thought to make the authorship of the letter sufficiently clear to the king.

337

Bibliography:

Previously unpublished. Copy *CT* 53, pl. 1 no. 3.

Discussion:

This text is strictly taken no letter or "report" but a prescription attached to a medicine sent to the court. However, it has been included here since many of the medical letters of the present edition are but similar prescriptions supplementing dispatchments of medicines; cf. *LAS* 246, 247, 251 and 253. The identity of the addressee remains obscure; it is not excluded that the king himself is in question, cf. *LAS* 26, 27 and 257. The prescription itself is quite in keeping with the directions found in recipe texts (cf. note on r1f), but is much more detailed than these.

Notes:

1. *maš-qit*: potion prepared from a mixture of various (up to 24) drugs; cf. Ritter, *Studies Landsberger* (1965) 314. The present spelling of the word (standing for /mašqîti/) has been taken over as such from the remedy texts, where it occurs very frequently (e.g. *BAM* 52:44, 67:9', 156:24, 164:4.25.28, 176:15 197:29), and accordingly does not any have relevance to the study of NA phono- and morphology.

3. *qar-ṭup-pi*: this NA variant of *qan ṭuppi* "(reed) stylus" it otherwise attested only in *4 R*^{2} 61 ii 28 ("I am Nabu, the lord of *qar-ṭup-pi*") and *KB* 6/1 268:4 ("[Nabû, the lord of] diptych and *qar-ṭup-pa-a-ti*"). In the present context, the word hardly means more than "a piece of reed"; cf. Hunger, *AOAT* 2 497:2 referring to a *qan ṭuppi* made of the stalk of "sweet reed".

4. *mu-naq-qi-te*: obviously a hapax legomenon in Akkadian, but cf. Bibl. *m*^{e}*naqqît* "sacrificial bowl" (Koehler-Baumgartner, *Lexicon* p. 540*a*). Since the verb *nqh* did not have the meaning "to libate" in Hebrew, the Bibl. word is probably a loan from Akkadian (where this meaning is well attested), and not vice versa.

r1. *pa-na-at NINDA*^{MEŠ} "before the bread": this expression corresponds to the prescription *lām* (var. *lā/balu*) *patān* "before (var. without) eating" of the remedy texts (e.g. *AMT* 8,1:12, *CT* 23 46 iv 6, *BKBM* Tf. I 3) and simply means that the medication had to be drunk on an empty stomach. Water (r3) figures as a very common drug-vehicle in remedy texts (e.g. *BKBM* Tf. I 8. 18) besides wine and beer (probably reserved for drugs having a more acrid taste).

r4. *lu kar su*: one verb *karāsu* meaning "to tie, fasten" is attested in OB and lexical texts (see *CAD* K 209*b* and *AHw* 447*b*), but in the present context such a meaning is obviously out of the question; one would rather expect a verb qualifying the temperature of the water (cf. A^{MEŠ} . . . *lu la ṣar-ḫu* "let the water not be hot", *LAS* 255r6-11). A meaning like "to be cool" would seem to fit well, especially in view of the fact that the verb *kaṣû* "to be cool, cold" is not attested in Neo-Assyrian; cf. *CAD* s.v. and note Gilg. XI 285, *i-mur-ma bu-ú-ra . . . šá ka-ṣu-ú* A^{MEŠ}-*šá* "he saw a well in which the water was cold", and *me-e* A^{MEŠ} *ka-ṣú-ú* "(If) the rain water is cold", *ACh* Adad 31:57, etc.

338

Bibliography:

Previously unpublished. Copy *CT* 53, pl. 126 no. 495.

Date:

Cf. note on "Rev." 4'.

[NB. According to collation, the order of the sides of this text is probably wrongly determined in Pt. I; in other words, the text probably begins with "Rev." 1 and ends in the date found in "Obv." 4'. The side order of Pt. I is retained in the following for the sake of convenience.]

Notes:

1'. Restore, perhaps, DINGIR^{MEŠ}-*n*[*i ša* LUGAL *be-lí-ja e-tap-šú*] "the gods [of the king, my lord, have taken action]", a phrase frequently met in NA letters referring to *unexpected* events (cf. e.g. *ABL* 1046:6f, 1093 r13f, 1360:2'ff and *Iraq* 35 22:7f.51f).

2' Possibly *šul mu* ⌜*gab-bi*⌝(-[*šú*?]) "total health" (collated); implications unclear.

3'. Probably *ina* ^{d}ALÀD *ša* LUGAL *be*-[*lí-ja ib-ta-laṭ*] "he has recovered thanks to the genius of the king [my lo]rd", cf. *LAS* 263 r11ff and 271:9f.

4'. There were only 2 leap years containing an intercalary Addāru within the period 674-666 from which most letters of the present edition date, viz. 673 and 668 (see App. A 1), but it is impossible to make out which of these (if either) is in question. Consequently, it also remains unclear whether the letter was addressed to Esarhaddon or Assurbanipal.

r3. *šum-ma 3-si*: obscure. If *3-si* stands for *3-su* (= *šalussu*) "one third of it" (cf. *ta-aṣ-bat-si* for *-su*, *ABL* 992 r4.6), the sense of the passage could be "If there is (even) one third of it (= the drug) <left>, send (it to me)", but even then the omission of the word *rēḫe* "is left" would be alarming. The imperative *šēbila* (pertaining to the king) is likewise unusual; one would rather expect a precative form, but cf. *LAS* 129 r19.25 and 171:22f.

r4. Probably *šùl-⌈mu⌉-ú* "is [PN] well?" (collated). Rest perhaps *mi-i-n[u (ša) šitini šarru bēlī lišpura]* "let the king, my lord, write how it is".

339+

Text:

Now joined to K.9776 (unp., join by myself 22.5.1974); part of the same tablet as K.13109 (= *LAS* 127; collated 27.5.1974). New transliteration on p. 377f.

Bibliography:

For K.13109 cf. Deller, *AOAT* 1 (1969) 59.

Copies:

K.7374 = *CT* 53, pl. 35 no. 97; K.9776 = ibid. pl. 106 no. 405; K.13109 = ibid. pl. 124 no. 487.

Writer:

Urad-Gula. This attribution can be regarded as virtually certain in light of the following evidence:

1) The *handwriting* is identical with that of *LAS* 223 and 225, and probably with that of *LAS* 224, too (pertinent data lacking). This is a very important point, for the hand in question is exceptionally distinctive; within the present collection of letters only the handwriting of *LAS* 239 makes a similar impression.[650]

2) The *introductory formula* contains features strongly pointing to Urad-Gula. First of all, the salutation (Obv. 2) occurs in this particular form (with a final *a-dan-niš*) only in the letters of U. (*LAS* 223:3, 225:3f) and Nabû-gāmil (227:2).[651] Secondly, the blessing ends with *[a-dan-niš a]-dan-niš lik-ru-bu* (Obv. 7), as in other letters of U. (223:5, 224:6, 225:6). Thirdly, while the present blessing formula does not recur identically anywhere else, it is closely paralleled by some blessings found in the letters of Adad-šumu-uṣur, the father and instructor of U., with whom the latter shared at least one blessing formula not attested elsewhere (cf. *LAS* 143:4ff with 225:4ff). But whereas Adad-šumu-uṣur's "long" blessings regularly began with the invocation of Aššūr, Sîn, Šamaš, (and Adad) (cf. 119-120, 122:3ff, 123:7ff, 125:3ff), these gods are markedly omitted in the present blessing which begins, as customary in the letters of U., with the invocation of Nabû and Marduk. Hence the writer is not Adad-šumu-uṣur but very plausibly Urad-Gula.

3) The *orthography* of the letter agrees with the conventions of Urad-Gula (cf. e.g. *be-lí-ia/ia* [Obv. 2.6.9] besides EN-*iá* [Obv. 11], as in *LAS* 223, and *la-a* [Obv. 10] besides *la* [Obv. 22'f, Rev. 3], as in *LAS* 224; *a-na-ku* [Rev. 1, not *ana-ku*], as in *LAS* 223).[652] Especially distinctive is the spelling *mi-e-nu* in Obv. 15', to be compared with *mi-mi-e-ni LAS* 224:12; as far as I have noticed, comparable spellings occur only in *LAS* 120 r1 (*mi-e-mi-i-ni*; from Adad-šumu-uṣur), *ABL* 951 r3 (*mi-mi-e-ni*; from [Urad-Gula?]) and 125:8 (*mi-mi-e-ni*; Gabbu-ana-Aššur). Otherwise the word was always spelled *mi/e-(i-)nu/i.*

4) *Style*: Note the frequent omission of the word *bēlī* "my lord" after LUGAL (Obv. 22'f. 31'. 33'. r2). This feature also occurs in other letters of Urad-Gula (cf. 223:12, 224:4.7.13.r13') but very seldom in the letters of other exorcists, with the exception of Nabû-nādin-šumi. For statistics see note on the writer of *LAS* 210.

5) Finally I would call attention to the reference to "the chief [exorcist/physician]" (LÚGAL [. .]) in Obv. 32'. This can be matched with *LAS* 224 r7'; and while it naturally does not *prove* or disprove anything, it at least makes it

---

650 The same "square" hand also occurs in *ABL* 951 and 1285. Were these letters also written by Urad-Gula? Orthographical and stylistic features are consistent with this possibility.

651 Salutations ending with a *double a-dan-niš* are attested in letters of Ikkāru (*LAS* 258-259), Nabû-tabni-uṣur (264) and Nergal-šumu-iddina (83).

652 Note, however, *ku-zip-pi* Obv.28', against TÚG*gu-zip-pi, LAS* 224 r10'.

likely that the writer was neither Adad-šumu-uṣur[653] nor the chief exorcist himself (Marduk-šākin-šumi), but one of their subordinates.

Addressee:
Esarhaddon. The author of the letter writes clearly in the capacity of a royal employee (cf. especially Obv. 21'f); and while it is known for certain that Urad-Gula served as exorcist at the court of Esarhaddon, it is equally certain that he did not have a position at court in the first years of Assurbanipal (see Appendix O and commentary to *LAS* 120). It seems possible, judging from *LAS* 121-122, that he was "rehabilitated" in the beginning of Assurbanipal's third year (666 BC), but there is no evidence (except, perhaps, for *LAS* 227) that he ever completely regained his former position.

Discussion:

This is one of the very few Akkadian (non-literary) texts dealing in detail with pregnancy and subsequent delivery, and it is therefore regrettable that it is so poorly preserved. The many gaps, coupled with other kinds of textual damage, make it difficult to give a continuous translation of even the best preserved passages, let alone to reconstruct in detail the events described in the tablet. A full evaluation of the letter is consequently not yet possible; a few general points may, however, be singled out for tentative discussion:

1) *The identity of the pregnant woman*: the concern shown by the king (cf. esp. Rev. 2) as well as the fact that the delivery was to take place in the palace (Rev. 4) suggest that a close relative of the king, most likely his wife, daughter or daughter-in-law, is in question; a concubine would hardly have received the same attention.

2) *The state of the pregnancy*: very advanced, to judge from the repeated references to the "basket" (27', r3.4); see pertinent notes. Against this background, the passage Obv. 16'-30' most naturally refers to (prophylactic) ceremonies performed in the temple of Gula against miscarriage. On the other hand, the broken passage Rev. 5-15 most probably dealt with exorcistic rituals performed at delivery and/or after it. See note to r8.

3) *Why such a wordy and detailed description* of an event that must have (in principle) been well-known to the king? And why does the writer constantly refer back to what the king, he himself, and others said on earlier occasions? This question is of crucial importance to the interpretation of the letter, and the only answer I can see is that *something went wrong at the delivery*, that is, either the baby or the mother, or both, were injured. If all had gone well, the writer would surely have contented himself with the usual statement "the mother and the baby are well" and the necessary compliments, cf. e.g. *LAS* 216f. By contrast, a wordy description like the present one sounds like an apology destined to prove that the writer had conscientiously done everything he could do, and was expected to do, and that he consequently could not be held responsible for what had happened. Note Obv. 24'ff: "*I* said: 'One has to proceed as follows . . . ; but we shall do as the king wanted'; afterwards PN_1 and PN_2 said: 'We shall [. . .]' They did this and that (and so *they* are to blame)." Note also Rev. 14: "[We are] now [performing] numerous (exorcistic) rituals" (scil. to make up for the injury caused?).

4) *What kind of injury* could be in question, then, if the above hypothesis is correct? I would primarily think of a malformed birth or an anomaly (not necessarily due to any fault of the medical personnel, since this is rather improbable in the case of a royal childbirth), perhaps with inherent lethal characteristics. Such an interpretation seems feasible not only from the viewpoint of the above analysis, but also considering the evidence of texts such as *LAS* 171 and 219.

Notes:

16'. *É* *dGu-la*: a reference to the temple of *Gula* in this context (as well as the significance attached to the worship of the goddess further down in the letter) is a bit surprising in that Gula was properly the goddess of medicine in general, with no special emphasis on pregnancy or childbirth, and one would rather expect a reference to the birth-goddess par excellence, Bēlet-ilī/Nintu.[654] Unless a visit to the temple of Gula was a customary event before

653 Who was a close associate of Marduk-šākin-šumi and hence scarcely would have referred to him by profession.

654 Cf. *Atraḫasīs* I 291ff, "Where the pregnant woman gives birth . . . , let the brick be in place for nine days, that Nintu, the birth-goddess, may be honoured; . . . without ceasing praise the birth-goddess, praise Kesh!", and ibid. S iii 15ff, "In the house of the pregnant woman in confinement, let the brick be in place for seven days, that Bēlet-ilī, the wise Mami, may be honoured." True, in *BMS* 6:71ff Gula seems to be equated with Bēlet-ilī.

childbirth, which (in the absence of additional evidence) seems unlikely,[655] the most natural explanation of the present passage is that the pregnant woman in question was either physically so built that a risky delivery was anticipated, or that her condition was such as to make imploration of the goddess of medicine appear otherwise desirable (overdue pregnancy, etc.). Notice the mention of the goddess at the end of an incantation purporting to ease delivery (INIM.INIM.MA MÍLA.R[A.AḪ.A.KÁM]), *BAM* 244 r70, and the use of "dust from the gate of the Gula temple" in a ritual against miscarriage (4 R^2 55,1:23 = Myhrman, *ZA* 16 184ff). On prophylactic rituals performed during the last months of pregnancy in general see Labat, *RlA* 3 178f.

23'. *a-na 2-i UD-me*: the same expression also in *ABL* 1217 r16' (collated); probably "on the following day", rather than "on the 2nd day", since the latter was normally written UD 2.KAM. Cf. note to *LAS* 210 r6.

25'f. d*Gu-la ša* [. .] d*Gu-la ša* ⸢EDIN⸣ *ša na-aḫ-li*: Gula of the steppe is known from *ADD* 1077 viii 30 (*ina* IGI d*Gu-la ša* EDIN) and *CT* 53 965 r8 (É d*Gu-la ša ṣe-e-*[*ri*]). Gula of the "wadi" is not otherwise known.

27'. *MA.SAB "basket"*: here (and further below) certainly referring to a basket in which the newborn baby was to be placed after delivery. Cf. *PBS* 5 100 iii 27ff, *ki-ma* I.dNIN.URTA-*ra-i-im-ze-ri-im i-wa-al-du* [28]*i-na* GIMA.SÁ.AB *il-qú-ú-šu-ma* [29]*a-na* É I.dEN:ZU-*ga-mil* DI.KUD *ub-lu-šu* "when PN was born, they picked him up in a basket and brought him into the house of PN_2, the judge", and note also *KAR* 90:10 (= Ebeling, *TuL* p. 117), referring to a basket (GIMA.SÁ.AB) in connection with a delivery ritual. The present spelling also in *ADD* 930 ii 18: 1 MA.SAB KÙ.UD "one silver basket" (inventory of temple property; cf. MA.SÁ.AB KÙ.GI *šá* d[. .] "the golden basket of DN", *ABRT* I 13:22; GIMA.SÁ.AB GUR_9 dBA.Ú, *BBR* 24 r6; and I MA.SÁ.AB DINGIR *na-ši ma-mit* DIB-*su* "If he carries the basket of a god, curse will seize him", Oppenheim *Dreams* 329:4). A comparison with Rev. 4 suggests that a basket belonging to a temple is in question, hence most probably the sacred basket of the goddess Gula herself (cf. Obv. 25'f); accordingly, the present passage probably described a ritual performed in the temple of Gula *before* the delivery, though the purpose of the ritual remains unclear.
[It is not excluded, of course, that the actual delivery was to take place in the temple; cf. note to r1. However, if this view is accepted, the interpretation of the rest of the letter causes difficulties. Cf. note to r8 and Discussion, 3].

r1. In the beginning of the line restore, perhaps, [*ul-d*]*a-at* "(this woman) [has given bir]th" (cf. *KAV* 1 vi 77); other restorations are, however, possible and even more probable, e.g. a verb describing the medical condition of the woman.

I.d*PA-ina+SÙḪ-K*[*AR*: perhaps identical with I.dPA-SÙḪ-KAR-*ir* LÚŠAMÁN.LÁ TUR, the copyist of the haruspical text *CT* 31 20 (Ass. script, no date).

r8. [d*NI*]*N.ŠI.KÙ*: an epithet of Ea, see Lambert, *Atraḫasīs* p. 148f. This is the only occurrence of this epithet in Assyrian letters, and it is therefore likely that the writer had some specific reason to use it here. A plausible explanation would be that he was describing the delivery anticipated in Rev. 1ff (cf. note to Obv. 27'), in the course of which magical ceremonies resembling those recorded in the Atraḫasīs myth were carried out. Cf. *Atraḫasīs* I 249ff (describing the birth of man): "They entered the house of destiny | Did prince Ea (*ni-iš-š*[*i-ku*] d*É-a*) and the wise Mami. | With the birth-goddesses assembled | He trod the clay in her presence. | She kept reciting the incantation, | Ea, seated before her, was prompting her . . . " That these ceremonies were to be observed by the humans also is implied by the continuation (p. 63, S iii 14ff). Note that out of the 55 mentions of Ea in the myth (*op. cit.*, p. 198), the god is called *niššīku* only in 5 instances (ibid., p. 190), and in 4 of these he is either involved in the creation of man or otherwise associated with the birth-goddess Bēlet-ilī/Nintu/Mami!

340

Bibliography:

(I) Waterman, *RCAE* 1278 (cf. IV 205, 270); Pfeiffer, *SLA* 339.
(II) Behrens, *ABB* (1906) 108.

---

[655] It is of course possible that "the house of Gula" had an idiomatic meaning corresponding to our "hospital" or "clinic"; but I am not aware of any further evidence supporting this possibility.

Discussion:

This text has two curious features which set it apart from all other letters of the collection. First, it is written in Babylonian script, though the dialect is Neo-Assyrian. Second, it consists of two separate messages, both of which, though stylistically utterly different, deal with exactly the same matter. The former of these (A 1 – B 4) is written in a relaxed, almost colloquial tone and addresses itself to a person spoken of in the second person singular; the later (B 5 – 8) is addressed to the king, in the same laconic, official style as the rest of the collection. Though the king could occasionally also be addressed in the second person (see note to *LAS* 121:24), the total lack of polite formulae in the former part makes it hard to believe that it was intended for the king; the same is implied by the fact that message 1 abounds in confidential utterances (such as "he doesn't know" [A 3.5], "let's find an excuse" [B 3], etc.), which were carefully avoided in message 2. But if the beginning of the text was not meant for the king, to whom then, and why were the two messages written on the same tablet? The best explanation I can find is that the *whole* text was actually written for a royal counselor who wanted to pass on some information to the king; message 1 would accordingly be the answer to certain question asked by the counselor on account of a royal query (which he had been unable to answer himself), and message 2 would simply represent a draft of the answer the counselor was supposed to give the king. This is admittedly a complicated solution, but then the text itself is fairly complicated and hardly lends itself to a simpler explanation, whatever that may be.

The problems posed by this curious text do not, however, end here. In particular, one wonders if there is any causal connection between the bird mentioned in A 1f (an evil omen? Cf. B 4 and note on A 1f), the rituals alluded to in the sequel (do A 3 and B 6 refer to apotropaic [*namburbi*] rituals performed in order to avert the evil portended by bird? This would seem likely in view of B 1f, see the relevant note; but is there any other evidence of *extispicies* [A 4f, B 7] performed on account of evil omens?), and the scene of the rituals (had the bird in question entered the Marduk temple? Cf. A 7ff); and who is meant by the remark "he doesn't know" in A 4f (the king himself? Were these remarks then meant as scornful)? Unfortunately, there is nothing in the text itself to elucidate these questions beyond what was suggested above, and as the text stands quite isolated from the other letters of the collection, there is no justification for further speculation about the matter.

Notes:

A 1. *eš-še-bu-u* MUŠEN: a bird of evil portent (cf. ^{d}NIN.BUL+BUL^{MUŠEN} = *iṣ-ṣur le-mut-ti* = [*e*]*š-še-bu*, Hg B 232 (*MSL* 8/2 p. 166); nin-na BUL = *eš-še-bu*^{MUŠEN} = MUŠEN *le-*[*mu-ut-tim*], Ea I 98; ^{d}DIN.BUL+BUL^{MEŠEN} = [MUŠEN] *le-mut-ti* = *eš-še-bu-u*, Ḫg D 345 (*MSL* 8/2, 176), [^{d}NIN.BUL+BUL^{MUŠEN} = *eš-še-b*]*u-u* = [*iṣ*]-⌈*ṣu-ru*⌉ ḪUL-*tú*, A I/2 332); also called "the message-bird" (*na-aš-par-tum*^{MUŠEN} = *eš-š*[*e-bu-u*], *RA* 17 140 K.4229:4'; cf. also *na-aš-par-tum* (*CT* 41 4 Rm.488:8ff) alternating with ^{d}NIN.BUL+BUL^{MUŠEN} (ibid. 1f), *iš-še-bu* (ibid. 4ff) and [MUŠEN] *le-mut-tum* (ibid. 11f)) by analogy with its homonym *eššebû* "ecstatic (with evil magical powers), prophet, conveyor of divine messages"; this latter name probably accounts for line 2 of the present text. The evil character of the bird suggests that the unspecified ritual alluded to in A 3 and B 5f was of apotropaic character, and the same is implied by the fact that this ritual was to be performed on the temple roof (cf. on B 1f) in the morning. For *eššebû*-omens see *CT* 39 27 r17ff, 41 4 (Rm. 488):1ff, 6:11, 7:35ff and 24 iii 9. – Identified as a "nocturnal bird related to the owl" in *CAD* E (1958) 371, but see Landsberger, *WO* 3 (1966) 265; cf. also Salonen, *Vögel* (1973) 163, and von Weiher, *ZA* 64 (1975) 293.

A 5. Ulūlu 2 is indeed almost unanimously classified as a favourable day in hemerological texts of the almanac type (cf. Labat, *RA* 38 (1944) 21 and Matouš, *Sumer* 17 (1961) 36). It is curious, however, that the 2nd day does not seem to be included among the "15 days (suitable) for extispicy each month (except Nisannu)" (*15* UD=MEŠ *šá* ḪAL-*ti šá* ITU-*us-su*) listed in *KAR* 151 r53 ff; the list begins with the 3rd and 5th day, and the small break at the head of it has almost certainly to be restored [UD 1.KÁM] on the analogy of the preceding entry (r52; list of the corresponding days of the month Nisannu).

A 6. *ni-ir-ḫu-uṣ*: possibly "we will get confident" (Pt. I) but, in view of the root vowel, rather "let us rinse" (*AHw* 943*a*). If so, what is the (omitted) object of the verb? The roof? Or, idiomatically, "hands" ("let's wash our hands of this")?

B 1f. Cf. Zimmern, *BBR* 1-20:1ff, [*e-nu-ma*] DUMU ^{LÚ}ḪAL SISKUR.SISKUR *ú-kan* . . . ^{29}UD ŠE.GA [*tu-u*]*q-ta-ad-da-aš* . . . . ^{55}[*la-am*] ^{d}Šam-*ši* (text: ^{d}*ši-šam*) *na-pa-ḫi ú-ri* (var. ÙR) *ta-šab-biṭ* A^{MEŠ} KÙ^{MEŠ} SÙ ^{56}*1* DUG$_{NÍG.NA}$ *ana* ^{IM}KUR.RA *ana* IGI ^{d}AMAR.UD GAR-*an* "[When] a haruspex is to perform a sacrifice . . . you cleanse yourself on an auspicious day . . . [Before] the sunrise, you sweep the roof, sprinkle holy water, place a censer toward the north before (the image of) Marduk . . . ." While the haruspical ritual mentioned in A 4f and B 7f thus evidently required that "the men go upon the roof of the temple", B 5f shows that it was primarily the unspecified ritual alluded to in A 3 that the writer has in mind here. This supports the hypothesis presented above (see on A 1) that the ritual in question was of apotropaic nature; cf. Caplice, *Or* NS 36 (1967) 34: 1ff, [NAM.BÚR.BI Ḫ]UL TU= MUŠEN *u* MUŠEN BAR-*i šá ana* É LÚ T[U] [2][*ina* UGU L]Ú GUB-*zu* ḪUL *šu-a-tu_4* LÚ NU SÁ.SÁ [3][*ina* UD] ŠE.GA *uq-ta-ad-da-aš* . . . [4]*ina* Á.GÚ.ZI.GA ÙR SAR [5]A KÙ.GA SÙ . . . "[Namburbi] for the evil of a dove or an(other) ill-portending bird which has entered a man's house (or) has hovered [over a m]an, that the evil may not affect the man. [On] a propitious [day] he is purified . . . In the morning you sweep the roof. You sprinkle pure water . . ." (etc.; see also *Or* NS 36 282f for another version of the same namburbi). Since both the haruspical ritual and the *namburbi* had to be performed early in the morning, it is probable that *ina kal-la-ma-ri* at the end of the line belongs to the present sentence and not to the following one, as assumed in Pt. I. For the word order cf. notes to *LAS* 214 r3' and 247: 16ff.

B 3f. My interpretation of this passage agrees with Behrens, *ABB* (1906) 108, q.v.

341

Bibliography:
Previously unpublished.

Copy:
CT 53, pl. 208 no. 939.

Note:
Against Pt. I, this text is not of the (horizontally oblong) report type; many lines have been lost at the beginning of Obv., and the curvature of the tablet indicates that only a couple of signs (at most) are missing at the end of each line. Obv. 5'ff reads: [5']*i-na-ṣu-[ru]* [6']*re-ḫu-ú-[ti]* [7']*ina am-ba-si* ⌈d⌉[DN . .] r[1] LÚ*di-da-bé-[e]* [2]*lu-šá-an-ši-[lu]* [3]*is-se-šú-nu li-[zi-zu]* "they keep watch (over [. . .] in the inner [. . .]); the rest are [. . .] in the game preserve of the god [. . .]. The apprentices (see note on *LAS* 85 r6) should do in like manner (and) assist them . . ."

342

Bibliography:
Previously unpublished. Copy *CT* 53, pl. 206 no. 933.

Writer:
Marduk-šākin-šumi. The content of the letter can be matched with *LAS* 188 r2ff, and the orthography is in perfect agreement with the conventions of Marduk-šākin-šumi (cf. [*i*]*n-na-me-ru-ú-ni* [not *-mer-u-ni*] with 172 r15; *iq-ṭi-bi-a* [not *-ṭí/ti_5-*] with 186 r7; [UD n].KÁM* [not KÁM/KAM] with 172 r13, 173:7.r10ff, 176 r5, etc.; and note especially *né-ep-pa-áš* [r2.4], against *né-pa-áš* in the letters of Adad-šumu-uṣur[656], Nabû-nādin-šumi and Urad-Gula[657]). The handwriting (e.g. the form of *ša* [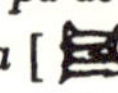, not 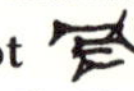 or ]) also agrees with that of M., to judge from the photograph of no. 180 published in *RCAE* IV pl. 8). Note finally that the writer was directly contacted by the chief eunuch.[658] This confirms that the chief exorcist, hence M., is in question, for a subordinate exorcist should have had to receive his orders either from the king or *through* the chief exorcist.

Date:
670 BC(?), if the text indeed is connected with *LAS* 188 (q.v.).

---

656 Cf. Appendix M 6; *né-pa-áš* 140 r1.3, 154:11, 167 r2, (*in-*)*né-pa-áš(-u-ni)* 147 r11, *e-pu-šu* 137 r10, 142 r9, *e-pu-šú* 152 r5; contra, *né-ep-pa-áš* 155:10, 156 r2, 159 r8' and *né-ep-pa-šú-u-ni* 156 r2.

657 *né-ep-pa-áš* otherwise only in the letters of Nabû-nāṣer.

658 = Aššur-nāṣir? Cf. note on 232 r1.

Discussion:

The ritual forming the subject of this "report" was certainly of the namburbi type (cf. e.g. *ABL* 367), though the identity of the portent counteracted remains obscure owing to the mutilation of the crucial word in Obv. 1. Note, however, that part of the ritual had to be performed on the river bank, a requirement not included in all namburbis; obviously, also, a *visible* thing (cf. Obv. 3) *contaminating* (188 r2) the house of the eunuchs was in question, hence most probably an animal (animals) or a plant. Suitable namburbis would be those against lizards (*Or* NS 34 116ff), ants (ibid. 123ff and *KAR* 337), or the *katarru*-fungus (*Or* NS 40 140ff), but the traces in Obv. 1 cannot be harmonized with any of these possibilities. They can be read ⸢*ka*⸣-*m*[*u-na-t*]*e* (plural of *kamūnu*, a fungus; cf. UZUDIR^{MEŠ}, *CT* 40 19 K.10390:10 and K.11729:3), but that is hardly acceptable as the relevant namburbi did not involve a trip to the river (see Caplice, *JNES* 33 [1974] 345ff).

Notes:

r1f. Read [UD n.KAM .]⸢x⸣ *dul*!-*li* ^{2}[*ina* UG]U!-⸢*šú-nu*⸣ *né-ep-pa-áš* "[on the . .th] we shall perform [the first half(?)] of the ritual on them".

r6. Cf. *LAS* 175:2'f, 187:7'ff, 271:8'f and 272:12f.

343

Bibliography:
Previously unpublished.

Writer:
Ištar-šumu-ēreš. This assignation is rendered certain by the spelling *šà-ṭir* (Obv. 2), which, though common in colophons of literary texts (see Hunger, *AOAT* 2 176), occurs in the present corpus only in the letters of Ištar-šumu-ēreš (1 r13, 12 r13[f] and 13 r15); the spellings *lu-ú-bi-lu*$_4$ (r9) and *le-e-pu-šú* (r8) are likewise characteristic of I. (see Appendix M 6), the former of these actually having parallels only in the letters of this writer (excepting *lu-ú-bi-lu-neš-šú*, *ABL* 564 r7 [a letter from the time of Sargon II]). Note also Obv. 2 *ki-i an-ni-i* (= 5 r4, 12 r13) and Rev. 10 *ga-mer* (= 19 r6', 230 r1; not *ga-me-er*), as well as the dividing lines following Obv. 1, 4 and 10 (cf. *LAS* 13-15; within the present corpus otherwise only in letters of Balasî, Nabû-aḫḫē-erība, and Akkullānu). The content of the letter is paralleled by *LAS* 5f and 29.

Addressee:
Probably Esarhaddon, judging from the reference to the king's sons in Obv. 7.[659] Cf. also *LAS* 72.

Notes:

3ff. Cf. Labat, *IE* § 38. The source of the present quotation is unknown.[660]

6. Possibly *né-ma-*[*a*]*l*!-*šú* "his prosperity", though the traces of the last sign(s) rather point to [*q*]*i*. The section beginning with this line seems to have contained a commentary to the preceding quotation, whereas the last section (Obv. 11ff) probably contained suggestions as to the manner in which the festival was to be celebrated. Details obscure.

11. *ḫu-lu*$_4$: a mistake for *kil*!-*lu*$_4$? Cf. 6 r1.

344-345

Bibliography:
(I) Waterman, *RCAE* 1428-1429.
(II) Kugler, *SSB* II (1909) 18.

---

659 On the analogy of the other letters of the collection it can, I think, be taken as granted that this reference pertains to the two (officially appointed) crown princes Assurbanipal and Šamaš-šumu-ukīn, not the royal offspring in general, though the latter possibility cannot of course be *categorically* rejected.

660 Probably *Enbu Bēl Arḫi*; certainly not *Iqqur Īpuš*.

Photographs:
RCAE IV pl. 14.

Writer:
Possibly Nabû'a (cf. below).

Discussion:

That these two texts are reports on the date of the vernal equinox (in two successive years? see below) is a matter that need not be specifically pointed out, but it is much less evident (1) *how* these dates were obtained and (2) *why* the dates had to be communicated to the king at all. It is clear, in view of the contemporary praxis of intercalation, that the dates cannot have been *computed* mathematically, as done in the Seleucid period,[661] but that direct *observations*, however in accurate, must be in question. Kugler (1909) thought that the dates were determined with the help of a *water clock*. Such an interpretation is not entirely impossible (cf. e.g. I *ina* ITUBÁR UD *15*.KÁM *3* MA.NA EN.NUN UD *3* MA.NA EN.NUN MI "on the 15th of Nisannu, 3 pounds (of water in a clepsydra) = a diurnal watch, 3 pounds (of water) = a nocturnal watch", *AJSL* 40 198:3 [Mul Apin II], and similar passages), but seems rather unlikely in view of the inaccuracy of the assumed method (as Kugler himself puts it (*loc. cit.*), "Wenn wir aber auch von der großen Ungenauigkeit des Verfahrens absehen, so bleibt doch bestehen, daß man auf diese Weise nicht das astonomische Äquinoktium erhalten konnte"); it is hard to believe that any experienced astrologer, even at that early period, would have been so ignorant of the defects of his instruments as to try to establish the *exact* length of the daylight by means of a water clock, not to speak of communicating a *specific* equinoctial date established in this way to the king, especially as he had in his disposal an instrument far better suited for that purpose: the *gnomon*. That this instrument was used by Assyrian astrologers is known for certain from the gnomon tables of Mul Apin (Weidner, *AJSL* 40 p. 198ff, cf. van der Waerden, *Anfänge der Astronomie* p. 80ff); by observing the direction of the shadow cast by the central (perpendicular) pointer of the instrument at sunrise (and comparing it with the corresponding direction at sunset) it is possible to determine with high precision the day when the sun sets exactly opposite the place it rises. This method of determining equinoxes and solstices was allegedly first used by the Greek Anaximandros (about 610-546),[662] but since Herodotus (II 109) explicitly states that "the sunclock (*polos*) and the sundial (*gnomon*) . . . came to Hellas from Babylonia", it is hardly to be doubted that the method as such was actually likewise an import from Mesopotamia.[663]

[Since the dates communicated in the present letters thus may well be reasonably accurate, they can be utilized for chronological purposes; it is, of course, impossible to *date* the letters exactly on such slight evidence, but one can at least point out the years in which the letters were *most likely* written. Supposing that the letters can be roughly placed between 681 and 646 BC,[664] the following years merit consideration:

Year	*Date of vernal equinox*[665]	*Difference from the dates given in LAS 344-345*
681	Nisannu 16	+ 1 days
679	Nisannu 8	+ 2
673	Nisannu 14	- 1
671	Nisannu 6	± 0 probable date of *LAS* 344
670	Nisannu 17	+ 2 probable date of *LAS* 345
663	Nisannu 4	- 2
662	Nisannu 15	± 0
660	Nisannu 8	+ 2
654	Nisannu 13	- 2
652	Nisannu 7	+ 1

661 Cf. O. Neugebauer, "Solstices and Equinoxes in Babylonian Astronomy during the Seleucid Period", *JCS* 2 (1948) 209ff.

662 Diogenes Laertios (ed. Cobet) II 1; cf. H. Diehls – W. Kranz, *Die Fragmente der Vorsokratiker* I s.v. Anaximandros.

663 Note that Anaximandros was a native of Miletos, like his contemporary Thales; that the latter owed his astronomical knowledge (if he had any) to Mesopotamian astrologers is beyond question.

664 Cf. Appendix 02.

665 The Assyrian dates given in this column are based on App. A2. The Julian date of the vernal equinox in the 7th cent. BC was March 28.

No letters of the present corpus can be placed in the years 681-675, 663-660 and 654-652; this leaves the years 673 or 670 as the most probable date of *LAS* 345, and 671 as the most probable date of *LAS* 344. Since the two letters are orthographically fairly consistent, it is tempting to see in them reports from two consecutive years, which would eliminate the year 673.][666]

The second question is more problematical. Obviously, the vernal equinox was *cosmologically* an important event, and hence may have been brought to the attention of the king for this reason alone, but it is difficult to see what *practical* significance its communication could have had. It certainly did not have anything to do with the New Year's festival, which was celebrated on days determined by the lunar calendar;[667] nor did it probably have any *calendrical* significance, unless it was used to determine the beginning of the solar year (which, according to the compendium Mul Apin, began 15 days before the vernal equinox; cf. the passage *AJSL* 40 198:3 quoted above). More evidence is needed before the question can be satisfactorily answered.

666 The handwriting of the scribe who wrote these letters very closely resembles the hand of Nabû'a (cf. *RCAE* IV pl.14 nos.90ff.), a scribe who was active ca. 670 BC (cf. *ABL* 817, written to the crown prince).

667 Cf. discussion on *LAS* 190.

ADDITIONAL TEXTS

346 (K 13083). Copy *CT* 53 pl. 122 no. 477.

A		(= Rev.?) Beginning lost		
	1'	⸢x⸣[	]	
	2'	*is-su-ur-*⸢*ri*⸣ LUGAL *b*[*e-li*	]	Perhaps the king, [my? lor]d
	3'	*ma-a šá ma-ḫi-ir-u-ni* [	]	[will say]: "[. . . . . .] what has
	4'	*a-na* ŠEŠ^{MEŠ}-*šú ša* [	]	been accepted", the king, my
	5'	DUMU ^{MEŠ} EN M[EŠ	]	(or our) lord [. . . . . . .] to the
	6'	LUGAL *be- li ni sa* [	]	brothers of [Assurbanipal?],
	7'	(blank) [	]	[your?] lordly sons.
		Balance lost		
B		(= Obv.?) completely broken away		

Judging from the orthography (*be-li, ma-ḫi-ir*), the writer of this fragment was probably Ištar-šumu-ēreš, though line 6' may indicate joint authorship. For DUMU^{MEŠ} EN$^{M[EŠ}$ cf. 171:17.

347 (K 14840). Transliteration collated by C.B.F. Walker.

A	1	] *ina* É.DIN[GIR	] in the temp[le
	2	*sa-ḫa*]*-ar u$_4$-me* [	at the tu]rn of the day [
	3	^{d}]DUMU.ZI *i-*[*bak-ki-u*	] Tammuz is [wailed
	4	UD 27.K]ÁM *pa-*[*šá-ru*	on the]th is the red[emption
	5	KÁ]M *ina s*[*a-ha-ar u$_4$-me*	on the]th at the t[urn of the day
	6	^{d}DUMU].ZI *ú-*[*kal-lu-mu*	Tammu]z is d[isplayed
	7	] DINGIR *i-*[	] the god is [
	8	]⸢*ep-pu-šú*⸣[	] they perform [
Edge	9	]⸢x⸣[	
B		completely broken away	

Commentary: Cf. *LAS* 6.

348 (83-1-18,713). Copy *CT* 53 pl. 209 no. 943.

Obv.	1	[*a-na*] LU[GAL EN-*ja*]	[To] the ki[ng, my lord],
	2	[ÌR-*k*]*a* ^{I}[15-MU-KAM-*eš*]	(from) you[r servant Ištar-šumu-
	3	[*lu šùl*]*-mu a-na* [LUGAL EN-*ja*]	ēreš: good hea]th to [the king,
	4	[^{d}P]A ^{d}AMAR.[UD]	my lord]. May [Na]bû (and) Mar-
	5	[*a-na* LUGAL] EN-*ja*	d[uk] bless [the king], my lord.
	6	[*lik- r*]*u- bu*	
	7	[*ina š*]*i- a- r*[*i*]	It is [not?] propitious
	8	[*a-na*] ⸢*ú*⸣- *ṣe-*⸢*e*⸣	[to] go out
	9	[*la-a? ṭ*]*a- a- b*[*a*]	[to]morrow.
	10	[. . . .*k*]*i ma-ṣ*[*i*]	[. . .] as long as
	11	[. . . . *d*]*a-ba-bi*	[. . . . . . s]peech
	12	[. . . . . . .] *ta n*[*a*]	[ ] . . .
		a few lines broken away	
Rev.		Beginning lost	
	1'	[. . .] *lak* [. . .]	
	2'	[*mi-i*]*nu š*[*a* LUGAL]	[wha]t is it th[at the king]
	3'	[*be-l*]*i* [*i-qab-bu-u-ni*]	[my lo]rd [says]?
		Remainder (7 lines) blank	

Commentary: The restoration of the name of the writer is based on the handwriting and the spelling [*be-l*]*i* in r3'. For the content, cf. *LAS* 176.

349 (82-5-22,92). Copy *CT* 53 pl. 47 no. 146; collated by C.B.F. Walker.

Obv.	1	[*a-na* LUGAL EN-*ja*]	[To the king, my lord],
	2	[ÌR-*ka* ^{Id}PA-PAP^{MEŠ}-S]U	[(from) your servant Nabû-aḫḫē-
	3	[*lu šùl-mu a-na* LUGAL EN]-⸢*ja*⸣	[erī]ba: [good health to the]
	4	[*a-dan-niš* ^{d}P]A ^{d}AMAR+UD	[king], my [lord. My Nabû and]
	5	[*a-na* LUGAL E]N-*ja*	Marduk bless [the king],
	6	[*lik- ru*]- *bu*	my [lo]rd.
	7	[*ina* UGU] ⸢A⸣.ŠÀ ⸢G⸣AL	[As to] the large field
	8	[*ša* ^{LÚ}*Áš-š*]*u-ra-aje*	[of the Ass]yrians
	9	[*ša* LUGAL] *be-lí iš-pur-an-ni*	[on which the king], my lord,
	10	[*ma-a* A].ŠÀ *id-di-mì-iq*	wrote to me: "It was a very
	11	*a-*⸢*dan*⸣*-niš* ^{ŠE}PAD^{MEŠ}	productive field; who is re-
	12	*man-nu ú-pa-sa-ak*	moving the grain?",
	13	^{LÚ}ENGAR^{MEŠ} *ša* ^{ŠE}NU[MUN]	the farmers who seeded
	14	*i- ru- šu- u- ni*	the fields
	15	*a- ka- an- ni*	do not revere
Edge	16	*ana* ^{d}IM [.] ⸢x⸣	Adad [. . . . . .]
	17	*la i-pal-*⸢*lu-ḫu*⸣	any more;
Rcv.	1	*ina lìb-bi šu-u*	that is why he let
	2	*i-šá-tú*⸢*ú*⸣*sa* [*a*]⸢*n*⸣-[*qit*]	a lightning strike down (and
	3	TA* *ma-ṣi* LUGAL	devastate the field). Accor-
	4	*be-lí iq-bu-u-ni*	ding as the king, my lord,
	5	LÚ*MAŠ.MAŠ *tak-pi-ti*	commands, an exorcist should per-
	6	*ú-ga-ri le-pu-*[*uš*]	form the (ritual called) "Purifi-
	7	ḪUL *mì*⸢*qit*$_4$⸣*ti* ⸢*i*⸣-[*šá-ti*]	cation of the Field", and he should at the same time [also] perform
	8	*is-se-niš le-pu-*[*uš-ma*]	the (apotropaion called) Evil
	9	*ša* LUGAL *be-lí iš-pur-*⸢*an-ni*⸣	of a Stroke of Lightning." (As
	10	*ma-a u*$_4$*-mu 1-en ki-ma*	to) the king's writing me:
	11	*ra-qa-ak ina pa-ni-ja*	"Visit me the first day I am
	12	*er-ba* ^{d}*Aš+šur* EN ^{d}PA	unoccupied", may Aššūr, Bēl
	13	UD^{MEŠ} GÍD.DA^{MEŠ} DÙG+GA *lìb-bi*	(and) Nabû give the king, my
	14	*a-na* LUGAL EN-*ja lid-di-nu*	lord, long days (and) happiness,
	15	⸢*aja*⸣*-bi-ka ina šá-pal*	(and) [may] they [bring] your
	16	[GÌR^{2}*-ku lu-šak-ni*]-⸢*šú*⸣	enemies to [submission] before [your feet].

Commentary: See on *LAS* 38. Rcv. 5f very probably refers to the ritual published by Caplice, *Or*NS 40 (1971) 155 as no. 50 of his corpus of namburbis.

350 (82-5-22,81)

Obv	1	*ša* LUGAL *be-li iš-pur-an-ni*	(As to) what the king, my lord,
	2	*ma-a* IM.DIRIG *dan-na-at*	wrote to me: 'The clouds were
	3	*ma-a a-ke-e ta- mu- ra*	thick, how did you observe
	4	*ki-i* DINGIR^{MEŠ} *a- ḫe- iš*	that the gods saw each other
	5	*e- mu- ru- u- ni*	(in opposition)?'
	6	*ina pa- an na- ma- ri*	– (the clouds) dispersed
	7	*iḫ- te- pe*	before daybreak
	8	*ki-ma ša a-na* LUGAL	(and) *when he whom* the king,
	9	*be-li-ia ú-du- u- ni*	my lord, *knows*
	10	*ra-man-šú uk-tal-lim*	revealed himself,

Rev	1	*30 ina* É *i-za-zu-u-ni*	we saw where the
	2	*né- ta- am- ra*	moon was standing.
	3	*am-mar ta-mar-ti-ni*	That amounts
	4	*i- ba- áš- ši*	to an observation (of the actual
	5	*ú-ma-a* LUGAL *be-li*	opposition). Now, doesn't the
	6	*la i-šam- me- e*	king, my lord, (indeed) hear
	7	*ki-i* UD *14*.KAM *a-ḫe-iš*	that they saw each other
	8	*e- ma- ru- u- ni*	on the 14th day?

Bibliography: Cf. Oppenheim, *Centaurus* 14 (1969) 120.[668]

Commentary: For a similar "report" see *RMA* 155 (from Nabû-iqîša); cf. also App. A and the texts mentioned ibid., fn. 2. The present text was almost certainly written by Ištar-šumu-ēreš, note the spelling *be-LI* in Obv. 1 and 9 and Rev. 5. – Regarding the interpretation of Obv. 8-10 note the following: Oppenheim's translation ("he revealed himself as if he knew the king, my lord", loc. cit.) is not acceptable since *kīma* in Neo-Assyrian was only used as a temporal conjunction ("when, after", etc.), never as a preposition ("as"); the relative clause beginning with *ša* must accordingly constitute the subject of the *kīma* clause, and consequently *ša* here has the meaning "he who". For the expression *ana . . . ūdûni* see note on 4:10; besides the translation "known to the king", one could also think of "(who) knows the king", taking *ana* as a nota accusativi. In either case, the sentence probably refers to the moon. Why such an oblique reference was chosen remains obscure. Perhaps *ki-ma* should be emended to *ki-i*!, after all, and the passage rendered as proposed by Oppenheim.

351 (83-1-18,247)

Obv	1	[UD *n*.KÁM *ša* ^{ITU}BÁR?]	[On the . . .th of Nisannu(?)]
	2	[u_4*-mu*] *ù mu-ši*	[the day] and the night
	3	*šit- qu- lu*	were in balance:
	4	*6* DANNA u_4*- mu*	12 hours of day,
	5	*6* DANNA *mu- ši*	12 hours of night.
	6	^{d}AG *u* ^{d}AMAR+UD	May Nabû and Marduk
Rev	1	*a-na* LUGAL *be-lí-*[*ni*]	bless the king,
	2	*lik- ru- bu*	[our] lord.

Commentary: See under *LAS* 344-345.

352 (*HAV* 256f)

Obv.	1	*a-na* LUGAL EN-⌜*j*⌝*a*	To the king, my lord,
	2	ÌR-*ka* ^{Id}*15*-SUM-A	(from) your servant Ištar-nādin-apli
	3	⌜L⌝ÚGAL *10-ti*	the foreman of (the collegium of)
	4	*ša* ^{URU}*Arba-ìl*	ten (scribes) of Arbela:
	5	⌜*lu*⌝*-u šùl-mu*	good health
	6	*a-na* LUGAL EN-*ja*	to the king, my lord.
	7	^{d}AG ^{d}AMAR+UD	May Nabû, Marduk,
	8	^{d}*15 ša* ^{URU}*Arba-ìl*	(and) Ištar of Arbela
	9	*a-na* LUGAL EN-*ja*	bless
	10	*lik-ru-bu ina* UD *29*	the king, my lord.
Rev.	1	*ma-ṣar-t*[*u*]	We kept watch
	2	*ni-ta-ṣa-ar*	on the 29th,
	3	^{d}30 *la né-mur*	(but) we did not see the moon.
		(blank space)	
	4	^{ITU}APIN UD *1*.KÁM	Araḫsamna 1 (October 12),
	5	*lim-mu* ^{I}PAP-DINGIR-*aja*	eponymy of Aḫī-ilāja (649 B.C.)

[668] This text was originally scheduled to the included in Oppenheim's edition of Sargonid astrological reports. However, since the text contains no omens and obviously belongs to the same category as *LAS* 317-345, its natural place is within the present volume. I am grateful to H. Hunger for communicating the text to me and agreeing to its inclusion here.

Commentary: Cf. *LAS* 93-99. Bibliography: C.F. Lehmann-Haupt, "Zwei unveröffentlichte Keilschrifttexte aus Kojundjyk", *Hilprecht Anniversary Volume* (Leipzig 1909), pp. 256-259 (photo p. 256, copy p. 257).

353 (K 10386). Copy *CT* 53 pl. 108 no. 411.

Obv.	1'	*ú mu* [	
	2'	*da* [	
	3'	ŠUB AŠ+TE GIN x[	The Foundation-of-the-Throne was firm [
	4'	SUḪUŠ EDIN *15* [ŠU.SI	the base of the right-hand surface
	5'	KASKAL *i-ši* UD x[	[of the Finger] had a Path; . . . [
	6'	DAGAL *2,30* ŠU.SI[	was wide; the left side of the Finger [. . .
	7'	DAGAL *2,30* ŠU.SI GIŠ[	was wide; the left side of the Finger . . [. . .
	8'	[ ]⸢TÙN ḪUL x⸣[	[ ] the Pocket . . . [
		Break of 4 lines	
Rev.		Beginning lost	*(Break)*
	3	[ ]⸢NA⸣[	
	4	⸢x x⸣ AN.T[A-*tum*	. . . . upward [. . . .
	5	*u* KI.TA-*tum* DU-[*ik*	and went downward; [. . .
	6	NU ZIR-*at* U+SAG BAR x[	was not . . . ; the Cap [. .] outside [. . .
	7	*ša* LUGAL *be-lí iq-bu-*[*u-ni*]	(As to) what the king, my lord,
	8	⸢*ma*⸣*-a* IdPA-SUM-MU DUMU [. . .]	sa[id]: "Did Nabû-nādin-šumi son
	9	⸢ *i*⸣*-te-li-li tak-*[*pir-tú* . . .]	of [PN] become pure?", the cle[an-
	10	(blank) [	sing ritual . . . .]
	11	[ ]⸢x⸣[	
		Balance destroyed	

Commentary: Judging from Rev. 7 ff and the format and curvatures of the fragment, this text was a letter and as such, the only extant haruspical letter from the Sargonid period containing omens derived from the exta. For similar letters from other periods, see Appendix Q1.

354 (K 1530). Copy *CT* 53 pl. 58 no. 184.

Obv.	1	[*a-na* LUGAL *be-lí-ja*]	[To the king, my lord,]
	2	[ÌR-*ka* IdIM-MU-PAP]	[your servant Adad-šumu-uṣur]
	3	[*lu šùl-mu a-na* LUGAL EN-*ja*]	[Good health to the king,]
	4	[dAG dAMAR+UD] *a-na* LU[GAL EN-*ja*]	[my lord. May Nabû (and) Marduk
	5	[*lik-*] *ru- bu*	bl]ess the k[ing, my lord.]
	6	*ša* LUGAL *be-lí iš-pur-an-ni*	(As to) what the king, my lord,
	7	*ma-a ina* UGU *a-da-an-ni*	wrote to me: "As to the time
	8	EN.NUN d⸢ASAR⸣.LÚ*.ḪI	of the 'watch of Asalluḫi',
	9	[*ša*] ⸢*taš*⸣*-pur-an-ni*	on which you wrote to me:
	10	[*ma-a* . . . *a*]*p-ta-làḫ*	'[. . . .]' – I am scared", [. . .
		Rest of Obverse destroyed	*(Break)*
Rev.		Beginning destroyed	
	1'	[ ]x	. . . . which] [4] 'kept [. . .]
	2'	[IAš+šur-GIN-B]ALMEŠ-*a*	[of? Aššur-mukīn-pa]lē'a
	3'	[I*30*-NUNUZ-G]IN-*in*	[(and) Sîn-perī-u]kīn,
	4'	[*ú*]*-kil-lu-ni*	[. . . . . .].
	5'	[ ]	
		Remainder uninscribed	

Commentary: The attribution of this fragment to Adad-šumu-uṣur is certain on the ground of the handwriting and the subject matter. The reference to the 'watch' of Asalluḫi (i.e. Marduk) remains unclear (cf. *LAS* 200), but no doubt an exorcistic treatment is in question (cf. *LAS* 161:8.10?). Rev. 2'f restored from 145:7ff.

355 (K 5488). Copy *CT* 53 pl. 75 no. 254.

Obv.		Beginning lost	
	1'	*ina* UGU *ri-in-ki*	As to the bath,
	2'	*mi- i- nu*	what is it
Rev.	1	*ša* LUGAL *be-lí*	that the king, my lord,
	2	⸢*i*⸣*-qab-bu-u-ni*	commands?
	3	[. .] ⸢*ú*⸣*-ma-a*	[. . .] now [. . .
		Balance lost	

Commentary: Cf. *LAS* 134. Hand of Adad-šumu-uṣur.

356 (K 15017). Copy *CT* 53 pl. 144 no. 608.

Obv.		Beginning lost	
	1'	⸢x⸣[ ]	
	2'	*a-na* [ ]	to [ ]
	3'	*e-pa-a-*[*še*]	perfor[m]
	4'	*liš-pu-ru* [ ]	let them send [ ];
	5'	*ba-si nu-*[*šá-aṣ-bit*]	we shall at once s[et about]
	6'	*né- p*[*u- uš*]	to perf[orm (it)].
	7'	⸢*ù*⸣ *š*[*a* LUGAL *be-lí*]	Furthermore, wh[at the king,
Edge	8'	[ ]	my lord, . . . (*Break*)]
	9'	[ ]	
Rev.	1	*a-na* [ ]	
	2	*re-e-šú* [*ni-iš-ši*]	
	3	*mì-i-nu š*[*a* LUGAL]	What is it th[at the king]
	4	*be-lí i-qa*[*b-bu-ni*]	my lord sa[ys]?
	5	UD *10*.KÁM* UD *11*[+n.KÁM*]	The 10th, 1[2th?],
	6	UD *15*.KÁM* [ ]	15th (and) [th] (are)
	7	⸢*a*⸣*-*[*na*]	[suitable] fo[r performing . . .
		Remainder lost	

Commentary: Writer probably Marduk-šākin-šumi. Cf. *LAS* 196.

357 (81-2-4,451). Copy *CT* 53 pl. 196 no. 897.

Obv.	1	[*a-na* LUGAL *be-lí-ja*]	[To the king, my lord,]
	2	[ÌR-*ka* ^{Id}AMAR+UD-GAR-MU]	[your servant Marduk-šākin-šumi]
	3	[*lu-u šùl-mu a-na* LUGAL EN-*já*]	[Good health to the king, my]
	4	[^{d}PA *u* ^{d}AMAR+UD *a-na* LUGAL EN-*já*]	[lord. May Nabû and Marduk]
	5	[*lik-r*]*u-bu ina* UG[U]	[ble]ss [the king, my lord].
	6	[*š*]*a* LUGAL *be-lí i*[*š-pur-an-ni*]	As to [. . . . .] on which the king
	7	[*mi-nu-u*]*m-ma aḫ-ḫur*	my lord w[rote to me, wh]at
	8	[*né-pu-uš*] *la-áš-šú*	else [shoud we do]?. There is
	9	[*ḫi-ṭu -r*]*a-a-ni*	no [danger . . . (*Break*)]
	10	[ ]*-eš*	
		Rest of Obverse destroyed	
Rev.		Beginning destroyed	
	1'	[*-l*]*am*	
	2'	[ ] *qí-ba-a-ni*	[ ] commandments(?)
	3'	[*lu l*]*a ú-kal-lu*	[ ] let them not keep
	4'	[*lu-š*]*ap-pi- ṭu*	[let them s]weep(?)
	5'	[ ]⸢Á[12]⸣*-šú* LUḪ-*s*[*i*]	[ ] let him wash his arms
	6'	[ ] DANNA [ ]	[ ] double-hour(s) [ ]
	7'	[*ina* IGI ^{d}E]N.LÍL *né-e*[*p-pa-áš*]	we sh[all perform before E]nlil
		Last line of Reverse destroyed	

Commentary: For the identification of the author, cf. commentary to *LAS* 149. Obv. 7 and Rev. 7' restored on the basis of 156:13 and 167 r1, respectively. For the rest cf. *LAS* 180ff and (for r.5') *LAS* 255.

358 (K 10908 + K.15645). Copy *CT* 53 pl. 109 no. 417, and pl. 160 no. 702.

A		B	
	Beginning destroyed		Beginning destroyed
1'	[^{GIŠ}*na-mul-lum*] : *n*[*a-mul-lu*]	1'	⌜x⌝[
2'	[^{GIŠ}ŠITÁ] : *kak-ku* : GI : ⌜*qa*⌝-[*nu-u*]	2'	*na-mar-k*[*u-*
3'	[^{GI}GUR.Ḫ]ÚB : *ḫúp-pu* : DUG : *ka*[*r-pa-tum*]	3'	IM.GÍD.DA [
4'	[ ] *zik-ri* DINGIR^{MEŠ} ^{d}AMA[R+UD]	4'	*a-ta-mar* x[
5'	[^{MUL}]APIN PAP *an-ni-ú* IM [ ]	5'	*ina pa-ni-i*[*a*
6'	*ša* ⌜*3*⌝-*šú-nu* ^{I}*Du-gul*-IGI-[ ]	6'	DUB^{MEŠ} ⌜x⌝[
7'	^{I}*Ki-ṣir-Aš+šur ki-lal-le-šú-*[*nu*]	7'	[........] ⌜*ni*⌝ [
8'	UR$_5$.RA : *i- šaṭ- ṭu- r*[*u*]	8'	[......] *áš ina* [
9'	*ú- b*[*a*]*-áš-šim man-za-za* [*an* DINGIR.DINGIR]	9'	[........] ⌜x⌝ [
10'	^{d}[*Be-e*]*l zik-ri* DINGIR^{ME}[^{Š} *ina še-mi-šú*]		Balance lost
	Balance of A destroyed		

Commentary: This fragment lists canonical tablets (A 1' = Ḫ̮ḫ̮ VI 1; A 2' = Ḫ̮ḫ̮ VII A 1 and VIII 1; A 3' = Ḫ̮ḫ̮ IX 1 (cf. *MSL* 7, 36!) and X 1; A 5' = MUL.APIN I 1; A 9' = En.El. V 1; A 10' = En.El. VI 1) copied for the library of Assurbanipal by scribes named Dugul-pān-[ili?] and Kiṣir-Aššur (A 6'f). The author is probably Akkullānu, cf. *LAS* 331 (the sign MEŠ written similarly in both texts; note also the separation marks). In A 10' one would expect either [^{d}AMAR]+UD or [AN.Š]ÁR (perhaps even [Be-l]um), but the traces (three vertical wedges) exclude these readings.

359 (Bu 91-5-9,81). Copy *CT* 53 pl. 214 no. 964.

Obv.	1	⌜*a-na* LUGAL EN- ⌜*j*⌝[*a*]	To the king, my lord, (from)
	2	Ì[R-*ka* ^{I}ÌR]-⌜^{d}⌝[*D*]*a-ga-n*[*a*]	[your ser]vant [Urad-D]āgān[a];
	3	*l*[*u*]-*u* ⌜*šùl*⌝-[*mu a*]-⌜*na* LUGAL *be-lí*⌝-[*ja*]	(etc.)
	4-5	indistinct traces only	
		Balance of Obverse destroyed	
Rev.		Beginning destroyed	
	1'	[*ṭ*]*up-šar-ru-t*[*i*]	scribal art [...........].
	2'	*ú-ma-a lu-ra-am-me* [ ]	Now, let me leave [.....];
	3'	*ú-la-a mi-nu ša* LUGAL [*be-lí*]	or what is it that the
	4'	*i- qab- bu- u- ni*	king, [my lord], says?

Commentary: The writer of this fragment is otherwise only known from a letter of Adad-šumu-uṣur (*LAS* 147).

360 (K 1595). Copy *CT* 53 pl. 60 no. 191.

Obv.		Beginning lost	
	1'	[.....]-⌜*šú-nu* x x⌝[.]	[.....] their [........]
	2'	[*ina* UGU]-*šú as-sa-kan*	I placed [upon] him (and)
	3'	[UZU^{MEŠ}-*šú*] *at-ta-ṣar*	observed [his flesh];
	4'	[*šùl?-mu?*] *la a-mur*	I did not see [any improvement?]
Edge	5'	[. .]⌜*x*⌝-*su-ma-a-ni*	[The ...]...s
	6'	[*ma-a*]'-*du*	[were nu]merous.
	7'	[L]Ú [*p*]*ar-šu-mu*	[An o]ld man
Rev.	1	[*dul-l*]*u la ú-da*	does not know [the wor]k(?)
	2	[. .]x *ma šu li* ⌜x⌝	(properly). [....] ....
	3	[. .]*a-ti ḫa-an-*[*na-ti*]	thes[e ....]s
	4	[. .]x ^{d}MAŠ.MAŠ [.. (.)]	[.......] Nergal [....]
	5	[. .] *a-du-na-k*[*an-ni*]	[.....] until n[ow]
		Remainder lost	

Commentary: If the restorations are correct, this may be a letter by Adad-šumu-uṣur (cf. Obv. 7'f with 126:14ff, 129 L.E. 1 and 144 r2f). For Obv. 2'ff cf. 235 r3, 239:4', etc.; the context seems to exclude such restorations as [EN.NUN] *at-ta-ṣar* [4] '[(d)*30/ 20*] *la a-mur.*

361 (K 1874). Copy *CT* 53 pl. 61 no. 196.

Obv.		destroyed	
Rev.	1	*ù am-mi-ú*	And (as to) that man,
	2	*a-nu-su gab-b*[*u*]	his whole equipment (and)
	3	*ku-zip-pi-šú ina pa-*⌈*ni*⌉-[*šú*]	his clothes are at his disposal.
	4	*ša* LUGAL EN *iš-pur-an-*[*ni*]	The king, my lord, wrote to me:
	5	*ma a-ta-a ki-i lìb-*[*bi-ka*]	"Why do you act arbitrarily?"
	6	*te-pa-áš a-k*[*e-e*]	(Yet) in what resp[ect have]
	7	*ki-i lìb-bi-ja e-*[*pu-uš*]	I [acted] arbitrarily?
	8	TI.LA-*ú-a šu*[*m-ma*]	By my (own) life, I [have] not
	9	[*ki-i l*]*ìb-bi-ja e-*[*pa-šú-ni*]	[acted ar]bitrarily [......
		Remainder lost	

Commentary: This fragment may be associated with *LAS* 224.

362 (82-5-22,1397). Copy *CT* 53 pl. 204 no. 924.

Obv.	1'	LU⌈GAL⌉ x[	the king [
	2'	*ma-a man-nu* $^{\text{I.}}$⌈^{d}⌉[. . .]	said: "Who is (this) [PN],
	3'	*ša* ^{GIŠ}*le-'a-a-ni am-mu-*[*te*]	who is inscribing those waxed
	4'	*šá* LUGAL EN-*ja i-šá-ṭar-u-ni*	tablets of the king, my lord?"
Rev.	1	*nu-uk is-su-ri*	I said: "Perhaps
	2	*ki-i ra-mì-ni-šú šu-ú*	he spoke to me as a private
	3	*iq-ṭi-bi-a nu-uk* ⌈*a-ni-nu*⌉	person; we
	4	*il-*⌈*la*⌉-[	..[.... "
		Rest destroyed	

363 (82-5-22,1775). Copy *CT* 53 pl. 204 no. 926.

Obv.		destroyed	
Rev.	1'	[.*an*]-⌈*na*⌉-*ka* [. . .]⌈x⌉	[..h]ere [........]
	2'	[*lu*]-*še-bi-lu-na-ši ni-iš-ṭur*	[let] (it) be sent to us for
	3'	[*ina*] UGU *šu-ub-te ina pa-an*	copying. We shall write (it)
	4'	[O Ú]R *ni-šá-ṭar re-eḫ-tu*	upon the seat in front of [...].
	5'	[O *i*]*na* UGU *ni-iš-ri 2-i*	the rest we shall write upon
	6'	[O] *ni-šá-ṭar nu-ga-mar*	another *nišru.*

364 (82-5-22,80). Copy *CT* 53 pl. 201 no. 916.

Obv.	1	^{ITU}NE UD 27.KÁM* KAŠ.SAG [BAL-*qí*]
	2	DINGIR^{MEŠ} ŠE.GA ^{MEŠ} [. . .]
	3	UD *29*.KÁM* *zi-né-e* GIŠIMMAR *ina* KÁ-*šú liz-*⌈*qup*⌉
	4	UGU EN INIM-*šú* GUB-*zu*
Rev.	1	(in Bab. script) [. .] *in* ^{d}AMA.ḪÉ.DÙ
	2	(in Ass. script) $^{\text{NA}_4}$ *as-ḫar šá te-qí-ti*

Obv.: On the 27th of Ābu one should [libate] fine beer, the gods will (then) be favourable [......]. On the 29th, one should plant midribs of the date palm at one's gate, one will (then) prevail over one's adversary.

Rev.: [1] [.....].. the god Amaḫedu (= Sumuqan). [2] *asḫar*-stone for daubing.

Commentary: The hemerological quotations in this note were probably extracted from the same source as those of *LAS* 69+71:12ff (cf. pertinent note; also RMA 151 r4ff); the source itself has not been preserved. The two lines of Rev. probably refer to items sent along with the note.

365 (K 7405). Copy *CT* 53 pl. 93 no. 350.

Obv.		destroyed	
Rev.	1'	[.]x[. . . . . .]	
	2'	⸢*i*⸣-[. . . . . .]	
	3'	⸢*ka*⸣-[. . . . .]	
	4'	[*i*]*na ma*[*š*- . . . . .]	
	5'	⸢*i*⸣-[. . . . . .]	
	6'	[*k*]*i-i ša* ⸢*a-na*⸣ x[. .]	Just as the [. . .]
	7'	[*i*]*na* URU*Ni-nu-*[*a*]	were performed (?)
	8'	⸢*e*⸣*-pa-šú- u-* [*ni*]	in Nineveh,
	9'	*ki-i ḫa-an-ni*[*m-ma*]	so will they
	10'	*ina* URU *Kal-* [*ḫa*]	be performed (?)
	11'	*ep- pu-* [*šú*]	in Calah.

Commentary: This fragment was probably written by Marduk-šākin-šumi, note the spellings *ḫa-an-NI*[*M-ma*] and *EP-pu-*[*šú*], and see App. M 6. The broken sign in r6' looks like L[Ú* or *k*[*a*; restorations such as L[Ú*ENGAR] or *k*[*a-a-šá*] would alter the translation to "just as the [farmer] was (or y[ou] were) treated in Nineveh, so will he (or they) be treated in Calah."

366 (K 5623). Copy *CT* 53 pl. 82 no. 298.

Obv.		beginning lost	
	1'	*ni-da-l*[*i-p(u-ni)*]	". . . we shall sit up (with
	2'	*ma-a* SAG.D[U-*su*]	him)"; (and) he said: "We should
	3'	*nu-gal-li-*[*ib* . (.)]	shear [his] head (and)
	4'	*ṣi-in-di* [. . .]	bind [the wound?] with [. . .]
	5'	*ni-ir-k*[*u-us*]	bandages."
	6'	*ú-* [*ma- a*]	Now,
Edge		uninscribed	what is it
Rev.	1	*mi-nu š*[*a* LUGAL *be-lí*]	th[at the king, my lord],
	2	*i-qa-b*[*u-u-ni*]	says?
		remainder blank	

Commentary: The extant lines of this fragment evidently quote words of a physician (cf. *CAD* Ṣ s.v. *ṣimdu*), but whether the writer himself was a physician is of course another matter. The medical term *dalāpu* (+ *isse*) "sit up (with a patient)" frequently occurs also in letters of exorcists.

367 (K 7373). Copy *CT* 53 pl. 90 no. 337.

Obv.	1	[*a-n*]*a* L[UGAL *be-lí-ia*]	To the k[ing, my lord,]
	2	[ÌR]-*ka* I⸢x⸣[. . . .]	your [servant PN].
	3	⸢d⸣AG dAM[AR+UD *a-na* LUGAL]	May Nabû (and) Ma[rduk]
	4	[*b*]*e-lí-ia lik-r*[*u-bu* . . .]	bl[ess the king], my lord.
	5	*ina* É KI.MAḪ *i*[*p* . . . (.)]	[. . . . .] in the burial chamber
	6	IdPA-BÀD-PAP EN [. . . .]	Nabû-dūru-uṣur, the [. . . .]
	7	*ša is-si-ia* [. . . .]	who with me [. . . . .]
	8	*a-mar lìb-bi* [. . . .]	contents (?) [. . . . .]
	9	É *ša* LUG[AL . . . . .]	the king's family [. . . . . . .].
	10	*ina sur-ri* [. . . . .]	Perhaps [. . . . .]
	11	*ip-taq-d*[*u* . . . . .]	they appoint[ed . . . .]
	12	I⸢d⸣x[. . . . .]	
		rest destroyed	

Rev. broken away

Commentary: This fragment is included because of its affinities with *LAS* 32. The identity of the writer remains obscure. The first broken sign of the name is not AN but BA or the like; the obvious restoration [Adad-šumu-uṣur] (cf. 32:3, and note the omission of the blessing formula, as in *LAS* 138, 148, 156 and 158) is hence out of the question.

368 (K 10373 + K 12947). Copy *CT* 53 pl. 39 no. 111.

Obv. 1 [*a-na* LUGAL] *be-lí- ja*
2 [ÌR-*ka*] ^{Id}AG-NUMUN-SUM-*na*
3 [*lu-u šùl-mu a*]-*na* LUGAL *be-lí-ja*
4 [^{d}*Aš+šur* ^{d}*30*] ^{d}UTU ^{d}AG ^{d}AMAR+UD
5 [*a-n*]*a* ⸢LUGAL *be*⸣-*lí-ja lik-ru-bu*
6 [*ṭ*]*u-ub lìb-bi ṭu-ub* UZU *a-na* LUGAL EN-*ja liš-ru-ku*
7 [*k*]*i-i* AN-*e u* KI-TIM ⸢LUGAL⸣ *be-lí lu-u da-a-ar*
8 ⸢d⸣15 *ša* ⸢URU*Arba*⸣-*ìl am-mar* ^{LÚ}KÚR^{MEŠ}-*ni*
9 [*ina* IGI LUGAL *be-lí-ja l*]*u-u tu-sa-ḫi-ip*
10 [*lu-u ta*]*š-kun*
Rev. 1 [ ]
2 [-*k*]*a*
3 [ ]-*kun*
4 [ ]- *du*
5-7 broken away, then in rough characters on dry clay:
8 [ ]⸢x⸣
9 [ ] ⸢*ad? ib?*⸣ *ḫu e 1* TÚG.DUL
10 [ ]⸢x⸣ *pa?-an* ^{d}EN*.KI
Edge 11 [ ]⸢*li? -li- su- um- ma*
12 [ ] *i- dáb- bu- ub*

[To the king], my lord, (from) [your servant] Nabû-zēru-iddina: [Good health t]o the king, my lord. May [Aššūr, Sîn], Šamaš, Nabû (and) Marduk bless the king, my lord; may they grant the king, my lord, happiness (and) physical health. May the king, my lord, live forever like Heaven and Earth. May Ištar of Arbela slay [before the king, my lord,] whatever enemies there are, may she put [. . . .(*Break, most probably containing further blessings*) . . .] . . . . . . in front of Enki [. . . . . .] a *lilissu*-drum [. . . . .] speaks [. . . .] .

Commentary: See after *LAS* 369.

369 (83-1-18,193 = *ABL* 1150)

Obv. 1 *a-na* LUGAL *be-lí- ja*
2 ÌR-*ka* ^{Id}AG-NUMUN- SUM-[*na*]
3 *lu-u šùl-mu a-na* LUGAL *be-lí-*[*ja*]
4 ^{d}*Aš+šur* ^{d}*30* ^{d}UTU ^{d}AG ^{d}[AMAR+UD]
5 *a-na* LUGAL *be-lí-ja lik-r*[*u-bu*]
6 *tu-ub lìb-bi ṭu-ub* UZU *a-na* LUGAL [EN-*ja liš-ru-ku*]
7 *ki-i* AN-*e u* KI-TIM LUGAL *be-lí* [*lu-u da-a-ar*]
8 ^{d}*30* ^{d}NIN.GAL ^{d}PA+KU *ṣu-ul-*[*le-e*]
9 *ša* LUGAL EN- *ja liš- mì-* [*u*]
10 *am-mar* ^{LÚ}KÚR^{MEŠ}-*ni ina* IGI [GÌR^{2}]
Rev. 1 [*ša*] LUGAL EN-*ja l*[*u!-sa-ḫi-pu*]
2 [ ] *liš-*[*ku-nu*]
3 [. .] *u bu* x[ ] *na* [ ]
4 [ ] SAG x[ ]
Remainder uninscribed

To the king, my lord, (from) your servant Nabû-zēru-iddina: Good health to the king, my lord. May Aššur, Sîn, Šamaš, Nabû (and) Marduk bless the king, my lord, (and) [may they grant] the king, my lord, happiness (and) physical well-being; may the king, my lord, [live forever] like Heaven and Earth; may Sîn, Nikkal (and) Nusku listen to the prayers of the king, my lord, (and) may they subdue under [the feet of] the king, my lord, whatever enemies there are . . . (*Rest broken and untranslatable*)

Commentary: The writer of these two letters is certainly identical with the son of Urad-Ea and the chief chanter (*kalamāhu*) of Assurbanipal known from colophons of literary texts and the list *ADD* 851 (App. N, nos. 11-13 and 26): note the reference to the *lilissu* drum and the god Enki in No. 368, and the invocation of the gods Sîn and Nikkal (whose chanter the priest Nabû-zēru-iddina was, like his father) in No. 369. Both letters, like *ADD* 851, probably date from about 650 BC.

370 (81-2-4,61). Copy *CT* 53 pl. 45 no. 139.

Obv. 1 [*a-na* DUMU-MAN *be*]- *lí-* *ja*
2 [ÌR-*ka* ^{I}Tab?- ni?]- *i*
3 [*lu* DI-*mu a-na* DUMU-MAN] *be-lí-ja*
4 [^{d}PA ^{d}AMAR+UD *a-na*] DUMU-MAN EN-*ja* ⌜*lik-ru*⌝-*bu*
5 [TA* *ṣe-ḫe-r*]*i-šú a-di ru-*⌜*bé-šú*⌝
6 [AD-*u-a* SAG A]D-*šú šá* DUMU-MAN *uk-te-*⌜*li*⌝
7 [. . . . *ina*] IGI-*šú it- ti-*⌜*ti*⌝-[*z*]*i*
8 ⌜*id-du-bu-ub*⌝[*m*]*a-a* LUGAL *be-lí* x[. . .]x
9 ⌜x⌝ *la ma* ⌜ x x x x x ⌝ *ni šú* ⌜x⌝[ ]
10 [*š*]*a ina* UGU$^{!}$-*in-ni* [ ]
11 [*de*]-*iq-tu* x[ ]
12 [.]⌜x⌝ É *us-s*[*a-*]
13 *a-na* ^{LÚ}GAL-ḪAL-*ti ip-*[*ti-q̮i-id-su*]
14 ⌜ x *mu*⌝ *ina* ŠÀ L[Ú]ÌR^{MEŠ} [*šá* LUGAL . . .]
15 ⌜^{LÚ}⌝*par-šá-*⌜*mu-te*⌝ *šá* É.G[AL]
16 ⌜^{LÚ}GAL⌝[. . . *b*]*i-ja* [ ]
17 [. . . . (.)]⌜ŠU+2⌝[ ]
18 [(.) . . .] *sap* [ ]
19 [. LUG]AL EN-*ja* [ ]
20 [*am*]-*mar IQ-*[*bu-u-ni*]
21 [*a-n*]*a qa-ti-šú* ^{d}UTU *us-sa-ḫiz-*[ ]
22 [*ma*]-⌜*a*⌝ *ur-di i-da-tu-u-a is-sa-ra-*[ ]
23 *a-*⌜*na-ku*⌝ *a-na ur-di-ja ṭa-ab-tu* [*le-pu-uš*]
24 [*ma-a*] *1-et : a-bu-tú ša ṭa-ab-ti* [ ]x x[ ]
25 [*re-d*]*u-tu ša um-ma-nu-ti* [*lap-qi-da-áš-šú*]
26 [*2-tú ṭa-a*]*b-te : a-di ina* KUR *Aš+šur*^{KI} [*šu-tu-ni*]
27 *l*[*u qur*]-*ba-an-ni is-* *s*[*i-niš*]
28 *ma-a ki-ma ṭa-ab-tu-uš la* ⌜*e*⌝-[*pu-u*]*š*
29 *ma-a ina pa-an* DINGIR^{MEŠ} *ma-ḫe-e-*$^{!}$*re*$^{!}$
30 ⌜*ta-ab*⌝-*tu e-ta- ap- šá- áš- šú*
31 *ù a-na a-a-ši ina* ŠÀ *ṭa-ab-ti šá* AD-*ja*
32 *u-nu* DUMU-MAN EN-*ja it-ta-na-an-ni*
Edge 33 ⌜*ù*⌝ DUMU-MAN *be-lí ri-ik-su ir-ta-*⌜*kas*⌝
34 *re-ḫa-a- te šá* DUMU-MAN EN-*ja a-t*[*a-kal*]
35 *ú-ma-a mi-i-nu* ⌜*ḫi*⌝-*ṭa-a-a ina* [IGI DUMU-MAN EN-*ja*]
Rev 1 *1-en* [NINDA^{MEŠ} *la*] *a-kal a-n*[*a*]-*ku* [ ]
2 TA* *bé-*[*et*]x *ik-lu-u-* *ni*
3 *lìb-bi it-*[*lu-q*]*u-ut a-* *dan-* *niš*
4 *ú-ma-a* [*an-nu-rig* DUMU-M]AN *be-lí ur-ta-ad-di*
5 *a-na* ^{I}x[^{SÍ}]^{G}ZA.GÌN.[SA$_{5}$ *u*]*s-sa-biš*

6 *ja-ú* DUMU-MAN [*be*]-*lí lìb-bi* ⸢x⸣[*u*]*k pa*
7 ⸢LÚ⸣ÌR^{MEŠ} *šá* LUGAL *šá* DUMU-MAN ⸢LÚÌR^{MEŠ} *šá* É⸣ AD-⸢*já*⸣
8 *a-ke-e lu-šá-pil* ⸢*ma*⸣-*a* ⸢*am*⸣-*mi- i*
9 ⸢*mi-i*⸣-*nu ṭa-ab-tu-šú nu-*[*u*]*k* DUMU-MAN
10 [*a-na a*]-*a-ši lu-šá-*⸢*ab*⸣-*ki* ⸢*a*⸣-[*na*]⸢x⸣^{MEŠ}-⸢*ku*⸣-*nu*
11 [ ]*x-a-ti-šá-ni* [*lu*]-*u ú-ka-ab-* <*bi-*>*di*
12 [*ana-ku un-za*]-*ar-ḫu šá* LUGAL *šá* DUMU-MAN
13 [*ina* ŠÀ *e-ṭu-t*]*e ka- ra- ak*
14 [ ]-⸢*u*⸣-*te šá* DUMU-MAN *ú-ka-bi-du-šú-u-ni*
15 [ ]x *ú-la-a qa-an-ni ma-ṣar-ti*
16 [*m*]*a-ṣar-ti šu- ú*
17 [LÚÌR *šá* DUMU]-MAN *a-na-ku* AD-*u-a* ŠU ⸢x⸣ *iš-di*
18 [ ]x *šar* [LU]GAL-[*u-t*]*e šu-ú*
19 [ ]*an-ni-*⸢*te*⸣[ ]*et-ka-an-ni*
20 [ ]⸢*ni ma* x⸣[ ]⸢x x x⸣
21 [ ]⸢x x⸣[ ]
22 [ ]*ḫu* x[ ]
23 [ ]⸢x⸣ *ka* x[ ]
24 ⸢*ù*⸣ [*t*]*up-pa-a-ni a-s*[*a-ṭar*]
25 [.] *me-me-ni* [.] *ku-*⸢*tal*⸣-*šú-nu i-*[ ]
26 [^{I} A]-*a ù* ^{I}*Na- ṣi- ru*
27 [ ]x *šu-un-nu* ⸢x⸣ *uk- ti- lu*
28 [*a-na-ku* T]A* ŠU^{2} AD-*ja as-sa-am-da*
29 [*ú-ma-a*] DUMU-MAN ^{LÚ}ÌR-*šú lil- tuk*
30 [ ]-*nu-u-te* IM^{MEŠ} *šá-ṭa-ru šá ú-ìl-ti*
31 [ ]⸢x x x *ja*⸣ *a-na-ku* DUMU-MAN *be-lí*
32 [*ki-i šá* Z]U-*'u-u-ni* ^{LÚ}ÌR-*šú le-e-pu-uš*
Edge 33 [DUMU]-LUGAL *be-lí*
34 [ ]⸢x *ri* x *ku* x⸣
L.E. 35 AD-*u-a šu-up-lu lìb-bi iṣ-ṣa-ab-t*[*a*
36 *in-nu-*⸢x⸣[

[To the crown prince], my lord, (from) [your servant . . .]ī. [Good health to the crown prince], my lord. May [Nabû and Marduk] bless the crown prince, my lord.
^{5}[From] his [chi]ldhood till his maturity, ^{6}[my father] took [care of] the father of the crown prince; ^{7}[steadily?] the stood in his presence, ^{8}and spoke: "The king, my lord, ^{9}will [. . . . .] ^{10}which is upon us [. . . . . . .]". ^{11} Kindness [. . . . .] ^{12}he made [. . . .] house [. . . . .] ^{13}(and) ap[pointed him] the chief haruspex. ^{14}Among the servants [of the king . . .] ^{15}(and) the elders of the palac[e . . . . . .] ^{16}the chief [. . . . . . *(break of 4 lines)* . . . . . .] ^{20}Everything that he (= my father) had s[aid . . . .] ^{21}Šamaš caused to . . . . to his hands. ^{22}(So) he (= the king) said: "My servant made my omens . . . . , ^{23} [let] me [do] my servant a favour. ^{24}The first piece of favour [is]: ^{25}[I will assign to him] the [lead]ership of scholars. ^{26}My [second fa]vour is: As long as [he is] in Assyria, ^{27} l[et him be n]ear me." Further[more] ^{28}he said: "If I didn't do him a favour, ^{29} would it be well-pleasing in sight of the gods?" ^{30}(So) he did him the (said) favour, ^{31}and myself, as part of the favour shown to my father, ^{32}he gave to the crown prince, my lord. ^{33}And the crown prince, my lord, drew up a contract ^{34}(entitling) me to have usufruct of the "leftovers' of the crown prince, my lord. ^{35}Now, what have I done wrong in [the eyes of the crown prince, my lord], $^{r.1}$ (that) I do not (get) a single [loaf of bread] to eat (and) . . . . [. . .]? ^{2}Ever sin[ce] they withheld [. . . . .], ^{3}my heart has been extremely s[a]d; ^{4}now [the crown p]rince, my lord, had added (to my misery), ^{5}(and) dressed [PN] in purple (robes); ^{6}as for my heart, the crown prince, my lord, [has made it . . . .]. $^{7-8}$How should he thus humiliate the servants of the king and the crown prince, the servants of my father's house, (that) they say (*or* he says): "That one, ^{9}what's his favour?" I (can only) say, "Let the crown prince ^{10}make me weep, (but) ^{11}he should have honoured you [. . . . .]." ^{12} [I, a s]ervant of the king and the crown prince, ^{13}have been left [in darkness]; ^{14}[the . . . . .] whom the crown prince has honoured, $^{15-6}$[is . . . .]. Or *is* [there no(?) gua]rd on duty? ^{17}I am [a servant of the crow]n prince; my father is [. . . . . *(break of 6*

lines) . . . .] [24]I have wr[itten] tablets [. . . . .] [25]anything [. . . . .]. [26][Apl]â and Nāṣiru [27]hold . . . . . [. . . . . .]; [28]I learned (my craft) from my (own) father. [29][Now], let the crown prince put his servant to a test: [30][. . . . .] tablets, to write a report, [31]I am [. . . . . .]. The crown prince, my lord, [32]may treat his servant [as he d]eems best. [33] [The crown] prince, my lord, [34][should know that] . . . . [35]depression has gripped my father [. . . . (*last line destroyed*)].

Commentary: The writer of this long, unfortunately badly damaged, petition remains unidentified, despite the fact that he explicitly identifies himself as son of the king's chief haruspex (obv. 13) and evidently was a trained haruspex himself (cf. r28ff, and notice the ref. to the haruspices [Apl]â and Nāṣiru [*LAS* 115] in r26). A tempting restoration of obv. 2 would be [^{I}*Tab-ni*]-*i* (cf. *LAS* 116 etc.), but other possibilities (Bānî, Sānî, Zīzî) exist. As the letter is addressed to the crown prince, it certainly dates from 672-669 BC, and probably should be placed in either 669 or 670, since obv. 20f seems to be an oblique reference to the conquest of Egypt (671 BC).

NEW JOINS

(1) *LAS 10 + unp.* (83-1-18,151 + 513). Collated by C.B.F. Walker.

Obv.	1	[*a-na* LUGAL EN-*ni*]	[To the king, our lord]
	2	[ÌR^{MEŠ}-*ka* ^{I}*Ba-la-si-i*]	[(from) your servants Balasî
	3	[$^{\text{I.d}}$PA-PAP^{MEŠ}-SU]	[(and) Nabû-aḫḫē-erība]:
	4	[*lu šùl-mu a-n*]*a* LUG[AL EN-*ni*]	[good health] to the ki[ng, our]
	5	[^{d}PA ^{d}]⌈AMAR⌉.[UD] *a-na* LU⌈GAL⌉	[lord. May Nabû and M]arduk
	6	EN-*ni lik-ru-b*[*u*]	bless the king, our lord.
	7	*ina* UGU *a-la-ki ša* URU[. .]	As to the trip to the city of
	8	*ša* LUGAL *be-li-ni*	[. . .], on which the king, our
	9	*iš-pur-an-na-ši-ni*	lord, wrote to us,
	10	*šum-ma* LUGAL *ina* É-*an-ni*	if the king keeps indoors,
	11	*ina* ^{ITU}DU$_6$ *ṭa-ba*	it is good to go
	12	*a-na a-la-ki*	in the month Tašrītu.
	13	*ú-la-a* L[UGA]L *i-qab-*⌈*bi*⌉	Or, (if) the king says:
	14	*ma-a la* [ ]x[ ]	"[I will] not [. . . . . . .
		balance of Obv. lost	(*Break*)
Rev.	1'	[*iq-b*]*u-*⌈*ú*⌉-[*ni*]	[As the king previously] sa[id],
	2'	⌈ITU⌉ *an-ni-*⌈*ú*⌉	the present month
	3'	*ur-ḫu*	
	4'	*da-ri-ir*	is intercalary.
	5'	*lu-u ra-am-mu*	The matter should be dropped
	6'	ITU *e-ri-ib-a-n*[*i*]	(and) the king make the trip (only)
	7'	LUGAL *lil-lik*	in the coming month.
	8'	*ka-qu-ru*[[x]] *liš-šiq*	Let him kiss the ground
	9'	UDU$^{\text{SISKUR.SISKUR MEŠ}}$	(and) perform
	10'	⌈*le-pu*⌉-*šu*	the sacrifices.
		last 5 lines destroyed	

(2) *LAS 34(+) 49* (K 1129 (+) 14679). Join verified by E. Sollberger.

Obv.	1	*a-na* LUGAL E[N-*ja*]	To the king, [my lo]rd,
	2	ÌR-*ka* ^{I}*Ba-l*[*a-si-i*]	(from) your servant Bal[asî]:
	3	*lu-u šùl-mu a-na* [LUGAL EN-*ja*]	good health to [the king, my lord.]
	4	[^{d}PA] ^{d}AMAR+UD *a-*[*na* LUGAL] EN-*ja*	[May Nabû] (and) Marduk bless

5	*[lik-ru-b]u ša* LUGAL *be-lí*	the king, my lord. (As to) what
6	*iš-pu-ra-an-ni ma-⌜a⌝*	the king, my lord, wrote to me:
7	*ina ḫa-ra-am-me ina pu-tu-u-a*	"From now on you will stay in
8	*ta-ti-ti-sa ma-a a-bu-tú*	my presence; is there anything
9	*i-ba-áš-ši ina pi-i-ku-nu*	you have to say?",
10	*a-bu-tu la- áš- šu*	there is nothing.
11	DINGIR^{MEŠ} GAL^{MEŠ} *ša* AN-*e* KI.TIM	May the great gods of heaven
	Rest as in Pt. I. Rev. 14ff uninscribed.	

(3) *LAS* 218 + 221 (K 950 + 14592). Join confirmed by C.B.F. Walker.

Obv.	1	*[a-n]a* LUGAL *[be]- lí- j[a]*	[T]o the king, m[y] lord,
	2	ÌR- *ka* $^{\text{I.d}}$AG- PAP- *i[r]*	(from) your servant Nabû-nāṣe[r]:
	3	^{d}AG *u* ^{d}AMAR+UD *a-na* LUGAL EN-*ia*	May the gods Nabû and Marduk
	4	*a-dan-niš a-dan-niš lik-ru-bu*	very much bless the king, my lord.
	5	*šùl-mu a-dan-niš a-dan-niš*	Aššur-mukīn-palēja is doing very,
	6	*a-na* $^{\text{I.d}}$*Aš+šur-mu-kin*-BAL^{MEŠ}-*ja*	very well, etc.
		etc., as in Pt.I	

The joins (2) and (3) did not add a single new word to the text of *LAS* 34 and 218 as edited in Pt. I, but they are important in confirming the connectness of the attribution of these letters to Balasî and Nabû-nāṣer. Cf. also below, join (4).

(3a) *LAS* 43(+?)55 (K 13174 + 83-1-18,154)

According to E. Sollberger (letter of Jan. 19, 1976), these two fragments "don't seem to belong to the same tablet". Their physical features are, however, very similar (cf. Pt. I, p. 332), and therefore the possibility of their being parts of the same tablet should not be overlooked. Granting this, the fragments should link up as follows:

(*LAS* 43)	6	^{d}PA ^{d}AMAR+UD *a-na* [LUGAL]	"May Nabû (and) Marduk b[less]
	7	EN-*ni l[ik-ru-bu ina* UGU]	the [king], our lord. [As to]
	8	M[UL . . *ša* LUGAL EN-*ni*]	the s[tar . . . concerning which
(*LAS* 55)	9	*[iš-pur]-an-na-ši-n[i]*	the king, our lord, w]rote to
	10	*[i-b]a-áš-ši ka-k[u-bu]*	us, it is indeed a star . . ."

(4) *LAS* 69 + 71 (K 1200 + Ki 1904-10-9,186). Collated by E. Sollberger.

Obv.	1	*⌜a-na⌝* LUGAL EN-*ja*	To the king, my lord, (from)
	2	ÌR-*ka* $^{\text{I.d}}$PA-PAP^{MEŠ}-SU	your servant Nabû-aḫḫē-erība:
	3	*lu šùl-mu a-na* LUGAL-EN-*ja*	good health to the king, my lord.
	4	^{d}PA ^{d}AMAR+UD *a-na* LUGAL	May Nabû (and) Marduk bless
	5	EN-*ja lik-ru-bu*	the king, my lord. As to
	6	*ina* UGU DUMU.LUGAL *ša* LUGAL	the crown prince concerning whom the
	7	*be-lí iš-pur-an-ni*	king, my lord, wrote to me saying that
	8	*[m]a-a* UD *⌜1*.KÁM*⌝ *š[a* ^{ITU}B]ÁR	the crown [prince should visit the ki]ng,
	9	*[m]a-a* DUMU.[LUGAL *ina* IGI LU]GAL	m[y lo]rd on the 1st o[f Nisannu],
	10	[E]N-*j[a lil-li-ka]*	(and asked), "[Is] the 1st day [au-
	11	*[ma-a* U]D *⌜1⌝*.K[ÁM* *ṭa-ba-a]*	spicious]?", (this is my reply):
	12	[I *ina* ^{IT}]UBÁR UD *1*.KÁM* LÚ *l[i-te-lil]*	'On the 1st of Nisannu one should
	13	*[l]i-te-bi-ib* ŠUG-*su*	c[leanse and p]urify [oneself], make
	14	*ku-ru-ma-at-su*	one's food offering to
	15	*a-na* ^{d}AMAR+UD *liš-kun*	the god Marduk,
	16	A^{MEŠ} KAŠ.SAG ZAG *u* KAB	libate water (and) first quality
	17	*ši-ka-ru i-mit-tú*	beer to the right and to the left,
	18	*liq-qí* LÚ BI *ki-ma* ^{d}*šá-maš*	(then) the man in question will
	19	*na-me-er*	shine like the divine sun.

Obv.	20	I UD 2.KÁM* *a-na* SILA NU DU	On the 2nd he should not go to the street
	21	I *ina* ^{ITU}BÁR UD 4.KÁM*	On the 4th of Nisannu
	22	*a-na* ^{d}AMAR+UD *liš-ken*	he should prostrate himself before Marduk
	23	ISKIM-BI *li-še-di*	(and) make his sign known;
	24	[*it-ta-šú*]!	
Edge	25	[M]U *ù*! (ḪUL) *iš-di-ḫu*	he will (then) be granted fame
	26	*iš-šak-kan-šú*	and prosperity.
Rev.	1	ISKIM.BI *li-še-di*	"He should make his sign known"
	2	*it-ta-šú*	(means):
	3	*ma-a de-en-šú ina* IGI DINGIR	'He should plead his case
	4	*lid-bu-ub*	before the god.'
	5	*šá-ni-it-tú a-bu-tú*	Another matter: The planet
	6	[M]^{UL}UDU.IDIM.GU$_4$.UD *ba-i-il*	Mercury is shining very bright-
	7	[*a-dan*]-*niš* DUMU.LUGAL *šu-u*	ly; it is (the star of) the crown
	8	[*du-un-qu*] *ša* KUR SU.BIR$_4$^{KI} ⸢*šu-u*⸣	prince. This is [advanta-
		šu-bar-ti	geous] to the country of Subartu,
	10	[*du-un-q*]*u ša* LUGAL *ša* DUMU.LUGAL	[advantag]eous to the king
	11	[*šu-u* DU]MU.LUGAL *ina* IGI LUGAL	and the crown prince. [If] the crown
	12	[EN-*ja ki-m*]*a er-ra-ba*	prince is to enter into the presence
	13	[*ṭa-a-ba a*]-⸢*na*⸣ *e-ra-ba*	of the king [my lord, it is (a) favour-
	14	[*ša*] ⸢LUGAL *be-lí iš*⸣ *pur* [*an-ni*]	able (moment)] to do (so). As
	15	[*ma*]-*a* ^{I}*Aš+šur-mu-kin*-BAL-*ja*	to the king, my lord's writing to
	16	[*ina* I]GI LUGAL EN-*ja lil-li-k*[*a*]	me that Aššur-mukīn-palēja
	17	[*ki-m*]*a* ^{MUL}*Dil-bat it-ta-mar*	should visit the king, he may come
	18	[*lil*]-*li-ka an-nu-rig*	as soon as Venus has become visible.
	19	[MU]^{L}*Dil-bat pa-ni-šú*	Venus is now on its way to (make)
	20	[*a-n*]*a du-un-qi is-sa-kan*	a lucky sign; [mean]while, the
	21	[*ina*] ŠÀ ^{ITU}BÁR *e-tar-ba*	month Nisannu has arrived; the
	22	[M]UL.LÚḪUN.GÁ *i-rab-bi*	constellation of Aries is setting
	23	*ug-da-ad-am-mar il-lak*	(and) will soon be completely
	24	LUGAL *be-lí uṣ-ṣu*-⸢*su*⸣	gone. Let the king, my lord, yet
Edge	25	*aḫ-ḫur lu-šá-ad-g*[*i-il*]	wait for its emergence,
	26	*ur-ke-e-et*	thereafter
	27	*lil-li-ka*	he may come.
L.E.	28	[ ]⸢ x x ⸣ *il*-[ ]	[*Break*]
	29	⸢^{d}⸣EN ^{d}PA [*né-mu-lu ša* ^{I}*Aš+šur-mu-k*]*in*-BA[L-*j*]*a*	May Bēl (and) Nabû [let] the king, my lord,
	30	*a-na* LUGAL EN-*j*[*a lu ḫal-li-mu*]	enjoy the prosperity of A.

(5) *LAS* 110 + 300 (83-1-18,61 + Ki 1904-10-9,59 [BM 99030]). Collated by E. Sollberger.

Obv.	1	[*a-na*] LUGAL *be- lí- ja*
	2	[ÌR-*ka*] ^{I}*Ak- kul- la- nu*
	3	[*lu-u š*]*ul-mu a-na* LUGAL *be-lí-ja*
	4	[^{d}AG] *u* ^{d}AMAR+UD *a-na* LUGAL EN-*já lik-ru-bu*
	5	[^{MUL}*Ṣal*]-*bat-a-nu ina* KASKAL *šu-ut* ^{d}EN*.LÍL *it-ti* GÌR^{2}.MEŠ
	6	[^{MUL}]ŠU.GI *it-tan-mar un-nu-ut pu-ṣu šá-kin*
	7	[^{IT}]^{U}GUD UD 26.KÁM *a-ta-mar a-du iš-qa-an-ni*
	8	[*ḫa*]-*ra-me-ma a-na* LUGAL EN-*já as-sap-ra pi-še-er-šu*
	9	[I M]^{UL}*Ṣal-bat-a-nu a-na* ^{MUL}ŠU.GI TE-*ḫi ina* KUR MAR.TU
	10	BAL-*tu*$_4$ GÁL-*ma* ŠEŠ ŠEŠ-*šú* GAZ-*ak*
	11	É.GAL NUN KAR-*a' ni-ṣir-ti* KUR *ana* KUR *šá-ni-tim-ma* È

Obv. 12 [Š]U.NIR KUR ḪUL^{MEŠ} LUGAL ŠÚ DINGIR^{MEŠ}-*šú ana* KÚR-*šú ú-saḫ-ḫa-ru-šú*

---

13 ḪUL *ša* KUR MAR *šu-u-tú* DINGIR^{MEŠ}-⌈*ka*⌉ *šum-ma kiš-šu-tu*$_4$
14 [*a*]*m-mar* ^{KUR}*Gim-ra-aje e-pu-*⌈*uš*⌉-[*u-n*]*i Aš+šur* DINGIR-*ka*
15 *la i-na-áš-šá-an-ni a-na* LUGAL EN-*já l*[*a id-da*]*n-*⌈*u-ni*⌉

---

16 [I] ^{MUL}MAN-*ma ana* ^{d}EN*.ME.ŠÁR.RA TE-*ḫi* ŠÀ KUR DÙG-*a*[*b* UN^{MEŠ} DAGAL^{MEŠ}]

---

17 I ^{MUL}MAN-*ma* ^{d}*Ṣal-bat-a-nu : du-un-qu ša* LUGAL EN-*já* [*šu-u-tú*]

---

18 I ^{MUL}*Ṣal-bat-a-nu um-mu-liš* KUR-*ḫa-ma* ŠE.ER.ZI^{MEŠ}-*šú* SI[G$_7$]
19 *ina* MU BI LUGAL NIM.MA^{KI} BA.ÚŠ
20 I ^{d}U+GUR *ina* IGI.DU$_8$.A-*šú ṣu-ḫur pu-ṣu šá-kin*
21 GIM MUL AN-*e ma-diš um-mul a-na* KUR URI^{KI} ARḪUŠ TUKU
22 Á ERIM.MU GUB-*az-ma* KÚR GAZ-*ak* ERIM KÚR *ina* IGI ERIM.MU NU GUB-*az*
23 *bu-ul* KUR URI^{KI} *par-ga-niš ina* EDEN NÁ-*iṣ* ŠEGIŠ.Ì
24 *u* ZÚ.LUM.MA SI.SÁ^{MEŠ} DINGIR^{MEŠ} *ana* KUR URI^{KI} ARḪUŠ TUKU^{MEŠ}
25 I *ina* ^{ITU}GUD ^{MUL}*Ṣal-bat-a-nu* IGI.LAL ^{MÍ}KÚR^{MEŠ} GÁL^{MEŠ}
26 *šal-pú-tì* ERIM *man- da*

---

27 ERIM *man- da* ^{LÚ}*Gim- ra- aje*

---

28 AN.MI *ša ina* ^{ITU}BARAG ^{d}UTU *iš-kun-u-ni*
29 *qaq-qa-ru ša* KUR SU.BIR$_4$^{KI} *la il-pu-ut*
30 *ù* ^{MUL}SAG.ME.GAR KI.GUB-*su us- sa- lim*
31 *15* UD^{MEŠ} DIRIG^{MEŠ} GUB-*iz* SIG$_5$ *šu-u-tú*

Edge 32 I ^{d}UTU *ina* ŠÀ *ni-di* KUR-*ḫa* EŠŠANA ŠÚR-*ma* ^{GIŠ}TUKUL *i-na-áš-ši*

---

33 KUR *Aš+šur* KUR URI^{KI}-*im-ma ša* LUGAL EN-*já*

Rev. 1 *ù ina* UGU ŠÈG^{MEŠ} *ša* MU.AN.NA *an-ni-ti*
2 *im-ṭu-u-ni* EBUR^{MEŠ} *la in-né-piš-u-ni*
3 *du-un-qu ša* TI.LA ZI^{2}.^{MEŠ} *ša* LUGAL
4 EN-*já šu-u-tú is-su-ri* LUGAL *be-lí i-qab-bi*
5 *ma-a ina* ŠÀ *mi-i-ni ta-a-mur qi-bi-'a-a*
6 *ina* ŠÀ *ú-ìl-ti ša* ^{d}*É-a-mu-šal-lim*
7 *ša a-na* ^{Id}MES-SUM-PAP^{MEŠ} EN-*šú iš-pur-u-ni šá-ṭir*
8 *šum-ma* ISKIM *ina* AN-*e* DU-*kam-ma pi-iš-šá-tu la ir-ši*
9 *šum-ma a-na ma-qa-at* ŠÈG^{MEŠ} *ib- ši- ka*
10 [E]ŠŠANA KASKAL^{MEŠ} *na-ki-ri šu- uṣ- bit*
11 [*e*]-*ma* DU-*ku i-kaš-šad* UD^{MEŠ}-*šú* GÍD.DA^{MEŠ}

---

12 [I *30 ina*] ^{ITU}SIG$_4$ UD *30*.KÁM IGI. LAL
13 [*ṭuḫ- d*]*u* MAR.TU^{KI} *Aḫ-la-mu-u* KÚ

---

14 [*an-na-ti*] ISKIM^{MEŠ} *ša* KUR MAR ḪUL^{MEŠ}
15 [. . ^{d}E]N* *u* ^{d}AG DINGIR^{MEŠ}-*ka*
16 [*šum-ma nak-ru-t*]*i ina* ŠU^{2} LUGAL EN-*já* [
17 [ŠUB]-*tì* ^{LÚ}K[ÚR^{MEŠ}]
18 [ ] x *a* [ ]
19 [ ]
20 [ ]
21 [ ]
22 [-*b*]*u-tum*
23 [ ]-*bu-u-ni*

Rev. 24 [-*b*]*u-nim-ma*
25 [ ] KU^{MEŠ} ŠUB^{MEŠ}
Remainder (about 6 lines) lost

[To] the king, my lord, (from) [your servant] Akkullānu: good health to the king, my lord. May [Nabû] and Marduk bless the king, my lord. [The planet M]ars has appeared in the path of the Enlil stars at the feet of Perseus; it is faint and of a whitish colour. I saw (it) on the 26th of Ajāru, when it had (already) risen high, (and) am subsequently sending the relevant interpretation to the king, my lord:

If Mars approaches Perseus, there will be a rebellion in the land of Amurru, brother will slay his brother. The palace of the nobleman will be plundered, the treasure of the country will go over to another country; the emblem of the land will be cast down, (and) the gods will deliver the king of the world to his enemy.

This portends misfortune to the land of Amurru. By your gods, verily your god Aššur will take away whatever power the Cimmerians have achieved (and) give it to the king, my lord.

If the star Šanumma approaches Enmešarra, the land will be happy (and) (its) population will increase. Šanumma (means) Mars; this portends good to the king, my lord.

If Mars lights up faintly (and) its glow is yellowish, the king of Elam will die in that year. If Nergal is small (and) whitish at his appearance, and is faint like a fixed star, he will have mercy on the land of Akkad. My army will stand (firm) and slay the enemy, the enemy army will not hold its ground before my army; the herds of Akkad will rest undisturbed in the pastures, sesame and dates will thrive, (and) the gods will have mercy on the land of Akkad. If Mars appears in the month of Ajāru, there will be hostilities (and) the Ummān-manda will be slain.

Ummān-manda (means) the Cimmerians.

The eclipse which the sun made in Nisannu did not touch the quadrant of Subartu. In addition, Jupiter retained its position (in the sky), it was visible for 15 more days. That is propitious.

If the sun lights up amidst a *nīdu*, the king will get angry (and) raise his weapon.

Assyria is the land of Akkad of the king, my lord.

And as to the rains which have been so scanty this year that no harvests were reaped, this is a good omen pertaining to the life (and) vigour of the king, my lord. Perhaps the king, my lord, will say: "Where did you see that, tell me!" In a report of Ea-mušallim, which he sent to Marduk-nadin-aḫḫē, his lord, it is written: "If a sign occurs in the sky and cannot be cancelled, if it happens to you that the rains become scanty, make the king take the road against the enemy: he will conquer whatever (country) he will go to, (and) his days will become long."

[If the moon] in the month Simānu appears on the 30th day, Arameans will consume the riches of Amurru.

[These] signs portending evil to Amurru [. . . .]. By Bēl and Nabû, your gods, [verily the enem]y will [fall] into the hands of the king, my lord [. . . . .] defeat of the enemy [. . . . .

(Remainder lost)

(6) [*LAS* 95 (K 14670) has now been joined to K 4719, a letter from a ^{LÚ}GAL *da-ni-ba-te*, and hence does not belong among the letters of Ištar-nādin-apli.]

(7) *LAS 127(+)339 + unp.* (K 7374 + 9776(+)13109). Personal collation.

Obv. 1 [*a-na* LUGAL *be-lí-ja* ÌR-*ka* ^{I}ÌR-^{d}*Gu-la*]
2 [*lu-u šùl-mu a-na*] ⸢LUGAL *be-lí-ja a-dan*⸣-[*niš*]
3 [^{d}AMAR+UD ^{d}*Zar-pa-ni-t*]*um* ^{d}AG ^{d}*Taš-me-tu*[*m*]
4 [^{d}*15 šá* ^{URU}NINA^{KI}] ^{d}*15 šá* ^{URU}*Arba-ìl* ^{d}MAŠ [O]
5 [^{d}*Gu-la* ^{d}U+GUR ^{d}*L*]*a-aṣ* DINGIR^{MEŠ} *ma-ḫa-z*[*i*]
6 [KUR *Aš+šur* KUR URI^{KI}] ⸢DÙ⸣-*šú-nu a-na* LUGAL *be-lí-*[*já*]

Obv. 7 [DUMU^{MEŠ}*-šú a-dan-niš a*]*-dan-niš lik-ru-bu* UD^{MEŠ} GÍD^{MEŠ}
8 [MU.AN.NA^{MEŠ} *da-r*]*a-a-te ṭu-ub lìb-bi ṭu-ub* UZ[U]
9 [*ši-bu-tu lit-t*]*ú-tu a-na* LUGAL *be-lí-já* [0]
10 [*lu-šab-bi-ú . . .*]x ^{d}*I*⌜5⌝ LUGAL *be-lí la-a ú-*[. .]
11 [*d*]*i* IGI[2] *ša* LUGAL E[N-*já*]
12 [ ]x *si-da-*[*a-te*]
13 [*b*]*i-la* [ ]
gap of a few lines
14' [ ]*a-ri-a*[*t*]
15' [ ]*-ni-ni ma-a mi-e-nu* [*ṭēnša?*]
16' [ ] É ^{d}*Gu-la i-na-šú-u-n*[*i*]
17' [*i*]*-ba-áš-ši ina* É [. .]
18' [ ]⌜x x⌝ *ig at-ta-ṣa ina bé-et*
19' [. . . . . .]⌜x⌝[. *a*]*t-ti-din ša* ⌜LUGAL⌝ *be-lí*
20' [. . . . .]*-ni ip-t*[*a*]*-*⌜*al*⌝*-ḫu* ⌜*šur-ši*⌝ *lìb-*⌜*bi* x⌝*-šu*
21' [*ki-i ša in*]*a* KA *e-gér-a-te* LUGAL *be-lí iš-pur-an-ni*
22' ⌜*bé-et*⌝[. . x]*+me šu-nu-u-ni la na-ṣa-ku-u a-na* LUGAL
23' *la ú-kal-li-mì a-na 2-i* u_4*-me* LUGAL *is-sa-al-a-ni*
24' *ma-a ša a-ri-at-u-ni te-pa-áš mu-uk ša* [. . .]
25' DINGIR^{MEŠ}*-ni i-pa-*[*la*]*-ḫa mu-uk* ^{d}*Gu-la ša* [. .]
26' ^{d}*Gu-la ša* ⌜EDIN⌝ *ša na-aḫ-li* x[. . .]
27' [*mu*]*-uk* ⌜x x x x x⌝ MÍPEŠ$_4$ MA.SAB x[. . . (.)]
28' [. . .]x ⌜*ak* x *ni mu-uk*⌝ [*ku-zip-p*[*i* . . . (.)]
29' [. . . . . .]*-uš-šú mu-ku ši-*[*i* . . . (.)]
Edge 30' [. . . *ta*]*-za-az ú-la-a qa-*⌜x⌝[. . .]
31' [*mu-ku a*]*-ni-nu ki-i ša* LUGAL *i*[*q-bu-u-ni*]
32' [*né-pu*]*-uš i-da-a-te* ^{LÚ}GAL.[MAŠ.MAŠ?]
33' [*a-na?* LU]GAL *iq-ṭi-pi ma-a* MÍ *ši-*[*i*]
Rev. 1 [.]x-⌜*at*⌝ *ma-a a-na-ku* ^{Id}PA-*ina*+SÙḪ-K[AR-*ir* . . .]
2 [LU]GAL *iq-ṭi-pi ma-a na-am-li-ka* UR-[. . .]
3 *ši-i la-mur* MA.SAB*-ma la ta-az-zi-*[*iz* (. .)]
4 *ina* ŠÀ É.GAL *i-tar-bu* MA.SAB TA* É ^{d}[Gu-la]
5 *na-ṣu-u-ni us-se-ši-bu* ⌜É? x⌝ [. . . . (.)]
6 [ ]⌜x x⌝[ ]
7 [ ]*-*⌜*làh*⌝
8 [^{d}NI]N.ŠI.KÙ
9 [ ]x *ni* [ ]*u ni*
10 [ ]x
11 [ ]⌜x x⌝[ ]x
12 [ ] *na*[*p-šal-tú* . .]IB *ú-maš-*[*šu*]*-u-ni*
13 [ ]*an-nu-ti* x[. .]*-du-u-ti is-s*[*a-* . .]
14 [ ]⌜*a*⌝*-mur ú-ma-a dul-la-a-ni ma-a*[*'-du-t*]*e*
15 [ ]x[.]⌜*ú* x⌝ *k*[*a* .]x*-u-ni* x[ ]
Remainder lost

[To the king, my lord, (from) your servant Urad-Gula:] The best of [health to] the king, my lord. May [Marduk (and) Zarpānīt]u, Nabû (and) Tašmētu, [Ištar of Nineveh] (and) Ištar of Arbela, Ninurta (and) [Gula, Nergal (and) L]āṣ, the gods of all the sacred cities [of Assyria (and) Babylonia] bless the king, my lord, [and his sons, very] very much. [May they sate] the king, my lord, with long days (of life), [ever-l]asting years, happiness (and) extreme [old] age. [Re . . . .](-)Ištar, the king, my lord, [did?] not [. . . . .]. The eyes of the king, [my lo]rd, [. . . . . . *(Break of a few lines)* . . . .] is pregnant [. . . . .] . . [15]saying: "What [is the news about her?]" [. . . . .] will bring [her? to?] the temple of Gula [. . . . .] indeed in the temple [? . . . .]. [18]I brought

[. . . . . . .] (and) gave [. . .] where [. . . . . . .]. [19] Those whom the king, my lord, [. . . . . . .] got afraid (*or:* revered [the god(s)]) (and/but) . . . . , [just as] the king, my lord, wrote in (his) letters; did I not bring (her) where their [. . . . is], and did I not show (it) to the king? The following day the king asked me: "The one who is pregnant, <what> will she do?" I answered: "Those who [attend her], revere the gods, Gula of [. . .], Gula of the steppe and the wadi [. . . . .] the pregnant woman will [. . .] the basket [. . . . .]", [28'] and continued: "[Her] robes [. . . . .]; she [will . . . . st]and, or alternatively [. . . . . .]; [31'] we shall do as the king t[old] (us to do)." Afterwards the chief [exorcist?] [33'] said [to? the k]ing: "This woman is [. . . .]; I and Nabû-ina-tēšî-ēṭer [shall . . . .]." [r2] The king said: "Take counsel; she is [. . . . .]. I want to see." The basket was not there (lit. standing); they entered the palace, brought the basket from the temple of [Gula], set (it) [. . . . .]
(Remainder lost, except for Rev. 8, where the god Niššiku (= Ea) is mentioned, and Rev. 14, "Now [we are performing] numerous rituals . . .")

APPENDIX A

ASSYRIAN CHRONOLOGY 681-648 BC

In the Sargonid period the public calendar year was composed of lunar months, which began when the thin crescent of the new moon was first visible in the sky at sunset. Since the lunar year was about eleven days shorter than the solar year (which regulated agricultural and religious activities), it was necessary at intervals to intercalate a thirteenth month, either a second Ulūlu (the sixth month) or a second Addāru (the twelfth month) in order that New Year's Day, Nisannu 1, should not fall much before the vernal equinox (March 28).[669]

To be able to reconstruct the chronology of this period and to correlate it with the Julian calendar, which is indispensable if the chronological indications found in the present letters are to be utilized in historical research, it is hence necessary to know 1) the specific years in which the intercalations were made and 2) the exact days on which the lunar crescent was monthly sighted in Assyria. Neither requirement can be fully satisfactorily met at present (the latter probably never). The list of identified leap years is still incomplete; only the period 680-650 is relatively well documented, and even there numerous leap years can be identified only on indirect evidence (e.g. consideration of the intercalation pattern). The dates of the appearance of the crescent must (save for a few isolated cases) be recovered by computation, and since it is known that cloudy weather often hampered reliable establishment of the 1st day in antiquity,[670] the results are bound to remain hypothetical no matter how good tables are used for the computation. Nevertheless, the possibilities at hand seem sufficient for a limited attempt at reconstruction along the lines set out by Parker and Dubberstein in their *Babylonian Chronology 626 B.C. – A.D. 75* (1956) and its predecessors. As a matter of fact, experience gained in applying the tables presented below for the identification of astronomical phenomena has shown that their error margin is of the order of one or two days at the most, and hence negligible in primarily historically oriented research.

1. Intercalary years 685-650

Year	Intercalary month	Evidence
684	Addāru	*ADD* 255 r.17'f (collated)
*681	*Ulūlu	inferred
678	{ Ulūlu (Assyria)	BT 118:4 (*Iraq* 25 86ff)
	{ Addāru (Babylonia)	BM 74497 (Landsberger, *BBEA* p. 31)
*676	*Addāru	inferred
673	Addāru	*ADD* 53:5 = *AR* 258:5; *RMA* 225 r2
670	Ulūlu	*LAS* 38, 190, 287, 289 (see resp. commentaries)
{ 668	Addāru (Assyria)	*RMA* 68 and 70[671]; *LAS* 325
{ 667	Ulūlu (Babylonia)	Driver, *JRAS CSpl* 1924, pl. 4f

[669] Cf. Parker + Dubberstein, *Babylonian Chronology* (1956) 1 ff. Note that both the necessity to intercalate and to begin a new month was before 383 BC established by direct observation, not by computation. The standardized intercalation cycle is attested with full certainty only from 367 BC on. For Assyrian royal orders concerning intercalation see *LAS* 190 and 287, and the relevant commentaries; note also *LAS* 10+, 38 and 325.

[670] Cf. *LAS* 96f, 100ff, 119, 323, 329; *ABL* 162; *RMA* 87A, 137, 139, 155, etc.

[671] These reports state that Mars had passed a stationary phase in Scorpio and was, by Du'ūzu 1, moving "forwards" (= eastward) in the said constellation. The stationary point in question is with certainty identifiable as that of June 20, 667 BC (see App. C3). If year 668 had not been intercalary in Assyria, Du'uzu 667 would have begun on June 5, a correlation wholly incompatible with the content of *RMA* 68 and 70.

Year	Intercalary month	Evidence
*665	*Addāru	inferred
*662	*Addāru	inferred
*659	*Ulūlu	inferred
657	*Addāru	*LAS* 110 (see commentary)
654	Addāru (Babylonia)	YBC 11309 (*JNES* 3 p. 44[13])
651	Ulūlu	*TCS* 5 129:7 (cf. *LAS* 109 r2ff)

2. Table for converting Assyrian dates into Julian ones[672]

ESARHADDON

Year	BC	Nis	Aja	Sim	Duz	Abu	Ulu	U II	Taš	Ara	Kis	Kan	Šab	Add	AII
Ac	*681*	3/13	4/12	5/11	6/10	7/9	8/7	9/6	10/5	11/5	12/4	1/2	2/1	3/3	
1	680	4/1	5/1	5/30	6/29	7/28	8/26		9/25	10/24	11/23	12/22	1/21	2/20	
2	679	3/21	4/20	5/19	6/18	7/17	8/16		9/14	10/14	11/13	12/12	1/11	2/9	
3	*678*	3/10	4/9	5/8	6/7	7/7	8/5	9/4	10/4	11/2	12/2	12/31	1/29	2/28	
4	677	3/28	4/27	5/26	6/25	7/24	8/23		9/22	10/22	11/20	12/20	1/18	2/16	
5	*676*	3/18	4/16	5/16	6/14	7/13	8/12		9/11	10/11	11/10	12/9	1/8	2/6	3/7
6	675	4/6	5/5	6/4	7/3	8/2	8/31		9/30	10/30	11/28	12/28	1/27	2/25	
7	674	3/27	4/25	5/24	6/23	7/22	8/20		9/19	10/19	11/17	12/17	1/16	2/14	
8	*673*	3/15	4/14	5/13	6/11	7/11	8/9		9/7	10/7	11/5	12/5	1/4	2/3	3/4
9	672	4/3	5/3	6/1	7/1	7/30	8/28		9/26	10/26	11/24	12/24	1/23	2/21	
10	671	3/23	4/22	5/21	6/20	7/20	8/18		9/16	10/16	11/24	12/13	1/12	2/10	
11	*670*	3/12	4/11	5/10	6/9	7/9	8/7	9/6	10/5	11/4	12/3	1/1	1/31	2/29	
12	669	3/30	4/28	5/28	6/27	7/26	8/25		9/24	10/23					

ASSURBANIPAL

Year	BC	Nis	Aja	Sim	Duz	Abu	Ulu	U II	Taš	Ara	Kis	Kan	Šab	Add	AII
Ac	669										11/22	12/21	1/20	2/18	
1	*668*	3/19	4/17	5/16	6/15	7/16	8/14		9/13	10/13	11/11	12/10	1/9	2/7	3/9
2	667	4/7	5/6	6/5	7/5	8/3	9/2		10/2	10/31	11/30	12/29	1/28	2/26	
3	666	3/28	4/26	5/25	6/24	7/23	8/22		9/21	10/20	11/19	12/19	1/17	2/16	
4	*665*	3/16	4/15	5/14	6/12	7/12	8/10		9/9	10/8	11/7	12/7	1/6	2/4	3/6
5	664	4/4	5/4	6/2	7/2	7/31	8/29		9/28	10/27	11/26	12/26	1/24	2/23	
6	663	3/25	4/23	5/23	6/21	7/20	8/19		9/17	10/16	11/15	12/15	1/13	2/12	
7	*662*	3/14	4/12	5/12	6/10	7/10	8/8		9/7	10/6	11/5	12/4	1/3	2/1	3/2
8	661	3/31	4/30	5/30	6/28	7/28	8/26		9/25	10/24	11/23	12/22	1/21	2/19	
9	660	3/21	4/19	5/19	6/17	7/17	8/16		9/14	10/14	11/12	12/12	1/10	2/9	
10	*659*	3/10	4/8	5/8	6/6	7/6	8/4	9/3	10/3	11/2	12/1	12/31	1/29	2/28	
11	658	3/29	4/27	5/27	6/25	7/25	8/23		9/22	10/22	11/21	12/20	1/19	2/17	
12	*657*	3/18	4/16	5/15	6/14	7/13	8/11		9/10	10/10	11/9	12/9	1/7	2/6	3/7

672 The dates in this table have been computed with the new moon tables of Karl Schoch in Lagdon + Fotheringham, *The Venus Tablets of Ammizaduga* (1928), and for the most part double-checked by means of P.V. Neugebauer's *Abgekürzte Tafeln des Mondes* (1905). The table itself is styled after the conventions of Parker + Dubberstein, *op. cit.*, p. 26ff. Thus the dates are given as civil days, from midnight to midnight, although the Mesopotamian day began in each case with the preceding sunset. The dates given are those of the first day of each month. Leap years are indicated by italics. In the interest of economy of space, months are designated by Arabic not Roman numerals, e.g. 4/5 = April 5. The Assyrian month names (see following note) are abbreviated to their first three letters.

Year	BC	Nis	Aja	Sim	Duz	Abu	Ulu	UII	Taš	Ara	Kis	Kan	Šab	Add	AII
13	656	4/6	5/5	6/3	7/3	8/1	8/30		9/29	10/29	11/27	12/27	1/26	2/25	
14	655	3/26	4/25	5/24	6/22	7/22	8/20		9/18	10/18	11/17	12/16	1/15	2/14	
15	*654*	3/16	4/14	5/12	6/12	7/11	8/10		9/8	10/7	11/6	12/5	1/4	2/3	3/4
16	653	4/2	5/2	5/31	6/30	7/29	8/28		9/26	10/26	11/24	12/24	1/22	2/21	
17	652	3/22	4/21	5/20	6/19	7/19	8/17		9/16	10/15	11/14	12/13	1/11	2/10	
18	*651*	3/11	4/10	5/10	6/8	7/8	8/6	9/5	10/5	11/3	12/3	1/1	1/31	3/1	
19	650	3/30	4/29	5/28	6/27	7/26	8/25		9/24	10/23	11/22	12/22	1/20	2/19	
20	*649*	3/19	4/17	5/17	6/15	7/15	8/13		9/12	10/12	11/10	12/10	1/9	2/7	3/9
21	648	4/7	5/6	6/5	7/4	8/2	9/1		9/31	10/30	11/29	12/29			

3. Table for converting Julian dates into Assyrian ones[673]

Year	Jan	Feb	Mar	Apr	May	Jun	Jul	Aug	Sep	Oct	Nov	Dec
681				I/20	II/20	III/22	IV/22	V/24	VI/26	VI$_2$/26	VII/28	VIII/27
680	IX/29	XI/1	XI/29	I/1	II/1	III/3	IV/3	V/5	VI/7	VII/7	VIII/9	IX/9
679	X/11	XI/12	XII/10	I/12	II/12	III/14	IV/14	V/16	VI/17	VII/18	VIII/19	IX/19
678	X/21	XI/22	XII/21	I/23	II/23	III/25	IV/25	V/26	VI/28	VI$_2$/28	VII/29	VIII/30
677	X/2	XI/4	XII/3	I/5	II/5	III/7	IV/7	V/9	VI/10	VII/10	VIII/11	IX/12
676	X/13	XI/15	XII/14	I/15	II/16	III/17	IV/18	V/20	VI/21	VII/21	VIII/23	IX/23
675	X/24	XI/25	XII/24	XII$_2$/26	I/26	II/28	III/28	IV/30	VI/2	VII/2	VIII/3	IX/5
674	X/5	XI/6	XII/5	I/6	II/7	III/9	IV/9	V/11	VI/13	VII/13	VIII/14	IX/15
673	X/16	XI/17	XII/16	I/18	II/18	III/20	IV/21	V/22	VI/24	VII/25	VIII/26	IX/27
672	X/28	XI/29	XII/27	XII$_2$/29	I/29	III/1	IV/1	V/3	VI/5	VII/6	VIII/7	IX/8
671	X/9	XI/10	XII/9	I/10	II/10	III/12	IV/12	V/13	VI/15	VII/16	VIII/17	IX/18
670	X/20	XI/21	XII/20	I/21	II/21	III/23	IV/23	V/24	VI/26	VI$_2$/26	VII/28	VIII/28
669	X/1	XI/2	XII/2	I/3	II/3	III/5	IV/5	V/7	VI/8	VII/8	VIII/10	IX/10
668	X/12	XI/13	XII/12	I/14	II/15	III/17	IV/17	V/17	VI/19	VII/19	VIII/20	IX/21
667	X/23	XI/24	XII/24	XII$_2$/24	I/25	II/27	III/27	IV/28	V/30	VI/30	VIII/2	IX/2
666	X/4	XI/5	XII/4	I/5	II/6	III/8	IV/8	V/10	VI/11	VII/11	VIII/13	IX/13
665	X/14	XI/16	XII/18	I/17	II/17	III/19	IV/20	V/21	VI/23	VII/23	VIII/25	IX/25
664	X/26	XI/27	XII/26	XII$_2$/27	I/28	II/29	III/30	V/2	VI/4	VII/4	VIII/6	IX/6
663	X/7	XI/9	XII/7	I/8	II/9	III/10	IV/11	V/13	VI/14	VII/15	VIII/17	IX/17
662	X/18	XI/20	XII/18									

4. List of eponyms 681-648[674]

681 Nabû-aḫḫē-ēreš
680 Danānu
679 Issi-Adad-anēnu
678 Nergal-šarru-uṣur
677 Abī-rām
676 Bambâ
675 Nabû-aḫḫē-iddina
674 Šarru-nūrī
673 Atar-ilī
672 Nabû-bēlu-uṣur
671 Kanūnāju
670 Šulmu-Bēl-lašme
669 Šamaš-kāšid-ajābī
668 Mar-larim
667 Gabbāru
666 Kanūnāju of the New Palace
665 Mannu-kı-šarri
664 Šarru-lū-dāri

---

673 This table is based on the preceding one and has been devised for the sake of convenience only. I = Nisannu, II = Ajāru, III = Simannu, IV = Du'ūzu, V = Ābu, VI = Ulūlu, VII = Tašrītu, VIII = Araḫsamna, IX = Kislīmu, X = Kanūnu, XI = Šabāṭu, XII = Addāru.

674 Based on Ungnad, "Eponymen", *RlA* 2, p. 264ff.

663 Bēl-na'id
662 Ṭāb-šār-Sîn
661 Arbīlāju
660 Gīr-ṣapūnu
659 Silim-Aššur
658 Ša-Nabû-šū
657 Lā-(a)bāši
656 Milki-rāmu
655 Awjānu
654 Aššur-nāṣir
653 Aššur-ilā'a
652 Aššur-dūru-uṣur
651 Sagab
650 Bēl-Ḫarrān-šadû'a
649 Aḫī-ilā'a
648 Bēlšunu

APPENDIX B

LUNAR CONSTELLATIONS

The Zodiac in our sense did not exist in Sargonid times, though its individual constellations had already been "known" for a long time.[675] Hence the positions of the sun, moon and the planets were not indicated by degrees with reference to 12 schematic signs of 30° each, as from the Neo-Babylonian period on,[676] but with reference to 17 zoomorphic constellations (and parts of their bodies) through which the planets and the moon passed in their orbits. These constellations are listed in the first tablet of the series Mul Apin:

[MULM]UL MULGUD.AN.NA MULSIPA.ZI.AN.NA MULŠU.GI 34 [MULZ]UBI MULMAŠ.TAB.BA. GAL.GAL MULAL.LUL MULUR.GU.LA 35 [MULA]B.S[ÍN MULZ]*i-ba-ni-tum* MULGÍR.TAB MULPA.BIL.SAG 36 [MULSUḪUR.MÁŠKU₆ MU]LGU.LA MULKUNMEŠ MULSIM.MAḪ 37 [MUL*A-nu-ni-t*]*um* MUL.LÚḪUN.GÁ 38 [PAP *an-nu-tum* DINGIRMEŠ *š*]*a ina* KASKAL d*30* GUBMEŠ*-ma* d*30 e-ma* ITU 39 [*pi-rik-šú-nu* DIB]MEŠ*-ma* TAGMEŠ*-šú-nu-ti*[677]

"The Pleiades, Taurus, Orion, Perseus, Auriga, Gemini, Cancer, Leo, Virgo, Libra, Scorpio, Sagittarius, Capricorn, Aquarius, the "Tails" (i.e. the two Fishes), SW Pisces, NE Pisces, Aries. These are the gods standing on the path of the moon, (the gods) through whose sectors the moon passes every month and whom he touches."[678]

The boundaries of these constellations certainly differed in *minor details* from their modern counterparts,[679] but taking into consideration the continuity of the astrological tradition (Ptolemy) it can be taken for granted that *on the whole* the shapes and extensions of the zodiacal constellations at least have remained unaltered through the millennia. With the help of the *Sterntafeln* of P.V. Neugebauer (1912),[680] the boundaries of these constellations valid in the Sargonid period can then be approximately defined as follows:

Aries (β - 41 Arietis)	354° - 7°
Taurus (σ - ζ Tauri)	16° - 46°
Pleiades	19° - 20°
Hyades	28° - 32°
Orion (α - γ Orionis)	47° - 53°
Perseus (α Persei - ι Aurigae)	11° - 33°
Auriga (α - ϑ Aurigae)	33° - 45°
Gemini (η - β Geminorum)	54° - 75°
Castor, Pollux	71°, 75°
Cancer (β + δ Cancri)	87° - 92°
Leo (λ - β Leonis)	102° - 141°
Regulus	115°
Virgo (β - μ Virginis)	142° - 187°
Spica	167°

675 Cf. B.L. van der Waerden, *AfO* 16 (1953) 216 ff.
676 Cf. van der Waerden, *Anfänge der Astronomie* (1968) 97ff.
677 BM 86378 iv 33-39 (*CT* 33 pl.8); restorations from AO 7540 iii 7-14 (Weidner, *AJSL* 40 189f).
678 For the identifications of the individual constellations see F. Gössmann, *Planetarium* (1950).
679 Cf. e.g. van der Waerden, *op. cit.* fig.7 (p. 66).
680 Necessary to eliminate the effects of the precession of equinoxes.

Libra (α^2 - τ Librae)	188° - 197°
Scorpio (ρ - G Scorpii)	201° - 224°
Antares	209°
Sagittarius (γ - ρ^1 Sagittarii)	230° - 251°
Capricorn (ξ^2 - δ Capricorni)	264° - 288°
Aquarius (β - c^2 Aquarii)	287° - 309°
Pisces (α - β Piscium)	313° - 353°
SW Fishes (ϵ - β Piscium)	313° - 343°
NE Fishes (β Andromedae - α Piscium)	343° - 353°

These values (corresponding to the situation in 670 BC) have been used in the preparation of the following tables (mainly covering the years 680-660 BC).

APPENDIX C

HELIACAL PHENOMENA OF MERCURY, VENUS, MARS AND JUPITER[681]

1. Mercury: Heliacal risings and settings for Babylon 681-663 BC

Year			Date		Place		
681	e	last	Apr	8 = Nis 27	18°	Taurus (Pleiades)	
	m	first	May	8 = Aja 27	17°	Taurus (Pleiades)	
	m	last	May	22 = Sim 12	33°	Taurus (Hyades)	
	e	first	Jun	21 = Duz 12	94°	Cancer	
	e	last	Aug	2 = Abu 25	145°	Virgo	
	m	first	Aug	25 = Ulu 19	132°	Leo	
	m	last	Sep	18 = U II 13	160°	Virgo	
	e	first	Nov	7 = Ara 3	239°	Sagittarius	
	e	last	Nov	23 = Ara 19	250°	Sagittarius	
	m	first	Dec	8 = Kis 5	236°	Sagittarius	
680	m	last	Jan	23 = Kan 22	285°	Capricorn	
	e	first	Feb	26 = Šab 26	348°	Pisces (NE)	
	e	last	Mar	9 = Add 7	0°	Aries	
							Ash 1
	m	first	Apr	15 = Nis 15	355°	Aries	
	m	last	May	5 = Aja 5	16°	Taurus/Perseus	
	e	first	Jun	4 = Sim 6	77°	Gemini (Pollux)	
	e	last	Jul	19 = Duz 21	128°	Leo	
	m	first	Aug	10 = Abu 14	116°	Leo (Regulus)	
	m	last	Aug	31 = Ulu 6	140°	Leo	
	e	first	Oct	24 = Ara 1	226°	Scorpio/Sagittarius	
	e	last	Nov	4 = Ara 12	235°	Sagittarius	
	m	first	Nov	22 = Ara 30	220°	Scorpio	
679	m	last	Jan	5 = Kan 15	267°	Capricorn	
	e	first	Feb	3 = Šab 14	319°	Pisces (SW)	
	e	last	Feb	28 = Add 9	343°	Pisces (NE)	
							Ash 2

681 Computed for the horizon of Babylon with the tables of Schoch (1928); for Nineveh an error of a day or two must be reckoned with. m(orning)/e(vening) first = first visibility in the morning, etc. For the correlations between Julian and Mesopotamian dates see App. A. The planetary longitudes which are not computable with the tables of Schoch (Mercury) are those given by Stahlman and Gingerich (1963).

Year			Date	Place		
						Ash 2
	m first	Mar	28 = Nis 8	336°	Pisces (SW)	
	m last	Apr	18 = Nis 29	0°	Aries	
	e first	May	18 = Aja 29	60°	Gemini	
	e last	Jul	3 = Duz 16	110°	Leo	
	m first	Jul	25 = Abu 9	99°	Cancer/Leo	
	m last	Aug	25 = Ulu 10	144°	Virgo	
	e first	Oct	15 = Ara 2	216°	Scorpio	
	e last	Oct	16 = Ara 3	217°	Scorpio	
	m first	Nov	6 = Ara 24	205°	Scorpio	
	m last	Dec	19 = Kis 1	249°	Sagittarius	
678	e first	Jan	19 = Šab 9	304°	Aquarius	
	e last	Feb	10 = Add 2	325°	Pisces (SW)	
	m first	Mar	2 = Add 22	314°	Pisces (SW)	
						Ash 3
	m last	Apr	2 = Nis 24	340°	Pisces (SW)	
	e first	May	2 = Aja 24	43°	Taurus/Auriga	
	e last	Jun	15 = Duz 9	91°	Cancer	
	m first	Jul	11 = Abu 5	83°	(Gemini –– Cancer)	
	m last	Jul	18 = Abu 12	89°	Cancer	
	e first	Aug	22 = Ulu 18	148°	Virgo	
	e last	Sep	30 = U II 27	201°	Scorpio	
	m first	Oct	21 = Taš 12	191°	Libra	
	m last	Nov	29 = Ara 28	230°	Sagittarius	
677	e first	Jan	2 = Kan 3	288°	Capricorn/Aquarius	
	e last	Jan	25 = Kan 26	308°	Aquarius	
	m first	Feb	6 = Šab 9	298°	Aquarius	
						Ash 4
	m last	Mar	18 = Add 20	297°	Aquarius	
	e first	Apr	16 = Nis 20	29°	Taurus (Hyades)	
	e last	May	28 = Sim 3	70°	Gemini (Castor)	
	m first	Jun	29 = Duz 5	78°	Gemini (Pollux)	
	m last	Jul	10 = Duz 16	88°	Cancer	
	e first	Aug	16 = Abu 24	155°	Virgo	
	e last	Sep	13 = Ulu 22	186°	Virgo/Libra	
	m first	Oct	5 = Taš 14	174°	Virgo	
	m last	Nov	13 = Ara 23	214°	Scorpio	
	e first	Dec	20 = Kan 1	279°	Capricorn	
676	e last	Jan	7 = Kan 19	292°	Aquarius	
	m first	Jan	21 = Šab 4	281°	Capricorn	
	m last	Mar	2 = Add 15	316°	Pisces (SW)	
						Ash 5
	e first	Mar	31 = Nis 14	13°	Perseus	
	e last	May	9 = Aja 24	52°	Orion	
	m first	Jun	18 = Duz 5	61°	Gemini	
	m last	Jun	21 = Duz 8	65°	Gemini	
	e first	Jul	23 = Abu 11	130°	Leo	
	e last	Aug	28 = Ulu 17	170°	Virgo (Spica)	
	m first	Sep	20 = Taš 10	158°	Virgo	
	m last	Nov	12 = Kis 3	228°	(Scorpio –– Sagittarius)	

	e	first	Dec 3 = Kis 25	261°	(Sagittarius — Capricorn)
	e	last	Dec 21 = Kan 13	276°	Capricorn
675	m	first	Jan 3 = Kan 26	264°	Capricorn
	m	last	Feb 15 = Add 10	303°	Aquarius
	e	first	Mar 16 = A II 10	359°	Aries
					Ash 6
	e	last	Apr 20 = Nis 15	32°	Taurus (Hyades)
	m	first	May 30 = Aja 26	40°	Taurus/Auriga
	m	last	Jun 4 = Sim 1	52°	Orion
	e	first	Jul 6 = Duz 4	111°	Leo
	e	last	Aug 12 = Abu 11	154°	Virgo
	m	first	Sep 4 = Ulu 5	142°	Leo/Virgo
	m	last	Sept 30 = Taš 1	168°	Virgo (Spica)
	e	first	Nov 8 = Ara 10	233°	Sagittarius
	e	last	Dec 3 = Kis 7	259°	(Sagittarius — Capricorn)
	m	first	Dec 17 = Kis 21	246°	Sagittarius
674	m	last	Feb 1 = Šab 6	299°	Aquarius
	e	first	Mar 1 = Add 5	346°	Pisces (NE)
					Ash 7
	e	last	Mar 31 = Nis 5	12°	Perseus
	m	first	May 10 = Aja 16	23°	Taurus
	m	last	May 15 = Aja 21	26°	Taurus
	e	first	Jun 14 = Sim 22	86°	Cancer
	e	last	Jul 28 = Abu 7	138°	Leo
	m	first	Aug 19 = Abu 29	126°	Leo
	m	last	Sep 10 = Ulu 22	148°	Virgo
	e	first	Nov 1 = Ara 14	231°	Sagittarius
	e	last	Nov 15 = Ara 28	244°	Sagittarius
	m	first	Dec 1 = Kis 15	230°	Sagittarius
673	m	last	Jan 16 = Šab 1	276°	Capricorn
	e	first	Feb 13 = Šab 29	328°	Pisces (SW)
	e	last	Mar 10 = Add 25	354°	Aries
					Ash 8
	m	first	Apr 12 = Nis 29	349°	Pisces (NE)
	m	last	Apr 27 = Aja 14	7°	Aries
	e	first	May 27 = Sim 15	69°	Gemini (Castor)
	e	last	Jul 12 = Abu 2	120°	Leo
	m	first	Aug 3 = Abu 24	109°	Leo
	m	last	Aug 23 = Ulu 15	133°	Leo
	e	first	Oct 17 = Ara 11	220°	Scorpio
	e	last	Oct 27 = Ara 21	229°	Sagittarius
	m	first	Nov 15 = Kis 11	213°	Scorpio
	m	last	Dec 29 = Kan 25	260°	(Sagittarius — Capricorn)
672	e	first	Jan 28 = Šab 25	315°	Pisces (SW)
	e	last	Feb 20 = Add 18	335°	Pisces (SW)
	m	first	Mar 16 = A II 13	325°	Pisces (SW)
					Ash 9
	m	last	Apr 11 = Nis 9	351°	Pisces (NE)
	e	first	May 11 = Aja 9	52°	Orion
	e	last	Jun 25 = Sim 25	103°	Leo
	m	first	Jul 18 = Duz 18	92°	Cancer
	m	last	Aug 7 = Abu 9	117°	Leo (Regulus)

Year			Date	Longitude	Position	
	e	first	Sep 26 = Taš 1	198°	Libra/Scorpio	
	e	last	Oct 9 = Taš 14	210°	Scorpio (Antares)	
	m	first	Oct 18 = Taš 23	209°	Scorpio (Antares)	
	m	last	Dec 10 = Kis 17	242°	Sagittarius	
671	e	first	Jan 12 = Kan 20	291°	Aquarius	
	e	last	Feb 3 = Šab 12	317°	Pisces (SW)	
	m	first	Feb 21 = Add 1	306°	Aquarius	
						Ash 10
	m	last	Mar 26 = Nis 4	336°	Pisces (SW)	
	e	first	May 9 = Aja 18	62°	Gemini	
	e	last	Jun 8 = Sim 19	83°	(Gemini –– Cancer)	
	m	first	Jul 5 = Duz 16	76°	Gemini (Pollux)	
	m	last	Jul 21 = Abu 2	99°	(Cancer –– Leo)	
	e	first	Aug 31 = Ulu 14	171°	Virgo	
	e	last	Sep 23 = Taš 8	195°	Libra	
	m	first	Oct 15 = Taš 30	182°	Virgo	
	m	last	Nov 21 = Kis 8	224°	Scorpio	
	e	first	Dec 27 = Kan 15	283°	Capricorn	
670	e	last	Jan 19 = Šab 8	300°	Aquarius	
	m	first	Feb 1 = Šab 21	290°	Aquarius	
						Ash 11
	m	last	Mar 12 = Nis 1	324°	Pisces (SW)	
	e	first	Apr 10 = Nis 30	22°	Taurus (Pleiades)	
	e	last	May 21 = Sim 12	62°	Gemini	
	m	first	Jun 25 = Duz 17	65°	Gemini	
	m	last	Jul 3 = Duz 25	80°	(Gemini –– Cancer)	
	e	first	Aug 7 = Ulu 1	146°	Virgo	
	e	last	Sep 7 = U II 2	180°	Virgo	
	m	first	Sep 30 = U II 25	167°	Virgo (Spica)	
	m	last	Oct 31 = Taš 27	202°	Scorpio	
	e	first	Dec 11 = Kis 9	268°	Capricorn	
669	e	last	Jan 1 = Kan 1	285°	Capricorn	
	m	first	Jan 14 = Kan 14	273°	Capricorn	
	m	last	Feb 25 = Šab 26	311°	(Aquarius –– Pisces)	
	e	first	Mar 24 = Add 25	6°	Aries	
						Ash 12
	e	last	Apr 30 = Aja 2	44°	Taurus	
	m	first	Jun 10 = Sim 14	52°	Orion	
	m	last	Jun 13 = Sim 17	58°	Gemini	
	e	first	Jul 14 = Duz 18	117°	Leo (Regulus)	
	e	last	Aug 20 = Abu 26	140°	Leo	
	m	first	Sep 12 = Ulu 19	163°	Virgo	
	m	last	Oct 11 = Taš 18	192°	Libra	
	e	first	Nov 26 = Kis 5	238°	Sagittarius	
	e	last	Dec 22 = Kan 2	265°	Capricorn	
668	m	first	Jan 4 = Kan 15	278°	Capricorn	
	m	last	Feb 9 = Šab 21	297°	Aquarius	
	e	first	Mar 9 = Add 20	352°	Pisces (NE)	
						Asb 1
	e	last	Apr 25 = Aja 9	17°	Taurus (Pleiades)	
	m	first	May 21 = Sim 6	31°	Taurus (Hyades)	
	m	last	May 24 = Sim 9	35°	Taurus/Auriga	

	e	first	Jun 23 = Duz 9	95°	(Cancer –– Leo)	
	e	last	Aug 5 = Abu 21	148°	Virgo	
	m	first	Aug 28 = Ulu 15	136°	Leo	
	m	last	Sep 20 = Taš 8	159°	Virgo	
	e	first	Nov 10 = Ara 29	241°	Sagittarius	
	e	last	Nov 26 = Kis 16	252°	Sagittarius	
	m	first	Dec 10 = Kan 1	239°	Sagittarius	
667	m	last	Jan 25 = Šab 17	284°	Capricorn	
	e	first	Feb 22 = Add 16	338°	Pisces (SW)	
	e	last	Mar 22 = A II 14	4°	Aries	
						Asb 2
	m	first	Apr 29 = Nis 23	7°	Aries	
	m	last	May 8 = Aja 3	22°	Taurus/Perseus	
	e	first	Jun 7 = Sim 3	80°	(Gemini – Cancer)	
	e	last	Jul 22 = Duz 18	130°	Leo	
	m	first	Aug 13 = Abu 11	119°	Leo	
	m	last	Sep 2 = Ulu 1	139°	Leo	
	e	first	Oct 26 = Taš 25	227°	(Scorpio –– Sagittarius)	
	e	last	Nov 7 = Ara 8	237°	Sagittarius	
	m	first	Nov 24 = Ara 25	223°	Scorpio	
666	m	last	Jan 8 = Kan 11	269°	Capricorn	
	e	first	Feb 6 = Šab 10	322°	Pisces (SW)	
	e	last	Mar 3 = Add 6	346°	Pisces (NE)	
						Asb 3
	m	first	Apr 1 = Nis 5	339°	Pisces (SW)	
	m	last	Apr 21 = Nis 25	1°	Aries	
	e	first	May 21 = Aja 26	66°	Gemini	
	e	last	Jul 5 = Sim 12	113°	Leo (Regulus)	
	m	first	Jul 27 = Abu 5	101°	Leo	
	m	last	Aug 17 = Abu 26	126°	Leo	
	e	first	Oct 10 = Taš 20	212°	Scorpio	
	e	last	Oct 20 = Ara 1	221°	Scorpio	
	m	first	Nov 9 = Ara 21	207°	Scorpio (Antares)	
	m	last	Dec 22 = Kan 4	253°	Sagittarius	
665	e	first	Jan 22 = Šab 6	307°	Aquarius	
	e	last	Feb 13 = Šab 28	328°	Pisces (SW)	
	m	first	Mar 5 = Add 22	317°	Pisces (SW)	
						Asb 4
	m	last	Apr 4 = Nis 20	348°	Pisces (NE)	
	e	first	May 4 = Aja 20	46°	Taurus/Orion	
	e	last	Jun 17 = Duz 6	95°	(Cancer –– Leo)	
	m	first	Jul 11 = Duz 30	85°	Cancer	
	m	last	Jul 30 = Abu 19	109°	Leo	
	e	first	Sep 15 = Taš 7	188°	Libra	
	e	last	Oct 2 = Taš 24	205°	Scorpio	
	m	first	Oct 23 = Aja 16	192°	Libra	
	m	last	Dec 2 = Kis 26	235°	Sagittarius	
664	e	first	Jan 5 = Kan 30	292°	Aquarius	
	e	last	Jan 27 = Šab 22	311°	(Aquarius –– Pisces)	
	m	first	Feb 12 = Add 9	298°	Aquarius	
	m	last	Mar 11 = A II 6	318°	Pisces (SW)	

					Asb 5
	e first	Apr 19 = Nis 22	32°	Taurus (Hyades)	
	e last	May 31 = Aja 28	74°	Gemini (Pollux)	
	m first	Jun 30 = Sim 29	71°	Gemini (Castor)	
	m last	Jul 13 = Duz 12	91°	Cancer	
	e first	Aug 21 = Abu 22	161°	Virgo	
	e last	Sep 15 = Ulu 18	188°	Libra	
	m first	Oct 7 = Taš 10	176°	Virgo	
	m last	Nov 16 = Ara 21	221°	Scorpio	
	e first	Dec 23 = Kis 28	282°	Capricorn	
663	e last	Jan 15 = Kan 21	290°	Aquarius	
	m first	Jan 24 = Šab 1	282°	Capricorn	
	m last	Mar 5 = Add 11	316°	Pisces (SW)	
					Asb 6
	e first	Apr 3 = Nis 10	16°	Taurus/Perseus	
	e last	May 12 = Aja 20	54°	Gemini	
	m first	Jun 21 = Duz 1	66°	Gemini	
	m last	Jun 25 = Duz 5	73°	Gemini (Castor + Pollux)	
	e first	Jul 27 = Abu 8	133°	Leo	
	e last	Jul 30 = Abu 11	138°	Leo	
	m first	Sep 22 = Taš 6	160°	Virgo	
	m last	Oct 22 = Ara 7	193°	Libra	
	e first	Dec 7 = Kis 23	267°	Capricorn	
	e last	Dec 23 = Kan 9	279°	Capricorn	
662	m first	Jan 5 = Kan 22	267°	Capricorn	

2. Venus: Heliacal risings and settings for Babylon 681-663 BC

Year		Date	Place	
681	m last	Dec 6 = Kis 3	242°	Sagittarius
680	e first	Jan 29 = Kan 28	310°	Aquarius
	e last	Oct 5 = Taš 11	205°	Scorpio
	m first	Oct 22 = Taš 28	195°	Libra
679	m last	Jul 6 = Duz 19	88°	Cancer
	e first	Sep 7 = Ulu 23	166°	Virgo (Spica)
678	e last	May 21 = Sim 14	56°	Gemini
	m first	May 30 = Sim 23	51°	Orion
677	m last	Feb 6 = Šab 9	300°	Aquarius
	e first	Apr 10 = Nis 14	20°	Taurus (Pleiades)
	e last	Dec 29 = Kan 10	276°	Capricorn
676	m first	Jan 1 = Kan 13	274°	Capricorn
	m last	Sep 21 = Taš 11	165°	Virgo (Spica)
	e first	Nov 19 = Kis 10	240°	Sagittarius
675	e last	Jul 24 = Duz 22	128°	Leo
	m first	Aug 8 = Abu 7	119°	Leo
674	m last	Apr 7 = Nis 12	357°	Aries
	e first	Jun 20 = Sim 28	88°	Cancer
673	e last	Mar 10 = Add 25	348°	Pisces (NE)
	m first	Mar 12 = Add 27	346°	Pisces (NE)
	m last	Dec 4 = Kis 30	240°	Sagittarius

672	e first	Jan 27 = Šab 24	309°	Aquarius
	e last	Oct 2 = Taš 7	203°	Scorpio
	m first	Oct 19 = Taš 24	194°	Libra
671	m last	Jul 3 = Duz 14	85°	Cancer
	e first	Sep 4 = Ulu 18	162°	Virgo
670	e last	May 19 = Sim 10	54°	Orion/Gemini
	m first	May 29 = Sim 20	48°	Orion
669	m last	Feb 5 = Šab 6	301°	Aquarius
	e first	Apr 8 = Nis 10	18°	Taurus (Pleiades)
	e last	Dec 27 = Kan 7	273°	Capricorn
	m first	Dec 30 = Kan 10	271°	Capricorn
668	m last	Sep 19 = Taš 7	163°	Virgo
	e first	Nov 18 = Kis 8	239°	Sagittarius
667	e last	Jul 21 = Duz 17	123°	Leo
	m first	Aug 7 = Abu 5	116°	Leo (Regulus)
666	m last	Apr 5 = Nis 9	354°	Aries
	e first	Jun 17 = Sim 24	84°	(Gemini — Cancer)
665	e last	Mar 8 = Add 25	345°	Pisces (NE)
	m first	Mar 10 = Add 27	344°	Pisces (NE)
	m last	Dec 2 = Kis 26	238°	Sagittarius
664	e first	Jan 25 = Šab 21	306°	Aquarius
	e last	Sep 31 = Taš 3	200°	Scorpio
	m first	Oct 17 = Taš 20	191°	Libra
663	m last	Jul 7 = Duz 17	91°	Cancer
	e first	Sep 5 = Ulu 18	165°	Virgo (Spica)

3a. Mars: Heliacal risings and settings for Babylon 681-650 BC

Year		Date	Place		Interval	m
681	e last	Jun 2 = Sim 23	80°.1	Gemini – Cancer		
	m first	Sep 3 = Ulu 28	138°.1	Leo	93d	+1.9
679	e last	Jul 3 = Duz 16	109°.2	Leo		
	m first	Oct 11 = Taš 28	177°.2	Virgo	102d	+1.8
677	e last	Jul 31 = Taš 9	140°.7	Leo		
	m first	Nov 26 = Kis 7	225°.7	Scorpio	119d	+1.5
675	e last	Sep 3 = Ulu 4	176°.1	Virgo		
674	m first	Mar 20 = Add 24	326°.1	Pisces (SW)	198d	+1.5
673	e last	Nov 21 = Ara 17	243°.7	Sagittarius		
672	m first	May 31 = Aja 29	28°.7	Taurus (Hyades)	191d	+1.5
670	e last	Feb 15 = Add 6	334°.0	Pisces (SW)		
	m first	Jun 25 = Duz 17	63°.0	Gemini	130d	+1.6
668	e last	Apr 11 = Nis 24	27°.4	Taurus (Hyades)		
	m first	Jul 28 = Abu 13	98°.4	Cancer – Leo	108d	+1.8
666	e last	May 21 = Aja 26	66°.6	Gemini		
	m first	Aug 23 = Ulu 2	126°.6	Leo	93d	+1.9
664	e last	Jun 18 = Duz 17	99°.0	Cancer – Leo		
	m first	Sep 24 = Ulu 27	161°.0	Virgo	98d	+1.9

662	e last	Jul 17 = Abu 9	128°0	Leo		
	m first	Nov 4 = Ara 28	205°1	Scorpio	110^d	+1.7
660	e last	Aug 19	161°4	Virgo		
659	m first	Jan 20	276°4	Capricorn	154^d	+1.5
658	e last	Oct 5	208°4	Scorpio (Antares)		
657	m first	May 2 = Aja 17	10°4	Aries/Perseus	210^d	+1.5
655	e last	Jan 15	303°7	Aquarius		
	m first	Jun 13	50°7	Orion	149^d	+1.5
653	e last	Mar 24	10°4	Aries/Perseus		
	m first	Jul 13	84°4	Cancer	111^d	+1.7
651	e last	May 7	54°0	Gemini		
	m first	Aug 13	116°0	Leo (Regulus)	98^d	+1.9

3b. Mars: Oppositions and stationary points for Babylon 681-650 BC

Year		Date	λ		β	m
680	a	Jul 28 = Abu 1	331°7	(SW Pisces)		
	opp.	Aug 27 = Ulu 2	326°7	(SW Pisces)	-5	-2.4
	b	Sep 20 = Taš 4	321°7	(SW Pisces)		
678	a	Sep 19 = U II 16	35°0	(Taurus)		
	opp.	Oct 26 = Taš 23	26°0	(Taurus)	0	-1.8
	b	Dec 1 = Ara 30	17°0	(Taurus)		
676	a	Oct 25 = Ara 15	76°5	(Gemini)		
	opp.	Dec 4 = Kis 26	66°5	(Gemini)	+3	-1.3
675	b	Jan 12 = Šab 5	56°5	(Gemini)		
674	a	Nov 30 = Kis 14	111°3	(Leo)		
673	opp.	Jan 8 = Kan 23	100°3	(Cancer – Leo)	+5	-1.1
	b	Feb 19 = Add 6	91°3	(Cancer)		
671	a	Jan 4 = Kan 12	144°7	(Virgo)		
	opp.	Feb 11 = Šab 20	135°7	(Leo)	+4	-1.3
	b	Mar 26 = Nis 4	126°7	(Leo)		
669	a	Feb 15 = Šab 16	182°6	(Virgo)		
	opp.	Mar 22 = Add 23	174°6	(Virgo)	+3	-1.7
	b	May 1 = Aja 3	166°6	(Virgo/Spica)		
667	a	Apr 5 = Add 29	233°8	(Sagittarius)		
	opp.	May 17 = Aja 12	227°8	(Scorp. – Sag.)	-3	-2.4
	b	Jun 20 = Sim 16	221°8	(Scorpio)		
665	a	Jun 23 = Duz 12	302°8	(Aquarius)		
	opp.	Jul 24 = Abu 13	296°8	(Aquarius)	-6	-2.6
	b	Aug 25 = Ulu 16	290°8	(Aquarius)		
663	a	Aug 31 = Ulu 13	15°5	(Perseus)		
	opp.	Oct 7 = Taš 21	7°5	(Aries)	-2	-2.0
	b	Nov 10 = Ara 26	359°5	(Aries)		
661	a	Oct 9	62°0	(Gemini)		
	opp.	Nov 20	52°0	(Orion)	+2	-1.4
	b	Dec 28	42°0	(Auriga)		

659	a	Nov 17	98°4	(Cancer – Leo)		
	opp.	Dec 26	88°4	(Cancer)	+4	-1.1
658	b	Feb 6	78°4	(Gemini – Cancer)		
657	a	Dec 20	132°2	(Leo)		
656	opp.	Jan 26	122°2	(Leo)	+5	-1.2
	b	Mar 12	112°2	(Leo)		
654	a	Jan 28	167°8	(Virgo/Spica)		
	opp.	Mar 6	158°8	(Virgo)	+4	-1.4
	b	Apr 17	149°8	(Virgo)		
652	a	Mar 20	210°5	(Scorpio)		
	opp.	Apr 22	204°5	(Scorpio)	0	-2.1
	b	May 29	198°5	(Libra – Scorpio)		
650	a	Jun 9	282°9	(Capricorn)		
	opp.	Jul 11	275°9	(Capricorn)	-6	-2.7
	b	Aug 10	272°9	(Capricorn)		

4a. Jupiter: Heliacal risings and settings (Babylon) 681-663 BC

Year		Date	Place		Interval
681	e last	Apr 25 = Aja 14	35°4	(Taurus)	
	m first	May 25 = Sim 15	42°4	(Auriga)	32,5^d
680	e last	May 29 = Aja 29	68°2	(Gemini)	
	m first	Jun 27 = Sim 29	75°2	(Gemini/Pollux)	28^d
679	e last	Jun 30 = Duz 13	100°5	(Leo)	
	m first	Jul 28 = Abu 12	106°5	(Leo)	28^d
678	e last	Jul 30 = Abu 24	130°9	(Leo)	
	m first	Aug 28 = Ulu 24	136°9	(Leo)	28^d
677	e last	Aug 29 = Ulu 8	159°3	(Virgo)	
	m first	Sep 26 = Taš 5	166°3	(Virgo/Spica)	28^d
676	e last	Sep 29 = Taš 19	191°0	(Libra)	
	m first	Oct 27 = Ara 17	198°0	(Libra)	28^d
675	e last	Oct 30 = Ara 1	222°3	(Scorpio)	
	m first	Nov 27 = Ara 29	229°0	(Sagittarius)	28^d
674	e last	Dec 3 = Kis 17	256°5	(Sag. – Capr.)	
673	m first	Jan 1 = Kan 16	262°5	(Capricorn)	28^d
672	e last	Jan 8 = Šab 5	291°5	(Aquarius)	
	m first	Feb 9 = Add 7	299°0	(Aquarius)	31,5^d
671	e last	Feb 16 = Šab 25	327°8	(SW Pisces)	
	m first	Mar 22 = Add 30	335°8	(SW Pisces)	34^d
670	e last	Mar 26 = Nis 15	4°2	(Aries)	
	m first	Apr 29 = Aja 19	12°5	(Perseus)	34^d
669	e last	Apr 30 = Aja 3	40°3	(Taurus)	
	m first	Jun 1 = Sim 3	47°3	(Orion)	32^d
668	e last	Jun 2 = Sim 18	72°9	(Gemini)	
	m first	Jul 1 = Duz 17	80°0	(Gemini – Cancer)	28^d

667	e last	Jul	4 = Sim 30	104°9	(Leo)	
	m first	Aug	1 = Duz 28	110°9	(Leo)	28[d]
666	e last	Aug	3 = Abu 12	134°4	(Leo)	
	m first	Sep	1 = Ulu 11	141°4	(Virgo)	28[d]
665	e last	Sep	2 = Ulu 24	164°6	(Virgo)	
	m first	Sep	30 = Taš 22	171°6	(Virgo)	28[d]
664	e last	Oct	3 = Taš 6	195°4	(Libra)	
	m first	Oct	31 = Ara 5	202°4	(Scorpio)	28[d]
663	e last	Nov	3 = Ara 19	227°0	(Scorp. – Sag.)	
	m first	Dec	1 = Kis 17	234°0	(Sagittarius)	28[d]

4b. Jupiter: Oppositions and stationary points (Babylon) 681-663 BC

Year		Date		Place		m
681	a	Sep	23 = U II 18	59°6	(Gemini)	
	opp.	Nov	30 = Ara 16	54°6	(Gemini)	-2.3
680	b	Jan	21 = Kan 20	49°6	(Orion)	
	a	Oct	26 = Ara 3	92°3	(Cancer)	
	opp.	Dec	22 = Kan 1	87°3	(Cancer)	-2.2
679	b	Feb	25 = Add 6	82°3	(Gemini – Cancer)	
	a	Nov	26 = Kis 14	123°4	(Leo)	
678	opp.	Jan	22 = Šab 12	118°4	(Leo)	-2.1
	b	Mar	26 = Nis 17	113°4	(Leo/Regulus)	
	a	Dec	27 = Kis 26	153°9	(Virgo)	
677	opp.	Feb	22 = Šab 25	148°9	(Virgo)	-2.0
	b	Apr	28 = Aja 2	143°9	(Virgo)	
676	a	Jan	25 = Šab 8	184°2	(Virgo)	
	opp.	Mar	24 = Nis 7	179°2	(Virgo)	-2.1
	b	May	28 = Sim 13	174°2	(Virgo)	
675	a	Feb	26 = Add 21	215°2	(Scorpio)	
	opp.	Apr	26 = Nis 21	210°2	(Scorpio/Antares)	-2.1
	b	Jun	29 = Sim 26	205°2	(Scorpio)	
674	a	Mar	27 = Nis 1	247°8	(Sagittarius)	
	opp.	May	30 = Sim 7	242°8	(Sagittarius)	-2.2
	b	Aug	2 = Abu 12	237°8	(Sagittarius)	
673	a	May	9 = Aja 26	282°1	(Capricorn)	
	opp.	Jul	5 = Duz 25	277°1	(Capricorn)	-2.3
	b	Sep	5 = Ulu 28	272°1	(Capricorn)	
672	a	Jun	15 = Sim 15	317°9	(SW Pisces)	
	opp.	Aug	10 = Abu 12	312°9	(SW Pisces)	-2.4
	b	Oct	11 = Taš 16	307°9	(Aquarius)	
671	a	Jul	22 = Abu 3	354°9	(Aries)	
	opp.	Sep	17 = Taš 2	349°9	(NW Pisces)	-2.4
	b	Nov	17 = Kis 4	344°9	(NW Pisces)	
670	a	Aug	27 = Ulu 21	30°0	(Taurus [Hyades])	
	opp.	Oct	23 = Taš 19	25°0	(Taurus)	-2.4
	b	Dec	23 = Kis 21	20°0	(Pleiades)	

669	a	Sep 28 = Taš 5	64°5	(Gemini)	
	opp.	Nov 24 = Kis 3	59°5	(Gemini)	-2.3
668	b	Jan 28 = Šab 9	54°5	(Gemini)	
	a	Oct 30 = Taš 18	96°8	(Cancer – Leo)	
	opp.	Dec 26 = Kan 15	91°8	(Cancer)	-2.2
667	b	Feb 28 = Add 23	86°8	(Cancer)	
	a	Nov 30 = Kis 1	127°8	(Leo)	
666	opp.	Jan 26 = Kan 29	122°8	(Leo)	-2.1
	b	Apr 1 = Nis 5	117°8	(Leo)	
	a	Dec 31 = Kan 13	158°1	(Virgo)	
665	opp.	Feb 26 = Add 11	153°1	(Virgo)	-2.0
	b	May 2 = Aja 18	148°1	(Virgo)	
664	a	Jan 30 = Šab 25	188°5	(Libra)	
	opp.	Mar 30 = A II 25	183°5	(Virgo)	-2.1
	b	Jun 2 = Sim 1	178°5	(Virgo)	
663	a	Mar 3 = Add 28	219°7	(Scorpio)	
	opp.	Apr 30 = Aja 8	214°7	(Scorpio)	-2.2
	b	Jul 4 = Duz 14	209°7	(Scorpio/Antares)	

APPENDIX D

SYNOPSIS OF PLANETARY POSITIONS AND PHASES, 680-663 BC[682]

Date	Venus	Mars	Jupiter	Saturn
680				
Jan 7 = Kan 6	Capricorn (282)	Scorpio (223)	Orion (50)	Taurus (26)
Feb 6 = Šab 6	SW Fishes (220) E	Sagittarius (244)	Orion (50)	Taurus (27)
Mar 8 = Add 6	Aries (357) E	Capricorn (264)	Orion (53)	Taurus/Hyades (30)
Apr 7 = Nis 7	Taurus (34) E	Capricorn (285)	Gemini (58)	Taurus (33)
May 7 = Aja 7	Gemini/Castor E	Aquarius (304)	Gemini (64)	Taurus (37)

682 This appendix, based on W. Stahlman's and O. Gingerich's *Solar and Planetary Longitudes for Years -2500 to +2000* (Wisconsin 1963), gives a panoramic view of the movements of the 4 major planets (Mercury excluded because of its rapid movement and short periods of visibility) in relation to the sun and the fixed stars, and is primarily intended to illustrate the astronomical discussions in the Commentary; despite its summariness, it can be profitably used for a preliminary identification of most planetary observations in the periods concerned, though a "final" identification of course requires much more accurate data. The tables contain the following information:
1. Planetary positions with reference to the zodiacal constellations and their most conspicuous stars (App.B) by 30-day intervals; the numbers in ellipses give the respective longitudes; + and - indicate position to the east and west of the given constellation, respectively;
2. Approximate intervals of invisibility, and heliacal risings and settings (cf. App.C), indicated by hatched boxes;
3. Retrograde periods and stationary points (cf. App.C), indicated by vertical lines at the left-hand margins of the planetary columns;
4. For Venus, visibility as evening/morning star, indicated respectively by the letters E and M in the Venus column.

Date	Venus	Mars	Jupiter	Saturn
Jun 6 = Sim 8	Leo (106) E	SW Fishes (323)	Gemini/Castor (71)	Taurus (41)
Jul 6 = Duz 8	Leo (140) E	SW Fishes (335)	Gemini (78)	Taurus (45)
Aug 5 = Abu 9	Virgo (172) E	SW Fishes (338)	Gemini+ (84)	Taurus (47)
Sep 4 = Ulu 10	Libra (197) E	SW Fishes (329)	Cancer (89)	Orion (48)
Oct 4 = Taš 10	Scorpio (205) E	SW Fishes (325)	Cancer (92)	Taurus (47)
Nov 3 = Ara 11	Libra (190) M	SW Fishes (330)	Cancer (92)	Taurus (45)
Dec 3 = Kis 11	Scorpio (201) M	NE Fishes (344)	Cancer (91)	Taurus (43)
679				
Jan 2 = Kan 12	Sagittarius (229) M	Aries (0)	Cancer (87)	Taurus (41)
Feb 1 = Šab 12	-Capricorn (262) M	Taurus/Pleiades (17)	Canc. – Gem. (83)	Taurus (41)
Mar 3 = Add 12	Aquarius (297) M	Taurus (35)	Canc. – Gem. (83)	Taurus (43)
Apr 2 = Nis 13	SW Fishes (332) M	Taurus (53)	Canc. – Gem. (85)	Taurus (46)
May 2 = Aja 13	Aries (8) M	Gemini/Castor (72)	Cancer (88)	Orion (49)
Jun 1 = Sim 14	Taurus (45) M	Cancer (90)	Cancer + (94)	Orion (53)
Jul 1 = Duz 14	Gem. – Canc. (82) M	Leo (109)	Leo (101)	Gemini (57)
Jul 31 = Abu 15	Leo (110)	Leo (128)	Leo (107)	Gemini (60)
Aug 30 = Ulu 15	Virgo (156)	Virgo (148)	Leo/Regulus (114)	Gemini (62)
Sep 29 = Taš 16	Libra (194) E	Virgo/Spica (169)	Leo (119)	Gemini (63)
Oct 29 = Ara 16	Sagittarius (232) E	Libra (189)	Leo (123)	Gemini (62)
Nov 28 = Kis 16	Capricorn (269) E	Scorpio/Ant. (210)	Leo (124)	Gemini (58)
Dec 28 = Kan 17	Aquarius (306) E	Sagittarius (232)	Leo (122)	Gemini (56)
678				
Jan 27 = Šab 17	SW Fishes (342) E	Sagittarius+(254)	Leo (119)	Gemini (55)
Feb 26 = Add 18	Taurus (16) E	Capricorn (276)	Leo/Regulus (115)	Gemini (56)
Mar 28 = Nis 19	Taurus (45) E	Aquarius (299)	Leo (114)	Gemini (58)
Apr 27 = Aja 19	Gemini (63) E	SW Fishes (321)	Leo/Regulus (115)	Gemini (61)
May 27 = Sim 21	Gemini (53)	SW Fishes (342)	Leo (118)	Gemini (65)
Jun 26 = Duz 20	Taurus (48) M	Aries (2)	Leo (124)	Gemini (69)
Jul 26 = Abu 20	Gemini (68) M	Taurus/Pleiades (20)	Leo (130)	Gemini/Castor (72)
Aug 25 = Ulu 21	Can. – Leo (99) M	Taurus/Hyades (33)	Leo (137)	Gemini/Pollux (75)
Sep 24 = U II 21	Leo (133) M	Taurus (35)	Virgo (143)	Gemini (77)
Oct 24 = Taš 21	Virgo (169) M	Taurus/Hyades (27)	Virgo (148)	Gemini (77)
Nov 23 = Ara 22	Scorpio (207) M	Taurus/Pleiades (18)	Virgo (152)	Gemini/Pollux (75)
Dec 23 = Kis 22	Sagittarius (244) M	Taurus/Pleiades (20)	Virgo (154)	Gemini/Castor (71)
677				
Jan 22 = Kan 23	Capricorn (282) M	Taurus/Hyades (31)	Virgo (153)	Gemini (69)
Feb 21 = Šab 24	SW Fishes (319)	Taurus (46)	Virgo (150)	Gemini (70)
Mar 22 = Add 24	Aries (356)	Gemini (61)	Virgo (145)	Gemini/Castor (71)
Apr 21 = Nis 25	Taurus (33) E	Gemini (79)	Virgo (144)	Gemini (73)
May 21 = Aja 25	Gemini (70) E	Cancer – Leo (96)	Virgo (145)	Gemini/Pollux (76)
Jun 20 = Sim 26	Leo (107) E	Leo/Regulus (115)	Virgo (148)	Gem. – Canc. (80)
Jul 20 = Duz 26	Virgo (143) E	Leo (134)	Virgo (153)	-Cancer (84)
Aug 19 = Abu 27	Virgo (179) E	Virgo (154)	Virgo (159)	Cancer (88)
Sep 18 = Ulu 27	Scorpio (214) E	Virgo (174)	Virgo/Spica (166)	Cancer (90)
Oct 18 = Taš 27	Sagittarius (246) E	Libra (195)	Virgo (172)	Cancer (91)
Nov 17 = Ara 27	Capricorn (273) E	Scorpio (217)	Virgo (178)	Cancer (91)
Dec 17 = Kis 28	Capricorn (282) E	Sagittarius (239)	Virgo (182)	Cancer (88)
676				
Jan 16 = Kan 28	Capricorn (266) M	Capricorn (263)	Virgo (184)	-Cancer (85)
Feb 15 = Šab 29	Capricorn (277) M	Capricorn (286)	Virgo (184)	Canc.–Gem. (83)
Mar 17 = Add 30	Aquarius (303) M	Aquarius (309)	Virgo (181)	Canc.–Gem. (84)

Date	Venus	Mars	Jupiter	Saturn
Apr 16 = Aja 1	SW Fishes (335) M	SW Fishes (332)	Virgo (177)	-Cancer (86)
May 16= Sim 1	Aries+ (9) M	Aries (354)	Virgo (174)	Cancer (89)
Jun 15 = Duz 2	Taurus (44) M	Taurus (15)	Virgo (175)	Cancer (92)
Jul 15 = Abu 3	Gem.-Canc. (81) M	Taurus (35)	Virgo (178)	Cancer – Leo (96)
Aug 14= Ulu 3	Leo (118) M	Taurus – Gem. (52)	Virgo (182)	-Leo (100)
Sep 13 = Taš 3	Virgo (156) M	Gemini (67)	Libra (188)	Leo (102)
Oct 13 = Ara 3	Libra (193)	Gemini/Pollux (76)	Libra (194)	Leo (104)
Nov 12= Kis 3	Sagittarius (231)	Gemini/Pollux (74)	Scorpio (201)	Leo (104)
Dec 12 = Kan 4	Capricorn (269) E	Gemini (63)	Scorpio (207)	Leo (103)
675				
Jan 11 = Šab 4	Aquarius (306) E	Gemini (53)	Scorpio (212)	-Leo (101)
Feb 10 = Add 5	NE Fishes (344) E	Gemini (62)	Scorpio (215)	Cancer – Leo (98)
Mar 12 = A II 6	Taurus/Pleiades (20) E	Gemini (73)	Scorpio (215)	Cancer – Leo (97)
Apr 11 = Nis 6	Gemini (55) E	Cancer (87)	Scorpio (213)	Cancer – Leo (98)
May 11= Aja 7	Cancer (88) E	Leo (104)	Scorpio/Antares (209)	Cancer – Leo (100)
Jun 10 = Sim 7	Leo/Regulus (116) E	Leo (121)	Scorpio (205)	Leo (103)
Jul 10 = Duz 8	Leo (131) E	Leo (140)	Scorpio (205)	Leo (107)
Aug 9 = Abu 8	Leo (118)	Virgo (159)	Scorpio (208)	Leo (111)
Sep 8 = Ulu 9	Leo (118) M	Virgo (180)	Scorpio (212)	Leo/Reg. (114)
Oct 8 = Taš 8	Leo (141) M	Scorpio (202)	Scorpio (218)	Leo (116)
Nov 7 = Ara 9	Virgo (173) M	Scorpio (224)	Scorpio (224)	Leo (118)
Dec 7 = Kis 11	Scorpio/Ant. (208) M	Sagittarius (247)	Sagittarius (232)	Leo (118)
674				
Jan 6 = Kan 10	Sagittarius (245) M	Capricorn (271)	Sagittarius (238)	Leo (116)
Feb 5 = Šab 10	Capricorn (281) M	Aquarius (294)	Sagittarius (243)	Leo (113)
Mar 7 = Add 11	SW Fishes (318) M	SW Fishes (318)	Sagittarius (247)	Leo (111)
Apr 6 = Nis 11	Aries (355) M	SW Fishes (340)	Sagittarius (248)	Leo (111)
May 6 = Aja 12	Taurus/Hyades (32)	Aries (2)	Sagittarius (247)	Leo (112)
Jun 5 = Sim 13	Gemini (69)	Taurus (24)	Sagittarius (243)	Leo/Reg. (115)
Jul 5 = Duz 13	Leo (106) E	Taurus (44)	Sagittarius (239)	Leo (118)
Aug 4 = Abu 14	Virgo (143) E	Gemini (63)	Sagittarius (238)	Leo (122)
Sep 3 = Ulu 15	Virgo (180) E	Gem. – Canc. (80)	Sagittarius (239)	Leo (125)
Oct 3 = Taš 15	Scorpio (217) E	Cancer – Leo (95)	Sagittarius (243)	Leo (128)
Nov 2 = Ara 15	Sagittarius+ (253) E	Leo (107)	Sagittarius (249)	Leo (130)
Dec 2 = Kis 16	Aquarius (289) E	Leo (111)	Sag. – Capr. (256)	Leo (131)
673				
Jan 1 = Kan 16	SW Fishes (321) E	Leo (104)	Capricorn (263)	Leo (130)
Feb 1 = Šab 17	NE Fishes (347) E	Cancer+ (93)	Capricorn (270)	Leo (128)
Mar 1 = Add 16	NE Fishes (357) E	Cancer (92)	Capricorn (276)	Leo (126)
Mar 31 = Nis 17	SW Fishes (336) M	Cancer – Leo (100)	Capricorn (280)	Leo (124)
Apr 30 = Aja 17	NE Fishes (348) M	Leo/Reg. (114)	Capricorn (282)	Leo (125)
May 30= Sim 18	Taurus (15) M	Leo (129)	Capricorn (282)	Leo (126)
Jun 29 = Duz 19	Orion (47) M	Virgo (147)	Capricorn (278)	Leo (129)
Jul 29 = Abu 19	Gem. – Canc. (81) M	Virgo (166)	Capricorn (274)	Leo (132)
Aug 28= Ulu 20	Leo (117) M	-Libra (187)	Capricorn (272)	Leo (136)
Sep 27 = Taš 21	Virgo (155) M	Scorpio/Ant. (209)	Capricorn (273)	Leo (139)
Oct 27 = Ara 21	Libra (193) M	Sagittarius (231)	Capricorn (276)	Virgo (142)
Nov 26= Kis 22	Sagittarius (231) M	Sagittarius (255)	Capricorn (282)	Virgo (143)
Dec 26 = Kan 22	Capricorn (268)	Capricorn (278)	Capricorn (288)	Virgo (144)

Date	Venus	Mars	Jupiter	Saturn
672				
Jan 25 = Šab 22	Aquarius (306)	Aquarius (302)	Aquarius (296)	Virgo (142)
Feb 24 = Add 23	SW Fishes (343) E	SW Fishes (325)	Aquarius (303)	Leo (140)
Mar 26 = A II 23	Taurus (20) E	NE Fishes (348)	Aquarius+(310)	Leo (138)
Apr 25 = Nis 23	Gemini (57) E	Aries (9)	SW Fishes (315)	Leo (137)
May 25 = Aja 22	Cancer (93) E	Taurus/Hyades (31)	SW Fishes (318)	Leo (139)
Jun 24 = Sim 24	Leo (127) E	Orion (51)	SW Fishes (319)	Leo (140)
Jul 24 = Duz 24	Virgo (160) E	Gemini/Castor (71)	SW Fishes (316)	Virgo (143)
Aug 23 = Abu 25	Libra (188) E	Cancer (89)	Aquarius+(311)	Virgo (146)
Sep 22 = Ulu 26	Scorpio (204) E	Leo (107)	Aquarius (309)	Virgo (150)
Oct 22 = Taš 27	Libra (192) M	Leo (122)	Aquarius (308)	Virgo (153)
Nov 21 = Ara 27	Libra (193) M	Leo (135)	Aquarius+(311)	Virgo (155)
Dec 21 = Kis 28	Scorpio (217) M	Virgo (144)	SW Fishes (316)	Virgo (156)
671				
Jan 20 = Kan 28	Sagittarius (249) M	Virgo (142)	SW Fishes (322)	Virgo (156)
Feb 19 = Šab 28	Capricorn (283) M	Leo (132)	SW Fishes (329)	Virgo (153)
Mar 21 = Add 29	SW Fishes (319) M	Leo (125)	SW Fishes (337)	Leo (151)
Apr 20 = Nis 29	Aries (354) M	Leo (130)	NE Fishes (343)	Leo (149)
May 20 = Aja 29	Taurus/Hyades (31)M	Leo (141)	NE Fishes (349)	Leo (150)
Jun 19 = Sim 30	Gemini (68) M	Virgo (157)	NE Fishes (353)	Leo (151)
Jul 19 = Duz 30	Leo (105)	Virgo (175)	Aries (355)	Virgo (153)
Aug 18 = Ulu 1	Virgo (142)	Libra (196)	Aries (354)	Virgo (156)
Sep 17 = Taš 2	Virgo (180) E	Scorpio (217)	NE Fishes (350)	Virgo (160)
Oct 17 = Ara 2	Scorpio (217) E	Sagittarius (239)	NE Fishes (346)	Virgo (163)
Nov 16 = Kis 3	Sag.–Capr. (255) E	-Capricorn (263)	NE Fishes (345)	Virgo (166)
Dec 16 = Kan 4	Aquarius (292) E	Capricorn (286)	NE Fishes (346)	Virgo (167)
670				
Jan 15 = Šab 4	SW Fishes (328) E	Aquar.–Fishes (310)	NE Fishes (350)	Virgo (168)
Feb 14 = Add 5	Aries (3) E	SW Fishes (333)	Aries (356)	Virgo (167)
Mar 16 = Nis 5	Taurus (35) E	Aries (355)	Aries (3)	Virgo (164)
Apr 15 = Aja 5	Gemini (58) E	Taurus (16)	Aries – Taur. (10)	Virgo (162)
May 15 = Sim 6	Gemini (57) E	Taurus (37)	Taurus (17)	Virgo (161)
Jun 14 = Duz 6	Taurus (43) M	Gemini (57)	Taurus (23)	Virgo (162)
Jul 14 = Abu 6	Gemini (58) M	Gemini/Pollux (77)	Taurus/Hyades (28)	Virgo (164)
Aug 13 = Ulu 7	Cancer (86) M	Cancer – Leo (96)	Taurus/Hyades (30)	Virgo (166)
Sep 12 = U II 7	Leo (120) M	Leo/Reg. (115)	Taurus/Hyades (31)	Virgo (170)
Oct 12 = Taš 6	Virgo (155) M	Leo (132)	Taurus (27)	Virgo (173)
Nov 11 = Ara 8	Libra (192) M	Virgo (149)	Taurus (23)	Virgo (176)
Dec 11 = Kis 9	Sagittarius (230) M	Virgo (164)	Taurus/Plei. (20)	Virgo (178)
669				
Jan 10 = Kan 10	Capricorn (267) M	Virgo (176)	Taurus (21)	Virgo (180)
Feb 9 = Šab 10	Aquarius (307)	Virgo (183)	Taurus (24)	Virgo (180)
Mar 10 = Add 11	SW Fishes (342)	Virgo (179)	Taurus/Hyades (29)	Virgo (178)
Apr 9 = Nis 11	Taurus/Plei. (19) E	Virgo/Spica (168)	Taurus (35)	Virgo (175)
May 9 = Aja 11	Gemini (56) E	Virgo (164)	Taurus (42)	Virgo (173)
Jun 8 = Sim 12	Cancer (93) E	Virgo (173)	Orion (49)	Virgo (173)
Jul 8 = Duz 12	Leo (129) E	Libra (188)	Gemini (55)	Virgo (174)
Aug 7 = Abu 13	Virgo/Spica (165) E	Scorpio (207)	Gemini (61)	Virgo (177)
Sep 6 = Ulu 13	Libra – Scorp.(200)E	Scorpio – Sag. (228)	Gemini (64)	Virgo (179)
Oct 6 = Taš 13	Sagittarius (234) E	Sagittarius (249)	Gemini (65)	Virgo (183)
Nov 5 = Ara 14	Capricorn (263) E	Capricorn (274)	Gemini (63)	Virgo (186)
Dec 5 = Kis 14	Capricorn (280) E	Aquarius (295)	Gemini (58)	Libra (189)

Date	Venus	Mars	Jupiter	Saturn
668				
Jan 4 = Kan 15	Capricorn (268) M	SW Fishes (318)	Gemini (55)	Libra (191)
Feb 3 = Šab 15	Capricorn (268) M	SW Fishes (340)	Gemini (55)	Libra (191)
Mar 5 = Add 16	Aquarius (291) M	Aries (2)	Gemini (57)	Libra (191)
Apr 4 = Nis 17	SW Fishes (322) M	Taurus (23)	Gemini (61)	Libra (188)
May 4 = Aja 18	Aries (356) M	Taurus (43)	Gemini (67)	Virgo (186)
Jun 3 = Sim 19	Taurus/Hyades (31)M	Gemini (63)	Gemini (73)	Virgo (184)
Jul 3 = Duz 19	Gemini (66) M	Gem. – Canc. (83)	Gem. – Canc. (80)	Virgo (185)
Aug 2 = Abu 18	Leo (104) M	- Leo (101)	Cancer (87)	Virgo (186)
Sep 1 = Ulu 19	Leo – Virgo (141) M	Leo (121)	Cancer (92)	Libra (189)
Oct 1 = Taš 19	Virgo (179)	Leo (139)	Cancer – Leo (96)	Libra (192)
Oct 31 = Ara 19	Scorpio (217)	Virgo (158)	Cancer – Leo (97)	Libra (196)
Nov 30 = Kis 20	Sagittarius (254) E	Virgo (176)	Cancer – Leo (96)	Libra – Scorpio (199)
Dec 30 = Kan 21	Aquarius (292) E	Libra (193)	Cancer (92)	Scorpio (201)
667				
Jan 29 = Šab 21	SW Fishes (330) E	Scorpio/Ant. (209)	Cancer (88)	Scorpio (202)
Feb 28 = Add 22	Aries (6) E	Scorpio (223)	Cancer (87)	Scorpio (203)
Mar 30 = A II 22	Taurus (42) E	Sagittarius (233)	Cancer (88)	Scorpio (201)
Apr 29 = Nis 23	Gemini/Pollux (75)E	Sagittarius (233)	Cancer (92)	Libra+(198)
May 29 = Aja 24	Leo (105) E	Scorpio (223)	Cancer – Leo (97)	Libra (197)
Jun 28 = Sim 24	Leo (126) E	Scorpio (221)	Leo (103)	Libra (196)
Jul 28 = Duz 24	Leo (122)	Scorpio – Sag. (228)	Leo (110)	Libra (197)
Aug 27 = Abu 25	Leo (122) M	Sagittarius (245)	Leo (117)	Libra – Scorpio (199)
Sep 26 = Ulu 25	Leo (130) M	Capricorn (264)	Leo (122)	Scorpio (201)
Oct 26 = Taš 25	Virgo (160) M	Capricorn (285)	Leo (126)	Scorpio (205)
Nov 25 = Ara 26	Libra (195) M	Aquarius (306)	Leo (128)	Scorpio/Ant. (209)
Dec 25 = Kis 26	Scorpio+(231) M	SW Fishes (328)	Leo (127)	Scorpio (211)
666				
Jan 24 = Kan 27	Capricorn (267) M	NE Fishes (348)	Leo (124)	Scorpio (213)
Feb 23 = Šab 27	Aquarius (304) M	Aries+(9)	Leo (120)	Scorpio (214)
Mar 25 = Add 28	SW Fishes (341) M	Taurus/Hyades (29)	Leo (118)	Scorpio (213)
Apr 24 = Nis 28	Taurus/Pleiades (19)	Orion (49)	Leo (119)	Scorpio (211)
May 24 = Aja 29	Gemini (55)	Gemini (68)	Leo (122)	Scorpio (208)
Jun 23 = Sim 30	Cancer (92) E	Cancer (87)	Leo (127)	Scorpio (207)
Jul 23 = Abu 1	Leo (129) E	Leo (107)	Leo (132)	Scorpio/Ant. (208)
Aug 22 = Ulu 1	Virgo/Spica (166) E	Leo (126)	Leo (139)	Scorpio (208)
Sep 21 = Taš 1	Scorpio (203) E	Virgo (145)	Virgo (146)	Scorpio (211)
Oct 21 = Ara 2	Sagittarius (239) E	Virgo (164)	Virgo (151)	Scorpio (214)
Nov 20 = Kis 2	Capricorn (275) E	Libra (185)	Virgo (156)	Scorpio (218)
Dec 20 = Kan 2	Aquarius (309) E	Scorpio (204)	Virgo (158)	Scorpio (221)
665				
Jan 19 = Šab 3	SW Fishes (338) E	Scorpio (224)	Virgo (158)	Scorpio (223)
Feb 18 = Add 3	NE Fishes (353) E	Sagittarius (243)	Virgo (155)	Scorpio (224)
Mar 19 = Nis 4	SW Fishes (338) M	-Capricorn (263)	Virgo (151)	Scorpio+(225)
Apr 18 = Aja 4	SW Fishes (340) M	Capricorn (281)	Virgo (149)	Scorpio (223)
May 18 = Sim 5	Aries (3) M	Aquarius (298)	Virgo (149)	Scorpio (221)
Jun 17 = Duz 6	Taurus (34) M	Aquarius (307)	Virgo (151)	Scorpio (219)
Jul 17 = Abu 6	Gemini (68) M	Aquarius (308)	Virgo (156)	Scorpio (218)
Aug 16 = Ulu 7	Leo (104) M	Aquarius (298)	Virgo (161)	Scorpio (219)
Sep 15 = Taš 7	Leo (140) M	Aquarius (299)	Virgo/Spica (168)	Scorpio (220)
Oct 15 = Ara 8	Virgo (178) M	Aquarius (308)	Virgo (175)	Scorpio (223)

Date	Venus	Mars	Jupiter	Saturn
Nov 14 = Kis 8	Scorpio (216)	SW Fishes (324)	Virgo (181)	Scorpio (227)
Dec 14 = Kan 8	Sag. – Capr. (254)	SW Fishes (341)	Libra (185)	Sagittarius (230)
664				
Jan 13 = Šab 8	Aquarius (291) E	Aries (359)	Libra (188)	Sagittarius (233)
Feb 12 = Add 9	SW Fishes (329) E	Taurus/Pleiades (18)	Libra (189)	Sagittarius (235)
Mar 14 = A II 9	Aries (6)E	Taurus (36)	Virgo (186)	Sagittarius (236)
Apr 13 = Nis 10	Taurus (43) E	Gemini (55)	Virgo (182)	Sagittarius (235)
May 13= Aja 10	Gem. – Canc. (79) E	Gemini/Pollux (74)	Virgo (179)	Sagittarius (233)
Jun 12 = Sim 11	Leo/Reg. (114) E	Cancer+(93)	Virgo (178)	Sagittarius (230)
Jul 12 = Duz 11	Virgo (147) E	Leo (112)	Virgo (181)	-Sagittarius (229)
Aug 11 = Abu 12	Virgo (177) E	Leo (131)	Virgo (185)	-Sagittarius (229)
Sep 10 = Ulu 13	Libra (198) E	Virgo (151)	Libra (191)	Sagittarius (231)
Oct 10 = Taš 13	Libra (195)	Virgo (171)	Libra (197)	Sagittarius (233)
Nov 9 = Ara 14	Virgo (186) M	Libra (191)	Scorpio (204)	Sagittarius (236)
Dec 9 = Kis 14	Scorpio (206) M	Scorpio (212)	Scorpio (211)	Sagittarius (240)
663				
Jan 8 = Kan 14	Sagittarius (236) M	Sagittarius (234)	Scorpio (215)	Sagittarius (243)
Feb 8 = Šab 16	Capricorn (270) M	Sag. – Capr. (256)	Scorpio (219)	Sagittarius (245)
Mar 9 = Add 15	Aquarius (305) M	Capricorn (278)	Scorpio (220)	Sagittarius (247)
Apr 8 = Nis 15	SW Fishes (341) M	Aquarius (299)	Scorpio (218)	Sagittarius (247)
May 8 = Aja 16	Taurus (17) M	SW Fishes (321)	Scorpio (214)	Sagittarius (246)
Jun 7 = Sim 16	Gemini (54) M	SW Fishes (341)	Scorpio (211)	Sagittarius (243)
Jul 7 = Duz 17	Cancer (91)	Aries (359)	Scorpio (210)	Sagittarius (241)
Aug 6 = Abu 18	Leo (128)	-Taurus (13)	Scorpio (211)	Sagittarius (240)
Sep 5 = Ulu 18	Virgo/Spica (165)	Taurus (17)	Scorpio (215)	Sagittarius (241)
Oct 5 = Taš 19	Scorpio (203) E	Aries+(8)	Scorpio (221)	Sagittarius (243)
Nov 4 = Ara 20	Sagittarius (241) E	Aries (0)	Scorpio (227)	Sagittarius (246)
Dec 4 = Kis 20	Capricorn (278) E	Aries (3)	Sagittarius (235)	Sagittarius (248)

APPENDIX E

SOLAR ECLIPSES AT NINEVEH 681-647 BC[683]

Year	Date		Time	B	M	E	PMA	Reported in
679	Jun 17	= Sim 30	Morning	6.28	7.41	8.55	0.68	*RMA* 272
669	May 27	= Aja 29	Sunrise		4.92*	5.27	0.17	*LAS* 28, 104, *RMA* 269
664	Aug 28	= Abu 29	Morning	7.54	8.33	9.12	0.25	
662	Jan 12	= Kan 29	Evening	15.59	16.81	16.86*	0.97	
661	Jun 27	= Sim 30	Afternoon	15.50	16.75	18.01	0.93	
657	Apr 15	= Nis 28	Forenoon	9.84	11.09	12.33	0.84	*LAS* 300+, *RMA* 277R
655	Aug 19	= Abu 29	Morning	7.25	7.71	8.17	0.09	
651	Jun 7	= Sim 29	Noon	10.67	12.50	14.32	0.72	*LAS* 83
650	Nov 21	= Ara 30	Evening	14.78	16.07	17.09*	0.93	
648	Apr 6	= Add 29	Forenoon	10.02	11.33	12.65	0.77	

683 This list is based on Kudlek + Mickler, *Solar and Lunar Eclipses of the Ancient Near East* (*AOATS* 1, 1971), where further details will be found. B = beginning, M = middle, E = end of eclipse (in local hours and their fractional parts); * = sunrise/sunset; PMA= maximal magnitude of occultation (0.10 = one 'finger').

APPENDIX F

LUNAR ECLIPSES (NINEVEH AND BABYLON), 681-647 BC

1. *List of eclipses*[684]

Year	Date (Jul = Ass)	Time (Hours = Watch)	Magnitude (in fingers)	Reported (or mentioned) in
681	Jan 27f = Šab 15	22^{h}95–02^{h}42 = Midnight	10	
681	Jul 22 = Duz 14	17^{h}99–21^{h}87 = Evening	10	
680	Jul 11f = Duz 14	22^{h}36–00^{h}06 = Midnight	2	
679	Jun 1 = Sim 14	01^{h}49–02^{h}82 = Midnight	1	RMA 272
678	May 22 = Sim 14	*17^{h}62–21^{h}08 = Evening	10	RMA 268 and 270
677	Nov 3 = Ara 14	18^{h}76–20^{h}03 = Evening	5	LAS 136:12
674	Sep 3f = Ulu 15	23^{h}11–02^{h}80 = Midnight	10	RMA 30, LAS 31
673	Feb 27 = Add 14	19^{h}09–20^{h}21 = Evening	4	RMA 272B
673	Aug 23 = Ulu 15	05^{h}98–06^{h}54*= Morning	3	
671	Jul 2 = Duz 14	19^{h}39–22^{h}65 = Evening	9	ABL 276, LAS 278
671	Dec 27f = Kan 15	23^{h}71–03^{h}40 = Midnight	5	ABL 137, LAS 185, 232, 279
670	Dec 17 = Kis 15	03^{h}55–04^{h}93 = Morning	1	RMA 85, LAS 41, 62
669	Jun 10 = Sim 14	01^{h}94–02^{h}73 = Morning	1	RMA 271, LAS 25, 77, 93, 234
667	Apr 21 = Nis 16	17^{h}72–20^{h}53 = Evening	10	LAS 40 and 61
667	Oct 15 = Taš 14	03^{h}81–05^{h}58 = Morning	10	RMA 272A and 273
666	Apr 10 = Nis 15	18^{h}90–21^{h}55 = Evening	5	LAS 298 and 299
666	Oct 4 = Taš 14	20^{h}17–22^{h}77 = Evening	6	
664	Feb 17 = Add 15	18^{h}63*–19^{h}28 = Evening	8	
664	Aug 13 = Abu 14	01^{h}17–04^{h}14= Morning	6	
663	Aug 2 = Abu 13	00^{h}83–04^{h}73 = Morning	10	
662	Jan 27 = Šab 14	00^{h}07–02^{h}11 = Midnight	3	
662	Jul 23 = Duz	05^{h}24–06^{h}31 = Morning	3	
661	Dec 6 = Kis	21^{h}21–00^{h}20 = Midnight	6	
660	Jun 1 = Sim	01^{h}08–03^{h}46 = Morning	10	
660	Nov 25 = Kis	20^{h}25–00^{h}11 = Eve-Midn	10	
659	May 22 = Sim	18^{h}46–20^{h}10 = Evening	10	
659	Nov 15 = Ara	02^{h}03–04^{h}58 = Morning	5	
657	Sep 24 = Taš	19^{h}23–21^{h}95 = Evening	7	
656	Mar 20 = Add II	18^{h}16*–19^{h}76 = Evening	10	
655	Mar 10 = Add	01^{h}68–04^{h}14 = Midn-Mor	5	
653	Jan 18 = Šab	22^{h}35–01^{h}45 = Midnight	9	
653	Jul 13 = Duz	02^{h}54–05^{h}63 = Morning	8	
652	Jul 2 = Duz	16^{h}98*–18^{h}63 = Evening	10	
650	May 13 = Aja	17^{h}30*–18^{h}60 = Evening	3	?LAS 80
650	Nov 5 = Ara	23^{h}52–02^{h}17 = Midnight	6	
649	May 1 = Aja	23^{h}51–03^{h}35 = Midn-Mor	10	
648	Apr 21 = Nis	01^{h}41–04^{h}36 = Morning	6	
648	Oct 15 = Taš	04^{h}92–05^{h}73*= Morning	6	

684 Based on Kudlek + Mickler, *Solar and Lunar Eclipses of the Ancient Near East* (*AOATS* 1, 1971), p. 146f.

2. *Graphic presentation of the lunar eclipses visible in Mesopotamia in years 680-664 BC*[685]

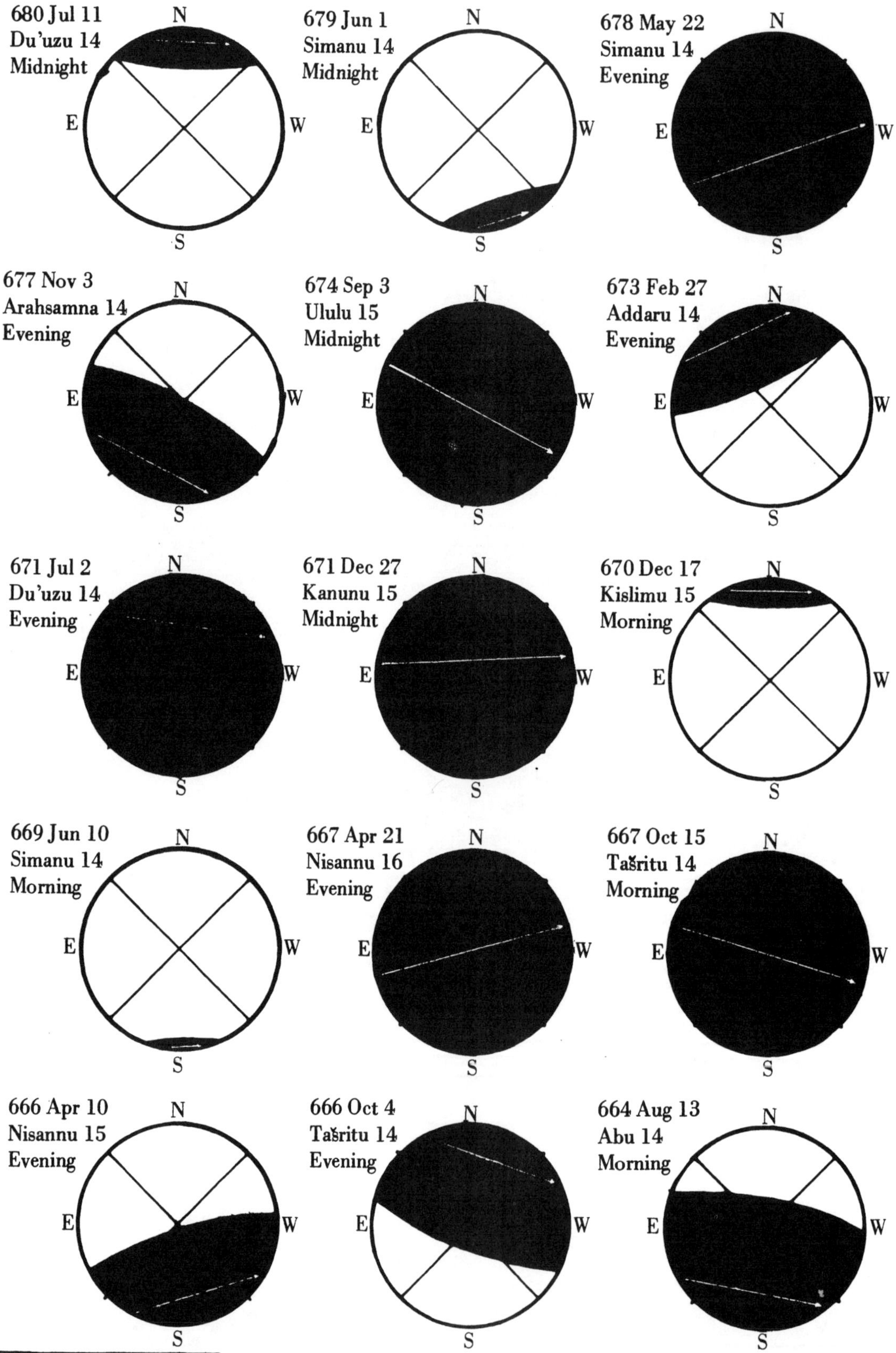

685 Based on the data of P.V. Neugebauer + O. Hiller, *Spezieller Kanon der Mondfinsternisse* (Kiel 1934). The drawings show the disc of the moon (divided into four quadrants after App. F4) in the middle of each eclipse; the dark areas represent the shadow of the earth and the vectors the direction in which the shadow moved in each case. The ends of the vectors indicate the entrance and exit angles of the eclipses, respectively.

3. *Visibility of Venus, Jupiter and Saturn during lunar eclipses 680 – 663 BC at Nineveh*[686]

Year	Eclipse	Venus		Jupiter		Saturn	
		Azimuth	Altitude	Azimuth	Altitude	Azimuth	Altitude
680 BC	-679 Jul 11						
	22^h	109°28	- 3°53	181°51	-31°25	216°43	-29°75
	24^h	130°48	-24°50	211°99	-24°17	240°70	-11°56
679 BC	-678 Jun 1						
	1^h	147°76	-23°91	202°68	-30°42	166°77	-29°53
	2^h	151°91	-25°24	217°30	-24°34	162°22	-29°03
678 BC	-677 May 22						
	18^h	101°78	16°89	47°68	68°33	98°80	24°39
	19^h	116°58	- 2°83	79°05	49°48	112°98	4°32
	21^h	134°69	-19°84	95°52	28°65	129°51	-13°56
677 BC	-676 Nov 3						
	19^h	51°15	9°97	128°78	-37°70	223°52	-15°88
	20^h	63°10	- 2°92	151°11	-47°64	236°69	- 4°09
674 BC	-673 Sep 3-4						
	23^h	125°49	-38°11	70°07	- 6°65	194°50	-33°17
	1^h	163°87	-52°39	86°58	-30°25	223°67	-21°28
	3^h	211°91	-48°92	107°45	-54°16	244°73	- 1°64
673 BC	-672 Feb 27						
	19^h	83°27	4°38	122°25	-68°50	276°50	41°04
	20^h	93°32	- 9°14	168°51	-76°61	289°98	54°22
671 BC	-670 Jul 2						
	19^h	126°83	- 7°88	225°21	-46°50	72°37	38°76
	23^h	168°76	-29°34	264°92	-10°81	103°27	- 0°19
	-670 Dec 27-28						
	24^h	102°90	-48°44	89°51	- 7°99	269°28	7°02
	3^h	215°11	-69°44	133°54	-49°27	312°76	48°42
670 BC	-669 Dec 17						
	4^h	278°47	-22°13	110°19	-13°04	297°86	32°84
	5^h	284°45	-13°48	117°84	-21°10	307°96	40°25
669 BC	-668 Jun 10						
	2^h	184°21	-30°12	233°42	-15°43	103°20	-12°68
	3^h	196°57	-28°39	241°55	- 7°37	111°16	-21°80
667 BC	-666 Apr 21						
	19^h	89°18	38°77	71°16	61°38	284°07	6°36
	21^h	105°17	15°70	96°62	38°35	304°54	27°60
	-666 Oct 15						
	4^h	267°52	17°38	274°83	39°49	254°44	36°78
	6^h	287°48	41°27	302°70	62°40	272°12	-12°90

[686] The data found in this appendix were generated with the help of a computer programme written by Mr. K. Koskenniemi of the Computing Centre of the University of Helsinki. Parameters used: Equinox = March 28; latitude (of Nineveh) = 36.50; longitude (of Nineveh) = 43.00; dates and times of eclipses as in App.F; planetary longitudes from Stahlman + Gingerich (1963); planetary latitudes = 0; theta = 5.752 radians.

Year	Eclipse	Venus		Jupiter		Saturn	
		Azimuth	Altitude	Azimuth	Altitude	Azimuth	Altitude
666 BC	-665 Apr 10						
	19^h	104°94	-18°58	341°71	73°36	276°82	-11°37
	22^h	140°36	-45°68	71°45	56°13	301°86	18°72
	-665 Oct 4						
	20^h	77°67	- 7°77	148°55	-36°01	83°48	-11°76
	23^h	106°01	-43°68	204°70	-38°27	114°55	-47°32
664 BC	-663 Aug 13						
	1^h	136°70	-44°05	128°64	-42°72	83°02	-20°56
	4^h	204°91	-50°37	197°42	-54°25	115°51	-56°07

4. *Interpretation of lunar eclipses*

4.1 *General principles*

ABL 1006 = *RMA* 168:3 ff (Munnabitu explaining the eclipse of May 22, 678 BC):

3 *šá* AN.MI ḪUL-*šú a-na* EN ITU EN UD-*mu* EN *ma-aṣ-ṣar-tu*$_4$ EN *taš-ri-tu*$_4$
4 *a-šar ú-šar-ru-ú ù a-šar* ^{d}*30* AN.MI *i-šaḫ-ḫa-ṭu-ma i-na-as-sa-ku*
5 ḪUL-*šú an-nu-tu*$_4$ *i-maḫ-ḫa-ru* ^{ITU}SIG$_4$ KUR MAR.TU^{KI} *ù*
6 *pu-ru-us-su a-na* ŠEŠ.UNU^{KI} *na-din* ḪUL *šá* UD *14*.KAM *šá qa-bu-ú*
7 UD *14*.KAM KUR NIM.MA^{KI} *taš-ri-tu*$_4$ *a-šar ú-še-er-ru-ú ul ni-i-du*
8 *mi-ni-tu* AN.MI-*šú a-na* UGU ^{IM}GÀL.LU *u* ^{IM}MAR.TU *il-ta-ḫa-aṭ*
9 ḪUL *šá* KUR NIM.MA^{KI} *u* KUR MAR.TU^{KI} *ul-tu* ^{IM}KUR.RA *u* ^{IM}SI.SÁ
10 KI-*šú im-mir* SIG$_5$ *šá Su-bar-tu*$_4$^{KI} *u* URI^{KI}-*i gab-bi-šú šá i-ri-mu*
11 *it-tu*$_4$ *šá ma-ta-a-ti gab-bi*

"The evil of an eclipse pertains to the lord of the MONTH, the lord of the DAY, the lord of the WATCH, and the lord of the QUADRANT where the Moon begins the eclipse and where he shifts and sheds it to: these take over the predicted evil.

The month of Simānu is Elam, and its 'decision' is given to Ur. The evil of the 14th day, as it is said: The 14th day is Elam. We do not know the quadrant where it began. The measurable eclipse drifted toward the South and the West, bad luck to Elam and Amurru; its disc started to clear from the East and the North, good luck to Subartu and Akkad. That it was covered completely means that the portent pertains to all the countries."

4.2. *Significance of the lunar quadrants*

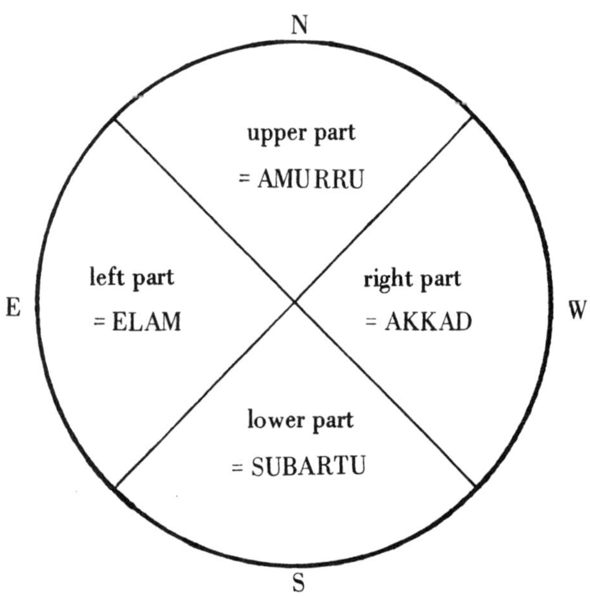

Cf. *ABL* 1006 = *RMA* 268:11 f (quoting the Great Star List *CT* 26 40 iv 23-26):
15 ^{d}*30* KUR URI^{KI} *2,30* ^{d}*30* / KUR NIM.MA^{KI} *e-la-a-ti* ^{d}[*30* KUR MA]R^{KI} *šap-la-a-ti* ^{d}*30* KUR SU.BIR$_4$^{KI}

"The right part of the Moon is Akkad, the left part of the Moon is Elam; the upper part of the Moon is Amurru, the lower part of the Moon is Subartu."

4.3 *The direction of the shadow*

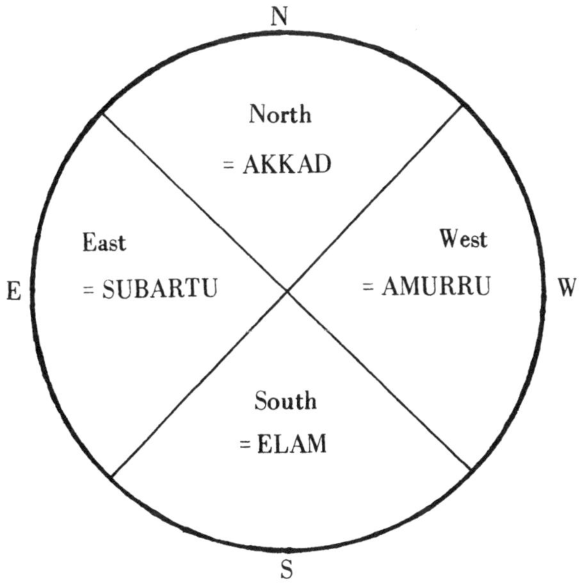

ACh 2 Suppl. 19:17':
[I ^{IM}GÀL.LU KUR NIM.MA^{KI} I]^{M}SI.SÁ KUR URI^{KI} ^{IM}KUR.RA SU.BIR$_4$^{KI} *u Gu-ti-i* ^{IM}MAR.TU KUR MAR.TU^{KI}

"The South is Elam, the North is Akkad, the East is Subartu, the West is Amurru."

Cf. also *ABL* 1006:8 ff, quoted above, and the passages quoted by Schott, *ZA* 47 (1941/2) 107.

4.4. *The month, day, and watch*

CT 26 41 vi 12 ff:

12	[^{ITU}BÁR ^{ITU}NE ^{ITU}]KAN	KUR URI^{KI}	"Nisannu, Ābu and Kislīmu	= Akkad;
13	[^{ITU}GUD ^{ITU}KI]N ^{ITU}AB	KUR NIM.MA^{KI}	Ajāru, Ulūlu and Ṭebētu	= Elam;
14	[^{ITU}SIG$_4$] ^{ITU}DU$_6$ ^{ITU}ZÍZ	KUR MAR.TU^{KI}	Simānu, Tašrītu and Šabāṭu	= Amurru;
15	[^{ITU}Š]U ^{ITU}APIN ^{ITU}ŠE	KUR SU.BIR$_4$^{KI}	Du'ūzu, Araḫsamna, Addāru	= Subartu."

ACh 2 Suppl. 19:12' ff:

12' [I AN.MI EN.NU]N AN.USÁN *a-na* KUR URI^{KI} : I AN.MI EN.NUN MÚRU.BA *a-na* KUR SU.BIR$_4$^{KI}
13' [I AN.MI EN.NUN U]D.ZAL.LI *a-na* KUR NIM.MA^{KI}: I ^{ITU}BÁR ^{ITU}NE ^{ITU}KAN KUR URI^{KI}
14' [I ^{ITU}GUD ^{ITU}KIN ^{ITU}AB KU]R NIM.MA^{KI} : I ^{ITU}SIG$_4$ ^{ITU}DU$_6$ ^{ITU}ZÍZ KUR MAR.TU^{KI}
15' [I ^{ITU}ŠU ^{ITU}APIN ^{ITU}ŠE KUR] SU.BIR$_4$^{KI} ^{ITU}^{MEŠ} *šá* AN.TA.LÙ ^{d}*30*
16' [I UD *13*.KAM KUR URI^{KI} UD *14*.K]AM KUR NIM.MA^{KI} UD *15*.KAM KUR MAR.TU^{KI} UD *16*.KAM KUR SU.BIR$_4$^{KI} UD^{MEŠ} *šá* AN.TA.LÙ ^{d}*30*

"An eclipse in the evening watch pertains to Akkad; an eclipse in the midnight watch pertains to Subartu; an eclipse in the morning watch pertains to Elam. Nisannu, Ābu, Kislīmu = Akkad; Ajāru, Ulūlu, Ṭebētu – Elam; Simānu, Tašrītu, Šabāṭu = Amurru, Du'ūzu, Araḫsamna, Addaru = Subartu: the months of the lunar eclipses.
The 13th day is Akkad; the 14th day is Elam; the 15th day is Amurru; the 16th day is Subartu: the days of the lunar eclipses."

Cf. also passages such as *RMA* 156 r2, 270 r10, 271:10, etc.

4.5 *The role of the planets*

ACh 2 Suppl. 29:14 (quoted in *LAS* 298 r10', *ABL* 1006 = *RMA* 168 r3f, and *RMA* 272 r11):

[I A]N.MI GAR-*ma ina* AN.MI BI ^{MUL}SAG.ME.GAR GUB *ana* LUGAL DI-*mu ki-mu-šú* IDIM SIG ÚŠ

"If an eclipse (of the moon) takes place and Jupiter is present (lit. stands) in that eclipse, the king will be well; a well-known important person will die in his stead."

ACh Šamaš 8:6 (cf. ibid. 22, 39, 56; 9:21, 39, 55, etc.)

[I AN.MI GAR-*ma* MUL*dili*]-*bat u* MULSAG.ME.GAR IGIMEŠ *ana* LUGAL DI-*mu ana* KUR ZI KÚR

"If an eclipse (of the sun) takes place and Venus and Jupiter are visible, the king will be well, but the country will be attacked by an enemy." (Nisannu; the entries for other months, listed above, are almost identically worded, the only variations being in the predictions concerning the country.)

APPENDIX G

SUNSET AND SUNRISE IN NINEVEH AND ASSUR[687]

Date	Sunset	Sunrise
Jan 0	16^h58^m	7^h16^m
Jan 10	17^h04^m	7^h17^m
Jan 20	17^h13^m	7^h16^m
Jan 30	17^h22^m	7^h11^m
Feb 9	17^h32^m	7^h04^m
Feb 19	17^h41^m	6^h53^m
Mar 1	17^h49^m	6^h42^m
Mar 11	17^h58^m	6^h28^m
Mar 21	18^h05^m	6^h13^m
Mar 31	18^h13^m	5^h58^m
Apr 10	18^h20^m	5^h43^m
Apr 20	18^h28^m	5^h28^m
Apr 30	18^h35^m	5^h14^m
May 10	18^h43^m	5^h02^m
May 20	18^h50^m	4^h52^m
May 30	18^h58^m	4^h44^m
Jun 9	19^h05^m	4^h38^m
Jun 19	19^h10^m	4^h37^m
Jun 29	19^h14^m	4^h38^m
Jul 9	19^h14^m	4^h41^m
Jul 19	19^h13^m	4^h47^m
Jul 29	19^h08^m	4^h55^m
Aug 8	19^h01^m	5^h04^m
Aug 18	18^h52^m	5^h12^m
Aug 28	18^h40^m	5^h21^m
Sep 7	18^h28^m	5^h29^m
Sep 17	18^h14^m	5^h38^m
Sep 27	18^h01^m	5^h47^m
Oct 7	17^h47^m	5^h56^m
Oct 17	17^h34^m	6^h04^m
Oct 27	17^h20^m	6^h14^m
Nov 6	17^h10^m	6^h25^m
Nov 16	17^h01^m	6^h35^m
Nov 26	16^h55^m	6^h47^m
Dec 6	16^h52^m	6^h56^m
Dec 16	16^h52^m	7^h06^m
Dec 26	16^h51^m	7^h11^m

687 Computed for the latitudes 35°.5-36°.6 by K. Koskenniemi, with the help of P.V. Neugebauer's *Tafeln zur astronomischen Chronologie III* (1925). The error for Babylon is 10 min at the most.

Diagram Showing the
Seasonal Variation of Daylight in Nineveh and Assur

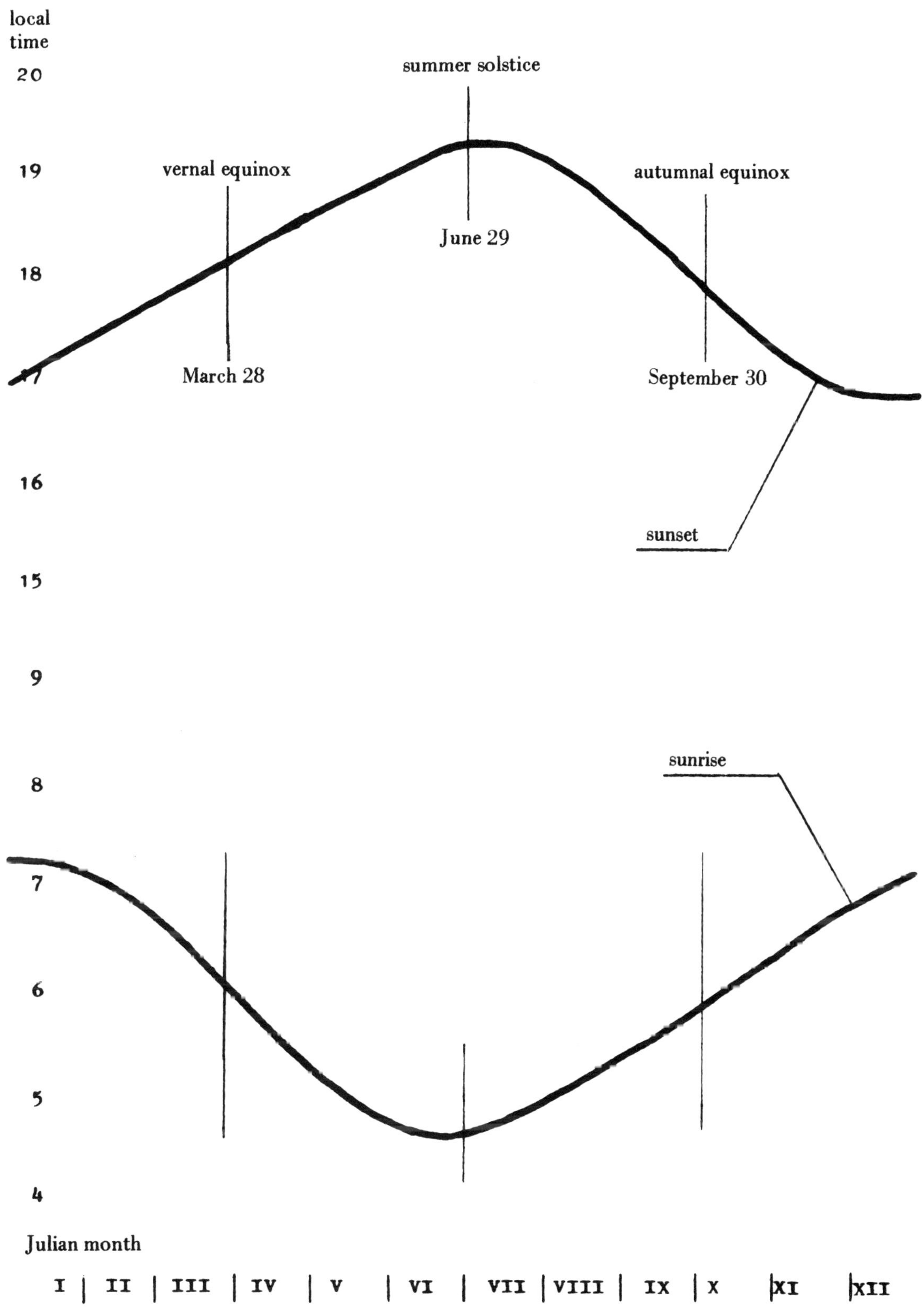

APPENDIX H

RISINGS AND SETTINGS OF SELECTED FIXED STARS[688]

1. *Heliacal risings and settings*

Star	Year 0 e last	Year 0 m first	Year -1000 e last	Year -1000 m first
α Arietis	Mar 20	Apr 13	Mar 13	Apr 6
Capella	May 18	Apr 28	May 8	Apr 22
Pleiades	Apr 10	May 18	Apr 3	May 13
Aldebaran	Apr 21	May 31	Apr 15	May 27
Bellatrix	Apr 27	Jun 23	Apr 22	Jun 21
Pollux	Jun 10	Jul 1	Jun 4	Jun 25
Betelgeuse	May 6	Jun 26	May 2	Jun 24
Procyon	May 31	Jul 17	May 28	Jul 14
Sirius	May 14	Jul 19	May 11	Jul 19
Regulus	Jul 10	Aug 11	Jul 5	Aug 5
δ Canis Maj.	May 9	Aug 5	May 8	Aug 5
γ Argus	May 10	Sep 7	May 12	Sep 7
Arcturus	Oct 26	Sep 26	Oct 26	Sep 18
Spica	Aug 28	Oct 3	Aug 22	Sep 27
α Librae	Sep 16	Oct 28	Sep 10	Oct 21
Antares	Oct 12	Nov 20	Oct 5	Nov 12
α Centauri	Jul 14	Nov 27	Jul 21	Nov 15
Vega	Jan 16	Nov 17	Jan 17	Nov 16
Athair	Dec 31	Dec 21	Dec 27	Dec 17
Deneb	Feb 10	Dec 14	Feb 9	Dec 15
Fomalhaut	Jan 6	Mar 22	Dec 25	Mar 10
α Persei	Apr 23	Mar 25	Apr 14	Mar 21

2. *Acronychal risings and cosmic settings*

Star	acr.ris.	cosm.set.	acr.ris.	cosm.set.
Regulus	Jan 16	Feb 5	Jan 9	Jan 29
Spica	Mar 11	Mar 28	Mar 5	Mar 22
Antares	Apr 28	May 11	Apr 21	May 5
Arcturus	Mar 6	May 21	Feb 27	May 22
Fomalhaut	Aug 21	Jul 29	Aug 12	Jul 19
Athair	Jun 1	Jul 23	May 29	Jul 21
Vega	Apr 30	Aug 5	Apr 28	Aug 8
Pleiades	Oct 4	Nov 7	Sep 27	Oct 31
Aldebaran	Nov 1	Nov 11	Oct 26	Nov 4
Betelgeuse	Nov 29	Nov 25	Nov 24	Nov 19
Capella	Sep 29	Dec 5	Sep 23	Nov 26
Sirius	Jan 1	Nov 26	Dec 30	Nov 23
Procyon	Dec 23	Dec 19	Dec 18	Dec 14

688 Based on Karl Schoch, *Planeten-Tafeln für Jedermann* (Berlin-Pankow, 1927), Sp. XLIV. Horizon of Babylon. The stars in Table 1 are arranged according to the Julian dates of the morning firsts, those of Table 2 according to the Julian dates of the cosmic settings (in year -2000).

APPENDIX I

THE CHRONOLOGY OF THE LETTERS

1. *Chronological list of datable letters*[689]

Date	Letter	Criteria
*674-09-03	*LAS* 31	A+
*674-10-23	30	AH
*674-12-11	32	+
674/3	33	+
672-02	328	A
?672-02-06	4	H
672-02-11	195	H
672-02-20	197	+
672-02-21	198	+
?672-02-21	3	H
672-04-10	1	H
672-04-18	2	H
?672-04-20	211	+
*672-05/6	129	H
672-*05/6*	132	H
672-08	182	AH
672	171	+
672/1	7	H
672/1	140	H
672/1	144	H
672/1	172	AH
*671-01-15	13	A
*671-03-25	67	A
671-03-28	344	A
*671-06	34	H
*671-06	59	H
671-07-06	278	A
671-07-*15*	57	+
671-07-*15*	58	+
671-07-22	276	H
671-08-*15*	134	+
*671-08-21	27	+
*671-09-05	26	A
*671-09-27	277	A
*671-09/10	249	+
*671-10-27	292	A
*671-12-25	185	AH
*671-12-27	232	AH+

Date	Letter	Criteria
*670-01-01	*LAS* 279	A
670-01	317	+
*670-02-10	218+	+
*670-*02/3*	280	+
670-03/4	281	H
670-03-28	345	A
*670-*04*	349	+
*670-*04*	38	A
?670-04-19	145	H
?670-04-19	332	+
*670-04-21	272	+
670-04-25	151	+
*670-04-30	273	+
*670-04/5	246	+
*670-04/5	247	H
670-04/5	248	+
670-04/5	130	+
*670-05-03	143	+
*670-05-04	51	A
670-*05*	180	+
*670-*05*	181	H+
*670-*05*	183	+
670-*05*	256	+
670-*05*	123	+
670-*05*	124	+
670-05/6	133	H+
?670-06-22	16	+
?670-06-25	147	H+
?670-07-06	148	H+
670-06/7	158	+
670-*06/7*	159	+
670-*06/7*	160	+
670-*06/7*	184	+
670-*06/7*	222	+
670-*06/7*	186	H+
670-*06/7*	187	+
670-*07*	188	+
670-08-04	208	+

[689] Cf. Introduction, p. XIIIff. Dates considered certain are marked with asterisks, those meant as approximate only are given in italics. A = astronomical, H = historical, C = chronological, + = association with other letters, D = eponym date.

Date	Letter	Criteria
670-*08*	*LAS* 285	+
670-08-24	170	H
670-*08/9*	284	AH
670-*08*	189	+
670-*08*	191	+
*670-08-07	170	AC
*670-08-12	287	+
*670-08	10+	A
670-10	72	+
670-11	196	+
*670-12-01	41	A
*670-12-16	62	A
670-12-17	101	A
*670-12-24	173	AH
*670-12-*31*	164	+
*669-01-03	174	+
669-01-05	175	+
*669-01-05	163	+
*669-01-05	176	+
*669-01-07	177	+
?669-01-23	269	A
669-*02*	288	H
669-02-15	146	H
*669-03-13	54	A
*669-03-*22*	45	A
*669-03-24	12	A+
?669-03-24	53	A+
*669-03-26	65	A+
*669-03-26	66	A+
*669-03-27	70	A+
*669-03-30	69+	A
*669-03-30	46	A
*669-04-07	106	A+
669-04-*15*	149	+
*669-04-*15*	233	A
669-*05*	294	H
669-05-16	29	H
*669-05-27	104	A
*669-05-28	28	A
669-06-*03*	234	A+
669-06	35	+
669-06-05	139	+
*669-06-08	137	+
*669-06-*08*	138	+
*669-06-08	289	A
*669-06-09	25	A
*669-06-10	77	AH
*669-06-10	93	AH
669-06-11	257	A+
*669-06-*12*	167	+
*669-06-*15*	152	+

Date	Letter	Criteria
*669-06-*15*	*LAS* 153	+
*669-06-*15*	154	+
*669-06-*15*	155	+
*669-06-*15*	156	+
*669-06-*20*	126	+
*669-06-*23*	136	A+
669-06-*25*	162	+
?669-06-*25*	242	+
*669-06-27	290	A
669-*06*	235	+
*669-07-06	291	A
*669-07-*06*	135	+
*669-07-*08*	166	+
669-*08*	142	+
669-*09*	19	H
669-*09*	150	+
669-*11*	21	H
669-*11*	230	H
669-*12*	18	H
670	94	H+
670	213	H
670	215	+
670	216	+
670	217	+
670	295	+
670/669	5	+
670/669	8	H
670/669	9	+
670/669	145	H
670/669	243	+
670/669	332	+
671/669	68	A
671/669	275	H
671/669	370	H
672 to 669	52	H
*672 to 669	127(+)339	H
*672 to 669	131	H
672 to 669	157	H
672 to 669	192	+
672 to 669	193	+
*672 to 669	201	H
672 to 669	209	H
*672 to 669	223	+
*672 to 669	224	H
*672 to 669	228	H
*672 to 669	236	+
*672 to 669	237	H
*672 to 669	238	H
672 to 669	240	H
*672 to 669	250	H
*672 to 669	251	+
*672 to 669	252	H

Date	Letter	Criteria
*672 to 669	*LAS* 253	H
*672 to 669	254	+
*672 to 669	255	+
*672 to 669	258	H
672 to 669	264	H
672 to 669	282	+
672 to 669	342	+
*672 to 669	343	H
*668-07-04	324	A
668-11-20	330	A
*667-01-30	325	A
*667-04-21	40	A
*667-04-21	61	A
*667-04-23	60	A+
*667-07-07	73	+
667-07	117	H
667-09-04	286	AH
667-10-15	63	A
*667-10-30	120	A
667-12-30	119	(A)+
*666-*04*	121	H+
*666-*04*	122	+
*666-*04*	125	+
*666-06-05	299	(A)+
666-06-17	111	A
*666-07-30	298	AH
667	*LAS* 114	H
666 to 668	318	H
666 to 668	321	H
666/665	301	+
666/665	308	+
665 to 660	309	+
665-01-01	302	+
657-04-15	329	A
*657-05-02	334	A
*657-05-15	110+	A
657 to 655	331	H
657 to 655	358	H
*651-06-07	83	A
*650-03-01	96	D
650-05-13	80	A+
*650-06-09	109	A
650	81	+
650	82	+
650	84	+
650	99	+
650	108	+
650	368f.	H
*649-01-21	97	D
*649-10-13	352	D
*648-07-05	98	D
*621-04-22	105	A

Total: 231

2. *List of undatable (or undated) letters*[690]

LAS 6, 11, 14, 15, (17), 20, (22), (23), (24), 36, 37, 39, 42, 43, (47), 48, (49), 50, (55), (56), 64, 74, (75), (76), (78), 79, 85, (86), 87, 88, 89, 90, 91, 92, 100, 102, 103, (107), 112, 113, 115, 116, (118), 128, 141, 161, (165), (168), (169), 178, 179, 194, 199, (200), (202), 203, 205, 206, 207, 209, 210, 212, 214, (220), (225), 226, (227), 229, 231, 239, 241, 243, 244, 259, (260), (261), (262), 263, 265, 266, 267, 268, 270, 271, (274), 283, 293, 296, 297, (303), 304, 305, 306, 307, 310, 311, 312, (313), 314, 315, 316, 319, 320, 322, 323, 326, 327, 333, 335, 336, 337, 338, 340, 341, 347, 348, 350, 351, 353, 354, 355, 356, 357, (359), 360, 361, 362, 363, 364, 365, 366, 367

Total: 131.

690 Virtually all the texts here listed should fall between the time brackets 674-665 and 657-648 holding for the rest of the collection, but they cannot be dated reliably for lack of tangible chronological data. The letters enclosed in parentheses contain introductory formulae only (± a couple of lines of fragmentary text).

3. *Chronological distribution of datable letters*

Year BC	Letters	Total
674	30 31 32	3
673/4	33	1
672	1 2 3 4? 129 132 171 182 195 197 198 211 328	13
671/2	7 140 144 172	4
671	13 26 27 34 57 58 59 67 134 185 232 249 276 277 278 292 344	17
670	10+ 16 38 41 51 62 72 94 101 123 124 130 133 143 147 148 151 158 159 160 164 170 173 180 181 183 184 186 187 188 189 190 191 196 208 213 215 216 217 218+ 222 246 247 248 256 272 273 279 280 281 284 285 287 295 317 345 349	57
669/670	5 8 9 145 243 332	6
669	12 18 19 21 25 28 29 35 45 46 53 54 65 66 69+ 70 77 93 104 106 126 135 136 137 138 139 142 146 149 150 152 153 154 155 156 162 163 166 167 174 175 176 177 230 233 234 235 242 257 269 288 289 290 291 294	55
669-671	68 275 370	3
669-672	52 127(+)339 131 157 192 193 201 219 223 224 228 236 237 238 240 250 251 252 253 254 255 258 264 282 342 343	27
668	324 330	2
668-666	318 321	2
667	40 60 61 63 73 114 117 119 120 286 325	11
666	111 121 122 125 298 299	6
665-666	301 308 309	3
665	302	1
657	110+ 329 334	3
657-655	331 358	2
651	83	1
650	80 81 82 84 96 99 108 109 368f.	10
649	97 350	2
648	98	1
621	105	1
	Grand total	231

4. *Chronological structure of the LAS Corpus*

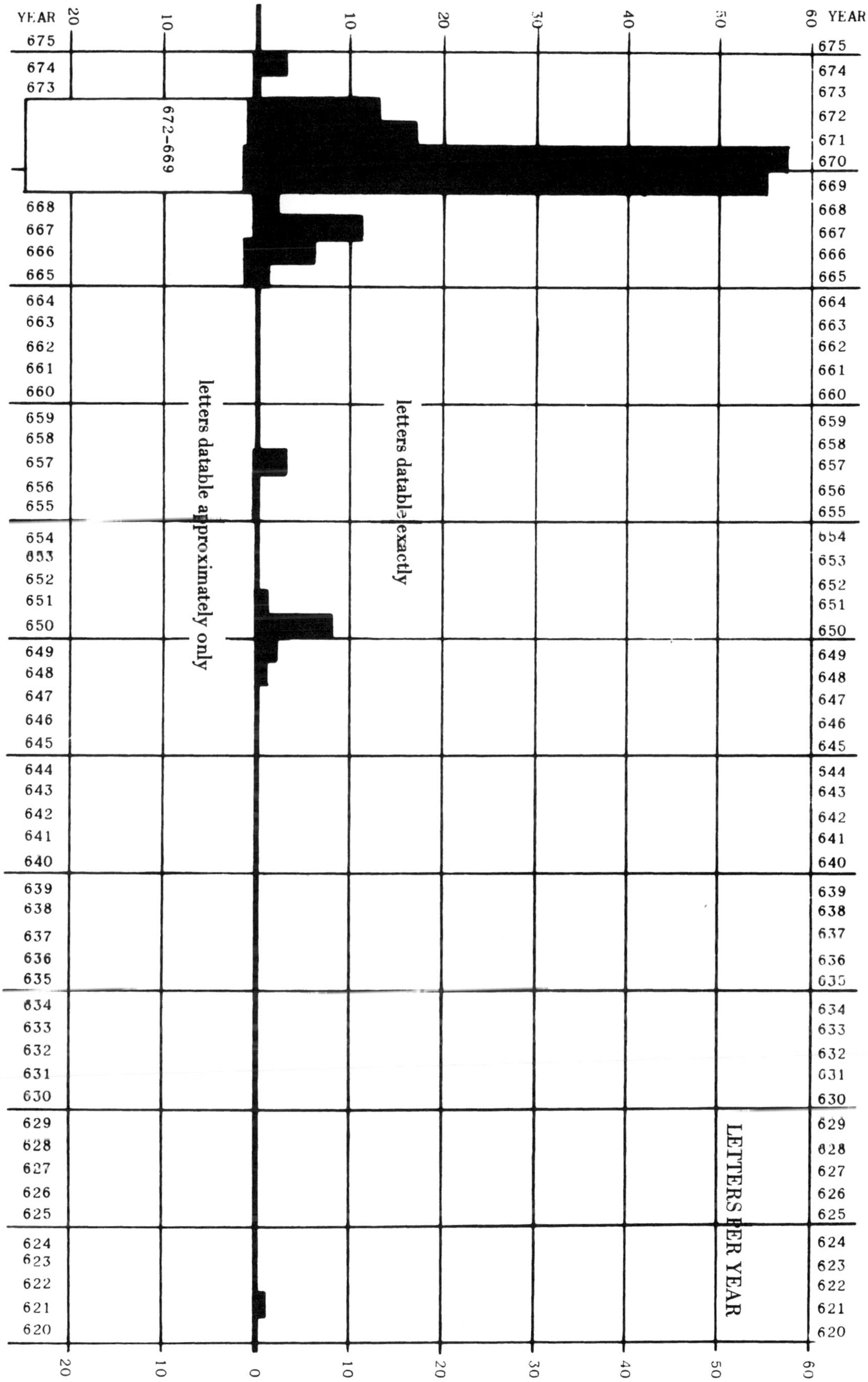

5. *Datable letters arranged by author and date*

Adad-aḫu-iddina	670-01	*LAS* 317
Adad-šumu-uṣur	674-09-03	31 (joint letter)
	674-12-11	32 (joint letter)
	672-05/6	129
	672-05/6	132
	671-08-15	134
	?670-04-19	145
	?670-04-19	332
	670-04-25	151
	670-05-03	143
	670-05/6	133
	670-06/7	159
	670-06/7	160
	670-08-24	170
	670-12-31	164
	669-01-05	163
	669-02-15	146
	669-04-15	233
	669-05-16	29
	669-06-05	139
	669-06-08	137
	669-06-08	138
	669-06-23	136
	669-06-25	162
	669-07-06	135
	669-07-08	166
	667-10-30	120
	667-12-30	119
	666-?04	121
	666-?04	122
	666-?04	125
Akkullānu	666-07-05	299
	666-07-05	298
	666 to 665	301
	666 to 665	308
	665-01-01	302
	665 to 660	309
	657-05-15	110+300
	appr. 655	331
Bābu-šumu-iddina	650-05-13	80
	appr. 650	81
Balasî	671-06	34
	671-07-15	57
	670-04	38
	670-05-04	51
	670-08-12	10+
	670-12-01	41
	669-03-13	54
	669-03-22	45

Balasî	669-03-26	*LAS* 66
	669-03-30	46
	669-06-03	234
	669-06	35
	668-07-04	324
	668-11-20	330
	667-01-30	325
	667-04-21	40
Ikkāru	672 to 669	258
Ištar-nādin-apli	650-03-01	96
	649-01-21	97
	649-10-13	352
	648-07-05	98
Ištar-šumu-ēreš	674-09-03	31 (joint letter)
	672-02-21	3
	672-04-10	1
	672-04-18	2
	672/1	7
	671-01-15	13
	671-08-21	27
	671-09-05	26
	672 to 669	343
	670/669	8
	669-03-24	12
	669-05-16	29
	669-05-28	28
	669-06-09	25
	669-11	21
	669-12	18
	668 to 666	318
	668 to 666	321
	657-04-15	329
Marduk-šākin-šumi	672-02-11	195
	672-02-20	197
	672-02-21	198
	672-08	182
	671-12-25	185
	670-05	181
	670-05	183
	670-06/7	184
	670-06/7	186
	670-06/7	187
	670-07	188
	670 08 07	190
	670-08	191
	670-11	196
	670-12-24	173
	670-12-31	164 (joint letter)
	669-01-03	174
	669-01-05	163
	669-01-05	175

Marduk-šākin-šumi	669-01-05	*LAS* 176
	669-01-07	177
	669-04-15	149
	669-05-16	29 (joint letter)
	669-05-28	28 (joint letter)
	669-06-23	136 (joint letter)
	669-07-08	166 (joint letter)
Marduk-šumu-uṣur	667	114
	667-07	117
Mār-Ištar	671-07-06	278
	671-07-22	276
	671-09-27	277
	671-10-27	292
	670-01-01	279
	670-02/3	280
	670-03/4	281
	670-08	285
	670-08-12	287
	670-08/9	284
	?670	295
	?669-02	288
	?669-05	294
	669-06-08	289
	669-06-27	290
	669-07-06	291
	667-09-04	286
Nabû-aḫḫē-erība	672-02	328
	671-03-25	67
	671-06	59
	671-07-20	58 (joint letter)
	670-04	349
	670-05-04	51 (joint letter)
	670-12-16	62
	669-03-13	54 (joint letter)
	669-03-26	65
	669-03-27	70
	669-03-30	69+71
	667-04-21	61
	667-04-23	60
	667-07-07	73
	667-10-15	63
Nabû-nādin-šumi	?672-04-20	211
	670-08-04	208
Nabû-nāṣir	670-02-10	218+221
	670-06/7	222
	670	215
	670	216
	670	217
	672 to 669	157
	672 to 669	219
	672 to 669	240

Nabû-šumu-iddina	674-09-03	*LAS* 31 (joint letter)
	669-06-10	77
rab-eširti of Arbela	670	94
	669-01-10	93
Nabû-tabni-usur	672 to 669	264
Nabû-zēru-līšer	674-09-03	31
	674-10-23	30
	674-12-11	32
	674/3	33
Nergal-šumu-iddina	651-06-07	83
Urad-Ea	674-09-03	31 (joint letter)
	670-04-21	272
	670-04-30	273
	669-01-23	269
	669-05-28	28 (joint letter)
	669-06-12	167 (joint letter)
Urad-Gula	672 to 669	223
	672 to 669	224
Urad-Nanâ	671-09/10	249
	670-04/5	247
	670-04/5	246
	670-06/7	222 (joint letter)
	669-06-11	257
	669-06-15	153
	672 to 669	250-255

APPENDIX J

DATABLE ASTROLOGICAL REPORTS[691]

1. *List of datable reports (arranged by publication number)*

Text		Writer	Chronological evidence	Date
RMA	21	Ištar-šumu-ēreš	e last of Mars at month's end	666-05-24
RMA	22	Nabû-iqbi	reference to conquest of KUR *ku-ú-ši* and KUR *mi-ṣir*	667
RMA	30	Nergal-ēṭir	prediction of lunar eclipse (Ulu)	674-09-03
RMA	33	Rāši-ili pānû	Mars stationary in Scorpio	667-06-20
RMA	37	Nergal-ēṭir	sighting of Moon (Add II); cf 225	672-03-04
RMA	44	[. . .]	Mercury in Aries (Add 30)	669-03-29
RMA	55	Balasî	Mercury visible (Add 30)	669-03-29
RMA	67	Šum-iddina	Venus + Saturn (Sim 1)	?675-05-21
RMA	68	Balasî	Mars stationary in Scorpio (Duz 1)	667-07-04
RMA	70	Nabû-aḫḫē-erība	Mars stationary in Scorpio (Duz 1)	667-07-04
RMA	85	Rāši-ili-pānû	lunar eclipse (Kis)	670-12-17
RMA	86	Nergal-ēṭir	Venus in front of Orion (Abu)	670-07-09
RMA	88	Balasî	Mars + Saturn in lunar halo on full moon day (Add 16)	669-03-15
RMA	89	Akkullānu	see *RMA* 88	669-03-15
RMA	90	Bēl-ušēzib	Saturn + Cancer in lunar halo	677 to 675
RMA	93	Ištar-šumu-ēreš	Jupiter + Cancer in luanr halo	668/7 or 656/5
RMA	94	Nabû-mušēṣi	Jupiter + Scorpio in lunar halo	664/3
RMA	95	Nabû-šum-iškun	Jupiter + Scorpio in lunar halo	675
RMA	98	Nabû-aḫḫē-erība	Mars + Saturn + Regulus in lunar halo	673-05-20
RMA	99	Šumāju	Mars + Saturn in lunar halo on full moon day (16th)	669-03-15
RMA	100	Urad-Ea	Mars + Saturn + Regulus in lunar halo	673-05-20
RMA	101A	Nabû-iqbi	Mars + Saturn in lunar halo; cf 99	669-03-15
RMA	102	Bāmāju	see *RMA* 101A	669-03-15
RMA	103	Nabû-aḫḫē-erība	see *RMA* 88	669-03-15
RMA	107	Rāši-ili panû	Mars + Saturn in lunar halo, full moon on 14th day	?669-03-15
RMA	109	rab-ṭupšarrī	Venus and Mercury setting	670-05, 668-09, or 667-02-21
RMA	112	[Nabû-aḫḫē-erība]	Venus approaching Scorpio, Mars in Pisces	667-12
RMA	114A	Zākir	Saturn + Cancer + Regulus in lunar halo	676 to 675
RMA	115C	Munnabitu	Saturn + Cancer in lunar halo	677 to 675
RMA	145	Rīmūtu	Jupiter passes Regulus thrice	678-03-26
RMA	151	Nabû-šum-iškun	(m first of) Mercury in Scorpio (Kis 14)	673-11-18
RMA	162	Nergal-ēṭir	Venus + Jupiter (Aia)	680 or 669
RMA	163	Nabû-aḫḫē-iddina	heliacal rising of Mercury in Cancer (Duz)	672-07-18

[691] Cf. Introduction, p. XV. Assyrian month names abbreviated as in App. A; + = in conjunction with; e = evening, m = morning (cf. App. C). Other abbreviations self-explanatory.

Text	Writer	Chronological evidence	Date
RMA 167	Šāpiku	Mars + Saturn (Add 16)	669-03-15
RMA 172	Ašarīdu pānû	Saturn + retrogr. Mars (Add 16)	669-03-15
RMA 174A	Rāši-ili	m last of Venus (Nis), Saturn in lunar halo	674-04-07 or 666-04-05
RMA 180	Nabû-[aḫḫē-erība]	Saturn + Regulus in lunar halo	674-04
RMA 183	Bēl-lē'i	e last of Jupiter (Ara 1)	675-10-30
RMA 184	[. . .]	e first of Mercury in Hyades (Nis)	677-04-16 or 664-04-19
RMA 185	Bāmāju	m first of Jupiter (Sim)	669-06-03
RMA 186	Nergal-ēṭir	m first of Jupiter (Aia)	670-04-29
RMA 187	Ašarīdu	m first of Jupiter in front of Cancer (*rēš šarrūti*)	680-06-27 or 668-07-04
RMA 187A	Ašarīdu pānû	m first of Jupiter near Pleiades (Aia)	670-05-03
RMA 189	Nabû-iqīša	m first of Jupiter in Leo (Ulu)	678-08-28
RMA 190	Nabû-šum-iškun	m first of Jupiter in Sagittarius (Ara)	675-11-27
RMA 190A	Aplâ	see *RMA* 190	675-11-27
RMA 191	[Nabû-aḫḫē-erība]	m first of Jupiter in Leo (not in Ulūlu)	667-08-01
RMA 195	Nabû-iqīša	Jupiter + Mars	679-06-11
RMA 195A	Nergal-ēṭir	(e last of) Jupiter + Venus (Kis 1)	674-11-17
RMA 196	Bulluṭu	m first of Jupiter (Sim)	669-06-03
RMA 196A	[. . .]	m first of Jupiter (Taš)	677-09-26 or 665-09-30
RMA 199A	Nergal-ēṭir	Mercury + Regulus (e first of ☿)	675-07-06
RMA 203	Aḫḫēšâ	m last of Venus (Nis); Orion in lunar halo	674-04-07
RMA 204	Nabû-aḫḫē-erība	m last of Venus (Nis)	666-04-05
RMA 205	Nabû-mušēṣi	see *RMA* 205	666-04-05
RMA 206	Ištar-šumu-ēreš	m last of Venus (Kan)	669-12-27
RMA 207	Šumāju	e first of Venus before Cancer (Sim)	666-06-17
RMA 207B	Nergal-ēṭir	see *RMA* 207	674-06-20
RMA 208	Nergal-ēṭir	e last of Venus; m first in Leo predicted	675-07-24
RMA 209	Nabû-aḫḫē-erība	e first of Venus + Mercury (Kis)	668-11-20
RMA 210	Ašarīdu	m first of Saturn in Leo (Abu)	675-08-13
RMA 211	Aplâ	(m) first of Venus in NE Pisces (Šab)	673-03-12
RMA 216	Ašarīdu pānû	m first of Saturn in Leo	675-08-13
RMA 218	Bēl-aḫḫē-irība	(m) first of Mercury in Pleiades (Aia 14)	674-05-10
RMA 219	Ašarīdu	e first of Mercury in Leo (Duz)	675-07-06
RMA 220	Ašarīdu panû	e first of Mercury (Ulu)	671-08-31 or 670-08-07
RMA 221	Ašarīdu	m first of Mercury in area of Virgo (Ulu)	675-09-04
RMA 222	Ṭābīja	(m) first of Mercury in Leo (Ulu)	668-08-28
RMA 223	[. . .]	e first of Mercury in Scorpio (Ara)	673-10-17
RMA 224	Nergal-ēṭir	m first of Mercury (Kis)	674-12-01 or 673-11-15
RMA 225	Nergal-ēṭir	e last of Mercury in SW Pisces (Add)	672-03-04
RMA 226	Nādinu	e first of Mercury in Pleiades (Nis)	670-04-10
RMA 227	Rāši-ili panû	(m) last of Mercury in Sagittarius, reference to crown prince (= Asb)	672-12-10
RMA 228	Nabû-mušēṣi	(e) last of Mercury near Regulus	666-07-05
RMA 231	Ašarīdu qatnu	m first of Mars in Gemini (Duz)	670-06-25

Text	Writer	Chronological evidence	Date
RMA 232	Bulluṭu	m first of Mars + Mercury in Gemini (Duz)	670-06-25
RMA 233	Nabû-iqbi	m first of Mars (Ulu)	666-08-23
RMA 234A	Balasî	Mars stationary in Leo	671-03-26
RMA 235	Akkullānu	Mars in Cancer, not retrograde (Abu)	672-08
RMA 235A	Bēl-šum-iškun	Mars 7 months in Gemini; lunar eclipse (Ara) affecting Subartu; repeated occultation of Jupiter; repeated full moon on 15th day	675-04
RMA 236	Bēl-nāṣir	Mars in Cancer, not retrograde	672-08
RMA 236A	Aḫḫēšâ	see *RMA* 236	672-08
RMA 236G	Nabû-aḫḫē-erība	Mars stationary in Sagittarius (Aia)	667-04-05
RMA 236H	Nabû-aḫḫē-erība	Mars passes Saturn	669-01-23
RMA 237	Nabû-aḫḫē-erība	Mars stationary in Leo	671-03-26
RMA 244A	Rāši-ili pānû	Mars reaches Cancer (not retrograde)	672-08
RMA 244C	Nabû-aḫḫē-erība	Saturn stationary in Libra	669-12, 668-06, or 667-06
RMA 246G	Nabû-aḫḫē-erība	m first of Mercury (Sim 16)	669-06-12
RMA 247A	[Rāsi-ili] pānû	Saturn retrograding from Scorpio to Libra	667-02
RMA 249A	Nabû-iqbi	fog in Šabāṭu (cf. LAS 325)	667-01-30
RMA 250	Ašarīdu pānû	see *RMA* 249A	667-01-30
RMA 250A	Rāši-ili pānû	see *RMA* 249A	667-01-30
RMA 256B	Balasî	Mars in Cancer (Abu), thunder	672-08
RMA 256C	Urad-Ea	thunder in Ābu, cf. *RMA* 256B	672-08
RMA 257	Ištar-šumu-ēreš	thunder in Ābu, king ill	672-08
RMA 258	Nabû-aḫḫē-erība	see *RMA* 256B	672-08
RMA 266B	Nabû-mušēṣi	m first of Jupiter in Leo	667-08-01
RMA 268	Munnabitu	lunar eclipse (Sim 14), Jupiter visible during eclipse	678-05-22
RMA 269	Rāši-ili pānû	solar eclipse (Aia 29)	669-05-27
RMA 270	[Ašarī]du	lunar eclipse (Sim 14, evening watch)	678-05-22
RMA 271	[. . .]	lunar eclipse (Sim 14, morning)	669-06-11
RMA 271A	Nabû-aḫḫē-erība	predicted nonoccurrence of lunar eclipse (Ulu 15)	673-08-23
RMA 272	Bēl-ušēzib	Venus in Sagittarius; Mars between Libra and Scorpio; Jupiter retrograding past Regulus; lunar eclipses predicted for Kislīmu and Simānu	679-11-26
RMA 272A	Akkullānu	lunar eclipse (Taš)	667-10-15
RMA 272B	Nergal-ēṭir	prediction of lunar eclipse (Add)	673-02-25
RMA 273	Rāši-ili pānû	prediction of lunar eclipse (Taš)	667-10-15
RMA 274	Bēl-ušēzib	potential (solar) eclipse at the end of Addāru following a (lunar) eclipse in Addāru	?673-03-13
RMA 274E	Nabû-aḫḫē-erība	predicted nonoccurrence of lunar eclipse (Duz)	670-09-19
RMA 274F	Nādinu	lunar eclipse (Aia 14)	?667-04-21
RMA 274G	Nabû-aḫḫē-erība	nonoccurrence of solar eclipse	670-12-02
RMA 277R	[Akkullānu]	solar eclipse (Nis 28, morning)	657-04-15
RMA p.lxxxv (Rm 193)	Zākir	lunar eclipse (Sim 14, evening)	678-05-22

TEXTS DATED BY EPONYM YEAR:

Text	Writer	Date
RMA 136S	[. . .] (Bab.)	710 BC
RMA 136B	anonymous (Ass.)	657 BC
RMA 264	Ištar-šumu-ēreš	657 BC

2. *Datable reports in chronological order*[692]

710 BC	**RMA* 136S	[...]
680-05 or 669-04	**RMA* 162	Nergal-īṭir
680-06-27 or 668-07	**RMA* 187	Ašarīdu s. Damqa
679-06-11	**RMA* 195	Nabû-iqīša of Borsippa
679-11-26	**RMA* 272	Bēl-ušēzib
678-03-26	**RMA* 145	Rīmūtu
678-05-22	**RMA* 268	Munnabitu
678-05-22	**RMA* 270	[Ašarī]du
678-05-22	**RMA* p.lxxxv (Rm 193)	Zākir
678-08-28	**RMA* 189	Nabû-iqīša of Borsippa
675-04	**RMA* 235A	Bēl-šum-iškun kalû
675-05-21	**RMA* 67	Šum-iddina
675-07-06	**RMA* 219	Ašarīdu
675-07-06	**RMA* 199A	Nergal-īṭir
675-07-24	**RMA* 208	Nergal-īṭir
675-08-13	**RMA* 210	Ašarīdu
675-08-13	**RMA* 216	Ašarīdu pānû
675-10-30	**RMA* 183	Bēl-lē'i āšipu
675-11-27	**RMA* 190	Nabû-šum-iškun
675-11-27	**RMA* 190A	Aplâ of Borsippa
675	**RMA* 95	Nabû-šum-iškun
674-04-07 or 666-04	**RMA* 174A	Rāši-ili s. Nurzānu
674-04	**RMA* 203	Aḫḫēšâ of Uruk
674-04	*RMA* 180	Nabû-aḫḫē-erība
674-05-10	**RMA* 218	Bēl-aḫḫē-irība
674-06-20	**RMA* 207B	Nergal-īṭir
674-09-03	**RMA* 30	Nergal-īṭir
674-11-17	**RMA* 195A	Nergal-īṭir
674-12-01 or 673-11	**RMA* 224	Nergal-īṭir
673-02-25	**RMA* 272B	Nergal-īṭir
673-03-12	**RMA* 211	Aplâ of Borsippa
673-03-13	**RMA* 274	Bēl-ušēzib
673-05-20	*RMA* 100	Urad-Ea
673-08-23	*RMA* 271A	Nabû-aḫḫē-erība
673-10-17	**RMA* 223	[...]
673-11-18	**RMA* 151	Nabû-šum-iškun
672-03-04	**RMA* 37	Nergal-īṭir
672-08	*RMA* 235	Akkullānu
672-08	**RMA* 236	Bēl-nāṣir
672-08	**RMA* 236A	Aḫḫēšâ of Uruk
672-08	*RMA* 256B	Balasî
672-08	*RMA* 256C	Urad-Ea
672-08	*RMA* 257	Ištar-šumu-ēreš
672-08	*RMA* 258	Nabû-aḫḫē-erība
672-12-10	**RMA* 227	Rāši-ili pānû
671-03-26	*RMA* 234A	Balasî
671-03-26	*RMA* 237	Nabû-aḫḫē-erība
671-08-31 or 670-08	**RMA* 220	Ašarīdu qatnu

---

[692] Texts by Babylonian writers indicated with asterisks.

670-04-10	**RMA* 226	Nādinu
670-04-29	**RMA* 186	Nergal-īṭir
670-05-03	**RMA* 187A	Ašarīdu pānû
670-06-25	**RMA* 231	Ašarīdu qatnu
670-06-25	*RMA* 232	Bulluṭu
670-07-09	**RMA* 86	Nergal-īṭir
670-09-19	**RMA* 274F	Nādinu
670-12	**RMA* 85	Rāši-ili pānû
670-12-02	*RMA* 274G	Nabû-aḫḫē-erība
669-01-23	*RMA* 236H	Nabû-aḫḫē-erība
669-03-15	*RMA* 88	Balasî
669-03-15	*RMA* 89	Akkullānu
669-03-15	*RMA* 99	Šumāju
669-03-15	**RMA* 101A	Nabû-iqbi of Cutha
669-03-15	*RMA* 102	Bāmāju
669-03-15	*RMA* 103	Nabû-aḫḫē-erība
669-03-15	**RMA* 107	Rāši-ili pānû
669-03-15	**RMA* 167	Šāpiku of Borsippa
669-03-29	*RMA* 55	Balasî
669-03-29	**RMA* 44	[. . .]
669-05-27	**RMA* 269	Rāši-ili pānû
669-06-03	*RMA* 185	Bāmāju
669-06-03	*RMA* 196	Bulluṭu
669-06-11	*RMA* 271	[. . .]
669-06-12	*RMA* 246G	Nabû-aḫḫē-erība
669-12-27	*RMA* 206	Ištar-šumu-ēreš
668-07-04 or 680-06	**RMA* 187	Ašarīdu s. Damqa
668-08-28	**RMA* 222	Ṭābīja
668-11-20	*RMA* 209	Nabû-aḫḫē-erība
667-01-30	**RMA* 250A	Rāši-ili pānû
667-01-30	**RMA* 249A	Nabû-iqbi of Cutha
667-01-30	**RMA* 250	Ašarīdu pānû
667-02	**RMA* 247A	Rāši-ili pānû
667-04-05	*RMA* 236G	Nabû-aḫḫē-erība
667-06-20	**RMA* 33	Rāši-ili pānû
667-07-04	*RMA* 68	Balasî
667-07-04	*RMA* 70	Nabû-aḫḫē-erība
667-07-05	*RMA* 228	Nabû-mušēṣi
667-08-01	*RMA* 191	[Nabû-aḫḫē-erība]
667-08-01	*RMA* 266B	Nabû-mušēṣi
667-10-15	*RMA* 272A	Akkullānu
667-10-15	**RMA* 273	Rāši-ili pānû
667-12	*RMA* 112	[Nabû-aḫḫē-erība]
666-04-05	*RMA* 204	Nabû-aḫḫē-erība
666-05-24	*RMA* 21	Ištar-šumu-ēreš
666-06-17	*RMA* 207	Šumāju
666-07-05	*RMA* 228	Nabû-mušēṣi
666-08-23	**RMA* 233	Nabû-iqbi
664 to 663	*RMA* 94	Nabû-mušēṣi
657-04	*RMA* 264	Ištar-šumu-ēreš
657-04-15	*RMA* 277R	[. . .]
657	*RMA* 136B	anonymous

3. *Datable reports arranged by author and date*[693]

Author	Date	Report
*Aḫḫēšâ of Uruk	674-04-07	*RMA* 203
	672-08	*RMA* 236A
Akkullānu	672-08	*RMA* 235
	669-03-15	*RMA* 89
	667-10-15	*RMA* 272A
*Aplâ of Borsippa	675-11-27	*RMA* 190A
	673-03-12	*RMA* 211
*Ašarīdu (no title)	678-05-22	*RMA* 270
	675-07-06	*RMA* 219
	675-08-13	*RMA* 210
(pānû)	675-08-13	*RMA* 216
	670-05-03	*RMA* 187A
	669-03-15	*RMA* 172
	667-01-30	*RMA* 250
(qatnu)	671-08-31 or 670-08	*RMA* 220
	670-06-25	*RMA* 231
(s. Damqa)	668-07-04 or 680-06	*RMA* 187
Balasî	672-08	*RMA* 256B
	671-03-26	*RMA* 234A
	669-03-15	*RMA* 88
	669-03-29	*RMA* 55
	667-07-04	*RMA* 68
Bāmāju	669-03-15	*RMA* 102
	669-06-03	*RMA* 185
*Bēl-aḫḫē-irība	674-05-10	*RMA* 218
*Bēl-lē'i āšipu	675-10-30	*RMA* 183
*Bēl-nāṣir	672-08	*RMA* 236
*Bēl-šum-iškun kalû	675-04	*RMA* 235A
*Bēl-ušēzib	679-11-26	*RMA* 272
	677 to 675	*RMA* 90
	?673-03-13	*RMA* 274
Bulluṭu	670-06-25	*RMA* 232
	669-06-03	*RMA* 196
Ištar-šumu-ēreš	672-08	*RMA* 257
	669-12-27	*RMA* 206
	668/667 or 656/655	*RMA* 93
	666-05-24	*RMA* 21
	657-04	*RMA* 264
*Munnabitu	678-05-22	*RMA* 268
	677 to 675	*RMA* 115C
*Nabû-aḫḫē-iddina	672	*RMA* 163

[693] Babylonian writers marked with asterisks.

Nabû-aḫḫē-erība	674-04-08	*RMA* 180
	673-05-20	*RMA* 98
	673-08-23	*RMA* 271A
	672-08	*RMA* 258
	671-03-26	*RMA* 237
	670-09-19	*RMA* 274E
	670-12-02	*RMA* 274G
	669-01-23	*RMA* 236H
	669-03-15	*RMA* 103
	669-06-12	*RMA* 246G
	668-11-20	*RMA* 209
	667-04-05	*RMA* 236G
	667-07-04	*RMA* 70
	667-08-01	*RMA* 191
	667-12	*RMA* 112
	666-04-05	*RMA* 204
*Nabû-iqbi	669-03-15	*RMA* 101A (of Cutha)
	667-01-30	*RMA* 249A (of Cutha)
	667-07 (ff)	*RMA* 22 (no title)
	666-08-23	*RMA* 233 (no title)
*Nabû-iqīša of Borsippa	679-06-11	*RMA* 195
	678-08-28	*RMA* 189
	667-07-05	*RMA* 228
Nabû-mušēṣi	667-08-01	*RMA* 266B
	666-04-05	*RMA* 205
	664 to 663	*RMA* 94
*Nabû-šum-iškun	675-11-27	*RMA* 190
	675	*RMA* 95
	673-11-18	*RMA* 151
*Nādinu	670-04-10	*RMA* 226
	667-04-21	*RMA* 274F
*Nergal-īṭir	680-05 or 669-04	*RMA* 162
	675-07-06	*RMA* 199A
	675-07-24	*RMA* 208
	674-06-20	*RMA* 207B
	674-09-03	*RMA* 30
	674-11-17	*RMA* 195A
	674-12-01 or 673-11	*RMA* 224
	673-02-25	*RMA* 272B
	672-03-04	*RMA* 37
	670-04-29	*RMA* 186
	670-07-09	*RMA* 86
*Rāši-ili (pānû)	672-12-10	*RMA* 227
	670-12-17	*RMA* 85
	669-03-15	*RMA* 107
	669-05-27	*RMA* 269
	667-01-30	*RMA* 250A
	667-02	*RMA* 247A
	667-06-20	*RMA* 33
	667-10-15	*RMA* 273
(s. Nurzānu)	674-04-07 or 666-04	*RMA* 174A

*Rīmūtu	678-03-26	*RMA* 145
*Šāpiku of Borsippa	669-03-15	*RMA* 167
Šumāju	669-03-15	*RMA* 99
	666-06-17	*RMA* 207
*Šum-iddina	?675-05-21	*RMA* 67
*Ṭābīja	668-08-28	*RMA* 220
Urad-Ea	673-05-20	*RMA* 100
	672-08	*RMA* 256C
*Zākir	678-05-22	Rm. 193 (*RMA* p.lxxxv)
	676 to 675	*RMA* 114A

APPENDIX K

SYNOPSIS OF THE HISTORICAL INFORMATION PROVIDED BY THE *LAS* CORPUS[694]

7th year of Esarhaddon (eponymy of Šarru-nūrī)

Ulu 15	=	Sep 3, 674	Total eclipse of the moon: substitute king enthroned in Nineveh (*LAS* 31)
Ara 5	=	Oct 23	Substitute king re-enthroned in Akkad. Esarhaddon warned of political ambitions of Ṣallāju of Bīt-Awukāni (*LAS* 30)
Kis 25	=	Dec 11	Substitute king dethroned and put to death (*LAS* 32)
Add 8	=	Feb 21, 673	Troops of Assyria storm Ša-amīlē in Bīt-Awukāni (*Chron.*)
Add 10	=	Feb 23	Ištar of Akkad returns from Elam and enters the city of Akkad (*Chron.*, cf. *LAS* 275)
Add 14	=	Feb 27	Partial eclipse of the moon *not* affecting Assyria (*RMA* 272B)

8th year of Esarhaddon (eponymy of Atar-ilī)

Kis-Kan	=	Nov-Dec, 673	Assyrians conquer and annex Šubria (Borger, *Ash* p. 104; *Chron.*)
Add 5/6	=	Feb 8/9, 672	King's wife dies (*Chron.*; *LAS* 195, 197-198; 4?; 132)

9th year of Esarhaddon (eponymy of Nabû-bēlu-uṣur)

Nis-Aja	=	Apr-May, 672	Esarhaddon settles his succession: Assur-banipal and Šamaš-šumu-ukīn are proclaimed heirs to throne, and allegiance is sworn to both (Wiseman, *VTE*; Streck, *Asb* p.2; *LAS* 129, 132, 171; cf. 1-3, 211?)
Abu	=	Aug, 672	Esarhaddon ill (*AGS* 99, *LAS* 282, *RMA* 257)

10th year of Esarhaddon (eponymy of Kanūnāju)

Nis	=	Mar/Apr, 671	Army of Assyria marches to Egypt (*Chron.*) [Note: King still in Nineveh on Nis 3 = Mar 25 according to *LAS* 67 and *RMA* 234A]
Duz 3	=	Jun 22	Assyrians defeat Egyptians in battle (*Chron.*)
early Duz	=	late Jun	Esarhaddon returns to Nineveh (*LAS* 34, 59)
Duz 14	=	Jul 2	Total eclipse of the moon predicting death of the king of Assyria but also, on the other hand, defeat of the king of Egypt; substitute king enthroned in Nineveh (*LAS* 278)
Duz 16, 18	=	Jul 5, 7	Egyptians defeated in two battles (*Chron.*)
Duz 22	=	Jul 11	Memphis taken and pillaged (*Chron.*)
Abu 2	=	July 22	Mār-Ištar receives precious stones for the crown of Nebo of Borsippa (*LAS* 276; cf. 57-58)
Ulu 4	=	Aug 21	Substitute king enthroned in Akkad (*LAS* 27, 26, 134, 249)

694 The purpose of this appendix is twofold: first, to *summarize* the historical information contained in the letters under study so as to make it more easily available to the historian, and second, to *correlate* this information with the evidence offered by other contemporary sources in order to show how the picture obtained through the chronological analysis of the letters fits in the general historical framework of the period. All information unessential from these points of view has been omitted. Thus, while the survey does contain some detail information, it should not be viewed as an attempt to reconstruct the entire course of history of the period of time concerned. For each event listed, the commentary should be consulted under respective letters. Dates are given in terms of both Julian and Assyrian calendar for the sake of convenience; for the correlations, see App. A. *Chron.* refers to entries in the Babylonian Chronicles (Grayson, *TCS* 5).

Taš 3	= Sep 19	Further battles in Egypt (*Chron.*)
Taš 12	= Sep 27	Restoration work under way in Uruk and Der (*LAS* 277)
Taš 22	= Oct 7	Substitute king dethroned and put to death in Akkad; restoration work carried out in Borsippa (*LAS* 292)
Kan 15	= Dec 27	Total eclipse of the moon; substitute king enthroned in Nineveh (*LAS* 185, 232)
Kan 20	= Jan 1, 670	Substitute king taken to Akkad and re-enthroned (*LAS* 279)
Add 1	= Feb 10	Prophylactic rituals performed for the royal family (*LAS* 218+)
Add	= Feb	Substitute king put to death; Šamaš-šumu-ukīn takes up residence in Babylonia (*LAS* 280)

11th year of Esarhaddon (eponymy of Šulmu-Bēl-lašme)

Nis	= March, 670	Conspiracy against Esarhaddon detected and crushed (*Chron.*; *LAS* 247, 133)
Late Nis	= early April	Restoration of Borsippa continued (*LAS* 281) Lightning burns crops in Assyria (*LAS* 38, 349)
Aja 10	= Apr 20	Akītu festival of Sin at Harran (*LAS* 272, 273)
Aja 22	= May 2	Esarhaddon falls ill (*LAS* 143, 51, 246, 247, 248, 180, 181, 183, 123, 124, 130)
Mid-Sin	= late May	Esarhaddon recovers (*LAS* 133, 159)
Duz 14	= Jun 22	Earthquake (*LAS* 16, 147-148; uncertain)
Duz/Abu	= Jun/Jul	Queen mother falls ill and recovers (*LAS* 159-160, 184, 222)
Abu	= July	Royal family exorcised (*LAS* 186-187, 208) Divine statues "renewed" (*LAS* 188; Borger, *Ash* p. 83f)
Ulu 3	= Aug 10	Dressing festival of Bēl at Babylon started but interrupted because of king's last-minute decision to intercalate a second Ulūlu (*LAS* 190, 285, 287)
Ulu 17	= Aug 24	Akītu of Ištar of Arbela (*LAS* 170; *Ash* p. 95; cf. *LAS* 10+ and 72)
Taš	= Oct	Reconstruction of [the sacred precincts of] Babylon under way; oath of loyalty imposed on Assyrian officials in Babylonia (*LAS* 284; *BBEA*)
Ara	= Nov	Cimmerians take an Assyrian city (*LAS* 196; uncertain)
Kis 15	= Dec 17	Partial eclipse of the moon (*LAS* 41, 62, 101; *RMA* 85)
Kis 24 through Kan 5 = Dec 26, 670, through Jan 5, 669		Entire royal family exorcised (*LAS* 163-164, 173-177); chariot of Marduk under construction (*LAS* 175)
Kan 23	= Jan 23, 669	Conjunction of Mars and Saturn (*LAS* 269; *RMA* 236H)
Šab	= Feb	King and crown prince [participate in the festival of Aššur] at Assur (*LAS* 146)
Add 14	= Mar 13	Conjunction of Mars and Saturn (*LAS* 54; *RMA* 88-89, etc.)
Add 23	= Mar 22	Crown prince (Šamaš-šumu-ukīn) due to visit the king (*LAS* 45)
Add 25	= Mar 24	Mercury rises heliacally: taken as a good omen from the viewpoint of the visit of the prince (*LAS* 12, 53, 46, 47, 65, 66, 69 l, 70)

12th year of Esarhaddon (eponymy of Šamaš-kāšid-ajābi)

Mid-Nis	= Mid Apr, 669	Mars retrogrades toward Spica: apotropaic rituals performed (to save the crops) (*LAS* 233, 146)
Early Aja	= early May	Strong floods (*LAS* 291, 294; Borger, *Ash* p. 7)
Aja 8	= May 6	Statue of Marduk departs for Babylon (*Ash* p. 7)
Aja 18	= May 16	Journey of the statue interrupted at Labbanat (*LAS* 29)
Aja 29	= May 27	Solar eclipse. Substitute king enthroned in Nineveh (*LAS* 104, 28)
Sim 5(?)	= Jun 1	Earthquake predicting misfortune to the king (*LAS* 234; 35; 137, 138)
Sim 12	= Jun 8	Jupiter rises heliacally after a long interval of invisibility: bad omen (*LAS* 289-290)
Sim 14	= Jun 10	Partial eclipse of the moon, bad omen to Assyria (*LAS* 25, 77, 93, 257)
Sim 19	= Jun 15	A junior member of the royal family (= the first-born son of the crown prince?) falls seriously ill (*LAS* 152-155, 167, 136)

Duz 10	=	Jul 6	Assyrian officials dismissed in Babylonia; Esarhaddon plans visiting Borsippa [and Babylon]; reconstruction work carried out in Cutha (*LAS* 291)
Duz 15	=	Jul 11	Substitute king put to death (*LAS* 135, 166)
Late Duz	=	late July	Festival of Tammuz (*LAS* 5-6)
Taš	=	Oct	Temple of Amurru (in Assur) restored (*LAS* 19)
Ara 10	=	Nov 1	Esarhaddon falls ill and dies on his way to Egypt (*Chron.*)
Ara	=	Nov	Queen mother holds the reins of Assyria (*ABL* 1239+; *LAS* 21, 230)
Kis 1	=	Nov 22	Assurbanipal ascends throne (*Chron.*)
1st year of Assurbanipal (eponymy of Mar-larim)			
Aja 24	=	May 10, 668	Bēl and gods of Akkad depart from Assur and arrive in Babylon; Nabu and gods of Borsippa go to Babylon (*Chron.*)
Duz 20	=	Jul 4	Heliacal risings of Jupiter, taken as good omen to the king (*LAS* 324)
2nd year of Assurbanipal (eponymy of Gabbāru)			
Nis 16	=	Apr 21, 667	Total eclipse of the moon. Not dangerous to the king (and consequently, not requiring the enthronement of a substitute king) since Jupiter visible during the eclipse (*LAS* 40, 60, 61)
Sim 16	=	Jun 20	Mars stationary in Scorpio: bad omen (*RMA* 33)
Duz 1	=	Jul 4	Troops mustered [for expedition to Egypt] (*LAS* 73; *RMA* 70; 68)
[Duz	=	Jul]	Assyrians march to Egypt, defeat Taharqa and install Necho on throne (*Chron.*; cf. *LAS* 117 and *RMA* 22)
Taš 14	=	Oct 15	Total eclipse of the moon (not "harmful" to king of Assyria) (*LAS* 63, *RMA* 272A)
Taš 30	=	Oct 30	Adad-šumu-uṣur petitions the king for his son Urad-Gula (*LAS* 120)
3rd year of Assurbanipal (eponymy of Kanūnāju of New Palace)			
Nis	=	April, 666	Assurbanipal reshapes his entourage (*LAS* 121, 122, 125)
Nis 15	=	Apr 10	Partial eclipse of the moon (*LAS* 299)
Duz 14	=	Jul 7	Substitute king enthroned in Akkad (*LAS* 298)

APPENDIX L

ADDRESSEES

1. "Farmer" (^{LÚ}ENGAR)

Text	Writer	Year
LAS 25	Ištar-šumu-ēreš	669
30	Nabû-zēru-lišir	674
31	Nabû-zēru-lišir et alii	674
77	Nabû-šumu-iddina	669
137	Adad-šumu-uṣur	669
138	Adad-šumu-uṣur	669
139	Adad-šumu-uṣur and Marduk-šākin-šumi	669
166	[Adad-šumu-uṣur] and Marduk-šākin-šumi	669
167	Adad-šumu-uṣur and Urad-Ea	669
235	[Adad-šumu-uṣur?]	
236	[. . .]	
257	[Urad-Nanâ]	669
334	NN	657

2. "Lord"

Text	Writer	Year
26	Ištar-šumu-ēreš	671
27	Ištar-šumu-ēreš	671
28	Ištar-šumu-ēreš et alii	669
337	NN	

3. Crown Prince

Text	Writer	Year
94	Head of the Scribes of Arbela	?670
130	Adad-šumu-uṣur	?670
131	Adad-šumu-uṣur	

4. Queen Mother

Text	Writer	Year
21	Ištar-šumu-ēreš	?669
230	Ištar-šumu-ēreš	?669

5. Palace Scribe

Text	Writer
79	Nabû-šumu-iddina

6. Various Scholars

Text	Writer
162	Farmer
226	King
242	[Farmer?]

Cf. also 320 and 340

All other letters addressed to the king

APPENDIX M

SENDERS

1. *List of letters with extant indication of authorship* (Total: 220)

1.1 One sender only (Total: 195)[695]

Name	Letter	Number of Letters	% of Total
Adad-ahu-iddina	317	1	0,5
Adad-šumu-uṣur	119 120 121 122 123 125 126 130 131 133 134 135 137 138 142 143 144 145 146 147 151 152 154 155 156 158 159 160 161 332*	30	15,4
Akkullānu	298 300 301 302 303 304 306 307 308 309 311 312 313 314 315 316	16	8,2
Bābu-šumu-iddina	80(*) 81(*)	2	1,0
Balasî (scribe)	35 36 38 39 40 41 42 44 45 46 47 48 49 50	14	7,2
Balasî (majordomo)	37	1	0,5
Bānî	263	1	0,5
Ikkāru	258 259 260 261	4	2,0
Ištar-nādin-apli	96(*) 97(*) 352(*)	3	1,5
Ištar-šumu-ēreš	1 2 3 4 5 7 8 9 12 13 15 16 17 18 19 20 21 22 23 24 25 26 27	23	11,8
Farmer	162	1	0,5
King	226	1	0,5
Marduk-šākin-šumi	172 173 174 176 177 178 179 180 181 182 183 186 191 195 197 198 199 200 201 202	21	10,8
Marduk-šumu-uṣur	113 114 117	3	1,5
Mār-Ištar	275 276 278 284 286 287 290 293 296	9	4,6
Nabû'a	88 89(*) 90(*) 92	4	2,0
Nabû-ahhē-erība	59 61 64 67 69 70 72 73 74 75 76	11	5,6
Nabû-ahhē-šallim	107	1	0,5
Nabû-gāmil	227	1	0,5
Nabû-nādin-šumi	203 204 205 206 207 208 209 211 212 213 214	11	5,6
Nabû-nāṣir	33! 215 217 220 221	5	2,6
Nabû-šumu-iddina	77(*) 78(*) 79	3	1,5
Nabû-tabni-uṣur	264	1	0,5
Nabû-zēru-iddina	368 369	2	1,0
Nabû-zēru-līšir	30	1	0,5

695 Reports (in letter form) indicated with asterisks.

Name	Letter	Number of Letters	% of Total
Nergal-šumu-iddina	82(*) 83(*) 84(*)	3	1,5
Rab-ešerti of Arbela	93(*) 94(*)	2	1,0
Scribes of Kalizi	85(*) 86(*)	2	1,0
Tabnî	118	1	0,5
Urad-Dagān	359	1	0,5
Urad-Gula	223 224 225	3	1,5
Urad-Ea	270 271 272 273 274	5	2,6
Urad-Nanâ	246 247 250 251 252 254 255 256	8	4,1

Joint letters (Total: 24)

	Senders	Letters
a)	Adad-šumu-uṣur + Marduk-šākin-šumi	139 163 164 165
b)	Adad-šumu-uṣur + Marduk-šākin-šumi + Nabû-nādin-šumi	169
c)	Adad-šumu-uṣur + Nabû-mušēṣi + Ištar-šumu-ēreš	170
d)	Adad-šumu-uṣur + Urad-Ea + Ištar-šumu-ēreš + Akkullānu	168
e)	Adad-šumu-uṣur + Urad-Ea	167
f)	Nabû-zēru-līšir + Adad-šumu-uṣur	32
g)	Nabû-zēru-līšir + Adad-šumu-uṣur + Nabû-šumu-iddina + Urad-Ea + Ištar-šumu-ēreš	31
h)	Ištar-šumu-ēreš + Adad-šumu-uṣur + Marduk-šākin-šumi	29
i)	Ištar-šumu-ēreš + Urad-Ea + Marduk-šākin-šumi	28
j)	Balasî + Nabû-aḫḫē-erība	51 52 53 54 55 56 57
k)	Nabû-aḫḫē-erība + Balasî	58
l)	Marduk-šumu-uṣur + Nāṣiru + Aqarâ	115
m)	Marduk-šumu-uṣur + Nāṣiru + Tabnî	116
n)	Nabû-nāṣir + Urad-Nanâ	222
o)	Ikkāru + [. . .]	262

a-b and j-o sent by men representing same or related (n) professions. The letters signed by scholars of diverse fields of specialization (c-i) either pertain to the substitute king ritual (e-g, i) or to cultic matters (c, h). The order of names is generally that of seniority and/or rank. Letters 139, 164, 165 authored by Marduk-šākin-šumi, 169 by Nabû-nādin-šumi, and 170 by Ištar-šumu-ēreš; in all other cases, the scholar heading the team of writers also wrote down the respective letter.

2. *List of letters lacking indication of authorship but assignable to definite writers* (Total: 123)[696]

Name	Letter	Number of Letters	% of Total	Corresponding % in List 1
Adad-aḫu-iddina		0	0,0	0,5
Adad-šumu-uṣur	124 129 132 136 140 141 148 150 171? 228 233 235? 333* 354 355? 360	16	13,1	15,4
Akkullānu	14 108? 109? 110 111? 299 305? 310? 331* 358?	10	8,2	8,2
Bābu-šumu-iddina		0	0,0	1,0
Balasî (scribe)	34 66 112 234 324* 325* 326* 330?*	8	6,6	7,2
Balasî (majordomo)		0	0,0	0,5
Bānî		0	0,0	0,5

[696] Reports (in letter form) indicated with asterisks.

Name	Letter	Numbers of Letters	% of Total	Corresponding % in List 1
Ikkāru		0	0,0	2,0
Ištar-nādin-apli	98* 99*	2	1,6	1,5
Ištar-šumu-ēreš	6 11 230 318* 319* 321* 322* 323* 329* 343* 346? 348 350*	13	10,7	11,8
Farmer	242?	1	0,8	0,5
King		0	0,0	0,5
Marduk-šākin-šumi	149 175 184 187 188 189 190 192 193 196 237 244? 342 356? 357 365	16	13,1	10,8
Marduk-šumu-uṣur	353?	1	0,8	1,5
Mār-Ištar	232? 277 279 280 281 282 283 285 288 289 291 292 294 295 297	15	12,3	4,6
Nabû'a	87 91* 344* 345* 351*	5	4,1	2,0
Nabû-abu-da''in	239	1	0,8	0,0
Nabû-aḫḫē-erība	60 62 63 65 68 71 328* 349	8	6,6	5,6
Nabû-aḫḫē-šallim		0	0,0	0,5
Nabû-gāmil		0	0,0	0,5
Nabû-nādin-šumi	218? 210 245? 335	4	3,3	5,6
Nabû-nāṣir	157 216 218 219 240 336	6	4,9	2,6
Nabû-šumu-iddina		0	0,0	1,5
Nabû-tabni-uṣur		0	0,0	0,5
Nabû-zēru-iddina		0	0,0	1,0
Nabû-zēru-līšir		0	0,0	0,5
Nergal-šumu-iddina		0	0,0	1,5
Rab-eširti of Arbela		0	0,0	1,0
Scribes of Kalizi	102(*)	1	0,8	1,0
Tabnî	370?	1	0,8	0,5
Urad-Dagan		0	0,0	0,5
Urad-Gula	127 238 339	3	2,5	1,5
Urad-Ea	268 269	2	1,6	2,6
Urad-Nanâ	153 248 249 253 257 265 266 267	8	6,6	4,1

(Joint letters:)

Adad-šumu-uṣur + Marduk-šākin-šumi	166
Balasî + Nabû-aḫḫē-erība	10+, 43

3. *List of fragments not assignable to definite writers* (Total: 27)

Text	Remarks
LAS 100	possibly by Ištar-nādin-apli
101	collegium of astrologers
103	very fragmentary
104	unsigned; conveys a report by Akkullānu
105	late (621 BC)
106	possibly by Nabû-mušēṣi
128	probably by Nabû-nādin-šumi
194	doubtful if a letter of a scholar
229	very fragmentary

Text	Remarks
LAS 231	lacks distinctive features
236	very fragmentary
241	possibly by Nabû-nādin-šumi
243	consists virtually of literary quotations only
320	unsigned
327	unsigned, omens only
334	probably NB in Assyrian script; unsigned
337	unsigned; possibly by Urad-Nanâ
338	possibly by Bānî
340	Assyrian in NB script
341	very fragmentary
347	possibly by Ištar-šumu-ēreš, very fragmentary
361	cf. *LAS* 224
362	uncertain if by a scholar
363	lacks distinctive features
364	unsigned, quotations only
366	very fragmentary
367	uncertain if by a scholar

4. *Totals of letters and reports assigned to definite authors*

Author	Name preserved (List 1)	Name restored (List 2)	Joint letters authored	Letters	Included in LAS (List 1-2)	Total from App. P	Reports	Total
Ištar-šumu-ēreš	23 +	5 +	3 =	31	8 +	33 =	41	72
Nabû-aḫḫē-ēriba	11 +	6 +	1 =	18	1 +	41 =	42	60
Adad-šumu-uṣur	29 +	15 +	2 =	46	2 +	2 =	4	50
Balasî	14 +	3 +	9 =	26	4 +	17 =	21	47
Marduk-šākin-šumi	21 +	17 +	5 =	43				43
Akkullānu	16 +	8	=	24	1 +	10 =	11	35
Mār-Ištar	9 +	15	=	24				24
Nabû'a	1 +	2	=	3	6 +	12 =	21	21
Nabû-mušēṣi					0 +	16 =	16	16
Nabû-nādin-šumi	11 +	3 +	1 =	15				15
Urad-Nanâ	8 +	6	=	14				14
Nabû-nāṣir	4 +	6 +	1 =	11				11
Bulluṭu					0 +	11 =	11	11
Urad-Ea	5 +	2	=	7	0 +	3 =	3	10
Bamāju					0 +	7 =	7	7
Šumaju					0 +	6 =	6	6
Marduk-šumu-uṣur	3 +	1 +	2 =	6				6
Urad-Gula	3 +	2	=	5				5
Ikkāru	4 +	0 +	1 =	5				5
Ištar-nādin-apli	5		=	5				5
Nabû-zēru-līšir	1 +	0 +	2 =	3				3
Nabû-šumu-iddina	3							3

Author	Name preserved (List 1)	Name restored (List 2)	Joint letters authored		Included in LAS (List 1-2)	Total from App. P	Total
	Letters				Reports		
Nergal-šumu-iddina	3						3
Scribes of Kalizi	2 +	1		= 3			3
Nabû-zēru-iddina	2						2
Bābu-šumu-iddina	2						2
Rab-ēsirti of Arbela	2						2
Tabnî	1 +	1		= 2			2
Bānî	1						1
Nabû-gāmil	1						1
Nabû-tabni-uṣur	1						1
Nabû-abu-da''in		1					1
Aššur-nāṣir						1	1
Aššur-šarrāni						1	1
Aššur-šumu-iddina						1	1
Nabû-aḫḫē-šallim	1						1
Urad-Dagān	1						1
Adad-aḫu-iddina	1						1
Balasî (majordomo)	1						1

5. *Introductory formulae*

Every letter of the corpus opens with an introductory formula, which may consist of the following four parts, or a combination of them:

(1) Address ("To [the king] my lord, your servant PN");
(2) Salutation ("Good health to [the king] my lord");
(3) Blessing ("May the gods [DNN] bless [the king] my lord");
(4) Wishes.

(1)-(3) are in principle obligatory, or at least present in most letters; (4) is optional in principle but forms an integral continuation of (3) in letters of certain writers. The address and salutation formulae are virtually identical in all letters; there is greater variation in the blessing formulae, and the wishes attached to the blessings vary from writer to writer, often even from letter to letter.

In principle, it can be said that each writer had his own, personal address conventions, which show relatively little variation within his own correspondence, but differ from the conventions of all other writers. The differences can be very small (orthographical only), for members of the same profession usually shared the same blessing formula (and in broad terms, even the same orthography), but they are definitely there. Hence, the forms of address attested in the letters of individual writers provide an important criterium for determining the authorship of letters with lost sender name but partially preserved address formula.

The attested formulae and the variations observable in them are presented below in a way making it possible to follow their distribution to individual writers.

5.1 Combinations of formulae

(Only cases deviating from the standard pattern 1+2+3 are listed.)

1+0+0 (salutation and blessing omitted): *LAS* 170 (Adad-šumu-uṣur et al.).

1+2+0 (blessing omitted): *LAS* 5 (Ištar-šumu-ēreš), 40 (Balasî), 61 (Nabû-aḫḫē-erība), 83 (Nergal-šumu-iddina), 168 (Adad-šumu-uṣur et al.), 260-261 (Ikkāru). See note on *LAS* 61:5 ff.

1+0+3 (salutation omitted)

a) regularly by	1) Nabû'a	(*LAS* 87-92; cf. 344 f., 351),
	2) Nabû-nāṣir	(*LAS* 33, 215-221; cf. 336);
	3) Nabû-šumu-iddina	(*LAS* 77-78);
b) occasionally by	4) Adad-šumu-uṣur	(*LAS* 138, 148, 156, 158);
	5) Marduk-šumu-uṣur	(*LAS* 115).

0+0+3 (blessing only): *LAS* 104, 331, 335, 336.

1+2+0+4 (address and salutation followed by wishes, no blessing):

a) regular, in letters of	1) Urad-Nanâ (*LAS* 246-257) and
	2) Bānî (*LAS* 263)
b) exceptional, in letters of	3) Urad-Gula (*LAS* 224)

1+2+3+4 (blessing formula amplified with wishes):

a) regular, in letters of 1) Mār-Ištar (*LAS* 275-296);

b) sporadic, in letters of 2) Balasî (*LAS* 36, 44, 54);

3) Nabû-aḫḫē-erība (75, 76);

4) Nabû'a (88);

5) Marduk-šumu-uṣur (117);

6) Tabnî (118);

7) Adad-šumu-uṣur (122, 123);

8) Marduk-šākin-šumi (184, 186-193, 195-196)

9) Nabû-nādin-šumi (212);

10) Urad-Gula (127 + 339),

11) Ikkāru (258, 259);

12) Nabû-tabni-uṣur (264).

5.2 Address

a-na LUGAL (LÚENGAR / DUMU.LUGAL / AMA-LUGAL) *EN-ja ÌR-ka PN*

"To the king (farmer / crown prince / king's mother) my lord, your servant PN"

This formula is standard in all letters. The only variation that occurs is in the orthography of the word /bēlīja/, which is attested in the following spellings (number of attestations in parentheses, writers with stable orthography italicized):

EN-*ja*: Adad-aḫu-iddina (1), Akkullānu (5), *Bābu-šumu-iddina* (2), *Balasî* (11), *Balasî 2.* (1), *Ištar-nādin-apli* (3), Ištar-šumu-ēreš (13), Marduk-šākin-šumi (1), Marduk-šumu-uṣur (2), Nabû'a (2), *Nabû-aḫḫē-erība* (10), Nabû-gāmil (1), Nabû-nāṣir (1), Nabû-nādin-šumi (6), Nabû-šumu-iddina (1), Nabû-zēru-lēšer (1), *Nergal-šumu-iddina* (3), *rab-ešerti of Arbela* (2), Urad-Nanâ (4).

EN-*já*: Adad-šumu-uṣur (1), Akkullānu (5), Marduk-šākin-šumi (1), *Mār-Ištar* (11), Nabû-šumu-iddina (1), Urad-Ea (2).

be-lí-ja: Adad-šumu-uṣur (21), Akkullānu (2), *Bānî* (1), *Ikkāru* (3), Ištar-šumu-ēreš (3), Marduk-šākin-šumi (11), Marduk-šumu-uṣur (1), Nabû'a (3), Nabû-nāṣir (3), Nabû-nādin-šumi (5), Nabû-tabni-uṣur (1), Urad-Gula (1), Urad-Nanâ (2).

be-lí-já: Adad-šumu-uṣur (1), Marduk-šākin-šumi (1), Marduk-šumu-uṣur (1), Urad-Ea (2).

be-li-ja/ni: Ištar-šumu-ēreš (2), Nabû-zēru-lēšer (2), Urad-Nanâ (1).

5.3 Salutation

lū šulmu ana šarri (etc.) bēlīja (adanniš (adanniš))

"Good (the (very) best of) health to the king (etc.) my lord"

This formula is attested in so many variant spellings and forms that the distribution of the individual variants can only be presented in the form of a table:

	Adad-aḫu-iddina	Adad-šumu-uṣur	Akkullānu	Bābu-šumu-iddina	Balasî	Bānî	Ikkāru	Ištar-nādin-apli	Ištar-šumu-ēreš	Marduk-šākin-šumi	Marduk-šumu-uṣur	Mār-Ištar	Nabû'a	Nabû-aḫḫē-erība	Nabû-gāmil	Nabû-nādin-šumi	Nabû-nāṣir	Nabû-šumu-iddina	Nabû-tabni-uṣur	Nabû-zēru-iddina	Nabû-zēru-lēšer	Nergal-šumu-iddina	rab-10 of Arbela	scribes of Kalizi	Tabnî	Urad-Ea	Urad-Gula	Urad-Nanâ
lu		11	1	x	4				x	1	1			9		1					x	x						3
lu-u	x	14	12		17	x	x	x		16	2	x		2	x	10			x	x			x	x		x	x	2
lu-ú		1																										
DI-mu		23	3		19	x	2	x	11	13	2	x		7	x	x			x	x	x	x	x	x		x	x	2
šul-mu	x	3	11	x	3		2		12	2	1			4														4
a-dan-niš						x				3																		1
ad-dan-niš																												6
a-dan-niš						x																						1
ad-dan-niš																												6
a-na	x	25	x	x	x	x	x	x	x	x	x	x		x	x	x			x	x	x	x	x	x		x	x	x
ana		3																										
LUGAL	x	22	x	x	x	x	x	x	x	x	x	1		x	x	x			x	x	x	2	x	x	x	x	›x	x
MAN		1										10										1						
EN-	x	10	13	x	x	x		x	19	15	1	x		x	x	8					x	x	x			2		x
be-lí-		14	3				x		2	8	2					4			x	x				x	x	1	x	
be-li-																												
ja		11	1	x	x	x	2	x	12	9	x			x	x	5			x	x	x	x	x		x	1	x	x
já	x	9	13				1		5	9		x				7										2		
a-dan-niš							x								x				x			1					x	
a-dan-niš							2												x			1						
caret							1															2						

x = exclusive attestation   11 (etc.) = number of attestations

5.4 Blessing

18 different blessing formulae are attested in the corpus. All of them follow the same basic pattern (*DNN ana šarri bēlīja likrubū* "may the gods DNN *bless* the king (etc.) my lord"), the difference between them lying in the gods invoked. Their number may vary between 2 and 20, though blessings involving more than 5 gods are rare. Normally only two gods are invoked, and then predominantly *Nabû and Marduk* (in this order). The blessing formula in which these gods figure alone is called *the standard blessing*, and is attested 177 times in letters of 22 different scholars representing four different professions (scribes, haruspices, exorcists and – with subsequent wishes – physicians). It has distinctive value only when the variations in detail are taken into consideration.

	Adad-šumu-uṣur	Akkullânu	Bābu-šumu-iddina	Balasî	Ikkāru	Ištar-šumu-ēreš	Marduk-šākin-šumi	Marduk-šumu-uṣur	Mār-Ištar	Nabû'a	Nabû-aḫḫē-erība	Nabû-gāmil	Nadû-nādin-šumi	Nabû-nāṣir	Nabû-šumu-iddina	Nabû-zēru-lēšer	Nergal-šumu-iddina	rab-10 of Arbela	scribes of Kalizi	Tabnî	Urad-Gula	Nabû-aḫḫē-šallim	
^{d}PA	4	6		x	1	7	13		x		x		10		x						x	x	^{d}PA
^{d}AG	20	9	x		1	15	4	x		x		x	3	x		x	x	x	x				^{d}AG
u	8	15				x	14	2	x	2			9	2		x	1						u
ù			x		1		2			2		x	2	2					1				ù
Ø	12	1		x	1		3	2		2	x		1		x		2	x	1		x	x	Ø
^{d}AMAR.UD	x	x	x	x	x	x	x	x	8	x	x	x	x	x	x	x	x	x	x		x	x	^{d}AMAR.UD
^{d}ŠÚ									1														^{d}ŠÚ
a-na	23	x	x	x	x	x	x	x	x	x	x	x	x	x	x	x	x	x	x	x	x	x	a-na
ana	3																						ana
LUGAL	23	x	x	x	x	x	x	x	2	x	x	x	x	x		x	x	x	x	x	x	x	LUGAL
MAN	1								9														MAN
EN-	7	x	x	x		x	18	2	x	4	x	x	4	1	x	x	x	x	Ø			x	EN-
be-lí-	20				x		7	1		2			7	2						x	2		be-lí
be-li-								1						1							1		be-li
ja	18	1	x	x	x	14	9	x		5	x		8	x	x	x	x	x		x	x	x	ja
já	7	15				3	11		x	1		x	1										já
a-dan-niš	7		1										1	2							x		a-dan-niš
Ø	23		1										12	2									Ø
a-dan-niš	7		1										7	3							x		a-dan-niš
Ø	23		1										4	1									Ø
lik-ru-bu	x	x	x	x	x	x	x	x	x	x	x	x	x	x	x	1	x	x	x		x	x	lik-ru-bu
li-ik-ru-bu																1							li-ik-ru-bu

The standard blessing. x = exclusive attestation
4 (etc.) = number of attestations

The remaining 17 formulae are more distinctive. They are attested in letters of 14 different writers, and not one of them is used by more than one writer. The most elaborate of them (invoking as many as 20 gods) appear in the letters of the exorcists Adad-šumu-uṣur (*LAS* 119-120, 122-123, 125-126, 130-131), Marduk-šākin-šumi (*LAS* 186), Urad-Gula (*LAS* 127+339), Nabû-nādin-šumi (*LAS* 128$^{?}$) and Nabû-nāṣir (*LAS* 222), who normally use the standard blessing, and clearly have a specific function related to the contents of the relevant letters. Six blessings serve as personal formulae of writers who do no appear to have used the standard blessing. In the following synopsis, these blessings (and the pertinent writers) are marked with asterisks.

	Gods invoked in blessing										Writer
*1.	Aššur	Sîn	Šamaš	Nabû	Marduk						*Nabû-zēru-iddina (*LAS* 368 & 369)
2.	Aššur	Sîn	Šamaš	Nabû	Marduk				ilāni rabûti ša šamê kaqqiri		Adad-šumu-uṣur (*LAS* 119, 130-131)
3.	Aššur	Sîn	Šamaš	Bēl	Nabû			Nergal			Adad-šumu-uṣur (*LAS* 120)
4.	Aššur + (Ninlil)	Sîn	Šamaš + Adad	Marduk + Zarpanītu	Nabû + Tašmētu	Ištar ša Nīnua + Ištar ša Arbail	Ninurta + Gula	Nergal + Lāṣ	ilāni rabûti ša šamê kaqqiri	ilāni rabûti ašibūti māt-Aššūr māt-Akkadî	Adad-šumu-uṣur (*LAS* 122 & 125)
5.	Aššur	Sîn	Šamaš + Adad + Nusku + Sagmegar + Dilibat	Marduk + Zarpanītu	Nabû + Tašmētu + Kaimānu + Šiḫṭu	Šarrat Nīnua + Šarrat Kidmūri + Šarrat Arbail	Ninurta + Gula	Nergal + Lāṣ	ilāni rabûti ša šamê kaqqiri	ilāni ašibūti māt-Aššūr. . . mātāti kališina	Adad-šumu-uṣur (*LAS* 123)
6.				Marduk + Zarpanītu	Nabû + Tašmētu	Ištar ša Nīnua + Ištar ša Arbail	Ninurta + Gula	Nergal + Lāṣ	ilāni māḫāzī māt-Aššūr māt-Akkadî kališunu		Urad-Gula (*LAS* 127+339)
7.	Aššur		Šamaš	Bēl + Zarpanītu	Nabû + Tašmētu	Ištar ša Nīnua + Ištar ša Arbail			100 šanāti		Marduk-šākin-šumi (*LAS* 186 f.)
8.	Aššur		Šamaš	Bēl u	Nabû						Marduk-šumu-uṣur (*LAS* 117)
9.	Aššur		Šamaš	Bēl	Nabû						Nabû'a (*LAS* 88)
10.	Aššur			Bēl	Nabû	!Šamaš					Balasî (*LAS* 50)
*11.	Aššur + Ninlil			Nabû	Marduk						*Adad-aḫu-iddina (*LAS* 317)
*12.				Nabû	Marduk	Ištar ša Arbail					*Ištar-nādin-apli (*LAS* 96-99, 352)
13.				Nabû u	Marduk	Ištar ša Nīnua + Ištar ša Arbail					Nabû-šumu-iddina (*LAS* 79)
*14.				Nabû	Marduk			Sîn u Nikkal (+ Nusku)			*Urad-Ea (*LAS* 268-274)
*15.				Bēl	Nabû						*Balasî 2. (*LAS* 37)
*16.							Ninurta u Gula				*Nabû-tabni-uṣur (*LAS* 264)
17.	Aššur	Sîn	Šamaš				Ninurta u Gula				Nabû-nāṣir & Urad-Nanâ (*LAS* 222)

Note that Ninurta and Gula are only invoked by exorcists and physicians (cf. below, sub 4.5). Most of the blessings starting with the invocation of Aššur (nos. 1-4, 8) are found in letters addressed to Assurbanipal; cf. discussion of *LAS* 129.

5.5 Wishes

The wish formulae attested in the corpus fall into two categories: wishes forming an integral, inseparable part of a writer's distinctive introductory formula, and ones that merely amplify the writer's standard formula(e). The former are generally short, consisting of only one sentence, while the latter tend to contain several sentences, whole clusters of wishes. The inventory of elements found in the formulae is relatively limited, but they can be combined in different ways to yield an almost unlimited variety of different wishes.

5.51 Wishes forming an integral part of the introductory formula

a) Attached to salutation

1. *Aššur Sîn Šamaš Bēl Nabû Nergal Ištar ša Nīnua Ištar ša Arbail balāṭu šalāmu ṭūb/ḫūd libbi ṭūb šēri u dūr/arāk ūmē ana šarri bēlīja liq/bbiū / šībūtu littūtu ana šarri bēlīja lūšabbiū / (išdī kussi šarrūti ša šarri bēlīja ana ūmē ṣâti lūkinnū)*: Marduk-šākin-šumi (*LAS* 189-193; cf. below, 10)
2. *Ninurta u Gula ṭūb libbi ṭūb šēri ana šarri bēlīja liddinū*: Urad-Nanâ (*LAS* 246-257) and Bānî (*LAS* 263)

b) Following "standard blessing"

3. *ūmē arkūti ṭūb libbi u ḫūd libbi ilāni rabûti ana šarri bēlīja lišrukū*: Mār-Ištar (*LAS* 275-297)
4. *ṭūb libbi ṭūb šēri ana šarri bēlīja lišrukū kī šamê u kaqqiri šarru bēlī lū dār*: Nabû-zēru-iddina (*LAS* 368-369)

5.52 Amplificatory wishes

a) In letters of exorcists

5. *ūmē arkūti šanāti darāti ṭūb libbi ṭūb šēri ana šarri bēlīja liddinū*: Nabû-nādin-šumi (*LAS* 212, following "standard blessing")
6. *ūmē arkūti šanāti darāti ṭūb libbi ṭūb šēri šībūtu littūtu ana šarri bēlīja lūšabbiū*. Urad-Gula (*LAS* 127+339, following blessing 6)
7. *ṭūb libbi ṭūb šēri ūmē arkūti šebê littūti palê ša nuhši ana šarri bēlīja liddinū šumu u zēru pir'u lillidu ana šarri bēlīja liqīšū zīmūka lišmuhū lirappišū ṣulūlī*: Adad-šumu-uṣur (*LAS* 122; blessing 4)
8. *ṭūb libbi ṭūb šēri ana šarri bēlīja liddinū*: Marduk-šākin-šumi (*LAS* 184; following standard blessing)
9. *Ištar ša Arbail ṭūb libbi ṭūb šēri ana šarri bēlīja lū taddin / šībūtu littūtu lū tušabbi / ūmē arkūti ana šarri bēlīja lū taqīš*: Marduk-šākin-šumi (*LAS* 195; following standard blessing)
10. *maṣṣār šulmi u balāṭi issi šarri bēlīja lipqidū / šībūtu littūtu ana šarri bēlīja lūšabbiū / išdī kussi šarrūti ša šarri bēlīja ana ūmī ṣâti lūkinnū / (nēmulu ša* RN *ša aḫḫēšu ana šarri bēlīja lūkallimū / mar-mar'=ēšunu šarru ina sīqīšu lintuḫ)*: Marduk-šākin-šumi (*LAS* 186-188; following blessing 7)
11. *ilāni ammar ša ūmu anniu šarru iplaḫūni ina dēni ša* RN_1 *u* RN_2 *adanniš adanniš lizzizzū*: Urad-Gula (*LAS* 224, following salutation)

b) In letters of physicians

12. *Ninurta u Gula ṭūb libbi ṭūb šēri ana šarri bēlīja liddinū*: Ikkāru (*LAS* 258, following standard blessing); cf. no. 2 above
13. *Bēl Nabû Bēlet-balāṭi ṭūb libbi ṭūb šēri ana šarri bēlīja liddinū*: Ikkāru (*LAS* 259, following standard blessing)

14. *Bēl u Nabû ūmē arkūti šanāti ma'dāti kussû ša darâti ṭūb libbi ṭūb šēri ana šarri bēlīja liddinū*: *LAS* 264 (Nabû-tabni-usur, following blessing 16)

c) In letters of scribes

15. *balāṭ ūmē rūqūti šībūtu littūtu ana šarri bēlīja liddinū*: Balasî (*LAS* 36 [after standard blessing] and 50 [after blessing 10])
16. *Aššur Bēl Nabû ṭūb libbi ḫūd libbi ana šarri bēlīja liddinū*: Balasî (*LAS* 44, following standard blessing)
17. *Aššur Bēl Nabû Sîn Nergal Nabû Marduk* } *Ištar ša Nīnua Ištar ša Arbail ūmē arkūti šanāti darâti ṭub libbi ḫūd libbi ana šarri bēlīja liddinū*: Nabû-aḫḫē-erība (*LAS* 75-76, following salutation)
18. *ṣumrāt libbi ana šarri bēlīja lūšakšidū*: Nabû'a (*LAS* 88; standard blessing)
19. *šulmu ša adanniš u ṭūb libbi liddinūnikka*: Akkullānu (*LAS* 14, standard blessing)

d) In letters of *kalû* chanters

20. *Ištar ša Arbail ammar nakarūtīni ina pān šēpē ša šarri bēlīja lū tusaḫḫip*: Nabû-zēru-iddina (*LAS* 368, following wish 4)
21. *Sîn Nikkal Nusku ṣullê ša šarri bēlīja lišmiū / ammar nakarūtīni ina pān šēpē ša šarri bēlīja lūsaḫḫipū*: Nabû-zēru-iddina (*LAS* 369, following wish 4)

e) In letters of haruspices

22. *[Aššur] Šamaš haṭṭi šarrūtīka [. . . .] lūṭībū*: Tabnî (*LAS* 118, following standard blessing)
23. *Sîn u Šamaš šulmu ša šarri bēlīja liš'ulū / Nabû u Marduk šumu u zēru ana šarri bēlīja liddinū / Ištar ša Nīnua Ištar ša Arbail kī ummi u ahāti littarrūka*: Marduk-šumu-uṣur (*LAS* 118, following blessing 8)

As can be seen from the above synopsis, the wish formulae listed under 4.52 have only limited distinctive value, since the wishes found in the correspondence of a given writer may considerably deviate from one another but, on the other hand, may closely resemble ones occurring in other persons' letters (cf., e.g., no. 6 with nos. 5 and 11). It may be noted, however, that wishes pertaining to the king's physical health (*ṭūb šēri*) are only found in the letters of physicians and exorcists, and that the verbs *šabbû* "to sate" (with *šībūtu* "old age"), *šarāku* "to bestow" and *qiāšu* "to grant" occur only in wish formulae of the latter.

6. *Distinctive features*

The following table presents a selection of contrastive orthographies, linguistic forms and other features that can be used for determining the authorship of letters lacking the name of the sender. The array of features presented is by no means inclusive — additional features are given in the commentaries on individual letters — but it should be fairly representative and give an idea of the possibilities for identifying writers through distinctive feature analysis. Only data found in letters with absolutely certain authorship are included.

The individual writers (top of the page) are grouped by profession and family relationship in order to make the orthographic and linguistic differences (or similarities) between members of the same profession and/or father and son stand out as clearly as possible. An x means that of the alternative spellings of a given feature, only the one so marked is attested in the writer's correspondence; in case two or more alternative spellings are attested, the relevant frequencies of occurrence are given.

	Scribes											Exorcists						Physicians				kalû		bārû		
	Ištar-šumu-ēreš	Nabû-zēru-lēšer	Balasî	Nabû-ahhē-erība	Nabû-šumu-iddina	Bābu-šumu-iddina	Nergal-šumu-iddina	Ištar-nādin-apli	Nabû'a	Mār-Ištar	Akkullānu	Adad-šumu-uṣur	Urad-Gula	Marduk-šākin-šumi	Nabû-nādin-šumi	Nabû-nāṣir	Nabû-gāmil	Urad-Nanâ	Bānî	Ikkāru	Nabû-tabni-uṣur	Urad-Ea	Nabû-zēru-iddina	Marduk-šumu-uṣur	Tabnî	Adad-ahu-iddina
a-dan-niš	x		x	x		x	x			x	x	x	x	x	x	x	x	3	x	x	x			x		
ad-dan-niš																		18								
a-di	x		1								3	1		x												
a-du			2	x						x	3	5			x	x		x								
a-he-'i-iš														x												
a-he-e-iš				x																						
a-he-iš									x	x		x	x					x								
a-ki	1			2						1		9				2		2								
a-ki-i															3											
ki-i	17		10							23	8	22		21	4			3		2		x		x		
ki			1	2								1		1												
i-na (vs. ina)		4										2						1								
ana (vs. a-na)	1		2								6	11		1		3						1				
ana-ku											5			4												
a-ni-nu/i		x	x							x		4	1	1												
a-ni-e/in-nu												1	3	1												
an-ni-u	x		1	x							x	5	2					1								
an-ni-i-u			3							x																
an-ni-ju-u																		7								
an-ni-'u-u																						x				
an-ni-i (Nom.)												1	1	x												
an-ni-e	2			5							1	4														
an-ni-i-e			x	1																						
an-ni-i (Gen.)	5									x	5	11	x	x								x				
an-ni(-im)-ma												x														
an-nim-ma	x													x												
a-sap-ra etc.		x								x		2	x			1										
as-sap-ra	x		x								x	4		x	x	1		x								x
be-lí	5	x	x	x		x	x	x	x	x	x	55	x	x	9	1	x	x	x	x	x	x	x	x	x	x
be-li	28															1										
EN (= bēlī)												1			1	1										
be-lí-ia	5								4		4	84	3	26	18	8		17	1	9		2	4	2	3	1
be-lí-iá											2	15		3	1					6		4		1		

	Scribes											Exorcists						Physicians				kalû		bārû		
	Ištar-šumu-ēreš	Nabû-zēru-lēšer	Balasî	Nabû-ahhē-erība	Nabû-šumu-iddina	Bābu-šumu-iddina	Nergal-šumu-iddina	Ištar-nādin-apli	Nabû'a	Mār-Ištar	Akkullānu	Adad-šumu-uṣur	Urad-Gula	Marduk-šākin-šumi	Nabû-nādin-šumi	Nabû-nāṣir	Nabû-gāmil	Urad-Nanâ	Bānî	Ikkāru	Nabû-tabni-uṣur	Urad-Ea	Nabû-zēru-iddina	Marduk-šumu-uṣur	Tabnî	Adad-ahu-iddina
be-li-ja/ni	3	2										1	1			1								1		
EN-ja	46	4	48	52	4	7	9	13	6		9	23		28	13	1	2	30	5			6	2	5		2
EN-já	10				2				1	101	41	20	1	25	7		2	1				5				1
e-pa-áš etc.	4			1	x	x				2	1	15	x	2	x			x		2						
ep-pa-áš	5		x	2						7	1	4		19		x				1		x				
glosses			2	16																						
iq-bu-u-ni			x							x	1	4	x	5				x								
iq-bu-ni												1		4												
i-qab-bu-ni											1			2												
i-sa-kan etc.		x								6		1						x					x			
is-sa-kan	x		x	x						7	x	1	x	x		x								x		
i-se-niš														1				x								
is-se-niš	x		x							x	x	x	x	6								x				
i-su-ri										x																
i-su-ur-ri																		x								
is-su-ri	x		x								x	x		x	x					x						
i-qab-bi-i-u etc.										x																
KAM	1								2			3		9												
KÁM	21				x	x	1	x	2	2	x	1	x	2	6			x		x		1				
KÁM*	3		x	x			1		1	19		7		16	3	x						1				
LÚ (det.)	x	x	x	2	x			x			34	24	x	11	x			2		x			x	x		x
LÚ* (det.)				1						82	3	4		1				7				x				
LUGAL	107	x	x	x	x	x	8	x	x	32	x	220	x	x	x	x	x	x	x	x	x	x	x	x	x	x
MAN	1						1			115		5														
le-mur etc.	1		9	x						5	2	5		x	1	x		x						x		
le-e-mur	7		1							3	2	6			1											
ma-hir										x	1	1		x												
ma-hi-ir	x		x	x							1	2					x	x		x						
mi-(i-)nu	6	1	1							x	6	x	x	7	2			1								
me-(i-)nu	3	1	5	x							1			6	1			1	x							
mu-uk			x									x		x	x			x								x
mu-muk																x										
nu-uk										x																

	Scribes											Exorcists						Physicians				kalû		bārû		
	Ištar-šumu-ēreš	Nabû-zēru-lēšer	Balasî	Nabû-ahhē-erība	Nabû-šumu-iddina	Bābu-šumu-iddina	Nergal-šumu-iddina	Ištar-nādin-apli	Nabû'a	Mār-Ištar	Akkullānu	Adad-šumu-uṣur	Urad-Gula	Marduk-šākin-šumi	Nabû-nādin-šumi	Nabû-nāṣir	Nabû-gāmil	Urad-Nanâ	Bānî	Ikkāru	Nabû-tabni-uṣur	Urad-Ea	Nabû-zēru-iddina	Marduk-šumu-uṣur	Tabnî	Adad-ahu-iddina
né-pe-še										x		x	x	x	x											
né-pe-ši																x										
pa-an	1	1	3							22	1	9			6	x		x		x		1				
IGI	9	1	6	x						1	4	7	x	x	2							3		x		
pi-šìr	x									x		x														
pi-še-er			x								x															
SAH = šàh														3				2								
šá (alone)	8	3	13	5								60		14	14			4		4						
ša-	2											1		2	3											
dšá-maš				x			x		2			4						x								
dUTU	x	x	x			x			2	x	x	17		x	x									x		
šá-ṭir			x											x	x											
šà-ṭir	x																									
šá-ṭi-ir																										
šum-ma	x	x	x	x							x	x	x	6		x		2		x						
šúm-ma										12								3								
šum-mu														8												
(lū) ṭa-(a-)ba												5						x								
(lū) ṭa-ab-šú														x		x										
(lū) DÙG.GA-šú										x		1														
ú-se-li etc.		x								x		2			2					x						
us-se-li	x		x								x	3	x	x	1			x		x						

APPENDIX N

BIOGRAPHICAL AND PROSOPOGRAPHICAL SOURCE MATERIALS

In addition to their own letters and reports, information on the lives and activities of the Assyrian scholars figuring in the corpus of letters under study is also found in other contemporary texts. These texts, insofar as known to the present writer, are collected in this appendix.[697] They fall into seven main categories: chronographic lists, colophons, private contracts, administrative records, oracle queries, and letters and reports. From the biographical point of view, the most important type of information (eponym dates, genealogies, professional identifiers) is primarily found in texts belonging to the first five of these genres. Letters and reports generally contain data valuable to prosopographical study only, even though they may occasionally also contain useful biographical information.

The material is arranged by text genre. Within each genre, texts featuring the same scholars are grouped together, if possible in chronological order. Each text is numbered consecutively, except for duplicates (or useless texts) which are distinguished with letters. In case a text refers to several scholars, it is presented in full once only, but cross-references to it are made in appropriate connections. To make it easier to locate references to writers of letters, an index of the relevant texts is given as a sort of table of contents to the text section.

Each entry in the text section contains the following information: 1. Place of publication and museum number of the source text; 2. type, general content and date of the document, insofar as determinable; 3. transliteration and 4. translation or paraphrasis of the passage(s) having bio- or prosopographical relevance. Some entries also contain a short discussion of the data found in the text. Presenting the source *in extenso* would have been senseless; the portions of text omitted are entirely irrelevant from the viewpoint of the present commentary.

The following texts are fully or partially quoted below (the numbers following the equal marks refer to the present appendix):

ABL	185 = 57	367 = 52	447 = 28	539 = 56	580 = 62	845 = 63	1109 = 77
	1217 = 59	1285 = 73	1373 = 47				
ADD	277 = 25	330 = 23a	331 = 17a	350 = 16	377 = 18	408 = 20	420 = 17b
	444 = 21	445 = 21a	447 = 23	448 = 17	470 = 19	473 = 22	502 = 23b
	640 = 24	709 = 4	769 = 27	833 = 25a	851 = 26	857 = 29	980 = 31
AfO 3	71 = 1						
AGS	6 = 33	35 = 35	36 = 35a	44 = 33a	48 = 39	51 = 32	88 = 33b
	91 = 40a	98 = 34	108 = 36	111 = 38a	119 = 38	124 = 37	145 = 40
AOAT 25	315 = 30						
BAK	299 = 9	344a = 6	344b = 7	348 = 10	498 = 14	499 = 11	500 = 12
	524 = 13						
BBEA	8 f = 65						

697 Texts referring to persons homonymous and contemporary but clearly not identical with the scholars in question were naturally left out of consideration. Some references to persons of doubtful identity (possibly, but probably not, pertinent) were however included (see nos. 10, 17, 22-24, 31, 53, 59 and 81).

BL	158 = 11						
Cat	p402 = 15	423 = 3	1416 = 26a				
KAV	182 = 1a						
LAS	40 = 55	104 = 54	120 = 79	121 = 80	122 = 72	125 = 64	151 = 78
	172 = 67	174 = 68	185 = 74	212 = 81	223 = 50	224 = 51	232 = 49
	238 = 69	242 = 61	249 = 48	263 = 70	321 = 75	335 = 76	341 = 58
	353 = 71						
PRT	17 = 33c	74 = 40b	106 = 41	110 = 42	111 = 43	121 = 45	122 = 46
	124 = 44						
3R	2,22 = 9	53,2 = 8	66 = 7a	*4R²* 9 = 6			
RMA	55 = 60						
Sm.	2116 = 53						
StOr 1	28ff = 14						
UVB 18	45 = 1b						
WO 4	217 = 66						
ZA 61	83 = 5						
ZA 62	101 = 2						

The writers of *LAS* figure in the following texts:

Adad-šumu-uṣur	2-4, 14, 16-17, 30, 47-53
Akkullānu	54-57
Balasî	58
Bānî	18-20
Ištar-nādin-apli	17(a-b), 59
Ištar-šumu-ēreš	1(a), 5-9, 17, 21, 26, 60-63
Marduk-šākin-šumi	10, 17, 21, 26, 64
Marduk-šumu-uṣur	20, 25a, 26, 32-46
Mār-Ištar	27, 31, 65-66
Nabû-aḫḫē-erîba	22(?), 60
Nabû-gāmil	67-69
Nabû-nādin-šumi	64, 70-72
Nabû-šumu-iddina	23(a)
Nabû-zēru-iddina	11-13, 26
Nabû-zēru-lišir	1(a), 5-7, 68-69, 73
Nergal-šumu-iddina	24(?), 26
Tabnî	36-37, 39-40
Urad-Ea	11-13, 29, 49, 67, 74-76
Urad-Gula	14-15, 25, 68, 77-80
Urad-Nanâ	81(?)

1. CHRONOGRAPHIC TEXTS (1-1b)

1. *AfO 3 (1926) 66ff* (Assur 14616c)

List of Assyrian kings and their scholars (*ummânu*). Ca. 640 BC. Rev.IV: "(When) Sennacherib was king of Assyria [and Babylon], ² Nabû-apla-iddina was his scholar. ³ [Two] yea[rs] (= 705-4) [Sennache]rib was ⁴ king of the land of Akkad. Thereafter, the inhabitants [of the land of A]kkad ⁵ rebelled (= 703-700), so ⁶ he placed Aššur-nādin-šumi, his son (text AD), on the throne (= 699-694). ⁷ (When) Sennacherib (was king of Assyria), Nergal-šēzib son of Gaḫul ⁸ (and) Mušēzib-Marduk son of Dakūri ⁹ were kings of the land of Akkad (= 693-689). [10] (When) Sennacherib was king of Assyria and Babylon (= 688-681), [11] BĒL-UPAḪḪIR and KALBU were his scholars. [12] (When) Esarhaddon son of Sennacherib was king of Assyria and Babylon (= 680-669). [13] NABÛ-ZĒRU-LĪŠIR and IŠTAR-ŠUMU-ĒREŠ were his scholars.

---

[14] (When) Assurbanipal ditto (was king of Assyria), Šamaš-šumu-ukīn ditto (= was king of Babylon, 668-647). [15] (When) Assurbanipal ditto, Kandalānu ditto (= 647-627). [16] IŠTAR-ŠUMU-ĒREŠ was his (= Assurbanipal's) scholar.

---

[17] 82 kings of Assyria from Erišu son of Ilušumma [18] till Assurbanipal son of Esarhaddon. [19] 98 kings of the land of Akkad [20] from Sumu-la-El till Kandalānu."

Lines 17ff imply a date of copying between 647 and 627 BC. The name of the scholar of Sargon lost in the break preceding the passage quoted is known from *Sg 8* 428 and *Iraq* 14 pl.23:6.10 (Nabû-šallimšunu; both texts dated 614 BC). For Sennacherib's scholar Kalbu see commentary to *LAS* 41; the other scholar of this king appears to have been a Babylonian, cf. Ki 1904-10-9,36 = BM 99007 (unp. astrological report, NB script, signed by Bēl-upaḫḫir, and referring to a meeting with the king in the town of Keramlis) and *RMA* 15 and 194 (NB script, signed by Ṭāb-ṣilli-Marduk son of Bēl-upaḫḫir).

Lines 10-16 in transliteration:

10 $^{\text{I.d}}$*30*-PAP^{MEŠ}-SU MAN KUR *aš+šur u* KÁ.DINGIR.RA[^{K}]^{I}
11 ^{I}EN-*ú-pa-ḫir* ^{I}*kal-bu um-ma-[ni]-šú*
12 ^{I}*aš+šur*-PAP-AŠ DUMU ^{I}*30*-PAP^{MEŠ}-SU MAN KUR *aš+šur u* KÁ.DINGIR.RA^{KI}
13 $^{\text{I.d}}$PA-NUMUN-SI.SÁ ^{I}15-MU-KAM-*eš* *um-ma-ni-šú*

---

14 ^{I}*aš+šur*-DÙ-A MIN $^{\text{I.d}}$GIŠ.ŠIR-MU-GI.NA MIN
15 ^{I}*aš+šur*-DÙ-A MIN ^{I}*kan-dil-a-nu* MIN
16 ^{I}*15*-MU-KAM-eš *um-man-šú*

1a *KAV 182* (Ph 4198 : Ass 13956dh)

Fragment of a kinglist including Aššur-etelli-ilāni (IV 7'), hence copied ca. 625 BC. Col. IV 1'ff (after three blank lines):

1' [ ] MAN KUR *aš+šur u* KÁ.DINGIR^{KI} ⌈$^{\text{I.d}}$⌉PA-*ba-ni*
2' [ ] ^{I}*kal-bu*
3' [ ] ^{I}EN-*ú-pa-ḫír*
4' [^{I}*aš+šur*-BAP-AŠ] MAN KUR *aš+šur u* KÁ.DINGIR^{KI} $^{\text{I.d}}$PA-NUMUN-GIŠ
5' [ ] ^{I}*aš+šur*-DÙ- A ^{I}*15*-MU-KAM-*eš*
6' [ ] ^{I} : ^{I} :
7' ^{I}*aš+šur-e-tel-li*-DINGIR^{MEŠ} (blank)

(Colophon)

1b *van Dijk, UVB 18 (1962) 44 ff* (W 20030,7)

List of antediluvian kings and their sages (*apkallu*), and selected historical kings and their scholars (*ummânu*). Dated Uruk, Ajaru 10, 147 SE = May 16, 165 BC. Rev. 18 ff:

18 [*ana tar-ṣi*] ^{Id}AG.NÍG.GUB-ŠEŠ LUGAL ^{I}*é-sag-gíl-ki-i-ni-ub-ba* ^{LÚ}*um-man-nu*
19 [*ana tar-ṣi*] ^{Id}*aš+šur*-ŠEŠ-SUM LUGAL ^{I}a-ba-^{d}ninnu-da-ri *um-man-nu*
20 [*šá* ^{LÚ}]*aḫ-la-mi-mu-ú i-qab-bu-ú* ^{I}*a-ḫu-'a-qa-a-ri*

"[Under] King Nebuchadnezzar I, Esangil-kīni-ubba was the Scholar;
[under] King Esarhaddon, ABA-NINNU-DARI was the Scholar, (the one)
[whom the] Arameans call AHIQAR." (+ Colophon)

This passage is clearly fictitious and of no historical value. Aba-ninnu-dari alias Mannu-kima-Illil-ḫatin, a MB scholar (cf. *5 R* 44 iii 9'), was possibly the author of the *Counsels of Wisdom* (*BWL* p. 96 ff; p. 106 K. 13770:1 read *um-ma-nu* DUMU!-[*šú i-mal-lik*]), the Babylonian archetype of the *Sayings of Ahiqar.*

2. COLOPHONS (2-15)

2. *ZA 62 (1972) 101* (ND 5427; here quoted from an unp. copy by Wiseman). Colophon of an [astrological?] omen text; colophon only preserved.

Rev. 1' [7-8 signs]⌈x⌉ *1* UŠ-TA.ÀM M[U.BI.IM]
2' [LIBIR.RA].BI.GIM AB.SAR.ÀM BA.AN.È
3' *ṭup-pi* $^{\text{I.d}}$IM-MU-ŠEŠ ^{LÚ}DUB.SAR
4' DUMU $^{\text{I.d}}$AG-*zu-qup*-GI.NA ^{LÚ}DUB.SAR
5' ŠÀ.BAL.BAL ^{I}*gab-bu*-DINGIR^{MEŠ}-*ni*-KAM-*eš* ^{LÚ}GAL-DUB.SAR

"Tablet of ADAD-ŠUMU-UṢUR the scribe, son of Nabû-zuqup-kēnu the scribe, descendant of Gabbu-ilāni-ēreš the chief scribe."

The tablet probably dates from the 8th century like the bulk of the literary tablets found in the Nabû temple of Calah.

3. *Bezold Cat II 423* (K 2223)

Unpublished astrological text, Assyrian script. The colophon mentions
$^{\text{I.d}}$IM-MU-*ú-ṣur* ^{LÚ}MAŠ.MAŠ MAN

"ADAD-ŠUMU-UṢUR the exorcist of the king."

4. *ADD 709* (83-1-18,321)

Draft of a royal inscription in report from referring to Esarhaddon as conqueror of Egypt and Kush (^{I}*aš+šur*-PAB]-AŠ MAN ŠÚ MAN KUR *aš* [2] [MAN] *kib-rat erbi-tim* . . . [6] . . . KUR*mu*]-*ṣur u ku-u-si*), hence dating from 671-669 BC. Contents obscure. The last line of the text (r2) reads:

[5-6 signs ^{I}]$^{\text{⌈d⌉}}$IM-MU-PAP "[. . . . .] ADAD-ŠUMU-UṢUR"

Rest of Reverse (ca. 4 lines) uninscribed.

For ADAD-ŠUMU-UṢUR see also 14.

5. *ZA 61 (1971) 83* (81-7-27,69)

6' [*ṭup-pi* ^{I}*15*-M]U-KAM-*eš* ^{LÚ}GAL-DUB.SAR^{MEŠ} *šá* ^{I}*aš+šur*-DÙ-A [. . .]
7' [DUMU $^{\text{I.d}}$AG-NUMU]N-SI.SÁ ^{LÚ}GAL-DUB. [SAR^{MEŠ} *šá* ^{I}*aš+šur*-PAB-AŠ . . .]
8' [4-5 signs] ⌈É⌉ ^{d}INNIN *šá qí-rib* UR[U^{NINA}^{KI} . . . .]

"[Tablet of IŠTAR-ŠU]MU-ĒREŠ the chief scribe of Assurbanipal [. . .],
[son of NABÛ-ZĒR]U-LĪŠIR the chief scr[ibe of Esarhaddon . . .],
[ ] the temple of Ishtar in [Nineveh]."

6. *4 R² 9* (K 2861+). Cf. Sjöberg, Nanna-Suen I 166ff; Hunger *BAK* 344a Bilingual hymn to the Moon god. Rev. 43 ff:

43 GIM-*ma* SUMUN-*šu šà-ṭir-ma* IGI.KÁR
44 *ṭup-pi* $^{\text{I.d}}$*15*-MU-KAM-*eš* ^{LÚ}GAL-DUB.SAR-*ri*
45 *šá* ^{I}AN.ŠÁR-DÙ-IBILA LUGAL ŠÚ LUGAL KUR *aš+šur*^{KI}
46 DUMU $^{\text{I.d}}$AG*-NUMUN-SI.SÁ ^{LÚ}GAL-GI.U

"Written according to its original and checked. Tablet of IŠTAR-ŠUMU-ĒREŠ the chief scribe of Assurbanipal, king of the world, king of Assyria, and son of NABU-ZĒRU-LĪŠIR the chief scribe."

7. *BAK 344* (K 3877)

Omen text. Rev. IV 16 ff:

16 *1 me 22* MU Š[ID.BI
17 *ṭup-pi* $^{\text{I.d}}$15-MU-KAM-*eš* ^{LÚ}GAL-DUB.SAR-*ri*
18 *šá* ^{I}AN.ŠÁR-DÙ-IBILA LUGAL ŠÚ LUGAL KUR *aš+šur*^{KI}
19 DUMU $^{\text{I.d}}$AG-NUMUN-SI.SÁ

"122 is the nu[mber of its] lines. Tablet of IŠTAR-ŠUMU-ĒREŠ the chief scribe of Assurbanipal, king of the world, king of Assyria, and the son of NABÛ-ZĒRU-LĪŠIR."

7a. *3R 66* (K 252)

Tākultu ritual for Assurbanipal. Col. XII 28' ff (after a division line and blank space of about two lines):

28'	[4 signs] DINGIR^{MEŠ}	[. . . . .] (of) the gods
29'	[3-4] GÁ	[. . . . .] . . . .
30'	[DUB ^{I}*15*]-MU-KAM	[Tablet of Ištar]-šumu-ēreš
31'	[^{LÚ}GAL]-⌜A. BA⌝	[the chief] scribe
	(Rest destroyed)	

8. *3R 53,2*

Astrological text, *pirišti ilāni* (= i - n a m g i š - ḫ u r a n - k i - a ?). Rev. 42ff:

42 [LIDIR.RA.DI].GIM AB.SAR.ÀM BA.AN.[È]
43 [*ṭup-pi* $^{\text{I.d}}$*iš*] *tar* MU KAM-*eš* ^{LÚ}A.[BA]
44 [DUMU? $^{\text{I.d}}$AG]-*zu-qup*-GI.NA ^{LÚ}A.[BA]

"Written according to its [original] and collated. [Tablet of IŠ]TAR-ŠUMU-ĒREŠ the scr[ibe], [son? of Nabû]-zuqup-kēnu the scr[ibe]."

See discussion sub 9.

9. *3R 2,22* (K 2670). = *BAK* 299

Third section (*pirsu*) of the series i - n a m g i š - ḫ u r a n - k i - a (cf. Hunger, ZA 62 [1972] 99f). Dated Kanūnu 30, eponymy of Manzarnê (= ca. January 22, 682 BC), 22nd year of Sennacherib. Rev. 5 ff:

I[M.GÍD.DA A.RÁ-*e*] ^{6} $^{\text{I.d}}$AG-*zu-qup*-GI.NA DUMU $^{\text{I.d}}$AMAR+UD-MU-BA-*šá* ^{LÚ}DUB.SAR [. . . (.)] ^{7} ^{LÚ}MAŠ.[MAŠ . .] ^{8} *a-na ta-mar-ti* $^{\text{I.d}}$INNIN-MU-KAM-*eš* DUMU-*ia ul-tu* $1\frac{1}{2}$ MU.AN.NA^{MEŠ}-[*šú?*] ^{9} *di-ig-la ú-kab-bir-ma za-mar ú-ba-aḫ-ḫi-iš-ma ab*-x[. .]

"*liginnu*-tablet with mathematical tables, by Nabû-zuqup-kēnu son of Marduk-šumu-iqīša, the scribe, [. . .] the exorc[ist]. For the perusal of my son IŠTAR-ŠUMU-ĒREŠ, ever since he was one and a half years old, I overtaxed(?) (my) eyesight, quickly . . .ed and [wrote(?) it]".

Considering the relatively late date of this colophon (the bulk of the tablets by Nabû-zuqup-kēnu date from the reign of Sargon, 716-704 BC, cf. *BAK* 293 ff), it is possible that the Ištar-šumu-ēreš mentioned here actually was not the son but the *grandson* of Nabû-zuqup-kēnu, and hence identical with the chief scribe son of Nabû-zēru-līšir of Nos. 5-7; note that According to *ABL* 1285 (No. 73 below), Nabû-zēru-līšir was brother of Adad-šumu-uṣur and hence son of Nabû-zuqup-kēnu (cf. No. 2). The word *maru* "son" would accordingly here have an affectionate connotation ("my child", referring to any male descendants of the speaker or young persons in general) rather than its literal meaning. Cf. the connotations of English "my son" and Hebrew *b*^{e}*nî*, referring to a younger fellow, disciple, reader or listener (Koehler + Baumgartner, *Lexicon* p. 133*a*), and note also *bnjw* "his grandsons" Gen. 32:1. This usage is also attested in Akkadian, see *AHw*. 616*b*.

10. *Borger, Ash § 58* (K 7862)

Inscription of Esarhaddon referring to the (planned) returnal of the statue of Marduk to Babylon (see sub *LAS* 29) and hence dating from 680 through 670 BC. Rev.IV 14ff:

14 [*i-n*]*a* UGU *ki-gal-li ša* ^{d}EN *šà-ṭir*
15 [GIM SU]MUN-*šú* AB.SAR-*ma bà-rì*
16 [DUB] $^{I.d}$AMAR+UD-GAR-MU ^{LÚ}ŠAMÁN.LÁ TUR
17 [A]⌈ x x x x ⌉ ^{LÚ}A.BA
18 [A]⌈ x x ⌉ A.BA A $^{I.⌈d⌉}$PA-PAP-*ir* A.BA

"Written on the pedestal of Bel; copied [from] the original and collated. [Tablet] of MARDUK-ŠĀKIN-ŠUMI the apprentice scribe, [son of] . . . . the scribe, [son of] . . . . the scribe, son of Nabû-nāṣir the scribe."

It is not impossible (though rather unlikely) that this Marduk-šākin-šumi was identical with the chief exorcist of Esarhaddon and Assurbanipal.

11. *Langdon, BL 158* (K 3238). = *BAK* 499

Penitential psalm to Nabû, series u k k i n - t a e š - b a r - r a t i l - l a . Rev. 6 ff:

6 GIM KA ^{GIŠ}*le*-[*'i-i la*]-*bi-ri*
7 *šá* É ^{1}MU-ḪÉ.GÁL UŠ.KU.MAḪ
8 $^{I.d}$AG-NUMUN-SUM-*na* ŠÚ ^{d}*30 u* LUGAL A ^{I}ÌR-^{d}*é-a*
9 [ŠÀ.BAL.B]AL ^{I}MU-ḪÉ.GÁL ŠÚ.MAḪ *iš-ṭur-ma í*[*b-rì*]

"According to the wording of an ancient writing-board of the house of Šumu-libši the *kalamāḫu*, NABÛ-ZĒRU-IDDINA the *kalû* of the Moon and the king, son of URAD-EA, and descendant of Šumu-libši, the *kalamāḫu*, wrote and collated."

12. *BAK* 500 (81-2-4,306)

Unpublished liturgical text. Rev. 6 ff:

6 *ki-i pi-i* ^{GIŠ}ZU-*'i* GABA.RI KÁ.DINGIR^{KI} *šá a*⌈ x x ⌉ *ku* ⌈ x ⌉ *šá* É ^{1}M[U]-HÉ.GÁL
7 UŠ.KU.MAḪ É.SAG.ÍL $^{I.d}$AG-NUMUN-SUM-*na áš-ta-lu-u* ^{d}*30* A ^{I}ÌR-^{d}*é-a*
8 UŠ.KU.MAḪ ^{d}EN.ZU *šà* ŠÀ ^{URU}*ḫar-ra-an* ŠÀ.BAL.BAL ^{I}MU-ḪÉ.GÁL
9 UŠ.KU.MAḪ É.SAG.ÍL *a-na* IGI.DU$_{8}$.A-*šú iš-ṭur-ma ib-ri*

"According to the wording of a writing board, copy of Babylon, . . . of the house of Šumu-libši, the *kalamāḫu* of Esangil, NABÛ-ZĒRU-IDDINA the *aštalû*-singer of Sîn, son of URAD-EA the *kalamāḫu* of Sin of Harran and descendant of Šumu-libši the *kalamāḫu* of Esangil, wrote and collated for his own perusal."

13. *BAK 524* (Sm 80)

Colophon only preserved:

1' GIM SUMUN-*šú* $^{I.d}$AG-NUMUN-SUM-*na*
2' A ^{I}ÌR-^{d}*é-a* ŠÚ.MAḪ *30 u* LUGAL
3' [*iš-ṭ*]*ur-ma íb-rì*

"Copied, and collated with the original, by NABÛ-ZĒRU-IDDINA son of URAD-EA, the *kalamāḫu* of Sîn and the king."

14. *StOr 1 (1925) 28 ff* (BM 79503). = BAK 498.

Copy of a bilingual votive inscription to Nabû originally written for Adad-apla-iddina, king of Babylon. Rev. 7 ff:

7 *11*.ÀM MU ŠID.BI.IM *šá* UGU *né-bé-ḫi šá* EN BÁR.SIPA^{KI}
8 LIBIR.RA.BI.GIM AB.SAR BA. AN. È
9 *i-na* UGU *ṭup-pi* GAZ^{MEŠ} *šà-ṭir a-me-ru la i-ṭa-pil ḫe-pa-a li-šal-lim*
10 DUB ^{I}ÌR- ^{d}*gu-la* ^{LÚ}MAŠ.MAŠ ME.EN
11 [DU]MU $^{I.d}$IM-MU-*ú-ṣur* ^{LÚ}*šá-an-gam-ma-ḫu*
12 *ša* [$^{I.d}$*aš*]+⌈*šur*⌉-PAB-AŠ MAN ⌈KUR⌉ *aš+šur*^{KI}

"11 is the number of its lines on the girdle of the lord of Borsippa. Copied from the original and collated, it was written on a damaged tablet. May the reader not mistreat (the tablet) but restore the breaks! Tablet of URAD-GULA the exorcist, son of ADAD-ŠUMU-UṢUR the *šangamāḫu* of Esarhaddon king of Assyria."

The provenience of this tablet is unknown (cf. Gadd, *StOr* 1 29; hardly Borsippa as conjectured ibid.). It may relate to the restoration of the cult of Nabû of Borsippa by Esarhaddon (cf. sub *LAS* 58, 276 and 281) and hence date from ca. 671 BC. For Adad-šumu-uṣur's title cf. *a-ši-pu šá-an-gam-ma-ḫu šá* d[*É-a*], Utukkū lemnūtu III 129 (*CT* 16 1ff.), and *a-ši-pu šá-an-gam-ma-ḫu mu-ul-lil par-ṣi šá Eri-du*$_{10}$ *a-na-ku*, Utukkū lemnūtu B 47 (*CT* 16 27ff.).

15. *K 2077* + K 3771 + K 11044 (unp., cf. Bezold, *Cat.* I 402)

Astrological text, Babylonian script, dated eponymy of Bēl-Harrān-šadû'a (650). Left edge, in NA script, reads as follows:

2 [....... ÌR]-⌈d⌉*gu-la* LÚ⌈A.ZU⌉	"[... URAD]-GULA the physician"
3 [....... *lim*]-*mu* I.dEN*-KUR-*u-a*	"[... epon]ymy of Bēl-šadû'a"

This may actually not be a colophon but rather a remark that the tablet had belonged to the collections of Urad-Gula before its incorporation in the royal library. If so, it may indicate the approximate date of Urad-Gula's death. For the titel "physician" here applied to Urad-Gula cf. No. 25.

3. CONTRACTS (16-25)

16. *ADD 350* = *AR 165* (83-1-18,335)

Sale of ground (buyer: Gazilu; seller: Išdī-Allā'a), dated Ulūlu 15, eponymy of Ša-Aššur-dubbu (707 BC). The witness list includes:

Rev. 12 I.dIM-MU-PAP "Adad-šumu-uṣur" (no title).

This tablet was found in Nineveh but the penalty clauses (cf. especially Rev. 2, *a-na* dMAŠ *a-šib* URU*kal-*[*ḫi*]) indicate that it was written in Calah. Cf. No. 2.

17. *ADD 448* = *AR 443* (K 1499)

Purchase of vineyards in the country of Izalla (buyer: Rēmanni-Adad, the charioteer of Assurbanipal), dated Šabāṭu 10, eponymy [of Kanūnāju of New Palace] = January 26, 665 BC. The witness list (Rev. 8 ff) opens with

8 IGI I*šum-ma-*⌈d⌉*aš+šur* LÚEN-NAM [...]
9 IGI I.dMAŠ.MAŠ-MAN-PAP LÚ3-*šú* [*dan-nu*]
10 IGI I*sa-si-i* LÚ*ḫa-za-nu* URU[NINA?]
11 IGI I.d*15*-MU-KAM-*eš* LÚGAL-[A.BA]
12 [IGI I].dIM-MU-PAP LÚGAL-[ ]
13 [IGI I*šu-ma*]-*a-a* DUMU I.[dPA-NUMUN-GIŠ]
14 [IGI I.dAMAR+UD-G]AR MU LÚ[GAL-MAŠ.MAŠ]

"Šumma-Aššur, the governor of [...]; Nergal-šarru-uṣur, the (king's) main shield-bearer; Sāsî, the mayor of [Nineveh?]; IŠTAR-ŠUMU-ĒREŠ, the chief [scribe]; ADAD-ŠUMU-UṢUR, the chief [...]; [Šumā]ju son of [Nabû-zēru-lišir]; [MARDUK-Š]ĀKIN-ŠUMI, the [chief exorcist]".

The following lines mention colleagues of Rēmanni-Adad well known from his other transactions (Šamaš-šarru-uṣur, Nabû-šēzib, Nabû-erība, Ištar-šumu-iddina). Scribe and date (Rev. 24 ff):

24 IGI I.d*15*-SUM-A LÚ[A.BA *ṣa-bit dan-ni-te*]
25 ITUZÍZ UD *10*.KÁM* *lim-mu* [I*ITU.AB-a-a* É-GIBIL]

The restoration of the eponym is based on the fact that IŠTAR-NĀDIN-APLI also functions as a public scribe in the following two documents, both dated late in the eponymy of Kanūnāju:

17a. *ADD 331 = AR 356* (83-1-18,461b)

Purchase of house (buyer: Rēmanni-Adad), dated Šabāṭu 1, eponymy of Kanūnāju of New Palace = January 17, 665 BC. Rev. 7 ff:

7 IGI I.d15-SUM-A LÚA.BA *ṣa-bit dan-ni-te*
8 ITUZÍZ UD *1*.KÁM* *lim-mu* IITU.AB-*a-a*
9 LÚEN-NAM É-GIBIL

17b. *ADD 420 = AR 100* (K 306) and its duplicate *ADD 421* (81-7-27, 28)

Purchase of landed estate (buyer: Rēmanni-Adad), dated Addāru 1, eponymy of Kanūnāju of New Palace = February 16, 665 BC. Rev. 7 ff (restored from 421 r14f):

7 IGI I.d*15*-AŠ-A LÚ*A.BA [*ṣa-bit dan-ni-te*]
8 ITUŠE UD *1*.KÁM* *lim-mu* IITU.AB-[*a-a*]
9 É- GIBIL

18. *ADD 377 = AR 399* (80-7-19,83)

Purchase of ground near the village of Dannai (URUŠE I*dan-na-a-a*). Buyer: [Rēmanni-Adad]; dated Kanūnu 17, eponymy of Šarru-lū-dāri = January 11, 663 BC. The witness list (Rev. 1'ff) mentions, among military officials also found as witnesses in other transactions by Rēmanni-Adad, in Rev. 5'

IGI IDÙ-*i* LÚ*2-u šá* LÚGAL-[A.ZU] "BĀNÎ, the deputy of the chief [physician]".

19. *ADD 470 = AR 168* (K 324)

Purchase of an entire village (URU*da-na-a-a . . . a-na gi-mir-te-šú*) by Rēmanni-Adad. Date: Kanūnu 25, eponymy of Bēl-na'di = January 8, 662 BC. The witness list includes influential magnates and military officials and mentions, in a context identical with that in No. 18,

IGI I*ba-ni-i* LÚ**2-u ša* LÚ*GAL-A.ZU "BĀNÎ, the deputy of the chief physician" (Rev. 19).

20. *ADD 408 = AR 415* (Bu 91-5-9,41)

Purchase of field (buyer: [Rēmanni-Adad]). Date lost but probably ca. 663 BC, cf. *ADD* 115-116 and 470 (No. 19). In the witness list are found, beside military officials also found in Nos. 18 and 19, "[MARDUK]-ŠUMU-UṢUR the chief haruspex and [BĀNÎ], the deputy of the chief physician" ([IGI I.dAMAR+UD]-MU!-PAP LÚGAL-ḪAL 8 [IGI I*ba-ni-i*] LÚ*2-u* LÚGAL-A.ZU, Rev. 7-8).

21. *ADD 444 = AR 445* (K 317)

Purchase of large landed estate (vineyards, cultivated fields, an oak grove, pastures, etc) in Sinjar. Buyer: Rēmanni-Adad. Dated Du'ūzu 26, eponymy of Gir-ṣapūnu = July 3, 660 BC. The witness list reads (Rev. 8 ff):

8 IGI I*si-lim-aš+šur* LÚ[SUKKAL *dan-nu*]
9 IGI ILUGAL-DINGIR-*a-a* L[ÚGAL-*ki-ṣ*]*ir*
10 *šá* LÚ*qur*-ZAG
11 IGI I.d*15*-MU-KAM-*eš* LÚGAL-A.BA
12 IGI I.dŠÚ-GAR-MU LÚGAL-MAŠ.MAŠ
13 IGI I.dAMAR+UD-MAN-PAP LÚDIB-KUŠPAMEŠ
14 *ša* MÍÉ.GAL

"Silim-Aššur, the [main *sukkallu*]; Šarru-ilā'i, the [command]er of the royal bodyguard; IŠTAR-ŠUMU-ĒREŠ, the chief scribe; MARDUK-ŠĀKIN-ŠUMI, the chief exorcist; Marduk-šarru-uṣur, the charioteer of the queen; (further: Mannu-kī-Aššur, the charioteer of the crown prince; Tardītu-Aššur, the shield-bearer of the crown prince; Nabû-zēru-iddina and Zēru-ukīn, charioteers; and Nabû-erība, the deputy of the royal equerry)."

21a. *ADD 445 = AR 446* (Bu 91-5-9,162)

Duplicate of No. 21. Rev. 6 ff:

6 IGI I15-MU-KAM-e[š LÚGAL-A.BA]
7 IGI I.dAMAR+UD-GAR-M[U LÚGAL-MAŠ.MAŠ]

For another contract mentioning IŠTAR-ŠUMU-ĒREŠ and MARDUK-ŠĀKIN-ŠUMI see No. 17. For a contract mentioning MARDUK-ŠUMU-UṢUR see No. 20.

22. *ADD 473 = AR 96* (83-1-18,331)

A sales document dated 698 BC, drawn up by "NABÛ-AḪḪĒ-ERĪBA the scribe, depositary of the tablet" (IGI I.dPA-PAPMEŠ-SU LÚ*A.BA 24 *ṣa-bit ṭup-pi*, Rev. 23 f).

Possibly, though unlikely, identical with the later astrologer of Esarhaddon and Assurbanipal. Same scribe also in *ADD* 43 (687 BC).

23. *ADD 477 = AR 61* (82-5-22,34)

Sale of persons and orchards (purchaser: Aḫī-ṭallī, the female prefect of Nineveh), dated Ajāru 1, 23rd year of Sennacherib, eponymy of Mannu-kī-Adad (683 BC). The witness list is headed by

IGI I.dPA-MU-AŠ LÚA.BA "NABÛ-ŠUMU-IDDINA the scribe" (Rev. 6).

It is possible, though uncertain, that this Nabû-šumu-iddina is identical with the *rab-eširti* of Nineveh figuring in *LAS* 31 and 77-79.

23a. *ADD 330 = AR 195* (83-1-18,337)

Purchase of house (buyer: Mannu-kī-Arbīl) dated Nisannu 24, eponymy of Banbâ, reign of Esarhaddon (= April 10, 676 BC). The witness list (Rev. 5 ff) is headed by

5	IGI IGÌR+2-*15* LÚ*A.BA	"Šēp-Ištar the scribe;
6	IGI I.dPA-MU-AŠ LÚ*A.BA	NABÛ-ŠUMU-IDDINA the scribe;
7	IGI I*ki-ṣir-15* LÚ*3.U$_5$	Kiṣir-Ištar the shield bearer
8	*ša* LÚ*GAL-KAŠ.LUL	of the chief cupbearer;
9	IGI 1NUMUN-d*15*	Zēr-Ištar."

The Nabû-šumu-iddina of this text should be identical with the one of No. 23, since the two texts have one further common witness (Zēr-Ištar; cf. INUMUN-*15* LÚGAL-UŠ.BARMEŠ, *ADD* 447 r8).

24. *ADD 640 = AR 45* (K 382)

Donation of people (as oblates) to the Ninurta Temple of Calah, dated Ulūlu 18, eponymy of Aššur-gimillī-tēre (= 641 BC according to Falkner). The text ends:

IGI I.dMAŠ.MAŠ-MU-AŠ A I.dPA-*mu*-SIG$_5$ 19 LÚA.BA *ṣa-bit dan-ni-te*

"NERGAL-ŠUMU-IDDINA son of Nabû-mudammiq, the scribe, depositary of the document" (Rev. 18 f).

The date makes it possible that this scribe is identical with the sender of *LAS* 82-84.

25. *ADD 277 = AR 62* (K 354)

Sale of people, dated Ajāru 12, eponymy of Nabû-aḫḫē-ēreš = April 25, 681 BC. The witness list (Rev. 3 ff) includes:

5 IGI IDÙG+GA-*i* LÚ**rak-[su]*
6 IGI IEN-PAP AŠ LÚ*GIŠ.GIGIR *na-[kam-te]*
7 IGI I.dPA-A-AŠ LÚ*A.BA
8 IGI IÌR-d*gu-la* LÚ**2-ú*
9 *ša* LÚ*GAL-A.ZU

"Ṭābnî, conscript; Bēl-aḫu-iddina, groom of *.akamtu*(-horses), Nabû-aplu-iddina, scribe; URAD-GULA, deputy of the chief physician."

A witness mentioned in Rev. 5 of this text (Mannu-kī-aḫḫē) also occurs in No. 23a (Rev. 10).

25a. *ADD* 833 (a roster of people) mentions [I.dAMAR].UTU-MU-PAP LÚGAL-ḪAL "MARDUK ŠUMU-UṢUR chief haruspex" (col. I 7). No date.

4. ADMINISTRATIVE RECORDS (26-31)

26. *ADD 851* (K 1276)

List of scholars attached to the court of Assurbanipal. Ca. 650 BC.[698]

Obv. I	1	^{I}*15*-MU-APIN-*eš*	IŠTAR-ŠUMU-ĒREŠ
	2	^{I}AŠ-PAP^{MEŠ}	Nādin-aḫḫē
	3	^{I}*ba-la-su*	Balāssu
	4	^{I}DÙ-*na-a-a*	Būnāju
	5	^{I}*ki-ṣir-*^{d}PA	Kiṣir-Nabû
	6	^{I}⌜UGUR⌝-MU!-AŠ	⌜NERGAL⌝-ŠUMU-IDDINA
	7	[^{I}DN]-KAR-*ir*	[DN]-ēṭir
	8	[PAP 7 A.BA]-UD-AN-BE	[total 7 scribes] of Enūma Anu Enlil
	9	[$^{\mathrm{I.d}}$AMAR+UD-G]AR-MU!	[MARDUK-Š]ĀKIN-ŠUMI
	10	[ ]⌜x⌝	[. . .]
	11	[^{I}*šu-ma*]-*a-a*	[Šumā]ju
	12	[^{I}. .]-*bu-u'*	[. .]bu'
	13	[^{I}*ku*]-*na-a-a*	[Ku]nāju
	14	[$^{\mathrm{I.d}}$]PA-*sa-kip*	Nabû-sākip
	15	[^{I}]*rém-u-tú*	Rēmūtu
	16	[^{I}]EN-*ú-še-zib*	Bēl-ušēzib
	17	[^{I}]^{d}PA-NUNUZ-GIŠ	Nabû-pir'u-līšir
	18	PAP *9*! MAŠ.MAŠ^{MEŠ}	total 9 exorcists
II	1	^{I}*a-qar-a*	Aqarâ
	2	^{I}*ba-ni-i*	Bānî
	3	^{I}*zi-zi-i*	Zīzî
	4	$^{\mathrm{I.d}}$ŠÚ-MU-PAP	MARDUK-ŠUMU-UṢUR
	5	$^{\mathrm{I.d}}$PA-SUM-A	Nabû-nādin-apli
	6	PAP *5* ḪAL^{MEŠ}	total 5 haruspices
	7	^{I}*qur-di-arba-ìl*	Qurdī-Arbīl
	8	$^{\mathrm{I.d}}$PA-*u-a*	Nabû'a
	9	$^{\mathrm{I.d}}$PA-PAP^{MEŠ}-TI	Nabû-aḫḫē-uballiṭ
	10	$^{\mathrm{I.d}}$MAŠ!-*bal-liṭ-su*	Ninurta-ballissu
	11	^{I}*as-qu-du*	Asqūdu
	12	^{I}*30*-MAN-PAP	Sîn-šarru-uṣur
	13	$^{\mathrm{I.d}}$PA-MU-AŠ	Nabû-šumu-iddina
	14	^{I}*bu-uk-lu*	Buklu
	15	^{I}*ṣi-ḫu-ru*	Ṣiḫūru
	16	PAP *9* A.Z[U]^{MEŠ}	total 9 physicians

[698] Cf. *ADD* 853 (list of governors), dated ^{ITU}AB UD *16*.KÁM (same date as in our document but no year); *ADD* 859 (= *ADD* 705, list of governors), dated ^{ITU}GUD UD *9*.KÁM* *lim-mu* ^{I}EN-KASKAL-KUR-*u-a* = May 7, 650 BC; *ADD* 943 (list of accessions to palace library), dated ^{ITU}ZÍZ UD *1*.KAM *lim-mu* ^{I}EN-*šú-nu* = January 28, 647 BC; and *ADD* 1053 (accessions to library), dated ^{ITU}ŠE UD *4*.KÁM* *lim-mu* ^{I}EN-*šú-nu* = March 1, 647 BC.

Rev III	1	I.dPA-NUMUN-AŠ	NABÛ-ZĒRU-IDDINA
	2	I*za-ki-ru*	Zākiru
	3	I*30*-TI-*su*-E	Sîn-balāssu-iqbi
	4	I.dPA-MAN-*a-ni*	Nabû-šarrāni
	5	I.dPA-EN-MUMEŠ	Nabû-bēl-šumāti
	6	I*mar-duk*	Marduk
	7	PAP *6* UŠ.KUMEŠ	total 6 chanters
	8	I.dIGI.DU-DÙ-PAPMEŠ	Nergal-bāni-aḫḫē
	9	IIS-PU-te	Ispute
	10	ISUḪUŠ-d*15*	Išdī-Ištar
	11	PAP *3 da-gíl*-MUŠEN	total 3 augurs
	12	I⌜*gi*?⌝-*ši-i*	Gišî
	13	I*ra-a'-si-i*	Ra'sî
IV	1	I*ṣi-ḫu-u*	Ṣiḫû
	2	PAP *3 ḫar-ṭi-bi*	total 3 dream interpreters
	3	I*ḫu-u-ru*	Ḫūru
	4	I*ni-mur-a-u*	Nimmura'u
	5	I*ṣu-u-a-ṣu*	Ṣu'aṣu
	6	[PAP] ⌜*3* A⌝.BAMEŠ	total 3 Egyptian
	7	*mu-ṣur-a-a*	scribes
	8	ITUAB UD *16*.KÁM	Kanūnu 16

Notes: (1) Section SCRIBE: Nādin-aḫḫē (I 2) also occurs in No. 28; for line 8 cf. Oppenheim, *Centaurus* 14 (1969) 100 and van Driel, *CA* 55[18].

(2) Section EXORCIST: I 9 -G]AR-MU! (copy NUMUN) not collated. Kūnāju, Rēmūtu and Bēl-ušēzib also occur in No. 28, Rēmūtu also in 26a; Nabû-pir'u-līšir probably = Pir'u in No. 28 r16. Restoration of I 11 conjectural. I 18 collated by van Driel, l.c.

(3) Section HARUSPEX: Cf. I*a-qar-a-a*, *PRT* 44 r15 (et passim); I[*b*]*a-ni-*[*i*], *PRT* 121 r2 (650 BC); I*zi-zi-i*, *PRT* 130 r4 and 131 r5 (both text Bab.); I.dPA-SUM-A ḪAL, *ADD* 980 i 10 (below No. 31). Omitted: Nīnuwāju (chief haruspex, *PRT* 116), Dannāja (*PRT* 110, etc.), Nergal-šarru-uṣur (*PRT* 124), etc.

(4) Section PHYSICIAN: Ninurta-ballissu, Sîn-šarru-uṣur, Buklu and Ṣiḫūru also occur in No. 26a, q.v. Note also I*bu-la*!-*lu* LÚA.ZU, *ADD* 417 r6.

(5) Section CHANTER: Except for Nabû-zēru-iddina, none of the chanters here mentioned seem to be otherwise known.

26a. *Bezold, Cat. IV 1416* (Sm 471)

List of exorcists and physicians; probably approximately contemporary with No. 26. Babylonian script.

Obv	1	I*na-ṣi-ru*	cf. No. 28 r4
	2	IEN-DÙ-*uš*	cf. No. 28 r17
	3	PAP *2* LÚMAŠ.MAŠMEŠ	
	4	I.dMAŠ-TIN-*su*	
Edge	5	I*ṣi-i-ḫur-ru*	
Rev	6	I.d*30*-MAN-PAP	
	7	I*bu-uk-lu*	
	8	PAP *4* LÚA.ZUMEŠ	

27. *ADD 769* (K 975)

List of persons, undated. Obv. 1-7: Aššur-bāni-aḫḫē, Nabû-rēšu-iši, Kalbu, Bānî, Qurdī-Adad, Urdu, total 6 Šelappeans. Obv. 8 ff:

Obv.	8	[IDÙ-*na*]-*a-a*	[Būn]āju
	9	[I*ba-l*]*a-su*	[Bal]āssu
Rev	1	I.dPA-MAN-PAPMEŠ-*šú*	Nabû-šar-aḫḫēšu
	2	I.dPA-*mu-še-ṣi*	NABÛ-MUŠĒṢI
	3	I*aš+šur*-MU-AŠ	Aššur-šumu-iddina
	4	IDUMU-*15*	MĀR-IŠTAR
	5	PAP *6* LÚ*A.BAMEŠ	total 6 scribes

Lines 8-9 restored from the SCRIBE section of No. 26 (I 3-4). Nabû-šar-aḫḫēšu is known from *ABL* 447 (No. 28) as a scribe working on the composition Bīt Marṣi; Nabû-mušēṣi is well known as deputy of the chief scribe (No. 29) and author of numerous astrological reports; Aššur-šumu-iddina is the author of the unp. astrological report K 985. In such context, it is extremely likely that the Mār-Ištar mentioned here was identical with the person who wrote *LAS* 275-297.

28. *ABL 447* (K 821)

Memorandum on works on the palace libraries of Nineveh. Undated, but probably late reign of Esarhaddon (ca. 670 BC). Cf. notes on Obv. 8-13, 14-19, and Rev. 2-7.

Obv	1	IEN-PAP-AŠ	Bēl-aḫu-iddina
	2	I*ṣal-la-a-a*	(and) Ṣallāju
	3	*an-nu-te 2*	these two are the ones
	4	*ša li-gìn-nu*	who are giving
	5	*i-qab-bu-ú-ni*	instruction.
	6	I*šá*-dPA-*šu-ú* [*la*] *qur-bu*	Ša-Nabû-šū is not present;
	7	*dul-lu ina* IGI I*ú-ku-me e-ta-mar*	he has found a job with Ukume.
	8	I.dMAŠ-ŠU DUMU LÚGÚ.EN.NA	Ninurta-gimillī the son of
	9	ÉŠ.GÀR *ug-da-mir*	the *šandabakku* has completed
	10	*si-par-ri* AN.BAR *šá-kin*	the series and has been put
	11	*ina* É *re-du-te*	in fetters. He is at the
	12	*ina* IGI I*ba-a-nu-ni pa-aq-qid*	custody of Bānūni in the Suc-
	13	*dul-lu ina* ŠU.2-*šú la-áš-šú*	cession Palace; he is doing
			no work (at the moment).
	14	I*ku-dúr-ru*	Kudurru (and)
	15	I*ku-na-a-a*	Kūnāju have completed
	16	UDUG.ḪUL.A.MEŠ	(the series)
	17	*ug-da-me-ru*	udug ḫul-a-meš.
	18	*ṭè-en-šú-nu*	Their report is
	19	*ina* IGI I*sa-si-i*	with Sāsî.
Rev	1	I.dAMAR+UD-LUGAL-*a-ni*	Marduk-šarrāni,
	2	I*su-la-a-a*	Sūlāju,
	3	I*ba-la-ṭu*	Balāṭu,
	4	I*na-ṣi-ru*	Nāṣiru
	5	I.d*30*-ŠEŠ-SUM-*na*	Sīn-aḫu-iddina,
	6	I*re-mu-tu*	Rēmūtu,
	7	IAŠ-PABMEŠ	Nādin-aḫḫē,
	8	IEN-*ú-še-zib*	Bēl-ušēzib,
	9	I.dPA-LUGAL-ŠEŠMEŠ-*šú*	Nabû-šar-aḫḫēšu
	10	*an-nu-te 9*	– these 9 are the ones
	11	*ša* TA* *um-ma-a-ni*	who are assisting
	12	*iz-za-zu-ú-ni dul-lu*	the masters and
	13	*ša* É LÚGIG	working on (the series)
	14	*ep-pa-šu-ú-ni*	Bīt Marṣi.

Rev	15	$^{I.d}$UTU-SUM-*na*	Šamaš-iddina,
	16	^{I}*pi-ir-'u*	Pir'u,
	17	^{I}EN-DÙ-*uš*	Bēl-ēpus
	18	*an-nu-te 3*	– these 3 are the ones
	19	*ša a-di ṭup-pi-šú*	who are going to complete
	20	ÉŠ.GÀR *ú-gam-ma-ru-ni*	the series as prescribed(?).

Obv. 8-13: The son of *šandabakku* mentioned here could well be identical with the DUMU ^{LÚ}GÚ.EN.NA *ša a-kan-nu ka-lu-ú* figuring in *CT* 54 22 (r2 f), a letter of Bēl-ušēzib dating from 675 BC (see Dietrich, *AOAT* 7 p. 65). ^{1}*ba-a-nu-ni* is probably identical with the exorcist (^{I}*ba-nu-ni* ^{LÚ*}MAŠ.MAŠ) known as the copyist of the *tamītu* IM 67692, r.III 30 (unp., courtesy W.G. Lambert).

Obv. 14-19: Cf. *ABL* 1257:6 ff (crown prince Assurbanipal to Esarhaddon, ca. 670 BC): *ina* UGU ^{I}*ku-na-a-a* ^{7} ^{I}*ku-dúr-ru šá* MAN EN *iq-bu-u-ni* ^{8} *ma-a šu-pur liš-ú-lu* ^{9} *a-na* ^{I}*sa-si-i* ^{10} *ma-a šu-tú* [*ṭè*]*-en-šú-*[*nu*] ^{11} *ú-da k*[*i-i*] *an-ni-i* ^{12} *is-sap-*[*ra ma-a* . . .] "As to Kūnāju and Kudurru, concerning whom the king, my lord, wrote as follows: 'Send word that they question Sāsî, he knows about them', he has written [to me as follows . . .]"; on Sāsî see note to *LAS* 115:12.

Rev. 2-7: Sūlāju is very probably identical with the homophonous person "kept in the *Māšartu* Palace of Nineveh by order of the king" according to BM 135586:37ff (ca. 670 BC, cf. *Iraq* 34 [1972] 21 ff). Nādin-aḫḫē and Rēmūtu are mentioned in two letters of Marduk-šākin-šumi (*LAS* 173 and 174), both dating from late 670 BC.

Rev. 13 É ^{LÚ}GIG: meant is naturally the diagnostic and prognostic series *Enūma āšipu ana bīt marṣi illiku* (Labat *TDP*).

29. *ADD 857* (K 1359 + K 13197)

List of people (primarily military) attached to the households of the queen mother (Naqīʾa/Zakūtu) and the crown prince (Assurbanipal). Not dated, but probably ca. 670 BC. Excerpts:

I	39	$^{I.d}$PA-*mu-še-ṣi*	^{LÚ}2-*u* GAL.A.BA	NABÛ-MUŠĒṢI, deputy chief scribe;
	40	^{I}ÌR-^{d}*é-a*	^{LÚ}UŠ.KU	URAD-EA, chanter;
II	9	^{I}ÌR-^{d}*na-na-a*	^{LÚ}*qur*-ZAG	Urad-Nanâ, bodyguard,
	40	^{I}*da-ni-i*	^{LÚ}A.BA	Danî, scribe;
	45	^{I}*la-qi-pu*	^{LÚ}*qur*-ZAG	Lā-qēpu, bodyguard;
	46	$^{I.d}$MES-MAN-PAP	LÚ DUMU-MAN	Marduk-šarru-uṣur ditto of the crown prince;
	47	^{I}*ar-ba-a-a*	^{LÚ}EN-NAM	Arbāju, provincial governor.

For II 9 cf. ^{I}ÌR-^{d}*na-na-a* ^{LÚ}*mu-šár-kis-ia* "Urad-Nanâ, my conscriptor", Borger *Ash* p. 114 ii 9. On Dānî, Marduk-šarru-uṣur and Arbāju see respectively notes on *LAS* 142, 190 and 113.

30. *AOAT 25 (1975) 315* (K 11922)

Catalogue of tablets donated by various scholars to the royal libraries of Nineveh. Obv. 2' reads (after a blank line):

[PAP] $^{I.d}$IM-MU-PAP	"All this (donated by) ADAD-ŠUMU-UṢUR".

Unfortunately the list of tablets is almost completely destroyed.

31. *ADD 980* (81-2-4,268)

List of acquisitions to the royal libraries of Nineveh. Not dated, but probably ca. 650 BC (cf. sub No. 26). Excerpts:

Obv. I	9'	PAP *1 me 28*! [DUB^{MEŠ}]	A total of 128 [tablets]
	10'	$^{I.d}$PA-SUM-A ḪAL	belonging to Nabû-nādin-apli
	11'	⸢A ^{I}⸣$^{.d}$*15*-BÀD	the haruspex, son of Ištar-dūrī.

Rev.III	2'	PAP *8* ^{I}x[.]$^{\ulcorner}$ x x $^{\urcorner}$	A total of 8 (tablets) belonging
	3'	A$^{!}$ ^{I}DUMU-[^{d}*15*] A.BA	to [. . .] son of MĀR-[IŠTAR] the
	4'	GAL *s*[*i-ma*]-$^{\ulcorner}$*a*$^{\urcorner}$-*t*[*e*]$^{!}$	scribe, ...

The restoration in III 3' is uncertain but not unlikely taking into consideration the rarity of names beginning with *Mār-*; cf. No. 27. For Nabû-nādin-apli (I 10') cf. No. 26 II 5. The unclear GAL-*si-ma-a-te* (III 4') is also attested in *ADD* 869 III 6' (*šá* GAL *si-ma-a-t*[*ú*]$^{!}$); both texts collated by Irving Finkel (January, 1978).

5. ORACLE QUERIES AND REPORTS (32-46)

32. *AGS 51* (83-1-18,557+563)

Query concerning [^{I}*m*]*i-it-ta-a* the city lord of [. . .], on behalf of Esarhaddon. Dated Kislīmu 16, eponymy of [. .] (probably ^{I}MAN-ZALÁG) = December 2, 674(?). Babylonian script. Signed by [. . . .] and MARDUK-ŠUMU-UṢUR ([^{I}]^{d}AMAR+UD-MU-*ú-ṣur*, L.E. 1) in the city of Calah.

33. *AGS 6* (K 11499)

Query concerning Kaštaritu, Cimmerians, Manneans and Medians, assigned by Aro, *RAI* XIV 114, to early 673 BC (text: Ajāru 6 through 12). Babylonian script. Signed by

[. . . ^{I}*n*]*a-ṣi-ru u* $^{I.d}$AMAR+UD-MU-*ú-ṣur* (Rev. 9).

33a. *AGS 44* (83-1-18,571)

Query concerning military expedition contemplated by Esarhaddon for the months of Šabāṭu and Addāru (all proper names lost). Babylonian script. Signed by

[. . . . . . .$^{I.d}$AMAR+UD]-MU-PAP ^{IT}[U. . . .] (Rev. 7; date lost).

33b. *AGS 88* (K 11432)

Query lost, omens only. Babylonian script. Signed by (Obv. 5)

[. . . . . . $^{I.d}$AMAR].UD-MU-ŠEŠ ^{I}*na-ṣi-ru* [. . . .]

33c. *PRT 17* (K 2663)

Contents obscure, Esarhaddon. Babylonian script. Dated Ajāru 27, signed by

[$^{I.d}$AMAR+UD-M]U-ŠEŠ *u* ^{I}*na-ṣi-ru* [. . . . .] (LE 2).

34. *AGS 98* (K 11477)

Subject matter obscure; Esarhaddon. Babylonian script. Signed by

LE	1	$^{I.d}$AMAR+UD-MU-ŠEŠ ^{I}*na-*[*ṣi-ru*	MARDUK-ŠUMU-UṢUR, Nā[ṣiru,
	2	$^{I.d}$EN*-DI-*im* ^{I}*a-qar-a* ^{I}[	Bēl-ušallim, Aqarâ, [
	3	$^{I.d\ulcorner}$EN*?$^{\urcorner}$-M[U]-BA-*šá* ^{I}[	$^{\ulcorner}$Bel$^{\urcorner}$-šumu-iqīša, [
	4	[ ]$^{\ulcorner}$ x x x $^{\urcorner}$[	[. . . .] . . . .[

According to Obv. 15, the extispicy concerned was performed in the *Mašartu* palace of Calah ($^{\ulcorner}$*ina* É.GAL *ma-šar-ti*$^{\urcorner}$ [^{UR}]^{U}*k*[*al-ḫ*]*a*). This may indicate that the text dates from 672 BC, cf. *AGS* 99 r8 (*lim-mu* $^{I.d}$A]G-EN-PAP *ina* É.GAL *ma-šar-te* ^{URU}*kal-ḫa*) and PRT 100 (dated *limmu* Nabû-bēlu-uṣur, Šabāṭu 3, in the city of *Kal-ḫa*).

35. *AGS 35* (K 11439)

Query concerning Scythians feared to attack Assyria through the passes of Hubuškia; Simānu through Du'ūzu (no eponym date). Assyrian script. The left edge reads:

1 ^{ITU}SIG$_4$ UD *22*.KÁM [. . . . . . .]
2 ^{I}*sa-ia* $^{I.d}$AMAR+UD-MU-PAP $^{\ulcorner}$*e*$^{\urcorner}$-[*tap-šú*]

35a. *AGS 36* (K 10149)

Same subject matter as in the preceding text; Simānu through Du'ūzu. Obverse in Babylonian, Reverse in Assyrian script. Signed by

[. . . $^{I.d}$AMAR+UD-MU]-PAB ^{I}⌜*su*⌝-*ki-nu* (Rev. 5).

36. *AGS 108* (K 11437)

Query concerning a potential rebellion against Esarhaddon, Addāru through Simānu (90 days); the relevant eponym year is not given, but because of the mention of Egypt and Cush in Obv. 12 only 671 and 670 can be in question. Accordingly, the query was almost certainly written in Addāru "671" (= February/March, 670 BC). Assyrian script. Signed by

1 $^{I.d}$AMAR+UD-MU-PAP ^{I}*na-ṣi-ru* ^{I}*tab-ni-i* [
2 ^{I}*u-qar-a* $^{I.d}$AMAR+UD-MU-DÙ ^{I}*ba-ni-*⌜*i*⌝[
3 ^{ITU}ŠE UD *16*.KÁM *ḫi-su-tú* ⌜x⌝[(LE 1-3)

37. *AGS 124* (82-5-22,425)

Sīḫu-bārtu query on behalf of Esarhaddon, dated Simānu 13 in the city of Tarbiṣu (L.E. 2; eponym year not given). Assyrian script; signed by

3 [$^{I.d}$AMAR]+UD-MU-PAP ^{I}*na-ṣ*[*i-ru*]
4 [*ù*] ^{I}*tab-ni- i* [0]

38. *AGS 119* (83-1-18,544)

Sīḫu-bartu query on behalf of Esarhaddon and Assurbanipal, the crown prince of the Succession Palace, concerning a person whose name is written on the attached papyrus and who is due to be appointed to a certain position, in order to find out whether he will make or instigate a rebellion against the royal house. Dated Addāru 2 (no eponym year given), in the city of [. . . . .] (^{ITU}ŠE UD *2*.KÁM* *ina* ^{UR}[U. . .], LE 3). In all probability, this query postdates the attempted coup d'état of 670, and hence dates from March 669 BC. The officiating haruspices (LE 1-2):

1 [$^{I.d}$A]MAR+UD-MU-PAP ^{I}*na-ṣ*[*i-ru* ^{I}*tab-ni-i*]
2 [$^{I.d}$P]A-PAP^{ME}-DI ^{I}*ba-l*[*a-su* . . . .] (cf. *LAS* 107!)

39. *AGS 48* (K 4268)

Query concerning a potential attack on Šubria by [Ur]sâ, king of Urarṭu (allied with the Cimmerians), very probably postdating by some years the Assyrian annexation of Šubria (673 BC); cf. *LAS* 196. Nisannu through Du'ūzu; Assyrian script. Signed by

1 $^{I.d}$AMAR+UD-MU-PAB ^{I}*na-ṣi-ru* ^{I}*tab-ni-*⌜*i*⌝ [
2 $^{I.d}$PA-*šal-lim* ^{I}*ba-la-su* ^{I}*su-ki-nu* ^{I}[
3 ^{I}*ku du-ru* ^{I}*ka-ṣi-i u* $^{I.d}$⌜ x ⌝[L.E. 1-3)

40. *AGS 145* (K 11521)

Query concerning a drug, dated Du'ūzu 22 (eponym year not given), in Adian. Babylonian script; colophon in in Assyrian script (LE 2 ff):

2 [$^{I.d}$AMAR+UD-MU-PAP ^{I}*na-ṣi-*[*ru*]
3 [^{I}*tab*]-*ni-i* $^{I.d}$PA-PAP^{MEŠ}-TI [0]
4 [^{I}. . .] $^{I.d}$PA-⌜*šub*⌝-*š*[*i*]

40a. *AGS 91* (81-2-4,191)

Query concerning a potential attack on [. . .]; date lost, Assyrian script. Obv. 14f (lower edge):

14 [. . . . . ^{I}]⌜^{d}⌝AMAR+UD-MU-PAP *e-tap-šú*
15 [. . . . .] UD *17*.KÁM

40b. *PRT 74* (K 14144)

Assyrian script, contents obscure. Left Edge, line 1, reads [. . . . .]-*a* I.dAMAR+UD-M[U-PAP

41. *PRT 106* (K 102)

Extispicy report concerning illness of the king (Assurbanipal), dated Ajāru 26, eponymy of Sagab = April 11, 651 BC. Assyrian script. Reporters: MARDUK-ŠUMU-UṢUR, Dannāja, Sîn-šarru-ibni (I.dŠÚ-MU-PAP IKALAG-*a* I*30*-MAN-DÙ ³ ENMEŠ-UMUŠ, Rev. 2'f).

42. *PRT 110* (K 396)

Extispicy report on obscure subject, dated Ābu 10, eponymy of Sagab = July 17, 651 BC. Babylonian script. The text ends (Rev. 9f): I.dŠÚ-MU-PAP IKALAG-*a* ḪALMEŠ ¹⁰ [. . .] *ina arba-ìl*KI DÙ "MARDUK-ŠUMU-UṢUR and Dannāja were the (officiating) haruspices; [the extispicy] was performed in Arbela."

43. *PRT 111* (81-7-27,136)

Extispicy report, dated Šabāṭu 4, eponymy of Sagab = February 3, 650 BC; Assyrian script. The purpose of the extispicy and the name of the reporter are stated on the reverse:

1'	[. . .] TARMEŠ *šá šá-an-nu-'i*	[In]definite [. . .], to be repeated;
2'	[*e-p*]*a-áš* ŠE ina UGU KUR	[re m]aking . . . against the land.
3'	[IT]UZÍZ UD *4*.KÁM* *lim* I*sa-gab*	(Date)
4'	[I.dAMA]R+UD-MU-PAP EN *ṭè-me*	Reporter: MARDUK-ŠUMU-UṢUR

44. *PRT 124* (K 3742 + K 4284)

Extispicy report concerning appointment of an official, dated Nisannu 23, eponymy of Bēl-Ḫarrān-šadû'a = April 21, 650 BC. Assyrian script. Reporter: MARDUK-ŠUMU-UṢUR ⌜son of(?)⌝ Nergal-šarru-uṣur (*šá* I.dAMAR+UTU-MU-PAP ⁸ ⌜A?⌝ I.dU+GUR-MAN-PAP EN-UMUŠ, Rev. 7f).

> The sign ⌜A⌝ in line 8 is uncertain and could also be read ⌜*ù*⌝ "and". Two officiating haruspices *do* bear patronyms in No. 45, though.

45. *PRT 121* (K 10532)

Extispicy report dated Tašrītu 8, eponymy of Bēl-Ḫarrān-šadû'a = October 1, 650 BC; content obscure. Assyrian script. Reported by Ilu-iṣbatanni son of [. . .] and Bānî son of MARDUK-ŠUMU-UṢUR (IDINGIR-DIB-AN-ni ⌜DUMU⌝ I[. .]x I[*b*]*a-ni-*[*i*] ⁴ DUMU I.dŠÚ-MU-PAP [L]ÚḪAL ENMEŠ [*ṭè-me*], Rev. 3'f).

46. *PRT 122* (K 1436 + K 1523)

Extispicy report concerning appointment of the priest of Anu, undated. Assyrian script. Rev. 10ff:

10 I.dŠÚ-MU-PAP *ina* UGU I*ba-ni-i*
11 DÙ-*áš* ISANGA-*u-te šá* d*a-num*

12 *šu-u gab-bi-šá-a-ma* TAG-*at*
13 TA* *a-a-ak aḫ-ḫur*
14 UZU.2MEŠ NU TAR-[*a*]*t*?

"MARDUK-ŠUMU–UṢUR; concerning Bānî; to exercise the priesthood of Anu. It (the extispicy) was enterily unfavourable . . ." (Rest unclear)

6. LETTERS (47-81)

47. *ABL 1373* (Ki 1904-10-9,15)

Letter of Bēl-ušēzib to Esarhaddon dating from about 678 BC (cf. Dietrich, *AOAT* p. 65). Refers to "ADAD-ŠUMU-UṢUR the brother of [Nabû-zēru-lišir]" (I.dIM-MU-ŠEŠ ŠEŠ [. . .], Rev. 4) in fragmentary context. Cf. below, Nos. 73 and 77.

48. *LAS 249* (K 1118)

Letter of [Urad-Nanâ] to Esarhaddon (671 BC). Obv. 3'ff: "As to the king's writing to me: 'Adjure ADAD-ŠUMU-UṢUR! Why did he say that the crown prince and Šamaš-šumu-ukīn should not go outdoors until Tašrītu 22?' . . . I had him adjured in the city of Akkad . . ."

49. *LAS 232* (K 1963)

[Mār-Ištar?] to Esarhaddon (late 671 BC). Obv. 6'ff: "On the 13th he went to [Calah] with the king's sons; on the 14th ADAD-ŠUMU-UṢUR returned to Nineveh [and spoke] to Aššur-nāṣir the chief [eunuch], Sāsî and URAD-EA as follows: 'Let him (= the substitute king) sit on the throne before the eclipse [takes place]'."

50. *LAS 223* (K 1026)

Urad-Gula to Esarhaddon, ca. 670 BC. Rev. 4'ff: "As to what the king said: 'Which exorcists are with you?', there are (only) Nabû-lē'ûtu, his son, and I. At present, ADAD-ŠUMU-UṢUR is coming to us, inspecting our work and instructing us; we are working in close collaboration . . ."

51. *LAS 224* (K 991)

Urad-Gula to Esarhaddon, ca. 670 BC. Mentions ADAD-ŠUMU-UṢUR twice, once (Rev. 17') as a servant of the king's father (= Sennacherib).

52. *ABL 367* (83-1-18,38)

Nergal-šarrani informs the king that lichen has been sighted on the walls of the Nabû temple and suggests that ADAD-ŠUMU-UṢUR perform an apotropaic ritual against the misfortune it predicts (NAM.BÚR.BI-*šú-nu* ^{7} *i-ba-áš-ši* ^{8} *dul-lu i-ba-áš-ši* ^{9} $^{\mathrm{I.d}}$IM-MU-PAP ^{10} *i-ši-'a-a-ri i-pa-áš* ^{11} TA*-*se-niš le-pu-uš*, Rev. 6-11). Date unclear, probably ca. 670 BC.

53. *Sm 2116* (unpublished)

Fragmentary royal letter (in Babylonian) referring to an ADAD-ŠUMU-UṢUR ($^{\mathrm{I.d}}$IM-MU-ŠEŠ, Obv.4'). This person is hardly identical with the scholar figuring in *LAS*; a much more suitable alternative is the Adad-šumu-uṣur (written $^{\mathrm{I.d}}$IM-MU-ŠEŠ) mentioned in a NB letter to Sargon II (*ABL* 1029 r7).

54. *LAS 104* (80-7-19,36)

Unsigned letter conveying the king a message from AKKULLĀNU (concerning a solar eclipse). 669 BC.

55. *LAS 40* (83-1-18,109)

Balasî to Assurbanipal (April 667 BC): "[AKKULL]ĀNU will read and explain the report on the lunar eclipse to the king" (Rev. 3'ff).

56. *ABL 539* (K 17)

Assurbanipal to a Babylonian ally (name lost), date unclear (cf. below). Rev. 10ff: *en-na a-du-u* ^{11} $^{\mathrm{I.d}}$AG*-SU $^{\mathrm{LÚ*}}$SAG-*iá* ^{I}U+GUR-MAN-PAP ^{14} $^{\mathrm{LÚ*}}$3.U$_{5}$-*iá* ^{I}*ak-kul-la-nu* $^{\mathrm{LÚ*}}$TU-É ^{15} *šá* AN.ŠÁR *it-ti ṭup-pi a-di-iá* ^{16} *ana pa-ni-ka al-tap-raš-šú-nu-ti* "At this very moment I am sending to you three officials carrying my treaty tablet: Nabû-erība, a eunuch of mine; Nergal-šarru-uṣur, my shield-bearer; and AKKULLĀNU, an 'enterer' of the temple of Aššur. (Please enter the treaty and I will make you great in the assembly of Babylonia)."

> Nabû-erība and Nergal-šarru-uṣur occur as witnesses in contracts of Rēmanni-Adad dating to 666-663 BC (cf. *ADD* 258 and 192+801; 420 and 421; 60; 448; 115 and 116; 247; 470 and 471).

57. *ABL 185* (K 1396)

Nabû-bēlšunu to Aššur-mudammiq. The latter is told to give AKKULLĀNU up to 3 pounds of silver for repair of the seats of Aššur and Mullissu (KUG.UD *lu-u 2* MA.NA *lu-u 3* MA.NA ^{5} *a-na bat-qi šá* KI.

TUSMEŠ 6 *ša* d*aš+šur ša* dNIN.LÍL 7 *am-mar* I*ak-kul-la-nu* 8 *e-ri-šu-ka-ni di-i-ni,* Obv. 4 ff). Date unclear.

58. *LAS 341* (83-1-18,721)

Fragmentary letter referring to BALASÎ in connection with apprentice scribes. Date unclear.

59. *ABL 1217* (82-5-22,108)

Letter informing the king (Esarhaddon) of a conspiracy, probably dating to early 670 BC (cf. sub *LAS* 247). Rev. 9 ff:

"May the name and seed of Sāsî and Bēl-aḫu-uṣur and the people who conspire with them be destroyed, and may Bēl and Nabû establish the name and seed of the king, my lord, forever! They should have a word with Ardâ who says that on the evening of the 27th the warden of the City and the scribe IŠTAR-NĀDIN-APLI (LÚ*šá*-UGU-URU I15-SUM-A LÚA.BA) said to Sāsî as follows: 'This is a [. . .] moment; [as soon as . . .] has gone, we shall [. . .] Aujānu the eunuch.' He also says that the scribe IŠTAR-NĀDIN-APLI and Nabû-ēṭir [should be interrogated] as follows: 'On the 28th, what did Sāsî [. . . .] on account of [. . . .]? [What kind of]discussion did Sāsî have with you and with the [warden of the City] on the following day? Why [have you not made public] whatever you he[ard]?' "

> The above rendering is based on a collated text. The scribe Ištar-nādin-apli mentioned in the text is certainly identical with the writer of Nos. 17-17b, but it is doubtful whether it can be identified with the scribe who wrote *LAS* 96-99 and 352.

60. *RMA 55 = ABL 993* (K 1335 + 80-7-19,335)

Balasî reporting to Esarhaddon (669 BC): "Yesterday IŠTAR-ŠUMU-ĒREŠ had an argument with NABÛ-AḪḪĒ-ERĪBA (about the planet Mercury) in the palace" (Obv. 6 ff).

61. *LAS 242* (K 13906) twice refers to IŠTAR-ŠUMU-ĒREŠ in fragmentary context.

62. *ABL 580* (K 1051)

Draft of a royal letter referring to the fashioning of cultic objects for a temple, possibly Esangil. Late Esarhaddon or early Assurbanipal. Obv. 9'ff: *ù ina* UGU AMEŠ KÙ.GI 10 *ša taq-bu-u-ni* r1 *a-na* I.dAMAR +UD-MAN-PAP 2 I.dAMAR+UD-SU I.dU+GUR-MAN-PAP 3 LÚ3-*šú* I*15*-MU-KÁM* 4 KIN-*ra* DUMEŠ BE DÙ-*še*! 5 SAG KÙ.GI-*ma i-na-áš-ši-u*! 6 *a-bu-ba-nim-ma am-mu-te em-mur* "And as to the golden waters which you spoke about, I have dispatched Marduk-šarru-uṣur, Marduk-erība, Nergal-šarru-uṣur the shield-bearer, and IŠTAR-ŠUMU-ĒREŠ; they will go and, if possible, make available the gold; they will also inspect (the quality) of those Deluge monsters."

> Lines 4-5 collated. Both Marduk-šarru-uṣur and Nergal-šarru-uṣur are well known as military officials of Esarhaddon and Assurbanipal (cf. notes on *LAS* 190 r12 and 291 r4; above, Nos. 29 and 56; both regularly occur in contracts of Assurbanipal's charioteer Rēmanni-Adad). Marduk-erība may be identical with the homonymous cohort commander of the chief eunuch (I.dAMAR+UD-SU LÚGAL-*ki-ṣir* GAL-SAG) mentioned in *ADD* 857 IV 11 (= No. 29).

63. *ABL 845* (K 671)

Kanūnāju and Mannu-kî-Libbi-āli to king (probably Esarhaddon) concerning building projects in Assur, Nineveh and Dūr-šarru-kēn. The letter ends (Rev. 6'f): *ina* UGU *re-ḫu-u-te a-na* I*15*-MU-APIN-*eš* 7 LUGAL BE-*ni ṭè-e-mu liš-kun*. "the king, our lord, should issue (appropriate) orders to IŠTAR-ŠUMU-ĒREŠ concerning the remaining . . ."

64. *LAS 125* (K 595)

Adad-šumu-uṣur to Assurbanipal (666 BC). Rev. 7ff:

"As to the matter about which the king my lord said: 'Ask NABÛ-NĀDIN-ŠUMI, he will tell', I have not been able to ask him since he has gone to Calah. And as to what the king my lord wrote: 'I have set MARDUK-

ŠĀKIN-ŠUMI free (of his obligations) so that he can assist you; notice my favour, (for) this is one', I know it is a favour . . ."

65. *BBEA 8 f.* (TSKM 21/676)

Letter of Šum-Iddina (the *šatammu* of Esangil) to Esarhaddon, probably written in August, 670 BC (cf. sub *LAS* 286). Obv. 3 ff: "I was about to leave to greet the king, my lord, when MĀR-IŠTAR came and declared: 'I shall inscribe the pedestals'. He was not pleased with anything, so I had to postpone my visit because of him. As soon as he is through with me, I shall come and kiss the feet of the king, my lord. The royal statues which MĀR-IŠTAR brought, saying: 'Have a look; the one which is best should stand (in the temple)' . . ."

66. *WO 4 (1968) 217* (81-2-4,417)

Small fragment assigned by Dietrich (l.c.) tentatively to Šum-iddina. MĀR-IŠTAR (IDUMU-d*15*) is mentioned in line 3 in connection with a message (*šipirtu*) from the [ki]ng.

67. *LAS 172* (K 626)

Letter of Marduk-šākin-šumi to Esarhaddon (ca. 672 BC). States that an apotropaic ritual had to be performed because the full moon day had fallen on the 13th, and proposes that "NABÛ-GĀMIL come and perform it according to my directions; he should also perform for URAD-EA." (Rev. 13 ff)

68. *LAS 174* (K 472)

Marduk-šākin-šumi to Esarhaddon (669 BC). Rev. 2 ff: [NABÛ]-GĀ[MIL] has come to Nineveh telling that Rēmūtu, the exorcist of the crown prince, has fallen ill. The king should choose one of 5 court exorcists mentioned by name (Nabû-rība-aḫu, Šumâ son of NABÛ-ZĒRU-[LĪŠIR], URAD-GULA, Nabû-lē'ûti and [Be]l-naṣir) to act as his replacement.

69. *LAS 238* (Bu 89-4-26,20)

[Urad-Gula] to Esarhaddon (ca. 670 BC). Obv. 10'ff: "The king knows that NABÛ-GĀMIL and Ninurta-aḫu-iddina are busy and that Sumāju son of NABÛ-ZĒRU-LĪŠIR is ill. If it is agreeable to the king, let Balāssu son of Nabû-aḫu-iddina be ordered to . . ."

70. *LAS 263* (K 512)

Bānî (deputy chief physician) to king (probably Assurbanipal): "In re NABÛ-NĀDIN-ŠUMI about whom the king wrote to me saying, 'Why do you lie?', would I lie to the k i n g , my lord? Your gods [Bēl] and Nabû made him recover!" (Obv. 8 ff)

71. *LAS 353* (K 10386)

Fragmentary letter quoting liver omens and answering a question of the king concerning NABÛ-NĀDIN-ŠUMI ("did he become purified", Rev. 8).

72. *LAS 122* (Rm 76)

Adad-šumu-uṣur to Assurbanipal (666 BC). In Rev. 26f, the writer refers to "Nergal-šarrāni and his brother NABÛ-NĀDIN-ŠUMI in very general terms.

For an additional reference to NABÛ-NĀDIN-ŠUMI in letters see No. 64.

73. *ABL 1285* (K 4267)

[Urad-Gula] to Assurbanipal, ca. 664 BC. Rev. 21 f: "My father divided six homers of field with his brother NABÛ-ZĒRU-LĪŠIR (I.dPA-NUMUN-GIŠ ŠEŠ-*šú*); I and my brother received three homers each, and we are two persons! At the same time, I have under the king's aegis purchased 5 or 7 people (whom I also have to support . . ."

The attribution of this letter to Urad-Gula is certain (detailed grounding will be given elsewhere). The father mentioned in the text is accordingly ADAD-ŠUMU-UṢUR (cf. Nos. 14

and 80). For further references to NABÛ-ZĒRU-LĪŠIR in letters see Nos. 68-69; cf. also *LAS* 13 r23 f.

74. *LAS 185* (K 602)

Marduk-šākin-šumi to Esarhaddon (671 BC): "I have today performed (the prayers and rituals set forth in) these 21 tablets on the river bank; URAD-EA will perform tonight on the roof of the palace." (Obv. 17 ff).

75. *LAS 321* (83-1-18,226)

[Ištar-šumu-ēreš] to Assurbanipal (ca. 667 BC). The king asks whether he has become "cleansed" through the offices of URAD-EA (Obv. 1f).

76. *LAS 335* (83-1-18,211)

[Nabû-nādin-šumi] to king (Esarhaddon or Assurbanipal), referring to a mission in Arbela. URAD-EA is mentioned in line 5 in conjunction with (the king's?) robes.

For further references to URAD-EA in letters see nos. 49 and 67.

77. *ABL 1109+* (K 15101 + 83-1-18,47)

Letter to Esarhaddon from Bēl-ušēzib, ca. 677-675 BC. Mentions URAD-GULA (^{I}ÌR-^{d}*gu-la*) in difficult but clearly political context (Rev. 5) together with ^{I}*Mar-di-ja* on whom see above, fn. 200.

The dating of the letter is based on the omens quoted in it; cf. App. J sub *RMA* 90.

78. *LAS 151* (K 666)

Adad-šumu-uṣur to Esarhaddon (670 BC). URAD-GULA donates a girl to the palace (Rev. 8ff).

79. *LAS 120* (82-5-22,171)

Adad-šumu-uṣur to Assurbanipal (667 BC). Petition for "URAD-GULA, a servant of the king, [whom] nobady has reminded the king of, [and who] therefore is falling from the hands of the king with a broken heart . . ." (Obv. 16ff)

80. *LAS 121* (K 183)

Adad-šumu-uṣur to Assurbanipal (667 or 666 BC). Renewed petition for Urad-Gula. Rev. 4ff: "Why must I and URAD-GULA be low-spirited and unhappy while all others are happy? The king has now made public his love of Nineveh in saying to the heads of the Families: 'Bring your sons to me, and let them stay in my entourage.' URAD-GULA is my son; he, too, should stay, together with them, in the entourage of the king, my lord."

For one further reference to URAD-GULA in letters see No. 68.

81. *LAS 212* (Rm 56)

Nabû-nādin-šumi to Esarhaddon or Assurbanipal. Refers twice to a certain URAD-NANÂ, both times in fragmentary and obscure context (Obv. 11, Rev. 9'). It is impossible to be sure whether this man is or is not identical with the physician who wrote *LAS* 246 ff.

APPENDIX O

CAREERS OF SCHOLARS

The purpose of this appendix is to present in an easily surveyable form the data available for defining the time limits within which the writers of the *LAS* were actively engaged in their professional work, both in order to document the *ranges of time* in which their correspondence must be placed and to show *how* the dates assigned to individual letters in the commentary actually fit in this chronological framework. For this purpose, the results obtained in the analysis of the *LAS* corpus (summarized in Appendix I) and the contemporary astrological reports (App. J) will be combined here with the biographical data presented in Appendix N, and re-presented in the form of a list showing all the dates and titles attested for each writer (Sect. 1) and a diagram giving a bird's-eye view of the time coverage and distribution of each career in relation to the others (Sect. 2). All dates are given in full Julian years; writers with only one extant letter and/or not known from other sources (Adad-aḫu-iddina, Balasî 2, Nabû-abu-da''in, Nabû-aḫḫē-šallim, Nabû-tabni-uṣur, Urad-Dagān) are not included in the survey.

The following special abbreviations and signs are used:

Sg	= reign of Sargon II	(721-705)
Sn	= reign of Sennacherib	(704-681)
Ash	= reign of Esarhaddon	(680-669)
Asb	= reign of Assurbanipal	(668-627)
+	= eponym date	
o	= approximate but reasonably certain date	
?	= identity with writer of letters uncertain	

Dates assigned to letters and reports written by the scholars themselves are recognizable from the absence of any special signs. References to scholars (and their activities) in letters are indicated with asterisks (*).

1. *List of attested dates and titles*

		Year	Source	Title/Activity
Adad-šumu-uṣur	+	707	*ADD* 350	
	o	Sg	*ZA* 62 101	LÚDUB.SAR
		Sn	*LAS* 224*	
	o	678	*ABL* 1373*	
		677	*LAS* 136*	exorcist
		674	*LAS* 31, 32	exorcist
		672	*LAS* 129, 132	
	o	671	*StOr* 1 28ff	LÚ*šá-an-gam-ma-ḫu* of Ash
		---	*Cat* 423	LÚMAŠ.MAŠ of the king
		671	*LAS* 134, 232[x], 249[x]	exorcist
		670	*LAS* 133, 143, 151, 159, 160,164, 170	exorcist
		669	*LAS* 29, 135-139, 146, 162, 163, 166, 233	exorcist
		667	*LAS* 119, 120	scribe
		666	*LAS* 121, 122, 125	
	+	665	*ADD* 448	LÚGAL-[. . .]

Name	Date		Reference	Title
Akkullānu	672		*RMA* 235	astrologer
	669		*RMA* 89, *LAS* 104*	astrologer
	667		*RMA* 272A, *LAS* 40*	astrologer
	666		*LAS* 298, 299	
	665		*LAS* 302	priest and astrologer
	o Asb		*ABL* 539	LÚTÚ-E *šá* AN.ŠÁR
	657		*LAS* 110+300	astrologer
	650	?	*LAS* 109	astrologer
Bābu-šumu-iddina	650		*LAS* 80	
Balasî	672		*RMA* 256B	astrologer
	671		*RMA* 234A, *LAS* 34	*ummânu* of crown prince
	670		*LAS* 10+, 41, 51	astrologer
	669		*LAS* 45, 46, 54, 66, 234	astrologer
			RMA 55, 88	astrologer
	668		*LAS* 324, 330	astrologer
	667		*LAS* 40, 325,*RMA* 68	astrologer
Bānî	+ 663		*ADD* 377	LÚ*2-u šá* LÚGAL-[A.ZU]
	+ 662		*ADD* 470	LÚ**2-u ša* LÚ*GAL-A.ZU
Ikkāru	late Ash		*LAS* 258	physician
Ištar-nādin-apli	o 670	?	*ABL* 1217*	LÚA.BA
	+ 665	?	*ADD* 331, 420, 421, 448	LÚA.BA
	+ 650		*LAS* 96	LÚGAL-*10-ti ša* LÚA.BAMEŠ *ša* URU*arba-ìl*
	+ 649		*LAS* 96, 352	ditto
	+ 648		*LAS* 98	LÚGAL-*10-ti ša* URU*arba-ìl*
Ištar-šumu-ēreš	+ 682	?	*3R* 2, 22	"son" of Nabû-zuqup-kēnu
	o 678		*LAS* 13*	deputy chief scribe?
	674		*LAS* 31	deputy chief scribe
	Ash		*AfO* 3 66ff	*ummânu* of Esarhaddon
	672		*LAS* 1-3, *RMA* 235	chief scribe
	671		*LAS* 13, 26, 27	chief scribe
	669		*LAS* 12, 18, 21, 25, 28, 29; *RMA* 55*, 206	chief scribe
	Asb		*AfO* 3 66ff	*ummânu* of Assurbanipal
	Asb		*ZA* 61 83	LÚGAL-DUB.SARMEŠ of Asb
	Asb		*4R*^{2} 9, *BAK* 344	LÚGAL-DUB.SAR-*ri* of Asb
	666		*RMA* 21	
	+ 665		*ADD* 448	LÚGAL-[A.BA]
	+ 660		*ADD* 444	LÚGAL-A.BA
	+ 657		*RMA* 264	
	o 650		*ADD* 851	head of [A.BA] UD-AN-BE
Marduk-šākin-šumi	Ash	?	Borger, *Ash* § 58	LÚŠAMÁN.LÁ TUR
	672		*LAS* 182,195,197,198	chief exorcist

		671	*LAS* 185	chief exorcist
		670	*LAS* 164,173,181,183, 184,186-188, 190, 191-196	ditto
		669	*LAS* 28,29,149,163, 166,174-17	ditto
		666	*LAS* 125*	ditto
	+	665	*ADD* 448	LÚGAL-[MAŠ.MAŠ]
	+	660	*ADD* 444	LÚGAL-MAŠ.MAŠ
	o	650	*ADD* 851	head of MAŠ.MAŠ^{MEŠ}
Marduk-šumu-uṣur	o	674	*AGS* 51	haruspex
	o	673	*AGS* 6	ditto
	o	672	*AGS* 98	chief haruspex
		670	*AGS* 108	ditto
	o	667	*LAS* 114	
	+	663	*ADD* 408	LÚGAL-ḪAL
	+	651	*PRT* 106, 110	ḪAL, EN *ṭè-me*
	+	650	*PRT* 111, 121, 124	ditto
	o	650	*ADD* 851	ḪAL
Mār-Ištar		671	*LAS* 276-278, 292	
		670	*LAS* 279-281,284-285, 287; *BBEA* 8f*	
		669	*LAS* 289-291	astrologer
		667	*LAS* 286	
		- - -	*ADD* 769	LÚ*A.BA
Nabû'a		671	*LAS* 344	
		670	*LAS* 345	
	late	Ash	*ABL* 817	
Nabû-aḫḫē-erība	+	698	? *ADD* 473	LÚA.BA
	+	687	? *ADD* 43	public scribe
		674	*RMA* 180	astrologer
		673	*RMA* 98, 271A	ditto
		672	*RMA* 258; *LAS* 328	ditto
		671	*RMA* 237; *LAS* 59,67	
		670	*RMA* 274E-G; *LAS* 101,51,62	ditto
		669	*RMA* 55*,103,236H, 246G, *LAS* 54,65, 69+71, 70	ditto
		668	*RMA* 209	ditto
		667	*RMA* 70,112,191,236G; *LAS* 60,61,63,73	ditto
		666	*RMA* 204	ditto
Nabû-gāmil	o	672	*LAS* 172*	exorcist
		669	*LAS* 174*	
Nabû-nādin-šumi		670	*LAS* 208	exorcist
		666	*LAS* 122*, 125*	

Nabû-nāṣir	670	*LAS* 218+, 222	exorcist
	o 670	*LAS* 215-217	ditto
Nabû-šumu-iddina	+ 683	*ADD* 477	^{LÚ}A.BA
	+ 676	*ADD* 330	^{LÚ}A.BA
	674	*LAS* 31	
	669	*LAS* 77	^{LÚ}GAL-*10-te ša* NINA^{KI}
Nabû-zēru-iddina	o 650	*ADD* 851	head of UŠ.KU^{MEŠ}
	- - -	*BL* 158	ŠÚ ^{d}*30 u* LUGAL
	- - -	*BAK* 500	*áš-ta-lu-u* ^{d}30
Nabû-zēru-līšir	Ash	*AfO* 3 66	*ummânu* of Esarhaddon
	Ash	*ZA* 61 83	^{LÚ}GAL-DUB.[SAR^{MEŠ}] of Esarhaddon
	Ash	*4R*² 9	^{LÚ}GAL-GI.U
	o 678	*LAS* 13*	chief scribe?
	674	*LAS* 30-32	chief scribe
Nergal-šumu-iddina	651	*LAS* 83	astrologer
	+ 641	? *ADD* 640	^{LÚ}A.BA
rab-eširti of Arbela	670	*LAS* 94	^{LÚ}GAL-*10-te sa* ^{URU}*arba-ìl*
	669	*LAS* 93	ditto
scribe of Kalizi	672	*LAS* 1*	
Urad-Ea	674	*LAS* 31	
	673	*RMA* 99	
	672	*RMA* 256C	
	671	*LAS* 185*, 232*	chanter
	670	*LAS* 272, 273	ditto (of Sîn)
	669	*LAS* 28, 167, 269	ditto
	late Ash	*ADD* 857	^{LÚ}UŠ.KU
	early Asb	*LAS* 321*	chanter
	- - -	*BAK* 500	UŠ.KU.MAḪ ^{d}EN.ZU
	- - -	*BAK* 524	ŠÚ.MAḪ *30 u* LUGAL
Urad-Gula	+ 681	*ADD* 277	^{LÚ}*2-u ša* ^{LÚ}GAL-A.ZU
	o 676	*ABL* 1109*	
	o 671	*StOr* 1 28ff	^{LÚ}MAŠ.MAŠ
	670	*LAS* 151*	
	669	*LAS* 174*	
	late Ash	*LAS* 223, 224	^{LÚ}MAŠ.MAŠ (223 r5'ff)
	667	*LAS* 120	discharged
	666	*LAS* 121*	ditto
	+ 650	K 2077+	^{LÚ}A.ZU
Urad-Nanâ	671	*LAS* 249	
	670	*LAS* 222, 246, 247	
	669	*LAS* 153, 257	

2. *Chronological distribution of individual careers*

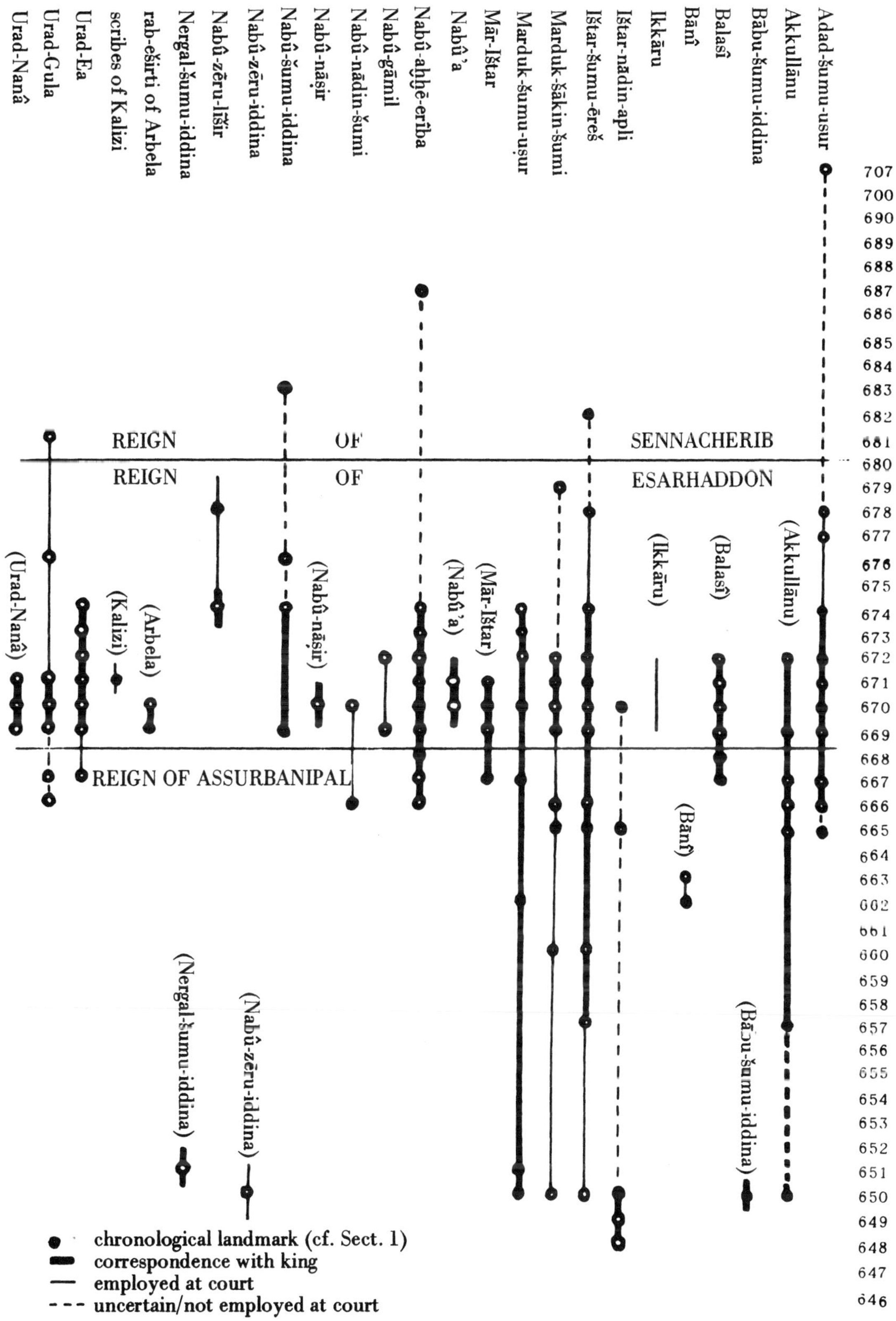

APPENDIX P

A SURVEY OF THE SUBJECT MATTERS COVERED BY THE CORRESPONDENCE

1. *Matters in which the SCHOLARS contacted the king*

1.1. *R e p o r t s* (*ṭēmu*)

1.11 Medical: condition of

(1-4) Queen mother: *LAS* 159-160 (Adad-šumu-uṣur to Ash)
LAS 184 (Marduk-šākin-šumi to Ash)
LAS 222 (Nabû-nāṣir and Urad-Nanâ to Ash)
(5-7) Crown prince: *LAS* 228 (Adad-šumu-uṣur to Ash)
LAS 252-253 (Urad-Nanâ to Ash)
(8-9) Assurbanipal and Šamaš-šumu-ukīn: *LAS* 172 and 237 (Marduk-šākin-šumi to Ash)
(10) Whole royal family: *LAS* 150 (Adad-šumu-uṣur to Ash)
(11) Šamaš-šumu-ukīn: *LAS* 258 (Ikkāru to Ash)
(12) Aššur-mukīn-palē'a: *LAS* 240 (Nabû-nāṣir to Ash)
(13) Aššur-mukīn-palē'a and Aššur-šarrāni-muballissu: *LAS* 218 (Nabû-nāṣir to Ash)
(14) Aššur-mukīn-palē'a and lakû: *LAS* 219 (Nabû-nāṣir to Ash)
(15) Aššur-mukīn-palē'a and lakû: *LAS* 250 (Urad-Nanâ to Ash)
(16) Aššur-mukīn-palē'a and Sîn-pirʾi-ukīn: *LAS* 352 (Adad-šumu-uṣur to Ash)
(17) Aššur-etel-šamê-erṣiti-muballissu: *LAS* 154 (Adad-šumu-uṣur to Ash)
(18) Sîn-pirʾi-ukīn: *LAS* 133 (Adad-šumu-uṣur)
(19-24) "Charge" of Šarrat Parṣī: *LAS* 123, 143, 151 (Adad-šumu-uṣur to Ash)
LAS 215-217 (Nabû-nāṣir to Ash)
(25-28) "Charge" of Rear Palace: *LAS* 126, 152, 154, 155 (Adad-šumu-uṣur to Ash)
(29) "Charge" of the house of Urad-Dagan: *LAS* 147 (Adad-šumu-uṣur to Ash)
(30) All "charges": *LAS* 188 (Marduk-šākin-šumi to Ash)
(31) Name lost: *LAS* 140 (Adad-šumu-uṣur to Ash)
(32-33) Ditto: *LAS* 249 (Urad-Nana to Ash), 336 (Nabû-nāṣir to Ash)
(34) lakû (Baby): *LAS* 254 (Urad-Nanâ to Ash)
(35) Unnamed patient suffering from hemorrhage: *LAS* (Urad-Nanâ to Ash)

1.12 Reports by scribes

a) Lunar observations

(36-46) Sighting of the crescent: *LAS* 91 (Nabû'a to Ash?)
LAS 96-99, 350 (Ištar-nādin-apli to *Asb*)
LAS 100, 102 (correspondents unidentified)
LAS 119 (Adad-šumu-uṣur to *Asb*)
LAS 323 (Ištar-šumu-ēreš to Asb?)
LAS 331 (Akkullānu to *Asb*, omens)
(47-55) Full moon: *LAS* 74 (Nabû-aḫḫē-erība to king, 13th day)
LAS 319 (Ištar-šumu-ēreš to Asb, omens)
LAS 85-86, 88-90 (Scribes of Kalizi und Nabû'a to king)
LAS 108, 302 (Akkullānu to ***Assurbanipal,*** omens)

b) Eclipses

(56-66) Lunar eclipse: *LAS* 40, 61 (Balasî and Nabû-aḫḫē-erība to *Asb*)
LAS 77 (Nabû-šumu-iddina to Ash)
LAS 80, 84 (Bābu-, Nergal-šumu-iddina to *Asb*)
LAS 93 (rab-eširti of Arbela to Ash)
LAS 105 (NN to *Sîn-šarru-iškun*)
LAS 234 (Balasî to Ash)
LAS 278-279, 286 (Mār-Ištar to Ash)
(67-71) Solar eclipse: *LAS* 83 (Nergal-šumu-iddina to *Asb*)
LAS 104 (NN quoting Akkullanu to Ash)
LAS 120 (Adad-šumu-uṣur to *Asb*)
LAS 290 (Mār-Ištar to Ash)
LAS 329 (Ištar-šumu-ēreš to *Asb*)
(72) Occultation of Jupiter: *LAS* 14 (Akkullānu to king)

c) Planetary and meteorological omens

(73-75) Heliacal rising of Jupiter: *LAS* 289-290 (Mār-Ištar to Ash)
LAS 324 (Balasî to *Asb*)
(76) Heliacal rising of Mercury: *LAS* 120 und 330 (Adad-šumu-uṣur and Balasî to *Asb*)
(77) Heliacal rising of Venus: *LAS* 111 (Akkullānu to *Asb*)
(78) Heliacal rising of Mars: *LAS* 110+300 (Akkullānu to *Asb*)
(79) Mars stationary in Capricorn: *LAS* 109 (Akkullānu to *Asb*)
Meteor; Dark sunrise (ibid.)
(80-83) Planets in relation to Moon and constellations: *LAS* 120 (Adad-šumu-uṣur to Asb), 277 and 291-292 (Mār-Ištar to Ash), 326 (Balasî to Asb?)
(84) Halo round Sun: *LAS* 328 (Nabû-aḫḫē-erība to Ash)
(85) Foggy weather: *LAS* 325 (Balasî to *Asb*)
(86) Scanty rainfall: *LAS* 110+300 (Akkullānu to *Asb*)
(87) Thunder: *LAS* 333 (Adad-šumu-uṣur)
(88) Earthquake: *LAS* 234 (Balasî to Ash)

d) Other portents

(89) Monstrous birth: *LAS* 327 (correspondents unclear)
(90) For entering Assur: *LAS* 92 (Nabûa to king)
(91) Sacrificial victim with 5 kidneys: *LAS* 281 (Mar-Ištar to Ash)

e) Varia

(92-93) *LAS* 344-345 (NN to Ash?) (Report on vernal equinox)
(94) Tablets copied for the royal libraries: *LAS* 358 (Akkullānu to Asb)

1.13 Exorcistic activities

(95-96) Performance of *Bīt Rimki* and related rituals: *LAS* 167 (Adad-šumu-uṣur + Urad-Ea to Ash), 185 (Marduk-šākin-šumi to Ash)
(97) Funeral rites: *LAS* 195 (Marduk-šākin-šumi to Ash)
(98) Ritual for attaining good dreams: *LAS* 219 (Nabu-nāṣir to Ash)
(99) Prophylactic rituals: *LAS* 218 (Nabû-nāṣir to Ash)
(100) Namburbi ritual involving king's robes: *LAS* 335 (Nabû-nādin-šumi to king)
(101) Handling of king's writings: *LAS* 198 (Marduk-šākin-šumi to Ash)

1.14 Chanter's activities

(102-3) *lilissu*-ceremonies at court: *LAS* 268-270 (Urad-Ea to Ash)
(104) *Akītu*-festival of Sin at Harran: *LAS* 273 (Urad-Ea to Ash)

1.15 Developments in Babylonia

(105-121) Letters of Mār-Issar: *LAS* 275-277, 279-284, 286, 288, 291-294, 297 (all to Ash; concerning substitute king ritual, matters, omens, etc.)
(122) Enthronement of substitute king: *LAS* 30 (Nabû-zēru-lišir to Ash)

1.2 *M e m o r a n d a* (*ḫissutu*)

1.21 Professional and practical matters

(123-30) Concerning performance of exorcistic (apotropaic, prophylactic, anti-witchcraft) rituals: *LAS* 67 (Nabû-aḫḫē-erība to Ash), 134, 140 (Adad-sumu-uṣur to Ash), 172, 177 (Marduk-šākin-šumi to Ash), 208 (Nabû-nādin-šumi to Ash?), 334 (NN to *Asb*)
(131-3) King's robes needed in expiatory and exorcistic rituals: *LAS* 271-272 (Urad-Ea to Ash), 342 (Marduk-šākin-šumi to Ash)
(134) King should appoint an exorcist to serve the crown prince: *LAS* 174 (Marduk-šākin-šumi to Ash; cf. 238)
(135) King should issue orders to help haruspices perform their duties: *LAS* 115 (Marduk-šumu-uṣur)
(136-7) King should don white robes: *LAS* 197 (Marduk-šākin-šumi to Ash), 304 (Akkullānu to Ash?)
(138) King should question a haruspex: *LAS* 113 (Marduk-šumu-uṣur to Ash)
(139) King should look at a recently completed writing board: *LAS* 319 (Issar-šumu-ēreš to *Asb*); cf. 305
(140) King should have the curriculum of (apprentice) haurspices revised: *LAS* 116 (Marduk-šumu-uṣur to king)

1.22 Chronological matters

(141) King should intercalate a second Addāru: *LAS* 325 (Balasî to *Asb*)
(142) King should adjust the beginning of a lunar month: *LAS* 119 (Adad-šumu-uṣur)

1.23 Cultic matters

(143-52) Timing of festivals and performance of religious ceremonies: *LAS* 6, 11, 343 (Issar-šumu-ēreš to Ash); 302, 306, 308, 312, 313 (Akkullānu to *Asb*); 190 (Marduk-šākin-šumi to Ash)
(153-7) Affairs of temples and the clergy: *LAS* 310-312, 315 (Akkullānu to *Asb*)

1.3 *C o u n s e l s* (*milku*)

(158-9) King should give up unhealthy fasting: *LAS* 51 and 143 (Balasî + Nabû-aḫḫē-erība and Adad-šumu-uṣur to Ash)
(160) King should have a substitute king enthroned: *LAS* 185 (Marduk-šākin-šumi to Ash)
(161) King should have a substitution ritual performed: *LAS* 299 (Akkullānu to *Asb*)

1.4 *R e q u e s t s f o r o r d e r s*

(162-69) Concerning exorcistic rituals: *LAS* 140, 355 (Adad-šumu-uṣur to Ash); 175, 178, 190. 195 (Marduk-šākin-šumi to Ash); 208 (Nabû-nādin-šumi to king); 336 (Nabû-nāṣir to Ash?)
(170) Concerning transport of Marduk's statue to Babylon: *LAS* 29 (Issar-šumu-ēreš, Adad-šumu-uṣur and Marduk-šākin-šumi to Ash)

(171) Concerning royal throne: *LAS* 317 (Adad-aḫu-iddina to Ash)
(172) Concerning edition of scholarly texts for the royal libraries: *LAS* 331 (Akkullānu to *Asb*)
(173) In unidentified matter: *LAS* 307 (Akkullānu to Asb?)

1.5 *Prescriptions, technical information*

(174-9) Medical prescriptions: *LAS* 247, 253, 265(+)266(+)267 (Urad-Nanâ to Ash); 258 (Ikkāru to Ash); 337 and 362 (correspondents unidentified)
(180-1) Instructions for performance of exorcistic rituals: *LAS* 137-138 (Adad-šumu-uṣur to Ash)
(182-4) List of auspicious days suitable for taking treaty oath: *LAS* 1-3 (Ištar-šumu-ēreš to Ash)
(185-6) List of tablets sent to king: *LAS* 151, 161 (Adad-šumu-uṣur to Ash)

1.6 *Denunciations*

(187-9) Concerning opponents of the king: *LAS* 30(Nabû-zēru-lišir to Ash), 133 (Adad-šumu-uṣur to Ash), 212 (Nabû-nādin-šumi to Ash?)
(190) Concerning colleagues: *LAS* 224 (Urad-Gula to Ash)

1.7 *Petitions*

(191-8) For rehabilitation or admission to royal service: *LAS* 117 (Marduk-šumu-uṣur to *Asb*), 120-121 Adad-šumu-uṣur to *Asb*, on behalf of his son), 227 (Nabû gāmil to king), 239 (Nabû-abu-da''in to king), 241, 264 (Nabû-tabni-uṣur to Ash), 370 ([Tabn]î to crown prince *Asb*)
(199-200) For financial help: *LAS* 36 (Balasî to king), 114 (Marduk-šumu-uṣur to *Asb*?)
(201-2) For excuse from corvée: *LAS* 85 (scribes of Kalizi to king), 248 (Urad-Nānâ to Ash; cf. 250)

1.8 *Blessings and thanks* (*ikribu*)

(203-4) On account of favours granted: *LAS* 123f (Adad-šumu-uṣur to *Asb*)
(205-6) On account of Assurbanipal's appointment as heir apparent: *LAS* 129, 131 (Adad-šumu-uṣur to Ash and Asb)

1.9 *Miscellanea*

(207) Request for a reply letter: *LAS* 301 (Akkullānu to *Asb*)
(208) Correction of a slip: *LAS* 176 (Marduk-šākin-šumi to Ash)

2. *Matters in which the KING contacted the scholars*

2.1 *Health of patients*

(1-11) King himself sick: *LAS* 180-183, 199, 357 (Ash to Marduk-šākin-šumi); 246, 247, 250, 255, 257 (Ash to Urad-Nanâ)
(12-23) Royal family: *LAS* 142, 144, 152, 156, 157, 171, 184, 211, 216, 251, 259, 339+ (Ash to Adad-šumu-uṣur, Marduk-šākin-šumi, Nabû-nāṣir, Nabû-nādin-šumi, Ikkāru, Urad-Gula, Urad-Nanâ)
(24) An exorcist: *LAS* 263 (Asb to Banî)

2.2 *Portents*

2.21 Evil

(25-34) Eclipses of the moon: *LAS* 25, 41, 42, 62, 87, 101, 278 (Ash to Ištar-šumu-ēreš, Balasî, Nabû-aḫḫē-erība, Nabû'a and Mār-Ištar); 63, 81, 82 (*Asb* to Nabû-aḫḫē-erība, Bābu-šumu-iddina and Nergal-šumu-iddina)

(35-38) Solar eclipses: *LAS* 28, 41, 42, 162 (Esarhaddon to Balasî and teams of scholars representing different disciplines)

(39) "Black" sun: *LAS* 64 (king to Nabû-aḫḫē-erība)

(40) Conjunction of Mars and Saturn: *LAS* 54 (Esarhaddon to Balasî and Nabû-aḫḫē-erība)

(41-43) Earthquake: *LAS* 16, 35, 147 (Ash to Ištar-šumu-ēreš, Balasî and Nabû-aḫḫē-erība)

(44-5) Lightning: *LAS* 38 and 349 (Ash to Balasî and Nabû-aḫḫē-erība)

(46-7) Monstrous births: *LAS* 39 and 205 (king to Balasî and Nabû-nādin-šumi)

(48-50) Ominous animals: *LAS* 15, 36, 340 (king to Ištar-šumu-ēreš, Balasî and NN)

(51-53) Retrograding planet: *LAS* 13, 149, 233 (Ash to Ištar-šumu-ēreš, Adad-šumu-uṣur and Marduk-šākin-šumi)

(54) Unidentified: *LAS* 44 (king to Balasî)

2.22 Good

(55-59) Visibility of Mercury and Venus: *LAS* 12, 53, 65, 66, 106 (Ash to Ištar-šumu-ēreš, Balasî and Nabû-aḫḫē-erība)

2.3 *Exorcistic rituals*

(60-72) Substitute king ritual: *LAS* 26-28 (Ash to Ištar-šumu-ēreš), 135-136, 139, 165, 166, 179 (Ash to Adad-šumu-uṣur and/or Marduk-šākin-šumi), 232 and 292 (Ash to Mār-Ištar), 298 (*Asb* to Akkullānu), 242 (addressee unidentified)

(73) Ritual to undo cultic offence: *LAS* 196 (Ash to Marduk-šākin-šumi)

(74-77) Apotropaic rituals (to counteract evil portents): *LAS* 203-205, 209 (king to Nabû-nādin-šumi)

(78-79) Prophylactic rituals (to protect from diseases): *LAS* 218 and 223 (Ash to Nabû-nāṣir and Urad-Gula)

(80-85) Rituals to undo evil sorcery: *LAS* 163-164, 173-174, 186-187 (Ash to Marduk-šākin-šumi)

(86) Medical rituals: *LAS* 172 (Ash to Marduk-šākin-šumi)

(87-89) Purification rituals: *LAS* 188 and 206 (Ash to Marduk-šākin-šumi and Nabû-nādin-šumi); *LAS* 353

(90-93) Unidentified: *LAS* 201, 210, 244 and 333

(94-96) Funeral rites: *LAS* 195, 198 (Ash to Marduk-šākin-šumi); 4 (Ash? to Ištar-šumu-ēreš)

2.4. *Chronology*

(97-99) Intercalating a month: *LAS* 38, 190, 287 (Esarhaddon to Balasî)

2.5 *Cultic matters*

(100-102) Timing of religious festivals and offerings: *LAS* 5, 72, 170 (Esarhaddon to Ištar-šumu-ēreš, Nabû-aḫḫē-erība and Adad-šumu-uṣur et al.)

(103-110) Construction of temples and fashioning of cultic objects: *LAS* 7-8, 18-19 (Ash to Ištar-šumu-ēreš), 57-58 (Ash to Balasî and Nabû-aḫḫē-erība), 276-277 (Ash to Mār-Ištar)

(111) Temple revenues: *LAS* 309 (*Asb* to Akkullānu)

(112-114) Affairs of the clergy: *LAS* 309, 312, 314 (Ash? and *Asb* to Akkullānu)

2.6 *Auspicious days for trips*

(115) King himself to travel: *LAS* 10 (Ash to Balasî and Nabû-aḫḫē-erība)

(116-129) King's sons: *LAS* 17, 45-47, 52, 69+, 70, 72, 145-146, 148, 243, 249, 332 (Ash to Ištar-šumu-ēreš, Balasî and Nabû-aḫḫē-erība, and Adad-šumu-uṣur)

2.7 *Favours granted*

(130-135) *LAS* 34, 59, 122, 125, 126, 349 (Ash to Balasî, Nabû-aḫḫē-erība, and Adad-šumu-uṣur)

2.8 *Personal problems*

(136-139) *LAS* 171, 318, 321, 354 (Ash and *Asb* to Adad-šumu-uṣur and Ištar-šumu-ēreš)

2.9 *Miscellanea*

(140) Auspicious days for mustering an army: *LAS* 73 (*Asb* to Nabû-aḫḫē-erība)
(141) Ditto, for obtaining good dreams: *LAS* 50 (king to Balasî)
(142) How to deal with eclipse reports: *LAS* 60 (*Asb* to Nabû-aḫḫē-erība)
(143-144) Visibility of fixed stars: *LAS* 43, 68 (king to Balasî and Nabû-ahhē-erība)
(145) Collection of tablets: *LAS* 226 (king to Urad-Gula)
(146-7) Reproaches: *LAS* 238 (Ash to Urad-Gula?), 361 (king to NN)
(148) Curse: *LAS* 9 (Ash? to Ištar-šumu-ēreš)
(149-50) Loyalty of servants: *LAS* 213, 214 (king to Nabû-nādin-šumi)
(151-52) Asking somebody through somebody else: *LAS* 125 and 207

2.10 *Broken or unclassifiable*

(153-163) *LAS* 20, 24, 76, 141, 158, 168, 235, 254, 261, 296, 322

3. *Number of reply letters vs. "spontaneously" sent letters*

Sender	Replies	Spontaneous	Unclassified
Adad-šumu-uṣur	23	22	1
Adad-šumu-uṣur et al.	6	1	1
Marduk-šākin-šumi	22	8	6
Ištar-šumu-ēreš	23	10	5
Akkullānu	4	19	1
Balasî	13	5	4
Balasî + Nabû-aḫḫē-erība	7	1	2
Mār-Ištar	6	14	3
Nabû-aḫḫē-erība	13	4	1
Urad-Nanâ	7	4	4
Nabû-nādin-šumi	11	2	0
Nabû-nāṣir (et al.)	3	6	0
Urad-Ea	0	6	1
Ikkāru	2	2	1
Marduk-šumu-uṣur	?1	5	0
Urad-Gula	2	1	1
Nabû-zēru-līšir	0	2	2
Nabu-zēru-iddina	0	0	2
Nabûa	1	5	0
Ištar-nādin-apli	0	5	0
Nabû-šumu-iddina	0	2	1
Nergal-šumu-iddina	1	2	0
Babu-šumu-iddina	1	1	0
scribes of Kalizi	0	3	0
rab-eširti of Arbela	0	1	1
Bānî	1	0	0
Nabû-abu-da' 'in	0	1	0
Nabû-gāmil	0	1	0
Nabû-tabni-uṣur	0	1	0
Adad-aḫu-iddina	0	1	0
Balasî (mayordomo)	0	1	0
Nabû-aḫḫē-šallim	0	0	1
Tabnî	0	1	1
Urad-Dagān	0	0	1
Others	6	14	13
King	1	0	0
Farmer	1	0	0
Total	155	151	53

4. *King's words quoted in the letters*

4.1 Commands

ESARHADDON addressing *exorcists*

(1) "Go and see [Sîn-pirḫî-ukīn and two patients in the New Palace]!" (*LAS* 142, Adad-šumu-uṣur)

(2) "Have those boy servants take [that medicine] first and let the prince drink it (only) later!" (*LAS* 144, Adad-šumu-uṣur)

(3) "Let the substitute king go to his fate [on the 15th], and let me perform my (purification) ritual on the 16th as before" (*LAS* 166, Adad-šumu-uṣur and Marduk-šākin-šumi)

(4) "Speak again to the Tur[tānu], as follows: 'You will be held responsible for the eclipse of the sun; perhaps . . . ' " (*LAS* 162, letter of Farmer to Adad-šumu-uṣur and Marduk-šākin-šumi)

(5) "Perform [the antiwitchcraft ritual] on the 24th! Send that they bring the Sumerian versions of the antiwitchcraft texts from Nineveh!" (*LAS* 173, Marduk-šākin-šumi)

(6) "Perform [the exorcisms of the month Ābu]!" (*LAS* 223, Urad-Gula)

(7) "Perform [the hand-lifting prayers to Mars] and also perform [. . .]!" (*LAS* 149, M[arduk-šākin-šumi])

addressing physicians

(8) "Sit up with [. . .]!" (*LAS* 259), Ikkāru)

addressing scribes

(9) "[Make the substitute king hear the omens] in front of Šamaš!" (*LAS* 27, Ištar-šumu-ēreš)

(10) "Watch whereto it . . .!" (*LAS* 13, Ištar-šumu-ēreš, referring to retrograding planet)

(11) "Let [the substitute king] 'sit' for a hundred days!" (*LAS* 292, Mār-Ištar)

(12) "The month of Ulūlu is intercalary; do not perform the rites in this month!" (*LAS* 287, Mār-Ištar); cf. *LAS* 190

UNIDENTIFIED (AS or ASB)

(13) "Perform [the universal namburbi ritual] tomorrow!" (*LAS* 204, Nabû-nādin-šumi)

(14) "Perform [the exorcisms against the Rabiṣu(-demon)]!" (*LAS* 209, Nabû-nādin-šumi)

(15) "Go and perform exorcisms for Šadītu!" (211, Nabû-nādin-š.)

(16) "You ask [him]!" (*LAS* 207, Nabû-nādin-šumi)

4.2 Requests

ESARHADDON *addressing exorcists*

(1) "Write me truthfully [about the child's condition]!" (*LAS* 216, Nabû-nāṣir)

addressing scribes

(2) "Write me a good month and a good day in which [the royal statues] may enter [Haran] and (determine) where they are to stand!" (*LAS* 7, Ištar-šumu-ēreš)

(3) "Look up a good day [for the cella of Nusku] and write down and send how it should be erected!" (*LAS* 8, Ištar-šumu-ēreš)

UNCERTAIN

(4) "Ask Bēl-nāṣir, Bēl-īpuš and other Babylonians whom you know [about the timing of the display ceremonies]!" (*LAS*

(5) "Discuss [the ritual] with Basî!" (*LAS* 205, Nabû-nādin-šumi)

(6) "Write me what the ritual involves!" (*LAS* 203, Nabû-nādin-šumi)

4.3 Queries

ESARHADDON *addressing exorcists*

(1) "Is this month propitious? The crown prince should enter into my presence; when would it be favourable?" (*LAS* 146, Adad-šumu-uṣur)

(2) "Is it favourable? Aššur-mukīn-palē'a should come up to visit me, and Sīn-pirḫī-ukīn should come with him; may he stay with his brother?" (*LAS* 145, Adad-šumu-uṣur)

(3) "How many days should [the substitute king] sit?" (*LAS* 139, Adad-šumu-uṣur)
(4) "I am being told that [the substitute king] should 'sit' until the 8th of Ulūlu; would it be possible to perform the *Bīt Salā' Mê*-ritual in Tašrītu?" (*LAS* 136, Adad-šumu-uṣur)
(5) "Why have you not answered my letter [inquiring about the interpretation and ritual of the earthquake]?" (*LAS* 147, Adad-šumu-uṣur)
(6) "What time should the maiden come in?" (*LAS* 139, Adad-šumu-uṣur and Marduk-šākin-šumi)
(7) "Can't you clarify which [people] are to come out [this time]?" (*LAS* 163, Adad-šumu-uṣur and Marduk-šākin-šumi)
(8) "Will you not enter? Will [the hierodule] not perform [the ritual] in your presence? Where shall they place the robes? For what purpose will the people be present?" (*LAS* 187, Marduk-šākin-šumi)
(9) "Where will the [apotropaic figurines] be buried?" (*LAS* 179, Marduk-šākin-šumi)
(10) "Is this the [tru]th?" (*LAS* 199, Marduk-šākin-šumi)
(11) "Will the [people] enter then? Or [. . .]" (*LAS* 244, ?Marduk-šākin-šumi]
(12) "What exorcists are with you?" (*LAS* 223, Urad-Gula)
(13) "What is the pregnant woman to do? Take counsel; she is [. . . .]" (*LAS* 339+, [Urad-Gula])
(14) "In the writing-board which you sent to me through Ṣalam-Bel there were phylacteries [. . . .]; and the pertinent ritual runs as follows: '. . . . . Fall of the heavens' What is this? The heaven exists forever . . ." (etc., *LAS* 226, royal letter to Urad-Gula)

addressing physicians

(15) "Adjure Adad-šumu-uṣur: Why did he say that the crown prince and Šamaš-šumu-ukin should not go outdoors before 22nd Tašrītu? Has he seen some omen?" (*LAS* 249, Urad-Nanâ)
(16) "Have you really been taking care of your own health?" (*LAS* 250, Urad-Nanâ)
(17) "Why can't you diagnose the nature of this illness of mine and cure it?" (*LAS* 246, Urad-Nanâ) [oral]

addressing scribes

(18) "[Will the moon make an eclipse?] And if it will, what is the word about it?" (*LAS* 25, Ištar-šumu-ēreš)
(19) "One of your colleagues wrote to me: 'Mercury will appear in Nisannu.' What month do you have now?" (*LAS* 12, Ištar-šumu-ēreš)
"When will you tell me (the significance of) 'Venus is stationary in the morning'?" (ibid.)
(20) "[Why] don't you ever tell me the truth? [When] will you give me explicit information [of this retrograding and its significance]?" (*LAS* 13, Ištar-šumu-ēreš)
(21) "Does(n't) 'passing between the legs of a man' (apply) to a thing's emerging from below a chariot?" (*LAS* 15, Ištar-šumu-ēreš) [uncertain if Esarhaddon]
(22) "What losses will follow from the omen interpretation 'The king will come to naught with his dignitaries'?" (*LAS* 35, Balasî)
(23) "Have you observed anything whatever in the sky?" (*LAS* 41, Balasî)
(24) "I am being told that Venus has appeared [so has it]?" (*LAS* 46, Balasî)
(25) "[Somebody has written to me:] 'Venus is visible'; what month do you have now?" (*LAS* 65, Nabû-aḫḫē-erība)
(26) "The crown prince [of Babylon] should come to visit the king on 1st of Nisannu; is the day favourable?" (*LAS* 69, Nabû-aḫḫē-erība)
(27) "I am being told that [the crown prince] should not go outdoors on the 1st [of Nisannu]; which date is safer, the 1st or the 4th?" (Balasî, *LAS* 46)
(28) "Is it ravourable for the crown prince to enter into the presence of the king?" (*LAS* 70, Nabû-aḫḫē-erība)
(29) "Mars is bright [so can the crown prince visit the king]?" (*LAS* 45, Balasî)
(30) "[Can] Aššur-mukīn-palē'a [visit me]?" (*LAS* 17, Ištar-šumu-ēreš)
(31) "I have heard [Mercury has been sighted] in Babylon, [is it true]?" (*LAS* 53, Balasî + Nabû-aḫḫē-erība)

(32) "Fire struck from the sky in Ḫariḫumba and burned the fields of the Assyrians, [what does this portend?]" (*LAS* 38, Balasî)
(33) "The field [of the Assyrians of Ḫariḫumba] was very productive, who is clearing away the corn?" (*LAS* 349, [Nabû-aḫḫē]-erība)
(34) "What [month] have you got as (the date of [its appearance]?" (*LAS* 106, referring to Mercury)

ASSURBANIPAL *addressing priest*

(35) "Which of the magnates have not agreed to deliver [the *dariu* and *ginû* offerings]?" (*LAS* 309, Akkullānu)

UNCERTAIN (ESARHADDON or ASSURBANIPAL)

(36) "How long should I wear [the white robes]?" (*LAS* 198, Marduk-šākin-šumi)
(37) "Did Nabû-nadin-šumi become (ritually) clean?" (*LAS* 351, [?Marduk-šumu-uṣur])
(38) "Why did you lie about Nabû-nadin-šumi?" (*LAS* 263, Bānî)
(39) "[Is an interpretation of an omen like this included] in (the series) Šumma Izbu?" (*LAS* 39, Balasî)
(40) "What is the apotropaion [against evil of earthquake]?" (*LAS* 16, Ištar-šumu-ēreš)
(41) "Is there any curse written there?" (*LAS* 9, Ištar-šumu-ēreš)
(42) "Why are you acting arbitrarily (with regard to his equipment)?" (*LAS* 259, [. . .])

QUEEN MOTHER NAQĪ'A

"What [. . . . .]" (*LAS* 230, Ištar-šumu-ēreš)

4.4 Personalia

ESARHADDON *addressing physicians*

(1) "How did the servants of former kings sit up with their masters (all the nights) and carry them in beds! How did they keep watch over them! [And how are you serving me!]" (*LAS* 247, Urad-Nanâ)
(2) "Why can't you diagnose the nature of this illness of mine and bring about its cure?" (*LAS* 246, Urad-Nanâ)
(3) "My [. . .] should be relieved; [once . . . is] finished, the rash will go away for good (lit. will go to rest for the rest of its days)" (*LAS* 255, Urad-Nanâ)

addressing exorcists

(4) "My arms and feet are without strength, I cannot open my eyes, I am lying prostrate" (*LAS* 180, Marduk-šākin-šumi)
(5) "Would [this fever affecting my eyes] be relieved!" (*LAS* 183, Marduk-šākin-šumi)
(6) "[This poultice] is very hot [yet I have chills]" (*LAS* 181, Marduk-šākin-šumi)
(7) "My heart is very sick; how did we act that I became so depressed because of this child of mine? you should have given away half your kingdom and have him cured. [As for my lordly sons], a mighty fire makes me weep and burns me" (*LAS* 171, ?[Marduk-šākin-šumi])
(8) "As to the time of the watch of Asalluḫi of which you wrote to me, I got scared [. . . .]" (*LAS* 352, [Adad-šumu-uṣur])

ASSURBANIPAL *addressing chief scribe*

(9) "Perhaps, now that they have placed the cross in my house, my word has been (or will be) wiser?" (*LAS* 318, Ištar-šumu-ēreš)
(10) "I was cleansed by Urad-Ea [from?] these [. . .]; . . . "words [. . . .] are tied upon me; — — — he who [knows about this] matter should speak up, is it true?" (*LAS* 321, Ištar-šumu-ēreš)

4.5 Words of favour

ESARHADDON

(1) "From now on you will stay in my entourage; if you have any wishes, just write me" (*LAS* 59, Nabû-aḫḫē-erība)
(2) "From now on you are part of my entourage; do you have anything to say?" (*LAS* 34, Balasî)
(3) "The first day I am unoccupied, enter into my presence!" (*LAS* 349, [Nabû-aḫḫē]-erība)

ASSURBANIPAL

(5) "May your heart become happy now, may you no more feel restless! I have assembled you, your nephews and the sons of your uncle(s), you will stay in my entourage" (*LAS* 122, Adad-šumu-uṣur)
(6) "May Aššur, Šamaš and my gods listen to these words you wrote to me. I did hear from my father that you are a loyal family, but now I know it of my own experience. Ask Nabû-nadin-šumi about that matter [not specified]. I have set Marduk-šākin-šumi free of duty, he will help you, notice my favour, (for) this is it" (*LAS* 125, Adad-šumu-uṣur)

4.6 Miscellanea

ESARHADDON

(1) "Let us intercalate the month Ululu" (*LAS* 190, Marduk-šākin-šumi)
(2) "That was not well read" (*LAS* 238, ?[Marduk-šākin-šumi])
(3) "The Ward of Rear Palace has vomited gall" (*LAS* 152, Adad-šumu-uṣur)
(4) "The crown prince will not go out" (*LAS* 148, Adad-šumu-uṣur) [perhaps hearsay]
(5) "There is plenty of *ṣurru* stone [available for the crown]" (*LAS* 58, Nabû-aḫḫē-erība + Balasî)
(6) "Itti-Marduk-balāṭu of Uruk has written to me that gold has indeed accumulated in the temple and that there is repair work to be done" (Mār-Ištar)

ASSURBANIPAL

(7) "A substitute statue 'sat' in the town of Akkad from the 14th of Du'ūzu till the 5th of Ābu" (*LAS* 298, Akkullānu)

UNCERTAIN (either ASH or ASB)

(8) "Today, tomorrow, and the day after tomorrow, these are the (days) of the display-festival" (*LAS* 5, Ištar-šumu-ēreš)
(9) *LAS* 20, fragmentary (Ištar-šumu-ēreš)

Total: 89

5.1 *References to future letters*

**LAS* 38 r13 *ki-ma* ^{MUL}SAG.ME.GAR ^{14} *it-ta-mar a-na* LUGAL EN-*ia* ^{15} *a-šap-pa-ra* (Balasî)
referring to *LAS* 51 (^{16} *ki-ma* SAG.DU ITU ^{17} ^{d}*30 it-ta-mar* . . . r^{4} *ú-ma-a* ^{5} ^{MUL}SAG.ME.GAR ^{d}*30 šu-u*)

LAS 41 r13 AN.MI (^{d}UTU) ^{14} NU GAR UD *27*.KÁM* ^{15} *tu-u-ra am-mar* ^{16} *a-šap-pa-ra* (Balasî)

LAS 44 r8 *di-ib-bi an-nu-ti* ^{9} UD-*mu an-ni-i-ú* ^{10} *a-na ḫa-sa-si* ^{11} *la ṭa-a-ba* ^{12} *ina ši-i-a-ri* ^{13} *a-šap-pa-ra* (Balasî)

**LAS* 14 r2 *a-bat-*[*su la-mur*] ^{3} *šum-ma ina* ŠÀ-*šú e-t*[*ar-ba*] ^{4} *pi-šìr-šú a-na* LUGAL E[N-*iá*] ^{5} *a-šap-pa-ra* (Akkullānu)
referring to *RMA* 192

LAS 13 r30 *a-na-ṣar* ^{30}[*mì*]-*i-nu šá ši-ti-ni a-na* LUGAL EN-*ia* ^{31} *a-šap-pa-ra* (Ištar-šumu-ēreš)

**LAS* 25 r6' *ù šum-ma is-sa-kan* $^{7'}$ *kaq-qu-ru* É *ú-la-pat-an-ni* $^{8'}$ *ù šá-a-ri a-li-ku* ^{9} *is-se-niš i-na-sa-ḫa* (Ištar-šumu-ēreš)
referring to *RMA* 271

**LAS* 54 r4' *an-nu-rig ni-na-ṣar* $^{5'}$ *a-na* LUGAL EN-*ni* $^{6'}$ *ni-šap-pa-ra* (Balasî and Nabû-aḫḫē-erība)
referring to *RMA* 88 and 103 (two days later)

LAS 61 r3 *ina ši-a-ri* ^{4} *ú-il-tú* ^{5} *ša* AN.MI *30* ^{6} *a-na* LUGAL EN-*ia* ^{7} *ú-še-ba-la* (Nabû-aḫḫē-erība; report not preserved)

LAS 64 r5 *re-eḫ-ti di-ib-bi* ^{6} *am-mur a-na* LUGAL ^{7} EN-*ia a-šap-pa-ra* (Nabû-aḫḫe-erība)

LAS 87:6 *ina* UGU *ma-ṣar-te* ^{7} *ša* LUGAL *be-lí* ^{8} *iš-pur-an-ni* ^{9} *ni-na-ṣar* r^{1} *ni-šap-pa-ra* (Nabû'a, several possibilities)

LAS 104:4 ^{d}UTU ^{5} *ina na-pa-ḫi-šu* . . . ^{7} AN.MI *i-sa-kan* ^{11} . . . *ma-a šum-ma ta-qab-bi* ^{12} *ma-a pi-šìr-šu* ^{13} *la-áš-ṭur* ^{14} *lu-še-bi-la-ka* (Akkullānu, not extant)

**LAS* 252 r18 *a-na ši-a-ri* ^{19} *le-ru-ub lu-saḫ-ki-im* (Urad-Nanâ), referring to *LAS* 251

LAS 278 r7' *ù ki-i šá* LUGAL *be-lí iš-pur-an-ni* ^{8} *ma-ṣar-tú ša* AN.MI ^{d}UTU *a-na-ṣar* ^{9} *šúm-ma is-sa-kan šúm-ma la iš-kun* ^{10} *mi-i-nu ša ši-ti-i-ni a-na* MAN EN-*iá* ^{11} *a-šap-pa-ra* (not extant)

LAS 324 r2 *i-da-a-ti ki-ma* ^{3} *it-tan-ta-ḫa* ^{3} *a-na* ^{MUL}AL.LUL *iq-ṭi-ri-ib* ^{4} *ú-il-tú šá-ni-tú a-na-as-sa-ḫa* ^{5} *a-na* LU=GAL EN-*ia ú-šá-áš-ma* (Balasî, promised report not extant)

LAS 338 Obv(!) 1, TA* ŠÀ *šam-me am-mi-*[*i* . . . .] ^{2} *áš-pur-ak-kan-ni* x[. . .] (unknown writer)

Balance:
5 identified
4 certainly not extant
6 possibly extant

5.2 *References to previous letters (identified)*

(1) *LAS* 290:14 *ina* UGU ^{MUL}SAG.ME.GAR ^{15} *ša i n a p a - n i - t i* ^{16} *a-na* MAN EN-*iá áš-pur-an-ni* ^{17} *nu-uk ina* KASKAL *šu-ut* ^{d}*A-nù* r^{1} *ina kaq-qar* ^{MUL}SIPA.ZI.AN.NA *it-ta-mar* [669-06-27]
referring to *LAS* 289 (8' *ina kaq-qar* ^{MUL}SIPA.ZI.AN.NA $^{9'}$ ^{MUL}SAG.ME.GAR *it-ta-mar* . . . $^{14'}$ I ^{MUL}SAG.ME.GAR $^{15'}$ *ina* KASKAL *šu-ut* ^{d}*A-nù* IGI-*ir* . . .) [669-06-08]

(2) *LAS* 298 r26' *ana-ku* i n a I G I - [t i] [27'] *lu* UD 12.KÁM *ša* ITUŠU *di-ib-bi an-nu-u-te a-na* LUGAL *be-lí-iá* [28'] *as-sap-ra* [666-07-30]
referring to *LAS* 299 [666-07-05],

(3) *LAS* 292:11' [*ina* UGU MUL*Ṣal-b*]*at-a-ni ša* i n a p a - n i - t i *a-n*[*a* . . . .] [12'] [MULPA.BIL.S]AG *iṭ-ḫu-u-ni* . . . [671-10-07]
referring to *LAS* 277 [671-09-27]

(4) *LAS* 176:5 *ina* UGU *dul-li* [6] *ša* i s - s u ḫ a - r a - a m - m e [7] *a-na* LUGAL EN*-iá áš-pur-an-ni* [8] *mu-uk a-na ši-a-ri* [9] *lu-ṣu-ni le-pu-šú* [671-12-18]
referring to *LAS* 163 [671-12-18]

(5) *LAS* 124:1 *an-ni-ú re-eḫ-ti* [2] *da-ba-a-bi šá* e - g í r - t i [3] p a - n i - i t - t i
referring to *LAS* 123

(6) *LAS* 125:9 *ina* UGU *ša* LUGAL *be-lí iš-pur-*[*an-ni*] [10] *ma-a da-ba-bu an-ni-u am-mar taš-*[*pur-an-ni*] [11] *Aš+šur* dUTU . . . *liš-mi-*[*ú*]
referring to *LAS* 122

(7) *LAS* 122:15 *ša* LUGAL EN LUGALMEŠ*-ni be-lí iš-pu-ra-an-ni* [16] *ma-a ú-ma-a lìb-ba-ka li-ṭi-ib-ka* [17] *ik-ka-ka aḫ-ḫu-ur lu la i kar-ru*
referring to *LAS* 121 (r4 *a-ta-a a-na-ku* TA* [1] ÌR-dGu-la [5] . . . *ik-ki-ni ku-ri lib-bi-ni* [6] *šá-pil*)

(8) *LAS* 46:6 *ina* UGU DUMU.LUGAL [*šá* LUGAL *be-lí*] [7] *i*[*š-p*]*ur-an-ni* [*ma-a iq-ṭi-bu-ni*] [8] *ma-a* UD *1*.KÁM* K[Á NU È], etc. [669-03-31],
referring to *LAS* 71 [669-03-30]

(9) *LAS* 12:6 *ša* LUGAL *be-li iš-pur-an-ni* [7] *ma-a 1-en ina* LÚ*ki-na-ta-ti-ku-nu* [8] *is-sap-ra ma-a* dUTU.IDIM [9] *ina* ITUBÁR IGI.LAL [669-03-24],
referring to *LAS* 70? [669-03-24?]

(10) *LAS* 66:6 *ina* UGU MUL[*Dil-bat*] [7] *ša* LUGAL *be-l*[*í iš-pur-an-ni*] [8] *ma-a iq-ṭi-*[*bu-u-ni*] [9] *ma-a it-*[*ta-mar*] [669-03-26]
referring to *LAS* 12 [669-03-24]

(11) *LAS* 65:6 [*ša a*]*-na* LUGAL EN*-ia iš-pur-an-ni* [7] [*ma-a* M]UL*Dil-bat nam-rat* [669-03-26],
referring to *LAS* 12 [669-03-24]

(12) *LAS* 198:6 *ina* UGU *ku-zip-pi* [7] BABBARMEŠ *ša be-lí iš-pur-an-ni* [8] *ma-a ki-i ma-ṣi* UDMEŠ [9] *lu-ke-'i-il*
referring to *LAS* 197

(13) *LAS* 166:6 *ina* UGU UD *15*.KÁM* [7] [*ša be-lí-ni*] *iq-bu-u-ni* [8] [*ma-a* LUGA]L *pu-u-ḫi a-na šim-ti* [9] [*lil-l*]*i-ki* . . . [669-07-11]
Farmer's words based on *LAS* 135 [669-07-10?]

(14) *LAS* 332 = appendix to *LAS* 145

(15) *LAS* 135:10 *ina* IGI AN.MI [11] dUTU *nu-us-sa-ad-gíl* [12] AN.MI dUTU *la iš-kun* (Adad-šumu-uṣur), referring (indirectly) to *LAS* 136 r2'f

(16) *LAS* 171:19 *a-na-ku-*⌜*ma*⌝ [20] [*ina*] ITU*Si-man-ni a-na* LUGAL [21] [*b*]*e-lí-i*[*a a*]*-sa*[*p*]*-ra* [22] *nu-uk lìb-ba-ka ṣab-ta* [23] *qab-le-e-ka ru-ku-us* (Ašu),
possibly referring to *LAS* 129 r19, DUMUMEŠ*-ka an-nu-te* SIG_5MEŠ *du-gu-ul* [20] *lìb-ba-ka lu ḫa-ad-di da-ba-bu* [21] *la* [S]IG_5 LUGAL *be-lí* TA* UGU *lìb-bi-šú* [22] [*lu-š*]*e-li ina lìb-bi te-ni-iš* (Adad-šumu-uṣur)

(17) *LAS* 173 r7 *ù ṭup-pa-a-ni am-mu-ti* [8] *ša* ÉŠ.GÀR *mé-e*[*ḫ*]*-ri* [9] *is-se-šú-ma lu-bi-la* (Marduk-šākin-šumi),
referring to *LAS* 164 r1

(18) *LAS* 177:6 *ina* UGU $UŠ_{12}$.BÚR.RU.[DA]*-a-ni* [7] *ša* i n a p a - n i - t i *ni-*[*ib-ṭi-lu-ni*] [8] *la nu-gam-me-*[*ru-u-ni*] [9] *la né -pu-šu-*[*u-ni*] (Marduk-šākin-šumi), referring to *LAS* 173, 176, etc.

(19) *LAS* 181:10 *la-a šu-tú* ^{11} *ṣu-ur-ḫe-e ma-a zu-ú-tú* ^{12} *ina lìb-bi li-ik-ru-ra* (Marduk-šākin-šumi), referring to *LAS* 246 r14f, *i -su-ur-ri zu-ú-tú* LUGAL ^{15} *i-kar-ra-ra ina lib-bi* (Urad-Nanâ)

(20) *LAS* 218:10 *ina* UGU *né-pi-ši ša* LU[GAL *be-lí*] ^{11} *iš-pur-an-na-ši-ni d*[*i-'u* ^{12} *šip-ṭu mu-ta-nu* . . . (Nabû-nāṣir);
king's order based on *LAS* 279 r14 (Mār-Ištar)

(21) *LAS* 273:9 ^{d}*30* ^{d}NIN.[GAL *it-tab-bu*] . . . ^{r1}'*i*[*k-tar-bu*] . . . ^{5}'*it-tan-nu* (Urad-Ea), referring (indirectly) to *LAS* 272:9, ^{d}*30 i-ta-bi* . . . ^{17} *i-kar-rab* . . . ^{r2} *i-da-an*

(22) *LAS* 282 r2' [*ù*] *ina* UGU [^{d}GAŠAN* *ša* ^{URU}*Ak-kad*. . . . . . .] ^{3}'[*ša i n a* p] *a - n i - t i a-*[*na* MAN EN-*iá áš-pur-an-ni*] ^{4}'[*nu*]-⌜*uk*⌝ *ina* É *a-k*[*i-ti* . . . .]
possibly referring to *LAS* 281 r24ff (both from Mār-Ištar)

(23) *LAS* 165:6 *ina* UGU ^{LÚ}TUR (or ^{LÚ}*tur-*[*ta-ni*]) ^{7} *š*[*a* LUGA]L *be-*[*lí-ni*] ^{8} [*iš-pur-an-na-ši-ni*] . . .
referring to *LAS* 162? (by "Farmer")

5.3 *Unidentified references to previous letters*

(1) *LAS* 291:17' *ina* UGU É.GAR$_{8}$ *ša* É ^{d}U+GUR ^{18}'*ša* GÚ.DU$_{8}$.A^{KI} *ša a-na* MAN [EN-*iá áš-pu*]*r-an-ni* ^{19}' *nu-uk a-na* x[. . . . .-r]u (Mār-Ištar)

(2) *LAS* 294:r11 ^{GIŠ}ÙR *am-mì-i-u* ^{11} [. . . *l*]*i-a ša ina pa-ni-ti a-na* MAN ^{13} [EN-*iá áš-pur-an*]-*ni nu-uk ina* ^{URU}*Ak-kad* ^{14} [*ni-zab-bil-šú*?] (Mār-Ištar)

(3) *LAS* 311:17 *ina* U[GU . . .] ^{18} *ša ina* ⌜É⌝ [*a-ki-t*]*t* ^{19} ^{DUG}*ḫa-ri-a-te* ^{20} [*ina* I]GI ^{GIŠ}BANŠUR LUGAL ^{r1} *ú-mal-lu-u-ni* ^{2} *ú-ma-a ba-aṭ-lu* ^{3} *iš-ka-nu-u-ni* ^{4} *ša a-na* LUGAL *be-lí-iá* ^{5} *áš-pu-ra-an-ni* ^{6} LUGAL *be-lí la-a iš-al* (Akkullānu)

(4) *LAS* 312 r18' *ù ina* UGU ^{LÚ}SANGA *ša* É ^{d}7.BI ^{19}'*ša* ^{URU}NINA *ša a-na LUGAL EN-ja* ^{20}'*áš-pur-a-ni mu-uk da-ba-bu ina pi-i-šú* ^{21}'*i-ba-áš-ši liš-ú-lu-šú* LUGAL *be-lí* ^{22}'*is-sap-ra ma-a lu qu-ru-ub* ^{23}'*a-di a-kan-ni* ^{24}'*me-me-e-ni la iš-al-šú*
(possibly referring to *LAS* 314)

(5) *LAS* 352:6 *ina* UGU *a-da-an-ni* ^{8} EN.NUN ^{d}ASAR.LÚ*.ḪI ^{9} [*ša*] *taš-pur-an-ni* ^{10} [*ma-a* . . . *a*]*p-ta-làḫ*
(= ref. to *LAS* 161 or 200?)

(6) *LAS* 106:4' *ù ša iq-*[*bu-u-ni a-na* LUGAL] ^{5}'[*m*]*a-a ina* $^{MUL.LÚ}$Ḫ[UN.GÁ IGI-*mar*]

(7) *LAS* 136:7 [*ina* UGU LUGAL *p*]*u-u-ḫi ša* LUGAL ^{8} [*be-lí iš-pur-a*]*n-ni ma-a iq-ṭi-bu-ni* ^{9} [*ma-a* EN UD] ⌜*8*⌝.KÁM *šá* ^{ITU}KIN ^{10} [*lu-šib*] (Adad-šumu-uṣur)

(8) *LAS* 217:10 *a-ki* LUGAL [*be-lí*] ^{11} *ina* ^{URU}*Tar-bi-ṣi* ^{12} [*šu-t*]*u-ni* ^{13} [*a-na* LU]GAL *be-lí-ia* ^{14} [*as-sa*]-*pa-ra* ^{mu}*muk* [^{15} *ša pi-qit*]-*te ša* ^{d}GAŠAN *par-ṣi* ^{r1} *šu-tu-šú de-eq-*⌜*tú*⌝ *am-rat* ^{2} *e-ge-ra-šú as-se-me* (Nabû-nāṣir)

(9) *LAS* 227 r6' *ù* [*ina* UGU] ŠEŠ-*ia* ^{7} *ša a-na* LUGAL *áš-pu-ra-an-ni* ^{8}'*la-a ma-ḫi-ir ina pa-ni-šú-nu* (Nabû-gāmil)

(10) *LAS* 246:11 *ina pa-ni-ti ina pa-an* LUGAL *aq-ṭi-bi* ^{12} SA.GIG *qó o šú la ú šá aḫ ki mì* (Urad-Nanâ, but not really pertinent since referring to oral communication; thus also *LAS* 277:9F)

(11) *LAS* 258:8 *nap-šal-a-ti qut-ari*$_{5}$ ^{9} *me-eli*^{MEŠ} *maš-qí-a-ti* . . . ^{13} *la gab-ri e-gír-ti a-mar* (Ikkāru), unless referring to *LAS* 265 (unlikely)

(12) *LAS* 276:5 *ina* UGU ^{NA_4} *gu-si-gu* ^{6} *ša a-na* MAN EN-*iá áš-pur-an-ni nu-uk* ^{7} *la na-aṣ-ṣu-u-ni* (Mār-Ištar)

APPENDIX Q

RELATED TEXTS[699]

1. *OLD BABYLONIAN LETTERS FROM MARI*

1.1 Letters to Jasmaḫ-Addu and Zimri-Lim[700] from the haruspex ASQŪDUM

(1) A 25 = Dossin, *CRRAI* 2 (1951) 46-48

Obv.	1	*a-[n]a be-lí-j[a]*	Say to
	2	*qí- bí- ma*	my lord:
	3	*um-ma aš-qú-du-um*	thus (says) Asqūdum,
	4	[Ì]R-*k[a]-a-ma*	your servant:
	5	[U]D *14*.KAM *an-ta-al-lu-[ú-u]m*	An eclipse of the moon oc-
	6	*ša* ^{d}*30 iš-ša-ki-in*	curred on the 14th, and the
	7	*ù na-aš-ku-un an-ta-al-[l]e-[e-e]m*	occurrence of that eclipse
	8	*[ša-a]-ti ma-ru-uṣ*	was ill-portending. I have
	9	*[te-re]-tim a-na šu-lum be-lí-ja*	performed extispicies con-
Edge	10	*ù šu-[lum] ḫ[a]-al-zi-im*	cerning the well-being of my
	11	*e- li- i- im*	lord and the well-being of
	12	*e-pu-úš-ma te-r[e-tum]*	the upper province, and the
Rev.	13	*ša- al- ma*	oracles were favourable.
	14	*i-na-an-na be-lí aš-ra-[nu-um]*	Now, let my lord have (exti-
	15	*[a-n]a šu-ul-mi-[šu]*	spicies) performed there for
	16	*ù šu-lum a-lim ma-ri*[KI]I	his well-being and the well-
	17	*[li]-še-pí-[iš]-ma*	being of the city of Mari, so
	18	*[li]-ib-bi be-lí-ja la i-na-ḫ[i-i]d*	that my lord's heart would not
	19	*[ù] me-ḫe-er ṭup-pí-j[a]*	be troubled. And let my lord
	20	*[be]-lí li-ša-bi-[lam-ma]*	send an answer to my tablet,
	21	*[li-ib-bi] li-nu-[uḫ]*	to reliefe my heart.

(2) *ARM(T)* 5 65

Obv.	1	*[a-na be-lí]-ja ja-áš-ma-aḫ-*^{d}IM	Say to my [lord]
	2	*qí- bí- ma*	Jasmaḫ-Addu:
	3	*um-ma aš-qú-du- um*	thus (says) Asqūdum,
	4	ÌR-*ka-a- ma*	your servant.
	5	*ki-ma ka-ša-di-ja- ma*	Upon my arrival
	6	*i-na tir-qa* KI	in Terqa,
	7	^{I}*ta-ri-im-ša-ki-im-ma*	Tarim-šakin also
	8	*ik-šu-dam-ma ki-a-am*	arrived and
	9	*a-ša-al-šu um-ma-a a-na-ku-ma*	I asked him als follows:
	10	*te-re-tim a-na šu-lum ma-a-tim*	"Did Zunān perform extispicies
	11	*ù a-al da-an-na-tim*	concerning the well-being of
Edge	12	^{I}*zu-na-an i-pu- úš*	the country and the fortified
	13	*šu-ú ki-ḫa-am i-pu-la-an-ni*	cities?" He answered as fol-
	14	*um-ma-mi ú-ul i-pu-úš*	lows: "He did not."

699 Texts included in this appendix are for economy of space given in transliteration and translation only, without commentaries. For editions and studies see Borger, *HKL*.

700 The addressee of Asqūdum's letters is specified by name only in *ARM* 5 65 (= below, no. 2). That most of his letters were addressed to Zimri-Lim is, however, made likely by the following seal inscription, quoted by Dossin in A. Parrot (ed.), *Studia Mariana* (1950), p. 42: *zi-im-r[i]-l[i-im]* / *ša-ki-in* ^{d}*da-g[an]* / *aš-qú-d[u-um]* / MÁŠ.ŠU.GÍD.GÍD "(to) Zimri-Lim, representative of Dagan, (from) Asqūdum, the haruspex."

Rev.	15	*i-na te-bi-ib- ti*	At the "clearing"
	16	ITU *an-ni-im it-ti-šu*	of this month I returned
	17	*a-na sa-ga-ra-tim*^{KI} *a-tu-ra-ma*	to Sagarātim with him and
	18	*te-re-tim a-na šu-lum a-lim*^{KI}	performed extispicies on the
	19	*sa-ga-ra-tim*^{KI} *a-na* ITU 6.KAM	well-being of the city of Sa-
	20	*e-pu-úš-ma te-re- tum*	garatim for six months, and
	21	*ša-al-ma ù ki- ma*	the oracles were favourable.
	22	*pa-ni-ja-ma ina* BÀD *be-lí-ja*	I am also going to perform
	23	*tir-qa*^{KI} *sú-ub-ri-im*^{KI}	(extiscpicies) in the wall(ed
	24	*ù ma-ri*^{KI} *e-pé-eš-ma*	cities) of my lord, Terqa, Sub-
	25	*ṭe*$_4$*-ma-am ga-am-ra-am*	rim and Mari, and shall
	26	*ma-aḫ-re-em- ma*	send a complete
	27	*a-na ṣe-er be-lí- ja*	preliminary report
	28	*a-ša-pa- ra- ma*	to my lord. [Furthermore],
Edge	29	[*ù*] *i-na sa-ga-ra-*[*t*]*im*	I [. . .]ed in Sagarātim at
	30	[*i*]*-na ni-iq wa-ar-ḫi-im*	the monthly sheep-offering and
	31	[*ù i*]*-na ni-iq be-lí-ja*	the sheep-offering of my lord,
	32	[ ]x- *ma*	making these observations:
L.E.	33	[*an*]*-ni-tam a-mu-ur-ma šu-me-el ú-ba-ni-im*	The left side of the Finger was open, and
	34	[*p*]*a-ṭe*$_4$*-er ú-ba-an ḫa-ši-i qa-ab-li-tum*	the middlemost Finger of the lungs was bent
	35	*a-na i-me-en na-dí ši-ir šu-mì-im be-lí lu ḫa-di*	to the right. A "flesh of fame"! My lord can be happy.

(3) *ARM(T)* 2 97

Obv.	1	⌜*a*⌝*-na be-lí- ja*	Say to
	2	*qí- bí- ma*	my lord:
	3	*um-ma aš-qú-du- um*	thus (says) Asqūdum,
	4	⌜ÌR⌝- *ka-a-ma*	your servant:
	5	*te-re-tim a-na šu-lum*	I have performed extispicies
	6	DUMU^{MEŠ} *ši-ip-ri*	for the well-being of the
	7	*e-pu-úš-ma la-ap-ta*	messengers, but the (oracles)
	8	*a-ta-ar e-pé-èš-šu-nu-ši-ma*	were unfavourable. I shall
	9	[*i*]*-nu-ma te-re-*⌜*tum*⌝	continue performing (sacri-
	10	⌜*iš*⌝*-ta-al-* ⌜*ma*⌝	fices), and as soon as the
Edge	11	⌜*a-ṭà-ar*⌝*-ra-sú-nu-t*[*i*]	oracles are favourable, I
	12	[*š*]*a-ni-tam aš-šum sa-a*[*g-bi*]	shall dispatch them. Another
Rev.	13	[*š*]*a ḫa-la-az ik-šu-u*[*d-ap-p*]*a-šu*	matter: apropos of the secu-
	14	*ù ḫa-ab-du-*⌜*ma*⌝*-*^{d}*da-gan*	rity troops of the districts of
	15	*mi-im-ma sa- ag- bu*	Ikšud-appašu and Ḫabdūma-
	16	*ú-ul ša-*⌜*ak*⌝*-nu*	Dagan, no security are stationed
	17	*ù ni-di mi-*⌜*im-ma*⌝ *ma-la*	there, and my lord himself
	18	*i-na ni-qí be-lí-ja*	knows what configurations
	19	*im-ta-na- qú- ta*	keep occurring in his sacrifices.
	20	*be-lí-ma i-di*	The security troops have been
	21	*a-na sa ag bi a-ḫu-um na-di*	neglected, and (that's why)
	22	*ù te-re-et né-pí-iš-tim*	the oracles pertaining to the
Edge	23	⌜*ša*⌝ *šu-*⌜*lum*⌝ *ḫa-al-zi-šu-nu*	well-being of their dističts
	24	[*la- ap*]- *ta*	unfavourable.

(4) *ARM(T)* 2 96

Obv.	1	*a-na be-lí-ja*	Say to

	2	*qí- bí- ma*	my lord:
	3	*um-ma aš-qú-du-um*	thus (says) Asqūdum,
	4	ÌR- *ka- a- ma*	your servant:
	5	*1* ^{TÚG}*mar-da-tam*	I asked my lord
	6	*be-lí e-⸢ri-iš⸣-ma*	for a curtain(?) but
Edge	7	*⸢ú⸣-ul id-di-nim*	he did not give me any.
	8	*⸢ki⸣-ma ka-ša-di-ia-ma*	Upon my arrival I sent
	9	*1* ^{LÚ}*a-ḫi-za- am*	a student
Rev.	10	*⸢a-na⸣ be-lí-ja ú-ša-re-em*	to my lord,
	11	*ù i-na-an-na ša-né-em*	and now I am sending
	12	*1* ^{LÚ}*a-ḫi-za-am uš-ta-re-em*	another student.
	13	*be-lí* $ṭe_4$*-ma-am*	Let my lord ask him
	14	*li-iš-ta-a-al-šu*	about the news; (and)
	15	*1 na-ṣí-ra-am*	let my lord assign him
	16	*ša a-ḫi-za-am i-re-de-em*	a guard to take the
Edge	17	*be-lí li-ip-qí-is-su*	student back to me.

For more letters by Asqūdum see *ARM* 2 95 and 98-100. These letters do not refer to haruspical matters, and are therefore not presented here.

1.2 Letters from the haurspex ERĪB-SÎN[701]

(5) A 1081 = Nougayrol, *JCS* 21 (1967) 227-229

Obv.	1	*a-na be-lí- ja*	Say to
	2	*qí- ⸢bí⸣- ma*	my lord:
	3	*um-ma e-ri-ib-*^{d}EN+ZU	thus (says) Erīb-Sîn,
	4	ÌR- *ka- a- ma*	your servant.
	5	*ṣa-bu-um ša be-lí-ja ša-lim*	The troops of my lord are well.
	6	ITU *ḫi-bi-ir-tim* UD 2.KAM BA.ZAL*-ma*	In the evening of the 2nd of
	7	*te-re-tim a-na ⸢šu-lum⸣ ṣa-bi-im*	Ḫibirtum I performed
	8	ITU *30* UD*-⸢mi ù⸣ 30 mu-še-tim*	extispicies on the well-being of
	9	*te-re-tim e-pu-úš- ma*	the troops for the full month.
	10	*i-na ma-aḫ-ri-ti-ja na-ap-la-su-um*	In my first extispicy, the Sight
	11	*ša-ki-in* KASKAL *ša-ki-in*	and the Path were there; the
	12	KÁ É.GAL*-lim ša-⸢lim⸣*	Palace Gate was normal; the
	13	*šu-u[l-m]u-um ša-ki-in*	Peace was there; the base of
	14	*iš-d[a* S]IPA *i-mi-tam*	the Shepherd was connected at
Edge	15	*ù šu-me-lam ra-ak-sa*	the right and left; the Finger was
	16	ŠU.SI *ša-al-ma- at*	normal; the Increase was strong;
	17	MÁŠ *ma- ag- ša- ar*	the lungs, the heart, and the
	18	*ḫa-šu-ú li-ib-bu-[u]m š[a-al-mu]*	upper parts were normal.
	19	*e-le-tu-ja ša-al-ma*	In my repeated inspection,
	20	*i-na pí-qí-ti- ja*	the Sight was there;
Rev.	21	*na-ap-la-su-um ša-ki-in*	the Path fell toward the
	22	KASKAL *a-na šu-ba-at šu-me-lim im-qú-ut*	left Seat;
	23	KÁ É.GAL-lim *ša-lim*	the Palace Gate was normal;
	24	*šu-ul-mu-um ša-ki-in*	the Peace was there; the base of

[701] The addressee of these letters was, judging from the references to Hammurapi, probably Zimri-Lim. Cf. Nougayrol, art.cit. 229[64].

25 *iš-da* SIPA *i-mi-tam na-as-ḫa*
26 *šu-me-lam ra- ak- sà*
27 *šu-me-lam* ŠU.SI *iḫ- pí*
28 MÁŠ *ma-ag-ša-ra- at*
29 *ḫa-šu-ú li-ib-bu-um ù e-le-tu-ja*
30 *ša- al- ma*
31 *te-re-tu-ja a-na* UD-*mi-ši-na*
32 *ša- al- ma*
Edge 33 *ša-ni-tam it-ti* DUMU^{MEŠ} MÁŠ.ŠU.GÍD.GÍD
34 *ša ḫa-mu-ra- pí*
35 *ú-ul i-ir-šu-ni-in-ni-ma*
36 *ù te-er-tam it-ti-šu-nu*
37 *ú-ul e-pé- eš- ma*
L.E. 38 *ù ṭe*$_4$*-em* ⌈*né-pé*⌉*-eš-ti-šu-nu*
39 *a-na ṣe-er* [*be-l*]*í- ja*
40 *ú-ul a-ša-pa-*⌈*ra*⌉*-am*

the Shepherd was disconnected at the right, but connected at the left; the left side was pierced by the Finger; the Increase was strong; the lungs, the heart, and the upper parts were normal. (Thus) my oracles were favourable for the period indicated. Another matter: the haruspices of Hammurapi did not invite (lit. "want") me, so I am not performing extispicies with them and cannot send a report of their activities to my lord.

(6) A 4222 = Nougayrol, *JCS* 21 (1967) 229-232

Obv. 1 *a-na be-lí-ja qí-bi-ma*
2 *um-ma e-ri-ib-*^{d}EN+ZU ÌR-*ka-*[*a-ma*]
3 *ṣa-bu-um ša be-lí-ja ša-lim aš-šum ṭe*$_4$*-em né-pé-*[*eš-ti-im*]
4 *ša šu-lum ṣa-bi-i*[*m š*]*a be-lí ú-wa-i-ra-an-ni-ma ú-*[. . .]
5 *i-na a-lim ḫa-al-ḫa-la* ^{KI}*ša-ap-la-nu-um* [. . .]
6 *te-re-tim a-na šu-lum ṣa-bi-im e-pu-uš-m*[*a*]
7 *i-na ma-a*[*ḫ-r*]*i-ti-ja na-ap-la-su-um ša-ki-in pa-*[*da-nu-um ša-ki-in*]
8 *šu-ba-at šu-me-li-im a-di 2-šu pa-ṭe*$_4$*-er* KÁ É.GAL-*l*[*im ša-lim*]
9 *pu-uz-ru-um ša-ki-in i-na er-ṣe-et šu-ul-mì-*[*im*]
10 ^{GIŠ}TUKUL *ša-ki-in-ma ma-áṣ-ra-aḫ* SIPA *i-na-aṭ-ṭ*[*à-al*]
11 *èš-da-a* SIPA *i-na*⟪i-na⟫ *ma-áṣ-ra-ḫi pa-ar-s*[*a*]*-ma*
12 *i-na* SAG *ra-ak-sa šu-me-lam ú-ul i-ku-n*[*a*]
13 SIPA *i-na dan-na-at šu-me-lim na-di i-na šu-me-*[*li-š*]*u pí-iṭ-rum*
14 *mì-ḫi-iṣ pa-an* ^{LÚ}KÚR *ša-ki-in mu-ud-d*[*a* ^{GIŠ}GU.Z]A *ka-pí-iṣ*
15 *ú-ba-nu-um a-na* É.GAL-*li-ša* ⌈ x x ⌉ [. .]x-*ku-ut*
16 *ḫa-šu-*⌈*ú*⌉ [
17 ⌈ x x ⌉ [

(Break of approximately 6 lines)

Rev. 1' [.]⌈ x x ⌉ [
2' ⌈*ša*⌉ *šu-me-el* ⌈*ú*⌉*-b*[*a-ni-im*
3' *ma-ad-da* ⌈^{GIŠ}⌉GU.ZA [
4' *šu-lum* MÁŠ *ša-ki-in ḫa-š*[*u-ú*

Say to my lord: thus (says) Erīb-Sîn, your servant: The troops of my lord are well. As to the report of the sacrifice which my lord ordered me to perform for the well-being of the troops, I performed extispicies for the well-being of the troops in the city of Ḫalḫal to the south of [. . .]. In my first extispicy, the Sight and the Path were there; the left Seat was split in two; the Palace Gate was normal; the Secret was there, in the area of the Peace there was a Weapon facing the duct of the Shepherd; the base of the Shepherd was disconnected from the duct, but connected with the head; it was unstable at the left. The Shepherd lay in the left Fortress. At its left there was a fissure. The Blow-in-the Enemy's-Face was there; the Fall-of-the-Throne was bent; the Finger was [. . .] toward its Palace; the lungs, [. . . . .].

of the left of the Finger [. . . .
the Fall-of-the Throne [. . . . . . .];
there was a *šulum-ṣibti*; the lungs,

	5' *e-le-tu ša-al-ma te-re-tum* x[	[heart] and upper parts were normal.
	6' *a-tu-ur qa-tam ša-ni-tam ki-a-am e-pu-uš*	The oracles [. . . .]. I returned and formulated
	šum-m[a ṣa-ab be-lí-ja]	another query as follows: "If the troops of my
	7' *ša a-na ṣe-er ḫa-am-mu-ra-pí iṭ-ru-du ṣa-ba-*	lord which he sent against Ḫammurapi
	am [*ša-ti*]	will not be captured, killed
	8' ^{I}*ḫa-am-mu-ra-pí la i-ba-ar la i-da-ak la*	assassinated or kept in
	uš-da-a[*k*]	evil and . . . captivity by
	9' *ki-li le-mu-un-tim ù sa-li-ma-tim la*	Hammurapi,
	i-ka-la-šu	will they, just as they marched out of the
	10' *ki-ma ba-al-ṭú-ma a-bu-ul ma-ri*^{KI} *ú-ṣú-nim*	gate of Mari safe and sound, enter
	11' *ba-al-ṭú-us-sú-nu a-bu-ul ma-ri*^{KI} *i-ru-bu*	the gate of Mari safe and sound?"
	12' *te-re-tim e-pu-uš-ma i-na ma-aḫ-ri-ti-ja*	I performed the extispicies, and in my first
	13' *na-ap-la-su ša-ki-in pa-da-nu-um ša-ki-i*[*n*	(extispicy), the Sight and Path were there;
	K]Á É.GAL *ša-lim*	the Palace Gate was normal;
	14' *pu-uz-rum ša-ki-*[*i*]*n šu-ul-mu-um* 2 AŠ [. . .]	the Secret was there; the Peace
	na-aṣ-ra-ap-t[*i* . .]	ditto, [. . .] facing the duct
	15' *i-na-ṭà-al èš-da-a* SIPA *i-mi-tam ra-a*[*k-sa*	[of the Shepherd]; the base of the
	šu-me-lam . . .]	Shepherd was connected at the right [. . . .],
	16' *mì-ḫi-iṣ pa-an* ^{LÚ}KÚR *ša-k*[*i-i*]*n* x x [. . . .]	the Blow-in-the-Enemy's-Face was there [. . .];
	17' *šu-me-el ú-ba-nim ḫe-pí* MÁŠ [	the left side of the Finger was broken; the In-
	18' *e-le-tu-ja ša-a*[*l-ma*	crease [. . . . . .] (and) the upper parts were
		normal.
	19' *i-na pí-qí-ti-ja* x[ ]	In my control extispicy, [. . . . .
	20' *pa-da-nu-um* ⌜*ša-ki*⌝-[*in*	the Path was there [. . .
	21' *šu-ba-at šu-me-l*[*im*	the left Seat [. . . .
	22' KÁ É.GAL-*lim* [*ša-lim*	the Palace Gate [was normal; . . .
	23' *i-mi-tam na-ás-ḫa* [	was loose at the right [. . . .
	24' *i-na šu-me-e*[*l*] x[	at the left side of [. . .
	25' *ša-at-q*[*a-a*]*t* x[	was cut [. . . .
	26' *mì-ḫi-iṣ pa-an* ^{LÚ}KÚR *ma-ad-da* ^{GI}[ŠGU.	the Blow-in-the-Enemy's-Face;
	ZA] *ša-ki-in*	the Fall-of-the-Throne was there;
L.E.	27' *ú-ba-nu ša-al-ma-at* MÁŠ *ma-ag-ša*<*-ra*>*-at*	the Finger was normal; the Increase was strong;
	28' *ḫa-šu-ú ša-al-ma* ŠÀ *ša-lim*	the lungs were normal; the heart
	29' *e-le-tu-ja ša-al-ma*	was normal, the upper parts were
II.	30' *te-re-tu-ja ša-al-ma l*[*i-ib-bi*]	normal. (All) my oracles were favourable;
	31' *be-lí-ja a-na ṣa-bi-šu* <*la*> *i-na-*[*ḫi-id*]	my lord should <not> be worried about his
		troops.

1.3 Letters from the haruspex IŠḪĪ-ADDU[702]

(7) A 860 = Nougayrol, *JCS* 21 (1967) 226-227

Obv.	1 *a-na be+lí- ja*	Say to my lord:
	2 *qí- bí- ma*	thus (says) Išḫi-Addu,
	3 *um-ma iš-ḫi-* ^{d}IM	your servant:
	4 ÌR- ⌜*ka*⌝*-a- ma*	I inspected the exta of the
	5 SILA$_4$ MÁŠ.ŠU.GÍD.GÍD *ša ma-ḫa-ar* ^{d}[.]	sacrificial lamb which was
	6 *ik-pu-pu te-er-ta-šu a-mu-u*[*r-ma*]	offered (lit. "bent") before
	7 *i-na te-er-tim ša-ti na-*[*ap-la-su-um*]	the god [. .]; in those exta,
	8 *i-na qa-qar ki-i*[*t-t*] *im* [*ša-ki-in*]	the Sight was in its normal

702 On this man see Finet, *RA* 53 (1959) 68.

	9	*pa-da-nu ša-ki-*⸢*in-ma*⸣ [ ]	place; the Path was there;
	10	*pu-iz-rum da-na-na-am ú-u*[*l i-šu*]	the Secret did not have a
Edge	11	KÁ É.GAL-*lim ša- lim* [O]	Fortress; the Palace Gate was
Rev.	12	*i-na ma-aṣ-*⸢*ra-aḫ*⸣ SIPA [O]	normal; in the duct of the
	13	^{GIŠ}TUKUL *ša-ki-in-ma pa-*⸢ x x ⸣[ ]	Shepherd there was a weapon
	14	*iš-da-an* SIPA *i-mi-*⸢*it-tam*⸣ [O]	and [. . .]; the base of the
	15	*sà-ar-ma šu-me-lam na-a*[*s-ḫa*]	Shepherd was cut off at the
	16	*da-an-n*[*a-at šu*]*-me-lim* ⸢ x x x ⸣[O]	right and loose at the left;
	17	*pa-*⸢ *aṭ*?⸣-[*ra*]- ⸢*at*⸣	the left Fortress was open [. . .]
•	18	*i-*⸢*mi-it-ti*⸣ [*ú*]*-ba-nim* ⸢*ša*⸣-[*at-qa-at*]	the right side of the Finger was c[ut];
	19	*šu-mì-il ú-*[*ba-nim*]	the left side of the F[inger was . .];
	20	*ṣí-ib-tum ma-*[*ag-ša-ra-at*]	the Increase was st[rong];
	21	*ḫa-šu-ú ša-a*[*l-ma*]	the lungs were nor[mal . . . . .],
	22	*ki-iṣ-rum i-m*[*i-it-tam*]	the Joint was [. . . to the ri]ght,
	23	*e-le-t*[*u*]	the upper parts [were . . . .].

(8) *ARM(T)* 2 134

Obv.	1	*a-na be-lí-ja qí-bí-ma*	Say to my lord: thus (says) Išḫī-Addu,
	2	*um-ma iš-ḫi-*^{d}IM ÌR*-ka-a-ma*	your servant: I and Ibbi-Amurru offered
	3	*a-na-ku ù ib-bi-*^{d}MAR.TU *a-na gi-ir-ri-im*	(a sacrifice) for the expedition of
	4	*ša* ÌR*-ì-lí-šu a-na aq-da-ma-tim*	Warad-ilīšu to this side of the river,
	5	*nu-uš-tam-ḫi-ir-ma te-re-tu-ni ú-ul* ⸢*ša-al*⸣*-ma*	but our oracles were not favourable.
	6	*te-re-tim ši-na-ti a-na ṣe-er be-lí-ja*	I am sending those oracles to my lord;
	7	*uš-ta-bi-lam a-na te-re-tim ši-na-ti*	my lord should pay much attention to
	8	*be-lí ma-di-iš li-qú-ul*	those oracles. Now, if my lord
	9	*i-na-an-na šum-ma be-lí i-qa-ab-bi*	so commands, I will see to
	10	*i-na* ^{GIŠ}MÁ *a-na ra-ka-ab* ^{MÍ}TUR^{MEŠ}	it that the girls make
Edge	11	⸢*lu*⸣- *pu- úš*	the trip in a boat;
	12	*ú-la-šu-ma be-lí ṣa-ba-am*	or if my lord can send here
	13	*ta-aq-ri- ba- tam*	an escort which could
Rev.	14	*ša a-di i-ma-a-ar*⸢KI⸣	accompany them to Imar,
	15	*ú-qa-ar-ra-bu i-ṭà-ar-ra-dam*	let him send (it) and
	16	*be-lí li-iṭ-ru-da-am- ma*	I will act (accordingly).
	17	*lu- pu- úš*	Whatever way, let my lord
	18	*an-ni-tam la* ⸢*an-ni-tam*⸣ [*b*]*e-lí li-iš-pu-ra-am*	write to me.

Several other Mari letters refer to haruspices and their activities, often in considerable detail (see e.g. *ARM* 1 85; 2, 22 and 139; 3, 80; 4, 54; 5, 83). These texts are not included in this appendix, however, since not written by haruspices themselves.

For Mari letters referring to physicians and/or medical matters see Finet, "Le médicins au royaume de Mari", *AIPHOS* 14 (1954/7) 123ff, note also *ARM* 2 127 and 10 129. None of these letters were written by physicians (or exorcists), and they are therefore not included here.

2. *OLD BABYLONIAN AND CASSITE REPORTS ON EXTISPICIES*

Altogether 35 texts of this category are known at present, 27 of them dating from the Old Babylonian period (reigns of Ammiṣaduqa and his successor Samsu-ditana) and the rest from Cassite times (reign of Burnaburiaš [II]). Since all these reports contain, in addition to date and occasional references to the person for whom the extispicy was performed,[703] only stereotype lists of features observed in the exta – much in the same way as in Texts above –, and since all of them are available in recent editions, it does not seem worth while quoting any of them in the present context. Nevertheless, a reference to the relevant publications appears desirable.

The reports are edited in the following articles:

A. Goetze, "Reports on acts of extispicy from Old Babylonian and Kassite times", *JCS* 11 (1957) 89-105 [23 texts];
J. Nougayrol, "Rapports paléo-babyloniens d'haruspices", *JCS* 21 (1967) 219-235 [11 texts];
I. Starr, "Extispicy reports from the Old Babylonian and Sargonid periods", *Finkelstein Memorial Volume* (1977), 201-208 [1 text].

3. *MIDDLE BABYLONIAN LETTERS*

3.1 Letters from the physician MUKALLIM

(1) Radau, *BE* 17/1 47 = Waschow, *MAOG* 10/1 (1936) 33f.

Obv.	1	[ÌR-*ka* ^{I}*mu- kal- lim*]	[Your servant Mukallim:]
	2	[*a-na*] ⸢*di*⸣-[*na-an be-lí-ja*]	[I am ready] to die (lit. "to go!")
	3	[*lu*]-*ul- li-* [*ik*]	[as my lord's substi]tute.
	4	[DU]MU.MÍ ^{I}*a-a- ri*	The daughter of Ajaru felt
	5	*i-na ba-ra-ri ki i'-i-*⸢*šu*⸣	much better in the evening,
	6	*iš-tu mu-šu me-še-li*	and having fallen asleep after
	7	*iš-tu* DUMU *šip-ri-ja*	midnight, after I dispatched
	8	*a-na mu-uḫ be-lí-ja áš-pu-*⸢*ra*⸣	my messenger to my lord,
	9	*ki it-ti- lu*	she did not wake up
	10	*a-di ša-*⸢*me*⸣*-e la-pa-ti*	until daybreak.
	11	[*u*]*l ig-ge-el- tu*$_4$	Nobody had put on
	12	[KE]ŠDA *ša mu-ši-ta*	the poultice which
Edge	13	*i-ṣa-am-mi-du-ši*	she has been dressed
Rev.	14	*ma-am-ma ul iṣ-m*[*i-i*]*d*	with (every) night.
	15	[*i-n*]*a ša-me-e la-pa-ti*	When she woke up
	16	⸢*ki ig*⸣*-ge-el-tu-ú*	at dawn, they (however)
	17	*na- aṣ- ma- at- ta*	put it on because
	18	*ki i-ri-šu iṣ-ṣa-an-du-ši*	she asked for it.
	19	*ù ša pa-na ma-a'-da*	But while she had been
	20	*i-né-'i- i- šu*	feeling very well before,
	21	*i-na-an-na ul i'-i-iš*	she did not feel well any more.
	22	[*ṭ*]*e-ma a-lam-ma-ad-ma*	I will learn (more) about
	23	[ ]x- *bi- ir- ma*	the situation, and then [. . .]
	24	[DUMU *šip*]*-ri-ja ú-š*[*e-ṣa-a*]	send off my messenger.

(2) Radau, *BE* 17/1 32 = Waschow, *MAOG* 10/1 p. 31f

Obv.	1	[ÌR]-*ka* ^{I}*mu-ka*[*l-lim*]	Your servant Mukallim:
	2	[*a-n*]*a di-na-an be-lí-*[*ja*]	I am ready to die as
	3	[*lu-u*]*l- li- ik*	my lord's substitute.
	4	[*a-na*] *na-a'-re-e na-a*['*-ra-ti*]	The male and female musicians,
	5	[MÍ]⸢*e*⸣*-ṭi-ir- ti*	(the lady) Eṭirtu, and the

---

703 E.g., a-na SILIM ^{MÍ}*be-el-ta-ni*, *Babyl.* 3 pl.9:3; *a-na šu-lum* ^{I}*ku-ub-bu-rum*, Szlechter, *TJA* pl.24:2; *ša ku-ub-bu-rum* UGULA D[AM]. QAR, ibid. pl.28:10. On the basis of the last two passages, it seems that the entry *ša* ^{d}EN+ZU-*a-ša-re-ed* in *YOS* 10 19:21 refers to the recipient of the oracles rather than the officiating haruspex (thus Goetze, ibid. p. 13).

6	[*ù*] ⸢É⸣ *be-lí-ja šu-u*[*l-mu*]	house of my lord are well.
7	[DUMU.MÍ ^{I}]*muš-ta-li*	The daughter of Muštālu
8	[*i-na*] *ši-mi-ti um-m*[*u*]	had an attack of fever
9	[*iṣ*]-*ṣa-ba-as-si-m*[*a*]	last night, and I gave
10	[*i-n*]*a na-*⸢*ma*⸣*-ri šam-ma á*[*š-qí-ši*]	her a drug in the morning.
11	[*u*]*m-ma-ša mi-*⸢*it*⸣*-ḫa-a*[*r*]	Her fever is balanced,
12	⸢*še-pa*⸣*-ša* *ka-* *ṣa-*⸢*a*⸣	her feet are cool, (and)
13	*ša pa-na i-*⸢*ge-en*⸣*-ni-*[*ḫu*]	though she was coughing before,
14	⸢*i-na-an-na*⸣ [*ul i-ge-en-ni-iḫ*]	she does not cough any more.
	Balance of Obverse lost	(Remainder fragmentary)
Rev.	Beginning lost	
1'	⸢x⸣[ ]	
2'	*iš*-[ ]	
3'	*a-*⸢*di ṣa*⸣*-at* U[D-*mi*]	
4'	*a-na šu-ul-m*[*i*]	
5'	[ ]⸢x x x x⸣[ ]	
6'-9'	destroyed	

(3) Lutz, *PBS* 1/2 71 = Waschow, *MAOG* 10/1 p. 34f.

Obv. 1	[ÌR-*ka* ^{I}*mu-kal-lim*]	[Your servant Mukallim]:
2	*a-na di-*⸢*na*⸣*-an be-lí-ja*]	I am ready to die as
3	*lu-ul-li-* [*ik*]	my lord's substitute.
4	*a-na na-a'-re* [*e*]	The male and
5	*na-a'-ra-* [*a- ti*]	female musicians,
6	^{MÍ}*e-ṭi-ir-*[*ti*]	Etirtu,
7	*ù* É *be-lí- ja*	and the house of my lord
8	*šu- ul- mu*	are well.
9	DUMU.MÍ ^{I}*a-a-ri*	The abscesses on the chest
10	*i-ša-ta-tu*$_4$ *ša ir-ti-š*[*a*]	of the daughter of Ajaru
11	*zu-ú-ta it-ta-da-a*	have secereted sweat (pus?)
12	*ša* DUMU.MÍ ^{I}*muš-*[*t*]*a-li*	those on the chest of the
13	*ša ir-ti-š*[*a*]*-ma*	daughter of Muštālu have
14	*zu-ú-ta it-ta-da-a*	likewise secreted sweat.
15	*ša* DUMU.MÍ ^{I}[*ku*]*-ri-i*	One of the [abscesses?]
16	*il-te-et* [ ]	of the daughter of Kūrî
17	⸢*ù*⸣ [ ]	and [. . . . . .]
	Balance of Obverse lost	(Break)
Rev. 1'	[*zu*]*-*⸢*ú*⸣*-ta it-*[*ta-da-a*]	[have se]creted sweat.
2'	[*ša*] DUMU.MÍ ^{I}DINGIR-*i*[*p-pa-áš-ra*]	Two (abscesses) on the chest
3'	*2 i+na ir-ti- ša*	of the daughter of Ilī-ippašra
4'	*zu-ú-ta it-ta-da-a*	have secreted sweat;
5'	*ša* DUMU.MÍ ^{I}ŠEŠ*-ni*	two on the chest of the
6'	*2 i+na ir-ti- šu*	daughter of Aḫūni
7'	*zu-ú-ta it-ta-da-a*	have secreted sweat.
8'	*ša* DUMU.MÍ ^{MÍ}*ba-ba-ti*	Those of the daughter of Babati
9'	*ù* ^{MÍ}*bi-* ⸢*it*⸣*- ti*	and Bitti
10'	*zu-ú-ta ul na-da-a*	have not secreted sweat;
11'	*a-na šu-ul-mi-ši-na*	their condition is
12'	*šu- ul- mu*	good.
13'	*8 na-at-*⸢*ba*⸣*- ki*	I sent (this message)
14'	⸢*uš*⸣*-ši ki at-b*[*a-ku*]	as soon as I had piled up
15'	[*al*]*- ta- pa- *[*ar*]	8 layers of the foundations.

(4) Radau, *BE* 17/1 31 = Waschow, *MAOG* 10/1 p. 30f

Obv.	1	[ÌR-*k*]*a* ^{I}*mu-kal-lim*	Your servant Mukallim: I am
	2	⸢*a-na di-na*⸣*-an be-lí-ja lu-ul-lik*	ready to die as my lord's sub-
	3	*a-na na-a'-re-e na-a'-ra-ti*	stitute. The male and female
	4	*ù* É *be-lí-ja šu- ul- mu*	musicians and the house of my
	5	^{MÍ}*e-ṭi-ir-ta li-pi-tu an-ni-tu*$_4$	lord are well. This disease
	6	*il- ta- pa- as-* ⸢*si*⸣	has (now) affected Eṭirtu, (but)
	7	*a-na* DUMU.MÍ ^{I}*ku-ri-i ù* ⸢DUMU.MÍ⸣ ^{I}ŠEŠ-*ni*	the daughters of Kūrî and Aḫūni
	8	*šu-ul-mu ši-ir-ši-na ṭa-ab*	are well and fine.
	9	*šum-ma be-lí i-šap-pa-ra*	If my lord so writes, they may
	10	*li-ṣa-nim-ma a-na iḫ-zi li-ši-ba*	go out and attend instruction.
	11	*ša* DUMU.MÍ ^{I}*muš-ta-li*	The abscesses of the daughter
	12	*i-ša-ta-tu ba- al- ṭa*	of Muštālu are healed, (and)
	13	*ša pa-na i-ge-en-ni-ḫu*	although she was coughing before
	14	*i-na-an-na ul i-ge-en-ni-iḫ*	she does not cough any more.
	15	*ša* DUMU.MÍ ^{I}DINGIR-*ip-pa-aš-ra*	The other abscess of the daughter
	16	*2 i-ša-tu ša uḫ-ḫu-ra-tu*$_4$	of Ilī-ippašra, which persisted,
	17	*ši-i-pa it- ta- di*	has turned to gray; her nostril,
	18	*ù na-ḫu-ri-ta-ša iṭ-ṭi-ba-aš-ši*	too, has become better.
	19	[*ša* ^{MÍ}]*bi- it- ti*	The [. . .] and back
Rev.	20	[ ]-*ša ù ša-šal-la-ša*	of Bitti
	21	[*ik-ka-l*]*a- ši*	hurt her.
	22	[DUMU.M]Í ^{I}*ḫu-ut-tir-me šu-ul-mu*	The daughter of Ḫuttirmu is well;
	23	[$^{\text{I.d}}$]⸢ x ⸣*-mu-bal-li- iṭ*	[DN]-muballiṭ
	24	*ma-áš-qí-ta i-na-di-in*	is providing the potion.
	25	⸢*ša aḫ*⸣*-la-mi- ti*	Half of the abscesses of the
	26	*mi-ši-il i-ša-ta-ti* [*uḫ*]*-ḫu-ra*	Aramean girl (still) persist.
	27	*ša* DUMU.MÍ ^{MÍ}*ba-ba-*[*ti*]	Of the abscesses of the daughter
	28	*i-ša-ta-tu ša ṣe-li-ša uḫ-ḫu-ra*	of Babati, those on her ribs
	29	*ù i-ge-en-ni- iḫ*	persist; she is coughing, too.
	30	*a-na be-lí-ja qí-*[*bí-m*]*a um-ma-a*	Say to my lord: thus (says)
	31	*la-am-zi-ni-*[*m*]*a* x[. . *š*]*a be-lí-ja*	Lamzini: (Rest fragmentary)
	32	*lu-uš-ni* x[ ] *ki* [ ]	
	33	*um-ma-a la ta-*[ ]	
	34	*du-ul-la ša* x[*lu-p*]*u-uš*	
	35	⸢*i*⸣*-na-an-na a-ma-*x[ ]*-li-ku*	
	36	[*g*]*a-ab-bi* É^{MEŠ} [ ]x-*ka*	
	37	*mi-*⸢*na*⸣*-a ep-p*[*u-uš*]x	
	38	*8*BÁN *3 qa* [ ]	
	39	⸢*me* x *ú*⸣ [ ]	
	40	⸢*a-di*⸣ [ ]	
Edge	41	⸢ x x x ⸣[ ]	

(5) Radau, *BE* 17/1 33 = Waschow, *MAOG* 10/1 p. 32f

Obv.	1	[ÌR-*ka* ^{I}*m*]*u-kal-l*[*im*]	Your servant Mukallim:
	2	[*a-na di-na-an*] *be-lí-ja*	I am ready to die as
	3	[*lu-ul*]*- lik*	my lord's substitute.
	4	[*a-na*] *na-a'-re-e na-a'-ra-a-ti*	The male and female musicians,
	5	[^{M}]^{Í}*e-ṭi-ir-t*[*i*] *ù* É *be-lí-ja*	Eṭirtu, and the house of my lord
	6	⸢*šu*⸣*- ul- mu*	are well.
	7	UD *27*.KÁM *ša mu-š*[*i-ti*]	On the night of the 27th

8	*iš-te-en a-ka-la it-ti pa-pa-si*	she was not able to finish a
9	*ú-ul ú-qá-at-ti*	single piece of bread with gruel;
10	*ba-ra-⌜ar⌝-tu$_4$ ki-i iq-tu-ú*	and when the evening watch ended,
11	*um-mu [i]ṣ-ṣa-bat-si*	she had an attack of fever.
12	⌜ x x x ⌝[.] *ki* ⌜x⌝ ^{d}IM	
13	[*-t*]*i-šu iš-ku-nu*	(Obv. 13 - Rev. 3 too fragmentary for
14	[ ]x-⌜*ra*⌝ *i-qá-ra*-x[ ]	translation)
15	[ ]⌜ x x ⌝-*ku-ti uḫ-ḫu-ra*	
16	[ ]-*tu$_4$ iṣ-ṣa-ba*[*t-si*]	
17	[MI]*qá-qá-d*[*a-ni-tu$_4$*]	
18	[ ]x[ ]	
	Balance of Obverse lost	
Rev.	Beginning lost	
1'	[ ]⌜*a*⌝-*na* x[ ]	
2'	[ ]x *si* [ ]	
3'	[ ] x UD *ša* ⌜ x ⌝[ ]	
4'	⌜*na-ap*⌝-*ḫa* [ ]	are inflamed [ ];
5'	*i-ša-ta-tu$_4$ zu-ta i*[*t-ta-da-ra*]	the abscesses have secreted sweat.
6'	UD *29*.KÁM *i-na* ^{d}UTU *na-pa-*[*ḫi*]	I sent off my messenger on the
7'	[D]UMU *šip-ri-*⌜*ja*⌝ *ul-te-*⌜*ṣa-a*⌝	29th at sunrise.
8'	⌜*ki*⌝-*i ša be-*⌜*lí*⌝ *iq-*⌜*ba*⌝-*a*	Just as my lord told me (to do),
9'	[*ṭ*]*e$_4$ e em mu-ši a-lam-ma-ad-*⌜*ma*⌝	I will keep checking and reporting
10'	[*i-n*]*a*⌜^{d}UTU *na*⌝-*pa-ḫi a* ⌜*ša*⌝-*ap-pa-*⌜*r*⌝*a*	the news of the night at sunrise,
11'	[*ṭe$_4$-e*]*-em* ⌜x⌝-*ma-nu a-*⌜*lam*⌝-*ma-ad-*[*m*]*a*	and (every) evening I will check
12'	[*i-na* ^{d}]UTU *ra-bé-e a-*[*ša-a*]*p-pa-ra*	and report the developments of the
13'	[ ]⌜ x ⌝ *ṭup-pa a-na* [*mu-uḫ*] *be-lí-ja*	day. [. . . . .] I dispatched the
14'	[*ul- te*]*- bi-* [*l*]*a*	tablet to my lord.

3.2 A letter from the physician [ ]-MUBALLIT

(6) Lutz, *PBS* 1/2 72 = Waschow, *MAOG* 10/1 p. 35ff

Obv.	1	[*a-na be-lí-ja qí-bi-ma*]	[Say to my lord]:
	2	[*um-ma-a* ^{I}DN*-mu-bal-li*]*-iṭ* ÌR*-ka-ma*	[thus (says) DN-muball]iṭ, your ser-
	3	[*a-na di-na-an be-lí-j*]*a lu-ul-lik*	vant: I am ready to die as my lord's
	4	[*aš-šum š*]*a be-lí iš-pu-ra-am*	substitute. [As to . . .] whom my lord
	5	[ ]⌜ x ⌝-*šu-*⌜*nu*⌝ *šu-ul-mu*	wrote me about, their [. . .] are well.
	6	[*š*]*a i-ra-as-su mar-ṣa-tu$_4$*	The patient whose chest is sick
	7	[*na*]*-aṣ-ma-at-ta e-te-iš-ḫ*[*u*]*-ma*	was prescribed a dressing, and
	8	*ú-ṣa-*[*a*]*m-ma- du š*[*u*]	is kept bandaged; he is also taking
	9	*ù ma-aš-qí-ta ša em-bu-ub ḫ*[*a-ši-i i*]*š-ta-na-at-ti*	a potion against tracheitis. And
	10	*ù ša-nu-ú ša i-ra-as-su i-*[ ]x-*ṣu*	the other one whose chest [. . . . . .]
	11	*šum-ma* LÚ *ki-ma iq-qí* ⌜ x ⌝[ ]	"If a man [. . .] like a door";[704]
	12	*na-aṣ-ma-ta-šu ki-i e-*[*si-ḫu*]	when I assigned a poultice for him,
	13	Ú *a-ši-i ba-t*[*i-iq*]	no *ašû* herb was available.
	14	*ù be-lí i-di-ki-i iš-te-en ša-a*[*m-mu*]	And my lord knows that if only a
	15	*ib-ba-ta-qu-ma la i-šal-li-i*[*m*]	single herb is missing, it will not
	16	*ḫa-za-an-na ki-i e-ri-šu* x[ ]	succeed. I asked the mayor to send
	17	*a-na* ^{LÚ}N[U.GI]^{Š}SAR *ki-i iš-ta-pa-ru* x[ ]x	word to a gardener, and [. . .].
	18	DUMU.MÍ ^{I}*muš-ta-li ša i-ga-an-ni-ḫu-ma la* [*id*]*-da-a*	The daughter of Muštālu who was
	19	*ma-aš-qá-ti* [*ša . .*]-⌜*ki*⌝ *ki-i aš-ta-*[*q*]*u-ú-ši*	coughing but not spitting out has
	20	*su-a-lam it-ta-da-a ù du-*x[ ]x-*ar*	started to expectorate after I gave

[704] Presumably a reference to a diagnostic text; unidentified.

21 [i+n]a-an-na ki-is ŠÀ-bi ir-ta-n[a-aš-ši]
22 ma-aš-qí-it ki-is ŠÀ-bi ki-i á[š-ta-qu-ú-ši]
23 iš-ta-na-at-ti Ú⌜ GUR$_5$! ⌝.U[Š]!
24 ù GIŠGEŠTIN.SUR.RA ba-ti-iq
25 be-lí li-še-bi-lam lu-uš-ta-aq-qí-ma
26 a-na ŠU NAM.<ER>ÍM.MA la i-tar-ši
27 DUMU.MÍ LUGAL ša um-mu iṣ-ṣa-na-ba-tu-ši
28 i-na-an-na i-na na-aṣ-ma-at-ti
29 ù ma-aš-qí-ti it- tu- aḫ
30 aš-šum Ú.ḪI.A ša a-na be-lí-ja aq-bu-ú
31 be-lí la i-ma- aš- ši
32 A.KAL nu-ḫu-ur-tim A.KAL [. . .]-ra Úpat-ra-nam
33 ša-am-mi ŠU-UL-ŠU-UL ša ki-iṣ ŠÀ-bi
34 Úpat-ra-nam Úme-er-gi-na-nu Úa-ra-ri-ja-nu
35 Únam-ruq-qu Úú-la-nu Úx[.]x-in-ni ŠÀ [
36 NUMUN ÚDILI Úkur-ka-nam Ú[. .]x
37 [. . .] NIM Úḫa-ša-na Úḫi-[. .]-ra-ni
38 [. . . .]⌜ x x x ⌝ le-si-iḫ-ma li-še-bi-lam-ma
39 [i-na] lu-ú šak-nu
40 [ ]x-ti an- na- ti
41 [ ]x am šu ú šá di i-na URUki-⌜ x x ⌝
42 [b]u um li ik ma li-il-qu-ni
43 [ ]x ša be-lí iq-bu-ú na-da-nam
44 [ ] ú-ul id-di-nam-m[a]
45 [ ]-⌜mi-iš⌝ ut-ta-na-ar-⌜x⌝
46 [i]š-pu-ra-am-ma

her [appropriate] potions; but [. . .] now she is constipated. I gave her a potion for constipation to drink, and she is taking it, (but) there is no *šarmadu* herb and drawn wine available. Let my lord send (some) so that I can have her drink, lest she develop a "hand of Curse". The princess who had repeated attacks of fever has now calmed thanks to the dressing and potion. As to the herbs of which I spoke to my lord, let my lord not forget about them. Let my lord set aside and send to me resin of asa foetida, resin of [. . .], *patrānu*, . . . herbs for constipation etc. (follows a list of 12 mostly unidentified medical plants), and let them be placed [in . . . . . .].

(The last lines of the letter are too fragmentary for translation.)

3.3 A letter from the physician ADAD-ŠAR-ILĀNI

(7) Radau, *BE* 17/1 36

Obv. 1 [ÌR-ka I.d]⌜ IM ⌝-LUGAL-DINGIRMEŠ
2 [a-na di-na-an be-lí-ja] lu-ul-lik
3 [a-na M]le-ṭi-ir-ti
4 [š]u- ul- mu
5 [ma-a']-di-iš šu-ul-mu
6 [ ]⌜ x ⌝-du-ú
Balance destroyed

[Your servant] Adad-šar-ilāni: I am ready to die [as my lord's substitute]. [. . . .], Etirtu (and) [. . . . .] are well; [. . . .] is very well.

For four more letters written by or to Middle-Babylonian physicians, see Radau, *BE* 17/1, nos. 4, 53 and 94, and Lutz, *PBS* 1/2 no. 82 (Waschow, *MAOG* 10/1, p. 37ff); these texts are too fragmentary for inclusion here. Two further letters dealing with medical matters (*BE* 17/1, nos. 21 and 22), also edited by Waschow (p. 39f), were not written by physicians and are therefore not given here.

For a MB letter possibly written by a haruspex and referring to physicians, see Lutz, *PBS* 1/2 no. 58 (Waschow, p. 21f).

4. *LETTERS TO SARGONID KINGS FROM BABYLONIAN SCHOLARS*[705]

SENDER	LETTER	CONTENTS
Aḫḫēšâ	K 4670 + BM 99229 (*CT* 54 60)	consecration of priests
	Sm 1186 (*ABL* 1062)	broken
Aplâ	K 523 (*ABL* 324)	salutation; to queen mother
Aqarâ	Bu 91-5-9,23 (*ABL* 1259)	petition
Ašarēdu	K 478 (*ABL* 254)	salutation; to queen mother
	K 552 (*ABL* 255)	acquisitions for royal library
	83-1-18,746 (*CT* 54 538)	
	83-1-18,869 (*ABL* 743)	broken
Ašarēdu qatnu	K 10736 (*CT* 54 221)	astrological matters
	83-1-18,869 (*ABL* 796 = *RMA* 274C)	astrological matters
Bēl-nāṣir	81-2-4,485 (*ABL* 765)	astrological matters
Bēl-ušēzib	K 772 (*ABL* 895 = *RMA* 274)	astrological matters
	K 1353 (*CT* 54 22)	astrological & political
	K 4684 (*CT* 54 63)	ditto
	K 6118 (*CT* 54 170)	political matters
	K 10120 + K 16127 (*CT* 54 359)	astrological matters
	K 13191 (*CT* 54 258)	astrological matters
	K 15101 + 83-1-18,47 (*CT* 54 294)	astrological & political
	Rm 280 (*CT* 54 441)	petition
	Rm 561 (*ABL* 1183)	astrological matters
	82-5-22,105 (*ABL* 1216)	astrological & political
	83-1-18,1 (*ABL* 1237)	ditto
	83-1-18,138 (*CT* 54 512)	
	83-1-18,394 (*CT* 54 523)	astrological
	Ki 1904-10-9,15 (*ABL* 1373)	astrological & political
Kudurru	K 154 (*ABL* 276)	magical & astrological
Marduk-šāpik-zēri	K 3034 + K 7655 (*CT* 54 57)	astrological omens; list of scholars
	K 5440a + 82-5-22,123 (*CT* 54 106)	resembles K 3034+
Munnabitu	K 5463 (*ABL* 928)	petition
Nabû-iqbi	K 7455 (*CT* 54 196)	broken
	Rm 198 (*ABL* 1410)	astrological matters
	81-2-4,91 (*CT* 54 463)	petition
	83-1-18,132 (*WO* 4 220 f)	petition
Nabû-šum-līšir	K 825 (*ABL* 263)	eclipse ritual, to queen mother
Nāṣiru	Bu 91-5-9,148 (*ABL* 1261)	petition; to crown prince
Nergal-īṭir	K 1055 (*ABL* 228)	petition
Ninurta-aḫ-iddin	K 22 (*ABL* 334)	acquisitions for royal library
	K 559 (*ABL* 335)	broken
Rāši-ili	K 474 (*ABL* 496)	cultic matters
	K 545 (*ABL* 497)	ditto
	K 646 (*ABL* 498)	ditto
	83-1-18,3 (*ABL* 475)	ditto
	Bu 91-5-9,39 (*ABL* 501)	denunciation
Rāši-ili son of Nurzānu	K 1002 (*ABL* 499)	petition
	K 1303 (*ABL* 500)	ditto, to crown prince
Šum-iddin	K 4789 (*ABL* 968)	construction of Esangil
	81-2-4,417 (*CT* 54 474)	broken
	83-1-18,32 (*CT* 54 506)	cultic matters
	TKSM 21/676 (*BBEA* 7 ff)	cultic & political matters

[705] Given in list form only for reasons stated in Pt.I, p.VIII.

SENDER	LETTER	CONTENTS
Tāb-ṣilli-Marduk	K 1393 (*ABL* 1448)	astrological matters
Zākir	K 467 (*ABL* 137)	ditto
	81-2-4,77 (*ABL* 702)	political matters
anonymous	83-1-18,7 (*ABL* 477)	astrological matters
name lost	K 895 (*ABL* 954)	petition
	K 5439a (*CT* 54 105)	astrological matters
	83-1-18,60 (*ABL* 1113)	astrological matters

5. *"ASTROLOGICAL" REPORTS TO SARGONID KINGS*[706]

5.1 *Assyrian writers*

Adad-šumu-uṣur	K 730 (*RMA* 135)	Sm 1179 (*RMA* 136F)
Akkullānu	K 694 (*RMA* 166)	Rm 208 (*RMA* 144B)
	K 747 (*RMA* 235)	83-1-18,191 (*RMA* 138A)
	K 1007 (*RMA* 87A)	83-1-18,205 (*RMA* 34)
	K 1304 (*RMA* 89)	83-1-18,228 (*RMA* 144)
	K 1406 (*RMA* 272A)	Bu 89-4-26,159 (*RMA* 36)
Aššur-nāṣir	K 920 (unp.)	
Aššur-šarrāni	K 775 (*RMA* 16)	Rm 207 (*RMA* 175)
Balasî	K 86 (*RMA* 91)	K 1301 (*RMA* 277F)
	K 703 (*RMA* 119)	K 1323+ (*RMA* 256B)
	K 706 (*RMA* 140)	K 1333 (*RMA* 270o)
	K 712 (*RMA* 88)	K 1335+ (*RMA* 55 = *ABL* 993)
	K 774 (*RMA* 68)	K 11046 (*RMA* 136Q)
	K 784 (*RMA* 8)	Sm 1027 (*RMA* 171)
	K 786 (*RMA* 254)	83-1-18,207 (*RMA* 274I)
	K 795 (*RMA* 138)	83-1-18,300 (*RMA* 208A)
	K 855 (*RMA* 234A)	
Bāmāju	K 92 (*RMA* 127)	83-1-18,246 (*RMA* 102)
	K 711 (*RMA* 99)	Bu 89-4-26,37 (*RMA* 81B)
	K 718 (*RMA* 161)	Bu 91-5-9,8 (*RMA* 156)
	K 871 (*RMA* 185)	
Bulluṭu	K 742 (*RMA* 196)	82-5-22,83 (*RMA* 4)
	K 787 (*RMA* 256A)	83-1-18,183 (*RMA* 76)
	K 1334 (*RMA* 114)	83-1-18,184 (*RMA* 77)
	K 1375 (*RMA* 229B)	83-1-18,185 (*RMA* 3)
	Rm 204 (*RMA* 131)	83-1-18,198 (*RMA* 232)
	81-2-4,133 (*RMA* 1)	
Ištar-šumu-ēreš	K 115 (unp., cf. *RMA* p.3[1])	K 3504 (*RMA* 198)
	K 124 (*RMA* 267)	Rm 195 (*RMA* 157D = *ABL* 1409)
	K 696 (*RMA* 7)	Rm 200 (*RMA* 159)
	K 697 (*RMA* 128)	Rm 212 (*RMA* 136P)
	K 728 (*RMA* 244)	80-7-19,57 (*RMA* 93)
	K 731 (*RMA* 206)	81-7-27,19 (*RMA* 257)
	K 733 (*RMA* 168)	82-5-22,55 (*RMA* 247)
	K 765 (*RMA* 255)	83-1-18,224 (*RMA* 21A)
	K 773 (*RMA* 136o)	83-1-18,287 (*RMA* 264)

706 This catalogue covers all "astrological" reports published in *RMA* as well as all unpublished texts of the same type identified to date (May, 1978).

(Ištar-šumu-ērēš)	K 788 (*RMA* 31)	Bu 91-5-9,14 (*RMA* 21)
	K 966 (*RMA* 277L)	Ki 1904-10-9,32 (unp.)
	K 1321 (*RMA* 252E)	Ki 1904-10-9,268 (unp.)
rab ṭupšarrī	K 693 (*RMA* 58)	80-7-19,56 (*RMA* 81)
	K 715 (*RMA* 259)	81-2-4,144 (*RMA* 109)
	K 779 (*RMA* 266)	Ki 1904-10-9,38 (unp.)
	Rm 203 (*RMA* 74)	Ki 1904-10-9,233 (unp.)
	Rm 211 (*RMA* 275)	
Nabû-aḫḫē-erība	K 692 (*RMA* 75)	Sm 1974 (*RMA* 62)
	K 705 (*RMA* 43)	81-2-4,79 (*RMA* 70)
	K 736 (*RMA* 139)	81-2-4,86 (*RMA* 209)
	K 740 (*RMA* 106)	81-2-4,109 (*RMA* 244C)
	K 748 (*RMA* 248)	81-2-4,287 (*RMA* 229)
	K 781 (*RMA* 180)	82-5-22,52 (*RMA* 96)
	K 782 (*RMA* 204)	82-5-22,79 (*RMA* 236H)
	K 839 (*RMA* 271A)	83-1-18,189 (*RMA* 54)
	K 864 (*RMA* 98)	83-1-18,190 (*RMA* 51)
	K 865 (*RMA* 274E)	83-1-18,197 (*RMA* 112)
	K 868 (*RMA* 238)	83-1-18,204 (*RMA* 212)
	K 877 (*RMA* 84)	83-1-18,227 (*RMA* 179)
	K 984 (*RMA* 274H)	83-1-18,236 (*RMA* 236G)
	K 1317 (*RMA* 191A)	83-1-18,297 (*RMA* 246G)
	K 1326 (*RMA* 252D = *ABL* 1447)	83-1-18,314 (*RMA* 81G)
	K 1508 (*RMA* 141)	83-1-18,317 (*RMA* 246A)
	K 2327 (*RMA* 236D)	83-1-18,320 (*RMA* 274G)
	K 8432 (*RMA* 57)	Bu 91-5-9,34 (*RMA* 246B)
	Sm 375 (*RMA* 103)	Bu 91-5-9,102 (*RMA* 237)
	Sm 1043 (*RMA* 258)	Ki 1904-10-9,53 (unp.)
	Sm 1073 (*RMA* 42)	
Nabû-mušēṣi	K 120a (*RMA* 94)	K 1318 (*RMA* 206A)
	K 704 (*RMA* 228)	K 14560 (unp.)
	K 710 (*RMA* 200)	K 14563 (unp.)
	K 719 (*RMA* 174)	Sm 1664 (*RMA* 6A)
	K 725 (*RMA* 205)	80-7-19,54 (*RMA* 61)
	K 767 (*RMA* 136E)	81-2-4,380 (*RMA* 244D)
	K 801 (*RMA* 118)	82-5-22,78 (*RMA* 217)
	K 866 (*RMA* 157)	83-1-18,310 (*RMA* 266B)
	K 876 (*RMA* 136L)	
Nabû'a of Assur	K 184 (*ABL* 817)	K 13116 (*ABL* 824)
	K 716 (*ABL* 819)	Rm 205 (*ABL* 825)
	K 720 (*ABL* 820)	82-5-22,37 (*ABL* 826)
	K 792 (*ABL* 821)	83-1-18,192 (*ABL* 827)
	K 802 (*ABL* 822)	Bu 91-5-9,6 (*ABL* 828)
	K 1368 (*ABL* 823)	Ki 1904-10-9,215 (unp.)
Šumāju	K 121 (*RMA* 207)	K 8960 (*RMA* 274D)
	K 695 (*RMA* 169)	83-1-18,222 (*RMA* 111)
	K 713 (*RMA* 80)	83-1-18,298 (*RMA* 246D)
Urad-Ea	K 853 (*RMA* 256C)	K 1405 (*RMA* 100)
	K 1383 (*RMA* 72)	
no name	K 727 (*RMA* 165)	DT 148 (*RMA* 129)
	K 743 (*CT* 40 21, ālu)	82-5-22,60 (*RMA* 9)
	K 798 (*CT* 28 37, ālu)	83-1-18,240 (*RMA* 136I)
	K 804 (*RMA* 40)	83-1-18,286 (*RMA* 136B)
	K 9572+ (*CT* 39 24, ālu)	

(no name)	82-5-22,82 (unp.)	Bu 89-4-26,3 (*RMA* 192)
name lost	K 777 (unp., izbu)	80-7-19,364 (*RMA* 274M)
	K 848 (unp., izbu)	81-2-4,108 (*RMA* 136)
	K 849 (*CT* 28 30)	81-2-4,504 (*RMA* 118A)
	K 854 (*RMA* 262)	82-5-22,54 (*RMA* 239)
	K 878 (*RMA* 130A)	82-5-22,84 (*RMA* 96A)
	K 994 (*RMA* 160A)	82-5-22,87 (*RMA* 277R)
	K 1320 (*RMA* 70A)	83-1-18,206 (unp.)
	K 1388 (*RMA* 6)	83-1-18,218 (*RMA* 194A)
	K 1535 (*RMA* 277G)	83-1-18,234 (*CT* 27 28)
	K 1970 (unp.)	83-1-18,236 (*RMA* 236G)
	K 6078 (*RMA* 155A)	83-1-18,292 (*RMA* 157A)
	K 12004+ (*RMA* 274K)	83-1-18,309 (*RMA* 277T)
	K 12176 (*RMA* 211A)	83-1-18,311 (*RMA* 96C)
	K 12369 (*RMA* 274L)	83-1-18,317 (*RMA* 246A)
	K 12469 (*RMA* 36A)	83-1-18,318 (*RMA* 277U)
	K 12555 (*RMA* 262B)	83-1-18,786 (*RMA* 196A)
	K 13170 (*RMA* 212A)	83-1-18,870 (*RMA* 144C)
	Sm 508 (*RMA* 277AC)	83-1-18,884 (*RMA* 277W)
	Rm 209(*RMA* 183A)	83-1-18,885 (*RMA* 81I)
	80-7-19,60 (*CT* 28 32)	Bu 89-4-26,61 (*RMA* 123A)
	80-7-19,154 (*RMA* 19A)	Bu 91-5-9,34 (*RMA* 246B)
	80-7-19,155 (*RMA* 229A)	Bu 91-5-9,38 (*RMA* 81A)
	80-7-19,343 (*RMA* 261)	Bu 91-5-9,58 (*RMA* 236C)

5.2 *Babylonian writers*

Aḫḫēšâ of Uruk	K 840 (*RMA* 13)	82-5-22,58 (*RMA* 125)
	K 1389 (*RMA* 252)	83-1-18,233 (*RMA* 236A)
	K 13087+ (*RMA* 203)	
Aplâ of Borsippa	K 758 (*RMA* 211)	K 1236 (*RMA* 277M)
	K 987 (*RMA* 190A)	K 1407 (*RMA* 79A)
(no title)	K 172 (*RMA* 46)	K 1385 (*RMA* 253A)
	K 714 (*RMA* 132)	81-2-4,82 (*RMA* 120)
	K 723 (*RMA* 197)	82-5-22,61 (*RMA* 265)
(title lost)	81-2-4,140 (*RMA* 2270)	83-1-18,312 (*RMA* 86A)
Ašarīdu 1) pānû (= 2)	K 861 (*RMA* 216)	81-2-4,105 (*RMA* 201)
	K 874 (*RMA* 27)	82-5-22,63 (*RMA* 170)
	K 1394 (*RMA* 187A)	83-1-18,174 (*RMA* 202)
	K 12388+ (*RMA* 32)	83-1-18,177 (*RMA* 87)
	Sm 86 (*RMA* 29)	Bu 89-4-26,18 (*RMA* 250)
	79-7-8,100 (*RMA* 172)	
2) son of Damqa	K 806 (*RMA* 187)	81-2-4,132 (*RMA* 221)
3) qatnu (= 4)	K 735 (*RMA* 231)	83-1-18,178 (*RMA* 220)
	K 1312 (*RMA* 136D)	
4) no title (= 3)	K 737 (*RMA* 133)	80-7-19,58 (*RMA* 210)
	K 753 (*RMA* 22B)	80-7-19,62 (*RMA* 81F)
	K 768 (*RMA* 249)	81-2-4,135 (*RMA* 242)
	K 873 (*RMA* 252A)	82-5-22,56 (*RMA* 219)
	K 955 (*RMA* 270)	83-1-18,175 (*RMA* 48)
	K 1338 (*RMA* 116A)	83-1-18,176 (*RMA* 252B)
	K 1340 (*RMA* 64A)	83-1-18,313 (*RMA* 216B)
	Sm 1232 (*RMA* 253)	

Bēl-aḫḫē-irība	K 902 (*RMA* 241)	81-2-4,84 (*RMA* 218)
Bēl-lēʾi son of Egibi,	K 188 (*RMA* 183)	K 1399 (*RMA* 24)
exorcist	K 734 (*RMA* 83)	83-1-18,775 (*RMA* 115F)
	K 761 (*RMA* 243)	
Bēl-nāṣir	K 808 (*RMA* 236)	82-5-22,1778 (*RMA* 253B)
	K 1207 (*RMA* 157C)	83-1-18,195 (*RMA* 18)
	81-2-4,81 (*RMA* 214)	83-1-18,296 (*RMA* 155B)
	82-5-22,69 (*RMA* 274P)	
Bēl-šum-iškun LÚkalû	K 700 (*RMA* 134)	83-1-18,232 (*RMA* 235A)
Bēl-upaḫḫir	Ki 1904-10-9,36 (unp.)	
Bēl-ušallim	K 6149 (*RMA* 277X)	
Marduk-šum-uṣur	K 1460 (*RMA* 252F)	
Munnabitu	K 769 (*RMA* 82)	K 1305 (*RMA* 115C)
	K 776 (*RMA* 63)	K 1398 (*RMA* 38)
	K 812 (unp.)	K 2085 (*RMA* 268 = *ABL* 1006)
	K 921 (*RMA* 274A)	
Nabû-aḫḫē-iddin of Dilbat	K 755 (*RMA* 158A)	
(no title)	K 794 (*RMA* 121)	83-1-18,244 (*RMA* 163)
	K 1373+ (*RMA* 143)	
Nabû-iqbi 1) of Cutha	K 744 (*RMA* 10)	82-5-22,72 (*RMA* 80A)
	K 789 (*RMA* 136M)	83-1-18,188 (*RMA* 249A)
	K 1329 (*RMA* 144E)	83-1-18,290 (*RMA* 101A)
	K 1380 (*RMA* 263)	
2) no title	K 18 (unp.)	81-2-4,273 (*RMA* 136H)
	K 699 (*RMA* 233)	82-5-22,51 (*RMA* 213)
	K 745 (*RMA* 177)	82-5-22,156 (unp.)
	K 933 (*RMA* 201A)	83-1-18,202+ (*RMA* 22)
	Rm 198 (*RMA* 19 = *ABL* 1410)	83-1-18,219 (*RMA* 20)
	80-7-19,154 (*RMA* 19A)	Bu 91-5-9,9 (*RMA* 110)
	81-2-4,141 (*RMA* 112B)	Ki 1904-10-9,39 (unp.)
Nabû-iqīša of Borsippa	K 756 (*RMA* 11)	82-5-22,48 (*RMA* 195)
	K 793 (*RMA* 153)	83-1-18,48 (*RMA* 155)
	K 900 (*RMA* 5)	83-1-18,186 (*RMA* 150)
	DT 304 (*RMA* 215A)	83-1-18,187 (*RMA* 49)
	81-2-4,104 (*RMA* 240)	83-1-18,241 (*RMA* 112A)
	81-2-4,107 (*RMA* 189)	83-1-18,299 (*RMA* 64)
Nabû-šum-iškun	K 19 (*RMA* 215)	81-2-4,102 (*RMA* 151)
	K 785 (*RMA* 95)	82-5-22,59 (*RMA* 230)
	K 791 (*RMA* 41)	83-1-18,200 (*RMA* 190)
	K 803 (*RMA* 17)	Bu 89-4-26,19 (*RMA* 277AD)
	80-7-19,55 (*RMA* 223A)	
Nādinu	K 1384 (*RMA* 274F)	81-2-4,89 (*RMA* 226)
	K 8393 (*RMA* 144D)	
Nergal-ēṭir	K 701 (*RMA* 14)	K 8861 (*RMA* 252C)
	K 702 (*RMA* 272B)	Sm 1062 (*RMA* 39)
	K 722 (*RMA* 78)	Rm 191 (*RMA* 146)
	K 729 (*RMA* 37)	Rm 194 (*RMA* 86)
	K 739 (*RMA* 98)	Rm 196 (*RMA* 162)
	K 741 (*RMA* 30)	Rm 197 (*RMA* 274Q)
	K 749 (*RMA* 277 = *CT* 27 45)	81-2-4,103 (*RMA* 35)
	K 763 (*RMA* 123)	81-2-4,136 (*RMA* 199A)
	K 783 (*RMA* 216C)	81-2-4,138 (*RMA* 52A)

(Nergal-ēṭir)	K 799 (*RMA* 137)	81-7-27,23 (*RMA* 208)
	K 842 (*RMA* 146A)	82-5-22,49 (*RMA* 69)
	K 856 (*RMA* 22A)	82-5-22,57 (*RMA* 186)
	K 901 (*RMA* 81K)	83-1-18,171 (*RMA* 154)
	K 907 (*RMA* 195A)	83-1-18,172 (*RMA* 243B)
	K 972 (*RMA* 225)	83-1-18,173 (*RMA* 79)
	K 1302 (*RMA* 277K)	83-1-18,208 (*RMA* 224)
	K 1306+ (*RMA* 144A)	83-1-18,221 (*RMA* 92)
	K 1309 (*RMA* 181A)	83-1-18,301 (*RMA* 277S)
	K 1322 (*RMA* 136T)	83-1-18,302 (*RMA* 149)
	K 1342 (*RMA* 207B)	Bu 91-5-9,7 (*RMA* 115D)
	K 1369 (*RMA* 157B)	1932-12-12,551 = BM 134556
	K 4708+ (*RMA* 199)	(unp.)
Rāši-ili 1) pānû	K 119 (*RMA* 182)	K 1310 (*RMA* 250A)
	K 752 (*RMA* 85)	K 1346 (*RMA* 96B)
	K 805 (*RMA* 164)	K 1395 (*RMA* 59)
	K 807 (*RMA* 148)	Sm 231 (*RMA* 273)
	K 809 (*RMA* 66)	81-2-4,83 (*RMA* 101)
	K 815 (*RMA* 269)	82-5-22,50 (*RMA* 65)
	K 843 (*RMA* 165A)	82-5-22,53 (*RMA* 60)
	K 850 (*RMA* 147)	83-1-18,230 (*RMA* 227)
	K 851 (*RMA* 244A)	83-1-18,242 (*RMA* 26)
	K 904 (*RMA* 46A)	83-1-18,243 (*RMA* 33)
	K 963 (*RMA* 245)	Bu 89-4-26,166 (*RMA* 107)
2) son of Nurzānu	K 698 (*RMA* 126)	K 1330 (*RMA* 174A)
	K 721 (*RMA* 130)	K 1331 (*RMA* 115E)
	K 811 (*RMA* 246)	82-5-22,74 (*RMA* 218A)
3) no title	K 875 (*RMA* 236B)	K 1594 (*RMA* 277B)
	K 973 (*RMA* 151A)	81-2-4,106 (*RMA* 173)
Rīmūtu	82-5-22,68 (*RMA* 265C)	83-1-18,245 (*RMA* 145)
Šāpiku of Borsippa	K 178 (*RMA* 117)	80-7-19,371+ (*RMA* 167)
	K 790 (*RMA* 265A)	81-2-4,134 (*RMA* 2)
	K 6184b (*RMA* 277A)	81-2-4,344 (*RMA* 262D)
Šumâ	83-1-18,216 (*RMA* 47)	
Šum-iddina	83-1-18,194 (*RMA* 67)	
Ṭābīja	K 1392 (*RMA* 243A)	83-1-18,181 (*RMA* 222)
	81-2-4,85 (*RMA* 12)	83-1-18,182 (*RMA* 71)
	83-1-18,179 (*RMA* 193)	Bu 89-4-26,11 (*RMA* 73)
	83-1-18,180 (*RMA* 260)	Ki 1904-10-9,28 (unp.)
Ṭāb-ṣilli-Marduk son of	K 754 (*RMA* 15)	K 1332 (*RMA* 194)
Bēl-upaḫḫir	K 1308 (*RMA* 11A)	K 1393 (*RMA* 52)
Zākir	K 770 (*RMA* 25)	80-7-19,155 (*RMA* 229A)
	K 1345 (unp., earthquake)	81-2-4,143 (*RMA* 251A)
	K 6077 (*RMA* 114A)	82-5-22,46 (*RMA* 234)
	K 8391 (*RMA* 272C)	82-5-22,67 (*RMA* 236E)
	DT 53 (*RMA* 253C)	83-1-18,196 (*RMA* 183B)
	Rm 193 (unp., cf. *RMA* p.lxxxv)	83-1-18,248 (*RMA* 122)
	Rm 201 (*RMA* 181)	Bu 89-4-26,8 (*RMA* 108)
	80-7-19,19 (*RMA* 267A = *ABL* 416)	Ki 1904-10-9,55 (unp.)
	80-7-19,59 (*RMA* 28)	
no name	82-5-22,89 (*RMA* 124)	Bu 91-5-9,161 (*RMA* 135A)

name lost

K 759 (*RMA* 184)
K 964 (*RMA* 207A)
K 967 (*RMA* 277I)
K 1300 (*RMA* 277H)
K 1307 (*RMA* 81H)
K 1311 (*RMA* 115B)
K 1314 (*RMA* 244B)
K 1316 (*RMA* 181B)
K 1324 (*RMA* 136C)
K 1336 (*RMA* 277D)
K 1339 (*RMA* 136 K)
K 1341 (*RMA* 56)
K 1344 (*RMA* 47A)
K 1347 (*RMA* 216A)
K 1557 (*RMA* 277C)
K 1586 (unp.)
K 1592 (*RMA* 116)
K 1593 (*RMA* 262C)
K 1599 (unp.)
K 1606 (*RMA* 85A)
K 1921+ (*RMA* 113)
K 1927 (*RMA* 64B)
K 1955 (*RMA* 211C)
K 5620 (unp.)
K 5723 (*RMA* 56A)
K 6182 (*RMA* 246E)
K 8407 (*RMA* 211B)
K 8704 (*RMA* 236F)
K 8713 (*RMA* 272)
K 12250 (*RMA* 211F)
K 12281 (*RMA* 265B)
K 12283 (*RMA* 23A)
Sm 694 (*RMA* 115)
Sm 885 (*RMA* 136U)
Sm 1327 (*RMA* 214A)
Rm 2,254 (*RMA* 237A)
Rm 2,345 (*RMA* 136S)
80-7-19,62 (*RMA* 81F)
80-7-19,63 (*RMA* 44)
80-7-19,65 (*RMA* 23)
80-7-19,176 (*RMA* 69A)
80-7-19,355 (*RMA* 277AB)
81-2-4,88 (*RMA* 223)
81-2-4,104 (*RMA* 240)
81-2-4,142 (*RMA* 243C)
81-2-4,145 (*RMA* 104)
81-2-4,321 (*RMA* 46B)
81-2-4,483 (*RMA* 136A)
82-3-23,112 (*RMA* 277Q)
82-5-22,64 (*RMA* 142)
82-5-22,65 (*RMA* 105)
82-5-22,66 (*RMA* 53)
83-1-18,203 (*RMA* 45)
83-1-18,212 (*RMA* 50)
83-1-18,214 (*RMA* 115A)
83-1-18,220 (*RMA* 160B)
83-1-18,225 (*RMA* 150)
83-1-18,296 (*RMA* 155B)
83-1-18,319 (*RMA* 211D)
83-1-18,322 (*RMA* 246C)
83-1-18,718 (*RMA* 262A)
83-1-18,774 (*RMA* 277V)
83-1-18,834 (*RMA* 211E)
83-1-18,881 (*RMA* 116B)
83-1-18,883 (*RMA* 277Y)
Bu 91-5-9,28 (*RMA* 136R)
Bu 91-5-9,29 (*RMA* 277Z)
Ki 1904-10-9,124 (unp.)

6. *LETTERS FROM THE NEO-BABYLONIAN AND PERSIAN PERIODS*

6.1 A letter from an astrologer to a colleague

UET 4 168 = Ebeling, *NB* 304

Obv	1	*ṭup-pi* ^{1}NÍG.GUB	A tablet from Kudurru
	2	*a-na* $^{1.d}$EN-*ri-man-ni* ŠEŠ-*šú*	to his brother Bēl-rīmanni:
	3	*ki-i uṣ-ṣu-ru* IM.DIRIG	the weather was cloudy
	4	*i-ba-áš-ši* AN.MI	while I was observing, did
	5	*it-taš-ki-na*	the eclipse take place?
	6	*ḫur-ṣa-am-ma šup-ra*	Send me a detailed report.
	7	*šá qa-bé-e li-gìn-ni-ka*	(Also) send a detailed
	8	*u ṭè-en-ka*	report of your teaching
Rev	9	x[ ] [tu?] *ka*	and your personal affairs,
	10	*šá* x[*ṣ*]*ir šá* ^{1}NUMUN-*tú*	your [. . . . .] and the [. . .]
	11	*ḫur-ṣa-am-ma šup-ra*	of Zērūtu.
		space of about 5 lines	

6.2 Orders of intercalation[707]

YOS 3 115

Obv.	1	*a-mat* L[UGAL]	A word from the king
	2	*a-na* ^{1}*kur-ban-ni*-^{d}[AMAR+UTU]	to Kurbanni-[Marduk]:
	3	*š*[*u-lu*]*m ia-a-ši*	I am well,
	4	Š[À-*b*]*a-ka lu-ú*	you can be happy.
	5	*ṭa- ab- ka*	
	6	*lu-ú ti- i- du*	For your information:
	7	ITU ŠE *a- ga- a*	I have intercalated this
	8	*šá* MU. *15.* KÁM	Addar of the 15th year
	9	*ud- di- ir- ri*	(540 BC, reign of Nabonidus)[708]

Clay, *YOS* 3 196

Obv	1	IM ⌜^{1}⌝NUMUN-*ia*	A tablet from Zērija
	2	*a-na* ^{1}*ki-na-a*	to Kīnâ
	3	*u* $^{1.d}$AG-ŠEŠ-MU ŠEŠ^{MEŠ}-*e-a*	and Nabû-aḫ-iddin, my brothers:
	4	^{d}EN *u* ^{d}AG *šu-lum u* TIN	may Bēl and Nabû ordain well-being
	5	*šá* ŠEŠ^{MEŠ}-*e-a liq-bu-ú*	and life for my brothers.
	6	*lu-ú ti-da-a'*	For your information:
	7	^{ITU}KIN *di-ri*	the month Ulūlu is intercalary.

Possible dates for this letter are year 2 or 9 of Cyrus (537 or 530 BC) or year 3 of Cambyses (527 BC); see Parker + Dubberstein, *Babylonian Chronology* (1956), p. 2.

Clay, *YOS* 3 15

Obv	1	IM ^{LÚ}⌜*qí*⌝-*pa-a-ni*	A tablet from the delegates
	2	*šá* É.SAG.Í⌜L⌝	of Esangil
	3	*a-na* ^{LÚ}ŠÀ.TAM *u* $^{1.d}$AG-ŠEŠ-MU	to the "bishop" and Nabû-aḫ-iddin,
	4	ŠEŠ^{MEŠ}-*e-nu*	our brothers:
	5	^{d}AG *u* ^{d}AMAR+UTU *a-na*	may Nabû and Marduk
	6	ŠEŠ^{MEŠ}-*e-nu*	bless our
	7	*lik- ru- bu*	brothers.
	8	*lu-ú ti-da-a'*	For your information: see, we are writing
	9	*a-mur ni-il-tap-rak-ku-nu-ši*	to (tell) you (that) the (current) month
	10	ITU *di-ir*	is intercalary.

Written in the reign of Cyrus or Cambyses (538 to 522 BC), see Parker + Dubberstein, *Babylonian Chronology* (1956), 1 f.

Clay, *YOS* 3 152

Obv	1	IM $^{1.d}$AMAR+UTU-ŠUR	A tablet from Marduk-ēṭir,
	2	^{1}*mu-še-zib*-^{d}AMAR+UTU	Mušēzib-Marduk,
	3	^{1}*ki-na-a* $^{1.d}$AMAR+UTU-MU-DÙ	Kīnâ, Marduk-šum-ibni,
	4	^{1}*mu-še-zib*-^{d}AMAR+UTU	Mušēzib-Marduk
	5	*u* $^{1.d}$AG- TIN- *iṭ*	and Nabû-uballiṭ
	6	*a-na* ^{LÚ} ŠÀ. TAM	to the "bishop",
	7	^{LÚ}TU. É ME[Š]	the temple enterers
	8	*u* ^{LÚ}*ki-niš-ti*	and the (lower) priesthood

707 Cf. commentary on *LAS* 287.

708 For the date of this document see Parker + Dubberstein, Babylonian Chronology (1956), p. 1.

	9	*šá* É. AN. NA	of Eanna,
	10	ŠEŠ-*e-ni* ^{d}AG *u* [^{d}AMAR]+UTU	our brothers: may Nabû and
	11	*a-na* ŠEŠ-*e-ni*	Marduk bless
	12	*lik- ru- bu*	our brothers.
Edge	13	*a- mat* LUGAL	The king has issued (the
	14	*ši- i*	following) order:
Rev	1	^{ITU}ŠE *di-ir*	the month of Addāru is intercalary;
	2	*par-ṣi-ku-nu*	perform your rites
	3	*ina* ^{ITU}ŠE *šá it-*⸢*ti*⸣	in the Addāru which
	4	^{ITU}BARAG [O]	merges with Nisannu
	5	*ṭi- bu- ú*	(i.e., Addāru II)
	6	*a-ki-i* IGI-*i*-[*ti*]	as previously.
	7	*ep- šá- a'*	We are writing
	8	*ki-i na-qut*-[*ti*]	(this) to you
	9	*ni-il-tap-rak-k*[*u-nu-ši*]	in all seriousness;
	10	*ina* UGU- *ḫi*	don't be neglectfull
	11	*la ta-šil-la-a'*	about it!

6.3 Royal order concerning *kalû* chanters

Clay, *YOS* 3 3 = Ebeling, *NBU* 3

Obv	1	*a-mat* LUGAL	A word from the king
	2	*a-na* $^{1.d}$NIN.URTA-LUGAL-⸢ŠEŠ⸣	to Ninurta-šar-uṣur,
	3	$^{1.d}$AG-*na-din-* NUMUN	Nabû-nādin-zēri
	4	*u* $^{1.d}$AMAR+UTU-KAR-ir	and Marduk-īṭir:
	5	*šu-lum ia-a-ši*	I am well;
	6	ŠÀ-*ba-ku-nu*	you can be
	7	*lu-u ṭa-ab-ku-nu-ši*	happy.
	8	UD-*mu ṭup- pi*	The very day you
Rev	9	⸢*ta*⸣- *m*[*u*]- ⸢*ru*⸣	see my tablet,
	10	*ḫa-* ⸢*an*⸣- *tiš*	quickly (see to it that)
	11	^{LÚ}UŠ. KU ^{MEŠ}	the chanters
	12	*a-na* UD.5.KÁM	reach me
	13	*šá* ^{ITU} ŠE	by the 5th
	14	*lik-šu-du-nu*	of Addāru.
	15	UD.⸢8⸣.KÁM	I shall offer
	16	*ḫa- ru- ú*	the *ḫarû* (libation)
	17	*a nam-din*	on the 8th.

ADDENDA AND CORRIGENDA

LAS 1 r5 for "be free" read "get free" (*li-ri-qu-u-nê*)

7 r7 restore *ina* [EGIR (^{d}*30*)] "behind (the moon god)"

8 r5 *ú-šá-an-ṣu-u*

11 r6 *ṭa-a-ba*

14:14f ⸢*a*⸣-[*bu-tú*] ^{15} *in!-nu-*⸢*u*⸣ [*ši-i*]"it is a matter concerning us"

r9 for "side of the moon" read "rear side of the moon"

15 r11 read *a-ḫu-lam-ma* ^{LÚ}*Na!-ba!-a-a-ti* and render: "Let us say *aḫulap* to the Nabateans! Why? Are they not enemy kings? They will not submit under the king's chariot."

21 r4' DÙG.G[A *lìb-bi*] ^{5} ḪÚL *lìb-bi* x[. . .]

26:8f read [^{MUL}*Ṣal*]-*ba*[*t!-a-n*]*u*! T[A*] ŠÀ *ir-ti* ^{9} [*ša* ^{MUL}GÍR.TAB *ú*]-*ṣa-a*, and render: "Mars is issuing from the breast of Scorpio"

r8' "I attached (the tablet) to the hem of his (garment)"

28:12 restore [*ma-a* UD *29*].KÁM*, and render: " 'A solar [eclipse occurred on the 29]th', [we shall] perform its [apotropaion]"

29:10 ^{LÚ}ÌR!^{MEŠ} "servants"

13ff "were preparing a strong horse harnessed in Kushite trappings for the triumphal entry (into Babylon) in the town of Labbanat"

30:11 ŠÉŠ

38:11 [*ina*] ⸢É⸣^{LÚ}*qa-tin-ni* LUGAL

r4 *i-šá-ti*

r17 *ú-gam-ma-ra*

39:5 *ina* UGU ⸢*ṭup!*⸣-[*pi*] "concerning the tablet"

9ff *1-en šu!-*[*ú*] / *ṭup-pu! ša* ⸢x x⸣ [*ina lìb-b*]*i* / *šá-aṭ-ṭa-ra-a-ni* "one particular tablet in which the . . . are written"

41 r9ff *ki-i ḫa-an-ni-i-e* ^{10} EN.NUN *šá* ^{d}UTU *2* ITU^{MEŠ} ^{11} *ni-na-aṣ-ṣar ina* UGU

42:13 "(the watch) is strong"

44 r4f read [u_4*-m*]*u an-ni-i-u* / [*l*]*a!-mì-i-ni* "this being an 'evil' day, I shall write again tomorrow"

50 r4f "he will answer you with a favourable oracle"

53 r10 *na-si-ki*!

59 r3f "the king went away until the 4th month"

60:12f "reports from all astrologers"

16 *ur-ke-e-et*

61:7 *la áš-pu-ra*

62:10' [*mu-šu*] not [u_4*-mu*]; translate accordingly

64 r11 *qa-bi*

65 r5 [*lu*]-*še-tì-iq-ú-neš-šú-*[*nu*]

r19 restore [*ár-ḫ*]*iš*, and render: "The king should not waver (but) [quick]ly promote him"

66 r6ff *ina šap-la* [$^{\text{MUL.LÚ}}$ḪUN.GÁ] ^{7} *ina pu-ut* ^{MUL}[UDU.IDIM.SAG.UŠ] ^{8} *li-is-hur* [^{MUL}UDU.IDIM. SAG.UŠ] "it (= Venus) should presently be situated under [constellation Aries], opposite the planet [Saturn]; [Saturn] is the star of the king"

66:2 [^{I}*Ba-la-si-i*] not [$^{\text{I.d}}$PA-PAP^{MEŠ}-SU]

67:12 restore *1-e*[*n* u_4*-me*] "during one [day]"

r1ff I MUL ^{d}[AM]AR+UD ^{2} MI-*ma* ⸢*it-ta*⸣*-n*[*a-mar*] ^{4} *ina* MU BI Á. [SÌG GÁL-*ši*] "If the star of Marduk is black but constantly visible, there will be *asakku* disease"

LAS 71 Crit. App. 14’: ḪUL scribal error for *ù*

73:6.11 *ma-šar-te* “muster”

79:9f *lik-ru-bu* ^{10}*lu-šal-li-mu-ka* “may (. . .) bless my lord, and may they keep you in good health”

80:8 *ziq-pu*

98:4 “moon” not “sun”

100:6’ “god” not “moon”

102:1’ff *lik-ru-b*]*u*! ^{2}*m*[*a*!*-ṣar*]-⸢*tú*! *šá*!⸣^{d}!*30*! $^{3'}$ *ni-ta-ṣar*

6’ff *ki-ma ip*[*-ta-šar* ^{d}*3*]*0* $^{7'}$*né-ta-m*[*ar (la) a-ki* ^{d}]*30*! $^{8'}$*šá* UD *29*.[KÁM* *šu*]*-u* “when (the clouds) dis-[persed], we saw [the m]oon; [it] was [(not) like the] moon of the 29[th day]. The 3rd day . . .”

106:1’ *in-na-m*[*ir*!*-u-ni*; render: “What do you have for [the month] in which it appe[ar]ed?”

3’ [*it-ta-mar*] “it appeared”

r3f *ù šu-*[*t*]*ú*! [*ina* ^{d}UTU.ŠÚ.A] ^{4}*in-nam-m*[*ar*! “but (Mercury) him(self) is visib[le as evening star]”

108:2’ NUN GABA.RI NU [TUKU . . .]

3’ *ša* ⸢*ta-mar-ti*⸣

109:5-13 “On the 29th of Ajāru, from the moment of daybreak until the day had advanced [n hours], the light of the sun was reduced. Its solution is as follows: ‘[If the sun l]ights up but does not intensify its radiance, the sun god is angry with the king of the land. If the sun is dark, the king of Akkad will die.’ ‘Its light is reduced, variant: dark’ (means) there is no [apotropaic ritu]al for the case.”

120:10 for “Virgo” read “Spica”
“There will be heavy rain (and) Adad will thunder”

122:12f insert: “May the grant the king, my lord, name and seed, offspring and progeny”

128 r10’ *iḫ-*⸢*te*!⸣*-ṭu-u*

129:8 ^{TÚG}*pi*!*-tu-tu*

130:6f “to the son of the king of the world, my lord”

136:9 [*ma-a a-du* UD] [*8*].KÁM “until the 8th of Ulūlu”

138 r1 delete *2* after ^{LÚ}ŠU.U.I

140:9 for “the god got up because of the sin” render: “a god has stood in the *pūt upni*”

145:18 for “Rev.” read “Edge”

146 r3 ⸢DUMU.LUGAL⸣

147:9 better “Chief *Cook*”

152 r3 “since he purged”

163:8ff “As to the people on whom the king, our lord, wrote to us: ‘Can’t you clarify which (of them) have gone out?’ those who have not performed (the ritual) should go out tomorrow (and) perform (it); the king our lord knows . . .”

164:9 possibly [*nu-t*]*a-as-si-ik* “[We a]ssigned”

11 possibly [EME].GI$_7$*-ti* “[Sum]erian (uššburrudas)”

r1 *ša mé-eḫ-ri* “the (incantations) of the antiphone (series)”

167:12 *šá ḫa-liq-ti* UZU! “the (ritual) of the (namburbi) Loss-of-Flesh”

r13 *šam-ḫír*

173:11ff “It took us 5-6 days even to get ready with the preparation of the figurines which the king saw (yesterday)”

r8 “refrain series” not “series Opponent”

174 r6 “Nabû-rība-aḫu” not “Nabû-murīb-aḫi”

175:5’ [*šá-n*]*i-ú-ti* “the others”

177 r2 *ug-da-d*[*am-mir(-u-ni)*]

179:9 *ma-a* ⸢*ina* KÁ.DIL⸣.ÀM *te-te-*⸢*mir*⸣ “bury (it) at the outer gate”

181:7ff “It is very hot’, it must be hot. To what purpose are we doing (this)? Didn’t he mean the heat when he said: ‘It should make him sweat’? But why . . .”

r3 for “bandages” read “(amulet) string”

183:6 [*ša*] ⸢*e*!⸣*-na*!*-a-te* “[of] eyes”

186:11 SUḪUŠ

187 L.E. [*ina tar-ṣi* ^{d}]UTU *ni-šak-kan* “we shall place (them) [before] Šamaš”

LAS	190 r3ff	[UD 7.K]ÁM* *ša* ^{ITU}DU$_6$ . . . [U]D 8!.KÁM* KÁ *pa-a-ti* "Bēl is dressed [on the 7]th of Tašrītu . . . the gate is kept open on the 8th"
	195:13	*šu-ru-up-t*[*ú šá* LUG]AL! "the (funeral) burnin[g (provided) by the ki]ng"
	198 r8f	"Bēl and Nabû have given the king a beautiful hand"
	199:7	restore [*ket-t*]*u*! and render: "Is this [the truth]?" Delete "servant" on next line
	r3ff	*ù šu*[*m!-ma*] "if he will not go safely and happily where he intends to go"
	204:8	"tomorrow" not "for tomorrow"
	206 r3	for "inspector" read "runner"
	208:9	*ṣip-pir-ra-a-te*
	r3	UD [*28/29*.KÁ]M "on [the 28/29t]h"
	r8	for "should (the ritual) be performed" read "should I perform (the ritual)"
	209:11	for "performed by me" read "which I had made"
	210 r1ff	r^{1} *qí-ba-a-ni* LUGAL ^{2}*li-ṣur ša i-šá-tú* ^{3}*la-pit-u-ni* LUGAL *la e-kal* ^{4}*ku-zip-pi ša ta-ri-ti* ^{5}LUGAL *ina* UGU-*šú i-na-áš-ši* ^{6}*a-na šal-ši*
	211:14f	"For what reason did Šumâ hurry from Calah . . ."
	r15f	"Why did he hasten to perform (it)?"
	215:6	*lik-ru-bu* not *lik-tu-nu*
	217 r2	for "kledon" read "oracle/utterance"
	218 r5	insert "a substitute figurine made of clay of garden ditch"
	r7	for "7 confederates of" read "5 *illat*-gods; the daughter of fat"
	r15	for *an-ni-u* restore *dul-lu*
	219 r4	for "weakling" read "Baby"
	r5ff	"until (. . .) your gods reckoned him among (grown-up) people"
	223:11	[SIG$_5$ SU]M^{MEŠ}-*šú*
	224 r10'	for "gap" read "shortage"
	232 r2f	[*id-du-bu-ub*] / *ma-a a-du la* AN.M[I *iš-kun-u-ni*] "[he spoke with them], saying: "Before the eclips[e occurs] . . ."
	233:9'	for "constellation Virgo" read "star Spica"
	10'	[ZI-*ut*] BURU$_5$ "invasion of locusts"
	r1'	[*šá-ru-r*]*i na-ši* "it is luminous"
	r2'	perhaps [. . . ḪU]L SU.BIR$_4$^{KI} "bad omen for Assyria"
	r3'	[. . *an*]-*nu-te ni-suḫ*$_4$ "we will extract these . . ."
	234:9	after "again" insert "at the command of Illil"
	r5	"Let them find out where the evil (portended by) the eclipse has materialized and eradicate it"
	235 r9	insert "[. . .] did not panic" (*la ig-ru-ur*) before "(When) the day arrived . . ."
	239:1'	for ⌜*ù*!⌝ read ⌜*ú*!⌝
	r4	I.^{d}AG-AD-KALAG!
	242:7'	⌜*a*!⌝-*sa-al*
	15'	LÚ *tur*-⌜*ta*!⌝-*nu*!
	244 r5ff	[. .] *ina* ŠÀ ⌜x⌝[.] ^{6}⌜^{d}PA⌝ *le-ru*-⌜*ub*⌝ ^{7}[*bé-e*]*l* LUGAL EN ^{8}⌜*e*⌝-*ru-ub*-⌜*ú-ni*⌝ "The king my lord should enter into the [. . .] of Nabû, (and) as soon as the king my lord has entered, he (= the god?) should come to meet him"
	246:9	*an-ni-ju-u*
	247:14ff	"Did the king my lord speak of his own men? All the ob[edient servan]ts who have remembered their orders are dying of throbbing heart because of this talk of the king. Aššur and the great gods bound . . ."
	r16	for ^{Ú}BU read ^{Ú}GÍD and delete the translation "chaff"
	r28	"I left as soon as the king my lord sent for me"
	248:13	for "let them do" read "let him do"
	L.E.	NA$_4$ *mu*-⌜*ṣa*!⌝
	249:4'	for "conjure" read "adjure"
	250:13	for "weakling" read "Baby"

LAS 251:8ff [*ina* UGU *li-ip-p*]*i* ^{9}[*ša* NUMUN] Ú[*mar*]*-ta-kal* (. . .) ^{11}[*ša a-n*]*a* MÚD KIR$_4$ *pa-*⌜*ra*⌝*-si* ^{12}[*a-ki an-ni*]*-e e-pu-šú* ^{13}[. . . .]x *ina* MÚD ^{GIŠ}ERIN ^{14}[*i-ḫi-qu i*]*na* ^{SÍG}*tab-re-e-bi* "[As to the tampo]ns [of *mar*] *takal* [seed] on which [the king] my lord wrote to me, [those which] are (intended) to stop nasal hemorrhage are prepared [as follo]ws: [they crush *martakal* seed, mix] (it) with cedar resin, [wra]p (the mixture) in red wool . . . ."

17 [*ina na-ḫi-ri i-š*]*ak-ku-nu* "insert (the tampons) [in the nostrils]". Thus also in Rev. 5 and 15(!)

r3 UZUBAL probably a mistake for ^{ŠEM}BAL "styrax"

r6 [. . . SAḪAR] *šá* ⌜*su-qi*⌝ *er-bet-ti* "[dust] from crossroads"

r14 [*ina* (ŠÀ) *ni*]*-ip-šú* "[in a t]uft of wool"

252:12 *i-da-te* not *i-da-at*

253 r2ff [*ina* ŠÀ *uz-ni*] *lu-na-ti-k*[*u i-da-te*] ^{4}*lu-qa-at-t*[*i-ru*] ^{5}*ki-ma uq-ṭa-t*[*e!-ru*] ^{6}*lu-sa-ḫi-ru* [*re-eḫ-ti* ÌxGIŠ] ^{7}*lu-na-ti-ku in*[*a* ^{SÍG}*tab-re-bi*], and translate the whole passage beginning Obv. 13 as follows: "Subsequently I am sending off (an assortment of) drugs to be fumigated. The *kanaktu* and *nikiptu* oil which I dispatched should be first dripped [into the ears], [thereafter] let them do the fumig[ation]. After they have fumi[gated], they should repeat (the procedure), drip [the rest of the oil] upo[n (a tuft of) red wool (and) insert (it)] into the ear(s) . . ."

254:11 for IGI^{2}*-šú* read PI!^{2}*-šú* and translate (beginning Obv. 8): "The child is much better. (As to) this abscess behind his ear, I fastened on it a plaster slackening against its tip. Yesterday . . . "

r5 for "clotted blood" read "pus"

255 L.E. better: "I set off [as soon as the king] wrote to me"

257:6f restore [ina UGU *bu-ul-ṭi*] ^{7}*ša pi-'a-ri*, and translate: "[As to the cure] of the blotches . . ."

258:18 for *eṣ*]*-ma!-a-te* rend *e*]*-na-a-te* "eyes"

264 r6 for "Nabû-murīb-aḫi" read "Nabû-rība-aḫu"

265 r4' restore *ša šu-gu-mé-*[*e* (PI^{2})] and translate: "salves, fumigations and potions for buzzing (ears)"

267 Reverse the order of sides and restore Rev.(!) 1: [DN$_1$ DN$_2$ *a-na* LUGAL EN*-ja*] *lik-ru-bu*

269:10 restore ^{d}[U]GU[R] "Nergal" (i.e., the planet Mars)

272:15 for ÉR.ŠÀ.ḪUN.GA read ÉR.ŠÀ.ḪUN.GÁ

276:7 read "It hasn't been brought" for "I hasn't . . ."

277:16 restore [*(ú)-šu-un-gal-l*]*i* "dragons"

r26ff restore [*le*]*-e-pu-š*[*u šu-mu ša* MAN EN*-já*] ^{27}*a-na da-ra-*[*a-ti liš-ku-nu*] ^{28}*a-na ma-ṣar-ti š*[*a* É.DIN=GIR^{MEŠ}], and translate: "Let them perform the work of the temple (and) [establish the name of the king, my lord,] for ever; [let] the king, my lord, [not neglect] the guard of [the temple]"

279 r4 for *ṣu-ra-a-ri* read *su-ra-a-ri*

280:13 for *šu-u u* ^{MÍ}É.GAL*-šú* read *šu-u* ^{MÍ}É.GAL*-šú*

281 r10ff read: [*lú-u*] *u-di i-*[*su-ri a-n*]*a* MAN EN*-já i-qab-bi-i-u* ^{11}*ma-a* TA* *la-bi-r*[*i* NÍG.ŠID^{MEŠ}] ⌜*la*⌝ *ú-pu-šú* ^{12}*i-sa-na-li-i-*[*u ina* (ŠÀ) *ti*]*-il-ti* ^{13}*ša ḫur-sa-an š*[*a* ^{I}*Bur-na-bu-r*]*i-ja-áš* ^{14}MAN K[Á.DI]NGIR^{KI} *q*[*a-bi ma-a ḫ*]*ur-sa-an* ^{15} L[Ú*]SI[PA^{MEŠ} NÍG.ŠID^{MEŠ} *ṭup-pa-šú a-na* MAN] EN*-já ú-se-bi-la*, and translate: "The king, my lord, [should] know (this). Perhaps they are telling the king, my lord: 'In olden times, [no accounts] (of oxen and sheep) were made.' (If so), they are cheating. [In] an ordeal proverb attributed to [Burnabur]ijaš, king of B[aby]lon, it is s[aid: "The (time of) accounting is] the ordeal of the sheph[erds].' I am dispatching [the relevant tablet to the king], my lord."

281:17f translate: "Supply, as in olden times, the regular ram offerings from the estates of the citizens of Borsippa!"

25ff "They turn the blesser's ungelded bulls to themselves from the (temple) gate, (and) have served (such bulls) on the table of Nabû"

r3ff better: "(But) all the citizens of Borsippa are complaining: "The oxen (and) sheep of Nabû are being concealed from the country!" Why do they . . ."

283:6 for AN.NE.SI read *an-ni-e*

r4' for KUR⌜*1*⌝*-*[*sa-na*] read KUR⌜*1*⌝*-*[*tú-'e*]. Thus also in r8'.

r6'f translate: "The inhabitants of Akkad are glazing (and) gilding kiln-fired bricks"

284:9 read ⌜*ša*⌝ for ⌜TA*⌝? and translate: "They should acquire (and) bring *elallu* limestone for the king mylord's stand in Esangil"

LAS 284:15 restore [*nu-uk* n *in*]*a+1*! KÙŠ-*aja*

18 perhaps [*ina* (ŠÀ) *uš-še i-š*]*ak-ku-nu* "they will be placed [in the foundations]"

22 for "conjured" read "adjured"

r11f better: "80 sheikhs have conspired with each other; no news of them has been heard"

r21 for [*ša*] ⌜É⌝.DINGIR read [TA* *p*]*a!-an* and translate: "[belon]ging to the Cuthaeans"

288:7' for "sprinkled" read "swelling"

12' restore [*na-piš-ta-šú gi-mi*]*l-ma*, and translate: "O Aššūr, save [the life of] the one who puts his trust in you"

289:3' restore MU[LŠU.GI] "Perseus"

r4 translate: "the gods will get angry, righteousness will be put to shame (*me-še-er ib-ba-áš-ši*), bright things . . . "

290 r3 for *ri-ib-si* read *ri-ip-si*

r6 after "it is on the path of the Anu stars" insert "and I sent the relevant interpretation to the king, my lord"

290 r9 for "Auriga" read "Chariot"

r11 cancel "retained (its course)" and leave ik-ri-im untranslated

291:5' for "high" read "narrow"

14'f translate: "let them glaze kiln-burnt bricks (and) brick up the quay(-wall) of Ezida"

r17 for "Scorpio" read "Leo"

292:2'ff restore *lu-ši-i*[*b ú-ma-a an-nu-rig*] 3'[*1*] ⌜*me*⌝ u_4-*me un-tal-li* LU[GAL-*us-su ga-am-rat*], and translate: "He should sit for a hundred days'. He has [just now] completed the hundred days, (and) [his] ki[ngship is finished]"

11'f restore [MUL*Ṣal-ba*]*t-a-ni ša ina pa-ni-ti a-n*[*a* . . .] 12'[MULPA.BIL.SA]G! *iṭ-ḫu-u-n*[*i*], and translate: "Mars which previously was approaching [Sagittari]us . . ."

4' for *iš-*[*pur-an-ni* read *iš-pur-*[*an-ni*

r3 for LÚ**sa-a*[*k-lu* read LÚ*sa-x[and cancel the translation "common man"

r4 read LÚ*SANGA *ša* dP[A

r7 read I*Si-i-li* KUR*Gam-*[*bu-la-aju*] and translate: "Sîli, a native of Gam[bulu]"

r8 read É *I!-ba-a*[*ju* "from the house of Ibâ"

r15 [*ina l*]*i-ba-a-ni ša* d*Ta*[*š!-me-*tu_4]

293:7 for "Bīt-Šarruku" read "Dūr-Šarruku"

294:12' for [*ú*]*-kal-la* read [*a*]*-kal-la*

298:23 better *at-ta aḫ-ḫur* "you are still [. . . . . .]"

302 r7' for "hearth" read "Kanūnu-festival"

304 r2'f restore [*lu-bi*]*l-u-né ku-zip-*[*pi*] 3'[*š*]*a* SÍG KUŠE.[SÍRMEŠ] "[let] them [brin]g me woolen garments and leather san[dals]"

308:12 for "wear" read "carry"

309:24f for "regular rations of emmer wheat" read: "regular deliveries of barley and emmer"

r1f read "cook" for "baker", "confectioner" (LÚSUM.NINDA) for "butler", and "baker" (LÚNINDA) for "miller"

r20 restore *i*[*p-ti-qi-su ke*]*t-tu* and translate: "Sennacherib ap[pointed] him to supervise their "bread'; indeed . . ."

310 r9 read ⌜LÚSANGA 2-*u*⌝ "assistant priest"

311:9 for "entered (the akītu-temple)" read "re-entered (Ešarra)"

r14 for *i ša ku nu* read *i-šá-ku-nu*

312:8f better: "If there is anything left of it, let them send (it) to me"

r25'f "(As to) the son of the priest of the Šamaš temple, his name is Zārî, (he is) the son of Nādin-apli"

314:9 for *iq-ti-*[*bi-a*] read *iq-ṭi-*[*bi-a*]

318:4 better: "The king, my lord, knows (that) on account of this (association) the cross is the badge of the crown prince". For *be-lí* read *be-li* (thus also in line 5).

r6 cancel the translation of *né-ra-ki-šá* ("its length")

r10 for *uš-ta-pal-u-ni* read *uš-ta-bal-u-ni*

LAS 319 r1f better: "The writing-board (edition) of *Enūma Anu Enlil* which we have written"

r6 read "3 stars each (month)" for "the stars, three of each"

322:2' read *áš-šú*! *ke-e-na-ti-ka* and translate: "because of your truthfulness"

5' read $^{\text{KU]R!}}$*Šu-me-ru* "Sumer"

r1 *ma*]*n!-gu!-u! šu!-u! tu-mu-lu*

r7]⸢*man*⸣!-*gi-ka*; cancel *nu* at the end of the line

323 r1 for DU^{MEŠ} read *iš kul* (collated; obscure)

324:6 restore [*ina* EGER ^{MUL}MAŠ.TAB.BA *in-na-mar-ma*] and translate: "Jupiter [is visible 'behind' Gemini]"

5 restore [^{MUL}MAŠ.TAB.BA GUB] and translate: "If Jupiter [stands] 'behind' [Gemini]"

9ff translate: "Now, as soon as I saw [its appearance], I wrote (this report) to the king, my lord. I shall afterwards, when it has risen higher (and) approached Cancer, extract (quotations for) another report . . . ."

10 for EN-*já* read EN-[*j*]*a*

325 r7 for "permanent" read "normal"

r9 for ITU.KÁM* read ^{ITU}ŠE!

326 reverse the order of sides

7 translate "sun is the star of the king" instead of "Saturn is (namely) the star of the king (too)"

r3 better: "If the sun stands above the moon (*or*) below . . ."

328:7f better: "This (prediction) was (also included) in the sign of Jupiter"

334:7 restore *i*[*n-na-mir-u-ni*] and translate: "which ap[peared] in the constellation Aries"

r2 for *ù*$_4$ read *ù*

335:5 for *iq-ṭi-bi* read *aq-ṭi-bi*

6 this line reads [T]A*! ⸢TÚG!*lu*⸣-[*bu-si* . . . .]; the passage Obv. 5f should accordingly be translated "I spoke about the clothes; Urad-Ea [. . . . . , came (?)] with the cl[othes . . ."

340:6 for *ne-er-ḫu-uṣ* read *né-er-ḫu-uṣ*

B 1ff better: "It may not be good to let the men go to the roof at dawn. Some pretext should be invented . . ."

341:6 the tablet reads ^{6}*re-ḫu-ú-*[*ti*] ^{7}*ina am-ba-si* ⸢d⸣[DN]

342:2 for LÚ read LÚ*. Thus also in line 4.

Revised text and translation of LAS 331

Obv.	1	[^{d}A]G *ù* ^{d}A[MAR+UD *a-na* LUGAL EN-ja *lik-ru-bu*
	2	[*ina* UGU D]UB^{MEŠ} ⸢*ša*⸣ [. . . . . (.)]
	3	[*ù* D]UB^{MEŠ} *a-ḫu-ú-*[*ti* . . . . . . (.)]
	4	[*ša*] ⸢*a*⸣*-na* LUGAL EN-*já a*[*q-bu-u-ni*]
	5	[*ú-ma*]*-a an-nu-rig na-ṣ*[*u-ni šum-ma ina* IGI LUGAL]
	6	[EN-*j*]*á ma-ḫi-ir lu-še-*[*ri-bu-šú-nu* LUGAL *be-lí*]
	7	[*le*]-⸢*e*⸣*-mur ḫa-ra-me-ma* [. . . . . .]
	8	[^{GIŠ}Z]U^{MEŠ} URI^{KI}*-ú- t*[*i* . . . . (.)]
	9	[^{GIŠ}ZU]^{MEŠ} *Aš+šur*^{KI}*-ú-ti* [. . . . (.)]
	10	[. . . D]UB^{MEŠ} *la-áš-ṭur* [. . . . .]
	11	[. . . T]A* *an-na-kám*-ma* ⸢*ú*⸣-[. . . .]
	12	[*LUGAL be-l*]*í* *li-* x[ ]
Edge		uninscribed
Rev.	1	[*ù ina* UGU *ša* L]UGAL *be-lí* [*iš-pur-an-ni*]
	2	[*ma-a* . . .] *li-* *in-* [. . .]
	3	[. . DUB^{MEŠ} *a-ḫ*]*u-ú-ti š*[*a aq-bu-u-ni*]
	4	[. . .]x-*šú-nu is-se-niš l*[*i* . . . .]
	5	[*ú-la-a*] *ina ṭup-pi šá-ni-im-*[*ma liš-ṭu-ru*]
	6	[*mi-i*]*-nu* *ša* LUGAL *be-lí* [*i-qab-bu-u-ni*]
		- -
	7	[^{d}30 *š*]*a in-na-mir-u-ni a-na šu*[*l-me* . . . . . .]
	8	[LUGAL *be*]*-lí ina* ^{GIŠ}ZU *le-e-*[*mur* . . . . . .]
	9	[*ši-t*]*i-ni la-mur* : I *30 ina* IGI.LAL-*šú* AG[A *a-pir* SAG.UŠ-*ma*]
	10	[. . .]x : I *30 ina* IGI.LAL-*šú* KI.GUB-*su* [GI.NA GUB-*iz*]
	11	[I *ina* UD].NÁ.ÀM ŠÈG ŠUR-*nun* [. . . . .]
	12	[*pi-šì*]*r-šú-nu* LUGAL *l*[*e-e-mur* . . . . .]

1 [May Na]bû and M[arduk bless the king, my lord. 2 As to] the tablets of [the series (named) . . . .] 3 [and] the apocryphal tablets [. . . . . .] 4 [of which] I s[poke] to the king, my lord, 5 they have now been brought. [If] it is acceptable [to the king], m[y lord], 6 let them b[ring them in, and let the king, my lord], 7 have a look. Later [. . . . .] 8 the Akkadian [writing-b]oards [. . . . . . .] 9 the Assyrian [writing-board]s [. . . . .] 10 [. . .] I shall write the tablets [. . . . .] 11 [. . .] from here [. . . . .] 12 let the king, my lord, [. . . . .]. (*Rev.*) 1 [And to the k]ing mylord's [writing to me:] 2 "They should be [. . .]", 3 should they at the same time [. . .] the apocryphal [tablets of wh]ich [I spoke]? 5 [Or should they write them] on a secondary(?) tablet (*ṭuppu šanumma*)? 6 [Wh]at is it that the king, my lord, [says]? 7 [The moon wh]ich has (just) appeared, [. . . . .] for goo[d . . .]. 8 Let the [king], my lo[rd], have a look at the writing-board, I shall see [whatever . . . .]. (The omens are as follows:) "If the moon at his appearance is wearing a crown [and remains stable . . .]"; "If the moon appears in his correct position"; "If it rains on the day of the moon's disappearance" [. . . . .]. 12 Let the king l[ook up] their in[terpretations . . . .].

ADDENDA AND CORRIGENDA, 1979-81

LAS 1 r19 — The date ist partly damaged and could also be read ⌜16⌝.

14 Date — The occultation referred to in this letter is datable to April 27, 676 BC, and will be studied in detail in an article currently in preparation by H. Hunger and myself. The writer of the letter is definitely Akkullānu not Ištar-šumu-ēreš: in addition to the arguments already presented, note that the alloform of SAG occurring in Obv.9 and 12 (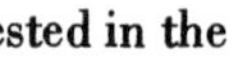) is not attested in the correspondence of Ištar-šumu-ēreš but occurs frequently in the letters and reports of Akkullānu (cf. *LAS* 298 r10, 307 r3 and 309 r10. 16.21; *RMA* 34:6.7, 144:3.9 and 235 r3).

15 Disc. — A punitive expedition against the Nabateans under Esarhaddon is reported in Assurbanipal's letter to Assur (Weippert, *WO* 7 [1976] 75:3-9) but not in Esarhaddon's own inscriptions; it should therefore have taken place quite late in his reign, probably either in 670 or 669.

21 r2' — For ^{d}NIN.LÍL = Mullissu see now S. Parpola, *CRRAI* 26 (1980), 174 and 177.

25 r3'f — *RMA* 271 was authored by Ištar-šumu-ēreš ($^{I.d}$[15-MU-KAM-*eš*]; note the form of SAG in Obv. 15 and cf. above, sub *LAS* 14) and hence very probably is the report promised in this letter.

30, 31 — (See at the end of the Addenda)

33 — The author is not Nabû-zēru-lēšer but Nabû-nāṣir ($^{I.d}$AG-PAP!-*ir*!), and the fragment may be part of the same tablet as *LAS* 216.

36 r9 — K. Kessler, *Untersuchungen zur historischen Topographie Nordmesopotamiens* (Tübingen 1980), p. 159 ff, rejects the location of the rab šāqê province proposed by Forrer, and would place it near 'Amādīyah, to the east of the abarakku province (p. 176). While Kessler certainly is right in pointing out that the key arguments on which Forrer based his proposal are erroneous, the evidence in the gross still favours, in my opinion, a location in the Tur Abdin region.

41 r6f — The date in these lines is not 26 but 28 (, collated from photo). In Rev.14, read UD *29*!.KÁM*.

60 r2 — ^{LÚ}ERIM^{MEŠ} could also be an ellipsis for *1-en* ^{LÚ}ERIM^{MEŠ} "one of the men", "a man"; cf. *1-en* URU^{MEŠ}-*ni-ja* "one of my cities" (*ABL* 1070:10') and *1-en* ^{URU}ŠE^{MEŠ}-*ja* "one of my villages" (*ABL* 1003:13'), and Aram. *ḥd mlkn* etc. (R. Degen, *Altaramäische Grammatik*, p. 104).

r5 — *qersu* is now also attested in OB Mari (*u$_4$-um gi-im-ki-im / qé-er-su-ú / iš-ša-ak-ka-nu*, *CRRAI* 26 p.142 ii 7-9). The West Semitic etymology considered is hence abortive.

85:3 — ^{URU}*Kàl-zi*: Cf. now also Postgate, *RlA* 5/7-8 (1980), p. 591.

115:12 — On Sāsî see now also Brinkman, *Or* NS 46 (1977) 314.

122 r11 — Note, however, that *šapāku* is obsolete in NA (where replaced by *t/dabāku*). The text should therefore probably be emended to read *liš-pu-ra*! "may (the king) send word (that)".

124 r10 — See also Hecker, *AOATS* 8 (1974), p. 69[3].

129:6 — A syllabic spelling *er-ṣu-tu* is attested in *KAR* 214 r.I 24 (*tākultu* rit. from the reign of Aššur-etel-ilāni). But this attestation does not imply that the word *erṣutu* existed in vernacular NA.

131:6 — *Bēt rēdûti* was not the SW Palace of Kuyunjik (rebuilt by Assurbanipal), as proven beyond doubt by the prisms (notably Assurbanipal's Prism A) found there; the equation *bēt šūti* = *bēt rēdûti* proved abortive upon checking. On ANŠE^{MEŠ} É *re-du-ti* (‖ ANŠE.(NITÁ)^{MEŠ} *bit-ru(-u)-ti*) see Weippert, *WO* 7 (1976) 83[134].

137 Bibl. Add Oppenheim, *Glass* (1970), p. 16a.

156:11 f Cf. also *a-ki-ma ina* ŠÀ *a-bi-te an-ni-te / qur-ba-ku* LUGAL *be-lí / a-na ši-ip-ṭi liš-kun-an-ni* "let the king, my lord, punish me, *if* I have anything to do with this matter", *ABL* 211 r15 ff.

158:6 f *a-na ḫur* also attested in *ABL* 1458 r6.

162:10 Read with Harper [*p*]*i-iq!-ta-a-te* and render "surely". *Piqtatti/piqtāti* appears to have been an adverb roughly synonymous with *issurri*; cf. OB *pīqat*, and correct *AHw*. 865b *piqittu* 3b.

171:11 *il-lu-ku-ú-ni*: perhaps better *il-lik!-ku-ú-ni* "that *could* not be done", cf. copy.

172 Date The form of SAG occurring in Obv. 15 (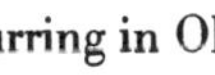) is in Marduk-šākin-šumi's correspondence otherwise attested only in *LAS* 195, 197 and 198, which are all fairly securely datable to early 672 BC. The reference to the (ominous) full moon observation in r13 ff makes this a very plausible date for the present letter, too (cf. commentary to *LAS* 74).

197 Date & Discussion: Note also that the word *šulmu* is spelled *šul-mu* both in *LAS* 195:3 and 198:3, but elsewhere in Marduk-šākin-šumi's correspondence consistently DI-*mu*, and that the peculiar form of SAG in *LAS* 195, 197 and 198 (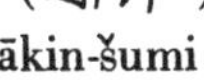) does not, with the exception of *LAS* 172 (cf. above), recur in other letters of Marduk-šākin-šumi (the sign is otherwise written either or  [188 r3, 342:2]).

206:11 *Zikkû*: Note *Zi-ik-ku-ú*^{KI}, *AOAT* 3/1 45 IV 3' and (partly damaged) 57 I 4 (Chagar Bazar/Tell Brak).

247 Photo: King, *Cat. Spl.*, Pl. I no. 13 (Obv. only)

252:14 Note *šum-mu ina pa-an* LUGAL [EN-*ja*] / *ta-ri-iṣ* (*CT* 53 891:8'f) for usual *šumma . . . maḫir* "if it is acceptable", and cf. *AHw*. 1327b.

r3 The existence of several *rab-mūgis* at a time is rendered beyond doubt by *ADD* 1036 iii 15 ff (LÚ*GAL-*mu-gi ša* ^{GIŠ}GIGIR, LÚ*GAL-*mu-gi ša* BAD-HAL-*li*); cf. also *ADD* 993 iii 6' and *GPA* 192 (showing that the *r.-m.* could be subordinate to a provincial governor). On the other hand, passages such as Jer. 39:13 & 19, *ABL* 1172+622:20, *AGS* 66 and 67, *CCENA* 21 ii 22 indicate that the *rab-mūgi* counted among the powerful officials ranking *between* the king and provincial governors in the Assyrian administrative hierarchy (turtānu, nāgir ekalli, rab-šāqê, sukkallu, sar=tinnu, mašennu/abarakku, rab-šarēši). Thus, there probably was one *rab-mūgi* par excellence (the *r.-m.* of the king) widely exceeding in power the (several) other *rab-mūgis* (of lesser potentates); cf. the analogous case of the king's abarakku/mašennu vs. other officials of the same title. The *rab-mūgi*'s constant association with chariotry, cavalry, horses, fodder etc. indicates that he was in command of a large contingent of cavalry and/or chariotry.

265(+). . .267 General remarks: Note also *LAS* 246:13ff probably referring to a tablet of medical contents sent along with the letter in question.

275:7 Concerning the location of Akkad it should be noted though that however tempting the recently proposed identification with Ishan Mizyad may seem archaeologically, it is hardly compatible with the textual evidence with points to a more northerly location, to the vicinity of Sippar. Note especially the Elamite inscription of Šutruk-nahhunte (König, *AfO* Bh.16, no. 28CI:6-10) where Akkad appears in a list of cities all situated withing a bare 40 kilometers from the mouth of the Diyala river (Dūr-Kurigalz[u], Sip[par], Ak[kad], Dūr-Šarr[ukku], Opis), and the other inscriptions of this ruler associating Akkad with Sippar and Ešnunna (ibid. nos. 22-24b); note also Unger, *RlA* I p. 62b. A location near Sippar would also account for the passage *LAS* 278:6-7 much better than one near Kish, because in the latter case the writer would be communicating to the king two eclipse observations made *virtually at the same latitude*, whereas in the former case the latitudinal difference between the three points of observation (Akkad, Borsippa, Nippur) would be almost equal. The chronicle and omen passages quoted by Weiss in support of a location near Babylon are not really relevant since they refer to (a sacrilegious act of) building a *replica* of Babylon near Akkad.

286 Date — Of the two possibilities considered (Ulūlu, 670 or 667), the former now seems more probable on the basis of an orthographic detail which had earlier escaped my attention: the spelling of the word *šarru* "king" in the salutation and blessing formula with the sign LUGAL. This is contrary to the standard orthography of Mār-Ištar, according to which the word concerned was in these formulae to be written with the sign MAN. There is only one further letter in the correspondence of Mār-Ištar displaying the same exceptional orthography, *LAS* 282. This letter can be confidently dated to the reign of Esarhaddon on the basis of the reference to Na'id-Marduk ibid., L.E. 1 (cf. note to *LAS* 30 r5), and its affinities with *LAS* 277 (written in Tašrītu/September, 671).

291:8'ff — A bridge of ships (*gi-iš-ra ša* GIŠ.MÁ) is also mentioned in *PBS* 1/2 54:30 (MB letter).

292 r9' — Opis cannot be equated with Seleucia since an administrative tablet from Tell Asmar to be published by R.M. Whiting implies that Upi was situated on the Tigris *north* of the mouth of the Diyala, exactly as also suggested by the classical sources.

308:11 — In the battle-ritual K 9912:8ff, ^{GIŠ}*pi-lag-gu* probably doesn't mean "spindle" but "lyre" since a further unpublished duplicate (K 10209 r19) writes the word logographically ^{GIŠ}BALAG.

309:15 — On the location of Tillê (= Tell Rumailan kabīr or Tell Ǧilāġa) see now in detail Kessler, *Untersuchungen* p. 9-15.

20 — ^{URU}*Par-nu-na*: to be read ^{URU}*Tam-nu-na*, see Kessler, *ZA* 69 (1979), 219f. Additional arguments in favour of the reading *Talmusu* for *RI-mu-su* are to be found ibid. Reade, *RA* 72 (1978) 157 ff criticizes the proposed identification of this site with Jerahiyah and suggests as a more likely alternative the mound of Gir-e-pan about 25 km NW of Jerahiyah.

311:10 — See also W.G. Lambert, "The great battle of the Mesopotamian religious year: The conflict in the akītu house", *Iraq* 25 (1963), 189f.

358:10' — Possibly to be restored ^{d}[EN.L]ÍL.

30, 31 — These two letters may also have been written in 679 BC. Note that if *LAS* 31 really is a report on an eclipse, as seems extremely likely in the light of *LAS* 28 and 77, then the fact that the letter is addressed to the "Farmer" actually implies that the eclipse in question had been immediately preceded by *another* eclipse (cf. *LAS* 25, 77 and 257). There were only two pairs of immediately successive eclipses in the reign of Esarhaddon: the lunar eclipse of June 1, -678 followed by a solar one on June 17, -678, and the solar eclipse of May 27, -668 followed by a lunar one on June 10, -668. Since the latter pair is out of the question for reasons stated in the commentary to *LAS* 30, the eclipse reported in *LAS* 31 would have to be the solar one of June 17, -678. The preceding lunar eclipse did indeed require the enthronement of a substitute king, though only in Nineveh (see Introduction, p. XXVIII), but the solar eclipse was almost total, and therefore would have called for a re-enthronement of the substitute in Babylonia, just as implied by *LAS* 30. While dating the letters to 674 BC still remains possible as well, the fact that the king is in these letters addressed as the "Farmer" makes the earlier date more attractive, since this form of address is otherwise only attested in substitute king rites triggered by *solar eclipses* (cf. App. L). The reference to Nikkal-iddina, Šamaš-ibni and Na'id-Marduk in 30 r3-5, taken in the commentary as a *terminus post quem*, would accordingly actually constitute a *terminus ante quem*.

INDICES

The numbers in the right-hand columns, unless otherwise indicated, refer to entries in the commentary (e.g., 308:7 = note on *LAS* 308 Obv. 7). d= date/discussion, n. = footnote. Cat. refers to entries in the catalogue of attested instances of the substitute king ritual, Introduction p. XXVIff.

1. TEXTS AND PASSAGES QUOTED[709] OR DISCUSSED

Akkadian

[709] Quotations from Mesopotamian literary or scientific texts found in the letters are indicated by asterisks. Texts quoted in extenso are italicized.

Aramaic

Bible

Classical

2. TEXTS EDITED UNDER "ADDITIONAL TEXTS"

3. GRAMMAR

Graphemics

Phonology

Morphology

Syntax

Style

4. LEXICON

5. NAMES[710]

Persons

[710] This index is selective only, since most of the names discussed in the commentary have already been listed in the indices to Pt. I.

Gods

Places

6. SUBJECT INDEX (IN SELECTION)

Astronomy and astrology

Medicine

Religion and cult

BIBLIOGRAPHY

Abusch, T. 1974 Mesopotamian anti-witchcraft literature: Texts and studies I: *JNES* 33, 259ff.

Aro, J. 1966 Remarks on the practice of extispicy in the time of Esarhaddon and Assurbanipal: *CRRAI* 14, 109ff.

Bayliss, M. 1973 The cult of dead kin in Assyria and Babylonia: *Iraq* 35, 115ff.

Behrens, E. 1906 *Assyrisch-babylonische Briefe kultischen Inhalts.* LSS 2/2. Leipzig

Biggs, R. 1969 Medicine in Ancient Mesopotamia: *History of Science* 8, 94ff.

Böhl, F. de Liagre 1953 *Opera Minora.* Groningen

Borger, R. 1954 *Studiën over inscripties en geschiedenis van Esarhaddon.* Diss. Leiden

1956 *Die Inschriften Asarhaddons. AfO* Bh 9. Graz

1971 Das Tempelbau-Ritual K 48+: *ZA* 61, 72ff.

1974 Die Beschwörungsserie *Bīt Mēsiri* und die Himmelfahrt Henochs: *JNES* 33, 183ff.

Bottéro, J. 1978 Le substitut royal et son sort en Mésopotamie ancienne: *Akkadica* 9, 2ff.

Brinkman, J. 1964 Mesopotamian chronology of the historical period: in: Oppenheim 1964, 335ff.

Caplice, R. 1965-1973 Namburbi texts in the British Museum: *Or* NS 34, 105ff.; 36, 1ff.; 39, 111ff., 40, 133ff. and 42, 508ff.

1974 The Akkadian Namburbi texts: An introduction: *SANE* 1/1. Malibu

Combe, E. 1908 *Histoire du culte de Sin en Babylone et Assyrie.* Paris

Contenau, G. 1947 *La magie chez les assyriens et les babyloniens.* Paris

Deller, K. 1959 *Lautlehre des Neuassyrischen.* Diss. Wien

1962a Zweisilbige Lautwerte des Typus KVKV im Neuassyrischen: *Or* NS 31, 7ff.

1962b Studien zur neuassyrischen Orthographie: *Or* NS 31, 186ff.

1964 Getreidekursangaben in neuassyrischen Rechtsurkunden: *Or* NS 33, 257ff.

(+ Parpola, S.) 1966 Die Schreibungen des Wortes *etinnu* "Baumeister" im Neuassyrischen: *RA* 60, 59ff.

(+ Parpola, S.) 1967 Progressive Vokalassimilation im Neuassyrischen: *Or* NS 36, 337f.

1969 Die Briefe des Adad-šumu-uṣur: *AOAT* 1, 45ff.

Denton, G. 1943 A new interpretation of a well-known Assyrian letter: *JNES* 2, 314f.

Dhorme, E. 1936/7 Quelques prêtres assyriens d'après leur correspondance: *RHR* 113, 125ff.; 116, 5ff.

1941 Rituel funeraire assyrien: *RA* 38, 57ff.

Dietrich, M. 1967/8 Neue Quellen zur Geschichte Babyloniens. (Ein Vorbericht. I-II): *WO* 4, 61ff. and 183ff.

1970 *Die Aramäer Südbabyloniens in der Sargonidenzeit* (700-648). *AOAT* 7. Kevelaer/Neukirchen-Vluyn

van Driel, G. 1969 *The Cult of Assur.* Assen

Ebeling, E. 1933 *Tod und Leben nach den Vorstellungen der Babylonier.* Berlin and Leipzig

1950 *Parfümrezepte und kultische Texte aus Assur.* Roma

1953 *Die akkadische Gebetsserie "Handerhebung".* Berlin

1954 *Stiftungen und Vorschriften für assyrische Tempel.* Berlin

1954-1956 Beiträge zur Kenntnis der Beschwörungsserie Namburbi: *RA* 48, 1ff., 130ff. and 178ff.; 49, 32ff., 137ff. and 178ff.; 50, 22ff. and 86ff.

Elman, Y. 1975 Authoritative oral tradition in Neo-Assyrian scribal circles: *JANES* 7, 19ff.

Fales, F. 1975 L'Ideologo Adad-šumu-uṣur: *ANL* 29, 453ff.

Falkner, M. 1954/6 Die Eponymen der spätassyrischen Zeit: *AfO* 17, 100ff.

Farber, W. 1973 *ina* KUŠ DÙ.DÙ(.BI) = *ina maški tašappi*: ZA 63, 59ff.

1977 *Beschwörungsrituale an Ištar und Dumuzi*. Wiesbaden.

Finet, A. 1954/7 Les médecins au royaume de Mari: *AIPHOS* 14, 123ff.

Forrer, E. 1921 *Die Provinzeinteilung des assyrischen Reiches*. Leipzig

Foster, B. 1974 Wisdom and gods in Ancient Mesopotamia: *Or* NS 43, 344ff.

Frank, C. 1925 Bīt mēsiri: *ZA* 36, 215ff.

Frankena, R. 1956 *Tākultu. De sacrale maaltijd in het Assyrische ritueel, met een overzicht over de in Assur vereerde goden*. Leiden

Frazer, J.C. 1927 *The Golden Bough*. Abr. edition. New York

Ginzel, F.K. 1899 *Spezieller Kanon der Sonnen- und Mondfinsternisse für das Ländergebiet der klassischen Altertumswissenschaft und den Zeitraum von 900 vor Chr. bis 600 nach Chr.* Berlin

Gössmann, F. 1950 *Planetarium Babylonicum*. Roma

Goetze, A. 1957 Reports on acts of extispicy from Old Babylonian and Kassite times: *JCS* 11, 89ff.

Grayson, A.K. 1975 *Assyrian and Babylonian Chronicles. TCS* 5. Locust Valley, N.Y.

Gurney, O.R. 1935 Babylonian prophylactic figures and their rituals: *AAA* 22, 31ff.

Hartman, L. 1962 The date of the Cimmerian threat against Ashurbanipal according to ABL 1391: *JNES* 21, 25ff.

Hartner, W. 1969 Eclipse periods and Thales: prediction of a solar eclipse – historical truth and modern myth: *Centaurus* 14, 60ff.

Hrouda, B. 1965 *Kulturgeschichte des assyrischen Flachbildes*. Bonn

Hulin, P. 1959 A hemerological text from Nimrud: *Iraq* 21, 42ff.

Hunger, H. 1968 *Babylonische und assyrische Kolophone. AOAT* 2. Kevelaer/Neukirchen-Vluyn

1972 Neues von Nabû-zuqup-kēna: *ZA* 62, 99ff.

(+ Reiner, E.) 1975 A scheme for intercalary months from Babylonia: *WZKM* 67, 21ff.

Jacobsen, T. 1975 Religious drama in ancient Mesopotamia: *Unity and Diversity* 65ff.

Jokinen, E. 1969 Lupus erythematosus disseminatus: *Duodecim* 85, 11ff.

King, L.W. 1896 *Babylonian magic and sorcery*. London

Kinnier Wilson, J.V. 1956 Two medical texts from Nimrud: *Iraq* 18, 130ff.

1962 The Nimrud catalogue of medical and physiognomical omina: *Iraq* 24, 52ff.

1965 An introduction to Babylonian psychiatry: *AS* 16, 289ff.

1972 *The Nimrud Wine Lists. CTN* 1. London

Klauber, E. 1913 *Politisch-religiöse Texte aus der Sargonidenzeit*. Leipzig

Knudtzon, J. 1893 *Assyrische Gebete an den Sonnengott für Staat und königliches Haus aus der Zeit Asarhaddons und Asurbanipals*. Leipzig

Köcher, F. 1966 Die Ritualtafel der magisch-medizinischen Tafelserie “Einreibung”: *AfO* 21, 13ff.

Kraus, F.R. 1935 *Die physiognomischen Omina der Babylonier. MVAeG* 40/2. Leipzig

1936 Ein Sittenkanon in Omenform: *ZA* 43, 77ff.

1936/7 Babylonische Omina mit Ausdeutung der Begleiterscheinungen des Sprechens: *AfO* 11, 219ff.

Krecher, J. 1966 *Sumerische Kultlyrik*. Wiesbaden

Kudlek, M. (+ Mickler,E.) 1971 *Solar and Lunar Eclipses of the Ancient Near East from 3000 B.C. to 0 with Maps. AOATS* 1. Kevelaer/Neukirchen-Vluyn

Küchler, F. 1904 *Beiträge zur Kenntnis der assyrisch-babylonischen Medizin. AB* 18. Leipzig

Kümmel, H.M. 1967 *Ersatzrituale für den hethitischen König. StBoT* 3. Wiesbaden

Kugler, F.X. 1907-1924 *Sternkunde und Sterndienst in Babel*. Münster

Kunstmann, W. 1932 *Die babylonische Gebetsbeschwörung. LSS* NF 2. Leipzig

Labat, R. 1939a *Le caractère religieux de la royauté assyro-babylonienne*. Paris

1939b *Hémérologies et ménologies d'Assur*. Paris

(Labat, R.) 1941 Un almanach babylonien (V R 48-49): *RA* 38, 13ff.

1946 Le sort des substituts royaux en Assyrie au temps des Sargonides: *RA* 40, 123ff.

1951 *Traité akkadien de diagnostics et pronostics médicaux.* Leiden

1952 Un calendrier cassite: *Sumer* 8, 17ff.

1957 Nouveaux textes hémérologiques d'Assur: *MIO* 5, 307ff.

1959 Asarhaddon et la ville de Zaqqap: *RA* 53, 113ff.

1961 Tabous de Tešrit et autres prescriptions: *Iraq* 23, 88ff.

1965 *Un calendrier babylonien des travaux, des signes et des mois (séries iqqur îpuš).* Paris

1967 Assyrien und seine Nachbarländer von 1000 bis 617 v.Chr.: *Fischer Weltgeschichte* 4 (Frankfurt a.M. and Hamburg), 7ff.

Laessøe, J. 1955 *Studies on the Assyrian Ritual and Series bît rimki.* Copenhagen

Lambert, W.G. 1957 Ancestors, authors and canonicity: *JCS* 11, 1ff.

1957/8 A part of the ritual for the substitute king: *AfO* 18, 109ff.

1959/60 The ritual for the substitute king – a new fragment: *AfO* 19, 119.

1960 *Babylonian Wisdom Literature.* Oxford

1962 A catalogue of texts and authors: *JCS* 16, 59ff.

1968 Literary style in first-millennium Mesopotamia: *JAOS* 88, 123ff.

(+ Millard, A.R.) 1969a *Atra-ḫasīs. The Babylonian Story of the Flood.* Oxford

1969b An eye-stone of Esarhaddon's queen and other similar gems: *RA* 63, 65ff.

1976 A late Assyrian catalogue of literary and scholarly texts: *AOAT* 25, 313ff.

Landsberger, B. 1915 *Der kultische Kalender der Babylonier und Assyrer. LSS* 6/1-2. Leipzig

1928/9 Das 'gute Wort': *MAOG* 4, 294ff.

1954 Babylonian scribal craft and its terminology: *PICO* 13, 123ff.

1965 *Brief des Bischofs von Esagila an König Asarhaddon.* Amsterdam

Langdon, S. 1913 *Babylonian Liturgies.* Paris

1914 *Tammuz and Ishtar.* Oxford

1921 The Assyrian catalogue of liturgical texts: *RA* 18, 157ff.

1925 A list of the known titles of Sumerian penitential psalms (eršaḫunga), arranged in alphabetical order: *RA* 22, 119ff.

1932 An unplaced fragment of the *Utukke limnuti* series: *JRAS* 1932, 557ff.

1935 *Babylonian Menologies and the Semitic Calendars.* London

Layard, A.H. 1849 *Nineveh and Its Remains.* London

1853 *Nineveh and Babylon.* London

Leichty, E. 1970 *The Omen Series Šumma Izbu. TCS* 4. Locust Valley, N.Y.

Lewy, H. 1952 Nitokris-Naqī'a: *JNES* 11, 264 ff.

Mallowan, M. 1966 *Nimrud and Its Remains.* London

Matouš, L. 1961 L'Almanach de Bakr-Awa: *Sumer* 17, 17ff.

Mayer, W. 1976 *Untersuchungen zur Formensprache der babylonischen "Gebetsbeschwörungen": Studia Pohl* S.M. 5. Roma

Meier, G. 1936/7 Beschwörung mittels eines Mehlkreises: *AfO* 11, 365ff.

1937 *Die assyrische Beschwörungssammlung Maqlû. AfO* Bh 2. Graz

1937/39 Die Ritualtafel der Serie "Mundwaschung": *AfO* 12, 40ff.

1939 Ein Brief des assyrischen Gelehrten Balasî: *Or* NS 8, 306ff.

1941/44 Die zweite Tafel der Serie bīt mēseri: *AfO* 14, 139ff.

Meissner, B. 1920-1925 *Babylonien und Assyrien.* Heidelberg

Moren, S. 1978 *The Omen Series "Šumma Alu": A Preliminary Investigation.* Diss. University of Pennsylvania, Philadelphia

Myhrman, D. 1902 Die Labartu-Texte, babylonische Beschwörungsformeln gegen die Dämonin Labartu *ZA* 16, 141ff.

Neugebauer, O. 1957 *The Exact Sciences in Antiquity.* 2nd ed. Providence

Neugebauer, P.V. 1912 *Tafeln zur astronomischen Chronologie I: Sterntafeln von 4000 v.Chr. bis zur Gegenwart.* Leipzig

1914 *Tafeln zur astronomischen Chronologie II: Tafeln für Sonne, Planeten und Mond.* Leipzig

1922 *Tafeln zur astronomischen Chronologie III: Himmels-Erscheinungen.* Leipzig

1929 *Astronomische Chronologie.* Leipzig and Berlin

1932/3 Genäherte Tafeln für Sonne und Planeten: *Astronomische Nachrichten* 248, No. 5397. Reprinted in Stahlman + Gingerich 1963, p. xix ff.

(+ Hiller, O.) 1934 *Spezieller Kanon der Mondfinsternisse.* Astronomische Abhandlungen. Ergänzungsheft zu den Astronomischen Nachrichten, Bd. 9, N. 2, S.B. 3. Kiel

Nötscher, F. 1928 *Haus- und Stadtomina der Serie šumma âlu ina mêlê šakin. Or* 31. Roma

1929/30 *Die Omen-Serie šumma âlu ina mêlê šakin. Or* 39-42 and 51-54. Roma

Nougayrol, J. 1967 Rapports paléo-babyloniens d'haruspices: *JCS* 11, 219ff.

Olmstead, A.T. 1923 *History of Assyria.* New York

Oppenheim, A.L. 1941 Idiomatic Accadian: *JAOS* 61, 251ff.

1944 Notes to the Harper letters: *JAOS* 64, 190ff.

1947 The shadow of the king: *BASOR* 107, 7ff.

1956 *The Interpretation of Dreams in the Ancient Near East.* Transactions of the American Philosophical Society N.S. 46/3. Philadelphia

1964 *Ancient Mesopotamia.* Rev. ed. (by E. Reiner) 1977. Chicago

1965 A note on the scribes in Mesopotamia: *AS* 16, 253ff.

1966 Analysis of an Assyrian ritual (KAR 139): *History of Religions* 5, 250ff.

1967 *Letters from Mesopotamia.* Chicago

1968 The eyes of the lord: *JAOS* 88, 173ff.

1969 Divination and celestial observation in the last Assyrian empire: *Centaurus* 14, 97ff.

1973 A note on *ša rēši*: *JANES* 5, 325ff.

1974 A Babylonian diviner's manual: *JNES* 33, 197ff.

von Oppelzer, T.R. 1887 *Canon der Finsternisse.* Denkschriften der Kaiserlichen Akademie der Wissenschaften, math.-naturwiss. Klasse, Bd. 52. Wien

Parker, R.
(+ Dubberstein, W.) 1956 *Babylonian Chronology 626 B.C. – A.D. 75.* Brown University Studies 19. Providence

Parpola, S. 1970 *Neo-Assyrian Toponyms. AOAT* 6. Kevelaer/Neukirchen-Vluyn

1971 *Letters from Assyrian Scholars to the Kings Esarhaddon and Assurbanipal, Part IIA: Introduction and Appendixes.* Diss. University of Helsinki

1972 A letter from Šamaš-šumu-ukīn to Esarhaddon: *Iraq* 34, 21ff.

1974 The alleged Middle/Neo-Assyrian verb **naṣṣ* and the Assyrian sound change *š* > *s*: *Assur* 1/1

Parrot, A. 1961 *Nineveh and Babylon.* London

Pfeiffer, R. 1923 Assyrian epistolary formulae: *JAOS* 43, 26ff.

1935 *State Letters of Assyria. AOS* 6. New Haven

Postgate, J.N. 1969 *Neo-Assyrian Royal Grants and Decrees. Studia Pohl* S.M. 1. Roma

1973 *The Governor's Palace Archive. CTN* 2. London

1974 *Taxation and Conscription in the Assyrian Empire. Studia Pohl* S.M. 3. Roma

Pritchard, J.B. (ed.) 1969 *Ancient Near Eastern Texts Relating to the Old Testament.* 3rd ed. Princeton

Rassam, H. 1897 *Asshur and the Land of Nimrod.* New York

Reiner, E. 1956 "Lipšur" litanies: *JNES* 15, 129ff.

1958 *Šurpu. A Collection of Sumerian and Akkadian Incantations. AfO* Bh 11. Graz

(Reiner, E.)	1961	The etiological myth of the "Seven Sages": *Or* NS 30, 1ff.
	1964	The phonological interpretation of a sub-system in the Akkadian syllabary: *Studies Oppenheim*, 167ff.
(+ Pingree, D.)	1975a	Observational texts concerning the planet Mercury: *RA* 69, 175ff.
(+ Pingree, D.)	1975b	*Babylonian Planetary Omens, Part I: Enūma Anu Enlil, Tablet 63: The Venus Tablet of Ammiṣaduqa. BM* 2/1. Malibu
Ritter, E.	1965	Magical expert (= *āšipu*) and physician (= *asû*): notes on two complementary professions in Babylonian medicine: *AS* 16, 299ff.
Schaumberger, J.	1935	*3. Ergänzungsheft* to Kugler 1907-1924, Münster
(+ Schott, A.)	1938	Die Konjunktion von Mars und Saturn im Frühjahr 669 v. Chr. nach Thompson, Reports Nr. 88 und anderen Texten: *ZA* 44, 271ff.
	1952	Die Ziqpu-Gestirne nach neuen Keilschrifttexten: *ZA* 50, 214ff.
	1955	Anaphora und Aufgangskalender in neuen Ziqpu-Texten: *ZA* 51, 237ff.
Schnabel, P.	1923	*Berossos und die babylonisch-hellenistische Literatur*. Leipzig
	1924	Die Saros-Periode der Finsternisse schon in der Sargonidenzeit bekannt: *ZA* 35, 297ff.
Schoch, K.	1927	*Planeten-Tafeln für Jederman.* Berlin-Pankow
	1928	Astronomical and calendrical tables. Appendix to S. Langdon and J.K. Fotheringham, *The Venus Tablets of Ammizaduga.* Oxford
Schott, A.	1936	Marduk und sein Stern: *ZA* 43, 124ff.
	1937a	Review of Waterman 1930-1936: *OLZ* 40, 293ff.
	1937b	Review of Pfeiffer 1935: *OLZ* 40, 358ff.
	1938	Nabû-aḫḫē-erība, der Astrologe mit den Silbenlesungen: *ZA* 44, 194ff.
(+ Schaumberger, J.)	1941/2	Vier Briefe Mâr-Ištars an Asarhaddon über Himmelserscheinungen der Jahre -670/668: *ZA* 47, 89ff.
Smith, S.	1925	The Babylonian ritual for the consecration and induction of a divine statue: *JRAS* 1925, 37ff.
von Soden, W.	1936a	Die Unterweltvision eines assyrischen Kronprinzen: *ZA* 43, 1ff.
	1936b	Texte zum assyrischen Begräbnisritual: *ZA* 43, 254ff.
	1936c	Leistung und Grenze sumerischer und babylonischer Wissenschaft: *Die Welt als Geschichte* 2, 411 ff. and 509 ff. – Reprint: Darmstadt 1965
	1939	Aus einem Ersatzopferritual für den assyrischen Hof: *ZA* 45, 42ff.
	1952	*Grundriß der akkadischen Grammatik*. AnOr 33. Roma
	1954	*Herrscher im alten Orient.* Berlin – Göttingen – Heidelberg
	1956	Beiträge zum Verständnis der neuassyrischen Briefe über die Ersatzkönigriten: *Fs Christian*, 100ff.
	1957	Zur Laut- und Formenlehre des Neuassyrischen: *AfO* 18, 121f.
	1959	Religiöse Unsicherheit, Säkularisierungstendenzen und Aberglaube zur Zeit der Sargoniden: *AnBi* 12, 356ff.
	1962	Der Nahe Osten im Altertum: *Propyläen-Weltgeschichte* 2 (Berlin), 41ff.
	1966-1977	Aramäische Wörter in neuassyrischen und neu- und spätbabylonischen Texten. Ein Vorbericht I-III: *Or* NS 35, 1ff; 37, 261ff; 46, 183ff.
Spaliger, A.	1974	Esarhaddon and Egypt: An analysis of the first invasaion of Egypt: *Or* NS 43, 295ff.
Stahlman, W.D. (+Gingerich, O.)	1963	*Solar and Planetary Longitudes for Years -2500 to +2000 by 10-day Intervals.* Madison
Starr, I.	1977	Extispicy reports from the Old Babylonian and Sargonid periods: *Finkelstein MV*, 201ff.
Streck, M.	1916	*Assurbanipal und die letzten assyrischen Könige bis zum Untergang Niniveh's. VAB* 7. Leipzig
Tallqvist, K.	1914	*Assyrian Personal Names. ASSFF* 43/1. Helsinki
	1938	*Akkadische Götterepitheta. StOr* 7. Helsinki

Thompson, R.C. 1900 *The Reports of the Magicians and Astrologers of Nineveh and Babylon.* London

1903-1904 *The Devils and Evil Spirits of Babylonia.* London

1923 *Assyrian Medical Texts.* London

Thorwald, J. 1967 *Macht und Geheimnis der frühen Ärzte.* München/Zürich

Thureau-Dangin, F. 1921 *Rituels accadiens.* Paris

Townend, B.R. 1938 An Assyrian dental diagnosis: *Iraq* 5, 82ff.

Ungnad, A. 1938 Eponymen: *RlA* 2, 412ff.

1941/4 Besprechungskunst und Astrologie in Babylonien: *AfO* 14, 251ff.

1943 Figurenzauber für den kranken König Šamaš-šumu-ukīn: *Or* NS 12, 293ff.

Virolleaud, C. 1908-1912 *L'Astrologie Chaldéenne.* Paris

Waschow, H. 1936 *Babylonische Briefe aus der Kassitenzeit. MAOG* 10/1. Leipzig

van der Waerden, B. 1953 History of the Zodiac: *AfO* 16, 216ff.

1966 *Die Anfänge der Astronomie.* Groningen

Waterman, L. 1930-1936 *Royal Correspondence of the Assyrian Empire.* Ann Arbor

Weidner, E. 1912 Zur babylonischen Astronomie: *Babyl.* 6, 8ff.

1914 *Handbuch der babylonischen Astronomie I. AB* 23. Leipzig

1923/4 Ein babylonisches Kompendium der Himmelskunde: *AJSL* 40, 186ff.

1939/40 Ein Segensgebet für Assurbanipal: *AfO* 13, 210ff.

1941/4 Der Tag des Stadtgottes: *AfO* 14, 340ff.

1941-1969 Die astrologische Serie Enûma Anu Enlil: *AfO* 14, 172ff. and 308ff.; 17, 70ff.; 22, 65ff.

1959/60 Ein astrologischer Sammeltext aus der Sargonidenzeit: *AfO* 19, 105ff.

Wiseman, D.J. 1955 Assyrian writing-boards: *Iraq* 17, 3ff.

1958 *The Vassal-Treaties of Esarhaddon. Iraq* 20/1. London

Ylvisaker, S. 1912 *Zur babylonischen und assyrischen Grammatik. LSS* 5/6. Leipzig

Zimmern, H. 1901 *Beiträge zur Kenntniss der babylonischen Religion. AB* 12. Leipzig.